RARE BOOKS

1983–84

Trends, Collections, Sources

Rare Books

1983–84

TRENDS, COLLECTIONS, SOURCES

Edited by Alice D. Schreyer

R. R. BOWKER COMPANY
New York and London, 1984

Dust jacket illustrations: Full-page miniature from the
Gospels of Henry the Lion, sold at Sotheby's, London,
on December 6, 1983, photograph courtesy of Sotheby
Parke-Bernet & Co.; John Dunlap 1776 broadside
printing of the Declaration of Independence, sold at Christie's,
New York, on April 22, 1983, courtesy of the new owner,
Chapin Library, Williams College; colophon page from the
Kelmscott *Chaucer*, part of a complete set of Kelmscott Press
books on vellum sold at Christie's, New York, on May 20,
1983, photograph courtesy of Christie, Manson & Woods;
Brideshead Revisited, In Our Time, Nineteen Eighty-Four, and
Ulysses, courtesy of Glenn Horowitz, Bookseller.

Designed by Philip Grushkin

Published by R. R. Bowker Company
205 East Forty-second Street, New York, N.Y. 10017
Copyright © 1984 by Xerox Corporation
Printed and Bound in the United States of America
ISBN: 0-8352-1756-6

CONTENTS

PREFACE

RARE BOOKS 1983–84: TRENDS, COLLECTIONS, SOURCES, the first in a projected series, combines an overview of recent developments in the field of rare books and manuscripts with information sources in this field. It provides for a specialized audience — collectors, dealers, rare book librarians, and scholars — a one-volume review and directory similar to *The Bowker Annual*, which has proved so useful for the library world. The rare books and manuscripts community is both diverse and interdependent and the purpose of this series is to enable its members to keep up with the trends and locate the collections and sources that constitute this dynamic and growing field.

During 1983 rare books and manuscripts were front-page news. Public attention was focused on the Hitler diary forgery and the record price at auction brought by the Gospels of Henry the Lion. Such isolated events afford a highly unbalanced picture of the field; unless placed in their broader context, they may distort not only the image but also the reality. In a series of essays, Part I builds a composite portrait of the present state of collecting, buying, selling, administering, and using collections of rare books and manuscripts.

The chapters on the antiquarian book trade, private collecting, and rare book libraries are based on interviews, questionnaires, informal conversations with colleagues, and personal reflections. Availability and price of desirable material are recurring themes; these factors are affected by inflation and the general state of the economy. A mood of reserved but increasing optimism is evident. Having survived very good and, more recently, very bad times, the field of rare books and manuscripts seems to be settling into a period of cautious confidence about the future. Imaginative and practical new directions in buying and selling by dealers, auction houses, and private and institutional collectors are emerging alongside the survival and revival of traditional fields and practices. The interaction among dealers, collectors, and librarians is forcefully documented in these chapters, which illuminate each other at the same time as they do the specific topics they consider.

The surveys of descriptive and analytical bibliography and scholarly editing, books about books, and periodical literature for book collectors, dealers, and librarians cover a broad range of scholarship and publishing. Independent research and cooperative projects, and the publishing based on these activities, are flourishing. The essays in Part II reveal how bibliographical scholarship and publishing identify new titles and call attention to new subject and chronological paths for collectors to pursue. The progress of the *Eighteenth Century Short Title Catalogue*, noted by several contributors, epitomizes these developments.

Progress and innovation are the hallmarks of issues in the news covered in Part III. Increasing technological and scientific expertise and cooperation among institutions in its application have resulted in improved techniques for providing access to and preserving rare and special materials. Automation is affecting the day-to-day operations of dealers and rare book libraries; collectors benefit from the variety and flexibility of approaches to bibliographic and holdings information, and may soon experiment with computer applications in their own libraries. Developments in the field of preservation have made archival quality storage materials and conservation treatment facilities much more widely available; collectors and dealers as well as librarians can now provide proper conditions for material in their care. The chapters on these topics provide a summary of developments together with information on sources and services.

The report on the Oberlin Conference on Theft documents an important step taken in 1983 to coordinate efforts in the area of security, an issue of increasing concern to dealers, collectors, and librarians. Activities of professional organizations, reports on educational developments, and continuing efforts to alter unfavorable legislation reflect growth and vitality. The history of books, an interdisciplinary and intercultural field, has received wide attention during the year. This approach, which combines a variety of ways of looking at books, for example, as physical objects and as social, cultural, and economic forces, demonstrates the importance of private and institutional collections, and the dealers who help form them, to contemporary education and scholarship.

Educational opportunities listed in Part IV range from formal academic programs and short-term fellowships to public lecture series. Part V brings together directories of selected rare book libraries and antiquarian book dealers, compiled by questionnaire, with listings of associations, auctioneers of literary property, and appraisers of books and manuscripts. This marketplace guide of the antiquarian trade serves as a convenient and useful reference for dealers, collectors, and librarians.

This book was enriched by the insight and expertise of several colleagues: Terry Belanger, William L. Joyce, William Matheson, and G. Thomas Tanselle. Their advice broadened the scope and sharpened the focus of the project; their enthusiastic and warm assistance made working on it a pleasure. Theresa Barry, who provided editorial assistance on the manuscript, and Iris Topel, who saw it through to production, were dedicated, precise, and supportive. Jean Peters served as editor's editor, compiler, and contributor—these roles only hint at her commitment to the project and the patience, grace, and skill with which she brought it to completion, for all of which I am extremely grateful.

Alice D. Schreyer
March 1984

NOTES
ON CONTRIBUTORS

TERRY BELANGER is Assistant Dean, Columbia University School of Library Service, founder and coordinator of Rare Book School, and coeditor of *Bibliography Newsletter.*

JOHN Y. COLE is Executive Director, Center for the Book in the Library of Congress.

STEPHEN PAUL DAVIS is a network specialist in the Network Development Office, Library of Congress. He is coauthor of *Standard Citation Forms for Rare Book Cataloging* (Washington, D.C.: Library of Congress, 1982) and author of "Computer Technology as Applied to Rare Book Cataloging," *IFLA Journal* 10 (Spring 1984).

JOHN FEATHER is a Lecturer in the Department of Library and Information Studies, Loughborough University, England, where he teaches a course on rare book librarianship.

JEROME P. FRANK is a free-lance writer with a special interest in the antiquarian book trade.

JOAN M. FRIEDMAN is Curator of Rare Books at the Yale Center for British Art and immediate past Chair of the Rare Books and Manuscripts Section, ACRL (ALA).

DAVID D. HALL is Professor of History, Boston University and Chair, Program in the History of the Book in American Culture, American Antiquarian Society.

CAROLYN HARRIS is Head, Preservation Department, Columbia University Libraries and Chair, Preservation of Library Materials Section, RTSD (ALA).

JOHN B. HENCH is Assistant Director for Research and Publication, American Antiquarian Society.

CAROL C. HENDERSON is Deputy Director, ALA Washington Office.

MARIE E. KOREY is Head, Rare Book Department, Free Library of Philadelphia, and served as moderator at the Oberlin Conference on Theft.

RICHARD LANDON is Head, Thomas Fisher Rare Book Library, University of Toronto, Canada.

KATHARINE KYES LEAB and **DANIEL J. LEAB** edit and publish *American Book Prices Current* and operate BAMBAM, a nonprofit database that lists stolen books and manuscripts.

WILLIAM MATHESON is Chief, Rare Book and Special Collections Division, Library of Congress.

ROBERT NIKIRK is Librarian of the Grolier Club, New York City.

JEAN PETERS is Manager, Research and Development, Book Division, R. R. Bowker Company.

KENNETH W. RENDELL is President of Kenneth W. Rendell, Inc., a firm that deals in autographs and manuscripts.

DEBORAH RISTEEN is Managing Editor, Society of American Archivists.

G. THOMAS TANSELLE is Vice President of the John Simon Guggenheim Memorial Foundation and President of the Bibliographical Society of America.

DANIEL TRAISTER is Curator of Special Collections, Van Pelt Library, University of Pennsylvania and coeditor of *Bibliography Newsletter.*

PETER M. VanWINGEN is Head, Reference and Reader Services Section, Rare Book and Special Collections Division, Library of Congress, and coauthor of *Standard Citation Forms for Rare Book Cataloging* (Washington, D.C.: Library of Congress, 1982).

REPORTS FROM THE RARE BOOK AND MANUSCRIPT FIELD

I

1

The Antiquarian
Book Trade

Jerome P. Frank and Jean Peters

AS THE NATION'S ECONOMY began strengthening in the latter half of 1983, antiquarian bookseller confidence, shaken by the effects of the recession the year earlier, began to return as sales of rare books, modern first editions, and manuscripts showed improvement described in terms that ranged from "gradual" to "dramatic." In fact, a number of antiquarian book dealers admitted that 1983 was their best year ever.

Although not all dealers were equally enthusiastic over their 1983 showing — some reported a flat year, with no change in sales volume compared with the year before and others were troubled by a falling off of mid-range sales — nevertheless, in a series of interviews with antiquarian booksellers across the country, it became increasingly clear that for a variety of reasons, the trade in general was filled with a confidence it hadn't felt for two years or more. Fears that library budget cuts would gravely diminish institutional buying were to a great extent allayed as curators and librarians found ways to continue to buy the important material they wanted, and, in cases where certain rare book libraries either seriously slowed or actually stopped purchases, other libraries moved in to fill the gap. At the same time, private collectors began playing an increasingly important role as dealers catered to a greater number of both young and seasoned collectors, many of whom were intent on capturing important and expensive items.

The optimism generated by the dealers was also reflected by their trade association, The Antiquarian Booksellers Association of America (ABAA), whose administrative assistant, Janice M. Farina, reported that each of the four regional ABAA book fairs — hosted last year by the Northern California, Middle Atlantic, Midwest, and New England chapters — was successful and that ABAA membership has been growing annually, with 1983 membership standing at 402. The number of bookstores in the United States selling antiquarian books also continues to grow, and has in fact more than doubled over the last decade — up from 902 stores in 1973 (*Ameri-*

can *Book Trade Directory,* 1973–1974, R. R. Bowker Company) to 1,810 in 1983 (the number of U.S. antiquarian bookstores listed in Chapter 26 of this book).

The satisfactory health of the antiquarian trade during 1983 was not achieved without complications, the nature and range of which varied from dealer to dealer and from bookselling area to bookselling area; and universally for dealers who sell in significant volume to foreign customers, 1983 was a bare landscape as a strong U.S. dollar, pitted against weaker foreign currencies, deterred many buyers from England and the Continent from even visiting the United States, let alone buying books from American dealers. However, even this situation was offset by the ability of American dealers to buy at favorable exchange rates abroad.

STRENGTHENING SALES ACTIVITY

In bookselling areas as diverse as fifteenth-century books and modern first editions, dealers reported improved sales in 1983, some ahead by as much as 20 percent over 1982. For the most part, sales to private collectors rose, university library sales held steady, and dealer-to-dealer sales dropped off. While sales volume was generally on the rise, its rate of increase varied significantly from one dealer to another in the same field. One bookseller of literary first editions described his sales as "brisk, substantially larger than 1982" and his customer range "broadened dramatically." Another in the same field reported only a leveling off. "I think what we're finding is a falling off from the go-go years of 1979 to 1981," this dealer declared, and ticked off what he said were two major signs: "A West Coast dealer in modern firsts, who has constantly done $35,000 at the Los Angeles book fair, now seems to be settling down to between $15,000 and $18,000 and that ratio probably holds for the fairs in Chicago, Boston and New York; and dealers do not run around from one to another buying stock, but rather buy cautiously, either with a client in mind or a book that's a sure thing." Yet another modern first dealer, whose firm's sales set a record in 1983, was troubled by what he sees as "inconsistencies" in the market. The "red flag," he said, "is the spottiness of business activity. On the one hand, we are selling more expensive books, but fewer customers can afford to buy them, and on the other, we see bald spots in our business caused by the disappearance of a number of customers who used to buy our mid-range books." Even gloomier, in spite of "better than level sales," was another modern first edition dealer who believes that "the tremendous number of 20th century authors being sold in our field, although bringing in big money now, will be impossible to give away in a couple of years."

However, a dealer in early printed Continental books, brimming with optimism for the future, reported "very active sales, especially during the second half of 1983." Although he reported prices continuing to rise, he added that they were not having an adverse effect on sales. The picture differed for a dealer in early English and American books, whose sales had surged 20 percent in 1983 as private collector sales rose, but overseas trade plummeted, dropping from 50 percent of total sales to 30 percent or less as a result of the strong U.S. exchange rate—"the dollar-forty pound prevents English dealers from buying in the U.S." But falloff of foreign business or not, this dealer's sales figures have shown a gradual rise since 1979, although in 1980 they leaped up because of an extraordinary profit on one item.

Similar optimism was echoed by a dealer in books, manuscripts, and drawings from the tenth century to the twentieth, who affirmed that 1983 was "one of the greatest years" in his business and for two reasons primarily: "There are many more people buying books than I have ever experienced in my whole career, and people are searching out and buying the high spots, even though prices are high."

More tempered were booksellers dealing in books-about-books, science and medicine, and illustrated books, all of whom reported a "gradual improvement" in sales over the previous year. The dealer in books-about-books was struck by the improvement in dealer confidence, "as reflected in their willingness to buy reference books for themselves." But, like the dealer in modern first editions, he too felt that the emphasis placed on high spots will have "a negative long-term effect on collecting, because it discourages the beginning collector." This dealer was quick to point out, however, that the books-about-books field is finally "starting to find some of the importance it should have had all along."

Yet pervading the optimism, almost paradoxically, is the booksellers' concern that mid-range books seem not to be moving, especially in the case of modern first editions. As one dealer put it, "I could sell a copy of Hemingway's *The Sun Also Rises* with one phone call and get anywhere from $3,500 to $6,000 for it, but a large portion of my non-highspot, bread-and-butter books have gotten soft. I suspect they were pushed too high too fast."

The result is that dealers are buying fewer of the mid-range books "unless they can be bought cheap," one dealer stated, adding, "We'll sell that stock to a dealer at a fraction of what we'd normally sell it for."

At the other end of the scale are the high-spot books, highly desirable, highly collectible works whose prices continue to rise year after year and for which demand usually outstrips supply. Prices are often so high that only the wealthy can afford them. Yet, even such books reach price plateaus from time to time, when demand slackens. Such was the case recently of a lovely book illustrated by Toulouse Lautrec that had been on the shelf of a dealer for three years. "Nobody wanted it," the bookseller recalled. "But now the economy has picked up and the supply of such books is shrinking so all of a sudden five people called me last year for the book, which I sold for $12,000."

This, together with other examples of "hot" books, denotes a healthy market. One dealer has worked out his own rule of thumb for determining the health of the antiquarian trade. He watches the price activity of a number of expensive, key works—he selects a group of ten books, which he calls "common rare books"—such as, in the literature category, the Kelmscott *Chaucer,* Johnson's *Dictionary,* and Joyce's *Ulysses.* Thus, when the Chaucer, which for a long time was an $8,000–$10,000 book in dealers' catalogues, rose to about $12,500 in 1983 and most recently to $15,000, he could judge the trade to be "healthy." He explained that he thinks these books are a better indication of the strength of the trade than the less expensive books—those, for example, under $150. In good condition at fair market value they are always salable because they have a wider market.

It does not pay to take the pulse of the trade on the basis of archival sales to institutions. As one dealer pointed out, archives, even in the case of a perfectly good second-tier author, are almost unsalable now. "In the 1960s, this kind of material was being gobbled up by such institutions as the University of Texas and Boston University. Today, it's difficult to find the institution with the purse to put anywhere from $50,000 to $100,000 into manuscripts and letters."

THE DILEMMA OF PRICES

Price was a two-pronged story in 1983: 15 to 20 percent of the top end of booksellers' stock continued to rise; the overall majority of books remained pretty much at the same level as they were in the previous two or three years. As one modern first edition dealer maintained, "I don't think that in either instance, prices had an appreciable or quantifiable effect upon sales."

However, it is debatable whether price played a deciding role in collecting in 1983. Some booksellers maintain that it did not; others cite chapter and verse to prove that price was a key element in decisions of collectors to buy or not to buy. Certainly booksellers were being more cautious in buying larger collections containing a number of "common" books because they could not afford to tie up cash in inventory that would not be appreciating in value enough to cover the high cost of money.

Dealers maintain that the rise in prices of the scarcer books tended to push some collectors out of the market, a fact not argued by a dealer in illustrated books, who saw higher prices keeping the average collector from buying his stock. "The fact is," he said, "they are becoming expensive for me to buy and it's a great pity because it's difficult for me to stock many of them." He cited the classic case of that trendy book *Jazz,* illustrated by Matisse, which in 1982 could have been bought for $25,000 and today is at least $40,000.

In a parallel situation, George Orwell was a classic case of inflated pricing within the modern first edition field. Orwell, in 1983, was perhaps one of the most sought-after authors. His *Nineteen Eighty-Four,* which in a fine dust jacket would have sold for between $200 and $300 in 1982, was priced between $600 and $800 in 1983. In this case, the price rise had nothing to do with scarcity, since the book was no less scarce in 1983 than it was 18 to 24 months before that. It had only to do with demand, and that was generated by an outside factor.

Another indication that the price situation had gotten out of hand in 1983, as some dealers firmly believe, was the price realized at the Frederic Dannay auction at Christie's in December, when Ernest Dowson's *Poems,* one of 30 copies on Japan vellum, copy number one inscribed to his publisher, brought $10,000. "If you had said earlier that the book would have sold for that price, people would have looked at you in disbelief," said one dealer. The fact is, the book sold far above what a consensus of dealers would have agreed was a reasonable price.

But what is a reasonable price? It is an almost unanswerable question. Price depends as much on the amount a dealer pays for a book as it does on how much a collector is willing to spend for it. One dealer in early English and American literature suggests that the range for the "normal" collector lies somewhere between $50 and $500. Another dealer notes that even $75 might be too much in the case of signed, limited editions of current authors. He insists that the prices and proliferation of these editions are causing many collectors to become less interested in certain authors, such as J. P. Donleavy, Joyce Carol Oates, and John Updike, who have so many signed, limited editions of their work that the normal collector cannot afford to continue to buy them.

Not all books rose in price in 1983. Even some high spots leveled off. In modern first editions, many post–World War II American writers from the 1950s to the present whose book prices kept rising during the 1960s and 1970s, were suddenly no longer collected. "People don't call us up as they did earlier to ask us for Donald

Barthelme, John Barth, Robert Coover or Thomas Berger, for example," one dealer noted, "although such writers as Walker Percy and Anne Tyler are exceptions."

The great standbys, like Hemingway's *In Our Time,* which recently sold for $4,500 at the Los Angeles Book Fair, and Faulkner's *Soldier's Pay,* which could probably bring $5,000 in a fine dust jacket, are expected to continue their upward climb, pausing every so often to plateau before the next rise.

Most dealers agree, however, that they have not seen any customer attrition that could be laid directly at the door of rising prices. "There is no question that some customers at a given moment simply stop buying books and they might in fact tell you that the reason they have stopped is because of the dramatic and precipitous rise in prices," a dealer in modern first editions commented. "I don't buy that," he added, "because I think that what oftentimes happens is that people who were buying books and committing a certain percentage of their disposable income to books encounter other circumstances in their lives that take precedence and necessitate a change in financial priorities."

THE MOST COLLECTED AUTHORS AND SUBJECTS IN 1983

"Stephen King is probably one of the most sought after authors in the last 20 years," was the startling assertion of a major dealer in antiquarian books of unusual value. "It's a matter of demand and the perception of the collector," the dealer said, trying to explain why an author of "pot boilers" had captured the imagination of so many collectors. "His books aren't really scarce because they were published in such large quantities," he noted. "How history will look upon Stephen King 50 years from now is more guesswork than anything else."

If this dealer was not mystified by the trend, one long-time bookseller of rare books and manuscripts was. He tells of the day when a long-time customer called him and asked him to obtain a copy of King's second novel. "I called a dealer who had the book and he quoted it to me at $100. I was stunned by the price. After all, it had only been published the year before in a typical large hardcover trade printing." Double checking, the dealer called a trusted source and was told that copies of the King book, depending on condition, would cost him anywhere from $100 to $200. "I couldn't grasp it," he said. "What has happened to the market!"

Another author who was highly collected in 1983 was Robert Penn Warren—especially his *All the King's Men.* "Although Warren is in his eighties," one bookseller explained, "he comes out with a book a year and is doing fantastic stuff." This dealer also pinpointed two other relatively lesser known authors who he said had made strong strides in 1983—Cormac McCarthy, who received a MacArthur grant for $60,000 a year for five years, and John Yount, author of four novels. He also noted that Seamus Heaney continued to be a favorite of collectors in 1983.

A first editions dealer stated that there was not much interest in women writers as such, but he singled out Margaret Atwood, who continues to be a widely collected writer less because of any feminist standard she may be carrying than for her position as Canada's preeminent woman writer.

A generalist rare book dealer said 1983 was a strong year for such standard authors as Charlotte Brontë, Jane Austen, Lewis Carroll, William Faulkner, John Steinbeck, Isaac Walton, and Ernest Hemingway, as well as such subjects as Cook's Voyages and early exploration. A bookseller of English and American literature indicated surprise at how many people collect dictionaries and books on chess and magic. In illustrated books, collectors were buying Art Déco books and color-woodblock books, particularly from Japan, as well as early illustrated books. In the field of early books, collectors were turning from incunables to acquiring just the leaves, and continued to collect the great continental presses as imprints.

THE RISING COST OF DOING BUSINESS

As the cost of doing business as an antiquarian bookseller continued to rise, it brought up the professional question of how much time and service the dealer should give his customers. Two sides are forming on the issue: On the one side are the dealers who hold tenaciously to the proposition that rare book dealing is a service business and that as such the dealer owes as much time as it takes to contribute to his customer's education, understanding, and collection building. On the other side are the dealers whose business is mainly in selling high spots, making a profit, and moving on to the next customer. "When a book dealer finds his customers dropping away, it probably is the dealer's own fault," argues one bookseller. "Dealers should be serving their customers. What they've done when they have followed after a richer customer, is neglect to serve their earlier customer in the way he or she was hopeful of or accustomed to being served. Consequently, it is the dealer who has betrayed that customer. I have no doubt about that and I hold those dealers responsible."

Another dealer offers another viewpoint: He maintains that "unlike most general antiquarian bookshops, the ones that sell the more valuable material find that five percent of their clients in number represent 75 percent to 80 percent of their gross sales. You can only spend so much time and energy on each person, so what we do is put the best energy into the people who we think have the best potential for sales."

He added that there is more competition for good customers because of the greater number of booksellers and the growing sophistication of the dealers' communication equipment, which gives them quick access to information.

The antiquarian bookseller normally carries a heavy expense burden that includes among other costs, rent, inventory, staff, and catalogue costs. Added to one West Coast dealer's usual expenses are the costs of seminars held since 1979 (but not in 1983) to introduce people to book collecting. "Although we charge $35 for a three-hour course to about 40 people," the dealer said, "the course is actually free because as they come into the class we give them a $35 gift certificate towards anything in the shop." The hope is, of course, that the "students" will catch the collecting fever.

An increase in the cost of doing business as a bookseller is being forced on the dealers who must leave their shops at 667 Madison Avenue in New York City in 1984 because the building is to be demolished. Among the dealers in the building are Black Sun Books, James Cummins Bookseller, House of Books Ltd, James Lowe Autographs, and Trebizond Rare Books. Because they all most likely will be paying considerably more for new office space, the 667 group will probably not be able to handle middle-to-low price merchandise on the premise that it doesn't move, it doesn't sell well at auction, and it takes up valuable space. One of the dealers who had been in the 667 Madison Avenue building for six years said that "the nature of dealing is changing for us." The change is the new approach to inventory. "Because people are more interested in important books that are going to have retail value," the bookseller said, "we will no longer handle the little-known authors, much as department stores don't handle merchandise they know they can't move. I don't think we looked at our business in that way before." He explained that when a dealer cannot move stock, it traditionally goes to auction. More often than not it becomes a loss factor.

Another change that will have a significant impact on rare book businesses is the advent of computerization specifically tailored to the rare book dealer. By using a computer, dealers will be able to produce catalogues more efficiently and quoting will become much easier, as will financial planning.

THE INSTITUTIONAL MARKET

Rare book libraries still have money to spend, most dealers agree, although without question their budgets have been eroded as the economy weakened over the past four years. This erosion has caused libraries to cut back their buying activities to some extent (it varies from library to library), to reduce staff, and to allocate what money they have not only to buying books, but also to such other activities as cataloguing and preservation. In some cases, libraries have dropped out of rare book and manuscript buying activities altogether; librarians frequently have less time to go through catalogues and supervisors are becoming more involved in administration, all of which militates against dealers' selling to libraries on the scale of the 1970s.

As grim as this sounds, dealers appear to agree that in a practical sense the changes are not affecting them dramatically. In fact, libraries new to these dealers have been ordering books they had not ordered before (one dealer reported that he has a small nucleus of libraries that order fairly often through catalogues). For example, some institutions have taken a firm stand on developing their children's book collections.

"I've been impressed at the activity of a lot of institutions and one of the strongest causes for it has been the creation and progress of the *Eighteenth Century Short Title Catalogue*," a dealer in children's literature states. "It certainly has made places like the British Library aware of their holdings and their deficiencies."

According to this dealer, the most notable institutional event to occur in 1983 in children's books was the bequest by Elizabeth Ball of the Ball Brothers Foundation of her remaining collection of children's books to the Lilly Library at Indiana University. The bequest comprises some 12,000 rare and important children's books, and makes the Lilly Library one of the most important research centers to be found between the two coasts for the study of children's literature. (New York has the J. Pierpont Morgan Library's collection of early children's books, Canada has the Osborne Collection at Toronto Public Library, and California has the UCLA collection of children's books.) The Lilly already had a remarkable group of children's "later" books, beginning with the 1865 *Alice in Wonderland,* but it did not have the early material, "so this was a perfect marriage."

One dealer in early English and American literature said he probably sold more in cash to libraries in 1983 than at any previous time, "partially because we've been expanding our dealing in literature quite a bit in the last couple of years, so we're selling a lot of institutions we didn't sell before." The bookseller remarked that some institutions that had been good and steady customers just went dry. "The most notorious example in the American book world is a university library that was an active buyer in the 1960s and 1970s in many fields," he declared. "It had been an important buyer of Western Americana. I was told that one of the reasons why this library dried up almost completely in the last couple of years was its lag in cataloguing. The administration rechanneled all the rare book budget into the cataloguing budget."

One generalist rare book dealer increased the number of library customers by making a point of going after them. "We called, wrote, and sent them special lists of books." Another bookseller with an extensive inventory of special-value early-to-late literature claims that there is still a lot of institutional money around for collections, but that it doesn't come from the same sources it used to. "I think a lot of them are seeking 'friends' money, donations, special gifts, or money from other places." This dealer said he sold as many $20,000 to $100,000 collections to institutions last year as he had in any other period. "It takes a little work and patience for a bookseller to understand which libraries have the funds and, more importantly, to have the right material to offer them." Dealers in books printed between 1500 and 1800 were also of the opinion that institutions were eager to buy the material they want. "We have at least 150 books on our shelves that are being considered by a library," one dealer noted. A dealer in modern American firsts, with two or three dozen libraries with whom he does business, last summer offered a "marvelous collection of letters and manuscripts to an institution for a price well into four figures. It took them about a month and a half but through the Friends of the Library they put together the money and bought it. There was no question that they were going to buy it; it was just a question of how they would do it."

THE PRIVATE COLLECTOR

With the diminished volume of sales to institutions, antiquarian dealers are working much more closely with private collectors. The activity of private collectors has risen considerably, as dealers report shifts in the percentage of their sales to institutions, private collectors, and dealers. For the most part, the greatest volume of sales at present is to the private collector; in one case it is as high as 86 percent private collector and 5 percent institutional, with the rest to dealers. On average, however, the percentages are closer to 50-50 or a shade over in favor of the private collector. Most dealers, particularly in the modern first edition field, show great interest in the collection building of one important collector who began buying modern first editions and literary manuscripts in 1982, when the trade was feeling the effects of the recession. He has been buying one copy of many books, according to a dealer in modern firsts, "but he hasn't even scratched the surface of possibility." So much money has been generated from this one customer that the revenues of many booksellers are wholly or substantially dependent on him. "They do not need or choose to consider that the rest of the world, minus one, is still out there buying books," added the dealer, who is himself a prime beneficiary of that customer.

Many of the booksellers are making their appeal to private collectors largely through catalogues. One dealer, who finds that most private collectors prefer the high spots, is buying—against his own preference and taste—such authors as Samuel Johnson, Dickens, and Mark Twain, even though he would rather, and in fact normally does, buy books by less standard authors.

But what happens, the booksellers ask themselves, when the moneyed collectors slow their buying or cut it out altogether? Their answer is a reassuring one, "There always seem to be more collectors to replace them."

BUILDING COLLECTIONS

Imprints, authors, Americana, baseball, hockey, travel, livres d'artistes, Kate Greenaway. As new collectors enter the antiquarian field, booksellers in all fields are ready with fresh ideas to present to willing customers, or are building *en bloc* collections for sale to institutions. Numbers of new collections are already in the building stage while others are simply ideas waiting to be embodied in collections.

Some antiquarian dealers favor forming collections that will be sold *en bloc* at a later date. The choice of subject is usually personal and represents something the dealer views as fun or of special interest. One bookseller collects publisher imprints, such as Copeland & Day and Stone & Kimball, and "odd publishers" like Nicholas Brown. But he is also building collections that appeal to his particular sports interests — baseball and ice hockey. He is also going to build one on football. As far as this dealer knows, there is at present no collection on the subject of ice hockey nor many books on ice hockey in any general collection.

Theater is one major area that is being considered by one dealer for collecting, and specifically within that subject, a single figure — novelist, poet, ballet master, critic — Lincoln Kirsten. The dealer's interest in Kirsten was generated by one of his customers, a young man at the University of Wisconsin, who introduced him to Kirsten as a great figure of the theater and one of the seminal figures of twentieth-century thought. "Kirsten edited *Hound and Horn* while he was at Harvard University and later in life was responsible for giving George Balanchine the opportunity to develop into one of the half-dozen great 20th century artists," this dealer noted.

One collecting area popular in 1983 was livres d'artistes, and a catalogue of a major collection was published during the year under the title, *The Book Beautiful and The Binding as Art*. The collection was sold in November *en bloc*. The handsome catalogue, with tipped-in color plates of the splendid bindings, was offered for sale in hard cover at $85 by John F. Fleming and Priscilla Juvelis, antiquarian book dealers in New York and Boston respectively, who offered the collection for sale. It was formed by Carlos Scherrer, a Buenos Aires businessman and the first important patron of the master binder Paul Bonet.

In the Americana field, people are collecting in more focused areas. Many are collecting states; others, railroad travel in the 1870s and 1880s, tourism, and the like. Particularly in Western Americana, several bibliographies have been catalysts for collecting, for example, the Wagner–Camp bibliography, *The Plains and the Rockies*. The late Warren Howell's new edition published in 1983 has revitalized interest in that subject.

In children's books, a specialist bookseller has noticed a resurgence in the past year of illustrator Kate Greenaway. From the beginning of the century to the late 1960s and the beginning of the 1970s there was much activity and interest in Greenaway collecting. Then, for a period of five or six years, there was a lull. Prices were stagnant, collectors had everything they wanted and new collectors found her drawings somewhat old fashioned. However, in 1983 a few new collectors were attracted by the nicely old-fashioned style; as a result, Kate Greenaway prices are rising.

But not only Greenaway has piqued the interest of children's book collectors. There is also a great interest in the illustrations of Maurice Sendak. "I think people have become aware of the long-term standing and importance that Sendak will have one day," the dealer said with confidence. "And certainly Sendak's reputation and following are as great if not greater overseas than they are here in the U.S."

A major collection being built by a bookseller in early English and American literature for a private collector is one defined as "social fiction." The collection will encompass literature from 1900 to 1950 and the books will describe in some way a time, or place, or social situation. "The most obvious example: Sinclair Lewis's *Babbitt* (on the high end of the literary scale), and *Stringtown on the Pike,* which described life in a small Kentucky town in 1910."

In general, good books are somewhat hard to find, but dealers firmly believe that there are plenty around to be bought. "Resourceful dealers can find them," say the booksellers. One dealer explains that he has no difficulty spending the money he has to spend on books every year. "I've done it by going farther afield, going on many buying trips around the country, and traveling in Europe, especially now, when the U.S dollar is strong." He went on buying trips to Europe five times last year "and, when you consider that the franc was four to the dollar in 1980 and 1981 and eight to the dollar now, it leaves a lot more room for buying books in France."

Supplying oneself with books is basically a matter of imagination, claims one dealer who has begun gathering together large numbers of theater archives. "New York is filled with archives and libraries that were generated by people who participated in the theater in the last 75 years and it is one of the most undercollected areas imaginable." The dealer began almost two years ago buying as much material as possible, all of it sitting in boxes in warehouses and all pertaining to the Broadway and Off-Broadway theater. He is also engaged in negotiations to buy the archives of The Living Theater. "I'm sure the price I buy it for, although in the absolute sense might be a healthy number of dollars, is going to be cheap compared to what the material is really worth," he added.

There is no question but that dealers are viewing new collections as a sensible way to drum up sales, either as a result of a single *en bloc* sale or as a way of strengthening inventory with attractive merchandise.

Auctions have always been a good source of new books, but according to most dealers, even that source is drying up somewhat. "For our kind of book," complained a dealer in early literature, "there are diminishing numbers of lots offered for sale. And the lots that are offered are less interesting, in less good condition and are generally less satisfactory than they used to be." This dealer recalled that Sotheby's actually gave him a refund for catalogues because they hadn't issued enough of them last year. "That was an alarming symptom in a way," he said. "The number of books we buy for stock in New York at Swann, Christie's and Sotheby's is going down and we're forced to look elsewhere for them. To some extent you compensate for this by raising prices, because prices go up as supply goes down, so in a way I suppose I shouldn't care, but I think it's more fun to be dealing in a greater variety of books."

As one dealer put it, when he described his purchase of a huge library with maybe 1,000 books in it (some quite rare and quite good), "It was a gentleman's library put together by a robber baron at the turn of the century and money was no object. You can still find the odd country library where you can find a lot of old books." He added that one might not find books from the fifteenth or sixteenth centuries there, but there will probably be books from the seventeenth century on. "If you just want to get old books, there's no problem. It's getting the quality that's the problem. Those are still available, too, if you are willing to pay for them."

SPECULATION: ITS TIME HAS ALMOST GONE

Dealers as a group appear to have little respect for the concept of speculation, which a dictionary defines as "engagement in risky business transactions on the chance of quick or considerable profit." It is almost a truism that when there are products of value controlled in an orderly way—as rare books are by their dealer-owners—speculators will appear with ideas for a quick kill. This was the case a few short years ago, when interest rates were going through the roof and high-priced books, which were rising in price from day to day, seemed like a speculator's dream. Even some ABAA members were carried away with the idea and in 1982 the organization held its New York regional book fair at the World Trade Center near the Wall Street area on the assumption that it would attract brokers and bankers, who, it was hoped, would see the merit of snapping up good books—expensive books—as a kind of investment portfolio. But brokers and bankers, being the sensible people that they are, do not invest in things they know nothing about. Since that time, with perhaps one or two exceptions, the speculators have folded their tents and quietly stolen away.

Some dealers deplore the idea of publicizing and pushing the concept of collecting for speculative reasons. One dealer thought it so shameful that he refused to exhibit at the World Trade Center. "An investment, to be a true investment, must have built in some degree of liquidity and it is non-existent in books," this dealer summed up.

Booksellers have always been reluctant to tie the words *collecting* and *investment* together, let alone *collecting* and *speculation.* Traditional or long-time booksellers thought that if collectors were interested in investing, they should go to their stockbrokers. "That made a lot of sense when books were much cheaper," one bookseller said, "but a lot of books are getting so expensive that people have to be conscious of the fact that if they are going to pay $500 and up for any collectible item, it has some potential to be worth more at some point in the future." He thinks it is unreasonable to suggest to anyone who buys a book that buying it as an investment is short-term. "Just the opposite is true, it is long-term. You don't buy a book now and put it on the market and expect to double the price next year. After all, the book was bought at a retail price. But the distinction is, that it is not unreasonable to expect that a profit of some sort might be made in, say, five years."

Generally, the antiquarian trade agrees that they meet no speculators and few investors. As one bookseller put it, "The people who buy expensive books and ask questions as to what the last copy sold for and whether they are getting fair market value, are intelligent. It's both unreasonable and unsophisticated not to deal with that aspect of the business."

AN OUTLOOK OF CONTINUED OPTIMISM

Most dealers agreed that 1984 will probably continue to build on the strengths displayed in 1983, both in the domestic and foreign markets. One bookseller who travels to Europe frequently reported making good European sales and said he believes the dollar will soon steady or drop and thus bring back some of the lost business from Europe. Other dealers, viewing the domestic market, voiced enthusiasm: "The high spots will keep going up," one dealer maintained.

"Very big. It started very big," enthused another.

"I'm extremely encouraged about the next two years," a third dealer said.

From their view of the future, it seemed clear that dealers had probably regained whatever confidence they may have lost during the recession period and were looking forward to an even better year.

The following members of the antiquarian book trade cooperated in supplying information for this chapter:

Bart Auerbach
Bart Auerbach Ltd.

Williston R. Benedict
Trebizond Rare Books

Mrs. Louis Henry Cohn
House of Books Ltd.

James Cummins
James Cummins Bookseller, Inc.

Janice M. Farina
Antiquarian Booksellers Association of
    America

Robert Fleck
Oak Knoll Books

John Fleming
John F. Fleming, Inc.

Walter Goldwater
University Place Book Shop

Glenn Horowitz
Glenn Horowitz—Bookseller

Peter B. Howard
Serendipity Books Inc.

T. Peter Kraus
Ursus Books Ltd.

James Lowe
James Lowe Autographs, Ltd.

Larry Moskowitz
Joseph the Provider—Books

Jeremy Norman
Jeremy Norman & Co. Inc.

William Reese
William Reese Company

Leona Rostenberg
Leona Rostenberg & Madeleine B. Stern—
    Rare Books

Justin Schiller
Justin G. Schiller, Ltd.

Fred Schreiber
E. K. Schreiber—Rare Books

Madeleine B. Stern
Leona Rostenberg & Madeleine B. Stern—
    Rare Books

Louis Weinstein
Heritage Bookshop, Inc.

Stephen Weissman
Ximenes: Rare Books, Inc.

Edith M. Wells
Antiquarian Booksellers' Center

Howard Woolmer
J. Howard Woolmer—Rare Books

2

Autographs and Manuscripts

Kenneth W. Rendell

THE YEAR 1983 has been an extraordinary one for the field of autograph and manuscript collecting. Several years ago, in writing a similar review, I stated that the publicity from the auction of the first part of the Philip D. Sang collection would probably never be surpassed. It has indeed been surpassed, and by a considerable amount. The year 1983 will be remembered as the year that our field of collecting received more public attention than ever before. It was almost as if the roof had been taken off our collecting community, and the public peered into our world of relatively undervalued material and our methods of authentication.

The year began with the domination of the auction market by a firm called the American Museum of Historical Documents. Its president, Todd Axelrod, previously unknown in the field, began to purchase nearly all autograph material of routine content by well-known Americans that was being offered at auction. His domination of the auctions caused many collectors and dealers to offer despairing prophecies, especially after he began to acquire letters with important content. Axelrod soon began visiting the dealers and, whenever possible, purchased virtually their entire stock of well-known Americana. He is the first investor to affect the autograph field seriously, and by April he had amassed several million dollars in acquisitions.

Little publicity outside of the autograph field had resulted from Axelrod's purchases when headlines throughout the Western nations bannered the discovery of the supposed Hitler diaries. It is unlikely that the popular news media will ever publish a bigger story involving the authentication of historical documents than the Hitler diaries. No other manuscripts could arouse the public attention that these did, and since the whole issue centered on whether or not they were authentic, the standards and methods used in the field of authenticity received unprecedented attention. The public, initially at least, certainly had cause to be concerned that people in the autograph field were not capable of definitively determining authenticity. If the Hitler diaries, for which $4.9 million was paid, and for which *Stern* magazine would receive $10 million in publication rights, could not be authenticated, then what assurance did collectors have in their purchases?

As the publicity over the forging of these diaries faded from the news, the details of Axelrod's future plans to sell shares of stock in his American Museum of Historical Documents were announced in a prospectus in August, 1983. A number of business magazines and newspapers, including *Fortune* and *Barrons,* published stories about his public stock offering, and his belief that framed autograph material could be sold at galleries in shopping centers in various wealthy cities at very substantial increases over the prices realized in the autograph market.

Public attention to the autograph and manuscript field continued almost unabated through the remaining months of the year with the discovery of an unknown fairy tale by Grimm, which had been available for years in a New York dealer's stock, and the sale of the Gospels of Henry the Lion in December for approximately $11,500,000, the highest price a single item has ever realized at auction.

Many events within the field were certainly of significance, including the effects of the improved economy and the competition among auction houses for autograph material, but the public attention and the possibility of its influences having a major effect on autograph collecting were certainly unprecedented and may portend what, for many, will be unwanted changes.

The autograph and manuscript field has always appeared to be a very undervalued area of collecting, waiting only for some form of public promotion to cause a sharp rise in prices and a decrease in availability. Many present collectors and dealers have believed that hordes of collectors would turn from coins, stamps, and other areas and begin collecting autographs if they were more readily available, and their authenticity and pricing better understood. With autograph material priced far less than other collectibles of comparable rarity and much less historical interest and importance, it does seem logical that a large number of new collectors would enter the field if they were aware of it. The present writer, however, has argued in various articles that this is unlikely to happen because of the general level of intelligence and sophistication required to collect and appreciate autograph material with historical content. Additionally, there are no meaningful price guides as there are in coin and stamp collecting and the quantity of autograph material available is not sufficiently large to warrant mass marketing. Gordon N. Ray, former president of the Grolier Club, wrote in "The World of Rare Books Re-examined" (*Yale University Library Gazette*) "[Autograph and manuscript collecting] is perhaps the most complex and sophisticated area of collecting . . . the operation of appraising the appeal of an offering . . . is one which brings into play every resource of knowledge, taste and intelligence at the command of the collectors . . . . Apart from the broad guidelines suggested by the sales of related material in the past, and such material is never really similar, the individual is on his own. He has none of the reference tools and comparative data that the book buyer can bring to bear in considering a purchase. . . ."

Mr. Axelrod's theory, if proven correct, would drastically change many areas of autograph and manuscript collecting. In the prospectus for the offering of common stock in his venture he writes: "The documents offered by the Company are presented in special framings to appeal to artistic tastes of potential customers who have not previously collected historical documents . . . its marketing strategy is novel among sellers of historical documents. This strategy is directed principally to persons not previously aware of the availability of such documents for purchase and is intended to be marketed in prestigious locations comparable to existing art galleries." While his basic concept is not unique, his method and scale of financing the concept are. Having spent slightly under $3 million as of August, he proposes to raise an additional $4.8 million through his public stock offering to buy more material. Branching out from his initial gallery on "The Strip" in Las Vegas, he plans to open galleries in Dallas, southern California, New York, San Francisco, Washington, Chicago, Los Angeles, Boston, Houston, and several other cities.

The effects of Mr. Axelrod's approximately $3 million in purchases as of mid-1983 were, indeed, significant. Dealers' stocks of Americana were drastically reduced and prices at auction rose by a large amount. If he is successful in raising the additional $4.8 million, he will be able to continue to remove a very substantial portion of the Americana offered for sale in the established autograph market. Hypothesizing further, should his chain of galleries come to fruition and become successful, he would require a quantity of autograph material that does not exist. After all, with his $3 million in purchases he has acquired stocks from dealers that took many years to accumulate. Similar quantities will not be available for many years.

Mr. Axelrod has undoubtedly based his optimistic forecast partly on the success of the two leading dealers who offer framed autographs to the public. Bob Tollett at B. Altman in New York City offers material through display ads in the *New York Times* and in a gallery-like setting on Fifth Avenue. Leon Becker, apparently the prototype for Mr. Axelrod's concept, has taken the art of designing mats and frames in accordance with the writer's personality or work to the ultimate degree. Mr. Becker, it should be noted, has a gallery in a shopping mall in an affluent southern California town. These two individuals, however, operate their businesses in a manner quite different from the one proposed by Mr. Axelrod. Their own knowledge and personalities are key elements to their success; they are dealing with clients, answering questions, and explaining authenticity and value. Perhaps more importantly, they do not view themselves as being outside the autograph market, and believe they must maintain levels of competency and service as well as prices comparable to other autograph dealers. In various interviews this fall, Mr. Axelrod indicated a large markup would be expected in his galleries, and since he has been paying relatively high sums for material at auction it would seem an impossibility for him to compete with established dealers in pricing. Perhaps the logical extension of Mr. Axelrod's concept is that, if successful on the large scale, he anticipates he will be buying virtually all of the Americana autograph material that dealers acquire; they therefore will not be competing with his galleries. As the year drew to a close it was not clear just how successful his stock offering plan had been. His purchases from dealers had clearly diminished and it will be 1984 before it is clear if this plan will be successful and to what degree.

Just what effect the Hitler diaries hoax will have on the Axelrod plan is also unclear. In many ways it certainly did not occur at a propitious time to engender confidence in autograph collecting on the part of prospective collectors. From the standpoint of the autograph field the most important issue with the Hitler diaries was not whether or not they were genuine, but rather how the process of authenticating historical documents was presented to the public. Within a few days of the first newspaper headlines and magazine cover stories, the whole issue turned to authenticity. *Newsweek,* for which I acted as a consultant, being brought in exactly one week before their first cover story, added "Are They Genuine?" as a subtitle to their issue entitled "Hitler's Secret Diaries." The question of authenticity was stressed in that first issue, but the principal emphasis both on the cover and in the text was on the content of the diaries. During the following two weeks literally dozens of newspaper reports concentrated on the authenticity question, finally putting the horse before the cart. Every television network had stories about the authenticity question and many major radio stations aired interviews on the subject. It was not just in the United States that this question received such attention. *Newsweek* warned me prior to leaving for Hamburg, Germany, to examine the diaries for *Stern* magazine, that the attention in this country was mild compared to what I would encounter in Europe. There the diaries would, if genuine, have a much greater impact on people because of Hitler's very direct influence on so much of the population. I was amazed to be followed around New York, to find television crews waiting for me, and to have so many requests for interviews that *Newsweek* had an office handle them for me. I was told that I would have legions of reporters following me and harassing me wherever I went. *Stern* also raised this issue and outlined a plan to have me arrive in a corporate jet at an odd hour and to put me up in a private house where I could not be located. There was indeed an emotional furor over the question of authenticity, putting this subject into the forefront of the news in a way in which it had never been before.

Two weeks after the first release of the news of the existence of the diaries both *Newsweek* and *Time* had cover stories proclaiming "FORGERY." *Time* magazine, in addition to reporting on the developments with the diaries, contained the most thorough and informative article ever to appear in the popular press concerning historical forgeries. *Newsweek* published a two-page report, with handwriting examples and comparisons, demonstrating how they were proven false.

Knowledgeable collectors were certainly unaffected by all of this publicity. They were aware from the *Newsweek* story that the authentication reports on which *Stern* had relied were not relevant to the diaries' authenticity. The public debate among historians and one autograph auctioneer was seen as a disgrace to all involved. Their methods, as described by them, were based on supposition, guesswork and assumption, when an examination of the original diaries would conclusively prove or disprove their authenticity. There was no need, except for immediate publicity, to speculate on the authenticity of the diaries and it was most unfortunate that those who were so publicly involved themselves did not reserve their opinions until the hard evidence, i.e. the diaries, had been examined. They certainly gave the world, for two weeks, the impression that authenticating historical documents was based on guesswork.

I am hopeful that the general public was left with the impression that the wrong people were shown the wrong material to authenticate and that once the actual diaries were examined it was absolutely and immediately clear that they were forgeries. The issue was not that it was difficult to authenticate them, but rather the journalistic question of publishing them before conclusively proving them authentic. A negative public reaction would most likely affect beginning rather than experienced collectors. If this proves to be the case, then it would certainly not bode well for selling framed autographs in shopping malls at prices significantly higher than those of established dealers. Anyone considering spending reasonably large sums would likely consult several dealers rather than rely on a chain of autograph galleries.

The events within the autograph field were certainly overshadowed during 1983 by these external happenings. The improved economy would have led to a general improvement in the autograph business even without the Axelrod purchases. A major trend from a business standpoint occurred when several auction houses that normally handled few autographs began to take much more active roles in the market. Both Swann Galleries and Phillips concentrated more on autographs in 1983, while the philatelic firm of Kelleher in Boston had several significant sales and then apparently decided to refocus their attention on an economically revived philatelic market. While Charles Hamilton Galleries, the leading autograph auction house, continued to auction diverse autograph material, some of the newer entries in the field concentrated on the more expensive and easier-to-catalogue material, thereby being able to offer lower commissions.

The year 1983 could be a pivotal year for the autograph field. The enormous publicity on the subject of authentication may aid or hinder Mr. Axelrod's plans to establish his chain of autograph galleries. The decisive role of authenticating historical documents has certainly brought attention to an area only rarely in the limelight, and the publication of the Grimm fairy tale has illustrated the important role that autograph and manuscript collecting plays in preserving and making available such works. It is certainly to be hoped that we do not reflect on 1982 as the last year when serious collectors could anticipate acquiring interesting material at reasonable prices without having to compete with casual autograph buyers at shopping malls.

3

The Auction Year

Katharine Kyes Leab

and Daniel J. Leab

IN AUCTION TERMS 1983 was, first and foremost, the year of Henry the Lion. The manuscript Gospels of Henry the Lion sold at Sotheby's in London on December 6, 1983, for £7,400,000 ($10,730,000) or with the buyer's premium, £8,140,000 ($11,920,000). Not Picasso, not Velasquez, not even Leonardo, but a magnificent twelfth-century illuminated manuscript has brought the highest price ever paid for a work of art at auction. Hermann J. Abs, former head and now honorary chairman of the Deutsche Bank, headed the West German consortium that purchased this treasure to return it to its homeland. The consortium was composed of the government of West Germany, the state of Lower Saxony, the state of Bavaria, and the Prussian Cultural Foundation of West Berlin, and it regarded the purchase as a mission. Speaking for the West German government, Interior Minister Friedrich Zimmerman stated: "German culture and German history are so uniquely manifested in the manuscript that its re-acquisition was a national task of prime importance." And the manuscript really is going home, for it is to reside in the Herzog August Library at Wolfenbüttel, not far from the monastery where it was created.

The man who commissioned this Gospel Book, Henry the Lion (ca. 1129–1195) was the only son of Henry the Proud, Duke of Saxony and Bavaria, and of Gertrude, daughter of the Emperor Lothair III. He was Duke of Saxony from 1142 and was the Guelph cousin and ally of the Emperor Frederick I, who restored Bavaria to him in 1156. Henry married Matilda, the daughter of Henry II of England, in 1168, by which time his own imperial plans were well underway. He obviously hoped to be the Barbarossa of the North, and he is known as the founder of such major German cities as Munich, Bremen, Lübeck, Hanover, and Hamburg. Henry's capital was Brunswick, and on his return from the Holy Land in January 1173 he ordered the rebuilding of Brunswick Cathedral and commissioned this Gospel Book to be placed in it. As Christopher de Hamel of Sotheby's points out in his catalogue, "above all the manuscript must be seen as the triumphant achievement of German imperial art: an outrageously lavish and expensive display of Ottonian grandeur, with the not insignificant political motive of presenting Henry the Lion as German king and emperor and (even above emperor) as the anointed of God." Indeed, Henry was not at all subtle in his propaganda efforts: One miniature depicts the coronation of Henry and Matilda by Jesus Christ.

Unfortunately for Henry, neither God nor Frederick Barbarossa seems to have accepted his vision, and by 1181 Henry was in exile in England. Before his death in August 1195, however, he had returned to reclaim Brunswick and Lübeck. Henry was the direct ancestor of most of the kings of Europe, beginning with his son, who became the Emperor Otto IV.

The Gospels of Henry the Lion, one of 19 known manuscripts produced at the Benedictine Abbey of Helmarshausen, near Brunswick, is the masterwork of the monk Herimann. The Gospel Book measures about 13½ by 10 inches and is composed of 226 leaves, including 41 full-page miniatures, 10 full-page carpet pages or interlaced initials, and over 1,500 illuminated initials. It is complete and, most remarkably, in superb condition, and its iconography is, in Mr. de Hamel's words, "so rich and elaborate that it will take generations of research to classify and explain." It contains the only contemporary portrait of Henry II of England and the earliest surviving picture of St. Thomas Becket, and it begins with a 20-line rhyming verse in Latin about the making of the manuscript, which provides the basis for localizing and attributing all other contemporary Helmarshausen books.

The Gospel Book also has an air of mystery about it. Its first disappearance was sometime before 1482, for it is not included in the earliest inventory of the Guelf Treasure in that year. Somehow it found its way to the Prague Cathedral, where, at the end of the sixteenth century it was rebound in a splendid binding that included an elaborate central rock crystal containing wrapped relics of Saint Mark and Saint Sigismund. The manuscript was purchased for the then huge sum of 10,000 thalers from the Prague Cathedral in 1861 by the King of Hanover, and in 1866 it was brought to the Schloss Cumberland at Gmuden in Austria. It disappeared again in the late 1930s and reappeared only at the occasion of its sale at Sotheby's. It is not known who consigned the manuscript to Sotheby's, though speculation on this point raged before the sale, almost to the point of obscuring the importance of the manuscript itself.

The sale of the Gospels of Henry the Lion was a triumph for Sotheby's (which made on the buyer's premium alone over $1 million in two minutes) and for Christopher de Hamel, the fine scholar who produced a catalogue for this sale that is altogether worthy of the magnificent manuscript it presents. From description to bibliography to the color reproductions of all the miniatures (for the first time anywhere), the catalogue reflects the auction process at its best — the public sale of a masterwork not only as an occasion to make money but also as an opportunity to serve scholarship.

The sale of the Gospels of Henry the Lion at a world-record price also capped a year in which Sotheby's moved from shakiness to stability, from losses to profits, and from a crumbling old order to the firm and sensible management of a Detroit group headed by real-estate developer Alfred Taubman. In the course of this renaissance, Sotheby's book and manuscript departments on both sides of the ocean underwent great changes. Books and manuscripts in London came under the direction of Roy

Davids, with Christopher de Hamel organizing Western and Oriental illuminated manuscripts and miniatures as a separate department. Creative cost-cutting was the order of the day, for brutal overheads in all departments in London and New York had been a major factor in putting Sotheby's into the red. Davids reorganized and reduced staff, and set up a system whereby each expert is responsible for a particular area, for example, maps or English literature. He also cut down catalogue production by inaugurating 1,001-lot sales and worked to achieve a higher per-lot price, which necessarily meant that more books were lotted up rather than being sold individually. Lotting up is a boon to the purchaser who can afford the lot, for the chances of finding an overlooked treasure are greater than when every book is examined carefully to be catalogued individually. The catch is in the ability to purchase the lot as a whole and to dispose of the remainder, and many dealers who in years past had purchased such books individually in the Sotheby's sales at Hodgson's Rooms found that they could not afford to bid for the lotted-up books.

At Sotheby's in New York the problem facing department head David Redden was somewhat different from that facing Roy Davids in London. Redden's task was to bring back the Sotheby New York book department to the point where it could compete with Stephen Massey of Christie's in New York, for Massey had a virtual lock on the upper end of the book and manuscript auction market in America. A superb administrator, Redden also proved to be a fine tactician who targeted specialized areas of the book and manuscript market that could be dominated, especially Americana and Judaica. If Las Vegas entrepreneur and dealer Todd Axelrod were engaged in building the largest and most expensive inventory of American autographs ever, then Mary-Jo Kline of Sotheby's would see to it that irresistible offerings were made at auction to meet the urgent demand by Axelrod and others for Americana. Kline is a new breed in terms of the American book and manuscript auction scene, for she is a well-known historian and the editor of the Aaron Burr papers. Sotheby New York's 1983 offerings in Americana included such rarities as an autograph letter of William Henry Harrison as president that sold for the astonishing price of $120,000 in April.

David Redden's other particular target for market capture was Judaica, and Sotheby's expert in this area, George Snyder, has made a well-organized specialty out of the chaotic and heretofore incompetently handled Judaica market in America. Among the manuscripts to pass through Mr. Snyder's hands in 1983 was the so-called Leipnik Haggadah. This beautifully preserved eighteenth-century vellum manuscript contains an illuminated title, 12 half-page, 5 quarter-page, and 44 small miniatures by Joseph ben David Leipnik, a brilliant illuminator who broke with the stylized tradition of imitating the engravings within the printed illustrated haggadot. Instead, he adorned his manuscripts with original miniatures that are masterpieces of eighteenth-century Jewish art. The Leipnik Haggadah first came to our attention in January 1970, when it was part of the Michael Zagayski collection. At that time the manuscript sold at Parke Bernet for $13,500. In the June 1983 sale masterminded by Mr. Snyder, it sold for $240,000. On this occasion, the 10 percent buyer's surcharge alone ($24,000) was almost twice what the manuscript itself brought in 1970, when there was no buyer's premium.

All of this activity at Sotheby's in New York did not mean, however, that Stephen Massey was suffering at Christie's. His 1983 sales included the Saks set of Kelmscott Press books on vellum and the Hewes-Johnston-Wood copy of the first printing of the Declaration of Independence.

Christie's had been selling books and manuscripts from the John A. Saks collection since November 1977 in both London and New York. The final portion of this library was sold at Christie's New York on May 20, 1983. Mr. Saks died just ten days later, but he had been able to enjoy the full recognition as expressed at public auction of the exceptionally fine collections he had built. In the last Saks sale a set of 49 vellum copies of Kelmscott Press works was sold as a single lot, a remarkable feat for several reasons. In 1898 Sydney Cockerell, then secretary of the Kelmscott Press and William Morris's executor, stated that "there are three complete vellum sets in existence, and the extreme difficulty of completing a set after the copies are scattered makes it unlikely that there will ever be a fourth." And, indeed, only 5 vellum copies were made of 2 Kelmscott publications, and there were only 6 to 8 vellum copies of 25 others. The odds against Mr. Saks's being able to form a complete set were enormous, but he managed to do just that in the period from 1935 to 1956. Christie's New York bravely and properly decided to offer the Saks set of Kelmscott Press books on vellum as a single lot even though a similar attempt to sell the Saks Ashendene Press works on vellum as a unit in November 1982 had failed. We now know that the reserve placed on the Kelmscott Press lot was $500,000, and the collection sold for $600,000 plus the buyer's premium of $60,000.

At the time of its sale on April 22, 1983, the Joseph Hewes–Samuel Johnston–Wood Family copy of the Declaration of Independence was the twenty-second known copy of the John Dunlap 1776 broadside printing and had not been recorded in Goff's 1976 census, *The John Dunlap Broadside*. It was the only copy of the first state of the broadside in private hands, and one of two copies bearing the D&C Blauw watermarks. Joseph Hewes, its original owner, was a signer of the Declaration of Independence representing North Carolina, and this document bears an endorsement in his hand on the verso. This association copy of the Declaration of Independence sold for the record price of $375,000, or $412,500 with surcharge.

Despite these and other successes, Stephen Massey also was faced with rising overheads and was holding fewer sales. Christie's in London, with a small department but blessed by the presence of the great bookman Hans Fellner, rolled along as it always does, setting records for natural history books on the way, though it too had to insist that consignors bring in quite expensive books to sell.

Just as General Motors produced fewer cars in 1983 but realized the greatest profits in its history, so Sotheby's and Christie's worked to cut costs by holding fewer sales but selling expensive books and manuscripts. The central administrations of these houses preferred that books worth less than, for example, $1,000 not be accepted for sale at auction, though the book departments bent the rules quite a bit here and there. This policy seems to work well for Sotheby's and Christie's but its implications for the book and manuscript market as a whole are somewhat murky.

Automotive labor leader Walter Reuther once said that you can save money by cutting labor costs, but who is going to buy your cars? Similarly, you can make more money by selling only very expensive books and manuscripts, but who is going to buy them? And indeed many more lots than usual were bought-in (meaning that they failed to reach their reserve price and thus were returned to their owners unsold) during 1983. Certainly there are enough buyers for the moment, but for the auction market to enjoy continued good health, the middle and lower ranges of the market must be served. Young dealers need materials with which to develop their stock; collectors need to be stimulated and brought along. And while the leading dealers did well this year, many others found that the books in their price range could not be bought at a Sotheby's or Christie's auction. The supply of single books available at auction has decreased greatly in London and New York. The cost of doing business has affected the auction process in other metropolitan areas as well: In Toronto, Canada Book Auctions regretfully closed its doors in mid-1983. This house was the successor to Bernard Amtmann's Montreal Book Auctions, and a note of sadness was struck in the final sale of March 16, for it contained the Bernard Amtmann Reference Library.

The problem of overhead and the need to sell big-ticket items does not have such telling effect on specialized book-auction houses in America, such as Swann and California Book Auction Galleries. To begin with, sales of books are not being compared by a central administration with sales of, for example, Old Master paintings. Swann, however, did lot-up more books by far in 1983, though it maintained its general excellence. California met the cost challenge in part by mining nontraditional areas such as science fiction. The Mark Marlow collection of fantasy and science fiction and similar sales at California Book attract buyers who are new to the book-auction rooms. A dozen Isaac Asimov entries, let alone 38 works of Robert A. Heinlein, would never have been found in the auction guide *American Book Prices Current* five years ago. It is fascinating to watch the major international auction houses become ever more conservative in their offerings, selling copies of the same high-priced, proven properties again and again, while California and other specialized houses become ever more innovative, reaching out to new buyers and into new areas in the hopes of solving the problem of the cost-price squeeze.

The most dramatic response to the cost-price problem was, however, the founding in 1983 of Bloomsbury Book Auctions in London by Sotheby alumni Lord John Kerr, Frank Hermann, and David Stagg. They set out to test the theory that a large market for less expensive books does exist but that the traditional venues can no longer serve it. Accordingly, they set up a lean operation in a building reportedly owned by one of the principals, arranged to hold auctions at a nearby hotel in Bloomsbury, and worked out a way to produce inexpensive but attractive catalogues. They are able to offer books in the £10 to £20 range, as well as higher-priced books. And they seem to be proving their point, lacking neither books to sell nor buyers for them.

Phillips, as usual, was a law unto itself. While everybody else was cutting down, Phillips in London held more book sales in 1983 than they had in 1982. Phillips sales were held in Oxford, Edinburgh, and New York as well. The London department seems to be selling ever more good autograph material, and the one-man New York department (Michael Robinson) was creative in combining its six sales with those of other departments to cut down on catalogue production costs.

In America, another answer to the problem of overhead is being provided by fast-growing regional auction houses. An example is the firm of Richard E. Oinonen in Sunderland, Massachusetts. Founded in mid-1980, this firm had reached sale number 66 by the end of 1983, many of these held in a hotel in Calvin Coolidge's hometown of Northampton, Massachusetts. Oinonen produces plain vanilla catalogues, and many of the books he sells are remnants of professorial libraries at $10 to $50 per book. The costs of doing business in Sunderland, Massachusetts, as opposed to doing business in New York, enable him to accept consignments of low-priced books and to make a profit selling them. Over the years he has also garnered such prizes as the reference library of John Kebabian, on Kebabian's retirement from the famous bookselling firm of H. P. Kraus, and, in 1983, the Emerson copy of the Revised Bay

Psalm Book, which Oinonen sold for $15,000. Other firms such as Waverly in Maryland and Hendsey in New Hampshire have similar stories to tell. Much of the future depends on such small regional auction venues if auction is to remain a major factor in the buying and selling of antiquarian books of all periods and prices.

Overall, 1983 was a year of contraction in the sale of books and manuscripts. Prices were high enough, but fewer sales were held, fewer single lots were available for purchase, and more lots were bought-in. But the problems that became so evident in 1983 also have provided opportunities for the innovators and experimenters in the auction field, who now are encouraged to try new areas and sales techniques that they never would have tried in palmier economic days. And there probably will never be another auction year with a more glorious ten minutes than the ten minutes on December 6, 1983, when Sotheby's sold the Gospels of Henry the Lion.

4

Private Collecting

Robert Nikirk

BOOK COLLECTING, as some of us learned of it in Wolf and Fleming's *Rosenbach,* is no more. Early books of the type sold by Dr. R. and eagerly bought through nearly a half century by his customers are simply not around in sufficient quantity. The Houghton sales at Christie's in 1979–1980 saw the last purely Rosenbachian collection dispersed, and when a leading bookseller can sell incomplete copies of early English poetry found in a basement to eager customers, we *know* an age has ended. But the scarcity of these books — English poetry and drama of the sixteenth and seventeenth centuries, with occasional high points of illustrated books of all periods, fine bindings, and so on — is only part of the answer. There has been a general shift in the educational consensus in the United States since the late 1960s. Not every educated person recognizes the names of the standard English and American poets, dramatists, and novelists through the end of the nineteenth century, let alone feels the desire to collect their first editions. This, combined with scarcity and high prices, has resulted in book collectors branching out in directions never before thought of. Book collecting in the past was often impelled by gratitude or respect for the writers who had enriched one's life. Although this impetus may still be true, the writers being collected certainly are different.

So who is spending disposable income on book collecting today? There is a vast middle level filled with all sorts of books, collectors with money to spend, and the imagination to spend it on some sort of book collecting — not a bad thing at all. What are they buying? The reflections on book collecting that follow are based upon my observations over a period of 26 years, first in the trade and for the last 14 years as librarian of the Grolier Club.

DETECTIVE AND SCIENCE FICTION

It is clear that, as a collecting field, detective fiction is here to stay. Once presented as an amusing byway in 1934 by John Carter, it is now a major field. Whereas no bookseller could earn a living exclusively from selling detective fiction until the 1970s, nowadays fat catalogues arrive regularly from all over the country. Serious literary criticism is constantly raising the level of acceptance of the detective novel. A

27

search for the ancestors of the detective novel in the late eighteenth and early nineteenth centuries can bring a collector into older company.

Another collecting area that developed in the 1970s as part of the interest in pop culture is science fiction and fantasy. Some colleges and universities now teach these subjects in English departments; as one bookseller put it to me: "People collect what they know and they know science fiction and fantasy writing." First editions in these fields are sought as avidly as Galsworthy ever was in the 1920s. In that period, Michael Sadleir and others helped preserve English Victorian civilization by collecting the popular three-decker novel and the yellowback at a time when Shakespeare quartos could be had on both sides of the Atlantic for the asking (and the price). If you were to mix all of Sadleir's collections into a sort of paté and then slice it, you would see nineteenth-century England in the strata. If you were to do the same with science fiction and fantasy writing today, would you see contemporary America? Whether or not one would, it is a lively area of book collecting. Once again, some of these collectors are looking backward to the roots of the genre, seeking such authors as Mary Shelley, Jules Verne, and H. G. Wells.

FIRST EDITIONS

Twentieth-century literature remains one of the broadest based of all collecting fields, especially works of the gods who have not been dead too long. F. Scott Fitzgerald, for instance, is eagerly sought, just as he is practically a living presence in the clothing business, advertising, and in Art Déco interior decoration. Ernest Hemingway has held his own; the predicted slip following his death did not occur. While you certainly hear less about him in critical writing today, he tells a good story and there are enough books to make a collection. William Faulkner, though a good deal less "easy" than Fitzgerald or Hemingway, commands plenty of attention in the first edition market. Many, many other American novelists are filling a share of the total picture. Collectors are, perhaps, playing that guessing game as to who will survive with a reputation intact when judged by the next generation.

Classic modern British writers are also popular among Americans, with great interest shown in Graham Greene, Somerset Maugham, and Evelyn Waugh. The ramifications on the first edition market of an important television series such as the splendid "Brideshead Revisited," based on Waugh's novel, were considerable: I was told that during the run of the series on television, a first edition of *Brideshead Revisited* was a much sought-after gift item.

One stimulus to the popularity of first editions of writers, especially of the twentieth century, seems to be the publication of a big, standard, and popular biography or a collection of letters. These are beacons for booksellers and collectors, and their production seems to be endless. The Bloomsbury group, especially Virginia Woolf, has reached virtual industrial status in both the scholarly and collecting worlds, to the point where some of us think we cannot tolerate another word. But then we are disarmed all over again by a fine memoir such as Frances Partridge's, or the 1983 biography of Vanessa Bell by Frances Spaulding. One reputation that was freshly burnished by a marvelous collection of letters was that of Flannery O'Connor. Try to find her first novel *Wise Blood*; some young booksellers have never even seen it.

Another writer once very well known throughout the English-speaking world who has had a remarkable revival because of recent books about her extraordinary private life is Vita Sackville-West. Interest awakened by her husband Harold Nicolson's diaries, her son Nigel Nicolson's *Portrait of a Marriage,* and the Virginia Woolf diaries and letters, was reinforced in 1983 by the long-awaited authorized biography by Victoria Glendinning. Thus several influences have produced a new market in her extensive corpus, whereas ten years ago many dealers in modern firsts did not even stock Sackville-West.

A case that deserves special mention is that of James Joyce. His 1982 centenary showed that interest in his work and life is still high, capped by Richard Ellmann's revision of his standard biography. At the Grolier Club's important exhibition on Joyce, we expected the age of the audience to be over 50. Not at all; the overwhelming number of visitors to the exhibition were in their 20s and 30s. Most of Joyce's first editions are out of the range of people with ordinary means, but for those who can afford him, Joyce is a much sought-after writer.

Difficult to chart but well worth considering is the effect of the women's movement on book collecting. There have always been some collectors of first editions of women writers and it is an area actively cultivated by some of the older women's colleges. As her 1974 centenary approached, Gertrude Stein came back into print in a scholarly Yale edition; this, and a lively interest in her unique personality, life, work, friendships, and influence, all led to an active market in her first editions. Women who were active in special areas and who wrote books—whether as doctors, Indian captives, or travelers—attract much interest today. Several large publishing projects are based on the works of women writers. Many of them are issuing in paperback novels of great merit that would never make it back on a hardcover list. This, in turn, has created a large new field of long-forgotten and now suddenly desirable first editions. The Virago Modern Classics is particularly rich in this regard. Elizabeth Taylor, Antonia White, Emily Eden, Mary Webb, and dozens of other novelists owe a new life to Virago. While it is true that a first edition collector cannot be said to have made a "discovery" by meeting a writer for the first time in a Virago paperback, this new sort of publishing project ought to be a taking-off point for dealers and collectors.

Analogous to the effect of television on Waugh was the truly extraordinary 1981 success of Glenda Jackson's film *Stevie,* about the life and poetry of the British poet and novelist Stevie Smith (d. 1971). Smith was little known in this country, and the movie produced a demand for her first editions that was totally unrequited. Oxford had even allowed her collected poems to go out of print, a situation that was not rectified until 1983. Stevie Smith has been born again in the poetic consciousness of this era, but her first editions are scarce. In a similar vein, sudden popularity at the end of her life marked the career of Barbara Pym (d. 1980), who between 1961 and 1977 published nothing. A rediscovery, through a *Times Literary Supplement* poll, subsequent paperback republication, three new hardcover novels, plus tremendous publicity, brought about a run on booksellers and book fairs for her first editions, requiring a supply that fell woefully short of its demand.

Modern poetry is a collecting area that, it is pleasant to report, is thriving. Those who hear the special voices of contemporary poets, let alone collect their first editions, have always been a small group, but they are extremely well informed, devoted, and vigorous in their support. Among the modern old masters, Ezra Pound is running strong, now outdistancing T. S. Eliot, W. B. Yeats, and others. Prices for standard Yeats items have changed little in 15 years, it is worth noting. Perhaps it has to do with the forthcoming centennial of Pound's birth and the critical commentary that continues to pour forth about him. His increasingly acknowledged influence on twentieth-century poetry, his long and controversial life, and his personality make him more appealing to some collectors than that fastidious fellow poet T. S. Eliot, who benefited most from Pound's critical advice.

Robert Frost is pretty much neglected, even though he is an easy read compared with Wallace Stevens, who is avidly sought. Perhaps it has to do with the revelations relating to his life and personality in the standard biography of Frost. The early works of such important poets as William Carlos Williams, Marianne Moore, Elizabeth Bishop, Robert Lowell, Sylvia Plath, and others are relatively scarce and have ready collectors.

Among living poets, most of whom could not by any stretch be termed an easy read, there is also great collecting interest. Scarce early works, periodical appearances, special limited signed editions, presentation copies, and perhaps an occasional autograph keep the chase spicy. Collectors of modern poets tend to collect more than one because of their limited production. For instance, a collection of Philip Larkin, generally conceded to be the most important poet in England today, would consist of four books of poetry, two novels, one book of jazz criticism, and collected essays. Thus one needs eight or ten poets to keep busy as a collector. Significant manuscript material by modern poets is hard to come by. Many collections of papers are bequeathed to institutional libraries and these same institutions vie with one another to get ownership of the papers before death. "Working manuscripts," that delight of collectors, are rarely seen and what they must often settle for takes the form merely of a signed typed letter.

Moving backward in time, there are some surprising developments alongside business-as-usual. The works of Rudyard Kipling and Anthony Trollope have returned to the first edition market. The approachability and the large output of these writers may help to account for this. Dickens has never been out of the picture; he writes a good plain story and there is a wealth of material to collect. His former reading audience is vastly diminished, but look what "Nicholas Nickleby" in the London and New York theater and on television has done for Dickens. Recently, he was even termed "the perfect writer for television."

The scarce and expensive firsts of Edgar Allan Poe are among the most sought-after American editions. Is it once again a combination of the storytelling combined with the facts of his life? Along these lines Herman Melville's life and work are of more interest to the late twentieth century than are Hawthorne's. There is also a whole range of nineteenth-century New England writers who are currently undervalued, including Whittier, Longfellow, and Lowell — all writers whose works occasioned pioneering American bibliographies and who enjoyed a brisk though small market even more than 100 years ago. In fact, these were the earliest American writers to be collected as "modern firsts."

AMERICANA

Americana and Western Americana are now off center stage and may be generally said to be undervalued, an eclipse that can be seen to have set in soon after the last Streeter sale in October 1969. Today there is plenty of material, ranging in subject from colonial New England, across the plains and Rockies, to California. The wealthy collecting personalities who formed huge collections of Americana and the bibliographers who served them by producing prodigious reference works are no longer around. And New York City is no longer the focus of the Americana trade since the retirements of such important dealers as the Eberstadts and Peter Decker. Today, Americana dealers are apt to be scattered across the land, many of them young dealers who are very well prepared and dedicated to their subject.

With Americana available, what we need is a new generation of young collectors moved by the story of the discovery, exploration, settlement, and growth of the United States. Admittedly, great early books are out of reach for the beginning collector. I would recommend starting a regional collection, especially if one is fortunate enough to have what are now termed roots and cares about them. For if one inquires into the motives of the important collectors of Americana of the past century, whose libraries not infrequently became the basis for major bibliographical works, one would find them to have been literally inspired by the epic story of the American experience.

BINDINGS

From splendid Renaissance examples to decorated cloth bindings of the past 150 years, bookbindings are receiving more attention than in the recent past. At the top of the market are European bindings from the late fifteenth to the late nineteenth centuries and French bindings of the 1920s and 30s. We have recently seen a few of these go beyond six figures, rising at last into the price range of the art market. These fine examples of the applied arts, as deserving of attention as silver or porcelain, have always been undervalued and the province of a handful of collectors and booksellers. But from the nadir of the Wilmerding sale of 1951, when magnificent examples of historic binding from the Grolier period through Dérôme and Padeloup went for a song, this area of the market is now performing well. The French bindings of the 1920s and 1930s mentioned above, especially those designed by Legrain, Bonet, and Martin, are surely at an all-time high.

The late nineteenth-century French bindings by such masters as Gruel, Marius Michel, and Meunier, astonishing virtuoso confections of gilding and inlay, have only recently come into focus again as fair game for collectors. Fifteen years ago the most elaborate of them could have been had for a sum in the low hundreds, whereas today a fine example costs at least a few thousand dollars. This generation's interest in Art Nouveau answers only part of the question of why there is such a demand for these bindings; a quest for superb handcrafted objects at reasonable prices may account for the active market.

Turn-of-the-century English bindings by Riviere, Sangorski and Sutcliffe, Bedford, and others, inlaid with enameled view plaques, miniature portraits, hair under isinglass, and other novelties of triumphant technique, are also back in favor. Bought as fancy gifts, or as starter sets by incipient bibliophiles, they never quite disappeared from the market.

There is a great deal of activity in publishers' trade bindings from about 1840 to 1940 because fine examples are affordable by the average collector. The elaborately stamped gift book of the mid-nineteenth century can still be found, and frequently not in bookshops. Other pictorial and gilt Victorian trade bindings are also popular, and searching for them adds exhilaration to visits to out-of-the-way secondhand bookshops of the sort you never tell your friends about.

Book covers with a designer's initials, or recognized as the work of a known designer, are rightly prized and will perhaps assist in the preparation of a major schol-arly publication on this subject some day. These designer books often belong to the Arts and Crafts period, that time of self-conscious reform of the excesses of the high Victorian gilt and pictorial stamping. Knowing your field can bring rewards. The collector with some knowledge of Bruce Rogers's style, for example, can spot his early work from the cover. Architects who turned their hand to book covers include Bertram Grosvenor Goodhue and Stanford White, who designed some 80 covers. The finely made trade book of post–World War I is also attracting collectors, and the books are well worth attention. The founders of the great American publishing houses of the twentieth century, now largely in the hands of conglomerates with other things on their minds, hired serious and excellent designers and there is still time to form impressive collections of their work. The rescue of a good-looking trade book of 1925 from a secondhand shop can be very satisfying. As always with bindings, the rule of fine condition is paramount, however.

OTHER COLLECTING FIELDS

Condition is important but harder to come by when searching for early paperback books. This new and worthwhile field has literary, sociological, and publishing his-tory aspects that are coming under increasing scholarly scrutiny, but not enough to spoil the fun of collecting. The nineteenth-century ancestors of the yellowback and the Tauchnitz editions are only part of the story. Charles Boni's Paper Books (designed by Elmer Adler), launched in September 1929 and ceased in 1931, are a real challenge to collectors. Penguin Books, one of the most widely collected paperback imprints, commenced in 1935, and Simon and Schuster's Pocket Books in 1938. It is hard to believe today how hesitant was the success of the paperback in the United States.

A growth industry of the 1970s, if ever there was one, is the field generally termed Books about Books. This includes bibliographies, essays about book collecting from all periods, private library catalogues, and antiquarian bookseller and certain types of book auction catalogues. Reference books on bindings are at a new high unto themselves. All these books were once found on a few shelves in a bookseller's shop and in only one part of an antiquarian catalogue, but today several booksellers make a living off nothing else. Long-established dealers, too, are not hesitant about han-dling books about books, and prices have risen about sixfold in a decade.

Collectors are also buying isolated auction catalogues of the eighteenth and nine-teenth centuries. Records of important sales are always interesting and sometimes of specialized reference use: one thinks of the catalogues of the Duke of Roxburghe, Beverly Chew, or Thomas Winthrop Streeter. But, for instance, a single, disbound, late eighteenth-century London sale catalogue of an unremarkable collection and with no bibliographical information to speak of for upward of $150? Here the in-crease over a decade is truly remarkable. It seems to me that these slim octavo listings have meaning only when combined in large research collections. Meanwhile, thou-sands of eighteenth-century English books are still within this price range, and with imagination one could build a worthwhile collection in contemporary bindings.

Collecting lives, with its ups and downs of fashion, prices, and availability. Every period is one of change, we are always told. With collectors eager to buy, at least in most areas, and booksellers eager to sell, in all areas, the scene is as diverse as ever.

5

Institutional Collections in the United States

William Matheson

IN THREE INFLUENTIAL papers written over a period of almost 20 years, Gordon Ray summarized the principal characteristics of the rare book world in the 1960s, 1970s, and 1980s. In his first article in the *Papers of the Bibliographical Society of America* (Second Quarter, 1965), Ray found that institutional libraries were the dominant purchasers of rare books and manuscripts, setting the pace for the market. By the time Ray published "The World of Rare Books Re-examined" in the *Yale University Library Gazette* (July 1974), the affluence of the 1960s had gone and institutional involvement in the rare book world had markedly diminished. Collectors and dealers had taken over the role that institutional libraries had played earlier. In a 1982 address to the Fellows of the Pierpont Morgan Library, *The Rare Book World Today* (New York: Pierpont Morgan Library, 1982), Ray found that rare book collections that were part of university libraries were in a particularly poor position, the privileged status of the rare book collections in two or three great libraries being seriously threatened.

When the editor of this volume suggested that in this chapter I survey activities and general concerns of rare book librarians, I reread Ray's first two articles and obtained from him a copy of his Pierpont Morgan Library talk. It seemed to me that if his assessments were correct, one would expect that rare book budgets would each year be falling further behind; that collectors, as they have moved into the space formerly occupied by libraries, would get in the way of whatever buying libraries can afford; that under more than 20 years of first library and then collector buying pressure the supply of certain books would be drying up; that in the face of rising prices institutions would be turning to less heavily worked fields; that some of these fields would contain materials individually costing less (preferably much less) than traditional rarities; that these collections might at the outset or in time bulk so large that they would present administrative and financial problems of a kind not previously encountered; that in a world in which the collector is predominant institutions might be expected to receive more gifts; that these gifts might determine new collecting specializations for the institutions to which they were presented; and that in a time of financial stringency libraries might be expected to be competing particularly energetically with fellow institutions.

In search of verification of these hypotheses I invited responses on these topics from 76 rare book librarians, whose collections are known to me, representing major university libraries, college libraries, independent research libraries, public libraries, and smaller university libraries. Though my questions were addressed in the main to printed materials, a number of my correspondents also responded on behalf of their manuscript operations. I have included responses on manuscripts when I received them and they were of general interest, but because of the nature of my questions and the fact that I directed the letters largely to heads of rare book collections, the information on manuscripts is sketchy and uneven. In my letter the topics and questions were listed in random order, as I did not want to impose a pattern on the responses. Though only one of my correspondents asked me not to quote what he had said (and in that single instance my correspondent asked that only one sentence be kept "off the record") I have omitted names in summarizing the responses to my questions. A listing of the 46 people whose replies were used is included at the end of this chapter. A further group apologized for being unable to respond and some simply sent printed materials: exhibition catalogues, press releases, acquisitions reports, unpublished and published annual reports, and the like.

The general picture of the library rare book world that emerges from these responses is considerably less austere than the one described in Ray's 1982 report, where the independent research library was seen to be in a more favorable position than rare book installations in hard-pressed academic institutions. Ray makes it clear that his 1982 talk was based on phone calls rather than the widely based survey of his earlier reports. It was also a piece prepared for the occasion in which his remarks about independent research libraries permitted him to end with richly deserved praise for an institution whose rare book activities stand out in any year, the Pierpont Morgan Library, and for its director, Charles Ryskamp. Ray also had only a limited amount of space to devote to libraries, because he again took on the larger world of the collector, dealer, and librarian. By restricting myself to the world of the rare book librarian and by including a wider range of kinds of libraries, I hoped to see whether the commonly accepted view of hard times is supported by the comments of people in the field. As will become clear, I got responses that documented the picture of hard times, especially in staffing (though since this was not one of the questions I asked, staff shortages emerged as a frequently mentioned additional concern). I also received a good many other letters painting a much rosier picture. My own view of the present situation in the rare book world has inevitably been colored by the state of health of the institution with which I am affiliated, the Library of Congress. In 1983 the dollar amounts available to the Rare Book and Special Collections Division for purchase (endowments, cash gifts, and budgeted funds) were by a generous margin the largest in the division's history and the resulting acquisitions of marked interest and variety. A good number of other libraries described institutional support that has permitted purchasing to move ahead energetically.

Though the topics I asked for responses on (as indicated in the headings throughout this chapter) were demanding enough, my correspondents often commented on further concerns. At the end of this chapter I will briefly discuss two additional concerns that seem to me to have general implications for libraries and the rare book world. In the course of the chapter I will also briefly describe some major gifts, purchases, and exhibitions reported by my correspondents.

Are Institutional Rare Book Budgets Increasingly Falling Behind?

The overwhelming response from my correspondents was that rare book budgets are not keeping up with inflation. Though my question did not specify whether I referred to the annual rate of inflation nationwide or to increases in book prices, the majority of my correspondents took my question to refer to book prices, which are seen to be increasing faster than the general rate of inflation. However, this state of affairs is not universally seen to be bad, as a comment from one of my correspondents makes clear:

> We are determined to live within our means, and in this day of easier access to rare books via microfilm (e.g., Research Publications back list, improved travel, *NUC Pre-1956,* better interlibrary cooperation, etc., etc.), we do not feel compelled to collect with catholicity. In fact, I'd say our awareness of our selectivity is increasing. The result is that we do not really feel our budget overstrained because we do not really set out to put it under strain. We try to let it do what it can for us, given today's market, our interests, and the constraints upon our Department's fund raising efforts imposed by the University.

Another institution reported that its special collections acquisitions budget is a "specified percentage of the library's total acquisitions budget and the latter has kept ahead of inflation throughout the [seven-year] period I have worked at [my university]." In one case support from other parts of the university has helped the budget situation:

> Since a good 25 percent of the titles coming into Special Collections are acquired by the various language and subject curators, we continue to be reasonably well supported. The book budget is carefully calculated to balance currency fluctuations and inflation with institutional needs and programs. In that context, the Provost has taken a thoughtful and considered approach to Library materials, and the Library as a whole has been able to maintain adequate buying levels. Cooperative arrangements . . . have further stretched acquisitions resources.

A curator who finds that "resources are not as plentiful as in the past" added, "When the need arises, we seem to be able to find the funds if the purchase can be justified." Friends of the Library groups and donors have made it possible for several institutions to keep purchasing, despite weak or nonexistent institutional budgets. However, in one institution having only endowment and gift funds, "The Library administration increased its charging of other costs to these restricted funds thereby reducing their accessibility for purchasing materials." A curator who buys very heavily in modern reference books remarked on the escalation in prices of books from scholarly presses, which he found "astounding."

How Powerful Is the Impact of the Private Collector on Library Buying?

This question brought forth more divergence of opinion than any other. Some correspondents dismissed the idea of competition, responding that "private collectors buy *for* us in the end," that libraries "profit significantly" from the private collector, or that "were it not for the private collector . . . there would . . . hardly be any rare book collection here." Noting that "private collectors have been the backbone of many institutional collections," another correspondent observed that:

> . . .collectors should be encouraged and helped by librarians whenever possible. Friends groups do a great deal for "established" collectors, but do we do enough for the young, beginning collectors? Do we make special efforts to identify them? To make them feel welcome? They are also the persons who might break new ground in collecting . . .

Another institution saw a less encouraging future:

> I would think the "new style" collector may be helping to inflate the prices of books. . . . When books are touted as investment properties and sold like any other *objet d'art,* obviously the price is going up beyond what a library can reasonably be expected to pay. And the conception of books as investment properties does not encourage the painstaking development of coherent collections that might be left to research libraries and form the basis of a useful, working collection.

This feeling of doubt about the future was underscored in another letter:

> . . . I suspect that collectors are no longer so eager as they once were to institutionalize their collections, and that the role of the collector in the building of an institution's collections may be declining.

Several correspondents noted "fierce" collector competition in the area of modern firsts and indicated their satisfaction that their institutions' interest lay elsewhere. A librarian from a university trying to build a modern literature collection reported "severe" competition from private collectors, to whom she had lost several small manuscript collections, and gave the following explanation of why some dealers in the modern literature field favor the private collector:

> . . . There is a chance [the collection] will come on the market and they can handle it again and institutions are not the steady customers they once were so we don't get enough quotes or advance copies of catalogs.

A vexed curator noted that it is in the field of modern firsts and literary manuscripts that the "private collector is reigning at the moment, and the impact on the library world . . . severe." He went on to say:

> A first in dust jacket of [William] Gaddis at $450 or James Merrill's *Short Stories* at $1,200 . . . is scarcely a research item, and the pricing of even minor figures has been quite unrealistic. We collect Bayard Taylor and E. C. Stedman because we have an endowment to do so, and I would expect our competition, especially for Stedman to be nil. However the going prices have increased to $150–$175. Taylor and Stedman are keeping pace with inflation in their way, but it is very hard on research-oriented libraries.

In framing the question about the impact of the private collector I had expected to receive multiple reports of collections lost to collectors. Only one other correspondent spoke of specific examples of competition:

> One very important reason for this upward trend in prices, I think, is the impact of wealthy private collectors who drive prices beyond all reason. This has occurred

to us in one area where we and only about three other institutions . . . have great strength. A single individual invaded the market in this area several years ago and has dominated it ever since. The prices he pays are so high that neither we nor the other institutions which collect in this field are competing.

Other reasons institutions gave for generally managing to avoid competition with collectors were that their collecting interests are "sufficiently obscure" so that they contend mainly with other institutions, and that they buy collections rather than individual high spots.

Is Good Material Drying Up?

The almost unanimous response to this question was, "I don't think good material is drying up at all," though one respondent immediately added, "although funds are." The sense of widespread availability comes across in the following comment on dealers' catalogues:

> [They] proliferate and have to be read on trips, in bed at night, at lunch, and while walking to work. I just counted the past several months' accumulation by my desk and this after distributing many to other librarians and faculty, and there are 110, many listing desirable material.

Though feeling that there is plenty of material out there to be bought, one person or another thought the following categories could be said to be drying up: Mormon Americana, Wing items, obviously famous works, illustrated editions of Ovid, and books on semeiology. Some who wrote recognized that their institutions' collections are so strong that it would be hard in any market to find books to fill the gaps.

One correspondent put forcefully what was implicit in responses from others:

> There is no question that earlier material is becoming more and more scarce, but one simply looks elsewhere when that's the case. When I stop finding "good material" then it is time to turn in my ALA card and move on to something else because I must be asleep on my feet. I have no problem spending my book budget.

Contrary to expectations, two of my correspondents noted that "some books have not increased or increased significantly" in price, though "finding them in quality examples is more difficult." More than one person observed that the sense of what constitutes good material is constantly expanding, in part because of the "increase in useful bibliographies and in bibliographical scholarship and consequent sophistication of dealers and curators" and in part because of a redefinition of "our ideas of what constitutes 'rare' material."

Are Some Areas So Overpriced and Worked Over That Institutions Are Avoiding Them?

Institutions with heavy concentrations of material in specific fields frequently responded that they intended to continue these specializations, "regardless of their current priciness but within . . . [their] ability to afford material." Further developing the same idea, a librarian from an institution having particularly defined collections observed:

If a library has . . . a commitment to certain areas . . . it cannot matter if the area is "exhausted," in a certain sense. . . . If things are wildly . . . overpriced we simply do not buy them; I am sure that we often pay more for many books than we ought, but we are in the business of acquiring material in certain well-defined areas and cannot stand and wait for the rare bargain. Since the long-term trend is toward higher prices my comfort is that whatever we buy today will cost more in the decades to come.

A representative of another institution having clear specializations responded to the question of "priciness" by saying:

I am, personally, not entirely certain what "overpriced" *means* any more. . . . Quite literally . . . the entire price structure for everything in our society seems to be undergoing a revolution that resembles the price revolution of the sixteenth century, and I don't know what standard of reasonableness to apply to anything.

Agreeing on the irrelevance of price as a determining factor in collection development, a representative of a major university wrote:

. . . The crucial issue for us is the nature of the need articulated by the faculty and our research constituency. The institution as a whole has demonstrated that it is prepared to support acquisitions in pricey fields where there is a definite need for those materials. . . .

Most of the people who responded to this question were less philosophical about price and designated the following areas in which their institutions were not collecting (when more than one person noted a field, the number is given in parentheses): modern firsts (4), history of science (3), early English literature (3), modern literary manuscripts (3), incunabula (3), illustrated books (3), early manuscripts, major color-plate books, Canadiana, revival of printing, illustrated modern press books, new press books, maps, science fiction, early calligraphy, natural history, *livres d'artiste*, Confederate imprints, Franklin, Darwin, and Jefferson. A representative of a well-known independent research library described withdrawing from fields that have grown too popular or pricey, "preferring to find new ones within our means." A director who "eschew[s] fashionable areas" described the following four "somewhat stubbly fields" his institution tries to "plow": pre-1861 American agriculture, natural history, education, and philosophy.

One librarian, looking to larger issues, observed that factors other than price may lead institutions to avoid collecting in certain areas:

The availability of holdings information through the NUC [National Union Catalog] and databases means that in a metropolitan area one can avoid costly duplication and readers can visit other libraries. . . . Major microfilm and facsimile publishing programs provide at least copies of many rare materials for scholars.

Carrying forward the same thought, a curator of an actively growing collection points out that the overpricing in many categories is being

"challenged" . . . by the publication of good facsimiles and microfilm collections. These . . . will never replace the originals, but for academic institutions that "need" research materials for scholars, there may well be more and more facsimiles and microfilm (and probably optical disk) publications available in the future.

Though most of my respondents directed their replies to overpricing, one new head picked up the words "worked over" in my question and observed wryly:

. . . I would be loathe to suggest that any of the areas in which we specialize is overworked. It is indeed my impression that all of them could stand far more serious scholarly attention than they now receive.

In the Face of Competition and High Prices Are Institutions Consciously Seeking to Move into New Collecting Areas?

The previous section's extensive listing of fields one library or another avoids could make bookdealers wonder what is left for some libraries to collect. Though a number of institutions reported changes in collecting policy, these shifts were more frequently into areas new for the institution rather than new or unusual for libraries. This moving out into relatively familiar territory followed from an often-expressed need to tie collection development to an institution's academic programs. A representative from a university with strong existing holdings wrote:

> . . . We collect to meet institutional needs and programs. To the extent that these change—and they do—we will move into new areas and perhaps out of older ones. New programs in science and technology and a general University commitment to bolster research in the humanities [have] opened up several fields for us which we are pursuing actively.

Another librarian in a similar university setting described the motivation for his trying to move into new collecting areas in this way:

> . . . The interests of students and faculty here are shifting. We are building our Spanish and Latin American material because of such a shift: for our general rare book collections we try to gather more social history.

The perception of a close relation between academic programs and special collections growth is equally true at a smaller university library where the curator is consulting with the faculty "to learn of their research interests and their students' needs."

Still, here as elsewhere, there is no consensus. Not all the university-based librarians who wrote feel that new areas of collecting specialization are desirable or inevitable. One of the institutions that has in the last 20 years had one of the largest budgets for book purchases reported that "no new directions are contemplated. . . . We have quite enough on our hands already." An institution that, to an outsider, seems to have carefully defined, if chronologically wide-ranging, collections is seen by its head as having "too much to keep up with in its rather diverse collecting areas deliberately to seek out new areas."

The principle of building on strength was put forward less frequently than I would have expected. A major independent research library, which does accept the principle, "rarely add[s] a new collecting field, preferring to build on established strength," though in this case the fact of having tremendously rich collections has not moved the institution to continue with "fields which have grown too popular or pricey. . . ." Indicating that "we are not seeking new areas in which to collect," a correspondent from a large university library stressed that his institution's policy has been "to build on strength, with some new but related areas that come naturally."

In one of the few letters that spoke of specific new possibilities, one enthusiastic curator asked the rare book world to:

> . . . look at the new fields—space travel, UFOs, topics once in the news every day such as Vietnam, and of course mystery and science fiction and fantasy, fad books like diet books, *ad infinitum*. . . . Surely every state university in this country should be collecting all the private press materials in their own states.

Other correspondents spoke of developing collections on the alternative press, postcard art, Dada, and genetics. Though I posed separate questions on new directions in collection development and on conscious efforts to move from overpriced and overworked fields into new collecting areas, the general sense of the responses is that not much is happening. However, a number of people spoke of the need for a "clearly thought out collection policy" and "newly defined directions within established emphases." One recently appointed curator commented on the financial implications of new collections, as perceived by the university administration:

> . . . My experience here suggests that, far from attempting to develop new areas of collecting interest, we have tended to retreat from accepting, even as gifts, collections that might force us into areas where we do not already have strong research materials on hand.

A veteran in the field did not need a crystal ball to come up with a view of the situation that agrees with the overall sense of the answers I received: "We are all pretty traditional in taste, and in subject interest. New authors for modern collectors, but not a lot of creative collecting among institutions."

Finally, another correspondent told me that he "usually do[es] not talk about new areas that we are developing." Presumably this curator feels that an imaginative new idea for collection development might quickly be taken up by other institutions and by private collectors. Possibly this is a view shared by others who wrote, accounting for the lack of specificity I have noted. This close-mouthed curator, himself head of a rare book program in a university library, described a view of collection development quite at variance with academic colleagues who tie their collection development closely to the curriculum:

> Whether or not all institutions are consciously seeking to move into collecting areas seems . . . to be less a matter of the institution than it is of the librarian or curator. The knowledge, vision, and energy of the person in charge may well be the key to developing new areas. Collection development policies are good, but people get books.

To What Extent Are Rare Book Installations Taking on Responsibility for Special Collections Having Research Potential but Very Little Market Value?

All rare book librarians in institutions with large and wide-ranging collections find themselves frequently having to say, when pressed to define a rare book, that even if an adequate definition could, in an inspired moment, be framed, that much of what is in their custody would not meet the definition. To get around this reality, the term "special collections" has come to replace or to be added to the names of many former rare book departments. The question I put to my correspondents assumed that virtually all rare book installations had groupings of materials, not individually valuable or necessarily difficult to obtain, but in the aggregate offering considerable potential for research. A staff member in one of the institutions to which I wrote found the question so incredible and the elitist implications of any other approach to collection building so distressing that he made it clear to his chief that his first reaction was not to respond at all. From the day 50 years earlier that his department was founded it has been accepting manuscript collections that exactly fill the description, and much of the strength of the collection can be traced to just such holdings.

In extenuation I should say that it seemed to me that to the extent that such material would be expected to cost relatively little, piece by piece at least, and that—by implication, given the realities of supply and demand—it would be little sought, it might present opportunities for consciously moving into new areas of collection development. The question, as this beginning makes clear, elicited a lively and divergent group of responses.

One curator, to what will undoubtedly be the incredulity of my irritated manuscript curator, saw no relevance to his situation:

> Special collections with research [potential] but little financial importance. I am not sure what these might be. Papers of local figures? Institutional archives? I cannot think of a collection we now have that would apply.

The head of a library not known for its collections of "lesser monetary value" responded to the concept by saying:

> Something as seemingly "worthless" as a full run of *TV Guide,* which will have, if it does not already, enormous research potential but certainly "little monetary value." I hope someone is collecting all the Harlequin romances and similar "junk." To sociologists, anthropologists, etc., of the future such stuff will be invaluable. Many of the most expensive items [my library] buys are so-called ephemera of the seventeenth and eighteenth centuries that nobody paid much attention to at the time. The sheer volume of the ephemera produced today makes it seem unlikely that it would ever be "rare"—but it could happen, especially considering the dreadful paper it's printed on.

Other institutional representatives described efforts to bring together collections dispersed at the time of receipt, now seen to have an integrity that makes them more useful when housed and serviced together, and major transfers from their libraries' open stacks:

> [My institution] has decided to treat all eighteenth century imprints as rare, and plans are being made to arrange for transfer to the Rare Books Division. . . . This is obviously a major development, and implementation of the new policy, which may entail the transfer of over 100,000 volumes from the main stacks, is being carefully planned.

The Library of Congress in early 1979 launched its first large-scale inventory of the General Collections in almost half a century. Recognizing that this inventory, which involves a comparison of every book against the shelf list, presented an opportunity not soon to be repeated, the Rare Book and Special Collections Division made a proposal, accepted by the library administration, that all pre-1801 books turned up in the inventory be transferred to the division's custody. The collection was at first housed in the security perimeters of the division but its size (30,000 volumes as of January 1984) has forced the division to move it to a somewhat less desirable area on decks at some distance from the Reading Room. In rescuing the collection and servicing it through the Rare Book Reading Room, the division has prevented the routine rebinding that was losing valuable evidence of binding structures, provenance, etc.; has markedly reduced the likelihood of theft; has instituted a kind of phased preservation of material formerly subjected to the hard life of the general stacks; and has given itself time to absorb the books into its collections and its catalogues.

The perception that books of earlier centuries having run-of-the-mill monetary value are frequently far more difficult to locate—and are in that sense "rarer"—than many accepted great rarities is far from new. Still, institutions have been slow to react to that knowledge. One of my correspondents, a recently appointed curator, described the situation at his library:

> We are slowly beginning to recognize a responsibility for materials now in the publicly accessible stacks that, because of age, fragility, irreplaceability, or other factors, are rendered liable to maltreatment if they are not used and read under supervision. Their monetary value is almost never a question for us; we do not . . . have a minimum dollar figure below which a stack book will not be transferred to Special Collections. . . . I would suspect, bearing in mind my own research orientation . . . this tendency is likely to increase; but eventually, of course, space limitations are going to pose us some delicate questions. On the whole . . . I think it fair to say that—long prior to my . . . arrival here—the Library had made a decision to place research value above monetary value in the specific issue of transfers from general to special collections; and that decision is one I am fully in agreement with.

Another curator expects this kind of moving of materials from the stacks into the rare book area to become more and more frequent "as major research collections age," but preferred "some indication of collection relevance and/or monetary value before assuming direct responsibility" for it. This correspondent saw an "out" in what she feels may become a more common feature in libraries, "a new storage facility where items can be designated as noncirculating—the facility is closed-stack with an on-site reading room."

Several librarians commented, not always with evident joy, on the responsibility that their rare book operations will increasingly have for pop culture. Though courses in pop culture "have no trouble in raising full enrollments . . . their trivia content brings trivia (trivial) requests to the library." A curator seeking an example of a category of book not now of academic interest proposed diet books and went on to say, "If you brought together all . . . the patent diet books since 1945 . . . would you not have a remarkable resource for students of various aspects of our society?" This librarian prophesied that rare book collections will be asked to take on more and more research collections of nontraditional material, ending up with the exhortation: "We must accommodate ourselves to the task or lose our claim to intellectual preeminence in the profession."

A rare book head who feels that rare book librarians are not taking enough responsibility for collections with lesser monetary value sees a problem:

> . . . The more ephemeral or less costly materials not yet gathered are difficult to find through regular channels precisely because there is little bibliographical control or established market for them. This means a library must be flexible enough to turn its curator loose to get out in the field to explore and locate such materials, but growing trends in administrative duties prevent such flexibility.

To round off this section and to put at rest the mind of the manuscript curator I referred to in its first paragraph, I would like to record that a number of correspondents wrote that they found the archives and papers their institutions have collected for years admirably fill their definition of research collections with little market value but large potential for scholarly research.

Have Institutions Acquired Any Collections So Large That They Present Administrative and Financial Problems?

Virtually all of the institutional representatives who responded to this question indicated that they had faced the problem of accepting or declining a collection that threatened to overtax the available space or the processing staff. Business archives and the papers of well-known political figures were frequently cited as the kinds of collections that present processing problems by virtue of their sheer size. One institution turned down a distinguished anthropologist's papers because "the Library would not have been able to accept and utilize that archive without several additional staff members."

Perhaps thinking back to the expansive days of the 1960s, a rare book head noted that in an earlier time getting a collection and then worrying about how to process and take care of it was not uncommon in special collections departments. Today, shrinking space and funds have forced people to think carefully before accepting enormous collections. Without specifying whether it applied to his situation this correspondent darkly noted that sometimes "the curator or librarian accepts a collection because higher administrators think, for a variety of reasons, it is a good idea." As an indication that others are also eyeing large collections carefully, an institutional representative described negotiations with an ongoing major learned society and noted that he hoped his institution wouldn't have to decline the donation, adding, "I think it would be irresponsible to take the archives and *then* be faced with the administrative and financial problems."

One head saw opportunities in accepting a large collection despite the "real headaches" that would follow. The resulting problems "might provide the stimulus to enlarge the library, something talked about for years. . . ." The head of a rare book library severely handicapped by staff shortages got her point across in ten words: "Any collection of any size poses a problem in processing." An independent research library described a solution others may be able to put to use. This institution quite successfully uses volunteers in its processing of large, complex collections. To make this possible the library provides training and supervision. My correspondent indicated that various projects involving 35 volunteers performing a wide range of tasks have been rewarding to the participants and beneficial to his institution. In another case the New York State legislature appropriated $250,000 to enable an institution to process the papers of a well-known senator. To the best of my correspondent's knowledge, this is the first time that a state legislature has helped to pay the expenses relating to the processing and housing of the papers of a U.S. senator.

The size of the collections some of my respondents described (1,200 cartons in one case) indicates the challenges processing sections face. One person, contending with a collection of trade catalogues, which represents for her institution a "major national responsibility," got her point across in only five words: "250,000 of anything presents problems." Despite the difficulties perceived, the general sense of the responses was positive, as indicated by a letter from a head faced with "a lot of material acquired in the last five years as part of an effort to enhance the rare book and manuscript collections":

Digesting this material will require internal and external funding, and I am optimistic about possibilities on both fronts. The acquisition of several large collections has, because of their very bulk, had a positive administrative effect in so far as they have encouraged us to think more in terms of non-traditional approaches to controlling them. The application of computer technology has been part of this approach; a re-examination of nostrums concerning rare book cataloging has been another.

To What Extent Do Gifts Determine New Collecting Specializations?

Fully aware of the importance of gifts to the development of the Library of Congress's rare book collections I had assumed that they were a determining factor in all rare book operations. That this is by no means the case is indicated by a response to this question, which I quote in full: "Gifts do not determine new collecting specializations." A curator in a large independent research library wrote, "We rarely take on a new field when we receive a gift," but qualified the statement, "unless purchase funds are included. . . ." In rejecting proffered materials, this same institution "often refer[s] out-of-scope gift offers elsewhere." The head of a large university rare book collection finds that "gifts can and have influenced collecting strategies" but notes that "the extent of the influence will be determined by the extent to which the gift coincides with institutional goals." When gifts are accompanied by endowments, "these can have an additional impact depending on their nature and size." Another major rare book installation recognizes that gifts entail a "commitment to continue developing that field," and its representative cited three collections that are currently actively being developed.

Amusingly, an institution that regretfully reported that it had "never gotten a large enough gift of books to bring up that question" is named for the donor whose collections today determine the direction of its growth. Another institution whose rare book collections are particularly identified with a recent gift doubted that future gifts, unless of great size, would determine collecting specializations: "We must hew to the curators' research and exhibit needs most of the time."

These exceptions aside, most of my respondents, many of them representing smaller rare book collections, found that gifts "obviously" determine collecting specializations and do so "a lot." One institution's holdings are a "collection of collectors' collections." A major independent research library with carefully defined collecting scope is managing to take in gifts and control its coverage by accepting "gifts of any sort with an understanding with a donor that we will deal with the material as best suits [us]. . . . We keep only the material that fits already established collecting policies."

Only two of my respondents spoke more than passingly of an institution's obligations and commitments to donors. I find this surprising, since in my work at the Library of Congress and earlier at Washington University in St. Louis I have seen great advantages to accepting and developing gifts. It is true that very few consequential book gifts cannot in some useful way be related to the very broad collecting responsibilities of an institution like the Library of Congress. In the recently launched series of separate custodial division acquisitions reports, one can see that the Rare Book and Special Collections Division of the Library of Congress makes a practice in reporting recent acquisitions to describe the larger collections they support (the division's 1980 report was published in 1982 and its report covering 1981–1982 in 1984). Because so many of the division's strengths are solidly based on gifts, these short descriptive essays acknowledge the contributions made by donors, living and dead, and have as their aim to revitalize gifts, many of which might with the passage of time otherwise disappear from public notice. If past donors are neglected or passed over, what inducement have prospective donors to turn over their collections to an apparently ungrateful institution?

Are Institutions Finding Themselves in Active Competition for the Same Collections?

In framing this question I took as a premise that if the supply of books was indeed shrinking that there might well be increasing competition for books and manuscripts, whether in the hands of collectors or in dealers' stocks. Most of my correspondents assumed that the question referred exclusively to gifts and to competition at the local level. One person saw this situation as so much a part of rare book operations that he led off: "[Competing] for the same donors. . . . What else is new?" The same sense of competition being a fact of rare book life came across in the comment: "[We compete] every time we go after a major gift; it's the nature of the trade, is it not?" A third rare book head finds institutional competition "unfortunate" but a "fact of life. . . ." Several curators described ways in which they are trying to deal with the situation at local levels. In one state:

> . . .Curators of several special collections meet frequently, out of which has developed cooperative collection development policies that are working. We continue to refine these policies. Such cooperation has been instrumental in reducing duplication; in advising potential donors about the best homes for their collections (no donor likes to be turned down flat, so a good suggestion is often accepted warmly); and in helping scholars use collections in other institutions.

A curator in another state described meetings at which institutions get together "to learn each other's collections and to reach informal agreements about collecting emphases." Though this has worked "fairly well" for printed books, "it doesn't work at all [for local history collecting] since that is usually a matter of the feelings of the donors." Within another state smaller historical societies and public libraries have become active collectors of manuscripts, offering more and more competition to a large, long-established institution. The competition is made even more threatening by the fact that "many donors like the idea of manuscripts remaining in the community to which they pertain." This correspondent reported competition even within his university, which has "allowed its Law School and Medical School each to begin an archives-manuscripts-rare books operation."

Some who wrote commented on competing at one time or another for the purchase of rare books and manuscripts. A particularly active rare book head found little competition from collectors or institutions in the purchase of collections: "There is more material than money around now." This same sense that the time is favorable, for some at least, emerged in a letter from an institution collecting Americana, the head of which finds the situation less difficult than it had been earlier, because "many of our colleagues have not had the funds to actively buy the kind of material that we do." The dealer is seen by one institution to be in the position of determining, in many cases, which of two competing institutions should be offered material first: "Dealers call this 'finding a good home.' "

In a city having two active rare book libraries with overlapping collections the staff talks "from time to time about material coming up at auction, to insure that we [are] not needlessly bidding against one another." Otherwise my correspondent buys:

> books in our period even if [the other library] does have them if they are "moderately" priced, say up to $500. . . . The realities of research require that we do acquire books that [the other library] may already have; much "discovery" comes from having a number of related texts at hand. Stopping one's work and driving across town . . . to look at a particular book that fits in with other books already at [our library] rather diverts one's creative and scholarly attention.

What Are the Major Gifts, Purchases, Exhibitions, and Celebrations of 1983?

When I accepted the editor's invitation to write about the activities of rare book libraries in 1983 I assumed that gathering information on purchases, gifts, exhibitions, and celebrations would be the easiest part of my assignment. The generosity of the response to my "questionnaire" soon made it clear how many other matters needed to come first in my summary and how comparatively little I would be able to cover in this section. To be in any way fair to those who took the time to provide so much valuable information, I have had to limit my coverage to the responding institutions. Even with that restriction I can do no more than touch on some of the highlights.

In this section the cloak of anonymity has no place. In one of the first letters I received, Helen Butz, reporting for the University of Michigan, articulated the problem I would face: " 'Major' is, of course, a relative term, depending on where one stands." That beauty is in the eye of the beholder should be no surprise, nor should I have been surprised by other characteristics of the responses. A curator familiar with a field, or who has recently done his homework, or who has in front of him a detailed description from a dealer, or who has been looking for a book for years to fill in a gap will understandably be excited by an acquisition. However, merely putting this book in an exhibit case or listing it with numerous other books in a general response to a letter isn't going to bring it alive for the viewer or for the reader running his eye down a list. As a great believer in the value of lively captions and descriptions that try to relate an acquisition to larger institutional goals, I felt an immediate, positive response to the report received within a few days of my mailing my letter from that veteran publicist, Edwin Wolf 2nd:

> The acquisitions I am most proud of are: Holbrook's *North American Herpetology,* Philadelphia, 1836–40 (all four volumes; LC lacks the last); Carson, *Illustrations of Medical Botany,* Philadelphia, 1847 (a vastly underrated color plate book); an unrecorded issue of Saur's Bible, Germantown, 1743; *Politicorum sive Civilis Doctrina Libri Sex,* Leyden, 1634 (Byrd of Westover's copy); Leslie, *A New and Exact Account of Jamaica,* London, 1739 (important addition to Afro-Americana); Franklin, *Mémoire sur la Vie,* Paris, 1818 (with MS corrections and additions made from the original AMS contemporaneously); Kircher, *Specula Melitensis,* Messina, 1638 (one of the very few books by Kircher we do not have); and over 3,500 aerial photographs of Philadelphia and vicinity by Virgil Kauffman, a pioneer in the field.

Wolf's brief, packed summary provides enough information to identify the book, gives the reader a clear idea of why the acquisition is important to the institution, and carries the personal stamp of the curator. Of course, I received other fine reports and single out Edwin Wolf's response only to make a point.

Some correspondents didn't distinguish between gifts and purchases, which takes us back to my earlier grumble about institutions' failing to give donors the credit and the attention they deserve. Curators who hadn't done as well as they might have wished in 1983 frequently sent me information for earlier years. Though I was glad to have these reports, my assignment is 1983 and it is to the activities of that year that I will turn.

One purchase of 1983 requires an exception to my policy of including only information received in response to my questionnaire. The July 12, 1983, *New York Times* described the New York Public Library's jubilation at obtaining a superb group of Herman Melville manuscripts: a 30-page "First Draught" of *Typee,* letters written by Melville, and 300 family letters. The *New York Times* article conveys the excitement and the importance of this acquisition: "Scholars' mouths are watering, says Public Library's president happily." Considering the rarity of Melville manuscript material, he had good reason to be happy.

Paul Koda reported that the University of North Carolina, Chapel Hill, has purchased an extensive collection of the books and manuscripts of Michael Sadleir, author, bibliographer, and publisher, including Sadleir's collection of the works of W. E. Henley, 124 books from Sadleir's publishing and bookselling library, and the remaining papers, manuscripts, proofs, letters, books, and ephemera. William Cagle, commenting on purchases for the Lilly Library of Indiana University, singled out as the "most exciting addition" the collection of Scottish books and manuscripts before the Union in 1707 acquired from the Scottish antiquarian booksellers Kulgin Duval and Colin Hamilton, "though the Vita Sackville-West/Harold Nicolson correspondence runs a close second." Decherd Turner, reporting for Texas, listed as his institution's "more memorable additions":

> *The Suite Vollard,* one hundred etchings created by Picasso between 1930 and 1937. The Kelmscott *Chaucer* printed on vellum. One of thirteen copies . . . Archival collections . . . of Samuel Beckett, J. Frank Dobie, Alfred Jarry, Timothy Leary, Nicholas Nabokov, Joanna Southcott, Dylan Thomas, Parker Tyler, and Tennessee Williams. Theatre Arts materials . . . , 3,400 television scripts, and the last section of the Gloria Swanson materials. Sections of personal libraries[:] . . . 125 copies from the personal library of Wyndham Lewis, and 250 volumes from the personal library of Edward Gordon Craig.

The University of Pennsylvania's major purchases primarily included additions to its Aristotle Collection; Emory University added books and manuscripts to its W. B. Yeats/Lady Gregory Collection; the Huntington Library purchased a history of early chemistry collection and works of the Fourth Earl of Chesterfield; the James Ford Bell Library made a "very significant" acquisition: Jan Huygen van Linschoten's *Itinerario, ofteschipvaert naer Oost ofte Portugaels Indien* (Amsterdam: Cornelius Claeszoon, 1595–1596); Washington University purchased one of ten copies, not for sale, of Robert Creeley's *Mabel; a Story,* with 12 original etchings by Jim Dine; the Gleeson Library of the University of San Francisco purchased William P. Barlow, Jr.'s collection of the Daniel Press, "perhaps the finest in the U.S."; the Free Library of Philadelphia added a December 6, 1839, letter of Edgar Allan Poe, written while he was living in Philadelphia. The University of Tulsa purchased a 2,400-volume nineteenth-century lending library of English fiction (mainly three-deckers) and the library of Sir Rupert Hart-Davis, strong in, among others, first editions and association copies of T. S. Eliot, William Plomer, Edmund Blunden ("the finest collection in private hands"), Siegfried Sassoon, Oscar Wilde, and Max Beerbohm. The task of summarizing major acquisitions is an invidious one, and I regret having to omit far too many acquisitions that are in anyone's definition major.

Stephen Ferguson, writing on behalf of Princeton University's diverse rare book collections, reported that "the past 12 to 18 months have provided such a harvest of accessions that we managed to put together an entire issue of the *Chronicle* on new acquisitions" (Autumn 1983 issue of the *Princeton University Library Chronicle*). Instead of the single, major acquisition typical of "millionth-volume" celebrations, the University of North Carolina at Chapel Hill received as its three-millionth volume 300 books produced and published by the Estienne family, the distinguished sixteenth-century printers. This truly "major" gift was made by the John Wesley and Anna Hodgin Hanes Foundation for the Study of the Origin and Development of the Book, which celebrated earlier landmarks in the library's history by important, single gifts. The Estienne Collection was formed by Fred Schreiber, a New York rare book dealer, whose detailed catalogue serves as a permanent record of his accomplishment in assembling the books.

Bryn Mawr College published a catalogue of a collection given to the library in 1983, *Bookbinding in America 1680–1910: From the Collection of Frederick E. Maser* (Bryn Mawr College Library, 1983). The Maser Collection contains more than 400 volumes ranging in date from the seventeenth to the twentieth century. James Hart, director of the Bancroft Library, forwarded a report from his rare book librarian, Anthony Bliss, describing a series of important gifts from Charlotte and Norman Strouse dealing with the art and history of the book. The Strouse gifts include a substantial grouping of books and ephemera relating to T. J. Cobden-Sanderson, the Doves Press, and the Doves bindery. The "star pieces" are 13 Cobden-Sanderson personal bindings. Bliss's report described other Strouse gifts: a complete collection of the Gregynog Press, an Ashendene Press Collection, including dozens of original woodblocks, and a collection of all the publications of the Kelmscott Press, as well as pre-Kelmscott Morris, material on Wm. Morris & Co., and Morrisiana.

Pennsylvania State received as its major gift a collection of Arnold Bennett. Princeton University was given a "beautiful copy of the Sha Nameh. This manuscript is certainly the most valuable single book given to the Library in the past 10 years." The George and Frances Ball Foundation gave the Lilly Library the Elizabeth W. Ball Collection of historical children's books, a portion of which was donated to the Morgan Library in the 1960s. The portion which Miss Ball retained, which has now been given to the Lilly Library, comprises 13,000 books and manuscripts. Washington University received as the gift of the mother of the contemporary American poet James Merrill copies of all his books inscribed to her and to his grandmother, including two rare modern books, *Jim's Book* and *The Black Swan*. Three manuscripts of "outstanding importance" came to the Pierpont Morgan Library as the bequest of Clara Sargent Peck, including a *Livre de la Chasse,* described in the library's press release as representing a "high point in the rich mediaeval tradition of picturing the hunt." The Morgan manuscript was made in Paris, about 1410, by the workshop of the Bedford Master and contains 87 painted miniatures. The three manuscripts were placed on display not long after their receipt, an unusual step for the Morgan and a further indication of their importance.

John Lancaster, writing from Amherst, reported that he and Ruth Mortimer, co-editors of the *Papers of the Bibliographical Society of America,* have commissioned a review article on exhibition catalogues in rare book libraries and collections. The article (not published at the time of this writing) found a "surprising number" of institutions that hadn't done any catalogues for years and other libraries that aren't names on the tips of people's tongues that had put out quite a few. As a generalization, "there seems to be a falling off in the production of such catalogues, and a tendency to use cheaper, slimmer checklists."

The exhibit that created perhaps the greatest rare book excitement in 1983 was *The Beinecke Rare Book and Manuscript Library: The First Twenty Years.* Gordon Ray's above-mentioned 1982 comment on the threat "to the privileged status of the rare book collections in two or three great libraries" was understood by this writer, and presumably by others, to include the Beinecke Library. The Beinecke Library exhibit and the brilliant invitational party that launched it constituted for many observers a double celebration: the successful completion of the first 20 years of the Beinecke Library and its being, as one of my correspondents put it, "back on the map in a big way."

The Folger Shakespeare Library celebrated its fiftieth anniversary with an exhibition and accompanying catalogue, *Gifts in Honor of the 50th Anniversary.* The Winter 1983 issue of the *Book Collector* describes some of the finest of the gifts received in commemoration of the event. The Humanities Research Center honored the centennial of the founding of the University of Texas at Austin by sending one of its volumes of the Gutenberg Bible on tour to 18 Texas towns. The entire issue of the *Library Chronicle,* new series, Number 24, is devoted to the Humanities Research Center's very popular exhibit *Gone with the Wind: A Legend Endures.* The Houghton Library's catalogue, *Luther 1483–1983* (Harvard College Library, 1983), was the most ambitious of the Luther exhibits mounted by the institutions reporting. The catalogue has at the end a "List of Sixteenth-Century Editions of the Works of Martin Luther in the Harvard University Library." The Morgan Library's principal exhibit of 1983 was *Holbein and the Court of Henry VIII,* featuring 70 drawings and one portrait miniature by Hans Holbein the Younger on loan from the collection of H. M. Queen Elizabeth II. The *APHA Letter,* Number 56, 1983, contains an account of a more specialized exhibit the Morgan mounted devoted to Belle da Costa Greene, the library's first director.

President and Mrs. Reagan attended the opening of the Library of Congress's major exhibit in 1983, *The American Cowboy.* United Technologies Corporation made possible the design and installation of the ambitious exhibit and the publication of its 228-page catalogue. A sentence from the exhibit's press release indicates the special character of the show and the challenges the exhibit staff faced in mounting the 370 pieces:

> Three-dimensional objects range from an 1866 chuck box and 1870s barbed wire to a 1940-style Seeburg Wall-o-matic jukebox (on which visitors will hear cowboy songs) and a pair of colorful porcelain cowboy boots made in 1980.

The University of Virginia continued its tradition of mounting a number of exhibits each year. In 1983 the library sent out keepsakes associated with exhibits of the work of Warren Chappell; "Formerly in the Possession of," an exhibit of books from the libraries of William Byrd II, Landon Carter, Thomas Jefferson, and their Virginia contemporaries; and "The Art of Lafcadio Hearn." The Bailey/Howe Library of the University of Vermont produced a catalogue for its exhibit of one of its principal special collections, *Charles Whittingham, Printer, 1795–1876,* and Ohio State University a catalogue for its centennial exhibition of the work of Dard Hunter, *The Compleat Bookman* (Ohio State University Libraries, 1983).

Additional Concern I: Book Fairs and Library Purchases

If the reports that appear in the trade journals of the almost total absence of librarians from antiquarian book fairs (at least as purchasers) seem to support the view that libraries are not buying, I think these statistics cannot be taken as a barometer of the rare book library field. Though this is not a question I asked, and though only one person commented (with some unhappiness) on antiquarian book fairs, I have over the years asked many colleagues how useful they find book fairs and have gotten an almost uniform response: "Not at all for buying books, though they are a good place to meet people and to get a sense of dealers' stocks." In my own case I cannot carry around the Library of Congress's holdings in my head and am reluctant to ask a dealer to take a book off display for the duration of the fair and then to quote it on the chance the library may not have it.

Because so much is said about other dealers buying all the good books and any bargains before a fair opens, there is also a psychological aspect of book fairs not to be overlooked. Unlike most private collectors, rare book librarians have wide collecting responsibilities and usually can pick and choose among possibilities. They also have obligations to their institutions not to pay more than the market justifies. My correspondents make it clear that in areas in which institutions have major strengths, the priciness of a field will not keep them from buying. However, the price of a *particular* book will hold back a rare book librarian and may especially do so at a book fair, as the need for instant decision is not advantageous to an institutional purchaser.

Where at a book fair does he or she find the auction records, dealers catalogues, and institutional files that indicate whether a price being asked is a favorable or an unfavorable one? Where can he or she determine how many libraries in his or her city or state have copies? Rather than assume that the dearth of library purchasers at book fairs indicates that librarians are lacking in energy, enthusiasm, and funds, I would say that book fairs are not for them nearly as promising an acquisitions medium as direct quotations, phone calls, visits to bookshops, and catalogues, to name four of the long-established avenues of communication between libraries and the antiquarian book trade.

Additional Concern II: Use of Rare Book Collections

Though my correspondents wrote me about a number of concerns not specifically addressed in my questions (preservation, automated cataloguing system changes and resulting time losses for cataloguers, administrators' willingness to provide money for new collections but not for staff to catalogue important existing resources, bibliographical control, and so on), an underlying concern, not always stated in these words, is "justifying our existence." Knowing that administrators frequently measure the success of a rare book operation by its use, my correspondents are "making an effort to bring in classes and groups," are "meeting with . . . faculty to learn of their research interests and their students' needs," are "collecting in additional areas," and are in general trying to broaden their base of support. A curator in a private university finds that use by her own faculty is poor and is trying to change that situation, recognizing that unless her department increases its use, "our arguments will fall on deaf administrative ears."

One of my correspondents criticized librarians who respond to their administrators' concerns about use by relying on "newest-is-best, more rather than how" philosophy. This concerned and outspoken curator finds that rare book librarians patronize "plain" librarians and talk glibly about "collection strengths" and "highspots" without addressing any of "the serious questions that might well be raised regarding the place of rare books in the academic library. . . . I don't see anyone doing damnall about any of them." In his October 1983 *Wilson Library Bulletin* article, "Rare Book Collections: The Need for Interpretation," Daniel Traister came to a similar conclusion: "I do not think we yet know ourselves what it is we want our collections to be or to do. What, then, can we say to others?"

On the evidence of what has been said so far, 1983 could, in this fundamental area, be seen as the year of questioning, not answering.

And yet there are people who are thinking seriously about the future use of their collections. One of my correspondents wonders if in regularly using the burgeoning (and clearly valuable) collections of facsimiles and microforms future scholars will become "satisfied" with these formats and get out of the habit of using originals. If certain skills are lost, the importance of originals will inevitably diminish. As foreign-language skills decline and are replaced by other skills like using a computer, how much will special collections operations, many of them solidly based on European books and manuscripts, suffer? What will it mean for the future use of special collections and of the skills needed to use them that fewer graduate students who traditionally use rare materials in areas like English, the classics, and foreign languages will be coming out of our universities? As the means of communication change because of television and computers, "will the scholarly 'value' of original books and texts diminish in the eyes of administrators, thereby reducing funds and accessibility even more?" The indicated need to build and rebuild constituencies may, in this thoughtful curator's eyes, be less important for:

> "use" statistics than it is for the future of scholarship to insure the handing down, in the best way possible, the past to the future. [This] may be the biggest challenge we face.

Surely that is the appropriate valedictory note on which to end.

Respondents Whose Replies Were Used in Writing This Report

Julius Barclay
University of Virginia

George M. Barringer
Georgetown University

John Buechler
University of Vermont

Helen S. Butz
University of Michigan

William R. Cagle
Indiana University

Edward C. Carter II
American Philosophical Society

D. Steven Corey
University of San Francisco

Ellen S. Dunlap
Rosenbach Museum and Library

David Farmer
University of Tulsa

Donald Farren
University of Maryland

Stephen Ferguson
Princeton University

Chad J. Flake
Brigham Young University

Joan M. Friedman
Yale Center for British Art

Johanna Goldschmid
San Francisco Public Library

Vesta Lee Gordon
University of Georgia

Holly Hall
Washington University

James D. Hart
University of California, Berkeley

Dean H. Keller
Kent State University

Paul S. Koda
University of North Carolina

Marie E. Korey
Free Library of Philadelphia

John Lancaster
Amherst College

Mary S. Leahy
Bryn Mawr College

Marcus A. McCorison
American Antiquarian Society

Charles W. Mann
Pennsylvania State University

Alexandra Mason
Kenneth Spencer Research Library
University of Kansas

Linda M. Matthews
Emory University

R. Russell Maylone
Northwestern University

Robert Nikirk
The Grolier Club

Frank Paluka
University of Iowa

John Parker
James Ford Bell Library
University of Minnesota

Nora J. Quinlan
University of Colorado at Boulder

Michael T. Ryan
Stanford University

John L. Sharpe III
Duke University

Samuel A. Streit
Brown University

Elizabeth A. Swaim
Wesleyan University

Lola L. Szladits
Berg Collection
New York Public Library

Robert A. Tibbetts
Ohio State University

Daniel Traister
University of Pennsylvania

Decherd Turner
University of Texas

Evert Volkersz
State University of New York at
    Stony Brook

Ellen B. Wells
Smithsonian Institution

James M. Wells
Newberry Library

Thomas M. Whitehead
Temple University

Edwin Wolf 2nd
Library Company of Philadelphia

Thomas F. Wright
William Andrews Clark Memorial Library
University of California, Los Angeles

Stanley Yates
Iowa State University

6

Institutional Collections in Canada

Richard Landon

In 1983 a book, albeit a rather special book, assumed its rightful place as the most valuable work of art ever sold at public auction. The price paid for the Gospels of Henry the Lion—£8.14 million ($11.7 million)—astonished even the most sanguine observers of the rare book and manuscript market, and the effect of such a price on the market in general will be a matter for much speculation and debate. We are told by economic forecasters that the recession is over, although, perhaps typically, the Canadian pundits have been more cautious than their U.S. colleagues; and it still remains a fact of life for collectors of books and manuscripts in Canada, whether institutional or personal, that the Canadian dollar is trading at approximately 80¢ in U.S. funds. Although the strength of the U.S. dollar compared to the major European currencies results in the Canadian dollar also being strong in an international sense, much of the material most desired by Canadian collectors is either available only from U.S. dealers or appears in British catalogues priced in U.S. funds. This specific weakness of the Canadian dollar erodes considerably the acquisition budgets of Canadian institutions.

It seems a cliché to say that Canada is a very large country, for in the context of rare books and manuscripts this is true only in the geographical sense. The rare book world in Canada is very small and very scattered. There are perhaps a dozen really significant institutional collections in Canada, concentrated for the most part in Toronto, Montreal, and Ottawa, with the rest scattered across the country. There are some very good collections of Canadiana, often focused on local history and literature, but few are of international scope and importance. Canada is a country of regions, divided not only by geographical distance but also by language, cultural tradition, and religious history. It is also a country obsessed in recent years by the definition of its identity. The basic question, expressed in an oversimplified way, has been "How are Canadians different from other nationalities, specifically Americans?"—a question neither very positive nor very easy to answer. When an agency of the federal government uses a phrase such as "of national importance" it is often understood as "of regional significance." These general circumstances make it extremely difficult for any single person to form valid opinions about what has been happening in the world of rare books and manuscripts in any general Canadian sense. The view from Toronto is not the same as the view from Vancouver or Quebec City or Halifax.

FUNDING THROUGH SPECIAL PROGRAMS

Institutional spending trends for antiquarian books and manuscripts are difficult to document. It seems generally true that university library collection budgets have come under great pressure from a combination of funding cutbacks and rising prices of new books and periodical subscriptions. One hears rumors of university libraries in both Canada and the United States that have ceased to acquire retrospective materials at all, but this kind of information does not appear in annual reports. Antiquarian book dealers maintain that there has been a sharp decrease in institutional spending over the past ten years; the number of institutions actively participating in the market has decreased and those still active spend less. Special collections departments have certainly had to rely more and more on outside funding of various kinds, and the percentage of regularly budgeted collection funds allocated to rare books and manuscripts has decreased.

Many of the significant institutional collections of books and manuscripts in Canada are owned by universities, and the responsibility for the control and financing of education in Canada, including higher education, rests with the provincial governments. Individual collections may have private endowments for acquisitions and depend a great deal on gifts of material and money to support their acquisitions programs, but the financial responsibility for processing, housing, and staffing the collections is that of the university through its system of provincial grants. All the universities in Canada have been seriously affected over the past several years by inflation, inadequate government support, and the reaction to the boom of the 1960s. Thus the rare books and special collections departments have suffered at least to the same degree as their parent institutions and, in some cases, have borne more than their share of fiscal stringency. This rather gloomy situation has not, however, rendered these collections stagnant. The skills, born of necessity, to develop new sources of funding and to exploit more carefully the traditional sources have been cultivated to some considerable effect.

The federal government of Canada does participate directly in the development of special collections through two programs. The Social Sciences and Humanities Research Council of Canada has established a Specialized Research Collections program to support the research collections of university libraries in the humanities and social sciences. Originally the guidelines specified that this funding would be available to strengthen further the strongest collections in the country that were of recognized national significance. If an institution, for instance, wished to apply for support of a collection of Renaissance Italian literature or a collection of the works of Samuel Johnson, it was incumbent upon the institution to demonstrate that its collection was the best one in Canada. Although this kind of demonstration was comparatively simple for some very specialized collections, it proved much more difficult for more general areas of research, and the old problem of "national significance" had to be faced.

The new guidelines have amended the concept of national significance to include collections of both local material and universal content and state explicitly that the term "national" is not meant to be understood in a political sense.* A specialized collection is stated as one recognized by its own library as a resource for graduate or comprehensive research. Thus two strong collections in the same field but located in different areas of the country may both be eligible for support. Practically, it seems that any institution, whether large or small, that possesses a decent special collection of books and can meet the application criteria is likely to receive a grant. These criteria include evidence of a continuing financial commitment to the collection by the institution, an understanding that the material purchased will be made available through cataloguing and be accessible to researchers, and an assurance that a significant number of faculty and students are working in the field. Each institution is limited to grants totaling $50,000 per year, although this amount could be in the form of one grant or several. Three years are allotted to spend the money, and a report of purchases must be submitted at the end of the grant period.

Most of the material acquired by institutions through this program consists of what might be loosely termed rare books. Indeed, the guidelines state explicitly that "rare books are considered by the Council to be the indispensable basis for research in many fields." The scope for purchase of manuscripts and archival material (other than large collections of papers) is much more restricted. The council will, however, consider manuscripts that are to be added to an already existing research collection of books and views with favor manuscript collections on microforms.

It is safe to say that every university in Canada has taken advantage of this program over the past few years and that even these comparatively small amounts of money have considerably encouraged institutional collecting. Often a collection that had atrophied because of funding cutbacks has been revived through a Specialized Research Collections grant, perhaps as much from the required institutional commitment as from the grant itself. In 1983, for example, the University of Toronto received a grant for the history of the physical sciences during the Renaissance, a field in which the university had been collecting extensively over the last 15 years.

Every special collections library in Canada collects Canadiana, often on a relatively large scale, and in this one area the Social Sciences and Humanities Research Council has also been much more restrictive. To collect Canadiana exhaustively, both history and literature, is the mandate of the National Library of Canada, a federally funded institution. Thus the council will not fund general Canadiana collections, although it will consider applications for strengthening specialized areas within the field of Canadiana.

The Social Sciences and Humanities Research Council also sponsors a program called Fleeting Opportunities, whereby support is offered to university libraries to acquire material that suddenly becomes available on the market and for which no budgetary provision has been made. Up to $10,000 per year, which must be matched by the institution, is available, and the same criteria apply as for the Specialized Research Collections grants. As desirable material becomes unexpectedly available almost every day, very little imagination is required for an institution to benefit from this program.

---

*Support to Specialized Collections: Guidelines . . . (Ottawa: Social Sciences and Humanities Research Council of Canada, 1983).

TAX INCENTIVES

Federal legislation also contributes indirectly to the growth of special collections in Canadian institutions, in a very important way, through tax incentives. In 1975 a Cultural Property Export and Import Act, analogous to legislation that has existed in many countries for some time, was established to protect the national cultural heritage.* Originally, the thrust of the legislation was aimed at preventing the export of Canadian art (particularly the arts of the native peoples), archeological artifacts, and the kinds of objects considered part of the national heritage. It also contains a provision whereby cultural property that meets the criteria for national importance — whether or not the property is explicitly Canadian — and is donated to an institution designated a Class A repository, enables the donor to obtain tax benefits up to 100 percent of taxable income with no capital gains tax applied. In addition, an individual who sells an important piece of cultural property to a designated institution is given relief from capital gains tax. The Control List, which is part of the act, contains a section called "Books, Records, Documents, Photographs, Films, Recordings" and sets out general criteria for the national importance of such material. Books and manuscripts, as well as other kinds of cultural property, are subject to the scrutiny of a Review Board, must have two independent evaluations if the object or collection is worth more than $5,000, and can be subject to the opinion of an expert examiner as to their national importance. Applications for certification of books and manuscripts are most often submitted for collections (including, for instance, the papers of living authors), and disputes are normally confined to the question of what constitutes fair market value of material for which an established market does not exist.

Cumbersome as the process sounds, in fact it works remarkably well, and the incentive for private collectors to donate books and manuscripts to institutions is a powerful one. The antiquarian book dealers objected to the legislation from the beginning on the grounds that it gave institutions an unfair advantage when dealing with private collectors. They continue to be incensed by the provision for capital gains relief for sales to designated institutions, a provision from which they are specifically excluded.

Individual Canadians can, of course, benefit from gifts-in-kind to any institution that can issue charitable receipts (normally up to 20 percent of taxable income), and books that might not qualify as cultural property of national importance are given to most institutions in this way. Indeed, it is possible for U.S. citizens to give material to Canadian institutions and receive U.S. tax relief, but only if the Canadian institution has a registered charitable association in the United States to act for it, for example, the University of Toronto Associates, Inc., in New York.

ACQUISITIONS AND COLLECTION DEVELOPMENT

With all this supportive legislation, what are the institutions doing themselves to enhance their collections, to make them known to interested scholars, and to preserve them for the scholars of the future? The collecting policies of special collections departments in universities, in municipal, provincial, and federal agencies, in public

---

*An Introduction to the Cultural Property Export and Import Act, prepared by Duncan Cameron (Ottawa: Department of Communications, 1980).

libraries, and in the few independent research institutions vary widely and often are not committed to paper. The trends, if they can be accurately described at all in Canada, seem to indicate that over the past decade a greater emphasis on special collections for research is discernible in institutions with large general collections, although the financial support for these collections often has to be sought outside the institutions. It has been noticed in the antiquarian book trade that during 1983 the pattern of purchasing has been altered from the regular and consistent buying of the past to the spending of larger amounts of money in short periods of time, and this is attributed to the phenomenon known as "institutional fall-in." Although the fiscal years of institutions vary considerably, unspent portions of budgets that remain toward the end of a fiscal year often cannot be carried over into the next year and must be spent quickly. The alert special collections librarian or archivist can often take advantage of this temporary embarrassment of riches through a prior knowledge about where desirable material might be located.

Canadian special collections departments make known the presence of their books and manuscripts to the local and international scholarly communities in the usual variety of ways. Machine-readable cataloguing from several institutions is put into databases and is available online or in the form of COM (computer output microform) catalogues. Many special collections departments, however, have substantial backlogs of uncatalogued books and files of unconverted records, and often special materials have to be searched for in the departments themselves. A special problem is the handling of ephemera, because although departments are more appreciative of the institutional responsibility to collect and preserve ephemera, few, if any, have developed adequate methods of arranging and listing them.

Exhibitions of special collections are used to an increasing extent as a method of making unfamiliar material known to the general community. Unfortunately, catalogues, with a few exceptions, are not produced for all exhibitions and their record is thus lost. Some libraries lend items to other institutions and achieve a wider exposure for their treasures. For example, the Thomas Fisher Rare Book Library of the University of Toronto has books displayed in exhibitions at four other institutions at the moment, including the Silk Roads, China Ships exhibition of the Royal Ontario Museum, which is currently touring North America.

The universal problem of the permanent preservation of the printed and manuscript cultural record is of particular concern in Canada because so many important Canadian books and pamphlets are printed on late nineteenth- and early twentieth-century paper. The problems are not, of course, confined to special collections departments and, indeed, are much exacerbated in large university research collections. A recent survey of the general collections of the University of Toronto revealed that 25 to 30 percent of the books are now brittle and thus virtually unusable. Research conducted at the National Library of Canada and the Canadian Conservation Institute, along with the extensive research projects of the United States and Great Britain, has resulted in the development of new methods of deacidification, but the problem remains overwhelming.

Since the early 1970s, Canadian institutions have been able to spend more of their available money in Canada because of the growth of its antiquarian book trade over the last 15 years. More of the kinds of books and manuscripts wanted by Canadian institutions can now be found in Canada, and the institutions are able to purchase them with Canadian dollars. Even with this advantage, most dealers would claim that the percentage of their total business done with institutions is much lower than it was ten years ago—reflecting both the decrease in institutional buying power and an increase in the number and seriousness of private collectors.

Canadiana in all its forms continues to be the focus of the special collections programs of most Canadian institutions. There are several outstanding collections, including those of the National Library of Canada, the Bibliotheque Nationale du Quebec, the Metropolitan Toronto Public Library, Dalhousie University, the University of British Columbia, and the University of Toronto, that continue to be well supported, and these collections can now be supplemented by the major microform project known as the Canadian Institute for Historical Microreproduction (CIHM) that began in 1978.* In brief, CIHM plans to produce microfiche copy for every piece of printed Canadiana produced before 1900 (and may eventually carry the project into the twentieth century). For this project, Canadiana has been defined in the widest possible way to include books and pamphlets with any substantial Canadian content, as well as those printed or published in Canada or written by Canadians. Some indication of the inadequacy of Canadian institutional collections, despite the concerted collecting efforts of many years, is CIHM's estimate that up to 40 percent of what it wishes to film will be available only outside Canada. This project, funded by the federal government, is now well under way and several thousand titles have been distributed to subscribers. Its aims are to make Canadiana more widely available to scholars and to assist in the preservation of the often fragile originals. Obviously, smaller institutions will be able to acquire instant collections of Canadiana, and the presence of the fiche editions is not likely to inhibit larger ones from collecting originals. An item can't be filmed unless the original exists and certain kinds of research can only be done by using originals.

THE ANTIQUARIAN BOOK TRADE

According to recently published interviews with a number of booksellers, the Canadian antiquarian book trade is relatively healthy, with more customers buying a greater variety of books than ever before.† Certainly the number of used and antiquarian booksellers increases each year and there are now approximately 70 used book stores in Toronto alone. At the same time the bookseller is subject to the same economic stresses as a person in any small business. The supply of books and manuscripts continues to outstrip the demand despite the age-old cries of collectors and dealers that there is nothing decent left to collect. Indeed, it is amazing how many really first-class books and manuscripts have recently appeared on the market (for example, de Bry's *Petite Voyages,* 1598–1607; Christian Huygens, *Horologium Oscillatorium,* 1673; and Johannes Kepler, *Astronomia Nova,* 1609), although the collector often questions whether he or she will ever have another chance at the purchase of particularly desirable items. Collecting is often a matter of creating opportunities and the most successful collectors, whether institutional or private, find that the right book appears when they have the money and the money appears when the right book

---

Canada's Printed Heritage: A Microfiche Collection and Preservation Project (Ottawa: Canadian Institute for Historical Microreproduction, 1983).

†As an example, see Paul Wilson, "The Touch," *Books in Canada* 12, no. 10 (December 1983): 7–11.

turns up. It is easy to acquire good books for an institution when you have the money; the challenge is acquiring them when you have none at all.

The year 1983 saw the close of Canada Book Auctions, the only auction house in Canada regularly to conduct auctions of books and manuscripts. The reasons for its failure after a number of years in business (it had previously been known as Montreal Book Auctions) are no doubt financially complex but ultimately come down to an inability to attract really good material for consignment. The only successful sales were those where a substantial group of desirable books in the same subject field was offered; the specter of yet another hundred lots of the same pieces of Canadiana failed to excite very spirited bidding. Toronto, at least, ought to be able to support regular book auctions, but for any venture to succeed the close cooperation of the antiquarian book trade will be required.

Book fairs, which proliferated in the 1970s, seem to have dwindled in importance as a marketing device over the past few years. The common complaints are that there are too many, they are too expensive to attend regularly, and the same books appear too often (for example, six copies of the first edition of *Origin of Species* at the same fair). The only genuine reasons for a rare books librarian to attend book fairs are to renew personal acquaintances in the trade, to discover new dealers, and to participate in the rich legacy of book trade gossip. It is difficult for a librarian to buy well at a fair, even one in the same city as the institution he or she represents. Almost any amount of money can be more effectively spent over the phone but the process is admittedly not as much fun. The Toronto Book Fair, one of the oldest in North America, has become in the last few years much more a local occasion, attracting fewer dealers from the United States and Great Britain than it used to. There are now annual fairs in Ottawa and Halifax, and a Vancouver Book Fair was successfully launched in 1983. These fairs are sponsored by the Antiquarian Booksellers Association of Canada, but there is at least one semiannual one-day book fair (in Toronto) that is privately promoted with some success, as it attracts a substantial number of small local dealers who do not belong to the association.

BIBLIOGRAPHICAL ORGANIZATIONS AND ACTIVITIES

Canada has few collecting or fine book societies, although the Alcuin Society of Vancouver has been producing special editions of Canadian texts since the mid-1960s. Recently a collectors' society, called the Amtmann Circle, after the late bookseller Bernard Amtmann, has been launched. It will attempt to bring together for lectures, exhibitions, and receptions private collectors, rare book librarians, and the producers of fine books. It will also attempt to be a national organization, a task that will prove its greatest challenge. The Bibliographical Society of Canada, a national organization with the same aims and objectives as other bibliographical societies, meets annually, publishes an annual volume of papers and a bulletin, and attempts to coordinate bibliographical activities in Canada. Its emphasis is on Canadiana and there is now in Canada an increasing number of retrospective bibliographical and textual projects concerned with Canadian literature and history.

Canadian special collections libraries participate, in company with their fellow institutions in other countries, in a number of international bibliographical projects. Most notable, perhaps, is the individual and cooperative effort to report holdings of eighteenth-century books and pamphlets to the *Eighteenth Century Short Title Cata-*

logue (*ESTC*) project. Forty-seven Canadian institutions, many with significant holdings, are now contributing records to *ESTC* in Baton Rouge. There is a Canadian ad hoc ESTC Committee, and Canadians participate in the affairs of the North American Advisory Committee and the International Committee.

Canadian special collections librarians don't meet together, in a formal sense, although very often they encounter each other at some of the meetings of the various organizations to which many of them belong. A few regularly attend the annual preconference of the Rare Books and Manuscripts Section of ACRL (Association of College and Research Libraries) but perhaps they ought to have their own organization.

From the perspective of 1983 the Canadian world of rare books and manuscripts appears active and flourishing. Although fewer institutions account for more of the public collecting than was true five or ten years ago, there seem to be more serious private collectors acquiring a much wider range of material than in the past. This is, of course, good news for the beleaguered institutions, as some of these collections will eventually find institutional homes and will enrich the scholarly resources of the nation. The intimate relationships between important private collectors and the major rare book libraries so common in the United States have not been cultivated as assiduously in Canada. This is changing, however, and what the Canadian antiquarian book world really requires for 1984 is a few more barons of business with serious interests in rare books and manuscripts and the belief that to spend freely is the sure and certain way to bibliophilic heaven.

7

Institutional Collections in Great Britain

John Feather

THE MOOD OF THE BRITISH rare book world has been strangely contradictory in 1983, as indeed it has been for several years. On the one hand, there is the optimism generated by the rapid progress of projects old and new in such fields as cathedral libraries, conservation, and the ubiquitous *Eighteenth Century Short Title Catalogue (ESTC);* on the other hand, in the publicly funded majority of rare book libraries there is the pervasive gloom of the shadows cast by financial restraints. The two moods are not wholly irreconcilable. This is a time of consolidation, when the great resources that are our heritage from the past are being husbanded more carefully and recorded in greater depth than ever before, with the computer scientist and the chemist making their contributions to this effort. The growth of collections, however, is slower than at any time since World War II. British universities are almost entirely dependent for their revenues on public funding; this is channeled to them in various ways, but all of the channels have begun to silt up in the past two or three years. Student numbers are being reduced as a matter of government policy, hence reducing the income from fees. At the same time, the universities' direct income from the central government, processed through the University Grants Committee, is also linked inter alia to student numbers, and hence it, too, has generally decreased in real terms. Universities have been obliged to reduce their staff, and although this has in most cases been achieved fairly painlessly through well-funded early retirement schemes, it has inevitably left great gaps. This situation, bad enough in itself, has been compounded by the "freezing" of posts that are theoretically still on the rosters. Finally, the government is pressuring the universities to increase their commitment to science and technology at the expense of the humanities and to emphasize what the Department of Education and Science regards as "useful" subjects.

Libraries have suffered badly from these retrenchments, perhaps disproportionately so, in the public sector as well as in the universities, and rare book departments have been among the hardest hit. Twenty years ago there was official endorsement for the view that the acquisition of research materials was an essential function of a uni versity library, but recently there has been a marked reluctance to encourage the use of public money for the purchase of older books, and strong support for the view that even when a library is offered a collection as a donation it should look at the costs of storage, processing, and servicing before accepting it. The long-term prospects are scarcely more cheerful. The decreased support for rare book collections is, at least in part, a reflection of decreased demand. Graduate research in the humanities, which has long been the mainstay of the use of rare books, is in decline. This situation has arisen partly from official pressure expressed both through the restriction of funds available for student finance and through direct pressure to reduce intake, and partly because research is no longer so attractive a proposition for a young arts graduate, since the academic profession is effectively closed to new entrants by the reduction of staffing establishments. Even before it was subjected to external factors, humanities research was changing, with a greater emphasis on more modern periods and sub-jects. These academic and political trends, all coinciding with the ever-rising costs of providing other library services, have had sad consequences: the limitation of acquisi-tions, reduced and demoralized staffs, and shortened hours of rare book rooms.

The interest in rare books remains strong despite all these problems. When the Library Association's Rare Books Group organized a residential course on seven-teenth-century books in July there were 52 participants, and the group's meetings generally attract good attendance. The same is true of the various bibliographical societies around the country, in which rare book librarians are prominent at every level. The Rare Books Group has also reached the final stages of an enterprise that has been one of its central concerns for ten years: a directory of rare book collections in Great Britain. Under the editorship first of the late Stanley Roberts and now of Moelwyn Williams, formerly Keeper of Printed Books at the National Library of Wales, a nationwide team of volunteers has compiled the first guide to the vast wealth of Great Britain's resources of early printed books. In the absence of a comprehensive national union catalogue, and with the compilation of such a catalogue unlikely in the foreseeable future, the *Directory* represents a major step forward in the published record of rare books in Great Britain. Publication, in a book of some 800 pages, is expected in the early months of 1984.

PRESERVATION ACTIVITIES

The *Directory* is merely one example of what I have called the process of consoli-dation. Perhaps the dominant topic in British rare book librarianship in 1983 has been the most fundamental of all: the preservation of the books themselves. The Brit-ish Library Research and Development Department has funded a major investigation of the book conservation situation in Great Britain. The Project Director was Dr. F. W. Ratcliffe, formerly Director of the John Rylands University Library of Manchester and now University Librarian at Cambridge. Ratcliffe, unlike so many chief librari-ans, is a committed advocate of the development of rare book collections and has translated his advocacy into action at both Manchester and Cambridge. The Conser-vation Project has conducted a survey of 418 libraries (of which an astonishing 332 responded to a questionnaire) to discover what is being done in this field, what is perceived to be needed, and, perhaps most important, the profession's attitude toward the whole issue of the conservation of library materials. The project has aroused great interest in the profession, and to that extent has in itself been a valuable exercise, quite apart from the information it has discovered and whatever actions it may subsequently inspire. Moreover, this interest has not been confined to the comparatively narrow world of the rare book librarian; the project, unlike so many similar research projects of this kind, has taken the trouble to publicize both its activities and its findings.

The Library and Information Services Council (LISC), the government's advisory body on libraries, convened a meeting of senior librarians and library educators in June, at which progress reports were presented and the feedback process initiated before the project was completed. In September, a two-day dissemination seminar was held in Cambridge, at which the draft report was subjected to searching examination, again by a group representative of all sides of the profession at its highest levels. The report itself, together with the papers presented at the Cambridge meeting, is to be published in the very near future and will become one of the fundamental documents of British rare book librarianship.

Already it is becoming clear that the British Library is prepared to extend its commitment in this field, both through the further development of its own programs in the Reference Division, where Dr. Richard Clements has been appointed Head of the Conservation Division, with a seat on the British Library Board, and through subventions from the Research and Development Department for further research and educational work. At the same time, there are encouraging signs that the library schools are willing to take seriously their obligation to ensure that the next generation of librarians is not as ignorant as their predecessors have been about the physical preservation of library materials, and that this educational effort will not be confined to those intending to specialize in the rare books field.

CATALOGUING PROJECTS

Progress has not been confined to the field of conservation. In a sense, the conservation crisis has arisen because of the huge increase in the use of rare book collections since 1945. With the library world ever more dominated by the cost-benefit analyses of public auditors, it is crucial that the present level of use is sustained and developed, and that collections are exploited as fully as is consistent with their continued long-term safety. Within the present financial and political circumstances, it is more important than ever to encourage the use of rare books. The Rare Books Group *Directory* is one major step in the right direction, for it will reveal the largely unknown strength of collections outside the golden triangle of London, Oxford, and Cambridge.

Cathedral Libraries Catalogue

One whole group of libraries whose full wealth of bibliographical treasures is about to be revealed in detail for the first time is that of the cathedrals of the Church of England. The compilation of a union catalogue of their pre-1700 holdings began in 1944, with a grant from the Pilgrim Trust. Miss M. S. G. Macleod (later Mrs. Hands) undertook it without help for ten years, resumed the work in 1966, and continued until not long before her death in 1979. By that time, the Bibliographical Society had become the sponsor of the project and had successfully sought funding from the British Academy. In the late 1970s, the British Library became heavily involved both in financing the final stages of the cataloguing and in the plans for eventual publication. After nearly 40 years the cathedral libraries catalogue, now under the editorship of David Shaw, is on the verge of completion. The first volume, covering English books up to 1700, is expected in 1984, with the second, listing the foreign material, and perhaps even more important in view of the weakness of bibliographical control of early continental printing, to follow before too long.

Eighteenth Century Short Title Catalogue

Of all the cataloguing projects, however, the most widely publicized has been the *Eighteenth Century Short Title Catalogue (ESTC)*; surely there cannot now be a rare book librarian in the world who has not heard of it. This great scheme, first conceived by Lars Hanson and Graham Pollard in the 1950s, and revived by the British Library in 1976–1977, is at last beginning to fulfill its promise. This has been the first full year in which *ESTC* has been available on BLAISE-LINE, the British Library Automated Information SErvice, which can be accessed in Great Britain via the public telephone network. BLAISE-LINE allows online searching of the *ESTC* file by author, title, publisher, place, date, and other fields. The user may also print through his own printer or order offline prints (which are a good deal cheaper than the costs of online printing) from the British Library. BLAISE-LINE is not inexpensive to use, but it is simple even for those unfamiliar with the principles of conducting an online search, and is widely available in Great Britain in both academic and public libraries. Moreover, the multiple access points to *ESTC* provide a highly flexible approach to the database, and will be of great value both to librarians and to users. The British Library has published, under the title *Searching the Eighteenth Century,* a group of papers that were given at a symposium held at London University during the fall; these papers show some of the potential uses of *ESTC* for eighteenth-century scholars. A brief guide, *Searching ESTC On-Line,* by R. C. Alston, the editor of *ESTC,* is available gratis from the British Library. In North America, online access to *ESTC* is possible through RLIN, the Research Libraries Information Network. More conventionally, *ESTC* is also available in microfiche, generated by COM printout from the database. This was published in December 1983 at a cost of £350 (£400 after March 1984). The microfiche, unlike the BLAISE-LINE database, is in author order only and contains only the British Library's own holdings, for the editorial work on other entries is still in progress, and new entries and locations continue to be added from other libraries. Each entry in *ESTC* is in UKMARC format, using AACR-2, modified by the *ESTC* team to take account of some of the physical peculiarities of handprinted books and to permit a more prolix use of the Note Area.

Meanwhile, the *ESTC* database continues to be enriched from libraries in Great Britain and around the world, and the parallel project in the United States (ESTC/NA) also flourishes. It is no secret that some reservations have been expressed from time to time about the *ESTC* project, partly because of the percentage of the limited funds available for rare book activities that it has consumed in the last six or seven years. Some of these criticisms remain as valid as they ever were, especially those relating to the form of entry that has been adopted, but it would be churlish to deny that benefits have accrued from the scheme. A great deal has been achieved in a comparatively short time, even though the principle of short-title cataloguing has been silently abandoned. But *ESTC,* an acceptable substitute, is within sight of completion, and the British Library now has what is probably the best catalogue of its eighteenth-century holdings of any library in the world. *ESTC* has heightened the general awareness of rare books, has trained many young people in the skills of cataloguing early printed materials, and has advanced techniques of automated record creation for rare books. All in all, the credit side of the account probably outweighs the debits, and we should be grateful to the British Library for its continued sponsorship of this expensive and complex program.

Nineteenth Century Short Title Catalogue

The eighteenth century being duly catalogued, or almost so, the nineteenth hoves into view; but if the *Eighteenth Century Short Title Catalogue* is a formidable undertaking, one for the nineteenth century must seem almost impossible. Such a project has nevertheless been initiated, under the chairmanship of John Jolliffe, Bodley's librarian, and, what is more remarkable, without public sponsorship of any kind. With private funding, AVERO (Eighteenth-Century) Publications of Newcastle-upon-Tyne proposes to produce a Nineteenth Century Short Title Catalogue (NSTC), beginning with the period 1801–1815. By working from catalogues, using highly abbreviated title entries, and making full use of both mainframe and microcomputers from the beginning, AVERO intends to publish the first volume (A–C, 1800–1815) in spring 1984. NSTC is in fact a descendant of *Eighteenth-Century British Books,* (*ECBB*), published by Dawsons, and its Executive Director is F. J. G. Robinson, who was P. J. Wallis's chief collaborator on *ECBB.* Full account has been taken of the valid criticisms of *ECBB* that occasionally surfaced among the barrage of prejudice by which its publication was greeted, and NSTC will represent another long step forward in recording the output of English printers and publishers.

Union Catalogue of Incunabula

These great projects, with six- or seven-figure funding, and the prestige of major national institutions behind them, naturally take the lion's share of attention. We should not neglect, however, the less fashionable but nevertheless invaluable achievements of those who work alone. One outstanding contribution to British rare book librarianship has been made by such a man. For many years Dennis Rhodes, an Assistant Keeper in the British Library Reference Division, has been working on a union catalogue of incunabula in all the libraries of Oxford other than the Bodleian. The fruits of his labors appeared during the year in a handsome and not overpriced volume (£40). Oxford's incunabula, which collectively are probably the third best collection in the world after those of the British Library and the Bibliothèque Nationale, have too long lain hidden. Rhodes has revealed the riches of the college and department libraries, and one can only hope that the Bodleian will feel inspired by his example to complete the long dormant catalogue of its own incunabula of which the foundations were laid, and the greater part of the superstructure built, by L. A. Shepherd some ten or more years ago. Meanwhile, Rhodes himself is hoping to compile a Goff-style catalogue of incunabula in all British libraries, and one can only admire his energy and wish him well in his efforts.

EXHIBITIONS

Union catalogues are essential tools for the custodians and users of rare books, and their compilation an integral part of their activities. Another duty that usually falls on the shoulders of the rare book librarian is that of organizing exhibitions. There is perhaps no better way of publicizing a rare book collection to the nonspecialist. A well-displayed exhibition can attract old and new users, potential benefactors, and even the sympathetic attention of members of the library committee. Anyone who has ever been involved in the planning of an exhibition knows how time consuming it can be; but it is time well spent. This year's crop in Great Britain has been as plentiful as ever, and a brief survey of a small selection will perhaps give a flavor of the rich variety of our libraries.

Anniversaries provide perhaps the best excuse for a major exhibition. Two this year had precisely that effect. William Hunter, physician to Queen Charlotte, died in 1783. Hunter was a major collector in true eighteenth-century style, with a house full of coins and medals, curiosities, prints, and *objets de vertu,* as well as superb collections of books and manuscripts. All of this he bequeathed to his alma mater, the University of Glasgow, where it has been kept together as the Hunterian Collection. During the summer, the bicentenary of Hunter's death was commemorated by an exhibition of 76 items from the collection at the University Library in Glasgow. The show was arranged by Jack Baldwin, the present custodian of the collection, who also compiled the excellent catalogue that accompanied it.

A hundred years after the death of Hunter, there occurred in London the death of a bearded German exile who for more than 30 years had been one of the most regular occupants of the recently completed Reading Room of the British Museum. Karl Marx was therefore a very proper subject for an exhibition in the museum's successor, the British Library. Throughout the summer, cases in the King's Library were devoted to early editions of his works, including, of course, perhaps the most famous book ever to be written in the Reading Room, *Das Kapital.* There was also a selection of very interesting manuscript material that illustrated his connection with the museum.

Exhibitions, like parties, do not need an excuse; they can be arranged and enjoyed for their own sakes. Nor are they the prerogative of national or university libraries. Indeed, some of the most enterprising are to be found in the provincial public libraries and museums. An excellent example was provided by the Portsmouth City Museums in the fall, with an exhibition of British wood engravings of the 1920s and 1930s. Both the period and the subject are attracting considerable interest. This engaging display includes not only the great private presses of the interwar years, notably Golden Cockerell and Gregynog, but also some of the excellent work done for the more enlightened trade publishers of the period, including that commissioned by Allen Lane for some of the early Penguin books. Like a number of provincial exhibitions, this is to go on tour and will be seen elsewhere in the country during 1984.

Another provincial exhibition which was seen in more than one place had its origin in one of the most enterprising museum services, that of Brighton. Entitled "The Inspiration of Egypt," it was concerned with the "Egyptian" style, which emerged in the aftermath of Napoleon's invasion of that country and subsequent British involvement in its affairs from the 1820s to the 1950s. Illustrated books played a key role in the dissemination of knowledge about the antiquities of Egypt, and they loom large in the exhibition.

The Bethnal Green Museum is the East London "branch" of the Victoria and Albert. It specializes in the history of childhood, and during the school holidays in the summer it mounted an enterprising display of penny dreadfuls and comics, covering the period from the middle of the nineteenth century to the present. In this case, the exhibits were on loan from the collection at the University of Oldenberg, in West Germany. The Victoria and Albert itself houses the National Art Library, and its book exhibitions should never be missed by bibliophiles visiting London. This year it mounted a superb exhibition of selected documents from county record offices in England and Wales, under the title "The Common Chronicle." Organized in collaboration with the Association of County Archivists, this was the first time such material had been brought together at the national level. The most spectacular exhibit was the Textus Roffensis, a twelfth-century cartulary from Rochester Cathedral.

Finally, we return to Scotland, where the National Library presented another magnificent exhibit during the summer. For a number of years, the library has mounted a major display as its contribution to the Edinburgh International Festival. This year it had the additional incentive of a meeting of the Association Internationale des Bibliophiles in the city in late September. The subject chosen was "The Eye of the Mind: The Scot and His Books," which surveyed several centuries of Scotland's bibliophilic history. The exhibits included many borrowed from other libraries and a notable group from private collections, some of which had never before been on public view.

THE ROLE OF THE BRITISH LIBRARY

It is clear that, despite all the problems that beset us, rare book librarianship in Great Britain is in surprisingly good health. What is disturbing is how long this can be maintained. Credit must, of course, go to the individuals around the country who continue to give their best in trying and discouraging circumstances, but, as the reader of this article will be aware, the British Library is ever more pervasive. This is as it should be, for one of its functions as a national library is to provide leadership. The British Library's own commitment to its rare book collections, and its willingness to support rare book activities elsewhere, has been vital in maintaining a high profile for rare book librarianship in the last few years and in enhancing the prestige of rare books in the library world as a whole. Alexander Wilson, Director-General of the Reference Division, publicly acknowledged the library's role and its concerns in a lecture he gave at Columbia University in New York City in April (reported in *BiN,* March–April 1983, pp. 23–26). Under the title "The Crisis in Rare Book Management: A United Kingdom Perspective," he dealt with the education of rare book librarians, the conservation of materials, and the management of collections. That there is a crisis there can be no doubt. The accumulated problems of decades, and even of centuries, are coming to a head at a time when financial resources are severely limited, and only firm and unequivocal action can save the books themselves and ensure that there are librarians properly qualified to guard and exploit them. If it is possible to express a limited optimism about the possibility that this may happen, it is not least because the British Library, both by exhortation and by example, is doing its utmost to preserve and maintain our national heritage of rare books.

REVIEW OF BIBLIOGRAPHICAL SCHOLARSHIP AND PUBLISHING

II

8

Descriptive and Analytical Bibliography and Scholarly Editing

G. Thomas Tanselle

A YEAR THAT BEGINS with the publication of a new volume of the *Bibliography of American Literature* (*BAL*) and ends with the appearance of two long-awaited works, Dan Laurence's bibliography of Shaw and the sequel to Carter and Pollard's *Enquiry*, would have to be regarded as a singularly eventful year for the field of bibliography. And the publication of these books by no means constituted the only significant bibliographical events of 1983. The vitality of the field was repeatedly demonstrated during the year, not least in the flourishing state of the bibliographical journals. The interrelationship of bibliography and textual criticism also continued to be illustrated through the year, both in lively discussion and in the steady production of additions to multivolume editions.

Members of the Bibliographical Society of America (BSA) attending its annual meeting on January 28, 1983, at the Morgan Library were greeted with the welcome news that Volume 7 of the *Bibliography of American Literature* was ready for publication; the first copy was presented on this occasion to Rosamunde Blanck, daughter of Jacob Blanck, the author of the first six volumes (see the account in the Society's *Papers* [*PBSA*], 2nd Quarter, 1983, pp. 256–257). Blanck's death in 1974 delayed work on the new volume, which covers 40 authors, from Paulding to Stockton; but that work has been completed with great care by Virginia L. Smyers and Michael Winship (Yale University Press). This is not the place for a detailed assessment of the strengths and weaknesses of the *BAL*; there are plenty of both (see Joel Myerson's review in *PBSA*, 1st Quarter, 1984, pp. 45–56). Its characteristics are in any case well known; suffice it to say that the standards of the *BAL* have been maintained or even elevated (it seems to me that more copies, from more collections, are now being examined). Michael Winship is pushing ahead with his work on the eighth, and final, volume; the bibliographical world is fortunate that this important project is in such capable hands.

Most works covering large numbers of books by many authors do not give as much attention to physical detail as does the *BAL*. To name an instance from 1983, the first volume of Laura Arksey, Nancy Pries, and Marcia Reed's *American Diaries: An Annotated Bibliography of Published American Diaries and Journals* (Gale Research), though a worthy enough enterprise, is really a checklist, exhibiting no interest in physical bibliography. Some library catalogues, on the other hand, even though they refer only to the copies in a particular collection, serve as bibliographies because of their careful attention to physical detail; one admirable example from 1983 is *The Newberry Library Catalog of Early American Printed Sheet Music* (3 vols., G.K. Hall), the splendid work of Bernard Wilson. Another catalogue of exceptional interest is *The Parkman Dexter Howe Library* (edited by Sidney Ives and handsomely published by the University of Florida), the first fascicle of which appeared in 1983, containing Roger E. Stoddard's "A Descriptive Catalogue of the Early New England Books." Future fascicles, to be prepared by other scholars, will take up the various author collections in the Howe library; Stoddard, with his exemplary signature collations and sensible annotations, has set a high standard for the series.

SINGLE-AUTHOR BIBLIOGRAPHIES

As for bibliographies of single authors, the biggest news is doubtless the publication of Dan H. Laurence's *Bernard Shaw: A Bibliography,* the latest (and, in two volumes, the largest) of the Soho Bibliographies (the series, now published by the Clarendon Press, has been active of late with the appearance in 1982 of David Gilson's impressive bibliography of Jane Austen). The product of some 25 years' research, the Shaw bibliography is full of detail about the publishing background of the recorded items, even many minor reprinted pieces. If Laurence does not quite succeed in his goal of making his bibliography "not merely informative but as pleasantly readable as if Shaw himself had been author rather than subject," one nevertheless appreciates the effort, for the aim is an important one. The work does have some shortcomings, particularly curious in light of the intelligence of the general approach: for example, there is no record of copies examined (but two locations where copies can be found are provided, when possible, for "scarce publications"); dust jackets are not normally described (for the odd reason that they "have never figured notably in the collecting of Shaw's works"); quasi-facsimile transcriptions do not—because of the printer's limitations, Laurence regretfully admits—distinguish large from small capitals; and the sequence of editions and impressions of a work is sometimes obscured by the lack of parallelism in their treatment.

Laurence's approach to bibliography, exemplified in the *Shaw,* was set forth more explicitly in his 1982 Engelhard Lecture at the Library of Congress, fittingly published in the year of his Shaw bibliography (as the ninth pamphlet in the Viewpoint Series of the Center for the Book in the Library of Congress). As its title, *A Portrait of the Author as a Bibliography,* suggests, Laurence's lecture emphasizes the concept of descriptive bibliographies as historical and biographical studies—in his words, as "the graphic recreation of the subjects' lives in the context of their professional business involvement and experience." Although this sensible point of view has received increasing attention in recent years, it is still not as widely understood as it ought to be, and this forceful statement of it is therefore welcome. Perhaps one should not quibble with so enlightened a piece, but it does at times falter: the ridicule directed at the obsessive pursuit of first-impression "points," for instance, is deserved, but it is not balanced by an explicit recognition of the positive value of such physical evidence; and the brief compliment paid to booksellers near the end does not make up for the earlier lack of attention to (or actual distrust of) their contributions. The occasional superficiality matters little, however, in comparison with the sanity of the essential argument and the value of having this expression of it.

The lack of uniformity within the Soho series is illustrated by another Soho volume of 1983, Richard Lancelyn Green and John Michael Gibson's *A Bibliography of A. Conan Doyle,* which employs peculiar definitions of such terms as "edition" and "issue" and uses an eccentric system of signature collation ("[A]4–R(4)," for example, means that A and R have four leaves each and B–Q have eight). At least it does recognize the importance of signature collation, and in general it is the product of a great deal of diligent research. Regrettably, signature collation is absent from another important bibliography of 1983, Donald Gallup's *Ezra Pound: A Bibliography,* a revision of the bibliography of 20 years ago, now published jointly by the Bibliographical Society of the University of Virginia and St. Paul's Bibliographies. But we have learned to accept such failings in exchange for the many virtues that any Gallup bibliography possesses. (St. Paul's, a series established four years ago by Robert Cross at Godalming, Surrey, has reprinted a number of important bibliographical works, often with new prefaces or addenda, and has occasionally, as here, published completely new editions.) Among the other 1983 author bibliographies that stand apart as serious works of bibliographical scholarship are three dealing with mid-twentieth-century writers: Keith Sagar and Stephen Tabor's *Ted Hughes: A Bibliography, 1946–1980* (Mansell—the first of a Mansell series), Terence A. Tanner's *Frank Waters: A Bibliography* (Glenwood, Ill.: Meyerbooks), and J. Howard Woolmer's *Malcolm Lowry: A Bibliography* (Woolmer/Brotherson—which follows the Pittsburgh series in showing photographs of title pages but not in providing signature collation).

SHORT-TITLE CATALOGUES

Another class of bibliographies, consisting of those large projects called "short-title catalogues," was in the news in 1983, as it had been for many years preceding, as a result of the ongoing work on the revision of Pollard and Redgrave's *A Short-Title Catalogue of Books Printed in England, Scotland, and Ireland, and English Books Printed Abroad, 1475–1640* (the STC) and Donald Wing's *Short-Title Catalogue . . . 1641–1700* (known as Wing) and on the production of a first record for the eighteenth century (ESTC). (These "catalogues" are "short-title" in that they do not attempt the detailed kind of description possible in a single-author bibliography; but they go beyond the standards of a simple checklist in their attention to physical details and their effort to distinguish editions.) Henry Snyder, North American director of ESTC, convened a meeting of his North American Advisory Committee at the New York Public Library on April 5, 1983. In a carefully prepared report, he showed that another three years' funding could see the recording of North American copies of British eighteenth-century imprints essentially completed. Marcus McCorison, director of the American Antiquarian Society, where the recording of American eight-eenth-century imprints is in progress, stated that this part of the project would be completed in late 1986. The most tangible results of the undertaking thus far relate to the holdings of the British Library (over 150,000 relevant items), all of which have now been reexamined and redescribed (or in many cases recorded for the first time) under the direction of Robin Alston. The resulting machine-readable catalogue is available in the United States through the Research Libraries Information Network (RLIN); it also forms a major microfiche publication (late 1983) by the British Library, *The Eighteenth Century Short Title Catalogue: Catalogue of the British Library Collections.* A great many works not previously listed in the British Museum *General Catalogue,* or not readily locatable there, have now been made accessible. Meanwhile, the process of adding to this file the holdings of some 500 libraries all over the world will continue, probably until the end of the decade.

In regard to the original, pre-1640, *STC,* the most pleasant way in recent years to keep abreast of its progress has been to attend the occasional lectures given by Katharine Pantzer, who is presently completing the work. (Volume 1, covering A–H, is expected in 1985; Volume 2, covering I–Z, was published in 1976.) One of these progress reports, which are also revealing demonstrations of the methods of analytical bibliography, was offered, among other bonuses, at the Columbia University School of Library Service during the inaugural and successful run of its Rare Book School (July–August 1983). (An earlier report, focusing on the English statutes, was presented at the 1980 Boston conference of the Association of College and Research Libraries [ACRL] Rare Books and Manuscripts Section and was published by R.R. Bowker Company in 1983 in the volume of conference papers, *Books and Society in History.*) Another STC, though labeled "A Preliminary Checklist" because it was based on the slips produced by WPA workers, is the record of American imprints from 1801 through 1819 published by Ralph R. Shaw and Richard H. Shoemaker (1958–1966); although work on later years has proceeded in other hands (and is now in the mid-1830s), the final, and extremely useful, volume of the 1801–1819 segment was published in 1983: Frances P. Newton's *American Bibliography . . . Printers, Publishers and Booksellers Index; Geographical Index* (Scarecrow Press).

Other large projects related to these short-title catalogues have recently been announced. For example, John Jolliffe (Bodley's Librarian) has set forth plans for a nineteenth-century short-title catalogue (NSTC), actually to run into the twentieth century (to 1918), under the direction of F. J. G. Robinson. It will consist of a union catalogue of the holdings of six libraries in Britain and Ireland and will provide access by subject, place of imprint, and title as well as by author. The first segment of the computer database, covering 1801-1815, is projected for completion in 1986. (Announcements appear, among other places, in the September 1983 number of the *Library,* p. 334, and in the Summer 1983 number of the *Newsletter* of Bodley's American Friends.) At the British Library, Lotte Hellinga is editing an incunable short-title catalogue (ISTC), a machine-readable record that was started with the entries from Frederick R. Goff's *Incunabula in American Libraries: A Third Census* (1964) and its *Supplement* (1972) and is now being augmented from other sources (at present it totals some 17,600 editions). Additions and corrections to Goff's census are being gathered by Paul Needham at the Morgan Library for inclusion in ISTC. (See his letter on this subject in the 4th Quarter, 1983 number of *PBSA,* pp. 497–498.) Another large-scale undertaking, but one with a different kind of focus, is the Early

Imprints Project (EIP) in Australia and New Zealand, which will record all pre-1801 imprints, wherever printed, that are now held in collections in Australia and New Zealand. More than a third of the estimated total of 150,000 items have been recorded; a general account of the project and some regional progress reports are printed in the 4th Quarter, 1982 number of the *Bulletin* of the Bibliographical Society of Australia and New Zealand and in the first number (January 1983) of the project's *Newsletter.*

ANALYTICAL BIBLIOGRAPHY

Although short-title catalogues and descriptive bibliographies are the products, in varying degrees, of the analysis of the physical evidence found in books, detailed studies in analytical bibliography generally find their principal outlet in the scholarly bibliographical journals. And those journals, it is pleasing to observe, are in a healthy condition at the moment. Their liveliness is obviously attributable in no small part to the caliber of their editors, and this survey would be remiss if it did not call attention to the recent shifts in editorship of the journals of the British and American bibliographical societies. From the first number of 1983, the *Library* has been edited by Mervyn Jannetta, with Lotte Hellinga and Ian Willison as book-review editors; from the first number of the previous year, *PBSA* has been edited by John Lancaster and Ruth Mortimer. (Another change involves a less venerable, but nevertheless indispensable, institution, the *Bibliography Newsletter* (*BiN*): as of the first number of 1983, Daniel Traister joins Terry Belanger as coeditor. With this appointment one can feel confident that *BiN*'s broad coverage of the bibliographical scene will not become any less incisive or outspoken.) If the two oldest of the major English-language bibliographical journals have changed editors, the other two are in the happy position of continuing under the capable hands of their distinguished editors of long standing: Nicolas Barker, who took over *The Book Collector* in 1965, following the death of John Hayward; and Fredson Bowers, who has edited *Studies in Bibliography* (Bibliographical Society of the University of Virginia) since the time he founded it in 1948 and who deserves congratulation on its thirty-fifth anniversary for the sustained excellence of its contents and the wide influence they have had.

It is clearly not feasible here to examine in detail the 1983 contents of these journals (or even to mention all the journals containing bibliographical analysis, a group that would include the publications of other bibliographical societies and of research libraries—for this purpose *see* Chapter 10, "Periodicals for Collectors, Dealers, and Librarians"); but reference to a few pieces will help to show the vitality of these publications. For example, Paul Needham has in recent months added substantially to his already major contributions to bibliographical scholarship. His brilliant article on "Johann Gutenberg and the Catholicon Press" (*PBSA*, 4th Quarter, 1982), which startlingly demonstrates that two-line slugs rather than movable types were used to print the *Catholicon,* was followed only nine months later by a thorough and highly critical analysis (*PBSA*, 3rd Quarter, 1983) of William B. Todd's 1982 Hanes Lecture (published by the University of North Carolina Library as *The Gutenberg Bible: New Evidence of the Original Printing*), in which Todd suggests that an error in the Texas copy of the Gutenberg Bible shows the setting to have been across the double-column page, not down each column individually. At about the same time, in a judicious review (*Fine Print,* July 1983) of Lotte Hellinga's *Caxton in Focus* (British Library,

1982) Needham made some important comments on the nature of analytical bibliography as history, concluding that "Without a knowledge of bibliography or codicology, it is impossible to write the history of the book, although such knowledge is not, by itself, sufficient for the task."

The study of incunabula was the subject of still another essay of uncommon interest in 1983: Richard N. Schwab, Thomas A. Cahill, Bruce H. Kusko, and Daniel L. Wick, in "Cyclotron Analysis of the Ink in the 42-line Bible" (*PBSA*, 3rd Quarter, 1983), explain how the cyclotron can be used to reveal—without damage to the material—the chemical makeup of ink and paper, thus opening exciting prospects for the analysis of various kinds of artifacts from all periods. A single number of the *Library* (September 1983) contains revealing analyses of problems produced by the differing methods of reprinting in two periods: B. J. McMullin ("The Bible and Continuous Reprinting in the Early Seventeenth Century") shows that, in the case of popular books, individual sheets might be reset as needed, with the result that there are no clear divisions between "editions" in the usual sense, since the sheet, not the volume as a whole, was the unit; and S. W. Reid ("The First Editions of *The Secret Agent*") provides an example of textual variants resulting from the reuse of an uncorrected Monotype roll rather than plates made from corrected type to produce a new impression. The 1983 volume of *Studies in Bibliography* offers two instances of analytical techniques applied to the physical evidence in manuscripts rather than printed books: Ralph Franklin's exemplary "The Emily Dickinson Fascicles" and Mary Hamel's "Scribal Self-Corrections in the Thornton *Morte Arthure*" (which demonstrates the importance of knowing the habits of individual scribes, just as one tries with printed books to ascertain the characteristics of individual compositors).

Perhaps the best-known work in the analytical bibliography of modern books is John Carter and Graham Pollard's 1934 exposure of T. J. Wise's forgeries, *An Enquiry into the Nature of Certain Nineteenth Century Pamphlets*, which employed evidence of typeface design and paper chemistry. In the half-century since its publication, a great deal of new information concerning Wise, his associates, and their activities has been uncovered, and Nicolas Barker has been at work consolidating this material for a number of years. Now he and John Collins have completed the work, and the result is a bibliographical landmark. The decision not to rewrite Carter and Pollard's classic text was a sensible one, and the first volume of the new work (published by the Scolar Press) is therefore a reprint of the *Enquiry,* with some corrections appended and a new epilogue, written by Carter and Pollard before their deaths, on the "Aftermath of 'An Enquiry.' " The second volume is Barker and Collins's *A Sequel to an Enquiry,* skillfully weaving together all the facts now known, including the details of H. Buxton Forman's complicity (and containing, among other appendixes, a list of the sales of the forgeries at auction from 1888 through 1920). (Three chapters of this work were printed, as a preview to the whole, in the *Book Collector* for Winter 1982 and Spring and Summer 1983). For a special limited issue of 80 copies, there is a third volume, a portfolio containing an original copy of the Brownings' *Two Poems* (1854)—from the surviving stock that descended from Harry and Maurice Buxton Forman to Percy Muir and then Laurie Deval—and a pamphlet on that pamphlet by Nicolas Barker, explaining that it may be "the *fons et origo* of the whole crime," the booklet that served as the model for the undertaking. The resulting three-volume work is a fitting monument to one of the most celebrated episodes of bibliophilic and bibliographical history. (The lasting value of John Carter's work is underscored not only by the reprinting of the *Enquiry* but by the recent reappearance of two other books of his: *Printing and the Mind of Man,* which he and Percy Muir edited in 1967, was reprinted in 1983 by Karl Pressler of Munich, with a new introduction by Muir, additional notes and corrigenda by Peter Amelung, and a revised index; the handlist of A. E. Housman, which Carter and John Sparrow published as one of the Soho Bibliographies in 1952, has been considerably revised by William White, and the resulting second edition was published in 1982 by St. Paul's Bibliographies as *A. E. Housman: A Bibliography.*)

TEXTUAL SCHOLARSHIP

Analytical bibliography is one of the tools that must be used by a scholarly editor in the process of establishing an author's text; and while editing must draw on other knowledge as well, the close connection between textual scholarship and bibliography is reflected in the considerable attention given to textual matters in the bibliographical journals. In the 1983 *Studies in Bibliography,* for instance, among various pieces of textual interest, there is Simon Cauchi's "The 'Setting Foorth' of Harington's Ariosto," which interestingly shows how book design can be used by an author as "an expressive means of communication. . . , modifying as well as reinforcing the verbal meanings of the text" and how it therefore must be regarded on some occasions as part of the text. I shall not venture to comment on, but will only record the presence of, my own article on "Classical, Biblical, and Medieval Textual Criticism and Modern Editing" in this same volume of *SB.* The connections between bibliography and editing were also recognized in the second biennial conference of the Society for Textual Scholarship, held in New York at the City University Graduate Center on April 21–24, 1983, with three sessions (involving about a dozen speakers) devoted to enumerative, descriptive, and analytical bibliography. (The first volume of *Text,* the transactions of the STS, containing some of the papers from the 1981 conference, is expected to appear early in 1984.)

Among the excellent sessions on textual matters at the 1983 conference, one—on "The Meaning of the Text"—may be singled out because it brought together several scholars who have recently made noteworthy statements about editing. Donald H. Reiman's effective opening remarks were in line with his judicious survey of the development of the editing of the Romantic poets in the Fall 1982 number of *Studies in Romanticism.* Hershel Parker's paper was another statement of a position he has been setting forth in a series of essays, urging editors to take the creative process more fully into account and to be more critical about admitting authorial revisions into the text. In a widely publicized article on Norman Mailer's revision of *An American Dream* (in the Winter 1981 number of *Bulletin of Research in the Humanities,* actually published in early 1983) and in a broader study of "The Determinacy of the Creative Process and the 'Authority' of the Author's Textual Decisions" (*College Literature,* Spring 1983), Parker cites examples to support the view that authors can lose "authority" over their texts, by making revisions not in tune with the creative process that produced the works, and that authors' revisions are therefore not always to be adopted. In contrast, Jerome J. McGann, who was the respondent to Parker's paper at the conference, believes that authors' intentions often cannot be disentangled from the social processes by which literary works are brought to the public, and he argues for a greater acceptance of the product of the publishing process. His position is set forth in a little book published in June, *A Critique of Modern Textual Criticism* (University of Chicago Press). It is a disappointing book, for its criticisms are often directed at straw-men and it fails to pursue the more interesting of the questions it raises. Both Parker and McGann challenge the concept of "final authorial intention" as it has sometimes been employed by recent editors, but they do so from nearly opposite directions. A thorough examination of their positions cannot be undertaken here; but it is clear from their work that the tradition of lively debate that has characterized modern textual criticism is by no means dead.

Of the editions of late 1982 and 1983, a few should be given special mention here. Late 1982 saw the appearance of the first three volumes of the Oxford Shakespeare, under the general editorship of Stanley Wells: *Henry V* (ed. Gary Taylor), *The Taming of the Shrew* (ed. H. J. Oliver), and *Troilus and Cressida* (ed. Kenneth Muir). The design of these volumes is excellent, but unfortunately the texts—in what can only be a futile effort—are modernized (Oxford has announced a companion series of unmodernized texts). The scholarship and commentary, however, are generally of a high order, though the editorial plan of the volumes strangely lacks uniformity (for instance, the statement of editorial principles is almost nonexistent in the *Troilus* but runs to six pages in *Henry V*—where we are told that quotations in the commentary are also modernized, for "If modernizing is valid for Shakespeare's text it is equally valid for passages quoted only to illuminate that text"). One of the prominent issues in Shakespearean textual criticism in recent years has been the extent to which variants in the early texts result from Shakespeare's own revisions; not surprisingly, this question enters all three of these volumes, with the editors at times arguing on behalf of revision. The central text for discussions of Shakespeare's revision has been *Lear,* and a substantial volume devoted to the subject appeared in 1983—*The Division of the Kingdoms: Shakespeare's Two Versions of* King Lear (Clarendon), a collection of 12 new essays edited by Gary Taylor and Michael Warren, including pieces by Steven Urkowitz (author of the 1980 Princeton book, *Shakespeare's Revision of* King Lear), Stanley Wells, Peter W. M. Blayney, and Randall McLeod. Blayney has also published within the year the first volume of another major work on *Lear, The Texts of* King Lear *and Their Origins* (Cambridge). The textual implications of the bibliographical evidence are largely reserved for his second volume; the present volume aims to set forth what can be learned about Nicholas Okes's printing shop and to examine in detail the printing of the *Lear* quarto through an extended analysis of the bibliographical evidence present in it. His work is the most sustained piece of bibliographical analysis since Charlton Hinman's *The Printing and Proof-Reading of the First Folio of Shakespeare* (1963) and does for quarto printing what Hinman did for folio. If much of this activity springs from a new generation of Shakespeareans, an older generation was active as well in 1982 and 1983, a point impressively demonstrated by Fredson Bowers's fine and characteristically thorough 14–page review (*Library,* September 1983) of Harold Jenkins's notable New Arden Edition of *Hamlet* (Methuen, 1982). (A nod should be made here to one other editorial event of 1983, whatever opinion one holds of the procedures followed in the Yale edition of Horace Walpole's correspondence: the appearance of a volume of additions and corrections and of five volumes of index brings to completion a vast undertaking that began publication 46 years ago.)

Additional volumes continue to appear in the various editions of writers and statesmen being prepared under the auspices of the Modern Language Association's Committee on Scholarly Editions and the National Historical Publications and Records Commission. For example, among these and related editions, new volumes of Charles Brockden Brown (Kent State), Dreiser (Pennsylvania), Franklin (Yale), Howells's letters (Twayne), Irving (Twayne), Washington (Virginia), and Wordsworth (Cornell) came out in 1983. An encouraging trend is that more such texts are beginning to be reprinted in forms that are accessible to a wider public. Although some of these editions (such as the Northwestern-Newberry Edition of Melville) have been published from the outset in paperback as well as hardcover, many have been available only in the expensive hardcover volumes sold largely to research libraries. One is therefore pleased to welcome the 1983 paperback printings of the first five volumes (originally published 1976–1978) of Jo Ann Boydston's edition of *The Middle Works* of John Dewey (Southern Illinois). (The editor should also be congratulated on continuing her enviable record by publishing in 1983 the last three of the 15 volumes of *The Middle Works*.) Similarly, the University of California Press is republishing, in a series called "The Mark Twain Library" (1982–   ), some of the Mark Twain texts established for the scholarly editions of Clemens's *Works* and *Papers* previously published by the Press. This handsome series (available in both hardcover and paperback) substitutes a brief section of "Explanatory Notes" for the extensive apparatus of the full scholarly editions and appends in each case an admirable "Note on the Text" (by Robert H. Hirst, general editor of the Mark Twain Project at the Bancroft Library) that not only explains the textual history of the work but also reports new information, corrections, or second thoughts that have surfaced since the publication of the earlier edition (always listing any changes made in the text). Although these volumes are intended for a general audience, scholars will thus need to refer to them as well.

The same can be said of the Library of America, the impressive series that began in 1982 (published by a nonprofit organization initially supported by the Ford Foundation and the National Endowment for the Humanities) with the aim of making reliable texts of American writing widely and permanently available in volumes of handsome design. By the end of 1983, 16 volumes had appeared: Hawthorne, Howells, Jack London (2 vols.), Melville, Stowe, Twain, and Whitman in 1982, and Henry Adams, Emerson, Irving, Henry James, Parkman (2 vols.), and second volumes of Hawthorne and Melville in 1983. Some of the texts come from first or early editions, others from recent scholarly editions; but the choices in every volume have resulted from careful study of the textual history of the works involved, and the notes and textual essays (though kept brief) report essential textual information and often supplement the earlier scholarly editions by noting additional facts and correcting (and listing) typographical errors. In broadly disseminating reliable texts, editions of this kind help to fulfill what is obviously one of the principal goals of textual scholarship.

9

Books about Books

Daniel Traister

FROM THE VARIED GROUP of books about books published between late 1982 and the end of 1983 encountered in the preparation of this survey, two themes emerge. I begin with these before turning to the individual works that will, of necessity, form the largest portion of this survey. Unless otherwise noted, the imprint date of books cited is 1983.

The first theme I impose on these books is from the outside: their *prices*. This is, or should be, a matter of considerable concern to anyone who reviews, reads, buys, or covets books. Prices are rising quickly and steeply. It is my opinion that they are about to outstrip — if they have not already done so — the ability of many to continue buying books.

Thus, Scolar distresses scholars by affixing an unbelievable price of £65 ($110) to its two-volume set of John Carter and Graham Pollard, *An Enquiry into the Nature of Certain Nineteenth Century Pamphlets,* and Nicolas Barker and John Collins's *Sequel.* Purchased alone, the *Sequel* is £40 ($70). *Aspects of French Eighteenth Century Typography* appeared over The Roxburghe Club's imprint for £120 — this from the pen of John Dreyfus, honored early in 1984 by the American Printing History Association for contributing to the spread of knowledge about printing history. The Pierpont Morgan Library's exhibition catalogue of late medieval and Renaissance French manuscript illumination, *The Last Flowering,* by John Plummer, costs $37.50 in paper covers, $89 cased. Even so tiny and unpretentious a work as Ian Philip's tale of the Bodleian Library's first two centuries costs £17.50 ($37.50) — this for a text of 113 pages and 17 plates.

Quite simply, such prices are frightening. They cannot further the interests or the needs of either authors or readers. Dreyfus's study, for example, is splendid; many people will want it, not simply to read once but to live and work with it over a long period of time. Yet the number of libraries, to say nothing of individuals, able to afford such a book, of concern to relatively few readers, is likely to prove minuscule. What physical requirements of the book's production, one wonders, necessitated such a price tag?

Some worrisome conclusions may be drawn from the tendency of books to return to the luxury market they left only in the last century; perhaps the most obvious is that the reliance of scholars upon libraries is going to increase (indeed, already has increased) as private scholarly collections become less frequently found as professorial toys and more commonly the preserve of the wealthy collector only. So long as such collectors exist and are interested, just so long will such specialized works continue to be published. Simultaneously, libraries—congenitally underfunded as almost all are—are already on the verge, and sometimes well over it, of failing their varied clienteles; prices such as these can only serve to hasten their collapse. I have no solutions to the problems these prices imply. But they are not going away; they are getting worse. They need attention from all interested communities in the book trade and book world—and soon.

BOOKS ON ILLUMINATED MANUSCRIPTS

The second of my themes emerges, I think, from the books themselves rather than my imposition upon them. For whatever reason, 1983 saw the appearance of a raft of studies of the illuminated manuscript book, Plummer's (mentioned above) among them. Perhaps the one that requires most attention is Robert G. Calkins, *Illuminated Books of the Middle Ages* (London: Thames and Hudson; Ithaca, N.Y.: Cornell University Press). Not many comparable texts exist in English, and Calkins has become the introduction of choice at a bound. His approach is topical, by various types of books that received illumination. He surveys the development of illumination from late antiquity through the High Middle Ages. He is constantly aware that the illuminations in which he is most interested are parts of books and thus associated with texts, words, to which they ought meaningfully to relate. His book is copiously and usefully illustrated. If it has any drawbacks, it is the perfunctoriness of its attention to nonreligious texts; and for the truly *introductory* study of the manuscript book, nonsplendid, nonilluminated manuscripts also deserve attention.

Were Calkins the only study of illuminated manuscripts to have appeared in 1983, the year still would have seen a notable addition to the literature of the field. Calkins was, however, part of a crowd. The Pierpont Morgan Library staged an exhibition of French manuscript art, 1420–1530, that opened in November 1982 and ran through January 1983. Its catalogue, John Plummer's *The Last Flowering* (New York: Pierpont Morgan Library, Oxford University Press, 1982), makes one sit up and take notice, just as the exhibition on which it is based tended to clear the cobwebs from one's eyes in a most cheering fashion. Plummer offers, as he remarks, but a "sampling" of French manuscript art: His catalogue—based not only on Morgan Library holdings but also on manuscripts at several other American repositories—is not an introduction to the field. But if his general remarks are very brief, it is because the bulk of his energies has gone into detailed and informative discussions of each illustration and the manuscript from which it is drawn.

From March through June, an exhibition of one institution's illuminated manuscripts was held at Harvard University; it too produced an important catalogue. Roger S. Wieck, *Late Medieval and Renaissance Illuminated Manuscripts 1350–1525 in The Houghton Library* (Cambridge, Mass.: Department of Printing and Graphic Arts, Harvard College Library), serves two purposes. First, full descriptions accompanied by illustrations are provided for the 50 manuscripts exhibited. Bindings and provenances are noticed—reminders that we are thinking about books as well as about art. (Plummer, by contrast, tends to be concerned with art historical rather than with more broadly bibliographical issues in the Morgan catalogue.) Second, 152 additional Harvard manuscripts are briefly listed, followed by small illustrations from each in a separate section. Thus Wieck provides both a record of the exhibition and a guide to Harvard's manuscript collection for the period. Indices by author and title, artist and scribe, previous owner, and century and country of origin — all enhance the usefulness of this product.

From October through early January of 1984, the J. Paul Getty Museum (Malibu, Calif.) exhibited *Renaissance Paintings in Manuscript: Treasures from the British Library*. A catalogue (London: British Library; New York: Hudson Hills Press) emerged from this exhibition, too. The show moved to the Pierpont Morgan Library in January, and was to head home to the British Library in May. The catalogue is divided by three national schools: Thomas Kren traces the Flemish tradition, Mark Evans the Italian, and Janet Backhouse the French. The authors do a bit of hopping around within these divisions; and Myra Orth and D. H. Turner also contribute to the volume. Rather brief surveys of the three schools are followed by more detailed treatments of about ten or so exemplars of each of them; illustrations are extensive. One might have expected a somewhat more secular tone in the illustrations of a volume devoted solely to Renaissance illumination than is found even in Plummer and in Wieck. But many of these late illustrations reflect a vital religious tradition, despite that tendency to direct its art "toward the individual" mentioned by Backhouse as characteristic of Renaissance illumination in her introduction to the French section of the catalogue. For its survey of the British Library's Renaissance manuscripts, as well as for its introduction to late manuscript illumination, this volume is a worthy adjunct to Plummer and Wieck.

The British Library's illuminated manuscripts attracted more detailed attention in three other 1983 publications. Lucy Freeman Sandler produced a study of *The Psalter of Robert De Lisle in the British Library* (London: Harvey Miller; New York: Oxford University Press), Arundel MS. 83 II, a fourteenth-century English manuscript of great beauty and interest. Discussion of both the complex history of the manuscript's creation — several hands worked on it, contrary to its first artist's apparent intentions — and of the intellectual program underlying the illustrations makes Sandler valuable not only for specialists but also for students. Twenty-five color plates, as well as a host of black-and-white illustrations, support Sandler's text. *The Hastings Hours: A 15th-Century Flemish Book of Hours*, with a preface and commentary by D. H. Turner, studies and extensively illustrates Add. MS. 54782 (London and New York: Thames and Hudson). Turner offers a brief biography of William, Lord Hastings, for whom the manuscript was made; comments on the book and its artist; describes selected illustrations; and provides in closing a detailed description of the work, noting, inter alia, the writing styles, binding, and provenance of the book. Rather more of a *jeu d'esprit*, but of remarkable beauty nonetheless, is a volume of reproductions of Add. MS. 24189, *The Travels of Sir John Mandeville*, with an introduction and commentary by Josef Krása (New York: George Braziller). This fifteenth-century Czechoslovakian manuscript is distinguished by unusual painting techniques and a distinctive use of color. Krása's long introduction explores both while also setting the manuscript into its literary and historical context.

Anthony Welch and Stuart Cary Welch wrote *Arts of the Islamic Book: The Collection of Prince Sadruddin Aga Khan* (Ithaca, N.Y.: Cornell University Press for The Asia Society, 1982) for an exhibition that opened at The Asia Society (New York City) in 1982 and was seen later during the year in Fort Worth and Kansas City. National schools serve to organize this catalogue. Manuscripts from the Arab region are followed by those from Ottoman Turkey, Iran, and India. But the tiny introductions to each school—Turkey gets a paragraph—indicate that the authors' primary interest is in detailed discussion of the specific illustrations they show from the Aga Khan's sumptuous collection.

"BIBLIOFICTIONS," AUTHORS, AND THE BOOK TRADE

One cannot leave the Middle Ages without at least mentioning one of the most startling publishing successes of 1983 and, though a fiction, a profoundly "bibliographical" book about books in almost every important sense, Umberto Eco's *The Name of the Rose* (San Diego, Calif.: Harcourt Brace Jovanovich; London: Secker and Warburg). William Weaver's translation from the Italian is superb; about the book, set largely in a monastic library with several interesting manuscripts ready to hand, one can only recommend it highly.

Eco's fiction illuminates the life of the book so vividly as to be almost unique in my experience. But other "bibliofictions" also ought to be more frequently regarded and read as books about books than is now normal practice, and I propose to single out two of them. British art historian Anita Brookner's *Look at Me* (New York: Pantheon) is a study of a librarian whose life is affected in peculiar ways by her association with books and writing. Brookner's novel is depressing; it is also superb. Very different is Philip Roth's *The Anatomy Lesson* (New York: Farrar, Straus & Giroux), the last in a trilogy that began with *The Ghost Writer* and continued with *Zuckerman Unbound* depicting the life of a writer in contemporary America. It is both brilliant fiction, scarifyingly funny, and a mine of information. *The Anatomy Lesson* (and the trilogy it concludes) vivifies the complex milieu in which modern American authors function, most particularly how they influence, and are influenced by, their audiences. It is an important book on the book.

It is also a novel that can profitably be read alongside several more conventional books about books from 1983. James L. W. West III, *The Making of* This Side of Paradise (Philadelphia: University of Pennsylvania Press), although primarily a study of the novel's textual history, looks at the beginning professional career of an author (F. Scott Fitzgerald) early in the twentieth century. Jerome J. McGann's *Critique of Modern Textual Criticism* (Chicago: University of Chicago Press) asks some important questions about the autonomy of the modern author—questions that West's study also raises—and hence about the significance of an author's intention for the establishment of his or her text. *Publishers Weekly Yearbook: News, Analyses, and Trends in the Book Industry* (New York: R. R. Bowker) offers a composite portrait of the book industry in 1983; it is the first in an anticipated annual series that will portray the world in which authors, publishers, printers, designers, and all the rest, work.

THE HISTORY OF BOOKS

My shift away from studies of the medieval illuminated manuscript to bibliofictions and some associated works suggests that I have left behind the second of my themes. I turn now to a few of the books that, united by no particular subject other than "the book," seem to me among the more important books on the book to have appeared during 1983.

Several collections might be mentioned first. The 1980 conference of the Rare Books and Manuscripts Section of the Association of College and Research Libraries (a division of the American Library Association) yielded a particularly rich harvest of essays tending to facilitate the domestication within the Anglo-American bibliographical community of continental approaches to *l'histoire du livre*. Edited by Kenneth E. Carpenter, who also chaired the conference, *Books and Society in History* (New York and London: R. R. Bowker) is an exceptionally important book from which many readers will profit. American, English, French, and German contributors include Elizabeth L. Eisenstein, John Feather, Henri-Jean Martin, and Paul Raabe. Its contributors' varied approaches to book history from the fifteenth through the twentieth centuries, combined with Robert Darnton's introduction to the field and an overview of the interconnections between many different forms of bibliographical study by G. Thomas Tanselle, give Carpenter's collection a stimulating quality and a significance that rank it among the year's most valuable publications.

One might note in passing that Eisenstein's 1977 work, *The Printing Press as an Agent of Change*, appeared in an abridgment under the title *The Printing Revolution in Early Modern Europe* from Cambridge University Press during the year. Raabe's Boston essay, urging librarians to practice scholarship concerned with both library history and the history of books, appears in Carpenter's volume in severely shortened form, but is found in a full version in *Essays in Honor of James Edward Walsh on His Sixty-fifth Birthday* (Cambridge, Mass.: Goethe Institute of Boston and Houghton Library). Other essays in the Walsh *festschrift* deal with a variety of bibliographical matters, many of them German, and other contributors include Philip Hofer, Ruth Mortimer, and Roger E. Stoddard. Yet another Boston conference participant, represented in Carpenter's volume by an essay other than the one he actually delivered, is Robert Darnton. *The Great Cat Massacre* contains the missing essay, and appeared in 1983 from Basic Books (New York), with a 1984 imprint. The general introduction to the emerging discipline of the history of the book by which Darnton *is* represented in Carpenter's collection also appeared during the year in the Summer 1982 issue of *Daedalus*, "Representations and Realities." Another issue of *Daedalus* relevant to students of the book is the Winter 1983 issue, "Reading: Old and New," which was reprinted by R. R. Bowker as *Reading in the 1980s*, with one additional essay.

The Early Illustrated Book: Essays in Honor of Lessing J. Rosenwald (Washington, D.C.: Library of Congress) is edited by Sandra Hindman. Its contents derive from a symposium sponsored by the library's Center for the Book and the Rare Book and Special Collections Division. Art historians and bibliographers are both represented in this well-illustrated and scholarly volume.

Another product of the growing concern for *l'histoire du livre* was published under the auspices of the American Antiquarian Society's Program in the History of the Book in American Culture. Edited by William L. Joyce and others, *Printing and Society in Early America* contains essays on the book trade, the interrelationship between books and culture, and the impact of printing. Its contributors include David D. Hall, Stephen Botein, and Robert B. Winans. The book offers impressive testimony to the vigor with which the American Antiquarian Society is calling attention to its institutional resources for students of book history.

Another primary concern of The Center for the Book is literacy. *Literacy in His-*

torical Perspective, published by the Library of Congress, will — as its title indicates — interest those historians of the book who have questioned the audience for printing in various periods and cultures. Edited by Daniel P. Resnick, the volume's contributions embrace early modern Europe, England and New England in the seventeenth century, nineteenth-century China, Russia, and America, and black Americans in recent times. Its authors include David Cressy and Thomas W. Laqueur. It may be pertinent to add that Cambridge University Press has made available a paperbound version of François Furet and Jacques Ozouf, *Reading and Writing: Literacy in France from Calvin to Jules Ferry.* A translation of the 1977 *Lire et écrire,* published as Cambridge Studies in Oral and Literate Culture, Number 5, the volume bears a 1982 imprint, but the paperback did not appear till mid-1983. So fundamental a study needs no recommendation here.

OTHER BOOKS ABOUT BOOKS

One of the great pleasures of 1983 — the caveat about its price earlier in my text notwithstanding — is Ian Philip's little volume, *The Bodleian Library in the Seventeenth and Eighteenth Centuries* (Oxford: Clarendon Press; New York: Oxford University Press). Philip's published version of his Lyell Lectures for 1981, the book is an utterly absorbing history of Bodley's first two centuries, richly anecdotal but impressively able to give an interpretation of the library's development, as well. It is apposite to notice here, with reference to the series of bibliographical lectures from which Philip's book springs, that Jonathan A. Hill (New York) has published *The Sandars and Lyell Lectures; A Checklist,* with an introduction by David McKitterick. Henry Morris's Bird & Bull Press printed the volume for Hill in a limited edition.

Another Oxford book is A. L. P. Norrington's *Blackwell's 1879–1979: The History of a Family Firm* (Oxford: Blackwell; U.S. distributer Blackwell North America). Blackwell's sells new and antiquarian books, and Norrington deals with both aspects of the firm's retail trade. It has also acted as a publisher, sometimes — as with the Shakespeare Head Press — producing highly collectible private press productions. Norrington addresses this aspect of the firm's affairs, too. His book is genial, but as a commissioned history it lacks that disinterestedness scholars occasionally claim to value.

Bookselling and publishing are also the subject of Noel Riley Fitch, *Sylvia Beach and the Lost Generation: A History of Literary Paris in the Twenties and Thirties* (New York and London: Norton). Sylvia Beach's Paris bookshop, Shakespeare and Company, sold works of Anglo-American literary modernism to expatriate Anglo-Americans and to the French. Not content with retail bookselling alone, Beach also published *Ulysses* in 1922. An often-told story, her career is exhaustively reexamined by Fitch in this readable book.

A volume that will go onto just about every reference shelf, along with John Carter's *ABC for Book Collectors* and *Glaister's Glossary of the Book,* is *The Bookman's Glossary,* whose sixth edition, edited by Jean Peters, appeared this year (New York and London: R. R. Bowker). Not quite so narrowly focused as Carter or *Glaister,* this work will appeal to librarians, publishers, and booksellers, as well as to collectors and historians. Its definitions are short and useful. While the sheer size of *Glaister* makes it a far richer resource for many topics, and Carter's style is (alas) inimitable, this is a welcome book.

Also welcome is the long-awaited study — originally hoped for from the pens of John Carter and Graham Pollard — *A Sequel to An Enquiry into the Nature of Certain Nineteenth Century Pamphlets: The Forgeries of H. Buxton Forman and T. J. Wise Re-Examined* (London and Berkeley: Scolar Press, distributed in the United States by University Press Books, Berkeley). As has already been mentioned, Scolar has published the *Sequel* as part of a two-volume work, the first a second edition of Carter and Pollard's *Enquiry*. This second volume, by Nicolas Barker and John Collins, will be necessary reading for just about everyone concerned with antiquarian and rare books and with the techniques of bibliographical detection. It is thus slightly disheartening that despite its virtues — which are many — the book must be used with some caution. Quite apart from its failure to attain what Barker and Collins rightly call "the classic quality" of *An Enquiry,* their work is marred by a problem that, while awkward for any scholarly study, is particularly awkward for a bibliographical work where accuracy even in matters of minute detail must be beyond reproach. *A Sequel*'s accuracy is not beyond reproach. An error in Harry Buxton Forman's birthdate emerges from internal evidence in the very first sentence of the first chapter; the next page misnames the author of the *Cours de philosophie positive.* This said, the volume adds significantly to our knowledge of the Wise-Forman forgeries. It adds, too, to our knowledge of the way in which typographic evidence may be utilized in bibliographical studies.

Dewey Ganzel's *Fortune and Men's Eyes: The Career of John Payne Collier* (Oxford and New York: Oxford University Press, 1982) will also interest students of literary forgery. His sympathetic approach to Collier has generated considerable controversy, though he does not entirely relieve Collier of the onus under which his reputation has languished since his own heyday.

That a book considered alongside a rash of studies of medieval manuscript illumination should nonetheless be, hands down, the most beautiful of all of the books mentioned in this survey is probably irrelevant to readers more interested in its contents than in a book's good looks. However, John Dreyfus's *Aspects of French Eighteenth Century Typography: A Study of Type Specimens in the Broxbourne Collection at Cambridge University Library* (Cambridge: Printed [by Cambridge University Press] for presentation to members of The Roxburghe Club, 1982) incarnates that most unlikely of combinations, the beautiful and the good. Dreyfus illuminates the French eighteenth-century typefounders' trade in a marvelously written work that educates its reader not only in its subject but also in the significance of the surviving evidence on which study of that subject is based (as, for instance, in his last chapter on type specimens). David McKitterick has appended to the volume a useful handlist of the 20 type specimens from Cambridge University Library's Broxbourne Collection, a gift to Cambridge by the late Albert Ehrman. The present volume was presented to The Roxburghe Club by his son, John Ehrman.

THE PRIVATE PRESS

Roderick Cave's *The Private Press* was published in a handsomely designed second edition in 1983 (New York and London: R. R. Bowker). Twelve years have passed since its first edition, and its author is now in New Zealand — an isolation from major currents in the private press world that travel and reading cannot entirely alleviate. But insularity alone does not account for Cave's treatment, for example, of

Walter Hamady's Perishable Press—viewed largely in terms of what Cave regards as Hamady's baneful influence on his *epigoni* rather than in terms demanded by the output of the press itself—or of Richard-Gabriel Rummonds's Plain Wrapper Press—about which Cave's reader learns that its products were, to Cave's way of thinking, overpriced. My inclination is to sympathize with that cost-consciousness; however, accompanied by little more, as though Rummonds's work were without aesthetic or historical significance of any kind (patently untrue), Cave's implied judgment is insufficient. In a study with historical and scholarly ambitions, editorializing is not a satisfactory substitute for analytical discussion of the work under consideration. I am also troubled by Cave's disinclination to make what I should have thought necessary distinctions between many different kinds of "private" printing, some of which are not really appropriate to this kind of book—wartime clandestine presses, for example, seem rather oddly out of place here. Moreover, the publisher has burdened Cave with one unnecessary technical problem: Too many of his photographs are grey. Yet it is on a more positive note that I would rather end this comment about a generally useful broad survey of the private press movement up to the very near present. Its readers are in the hands of a guide who has done an enormous amount of looking at all sorts of privately printed books and cares very deeply about what he has seen.

The private press was also celebrated in 1983 by the appearance of a catalogue for an exhibition held in New York City's Grolier Club in 1978–1979. The catalogue appeared in a format that, while it surely complemented the nature of the books exhibited, simultaneously guaranteed it a limited, generally exclusive circulation. Organized by Ruth E. Fine of the National Gallery of Art and William Matheson of the Library of Congress, *Printers' Choice: A Selection of American Press Books, 1968–1978* represented a landmark effort to evaluate and appraise the American private press scene. With introductory words and brief histories of the presses by Fine and Matheson, as well as bibliographical descriptions by W. Thomas Taylor, the catalogue appeared in an edition of 325 copies printed by Texas printer David Holman at his Wind River Press (Austin, Tex.: W. Thomas Taylor). A section of photographs shows some of the printers, usually at their press or setting type. In addition, a good number of sample sheets of the printers' joyously diverse work is bound in. These range from the classical chastity of Lillian Marks and Patrick Reagh at The Plantin Press, through the eclectic and witty Bird & Bull Press of Henry Morris, the brash flamboyance of Andrew Hoyem's Arion Press, and on to the playfully idiosyncratic Perishable Press of Walter Hamady. One may quibble about some of the book's details—the description, for instance, of Toby Olson's *Fishing,* an exceptionally complicated Perishable Press book, is not at all one from which a bibliographer could plausibly "reconstruct" what that work looks like. Yet this is a magnificent publication and an important one, even if it is regarded as nothing but the record of a major exhibition—and it is much more than that.

Nonetheless (if I may make one more turn here) I am finally tempted to suggest that a reader interested in the American private press at the present time might, for about one-thirtieth the cost of *Printers' Choice,* read about it to great advantage in a cheaply produced paperbound publication offset from typescript from Columbia University's School of Library Service, *Proceedings of The Fine Printing Conference at Columbia University, Held May 19–22, 1982* (New York, 1983). The combative voices transcribed from tapes of the Columbia Fine Printing Conference are scruffy—and alive. Their concerns—aesthetic and practical, literary and bibliographical—are the concerns of the American private press movement at this time, and their expression sheds a raking, and frequently amusing, light on the scene.

One more publication of interest to students of the private press is John J. Walsdorf, *William Morris in Private Press and Limited Editions: A Descriptive Bibliography of Books by and about William Morris, 1891–1981* (Phoenix, Ariz.: Oryx Press). This book offers a bibliographical approach to the study of Morris's influence on the book arts, and is the reflection as well of one man's — Walsdorf's — collecting passion. It is an idiosyncratic but interesting work, and likely to prove useful to those concerned with the Morris revival.

BOOK ARTS

The book arts were further studied in 1983 by Phoebe Jane Easton, *Marbling: A History and a Bibliography* (Los Angeles: Dawson's Book Shop). Her book appeared in an edition of 850 copies printed by Joseph Simon and Lillian Marks. Easton's comprehensive survey clearly describes marbling techniques as well as providing a discussion of the history of the craft in a variety of cultures. Her extraordinarily intelligent work also discusses collections in which special materials related to the history of marbling are located (the Free Library of Philadelphia, for example). Equally admirable, she briefly describes many of the men and women who are walking resources for the study of marbling (Niyazi Sayin in Turkey, for instance, or Norma Rubovits and Richard J. Wolfe in the United States). This is a valuable addition to the literature on the book arts.

Another book on marbling appeared in 1983, this by one of Easton's resource people, Richard J. Wolfe: *On Improvements in Marbling the Edges of Books and Paper: A Nineteenth Century Marbling Account Explained and Illustrated with Fourteen Original Marbled Samples* (Newtown, Pa: Bird & Bull Press). Wolfe reprints an article originally printed in the *Journal of the Franklin Institute* (n.s. 3:4, April 1829). That article was one aspect of a movement intended to encourage American economic as well as political independence of Europe through promotion of local industry. A translation from a French original, it provided — as Wolfe's useful introduction remarks — the bulk of the information about marbling processes available in this country until the 1856 appearance of James Nicholson's *Manual on the Art of Bookbinding*. Wolfe not only provides the introduction, he also includes samples of marbled papers to supplement his text.

Other book arts, notably binding and illustration, are the province of the one sale catalogue I mention in this survey. A collection of *livres d'artistes* offered jointly by John F. Fleming (New York) and Priscilla Juvelis (Boston) was catalogued by Peter A. Wick and published in an edition of 750 copies (plus 100 copies for the collaborators) as *The Book Beautiful and The Binding as Art*. Numerous color photographs of both bindings and illustrations are tipped into the book, and some black-and-white illustrations also appear in the text. As a record of fine twentieth-century bookmaking, almost entirely French, as well as of the collection of one Carlos Scherrer and his unnamed "successor," this is a useful as well as an attractive volume.

LIBRARY EXHIBITION CATALOGUES

This survey has surely neglected a great many publications that ought to have come my way but did not, or that — written in languages other than English — were outside its scope. Some of these—*Histoire de l'édition française* (Paris: Promodis), volume 1 of a series under the general editorship of Henri-Jean Martin—deserve considerable attention. The situation with exhibition catalogues is even more doubtful. Of these all too ephemeral publications, I have almost certainly seen the merest fraction of what must have appeared in 1983. However, even about most of those I have seen there is little to say other than that they appeared, and add to our knowledge about their subjects and the libraries or other institutions that issued them.

There are a few exceptions, including Plummer and Wieck, already mentioned above. One other that belongs in their company is *Bookbinding in America 1680–1910 from the Collection of Frederick E. Maser,* with an essay by Willman Spawn, issued by the Bryn Mawr College Library (Bryn Mawr, Pa.). Both the exhibition and its catalogue offer a quick survey of American bookbindings, judiciously selected from Maser's collection and exquisitely shown. The catalogue is one that will sit happily alongside the Morgan Library's catalogue of Michael Papantonio's American bookbindings as a new source of light on this dark area of American bookmaking history.

Physically less imposing than the Bryn Mawr catalogue, but intellectually a very happy achievement, is *Luther*, a catalogue of the printed and manuscript materials displayed at The Houghton Library, Harvard University, during an exhibition honoring the five hundredth birthday of Martin Luther. Heavily illustrated, the catalogue contains a complete photographic reproduction of a 1517 edition of Luther's 95 theses; it also lists all sixteenth-century editions of Luther's works at Harvard. Muhlenberg College (Allentown, Pa.) also celebrated Luther's quincentenary with an exhibition that produced a catalogue: *Imagery and Ideology: Early Lutheran Art,* with an extended essay by Carol L. Neuman de Vegvar, will interest those concerned with the graphic arts of the late fifteenth and early sixteenth centuries, some, of course, used in books.

Some libraries use catalogues to celebrate themselves. *The First Twenty Years* honors Yale University's Beinecke Library on its own twentieth birthday, and—on the evidence of the catalogue alone, to say nothing of my own experiences as a satisfied user—Beinecke has lots to celebrate. The catalogue indicates quite successfully the vast range of collecting interests and the quantity of sheer intelligence that have gone into Beinecke's building since its opening in 1963. It was published by the Yale University Library (New Haven, Conn.). The Folger Shakespeare Library (Washington, D.C.) published a catalogue in 1983 of *Gifts in Honor of the 50th Anniversary.* A very impressive catalogue, with notes by astronomer and bibliophile Owen Gingerich, was issued by The Houghton Library in conjunction with a commencement exhibition at Harvard: *Collectors Choice: A Selection of Books and Manuscripts Given by Harrison D. Horblit to the Harvard College Library* is a short course in some of the manuscript and printed monuments of the history of science.

Book collecting and bookselling were the topics of an exhibition held at Philadelphia's Rosenbach Museum and Library and, later, at The Library of Congress. *Rosenwald and Rosenbach: Two Philadelphia Bookmen* (Philadelphia: Rosenbach Museum and Library) was the resultant catalogue, written by Kathleen T. Hunt, with a charming introduction memorializing Lessing J. Rosenwald by his fellow Philadelphian and collector Seymour Adelman. The exhibition, drawn from the Rosenwald Collection now housed at The Library of Congress, offered a partial survey of the relationship between Rosenwald and bookseller A. S. W. Rosenbach that helped in the development of the Rosenwald Collection.

Older books were included in two midwestern exhibitions that both produced catalogues. *Ars Librorum Medicorum per Quinque Saecula . . . Selections from the John Martin Rare Book Room of the Health Sciences Library* was exhibited in Iowa City by The University of Iowa Museum of Art; its catalogue offers a record of medical books from a 1476 Pietro d'Abano on through a 1934 Antonio Egas Moniz publication of a cerebral angiograph. Indiana University's Lilly Library exhibited and published a catalogue of cookbooks: *Une Affaire de Goût: A Selection of Cookbooks: 1475 to 1873* (Bloomington, Ind., Lilly Library Publication 35). Pegram Harrison wrote the catalogue, which is well illustrated. *Germantown and the Germans* was an exhibition mounted in Philadelphia by The Library Company of Philadelphia and the Historical Society of Pennsylvania; its catalogue uses many older printed and manuscript documents in illustrating the history of German settlement of the Philadelphia suburb (now part of the city), begun in 1683, and includes some bibliographical discoveries of interest even to those not particularly concerned with the history of that region — "the heretofore unrecognized first type specimen printed in America," as the catalogue states, from the press of German-American printer Christopher Saur. Many eighteenth-century graphic forms — maps, plans, and engravings — provide material for an exhibition at the Yale Center for British Art catalogued by Kimerly Rorschach, *The Early Georgian Landscape Garden* (New Haven, Conn.). Margaret Sax saw into print *A Little Learning: School Books in America from Colonial Times to the End of the Nineteenth Century,* based on an exhibition at Trinity College (Hartford, Conn.), where the Watkinson Library has continuously issued inexpensive but intelligent records of its exhibitions. In Providence, R.I., Brown University's John Carter Brown Library published two catalogues: Everett C. Wilkie, Jr., *The Spanish Church and the New World in the Golden Age,* and Ilse Kramer's *Die wunderbare Neue Welt: German Works in The John Carter Brown Library.* Mildred K. Abraham, *Formerly in the Possession Of: Books from the Libraries of William Byrd II, Landon Carter, Thomas Jefferson, and Their Virginia Contemporaries,* was issued by the Department of Rare Books, University of Virginia Library, Charlottesville. Berniece Webber's *Canada in Maps, from Early Times to the Present,* appeared from the Thomas Fisher Rare Book Library at the University of Toronto. Like Trinity College's Watkinson Library, Toronto's Thomas Fisher makes it an agreeable habit to issue unpretentious, inexpensive records of all its exhibitions; they are worth seeking out.

The print and photographic collections of The Library Company of Philadelphia were celebrated in *Philadelphia ReVisions: The Print Department Collects.* Kenneth Finkel's catalogue of the exhibition appeared from The Library Company in 1983. Typographers will particularly appreciate the centerfold in *The Fat and the Lean: American Wood Type in the 19th Cent.* [sic], Elizabeth M. Harris's nice catalogue commemorating an exhibition in the Hall of Printing and Graphic Arts of The National Museum of American History (Washington, D.C.: Smithsonian Institution). The work of Charles Whittingham and The Chiswick Press is recalled in an exhibition at the University of Vermont's Bailey/Howe Library that produced *Charles Whittingham, Printer* (Burlington, Vt.). The catalogue, by John Buechler, is prefaced by a foreword from Mills College's Janet Ing. H. B. de Groot, with Susan Douglas-Drinkwater, produced *Blake and the Ancients* from Toronto's Thomas Fisher Rare Book Library (with University College also participating in the publication); Richard G. Landon produced, also from the Thomas Fisher, *1883: Echoes of the Year.*

Charles Kemnitz's *James Joyce at 101: An Exhibition* (Tulsa, Okla.: McFarlin

Library, University of Tulsa) records with nice illustrations a great deal of Joyce exhibited at Tulsa in 1983. Modernism was also the focus of an exhibition at Yale's Beinecke Library, with a catalogue by Marjorie G. Wynne and Luce Marinetti Barbi, celebrating *F. T. Marinetti and Futurism.* Associated with that exhibition was a 300-copy translation of Marinetti's *Manifesto of Futurism* (from *Le Figaro,* February 20, 1909), printed at Yale's Silliman College Press for the Yale Library Associates. A separately issued reprint from *Books at Iowa,* Number 39 (November 1983), is Timothy Shipe's introduction to *The Dada Archive* at The University of Iowa (Iowa City). Three more catalogues from Toronto's Thomas Fisher Rare Book Library merit mention in this section on catalogues devoted to recent times: Alan J. Horne, *The Revival of Wood Engraving: English Illustrated Books 1915–1950*; D. E. Moggridge, *John Maynard Keynes 1883–1946*; and Margery Pearson, *The Black Art: An Exhibition of British Private Press Books.*

And last of all the catalogues I want to mention, concluding this survey, is one from the University of Wisconsin's Elvehjem Museum of Art (Madison): *Breaking the Bindings: American Book Art Now. An Exhibition of Creative Bookmaking Produced in the United States since 1980.* Katherine Harper Mead's foreword remarks that this exhibition, organized for her museum by Wisconsin professor Walter Hamady (mentioned earlier in this survey in connection with his Perishable Press), "breaks new ground as it invites us to take a fresh look at what the book can be and to review traditional definitions we had perhaps too complacently accepted." New ground — and bindings — are indeed broken in this exhibition of the post-book book. Its catalogue makes an appropriate conclusion to this survey, indicating the range of the year's books about books. The course from illuminated manuscripts through these broken bindings has proven to be enormously exhilarating.

10

Periodicals for Collectors, Dealers, and Librarians

Peter M. VanWingen

PERIODICALS RELATING to rare books are addressed to a diverse audience that includes a commercial trade, a profession, scholarly disciplines, and a knowledgeable lay public. This variety makes the periodicals on the whole more readable than the scientific and learned journals often met in other fields. In order for cross-pollination to work, reporting must come from all sides. The collector can raise points of interest for the bookseller and the librarian. The academic researcher can uncover collections and collecting areas unknown to dealers, librarians, and collectors. Librarians can describe their collections and report recent discoveries made in their institutions. Notes and comments form an important element in rare book periodicals and these items must often be pieced together by the reader to get a view of the whole field. Periodical literature gives the reader the most current knowledge available, and rare book collectors, dealers, and librarians should read these journals assiduously.

The discussion that follows focuses on the scope, editorial policies, and contents of a selection of periodicals published in 1983. At the end of the essay an even broader range of periodicals is classified by area of interest. This is followed by one alphabetical sequence containing subscription information for all of the journals in the classified subject listing as well as those mentioned in the essay. This is not a comprehensive review; rather it presents the most important periodicals in the field along with representative examples of other journals encompassed in that omnibus term "rare books."

Any discussion of periodicals in this field must begin with four journals—*The Book Collector, The Library, Papers of the Bibliographical Society of America (PBSA)*, and *Studies in Bibliography (SB)*—which have gained eminence through longevity, regular frequency, and scholarship. Of these, *The Book Collector* probably cuts a wider swath and has a greater appeal than the other three journals, which are all associated with bibliographical societies, and it strikes a fine balance between scholarly research and personal recollections. Whether reporting discoveries in the bibliographical world or presenting biographies of collectors, the articles are always readable. The Spring 1983 issue carried a sparkling overview of Douglas Cleverdon's 60 years in the book world followed by Cleverdon himself writing on "Stanley Morison and Eric Gill, 1925–1933." Mirjam M. Foot's regular series on "English and Foreign Bookbindings" continued throughout the year. The Winter 1982 and Spring and Summer 1983 issues brought a three-part preview of *A Sequel to An Enquiry into the Nature of Certain Nineteenth Century Pamphlets.*

The journals of the major bibliographical societies also tend to cut across most areas of interest in the field of antiquarian books, but the articles usually have a scholarly and research orientation. A new editorial team joined the *Papers of the Bibliographical Society of America* in 1982. After 15 years of service William B. Todd and Ann Bowden retired as editors and their places were ably filled by John Lancaster of Amherst College and Ruth Mortimer of Smith College. In recent issues new editorial policies can be seen: The editors coordinate book reviewing, the news section was dropped for lack of timeliness, and a trend toward long review essays gives reviewers a chance to explore fully a book or a set of books on a given topic. Paul Needham's review essay (Third Quarter, 1983) of William Todd's work on the Gutenberg Bible is a model of this form. The work of Gutenberg also came under close scrutiny in the Second Quarter of *PBSA* in an article entitled "Cyclotron Analysis of the Ink of the 42-Line Bible" by Richard N. Schwab, Thomas A. Cahill, Bruce H. Kusko, and Daniel L. Wick. The authors describe their studies of ink using a particle accelerator and demonstrate the progress possible when twentieth-century scientific techniques are applied to fifteenth-century books. The Fourth Quarter issue broke new ground with four pages of color plates used to illustrate "Composite Imaging: A New Technique in Bibliographic Research" by Paul R. Sternberg and John M. Brayer.

The journal of the Bibliographical Society (England), *The Library,* changed editorship with its 1983 issues. Mervyn Jannetta became editor, and Lotte Hellinga and Ian Willison were appointed joint review editors. The journal's long tradition of scholarly articles with a bias toward English-language materials continues. In addition to articles the journal carries bibliographical notes, correspondence, and book reviews. The signed reviews are supplemented by short reviews of recent books and contents notes of selected bibliographical periodicals. Though these necessarily are not current they serve as useful reminders or indexes.

Studies in Bibliography completes the triad of major society publications. Published annually by the Bibliographical Society of the University of Virginia and edited for the past 35 years by Fredson Bowers, *SB* reflects the society's and the editor's strong interest in linking bibliography with textual criticism. The two lead articles in the 1983 volume are representative of *SB*'s contents: "The Emily Dickinson Fascicles" by R. W. Franklin and "Classical, Biblical, and Medieval Textual Criticism and Modern Editing" by G. Thomas Tanselle.

Usually all periodicals relating to rare books carry book reviews, but some of the general book reviewing media also carry reviews of these works. One that deserves special mention is *The Times Literary Supplement* (*TLS*), which has had a long tradition of reviewing books relating to bibliography. Although the entire back page is seldom given over to bibliography as it once was, the reviews that are carried in *TLS* remain influential, focusing on important books considered by leading authorities.

Timeliness of reviews is always a problem with the quarterly journals. The newsletter approach of *BiN: Bibliography Newsletter* rectifies this with short notices and reviews of many new books. The highly personal points of view about new books come from one or both of the editors (Daniel Traister joined Terry Belanger during the past year). In addition, *BiN* covers events and issues in the world of antiquarian books and rare book libraries in a style that is always refreshing. The long lists of remaindered books that are carried in each issue of *BiN* are a must for the impecunious collector.

This essay and the appended list of journals concentrate on English-language periodicals. A few journals have been included in the list because they consistently carry English-language pieces even though they are not English-language journals. *Gutenberg-Jahrbuch* represents this category. However, one journal, *Quaerendo,* takes a slightly different tack. Though published in the Netherlands, *Quaerendo* considers itself an English-language journal (articles in French and German have summaries in English); yet the emphasis of the articles and reviews rests clearly on European books and libraries. This unique viewpoint provides coverage of important bibliographical projects and introduces to English-language readers European libraries and collections that might not otherwise be accessible to them.

Bookselling and book collecting are, of course, inseparable, and the periodicals from both sides of the business contain articles of equal interest to all parties. *American Book Collector,* a lively, popular magazine for collectors, includes feature articles, book reviews, catalogues received, a news column—"Business of Books"—and a review of press books (under the direction of Richard Gabriel-Rummonds). Every issue contains a bibliographical checklist of an author. A review of *American Book Prices Current 1982* in the December 1983 issue demonstrated an aggressiveness not often encountered in its pages. *Antiquarian Book Monthly Review* aims at both the collector and the bookseller with slightly more emphasis on the trade. Feature articles as well as regular columns on auctions, catalogues, and visits to bookshops and Philip Jaggard's long-running series on "Rum Customers" make good reading for anyone concerned with the English antiquarian book trade. George Sims's articles, such as those on Richard Aldington (December 1982 and January 1983), based on his years in the trade, provide some revealing insights into conditions for writing and selling books in the mid-twentieth century. The September 1983 issue (vol. 10, no. 9) carried an article by Margaret Hey on "Foxing: Some Unanswered Questions."

Antiquarian bookselling in America has two journals. *AB Bookman's Weekly* has appeared regularly since 1948. Each issue combines book world news, obituaries, reviews, and essays (some keyed to special issues, for example, the December 12 "theme" issue on music), with lists of books wanted by dealers and for sale by dealers and individuals. A less well-known journal comes from the American Antiquarian Booksellers Association (ABAA). Entitled the *Rare Professional Bookseller,* this journal focuses exclusively on antiquarian bookselling with reports on various ABAA chapter meetings and news about the trade. Number 5 (appearing in 1983) contained anecdotal articles, such as "The Bookseller's Apprentice" by George Goodspeed and "Walter R. Benjamin and the Autograph Trade at the Turn of the Century" by Lester J. Cappon. A section called "Members' Forum" reprints articles on the trade written by ABAA members but originally published elsewhere. News notes, book reviews, and especially "Counsel's Column" by Lawrence I. Fox have interest for the entire antiquarian book field.

Journals dealing with rare books are often as well made as the books their readers collect and sell. Few other fields can boast of such high-quality production standards for their current literature. Fine appearance often takes precedence over timeliness, yet readers appreciate (even demand) quality, for they tend to keep these journals in their collections as reference tools. As one would expect, journals concerned with typography and printing set the standard for all the others. The *Journal of the Printing Historical Society* represents journal quality at its highest. Since 1964 the society has published an annual journal that is distinguished in appearance and invariably carries articles of high importance. The unmistakable attention paid to design and editorial details comes through in every issue. Publication delays have caused the journal to fall behind; during the past year members received Number 15, which is dated 1980/81. The four articles in that latest offering represent the journal's interest over the years in the history of practical printing and typography: Nicolete Gray on "Slab-serif Type Design in England 1815–1845"; Michael Treadwell on "The Grover Typefoundry"; a facsimile with commentary by Gwyn Walters on "The Account Book, 1826–1836, of the Reverend John Parry, Printer and Publisher of Chester"; and, continuing a long tradition of articles about printing presses, John E. Smart describes "The Wooden Common Press at the Science Museum, London." In addition, the society publishes a quarterly *Bulletin*. Ten numbers have appeared since 1980. The *Bulletin* gives news about the society's events and contains book reviews that are much more current than is possible in the annual *Journal*.

Printing History, a publication of the American Printing History Association (APHA), has become the American counterpart of the *Journal of the Printing Historical Society.* Number 10 (vol. 5, no. 2) reached members at the end of 1983. The journal carries articles, published versions of papers presented at APHA's annual conferences, and book reviews. The success of the editor, Susan Thompson, in making this journal useful for printing historians has brought great credit to her and to the association. The latest issue reports that with the second number of 1983, Dr. Thompson will step down as editor and Anna Lou Ashby will replace her.

Over the years the *Proceedings of the American Antiquarian Society* has published articles of interest on the history of the book. This year the American Antiquarian Society (AAS) committed itself even further to this field through the creation of the Program in the History of the Book in American Culture. In November 1983 the Program issued its first number of a semiannual newsletter entitled *The Book*. The editor states: "Although the primary purpose of *The Book* will be to publish news of the AAS Program, we want to include news of related activities from other quarters, space permitting."

Project newsletters flourish: The Eighteenth Century Short Title Catalogue project has *Factotum;* the recently begun Nineteenth Century Short Title Catalogue already has a newsletter; and the Early Imprints Project in Australia and New Zealand publishes its *Newsletter.*

The splendidly eclectic *Visible Language: The Research Journal Concerned with All That Is Involved in Our Being Literate* defies any subject categorizing. Until 1970 this journal, edited then as now by Merald E. Wrolstad, was entitled *Journal of Typographic Research.* As the new title indicates, the scope has broadened. The special issues in particular reveal Wrolstad's view of his territory. The Spring 1982 special issue dealt with the topic "Understanding the Symbolism of Mathematics." A recent special issue (Winter 1983) was devoted to calligraphy. Guest editor Gunnlauger S. E. Brien invited about three dozen calligraphers to answer on two pages in their own hands the question "What are the parts of your work which give you the most trouble?" The answers, from the pens of Michael Harvey, Kris Holmes, and Sheila Waters, among many others, describe such problems as the letter *R,* space, drawing lines, inconsistencies in ink, and photographic reductions. Regular issues include articles on typography, reading and literacy, and design. Book reviews are often included.

Trade journals of the printing and papermaking industries sometimes carry articles of historical interest. Over the years *Printing Impressions* has run articles on the history of type design by Alexander Lawson. The specialist will want to consult *Graphic Arts Literature Abstracts* for articles appearing in these types of journals. For its sheer high energy most readers will find *Upper and Lower Case: The International Journal of Typographics* irresistible. The multitudinous typefaces shown and described, along with articles of general interest about bookmaking, are always entertaining. The September 1983 issue initiated a series on "Typographic Milestones" by Allan Haley. The first in the series was on Morris Fuller Benton, with the promise of future articles devoted to Baskerville, Goudy, Gill, and Dwiggins.

When Sandra Kirshenbaum founded *Fine Print: A Review of the Book Arts* in 1975 she filled an obvious gap by reporting news about fine printing, listing new productions from private presses, and featuring the printers themselves. These features continue, but *Fine Print* has become much more than a current private press periodical. Indeed, printing, papermaking, binding, typefounding, and illustration from all periods are covered with a vitality that demands cover-to-cover reading. A sampling of issues for 1983 makes this clear: Number 2 (April) carried an article by Stephen O. Saxe on "The Romance of Wood Type," a feature story on a binding by Donald Etherington, and Vivian Ridler's appreciation of Harry Graham Carter, 1901–1982. Number 3 (July) presented a series of articles on paper, including an anthology of "Thoughts on Western Book Papers" (contributions by Timothy Barrett, Howard and Kathryn Clark, Gary Frost, and others), "Some Early American Mouldmakers" by John Bidwell, and Will H. Powers's "Paper Report: Mohawk Letterpress." In Number 4 (October) the variety continued with articles on "Techniques of Marbling in Early Indian Paintings" by Christopher Weiman, a report on the International Paper Conference held in Kyoto, Japan, and the first in a series of articles on American craft binders by W. Thomas Taylor.

The Quarterly Journal of the Library of Congress (QJ) terminated publication with the December 1983 issue. For 40 years the *Quarterly Journal* served as a valuable guide to the vast collections of that library. Articles published in its final year included "The Bollingen Foundation: Ezra Pound and the Prize in Poetry" by William McGuire (Winter 1983), "Artist in the Library" by Will Barnet (Summer 1983), and "Amassing American 'Stuff': The Library of Congress and the Federal Arts Projects of the 1930s" by John Y. Cole (Fall 1983).

In spite of this demise, the list that follows shows that library journals thrive and prosper. Those considered here are produced by libraries to serve scholarly research and public relations ends. Many act as the communication vehicle between the library and "friends" groups. Most, of course, concentrate on the collections of the issuing institution. In format they range from sizable volumes to two-leaf newsletters. A remarkable range of topics receives coverage.

Though the *British Library Journal* has only completed its ninth year, it has already become one of the best in this genre. Its combination of scholarly articles and brief notices about recent acquisitions works very successfully. Of particular recent interest was the Spring 1983 issue (vol. 9, no. 1), which contained an article on

"Printing with Gold in the Fifteenth Century" by Victor Carter, Lotte Hellinga, and Tony Parker, with photographs (some in color) by Jane Mullane. The clarity of the explanations and the precision of the photographs made this complicated subject understandable. The same issue carried Janet Ing on "The Mainz Indulgences of 1454/5: A Review of Recent Scholarship," Eberhard König's "A Leaf from a Gutenberg Bible Illuminated in England," and W. J. Partridge on "The Use of William Caxton's Type 3 by John Lettou and William de Machlinia in the Printing of Their *Yearbook 35 Henry VI,* c. 1481–1482." In this last piece, Partridge, a printer, brings his practical trade experience to a bibliographical inquiry. The journal prints frequent contributions of Dennis E. Rhodes of the British Library staff. The Autumn issue carried two of his short, focused bibliographical pieces — "A Mysterious Italian Newsletter of 1517" and "An Anonymous Guidebook to Rome, 1677."

The *Bodleian Library Record* brings much local institutional news, a welcome feature especially for overseas users of that library. Articles concentrate on the Bodleian's holdings and history. The May 1983 issue included Milton McC. Gatch's piece on "Humfrey Wanley's Proposal to the Curators of the Bodleian Library on the Usefulness of Manuscript Fragments from Bindings," which presents a seventeenth-century (the earliest?) advocacy for the preservation of fragments from bindings. Finally, dedicated periodical readers will want to follow the contents of *The Bulletin of the John Rylands University Library of Manchester.* Many of the articles deal with impenetrable issues of biblical criticism; however, pieces occasionally have broader interest. The Spring 1983 issue (vol. 65, no. 2) carried a compelling article by Meridel Holland entitled "Robert Curzon, Traveller and Book Collector."

The number of North American libraries with journals and newsletters is legion. The appended subscription list makes no attempt at comprehensiveness. Most contain "news and notes" sections, which are always worth browsing through, and several include in-depth articles about collections. The *Harvard Library Bulletin* leans especially toward scholarly reporting. The Spring 1983 issue (vol. 31, no. 2) shows the extent of the journal's commitment to scholarship: "Realities and Dreams; Images of the World in Israeli Children's Literature" by Bernard Dov Cooperman, "Samuel Johnson and the Campaign to Save William Dodd" by A. D. Barker, "Speaking of Emerson: Two Unpublished Letters Exchanged between John Jay Chapman and Elliot Cabot" by Nancy Craig Simmons, and "French Illuminated Manuscripts in the Houghton Library: Recent Discoveries and Attributions" by Roger S. Wieck.

Many gems turn up in these far-flung library periodicals. The Winter 1983 issue (vol. 4, no. 2) of *Kentucky Review* ran a delightful article by Harry Duncan entitled "My Master Victor Hammer." *Bancroftiana,* published occasionally by the Friends of the Bancroft Library, often notes the progress of the Mark Twain Project. The September 1983 issue reports on efforts to locate early English editions of *The Adventures of Huckleberry Finn* — "after an extensive search only one copy of the first English edition has been found that bears features showing that it was *not* among those first issued, and no copy of the second or third English editions has been located." In Number 9 of *HRC Notes* (March 1983), Decherd Turner, Director of the Humanities Research Center (HRC) at the University of Texas at Austin, devoted the whole issue to defining "What is the HRC?" In a way all library journals and newsletters are attempting to define their institutions and by so doing can provide very useful information.

Periodicals relating to manuscripts and binding should not go unnoticed by those interested in antiquarian books. *The American Archivist,* published by the Society of American Archivists, often contains topical articles. The Spring 1983 issue (vol. 46, no. 2) carried a piece by Michael J. Crawford on "Copyright, Unpublished Manuscript Records, and the Archivist," and the Summer issue (vol. 46, no. 3) included "Tax Appraisals of Manuscript Collections" by Kenneth W. Rendell. *Manuscripts,* the quarterly publication of the Manuscript Society, has informative articles and also runs three regular series that help give a clear overview of manuscript collecting: "Auction Trends" by Earl Moore, "News Notes" by Paul G. Sifton, and "Collector's Showcase," which presents short views of private and institutional manuscript collections.

Conservation and bookbinding periodicals can quickly run into highly technical areas. *The Abbey Newsletter* and the *Guild of Book Workers Newsletter* both serve as valuable guides to current conservation and bookbinding activities. The most beautiful of the binding periodicals is *The New Bookbinder* published by Designer Bookbinders. The volume received in 1983 had a masterful appreciation of the work of Roger Powell by Nicholas Pickwoad entitled "Powell Multiscient."

Rare book librarianship does not have a separate, full-scale journal. News and articles dealing with aspects of library operations are sometimes carried in more general library literature. This occurred during 1983 in the *Wilson Library Bulletin* (October 1983), which ran five articles on the scope and functions of rare book libraries: "Rare Books in Large Libraries: The Library of Congress" by Peter VanWingen, "Rare Books for Research: Separately Housed Collections" by John Bidwell, "Manuscripts and Books in an Undergraduate Library" by Ruth Mortimer, "Special Collections: The Museum Setting" by William Keller, and "Rare Book Collections: The Need for Interpretation" by Daniel Traister.

The number of periodicals accumulated for this short survey testifies to the vitality of journalism in the field of antiquarian books. Few people in this field will regularly read all of the titles in the checklist at the end of this article, and even in this lengthy listing many items have been omitted. Still the list indicates the range of publications available. Those avid readers for whom the cost of being informed is never too high may be taken aback to know that the dollar value of the list (not including elected memberships) now stands at $2,238.95.

PERIODICALS CLASSIFIED BY SUBJECT

Antiquarian Bookselling and Book Collecting

AB Bookman's Weekly
American Book Collector
American Book Prices Current
American Society of Bookplate Collectors and Designers Yearbook
Antiquarian Book Monthly Review
Biblionews and Australian Notes and Queries: Journal for Book Collectors
Book Auction Record

Book Club of California Quarterly News Letter
The Book Collector
The Book Collector's Ephemeron
Bookman's Price Index
The Bookplate Journal
Ephemera News
The Grolier Club Gazette
Miniature Book News
Private Library
The Professional Rare Bookseller: Journal of the Antiquarian Booksellers Association of America

Archives and Manuscripts

The American Archivist
Archives
Manuscripts
Scriptorium: International Review of
    Manuscript Studies

Bibliography and Textual Criticism

Analytical and Enumerative Bibliog-
    raphy
The Bibliographical Society of Austra-
    lia and New Zealand Bulletin
Bibliotheck: A Scottish Journal of
    Bibliography and Allied Topics
BiN: Bibliography Newsletter
Bulletin of Research in the Humanities
Early Imprints Project in Australia and
    New Zealand Newsletter
Factotum
Gutenberg-Jahrbuch
The Library
Nineteenth Century Short Title Cata-
    logue Newsletter
The Papers of the Bibliographical
    Society of America
The Papers of the Bibliographical
    Society of Canada
Quaerendo
Studies in Bibliography
Studies in Bibliography and Booklore
Times Literary Supplement

Conservation and Bookbinding

AIC Newsletter
Abbey Newsletter
Guild of Book Workers Journal
Guild of Book Workers Newsletter
Journal of the American Institute for
    Conservation
The New Bookbinder: Journal of
    Designer Bookbinders
Restaurator: International Journal for
    the Preservation of Library and
    Archival Material

Library Journals

Annual Report of the Library Com-
    pany of Philadelphia
Bancroftiana

Bibliotheca (Friends of the Library of
    the University of Pennsylvania)
Books at Brown
Books at Iowa
British Library Journal
Bulletin of the John Rylands University
    Library at Manchester
Columbia Library Columns
Folger Library Newsletter
Harvard Library Bulletin
Humanities Research Center Notes
Huntington Library Quarterly
Indiana University Bookman
The Kentucky Review
Library Chronicle
Newberry Newsletter
Osler Library Newsletter
Princeton University Library Chronicle
Quarterly Journal of the Library of
    Congress
Quarto
Yale University Library Gazette

Publishing, Distribution, and Reading Books

The Book: Newsletter of the Program
    in the History of the Book in Ameri-
    can Culture
Dime Novel Round-Up
Gulden Passer/Compas D'Or
Horn Book Magazine
Journal of Library History
Paperback Quarterly: Journal of
    Mass-Market Paperback History
Proceedings of the American Antiquar-
    ian Society
Publishers Weekly
Publishing History
Scholarly Publishing
Small Press

Typography, Printing, and Paper

Albion: A Journal for Private Press
    Printers
American Printing History Association
    Letter
Book Arts Review
British Printer
Bulletin of the International Associa-
    tion of Paper Historians
The Devil's Artisan: A Journal of the
    Printing Arts

Fine Print
Graphic Arts Literature Abstracts
Journal of the Printing Historical
    Society
Matrix
Paper

Penrose Annual
Printing Historical Society Bulletin
Printing History
Printing Impressions
Upper and Lower Case
Visible Language

PERIODICALS WITH SUBSCRIPTION INFORMATION

AB Bookman's Weekly
PO Box AB
Clifton, NJ 07015
(weekly $35)

AIC Newsletter
American Institute for Conservation of
    Historic and Artistic Works
3545 Williamsburg Lane NW
Washington, DC 20008
(quarterly   with membership; associate
    $35; professional associate $45; institu-
    tion $60)

Abbey Newsletter
c/o School of Library Service
516 Butler Library
Columbia University
New York, NY 10027
(6 issues/year   individual $20; institution
    $25)

Albion: A Journal for Private Press Printers
26 West Hill
Hitchin, Hertfordshire
England
(United States: R. T. Risk, Bennington Rd,
    Francestown, NH)
(3 issues/year   £2 UK; £2.50 Europe; £3
    elsewhere)

The American Archivist
Society of American Archivists
330 S Wells
Suite 810
Chicago, IL 60606
(quarterly $30)

American Book Collector
Moretus Press
274 Madison Ave
New York, NY 10016
(bimonthly   individual $18.50; institution
    $23.25)

American Book Prices Current
PO Box 236
Washington, CT 06793
(annual $89.95)

**American Printing History Association
    Letter**
PO Box 4922 Grand Central Sta
New York, NY 10163
(6 issues/year   membership: individual
    $15; institution $20)

**American Society of Bookplate Collectors
    and Designers Yearbook**
605 N Stoneman Ave, No. F
Alhambra, CA 91801
(irregular $25)

Analytical and Enumerative Bibliography
Bibliographical Society of Northern Illinois
Founders Memorial Library
Northern Illinois University
DeKalb, IL 60115
(quarterly $17)

**Annual Report of the Library Company of
    Philadelphia**
Library Co of Philadelphia
1314 Locust St
Philadelphia, PA 19107
(annual   membership: $20 first year, $8
    thereafter)

Antiquarian Book Monthly Review
ABMR Publications Ltd
52 St. Clement's St
Oxford OX4 1AG
England
(monthly   £6; $18 US)

Archives
British Records Association
Archives Account
c/o Mrs. M. J. Post
The Charterhouse
Charterhouse Sq
London EC1M 6AU
England
(semiannual   £8)

Bancroftiana
Friends of the Bancroft Library
University of California
Berkeley, CA 94720
(occasional   membership $35)

Bibliographical Society of Australia and New Zealand Bulletin
Helen Thomson, Secretary
6 Sherbourne Rd
Medindie Gardens
S.A. 5081
Australia
(quarterly   individual $A10; institution $A12.50)

Biblionews and Australian Notes and Queries: A Journal for Book Collectors
Book Collectors Society of Australia
64 Young St
Cremorne, NSW 2090
Australia
(quarterly $A10)

Bibliotheca
Friends of the Library of the University of Pennsylvania
Van Pelt Library/CH
Philadelphia, PA 19104
(occasional   membership $25)

Bibliotheck: A Scottish Journal of Bibliography and Allied Topics
Library Association, Scottish Group
National Library of Scotland
Edinburgh EH1 1EW
Scotland
(3 issues/year   £5; $12.50 US)

BiN: Bibliography Newsletter
21 Claremont Ave
New York, NY 10027
(irregular, approx. 6 issues/year $15)

Bodleian Library Record
Oxford University Press
Walton St
Oxford OX2 6DP
England
(semiannual $10)

The Book: Newsletter of the Program in the History of the Book in American Culture
American Antiquarian Society
185 Salisbury St
Worcester, MA 01609
(semiannual   free)

Book Arts Review
Center for Book Arts
15 Bleecker St
New York, NY 10012
(quarterly   membership $20)

Book Club of California Quarterly News Letter
545 Sutter St
San Francisco, CA 94102
(quarterly   elected membership $40)

The Book Collector
The Collector Ltd
90 Great Russell St
London WC1B 3PY
England
(quarterly   £16.50; $37.50 US)

The Book Collectors Ephemeron
Book Collectors Club of Los Angeles
Jody Steinfeld, Secretary
Huntington Library
San Marino, CA 91108
(occasional   membership $25; corresponding member $15)

Bookman's Price Index
Gale Research Co
Book Tower
Detroit, MI 48226
(irregular $115 per vol.)

The Bookplate Journal
Bookplate Society
9 Lyndale Ave
London NW2
England
(irregular   £10)

Books and Libraries at the University of Kansas
University of Kansas Libraries
Lawrence, KS 66045
(irregular   free)

Books at Brown
Friends of the Library
Brown University
PO Box A
Providence, RI 02912
(annual $10)

Books at Iowa
Friends of the University of Iowa Libraries
University of Iowa
Iowa City, IA 52242
(semiannual   membership $10)

British Library Journal
Oxford University Press
Walton St
Oxford OX2 5DP
England
(semiannual   £14; $38 US)

British Printer
Maclean-Hunter Ltd
76 Oxford St
London W1N OHH
England
(monthly   £20)

Bulletin of Research in the Humanities
Publishing Center for Cultural Resources
625 Broadway

New York, NY 10012
(4 issues/year   individual $15; institution
   $20)

**Bulletin of the John Rylands University
   Library of Manchester**
John Rylands University Library
Manchester M3 3EH
England
(quarterly   £16)

Columbia Library Columns
Friends of Columbia University Libraries
Butler Library
Columbia University
New York, NY 10027
(3 issues/year $7.50)

**The Devil's Artisan: A Journal of the Print-
   ing Arts**
215 College St
Apt 248
Toronto, ON M5T 1R1
Canada
(3 issues/year $6)

Dime Novel Round-Up
Edward T. LeBlanc
87 School St
Fall River, MA 02720
(bimonthly $10)

**Early Imprints Project in Australia and
   New Zealand**
c/o Trevor Mills
State Library of Victoria
Melbourne
Australia
(occasional   free)

Ephemera News
Ephemera Society of America Inc
PO Box 943
Hillsboro, NH 03244
(quarterly $25)

Factotum
British Library
Reference Division
Great Russell St
London WC1B 3DG
England
(3–4 issues/year   free)

Fine Print
PO Box 3394
San Francisco, CA 94119
(quarterly   individual $30; institution $36)

Folger Library Newsletter
Folger Shakespeare Library
201 E Capitol St SE
Washington, DC 20003
(5 issues/year $5)

Graphic Arts Literature Abstracts
Graphic Arts Research Center
Rochester Institute of Technology
One Lomb Memorial Dr
Rochester, NY 14623
(monthly $34)

The Grolier Club Gazette
47 E 60 St
New York, NY 10022
(occasional   with elected membership)

Guild of Book Workers Journal
521 Fifth Ave
New York, NY 10175
(2 issues/year $10)

Guild of Book Workers Newsletter
521 Fifth Ave
New York, NY 10175
(6 issues/year; available by membership
   only)

Gulden Passer/Compas D'Or
Antwerp Bibliophile Society
Museum Plantin-Moretus
Vrijdammarkt 22
B-2000 Antwerp
Belgium
(annual $13)

Gutenberg-Jahrbuch
Gutenberg-Gesellschaft
Liebfrauenplatz 5
6500 Mainz
West Germany
(annual   DM40)

Harvard Library Bulletin
Harvard University Library
Cambridge, MA 02138
(quarterly $25)

Horn Book Magazine
Horn Book Inc
Park Square Bldg
31 St. James Ave
Boston, MA 02116
(bimonthly $23; foreign $26)

Humanities Research Center Notes
PO Box 7219
Austin, TX 78712
(occasional   free)

**Huntington Library Quarterly: A Journal
   for the History and Interpretation of
   English and American Civilization**
Huntington Library, Art Gallery and Botanical Gardens
San Marino, CA 91108
(quarterly $15)

IPH Information: Bulletin of the International Association of Paper Historians
Bollwerk Strasse 74
CH-4102 Binningen
Switzerland
4 issues/yr   30 Swiss Fr)

Indiana University Bookman
Indiana University Library
Bloomington, IN 47401
(irregular $10)

Journal of Library History, Philosophy and Comparative Librarianship
University of Texas Press
PO Box 7819
Austin, TX 78712
(quarterly   individual $18; institution $24)

Journal of the American Institute for Conservation
American Institute for Conservation of Historic and Artistic Works
3545 Williamsburg Lane NW
Washington, DC 20008
(biannual $20)

Journal of the Printing Historical Society
Printing Historical Society
St. Bride Institute
Bride Lane, Fleet St
London EC4
England
(annual   membership £8)

The Kentucky Review
University of Kentucky Library Association
University of Kentucky Libraries
Lexington, KY 40506
(3 issues/year $10)

The Library
The Bibliographical Society
Oxford University Press
Walton St
Oxford OX2 6DP
England
(quarterly   £18; $30)

Library Chronicle
University of Texas at Austin
Humanities Research Center
PO Box 7219
Austin, TX 78712
(quarterly $20)

Library History
Library Association, Library History Group
7 Ridgemont St
London WC1E 7AE
England
(semiannual   £4; $12 US)

Manuscripts
Manuscript Society
350 N Niagara St
Burbank, CA 91805
(quarterly $20)

Matrix
The Whittington Press
Manor Farm
Andoversford, Gloucestershire
England
(biannual   price varies)

Miniature Book News
12 Dromara Rd
St. Louis, MO 63124
(quarterly $10)

The New Bookbinder: Journal of Designer Bookbinders
Designers Bookbinders
6 Queen Sq
London WC1N 3AR
England
(annual   £12; outside Europe £15)

Newberry Newsletter
Newberry Library
60 W Walton St
Chicago, IL 60611
(4 issues/year   free)

Newsletter of the Library Association, Rare Book Group
c/o Miss J. Archibald
British Library
Great Russell St
London WC1B 3DG
England
(semiannual   £1; $3.50 US)

Nineteenth Century Short Title Catalogue Newsletter
20 Great North Rd
Newcastle upon Tyne NE2 4PS
England
(irregular   free)

Osler Library Newsletter
McGill University
Osler Library
3655 Drummond St
Montreal, PQ H3G 1Y6
Canada
(3 issues/year   free)

Paper
Benn Publications, Ltd.
25 New Street Sq
London EC4A 3JA
England
(semimonthly   £26)

Paperback Quarterly: Journal of Mass-
Market Paperback History
1710 Vincent St
Brownwood, TX 76801
(quarterly $12)

The Papers of the Bibliographical Society of
America
Bibliographical Society of America
PO Box 397 Grand Central Sta
New York, NY 10163
(quarterly membership $20)

The Papers of the Bibliographical Society of
Canada
Bibliographical Society of Canada
PO Box 1110
Sta B
London, ON N6A 5K2
Canada
(annual membership $20; institution $30)

Penrose Annual: International Review of
the Graphic Arts
Northwood Publications Ltd
Elm House
10-16 Elm St
London WC1X 0BP
England
(annual £12.50)

Princeton University Library Chronicle
Friends of the Princeton University Library
Princeton, NJ 08544
(3 issues/year $15)

Printing Historical Society Bulletin
St. Bride Institute
Bride Lane, Fleet St
London EC4
England
(quarterly membership £8)

Printing History
American Printing History Society
PO Box 4922, Grand Central Sta
New York, NY 10163
(semiannual membership: individual $15;
institution $20)

Private Library
Private Libraries Association
Ravelston, South View Rd
Pinner, Middlesex
England
(United States: W. A. Klutts, 145 E Jack-
son, PO Box 289, Ripley, TN 38063)
(quarterly £12.50; $24 US)

Proceedings of the American Antiquarian
Society
185 Salisbury St
Worcester, MA 01609
(semiannual $30)

Professional Rare Bookseller: Journal of the
Antiquarian Booksellers Association of
America
50 Rockefeller Plaza
New York, NY 10020
(occasional $7.50 per issue)

Publishers Weekly
R. R. Bowker Co
205 E 42 St
New York, NY 10017
(weekly $68)

Publishing History
Chadwyck-Healy Ltd
20 Newmarket Rd
Cambridge CB2 1NB
England
(United States: 623 Martense Ave, Teaneck,
NJ 07666)
(semiannual £10)

Quaerendo
E. J. Brill
Postbus 9000
2300 PA Leiden
The Netherlands
(quarterly fl. 84)

Quarto
Clements Library Associates
William L. Clements Library
University of Michigan
Ann Arbor, MI 48104
(quarterly $25)

Restaurator: International Journal for the
Preservation of Library and Archival
Material
Munksgaard, Noerre Soegade
DK-1370 Copenhagen K
Denmark
(irregular DKr.290)

Scholarly Publishing
University of Toronto Press
Toronto, ON M5G 1A6, Canada
(quarterly individual Can. $12.50; insti-
tution Can. $25)

Scriptorium: International Review of
Manuscript Studies
Cultura
Hoenderstraat 22
B-9200 Wetteren
Belgium
(semiannual 3000 Fr.)

Small Press
R. R. Bowker Co
205 E 42 St
New York, NY 10017
(bimonthly $18)

Special Collections
Haworth Press
28 E 22 St
New York, NY 10010
(quarterly individual $38; institution $95)

Studies in Bibliography
Bibliographical Society of the University of
Virginia
University of Virginia Library
Charlottesville, VA 22901
(annual membership $15)

Studies in Bibliography and Booklore
Hebrew Union College Library
JIR
3101 Clifton Ave
Cincinnati, OH 45220
(occasional $9)

Times Literary Supplement
Times Newspapers Ltd
PO Box No. 7
New Printing House Sq
Gray's Inn Rd
London WC1X 8EZ
England
(weekly $45; £22)

**Transactions of the Cambridge Bibliograph-
ical Society**
Cambridge Bibliographical Society
University Library
West Rd
Cambridge CB3 9DR
England
(occasional $15; £6)

**Visible Language: The Research Journal
Concerned with All That Is Involved in
Our Being Literate**
PO Box 1972 CMA
Cleveland, OH 44106
(quarterly individual $15; institution $25)

Wilson Library Bulletin
H.W. Wilson Co
950 University Ave
Bronx, NY 10452
(monthly $22)

Yale University Library Gazette
Yale University Library
New Haven, CT 06520
(quarterly $14)

ISSUES AND
PROGRAMS
IN THE NEWS

11

Recent Work in Automation and Rare Books

Stephen Paul Davis

THOSE INVOLVED IN AUTOMATION have grown fond of the phrase "state of the art" to describe their brightest and shiniest new electronic wonders. The present state of the art in U.S. libraries may soon include such innovations as optical disk jukeboxes, page-image-transfer capability, multiple-font optical character recognition equipment, and local area networks. And while it is not impossible that these new technologies will play a role in rare book libraries of the future, for the moment such libraries remain comfortably behind the cutting—and what some have pointed out is often the bleeding—edge of technology.

During the past few years rare book librarians have, at a slow but steady pace, made substantial progress in developing appropriate national standards so that computer-assisted cataloguing will meet the special needs of their collections. These standards have allowed a large number of special collections to begin to use the automated support of the national bibliographic utilities, OCLC, RLIN, and WLN (the Online Computer Library Center, the Research Libraries Information Network, and the Washington Library Network; for definitions of these and other terms, see Glossary at the end of this chapter) with the knowledge that essential specialized bibliographic information can be accommodated in their automated catalogue records, even if not yet retrievable online. During 1982 and 1983, two important new standards were published, and work proceeded on a third. In addition, many more institutions began exploring the use of in-house or local computer capabilities and vendors of library computer services to help provide direct support for patron use of their collections. Two large-scale computer-assisted bibliographic projects, the *Eighteenth Century Short Title Catalogue* and the United States Newspaper Project, passed major milestones, and at least one began to demonstrate the solid contributions to research and scholarship that may be had from the well-planned use of computer capabilities.

ADVANCES IN STANDARDS

Genre Terms

During 1983, the Standards Committee of the Rare Books and Manuscripts Section (RBMS) of the Association of College and Research Libraries (ACRL) completed and published its long-anticipated standard for recording genres of rare printed materials in catalogue records.* A standard for genre terms had first been proposed in 1979 by an ad hoc committee of the Independent Research Libraries Association (IRLA),† and the draft published by IRLA as part of its final report contained about 140 terms, with only a few cross-references and no real principles of application. The RBMS thesaurus, building on the earlier list, contains nearly 350 terms and has an extensive cross-reference structure. A set of guidelines for application has also been provided.

Genre Terms should provide a major new tool for rare book libraries using either automated or manual bibliographic tools. The concept of "genre" in this list encompasses the intellectual and physical types of publications for which libraries often maintain special files. The thesaurus is predicated on the principle that genre access should be kept distinct from subject access, though traditional library cataloguing has tended to combine the two.

The new list was constructed according to the thesaurus-building principles of the American National Standards Institute (ANSI) (hence the UF for "Used For," RT for "Related Term," BT for "Broader Term," etc.) and, when implemented, will allow individual special collections to increase direct access to categories of materials held. The following selected entries from *Genre Terms* will serve to clarify what is being standardized here:

Acting editions
  [Use for plays with extensive
  printed production information.]
  UF Acting versions
  RT Promptbooks

Broadsides
  [Use for types of texts normally
  printed in broadside form.]
  UF Handbills
  NT Broadside poems
  RT Playbills

Confessions
  RT Autobiographies
      Diaries
      Memoirs

Dime novels
  RT Penny dreadfuls

Library catalogues
  UF Catalogues, Library
  BT Catalogues

Science fiction
  BT Fiction
  RT Fantasy literature
      Imaginary voyages

Yellowbacks
  UF Railway novels
  BT Fiction

---

*Association of College and Research Libraries. Rare Books and Manuscripts Section. Standards Committee. *Genre Terms: A Thesaurus for Use in Rare Book and Special Collections Cataloguing* (Chicago, 1983).
†*Proposals for Establishing Standards for the Cataloguing of Rare Books and Specialized Research Materials in Machine-Readable Form: Final Report* (Worcester, Mass.: Independent Research Libraries Association, December 1979), pp. 30–33.

Major literary genres are included, and the list encompasses modern genres as well as genres appropriate to older materials. The authors of this standard make clear in the introduction that not all libraries will want to use all the terms in the list; each institution will need to determine which aspects of its collections it would like to emphasize.

A field in the MARC format (the *MA*chine *R*eadable *C*ataloguing format—the data format for machine-readable bibliographic data most widely used in library automation) has already been defined for this kind of heading, and those libraries that are members of bibliographic utilities should be able to use it in the near future for producing overprinted headings on cards. Users of RLIN will be able to search their own records and those of other institutions online by using this new kind of access point.

A lengthy supplementary genre thesaurus solely for liturgical genres, prepared in draft form by Patrick Russell (Bancroft Library, University of California at Berkeley) for the Standards Committee, has been tabled until additional expert help can be found to complete it.

Standard Citation Forms

Toward the end of 1982, the Library of Congress published a new standard for recording citations to bibliographies and catalogues used in rare materials cataloguing.* This work, too, was based on that of the IRLA ad hoc committee and subsequently sponsored by the RBMS Standards Committee, and grew out of the desire both to clarify and simplify practice in this area. Users of both libraries' and dealers' catalogues can sometimes have difficulty in identifying cryptic citations to bibliographies, leading to uncertainty in identifying the work being described. *Standard Citation Forms* lists and provides recommended citations for some 400 bibliographies and catalogues commonly used in rare book cataloguing at the Library of Congress and elsewhere and, in addition, sets out a few basic guidelines for citing works not appearing in the list. No longer will librarians, book dealers, and collectors need to guess which of Claus Nissen's bibliographies on zoological illustration is intended by the terse "Nissen." Instead, the following standard forms should clarify the situation:

> Nissen, C. Illustrierte Vogelbücher
> Nissen, C. Schöne Fischbücher
> Nissen, C. Schöne Vogelbücher
> Nissen, C. Zoologische Buchillustration

Besides helping the uninitiated to interpret unfamiliar references, a further benefit from introducing a little more explicitness and consistency into such citations will be granted those libraries with access to flexible automated systems. An online or "batch" computerized request for catalogue records containing a particular citation should be a powerful new kind of search capability, providing subject, geographical, or chronological access corresponding to the nature of the bibliography or catalogue referenced. The MARC format also contains a special tag for this kind of standard

---

*Peter VanWingen and Stephen Paul Davis, *Standard Citation Forms for Published Bibliographies and Catalogs Used in Rare Book Cataloging* (Washington, D.C.: Library of Congress, 1982).

citation form, and the three major bibliographic utilities (RLIN, OCLC, and WLN) support the input of this field, though not online access to it. Because the effectiveness of this kind of search is contingent on the presence of the standard citation in all applicable records—also the case with regard to the genre terms discussed above—libraries having the resources may wish to plan a program of upgrading existing MARC records to include this information against the day when it will be searchable.

Thesaurus of Terms for Publishing/Physical Aspects of Printed Works and for Provenance

Yet another thesaurus, or more likely a set of thesauri, is currently under development by the RBMS Standards Committee in order to standardize access terminology for aspects of publishing and bookselling, paper and papermaking, printing processes, type, typefaces and ornaments, illustration methods, binding, and provenance. This thesaurus parallels *Genre Terms* and will contain terms such as the following:

> Counterfeits
> Made-up copies
> Watermarks—Goat
> Press proofs
> Type ornaments—Fleurons
> Drypoint
> Stereoscopic view
> Binders—Stamps—Sangorski & Sutcliffe
> Bookplates—Memorials—Spaulding, Stephen

This thesaurus will probably not be finished for a year or two, both because of the difficulties inherent in such a task as well as the inefficiencies of preparing standards long distance. The Standards Committee welcomes expert help in reviewing drafts of its standards, and with these thesauri in particular will seek widespread comment during their preparation.

Even in advance of the availability of this standard, a special field has been defined in the MARC formats for this kind of information, though it has not yet been implemented by the bibliographic utilities.

Rare Serials

A program of the ACRL RBMS group called MASC—"MARC for Special Collections"—at the 1983 annual meeting of the American Library Association in Los Angeles focused on questions of cataloguing and achieving automated access to rare serials. This program may have been the first ever on these subjects, and it brought out some genuinely new perspectives. Joseph E. Macmanus, American Antiquarian Society, in a perceptive paper on the topic, expressed the view that rare serials may actually require individual, issue by issue cataloguing to bring out both their unique bibliographical aspects and subject content. By contrast, most rare materials collections now provide only "collected set" cataloguing for serials, with occasional notes to bring out special features of particular issues. Stephen Davis, Library of Congress, discussed how such a requirement might be accommodated in an automated system, particularly within the context of the MARC Holdings Format, which the bibliographic utilities are now making plans to implement; and the provisions of the new MARC record-linking technique (via field 773), which will allow for what traditionally has been called "analytic cataloguing"—something that until now has been impossible to do in most automated library systems.

Leaving aside the problem of the resources that would be required for such detailed description, it is worth considering whether this approach might not be appropriate for selected rare serials—those meriting such attention either by virtue of their bibliographical nature or subject content. The bibliographic utilities may be able to support the input of such information, but it is uncertain how readily they will allow online access to it. A more flexible retrieval system, however, would be able to access records for individual issues, perhaps by the name of the contributor or by special subjects emphasized in the issue.

The ACRL RBMS Standards Committee, working in a similar vein, established a Rare Serials Subcommittee that, during 1983, drafted a proposal to the Library of Congress and the CONSER (Conversion of Serials) Coordinating Committee requesting that certain, more detailed descriptive conventions—paralleling those now available for rare books*—also be allowed for rare serials cataloguing.

COMPUTER–ASSISTED BIBLIOGRAPHICAL PROJECTS

A fair number of individual institutions have undertaken computer-assisted bibliographic projects over the last several years to support research and publication in the area of old and rare materials. Because it would be impossible to describe them all in this kind of essay, only the two largest such projects will be mentioned here.

Eighteenth Century Short Title Catalogue

As has been the case almost from its inception, the *Eighteenth Century Short Title Catalogue (ESTC)* project continues to lead the way in showing how the computer can benefit bibliographical and historical research. During 1983 the online *ESTC* file remained available in the United States via RLIN; in Great Britain, it is available through the British Library's BLAISE system. In addition, the British Library passed a major project milestone this year when it used the *ESTC* database to produce a first edition of the catalogue in microfiche. The microfiche edition, which may be purchased directly from the British Library, will provide many libraries with their first look at the file and should prove to be a major new research tool in its own right, even though it still reflects largely the British Library's own eighteenth-century holdings. (A later edition will include unique holdings and locations from other libraries in Great Britain and around the world.)

However useful the microfiche edition, the online version of the *ESTC* provides still more exciting opportunities for exploring the potential of automated access to a large retrospective database. Many U.S. libraries are not aware that they can open "dial-up" accounts to search the *ESTC* and other RLIN files even if they are not RLIN members. All that is required is a standard terminal with a telephone modem. Users

---

*As exemplified in *Bibliographic Description of Rare Books* (Washington, D.C.: Library of Congress, 1981).

of the database will find that, despite the lack of subject headings in *ESTC* records, RLIN retrieval software will allow kinds of searches that were previously impossible or immensely more difficult in traditional bibliographies or card catalogues. Some of the kinds of research that a file like the *ESTC* can support are described in the new publication *Searching the Eighteenth Century* (London: British Library, 1983). This excellent collection of essays, edited by Michael Crump and Michael Harris, is based on papers originally presented at the Symposium on the Eighteenth Century Short Title Catalogue, held in 1982, and should help convert those who still doubt the value of computer-assisted bibliography.

In the fall of 1983, the Library of Congress made plans to include the American Antiquarian Society (which is responsible for cataloguing U.S. imprints for the *ESTC* project) and the ESTC/North America office at Louisiana State University in the first group of libraries selected to participate in the Linked Systems Project (LSP), scheduled to begin in 1984–1985. This project will allow RLIN, WLN, and the Library of Congress to share information among their three systems through an advanced telecommunications facility. Initially, this link will be exploited chiefly for the exchange of name authority records, allowing AAS and ESTC/NA to contribute name headings for eighteenth-century works to the nationwide authorities database. Staff from AAS and ESTC/NA have already received special training at the Library of Congress in the creation of standard MARC authority records.

United States Newspaper Project

In a major effort to inventory U.S. newspapers from 1690 to the present, the National Endowment for the Humanities has given nearly $1 million to a number of institutions that will enter bibliographic records for old and rare newspapers into the CONSER/OCLC database. Participating institutions include the American Antiquarian Society, the Center for Research Libraries, Western Reserve Historical Society, New York State Library, the Virgin Islands Department of Conservation and Cultural Affairs, the Library of Congress, and the state historical societies of Kansas, Montana, New York, and Wisconsin; the Library of Congress will also provide technical support.

This project will eventually result in the creation of some 300,000 records for U.S. newspapers; it will also involve the preservation microfilming of selected newspapers that are found to be in advanced states of deterioration. As with other CONSER records, the Library of Congress will make tapes of them available through its Cataloging Distribution Service so that the data may be accessed through RLIN, WLN, and other automated systems.

USE OF COMPUTERS TO SUPPORT
DIRECT SERVICE TO READERS

The use of the computer to support direct patron access continues to lag behind its use for cataloguing and other technical services applications. In certain areas, such as in the production of offline printed products, the use of automated support is already routine in many institutions; in many other areas, such as online public access, use of the computer is still in its infancy.

Bibliographic Utilities

At present, none of the major bibliographic utilities is well suited to providing online public access to patrons of special collections, and this seems unlikely to change in the near future. OCLC lacks the capability to perform subject searches, not to speak of more esoteric kinds of access, such as access by date of publication or by genre. OCLC also reflects only a master record for each item, omitting copy-specific information, such as call number, physical characteristics, or provenance, except that of the first institution to catalogue the item.

RLIN, on the other hand, does provide many important features for special collections, such as retrieval by subject and by certain special fields, and retention of copy-specific information for each institution's copy. However, many librarians feel that RLIN is not well suited for public access; the system is seen as a little too complicated for the average user, requiring continuous staff guidance for efficient use. Further, neither OCLC nor RLIN was designed to support the heavy demand on computer resources that would accompany their widespread use for direct patron access.

Many libraries do put OCLC or RLIN terminals in the public service area, but have reference staff mediate searches. This amounts to using the RLIN or OCLC terminal as a backup or enhancement to other bibliographic tools—chiefly the card catalogue—but in no way as a replacement.

Local Online Catalogues

Online public-access catalogues are a reality in only a few institutions, though they are under development in many more. Generally, only the largest institutions, such as university systems, can support the development or purchase of such a capability. The systems that exist at present are nearly all mainframe or mini-based—that is, they require relatively large and expensive computer facilities to run on and systems staff to maintain them. Further, they are normally oriented to the needs of general collections and tend not to support the particular requirements of special collections, such as access by genre, place of publication, date of publication, name of collection, physical features, and the like. In short, most existing online public access catalogues are not particularly suited to rare book collections.

OCLC did announce in 1983 that it would be adapting Integrated Library System software (originally developed by the National Library of Medicine) as the basis for its local library system project, whereby the database of a consortium or library system would be maintained locally on a minicomputer for such applications as online patron access; RLIN is also planning to move in the same direction. These new developments may ultimately be of benefit to rare book and special collections, but it will be important in the interim for individual libraries and the special collections community as a whole to articulate their needs to those who are planning and implementing these systems at the local level.

Microcomputers

Increasingly, special collections are turning their attention to the microcomputer and its possible use as a new bibliographic tool. It is already feasible, for example, to store specialized information using a microcomputer and then retrieve it in ways that are not possible through the bibliographic utilities. For example, it is possible to create brief catalogue records for a collection of books and to index them by the date of publication, genre, illustration technique, name of donor, and so on. Retrieval could be done by a single access point (for example, a name) or by combinations of access points (for example, a name and a date), and the results used to form additional files or to print out a mini-bibliography. Microcomputer systems hold out the prospect of enhancing—though not yet replacing, the retrieval capabilities available through the bibliographic utilities. It should be emphasized that there are storage limitations in using microcomputers and that online retrieval is not always fast. Still, microcomputers continue to decrease in price and increase in storage capability, and—most significantly for special collections—they allow for a customized approach to the creation of bibliographic tools.

At least two of the systems developed for general library applications may prove of value in special collections. The first is Golden Retriever, available from CLASS (1415 Koll Circle, Suite 101, San Jose, Calif. 95112). It runs on a standard microcomputer supporting CP/M or TRSDOS (such as HP125 or Radio Shack Model II), with 64K of memory, and provides flexible indexing, storage, and retrieval of data. Golden Retriever also supports the downloading of MARC records for further manipulation. The STAR System, available from Cuadra Associates (1523 Sixth St., Suite 12, Santa Monica, Calif. 90401) runs only on the Alpha MICRO, a 16-bit micro with 96K of memory and a hard disk drive. It is somewhat more powerful, but also more expensive than Golden Retriever. Both of these systems could be used to index types of information to which the bibliographic utilities do not provide access.

An interesting software package designed strictly for the production of bibliographies, called The Personal Bibliographic System, has been developed under grants from the Council on Library Resources, OCLC, Inc., and other agencies, and is available from Personal Bibliographic Software, Inc. (PO Box 4250, Ann Arbor, Mich. 48106) for about $250. This software runs on Apple II, Apple IIe, and the IBM-PC; future plans call for versions to run on the Radio Shack TRS-80 model II, the IBM Displaywriter, and others. This kind of software seems particularly useful for institutions producing bibliographies and finding lists on a regular basis. It allows the copying (downloading) of MARC records from OCLC, RLIN, or WLN, and automatically formats them into "bibliography style" citations according to the ANSI standard for bibliographic references. It also allows for the addition of annotations to records, modification of data, and input of additional records, such as those for analytics.

One can imagine using a system like this to support the production of scholarly bibliographies, perhaps even by visiting scholars or researchers who are willing to learn the system. It may also be possible to find a vendor who can use the output from such a system to drive automated photocomposition equipment to produce a high-quality printed bibliography.

Many similar systems suitable for use in special collections will doubtless be available in the future, including software developed in-house by enterprising librarians. A principal consideration for those developing such systems should be their capability to download MARC records from a bibliographic utility for use either in an online patron-access catalogue, or a bibliography system such as the one described above. Libraries should probably avoid systems that require the original creation of catalogue records in a format other than MARC. The MARC format is the basis for the exchange of machine-readable records nationally and internationally, and the use of a format other than MARC makes it nearly impossible to collaborate with other institutions bibliographically, to change vendors, or even to use the same database for a variety of applications. The ideal system model for the time being would seem to involve (1) the creation of full MARC catalogue records for all of an institution's materials through a bibliographic utility or other MARC-based system; (2) permanent maintenance of an institution's MARC records by a regional network, such as SOLINET, or by a vendor of library computer services (compare the list of such vendors given below under "Offline Products"); and (3) the transfer or downloading of full or partial MARC records into local systems for various applications.

The extent to which microcomputers are now on the minds of those working in rare book and special collections libraries may be seen in the welcome course to be offered by the Columbia University School of Library Service's Rare Book School during the summer of 1984 entitled "Microcomputers for Rare Book Libraries" (John Bidwell, UCLA, instructor). Those who are able will certainly want to take advantage of such opportunities for gathering current information in this fast-changing area.

Offline Products

Because of the special access requirements of rare materials collections in general and of individual special collections in particular, some institutions have decided that certain of their needs can best be met by offline, or batch, processing. This approach involves creating MARC records, with special access fields and the like through one of the bibliographic utilities, and then providing a copy of the MARC records in tape form to a vendor of computer services to maintain as a database. The vendor can then produce special printed products for the library, such as photocomposed catalogues or bibliographies, microfiche catalogues, finding lists, or statistics. Some vendors will also allow the institution to request occasional or routine special searches of their database. As an example of the last possibility, an institution might request that the vendor produce a monthly cumulative finding list of all of its illustrated books, arranged by type of illustration and subarranged by the name of the illustrator.

This use of a vendor of library computer services may, in the short- to medium-range future, be the solution to the problem of the lack of searching flexibility of the larger bibliographic systems and their inability to provide the kinds of special access needed in rare materials collections. And, because this approach usually results in printed products, it has the advantage of being more acceptable to many of the users of such collections. Until the flexibility of online systems has substantially increased and the cost decreased, the use of offline computer support may be the wiser and more cost-effective, if less glamorous, means of using an institution's expensive, detailed MARC records for research purposes, particularly for those institutions that do not wish to be on the absolute cutting edge of technology.

There are a number of vendors that can perform various kinds of database maintenance services, including Autographics (751 Monterey Pass Rd., Monterey Park, Calif. 91754), Computer Company (1905 Westmoreland St., Richmond, Va. 23230), General Research Corporation (P.O. Box 6770, Santa Barbara, Calif. 93111), Inforonics, Inc. (550 Newtown Rd., Littleton, Mass. 01460), MARCIVE, Inc. (P.O. Box 12408, San Antonio, Tex. 78212), Science Press (P.O. Box 378, Sterling, Va. 22170), and Library Systems and Services (General Motors Bldg., 1395 Piccarel Dr., Suite 100, Rockville, Md. 20850). This is not a complete list, and additional vendors may be located by asking colleagues or visiting exhibits at library association conventions. Libraries may not get the performance they want and need from university computing centers and local data processing firms, particularly if these organizations do not support the MARC format or the American Library Association character set (containing diacritics, special characters, and so on). It is impossible to overemphasize the long-term importance of creating and maintaining a special collection's master database in the MARC format.

In conclusion, one is justified in saying that rare book and special collections libraries continue to make progress in rendering computers more hospitable to their needs, but that the battle is not yet won. The best strategy for further gains is to continue to work for national standards in the area of computerized rare book information and to lobby for on- and offline systems that are more suited to the needs of rare materials collections. In some cases it may be useful to approach vendors of library computer services in informal consortia of like-minded institutions to help reduce costs and provide an incentive for vendors to develop more hospitable systems.

For the time being, however, most rare materials librarians will want to concentrate on putting as many of their new and retrospective catalogue records into machine-readable form as possible, following appropriate new standards — such as the *Anglo-American Cataloguing Rules,* * *Bibliographic Description of Rare Books,* and the MARC format — and wait until the technology of online catalogues and library microcomputer systems has advanced a bit further before spending too much time or money on what is still, after all, a relatively new technology.

GLOSSARY

This short glossary lists a few of the terms used in this chapter that may be unfamiliar to some readers.

AACR2 — Anglo–American Cataloguing Rules, Second Edition. *AACR2* is the set of cataloguing rules that, since 1981, has been used by most major libraries in the United States, Great Britain, Canada, and Australia, as well as by many other libraries worldwide. To provide further guidance for the cataloguing of rare books under *AACR2,* the Library of Congress prepared *Bibliographic Description of Rare Books* (Washington, D.C.: Library of Congress, 1981; available from the LC Cataloging Distribution Service).

ACRL RBMS Standards Committee. The Standards Committee of the Rare Books and Manuscripts Section of the Association of College and Research Libraries of the American Library Association. The Standards Committee has so far focused chiefly on bibliographic and computer standards relating to special collections.

ANSI — American National Standards Institute. A U.S. standards organization engaged in developing voluntary standards in all fields. American National Standards Committee Z39 is the part of ANSI dealing with standards in library and information sciences and related publishing practices.

---

*2nd ed. (Chicago: American Library Association, 1978).

Bibliographic utility. A generic term used to refer to the three largest library computer networks, OCLC, RLIN, and WLN (qq.v.). The bibliographic utilities variously provide support for online cataloguing, online retrieval, production of catalogue cards, production of computer output microform catalogues, acquisitions and ordering (for current materials), serials check-in, and other library functions. Cf. Network.

BLAISE — British Library Automated Information Service. The general name for the automated information services offered by the British Library. In many ways, BLAISE is similar to a U.S. bibliographic utility.

CONSER — Conversion of Serials. A cooperative effort by the North American library community to build a computerized database of consistent serials cataloguing information. The master CONSER file resides on OCLC, but is distributed in tape form by the Library of Congress.

Download. To transfer or copy a record from one system to another, usually from a larger external database to a smaller local system. OCLC, RLIN, and WLN allow downloading of records for local library use.

ESTC — Eighteenth Century Short Title Catalogue. A worldwide effort to create a bibliographic database of all eighteenth-century books published in English or in an English-speaking country, catalogued in the MARC format according to *AACR2*. *ESTC* has its headquarters in the Reference Division of the British Library; in the United States, *ESTC* is based at the ESTC/NA office at Louisiana State University. The American Antiquarian Society in Worcester, Mass., is cataloguing U.S. imprints for the *ESTC*.

LSP — Linked Systems Project. A cooperative project of the Library of Congress, RLIN, and WLN that will allow bibliographic information to be transmitted online between dissimilar computer systems. LSP has involved the implementation of a new telecommunications protocol that will eventually be usable by any computerized library system. LSP has been supported by funds from the Council on Library Resources under its Bibliographic Services Development Program.

MARC format — MAchine Readable Cataloging format. A data format designed to communicate bibliographic information in machine-readable form. It is the basis for the processing and communication of nearly all library-related computerized bibliographic information in the United States. The basic MARC structure is also used internationally for the exchange of bibliographic records. The authoritative description of the U.S. MARC format is *MARC Formats for Bibliographic Data* (Washington, D.C.: Library of Congress, Cataloging Distribution Service, 1980–   ).

MASC — MARC for Special Collections. An ACRL RBMS information exchange committee that meets at the annual American Library Association conventions.

Network. Two or more entities engaged in organized, computer-supported information exchange through telecommunications links.

OCLC, Inc. — Online Computer Library Center. Formerly known as the Ohio College Library Center, OCLC, Inc., is the largest bibliographic utility, maintaining a database of over nine million records (as of the end of 1983). OCLC supports online cataloguing and retrieval, the production of catalogue cards and computer transaction tapes, interlibrary loan, acquisitions/ordering, and other library-related functions. Many special collections and research libraries are members of OCLC. Address: 6565 Frantz Rd., Dublin, Ohio 43017. Cf. RLIN, WLN.

Offline. Offline, or "batch," retrieval is the capability of searching a computerized file indirectly, by placing a request first and receiving a response at a later time; it may not involve interacting directly with the computer. Offline retrieval can be considerably less expensive than online retrieval and can make possible searches and kinds of output that would be prohibitively expensive if performed online. Many vendors of computer services offer offline retrieval to their customers. Cf. Online.

Online. In the context of this chapter, "online" generally refers to "online retrieval," which is the capability of searching a computerized file or database and receiving an immediate response. Online retrieval involves direct interaction with the computer. Cf. Offline.

RLIN – Research Libraries Information Network. RLIN is the bibliographic utility used as the information system of the Research Libraries Group (RLG), a consortium of major U.S. research libraries. RLIN attempts to aim its services and programs at the special needs of research libraries. It supports most of the same library functions as OCLC, but also allows libraries to view their own local records online and perform searches by specialized access points. Address: Research Libraries Group, Inc., Jordan Quadrangle, Stanford, Calif. 94305. Cf. OCLC, WLN.

SOLINET. Formerly called the Southeast Library Network. One of a number of regional library networks that serve as middlemen between individual libraries and OCLC (q.v.). Other regional networks include AMIGOS, CAPCON, FEDLINK, NELINET, and SUNY/OCLC, among others.

Telephone modem. An electronic device that enables computerized information to be reliably transmitted over ordinary telephone lines.

WLN – Washington Library Network. WLN is a bibliographic utility administered by the Washington State Library, but having members in many northwestern states. WLN offers the same kinds of automated support to libraries provided by OCLC and RLIN and, in addition, can provide automated authority control, microfiche catalogues, and other enhanced services. WLN prefers to provide direct access to the Northwest region only and to sell its software to libraries in other parts of the country for use in internal automation or regional networking. Address: Washington State Library, AJ–11, Olympia, Wash. 98504. Cf. OCLC, RLIN.

12

Trends in the Preservation of Rare and Special Materials

Carolyn Harris

IT HAS BEEN generally recognized for some time that rare books and manuscripts need special attention if they are to be preserved, and the preservation techniques are well developed. The word "increasing" could be used to sum up the trends in 1983: increasing scientific research and development; an increasing number of grants to implement programs and improve environmental conditions; increasing support for publications; an increasing number of educational programs, seminars and conferences; and increasing attention to the identification of national priorities. The growing awareness of the need for preservation has resulted in major programs in research libraries and in concern on the part of collectors and dealers to provide proper protection for material in their care.

The terms "preservation" and "conservation" should be defined for the purposes of this article. Preservation refers to activities that extend the life of an item, for example, storage conditions, and the replacement of items with longer-lived copies or alternate formats that preserve intellectual content but not physical form. Conservation implies physical treatment of the materials, including restoration of rare and valuable items.

SUPPLIES

Nondamaging supplies and storage materials are increasingly available to libraries, collectors, and dealers. Most library supply houses, such as Gaylord Brothers, Inc., Hollinger Corporation, and University Products, offer polyester envelopes, acid-free papers, boxes, pamphlet binders, map folders, and other nondamaging storage materials. Conservation Resources International produced an acid-free but nonbuffered photographic storage envelope when it was found that the buffering tarnished silver. The firm also offers a "lig-free" board, manufactured so that the acidic lignin is not present and long-term freedom from acid is ensured. Light Impressions has a large line of photographic storage supplies available; Process Materials, Inc., produces acid-free papers and boards; and TALAS has one of the most comprehensive lines of conservation supplies. Protective enclosures are being offered by many commercial library binders, including Information Conservation, Inc., in Horsham, Pa., and Bridgeport National Bindery, Inc., in Agawam, Mass. The book boxes, made of acid-free board to the specific size of each book for reasonable prices, are useful to those who do not have box-making facilities. Encapsulation supplies—Mylar, double-stick tape, and ultrasonic polyester welders—are also widely available. Supplies are continually being improved, and periodical literature and suppliers' catalogues should be watched closely for the latest information. For addresses of suppliers, see the list at the end of this chapter.

PUBLICATIONS

Information on preservation and conservation is also increasingly available. Two newsletters full of important and timely information are *CAN, the Conservation Administrators' Newsletter,* published at the University of Tulsa, in its fourth year; and *The Abbey Newsletter,* published by Ellen McCrady, and recognized as the most important information source in the profession, both for conservators and preservation administrators. In print in 1983 are several other useful publications. To identify trained conservators for treatment work, the American Institute for Conservation and the Guild of Book Workers are helpful. Both organizations publish a directory of members. Another source, *The Directory of American Book Workers,* is also available, although it is important to remember that this is a self-selected directory.

Major resource books published recently include the Research Libraries Group (RLG) *Preservation Manual,* describing the RLG Preservation Program, the technical standards for the cooperative microfilming project. Other published resources on preservation topics are the Association of Research Libraries' *Preservation Planning Resource Notebook,* a compilation of useful information and articles; *The Preservation Challenge* by Carolyn Clark Morrow (Knowledge Industry Publications, 1983), a good description of a complete preservation program; and *Conservation in the Library, A Handbook of Use and Care of Traditional and Non-Traditional Material,* edited by Susan Swartzburg (Greenwood, 1983). Three how-to manuals—*Conservation Treatment Procedures* by Carolyn Clark Morrow (Libraries Unlimited, 1982); *The Design and Construction of Boxes for Rare Books* (Library of Congress, 1982); and *The Library Materials Preservation Manual* by Hedi Kyle (N.T. Smith, 1983)— are now available. George Cunha has brought out a new edition of his *Libraries and Archives Conservation* (Scarecrow Press, 1983), bringing it to the 1980s and beyond. The first dictionary of descriptive terms in *Bookbinding and the Conservation of Books,* edited by Matt Roberts and Don Etherington (Library of Congress, 1982), is available from the Government Printing Office. The Library of Congress Preservation Leaflet Series, available from the National Preservation Office of the Library of Congress, gives general information on topics such as bibliographic sources, marking manuscripts, and the preservation of newsprint. The Society of American Archivists has published three manuals addressing preservation: *Exhibits, Reprography,* and *Conservation.* A bibliography of preservation monographs in print is available from the Resources and Technical Services Division of the American Library Association. Margaret Byrnes's essay on preservation developments in 1982, published in *LRTS* (July/September 1983), is a good source for earlier bibliographical information. Other library literature and popular media have also begun to cover preservation topics. Two examples are the series by Anthony Amodeo in the *College and Research Libraries News* (which has included such useful articles as "Helpful Hints for Moving and Shifting Collections," "Preventing Damage," and "Photocopying without (Much) Damage") and the Preserv/Conserv/ation Column in *American Libraries.*

CONSERVATION TREATMENT FACILITIES

The number of available conservation treatment facilities is also growing. A recently organized Association of Cooperative Conservation Centers consists of 13 centers—for addresses see the list at the end of this chapter—which collectively serve most of the nation:

The Balboa Art Conservation Center
The Center for Conservation and Technical Studies
The Center for Conservation of Art and Historic Artifacts
The Conservation and Collections Care Center
Intermuseum Conservation Association
Kansas Museum of History Regional Center Laboratories
Maine State Museums Regional Conservation Center
Northeast Document Conservation Center
Pacific Regional Conservation Center
Rocky Mountain Regional Conservation Center
State of Alabama Conservation Laboratory
Upper Midwest Conservation Association
Williamstown Regional Art Conservation Center

The Chicago Conservation Center has recently opened, and major grant-funded information programs are being implemented in the Midwest (the Midwest Cooperative Conservation Program and the Illinois Cooperative Conservation Program). Most of these centers offer consulting services, treatment facilities, and information on the conservation of art works and books to libraries, collectors, and dealers. Several major research libraries have begun in-house treatment programs; they include the Humanities Research Center at the University of Texas at Austin, the University of California at Berkeley, and the University of Michigan.

RESEARCH AND PROGRAMS

Of particular interest is the continuing examination of standard conservation procedures. Research into leather treatment, dust cloths, and thymol and ethylene oxide fumigation has caused rethinking of procedures. Another research development is the face-up photocopier. The Library Technology Project has let a contract for the development of such a copier or added equipment for existing copiers.

Although disasters were widely discussed and disaster preparedness plans implemented this year, there were few major disasters. One disaster, which resulted in an improvement of techniques, was a flood in the San Diego Central Library in December 1982. The newspaper storage room was flooded and hundreds of irreplaceable issues were wetted. The Convair Division of General Dynamics Corporation offered to assist in recovery. After the volumes were frozen, they were pressed in a large press used to bond metal parts and dried under a partial vacuum at a temperature of 160° to 170° F. This gentle heat and vacuum took out the moisture, but only dried the book to its normal 6 percent moisture content, so the paper was not embrittled in the process.

That the preservation of embrittled materials sometimes necessitates preservation of the intellectual content and not the object itself had been recognized long before 1983, but this year major steps were taken to meet this need. The Research Libraries Group Preservation Program, with funding from the National Endowment for the Humanities and the Mellon Foundation, has taken on the responsibility for the preservation on microfilm of U.S. imprints and Americana printed between 1876 and 1900. Seven participating libraries are filming in distinct subject areas such as language and literature, history, trans-Mississippi West, social science, dime novels, and poetry. The implementation of this program involved setting guidelines and standards for microfilming projects. In addition to preserving more than 20,000 volumes, the guidelines provide the basis for a national preservation microfilming effort. This program has also involved sharing of information to prevent duplication of effort, building on the *National Register of Microform Masters*. The Association of Research Libraries in 1983 initiated coordination of cooperative cataloguing to provide online bibliographic access to large microform sets available from commercial sources, primarily through the OCLC system.

Other means of preserving brittle materials are being tested by the Library of Congress. Optical disks, high density storage media, are being used to store and provide access to both new materials (to prevent future preservation problems) and older materials. Analog videodisks are being used to provide access to graphic, photographic, and motion picture materials, and digitized optical disks to contemporary periodicals. The experiment will provide information for future use of these media, including the medium's own preservation characteristics, its costs, copyright issues, and feasibility for libraries. Videodisks are being used to provide access to Smithsonian photographs, the collection of the Eastman House Museum, and others, offering exciting possibilities of viewing while limiting the handling of rare materials.

Preventing future preservation problems has also been a high priority in 1983. Prevention has been approached from two directions: encouraging publishers to use permanent paper and the deacidification of new materials to slow down their inevitable decay. The Council on Library Resources Committee on the Longevity of Books published guidelines on the use of permanent paper, which formed the basis of an ANSI Standard on Permanent Paper. There has been cooperation on the part of publishers: The American Library Association is publishing all monographs on permanent paper, and most university presses, as well as several trade publishers, have begun to use paper that meets the standard.

Mass deacidification, the neutralization of acid in paper and the deposit of buffers to prevent future acid attack in many books at one time, has long been a dream of the preservation community. The Library of Congress is now testing a process using diethyl zinc as the deacidification agent. A large-scale test was done this year. The process was successful, and the few problems identified in the experimental testing have been solved by Library of Congress scientists. A large production facility has been designed, and construction will begin in 1984 if funding is appropriated by the U.S. Congress.

Information on preservation and conservation was conveyed to various audiences in many ways in 1983. The American Library Association Preservation of Library Materials Section and the Library of Congress invited library administrators to hear about programs that are in place and means of preservation funding. This was the first in a series of seminars to be continued with midlevel library managers in 1984 and technicians in 1985. Major conferences were held during the year: The Fumigation of Library Materials, sponsored by the Massachusetts Institute of Technology and *Technology and Conservation Magazine*; Excellence in Fine Binding, sponsored by the Guild of Book Workers; The Structure of Cellulose, sponsored by the Book and Paper Group of the American Institute for Conservation; Commercial Binding, sponsored by the Preservation of Library Materials section of the American Library Association; two conferences on the Preservation of Photographic Materials, sponsored by the Northeast Document Conservation Center and the Rochester Institute of Technology; and the Treatment of Book Leaves, and Binding Styles, sponsored by the Humanities Research Center. The Society of American Archivists continued its workshop series on the preservation of archival materials and extended them to photographic collections. Meckler Publishing sponsored the third annual Preservation and Optical Disk Conference.

Formal educational programs are still rare in library preservation and conservation. Columbia University's School of Library Service is currently the only degree program for conservators of book and paper artifacts. The first class of conservators entered its third year of internship. The preservation administration program continues to attract strong students. Students from the first class of preservation administrators are employed in the New York Public Library Conservation Division, the Midwest Cooperative Preservation Program, and Columbia University's Avery Library. Other library schools are offering an increased preservation component in their degree programs. Twenty-three library schools are listed in the 1981 edition of the *Preservation Education Flyer* as having a course in preservation, including the Simmons program in conjunction with the Northeast Document Conservation Center, Rutgers, Case Western Reserve, and the universities of Alabama, Hawaii, Chicago, and Denver. These programs have been augmented by a Mellon-funded internship program in preservation administration. Five libraries—the New York Public Library, Stanford, Yale, Columbia, and the Library of Congress—are, or will be, offering one-year internships over the next three years.

Granting agencies are becoming increasingly generous to preservation programs. Thirteen Independent Research Libraries were awarded a National Endowment for the Humanities (NEH) Challenge Grant totaling $5.3 million in 1983; nine of those libraries are using the funds for improved preservation and environmental control. The New York Public Library was awarded $750,000 from the Mellon Foundation for improvement of microform and conservation laboratories, and private money was received to endow the ongoing activities. Internships for paper conservators and preservation administrators have been funded by the Mellon Foundation. RLG Master Negative Reconversion activities and the Cooperative Preservation Microfilming Project were funded jointly by NEH and Mellon. The Office of Education Title IIC grants and LSCA have funded preservation activities in the Midwest, at the University of Michigan, and at Avery Library, Columbia University, among others. Many private and public grants have funded local preservation projects.

At the tenth anniversary celebration of the Northeast Document Conservation Center, Pamela Darling, a preservation pioneer now developing the Library of Congress National Preservation Office and teaching in the Columbia University School of Library Service Preservation Program, compared a national preservation program to the street map of Washington, D.C.: a network of nodes connected by communication channels, some straight and some diagonal. Communication travels between these varied nodes, as is necessary. The nodes—leadership roles taken by the Library of Congress, the Association of Research Libraries, the Research Libraries Group, and the infrastructure of local, state, and regional programs—were strengthened this year, and major programs were put into place to ensure the preservation of rare and fragile materials.

A SELECTED LIST OF PRESERVATION SUPPLIERS

This list is by no means complete; other library and conservation supply houses and commercial library binders offer comparable products.

Bridgeport National Bindery Inc
PO Box 289
Agawam, MA 01001
413-789-1981

Conservation Resources International Inc
1111 N Royal St
Alexandria, VA 22314
703-549-6610

Gaylord Brothers
PO Box 4901
Syracuse, NY 13221
315-457-5070

Hollinger Corp
PO Box 6185
3810 S Four Mile Run Dr
Arlington, VA 22206
703-671-6600

Information Conservation Inc
935 Horsham Rd
Horsham, PA 19044
215-674-0486

Process Materials Corp
301 Veterans Blvd
Rutherford, NJ 07070
201-935-2900

TALAS
213 W 35 St
New York, NY 10001
212-736-7744

University Products Inc
PO Box 101
South Canal St
Holyoke, MA 01041
800-628-1912

ADDRESSES FOR CONSERVATION TREATMENT FACILITIES

The Balboa Art Conservation Center
 PO Box 3755
San Diego, CA 92103
714-236-9702

The Center for Conservation and Technical
 Studies
Fogg Museum, Harvard University
32 Quincy St
Cambridge, MA 02138
617-495-2392

The Center for Conservation of Art and Historic Artifacts
612 Spruce St
Philadelphia, PA 19106
215-545-0613

The Conservation and Collections Care
 Center
Division for Historic Preservation
New York State Parks and Recreation
Peebles Island
Waterford, NY 12188
518-237-8090

Intermuseum Conservation Association
Allan Art Building
Oberlin, OH 44074
216-775-7331

Kansas Museum of History Regional Center
Laboratories
Kansas State Historical Society
120 West 10th St
Topeka, KS 66612
913-296-4782

Maine State Museums Regional Conservation Center
Regional Conservation Center
State House
Augusta, ME 04330
207-289-2301

Northeast Document Conservation Center
Abbot Hall, 24 School St
Andover, MA 01810
617-470-1010

Pacific Regional Conservation Center
1355 Kalihi St
Honolulu, HI 96819
808-847-3511

Rocky Mountain Regional Conservation Center
University of Denver
University Park
Denver, CO 80208
303-753-3218

State of Alabama Conservation Laboratory
Birmingham Museum of Art
2000 8th Ave North
Birmingham, AL 35203
205-254-2565

Upper Midwest Conservation Association
The Minneapolis Institute of Arts
2400 Third Ave South
Minneapolis, MN 01267
612-870-3120

Williamstown Regional Art Conservation Center
Clark Art Institute
225 South St
Williamstown, MA 01267
413-458-5741

13

The Oberlin Conference on Theft

Marie E. Korey

THE ALARMING INCREASE in the theft of valuable books and manuscripts has been a matter of grave concern to librarians, archivists, and antiquarian booksellers. In recent years, each of these constituencies has attempted to combat the problem, usually working independently of the other. The Society of American Archivists (SAA) set up a security system; published *Archives and Manuscripts: Security,* edited by Timothy Walch, in 1977; and began circulating a registry of stolen manuscripts to its members. SAA also sponsored a conference on security, held in Detroit in 1979, the proceedings of which were published and are available from the society.

The Rare Books and Manuscripts Section (RBMS) of the Association of College and Research Libraries (ACRL) of the American Library Association (ALA) established a Security Committee that developed guidelines for the security of rare book, manuscript, and other special collections. Included in these guidelines are recommendations for the marking of rare books, manuscripts, and other special collections in a permanent fashion. The RBMS guidelines were published in the March 1982 issue of *College & Research Libraries News* and were adopted as official ACRL guidelines in July 1982.

During his term of office (1980–1982) as president of the Antiquarian Booksellers Association of America (ABAA), John H. Jenkins worked to establish a security system that enlisted the cooperation of librarians, archivists, booksellers, the Federal Bureau of Investigation, and the U.S. Customs Agency. The creation of Bookline Alert: Missing Books and Manuscripts (BAMBAM) by Daniel Leab and Katharine Kyes Leab in 1981 as a nonprofit database operated by the editors of *American Book Prices Current* provided a single, central location for records of missing books and manuscripts. Losses can be reported instantly to this computer-assisted alerting system, and questionable items offered for sale can be checked to see if they are reported as missing. BAMBAM is also available in printed form.

While rare book and manuscript librarians, archivists, and antiquarian book-sellers were developing these protective measures, the vulnerability of the general collections of research libraries was dramatized by the apprehension of James R. Shinn in April 1981 by William A. Moffett, director of libraries at Oberlin College. Shinn was subsequently linked to the theft of $750,000 worth of valuable books from the open stacks of some 40 libraries throughout the country. He jumped the $40,000 bail posted after his arrest in Oberlin, but eventually was apprehended at Muhlenberg College Library in Allentown, Pa.; he was later tried and convicted.

Shinn's activities in the open stacks of research libraries highlighted problems that were not adequately addressed by either the SAA security manual or the RBMS security guidelines, as both documents are concerned with closed-stack collections with restricted access. The Shinn affair also emphasized the need for even greater communication and cooperation among librarians, booksellers, and the law enforcement agencies than had been achieved by the ABAA security system. Concerned about these matters, William A. Moffett suggested to Robert Wedgeworth, executive director of ALA, that the time was ripe for a conference of the members of the ALA, ABAA, SAA, and law enforcement agencies. In January 1982, Moffett's proposal was referred to Ellen Dunlap, chair of the ALA-SAA Joint Relations Committee, who outlined a tentative program for a conference to be held in the fall of 1983 and enlisted the support of both associations.

An ad hoc committee, consisting of members of RBMS, SAA, and ABAA, met in July 1982 to begin planning an invitational conference, modeled somewhat on the De-accessioning Conference held at Brown University in 1981. Members of the Committee were Terry Belanger (School of Library Service, Columbia University), Ellen Dunlap (at that time, at the Humanities Research Center, University of Texas at Austin; now director, Rosenbach Museum and Library), Joan M. Friedman (Yale Center for British Art), Peter E. Hanff (Bancroft Library, University of California at Berkeley), Katharine Kyes Leab (editor, *American Book Prices Current*), William A. Moffett (Oberlin College Library), Peter J. Parker (Historical Society of Pennsylvania), Daniel Traister (University of Pennsylvania), and Elisabeth Woodburn (president, Antiquarian Booksellers Association of America). Ellen Dunlap later withdrew from the committee, and Marie E. Korey (Rare Book Department, Free Library of Philadelphia) joined it to serve as moderator. Oberlin College Library was chosen as the site for the conference, which was scheduled for late September 1983.

A grant from the H. W. Wilson Foundation, received in January 1983, provided the necessary funding for the Oberlin Conference on Theft. Plans for the program were finalized by June and invitations were sent to representatives of Interpol, the FBI, the Lorain County (Ohio) Prosecuting Attorney's Office, Mexico's Secretaria de Relaciones Exteriores, Canada's Department of Communications, and the legal staffs of the American Library Association, the Antiquarian Booksellers Association of America, the House Judiciary Committee, and the Smithsonian Institution, as well as to librarians, archivists, library administrators, security officers, and antiquarian booksellers.

The conference was organized as a series of working sessions focusing on the following issues: the prevention of theft, institutional responses to theft (and the associated public relations problems), existing laws and enforcement procedures, the establishment of ownership of recovered stolen property, legislation giving explicit protection to libraries and archives, and the establishment of agencies for national and international communication regarding the theft of such materials.

In his opening remarks, Lawrence W. Towner (president, Newberry Library, Chicago) deplored the current epidemic of library theft that imperils the "republic of letters" and threatens to destroy the atmosphere of trust once characteristic of American cultural institutions. Librarians themselves must assume much of the blame for this situation, Towner asserted, because they all too frequently have failed to pursue effective measures to prevent library theft.

Conference participants were united in recommending specific steps that institutions can initiate prior to theft to improve their security and other steps that increase the chances of recovering stolen material in the event of a theft. Restriction of access to materials, positive identification of readers, and the visible and indelible marking of all books and manuscripts were strongly recommended as preventive measures. Peter Hanff urged that marking be done systematically and that a record of library markings be retained as a means of identifying property in the event of a theft. Accurate catalogue records that provide specific identification for each book or manuscript should also be maintained for the same purpose. Katharine Leab pointed out that the failure of libraries to record their own markings and retain copy-specific information sometimes makes it difficult to achieve the return of books that police have recovered.

Maximizing publicity in the event of a theft was another major emphasis of conferees. Laurence Witten, a former president of ABAA, pointed out that booksellers cannot hope to identify as stolen property books or manuscripts that have not been reported as missing. He added that librarians who do not immediately consult with the book trade are denying themselves expertise in the evaluation and appraisal of stolen goods. Without reliable dollar values for materials reported as stolen, law enforcement agents, unfamiliar with the value or significance of old books and manuscripts, may be reluctant to pursue an investigation.

Jan Snyder, news officer at the University of Pennsylvania, suggested that libraries can control the reaction to theft if they take an open approach with the press and the public. Snyder set forth some general rules for "crisis public relations": Prepare a statement for the media; designate a single spokesperson to deal with the media; give reporters enough information to write their stories, but don't offer details of security systems or engage in speculation; and prepare in advance a telephone listing of donors and contacts to notify immediately when a crisis occurs.

Lawyers and law enforcement agents also stressed the importance of following through with prosecution once thieves are apprehended. If book theft is not now a high priority in law enforcement circles, that is in part the fault of libraries for failing to prosecute in the past. Barbara Kammerman, assistant counsel for the U.S. House Judiciary Committee Criminal Justice Subcommittee, suggested that as judges see more prosecution of book thefts, convictions and sentences will increase. FBI agent Mike Bartley warned that law enforcement officials will be unwilling to pursue book thieves if libraries won't prosecute them.

The importance of a good working relationship with local law enforcement personnel, well in advance of any theft, was also emphasized. Librarians were urged to familiarize themselves with the laws in their jurisdictions. Gregory A. White, Lorain County prosecuting attorney, suggested that local prosecuting attorneys be asked what librarians can do to apprehend and detain suspected thieves.

One of the steps recommended by Peter Parker was to organize support for adoption by state legislatures of laws extending explicit protection to libraries and archives. Only nine states have laws exempting library employees from liability for detaining persons suspected of theft or mutilation; only 17 have any laws relating to book theft. Robert Dierker, assistant general counsel of the Smithsonian Institution, suggested that legislation should include the right for librarians to seize and search suspects, immunity for librarians from false arrest, and provisions for restitution to book dealers.

The establishment of a national registry of library markings and a national security office that could serve as a clearinghouse for information on theft and all forms of security was strongly urged by Katharine Leab. As outlined by Leab, the National Security Office would provide reference services, database management, and advice and arbitration in matters of appraisal and ownership of materials. The Library of Congress was suggested as the best location for the National Security Office.

The conference proceedings, together with the guidelines on preventing and dealing with library theft developed at the conference, will be published in 1984. Members of the conference planning committee will pursue ways of funding and implementing the National Security Office. Ongoing efforts to deal with the problems of theft by units within SAA and ALA will continue, and it is hoped that a second conference will address university as well as library administrators.

14

Restoring Tax Incentives for Manuscript Donations

Carol C. Henderson

PRIOR TO THE TAX REFORM ACT of 1969, an author or artist who donated literary, musical, or artistic compositions or papers to a library or museum could take a tax deduction equal to the fair market value of the items at the time of the contribution. The reform provision enacted in P.L. 91-172 was intended to prevent public officials from receiving a tax advantage from donating papers created with public funds to nonprofit institutions. The language, however, was overbroad and removed the deduction from all authors and artists. Collectors of such work could still take a fair market value tax deduction for qualified donations, but artists and authors were limited to deducting only the cost of the materials used to produce the composition.

The unintended result was that donations of manuscripts to libraries were drastically reduced, as documented in surveys conducted by Norman Tanis, Library Director at California State University, Northridge. The decline has been most severe at those institutions specializing in original works of contemporary literature, art, and music. Before 1969, such institutions often sought out donors who gave materials on a continuing basis. Such an arrangement actually minimized the loss of tax revenue since donations more often occurred before the materials increased in value, and ensured that the materials were preserved and accessible. Where donors have deposited materials in libraries since 1969, they are often placed "on deposit," under conditions set by contract with the donor.

Under the current tax situation, manuscripts of minor figures or early works of authors who later become famous may turn to dust in attics or be carelessly discarded or destroyed. Well-known authors are more likely to sell their manuscripts to the highest bidder, a situation in which few libraries have funds to compete. Collections may be sold piecemeal to dealers or private collectors. An author's work may be split up in several different private collections in widely separate locations. The papers of a writer identified with a particular state or region may be located across the country or may be sold abroad.

The library, museum, and arts communities pressed for restoration of the tax deduction, except for the papers of public officials, in the years since 1969, often making considerable progress, but never getting a corrective measure all the way through the legislative process and into law. A unifying force among the artist, author, composer, library, and museum communities in many of these efforts was the Council of Creative Artists, Libraries, and Museums under the leadership of composer Elie Siegmeister. In 1979 the delegates to the White House Conference on Library and Information Services, two-thirds of whom were lay citizens not connected with libraries, recommended that Congress restore the tax deduction. Congressional hearings on the issue were held later that year, at which a U.S. Department of the Treasury spokesman testified in opposition to pending legislation.

In 1981 the American Association of Museums, the American Library Association (ALA), the Association of Research Libraries (ARL), and several arts organizations intensified their efforts to get legislation passed. In October, 1981, the Presidential Task Force on the Arts and Humanities, concerned that the Economic Recovery Tax Act (P.L. 97-34) would have the unintended effect of reducing private giving to the arts and humanities and responding to President Reagan's request to suggest ways to increase private sector support, made several tax recommendations. The first of these was to restore the fair market value tax deduction so that authors, artists, and composers would receive the same tax treatment as a result of charitable contributions of their works as collectors or other donors giving a purchased work or manuscript.

At Senate hearings in November, 1981, witnesses supporting a tax deduction included two members of the Presidential Task Force—Librarian of Congress, Daniel Boorstin, and Folger Shakespeare Library board member, Gordon Hanes—and representatives of ALA; ARL; the Council of Creative Artists, Libraries, and Museums; the American Arts Alliance; the American Association of Museums; and the Authors League of America. Other organizations that have been supportive include the Independent Research Libraries Association, the Society of American Archivists, and the Association of American Publishers.

The Treasury Department was invited to testify at these hearings, but declined to do so. The administration's position on the tax deduction appeared to be changing, and the momentum generated in 1981 carried over to the following year. A bill (S. 2225) introduced by Sen. Max Baucus (D-MT) attracted 25 cosponsors, including a majority of the Senate Finance Committee members, and was approved by the committee in September 1982. However, certain conditions were added in committee. The prospective donor must obtain a written appraisal done within one year of the contribution by a qualified third party, and attach a copy of the appraisal to the income tax return. The donee must use the contribution for a purpose related to its tax-exempt function and provide the donor a written statement to that effect. The small number of very wealthy individuals to whom the alternative minimum tax applies would not be able to deduct the excess of fair market value over basis (the cost of materials).

The amended provision was brought up on the Senate floor briefly in October and again in December when a further amendment was added, but not brought to a vote. The new modification would limit the deduction to 50 percent of adjusted gross income, defined as "income from all property created by the taxpayer which is similar to the qualified artistic charitable contributions." This limitation would mean authors could claim a deduction only from income earned from the sale of written works or from royalties or rights from such works, and not from income from teaching or lecturing.

In 1983, the affected communities and congressional sponsors agreed on revised legislation that was introduced by Sen. Max Baucus and Rep. Thomas Downey (D-NY), the new Chairman of the Congressional Arts Caucus. The identical bills (S. 427 and H.R. 1285) include the following safeguards against abuse: (1) the property must have been created at least one year prior to its donation, (2) a written appraisal of the fair market value of the property must be made within one year of donation, (3) the use of the donation must relate to the institution's primary tax-exempt function, (4) donations would be limited to "50-percent charities," such as public libraries, public museums, and universities, and (5) high income individuals using the alternative minimum tax would not be eligible for the deduction. As before, papers of public officials would not be eligible.

These bills are still pending in 1984. However, momentum seems to have slowed, affected by publicity over inflated appraisals in other areas of donations and concern about growing deficits, despite revision of the bills to head off possible abuses, considerable publicity given the legislation by its House sponsor, and a major effort by library, museum, and arts groups. The administration's tenuous support, or at least neutrality, evaporated as shown by a related incident.

Sen. Daniel Moynihan (D-NY), long a supporter of restoring tax incentives for donations of art and manuscripts, introduced a tax bill (S. 2123) in November, 1983, based on proposals to encourage charitable contributions developed in October by the President's Committee on the Arts and Humanities in conjunction with the Treasury Department. A taxpayer could deduct the value of certain charitable gifts from up to 75 percent of adjusted gross income, up from the current 50 percent. A taxpayer could also carry over for 15 years (up from 5) charitable contributions exceeding 75 (up from 50) percent of adjusted gross income.

The third provision of the bill was worrisome to many potential donee institutions. It would require that noncash gifts be held for at least five years by the taxpayer before any appreciated value could be deducted. The provision would, if passed, apply currently to collectors of manuscripts and artwork, and if the tax deduction for authors and artists was restored, would apply to them as well.

After hearing concerns from some nonprofit institutions and after the Treasury Department changed its mind about the first two provisions and supported only the third, which was not actually an incentive to charitable contributions at all, Sen. Moynihan backed off from support of the President's committee recommendations. Efforts in both Senate and House to attach the "5-year hold" provision to larger tax bills failed.

Problems of perceived abuse, however, are likely to recur in any attempts to restore a tax incentive for authors and artists to donate their creations to libraries and museums.

15

Rare Book School, 1983

Terry Belanger

IN THE SUMMER OF 1983, Columbia University's School of Library Service (SLS) sponsored for the first time a four-week summer institute called Rare Book School (RBS). The program comprised eight noncredit courses of interest to research librarians and antiquarian booksellers. Courses, each led by two instructors, lasted for one five-day week, and two courses ran concurrently each week. The program was a success both financially and intellectually: It attracted nearly 200 applicants, of which 122 were selected, and elicited positive student evaluations of all eight courses.

Throughout the regular school year, SLS has several closely related programs in rare books and special collections, conservation, and preservation administration, with courses taught by (among others) Paul N. Banks, Gary Link Frost, Susan O. Thompson, Pamela W. Darling, Gerald Gottlieb, and myself. The conservation and preservation administration programs are relatively new (they began to admit students in the fall of 1981). The rare book and special collections program, which trains students for work in rare book, manuscript, archives, and other special collections in academic and research libraries, and for work in the antiquarian book trade, has for more than a decade been the largest and best known program of its kind in the United States.

As coordinator of the rare book program at Columbia, I have tried to stay in touch with as many of our graduates as possible. Many of them regularly return to New York City for such professional meetings as the American Printing History Association annual conference, held at the end of September, and the annual meeting of the Bibliographical Society of America, held at the end of January. Over the years, various of my former students have said, rather wistfully, that they wish they could come back to SLS and take some of our newer courses in rare books — or retake some of the old ones, now that they know what they're doing! Often, as they have gone on to more responsible jobs within the field over the years since their graduation, they have found themselves looking after collections about which they have little previous subject knowledge or bibliographical expertise.

The idea of a summer institute offering short, intensive courses in various areas of interest to rare book librarians and antiquarian booksellers took its original shape in this context: a chance for Columbia graduates and others in the field of rare books and special collections to learn more about various aspects of the history and care of books and other materials, through the provision of various one-week summer courses taught in each case by prominent subject specialists.

Having received permission from Richard L. Darling, dean of SLS, to begin a non-credit summer school for rare books, I sent out a questionnaire in November 1982, to about 400 former students, friends, and acquaintances in the field, soliciting advice about desirable courses: If you were free to come to Columbia to take a course in some aspect of rare books (I asked), what course would you want? The returns provided the basis for the construction of eight courses:

> Interpreting rare books and manuscripts to their communities, taught by John Parker (professor and curator, James Ford Bell Library, University of Minnesota/Twin Cities) and Daniel Traister (assistant curator for special collections, Van Pelt Library, University of Pennsylvania)
>
> The nineteenth-century book, taught by Michael Turner (head, Conservation, Bodleian Library, Oxford University) and Michael Winship (editor, *Bibliography of American Literature*)
>
> The study of incunabula, taught by Paul Needham (Keeper of Printed Books and Bindings, Pierpont Morgan Library) and Felix de Marez Oyens (president, L. C. Harper, Inc.)
>
> Comparative historical bookbindings and their preservation, taught by Sue Allen (a bookbinding historian), Christopher Clarkson (conservator, Bodleian Library, Oxford University), and Gary Link Frost (SLS)
>
> The sixteenth-century book, taught by Nicolas Barker (Deputy Keeper, British Library Reference Division) and Ruth Mortimer (curator of rare books, Smith College Library)
>
> Rare book cataloguing, taught by John Lancaster (special collections librarian and archivist, Amherst College) and Earl Taylor (chief of cataloguing, John Carter Brown Library)
>
> Preservation for rare book librarians and archivists, taught by Pamela W. Darling (SLS) and Carolyn Harris (head, Preservation Department, Columbia University Libraries)
>
> Book illustration to 1860: techniques in context, taught by Joan Friedman (curator of rare books, Yale Center for British Art) and myself.

The assembling of the necessary faculty to teach in the Rare Book School proved to be a much simpler task than I had anticipated. Almost everyone I asked to teach for me accepted my invitation, even though a number of them had never taught before and almost none had previously been concerned in a team-teaching venture — necessary here because of the concentrated nature of the courses, each of which offered about 25 hours of instruction over five days.

The chief difficulty with the 1983 Rare Book School was its timing. Having secured permission to run the school only in November of 1982, and needing December to assemble a faculty and course descriptions, I was in a position to begin advertising the school only in January 1983, less than six months before the first course would begin. Most of the enrollees of the school, I knew, would be rare book and other research librarians who would in many cases need to secure permission from their supervisors to attend and would in addition need to apply for financial subvention to offset (or help offset) the costs of transportation, tuition, and living expenses while in New York City (we offered air-conditioned dormitory housing at $20 per night). Library budgets like other academic budgets tend to solidify many months in advance of the spending, and the earlier one applies for money from them the greater the likelihood of its being forthcoming. To ask potential students to go to their bosses in January or later for money to attend school in July was more, I was afraid, than many persons would be even willing to attempt.

Still, there was only one way of finding out what would happen. The 1983 Rare Book School brochures came back from the printer in mid-January, and I began sending them out immediately. In this endeavor I was aided by two circumstances. My own *Bibliography Newsletter* (*BiN*) then had a subscription list of about 700 names, and I could enclose the Rare Book School brochure with the next issue of this newsletter, whose subscribers tend to be very active in the book world. Furthermore, SLS had entered the word processing age more than a year earlier, and by early 1983, I had a coded, word-processed list of more than 800 names (excluding *BiN* subscribers, who are recorded on a different system) to draw upon for my publicity campaign. I sent copies—in a good many cases multiple copies—of the brochure out to my SLS general mailing list. I placed full-page advertisements in *AB Bookman's Weekly, C & R L News,* and the *American Book Collector* (these appeared in March and April). I began folding into my master word processor mailing list additional names furnished by the membership lists of various bibliographical and other research and library societies. After consulting the *American Library Directory,* I wrote to the directors of libraries that had rare book, special collections, or archives departments, suggesting that they send one of their staff members to the school. I added the names of the members of various bibliographical social clubs—and so on. In all, I had made 8,000 copies of the brochure advertising the 1983 Rare Book School, and most of them were used for these direct mailings.

As I watched the brochures go out, I had no sure way of knowing what kind of response I would have, how many persons would want to come to New York City in July to study, for instance, bookbinding structure. However, when the responses were in we received for five of the eight courses offered far more applications than there were places, with the greatest number of applications received for the bookbinding and cataloguing courses. We ended up with 121 paying students for a 95 percent enrollment. (One full scholarship was given to a New York Public Library employee in thanks for the library's letting us use its facilities for certain class sessions.) Attendance by course is shown in Table 1.

The school itself was a considerable success—in part because of excellent students who in most cases had several years or more of professional experience in some aspect of rare books or related work and who were very eager indeed to learn, and in part because of knowledgeable and enthusiastic instructors who adapted quickly to the challenges of team teaching and long and intense classroom hours.

Two courses ran simultaneously for each of the four weeks of the 1983 Rare Book School, usually beginning at about 9:30 A.M. and (with breaks for coffee and lunch) running till late afternoon. In several instances I found myself breaking into classrooms at 5:45 P.M., to insist that the class finally stop for the day, so that its students

Table 1. Attendance at RBS 1983 by Course

Course	Enrollment
Interpreting Rare Books and Manuscripts to Their Communities	6
The 19th-Century Book	19
The Study of Incunabula	17
Comparative Historical Bookbindings and Their Preservation	19
The 16th-Century Book	18
Rare Book Cataloguing	20
Preservation for Rare Book Librarians and Archivists	11
Book Illustration to 1860: Techniques in Context	12

could have some kind of break before the evening's entertainment; for in addition to the formal daytime classes we offered two or three evening lectures on bibliographical subjects each week, of sufficient general interest to appeal to both classes then in residence. Also invited to these lectures were the Friends of the Book Arts Press, a group of about 150 persons principally in the New York City area who support the rare book program at the School of Library Service with annual contributions and who in return receive special announcements about public lectures on bibliographical subjects at SLS. Over the four weeks, we offered evening lectures by Edwin Wolf 2nd (Library Company of Philadelphia), John Bidwell (Clark Library, UCLA), Willman Spawn (American Philosophical Society), William H. Scheide, Chistopher Clarkson, Katharine F. Pantzer (*Short Title Catalogue* revision, Houghton Library, Harvard), Katharine Kyes Leab (*American Book Prices Current*), Nicolas Barker, and Eleanor M. Garvey (Houghton Library, Harvard).

The Friends of the Book Arts Press turned up in good numbers for these lectures, which typically drew 50 to 60 persons. The formal lectures were in each case followed by receptions, so that Rare Book School students could improve their acquaintance with each other and meet some of the local bibliographical professionals. These receptions and a great deal of the other business of keeping Rare Book School afloat were ably handled by SLS student Arnold Arcolio (now working at the Huntington Library in San Marino).

An analysis of the students who attended RBS 1983 indicates that about 30 percent were from the greater New York City area, 40 percent lived outside New York but in the East, and the remaining 30 percent lived west of the Mississippi. The students were asked whether they were given time off from work to attend RBS, whether their institutions paid their tuition, and whether they received financial assistance for their travel expenses and/or room and board. Their responses (see Table 2) show that the courses most heavily subsidized by students' institutions were those dealing with various aspects of rare book librarianship, whereas the courses dealing with historical periods were primarily attended by students paying their own way. (About a dozen book dealers or book collectors took one or another of these period courses, somewhat skewing the figures.) We had to turn away qualified students for six of the eight courses offered, including all three of the period courses, an encouraging sign for our first year in this business and one that, indeed, suggests considerable expansion of RBS in 1984.

Table 2.   Percentage of Students Whose Institutions
Subsidized Their Attendance at RBS 1983

Course	Paid Leave	Tuition	Travel	Room and Board
Preservation	90	80	60	50
Rare Book Cataloguing	89	82	47	37
Book Illustration	75	58	33	17
Interpreting Rare Books	66	50	50	50
Bookbinding	58	35	12	6
The 19th-Century Book	44	28	17	17
The 15th-Century Book	29	24	18	12
The 16th-Century Book	25	6	6	6

The 1983 Rare Book School offered eight courses over four weeks; the 1984 Rare Book School will offer 20 different courses (three of them given twice) over six weeks.

(For a complete list of 1984 courses offered, *see* Chapter 21.) The approximately 300 students who will, I hope, be impelled to attend the school will have the opportunity to take rare book courses dealing with fields ranging from music, children's literature, letterforms, textual editing, and exhibitions to microcomputers.

16

The Program in the History of the Book in American Culture at the American Antiquarian Society

David D. Hall and John B. Hench

THE AMERICAN ANTIQUARIAN SOCIETY (AAS) in 1983 established a Program in the History of the Book in American Culture. The program is composed of a number of scholarly activities, including an annual lecture series, workshops and seminars, conferences, publications, and residential fellowships. Some of these activities are already underway; others will be implemented over the next several years.

By inaugurating this program, the American Antiquarian Society intends to grasp two opportunities. The first is to stimulate and give direction to a developing field of inquiry, one that has only recently begun to emerge from the work of European scholars. In bringing this new field to the attention of Americans, and in applying its methods and approaches to American materials, the program will take advantage of the circumstance that the history of the book is inherently a crossroads. It is a means of linking specialties that hitherto existed in isolation. It is as well a means of bringing the broader questions of social and intellectual history into fruitful juncture with textual studies and the history of printing. The program will work to show how different approaches impinge on one another, and how, indeed, "the history of books in this unified sense," in the words of G. Thomas Tanselle, "is central to humanistic study." In short, the program will pose, and attempt to meet, a major intellectual challenge: to work toward a history of the book that relates this field of inquiry closely to economic, social, and cultural history, while at the same time making clear the central role of printing and publishing in the making of culture and society.

The second opportunity to which the program is addressed is the need for advanced interdisciplinary training in the humanities. As a major research center, the American Antiquarian Society can provide a breadth of resources in its field that few colleges and universities can equal. The holdings of the AAS library are unrivaled in the area of American imprints through the year 1876. The library also includes outstanding collections of manuscripts, graphic arts materials, and secondary printed materials relating to American history and culture through the centennial year. Moreover, the Program in the History of the Book can be crucial in helping scholars to expand the boundaries of their competence, in fostering interdisciplinary approaches, and in bringing into concert persons from a wide variety of fields. The program is dedicated to encouraging creative learning at every level, from Ph.D. candidates to senior faculty.

Some 25 years ago the French historian Lucien Febvre called for a reassessment of the role of the book in early modern European society. Febvre and Henri-Jean Martin sketched some of the possibilities for such a history in *L'Apparition du Livre* (1958). With the field thus newly energized, a number of important works have come forth in the intervening years. Among the earlier contributions are two volumes of essays, *Livre et Société* (1965 and 1970) and the refounding of the *Revue Française d' Histoire du Livre* (1971). In rediscovering the significance of the "Bibliothèque Bleue," Robert Mandrou and Genevieve Bollème seemed to demonstrate how social history — in this instance recovering the mental world of a semiliterate peasantry — could be integrated with the history of the book. That process of integration was forwarded by Natalie Z. Davis in her essay "Printing and the People" (*Society and Culture in Modern France*, 1975); by Elizabeth Eisenstein, most notably in her book *The Printing Press as an Agent of Change* (2 vols., 1979; abridged edition, published under the title *The Printing Revolution in Early Modern Europe*, 1983); and by Robert Darnton in a series of contributions culminating in *The Business of Enlightenment* (1979), *The Literary Underground of the Old Regime* (1982), and *The Great Cat Massacre and Other Episodes in French Cultural History* (1984). International research in the history of the book stimulated a conference sponsored by the Rare Books and Manuscripts Section of the Association of College and Research Libraries in 1980, papers from which were published in 1983 as *Books and Society in History*, edited by Kenneth E. Carpenter. In the early 1980s, historians from both Europe and America were collaborating on a three-volume *Histoire de l'Édition Française* under the general editorship of Roger Chartier and Henri-Jean Martin. Volume I, which covers the period from the Middle Ages to the seventeenth century, appeared in 1983. All in all, the new historians of the book have transformed our understanding of popular belief and of the cultural boundaries that divided one group from another in early modern Europe. They have altered our perception of the rise and spread of intellectual and social movements. Most recently, a new understanding of literacy — focused on the act of reading — has begun to emerge out of the fusion of literary, bibliographical, and historical approaches.

The purpose of the Program in the History of the Book in American Culture is to promote this same collaboration and to pose the same kinds of questions, but with respect to American materials and in an American historical setting. In the United States we are well advanced toward a comprehensive bibliography of American imprints. The works of Evans, Bristol, Shaw, Shoemaker, and many others laid a sound foundation of this sort, which in turn has facilitated the present work of creating a machine-readable record of early American imprints by the North American Imprints Program at the American Antiquarian Society. Progress toward collaboration by scholars from different disciplines and, more importantly, toward recasting of the subject, has not been as substantial. AAS made a step in this direction in 1980 by sponsoring a conference on "Printing and Society in Early America," which was attended by historians, literary scholars, bibliographers, and librarians from the United States and abroad. The society was sufficiently encouraged by the potential in the field that this conference suggested to plan and establish the Program in the History of the Book in American Culture. The program will pursue research and interpretation in several directions. These will include, but not be limited to, the history of reading; writers in the marketplace; popular religion and popular belief; the influence that the book arts and crafts, including typographical design, had on the ways texts were transmitted and perceived; and the relationships between printing and certain social and political movements.

Ideas developed in the program will achieve permanent form through a series of publications, the most important of them being a collaborative history of the book in America (to be published in the early 1990s) that will synthesize relevant scholarship, while opening and exploiting new lines of inquiry.

The program will pursue several other means of achieving its goals as well. It will offer short-term workshops on problems and methodologies in the history of the book and its associated crafts and trades. To staff these workshops, the program will draw on leading scholars from Europe and America. The program will sponsor periodic conferences, each of which will bring together persons from different disciplines. A conference focusing on needs and opportunities for further research in the field of the book in American culture is scheduled to be held at the American Antiquarian Society in the fall of 1984. This invitational conference will bring together some three dozen scholars from around the country and abroad and from a variety of disciplines and professional fields to survey the work already accomplished and to suggest promising avenues for future research. Among the topics scheduled for examination are the printing trade and allied crafts (technologies and labor practices), publishing networks of distribution, readers and reading, the religious press, the book in popular culture, the nineteenth-century newspaper, the book and forms of expertise, the morphology of the book, bibliography and textual studies, and social history and the book. The society expects that the conference will help set a more specific research agenda for work leading to the collaborative history of the book planned for the next decade.

In part depending on the needs and possibilities for interinstitutional collaboration with colleges and universities in New England, the program will offer semester-long seminars, not available in other institutions, to faculty and graduate students in history, English and American literature, American studies, and other relevant disciplines. Apart from courses and conferences, the program will sponsor several short- and long-term research fellowships for persons who are pursuing research on the history of the book. Three categories of fellowships are planned for the program. A major fellowship will provide the funds to bring a senior scholar to AAS for an entire academic year, or, alternately, to provide stipends for two such scholars each to spend at least a semester in residence. Also, an annual fellowship for a young scholar at work on a doctoral dissertation in the field of American book history is planned. Such a fellowship would enable a Ph.D. candidate to establish a residency in the society's library during the most crucial year of research on the dissertation. This plan is motivated in part by the society's desire to foster the recruitment, in however modest a fashion at first, of a new generation of scholars who may be expected to make the field of American book history their field. The third category of residential fellowships will be a series of three to five short-term fellowships to enable scholars from a variety of disciplines to work among relevant AAS collections for periods of two or three months.

The AAS's Program in the History of the Book in American Culture is already underway. The program is administered within the society's department of research and publication, which is headed by John B. Hench, assistant director for research and publication. Chairman of the program is David D. Hall, professor of history at Boston University, a member of AAS, and co-editor of and contributor to the society's book *Printing and Society in Early America,* published in June 1983. This collection of original essays, an outgrowth of the 1980 AAS conference, is the first in a series of publications that the program will sponsor. An Advisory Board, international in its membership, and an Executive Committee have been named. The members of the Executive Committee are: G. Thomas Tanselle (chairman), Vice President, John Simon Guggenheim Memorial Foundation; Bernard Bailyn, Adams University Professor of History, Harvard University; John Bidwell, Reference/Acquisitions Librarian, William Andrews Clark Memorial Library, University of California, Los Angeles; Kenneth E. Carpenter, Research and Publications Librarian, Harvard University Library; Robert Darnton, Professor of History, Princeton University; Stephen Nissenbaum, Professor of History, University of Massachusetts, Amherst; Roderick D. Stinehour, President, Meriden-Stinehour, Inc.; Larzer Ziff, Caroline Donovan Professor of English, Johns Hopkins University.

Serving on the Advisory Board are: Thomas R. Adams, John Hay Professor of Bibliography, Brown University; James F. Beard, Professor of English, Clark University; Terry Belanger, Assistant Dean, School of Library Service, Columbia University; Stephen Botein, Associate Professor of History, Michigan State University; Richard D. Brown, Professor of History, University of Connecticut; Roger Chartier, Maitre Assistant, l'Ecole des Hautes Etudes en Sciences Sociales; John Y. Cole, Executive Director, Center for the Book, Library of Congress; Richard Crawford, Professor of Music, University of Michigan; Gaylord Donnelley, Honorary Director, R. R. Donnelley and Sons; Everett Emerson, Professor of English, University of North Carolina, Chapel Hill; Bernhard Fabian, Professor, Englisches Seminar, Westf. Wilhelms-Universität (Federal Republic of Germany); William J. Gilmore, Associate Professor of History, Stockton State College; Oscar Handlin, Professor of History and Librarian, Harvard University; Elizabeth Harris, Curator, Graphic Arts Division, Smithsonian Institution; Jeremiah Kaplan, President, Macmillan Publishing Company; David Kaser, Professor of Library Science, Indiana University; Linda K. Kerber, Professor of History, University of Iowa; Marie E. Korey, Rare Book Librarian, Free Library of Philadelphia; Richard Landon, Head, Thomas Fisher Rare Book Library, University of Toronto; D. F. McKenzie, Professor of English, Victoria University of Wellington (New Zealand); Mary Beth Norton, Professor of History, Cornell University; Rollo G. Silver, historian of printing, Boston; Roger E. Stoddard, Associate Librarian, Houghton Library; Michael L. Turner, Head of Conservation, Bodleian Library; John William Ward, President, American Council of Learned Societies; James M. Wells, formerly Vice President, Newberry Library; Robert M. Weir, Professor of History, University of South Carolina; Edwin Wolf 2nd, Librarian, Library Company of Philadelphia.

Among other recent activities of the program is the establishment of a series of annual lectures in the field, named the James Russell Wiggins Lectures in the History of the Book in American Culture. The first of these lectures was held at AAS on November 9, 1983, with David Hall, program chairman, delivering a paper entitled "On Native Ground: From the History of Printing to the History of the Book." Beginning with Isaiah Thomas's *History of Printing in America,* Hall traced the rise of American printing history through the generation of Joseph Sabin and John Russell Bartlett and the achievements of Charles Evans, Clarence Brigham, and Wilberforce Eames to Lawrence Wroth's *The Colonial Printer.* Divergent themes converged in Wroth's study: the utilitarian and the democratic, in contrast with aesthetic standards of high quality. The same tension, Hall suggested, could be seen in the emerging history of American literature, from the Duyckincks and Moses Coit Tyler to *The Literary History of the United States* and F. O. Matthiessen's *American Renaissance.* Was "literature" to include such lowly artifacts as the almanac, or only the great masters; and must ours be a *native* literature? Hall proposed that the history of the book in America would turn away from aesthetic, nativist, and other limiting criteria in favor of a broad understanding of literature, printing, and society. In closing, he sketched several themes and topics that would characterize the history of the book: a concern for popular culture, viewed not as literary trash but as a complex arena of conservative and radical forces; the history of reading; the text as artifact; and an understanding of social forces that acknowledges the ambivalences of power. Hall's lecture will be published in April 1984 both in the *Proceedings of the American Antiquarian Society* and as a separate pamphlet that will be distributed by the society's book distributor, the University Press of Virginia.

On November 28, the program sponsored two appearances by Dr. Paul Raabe, the director and librarian of the Herzog August Bibliothek in Wolfenbüttel, West Germany. The library that Raabe directs is a major European center for the study of the history of the book. The program has also published the first issue of a newsletter, *The Book.* The purpose of the newsletter is to inform readers of the activities of the program and related activities elsewhere. Also to be published, in addition to news, will be research notes, book notes, and other short features that give some view of substantive work being done in this area. The editors of *The Book* welcome contributions of news, notes, and comment. For the time being at least, subscriptions to *The Book* will be given gratis to all those requesting them. News and subscription requests may be addressed to John B. Hench at the American Antiquarian Society, 185 Salisbury St., Worcester, Mass. 01609.

Those of us concerned with the development of the Program in the History of the Book in American Culture have been highly gratified by the response the program has received from scholars in a wide variety of disciplines, from bibliographers, and from librarians. In the society's view, the establishment at AAS of the Program in the History of the Book in American Culture is a natural outgrowth of the society's past and present interests and will build on the very strengths of its research collections and research interests. At the same time the society is anxious to establish links with other institutions in the United States and abroad with similar interests. A new, imaginative, and interdisciplinary approach to the history of the book in American culture promises to enrich the study of the humanities in America for many years to come.

17

The Center for the Book

in the Library of Congress

John Y. Cole

THE CENTER FOR THE BOOK in the Library of Congress was created by Act of Congress in 1977 to focus national attention on the importance of books, reading, and the written word. The role of books in contemporary society, reading promotion, and the interdisciplinary study of the history of books are its three major interests. An informal, voluntary organization funded primarily by private contributions, the center brings together members of the book, educational, and business communities for projects and symposia. Drawing on the collections and specialists of the Library of Congress, it also sponsors publications, lectures, exhibits, and events that enhance the role of the book in society.

Many of the projects relating to rare books and manuscripts sponsored by the Center for the Book emphasize the rich collections of the Library of Congress. For example, *The Early Illustrated Book: Essays in Honor of Lessing J. Rosenwald* (1982) focuses on fifteenth- and sixteenth-century Dutch and Flemish books, landscape, and the works of Vergil, three special strengths of the Rosenwald Collection in the library's Rare Book and Special Collections Division. The volume was edited by art historian Sandra Hindman. The *1812 Catalogue of the Library of Congress: A Facsimile* (1982) is the last record of the library's collection before its destruction in 1814, when British troops burned the Capitol. This reprint includes an essay about the collection's significance by Robert A. Rutland, editor of *The Papers of James Madison,* and contains indexes to authors, titles, places, and dates of publication compiled by consultant Lynda Corey Claassen.

The Center for the Book also hosts symposia on important subjects of interest to both historians and contemporary policymakers. *Literacy in Historical Perspective* (1983), edited by historian Daniel P. Resnick, is based on a symposium cosponsored by the center and the U.S. National Institute of Education. Historical essays about literacy in Europe, the United States, China, and Russia are included in the volume, along with a bibliographical essay.

The Center for the Book occasionally hosts visiting scholars. The first was Elizabeth Eisenstein, professor of history at the University of Michigan and author of *The Printing Press as an Agent of Change.* Marianna Tax Choldin of the University of Illinois at Urbana-Champaign was a visiting scholar at the center during the first half of 1983. She carried out her own research about Soviet censorship of foreign books and participated in the center's symposia program.

In May 1983, the executive director represented the Center for the Book at an international symposium on the study of the history of books held at the Herzog August Bibliothek in Wolfenbüttel, Federal Republic of Germany. Later in the month the center hosted a meeting at the Library of Congress to discuss the future of two cooperative bibliographic projects of special interest: the compilation of a guide to archival resources for the study of U.S. publishing history and the indexing of the copyright records for 1790–1870, most of which are in the library's Rare Book and Special Collections Division.

In June, Alice D. Schreyer joined the Center for the Book as a consultant to prepare a guide to the resources of the Library of Congress for the study of the history of books. She is identifying and describing resources from most of the library's major custodial collections, including those in the Copyright Office, the Law Library, and the Geography and Map, Manuscript, Music, Prints and Photographs, and Rare Book and Special Collections divisions. The guide will be published by the Library of Congress in 1985.

The Englehard lecture series on the book, sponsored by the Center for the Book with funds contributed by Mrs. Charles W. Engelhard, consists of public talks that consider books in their many roles — as physical objects, as exemplars of the graphic and typographic arts, as transmitters of ideas, as influences on society, and as a collecting field. Since the start of the series in 1976, the lecturers have been Nicolas Barker, Philip Hofer, Elizabeth Eisenstein, Edwin Wolf 2nd, Ian Willison, and Robert Darnton; several of the lectures have been published by the Library of Congress. In 1983 the seventh Engelhard lecture, *A Portrait of the Author as a Bibliography,* by Dan H. Laurence, was published. The series continued in late 1983 with lectures by two Californians. In November, James D. Hart, director of the Bancroft Library at the University of California at Berkeley, delivered an illustrated lecture on "Fine Printing: The San Francisco Tradition." Book collecting was the subject of the other lecture, offered in December by William Barlow, Jr., of Oakland, Calif. In April 1984, Anthony Rota of Bertram Rota, Ltd., Booksellers, London, England, presented an Engelhard lecture titled "Points at Issue: A Bookseller Looks at Bibliography." In the spring of 1985, John P. Feather of the School of Library and Information Studies, Loughborough University, England, will lecture about the history of books as a field of study.

Special events scheduled in 1984 include a program marking the centennial of the Association of Book Travelers and, in October, an international symposium about the history and the influence of atlases. Titled "Images of the World: The Atlas through History," this two-day event will be cosponsored with the Geography and Map Division of the Library of Congress.

Two publications dealing with the history of books will be published in late 1984 or early 1985. "Books in Action: The Armed Services Editions," based on discussions at the fortieth anniversary celebration of the Armed Services Editions (ASE), includes essays by historians and ASE collectors Michael Hackenberg and Matthew Bruccoli and an author index to the 1,324 volumes in the series. The second publication will be by Paul Needham, curator of printed books at the Morgan Library. In 1980, Needham discovered an unrecorded indulgence printed by William Caxton in the Rosenwald collection in the library's Rare Book and Special Collections Division. The Center for the Book has commissioned a publication based on this discovery.

18

Rare Books and Manuscripts Section, Association of College and Research Libraries

Joan M. Friedman

THE RARE BOOKS and Manuscripts Section (RBMS), a unit of the Association of College and Research Libraries (ACRL), in turn a division of the American Library Association (ALA), is the primary professional association of rare books and special collections librarians in America. Its place within the structure of ALA ensures that it provides not only a focus for the concerns of those involved with antiquarian books but also a channel of communication with the rest of the library world. In recent years this double role has proved not only workable but also of immense value to special collections librarians. There are nearly 1,300 personal members of RBMS. The current officers are listed at the end of this chapter.

The section is best known to the greatest numbers of its constituents for the annual conferences it sponsors, generally just prior to the annual meeting of ALA. In 1983, for the first time, RBMS's annual conference took place just after the ALA meeting in Los Angeles. This postconference was organized by Thomas Wright, librarian of UCLA's Clark Library. The venue was the UCLA campus, a relaxed setting well suited to encouraging congeniality among colleagues.

The theme of the postconference was "The Enemies of Books Revisited"; over the course of three days participants considered some of the practical limitations facing those who will care for special collections in the last quarter of the twentieth century.

Keynote speaker Roger Stoddard of Harvard's Houghton Library inspired the assembly, not so much with a recital of the institutional indifference and financial constraints known only too well to most of us, but rather with a moving invocation for librarians to look to themselves first when seeking to improve the resources for scholarly research. He offered as a model the Talmud's 48 qualifications to be worthy of the crown of the Torah. These range from "study," "the heart's attention," and "patience" to "exactness with colleagues," "loving correction," and "quoting each word in the name of its source." His words held much relevance for today's custodians of learning.

In 1984, RBMS will sponsor a preconference in Austin, Tex., June 19–22, just prior to the ALA annual meeting in Dallas. The theme will be "Collecting the Twentieth Century," and among the speakers will be Donald Gallup and Michael Holroyd. James Green of the Library Company of Philadelphia has planned an exciting program.

More than 200 librarians, collectors, and booksellers attended the 1983 RBMS postconference, but nearly 70 members of the section also participate in its increasingly significant committee work. Most of this business is conducted at ALA's annual and midwinter meetings. There are now some 13 active RBMS committees engaged in such tasks as the preparation of guidelines for practice in the field and the planning of conferences and programs.

One of the hardest-working committees of RBMS is the Standards Committee, which, since 1979, has been developing uniform standards for the cataloguing of rare books and special collections in machine-readable form. Its efforts have been instrumental in persuading the national bibliographical networks to which most research libraries subscribe to accommodate the special files and fuller descriptions that rare book libraries have traditionally tried to provide. During 1983, under the chairmanship of John Lancaster of Amherst College, the committee completed and published a thesaurus of terms for "genres" of publications (such as "almanac" or "play"). Work has begun on another thesaurus for terms concerning the physical makeup of books (such as bookbinding terms), and assistance has been provided to non-RBMS groups working in overlapping areas, such as the graphic arts.

The Security Committee, under Peter Hanff of Berkeley's Bancroft Library, also had a busy year. Committee members undertook a survey of research libraries' security procedures, hoping to determine what impact the section's published guidelines might have had in this area. The immediate effect of this survey in many cases was to inform the libraries questioned that these guidelines do exist! The committee also played a role in sponsoring the Oberlin Conference on Theft, reported on in Chapter 13. A task to be begun in 1984 is the preparation of a handbook of library security.

The Continuing Education Committee has traditionally been responsible for organizing the seminars that are such a useful feature of RBMS conferences. At UCLA, there were sessions on preparing exhibitions, the use of publications for public relations, and the legal aspects of librarian-book collector relations, among other practical topics. The committee, under the leadership of Alice Schreyer of the Library of Congress's Center for the Book, is planning additional intriguing sessions for the 1984 preconference. Members are also at work on several publications for the use of librarians and their patrons. One, tentatively entitled "What to Do with My Old Books" (a revision of a pamphlet formerly issued by the American Library Association), has also formed the basis for a program at the ALA annual meeting in Dallas.

Other committees have been addressing other issues: the problems of transferring materials from general stacks of libraries to special collections departments; the issues of professional ethics facing today's rare book librarians; and means of communicating better with members of the section. With the latter aim in mind, the section has established a newsletter, the first issue of which is to go out to the membership in 1984.

During 1983, several new RBMS committees were established. At the request of some members, a group was appointed to survey manuscripts curators and make recommendations as to how the section might better accommodate the *M* in its acronym. The completed survey indicates a need for a focus on manuscripts different from that offered by the Society of American Archivists. Clifton Jones of Southern Methodist University, chair of the committee, will report its recommendations to the section in June.

Another new committee, under the leadership of Ann Gwyn of Johns Hopkins University, has been investigating the possibility of the section's offering an annual award for the best exhibition catalogues published by rare books and special collections libraries. It, too, will be making a final report in Dallas in June.

The Publications Committee has been established to coordinate and facilitate the various printed matter that the expanded activities of RBMS have engendered. These include committee guidelines, informational booklets, conference proceedings, the newsletter, and, it now seems possible, a journal of rare books and special collections librarianship.

RBMS, as the foregoing testifies, is an active and diverse group. The expansion of activities and concerns in recent years has created a real need for more participants; at the same time the section has shown itself to be receptive to ideas for additional projects.

RBMS CURRENT OFFICERS

Chair
Stephen Ferguson
Firestone Library 1-17-D
Princeton University
Princeton, NJ 08540

Vice Chair, Chair-Elect
Lynda Claassen
Special Collections
Central University Library C-075-5
University of California, San Diego
La Jolla, CA 92093

Immediate Past Chair
Joan M. Friedman
Yale Center for British Art
PO Box 2120, Yale Sta
New Haven, CT 06520

Secretary
Anthony Bliss
Bancroft Library
University of California, Berkeley
Berkeley, CA 94720

Members-at-Large
Donald Farren
Special Collections
McKeldin Library
University of Maryland
College Park, MD 20742

Peter VanWingen
Rare Book & Special Collections Division
Library of Congress
Washington, DC 20540

Jennifer Lee
John Hay Library
Brown University
Providence, RI 02912

19

The Society of American Archivists

Deborah Risteen

THE SOCIETY OF AMERICAN ARCHIVISTS (SAA) is a professional association of individuals and institutions interested in the preservation and use of archives and manuscripts. SAA's 3,000 members represent archival repositories of many types—college and university, religious, government, and business among the most prominent. The officers and council members for 1983–1984 are:

Officers 1983–1984

David B. Gracy II, President
Texas State Archives

Andrea Hinding, Vice President
University of Minnesota

Paul H. McCarthy, Jr., Treasurer
University of Alaska

Council Members 1983–1984

Kenneth W. Duckett
University of Oregon

John A. Fleckner
Smithsonian Institution

Robert Gordon
Public Archives of Canada

Larry J. Hackman
New York State Archives

Edie Hedlin
National Archives and Records Service

Linda Henry
National Archives and Records Service

Sue E. Holbert
Minnesota Historical Society

William L. Joyce
New York Public Library

Virginia C. Purdy
National Archives and Records Service

Executive Director

Ann Morgan Campbell

The year 1983 was a very busy one for SAA. The society is active in continuing education for archivists and in 1983 sponsored workshops from Fairbanks to Washington, D.C. Among the topics addressed by these workshops were management for archivists, business archives, conservation, machine-readable records, administration of photographic collections, oral history, tribal archives, and how to start an archives. The workshops on conservation and photographic collections are part of SAA's Basic Archival Conservation Program, funded by the National Endowment for the Humanities. That program also includes a photographic consultant service to assist repositories in evaluating the needs of their photographic holdings.

In addition to the quarterly journal *The American Archivist* and the bimonthly *SAA Newsletter,* the society published several new titles in 1983. *Archives & Manuscripts: Conservation,* by Mary Lynn Ritzenthaler, is the newest addition to SAA's Basic Manual series. It covers such topics as causes of deterioration, creating a suitable environment, and storage of archival materials, as well as illustrated instructions to several basic conservation practices. The *Education Directory* contains listings of archival courses and institutes in the United States and Canada. *College & University Archives Guidelines* is a booklet containing guidelines in the areas of administration, personnel, facilities and equipment, supporting services, and records management. A bibliography entitled *Information Management, Machine-Readable Records, and Archival Administration* was also published in 1983.

The society began work on several important projects in 1983. The Task Force on Archives and Society was created to address the image/perceptions that people outside the archival profession hold of archivists and their work. The task force will recommend ways that the archival profession can increase public awareness, understanding, appreciation, and support of archives.

SAA's Task Force on Goals and Priorities drafted a statement of missions and goals for the archival profession, which is currently under review by the membership of the society. Three main goals were identified by the task force: the ongoing identification and retention of only those records of enduring value to society; the responsible administration of archival records to ensure their availability under appropriate conditions; and the maximum use of archival records for the benefit of society.

A study group was formed in 1983 to draft a definition of an archivist. This is viewed as an important step toward the consideration of certification of archivists, accreditation of archival education programs and/or repositories, and determination of who is qualified to serve as an archival consultant. A draft of the study group's definition is currently under review.

In 1983, SAA received funding from the Everett McKinley Dirksen Congressional Leadership Research Center to support initial efforts to develop guidelines for members of Congress and their staff on the administration of current records and their eventual deposit in archival institutions.

SAA continued throughout 1983 to be involved in efforts to gain independence for the National Archives and Records Service (NARS) from the General Services Administration (GSA). Bills authorizing such a separation are pending in both houses of Congress. Supporters of the National Archives believe that independence is important because (1) the basic missions of NARS and GSA are incompatible; (2) the records of the nation need protective independence from partisan political influence, which they do not get under GSA; and (3) NARS's lack of authority over budget, program priorities, and personnel management as part of GSA severely handicaps its authority to care for the records of government.

Archivists, manuscript dealers and appraisers, and historians found themselves in the media spotlight in spring 1983 as the West German magazine *Stern* began publication of the "Hitler Diaries." After examination by West German archivists, the materials were termed "a blatant, grotesque, and superficial forgery" by Hans Booms, head of the German Federal Archives. Booms reported that 7 of the 62 volumes were written on paper made some time after 1955. American manuscript dealer Kenneth Rendell, hired by *Newsweek* magazine to determine the diaries' authenticity, compared individual letters of the alphabet in authentic Hitler documents with those in the diaries and concluded that "the initial and final installments of the so-called Hitler diaries were not only forgeries, they were bad forgeries."

Konrad Fischer, a Stuttgart dealer in Nazi and Hitler memorabilia, admitted forging the diaries in a confession signed "Respectfully, Adolph Hitler." Also implicated in the fraud was Gerd Heidemann, the *Stern* reporter who had uncovered the "diaries" for the magazine.

EDUCATIONAL OPPORTUNITIES

IV

20

Fellowships and Lectures

FELLOWSHIPS

AMERICAN ANTIQUARIAN SOCIETY, AL-
BERT BONI FELLOWSHIP. An award de-
rived from a gift from the Readex
Microprint Corporation (founded by
Albert Boni) and given to a qualified
scholar working in the fields of early
American bibliography or printing and
publishing history. The award allows
the recipient to work in the society's library from one to two months. Further
information is available from John B.
Hench, Asst. Dir. for Research and
Publication, American Antiquarian Society, 185 Salisbury St., Worcester, MA
01609.

1983: Ronald J. Zboray, Pace University. "A Fictive People."

The American Antiquarian Society
offers other more general short-term
fellowships, which, although not restricted to work in the fields of bibliography or printing and publishing
history, are available to scholars working in these fields.

BIBLIOGRAPHICAL SOCIETY OF AMER-
ICA, RESEARCH FELLOWSHIPS. Short-
term fellowships established in 1983 to
underwrite costs of transportation and
living expenses associated with the
study of the history of books and printing. For further information, applicants should write to Executive
Secretary, Bibliographical Society of
America, Box 397, Grand Central Station, New York, NY 10163.

1983: C. Paul Christianson, The
College of Wooster (Ohio). "London

Bridge records and the medieval book
trade."

Andrew S. Cook, India Office Library and Records (England). "Bibliography of Alexander Dalrymple's
publications (1767–1808)."

Daniel Eisenberg, Florida State
University. "Cervantes' library."

Robert Emmet McLaughlin, Yale
University. "Printing's impact upon religion in Germany 1500–1520."

Allen H. Reddick, Columbia University. "Examination of the annotated
partial copy of Johnson's 'Dictionary'
in the British Library and its relationship to the Sneyd-Gimbel copy at Yale
University."

Andrea J. Tucher, New York University Graduate School of Arts and
Science. "The power press as an agent
of change."

David L. Vander Meulen, University of Wisconsin. "A descriptive bibliography of Alexander Pope's 'Dun-
ciad.' "

CAMBRIDGE UNIVERSITY (ENGLAND),
MUNBY FELLOWSHIP. Founded in 1977
in memory of Alan Noel Latimer
Munby, bibliographical scholar and Librarian of King's College, Cambridge,
for bibliographical research based primarily on the collections of the libraries
of Cambridge. The fellowship is tena-
ble for one academic year. For further
information applicants should write to
the Deputy Librarian, Cambridge University, West Road, Cambridge, England CB3 9DR.

1983–1984: B. J. McMullin. "Aspects of the Bible trade in Britain in the 17th and 18th centuries."

1985–1986: F. Korsten. "Thomas Baker (1656–1740)."

Note: Research libraries offering general fellowships in historical/literary/bibliographical topics include the John Carter Brown Library (Providence, RI); William Andrews Clark Library (UCLA); Huntington Library (San Marino, CA); and the Newberry Library (Chicago).

LECTURES

ENGELHARD LECTURES ON THE BOOK (The Center for the Book in the Library of Congress). Established in 1976 with funding from Mrs. Charles Engelhard. The lectures are frequently published by the Center for the Book.

1983: James D. Hart. "Fine Printing: The San Francisco Tradition."

1983: William P. Barlow, Jr. "Book Collecting."

1984: Anthony B. Rota. "Points at Issue: A Bookseller Looks at Bibliography.".

1985: John P. Feather. "The History of Books as a Field of Study."

HANES LECTURES (University of North Carolina at Chapel Hill). Established in 1980 and sponsored by the Hanes Foundation for the Study of the Origin and Development of Books, the University Library, and the Rare Book Collection. The lectures are published by the Rare Book Collection.

1983: Fred Schreiber. "The Hanes Collection of Estienne Publications: From Book Collecting to Scholarly Resource."

1984: Alan Fern. "Off the Wall: Research into the Art of the Poster."

LYELL LECTURES (Oxford University, England). A readership in "the science of books and manuscripts" founded under the terms of the will of James Patrick Ronaldson Lyell in 1952. For a complete list of the lectures through 1982–1983 and the places where they

have been published, see *The Sandars and Lyell Lectures: A Checklist;* with an Introduction by David McKitterick (New York: Jonathan A. Hill, 1983).

1983–1984: Robert Shackleton
1984–1985: Gordon N. Ray
1985–1986: Edwin Wolf, 2nd

PANIZZI LECTURES (The British Library). A bibliographical lecture series endowed in 1983 to honor Sir Anthony Panizzi, the 19th-century Principal Librarian of the British Museum. The lectures will begin in 1985 and are expected to be published after their oral presentation.

1985: D. F. McKenzie (topic to be announced).

1986: T. A. Birrell. "The Old Royal Library."

A. S. W. ROSENBACH LECTURES IN BIBLIOGRAPHY (University of Pennsylvania). Established in 1930 to perpetuate the memory of the American antiquarian bookseller and bibliographer. The lectures are frequently published by the University of Pennsylvania Press.

1983: James L. W. West III. "The Profession of Authorship in America, 1900–1950."

1985: Ruth Mortimer. "Sixteenth-Century French Architectural Ornamentation and Its Use in Book Design."

1986: Terry Belanger. "The History of Rare Book Librarianship in America, 1876–1986."

1987: G. Thomas Tanselle. "Textural Criticism and Literary Editing."

SANDARS LECTURES (Cambridge University, England). A Readership in Bibliography established in 1894 under the terms of the will of Samuel Sandars. For a complete list of the lectures through 1982–1983 and the places where they have been published, see *The Sandars and Lyell Lectures: A Checklist;* with an Introduction by David McKitterick (New York: Jonathan A. Hill, 1983).

1983–1984: Peter Isaac

JAMES RUSSELL WIGGINS LECTURE IN THE HISTORY OF THE BOOK IN AMERICAN CULTURE (American Antiquarian Society). Established in 1983 from an endowment funded by friends of James Russell Wiggins, former editor of the *Washington Post*, former U.S. Ambassador to the United Nations, and President of the American Antiquarian Society, 1970–1977. The lectures will be published in the *Proceedings of the American Antiquarian Society* and also issued as a separate pamphlet by the society and distributed by the University Press of Virginia.

1983: David D. Hall: "On Native Ground: From the History of Printing to the History of the Book."

1984: James M. Wells (topic to be announced).

21

Programs and Courses

UNITED STATES

ALABAMA

UNIVERSITY OF ALABAMA. Graduate School of Library Service. PO Box 6242, University 35486. Tel: 205-348-4610. *Dean:* James D Ramer. *Specialized courses:* Descriptive Bibliography; History of Books & Printing; Rare Books

ARIZONA

UNIVERSITY OF ARIZONA. Graduate Library School. 1515 E First St, Tucson 85721. Tel: 602-626-3565. *Director:* Ellen Altman. *Specialized courses:* History of Books & Printing

CALIFORNIA

SAN JOSE STATE UNIVERSITY. Division of Library Science. Washington Sq, San Jose 95192. Tel: 408-277-2292. *Director:* Guy A Marco. *Specialized course:* History of Books

UNIVERSITY OF CALIFORNIA, BERKELEY. School of Library & Information Studies. Berkeley 94720. Tel: 415-642-1464. *Dean:* Michael K Buckland. *Specialized courses:* History of Books & Printing

UNIVERSITY OF CALIFORNIA, LOS ANGELES. Graduate School of Library & Information Science. 405 Hilgard

Ave, 120 Powell Library, Los Angeles 90024. Tel: 213-825-4351. *Dean:* Robert M. Hayes. *Specialized courses:* Analytical Bibliography; Historical Bibliography; History of Books; Printing for Bibliographers

UNIVERSITY OF SOUTHERN CALIFORNIA. School of Library & Information Management. University Park, Los Angeles 90089. Tel: 213-743-2548. *Dean:* Roger C Greer. *Specialized courses:* Archives; History of Printing

COLORADO

UNIVERSITY OF DENVER. Graduate School of Librarianship & Information Management. Denver 80208. Tel: 303-753-2557. *Dean:* Bernard Franckowiak. *Specialized courses:* History of Books & Printing. The Graduate School of Librarianship & Information Management holds in cooperation with *AB Bookman's Weekly* an Out-of-Print & Antiquarian Book Market Seminar/Workshop. The sixth annual workshop will be held August 12–17, 1984. Program highlights will include: Survey of the Antiquarian Book Trade & the Out-of-Print Market; Economics of the Antiquarian Book Trade; The Generalist & Specialist Dealer; Bibliographic Description; Information Systems for Bibliographic Description; Appraisals; Compiling & Reading Bookseller Catalogues; The Auction Market for Antiquarian Books; Procedures & Problems in Acquiring Rare & Out-of-Print Materials; Care & Preservation of Rare & Antiquarian Books; Computer Systems for the Antiquarian Book Business; How to Establish & Manage an Antiquarian Bookstore

CONNECTICUT

SOUTHERN CONNECTICUT STATE UNIVERSITY. School of Library Science & Instructional Technology. 501 Crescent St, New Haven 06515. Tel: 203-397-4530. *Acting Dean:* Emanuel T Prostano. *Specialized courses:* History of Books & Printing

DISTRICT OF COLUMBIA

CATHOLIC UNIVERSITY OF AMERICA. School of Library & Information Science. 620 Michigan Ave NE, Washington 20064. Tel: 202-635-5085. *Dean:* Elizabeth W Stone. *Specialized courses:* Archives; History of Books & Printing; Rare Books

FLORIDA

FLORIDA STATE UNIVERSITY. School of Library & Information Studies. Tallahassee 32306. Tel: 904-644-5775. *Dean:* Harold Goldstein. *Specialized course:* History of Books

UNIVERSITY OF SOUTH FLORIDA. Graduate Department of Library, Media & Information Studies. College of Education—HMS 301, 4202 Fowler Ave, Tampa 33620. Tel: 813-974-3520. *Chairperson:* John A McCrossan. *Specialized courses:* History of Books & Printing

GEORGIA

EMORY UNIVERSITY. Division of Library & Information Management. Atlanta 30322. Tel: 404-329-6840. *Di-*

rector: A Venable Lawson. *Specialized courses:* History of Books & Printing

HAWAII

UNIVERSITY OF HAWAII. Graduate School of Library Studies. 2550 The Mall, Honolulu 96822. Tel: 808-948-7321. *Dean:* Miles M Jackson. *Specialized course:* Rare Books

ILLINOIS

ROSARY COLLEGE. Graduate School of Library & Information Science. 7900 W Division St, River Forest 60305. Tel: 312-366-2490. *Dean:* Richard Li. *Specialized courses:* Archives; Rare Books

UNIVERSITY OF CHICAGO. Graduate Library School. 1100 E 57 St, Chicago 60637. Tel: 312-962-8272. *Dean:* W Boyd Rayward. Program on the theory & practice of the care of historical resources within the research library, including rare books, manuscripts & archives. *Specialized courses:* Archives & Manuscripts; Bibliographical Analysis; Institutionalizing the Past, An Introductory Course. Related courses are offered on the history of the book & the diffusion of knowledge

UNIVERSITY OF ILLINOIS. Graduate School of Library & Information Science. 410 David Kinley Hall, 1407 W Gregory Dr, Urbana 61801. Tel: 217-333-3280. *Dean:* Charles H Davis. *Specialized courses:* Archives; History of Books; Music Rare Books

INDIANA

INDIANA UNIVERSITY. School of Library & Information Science. University Library, Bloomington 47405. Tel: 812-335-2848. *Dean:* Herbert S White. *Specialized courses:* Archives; History of Books; Rare Books

KENTUCKY

UNIVERSITY OF KENTUCKY. College of Information & Library Science. 459

Patterson Office Tower, Lexington 40506. Tel: 606-257-8876. *Dean:* Timothy W Sineath. *Specialized courses:* History of Books & Printing

MARYLAND

UNIVERSITY OF MARYLAND. College of Library & Information Services. College Park 20742. Tel: 301-454-5441. *Acting Dean:* Anne S MacLeod. *Specialized courses:* Archives & Manuscripts; History of Books & Printing; Rare Books

MASSACHUSETTS

SIMMONS COLLEGE. Graduate School of Library & Information Science. 300 The Fenway, Boston 02115. Tel: 617-738-2264. *Dean:* Robert D. Stueart. *Specialized courses:* History of Books & Printing

MICHIGAN

UNIVERSITY OF MICHIGAN. School of Library Science. 580 Union Dr, Ánn Arbor 48109. Tel: 313-764-9376. *Dean:* Russell E Bidlack. *Specialized courses:* Archives; History of Books & Printing

WAYNE STATE UNIVERSITY. Division of Library Science. 315 Kresge Library, Detroit 48202. Tel: 313-577-1825. *Director:* Robert E Booth. *Specialized courses:* Archives; History of Books & Printing

WESTERN MICHIGAN UNIVERSITY. School of Librarianship. Kalamazoo 49008. Tel: 616-383-1849. *Interim Director:* Laurel Grotzinger. *Specialized courses:* Archives; Rare Books

MINNESOTA

UNIVERSITY OF MINNESOTA. Library School. 419 Walter Library, 117 Pleasant St SE, Minneapolis 55455. Tel: 612-373-3100. *Director:* George D'Elia. *Specialized courses:* History of Books & Printing; Rare Books

MISSISSIPPI

UNIVERSITY OF MISSISSIPPI. Graduate School of Library & Information Science. University 38766. Tel: 601-232-7440. *Acting Director:* Stephen B Schoenly. *Specialized courses:* History of Books & Printing

UNIVERSITY OF SOUTHERN MISSISSIPPI. School of Library Service. Box 5146, Southern Sta, Hattiesburg 39406. Tel: 601-266-4228. *Dean:* Onva K Boshears Jr. *Specialized courses:* History of Books & Printing

MISSOURI

UNIVERSITY OF MISSOURI. School of Library & Informational Science. 104 Stewart Hall, Columbia 65211. Tel: 314-882-4546. *Dean:* Edward P Miller. *Specialized courses:* History of Books & Printing; Rare Books

NEW YORK

COLUMBIA UNIVERSITY. School of Library Service. 516 Butler Library, New York 10027. Tel: 212-280-2292. *Dean:* Richard L Darling. *Specialized courses:* Archives; Descriptive Bibliography; History of Books & Printing; Rare Books. The School of Library Service sponsors an extensive summer program in the study of rare books, called Rare Book School (RBS). In 1984, RBS will meet from July 9 through August 17, & the following courses will be offered: Medieval Bookbinding Structures; The Study of Incunabula; The Handmade Book, 1450–1550; Type, Lettering & Calligraphy, 1450–1830; The Illustrated Book in c16 France & Italy; Rare Materials in Music, 1500–1900; The Study of American Bookbindings, 1660–1830; The c18 English Book; Book Illustration to 1860; Historical Children's Literature, 1770–1900; Publishers' Bindings, 1780–1910; The c19 English & American Book; Scholarly Editing; Theory & Practice of Conservation Bookbinding; Introduction to Archives for Special Collections Librarians; Introduction to Rare Book Librarianship for Archivists; Special Collections Development; Rare Book Exhibitions; Rare Book Cataloging; Microcomputers for Rare Book Libraries.

LONG ISLAND UNIVERSITY. Palmer School of Library & Information Science. C W Post Center, Greenvale 11548. Tel: 516-299-2855, 2856. *Dean:* Ralph J Folcarelli. *Specialized courses:* Archives; History of Books & Printing; Rare Books

QUEENS COLLEGE. Graduate School of Library & Information Studies. 64-15 Kissena Blvd, Flushing 11367. Tel: 212-520-7194, 7195. *Director:* Richard J Hyman. *Specialized courses:* History of Books & Printing

ST JOHN'S UNIVERSITY. Division of Library & Information Science. Grand Central & Utopia Pkwys, Jamaica 11439. Tel: 212-990-6161 ext 6200. *Director:* Mildred Lowe. *Specialized courses:* History of Books & Printing

STATE UNIVERSITY OF NEW YORK, ALBANY. School of Library & Information Science. 135 Western Ave, Albany 12222. Tel: 518-455-6288. *Dean:* Richard S Halsey. *Specialized courses:* History of Books & Printing; Rare Books

SYRACUSE UNIVERSITY. School of Information Studies. 113 Euclid Ave, Syracuse 13210. Tel: 315-423-2911. *Dean:* Evelyn Daniel. *Specialized courses:* Archives; Rare Books

NORTH CAROLINA

UNIVERSITY OF NORTH CAROLINA. School of Library Science. 100 Manning Hall 026A, Chapel Hill 27514. Tel: 919-962-8366. *Dean:* Edward G Holley. *Specialized courses:* History of Books & Printing; Rare Books

OHIO

CASE WESTERN RESERVE UNIVERSITY. Matthew A Baxter School of Informa-

tion & Library Science. 10950 Euclid Ave, Cleveland 44106. Tel: 216-368-3500. *Dean:* Phyllis A Richmond. *Specialized courses:* Archives & Manuscripts; History of Books & Printing

KENT STATE UNIVERSITY. School of Library Science. Kent 44242. Tel: 216-672-2782. *Dean:* A Robert Rogers. *Specialized courses:* Archives; Rare Books

PENNSYLVANIA

CLARION STATE COLLEGE. School of Library Science. 836 Wood St, Clarion 16214. Tel: 814-226-2271. *Dean:* Elizabeth A Rupert. *Specialized courses:* History of Books & Printing

DREXEL UNIVERSITY. School of Library & Information Science. Philadelphia 19104. Tel: 215-895-2474. *Dean:* Guy Garrison. *Specialized courses:* History of Books; Rare Books

UNIVERSITY OF PITTSBURGH. School of Library & Information Science. 135 N Bellefield Ave, Pittsburgh 15260. Tel: 412-624-5230. *Dean:* Thomas J Galvin. *Specialized courses:* Archives & Manuscripts; History of Books & Printing; Rare Books

RHODE ISLAND

UNIVERSITY OF RHODE ISLAND. Graduate Library School. 74 Lower College Rd, Rodman Hall, Kingston 02881. Tel: 401-792-2878, 2947. *Dean:* Bernard S Schlessinger. *Specialized courses:* Archives; History of Books & Printing

SOUTH CAROLINA

UNIVERSITY OF SOUTH CAROLINA. College of Library & Information Science. Columbia 29208. Tel: 803-777-3858. *Dean:* F William Summers. *Specialized course:* History of Printing

TEXAS

UNIVERSITY OF TEXAS. Graduate School of Library & Information Science. PO Box 7576, University Sta, Austin 78712. Tel: 512-471-3821. *Acting Dean:* Ronald E Wyllys. *Specialized courses:* Archives; History of Books & Printing; Rare Books

UTAH

BRIGHAM YOUNG UNIVERSITY. School of Library & Information Sciences. Rm 5042 HBLL, Provo 84602. Tel: 801-378-2977. *Director:* Nathan M Smith. *Specialized course:* Rare Books

WASHINGTON

UNIVERSITY OF WASHINGTON. School of Librarianship. 133 Suzzallo Library, FM-30, Seattle 98195. Tel: 206-543-1794. *Director:* Margaret Chisholm. *Specialized courses:* Archives; History of Books & Printing

WISCONSIN

UNIVERSITY OF WISCONSIN–MADISON. Library School. 4236 Helen White Hall, 600 N Park St, Madison 53706. Tel: 608-263-2900. *Director:* Jane Robbins-Carter. *Specialized courses:* Archives; History of Books & Printing; Rare Books

CANADA

ALBERTA

UNIVERSITY OF ALBERTA. Faculty of Library Science. Edmonton T6G 2J4, Canada. Tel: 403-432-4578. *Dean:* William J Kurmey. *Specialized courses:* History of Books & Printing

BRITISH COLUMBIA

UNIVERSITY OF BRITISH COLUMBIA. School of Librarianship. 831-1956 Main Mall, Vancouver V6T 1Y3, Canada. Tel: 604-228-4991 ext. 604. *Director:* Basil Stuart-Stubbs. *Specialized courses:* History of Books & Printing; Rare Books

NOVA SCOTIA

DALHOUSIE UNIVERSITY. School of Library Service. Halifax B3H 4H8, Canada. Tel: 902-424-3656. *Director:* Norman Horrocks. *Specialized courses:* Archives; History of Books; Rare Books

ONTARIO

UNIVERSITY OF TORONTO. Faculty of Library & Information Science. 140 St George St, Toronto M5S 1A1, Canada. Tel: 416-978-3202. *Dean:* Katherine H Packer. *Specialized courses:* Archives; History of Books & Printing; Rare Books

UNIVERSITY OF WESTERN ONTARIO. School of Library & Information Science. London N6G 1H1, Canada. Tel: 519-679-3542. *Dean:* William J. Cameron. *Specialized courses:* Archives; History of Books & Printing; Rare Books

QUEBEC

McGILL UNIVERSITY. Graduate School of Library Science. 3459 McTavish St, Montreal H3A 1Y1, Canada. Tel: 514-392-5934. *Director:* Hans Möller. *Specialized courses:* Archives; History of Books & Printing; Rare Books

UNIVERSITE DE MONTREAL. École de Bibliothéconomie. C P 6128, Montreal H3C 3J7, Canada. Tel: 514-343-7400. *Director:* Richard K Gardner. *Specialized courses:* Archives; History of Books

DIRECTORY OF
COLLECTIONS
AND SOURCES

V

22

Associations

This selected list of associations of interest to book collectors, antiquarian booksellers, and rare book librarians provides names, addresses, and contacts. Organizations in which membership is invitational have not been included.

ALCUIN SOCIETY. Members: 350. W. G. Chappell, *Secy.* Box 3216, Vancouver, BC, Canada V6B 3X8. Tel: 604-688-2341.

AMERICAN PRINTING HISTORY ASSOCIATION. Members: 1200. E. H. Pat Taylor, *Pres.* Box 4922, Grand Central Station, New York, NY 10163.

AMERICAN SOCIETY OF APPRAISERS. Members: 5000. Dexter D. MacBride, *Exec. VP.* Dulles International Airport, Box 17265, Washington, DC 20041. Tel: 703-620-3838.

AMERICAN SOCIETY OF BOOKPLATE COLLECTORS AND DESIGNERS. Members: 250. Audrey Arellanes, *Dir.* 605 North Stoneman Ave., No. F, Alhambra, CA 91801. Tel: 213-283-1936.

ANTIQUARIAN BOOKSELLERS ASSOCIATION (International). Bridget Cumings, *Secy.* Book House, 45 East Hill, London SW18 2QZ, England. Tel: 01-870-8259.

ANTIQUARIAN BOOKSELLERS ASSOCIATION OF AMERICA, INCORPORATED. Members: 402. Janice M. Farina, *Admin. Asst.* 50 Rockefeller Plaza, New York, NY 10020. Tel: 212-757-9395.

ANTIQUARIAN BOOKSELLERS ASSOCIATION OF CANADA. 763 Bank St., Ottawa, ON, Canada K1S 3V3.

THE BIBLIOGRAPHICAL SOCIETY. MRS. MIRJAM FOOT, *Hon. Secy.* British Library Reference Division, Great Russell St., London WC1B 3DG, England; William H. Bond, *Hon. Secy. for America.* Houghton Library, Harvard University, Cambridge, MA 02138.

BIBLIOGRAPHICAL SOCIETY OF AMERICA. Members: 1400. Irene Tichenor, *Exec. Secy.* Box 397, Grand Central Station, New York, NY 10163. Tel: 212-638-7957.

BIBLIOGRAPHICAL SOCIETY OF THE UNIVERSITY OF VIRGINIA. Members: 1000. c/o Ray W. Frantz, Alderman Library, University of Virginia, Charlottesville, VA 22901. Tel: 804-924-7013.

THE EPHEMERA SOCIETY OF AMERICA, INC. Members: 500. Calvin P. Otto, *Pres.* 124 Elm St., Bennington, VT 05201. Tel: 802-442-9916.

INTERNATIONAL LEAGUE OF ANTIQUARIAN BOOKSELLERS. Jacques Van der Heyde, *Gen. Secy.* Rue du Chêne 21, 1000 Brussels, Belgium.

THE MANUSCRIPT SOCIETY. Members: 1200. David R. Smith, *Exec. Dir.* 350 North Niagara St., Burbank, CA 91505.

PRINTING HISTORICAL SOCIETY. Members: 1000. Christopher Hicks, *Hon. Secy.* St. Bride Institute, Bride Lane, Fleet St., London EC4, England; David Pankow, *Hon. Secy. for America.* School of Printing, Rochester Institute of Technology, 1 Lomb Memorial Dr., Rochester, NY 14623. Tel: 716-475-2728.

PRIVATE LIBRARIES ASSOCIATION. Members: 1200. John Allison, *Hon. Membership Secy.* 5 Criffel Ave., Streatham Hill, London SW2 4AY, England; William A. Klutts, *Hon. Membership Secy. for America.* 145 East Jackson, Box 289, Ripley, TN 38063.

RARE BOOKS AND MANUSCRIPTS SECTION, ASSOCIATION OF COLLEGE AND RESEARCH LIBRARIES (ALA). Members: 1300. c/o ACRL, 50 East Huron St., Chicago, IL 60611. Tel: 312-944-6780.

RARE BOOKS GROUP, LIBRARY ASSOCIATION. Katherine Swift, *Hon. Secy.* St. Anne's College, Oxford OX2 6HS, England.

THE SOCIETY OF AMERICAN ARCHIVISTS. Members: 3000. Ann Morgan Campbell, *Exec. Dir.* 600 South Federal, Suite 504, Chicago, IL 60605. Tel: 312-922-0140.

SOCIETY OF SCRIBES. Members: 1500. Sally Bowen, *Pres.* Box 933, New York, NY 10150.

SOCIETY OF SCRIBES AND ILLUMINATORS. Members: 950. Susan Cavendish, *Hon. Secy.* c/o BBC, 43 Earlham St., London WC2H 9LD, England.

23

Auctioneers

of Literary Property

Americana Mail Auction
George Rinsland
4015 Kilner Ave
Allentown, PA 18104
  Tel 215-395-3939

Amherst Auction Galleries
Junction Rtes 116 & 63
North Amherst, MA 01002
  Tel 413-253-9914

Auction Marketing Network
122 W Main St
New Paris, OH 45347
  Tel 513-437-0263

California Book Auction Galleries
1749 N La Brea Ave
Los Angeles, CA 90046
  By appt only

California Book Auction Galleries
358 Golden Gate Ave
San Francisco, CA 94102
  Tel 415-775-0424

Christie, Manson & Woods
502 Park Ave
New York, NY 10022
  Tel 212-546-1000

Connecticut Book Auction Gallery
251 Carroll Rd
Fairfield, CT 06430

Douglas Auctioneers
Rte 5
South Deerfield, MA 01373
  Tel 413-665-2877

DuMouchelles
409 E Jefferson Ave
Detroit, MI 48226
  Tel 313-363-6255

Samuel T Freeman & Co
1808 Chestnut St
Philadelphia, PA 19103
  Tel 215-563-9275

C E Guarino
Box 49
Denmark, ME 04022
  Tel 207-452-2123

Charles Hamilton Autographs Inc
200 W 57 St
New York, NY 10019
  Tel 212-245-7313

Hanzel Galleries
1120 S Michigan Ave
Chicago, IL 60605
  Tel 312-922-6234

Harris Auction Galleries
873–875 N Howard St
Baltimore, MD 21201
  Tel 301-728-7040

Hendsey Auctioneers Inc
N River Rd, Box 60
Epping, NH 03042
 Tel 603-679-2428

Leslie Hindman Auctioneers
225 W Ohio St
Chicago, IL 60610
 Tel 312-670-0010

James D Julia Auctioneers
Rte 201, Skowhegan Rd
Fairfield, ME 04937
 Tel 207-453-9725, 453-9493

Lazy Day Galleries
26 E Mt Pleasant Ave
Livingston, NJ 07039
 Tel 201-996-9404

Joseph Lepczyk
Box 751
East Lansing, MI 48823
 Tel 517-332-8581 (numismatics)

William D Longo Assoc, Auctioneers
 & Appraisers
14 W Natick Rd
Warwick, RI 02886
 Tel 401-737-8160

David W Mapes Inc
1600 Vestal Parkway W
Vestal, NY 13850
 Tel 607-754-9193

Northwest Auction Gallery
231 Burlington
Clarendon Hills, IL 60514

Richard E Oinonen
School St
Sunderland, MA 01375
 Tel 413-665-3275

Phillips Auctioneers — New York
406 E 79 St
New York, NY 10021
 Tel 212-570-4842

Plandome Book Auctions
Box 395
Glen Head, NY 11545
 Tel 516-671-3209

George Rinsland. *See* Americana Mail
Auction

Rose Galleries
1123 W County Rd B
Roseville, MN 55113
 Tel 612-484-1415

K C Self Jr, Auctioneer
213 Bean Ave
Los Gatos, CA 95030
 Tel 408-354-4238

Shields Book Auction
650 Spring St
Danville, VA 24541
 Tel 804-793-1833

Robert W Skinner Inc
Rte 117
Bolton, MA 01740
 Tel 617-779-5528

William A Smith Inc
Rte 12
Plainfield, NH 03781
 Tel 603-675-2549

Sotheby Parke-Bernet
1334 York Ave
New York, NY 10021
 Tel 212-472-3592

Southeast Book Auction Service
432 N Eustis St
Eustis, FL 32726
 Tel 904-357-7145

Stremmel Auctions
2152 Prater Way
Sparks, NV 89431
 Tel 702-331-1035

Swann Galleries Inc
104 E 25 St
New York, NY 10010
 Tel 212-254-4710

Waverly Auctions
c/o Quill & Brush
7649 Old Georgetown Rd
Bethesda, MD 20814
 Tel 301-951-0919

Weiss Auctioneers & Appraisers
North Leverett, MA 01054
 Tel 413-367-9952

Samuel Yudkin & Associates
1125 King St
Alexandria, VA 22314
 Tel 703-549-9330

24

Appraisers of Books
and Manuscripts

UNITED STATES

ALABAMA

William M Boulton, 4003 Medford Dr
SE, Huntsville, 35802.
Tel 205-881-5021

Cather & Brown, Antiquarian Books,
3109 7th Ave S, Birmingham, 35233.
Tel 205-322-3631

The Haunted Bookshop, 214 St Francis
St, Mobile, 36602. Tel 205-432-6606

ARIZONA

Antiquarian Shop, 4246 N Scottsdale
Rd, Scottsdale, 85251. Tel 602-947-
0535

Bisbee Book Stall, PO Box 73, Bisbee,
85603. Tel 602-432-4249

Van Allen Bradley, Inc, PO Box 4130,
Hopi Station, Scottsdale, 85261. Tel
602-991-8633

L E Gay Southwest Books, Box 319,
Alpine, 85920. Tel 602-339-4341

Guidon Books, 7117 Main St, Scottsdale, 85251. Tel 602-945-8811

Harold J Mason Inc, PO Box 32363,
Phoenix 85064. Tel 602-956-6269

Bonita Porter—Books, PO Box 1765,
Litchfield Park, 85340. Tel 602-242-
9442

The Ravenstree Co, PO Box 10552,
Yuma, 85364. Tel 602-785-4003

Readex Book Exchange, PO Box 1125,
Carefree, 85377. Tel 602-488-3304

Russ Todd, Book Scout, 4201 E Beryl
Lane, Phoenix, 85028. Tel 602-996-
7277

ARKANSAS

House of Books—South Star Books, 518
W Dickson St, Fayetteville, 72701.
Tel 501-442-7452

Marshall Vance—Publisher-Bookseller,
1102 N Division, PO Box 27, Forrest
City, 72335. Tel 501-633-1980

CALIFORNIA

Acoma Books, PO Box 4, Ramona,
92065. Tel 619-789-1288

Adams Angling Books & Paraphernalia,
1170 Keeler Ave, Berkeley, 94708.
Tel 415-849-1324

A Different Light, 4014 Santa Monica
Blvd, Los Angeles, 90029. Tel 213-
668-0629

The Albatross Bookstore, 166 Eddy St,
San Francisco, 94102. Tel 415-885-
6501

American Comic Book Co, 12206 Ventura Blvd, PO Box 1809, Studio City,
91604. Tel 213-980-4976

American Fragments, 7127 Hollister,
Goleta, 93117. Tel 805-964-8196

Argonaut Bookshop, 786-792 Sutter St,
San Francisco, 94109. Tel 415-474-
9067

Argus Books & Graphics, 1714 Capitol Ave, Sacramento, 95814. Tel 916-443-2223

Arkadyan Books & Prints, 926 Irving St, San Francisco, 94122. Tel 415-664-6212

Ark Bookshop, 1703 University Ave, Berkeley, 97403. Tel 415-841-2853

Aviation Bookmobile Mil-Air Photos & Books, PO Box U, Norwalk, 90650. Tel 213-863-5028

Beers Book Center, 1013 14th St, Sacramento, 95814. Tel 916-443-9148

Bennett & Marshall, 8205 Melrose Ave, Los Angeles, 90046. Tel 213-653-7040

Roy Bleiweiss Fine Books, 92 Northgate Ave, Berkeley, 90064. Tel 415-548-1624

Blitz Books, PO Box 1076, Weaverville, 96093. Tel 916-623-5430

Bolereim Books 931 Judah, San Francisco, 94122. Tel 415-665-6110

Book Attic, 10239 Fair Oaks Blvd, Fair Oaks, 95628. Tel 916-961-3703

The Book Baron, 1236 S Magnolia Ave, Anaheim, 92804. Tel 714-527-7022

The Book Cellar, 124 Orangefair Mall, Fullerton, 92632. Tel 714-879-9420

Book Company, 1328 N Lake Ave, Pasadena, 91104. Tel 213-798-4630

The Book Harbor, 201 N Harbor Blvd, Fullerton, 92632. Tel 714-738-1941

The Bookie Joint, 7246 Reseda, Reseda, 91335. Tel 213-343-1055, 345-2083

The Book Nest, 366 2nd St, Los Altos, 94022. Tel 415-948-4724

The Book Stop, 3369 Mt Diablo Blvd, Lafayette, 94549. Tel 415-284-2665

Bookstore on Main Street, 213 Main St, Seal Beach, 90740. Tel 213-598-1818

Book Village, 1766 E Colorado Blvd, Pasadena, 91106. Tel 213-793-7780

Meyer Boswell, Books, 982 Hayes St, San Francisco, 94117. Tel 415-346-1839

The Brick Row Bookshop, 278 Post St, Suite 303, San Francisco, 94108. Tel 415-398-0414

California Book Auction Galleries, 1749 N La Brea Ave, Los Angeles, 90046. Tel 213-850-0424; 358 Golden Gate Ave, San Francisco, 94102. Tel 415-775-0424

Canterbury Bookshop, 8344 Melrose Ave, Los Angeles, 90069. Tel 213-653-9467

Caravan Bookstore, 550 S Grand Ave, Los Angeles, 90071. Tel 213-626-9944

Celestial Books, Box 1066, La Canada, 91011, Tel 213-790-4984

Chimney Sweep Books, 220-A Mt Hermon Rd, Scotts Valley, 95066. Tel 408-438-1379

Arthur H Clark Co, 1264 S Central Ave, PO Box 230, Glendale, 91209. Tel 213-245-9119

Louis Collins Books, 1083 Mission St, San Francisco, 94103. Tel 415-431-5134

Comic World, 3766 Burns St, Joshua Tree, Palm Springs, 92252. Tel 619-366-9304

W & V Dailey, 8216 Melrose Ave, PO Box 69812, Los Angeles, 90069. Tel 213-658-8515

Danville Books, 176 S Hartz Ave, Danville, 94526. Tel 415-837-4200

Davis & Schorr — Art Books, 1547 Westwood Blvd, Los Angeles, 90024. Tel 213-477-6636

Dawson's Bookshop, 535 N Larchmont Blvd, Los Angeles, 90004. Tel 213-469-2186

Dianco International, 390 Tennessee Ave, Mill Valley, 94941. Tel 415-383-4071

Frank A Douglas, Law Books, 1006 Rossi Way, San Mateo, 94403. Tel 415-345-5808

Drew's Bookshop, 31 E Canon Perdido St, PO Box 163, Santa Barbara, 93102. Tel 805-966-3311

J S Edgren, PO Box 326, Carmel, 93921. Tel 408-625-2575, 624-3611

Eldorado Books, PO Box 14-036, San Francisco, 94114. Tel 415-552-8122

Ethnographic Arts Publications, 1040 Erica Rd, Mill Valley, 94941. Tel 415-383-2998, 332-1646

Family Bookstore, 6725 Comstock Ave, Whittier, 90601. Tel 213-696-2683

Ferndale Books, 405 Main St, PO Box

1034, Ferndale, 95536. Tel 707-786-9135

A S Fischler — Rare Books, 604 S 15th St, San Jose, 95112. Tel 408-297-7090

David Forbes, 1330 Leavenworth St, San Francisco, 94109

Fowler-Mills Galleries, 210 Pier Ave, Santa Monica, 90405. Tel 213-392-3313

Edwin V Glaser Rare Books, PO Box 1765, Sausalito, 94965. Tel 415-332-1194

Golden Hill Antiquarian Books & Antiques, 2456 Broadway, San Diego, 92102. Tel 619-236-9883

Gull Bookshop, 1547 San Pablo Ave, Oakland, 94612. Tel 415-834-8108

Haight Street Bookshop, 1682 Haight St, San Francisco, 94117. Tel 415-864-9636

Hammon's Archives & Artifacts, 1115 Front St, Sacramento, 95814. Tel 916-446-1782

James Hansen Books, 3514 Highland, Carlsbad, 92008. Tel 619-729-3383

Happy Booker, 4645 N Sierra Way, San Bernardino, 92407. Tel 714-883-6110

Harmon Books, 964 Chapel Hill Way, San Jose, 95122. Tel 408-297-2810

Doris Harris Autographs, 5410 Wilshire Blvd, Los Angeles 90036. Tel 213-939-4500

Hennessey & Ingalls Inc, 10814 W Pico Blvd, Los Angeles, 90064. Tel 213-474-2541

Heritage Bookshop Inc, 847 N La Cienega Blvd, Los Angeles, 90069. Tel 213-659-3674

Hollywood Book City, 6625-31 Hollywood Blvd, Los Angeles, 90028. Tel 213-466-2525, 466-1049

J & J House, Booksellers, Box 20734, San Diego, 92120. Tel 619-265-1113

John Howell — Books, 434 Post St, San Francisco, 94102. Tel 415-781-7795

Paul Hunt, PO Box 2713, Los Angeles, 90051. Tel 213-845-1563

The Invisible Bookman, 97 Franciscan Way, Berkeley, 94707. Tel 415-524-7823

Joseph the Provider Books, 903 State St, Santa Barbara, 93101. Tel 805-962-6862

Joyce Book Shops, Box 310, Martinez, 94553. Tel 415-228-4462

L S Kaiser Books — Chimney Sweep Books, 220-A Mount Hermon Rd, Scottsvalley, 95066. Tel 408-438-1379

George Robert Kane Books, 252 3rd Ave, Santa Cruz, 95062. Tel 408-426-4133 (by appt)

Kenneth Karmiole Bookseller, 2255 Westwood Blvd, Los Angeles, 90064. Tel 213-474-7305

Howard Karno Books, Inc, PO Box 431, Santa Monica, 90406. Tel 213-458-1619

Samuel W Katz, 10845 Lindbrook Dr 6, Los Angeles, 90024. Tel 474-6910 (appt only)

Peg & Don Kenyon Books, 408 DeAnza Heights Dr, San Dimas, 91773. Tel 714-599-1651

Kestrel Books, 1 W Carmel Valley Rd, PO Box Q, Carmel Valley, 93924. Tel 408-659-4534

George Frederick Kolbe Fine Numismatic Books, PO Box Drawer 1610 A, Crestline, 92702

Krown & Spellman, Booksellers, 2283 Westwood Blvd, Los Angeles, 90064. Tel 213-474-1745

Robert Kuhn Antiques-Autographs, 720 Geary St, San Francisco, 94109. Tel 415-474-6981

Lake Law Books, 142 McAllister St, San Francisco, 94102. Tel 415-863-2900

La Mesa Bookstore, 8209 Broadway, La Mesa 92041. Tel 619-464-3802

Robert P Lang, 2008 Prince Albert Dr, Riverside, 92507

James G Leishman, Bookseller, PO Box A, Menlo Park, 94025. Tel 415-332-7034

Barry R. Levin Science Fiction & Fantasy Literature, 2253 Westwood Blvd, Los Angeles, 90064. Tel 213-474-5611

Harry A Levinson Rare Books, PO Box 534, Beverly Hills, 90213. Tel 213-276-9311

R E Lewis Inc, PO Box 1108, San Rafael, 94902. Tel 415-461-4161

Wade Lillywhite Books, 2521-F N Grand Ave, Santa Ana, 92701. Tel 714-997-1384 (by appt only)

Lion Bookshop, 3427 Balboa, San Francisco, 94121. Tel 415-221-5522, 221-5529

Jack London Bookstore, 14300 Arnold Dr, PO Box 337, Glen Ellen, 95442. Tel 707-996-2888

Long Beach Museum of Art Bookshop & Gallery, 2300 E Ocean Blvd, Long Beach, 90803. Tel 213-439-2119

Laurence McGilvery, PO Box 852, La Jolla, 92038. Tel 619-454-4443

John Makarewich, Books, PO Box 7032, Van Nuys, 91409

Robert W Mann Rare Books, 743 E St, San Diego, 92101. Tel 619-233-8568

Milestone Autobooks, 3524 W Magnolia, Burbank, 91505. Tel 213-849-1294

Robert Mitchell — Books, PO Box 3121, Fremont, 94539

Moe's Books, 2476 Telegraph Ave, Berkeley, 94704. Tel 415-849-2087

Monroe Books, 809 E Olive, Fresno, 93728. Tel 209-441-1282

J B Muns, Books, 1162 Shattuck Ave, Berkeley, 94707. Tel 415-525-2420

Maurice F Neville Rare Books, 835 Laguna St, Santa Barbara, 93101. Tel 805-963-1908

Niles & Silver, 1213 Pine St, Santa Monica, 90405. Tel 213-392-9791

Jeremy Norman & Co Inc, 442 Post St, San Francisco, 94102. Tel 415-781-6402

The Novel Experience, 880 Buchon St, San Luis Obispo, 93401. Tel 805-544-1549

Ostby's Americana, 8758 Park Ave, PO Box 89, Bellflower, 90706. Tel 213-925-7767

Otento Books, 3817 5th Ave, San Diego, 92103. Tel 619-296-1424

Pellucidar Fine Books, 2441 Shattuck Ave, Berkeley, 94704. Tel 415-845-3127

Peninsula Antiquarian Booksellers, 506½ W Balboa Blvd, Balboa, 92661. Tel 714-675-1990

Robert Perata Books, 3170 Robinson Dr, Oakland 94602. Tel 415-482-0101

Peri Lithon Books, PO Box 9996, San Diego, 92109. Tel 619-488-6904

Perry's Antiques & Books, 1863 W San Carlos, San Jose, 95128. Tel 408-286-0426

Pettler & Lieberman, Booksellers, 7970 Melrose Ave, Los Angeles, 90046. Tel 213-651-1568

Ralston Popular Fiction, PO Box 4174, Fullerton, 92634. Tel 714-990-0432

Ranch Book Shop, PO Box K, 6030 La Flecha, Rancho Santa Fe, 92067. Tel 619-756-2265

Randall House, 185 Post St. Suite 301, San Francisco, 94108. Tel 415-781-2218

Rare Oriental Book Co, *See* Jerrold G Stanoff

O P Reed, Jr, 21536 Rambla Vista, Malibu, 90265. Tel 213-456-6160, 652-5500

Regent Street Books, 2747 Regent St, Berkeley, 94705. Tel 415-548-8459

John Roby, 3703 Nassau Dr, San Diego, 92115. Tel 619-583-4264

B & L Rootenberg Fine & Rare Books, PO Box 5049, Sherman Oaks, 91403, Tel 213-788-7765

Bernard M Rosenthal, Inc, 251 Post St, San Francisco, 94108. Tel 415-982-2219

Ross Valley Book Co Inc, 1407 Solano Ave, Albany, 94706. Tel 415-526-6400

J Roth Bookseller, 9427 W Pico Blvd, Los Angeles, 90035. Tel 213-557-1848

Rudolph Wm Sabbot, Natural History Books, 5239 Tendilla Ave, Woodland Hills, 91364. Tel 213-346-7164

Sand Dollar Books, 1222 Solano Ave, Albany, 94706. Tel 415-527-1931

Sarkis Shmavonian Books & Prints, 1796 Shattuck Ave, Berkeley, 94709. Tel 415-843-5910

The Scriptorium, PO Box 1290, Beverly Hills, 90213. Tel 213-275-6060, 278-4200

Sebastopol Bookshop, 133 N Main St,

Sebastopol, 95472. Tel 707-823-9788

Serendipity Books, 1790 Shattuck Ave, Berkeley, 94709. Tel 415-841-7455

Florian Shaskey, 1030 Colorado Ave, Palo Alto, 94303

The Silver Door, PO Box 3208, Redondo Beach, 90277. Tel 213-379-6005

Silvergate Books, 6156 Camino Largo, San Diego, 92120. Tel 619-582-6737

Martin A Silver Musical Literature, 643 Willowglen Rd, Santa Barbara, 93105. Tel 805-687-4198

Sonoma Auto Books, 720 Sebastopol Rd, Santa Rosa, 94501. Tel 707-576-1111

Southbay Bookstore, 1489 Plaza Blvd, National City, 92050. Tel 714-474-4444

Jerrold G Stanoff, Rare Oriental Book Co, PO Box 1599, Aptos, 95003. Tel 408-724-4911

Christophe Stickel, Fine Books & Autographs, 5 Surrey St, San Francisco, 94131. Tel 415-334-0636 (by appt)

Sun Dance Books, 1520 N Crescent Heights, Los Angeles, 90046. Tel 213-654-2383

Jeffrey Thomas, Fine & Rare Books, 49 Geary St, Suite 215, San Francisco, 94102. Tel 415-956-3272

Three R's Productions, 302-A W Main St, Grass Valley, 95945. Tel 916-273-9874

Tolliver's Books, 1634 Stearns Dr, Los Angeles, 90035. Tel 213-939-6054

Town & Gown Book Co, PO Box 190, Dutch Flat, 95714. Tel 916-389-2363 (by appt)

Transition Books, 445 Stockton St, San Francisco, 94114. Tel 415-391-5161

Trophy Room Books — Big Game Hunting Books, 4858 Dempsey Ave, Encino, 91436. Tel 213-784-3801

Vagabond Books, 2076 Westwood Blvd, Los Angeles, 90025. Tel 213-475-2700

Valley Book City, 5249 Lankershim Blvd, North Hollywood, 91601. Tel 213-985-6911

Graeme Vanderstoel, Box 599, El Cerrito, 94530. Tel 415-527-2882

Wahrenbrocks Book House, 726 Broadway, San Diego, 92101. Tel 619-232-0132

Stephen White's Gallery of Photography, 752 N La Cienega Blvd, Los Angeles, 90069. Tel 213-657-6995

William P Wreden, Books & Manuscripts, PO Box 56, Palo Alto, 94302. Tel 415-325-6851

Zeitlin & Ver Brugge Booksellers, 815 N La Cienega Blvd, Los Angeles, 90069. Tel 213-652-0584

COLORADO

A Bookscout's Den, 1238 E Colfax Ave, Denver, 80218. Tel 303-831-1431

Abaco Books, 5924 E Colfax Ave, Denver, 80220. Tel 303-333-1269

Bookland, 9262 W 58th Ave, Arvada, 80002. Tel 303-424-4070

W J Bookunter, PO Box 2795, Denver, 80201. Tel 303-757-0160

Butterfield's, 210 University Blvd, Suite 760, Denver, 80206

The Cache, 7157 W US 34, Loveland, 80537. Tel 303-667-1081

Henry A Clausen Bookshop, 224½ N Tejon St, Colorado Springs 80903. Tel 303-634-1193

The Collective — Millet & Simpson Antiquarian Booksellers, 130 S Union, Pueblo, 81003. Tel 303-542-4462

Collectors' Center, Rare Books, 609 Corona St, Denver, 80218. Tel 303-831-7237

The Court Place Antiquarian Bookshop, 3827 W 32nd Ave, Denver, 80211. Tel 303-455-0317

General Adjustment Bureau, 620 Sherman, Denver, 80203

Richard Goff, 425 Walnut Ave, Grand Junction, 81501

Mary Gustafson, 531 Main St, Grand Junction, 81501

The Hermitage Antiquarian Bookshop, 2817 E 3rd Ave, Denver, 80206. Tel 303-388-6811

Al Jolson, 523 Guaranty Bank Bldg, Denver, 80202. (Law libraries only)

The King's Market — Books & Prints,

1021 Pearl St, Suite D, PO Box 709, Boulder, 80306. Tel 303-444-8484

Kenton Lewis, 439 Main St, Grand Junction, 81501

Fred A Rosenstock — Books & Arts, 1228 E Colfax Ave, Denver, 80218. Tel 303-832-7190

Richard J Schwann, 1259 Gunnison, Grand Junction, 81501

Suncircle Books, PO Box 607, Fort Collins, 80522

Unique's of Denver, 329 14th St, Denver, 80202

CONNECTICUT

Angler's & Shooter's Bookshelf, Goshen, 06756. Tel 203-491-2500

The Antiquarium, 66 Humiston Dr, Bethany, 06525. Tel 203-393-2723

Antique Books, 3651 Whitney Ave, Hamden, 06518. Tel 203-281-6606

Lee Ash, 66 Humiston Dr, Bethany, 06525. Tel 203-393-2723

Deborah Benson Bookseller, River Rd, West Cornwall, 06796. Tel 203-672-6614

Preston C Beyer, Fine Literary Property, 752A Pontiac Lane, Stratford, 06497. Tel 203-375-9073

The Book Block, 8 Loughlin Ave, Cos Cob, 06807. Tel 203-629-2990 (by appt)

Branford Rare Book & Art Gallery, 221 Montowese St, Box 56, Branford, 06405. Tel 203-488-5882

Richard Cady Rare Books, Glenville Sta, PO Box 12, Greenville, 06830. Tel 914-937-6606

Cartographics, PO Box 67, North Stonington, 06359. Tel 203-535-3152

Colebrook Book Barn, Rte 183, Box 108, Colebrook, 06021. Tel 203-379-3185

Country Lane Books, 38 Country Lane, Collinsville, 06022. Tel 203-693-2245

Coventry Bookshop, 1159 Main St, PO Box 36, Coventry, 06238. Tel 203-742-9875

John S Craig, Photographic Historian, Box 656, Norfolk, 06058. Tel 203-542-5479

The Current Company, PO Box 46, Bristol, 02809. Tel 401-253-7824

Elliot's Books, Out of Print Specialists, Forest Rd, Box 6, Northford, 06472. Tel 203-484-2184

Barbara Farnsworth, Bookseller, Rte 128, West Cornwall, 06796. Tel 203-672-6333, 672-6571

Avis & Rockwell Gardiner, 60 Mill Rd, Stamford, 06903. Tel 203-322-1129

Lawrence F Golder Rare Books, PO Box 144, Collinsville, 06022. Tel 203-693-8110, 693-8631

David Ladner Books, PO Box 6179, Whitneyville, 06517. Tel 203-288-6575

Kathleen & Michael Lazare, PO Box 117, Sherman, 06784. Tel 203-354-4181

Lion's Head Books, Academy St, Salisbury, 06068. Tel 203-435-9328

McBride First Editions, 157 Sisson Ave, Hartford, 06105. Tel 203-523-7707

Hugh Miller, Bookseller, 216 Crown St, Room 506, New Haven, 06510. Tel 203-481-6309

Old Book & Photo — Russell Norton, PO Box 1070, New Haven, 06504. Tel 203-562-7800

Park Road Bookshop, 258 Park Rd, West Hartford, 06119. Tel 203-232-3001

Wyman W Parker, 330 Pine St, Middletown, 06457

Pharos Books — Fine First Editions, PO Box 17, New Haven, 06513. Tel 203-562-0085 (by appt only)

The Raven Bookshop, 40 W Broad St, Pawcatuck, 06379. Tel 203-599-3535

William Reese Co, 409 Temple St, New Haven, 06511. Tel 203-789-8081

Cedric L Robinson, Bookseller, 597 Palisado Ave, Windsor, 06095. Tel 203-688-2582

Scarlet Letter Books & Prints, Candlewood Mountain Rd, New Milford, 06776. Tel 203-354-4181

Barry Scott, PO Box 207, Stonington, 06378. Tel 203-535-2643

Whitlock Farm Booksellers, 20 Sperry Rd, Bethany, 06525. Tel 203-393-1240

Whitlock's Inc. 17 Broadway, New

Haven, 06511. Tel 203-562-9841

Laurence Witten Rare Books, 181 Old Post Rd, PO Box 490, Southport, 06490. Tel 203-255-3474

Charles B Wood III Inc, Antiquarian Booksellers, The Green, South Woodstock, 06267. Tel 203-928-4041

John Woods Books (Out of Print), 1117 Main St, Coventry, 06238. Tel 203-742-7457

DELAWARE

Attic Books, 1175 Pleasant Hill Rd, Newark, 19711. Tel 302-738-7477

Dale A Brandreth, Books, White Briar, Hockessin, 19707. Tel 302-239-4608

Greenwood Bookshop Inc, 110 W 9th St, Wilmington, 19801. Tel 302-654-6237

Hollyoak Book Shop, 300 E Delaware Ave, Wilmington, 19809. Tel 302-798-2708

Oak Knoll Books, 414 Delaware St, New Castle, 19720. Tel 302-328-7232

DISTRICT OF COLUMBIA

Booked Up Inc, 1209 31st St NW, Washington, 20007. Tel 202-965-3244

William F Hale Books, 1222 31st St NW, Washington, 20007. Tel 202-338-8272

Illustrated Antiques, 1222 31st St NW, Washington, 20007. Tel 202-333-6359

Jefferson Law Book Co, 1411 G St NW, Suite 1002, Washington, 20005. Tel 202-638-6620

Lloyd Books, 1346 Connecticut Ave NW, Suite 719, Washington, 20036. Tel 202-785-3826

The Old Print Gallery, 1220 31st St NW, Washington, 20007. Tel 202-965-1818

Second Story Books, 3236 P St NW, Washington, 20007. Tel 202-338-6860

Willis Van Devanter, PO Box 32426, Calvert Sta, Washington, 20007

Yesterday's Books, 4702 Wisconsin Ave NW, Washington, 20016. Tel 202-363-0581

FLORIDA

Aceto Bookmen, 5721 Antietam Dr, Sarasota, 33581. Tel 813-924-9170

Books & Things, 473 NE 20th St, Boca Raton, 33431. Tel 305-395-2227

The Booktraders, Inc, PO Box 9403, Winter Haven, 33883. Tel 813-299-4904

Book Warehouse Inc, 2010 Ponce De Leon, Coral Gables, 33134. Tel 305-448-3223

Brasser's Books, 8701 Seminole Blvd, Seminole, 33542. Tel 813-393-6707

Demerara Book Service, 13018 SW 85th Rd, Miami, 33156. Tel 305-238-8761

Downtown Bookshop, 100 E Adam St, Jacksonville, 32202. Tel 904-356-9271

Farleys Old & Rare Books, 5855 Tippen Ave, Pensacola, 32504. Tel 904-477-8282.

Florida Bookstore, 1614 W University Ave, PO Box 14076, Gainesville, 32604. Tel 904-376-6066

Alla T Ford Rare Books, 114 S Palmway Ave, Lake Worth, 33460. Tel 305-585-1442

Harbar Book Exchange, 916 E Semoran Blvd, Casselberry, 32707. Tel 305-834-0153

Historical Bookshelf Ltd, 4210 SW 3rd St, Plantation, 33317. Tel 305-583-2378

Robert A Hittel, Bookseller, 3020 N Federal Hwy, Bldg 6, Fort Lauderdale, 33306. Tel 305-563-1752

Lighthouse Books, 148 Central Ave, Saint Petersburg, 33701. Tel 813-822-3278

The Old Bookshop, 3142 Beach Blvd, Jacksonville, 32207. Tel 904-398-6163; 113 N County Rd, Palm Beach, 33480. Tel 305-833-3920, 585-0395

Raintree Books, 432 N Eustis St, Eustis, 32726. Tel 904-357-7145

Wallace A Robinson, 461 12th Ave N, Saint Petersburg, 33701. Tel 813-823-3280 (by appt)

Tappin Book Mine, 705 Atlantic Blvd, Atlantic Beach, 32233. Tel 904-246-1388

GEORGIA

Harvey Dan Abrams—Bookseller, 30703 Peachtree Rd, Atlanta, 30341. Tel 404-233-6763

Arnolds' Archives, Emory Village, 1579 N Decatur Rd NE, Atlanta, 30307. Tel 404-377-2665.

Book Search Service, 36 Kensington Rd, Avondale Estates, 30002. Tel 404-294-5398

Julian Burnett Books, PO Box 229, Atlanta, 30301. Tel 404-252-5812

Concord Book Service, Box 13672, Atlanta, 30324

Downs Book, 774 Mary Ann Dr, Marietta, 30067. Tel 404-971-1103

Jaqueline Levine Books, 107 E Oglethorpe Ave, Savannah, 31401. Tel 912-233-8519

David McCord Books, 1069 Juniper St NE, Atlanta, 30309. Tel 404-874-7761

The Old Book Scout — Jim McMeans Books, 4175 Roswell Rd, Atlanta, 30342. Tel 404-257-1012

Old New York Bookshop, 1069 Juniper St NE, Atlanta, 30309. Tel 404-881-1285

Whistles in the Woods, Rte 1, Box 265A, Rossville, 30741. Tel 404-375-4326

Yesteryear Bookshop, 256 E Paces Ferry Rd NE, Atlanta, 30305. Tel 404-237-0163

HAWAII

Aldamar World of Books, 409 N King St, Honolulu, 96817. Tel 808-533-1333

Pacific Book House, Kilohana Sq, 1016 Kapahula Ave, Honolulu 96816. Tel 808-737-3475

Prints Pacific, RR 1, PO Box 276, Wailuku, 96793. Tel 808-244-9787 (by appt)

Tusitala Bookshop, 116 Hekili St, Kailua, 96734. Tel 808-262-6343

IDAHO

The Bookshop Inc, 908 Main St, Boise, 83702. Tel 208-342-2659

ILLINOIS

Abraham Lincoln Bookshop, 18 E Chestnut St, Chicago, 60611. Tel 312-944-3085

Richard Adamiak, 1545 E 60th St, Chicago, 60637. Tel 312-955-4571

Norma K Adler Books, 59 Eastwood Dr, Deerfield, 60015. Tel 312-945-8575

The Athenaeum, 1814 Central St, Evanston, 60201. Tel 312-475-0900

Richard S Barnes & Co, Books, 821 Foster St, Evanston, 60201. Tel 312-869-2272

Barrington Old Bookshop, 310 W Northwest Hwy, Barrington, 60010. Tel 312-381-6698

Mary Beth Beal, 3919 N Claremont Ave, Chicago, 60618. Tel 312-539-0105

Herbert Biblo Bookseller, 5225 Blackstone Ave, Chicago, 60615. Tel 312-643-2363

Book Barn, RR 1, Walnut, 61376. Tel 815-379-2581

Bookman's Alley, 1712 Sherman Ave, Evanston, 60201. Tel 312-869-6999

James M W Borg Inc, 8 S Michigan, Chicago, 60603. Tel 312-236-5911

James Dowd—Bookseller, 38 W 281 Toms Trail Dr, Saint Charles, 60174. Tel 312-584-1930

Hamakor Judaica, Inc, 6112 N Lincoln Ave, Chicago, 60659. Tel 312-463-6186

Hammil & Barker, 400 N. Michigan Ave, Suite 1210, Chicago, 60611. Tel 312-644-5933

Thomas J Joyce & Co, PO Box 561, Geneva 60134. Tel 312-232-6383, 232-6388

E F Keenan—Books, 506 North Ave,

Lake Bluff, 60044. Tel 312-234-5054

Leiden Gallery, 1045 Morrison Lane, Northbrook, 60062. Tel 312-291-0919

John Wm Martin Bookseller, 436 S 7th Ave, La Grange, 60525. Tel 312-352-8115

Kenneth Nebenzahl Inc, 333 N Michigan Ave, Chicago, 60601. Tel 312-641-2711

Ruth Putnam, 306 S McLean St, Bloomington, 83223

Richard Owen Roberts, Booksellers, 205 E Kehoe Blvd, Wheaton, 60187. Tel 312-668-1025

Paul Romaine — Books, 635 W Grace 1104, Chicago, 60613. Tel 312-348-7551

Sotheby Parke Bernet, Inc, 840 N Michigan Ave, Chicago, 60611. Tel 312-280-0185

Harry L Stern, Ltd, 620 N Michigan Ave, Chicago, 60611. Tel 312-787-4433

Stonehill's Antiquarian Books, 806 Richard Lane, PO Box 5015, Sta A, Champaign, 61820. Tel 217-359-2607

Titles Inc, 1931 Sheridan Rd, Highland Park, 60035. Tel 312-432-3690

Veloce Publications, Box 8234, Chicago, 60680. Tel 312-288-8139

Weingarten Book Service, 614 Forest Ave, Evanston, 60202. Tel 312-869-4130

Mary F Wendell Books, 135 E Lincoln, White Hall, 62092. Tel 217-374-2091

INDIANA

A & OP Fort Wayne Bookshop, 1412 Delaware Ave, Fort Wayne, 46805. Tel 219-424-1058

Back Tracts Inc, PO Box 3008, Indianapolis, 46220. Tel 317-257-3686

Barnette's Books, 22727 Adams Rd, South Bend, 46628. Tel 219-272-9880

Between The Lines, 1400 E 3rd St, Bloomington, 47401. Tel 812-332-4440

The Book Stack, 112 W Lexington Ave,

Elkhart, 46516. Tel 219-293-3815

Caveat Emptor, 208 S Dunn St, Bloomington, 47401. Tel 812-332-9995

Christopher's Book Room, 105½ N Dunn St, PO Box 1061, Bloomington, 47402. Tel 812-333-5774

Erasmus Books, 1027 E Wayne, South Bend, 46617. Tel 219-232-8444

Forest Park Bookshop, 1412 Delaware Ave, Fort Wayne, 46805. Tel 219-424-1058

Hoosier Bookshop, 3820 E 61st St, Indianapolis, 46220. Tel 317-257-0888

Mason's Rare & Used Books, 264 S Wabash St, Wabash, 46992. Tel 219-563-6421

Richard's Readers, RR 1, Box 260A, Tennyson, 47637. Tel 812-362-8462

Gary L Steigerwald Bookseller, 1500 Maxwell Lane, PO Box 1951, Bloomington, 47402. Tel 812-339-8220

Sycamore Books, 311 Iowa, Clayton, 46118. Tel 317-539-4993

IOWA

William A Graf — Books, 717 Clark St, Iowa City, 52240. Tel 319-337-7748

Mike Maddigan, PO Box 824, Cedar Rapids, 52406. Tel 319-363-4821

The Source Bookstore, 232 W 3rd St, Davenport, 52801. Tel 319-324-8941

KANSAS

David Dary Western Books, 1101 W 27th St, Lawrence, 66044. Tel 913-843-5268

T N Luther Books, Box 6083, Shawnee Mission, 66207. Tel 913-381-9619

Nemaha Booksellers, Goff, 66428. Tel 913-939-2130

KENTUCKY

Glover's Books, 397 Virgina Ave, Lexington, 40504. Tel 606-253-0614

The Mount Sterling Rebel, PO Box 481, Lexington, 40353. Tel 606-498-5821

Philatelic Bibliopole, PO Box 36006,

Louisville, 40233. Tel 502-451-0317

The Sail Loft Inc, 269 Cassidy Ave, Lexington, 40502. Tel 606-266-6348

Shawk's Green Dome Antiques, 3288 Georgetown Rd, PO Box 11253, Lexington, 40574. Tel 606-255-9716

S-T Associates, 1317 Cherokee Rd, Louisville, 40204.

LOUISIANA

Claitor's Law Books & Publishing Division, 3165 S Acadian Thruway at I-10, PO Box 3333, Baton Rouge, 70821. Tel 504-344-0476

Taylor Clark's Inc, 2623 Government St, Baton Rouge, 70806. Tel 504-383-4929

Richard Klenk, 1761 Cloverdale Ave, Baton Rouge, 70808

Wilbur Meneray, 7314 Zimple St, New Orleans, 70118

John Richard, EBR Parish Library, 7711 Goodwood Blvd, Baton Rouge, 70806

Ray Samuel, 2727 Prytania St, New Orleans, 70130

MAINE

Book Cellar, 36 Main St, Freeport, 04032. Tel 207-773-4200

Carlson & Turner Books, 241 Congress St, Portland, 04101. Tel 207-773-4200

Nathan Copeland, Bookseller, 72 Groveside Rd, Portland, 04102. Tel 207-773-3647

Cross Hill Books, PO Box 798, Bath, 04350. Tel 207-443-5652

Country Book Room, Rte 302 & Pope Rd, 1 Pope Rd, Westbrook, 04092. Tel 207-892-6518

Harland H Eastman, Books & Prints, 66 Main St, PO Box 276, Springvale, 04083. Tel 207-324-2797

Douglas N Harding, 60 Post Rd, Box 184, Wells, 03061. Tel 207-646-8785

The Mathom Bookshop & Bindery, Blinn Hill Rd off Rte 27, PO Box 161, Dresden, 04342. Tel 207-737-8806

F M O'Brien Old Book Shop, 38 High St, Portland, 04101. Tel 207-774-0931

Charles L Robinson Rare Books, The Pond Rd, Manchester, 04351. Tel 207-622-1885

The Sail Loft Inc, Box 278, Newcastle, 04553. Tel 207-563-3209

Southwest Harbor Antiques Gallery, Box 732, Southwest Harbor, 04679. Tel 207-244-3162

F P Wood Books, 256 Main St, PO Box 365, Springvale, 04083. Tel 207-324-8319

MARYLAND

Marilyn Braiterman, 20 Whitfield Rd, Baltimore, 21210. Tel 301-235-4848

Chirurgical Bookshop, 1211 Cathedral St, Baltimore, 21201. Tel 301-539-0872, Ext 235

Curlander's Law Books Ltd, 525 N Charles St, PO Box 3245, Baltimore, 21201. Tel 301-261-2392

Q M Dabney & Co, 11910 Parklawn Dr, Rockville, 20852. Tel 301-881-1470

Deeds Bookshop, 8012 Main St, PO Box 85, Ellicott City, 21043. Tel 301-465-9419

P William Filby, 8944 Madison St, Savage, 20763

Firstborn Books, 1007 E Benning Rd, Galesville, 20765. Tel 301-867-7050

Carl B Frushon, Ltd, PO Box 14, Monkton, 21111. Tel 301-329-6465

John Gach Books Inc, 5620 Waterloo Rd, Columbia, 20145. Tel 301-465-9023

Harris Auction Galleries, 873 N Howard St, Baltimore, 21201. Tel 301-728-7040

Hirschtritt's "1712," 1712 Republic Rd, Silver Spring, 20902. Tel 301-649-5393

Imagination Books, 946 Sligo Ave, Silver Spring, 20910. Tel 301-589-2223

Frank & Laurese Katen, PO Box 4047, Colesville Sta, Silver Spring, 20904. Tel 301-384-9444, 384-9449

Kelmscott Bookshop, 32 W 25th St,

Baltimore, 21218. Tel 301-235-6810

Kensington Used Bookshop, 10417 Armory Ave, Kensington, 20795. Tel 301-949-9411

Main Street Books, 185 Main St, Annapolis, 21401. Tel 301-268-3321

The Old Printed Word, 3746 Howard Ave, Kensington, 20895. Tel 301-949-7350

Quill & Brush Bookstore, 7649 Old Georgetown Rd, Bethesda, 20014. Tel 301-951-0919

Second Story Books, 7730 Old Georgetown Rd, Bethesda, 20014. Tel 301-656-0170

Willis Van Devanter Books, 19558 Fisher Ave, PO Box 277, Poolesville, 20837. Tel 301-972-7298 (by appt)

MASSACHUSETTS

Ahab Rare Books, 5 John F Kennedy St, Suite 401, Cambridge, 02138. Tel 617-547-5602

Kenneth Andersen — Books, 38 Silver St, Auburn, 01501. Tel 617-832-3524

The Antiquarian Scientist, PO Box 602, Amesbury, 01913. Tel 617-388-2314

ARS Libri Ltd, 286 Summer St, Boston, 02210. Tel 617-357-5212

Artistic Endeavors, 24 Emerson Pl, Boston, 02114. Tel 617-227-1967

Astronomy Books, Box 217, Bernardston, 01337. Tel 413-648-9500

Book & Tackle Shop, 29 Old Colony Rd, Chestnut Hill, 02167. Tel 617-965-0459

The Book Bear, West Main St, PO Box 663, West Brookfield, 01585. Tel 617-867-8705

The Book Collector, 375 Elliot St, Newton, 02164. Tel 617-964-3599

Boston Book Annex, 906 Beacon St, Boston, 02215. Tel 617-266-1090

Osee H Brady Books, 12 Elm St, Assonet, 02702. Tel 617-644-5073

Brattle Book Store, 25 West St, Boston, 02111. Tel 617-542-0210

Bromer Booksellers Inc, 607 Boylston St, Boston, 02116. Tel 617-247-2818

Maury A Bromsen Associates Inc, 770 Boylson St, Boston, 02199. Tel 617-266-7060 (by appt only)

Brookline Village Books & Prints, 23 Harvard St, Brookline, 02146. Tel 617-734-3519

Roger F Casavant, 88 Dudley Rd, Wayland, 01778. Tel 617-653-4104

J P Dwyer Inc, 30 Pleasant St, Northampton, 01060. Tel 413-584-7909

Elmcress Books, 587 Bay Rd, Hamilton, 01936. Tel 617-468-3261

Barbara L Feret, 136 Crescent St, Northampton, 01060. Tel 413-586-6365

Steve Finer — Books, PO Box 365, Turner Falls, 01376. Tel 413-863-2375

Michael Ginsberg Books, Inc, PO Box 402, Sharon, 02067. Tel 617-784-8181

Goodspeed's Book Shop Inc, 7 Beacon St, Boston, 02108. Tel 617-523-5970

Grolier Book Shop, 6 Plympton St, Cambridge, 02138. Tel 617-547-4648

Hingham Book House, 112 North St, Hingham, 02043. Tel. 617-749-1651

Horse in the Attic Bookshop, 52 Boylston St, Brookline, 02147. Tel 617-566-6070

Howland & Co, 100 Rockwood St, Jamaica Plain, 02130. Tel 617-522-5281

Hurst & Hurst, 53 Mt Auburn St, Cambridge, 02138. Tel 617-491-6888

Irene's Bookshop, 49 W Broadway, Gardner, 01440. Tel 617-632-5574

Priscilla Juvelis Inc, 89 Beacon St, Boston, 02108. Tel 617-367-8452

Edward J Lefkowicz, PO Box 630, Fairhaven, 02719. Tel 617-997-6839

Philip Liozinski, Scholarly Books, 1504 Drift Rd, Westport, 02790. Tel 617-636-2044

Lord Randall Book & Print Shop, 22 Main St, Marshfield, 02050. Tel 617-837-1400, 834-8330

J & J Lubrano, Main St, PO Box 47, South Lee, 01260. Tel 413-243-2218

Robert F Lucas, PO Box 63, Blandford, 01008. Tel 413-848-2061

M & S Rare Books, Inc, 45 Colpitts Rd, PO Box 311, Weston, 02193. Tel 617-891-5650

Peter L Masi — Books, 17 Central St, PO

Box B, Montague, 01351. Tel 413-367-2628

Robert L Merriam, Newhall Rd, Conway, 01341. Tel 413-369-4052

Million Year Picnic, 99 Mt Auburn, Cambridge, 02138. Tel 617-492-6763

George Robert Minkhoff, Inc, Rowe Rd, RFD 3, Box 147, Great Barrington, 01230. Tel 413-528-4575

Howard S Mott, Inc, S Main St, Sheffield, 01257. Tel 413-229-2019

Murray Books, PO Box 477, Wilbraham, 01095. Tel 413-596-3801, 596-9372

Neath the Elms, 235 Washington St, Marblehead, 01945. Tel 617-631-6222

Newburyport Rare Books, 32 Oakland St, Newburyport, 01950. Tel 617-462-7398 (by appt only)

David D Newell, RFD Steady Lane, Ashfield, 01330

The Open Creel, 25 Breton St, Palmer, 01069. Tel 413-283-3960

Robert & Barbara Paulson Books, Allen Coit Rd, Huntington, 01050. Tel 413-667-3208

The Printer's Devil, 1 Claremont Ct, Arlington, 02174. Tel 617-646-6762

The Rendells, Inc, 154 Wells Ave, Newton, 02159. Tel 617-965-4670

Paul C Richards—Autographs, High Acres, Templeton, 01468. Tel 617-939-8981

M Douglas Sackman, PO Box 308, Deerfield, 01342. Tel 413-774-3507

John R Sanderson, PhD-Antiquarian Books, Box 285, Stockbridge, 01262

Second Fiddle Bookshop, 62 Elm St, Sturbridge, 01550. Tel 347-7564, 765-0370

Second Floor Books, 47 North St, Pittsfield, 01201. Tel 413-442-6876

Second Life Books, Upper E Hoosac St, Adams, 01220. Tel 413-743-4561

Robert W Skinner, Main St, Bolton, 01740. Tel 617-779-6641

Sotheby Parke Bernet, Inc, 232 Clarendon St, Boston, 02116. Tel 617-247-2851

Starr Book Co Inc, 186 South St, Boston, 02111. Tel 617-542-2525

Peter L Stern, PO Box 160, Sharon, 02067. Tel 617-784-7618

Taste of Honey Bookstore, 1749 N Main St, Fall River, 02720. Tel 617-679-8844

Isaiah Thomas Books & Prints, 980 Main St, Worcester, 01603. Tel 617-754-0750

Twice Sold Tales, W Main St, PO Box 725, Wellfleet, 02667. Tel 716-349-9517

University Book Exchange, PO Box 28, Lowell, 01853. Tel 617-454-7108

University Book Reserve, 75 Main St, Hull, 02045. Tel 617-925-0005, 925-0570

Francis G Walett, 12 Pine St, North Abington, 02351

Weiss Auctioneers & Appraisers, North Leverett, 01054. Tel 413-367-9952

Anthony G Ziagos Bookseller, Box 28, Lowell, 01853. Tel 617-454-7108

MICHIGAN

Don Allen, PO Box 3, Three Oaks, 49128. Tel 616-756-9218

James M Babcock Bookseller, 5055 Point Tremble Rd, Algonac, 48001. Tel 313-794-2227

Bicentennial Bookshop, 820 S Westnedge, Kalamazoo, 49008. Tel 616-345-5987

Bohling Book Co, PO Box 215, Lawton, 49065. Tel 616-624-6002

Book World, PO Box 472, Petoskey, 49770. Tel 616-347-0480

John Cumming, 465 Hiawatha Dr, Rte 2, Mount Pleasant, 48858

Curious Bookshop, 307 E Grand River Ave, East Lansing, 48823. Tel 517-332-0112

The Dawn Treader Book Shop, 525 E Liberty, Ann Arbor, 48104. Tel 313-995-1008

Entropy Books, 31 Oakland Park Blvd, Pleasant Ridge, 48069. Tel 313-546-6078 (by appt only)

Exnowski Enterprises, 31512 Reid Dr, Warren, 48092. Tel 313-264-1686

Gem Wave Books, 1324 Milton SE,

Grand Rapids, 49506. Tel 616-459-4705

Global Book Research, PO Box 153, Belding, 48809. Tel 616-794-3992

Grub Street—A Bookery, 17194 E Warren, Grosse Pointe Park, 48230. Tel 313-882-7143

Hartfield Fine & Rare Books, 117 Dixboro Rd, Ann Arbor, 48105. Tel 313-662-6035

House of Trivia, 136 E Middle St, Williamston, 48895. Tel 517-655-1136

Keramos, PO Box 7500, Ann Arbor, 48107. Tel 313-429-7864

John K King Books, PO Box 363-A, Detroit, 48232. Tel 313-961-0622

Leaves of Grass, 2433 Whitmore Lake Rd, Ann Arbor, 48013. Tel 313-995-2300

Bernard A Margolis—Books, 1565 Arbor Ave, Monroe, 48161. Tel 313-243-5213

Memory Aisle, 1509 Lake Dr, Grand Rapids, 49506. Tel 616-456-5908

Much Loved Books, PO Box 2005, Southfield, 48037. Tel 313-355-2040

Einer Nisula—Rare Books, 1931 Osage Dr, Okemos, 48864. Tel 517-349-0495

Phillip J Pirages Rare Books, 315 N Prospect, Kalamazoo, 49007. Tel 616-345-7220

L A Rubin Books, 250 Martin St, Birmingham, 48011. Tel 313-646-6190, 646-4138

J E Sheldon, Fine Books, 421 E Madison, Hastings, 49058. Tel 616-948-2131

State Street Bookshop, 316 S State St, Ann Arbor, 48104. Tel 313-994-4041

George Tramp Books, 709 2nd St, Jackson, 49203. Tel 517-784-1057 (by appt)

Richard Weiderman, PO Box 209, Cedar Springs, 49519. Tel 616-245-8812

West Side Bookshop, 113 W Liberty, Ann Arbor, 48103. Tel 313-995-1891

The Wine & Food Library, 1207 W Madison, Ann Arbor, 48103. Tel 313-663-4894

MINNESOTA

Biermaier's B H Books, 809 SE 4th St, Minneapolis, 55414. Tel 612-378-0129

The Book House Booksellers, 429 SE 14th Ave, Minneapolis, 55414. Tel 612-439-8944

The Bookmailer, 2730 W Broadway, Minneapolis, 55411. Tel 612-588-2830

China Book Gallery, PO Box 19324, Minneapolis, 55419. Tel 612-926-6887

Ken Crawford Books, 2735 E 18th Ave, North Saint Paul, 55109. Tel 612-777-6877

James & Kristen Cummings, 639 E Lake St, Wayzata, 55391.

Dinkytown Antiquarian Bookshop, 1316 SE 4th St, Minneapolis, 55414. Tel 612-378-1286

James & Mary Laurie, Booksellers, 251 S Snelling, Saint Paul, 55105. Tel 612-699-1114

Leland N Lien, Bookseller, 413 S 4th St, Minneapolis, 55415. Tel 612-332-7081

Melvin McCosh Bookseller, 26500 Edgewood Rd, Excelsior, 55331. Tel 612-474-8084

Harper McKee Bookseller, 449 W 7th St, Saint Paul, 55102. Tel 612-227-5771

Oudal Bookshop, 315 S 9th St, Minneapolis, 55402. Tel 612-332-7037

Scientia, Books in Science & Medicine, Box 14042, Minneapolis, 55414. Tel 612-379-7463 (by appt)

MISSISSIPPI

William M Hutter, Rte 3, Box 123, Ocean Springs, 39564. Tel 601-875-3150

John Kelly, Box 5148 Southern Sta, Hattiesburg, 39406

Terry Latour, Box 5148 Southern Sta, Hattiesburg, 39406

Nouveau Rare Books, 5005 Meadow Oaks Park Dr, PO Box 12471, Jackson, 39211. Tel 601-956-9950 (by appt)

Henry Simmons, Box 5148 Southern Sta, Hattiesburg, 39406

MISSOURI

ABC Theological Index, Box 2786 CSS, Springfield, 65803. Tel 417-833-2019

Addison's Bookstore, 314 E Commercial, Springfield, 65803. Tel 417-862-8460

Amitin's Bookshop, 711 Washington Ave, Saint Louis, 63101. Tel 314-421-9208, 421-2426

The Bookseller — Columbia, 27 N 9th, Columbia, 65201. Tel 314-874-4100

Columbia Books, PO Box 27, Columbia, 65201. Tel 314-449-7417

R Dunaway, Bookseller, 6138 Delmar Blvd, Saint Louis, 63112. Tel 314-725-1581

Anthony Garnett — Fine Books, PO Box 4918, Saint Louis, 63108. Tel 314-367-8080

Glenn Books Inc, 1227 Baltimore, Kansas City, 64105. Tel 816-842-9777

D Halloran Books, 7629 Wydown Blvd, St Louis 63105. Tel 314-863-1690

Hall's Bookshop, 202 Taylor Ave, Crystal City, 63019

Grunewald Klaus — Bookdealer, 807 W 87th Terr, Kansas City, 64114. Tel 816-333-7799

H L Prosser Bibliophile, Professional Appraiser & Collector, 1313 S Jefferson Ave, Springfield, 65807. Tel 417-866-5141

Harry B Robinson Book Search Service, 915 Texas Ave, Columbia, 65202. Tel 314-449-1611

D Scudder, Books, 6343 N Rosebury, Clayton, 63105. Tel 314-721-0799

David R Spivey Fine Books & Prints, 900 Manheim Rd, Kansas City, 64109. Tel 816-531-6088

MONTANA

Barjon's Books & Graphics, 2516 1st Ave N, Billings, 59101. Tel 406-252-4398

Bay Books & Prints, PO Box 426, Bigfork, 59911. Tel 406-837-4646

The Book Exchange, Holiday Village S/Ctr, Missoula, 59801. Tel 406-728-6342

H-P (Hardback-Paperback) Bookstore, 508 2nd Ave N, Box 1445, Great Falls, 59403. Tel 406-454-1393

Thomas Minckler Art & Books, 111 N 30th, Billings, 59101. Tel 406-245-2969

NEBRASKA

Book Barn, RR 1, Box 304H, South Sioux City, 68776. Tel 402-494-2936

D N Dupley, Book Dealer, 9118 Pauline St, Omaha, 68124. Tel 402-393-2906

Richard Flamer Bookseller, PO Box 3668, Omaha, 68103. Tel 402-553-8201

Mostly Books, 1025 S 10th St, Omaha, 68108. Tel 402-345-0999

Niobrara Books, PO Box 2664, Lincoln, 68502

1023 Booksellers, 4811 Leavenworth St, Omaha, 68103

NEVADA

Book Stop III, 3732 E Flamingo Rd, Las Vegas, 89121. Tel 702-456-4858

Donato's Fine Books, 2202 W Charleston Blvd, Suite 9, Las Vegas, 89102. Tel 702-702-5838

Five Dog Books, 606 W Plumb Ln, Reno, 89509. Tel 702-826-0650

Unique Book Stall, 912 S Virginia St, Reno, 89502. Tel 702-786-2631

NEW HAMPSHIRE

Book Farm, Concord Rd, Box 515, Henniker, 03242. Tel 603-428-3429

Edward C Fales Old & Rare Books & Manuscripts, Turnpike Rd, Box 56, Salisbury, 03268. Tel 603-648-2484

J & J Hanrahan, 62 Marcy St, Portsmouth, 03801, Tel 603-436-6234

Homestead Bookshop, Rte 101, E Main St, PO Box 90, Marlborough, 03455. Tel 603-876-4610

David L O'Neal Antiquarian Booksellers

Inc, 263 Elm Hill Rd, Peterborough, 03071. Tel 603-824-7489

Robert M O'Neill, Rare Books, Main St, Warner, 03278. Tel 603-456-3260

Sykes & Flanders, PO Box 86, Weare, 03281. Tel 603-529-7432

NEW JERSEY

Bauman Rare Books, 14 S LaClede Pl, Atlantic City, 08401. Tel 609-344-0743

A Bookmans Old Print Shop, Box 331, Maplewood, 07040 (maps)

The Bookstore at Depot Square, 8 Depot Square, Englewood, 07631. Tel 201-568-6563

The Chatham Booksellers, 8 Green Village Rd, Madison, 07940. Tel 201-822-1361

Joseph J Felcone Inc, Rare Books, Box 366, Princeton, 08540. Tel 609-924-0539

Heinoldt Books, 1325 W Central Ave, Egg Harbor City, 08215. Tel 609-965-2284

Hobbit Rare Books, 305 W South Ave, Westfield, 07090. Tel 201-654-4115

David Holmes, 322 Collings Ave, Collingswood, 08108

Arthur E Jones, 24 Rose Ave, Madison, 07940

La Scala Autographs Inc, PO Box 268, Plainsboro, 08536. Tel 609-799-8523

The Old Bookshop, 75 Spring St, Morristown, 07960. Tel 201-538-1210

Old York Books, 77 Church St, New Brunswick, 08901. Tel 201-249-0430

Paper & Ink Bookshop, 44 Beech Ave, Berkeley Heights, 07922

Past History, 136 Parkview Terrace, Lincroft, 07738. Tel 201-842-4545

Princeton Antiques Bookservice, 2915-17-31 Atlantic Ave, Atlantic City, 08401-6395. Tel 609-344-1943

Rare Book Co, PO Box 957, Freehold, 07728. Tel 201-780-1393

Richardson Books, 209 Stratford Ave, Camden, 08108. Tel 609-854-3348

Albert Saifer, 102 Longview St, West Orange, 07052. Tel 201-753-5701

Patterson Smith, 23 Prospect Terrace, Montclair, 07042. Tel 201-744-3291

Wangner's Bookshop & Book Search, 9 Midland Ave, Montclair, 07042. Tel 201-744-4211

Witherspoon Art & Bookstore, 12 Nassau St, Princeton, 08540. Tel 609-924-3582

Elisabeth Woodburn, Booknoll Farm, Hopewell, 08525. Tel 609-466-0522

NEW MEXICO

Abacus Books, PO Box 5555, Santa Fe, 87502. Tel 505-983-6434

Tom Davies Bookstore, 218 Central SW, Albuquerque, 87102. Tel 505-247-2072

De La Pena Books, 322½ Camino Cerrito, Santa Fe, 87501. Tel 505-982-1299

Richard Fitch, 2324 Calle Halcon, Santa Fe, 87501. Tel 505-982-2939

La Galeria De Los Artesanos, 220 N Plaza, PO Box 1657, Las Vegas, 87701. Tel 505-425-8331

Great Southwest Books, 960 Camino Santander, Santa Fe, 87501. Tel 505-983-1680

Lane's Repository, 10412 Chapola Pl NE, Albuquerque, 87111 (maps)

Margolis & Moss, PO Box 2042, Santa Fe, 87501. Tel 505-982-1028

Nicholas Potter, Bookseller, 203 E Palace Ave, Santa Fe, 87501. Tel 505-983-5434

Jack D Rittenhouse, Books, PO Box 4422, Albuquerque, 87196. Tel 505-255-2479

The Santa Fe Bookseller, 203 W San Francisco St, Santa Fe, 87501. Tel 505-983-5278

Paul Sternberg, 6623 Elwood NW, Albuquerque, 87107

Woodstock Ink, PO Box 492, Placitas, 87043

NEW YORK

Abrahams Magazine Service, 56 E 13th St, New York 10003. Tel 212-777-4700

Academy Bookstore, 10 W 18th St, New York, 10011. Tel 212-242-4848

Acanthus Books, 46 W 87th St 4B, New York, 10024. Tel 212-787-1753 (by appt)

Adirondack Yesteryears Inc, PO Drawer 209, Saranac Lake, 12983. Tel 518-891-3206

Agatherin—Historical Paper, PO Box 175, Wynantskill, 12198. Tel 518-674-2979

Alicat Gallery, 64 Ludlow St, Yonkers, 10705. Tel 914-963-4794

Jerry Alper Inc, 274 White Plains Rd, PO Box 218, Eastchester, 10707. Tel 914-793-2100

American Library Service, PO Drawer A, New City, 10956

Ampersand Books, PO Box 674, Cooper Sta, New York, 10276. Tel 212-674-6795

Appelfeld Gallery, 1372 York Ave, New York, 10021. Tel 212-988-7835

W Graham Arader, III, 23 E 74th St, Suite 5A, New York, 10021. Tel 212-628-3668

Argosy Bookstore Inc, 116 E 59th St, New York, 10022. Tel 212-753-4455

Richard B. Arkway Inc, 144 E 61st St, New York, 10021. Tel 212-475-6777 (maps)

Frederick Arone, Railroad Items, 377 Ashford Ave, Dobbs Ferry, 10522. Tel 914-693-5858

G S Askins Bookseller, PO Box 386, New Lebanon, 12125. Tel 518-794-8833

Bart Auerbach, Ltd, 411 West End Ave, New York 10024. Tel 212-724-4054

Austin Bookshop, 82-60 A Austin St, Box 36, Kew Gardens, 11415. Tel 212-441-1199

Barlenmir House Bookstore, 413 City Island Ave, Bronx 10464. Tel 212-885-2120

C Virginia Barnes—Bookseller, PO Box 112, Cathedral Sta, New York 10025

Barnstable Books Inc, Rm 506A, 799 Broadway, New York 10003. Tel 212-473-8681

J N Bartfield Books Inc, 45 W 57th St, New York, 10019. Tel 212-753-1830

Bayview Books & Bindery, PO Box 208, Northport, 11768. Tel 516-757-3563

Walter R Benjamin Autographs Inc, PO Box 255, Scribner Hollow Rd, Hunter, 12442. Tel 518-263-4133

Carl Sandler Berkowitz, PO Box 573, Chester, 10918. Tel 914-469-4231

F A Bernett Inc, 2001 Palmer Ave, PO Box 948, Larchmont, 10538. Tel 914-834-3026

Berry Hill Bookshop, Rte 12-B, RD Box 118, Deansboro, 13328. Tel 315-821-6188

Black Sun Books, 667 Madison Ave, New York, 10021. Tel 212-688-6622

Blue Fox Used Books & Records, 104 N Aurora St, Ithaca, 14850. Tel 617-272-5186

Bonmark Books Inc, 182 Old Country Rd, Levittown, 11801. Tel 516-938-9000

The Book Barn, 237 S Main St, Canandaigua, 14424

The Book Chest, Inc, 19 Oxford Pl, Rockville Centre, 11570. Tel 516-766-6105

The Book Gallery, Box 26, Gedney Station, White Plains, 10605. Tel 914-949-5406

The Bookworm, 18 W Market, PO Box 263, Corning, 14830. Tel 607-962-6778

William G Boyer, Box 70, Planetarium Sta, New York, 10024

Warren F Broderick—Books, PO Box 124, Lansingburg, 12182. Tel 518-235-4041

Robert K Brown, 120 E 86th St, New York 10028. Tel 212-410-4223

Buffalo Bookstore 1811, Century Mall, Northtown Plaza, 3131 Sheridan Dr, Buffalo, 14226. Tel 716-835-9827

Richard Cady, Rare Books, (see CT)

Caravan—Maritime Books, 87-06 168th Pl, Jamaica, 11432. Tel 212-526-1380

Carnegie Bookshop Inc, 30 E 60th St, New York, 10022. Tel 212-755-4861

Carney Books, 44 Elm St, Oneonta, 13820. Tel 607-432-5360

John Cashman Books, 327 Sea Cliff Ave, Sea Cliff, 11579. Tel 516-676-6088

Chip's Booksearch, PO Box 123 Planetarium Station, New York, 10024. Tel 212-362-9336

Roy W Clare—Antiquarian & Uncommon Books, PO Box 136, Getzville, 14068. Tel 716-688-8723

Collectors Antiques Inc, 286 A Main St, Port Washington, 11050. Tel 516-883-2098

James Cummins Bookseller, Inc, 667 Madison Ave, Suite 1005, New York, 10021. Tel 212-371-4151

L W Currey Rare Books, Inc, Church St, PO Box 187, Elizabethtown, 12932. Tel 518-873-6477 (by appt only)

Howard C Daitz—Photographica, Box 530, Old Chelsea Station, New York, 10013. Tel 212-929-8987

Denning House, Orrs Mills Rd, PO Box 42, Salisbury Mills, 12577. Tel 914-496-6771

Richard E Donovan, 305 Massachusetts Ave, Endicott, 13760. Tel 607-785-5874

Editions, Rte 28A, Boiceville, 12412. Tel 914-657-7000

El Cascajero, The Old Spanish Book Mine, 506 La Guardia Pl, New York, 10012. Tel 212-254-0905

Elgen Books, 336 De Mott Ave, Rockville Centre, 11570. Tel 516-536-6276

Estate of Herbert K Goodkind, 25 Helena Ave, Larchmont, 10538. Tel 914-834-1448

Europe Unie Books, 60 Reynolds St, Staten Island, 10305. Tel 212-273-0475

Ex Libris, 160A E 70th St, New York, 10021. Tel 212-249-2618

Fantasy Archives, 71 8th Ave, New York, 10014. Tel 212-929-5391

Far Country Bookstore, 79 Central Ave, Albany, 12206. Tel 518-465-2755

Don Fay—Books, 4329 Avon-Caledonia Rd, Caledonia, 14423. Tel 716-226-2288

Lawrence Feinberg—Rare Books & Manuscripts, 68 Ashford St, Brooklyn, 11207. Tel 212-235-7106

Leonard Fox Ltd, 667 Madison Ave, New York, 10021. Tel 212-888-5480

Lorraine Galinsky, 46 Glen Way, Cold Spring Harbor, 11724. Tel 516-692-4315

Ralph D Gardner, 135 Central Park W, New York, 10023. Tel 212-877-6820

Genealogists Bookshelf, Box 468, New York, 10028. Tel 212-879-1699

Genesee Bookshop, 2420 Monroe Ave, Rochester, 14618, Tel 716-442-3620

Harold Graves, 500 Kappock St, Riverdale, 10463

Paulette Greene, 140 Princeton Rd, Rockville Centre, 11570. Tel 516-766-8602

Greenwich Books Ltd, 127 Greenwich Ave, New York, 10012. Tel 212-242-3095

Gryphon Bookshop, 216 W 89th St, New York, 10024. Tel 212-362-0706

Anton Gud, 41-22 Judge St, Elmhurst, 11373

Renate Halpern Galleries, Inc, 325 E 79th St, New York, 10021. Tel 212-988-9316

Hammer Mountain Book Halls, 841 Union St, Schenectady, 12308. Tel 518-393-5266

C F Heindl Books, PO Box 8345, Rochester, 14618. Tel 716-271-1423

Morris Heller, RD 1, Box 87, Swan Lake, 12783. Tel 914-583-5879

Hennesseys Bookstore, 4th & Woodlawn, Saratoga Springs, 12866. Tel 518-584-4921

J N Herlin, Inc, 68 Thompson St, New York, 10012. Tel 212-431-8732

Daniel Hirsch, PO Box 315, Hopewell Junction, 12533. Tel 914-462-7404 (by appt)

Glenn Horowitz, Bookseller, 141 E 44th St, New York, 10017. Tel 212-557-1381

House of Books Ltd, 667 Madison Ave, New York, 10021. Tel 212-755-5998

House of El Dieff Inc, 139 E 63 St, New York, 10021. Tel 212-838-4160

John C Huckans Rare Books—Pan American Books, PO Box 270, Cazenovia, 13035. Tel 316-655-8499, 655-9654

International Books & Periodicals, 46-41 Overbrook St, Douglaston, 11362. Tel 212-729-5655, 224-4567

International University Booksellers,

Inc, 30 Irving Pl, New York, 10003. Tel 212-254-4100

Janus Books, 36 Wyoming Dr, Huntington Station, 11746. Tel 516-271-6454

Harmer Johnson Books Ltd, 667 Madison Ave, Suite 906, New York, 10021. Tel 212-752-1189

Kim Kaufman Bookseller, 1370 Lexington, Suite 2F, New York, 10028. Tel 212-369-3384

Kew Books, 667 Madison Ave, New York, 10021. Tel 212-308-4014

La Tienda El Quetzal, PO Box 246, Troy, 12180. Tel 518-271-7629

Lee & Lee Booksellers Inc, 424 Broome St, New York, 10013. Tel 212-226-3460

Librarium, Black Bridge Rd, RD 190, East Chatham, 12060. Tel 518-392-5209

William B Liebmann, 5700 Arlington Ave, Riverdale, Bronx, 10471. Tel 212-548-6014

Littwin & Feiden, 124 Prospect Ave, Mamaroneck, 10543. Tel 914-698-6504

The London Bookshop, 456 Madison Ave, Albany, 12208. Tel 518-436-1425

James Lowe Autographs, 30 E 60th St, Suite 907, New York, 10022. Tel 212-759-0775

Lyrical Ballad Bookstore, 7 Philadelphia St, Saratoga Springs, 12866. Tel 518-584-8779

Mahoney & Weekly, Booksellers, 513 Virginia St, Buffalo, 14202. Tel 716-856-6024

Maiden Voyage Books, One 5th Ave, New York, 10003. Tel 212-260-5131

Mason Fine Prints, Quaker Ridge Dr, Glen Head, 11545

The Military Bookman, 29 E 93rd St, New York, 10028. Tel 212-348-1280

S Millman, Box 23, New Lots Sta, Brooklyn, 11208. Tel 212-649-0111

Arthur H Minters Inc, 84 University Pl, New York, 10003. Tel 212-989-0593

Edward J Monarski Antiquarian Books, 1050 Wadsworth St, Syracuse, 13208. Tel 315-455-1716

Willis Monie Books, RD 1, Box 336, Cooperstown, 13326. tel 607-547-8363

Bradford Morrow Bookseller, 33 W 9th St, New York, 10011. Tel 212-477-1136

North Shore Books Ltd, PO Box 334, Huntington, 11743. Tel 516-271-5558

Nudel Books, 135 Spring St, New York, 10003. Tel 212-966-5624 (by appt only)

Oceanic Primitive Arts, 88 E 10th St, New York, 10003. Tel 212-982-8060

Emil Offenbacher, 84-50 Austin St, Box 96, Kew Gardens, 11415. Tel 212-849-5834

Olana Gallery, Drawer 9-F, Brewster, 10509. Tel 914-279-8077

Once Upon A Time Books, 28 Lincoln Ave, Roslyn Heights, 11577. Tel 516-621-4637

Page One Books, PO Box B, Buffalo, 14240

Pan American Books, Box 270, Cazenovia, 13035

N & N Pavlov, 37 Oakdale Dr, Dobbs Ferry, 10522. Tel 914-693-1776

Phillips Auctioneers, New York, 406 E 79th St, New York, 10021. Tel 212-570-4830

Phoenix Bookshop, 22 Jones St, New York, 10014. Tel 212-675-2795

Quality Book Service—T Emmett Henderson, 130 W Main St, Middletown, 10940. Tel 914-343-1038

The Question Mark, PO Box 9107, Albany, 12209. Tel 518-465-8135

Richard C Ramer, Old & Rare Books, 225 E 70th St, New York, 10021. Tel 212-737-0222, 737-0223

Kevin T Ransom—Bookseller, PO Box 176, Amherst, 14426. Tel 716-839-1510

Riverow Bookshop, 204 Front St, Owego, 13827. Tel 607-687-4094

Riverrun, 7 Washington Ave, Hastings-on-Hudson, 10706. Tel 914-478-4307

Rockland Bookman, Washington St, Cattaraugus, 14719. Tel 716-257-9504

Leona Rostenberg & Madeleine B Stern—Rare Books, PO Box 188,

Gracie Sta, New York, 10028. Tel 212-831-6628

Sigmund Rothschild, 27 W 67th St, New York, 10023

J B Rund, PO Box BB, Old Chelsea Sta, New York, 10113

William Salloch, Pines Bridge Rd, Ossining, 10562. Tel 914-941-8363 (by appt only)

Howard Schickler, Gracie Sta, PO Box 1298, New York, 10028. Tel 212-674-1953

Justin G Schiller Ltd, PO Box 1667, FDR Sta, New York, 10150. Tel 212-832-8231

E K Schreiber, 135 E 65th St, New York, 10021. Tel 212-772-3150

7 Terrace Drive, 7 Terrace Dr, Hastings on Hudson, 10706. Tel 212-777-4700

Nathan Simons, 1816 Seminole Ave, Bronx, 10461. Tel 212-863-4328

Sydney R Smith, Sporting Books, Canaan, 12029. Tel 518-794-8998

Sotheby Parke Bernet, Inc, 1334 York Ave, New York, 10021. Tel 212-472-3592

Southampton Book Co, S Main St, PO Drawer O, Southampton, 11968. Tel 516-283-1612

South Shore Book Reserve, Box 768, Southampton, 11968. Tel 516-283-5347

Springwater Books & Antiques, PO Box 8, Springwater, 14560. Tel 716-669-2450

Sterling Valley Antiquities, at Homestead Antiques, Rte 57, Syracuse, 13203. Tel 315-652-5477

Richard Stoddard, Performing Arts Books, 90 E 10th St, New York 10003. Tel 212-982-9440

Paul A Stroock, 35 Middle Lane, PO Box 126, Jericho, 11753. Tel 516-433-9018

Supersnipe Comic Book Euphorium & Art Gallery, 1617 2nd Ave, New York, 10028. Tel 212-879-9628

Victor Tamerlis, 911 Stuart Ave, Mamaroneck, 10543. Tel 914-698-8950

Temares Family Books, 50 Heights Rd, Plandome, 11030. Tel 516-627-8688

Timothy Trace, Red Mill Rd, Peekskill, 10566. Tel 914-528-4074

Trojan Books, 186 River St, Troy, 12180. Tel 518-271-6925

Peter Tumarkin Fine Books, Inc, 310 E 70th St, New York, 10028. Tel 212-348-8187

Breck Turner, 117 Main St, Lake Placid, 12946. Tel 518-523-9096

United States Games Systems Inc, 38 E 32nd St, New York, 10016. Tel 212-685-4300

University Place Bookshop, 821 Broadway, New York, 10003. Tel 212-254-5998

Ursus Books Ltd, 1011 Madison Ave, New York, 10021. Tel 212-772-8787

Victoria Bookshop, 303 5th Ave, Rm 809, New York, 10016. Tel 212-683-7849

Bernice Weiss — Rare Books, 36 Tuckahoe Ave, Eastchester, 10707. Tel 914-793-6200

Wildwood Enterprises, Box 560, Old Forge, 13420. Tel 315-369-3397

The Witkin Gallery, 41 E 57th St, New York, 10022. Tel 212-355-1461

Xerxes Books, PO Box 428, Glen Head, 11545. Tel 516-671-6235

Ximemes: Rare Books Inc, 19 E 69th St, New York, 10028. Tel 212-744-0226

Yankee Peddler Bookshop, East Lake Rd, Pultneyville, 14538. Tel 315-589-2063

Roy Young Bookseller, 145 Palisade St, Dobbs Ferry, 10522. Tel 914-693-6116

Margaret Zervas Rare Books, Box 562, Manhasset, 11030. Tel 516-767-0907

Irving Zucker Art Books, 256 5th Ave, New York, 10001. Tel 212-679-6332

NORTH CAROLINA

The Ancient Page, 64 Haywood St, Asheville, 28803. Tel 704-254-1177

Michael E Bernholz Antiques & Books, 1 Sycamore Dr, Chapel Hill, 27514. Tel 919-929-3533

Broadfoot's Bookmark, Rte 3, Box 318, Wendell, 27591. Tel 919-365-6963

Carolina Bookshop, 1601 E Independence Blvd, Charlotte, 28205. Tel 704-375-7305

Cattawba River Books, Rte #10, Box 120, Morganton, 28655. Tel 704-433-5478

Old Galen's Books, Box 3044, Durham, 27705. Tel 919-489-6246

Pathway Christian Bookstore, Willow Dr—School Rd, Hwy 27 E, PO Box 643, Locust, 28097. Tel 704-888-6257

Super Giant Books, 38 Wall St, Asheville, 28801. Tel 704-253-2103

NORTH DAKOTA

Dacotah Book Co, 3107 Winnipeg Dr, Box 512, Bismarck, 58501. Tel 701-223-7315

OHIO

Acres of Books, 633 Main St, Cincinnati, 45202. Tel 513-721-4214

Barbara Agranoff Books, Box 6501, Cincinnati, 45206. Tel 513-281-5095

Akron Books, 571 Malvern Rd, Akron, 44303. Tel 216-867-8784

The Asphodel Book Shop, 17192 Ravenna Rd, Rte 44, Burton, 44021. Tel 216-834-4775

Attenson Antiques & Books, 2219 Noble Rd, Cleveland, 44112. Tel 216-381-8788

The Bookery, 34 N Broad St, Fairborn, 45324. Tel 513-879-1408

Bookphil Book Search Service, 3987 Main St, Hilliard, 43026. Tel 614-876-0442

The Bookseller Inc, 521 W Exchange St, Akron, 44302. Tel 216-762-3101

The Book Store, 97 N High St, Columbus, 43215. Tel 614-224-4877

Doris Davis Books, 271 Streetsboro St, Hudson, 44236. Tel 216-653-5780

De Anima: Books in Psychology, 122 E Evers, Bowling Green, 43402. Tel 419-352-8533

Duttenhofer's Book Treasures, 214 W McMillan, Cincinnati, 45219. Tel 513-381-1340

Robert G Hayman, Box 188, Carey, 43316. Tel 419-396-6933

Susan Heller Books, Box 22723, Cleveland, 44122. Tel 216-283-2665 (by appt only)

Michael R Hurwitz, 151 N High St, Columbus, 43215. Tel 614-221-6610

Peter Keisogloff Books, 53 The Arcade, Cleveland, 44114. Tel 216-621-3094

McClintock Books, PO Box 3111, Warren, 44485. Tel 216-394-3398

Jack Matthews, Box 114, Athens, 45701. Tel 614-593-8915

Miran Arts & Books, 2824 Elm Ave, Columbus, 43215. Tel 614-236-0002

Morningside Bookshop, PO Box 1087, Dayton, 45410. Tel 513-461-6736

Paul H North Jr, 81 Bullitt Park Pl, Columbus, 43209. Tel 614-252-1826

The Odyssey Shop, 1743 S Union, Alliance 44601. Tel 216-821-9958

Ohio Bookhunter, 564 E Townview Ctr, Mansfield, 44907. Tel 419-526-1249

Ohio Book Store, 726 Main St, Cincinnati, 45202. Tel 513-621-5142

Owl Creek Books, 309 W Vine St, Mount Vernon, 43050. Tel 614-397-9337

Professional Books Service, PO Box 366, Dayton, 45401. Tel 513-223-3734

Publix Book Mart, 1310 Huron Rd, Cleveland, 44115. Tel 216-621-6624

Radiographics Books, Box 18492, Cleveland Heights, 44118. Tel 216-943-6374

Jerry Ray Books, 1306 N Orleans, Bowling Green, 43402. Tel 419-352-5321

Richardson, 7632 Manor Rd, Mentor Lake, 44060. Tel 216-257-4191

Robert Richshafer, 4606 Williamsburg Rd N, Cincinnati, 45215

Irving M Roth, Antiques, 89 Whittlesey Ave, Norwalk, 44857. Tel 419-668-2893

L J Ryan—Scholarly Books, PO Box 243, Columbus, 43216. Tel 614-258-6558

Josph Scheetz—Antiquarian Books, 6236 Foxridge Dr, Youngstown, 44512. Tel 216-758-0427

Karen Wickliff Books, 2579 N High St, Columbus, 43202. Tel 614-263-2903

Wesley C Williams, 2214 Deminston Dr, Cleveland, 44106

John T Zubal Inc, 2969 W 25th St, Cleveland, 44113. Tel 216-241-7640

OKLAHOMA

A Points Northe, 3630 NW 22nd, Oklahoma City, 73107. Tel 405-949-0675

Ada Book Stall, 301 W 12th, Ada, 74820. Tel 405-332-8062

Aladdin Book Shoppe, 2037 NW 23rd, Oklahoma City, 73106. Tel 405-528-0814

Ron Bever, Rt 3, Box 243-B, Edmond, 73034. Tel 405-478-0125

Book Stall, 1110 W Main, Norman, 73069. Tel 405-329-6787

Lawton Book Stall, 1832 NW 52nd, Regency Sq S/Ctr, Lawton, 73505. Tel 405-248-3111

The Oklahoma Bookman, 1107 Foreman Rd NE, Yukon, 73099

Shawnee Book Stall, 702B W Ayre, Shawnee, 74801. Tel 405-275-5714

OREGON

Antiques & Artifacts, 20457 Hwy 126, Noti, 97461. Tel 503-935-1619

Authors of the West, 191 Dogwood Dr, Dundee, 97115. Tel 503-538-8132

Book Fair, 1409 Oak St, Eugene, 97401. Tel 503-343-3033

Holland's Bookstore, 3522 SE Hawthorne, Portland, 97214. Tel 503-232-3596

Robert Hoyt Associates, 2343 NW Irving St, Portland, 97210

The Ken-L-Questor, Rte 4, Box 279, Newberg, 97132. Tel 503-538-2051

The Manuscript, 223 High St NE, Salem, 97301. Tel 503-370-8855

J Michaels Books, 376 E 11th, Eugene, 97401. Tel 503-342-2002

Old Oregon Bookstore, 525 SW 12th, Portland, 97205. Tel 503-227-2742

Ernest L Sackett, 100 Waverly Dr, Grants Pass, 97526. Tel 503-476-6404

Charles Seluzicki—Fine Books, PO 12367, Salem, 97309. Tel 503-362-9606

PENNSYLVANIA

William H Allen Bookseller, 2031 Walnut St, Philadelphia, 19103. Tel 215-563-3398

The Americanist, 1525 Shenkel Rd, Pottstown, 19464. Tel 215-323-5289

W Graham Arader III, 1000 Boxwood Ct, King of Prussia, 19406. Tel 215-825-6570, 688-4565

Baldwin's Book Barn, 865 Lenape Rd, West Chester, 19380. Tel 215-696-0816

Deanna Beeching, Bookseller, 603 N Front St, Harrisburg, 17101. Tel 717-236-2656

The Book Mark, 2049 Rittenhouse Sq W, Philadelphia, 19103. Tel 215-735-5546

Bernard Conwell Carlitz, 1901 Chesnut St, Philadelphia, 19103. Tel 215-563-6608

The Epistemologist, Scholarly Books, PO Box 63, Bryn Mawr, 19010. Tel 215-527-1065

The Family Album, Rd 1, Box 42, Glen Rock, 17327. Tel 717-235-2134

Do Fisher Books & Antiques, 2020 Roosevelt Ave, Williamsport, 17701. Tel 717-323-3573

Carl B Frushon, Ltd, 75 Acco Rd, York, 17403. Tel 717-329-6465

The Gateway, Ferndale, 18921. Tel 215-847-5644

Michael Gibbs, Books, PO Box 883, State College, 16801

Graedon Books Inc, RD 1, New Hope, 18938. Tel 215-794-8351

Terry Harper, Bookseller, PO Box 103, Rouseville, 16344. Tel 814-676-6728

F Thomas Heller Books, PO Box 356, Swarthmore, 19081. Tel 215-543-3582

Hive Of Industry, PO Box 602, Easton, 18042. Tel 215-258-6663

Hoffman Research Services, Box 342, Rillton, 15678. Tel 412-446-3374 (by appt)

Hughes', 2410 N Hills Dr, Williamsport, 17701. Tel 717-326-1045

James S Jaffe, Rare Books, PO Box 90, Bryn Mawr, 19010. Tel 215-527-5421 (by appt)

Lincoln Way Books, 136 Lincoln Way West, Chambersburg, 17201. Tel 717-264-7120

Lock Stock & Barrel Shop, Rd One, Dalton, 18414. Tel 717-945-5123, 344-5561

Thomas Macalusco Rare & Fine Books, PO Box 133, Kennett Square, 19348. Tel 215-444-1063

Bruce McKittrick, 2240 Fairmount Ave, Philadelphia, 19130. Tel 215-235-3209

George S MacManus Co, 1317 Irving St, Philadelphia, 19107. Tel 215-735-4456

Miscellaneous Man, PO Box 1776, New Freedom, 17349. Tel 717-235-4766

Mitchell's Bookshop, 296 N Main St, Doylestown, 18901. Tel 215-348-4875, 348-3319

Earl Moore Associates, Inc, PO Box 243, Wynnewood, 19096. Tel 215-649-1549

Photopia, 1728 Spruce St, Philadelphia, 19103

William H Powers, RD 3, Export, 15632. Tel 412-327-6886

Quadrant Book Mart, 20 N 3rd St, Easton, 18042. Tel 215-252-1188

S & D Bookstore Inc, 16 S 11th St, Indiana, 15701. Tel 412-465-2795

Schoyer's Books, 1404 S Negley Ave, Pittsburgh, 15217. Tel 412-521-8464

D Sedenger Galleries, PO Box 189, Huntingdon Valley, 19006. Tel 215-947-2806

R F Selgas Sporting Books, PO Box 227B, Hershey, 17033. Tel 717-534-1868

Charles Sessler, 1308-1310 Walnut St, Philadelphia, 19107. Tel 215-735-1086

Stephen Shuart Photographic Books, PO Box 419, Kane, 16735. Tel 814-837-7786

Carol Soffa, Box 4287, Philadelphia, 19144

Sotheby Park Bernet, Inc, 1630 Locust St, Philadelphia, 19130. Tel 215-735-7886

Geoffrey Steele Inc, Lumberville, 18933. Tel 215-297-5187

William Thomas — Bookseller, Box 331, Mechanicsburg, 17055. Tel 717-766-7778

The Tuckers, 2236 Murray Ave, Pittsburgh, 15217. Tel 412-521-0249

Benjamin W Turner Jr, Bookseller, PO Box 262, Point Pleasant, 18950. Tel 609-397-0954

Carmen Valentino, 2956 Richmond St, Philadelphia, 19134. Tel 215-739-6056

J Howard Woolmer — Rare Books, Marienstein Rd, Revere, 18953. Tel 215-847-5074

RHODE ISLAND

Don E Burnett, PO Box 178, East Greenwich, 02818. Tel 401-884-6181

The Cartographer, 168 Governor St, Providence, 02906

Patrick T Conley — Books, 45 Windsor Rd, Cranston, 02905. Tel 401-785-0169

Fortunate Finds Bookstore, 16 W Natick Rd, Warwick 02886. Tel 401-737-8160

Iron Horse Comics & Collectibles, 834 Hope St, Providence, 02906. Tel 401-521-9343

Nicholas Olsberg, 31 Walnut St, Newport, 02840

Sign Of The Unicorn Bookshop, Box 297, Peace Dale, 02883. Tel 401-789-8912

The Wayside Bookshop, Box 501, Westerly, 02891. Tel 401-322-1698

Frank J Williams, Lincolniana, RFD Hope Valley Rd, Hope Valley, 02832

SOUTH CAROLINA

The Attic, Inc, PO Box 128, Hodges, 29653. Tel 803-374-3013

Norm Burleson Bookseller, 104 First Ave, Spartanburg, 29302. Tel 803-583-8845

The Good News Center, 5131 Dorchester Rd, Charleston, 29405. Tel 803-552-3302

Hampton Books, Rt 1, Box 202, Newberry, 29108. Tel 803-276-6870

Noah's Ark Book Attic, Stony Point Rte

2, Greenwood, 29646. Tel 803-374-3013

Old Mill Books, Box 12353, Charleston, 29412. Tel 803-795-7177

Woodspurge Books, PO Box 18404, Spartanburg, 29318. Tel 803-585-4210

SOUTH DAKOTA

Dakota Books, 505 Main St, Webster, 57274. Tel 605-345-3033, 486-4695

TENNESSEE

The Book Shelf, 3765 Hillside Dr NE, Cleveland, 37311. Tel 615-472-8408

Burke's Bookstore Inc, 634 Poplar Ave, Memphis, 38105. Tel 901-527-7484

Elders Bookstore, 2115 Elliston Pl, Nashville, 37203. Tel 615-327-1867

F M Hill Books, PO Box 1037, Kingsport, 37662. Tel 615-247-8740

Mid-America Books, 105 S Court, Memphis, 38103. Tel 901-527-0482

TEXAS

Antiquarian Book Mart, 3127 Broadway, San Antonio, 78209. Tel 512-828-4885

W Graham Arader, III, 2800 Virginia Ave, Houston, 77098. Tel 713-527-8055

Attals Southwest Gallery, 3310 Red River, Austin, 78705. Tel 512-476-3634

Big D Books & Comics, 1516 Centerville, Dallas, 75228. Tel 214-328-0130

Frank M Blackburn, One Windwood Place, Canyon, 79015

Louis V Boling, 3413 Tiger Lane, Corpus Christi, 78415. Tel 512-852-1131

A Book Buyer's Shop, 711 Studewood, Houston, 77007. Tel 713-868-3910

Books Etc, 4912 Camp Bowie Blvd, Fort Worth, 76107. Tel 817-731-9162

The Book Worm, 4707 Blanco Rd, San Antonio, 78212. Tel 512-342-4258

Joshua David Bowen, 1037 S Alamo,

San Antonio, 78210. Tel 512-227-1771

Detering Book Gallery, 2311 Bissonet, Houston, 77006. Tel 713-526-6974

Fletcher's Books, Main St, Box 65, Salado, 76571. Tel 817-947-5414

Frontier America Corp, Box 3698, Bryan, 77805. Tel 713-846-4462

David Grossblatt, Bookseller, Box 30001, Dallas, 75230. Tel 214-373-0218, 361-4320

Gutenberg's Folly: Rare & Scholarly Books, 627 E Guenther, San Antonio, 78210. Tel 512-222-8449

Michael Heaston, 5614 Wagon Train Rd, Austin, 78749

The Jenkins Co, Rare Books, PO Box 2085, Austin, 78768. Tel 512-444-6616

Kingston Bookstore, 118 Sayles, Abilene, 79605. Tel 915-672-8261, 677-5153, 672-8152

Libros Latinos, PO Box 1103, Redlands, 92373. Tel 714-793-8423

John R Mara Law Books, 5628 Richmond Ave, Dallas, 75206. Tel 214-821-1979

John W Marx, 4212 18th, Lubbock, 79416

Tom Munnerlyn, Books, PO Drawer 15247, Austin, 78761. Tel 512-926-5876

Marian Orgain, 1618 Milford, Houston, 77006

John R Payne, 2205 Bridle Path, Austin, 78703

Thomas Payne, 2205 Bridle Path, Austin, 78703

Joe Petty — Books, 1704 Park, Victoria, 77901. Tel 512-573-3320

William Simpson Questioned Document Examiner, 4001 S Main, Houston, 77006

Sotheby Parke Bernet, Inc, 2501 River Oaks Blvd, Houston 77019. Tel 713-528-2863

W Thomas Taylor — Bookseller, 708 Colorado, Suite 704, Austin, 78763. Tel 512-451-5406

T W Tingle Rare & Out-of-Print Books, 3012 Headly Dr, Austin, 78745. Tel 512-433-6690

Ray S Walton — Rare Books, 1310 W

42nd St, Austin, 78703. Tel 512-476-9513

Jerry Williams, 700 19th St, Canyon 79015

Zane Grey's West, Drawer A, Keene, 76059. Tel 817-641-8536

UTAH

Cosmic Aeroplane Books, 258 E 1st St, Salt Lake City, 84111. Tel 801-533-9409

Scallawagiana Books, PO Box 2441, Salt Lake City, 84110. Tel 801-487-7184

Sam Weller's Zion Bookstore, 254 S Main St, Salt Lake City, 84101. Tel 801-328-2586

Walt West Books, 1355 Riverside Ave, Provo, 84604. Tel 801-377-1298

VERMONT

Richard H Adelson Antiquarian Bookseller, Cloudland Rd, North Pomfret, 05053. Tel 802-457-2608

Armand Beliveau, RD 2, Williston, 05495. Tel 802-482-2540

Bygone Books Inc, 91 College, Burlington, 05401. Tel 802-862-4397

The Country Bookshop, RFD 2, Plainfield, 05667. Tel 802-454-8439

F P Elwert, Box 254, Rutland, 05701. Tel 802-773-3417

Green Mountain Books & Prints, PO Box 74, Sutton, 05851. Tel 802-626-5051

Haunted Mansion Bookshop, Rte 103, Cuttingsville, 05738. Tel 802-492-3337, 492-3462

Ken Leach, 16 Elm St, Box 78, Brattleboro, 05310. Tel 802-257-7918

William Parkinson, PB Box 397, Shelburne, 05482. Tel 802-482-3113

Tuttle's Antiquarian Books Inc, Box 541, Rutland, 05701. Tel 802-773-8930.

VIRGINIA

Auld Stone Bookshop, RFD 1, Box 200, Glasgow, 24555. Tel 703-258-2582

The Bookpress Ltd, PO Box KP, Williamsburg, 23187. Tel 804-229-1260

Bookworm & Silverfish, PO Box 639, Wytheville, 23482

Charles P Cella, Jr, Rte 2, Box 3, Powhatan, 23129

Collector's Old Bookshop, 707 E Franklin St, Richmond, 23219. Tel 804-644-2097

Daedalus Bookshop, 121 4th St NE, Charlottesville, 22901. Tel 804-293-7595

Ghent Bookworm, 1407-1409 Colley Ave, Norfolk, 23517. Tel 804-627-2267

Franklin Gilliam: Rare Books, 112 Fourth St, NE, Charlottesville, 22901. Tel 804-979-2512

Great Bridge Books, Inc, 404 Woodford Dr, Chesapeake, 23320. Tel 804-482-1666

Heartwood Used Books, 5 & 9 Elliewood Ave, Charlottesville, 22903. Tel 804-295-7083

Hilton Village Bookshop, 10375 Warwick Blvd, Newport News, 23601. Tel 804-595-5866

The Manuscript Co of Springfield, Box 1151, Springfield, 22151. Tel 703-256-6748

The Memorabilia Corner, PO Box 15052, Norfolk, 23511-0052. Tel 804-467-4256

W B O'Neill—Old & Rare Books, 11609 Hunters Green Ct, Reston, 22091. Tel 703-860-0782

Richmond Bookshop, 808 W Broad St, Richmond, 23220. Tel 804-644-9970

Henry Stevens, Son & Stiles, Antiquarian Booksellers, PO Box 1299, Williamsburg, 23185. Tel 804-220-0925

Waverly K Winfree, 6105 Hokie Court, Richmond, 23234

Samuel Yudkin & Associates, 1125 King St, Alexandria, 22314. Tel 703-549-9330

WASHINGTON

Beatty Bookstore, 1925 3rd Ave, Seattle, 98101. Tel 206-624-2366

The Book Store, 108 E 4th Ave, Olympia, 98501. Tel 206-754-7470

M Taylor Bowie Bookseller, 2613 5th Ave, Seattle, 98121. Tel 206-682-5363

Churchill's Book Lover's Haunt, 125 S 2nd, Yakima, 98901. Tel 509-453-8207

Crucible Bookshop, 5525 University Way NE, Seattle, 98105. Tel 206-525-3737

Culpepper & Hanson Bookseller, 741 St Helens St, Tacoma, 98402. Tel 206-622-4719

Fox Book Co, 1140 Broadway, Tacoma, 98402. Tel 206-627-2223

David Ishii Bookseller, 212 1st, S, Seattle, 98101. Tel 206-624-2366

McDuffie's Books, Box 14557, Opportunity, 99214. Tel 509-928-3623

P T Mallahan Bookseller, 307 130th SE, Bellevue, 98005. Tel 206-454-1663

Robert W Mattila Bookseller, Pioneer Sq Sta, PO Box 4040, Seattle, 98104. Tel 206-622-9455

Edward D Nudelman Children's & Illustrated Antiquarian Books, PO Box 20704 Broadway Sta, Seattle, 98102. Tel 206-782-2930

The Old Book Home, PO Box 18777, Spokane, 99208. Tel 509-838-6017

Old Seattle Paperworks, 1501 Pike Pl, Suite 424, Seattle, 98101. Tel 206-623-2870

Pegasus Books & Press, PO Box 1350, Vashon Island, WA, 98070. Tel 206-567-5224 (appt only)

John L Polley — Bookseller, 2231 2nd Ave, Seattle, 98121. Tel 206-625-1533

The Shorey Bookstore, 110 Union St, 98101. Tel 206-624-0221

George H Tweney, Books, 16660 Marine View Dr SW, Seattle, 98166. Tel 206-243-8243

R M Weatherford — Books, 10902 Woods Creek Rd, Monroe, 98272. Tel 206-794-4318

WEST VIRGINIA

The Bishop of Books, 117 15th St, Wheeling, 26003. Tel 304-232-8801

Inland River Books, PO Box 87, Washington, 26181. Tel 304-428-4948

Stroud Theological Booksellers, Star Rte, Box 94, Pembroke Rd, Williamsburg, 24991. Tel 304-645-7169

WISCONSIN

The Antiquarian Shop, PO Box L, Stevens Point, 54481. Tel 715-341-3351

Bob's Bookshop, 227 E College Ave, Appleton, 54911. Tel 414-731-3531

Raymond Dworczyk, Rare Books, 2114 W Rogers St, Milwaukee, 53204. Tel 414-383-2659

Just Books, 216 N Water St, Milwaukee, 53202. Tel 414-278-8478

The Old Book Corner, 1815 Park Ave, Racine, 53403. Tel 414-632-5195

Renaissance Bookshop Inc, 834 N Plankinton, Milwaukee, 53203. Tel 414-271-6850

Spaightwood Galleries, 1150 Spaight St, Madison, 53703. Tel 608-255-3043 (by appt)

Trine Book Service, 2581 University Ave, Madison, 53705. Tel 608-231-3414

Yesterday's Memories Book & Old Record Shop, 5406 W Center St, Milwaukee, 53210. Tel 414-444-6210

CANADA

ALBERTA

Tom Williams Books, Box 4126, Sta C, Calgary, T2T 5M9. Tel 403-264-0184

BRITISH COLUMBIA

J F Ahrens Bookshop, 756 Davie St, Vancouver, V6Z 1B5. Tel 604-683-2014

Colophon Books, 407 W Cordova St, Vancouver, V6B 1E5. Tel 604-685-4138

The Haunted Bookshop, 822 1/2 Fort St, Victoria, V8W 1H6. Tel 604-382-1427

Johnson & Small Booksellers, Law Chambers, 45 Bastion Sq, Victoria, V8W 1J1. Tel 604-382-1144, 383-4366

Stephen C Lunsford Books, PO Box 86773, North Vancouver, V7L 4L3. Tel 604-988-1469

Sotheby Parke Bernet, Inc, 2321 Granville St, Vancouver, V6H 3G4. Tel 604-736-6363

Venkatesa Books, Box 524, Tofino, V0R 2Z0

MANITOBA

Antiquarian Books, 31 D'Arcy Dr, Winnipeg, R3T 2K4. Tel 204-269-6930

Comic World, 389 Portage Ave, Winnipeg, R3B 2C5. Tel 204-943-1968

NEW BRUNSWICK

Arctician Books, PO Box 691, Fredericton, E3B 5B4. Tel 506-457-0544

NOVA SCOTIA

L S Loomer Antiquarian Books, PO Box 878, Windsor, B0N 2T0.

Nautica Booksellers, 1579 Dresden Row, B3J 2K4. Tel 902-429-2741

Schooner Books Store, 5378 Inglis St, Halifax, B3H 1J5. Tel 903-423-8419

Thoth's Bookshops Ltd, Box 749, Wolfville, B0P IX0. Tel 902-542-2640

ONTARIO

About Books, 280 Queen St W, Toronto, M5V 2A1. Tel 416-593-0792

Attic Books, 388 Clarence St, London, N6A 3M7. Tel 519-432-6636

Avenue Bookshop, 101 4th Ave, Ottawa, K1S 2L1. Tel 613-233-0966

Book Shop, 134 Jame St N, Hamilton, L8R 2K7. Tel 416-526-9185

The Bookstore, 228 Charlotte St, Peterborough, K9J 2T8. Tel 705-748-1230

City Lights Bookshop, 356 Richmond St, London, N6A 3C3. Tel 519-679-8420

Great Northwest Book Co, 338 Jarvis St, Toronto, M4Y 2G6. Tel 416-964-2089

Dora Hood's Book Room Ltd, 34 Ross St, Toronto, M5T 1Z9, Tel 416-979-2129

Terrence Kohls Books, 193 Victoria, Pembroke, K8A 4K2. Tel 613-735-0001

Kuska House, PO Box 1507, Kingston, K7L 5C7. Tel 613-546-7666

D & E Lake Ltd Old & Rare Books, 106 Berkeley St, Suite 302, Toronto, M5A 2W7. Tel 416-863-9930

J Patrick McGahem — Books Inc, 783 Bank St, Ottawa, K1S 3V5. Tel 613-233-2215

David Mason Books, 638 Church St, Toronto, M4Y 2G3. Tel 416-922-1712

William Matthews, Bookseller, 46 Gilmore Rd, Fort Erie, L2A 2M1. Tel 416-821-7859

Mostly Mysteries Books. 398 Saint Clair Ave E, Toronto, M4T IP5. Tel 416-485-4373

Movements In Time Ltd, Box 6629, Station A, Toronto, M5W 1X4. Tel 416-883-1924

North Toronto Coins Ltd, 3234 Yonge St, Toronto, M4N 2L4. Tel 416-489-5949

Old Favorites Bookshop Ltd, 250 Adelaide St W, Toronto, M5H 1X8. Tel 416-977-2944

Pomona Book Exchange, Hwy 52, Rockton, L0R 1X0. Tel 519-621-8897

Sotheby Parke Bernet, Inc, 156 Front St W, Toronto, M5J 2L6. Tel 416-596-0300

Sportsman's Cabinet, Box 15, Manotick, K0A 2N0. Tel 613-692-3618

Steven Temple, 308 Queen St W, Toronto, M5T 2W1. Tel 416-593-0582

Arthur Wharton Books, 308 Queen St W, PO Box 263, Sta B, Toronto, M5T 2W1. Tel 416-593-0582

QUEBEC

Michel Brisebois Librarie, Dorchester W, Montreal, H3B 3J7. Tel 514-875-5210

I Ehrlich, Box 994, Sta B, Montreal, H3B 3K5. Tel 514-842-7000

Helen R Kahn Antiquarian Books, PO Box 323, Victoria Sta, Montreal, H3Z 2V8

Librairie D'Antan, 1995 Baile, Montreal, H2Y 2V8. Tel 514-989-5124

Librairie Quebecoise, 1417 Amherst, Montreal, H2L 3L2. Tel 514-523-3305

William P Wolfe Rare Books, Pointe Claire, PO Box 1190, Montreal H9S 5K7. Tel 514-697-1630

SASKATCHEWAN

Northland Books, 813 Broadway Ave, Saskatoon, S7N 1B5. Tel 306-242-9466

Richard Spafford—Books, 3036 13th Ave, Regina, S4T 1N9. Tel 306-527-0844

Victoria Book Exchange, 922 Victoria, Regina, S4N 0R7. Tel 306-352-3067

25

Rare Book and

Manuscript Libraries

Listings of rare book and manuscript libraries in the United States and Canada are arranged geographically. Independent research libraries whose names do not reflect their locations, and other rare book collections whose names differ from those of their parent institutions, can be found in the name index at the end of this chapter.

UNITED STATES

ALABAMA, Birmingham

BIRMINGHAM PUBLIC LIBRARY. Tutwiler Collection of Southern History & Literature. 2020 Park Place, Birmingham 35203. Tel: 205-254-2534. Virginia K. Scott, *Department Head.* **Staff:** Yvonne Crumpler, *Assistant Librarian.*

Holdings: Bks 3000. **Scope:** Significant Alabama imprints, books on travel in the South & Southeast from the 18th & 19th centuries & major works on Indians in the South. **Subjects:** Regional—Southeast United States; Travel & Exploration (southern states). **Budget:** $3000 per year. **Access Policy:** Open to public; no photocopying.

ALABAMA, University

UNIVERSITY OF ALABAMA. William Stanley Hoole Special Collections Library. PO Box S, University 35486. Tel: 205-348-5512. Joyce H. Lamont, *Head, Special Collections & Programs.*

Scope: Collection contains material related to Alabama & the deep South, rare editions, confederate imprints, pamphlets, maps, archives of the University & Alabama state publications. Important collections include first editions of Sir Walter Scott, Lafcadio Hearn & Robinson Jeffers; World War II Armed Services Editions of paperback books. **Access Policy:** Open to the public by appointment.

ALASKA, Anchorage

ANCHORAGE MUNICIPAL LIBRARIES. Alaskana Collection. 524 W Sixth Ave, Anchorage 99501. Tel: 907-264-4481. Michael Catoggio, *Supervisor.*

Holdings: Bks 7000. **Scope:** Comprehensive collection of published Alaskana—historical & current. Archives & manuscripts collection will commence in 1985–1986. **Budget:** $15,000 per year. **Access Policy:** Open to public.

ALASKA, Fairbanks

UNIVERSITY OF ALASKA. Elmer E. Rasmuson Library, Alaska & Polar Regions Department. Fairbanks 99701. Tel: 907-474-7227. Paul McCarthy, *Head & Archivist*. Staff: Marvin W. Falk, *Curator of Rare Books;* Betsy Harding, *Indexer.*

Holdings: Bks 3500; Mss 6200 cu ft; extensive rare map collection; over 100,000 historical photographs of Alaska. Scope: Specialized collection on Alaska & the polar regions in all languages. Manuscript collection limited to Alaska. Subjects: Alaska Politics & Business; History of Alaska & Polar Regions & Russian America; Regional—Alaska & Polar Regions; Travel & Exploration; Oral History. Budget: $50,000 per year. Access Policy: Open to public.

ALASKA, Juneau

ALASKA HISTORICAL LIBRARY. Division of State Libraries & Museums. Pouch G, Juneau 99811. Tel 907-465-2926. Phyllis DeMuth, *Librarian.* Staff: Verda Carey, *Librarian.*

Holdings: Bks 24,000; Mss 250 ln ft; 92,000 photographs. Scope: Alaska/Arctic research collection of books, manuscripts, photographs, films, video & microfilms. Published Guides: *A Guide to the Russian Holdings in the Alaska Historical Library; A Guide to the Dolgopolov Collection; A Guide to the Alaska Packers Association Records.* Subjects: Travel & Exploration; Early Voyages/Explorations of Alaska; Arctic Regions; Manuscripts, Diaries & Journals on Ethnology, Mining, Canneries, Russian Orthodox Church in Alaska. Access Policy: Open to public.

ARIZONA, Tucson

UNIVERSITY OF ARIZONA. Library, Special Collections. Tucson 85721. Tel: 602-621-6423. Louis A. Hieb, *Head Librarian.* Staff: David Robrock, *Special Collections Librarian;* Phyllis Ball, *Manuscripts Librarian.*

Holdings: Bks 85,000; Mss 1400 ln ft; 30,000 documentary photographs. Published Guides: Todd Mills, "Western Manuscripts in the University of Arizona Library," *Arizona and the West* 22 (1980). Subjects: Restoration Drama; 18th-, 19th- & 20th-century English & American Authors (especially Yeats & Conrad); History of Science (especially astronomy & optics); Regional—Arizona, Southwest; Science Fiction; Mystery Fiction; Black Sparrow Press Archives. Budget: $100,000 per year. Access Policy: Open to public.

ARKANSAS, Fayetteville

UNIVERSITY OF ARKANSAS. Mullins Library, Special Collections. Fayetteville 72701. Tel: 501-575-5576, 5577. Michael Dabrishus, *Head.* Staff: Deborah K. McAnallen, *Special Collections Librarian;* Ethel C. Simpson, *Arkansas & Regional Studies Bibliographer;* E. Betty Austin, N. T. Ernst, Ellen C. Shipley, *Technical Assistants III.*

Holdings: Bks 2528; Mss 4500. Scope: Holdings center on Arkansas & the surrounding region. Arts collections include papers of Arkansas writers John Gould Fletcher, Charles Morrow Wilson & Francis Gwaltney, as well as Ezra Pound correspondence & the papers of architect Edward Durrell Stone. Special collections include the Haldeman-Julius Little & Big Blue Books. Subjects: Literature 1900 to present; Regional—Arkansas. Access Policy: Open to public.

CALIFORNIA, Berkeley

UNIVERSITY OF CALIFORNIA. The Bancroft Library. Berkeley 94720. Tel: 415-642-3781. James D. Hart, *Director.* Staff: Anthony S. Bliss, *Rare Books Librarian;* Estelle Rebec, *Head, Manuscripts Division;* Robert Hirst, *Editor, The Mark Twain Papers;* William M. Roberts, *University Archivist;* Irene

Moran, *Head, Public Services;* Robin E. Rider, *History of Science & Technology;* Peter E. Hanff, *Coord., Tech. Serv.;* Willa K. Baum, *Regional Oral History.*

Holdings: Bks 325,000; Mss 44,000,000 items; 2,000,000 photographs. **Scope:** History of western North America, particularly from the western plains states to the Pacific Coast & from Alaska to Panama, with greatest emphasis on California & Mexico; Mark Twain's notebooks, correspondence & other manuscripts, first editions & other materials; rare European, English & American imprints; fine printing of all periods, with emphasis on English & American typography; collections of major English, American & European authors; modern poetry; fine bindings; medieval manuscripts; papyri. **Published Guides:** *A Guide to Manuscript Collections in the Bancroft Library* (University of California Press, 1964, 1972); *Catalogue of The Bancroft Library* (G. K. Hall). **Subjects:** Americana; Books about Books; Ephemera; History; History of Mathematics; History of Science; Illustrated Books; Incunabula; Literature pre-1640 to present; Press Books; Theater & Performing Arts; Travel & Exploration; Pictorial Collections Documenting California & the West. **Budget:** $240,000. **Access Policy:** Open to adults with two pieces of identification.

CALIFORNIA, Claremont

FRANCIS BACON FOUNDATION INC, THE FRANCIS BACON LIBRARY. 655 N Dartmouth Ave, Claremont 91711. Tel: 714-624-6305. Elizabeth S. Wrigley, *Director.* **Staff:** Thelma S. Davies, *Special Collections Librarian;* Jackie L. Bellows, *Technical Services Librarian;* Michele A. Moss, *Library Assistant.*

Holdings: Bks 10,800; Mss 25 ln ft; maps; pictures; correspondence; 110 pamphlet files. **Scope:** Collection consists of books, pamphlets, manuscripts & photographs (primarily 16th & 17th century); cryptology (16th cen-

tury to present); Emblem literature (16th & 17th century); Lee-Bernard Collection (American political theory of 18th century); Shakespeare-authorship-controversy books, photos, clippings & correspondence; American literary manuscripts; [Walter Conrad] Arensberg Archives (6 collections covering family correspondence, legal documents, correspondence with American literary figures, French poets & painters & anti-Shakespeareans). **Published Guides:** *Census of Aldine Editions in California* (Stanford Univ Press, 1974). **Subjects:** Americana; History (Tudor & Stuart; Early American); History of Medicine & Science (16th & 17th century); Law (16th & 17th century); Literature pre-1640–1800. **Budget:** $70,000 per year. **Access Policy:** Open to public for reading & reference only.

CALIFORNIA, Davis

UNIVERSITY OF CALIFORNIA, DAVIS. Library, Department of Special Collections. Davis 95616. Tel: 916-752-1621. Donald Kunitz, *Head.* **Staff:** C. Daniel Elliott, *Assistant Head.*

Holdings: Bks 35,000 (includes 15,000 off-campus); Mss 4000 (includes printed ephemera). **Subjects:** Agricultural Technology, Viticulture & Enology, Apiculture (1500–present); English History (17th century); American Poetry (1946–present); English Poetry (19th century); American Theater (20th century); Western Americana (20th century). **Budget:** $20,000 per year. **Access Policy:** Open to public.

CALIFORNIA, Hayward

CALIFORNIA STATE UNIVERSITY, HAYWARD, Library, Floyd R. Erickson Special Collections Room. Hayward 94542. Tel: 415-881-3664. Ronald L. Sparks, *Librarian.*

Holdings: Bks 11,000; Mss 15 ln ft; original botanical prints by Henry Evans. **Scope:** Includes early imprints, modern fine press, early travel, contemporary poetry. **Subjects:** Press Books; Regional—San Francisco Bay Area Poetry; Travel & Exploration; Marco Polo Collection. **Budget:** $7000 per year. **Access Policy:** Open to public.

CALIFORNIA, La Jolla

UNIVERSITY OF CALIFORNIA, SAN DIEGO. Mandeville Department of Special Collections. La Jolla 92093. Tel: 619-452-2533. Lynda Corey Claassen, *Head.* **Staff:** Michael Davidson, *Curator of Archive for New Poetry;* Roy Ritchie, *Curator of Manuscripts.*
Holdings: Bks 75,000; Mss 600 ln ft; 1000 tape recordings. **Published Guides:** *The Hill Collection of Pacific Voyages* (UCSD). **Subjects:** History; History of Science; Literature pre-1640 to present; Regional—Baja California; Travel & Exploration; Mystery & Detective Fiction; Pacific Voyages; Cultures of the Pacific Rim & Islands; Spanish Civil War; English-Language Poetry (since 1945); Early Modernist Works; Science & Public Policy; Theosophy; Hispanic Cultures & Literature; General Humanities. **Budget:** $60,000 per year. **Access Policy:** Open to public.

CALIFORNIA, Long Beach

CALIFORNIA STATE UNIVERSITY, LONG BEACH. Library, Special Collections & Archives. 1250 Bellflower Blvd, Long Beach 90840. Tel: 213-498-4087. John Ahouse, *Librarian.* **Staff:** Robert Brasher, *Assistant Librarian.*
Holdings: 15,000 Bks; Mss 300 ln ft; 400 art prints; 150 original photographic prints. **Subjects:** California History; Modern First Editions, Abolition Movement; Radical Politics in California; Local History; Institutional History; Photography; Art Prints. **Access Policy:** Apply to librarian.

CALIFORNIA, Los Angeles

LOS ANGELES PUBLIC LIBRARY. Collection Development Department. 630 W Fifth St, Los Angeles 90071. Tel: 213-626-7555 ext 207. Romaine Ahlstrom, *Manager.*
Holdings: Bks 7000. **Published Guides:** Los Angeles Public Library since 1872 (catalogue). **Subjects:** Travel & Exploration; History of Mexico (19th century); California Cookery; Exploration of the West, Natural History; Fine Press. **Budget:** $18,000 per year. **Access Policy:** Apply to manager.

SOUTHWEST MUSEUM. Braun Research Library, Rare Books & Manuscript Collection. PO Box 128, Highland Park Sta, Los Angeles 90042. Tel: 213-221-2164. Daniela Moneta, *Librarian.*
Holdings: Bks 50,000; Mss 550 ln ft; 100,000 historic photographs. **Subjects:** Americana; Books about Books; Ephemera; Fine & Applied Arts; History; History of Science (Anthropology); Literature 1900 to present; Natural History; Press Books; Regional—Southwest, California, Arizona; Travel & Exploration; Anthropology; Archaeology; American Indian Studies; Mexican Imprints; Western Americana. **Budget:** $25,000 per year. **Access Policy:** Apply to librarian; photocopying not permitted.

UNIVERSITY OF CALIFORNIA, LOS ANGELES. The Art Library, Elmer Belt Library of Vinciana. 2250 Dickson Art Center, Los Angeles 90024. Tel: 213-825-3817. Joyce Pellerano Ludmer, *Head Librarian.* **Staff:** Raymond Reece, *Public Services Librarian.*
Holdings: 9000 volumes. **Scope:** Leonardo da Vinci & the Italian Renaissance. **Published Guides:** Francis L. Finger, *Catalogue of the Incunabula in the Elmer Belt Library of Vinciana* (1971). **Subjects:** Fine & Applied Arts; Incunabula; Regional—Italy, 1400–1600. **Access Policy:** Open to public for reference.

UNIVERSITY OF CALIFORNIA, LOS ANGELES. Biomedical Library, History & Special Collections Division. Los Angeles 90024. Tel: 213-825-6940. Victoria Steele, *Head.*

Holdings: Bks 36,000 (13,000 rare, 23,000 support); Mss 36 ln ft; pamphlet file; prints & portraits file; museum objects; slides. **Scope:** The history of the health & life sciences, which encompasses, in the health sciences, dentistry, medicine, neurology, nursing, ophthalmology, pharmacology, psychiatry; in the life sciences, biology, botany, ornithology, zoology. **Published Guides:** *The John A. Benjamin Collection Catalogue & First Supplement* (UCLA Library, 1968). **Subjects:** History of Medicine. **Budget:** $60,000 per year. **Access Policy:** Open to public, supervised use.

UNIVERSITY OF CALIFORNIA, LOS ANGELES. William Andrews Clark Library. 2520 Cimarron St, Los Angeles 90018. Tel: 213-731-8529. Thomas F. Wright, *Librarian.* **Staff:** John Bidwell, *Reference/Acquisitions Librarian;* Carol Briggs, *Manuscript Cataloguer & Archivist;* Pat McCloskey, *Head Cataloguer.*
Holdings: Bks 80,724; Mss 125 ln ft; Archives 225 ln ft; maps; graphic works. **Scope:** Primary collection, defined as "English Cultural Life" (1640–1750), includes music & all other areas except medicine. **Published Guides:** *Dictionary Catalog of W. A. Clark* (G. K. Hall, 1974, 15v.) **Subjects:** Books about Books; History; History of Science; Literature 1640–1800; Press Books; Regional—Montana; Religion; Travel & Exploration; John Dryden; Oscar Wilde. **Access Policy:** Valid research projects, identification required.

UNIVERSITY OF CALIFORNIA, LOS ANGELES. Research Library, Department of Special Collections. 405 Hilgard Ave, Los Angeles 90024. Tel: 213-825-4879, 4988. David S. Zeidberg, *Head.* **Staff:** James Davis, *Rare Books, Literary Manuscripts;* Hilda Bohem, *Ephemera, Photographica, Public service.*
Holdings: Bks 160,000; Mss 18,000,000 items. **Scope:** Collections that support UCLA teaching & re-search programs in the humanities & social sciences. **Subjects:** Children's Literature; Ephemera; Illustrated Books; Incunabula (Venetian); Regional—California; Travel & Exploration; 19th-century British Fiction; Early Venetian Imprints (including Aldine & Giunta); Popular Literature; D. H. Lawrence; Henry Miller; Anaïs Nin; Gertrude Stein; Richard Nuetra; Orsini Family Archives; Ralph Bunche; Black American Fiction; Japanese-American Research Project; Captain James Cook; Maria Edgeworth; Spinoza; Photography; California Cookbooks; Local Imprints; Los Angeles *Daily News* Morgue; Norman Douglas; The Poetry Bookshop; Tauchnitz Editions; Fictitious Imprints; Mountaineering; Early English-Language Children's Books. **Budget:** $279,000 per year. **Access Policy:** Readers must register.

CALIFORNIA, Pasadena

CALIFORNIA INSTITUTE OF TECHNOLOGY. Millikan Library, Institute Archives. 1202 E California Blvd, Pasadena 91125. Tel: 213-356-6433. Judith R. Goodstein, *Archivist.*
Holdings: Bks 2500; Mss 500,000; landmark scientific equipment; scientific photographs; rare maps; scientific illustrations. **Scope:** History of astronomy & physics since 1543; small collections of science landmark books & prints in chemistry, mathematics & geology; history of astronomy books. **Published Guides:** *The Robert Andrews Millikan Collection at the California Institute of Technology* (Caltech, 1977); *The Theodore von Karman Collection at the California Institute of Technology* (Caltech, 1981). **Subjects:** History of Mathematics & Science; Illustrated Books. **Access Policy:** Not open to public.

CALIFORNIA, Riverside

UNIVERSITY OF CALIFORNIA, RIVERSIDE. University Library, Special Collections. PO Box 5900, Riverside

92517. Tel: 714-787-3233. Clifford R. Wurfel, *Librarian*. **Staff:** Araxie Churukian, *Assistant Librarian;* George Slusser, *Curator, Eaton Collection of Science Fiction.*

Holdings: Bks 30,000; Mss 300 ln ft; 50 ln ft photographs. **Published Guides:** *The Sadakichi Hartmann Papers—1980; Dictionary Catalog of the J. Lloyd Eaton Collection* (G. K. Hall, 1982). **Subjects:** History; History of Science; Literature 1640 to present; Natural History; Regional—Southern California; Science Fiction; Citrus & Sub-Tropical Agriculture; Music Theory; Paraguayan History; Thomas Hardy Dramas; Ezra Pound; British Religious & Political History (17th–18th centuries); Paris (19th century); Utopias (19th–20th centuries); British Literature (1860–1960); American Boys' Books. **Budget:** $25,000 per year. **Access Policy:** Open to public.

CALIFORNIA, Sacramento

CALIFORNIA STATE LIBRARY. Reference Center, Rare Book Collection. PO Box 2037, Sacramento 95809. Tel: 916-322-4570. Irene Stone, *Supervising Librarian*.

Holdings: Bks 5000. **Scope:** Miscellaneous collection of rare books with strengths in art & illustrated books, voyages & travel & Americana. **Access Policy:** Open to the public.

CALIFORNIA STATE LIBRARY. Special Collections Branch, California Section. PO Box 2037, Sacramento 95809. Tel: 916-324-4873. Gary F. Kurutz, *Program Manager*. **Staff:** Thomas Fante, *Senior Librarian;* Tere Silva, *Preservation Officer;* Richard Terry, D. Geraldine Davis, *Processing Librarians;* John Gonzales, Sibylle Zemitis, *Reference Librarians*.

Holdings: Bks 20,000; Mss 600 ln ft; 150,000 photographs; 5000 maps; 1000 prints & posters; 70,000 reels of film; 8000 volumes of newspapers & massive collection of ephemera. **Scope:** California history from pre-historic period to the present; includes strong collection of California fine press. California manuscripts emphasize pioneer period, San Francisco & Sacramento area business, economic & political history. **Published Guides:** Gary F. Kurutz, *Fifty Treasures of the California State Library;* Thomas M. Fante, *Fragments of California's Past; The Manuscript Collections of the State Library's California Section* (all published by Calif. State Library, 1982). **Subjects:** Americana; Books about Books; Ephemera; Fine & Applied Arts; History; History of Science; Illustrated Books; Incunabula; Law; Literature 1640–1800; Natural History; Press Books (California only); Regional—Californiana & US local history; Religion; Theater & Performing Arts (California); Travel & Exploration; History of Western Photography. **Budget:** $15,000 per year. **Access Policy:** Open to the public. (See also Sutro Library branch in San Francisco.)

CALIFORNIA STATE RAILROAD MUSEUM LIBRARY. 111 I St, Sacramento 95814. Tel: 916-323-8073. Stephen E. Drew, *Curator*. **Staff:** Walter P. Gray III, *Archivist;* Ellen Schwartz, *Librarian*.

Holdings: Bks 4500; Mss 6000 ln ft; 1,000,000 photographs. **Scope:** Railroad history, 1830 to present, with emphasis on operating companies in Trans-Mississippi West & North American Railroad technology. **Subjects:** History of Technology; Western Railroad History. **Budget:** $5000 per year. **Access Policy:** Open to public for research.

CALIFORNIA, Saint Helena

THE SILVERADO MUSEUM. PO Box 409, Saint Helena 94574. Tel: 707-963-3757. Ellen Shaffer, *Curator*.

Holdings: 7600 including books, manuscripts, letters, photographs, sculptures, paintings, memorabilia. **Subjects:** Robert Louis Stevenson & his immediate circle, including Fanny

Stevenson & Isobel Osbourne Field (formerly Isobel Strong), 1850 to present. **Access Policy:** Open to public; rare material available to qualified research workers.

CALIFORNIA, San Diego

SAN DIEGO PUBLIC LIBRARY. Wangenheim Room. 820 E St, San Diego 92111. Tel: 619-236-5807. Eileen Boyle, *Librarian.*

Holdings: Bks 7000; Mss 3 ln ft; 3 writing implements; 101 Hogarth prints; books in various formats ranging from Babylonian tablets & papyrus to cassettes. **Scope:** Illustrates the development of the book through the ages in its various aspects — papermaking, bookbinding, book illustration, the history of printing. **Published Guides:** "The Wangenheim Room" (San Diego Public Library). **Subjects:** Books about Books; Illustrated Books; Incunabula; Press Books. **Budget:** $1000 per year. **Access Policy:** Open to public.

SAN DIEGO STATE UNIVERSITY. Library, Special Collections. San Diego 92182. Tel: 619-265-6791. Douglas Cargille, *Librarian.* **Staff:** Sharon L. Johnson, *Library Assistant.*

Holdings: Bks 23,000; Mss 105 ln ft. **Scope:** Emphasis on bookbinding, 18th- & 19th-century literature, theater & drama. **Subjects:** Books about Books; History of Mathematics, Medicine & Science; Literature 1800–1900; Natural History; Regional — Southwest Americana; Theater & Performing Arts; Astronomy; Desi Arnaz Film Collection; Ernst Zinner Collection (early rare astronomical works); Reginald S. Davis Collection (orchids); Papers of Jan Lowenbach (Czechoslovakian composer). **Access Policy:** Open to public.

CALIFORNIA, San Francisco

CALIFORNIA HISTORICAL SOCIETY LIBRARY. 2099 Pacific Ave, San Francisco 94109. Tel: 415-567-1848. Bruce L. Johnson, *Director.* **Staff:** Douglas M. Haller, *Curator of Photographs;* Stephen J. Fletcher, *Assistant Curator of Photographs;* Waverly L. Lowell, *Curator of Manuscripts;* Sandra McCoy Larson, *Archivist;* Glenn E. Humphreys, *Curator of the Kemble Collection;* Joy Berry, Jocelyn Moss, Judy Sheldon, *Librarians;* Gerald D. Wright, *Genealogy Librarian.*

Holdings: Bks 45,000; Mss 1500 ln ft; photographs 571 ln ft; pamphlets 154 ln ft; sheet music 12 ln ft; maps/posters 115 oversize drawers. **Scope:** Subjects covering California & the West. Archives include those of ACLU-Northern California, California Tomorrow, League of Women Voters, the Peoples Temple of the Disciples of Christ & the archives of the *San Francisco Chronicle.* **Published Guides:** Diana Lachatanere, *Preliminary Listing of the San Francisco Manuscript Collections in the Library of the California Historical Society* (CHS, 1980). **Subjects:** Books about Books; Children's Literature (California); Ephemera; Fine & Applied Arts; History; Illustrated Books; Law; Literature 1850 to present; Press Books; Regional — Western US; Theater & Performing Arts; Travel & Exploration; Pacific Coast Voyages; Spanish/Mexican Era; California Gold Rush; Transportation Development; 19th-century Industries. **Access Policy:** Apply to director.

SAN FRANCISCO PUBLIC LIBRARY. Rare Books & Special Collections. Civic Center, San Francisco 94102. Tel: 415-558-3940. Johanna Goldschmid, *Curator.* **Staff:** Sue Taylor, *Curator, Harrison Collection.*

Holdings: Bks 31,000. **Scope:** Grabhorn Collection on the History of the Printed Book, which includes examples of printing (1471 to present); Harrison Collection of Calligraphy & Lettering; Schmulowitz Collection of Wit & Humor. **Subjects:** Books about Books; Incunabula; Press Books. **Budget:** $10,000 per year. **Access Policy:** Open to public.

SAN FRANCISCO STATE UNIVERSITY. J. Paul Leonard Library, Frank V. de Bellis Collection of the California State University. 1630 Holloway Ave, San Francisco 94132. Tel: 415-469-1649. Serena de Bellis, *Librarian.* **Staff:** Rose Grabstein, *Consultant for Archaeology;* Eleanor Selfridge-Field, *Consultant for Musicology.*

Holdings: Bks 12,500; Mss 50 ln ft; 10,000 music scores; 25,000 archival sound recordings, periodicals, prints, drawings, microfilms, artifacts, coins. **Scope:** A library-museum of Italian authors & subjects representing the civilization of ancient & modern Italy, particularly in the areas of history, literature, fine arts & music. **Published Guides:** *The Frank V. de Bellis Collection* (1967); *Etruscan, Roman & Greek Artifacts in the Frank V. de Bellis Collection* (1976). **Subjects:** (As pertaining to Italy) Books about Books; Fine & Applied Arts; History; Illustrated Books; Incunabula; Literature pre-1640 to present; Press Books; Regional—Italy; Theater & Performing Arts; Music Treatises (16th–19th centuries); Music Scores (mss, 15th–19th centuries & printed, 16th–20th centuries). **Access Policy:** Open to adults with valid identification for serious study.

SUTRO LIBRARY (a branch of California State Library). 480 Winston Dr, San Francisco 94132. Tel: 415-557-0421. Gary Kurutz, *Program Manager.* **Staff:** Eleanor Capelle, *Senior Librarian;* Frank Glover, *Reference Librarian;* Tere Silva, *Preservation Officer.*

Holdings: Bks 75,000; Mss 40 ln ft. **Scope:** Rare book collection of Adolph Sutro, former mayor of San Francisco, comprising Mexican pamphlets, government documents, manuscripts, broadsides & periodicals on the history of Mexico, 1800–1875; rare early English pamphlets including the Sir Joseph Banks Collections; 13th- & 14th-century Yosemite Hebrew manuscripts; Fine Printing; Incunabula such as *The Nuremberg Chronicle;*

first four folios of Shakespeare. **Published Guides:** *Anatomy of a Library; Catalogue of Sutro Library Hebraica Collection.* **Subjects:** Americana; Economics; History; Illustrated Books; Literature pre-1640–1800; Regional—Great Britain, United States except California; Religion; Theater & Performing Arts; Mexican History; Genealogy; Natural History; History of Science & Technology; History of Medicine; Description & Travel. **Budget:** $10,000 per year. **Access Policy:** Open to the public.

UNIVERSITY OF CALIFORNIA, SAN FRANCISCO. The Library, Special Collections. San Francisco 94143. Tel: 415-666-2334. Nancy Whitten Zinn, *Head.*

Holdings: Bks 10,000; Mss 150; artifacts, illustrations/photographs. **Scope:** Collection supports research & teaching in the history of health sciences, dentistry, medicine, nursing, pharmacy, hospitals & basic sciences. **Subjects:** History of Medicine; Regional—California; Californiana (health related); Anesthesiology; Obstetrics & Gynecology; Toxicology & Forensic Medicine; Surgery & Anatomy. **Budget:** $10,000 per year. **Access Policy:** Open to public.

UNIVERSITY OF SAN FRANCISCO. Richard A. Gleeson Library, Donohue Rare Book Room. San Francisco 94117. Tel: 415-666-6718. D. Steven Corey, *Special Collections Librarian.*

Holdings: Bks: 15,000; Mss 200 ln ft. **Subjects:** Books about Books; Ephemera; Illustrated Books; Incunabula; Literature 1640–1900; Press Books; Religion; L. Frank Baum & Oziana. **Budget:** $30,000–$40,000 per year. **Access Policy:** Open to public.

CALIFORNIA, San Marino

THE HUNTINGTON LIBRARY, ART GALLERY & BOTANICAL GARDENS. 1151 Oxford Rd, San Marino 91108. Tel: 818-792-6141. Daniel H. Woodward,

Librarian. **Staff:** Mary Robertson, *Curator of Manuscripts;* Alan Jutzi, *Curator of Rare Books.*

Holdings: Bks 336,464; Mss 2,500,000; 252,822 reference books. **Scope:** Concentration of Anglo-American literature & history from the Renaissance through the 19th century. Selected authors & areas of history in 20th century; continental imprints; small collection of English & European medieval manuscripts from the 12th–15th centuries. **Published Guides:** Available in 1984 from library. **Subjects:** Americana; Books about Books; Children's Literature; Economics; Ephemera; Fine & Applied Arts; History; History of Mathematics; Medicine & Science; Illustrated Books; Incunabula; Law; Literature pre-1640 to present; Natural History; Press Books; Regional — California & the American West, England (& individual English counties); Religion; Theater & Performing Arts; Travel & Exploration. **Access Policy:** Open to qualified scholars.

CALIFORNIA, Santa Barbara

UNIVERSITY OF CALIFORNIA, SANTA BARBARA. Library, Department of Special Collections. Santa Barbara 93106. Tel: 805-961-3420. Christian F. Brun, *Head & University Archivist.*

Holdings: Bks 150,000; Ms 301,756; Trade Catalogue Collection 200,000 items. **Scope:** William Wyles Collection — Civil War, Lincoln; Skofield Printers Collection — fine printing, history of printing; modern English & American author collection; Darwin & Evolution Collection; Marie Stopes Birth Control Collection; Chase Community Development & Conservation Collection; Romaine Trade Catalogue Collection. **Published Guides:** *UCSB Library Department of Special Collections* (pamphlet); *A Checklist of Manuscripts;* Jay Monaghan, *William Wyles & the William Wyles Collection.* **Subjects:** Books about Books; History; Illustrated Books; Literature 1900 to present; Press Books; Regional — California & Southwest; Religion; Evolution; Circus; Censorship. **Access Policy:** Apply to head.

CALIFORNIA, Santa Cruz

UNIVERSITY OF CALIFORNIA, SANTA CRUZ. McHenry Library, Special Collections. Santa Cruz 95064. Tel: 408-429-2547. Rita Bottoms, *Head.* **Staff:** Jerry James, *Bibliographer for Literature;* Christine Bunting, *Head of Slide Library/Art Bibliographer;* Margaret Felts, *Bibliographer for South Pacific.*

Holdings: Mss 60 ln ft. **Subjects:** Books about Books; Ephemera; Fine & Applied Arts; History; Literature 1900 to present; Press Books; Regional — Santa Cruz, California; Thomas Carlyle; Santa Cruziana; Contemporary Literature; Kenneth Patchen; Edward Weston Photographs; Lick Observatory Rare Books; Fine Press; Robert Heinlein Archive; Californiana; Trianon Press Archive; South Pacific. **Budget:** $8750. **Access Policy.** Open to public, appointment necessary.

CALIFORNIA, Stanford

STANFORD UNIVERSITY LIBRARIES. Department of Special Collections. Stanford 94305. Tel: 415-497-4054. Michael T. Ryan, *Director.*

Holdings: Bks 100,000; Mss 6,000,000 items; prints; photographs; maps. **Scope:** Collection ranges from the third century BC papyri fragments through representative examples of early printed books to modern literary manuscripts. **Subjects:** Books about Books; Children's Literature; History; History of Science; Illustrated Books; Literature 1800 to present; Press Books; Regional — California; Theater & Performing Arts. **Access Policy:** Open to qualified researchers.

COLORADO, Boulder

UNIVERSITY OF COLORADO AT BOULDER. Norlin Library, Special Collections. Campus Box 184, Boulder 80309. Tel: 303-492-6144. Nora J. Quinlan, *Head.* **Staff:** Carol Klemme, *Cataloguer.*

Holdings: Bks 30,000; Mss 560 ln ft. **Scope:** Rare books & manuscripts as well as special subject collections. Includes 17th-, 18th-, 19th- & 20th-century English literature, illustrated books, Colorado literature, mountaineering, John McDonald, etc. **Published Guides:** Flyer available in 1984. **Subjects:** Books about Books; Children's Literature (Epsteen); Economics (Leavens); Fine & Applied Arts; History (Willard, Creighton); History of Mathematics (Kemper); Illustrated Books (Creamer); Literature 1900 to present; Press Books (Goldman); Regional—Colorado Literature; Travel & Exploration; Seiffert Collection; Huxley Collection; Masefield Collection; Mountaineering Collection; Works of the Press at Colorado College; Meteorology Collection; Jean Stafford Collection; John McDonald Collection. **Budget:** $30,000 FY 1983-1984. **Access Policy:** Open to public.

COLORADO, Denver

COLORADO HISTORICAL SOCIETY. Printed Books & Ephemera & Manuscripts Departments. 1300 Broadway, Denver 80203. Tel: 303-866-3682. Katherine Kane, *Acting Curator, Books;* Lee Scamehorn, *Curator, Manuscripts.* **Staff:** Alice Sharp, *Cataloguer, Books;* Margot West, *Assistant Curator, Manuscripts.*

Holdings: Bks 40,000; Mss 3000 ln ft. **Scope:** Books: Colorado & the West. Manuscripts: business, social, political papers, diaries, corporate reports, personal papers. **Published Guides:** calendars; guide to manuscripts. **Subjects:** Ephemera; History; Regional—Rocky Mountain Area; Colorado History. **Access Policy:** Open to public for reference use.

CONNECTICUT, Hartford

CONNECTICUT HISTORICAL SOCIETY. Library. One Elizabeth St, Hartford 06105. Tel: 203-236-5621. **Staff:** Ruth Blair, *Manuscript Cataloguer.*

Holdings: Bks 35,000; Mss 1400 ln ft. **Scope:** Connecticut imprints; sermons; children's books; almanacs; Americana/personal correspondence; letterbooks, diaries, account books of Connecticut people; town records; business, labor, financial, educational & club records. **Subjects:** Americana; Children's Literature; Ephemera; History; Regional—Connecticut & New England; Religion (sermons). **Budget:** $60,000 per year. **Access Policy:** Apply to curator.

THE STOWE-DAY FOUNDATION. The Stowe-Day Library. 77 Forest St, Hartford 06105. Tel: 203-522-9258, 9259. Diana Royce, *Librarian.* **Staff:** Roberta Bradford, *Assistant Librarian;* Thomas Harkins, *Manuscript Cataloguer.*

Holdings: Bks 15,000; Mss 150,000 items; 7500 photographs. **Scope:** 19th-century Americana with particular interest in Harriet Beecher Stowe, Mark Twain, Charles Dudley Warner, William Gillette, the family of Lyman Beecher; decorative arts; landscape design; architecture; black history; the woman suffrage movement. **Published Guides:** *The Papers of Harriet Beecher Stowe* (Stowe-Day Foundation, 1977); *The Isabella Beecher Hooker Project* (Stowe-Day Foundation, 1979). **Subjects:** Americana; Ephemera; Fine & Applied Arts; History; Literature 1640-1900; Regional—Connecticut & Hartford; Religion; Theater & Performing Arts. **Access Policy:** Open to public.

TRINITY COLLEGE. Watkinson Library. 300 Summit St, Hartford 06106. Tel: 203-527-3151 ext 307. Ralph S. Emerick, *Librarian.* **Staff:** Jeffrey H. Kaimowitz, *Curator;* Margaret F. Sax, *Associate Curator;* Karen Clarke, *Assistant Curator for Ornithology Collection.*

Holdings: Bks 162,500; Mss 100,000 items. **Published Guides:** *Edwin Arlington Robinson: A Bio-Bibliography* (1969); *The Robert Frost Collection in the Watkinson Library*

(1974); *The Allerton C. Hickmott Ashendene Press Collection at Trinity College* (1979); *Ornithological Books in the Library of Trinity College, Hartford. Including the Library of Ostrom Endens* (1983). **Subjects:** Americana; Books about Books; Children's Literature; Ephemera; History; Illustrated Books; Incunabula; Literature pre-1640 to present; Natural History; Press Books; Religion; Travel & Exploration; Maritime History; Horology; Ornithology; Sir Walter Scott; Walton: Compleat Angler. **Budget:** $25,000 per year. **Access Policy:** Open to public.

CONNECTICUT, Middletown

WESLEYAN UNIVERSITY LIBRARY. Special Collections & Archives. Middletown 06457. Tel: 203-347-9411 ext 2456. Elizabeth Swaim, *Special Collections Librarian and University Archivist.*
   Holdings: Bks 20,000; Mss 50 ln ft. **Scope:** A general collection supporting an undergraduate level liberal arts curriculum, ranging from incunabula to 20th century books, with strengths in history of printing, English and American literature & civilization, Methodistica, and social credit. **Published Guides:** Brochure available from the library. **Access Policy:** Open to the public by appointment.

CONNECTICUT, New Britain

CENTRAL CONNECTICUT STATE UNIVERSITY. Elihu Burritt Library, Special Collections Department. Wells St, New Britain 06050. Tel: 203-827-7524. Frank Gagliardi, *Associate Director of Library Services.*
   Holdings: Bks 13,002; Mss 100 ln ft. **Subjects:** Books about Books; Children's Literature; Illustrated Books; Press Books; Walter Hart Blumenthal; Frederic W. Goudy; Daniel Webster; Thomas Hardy; Bruce Rogers; Records of the First Church of Christ, New Britain, 1754-1930; University Archives 1849 to present; Dutch Children's Book Collection; Middletown & Berlin Turnpike Company Papers,

1806-1858. **Budget:** $2500 per year. **Access Policy:** Open to qualified researchers.

CONNECTICUT, New Haven

YALE CENTER FOR BRITISH ART. Rare Books Department. PO Box 2120 Yale Sta, New Haven 06520. Tel: 203-432-4099. Joan M. Friedman, *Curator.* **Staff:** Elisabeth Fairman, *Catalogue Librarian.*
   Holdings: Bks 22,000; Mss 24 ln ft. **Scope:** English illustrated books; the fine arts in England (1700-1850); British topography. **Published Guides:** J. R. Abbey, *Life in England; Scenery of Great Britain; Travel* (Yale Center for British Art, 1953-1957); *Selected Paintings, Drawings and Books* (1977). Leaflet available from library. **Subjects:** Fine & Applied Arts; Illustrated Books; Incunabula; Regional—Great Britain; Travel & Exploration; Color Printing. **Access Policy:** Open to public.

YALE UNIVERSITY. Beinecke Rare Book & Manuscript Library. PO Box 1603A, Yale Sta, New Haven 06520. Tel: 203-436-8438. Ralph W. Franklin, *Director.* **Staff:** Marjorie G. Wynne, *Research Librarian;* Patricia M. Howell, *Public Services/Reference Librarian;* Suzanne Rutter, *Technical Services Librarian;* Halyna Lobay, *Bibliographic Librarian;* David Schoonover, *Curator, Collection of American Literature;* Christa Sammons, *Curator, German Literature Collection;* Stephen R. Parks, *Curator, Osborn Collection & Pre-1800 Manuscripts;* George A. Miles, *Curator, Western Americana Collection.*
   Holdings: Bks 500,000; Mss 10,500 ln ft. **Scope:** Beinecke Rare Book & Manuscript Library contains the principal rare books & literary manuscripts of Yale University & serves as a center for research by students, faculty & other serious readers, whether connected with Yale or not. The library contains five major collections: the General Collection of Rare Books & Manuscripts, the Collection

of American Literature, the Collection of Western Americana, the German Literature Collection & the Osborn Collection of English literary & historical manuscripts. **Published Guides:** *The Beinecke Rare Book and Manuscript Library: A Guide to Its Collections* (Yale University Library, 1974). **Subjects:** Americana; Books about Books; Children's Literature; Economics; Fine & Applied Arts; History; History of Science; Illustrated Books; Incunabula; Law; Literature pre-1640 to present; Natural History; Press Books; Regional—Western America & Tibet; Religion; Theater & Performing Arts; Travel & Exploration; Pre-1600 Manuscripts; Papyri; Near Eastern Manuscripts; Judaica; Black Literature to present; Playing Cards. **Access Policy:** Open to adults for scholarly research; photo-identification required.

YALE UNIVERSITY. Medical Library. Medical Historical Library. 333 Cedar St, New Haven 06510. Tel: 203-785-4354. Ferenc Gyorgyey, *Historical Librarian.* **Staff:** Thomas Falco, *Assistant Historical Librarian;* Ellen Danforth, *Cataloguer of Streeter Collection of Weights and Measures;* Susan Wheeler, *Cataloguer of Fry Medical Print Collection.*

Holdings: Bks 60,000; 2000 prints; 3000 items in Weights and Measures Collection. **Scope:** Rare books in the history of medicine, including 313 incunables and some landmark books in the history of general science. **Published Guides:** *The Harvey Cushing Collection of Books and Manuscripts* (Schuman, 1943). **Subjects:** Americana; History of Medicine; History of Science; Illustrated Books; Incunabula; Natural History; Anatomy; Anesthesia; Inoculation and Vaccination; Ichthyology; the works of Hippocrates, Vesalius, and William Harvey. **Access Policy:** Open to qualified researchers by appointment.

CONNECTICUT, New London

CONNECTICUT COLLEGE LIBRARY. Mohegan Ave, New London 06320. Tel: 203-447-7622. Mary Kent, *College Librarian.* **Staff:** W. James MacDonald, *Reference Librarian;* Mary T. Odyniec, *Associate Reference Librarian;* Marian Shilstone, *Collection Development Librarian.*

Holdings: Bks: 11,000; Mss 20 boxes; 150 broadsides. **Scope:** Chiefly arts & humanities but inclusive of all the liberal arts. **Subjects:** Americana; Books about Books; Children's Literature; Fine & Applied Arts; Literature 1900 to present; Press Books; Regional—New London County & Connecticut; Religion; Travel & Exploration; American Woman's Collection (papers of several prominent figures, including Prudence Crandall, Belle Moskowitz, Lydia Sigourney, Alice Hamilton & Frances Perkins); Wyman Ballad Collection (350 volumes from the Library of Loraine Wyman). **Budget:** $2500 per year. **Access Policy:** Open to public.

DELAWARE, Wilmington

ELEUTHERIAN MILLS HISTORICAL LIBRARY. PO Box 3630 Greenville, Wilmington 19807. Tel: 302-658-2400. Heddy A. Richter, *Head, Imprints Department.* **Staff:** Nina Walls, *Cataloguer;* Nannie W. Brightwell, *Catalogue Specialist;* Michael H. Nash, *Curator, Archives & Manuscripts Dept;* Dorothy Jenner, Christopher Baer, *Archival Specialists.*

Holdings: Bks 16,000; Mss 22,000. **Scope:** Extensive collection of business, economic & technological history of the Middle-Atlantic region excluding New York State. Manuscripts include business archives from I. E. du Pont de Nemours & Co, Sun Oil Co & Sperry Corp. Imprints include early American technology in depth & large collection of trade catalogues. **Published Guides:** J. B. Riggs, *A Guide to Manuscripts in the Eleutherian Mills Historical Library* (1970, Supplement 1978). **Subjects:** Regional—US Middle-Atlantic history; US Economic History & Conditions; History of Technology & Transportation; Explosives

& Pyrotechnics; Manufacturers; French Revolution. **Budget:** $12,000–$15,000 per year. **Access Policy:** Open to public for research upon approval of written application.

DELAWARE, Winterthur

H. F. DU PONT WINTERTHUR MUSEUM. Library. Winterthur 19735. Tel: 302-656-8591 ext 315, 227. **Staff:** Beatrice Taylor, Barbara Adams, *Downs Collection Librarians;* Frank H. Sommer, *Belknap Librarian;* Eleanor Thompson, *Librarian, Collection of Printed Books & Periodicals;* Edward McKinstry, *Associate Librarian.*
  Holdings: Bks 15,000; Mss 70,260 lots; 5000 microfiche cards; 3430 microfilm reels; 1400 photostats. **Scope:** Early American culture, especially architecture, painting & decorative arts & its European origins before 1914. **Published Guides:** *The Winterthur Museum Libraries Collection of Printed Books & Periodicals; Rare Book Catalogue,* vols VIII & IX (Scholarly Resources, 1974). **Subjects:** Americana; Books about Books; Children's Literature; Economics; Ephemera; Fine & Applied Arts; Illustrated Books; Natural History; Travel & Exploration; Design Books for Architecture & Decorative Arts; Drawing Books; Trade Catalogues; Sports; Gardens. **Access Policy:** Open to public.

DISTRICT OF COLUMBIA

CATHOLIC UNIVERSITY OF AMERICA. John K. Mullen of Denver Memorial Library, Rare Books & Special Collections. Washington 20064. Tel: 202-635-5091. Carolyn T. Lee, *Curator.*
  Holdings: Bks 50,000; Mss 100. **Scope:** Theology & canon law; church history; travel books; Irish culture; botany; Catholic Americana (19th century; parish histories); catechisms. **Subjects:** Americana; Ephemera; History; History of Science; Illustrated Books (pre-20th century); Incunabula; Law (canon law); Literature 1640 to present; Natural History; Religion; Travel & Exploration; Knights of Malta; Henry James; Fine Bindings (15th–20th century); Gilt & Marbled Papers; Clementine Library of the Albani Family of Urbino (including Jansenism & Law, 1473–1800). **Access Policy:** Open to public by appointment.

FOLGER SHAKESPEARE LIBRARY. 201 E Capitol St, Washington 20003. Tel: 202-544-4600. Philip A. Knachel, *Acting Director.* **Staff:** Lilly Lievsay, *Curator of Books & Head, Cataloguing Department;* Laetitia Yeandle, *Curator of Manuscripts;* Elizabeth Niemyer, *Acquisition Librarian;* Nati H. Krivatsy, *Reference Librarian.*
  Holdings: Bks 223,570; Mss 50,000 vols; 1000 reels of microfilm. **Scope:** Shakespeare (books, playbills, art, promptbooks); history of English & Western civilizations in 16th & 17th centuries; history of the theater in England especially 16th–18th centuries; Renaissance drama, history & literature. **Published Guides:** *Catalog of Printed Books of The Folger Shakespeare Library* (G. K. Hall, 1970, supplements 1976 & 1981); *Catalog of Manuscripts of the Folger Shakespeare Library* (G. K. Hall, 1971); *The Widening Circle: The Story of the Folger Library* (1976). **Subjects:** History; Literature pre-1640–1800; Religion; Theater and Performing Arts; Shakespeareana. **Access Policy:** Open to post-PhD scholars & PhD candidates.

GALLAUDET COLLEGE. Library, Gallaudet Archives. 800 Florida Ave, Washington 20002. Tel: 202-651-5582. David L. de Lorenzo, *Archivist & Special Collections Librarian.*
  Holdings: Bks 6753; Mss 365 ln ft; deaf periodicals (pre-1900) 206 ln ft. **Scope:** Rare books: deaf people, deafness, education of the deaf, linguistics, sign language, hearing loss, vocalism, oralism, psychology & sociology of the deaf. Manuscripts: deaf people & hearing people involved with research of the deaf & deafness. **Subjects:** Americana; Fine & Applied Arts; History;

History of Medicine; Linguistics; Sociology; Literature 1640–1800; Religion; Deafness; Deaf People; Minorities. **Access Policy:** Open to public.

GEORGE WASHINGTON UNIVERSITY. Gelman Library, Special Collections Division. 2130 H St NW, Washington 20052. Tel: 202-676-7497, 7549. *Staff:* Suellen M. Towers, Sandra L. Powers, *Assistant Curators;* Mary Faith Pankin, *Special Collections Cataloguer;* Frances A. McDonnell, *Special Projects.*

Holdings: Bks 40,000; Mss 1500 ln ft; 700 maps; 400 prints & drawings; 1200 photographs. **Scope:** Printed materials & manuscripts (15th century to present). **Subjects:** Americana; Books about Books; Fine & Applied Arts; Regional — Washington & Mid-Atlantic States; Theater & Performing Arts; Labor History; Transportation History; Historic Preservation. **Access Policy:** Open to registered researchers with valid identification, for reference only.

GEORGETOWN UNIVERSITY. Joseph Mark Lauinger Memorial Library, Special Collections Division. 37th & O Sts NW, Washington 20057. Tel: 202-625-3230. George M. Barringer, *Librarian.* Nicholas B. Scheetz, *Manuscripts Librarian;* Jon K. Reynolds, *University Archivist;* L. Carl Chamberlain, *Rare Books Cataloguer.*

Holdings: Bks 62,500; Mss 7000 ln ft; 125,000 photographs; 6000 audiotapes; 2500 original editorial cartoons; 5000 prints & drawings. **Scope:** Americana, English & American Literature, linguistics, political science, diplomacy, foreign affairs & intelligence, Jesuits in America. **Published Guides:** *Scholar's Guide to Intelligence Literature* (University Publications of America, 1983). **Subjects:** History; Illustrated Books; Incunabula; Literature 1800 to present; Press Books; Regional — Washington, DC & Maryland; Religion; Travel & Exploration; Russell J. Bowen Collection of Intelligence Literature; Charles Dickens; A. C. Swinburne; Graham Greene; Evelyn Waugh; US Congress. **Budget:** $15,000. **Access Policy:** Open to public.

HOWARD UNIVERSITY. Moorland-Spingarn Research Center, Manuscript Division. 500 Howard Place, Washington 20059. Tel: 202-636-7479, 7480. Thomas Battle, *Curator of Manuscripts.* **Staff:** Karen L. Jefferson, *Senior Manuscript Librarian;* Deborah Richardson, *Music Librarian;* Marcia B. Bracey, *Prints & Photographs Librarian;* Elinor D. Sinnette, *Oral History Librarian.*

Holdings: Mss 6000 ln ft; Oral History: 700 tapes & transcripts; 20,000 prints & photographs; 35,000 pieces of sheet music. **Scope:** 400 collections documenting various professional & organizational activities of Black Americans in the United States. **Published Guides:** *Guide to Processed Collections in the Manuscript Division of the Moorland Spingarn Research Center* (Moorland-Spingarn, 1983); *The Glenn Carrington Collection: A Guide to the Books, Manuscripts, Music, and Recordings* (Moorland-Spingarn, 1977). **Subjects:** Literature 1900 to present (Harlem Renaissance period); Regional — Washington, DC local history; Medicine; Law; Higher Education; Civil Rights; Journalism. **Access Policy:** Open to public by appointment.

HOWARD UNIVERSITY. Moorland-Spingarn Research Center, Spingarn Collection. 500 Howard Place, Washington 20059. Tel: 202-636-7239. James P. Johnson, *Chief Librarian.*

Holdings: Bks 12,700. **Scope:** Books by people of African descent, 16th to 20th century, from an Afro-centric viewpoint. **Published Guides:** *Dictionary Catalog of the Arthur B. Spingarn Collection of Negro Authors* (G. K. Hall, 1970). **Subjects:** History; Literature 1800 to present; Regional — Africa & Caribbean; Travel & Exploration; Afro-Americans. **Access Policy:** Open to the public.

LIBRARY OF CONGRESS. Manuscript Division. 110 First St SE, Washington 20540. Tel: 202-287-5000. James Hutson, *Chief.*

Holdings: 10,000 collections; 40,000,000 items. **Scope:** The collections cover the entire range of American history, from colonial times to the present. They include the papers of most of the presidents from George Washington through Calvin Coolidge & the papers of many political, diplomatic, military, judicial, scientific, literary & cultural figures, as well as the records of a number of national organizations. **Published Guides:** *Handbook of Manuscripts* (1918); *List of Manuscript Collections in the Library of Congress to July 1931; List of Manuscript Collections in the Library of Congress, July 1931 to July 1938; Library of Congress Acquisitions: Manuscript Division* (1979–); various calendars, indexes, registers. **Subjects:** Americana; Economics; History; History of Medicine & Science; Law; Literature 1900 to present; Natural History; Regional — United States & Caribbean; Theater & Performing Arts; Travel & Exploration. **Access Policy:** Apply to chief.

LIBRARY OF CONGRESS. Rare Book & Special Collections Division. 110 First St SE, Washington 20540. Tel: 202-287-5434. William Matheson, *Chief.* **Staff:** Leonard N. Beck, *Subject Collections Specialist;* James Gilreath, *American History Specialist;* Peter M. VanWingen, *Head, Reference & Reader Services Section;* Don C. Marcin, *Head, Processing Section;* Kathleen T. Hunt, *Librarian for the Rosenwald Collection.*

Holdings: Bks 329,898; Mss 17,287 ln ft; 219,962 broadsides, playbills, pamphlets, title pages, etc. **Scope:** Over a half million books, broadsides & pamphlets with long-term scholarly importance for European & American arts & sciences. **Published Guides:** *The Rare Book Division: A Guide to Its Collections & Services* (1974); Annette

Melville, *Special Collections in the Library of Congress* (1980); *The Lessing J. Rosenwald Collection: A Catalogue of the Gift* (1977). **Subjects:** Americana; Books about Books; Children's Literature; Ephemera; Fine & Applied Arts; History; History of Science; Illustrated Books; Incunabula; Literature pre-1640 to present; Natural History; Press Books; Regional — Washington, DC; Religion; Travel & Exploration; Discovery & Exploration of the Americas; Establishment & Growth of American Politics & Culture to the present; History of the Book & Book Illustration; European Printing, 1450–1600; English Printing, 1476–1640; Cervantes; Whitman; Gastronomy; Bibles; Dime Novels; Early Russian & Bulgarian Imprints. **Budget:** $50,000 per year. **Access Policy:** Users must be 18 years old or over.

NATIONAL SOCIETY DAUGHTERS OF THE AMERICAN REVOLUTION. Office of the Historian General / Americana Collection. 1776 D St NW, Washington 20006. Tel: 202-628-1776 ext 256. Elva B. Crawford, *Archivist.*

Holdings: Bks 5000; newspapers; currency. **Scope:** Principally 18th- & early 19th-century printed books, newspapers, account books, diaries & miscellaneous manuscripts focusing on early America (pre-1830). Also collections of signatures of famous people: United States presidents, first ladies, signers of the Declaration of Independence, etc. **Subjects:** Americana. **Access Policy:** Apply to archivist.

SMITHSONIAN INSTITUTION LIBRARIES. Special Collections Branch. Washington 20560. Tel: 202-357-1568, 1577. Ellen B. Wells, *Chief.*

Holdings: Bks 30,000; Mss 30 ln ft; 300 medals; 2000 portrait prints of scientists. **Scope:** American Trade Catalogues (manufacturing, retail & horticultural); International Industrial & Trade Exhibition Publications. Special collections are housed in & reflect the collection goals of the following museums: Cooper-Hewitt Museum of

Design, National Museum of American History, National Museum of Natural History & National Air & Space Museum. **Subjects:** Applied Arts; Children's Literature; History of Mathematics & Science; Incunabula (scientific); Natural History; Engineering/Technology. **Budget:** $20,000 per year. **Access Policy:** Open to public by appointment.

FLORIDA, Gainesville

UNIVERSITY OF FLORIDA LIBRARIES. Special Collections. 531 Library W, Gainesville 32611. Tel: 904-392-0321. Sidney Ives, *Librarian for Rare Books & Manuscripts*. **Staff:** Carmen Russell, *Assistant for Rare Books & Manuscripts*.
Holdings: Bks 40,000; Mss 600 ln ft. **Scope:** 19th-century American literature; 17th–18th century English literature; Victorian theology; modern British & American poetry; Irish literary revival. **Subjects:** Books about Books; History; Literature pre-1640 to present; Press Books; Regional — New England Authors; Religion; Theater & Performing Arts. **Access Policy:** Open to public.

FLORIDA, Miami

MIAMI-DADE PUBLIC LIBRARY SYSTEM. Florida Collection. One Biscayne Blvd, Miami 33231. Tel: 305-579-5001. Samuel J. Boldrick, *Librarian*.
Holdings: Bks 5500; Mss 40 ln ft; 5600 microfilm reels; 17,500 photo images. **Scope:** Books about Florida history from mid-1500s to present; manuscripts of books by Florida authors; photographs of Southern Florida 1890s to late 1940s; Seminole Indian Wars; Spanish-American War; Cuba. **Subjects:** Americana; History & Discovery; Regional — Florida & Caribbean. **Access Policy:** Open to public.

FLORIDA, Tallahassee

FLORIDA STATE UNIVERSITY. Robert Manning Strozier Library, Special Collections Department. Tallahassee 32306. Tel: 904-644-3271. Opal M. Free, *Head*. **Staff:** Susan Hamburger, *Associate University Librarian;* Burton Altman, *Associate University Librarian, Pepper Collection;* Shirley Fogle, *Manuscript Collections*.
Holdings: Bks 53,000; Mss 1278 ln ft; 25 clay tablets; 32 ostraka; 25 papyri. **Scope:** Rare books: books printed before 1800; Confederate imprints, 1860–1865; all Florida imprints through 1850; fine printing, illustrations, or binding; private press books; fore-edge paintings; limited editions; autographed or association copies; first or early editions of significance, especially American or British. Manuscripts: North Florida region — business records to early 1900s, family records, personal papers and memorabilia of Florida governors, supreme court justices, circuit judges; literary manuscripts — Florida authors & Florida State University faculty. **Published Guides:** Donald D. Horward, *The French Revolution & Napoleon Collection at Florida State University: A Bibliographical Guide* (Friends of the Florida State University Library, 1973). **Subjects:** Americana; Books about Books; Fine & Applied Arts; Illustrated Books; Incunabula; Literature pre-1640 to 1800; Natural History; Press Books; Regional — Florida; Religion (early bibles); Travel & Exploration; Herbals; French Revolution & Napoleon; Childhood in Poetry. **Access Policy:** Identification required.

FLORIDA, Tampa

UNIVERSITY OF SOUTH FLORIDA LIBRARY. Special Collections Department. Tampa 33520. Tel: 813-974-2731. J. B. Dobkin, *Librarian*. **Staff:** Paul Camp, *Assistant Librarian*.
Holdings: Bks 55,000; Mss 762 ln ft; maps (several thousand); 10,000 photographs. **Scope:** Exhaustive coverage of Floridiana; juvenile & adult 19th-century American literature; American Boys & Girls series; dime

novels; rare botanical works. **Subjects:** Americana; Children's Literature; History (Florida); Regional — Floridiana. **Budget:** $35,000 per year. **Access Policy:** Open to public.

GEORGIA, Athens

UNIVERSITY OF GEORGIA LIBRARIES. Special Collections Division. Athens 30602. Tel: 404-542-7123. Vesta Lee Gordon, *Assistant Director for Special Collections.* **Staff:** Robert M. Willingham Jr, *Curator of Rare Books & Manuscripts;* Mary Ellen Brooks, *Rare Book Bibliographer;* J. Larry Gulley, *Manuscript Librarian;* Joseph Cote, *Curator of Georgia Collection;* John Edwards, *University Archivist;* Sheryl Vogt, *Curator, Russell Library.*
Holdings: Bks 75,000; Mss 20,460. **Scope:** General rare books strong in Southern history, 19th-century literature & natural history; Confederate imprints; British local history; Georgiana, printed & mss; historical & literary mss; 20th-century political papers & university archives. **Subjects:** Ephemera; Press Books; Regional — Georgia & South; Theater & Performing Arts. **Budget:** $90,000 per year. **Access Policy:** Open to public.

GEORGIA, Atlanta

EMORY UNIVERSITY. Robert W. Woodruff Library, Special Collections Department. Atlanta 30322. Tel: 404-329-6887. Linda M. Matthews, *Head.* **Staff:** Virginia J. H. Cain, *Processing Archivist;* Richard H. F. Lindemann, *Reference Archivist & Department Head.*
Holdings: Bks 16,000; Mss 3847 ln ft. **Scope:** Rare books: strengths in 18th- & 19th-century British literature, Anglo-Irish literature (especially W. B. Yeats & Lady Gregory), Southern Americana, Confederate imprints. Manuscripts: primarily 1850 to present with major collecting areas in southern history & politics, southern journalists, Civil War, history of Methodism (Wesley manuscripts), Commu-nist party of the United States, Anglo-Irish literary manuscripts & southern literary manuscripts. **Published Guides:** "The Robert W. Woodruff Library, Special Collections"; "Manuscript Sources for Women's History: A Descriptive List of Holdings" (1978); "A Guide to Manuscript Sources . . . Relating to Atlanta" (1978); "Guide to the Charles Holmes Herty Papers" (1981); John Hill Hewitt, *Sources and Bibliography* (1981); Ronald Schuchard, "The Lady Gregory-Yeats Collection at Emory University." **Subjects:** Americana; History (southern); Incunabula; Literature 1640 to 1900 (British); Regional — South (primarily Georgia) & Belgium; Religion (Methodism); French Revolution Pamphlets; History & Culture of Belgium (concentrating on literature & fine arts). **Access Policy:** Registration & identification required.

GEORGIA STATE UNIVERSITY. William Russell Pullen Library, Special Collections Department. PO Box 1027, GSU, Atlanta 30303. Tel: 404-658-2476, 2477. Les Hough, *Director.* **Staff:** Joe Constance, Chris Paton, Robert Dinwiddie.
Holdings: Bks 1500; Mss 700 ln ft. **Scope:** Rare book collection emphasizes American labor history, 18th- & 19th-century Georgia history & literature, first editions of works by noted American & British authors, incunabula. **Subjects:** History; Illustrated Books; Literature 1900 to present; Regional — the South (especially Georgia). **Access Policy:** Open to public.

HAWAII, Honolulu

BISHOP MUSEUM LIBRARY. PO Box 19000A, Honolulu 96819. Tel: 808-847-3511 ext 148. Cynthia Timberlake, *Head Librarian.* **Staff:** Marguerite Ashford, *Associate Librarian;* Janet Short, *Catalogue Librarian;* Robert Benedetto, *Archivist.*
Holdings: Bks 45,000; Mss 3500 ln ft. **Scope:** Natural history, cultural history of the Pacific with strong emphasis

on Hawaiiana, early voyages, expedition reports & Bishop Museum staff manuscripts. **Published Guides:** *Catalog of the Bernice P. Bishop Museum Library* (Hall, 1963–1967). **Subjects:** History of Science; Illustrated Books; Natural History; Regional—Hawaii & the Pacific; Travel & Exploration. **Access Policy:** Open to public on Wednesday; other times by appointment.

IDAHO, Moscow

UNIVERSITY OF IDAHO. Library, Department of Special Collections. Moscow 83843. Tel: 208-885-7951. Stan Shepard, *Head.* **Staff:** Judith Nielsen, *Manuscripts Assistant;* Ralph Nielsen, *Cataloguing Assistant.*

Holdings: Bks 27,000; Mss 1350 ln ft; 50,000 photographs. **Published Guides:** All by Charles A. Webbert, *Scottiana Idahoensis* (University Press of Idaho, 1978); *Checklist of Western Americana in the University of Idaho Library* (1970); *The Basque Collection: A Preliminary Checklist* (1971); *Checklist of the Publications of Caxton Printers, 1903–1973* (1974). **Subjects:** Regional—Idaho & Pacific Northwest; Spanish Basque; Sir Walter Scott; Ezra Pound. **Budget:** $5000 per year. **Access Policy:** Open to public for research.

ILLINOIS, Carbondale

SOUTHERN ILLINOIS UNIVERSITY. Morris Library, Special Collections. Carbondale 62901. Tel: 618-453-2516. David V. Koch, *Curator & University Archivist.* **Staff:** Louisa Bowen, *Curator of Manuscripts;* E. Jane Lockrem, *Assistant Rare Books Librarian;* Shelley Cox, *Rare Books Cataloguer;* Anne Sims, *Assistant University Archivist.*

Holdings: Bks 40,000; Mss 3000 ln ft. **Scope:** Primarily 20th century in the areas of modern philosophy, American & British expatriatism, James Joyce, Irish literary renaissance, proletariat theater, southern Illinois history, press freedom, fine printing/private presses. **Published Guides:** Steven Lund, *James Joyce . . . at Southern Illinois University* at Carbondale (Whitson, 1983); John Presley, *Robert Graves . . . at Southern Illinois University at Carbondale* (Whitson, 1976); *Guide to the Philosophy Manuscript Collections* (Morris Library, 1983); Ian MacNiven, "The Lawrence Durrell Collection at Southern Illinois University at Carbondale" (PhD dissertation, 1976); Jurgen Stein, "The Erwin Piscator Collection at Southern Illinois University at Carbondale" (PhD dissertation, 1972); *ICarbS* magazine (1973–present). **Subjects:** Americana; Books about Books; Children's Literature; Ephemera; History; Law; Literature 1900 to present; Press Books; Regional—Illinois; Religion; Theater & Performing Arts; Irish Literature (1865 to present). **Access Policy:** Open to qualified scholars.

ILLINOIS, Chicago

THE CHICAGO PUBLIC LIBRARY. Special Collections Division. 78 E Washington St, Chicago 60602. Tel: 312-269-2926. Laura Linard, *Curator & Archivist.* **Staff:** Robert Marshall, *Senior Archival Specialist;* Constance Gordon, *Cataloguing Specialist.*

Holdings: Bks 28,771; 250 historic artifacts. **Scope:** Major holdings are the Civil War & American history research collection & the Chicagoana collection (Chicago authors & imprints, theater history, World's Columbian Exposition); book arts & history. **Published Guides:** *Treasures of the Chicago Public Library* (1977). **Subjects:** Books about Books; History; Literature 1900 to present; Theater & Performing Arts; Chicago Authors & Imprints. **Access Policy:** Open to public.

THE JOHN CRERAR LIBRARY. See University of Chicago. Library, Department of Special Collections.

DEPAUL UNIVERSITY. Library, Special Collections/University Archives. 2323 N Seminary, Chicago 60614. Tel: 312-321-7940. Kathryn DeGraff, *Librarian.*

Holdings: Bks 8000; Mss 100 ln ft; 1000 volumes of university archives.

Scope: Rare books; incunabula; Irish materials; some fine printing; Napoleon (biographical material, detailed campaign accounts, history of the era); Dickens (first editions, illustrated editions); sporting books (19th-century British upper-class leisure activities). **Access Policy:** Open to public for research.

THE NEWBERRY LIBRARY. Department of Special Collections. 60 W Walton, Chicago 60610. Tel: 312-943-9090. Jean Donaldson, *Librarian.* **Staff:** Diana Haskell, *Curator, Modern Manuscripts;* Lucille Wehner, *Reference Librarian;* John Aubrey, *Reference Librarian;* Carolyn Sheehy, *Modern Manuscripts Assistant.*
  Holdings: Bks 302,000; Mss 5250 ln ft. **Scope:** Books—humanities of the Western World from earliest times to 1900. Manuscripts—as related to books, modern literary & regional materials & dance history. **Published Guides:** *Dictionary Catalogue of the History of Printing from the John M. Wing Foundation* (G. K. Hall, 1961; Supp. 1970, 1981); *Dictionary Catalogue of the Edward E. Ayer Collection of Americana and American Indians* (G. K. Hall, 1961; Supp. 1970, 1980). Information on other guides available through Newberry bookshop. **Subjects:** Americana; Books about Books; History; Incunabula; Literature pre-1640–1800; Press Books; Religion; History of Printing; American Indians; Western Expansion beyond the Mississippi; Maps; Railroads. **Access Policy:** Open to public.

UNIVERSITY OF CHICAGO. Library, Department of Special Collections. 1100 E 57 St, Chicago 60637. Tel: 312-962-8705. Robert Rosenthal, *Curator.* **Staff:** Jeffrey Abt, *Conservator & Exhibits Coordinator;* Daniel Meyer, *Assistant University Archivist;* Sem C. Sutter, *Assistant Rare Books Bibliographer.*
  Holdings: Bks 215,000; Mss 7,000,000 pieces. **Scope:** The rare book collections are particularly strong in American, English & Continental literature, history of science & medicine & history of religion. The science holdings include the rare book collections of the John Crerar Library. Manuscript resources include the university archives, an extensive collection of New Testament manuscripts, collections of English & Italian legal documents & personal papers of leading scientists & social scientists. **Subjects:** Americana; Books about Books; Children's Literature; Economics; Fine & Applied Arts; History; History of Mathematics, Medicine & Science; Illustrated Books; Law; Literature pre-1640 to present; Natural History; Press Books; Regional—Ohio River Valley; Religion; Theater & Performing Arts; Travel & Exploration; Lincolniana; German Almanache & Taschenbücher; Manuscript Catalogues & Works on Paleography; Drama (especially English, American, Italian & Dutch); German Fiction, 1750–1850; Theology. **Access Policy:** Open to public.

UNIVERSITY OF ILLINOIS AT CHICAGO. University Library, Special Collections Department. PO Box 8198, Chicago 60680. Tel: 312-996-2756. Gretchen Lagana, *Librarian.* **Staff:** Robert Adelsperger, Mary Anne Bamberger, *Assistant Librarians.*
  Holdings: Bks 55,000; Mss 9200 ln ft. **Scope:** Chicago—historical & contemporary. **Published Guides:** "Special Collections in the University Library," *UIC Reporter* 1, no 1 (1983). **Subjects:** Americana; Economics; Fine & Applied Arts; History; History of Medicine; Literature 1900 to present; Regional—Chicago & the Midwest; Theater & Performing Arts; Women's History; Slavery & Antislavery (British & American); Urban History; Social Welfare. **Access Policy:** Apply to librarian.

ILLINOIS, Evanston

NORTHWESTERN UNIVERSITY. Library, Special Collections Department. 1937 Sheridan Rd, Evanston 60201. Tel: 312-492-3635, 3177. R. Russell Maylone, *Curator.* **Staff:** Sarah Sherman, *Assistant Curator & Head, Women's Collection.*

Holdings: Bks 190,000; Mss 500,000 items; 5000 posters; 1300 photographs. **Scope:** Collection consists of books, posters, pamphlets, photographs, serials. Primary collecting areas include Art Nouveau, European, English, American books & periodicals of the 19th & 20th centuries & women's liberation materials. **Subjects:** Fine & Applied Arts; Illustrated Books; Literature 1640 to present; Press Books; Religion (Deism); Theater & Performing Arts; Avant-Garde in Europe, Turn-of-the-Century (Dada, Surrealism, Futurism, Expressionism); Siege & Commune of Paris, 1870–1871. **Access Policy:** Open to public.

ILLINOIS, Galesburg

KNOX COLLEGE. Seymour Library. Galesburg 61401. Douglas L. Wilson, *Director.* **Staff:** Lynn Harlan, *Curator of Archives;* Mary Elizabeth Willey, *Special Collections Librarian.*

Holdings: Bks 12,000; Mss 235 ln ft. **Subjects:** Americana; Ephemera; History; Literature 1900 to present; Regional—Northwest; Civil War; Galesburg & Western Illinois; Hemingway. **Budget:** $2000 per year. **Access Policy:** Open to public for research.

ILLINOIS, Rock Island

AUGUSTANA COLLEGE LIBRARY. Special Collections. Rock Island 61201. Tel: 309-794-7317. John Caldwell, *Director.* **Staff:** Marjorie M. Miller, *Librarian.*

Holdings: Bks 5523; Mss 565 ln ft. **Scope:** History of the upper Mississippi Valley, 18th–20th centuries; North American Indians, 18th–20th centuries; reformation imprints; incunabula; English & American literature, 18th–20th centuries; revolutionary period in European history, 1789–1848. **Subjects:** Children's Literature; Illustrated Books; Incunabula; Literature 1640 to present; Regional—Upper Mississippi Valley; Religion (reformation imprints); Travel & Exploration (North American); Rock Island County History; Sac & Fox Indian Tribes; Black Hawk War; Early Quad City Industries; Cook Books (18th & 19th centuries); Revolutionary Period in European History (1789–1848); Augustana College History; Local Authors (Illinois & Iowa). **Access Policy:** Open to public for research.

ILLINOIS, Springfield

ILLINOIS STATE HISTORICAL LIBRARY. Manuscripts Section. Old State Capitol, Springfield 62706. Tel: 217-782-4836. Roger D. Bridges, *Head, Library Services.* **Staff:** Laurel Bowen, *Curator of Manuscripts;* Cheryl Schnirring, *Assistant.*

Holdings: Mss 10,500 ln ft. **Subjects:** Americana; History; Regional—Illinois & Midwest; Religion; Lincolniana. **Budget:** $5000 per year. **Access Policy:** Open to public.

ILLINOIS, Urbana

UNIVERSITY OF ILLINOIS AT URBANA-CHAMPAIGN. Library, Rare Book Room/Illinois Historical Survey/University Archives. 1408 W Gregory Dr, Urbana 61801. Tel: 217-333-3777. N. Frederick Nash, *Librarian.* **Staff:** Mary S. Ceibert, *Assistant Librarian.*

Holdings: Bks 214,698; Mss 598 cu ft. **Scope:** Milton Collection; works influencing Milton & Shakespeare represented by 16th- & 17th-century religious, history & literary books; incunabula; history of geology; British historical, economic & literary works of the 18th century; emblem books; Wells & Sandburg collections. **Published Guides:** *Catalog of the Rare Book Room, University of Illinois at Urbana-Champaign* (Hall, 1978); *Incunabula in the University of Illinois Library* (University of Illinois Press, 1979). **Subjects:** History (16th- &

17th-century English); History of Science (geology); Illustrated Books (emblem books); Incunabula; Literature 1640–1800; Stage Scenery & Design. **Access Policy:** Open to public.

INDIANA, Bloomington

INDIANA UNIVERSITY. Lilly Library. Bloomington 47405. Tel: 812-335-2452. William R. Cagle, *Librarian*. **Staff:** L. C. Rudolph, *Curator of Books;* Saundra B. Taylor, *Curator of Manuscripts*.

Holdings: Bks 335,000; Mss 16,000 ln ft; 100,000 pieces of sheet music. **Scope:** Ranges widely over the humanities with emphasis on American & British literature & history, 1640 to present; European expansion (especially Spanish, Dutch & Portuguese empires) & including smaller collection of French & German literature; history of science & medicine; history of painting. **Subjects:** Americana, Children's Literature; History; Incunabula; Literature 1840 to present; Theater & Performing Arts; Travel & Exploration; American Sheet Music; Genetics (history of); Publishing History; Cookery Books (1475–1900). **Budget:** $550,000. **Access Policy:** Open to public.

INDIANA, Indianapolis

INDIANA HISTORICAL SOCIETY LIBRARY. Rare Books, Bibliographic Services & Manuscripts, Manuscripts Department. 315 W Ohio St, Indianapolis 46202. Tel: 317-232-1879. Leigh Darbee, *Head, Bibliographic Services, Rare Books;* Eric Pumroy, *Head, Manuscripts Department*. **Staff:** Constance McBirney, *Manuscripts Librarian;* Donald West, *Program Archivist;* F. Gerald Handfield, *Library Field Agent*.

Holdings: Bks 15,000; Mss 2000 ln ft. **Scope:** Books: early travel accounts, local history; manuscripts: 19th-century politics, social service agencies, architectural firms. **Published Guides:**

"Indiana & the Old Northwest" (1980). **Subjects:** Regional—Indiana & the Old Northwest; Travel & Exploration (books); William Henry Harrison, Lew Wallace; Civil War; Social Welfare Organizations; Northwest Territory. **Budget:** $55,000 per year. **Access Policy:** Open to public.

INDIANA, Muncie

BALL STATE UNIVERSITY. Alexander M. Bracken Library, Special Collections. Muncie 47306. Tel: 317-285-5078. David C. Tambo, *Head*. **Staff:** Nancy Turner, *Technician*.

Holdings: Bks 9269; Mss 2500 ln ft; 850 local historical maps; 7000 prints & negatives; 200 reels & cassettes of oral history; 500,000 ft of film. **Scope:** Rare books, 13th century to present; modern literature (John Steinbeck, Aldous Huxley, contemporary poetry); Ku Klux Klan Collection; Nazi Collection; University Archives; Stoeckel Archives, with local history materials, including local government records & manuscripts; Center for Middletown Studies. **Published Guides:** Juanita Smith, "The Steinbeck Collections in Honor of Elizabeth R. Otis at the Alexander M. Bracken Library, Ball State University," *Steinbeck Quarterly* 11, no 3/4 (Summer–Fall 1978); update in *Steinbeck Monograph Series,* no 11 (1981). **Subjects:** History; Literature 1900 to present; Contemporary Poetry; Middletown Collections (relating to the study of Muncie as Middletown, USA). **Access Policy:** Open to public.

INDIANA, Notre Dame

UNIVERSITY OF NOTRE DAME. University Libraries, Department of Rare Books & Special Collections. 102 Memorial Library, Notre Dame 46556. Tel: 219-239-6489. Anton C. Masin, *Head*.

Holdings: Bks 25,000; Mss 30 ln ft. **Published Guides:** James A. Corbett, *Catalogue of the Medieval & Renais-*

sance *Manuscripts of the University of Notre Dame* (University of Notre Dame Press, 1978); Anton C. Masin, *Incunabula Typographica: Catalog of Fifteenth-Century Books* (University of Notre Dame Press, 1979). **Subjects:** Americana; Illustrated Books; Incunabula; Literature pre-1640 to present; Press Books; Religion; G. K. Chesterton; Dante; International Sports & Games; Descartes; Botany; Orchidology. **Access Policy:** Apply to head.

INDIANA, Terre Haute

INDIANA STATE UNIVERSITY. Cunningham Memorial Library, Department of Rare Books & Special Collections. Terre Haute 47809. Tel: 812-232-6311 ext 2862, 2863. Lawrence J. McCrank, Sr, *Librarian & Head.* **Staff:** J. Thomas Brown, *University Archivist;* Robert Carter, *Bibliographer & Reference Librarian;* Frances Kepner, *Rare Books & Special Collections Cataloguer.*
   Holdings: Bks 24,000; Mss 487 ln ft; 15,000 photographs & prints. **Scope:** Dictionaries & lexicography, 15th century to present, with emphasis on English & Western European languages & classics; Eugene Debs Collection on labor & social history, 1880–1940; travel & exploration, especially European expansion, immigration across northern United States; Indiana history & literature with focus on Wabash Valley regional materials; books about books and book arts; American education classics & representative textbooks. **Published Guides:** Brochures available from library; *A Checklist of the Cordell Collection of Dictionaries in the Cunningham Memorial Library* (Indiana State University, 1971); *A Short-Title Catalogue of the Warren N. & Suzanne B. Cordell Collection of Dictionaries, 1475–1900* (Indiana State University, 1975). **Subjects:** History (social & labor); Literature 1640 to present; Regional— Indiana; Travel & Exploration; Indiana State University Archives; Dictio-

naries & Lexicography; Labor & Social History (socialism & Debs); American Education in the Midwest. **Budget:** $14,000 to $17,000 per year. **Access Policy.** Open to public.

IOWA, Ames

IOWA STATE UNIVERSITY. Library, Department of Special Collections. Ames 50011. Tel: 515-294-6672. Stanley Yates, *Head.* **Staff:** Laura Kline, *Librarian;* Isabel Matterson, *Curator of Manuscripts.*
   Holdings: Bks 11,358; Mss 1,933.58 ln ft; 8000 films. **Published Guides:** *Guide to the Manuscript Collections in the ISU Library.* **Subjects:** History of Science; Illustrated Books; Natural History; Travel & Exploration; History of Technology; Agriculture; Entomology; Botany; Iowa Private Presses. **Access Policy:** Open to public for research.

IOWA, Cedar Rapids

GRAND LODGE OF IOWA, AF & AM. Iowa Masonic Library & Museum. PO Box 279, Cedar Rapids 52406. Tel: 319-365-1438. Tom Eggleston, *Grand Secretary-Librarian.* **Staff:** Bill Durow, *Assistant Librarian.*
   Holdings: Bks 100,000. **Scope:** Extensive collection on freemasonry. **Subjects:** Americana; History; Regional— Iowa History; Religion; Freemasonry. **Access Policy:** Open to public for research; no photocopying.

IOWA, Iowa City

STATE HISTORICAL SOCIETY OF IOWA. Library Manuscript Collection. 402 Iowa Ave, Iowa City 52240. Tel: 319-338-5471. Peter H. Curtis, *Head Librarian.* **Staff:** David Kinnett, *Manuscripts Librarian;* Mary Bennett, *Manuscripts Assistant.*
   Holdings: Bks 5000; Mss 2250 ln ft; 100,000 photographs; 5000 maps. **Scope:** Comprehensive collection of rare Iowa history books, photographs

& maps; papers of several governors, religious groups, labor unions, businesses. **Subjects:** Iowa History; Genealogy. **Access Policy:** Open to public.

UNIVERSITY OF IOWA LIBRARIES. Special Collections Department. Iowa City 52242. Tel: 319-353-4854. Frank Paluka, *Head.* **Staff:** Robert A. McCown, *Manuscripts Librarian;* Earl M. Rogers, *Curator of Archives.*

Holdings: Bks 60,000; Mss 10,000 ln ft. **Scope:** Fifteen separately designated collections of rare books & 430 inventoried collections of papers. **Published Guides:** Boyd K. Swigger, *A Guide to Resources for the Study of the Recent History of the United States . . .* (1977); *The Wallace Papers: An Index . . .,* 2 vols (1975); O. M. Brack & D. H. Stefanson, *A Catalogue of the Leigh Hunt Manuscripts in the University of Iowa Libraries* (1973); semiannual issues of *Books at Iowa* (1964–). **Subjects:** Children's Literature; History of Science (hydraulics); Literature 1800–1900; Press Books; Regional—Iowa Authors; Theater & Performing Arts (Chautauqua); Music; Agriculture; Women's History; Progressive Party, 1948; Political Cartoons (Ding Darling). **Access Policy:** Open to public.

KANSAS, Lawrence

UNIVERSITY OF KANSAS LIBRARIES. Kenneth Spencer Research Library, Department of Special Collections. Lawrence 66045. Tel: 913-864-4334. Alexandra Mason, *Librarian.* **Staff:** William L. Mitchell, *Associate Librarian & Conservator;* Sally Haines Hocker, *Associate Librarian;* Ann Hyde, *Curator of Manuscripts;* Joseph A. Springer, *Assistant Librarian;* Ann E. Williams, *Associate Librarian.*

Holdings: Bks 175,000; Mss 1300 ln ft; 900 antiquarian maps. **Scope:** Printed matter: European continental imprints (15th–17th centuries); British imprints (17th–18th centuries—espe-

cially literature, history, economic & social history); British periodicals & newspapers (17th & 18th centuries); natural history (birds & medicinal botany); Anglo-Irish culture; science fiction; Frank Lloyd Wright; Central America. Manuscripts: 10th century to present, especially Great Britain, Italy, France. **Published Guides:** Alexandra Mason, *A Guide to the Collections* (1972). **Subjects:** Books about Books; Children's Literature; Economics; History; History of Science; Incunabula; Law; Literature pre-1640 (non English); Literature 1640 to present (Yeats, Joyce, Mencken, Rilke); Natural History; Travel & Exploration; Linnaeus; Cervantes; Guatemala; Ireland; Charles V (Holy Roman emperor); Pre-Raphaelites; Tennyson; French Revolution; Science Fiction. **Access Policy:** Open to public for research.

KANSAS, Manhattan

KANSAS STATE UNIVERSITY LIBRARIES. Special Collections Department. Manhattan 66506. Tel: 913-532-6516. Antonia Pigno, *Coordinator.* **Staff:** John Vander Velde, *Librarian.*

Holdings: Bks 20,000. **Scope:** Basic general collection of rare books with emphasis on cookery & 20th-century literature. **Published Guides:** William P. Williams, *A Descriptive Catalogue of Seventeenth-Century Religious Literature in the Kansas State University Library* (1966); G. A. Rudolph, *The Kansas State University Receipt Book & Household Manual* (1968); G. A. Rudolph & Evan Williams, *Linnaena* (1970). **Subjects:** Literature 1900 to present; Regional—Kansas; Historical Cookery; Linnaena Collection; Poultry Collection. **Budget:** $10,000 per year. **Access Policy:** Open to public for research.

KANSAS, Topeka

KANSAS STATE HISTORICAL SOCIETY. Manuscript Department. 120 W Tenth

Ave, Topeka 66612. Tel: 913-296-4793. Patricia A. Michaelis, *Curator.* **Staff:** Bob Knecht, *Assistant Curator.* **Holdings:** Mss 9200 ln ft. **Scope:** Kansas, Plains states & Western United States. Included are significant holdings on Indians & Indian missions, agriculture, Civil War, territorial period, railroads, the military, political & literary figures. **Published Guides:** Guides to microfilmed collections: Anderson family; Joseph Little Bristow; John Stillman Brown family; Thomas Ewing, Jr; Thaddeus Hyatt; Chester I. Long; Isaac McCoy; Jotham Meeker; New England Emigrant Aid Company; John G. Pratt; Charles & Sara T. D. Robinson private papers. **Subjects:** History; Regional—Kansas & the West. **Access Policy:** Open to public.

KANSAS, Wichita

WICHITA STATE UNIVERSITY. Ablah Library, Department of Special Collections. PO Box 68, Wichita 67208. Tel: 316-689-3590. Michael Kelly, *Curator.*

Holdings: Bks 3000; Mss 674 ln ft; 250 maps; photos; original editorial cartoons. **Scope:** The rare book collection includes examples of incunabula, fine printing, binding & illustration. The manuscript collection includes personal papers, corporate archives, photographic collections & graphic art having 19th- and 20th-century local & regional importance. **Published Guides:** *Catalog of the Maurice M. & Jean Tinterow Collection of Works on Mesmerism, Animal Magnetism, and Hypnotism; The R. T. Aitchison Collection of Old & Rare Books.* **Subjects:** History; Regional—Kansas & Midwest; Antislavery Materials, Including the William Lloyd Garrison Papers; Aviation; 19th- & 20th-Century Congressional Papers; Radical Pamphlet Collection; Editorial Cartoons; German Pamphlet Collection; Hypnotism, Mesmerism, Animal Magnetism; Kansas Historical Maps. **Access Policy:** Open to public for research.

KENTUCKY, Lexington

UNIVERSITY OF KENTUCKY LIBRARIES. Special Collections & Archives. King Library North, Lexington 40506. Tel: 606-257-8371; 8611. William Marshall, *Assistant Director, Special Collections & Archives.* **Staff:** James Birchfield, *Assistant Director for Collection Development.*

Holdings: Bks 30,000; Mss 6000 cubic ft; 650,000 photographs; 800 maps; 6000 posters. **Scope:** Collection includes Kentuckiana collection (books & manuscripts about Kentucky or by Kentucky authors, 18th century to present); 18th & 19th century American & English literature, with emphasis on the romantic period; Milton collection; history of books & typography. Manuscript collection includes papers of Robert Penn Warren, John Fox, Jr., Thomas Merton, Harriet Arno, James Lane Allen, James Still & John Jacob Niles; 20th-century political papers. **Subjects:** Americana; Books about Books; Children's Literature; Economics; Ephemera; Fine and Applied Arts; History; History of Medicine; Illustrated Books; Incunabula; Literature 1640 to present; Natural History; Press Books; Regional—Kentucky and Ohio Valley; Travel and Exploration. **Budget:** $25,000 per year. **Access Policy:** Open to the public.

KENTUCKY, Louisville

THE FILSON CLUB, INC. 118 W Breckinridge St, Louisville 40203. Tel: 502-582-3727. Martin F. Schmidt, *Director.* **Staff:** Dorothy C. Rush, *Librarian;* James R. Bentley, *Curator of Manuscripts.*

Holdings: Bks 40,000; Mss 1,000,000 items. **Scope:** Early Kentucky history & genealogy; pioneer, antebellum, Civil War & later; manuscript collections for Kentucky; printed materials on Kentucky history, literature & imprints; Ohio Valley. **Subjects:** Americana; Ephemera; History; Regional—History of Kentucky & Surrounding States; Kentucky Theater Programs, Broadsides, Menus & Invitations; Sheet Music (by, about, or printed in Kentucky); Kentucky Portraits. **Budget:** $12,500 per year (manuscripts). **Access Policy:** Open to public for research.

KENTUCKY, Richmond

EASTERN KENTUCKY UNIVERSITY. John Grant Crabbe Library, John Wilson Townsend Room. Richmond 40475. Tel: 606-622-1792. Ernest E. Weyhrauch, *Director.* **Staff:** Sharon Brown McConnell, *Curator;* Tawanna Ray, *Library Assistant II.*
Holdings: Bks 15,500; Mss 16 ln ft. **Scope:** Books written by Kentuckians or about Kentucky & Kentuckians. **Subjects:** History; Literature 1640 to present; Genealogical Material of Kentucky & Surrounding Areas. **Budget:** $10,000 per year. **Access Policy:** Open to public for research.

LOUISIANA, Baton Rouge

LOUISIANA STATE UNIVERSITY. Troy H. Middleton Library, Department of Archives & Manuscripts. Baton Rouge 70803. Tel: 504-388-2240. M. Stone Miller, Jr, *Head.* **Staff:** Gisela J. Lozada, *Research Archivist;* Thomas E. Price, *Registrar of Manuscripts.*
Holdings: Mss 4.5 million items. **Scope:** Original research materials pertaining to Louisiana, southwestern Mississippi & the Lower Mississippi River Valley from 1700 to present. **Published Guides:** "Archives & Manuscripts, Louisiana State University," in *A Guide to the History of Louisiana* (departmental brochure, 1982). **Subjects:** Americana; Economics; Ephemera; History; Law; Literature 1640 to present; Regional—Louisiana, Mississippi, Lower Mississippi River Valley; Religion; Plantation Society & Economy; Slavery; Agriculture (cotton & sugar); Civil War & Reconstruction; Steamboats & Transportation on western waters; Banking & Other Business

History. **Access Policy:** Open to qualified researchers with valid identification.

LOUISIANA STATE UNIVERSITY. Troy H. Middleton Library, The E. A. McIlhenny Natural History Collection. Baton Rouge 70803. Tel: 504-388-6934. Kathryn N. Morgan, *Curator.*
Holdings: Bks 4500. **Scope:** Both scientific & finely illustrated works on natural history from 1486 to the present. Particular strengths in botany & ornithology. **Published Guides:** *Catalogue of the E. A. McIlhenny Natural History Collection* (1984). **Subjects:** Natural History. **Access Policy:** Open to public for research.

LOUISIANA STATE UNIVERSITY. Troy H. Middleton Library, Rare Book Room. Baton Rouge 70803. Tel: 504-388-2575. Evangeline Mills Lynch, *Librarian & Head.* **Staff:** Ruth Murray, *Associate Librarian.*
Holdings: Bks 16,384. **Scope:** Contains books & pamphlets representing all fields of knowledge with the exception of natural history. Works range from incunabula to modern fine presses. **Subjects:** Books about Books; Economics; Press Books; Regional—Lower Mississippi Valley, Deep South, Caribbean Area & Gulf of Mexico Countries; Travel & Exploration; Chess; Poker; Lincoln; Crayfish. **Access Policy:** Open to public, valid identification required.

LOUISIANA, New Orleans

THE HISTORIC NEW ORLEANS COLLECTION. Research Library & Manuscripts Division. 533 Royal St, New Orleans 70130. Florence M. Jumonville, *Head Librarian, Rare Books;* Susan T. Cole, *Curator of Manuscripts.* **Staff:** Pamela D. Arceneaux, Judith L. McMillan, *Reference Librarians, Rare Books;* Catherine C. Kahn, *Registrar of Manuscripts;* Alfred E. Lemmon, Mark D. Luccioni, *Cataloguers of Manuscripts.*
Holdings: Bks 12,000; Mss 6000 ln

ft; pamphlets 45 ln ft. **Scope:** Materials relating to all aspects of Louisiana culture, history, literature, architecture. **Published Guides:** *Guide to Research at the Historic New Orleans Collection* (1980). **Subjects:** Regional—Louisiana. **Access Policy:** Open to public.

LOUISIANA HISTORICAL CENTER. (Mailing: Louisiana State Museum, 751 Chartres St, New Orleans 70116.) 400 Esplanade Ave, New Orleans, 70116. Tel: 504-568-8214. Joseph D. Castle, *Curator of Maps, Manuscripts & Rare Books.*
　　Holdings: Bks 30,000; Mss 743 ln ft; maps; colonial judicial documents. **Scope:** Regional history with emphasis on Louisiana. Rare books include many dealing with exploration & travel from the mid-17th–19th century. Manuscripts include 500,000 pages of the French Superior Council Records, 1714–1769 & the Judicial Records of Spanish Louisiana, 1769–1803. Also family records from early 19th century through present dealing with Louisiana history. **Subjects:** Fine & Applied Arts; History; Law; Regional—Louisiana & Borderlands Area; Theater & Performing Arts (music); Travel & Exploration. **Access Policy:** Open to public; no photocopying.

MAINE, Brunswick

BOWDOIN COLLEGE LIBRARY. Special Collections. Brunswick 04011. Tel: 207-725-8731 ext 288. Dianne M. Gutscher, *Curator.*
　　Holdings: Bks 45,000; Mss 450 ln ft; 500 maps; large collection of photographs of the area, mostly 19th century. **Scope:** Collections pertain to alumni or to the history of Maine & Bowdoin College & include the books & manuscripts of the H. W. Longfellow & Nathaniel Hawthorne collections (both were members of Bowdoin's class of 1825); the Abbott collection, consisting of the books & papers of Jacob, John S. C., Edward & Lyman Abbott; the papers of Civil War Generals Oliver Otis Howard (Bowd. 1850) & Joshua L. Chamberlain (Bowd. 1852), as well as those of William Pitt Fessenden (Bowd. 1823), who was Lincoln's secretary of the treasury; the papers & library of Donald B. MacMillan (Bowd. 1898) & the papers of Captain Robert A. Bartlett, shipmaster for Robert E. Peary (Bowd. 1877). Significant collections of printed works include the library of James Bowdoin & collections of Mosher Press books & those of the Anthoensen Press. **Published Guides:** "Hawthorne-Longfellow Library: A Catalogue of Endowed Funds & Selected Special Collections," *Bowdoin College Bulletin,* no. 388 (March 1973). **Subjects:** Children's Literature; Literature 1640 to present; Press Books; Regional—Maine; Arctic Exploration; French Language & Literature. **Access Policy:** Open to public.

MAINE, Portland

MAINE HISTORICAL SOCIETY. Manuscripts Section. 485 Congress St, Portland 04101. Tel: 207-774-1822, 774-1430. Thomas L. Gaffney, *Curator of Manuscripts.* **Staff:** Lisa C. Fink, *Manuscript Assistant.*
　　Holdings: Mss 1500 ln ft. **Scope:** 1492 to present; Maine maps, architectural drawings, locomotive & marine drawings, diaries, personal correspondence, family genealogies, records, church records, town records, proprietors' records, justice dockets, sheriffs' papers & jailors' records of Cumberland County, logbooks, railroad & streetcar records. **Published Guides:** Elizabeth Ring, ed., *A Reference List of Manuscripts Relating to the History of Maine.* **Subjects:** Americana; Economics; Ephemera; History; Regional—Maine. **Access Policy:** Open to public.

MAINE, Waterville

COLBY COLLEGE LIBRARY. Special Collections. Waterville 04901. Tel: 207-

873-1131 ext 2284. Fraser Cocks, *Curator.*
Holdings: Bks 29,800; Mss 450 ln ft; deceased alumni file: 1000. **Scope:** Late 19th- & early 20th-century British & American poetry & prose; contemporary American poetry; Irish Literary Renaissance; post-1945 Irish poetry & fiction. **Published Guides:** *James Augustine Healy Collection of Nineteenth and Twentieth Century Irish Literature.* **Subjects:** Edwin Arlington Robinson; Thomas Hardy Collection; Bern Porter, Collection of Contemporary Letters; Irish Literature, 1880–. **Budget:** $8000 per year. **Access Policy:** Open to public.

MARYLAND, Baltimore

JOHNS HOPKINS UNIVERSITY. Milton S. Eisenhower Library, Special Collections Division. Charles & 34th Sts, Baltimore 21218. Tel: 301-338-8348. Ann S. Gwyn, *Assistant Director.* **Staff:** Carolyn Smith, *Bibliographer;* Judith Gardner-Flint, *Senior Cataloger;* Susan Mottu, *Cataloger.*
Scope: Book collections are strong in the humanities, particularly literature & architecture. **Published Guides:** *Special Collections, Milton S. Eisenhower Library, Johns Hopkins University* (1982). **Subjects:** German Literature (18th & early 19th centuries); English Literature; Development of Graduate Education at the Johns Hopkins University (manuscript collection); Economics; American Sheet Music. **Access Policy:** Open to members of the Hopkins community & to others by application.

JOHNS HOPKINS UNIVERSITY. Milton S. Eisenhower Library, Special Collections Division, John W. Garrett Library. 4545 N Charles St, Baltimore 21210. Tel: 301-338-7641. Ann S. Gwyn, *Assistant Director.* **Staff:** Jane Katz, *Garrett Librarian.*
Scope: Book collections are strong in the humanities, particularly literature & architecture. **Published Guides:**
John Work Garrett & His Library at Evergreen House (privately printed, 1944); *Special Collections, Milton S. Eisenhower Library, Johns Hopkins University* (1982); *The Fowler Architectural Collection of the Johns Hopkins University,* reprint ed (Research Publications, 1982). **Subjects:** English Literature; Architecture (early works on classical & Renaissance architecture). **Access Policy:** Open to public but appointment suggested.

JOHNS HOPKINS UNIVERSITY. Milton S. Eisenhower Library, Special Collections Division, George Peabody Library. 17 E Mt Vernon Place, Baltimore 21202. Tel: 301-659-8197. Ann S. Gwyn, *Assistant Director.* **Staff:** Lyn Hart, *Peabody Librarian;* Robert M. Bartram, *Reference Librarian.*
Scope: 19th-century scholarly literature; also strong in British & European genealogy. **Published Guides:** *Surprises and Delights from a Century of Collecting: Catalogue of the Exhibition . . . in Honor of the Centenary of the Peabody Library* (Enoch Pratt Free Library, 1978). **Subjects:** Literature; History; Genealogy. **Access Policy:** Open to public.

MARYLAND HISTORICAL SOCIETY. Museum & Library of Maryland History, Manuscripts Division. 201 W Monument St, Baltimore 21201. Tel: 301-685-3750 ext 50. Donna M. Ellis, *Manuscripts Librarian.* **Staff:** Karen A. Stuart, *Assistant Manuscripts Librarian.*
Holdings: Mss 4200 ln ft. **Scope:** Covers whole spectrum of Maryland history from the Calvert family (Maryland colonial proprietors) of the 16th century to the papers of political & social leaders, businesses, civic, literary & social organizations, family histories & genealogies. There is a concentration of material from the 18th & 19th centuries with a growing number of records from the 20th century. Most of the collections are private & not the official state or local records. **Published Guides:** Avril J. M. Pedley, *The Manu-*

scripts Collections of the Maryland Historical Society (Maryland Historical Society, 1968); Richard J. Cox & Larry E. Sullivan, Guide to the Research Collections of the Maryland Historical Society (Maryland Historical Society, 1981). Subjects: Economics; Fine & Applied Arts; History; Regional — Maryland; Religion; Theater & Performing Arts; Travel & Exploration; Family History/Genealogy. Access Policy: All researchers are screened by Division; undergraduates must have letter of introduction from faculty; high school & below not admitted.

MARYLAND, Bethesda

NATIONAL LIBRARY OF MEDICINE. History of Medicine Division. 8600 Rockville Pike, Bethesda 20209. Tel: 301-496-5405. Dr. John L. Parascandola, Chief. Staff: Dr. James H. Cassedy, Historian; Peter Krivatsky, Curator of Rare Books; Dorothy T. Hanks, Reference Librarian; Carol Clausen, Cataloguer; James Kopp, Editor, The Bibliography of the History of Medicine; Manfred Waserman, Curator of Modern Manuscripts; Lucinda Keister, Head, Prints & Photographs Collection.
Holdings: Bks, pamphlets, dissertations 500,000; Mss 1000 collections, 1,000,000 items; Prints & Photographs Collection — 60,000 portraits. Scope: Emphasis of collection is on 16th to early 19th-century medicine & paramedical sciences, which includes early botany, chemistry, zoology & witchcraft as the forerunner of modern-day psychology & psychiatry. Published Guides: Catalogue of the 16th Century Printed Works in the National Library of Medicine (1967); Short Title Catalogue of 18th Century Printed Works in the National Library of Medicine (1979). Access Policy: Open to the public.

MARYLAND, College Park

UNIVERSITY OF MARYLAND LIBRARIES. Special Collections Division. McKeldin Library, College Park 20742. Tel: 301-454-4020. Donald Farren, Assoc. Dir. of Libraries for Special Collections.
Holdings: Bks 75,000; Mss 5000 cubic ft; 15,000 photographs; 700 maps. Scope: Rare books in a wide range of scholarly fields. Personal papers & textual manuscripts of American & English authors of the modern period. Personal & family papers & the records of organizations, many of direct Maryland interest. Archives of Japanese publications (periodicals, newspapers & books) of the period of the Allied Occupation, 1946–1949. Subjects: Books about Books; History; Literature 1900 to present; Regional — Maryland & Chesapeake Bay; French Drama, 18th & 19th centuries; Spanish Plays, 18th & 19th centuries; German Expressionism, 1910–1930; The Savoy, 1500–1900; Slavery pamphlets; Papers of Katherine Anne Porter; Papers of Djuna Barnes. Access Policy: Open to the public.

MASSACHUSETTS, Amherst

AMHERST COLLEGE LIBRARY. Special Collections/Archives. Amherst 01002. Tel: 413-542-2299. John Lancaster, Librarian & Archivist. Staff: Joanne Dougherty, Assistant Archivist.
Holdings: Bks 65,000; Mss 2000 ln ft. Scope: General teaching & research collection with strengths in acting editions (Samuel French, Inc); modern English & American poetry & drama; lepidoptera; history of Amherst College. Subjects: History; Literature 1900 to present; Theater & Performing Arts; Underground/Alternative Press Newspapers 1968–1980; Emily Dickinson. Budget: $10,000 per year. Access Policy: Open to public.

UNIVERSITY OF MASSACHUSETTS LIBRARY. Special Collections & Rare Books; Archives & Manuscripts. Amherst 01003. Tel: 413-545-2780 (manuscripts); 545-0274 (rare books). John D. Kendall, Head.
Holdings: Bks 12,000; Mss 575 ln ft; maps; audio- & videotapes; films;

photographs. **Scope:** General teaching & research collections, including Russell K. Aslpach Yeats Collection, Federal Land Bank Collection (atlases & cartography of the northeastern United States), Wallace Stevens Collection, W. E. B. DuBois Collection, Horace Mann Bond Papers, Harvey Swados Papers, Robert Francis Papers, Linguistic Atlas of New England Papers, Renaissance Diplomatic Documents 1450–1500. **Published Guides:** Robert W. McDonnell, *The Papers of W. E. B. DuBois* (Microfilming Corp. of America, 1981); Barbara S. Meloni, Rita Norton & Katherine Emerson, *The Horace Mann Bond Papers* (Univ. of Mass. Lib., 1982); Peter Brazeau, "Wallace Stevens at The University of Massachusetts: A Check List of an Archive," *The Wallace Stevens Journal* 2 (Spring 1978). **Subjects:** History; Natural History; Regional—Massachusetts, New England. **Access Policy:** Open to public.

MASSACHUSETTS, Boston

THE BOSTON ATHENAEUM. Rare Book Collection. 10½ Beacon St, Boston 02108. Tel: 617-227-0270. Cynthia English, *Head of Reference Department*. **Staff:** Lisa Backman, Stephen Nonack, *Reference Librarians*.
Holdings: Bks 30,000; Mss 150 ln ft. **Scope:** Incunabula & 16th century books; 17th–19th century tracts; Confederate imprints; George Washington's Library; 18th–19th century books on European art & architecture; 17th–19th century New England maps; papers of Isaac Hull, Ezekiel Price, other local figures, mostly 19th century. **Published Guides:** *The Reader's Guide to the Boston Athenaeum;* Marjorie Crandall, *Confederate Imprints: A Check List* (1955); *A Catalogue of the Washington Collection in the Boston Athenaeum* (1900). **Subjects:** Americana; Books about Books; Children's Literature; Fine & Applied Arts; History; Illustrated Books; Literature 1640–1800; Press Books; Regional—Boston, New England; Travel & Exploration. **Access Policy:** Open to members and qualified researchers.

BOSTON PUBLIC LIBRARY. Department of Rare Books & Manuscripts. PO Box 286, 666 Boylston St, Boston 02117. Tel: 617-536-5400. Laura V. Monti, *Keeper of Books & Manuscripts.* **Staff:** Ellen M. Oldham, *Assistant Keeper of Rare Books;* Roberta Zonghi, *Librarian II;* Gail Fiphian, *Librarian I.*
Holdings: Bks 500,000; Mss 1,000,000 items. **Published Guides:** Brochure available from the library. **Subjects:** Americana; Books about Books; Children's Literature; History of Mathematics; Illustrated Books; Incunabula; Literature pre-1640 to present; Natural History; Press Books; Religion; Theater & Performing Arts; Travel & Exploration; Landscape Architecture; Astronomy. **Access Policy:** Open to qualified researchers by appointment.

BOSTON UNIVERSITY. Mugar Memorial Library, Department of Special Collections. 771 Commonwealth Ave, Boston 02215. Tel: 617-353-3696. Howard B. Gotlieb, *Director.* **Staff:** Katherine Cain, *Book Selector;* Margaret R. Goostray, *Assistant Director;* Nancy L. Noel, *Curator, Nursing Archives.*
Holdings: Bks 70,914; Mss 15,000 ln ft. **Scope:** 15th- to 20th-century manuscripts & books with special emphasis on 19th- & 20th-century English & American literature; American colonial imprints; military history with special emphasis on the US Civil War & Abraham Lincoln; Bibles & Books of Common Prayer; 20th-century manuscript collections of authors, actors, musicians, journalists, mystery writers, cartoonists with their printed works. **Published Guides:** *Special Collections at Boston University* (Boston University Libraries, 1981). **Subjects:** Americana; Books about Books; History; Literature 1640 to present; Press Books; Theater & Performing Arts; Travel & Exploration (primarily African); History of Nursing (American, 1870s to present); Music (19th & 20th

centuries); Mystery & Detective Novels; Bibles & Books of Common Prayer. **Access Policy:** Open to public.

FRANCIS A. COUNTWAY LIBRARY OF MEDICINE (Incorporates the Boston Medical Library & the Harvard Medical Library). Rare Books Department. 10 Shattuck St, Boston 02115. Tel: 617-732-2170. Richard J. Wolfe, *Curator of Rare Books & Manuscripts & Joseph Garland Librarian of the Boston Medical Library.*

Holdings: Bks & pamphlets 250,000; one of the largest collections of manuscripts relating to medicine in the United States; medical illustration, iconography, numismatics & prints. **Scope:** Collection encompasses rare medical literature, including all the landmark books in medicine & the world's largest collection of medical incunabula; manuscripts date from the 13th century to the present. Non-medical books include literature & travel accounts by physicians. **Subjects:** History of Medicine & Science; Illustrated Books; Incunabula; Literature 1640 to present; Natural History; Anatomy; Geology; Psychiatry. **Access Policy:** Open to qualified researchers.

GRAND LODGE OF MASONS. Library. 186 Tremont St, Boston 02111. Tel: 617-426-6040 ext 131. Roberta Hankamer, *Librarian.* **Staff:** K. Ruland, *Archives;* John M. Sherman, *Historian.*

Holdings: Bks 65,000. **Scope:** Freemasonry & related studies. **Published Guides:** *A Short List of Books on Freemasonry.* **Subjects:** John Paul Jones Letters & Artifacts; Paul Revere Collection; Isaiah Thomas Masonic Correspondence & Letterbooks; Freemasonry Worldwide; Antimasonry (especially US). **Access Policy:** Open to public.

MASSACHUSETTS HISTORICAL SOCIETY. Library. 1154 Boylston St, Boston 02215. Tel: 617-536-1608. John D. Cushing, *Librarian.* **Staff:** Mary Cogswell, *Books;* Robert Sparks, *Manuscripts;* Peter Drummey, *Manuscripts.*

Holdings: Bks 50,000 (rare); Mss 6000 ln ft; 10,000 broadsides; 5000 maps. **Scope:** Rare books: pre-1820 Americana, especially New England. Manuscripts: family papers, chiefly from Massachusetts, 1628–1980. **Published Guides:** Catalogue of manuscripts in 9 folio volumes (G. K. Hall). **Subjects:** Americana; History; Law; Regional—New England; Religion. **Access Policy:** Open to public.

NORTHEASTERN UNIVERSITY. Robert Gray Dodge Library, University Archives/Special Collections Department. 360 Huntington Ave, Boston 02115. Tel: 617-437-2351. Andrew M. Calo, *University Archivist.*

Holdings: Bks 4500; correspondence; historical leaves. **Scope:** Collection reflects the academic needs of the institution. Material is acquired within fields of major academic interest such as literature, engineering, political science, transportation & economics. **Published Guides:** *Guide to the Rare Books; Inventory of the Volpe Papers.* **Subjects:** Americana; Books about Books; Economics; Ephemera; Fine & Applied Arts; History; History of Mathematics; History of Medicine; History of Science; Illustrated Books; Law; Literature pre-1640 to present; Natural History; Press Books; Regional—New England; Religion; Theater & Performing Arts; Travel & Exploration. **Access Policy:** Material circulates with permission of archivist.

SIMMONS COLLEGE LIBRARIES. The Colonel Miriam E. Perry Goll College Archives. 300 The Fenway, Boston 02115. Tel: 617-738-3141, 2242. Megan Sniffin-Marinoff, *College Archivist.* **Staff:** Martha Davidson, *Assistant Director for Technical Services.*

Holdings: Bks 3100; Mss 144 ln ft. **Scope:** Knapp Collection—19th- & early 20th-century American & European children's books; Nursing Collection—20th-century public health nursing & nursing education; Moreland/Ramsey Collections—19th- & 20th-century European & American social welfare; Simmons College—pertaining to the history of Simmons College. **Published Guides:** Robin Carlaw & Megan Sniffin, "Inventory to the Simmons College School of Public Health Nursing-School of Nursing Records, 1902–1970" (1983). **Subjects:** Children's Literature; Social Welfare (European & American, 19th & 20th century); Nursing, Public Health & Education. **Budget:** $10,000. **Access Policy:** Open to public.

MASSACHUSETTS, Cambridge

HARVARD UNIVERSITY. Houghton Library. Cambridge 02138. Tel: 617-495-2441. Lawrence Dowler, *Associate Librarian of Harvard College Library.* **Staff:** Roger E. Stoddard, *Associate Librarian;* Rodney G. Dennis, *Curator of Manuscripts;* Eleanor M. Garvey, *Curator of Printing and Graphic Arts;* Jeanne T. Newlin, *Curator of the Harvard Theater;* James E. Walsh, *Keeper of Printed Book Collection.*
Holdings: Bks 450,000; Mss 25,000 ln ft. **Scope:** Rare books & manuscripts in all fields, with some emphasis on literature, history & typography. **Subjects:** Americana; Books about Books; History: History of Mathematics & Science; Illustrated Books; Incunabula; Literature pre–1640 to present; Natural History; Press Books; Religion; Theater & Performing Arts. **Budget:** $225,000 per year. **Access Policy:** Open to public.

HARVARD UNIVERSITY ARCHIVES. Harvard University Library. Cambridge 02138. Tel: 617-495-2462. Harley P. Holden, *Curator.* **Staff:** Clark A. Elliott, *Associate Curator;* Barbara Meloni, Lucy Manzi, *Curatorial Associates;* Robin McElheny, *Curatorial Associate for Visual Collections;* Richard Haas, *Records Management Officer.*
Holdings: Mss 32,000 ln ft; broadsides; plans; photographs; motion picture films; clippings; pamphlets. **Scope:** All items relate to Harvard University, including official records, personal/professional papers of faculty, records of student organizations & publications by & about various aspects or offices of the university; biographical files. **Published Guides:** *A Descriptive Guide to the Harvard University Archives* (1974); *User's Guide;* listed in *Directory of Archives and Manuscript Repositiories at Harvard University and Radcliffe College* (1983). **Subjects:** Education; Political History; Biography; Student Academic & Social Life. **Budget:** $316,000 per year. **Access Policy:** Apply to curator.

MASSACHUSETTS INSTITUTE OF TECHNOLOGY LIBRARIES. Institute Archives & Special Collections. 77 Massachusetts Ave, Cambridge 02139. Tel: 617-253-5136. Helen W. Slotkin, *Institute Archivist, Head of Special Collections.* **Staff:** Kathleen Marquis, *Reference Archivist;* Donna Webber, *Assistant Archivist.*
Holdings: Bks 8000; Mss 4400. **Scope:** Emphasis primarily on history of technology with lesser strength in the history of science. Other strong areas are naval architecture & animal magnetism. The Institute Archives is primarily a repository for the MIT archival records & personal & professional papers of the faculty. **Subjects:** History of Science & Technology. **Access Policy:** Open to the public.

MASSACHUSETTS INSTITUTE OF TECHNOLOGY MUSEUM—HART NAUTICAL COLLECTIONS. Institute Archives & Special Collections, MIT Library. Room 14N-118, Massachusetts Institute of Technology, Cambridge 02139. Tel: 617-253-5136. Helen Slotkin, *Institute Archivist.* **Staff:** John W. Waterhouse, *Curator;* Donna Webber, *Assistant Archivist.*
Holdings: Bks 2000; 40,000 ship's plans. **Scope:** History of ship design & construction. Books are mainly technical works from the later half of the 19th century to the present. **Subjects:** History of Ship Design & Construction. **Budget:** $1000 per year. **Access Policy:** Open to public.

MASSACHUSETTS, Deerfield

THE MEMORIAL LIBRARIES. The Pocumtuck Valley Memorial Association Library & Henry N. Flynt Library of Historic Deerfield, Inc. PO Box 53, Deerfield 01342. Tel: 413-774-5581 ext 125. David R. Proper, *Librarian*.

Holdings: Bks 15,000–18,000; Mss 200–300 ln ft; photographs; maps; clippings; architectural drawings & plans. **Scope:** Especially strong in materials about Deerfield, the Connecticut River Valley of Massachusetts & New England. There are significant holdings of local history, genealogy & works by regional authors, as well as collections on the decorative arts, particularly early American & especially of New England, 17th to 19th centuries, American cultural history, museum studies & methodology, historiography & bibliography. In connection with a strong interest in the Connecticut Valley, the Libraries hold valuable collections of family letters & papers, about 400 manuscript accounts & daybooks & a significant number of diaries. **Access Policy:** Open to public for research; limited copying.

MASSACHUSETTS, New Bedford

OLD DARTMOUTH HISTORICAL SOCIETY. Whaling Museum Library. 18 Johnny Cake Hill, New Bedford 02740. Tel: 617-997-0046. Virginia M. Adams, *Librarian*. **Staff:** Judith M. Downey, *Manuscript Cataloguer*; Robert Hauser, *Conservator*.

Holdings: Bks 15,000; Mss 750 ln ft; 1800 reels microfilm; 650 maps; 500 bound periodical volumes. **Scope:** Focus on history of American whaling & local history; over 1000 manuscript logbooks. **Subjects:** Regional—Southeastern Massachusetts; Travel & Exploration; Whaling. **Budget:** FY 1982 $24,000. **Access Policy:** Open to public.

MASSACHUSETTS, North Andover

MERRIMACK VALLEY TEXTILE MUSEUM. Library. 800 Massachusetts Ave, North Andover 01845. Tel: 617-686-0191. Clare M. Sheridan, *Librarian*. **Staff:** Patricia Markey, *Rare Book Cataloguer*; Eartha Dengler, *Serials Cataloguer*; Dorothy Truman, *Archivist*; Marion Hall, *Print Collection*.

Holdings: Bks 2500 (rare books only), entire collection 35,000; Mss 2000 ln ft; print collection including textile ephemera 30,000 images. **Scope:** Collection of printed volumes deals with the technology of textile machinery & the manufacture of textiles both in North America & Europe from earliest times to modern era. The manuscript collections consist of business records of textile manufacturing & textile machinery companies, land & waterpower corporations & individual chemists, weavers, dyers, inventors & fiber scientists. The print collection includes paintings, drawings, engravings, lithos, photographs & blueprints relating to above. **Published Guides:** Wright, *Merrimack Valley Textile Museum: A Guide to the Manuscript Collection* (Garland, 1983); *A Checklist of Prints, Drawings & Paintings in the Merrimack Valley Textile Museum; Textile Technology Prints: Merrimack Valley Textile Museum*. **Subjects:** Americana/Local History/Textile Related; Ephemera/Textile Related; History/Textile Industry, American; Regional—New England/Textile Industry. **Budget:** $4000 per year. **Access Policy:** Appointment required.

MASSACHUSETTS, Northampton

SMITH COLLEGE. Rare Book Room. Northampton 01063. Tel: 413-584-2700 ext 602. Ruth Mortimer, *Curator of Rare Books*. **Staff:** Ritsuko Ozawa, *Assistant Curator*.

Holdings: Bks 15,000; Mss 8500.

Scope: Wide-ranging general collection with emphasis on printed books, incunabula to modern fine printing. **Published Guides:** Brochure available from library. **Subjects:** Children's Literature; Economics; Fine & Applied Arts; History of Mathematics; History of Science; Illustrated Books; Incunabula; Literature pre-1640 to present; Press Books; Regional—Northampton printing; Travel & Exploration; Botany; English Drama, 17th & 18th centuries; Irish Literary Renaissance; Sylvia Plath Collection (books & manuscripts). **Access Policy:** Open to the public, appointment recommended.

MASSACHUSETTS, Norton

WHEATON COLLEGE LIBRARY. Archives & Special Collections. Norton 02766. Tel: 617-285-7722 ext 513. Zephorene L. Stickney, *Archivist & Curator.*

Holdings: Bks 7300; Mss 580 ln ft; 50 cu ft costumes, paintings, objects. **Scope:** Archives consist of administrative records of Wheaton Female Seminary & Wheaton College, including correspondence, reports & publications. Rare book collections include books by & about Lucy Larcom & her personal library; rare books & fine bindings; the Wheaton Female Seminary Library as it existed in 1912; Paul H. Smart Collection of Private Press Books, especially strong in Bruce Rogers & Doves Press; books by Wheaton alumnae, faculty & staff; Samuel Valentine Cole Collection of English & American literature & poetry. **Subjects:** History; Literature 1640–1800; Press Books; Archival Collections for the History of Women's Education.

MASSACHUSETTS, Plymouth

PILGRIM SOCIETY LIBRARY. Pilgrim Hall, 75 Court St, Plymouth 02360. Tel: 617-746-1620. Caroline D. Chapin, *Curator of Books & Manuscripts.*

Holdings: Bks 12,000; Mss 150 ln ft; 300 maps; 600 photographs. **Scope:** Collection focuses on Pilgrim history & the history of Plymouth Colony. The rare book collection contains one of the most complete groupings of books that were printed and/or read by the Pilgrims. **Published Guides:** Charlotte S. Price, *Guide to the Pilgrim Society Manuscripts Collection* (1975); Lawrence D. Geller, *The Books of the Pilgrims* (1975); Jeanne M. Mills, *Checklist of Rare Book Collections* (1981). **Subjects:** Regional—Plymouth. **Budget:** $1000 per year. **Access Policy:** Appointment required.

MASSACHUSETTS, Waltham

AMERICAN JEWISH HISTORICAL SOCIETY. Lee M. Friedman Memorial Library. 2 Thornton Rd, Waltham 02154. Tel: 617-891-8110. Nathan M. Kaganoff, *Librarian.* **Staff:** Donald Altschiller, *Assistant Librarian.*

Holdings: Bks 70,000; Mss 6,000,000 items. **Scope:** American Jewish history. **Subjects:** Religion; Ethnic History. **Budget:** $15,000 per year. **Access Policy:** Open to public for research.

BRANDEIS UNIVERSITY LIBRARIES. Special Collections. 415 South St, Waltham 02254. Tel: 617-647-2513, 2520. Victor A. Berch, *Librarian.* **Staff:** Susan E. Rainey, *Cataloguer.*

Holdings: Bks 75,000; Mss 400 ln ft. **Subjects:** Children's Literature; History of Mathematics; History of Science; Literature 1900 to present; Travel & Exploration; Spanish Civil War; Leonardo da Vinci; Judaica. **Access Policy:** Open to public, but some material is restricted.

MASSACHUSETTS, Wellesley

WELLESLEY COLLEGE. Margaret Clapp Library, Special Collections. Wellesley 02181. Tel: 617-235-0320 ext 2129. Ann Anninger, *Librarian.*

Holdings: Bks 25,000; Mss 40 ln ft. **Scope:** Robert & Elizabeth Barrett

Browning collection; strong English poetry collection; Italian collection, 15th–17th centuries; slavery & Reconstruction collection; juvenile collection; North American languages collection; book arts collection; Ruskin collection. **Published Guides:** George Herbert Palmer, *A Catalogue of Early & Rare Editions of English Poetry Collected & Presented to Wellesley College* (Riverside Press, 1923); Margaret Hastings Jackson, *Catalogue of the Frances Taylor Pearsons Plimpton Collection of Italian Books and Manuscripts in the Library of Wellesley College* (Harvard University Press, 1929); Wendy Ball and Tony Martin, *Rare Afro-Americana: A Reconstruction of the Adger Library* (G. K. Hall, 1981). **Access Policy:** Two current identifications required.

MASSACHUSETTS, Williamstown

WILLIAMS COLLEGE. Chapin Library. Stetson Hall, PO Box 426, Williamstown 01267. Tel: 413-597-2462. Robert L. Volz, *Custodian*. **Staff:** Wayne G. Hammond, *Assistant Librarian*.

Holdings: Bks 25,000; Mss 20 ln ft. **Scope:** General collection of rare books & manuscripts, unrestricted as to time period or subject matter, which supports, through original source materials, the liberal arts curriculum of Williams College. **Published Guides:** *A Short-Title List of the Books in the Chapin Library* (1939). **Subjects:** Americana, Books about Books; History; History of Science; Illustrated Books; Incunabula; Literature pre-1640 to present; Natural History; Press Books; Religion; Travel & Exploration. **Budget:** $10,000 per year. **Access Policy:** Open to public.

MASSACHUSETTS, Worcester

AMERICAN ANTIQUARIAN SOCIETY. 185 Salisbury St, Worcester 01609. Tel: 617-755-5221. Marcus A. McCorison, *Director & Librarian*. **Staff:** Frederick

E. Bauer, *Associate Librarian;* John B. Hench, *Assistant Director for Research & Publication;* Nancy H. Burkett, *Head, Readers' Services;* Georgia B. Bumgardner, *Curator of Graphic Arts;* Joyce Ann Tracy, *Curator of Newspapers & Serials;* Kathleen A. Major, *Keeper of Manuscripts;* Richard C. Baker, *Chief Conservator;* Alan N. Degutis, *North American Imprints Program;* Judy L. Larson, *Catalogue of American Engravings.*

Holdings: Bks 620,000; Mss 2215 ln ft; 110,175 microform units; 28,000 broadsides & ephemera; 10,500 maps; 10,000 prints; 65,000 sheet music; 35,000 bookplates; 550 current periodicals. **Scope:** Materials printed in the United States & Canada, 1639–1876, & secondary materials that explicate American history & culture of the period. **Published Guides:** *A Dictionary Catalogue of American Books Pertaining to the 17th through 19th Centuries in the Library of the American Antiquarian Society* (Greenwood, 1971); *Catalogue of the Manuscript Collections of the American Antiquarian Society* (G. K. Hall, 1979). **Subjects:** Americana; Books about Books; Children's Literature; Economics; Ephemera; Fine & Applied Arts; History; History of Medicine; History of Science; Illustrated Books; Literature 1640–1876; Natural History; Religion; Theater & Performing Arts; Travel & Exploration; US & Canadian Experience Prior to 1877; Printing History. **Budget:** $243,400 (1983). **Access Policy:** Positive identification required; preliminary letter preferred; not open, except under unusual circumstances, to undergraduates.

MICHIGAN, Ann Arbor

UNIVERSITY OF MICHIGAN. William L. Clements Library. Ann Arbor 48109. Tel: 313-764-2347. John C. Dann, *Director*. Arlene P. Shy, Richard W. Ryan, Galen R. Wilson, *Curators*.

Holdings: Bks 60,000; Mss 230 ln ft; sheet music; newspapers; prints.

Scope: Primary source materials for study of American discovery, exploration & history, 1492–1900. **Published Guides:** Howard H. Peckham, *History of the William L. Clements Library, 1923–1973* (1973); Christian Brun, *Guide to the Manuscript Maps in the W. L. Clements Library* (1959); G. K. Hall *Guides to Books,* 7 vols. (1970) and *Maps,* 4 vols. (1972); Arlene W. Shy, *Guide to Manuscript Collections* (1978). **Subjects:** Americana (all aspects). **Access Policy:** Open for qualified, serious scholarship.

UNIVERSITY OF MICHIGAN. Libraries, Department of Rare Books & Special Collections. Ann Arbor 48109. Tel: 313-764-9377. Robert J. Starring, *Head.* **Staff:** Helen S. Butz, Mary Ann Sellers, *Rare Book Librarians;* Kathryn L. Beam, *Manuscript Librarian;* Edward C. Weber, *Head, Labadie Collection;* Ruth Anne Okey, *Adminstrative Librarian, Labadie Collection.*

Holdings: Bks & pamphlets 94,120; Mss (modern) 333.5 ln ft; 8255 serial titles; 7000 pieces of papyri; 244 medieval & Renaissance manuscripts; 1120 Islamic & Oriental manuscripts; 2895 posters & broadsides; 43,924 photos; 1941 prints; 3985 bookplates; 192 tapes, cartridges, etc; 1032 microforms; 30,500 leaflets, flyers, etc. **Scope:** World-renowned collection of papyri; modern manuscripts strongest in Swinburne & American literary figures; incunabula (450 titles); history — emphasis on British; English drama to 1850 & 19th century American drama; Shakespeare (9300 volumes); imaginary voyages; history of science; military art & science; Worcester Philippine collection; polar expeditions; documents of Weimar Republic & Nazi periods; Oneida Community. Labadie Collection: originally anarchist materials; now all social protest literature, 1870 to present. **Subjects:** Economics; History; History of Mathematics & Science; Illustrated Books; Incunabula; Literature 1640 to present; Religion;

Theater & Performing Arts; Travel & Exploration. **Budget:** $80,000 per year. **Access Policy:** Apply to head.

UNIVERSITY OF MICHIGAN. Michigan Historical Collections. Bentley Historical Library, 1150 Beal Ave, Ann Arbor 48109. Tel: 313-764-3482. Francis X. Blovin, Jr, *Director.* **Staff:** William K. Wallach, *Assistant Director;* Marjorie Barritt, Frank Boles, *Assistant Archivists for University Records;* Leonard Coombs, *Curator of Printed Works;* James Craven, *Conservator;* May Davis Hill, *Curator of Photographs;* Thomas E. Powers, *Curator of Manuscripts;* Mary Jo Pugh, *Reference Archivist;* Kenneth P. Scheffel, *Field Representative.*

Holdings: Bks 45,000; Mss 18,000 ln ft; 500,000 photos; 3500 maps. **Scope:** Collections relate chiefly to the history of Michigan & the University of Michigan. Strengths include temperance & prohibition movement; US-Philippine relations; US-China relations; history of business; church history; immigration history. **Published Guides:** Thomas E. Powers & William H. McNitt, *Guide to Manuscripts in the Bentley Historical Library* (1976). The library has also issued 10 subject guides. Those in print focus on pacifism & conscientious objection, athletics, Native Americans, the clergy, underground press & American-Philippine relations. **Subjects:** History; Regional — Michigan; Religion; Temperance & Prohibition; American-Philippine Relations; US-China Relations; 20th-Century Politics & Government; Civil War; Lumbering; Conservation; Women's History; Black History; Pacifism; Journalism; Medicine; Agriculture; Immigrant Groups in Michigan; Higher Education; US Intellectual History. **Budget:** $2800 per year. **Access Policy:** Open to public.

MICHIGAN, East Lansing

MICHIGAN STATE UNIVERSITY. Library, Special Collections. East Lansing

48824. Tel: 517-355-3770. Jannette Fiore, *Head*. **Staff:** Ann Tracy, *Assistant*.

Holdings: Bks 145,000; Mss 65 ln ft. **Scope:** Collections are meant to meet the university's curricular needs & to strengthen the major subject fields. **Published Guides:** Jannette Fiore, *The Russell B. Nye Popular Culture Collection: A Descriptive Guide* (1978). **Subjects:** History; History of Medicine & Science; Illustrated Books; Literature pre-1640 to present; Natural History; Africana (Sub-Saharan); Popular Culture; Veterinary Medicine; American Radicalism; Facsimiles of Illuminated Manuscripts. **Access Policy:** Open to public.

MICHIGAN, Grand Rapids

CALVIN COLLEGE AND SEMINARY LIBRARY. Heritage Hall—Colonial Origins. 3207 Burton St SE, Grand Rapids 49506. Tel: 616-957-6313. Herbert J. Brinks, *Curator*. **Staff:** Zwanet C. Janssens, *Research Archivist*.

Holdings: Bks 3751; Mss 1238 ln ft; 2472 microfilm reels; 1108 sound tapes. **Scope:** Archives, manuscripts & other records of the Christian Reformed church, its leaders, its closely related institutions & its Dutch origins. **Subjects:** History; Regional—Western Michigan; History of Christian Reformed Church; Dutch Immigrant Letter Collection; Dutch-Language Books, Pamphlets & Newspapers Printed in America, 1839–1948. **Budget:** $15,000 per year. **Access Policy:** Limited hours.

CALVIN COLLEGE AND SEMINARY LIBRARY. H. H. Meeter Center for Calvin Studies. 3207 Burton St SE, Grand Rapids 49506. Tel: 616-957-6089. M. Howard Rienstra, *Director*. **Staff:** Peter De Klerk, *Curator*.

Scope: 16th-century imprints of John Calvin, anti-Calvin treaties, works of Beza & others in Geneva & Calvinist tradition. **Published Guides:** "The Meeter Center for Calvin Studies: An Introduction" (October 1983). **Sub**jects: Religion. **Budget:** $16,000 per year. **Access Policy:** Open to public.

MICHIGAN, Kalamazoo

KALAMAZOO COLLEGE. Upjohn Library. 1200 Academy St, Kalamazoo 49001. Eleanor H. Pinkham, *College Librarian*.

Holdings: Bks 3000. **Subjects:** History of Books & Printing; Ornithology; History of Science; History of Private Presses. **Budget:** $5000 per year. **Access Policy:** Restricted hours; valid identification required.

MICHIGAN, Monroe

MONROE COUNTY LIBRARY SYSTEM. Rare Books & General George Armstrong Custer Collection. 3700 South Custer Rd, Monroe 48161. Tel: 313-241-5277. Bernard A. Margolis, *Director*. **Staff:** Karen Stoll, *Curator, Custer Collection;* Marie Duber Chulski, *Head of Reference & Information Services*.

Holdings: Bks 20,000; Mss 10 ln ft. **Scope:** Custeriana collection: includes all manner of material related to General George Armstrong Custer, the Battle of the Little Big Horn & related topics. Michigan and local history: includes materials related to Monroe; War of 1812. **Published Guides:** *General George Armstrong Custer: A Bibliography of Cataloged Materials in Special Collections of the Billings Public Library & Monroe County Library System* (1976). **Subjects:** Americana; Regional—Michigan; General George Armstrong Custer; Battle of the Little Big Horn; Indian Wars of America; American Indians. **Budget:** $15,000 per year. **Access Policy:** By appointment only.

MINNESOTA, Collegeville

ST. JOHN'S UNIVERSITY. Alcuin Library, Rare Book Room. Collegeville 56321. Tel: 612-363-2119. Bro Richard Oliver, OSB, *Librarian*.

Holdings: Bks 5500; Mss 3 ln ft; 110 manuscript facsimiles. **Scope:** Items in collection date from 1470 to present; heavy concentration in 18th-century German Catholic theology in distinctive pigskin bindings. Strong in Benedictina (especially Maurist editions) & liturgical works. Classics well represented. **Published Guides:** Ronald W. Roloff, *St. John's University Library: An Historical Evaluation* (1953). **Budget:** $6000 per year. **Access Policy:** By appointment.

MINNESOTA, Minneapolis

MINNEAPOLIS PUBLIC LIBRARY & INFORMATION CENTER. Athenaeum. 300 Nicollete Mall, Minneapolis 55401. Tel: 612-372-6522. Richard J. Hofstad, *Librarian.*
Holdings: Bks 16,000. **Scope:** Collection is strong in natural history, early American exploration & travel, the North American Indian & fine illustrated books. **Subjects:** Americana; Illustrated Books; Literature 1800–1900; Natural History; Travel & Exploration. **Budget:** $20,000 per year. **Access Policy:** Valid identification required.

UNIVERSITY OF MINNESOTA LIBRARIES. James Ford Bell Library. Wilson Library-472, 309 19th Ave S, Minneapolis 55455. Tel: 612-373-2888. John Parker, *Curator.* **Staff:** Carol Urness, *Assistant Curator.*
Holdings: 10,000 books, maps & manuscripts. **Scope:** Original source materials for the history of European overseas expansion prior to 1800. **Published Guides:** *The James Ford Bell Library* (G. K. Hall, 1981). **Subjects:** Americana; Economics; History; Incunabula; Law; Natural History; Religion; Travel & Exploration; Missionary Activities; Colonial History; International Commerce; Geography. **Access Policy:** Open to the public by appointment.

UNIVERSITY OF MINNESOTA LIBRARIES. Bio-Medical Library, Owen H. Wangensteen Historical Library of Biology & Medicine. Diehl Hall, 505 Essex St SE, Minneapolis 55455. Tel: 612-373-5586. Judith Overmier, *Head.* **Staff:** Brian Mulherne, *Archivist.*
Holdings: Bks 35,000. **Scope:** Research materials in the health sciences, including books & manuscripts (15th century through 1920); 20th-century archives; museum objects of 19th & 20th centuries. **Published Guides:** Brochure available from the library. **Subjects:** Biology; Surgery; Pathology; Anatomy. **Budget:** $80,000 per year. **Access Policy:** Open to the public.

UNIVERSITY OF MINNESOTA LIBRARIES. O. Meredith Wilson Library, Special Collections & Rare Books. 309 19 Ave S, Minneapolis 55455. Tel: 612-373-2897. Austin J. McLean, *Curator.* **Staff:** John R. Jenson, *Assistant Curator.*
Holdings: Bks 100,000; Mss 100 ln ft. **Scope:** Early printed books to the present. **Sujects:** History; Literature 1640 to present; Press Books; Religion. **Budget:** $10,000 per year. **Access Policy:** Identification required.

MINNESOTA, Northfield

ST. OLAF COLLEGE. Howard & Edna Hong Kierkegaard Library. Northfield 55057. C. Stephen Evans, *Curator.* **Staff:** Howard V. Hong, *Associate Curator.*
Holdings: Bks 7500; 195 microfilm reels of all extant journals & papers of Søren Kierkegaard. **Scope:** Substantial reconstruction of Søren Kierkegaard's library (same editions); complete set of first editions of Kierkegaard's works, subsequent Danish editions of works, various English, German, French & Italian editions of works, all editions of Kierkegaard's journals & papers; extensive collections of secondary, lexical, historical & bibliographic works pertaining to Søren Kierkegaard. **Subjects:** Religion; Søren Kierkegaard; Philosophy (19th-century north European). **Budget:** $13,000 per year.

Access Policy: Open to qualified researchers.

MINNESOTA, Saint Paul

COLLEGE OF SAINT THOMAS. O'Shaughnessy Library, Department of Special Collections. 2115 Summit Ave, Saint Paul 55105. Tel: 612-647-5726, 5796. John B. Davenport, *Librarian.* Staff: Ann Miller, *Assistant.*
Holdings: Bks 6733; Mss 554 ln ft. Scope: Manuscripts: archives of the College of Saint Thomas. Books: Celtic collection & other rare books. Subjects: Celtic Collection (Irish, Scottish & Welsh history, language & folklore). Budget: $4000 per year. Access Policy: Archives open to public; rare books upon written application.

MISSISSIPPI, Hattiesburg

UNIVERSITY OF SOUTHERN MISSISSIPPI. William David McCain Graduate Library, Sam Woods Rare Book Collection. PO Box 5148, Southern Sta, Hattiesburg 39406. Tel: 601-266-4347. Terry Latour, *Curator for Special Collections.* Staff: John Kelly, *Curator for Special Collections;* Henry Simmons, *Curator for Mississippiana.*
Holdings: Bks 5500; Mss 2100 ln ft (de Grummond); 1800 archives. Subjects: Americana; Children's Literature; History; Illustrated Books; Incunabula; Literature 1640 to present. Budget: $5000 per year. Access Policy: Apply to curator.

MISSISSIPPI, Jackson

MISSISSIPPI DEPARTMENT OF ARCHIVES & HISTORY. Archives & Library Division. PO Box 571, Jackson 39205. Tel: 601-359-1424. Madel Morgan, *Director.* Staff: Anne Lipscomb, *Head Librarian;* William Hanna, *Curator, Manuscripts and Special Collections.*
Holdings: Bks 38,000; Mss 3000 cu ft; 25,000 photographs & maps. Scope: Books, manuscripts & other items pertaining to the state of Missis-

sippi (including colonial & territorial times) & to all inhabitants. Published Guides: Books are included in *Mississippiana Union Catalog,* vol. 1 (Mississippi Library Commission, 1970). Subjects: Regional — Mississippi. Access Policy: Open to public.

MISSOURI, Columbia

STATE HISTORICAL SOCIETY OF MISSOURI. 1020 Lowry St, Columbia 65201. Tel: 314-882-7083. Richard S. Brownlee, *Administrator.*
Holdings: Bks 432,000; Mss 17,500 ln ft; 27 million pages of Missouri newspapers on microfilm. Scope: Historical works relating to Missouri & the Trans-Mississippi West; works of Missouri authors; Western Americana; accounts of travels & explorations in the Midwest, South & Trans-Mississippi West. Subjects: Americana; Children's Literature (Missouri); History; Regional — Trans-Mississippi West; Religion (Methodism); Mark Twain; Western Americana; Eugene Field Collection; American Methodism. Access Policy: Apply to librarian.

UNIVERSITY OF MISSOURI-COLUMBIA. Ellis Library, Special Collections. Columbia 65201. Tel: 314-882-7461. Margaret Howell, *Head.*
Holdings: Bks 31,000. Scope: General collection with strengths in illustrated books, philosophy, natural history, history of books & printing. Published Guides: *Thomas Moore Johnson Collection; The Friends of the University of Missouri Libraries & State Historical Society Gifts to the Rare Book Room.* Subjects: Books about Books; Illustrated Books; Natural History; Press Books; Philosophy (Plato & the Neo-Platonists). Budget: $3000 per year. Access Policy: Open to public.

MISSOURI, Kansas City

LINDA HALL LIBRARY. History of Science Collection. 5109 Cherry St, Kan-

sas City 64110. Tel: 816-363-4600. Bruce Bradley, *Bibliographer.* **Staff:** William B. Ashworth, *Consultant.*
Holdings: Bks 4000. **Scope:** Collection of rare & early printed materials covering all areas of science & technology except medicine. **Published Guide:** Brochure & exhibition catalogues available from the library. **Access Policy:** Open to the public.

UNIVERSITY OF MISSOURI-KANSAS CITY LIBRARY. Joint Collection, University of Missouri Western Historical Manuscript Collection & the State Historical Society of Missouri Manuscripts. 5100 Rockhill Rd, Kansas City 64112. Tel: 816-276-1543. Gordon Hendrickson, *Associate Director for Joint Collection.* **Staff:** David Boutros, *Manuscript Specialist.*
Holdings: Mss 2318.5 ln ft; 48 microfilm rolls; 36,500 aperture cards for architectural drawings. **Subjects:** Americana; Regional—Western Missouri & Kansas City; Architecture; American Music. **Access Policy:** Open to public.

MISSOURI, Saint Louis

CONCORDIA HISTORICAL INSTITUTE. Rare Books Department & Archives/ Manuscripts Department. 801 De Mun Ave, Saint Louis 63105. Tel: 314-721-5934 ext 320. Aug. R. Suelflow, *Director.* **Staff:** Kurt A. Bodling, *Reference and Research Assistant.*
Holdings: Bks 3500; Mss 2308 ln ft. **Scope:** Theological, devotional & religious works that have had an influence on the growth of Lutheranism worldwide; Bibles and hymnals. **Subjects:** Religion. **Access Policy:** Apply to director.

MISSOURI HISTORICAL SOCIETY. Research Library & Archives. Jefferson Memorial Bldg/Forest Park, Saint Louis 63112. Tel: 314-361-1424. Stephanie A. Klein, *Librarian-Archivist.* **Staff:** Peter Michel, *Manuscript Processor;* Jean D. Streeter, Charles A.

Lindbergh, *Archivists;* Janice L. Fox, *Researcher in Residence.*
Holdings: Bks 1000; Mss 1500 ln ft; **Scope:** American fur trade; history of Saint Louis & Missouri; Lewis & Clark expedition; Louisiana Territory; Missouri & Mississippi rivers; westward expansion; genealogy & family history (Missouri & connecting states). **Published Guides:** *A List of Manuscript Collections in the Archives of the Missouri Historical Society, Saint Louis; In Her Own Write: Women's History Resources in the Library & Archives of the Missouri Historical Society.* **Subjects:** Chouteau Collection; Clark Family Papers; Kate Chopin Papers; David R. Francis Papers; Hamilton R. Gamble Papers; William Torrey Harris Papers; William Carr Lane Papers; Louisiana Purchase Exposition Papers; Merchants Exchange (Saint Louis) Papers; New Madrid Archives; Saint Louis (Missouri) Archives (1764–1804); Dexter P. Tiffany Papers; Numerous Other Collections Dealing with Saint Louis; Lindbergh Papers (1827–1969; bulk of the collection covers 1927–1945). **Access Policy:** Nonmembers pay daily fee.

SAINT LOUIS MERCANTILE LIBRARY. PO Box 633, Saint Louis 63188. Tel: 314-621-0670. Elizabeth Kirchner, *Director/Librarian.* **Staff:** Mary Mewes, *Reference and Research;* Susan Schucart Finley, *Restoration and Binding.*
Holdings: Bks 50,000. **Scope:** Western Americana; alchemy dating back to 17th century; Chauteau & Bissell manuscripts; Zebulon Pike papers; Audubon elephantine folios & Audubon quadrapeda. **Subjects:** Americana; History; Incunabula; Literature 1800–1900; Natural History; Regional—Early Saint Louis & Missouri; Travel & Exploration; Early Missouri & Illinois Newspapers, 1817–1900; Civil War. **Budget:** $50,000 over 5-year period. **Access Policy:** Library membership.

SAINT LOUIS PUBLIC LIBRARY. Carol McDonald Gardner Rare Book Room.

1301 Olive St, Saint Louis 63103. Tel: 314-241-2288 ext 381. Julanne Good, *Supervisor.* **Staff:** Martha Riley, *Rare Books Librarian.*

Holdings: Bks 6300; Mss 6.5 ln ft. **Scope:** Current areas of acquisition center on Saint Louis–related materials, including Saint Louis authors & early imprints & reference materials on care of books, book arts & book collections. **Subjects:** Books about Books; Natural History; Regional—Missouri & Saint Louis; Saint Louis Authors; Leonard Blake Collection (Bewick Woodcuts); New Jersey Werner Typographic Collection; Early Saint Louis & Missouri Imprints; William Marion Reedy Collection of First Editions of Authors Having Some Association with Reedy and *Reedy's Mirror;* William K. Bixby Publications & Association Items; Saint Louis Public Library Archives. **Budget:** $5573 per year. **Access Policy:** Open to public.

UNIVERSITY OF MISSOURI-SAINT LOUIS. Thomas Jefferson Library, Special Collections. 8001 Natural Bridge Rd, Saint Louis 63121. Charles A. Hamaker, *Head of Collection Development Division.*

Holdings: Bks 5000. **Scope:** Utopian literature in English & American imprints (1000 volumes); Ernest Augustus collection (duke of Cumberland, later king of Hanover; 600 volumes from the family library); also Missouri imprints, especially Saint Louis. **Subjects:** Utopian Literature (American & British). **Access Policy:** Open to public.

WASHINGTON UNIVERSITY. Olin Library, Special Collections. Saint Louis 63130. Tel: 314-889-5495. Holly Hall, *Head.* **Staff:** Ida Holland, *Rare Books Cataloguer;* Timothy D. Murrary, *Curator of Manuscripts;* Beryl Manne, *University Archivist.*

Holdings: Bks 35,000; Mss 651 cu ft; archives & historical papers 4200 cu ft. **Scope:** Modern literature collection: first, limited, variant & uncommon editions; correspondence, worksheets, notebooks & ephemera of selected American & British authors. History of printing collection. The Semeiology collection documents the early history of communications & is concerned with the study of signs & symbols. Topics covered include cryptography, codes & ciphers, artificial memory, decipherment of unknown languages, universal languages & early development in stemography, Braille & various languages of the deaf & mute. 16th-century French literature collection: focuses on Pierre de Ronsard & his circle & includes titles that Ronsard might have had occasion to consult; also includes the working papers, pertinent correspondence & annotated texts of Paul Laumonier, the Ronsard scholar. Also rare books & manuscripts for most areas in which the university teaches & conducts research. **Subjects:** Books about Books; Ephemera; Illustrated Books; Literature 1800 to present; Press Books; Regional—St. Louis Area. **Access Policy:** Open to public.

MONTANA, Missoula

UNIVERSITY OF MONTANA. Maureen & Mike Mansfield Library, K. Ross Archives/Special Collections. Missoula 59812. Tel: 406-243-2053. Dale L. Johnson, *Archives & Manuscripts;* Katherine Schaefer, *Special Collections.*

Holdings: Bks 2000; Mss 6500; 30,000 photographs; 800 oral history tapes. **Scope:** Rare books cover all subject areas with emphasis on Montana & the Northwest, Indians, Geoffrey Chaucer & his age. Manuscripts cover Montana & US history; local, state & national political figures; business history; lumber industry history; manuscripts of Montana authors; University of Montana Archives. **Budget:** $4000 per year. **Access Policy:** Open to public.

NEBRASKA, Lincoln

UNIVERSITY OF NEBRASKA-LINCOLN LIBRARIES. Love Library, University

Archives & Special Collections Division. Lincoln 68588. Tel: 402-472-2531. Joseph G. Svoboda, *Head and University Archivist*. **Staff:** Elsie Thomas, *Assistant*.

Holdings: Bks 60,000; Mss 4000; 2000 maps, posters, etc. **Published Guides:** Descriptive brochures available from library. **Subjects:** Americana (Western); Folklore; American Railroads; Russian History (19th & 20th centuries); World War II; Czech Heritage; Nebraskana. **Access Policy:** Open to public.

NEBRASKA, Omaha

UNIVERSITY OF NEBRASKA AT OMAHA. University Library. Omaha 68182. Tel: 402-554-2514. Mel Bohn, *Humanities Reference Librarian*. **Staff:** Carole Larson, *Social Sciences Reference Librarian*.

Holdings: Bks 6000. **Subjects:** Press Books; Regional—Omaha; Cummington Press Collection. **Budget:** $5000 per year. **Access Policy:** Open to public.

NEVADA, Reno

NEVADA HISTORICAL SOCIETY. 1650 N Virginia St, Reno 89503. Tel: 702-789-0190. Eric N. Moody, *Curator of Manuscripts*. **Staff:** Lee Mortensen, *Librarian*.

Scope: Lumber, mining, transportation & communication in Nevada & western United States; Nevada history. **Access Policy:** Open to public.

NEW HAMPSHIRE, Concord

NEW HAMPSHIRE HISTORICAL SOCIETY. 30 Park St, Concord 03301. Tel: 603-225-3381. R. Stuart Wallace, *Manuscripts Librarian*. **Staff:** William Copeley, *Associate Librarian*.

Holdings: Bks 2000; Mss 1000 ln ft. **Scope:** New Hampshire history, 1700–1900. **Subjects:** Fine & Applied Arts; Regional—New Hampshire. **Budget:** $2000 per year. **Access Policy:** Apply to librarian.

NEW HAMPSHIRE STATE LIBRARY. General Reference Collection. 20 Park St, Concord 03301. Tel: 603-271-2144. Stella J. Scheckter, *Director of Reference & Loan Division*.

Scope: Book collection includes an estimated 200–300 pre-1800 imprints, mostly religious sermons, literary works, history & travel & medical books & a collection of juveniles ranging from 1700s through 1930 (5000 volumes). Manuscript collection is limited to papers of some former New Hampshire governors & a Supreme Court justice. **Access Policy:** Apply to division director.

NEW HAMPSHIRE, Hanover

DARTMOUTH COLLEGE LIBRARY. Special Collections. Hanover 03755. Tel: 603-646-2037. Stanley W. Brown, *Chief & Curator of Rare Books*. **Staff:** Philip N. Cronenwett, *Curator of Manuscripts;* Kenneth C. Cramer, *Archivist*.

Holdings: Bks 70,000; Mss 6600 ln ft; many uncatalogued items, ephemera, etc. **Scope:** American & British 19th- & 20th-century literature, including Robert Frost, Kenneth Roberts, Rupert Brooke, Erskine Caldwell, Edward Verrall Lucas, Vilhjalmur Stefansson; fine printing & printing history; Americana, especially local & New Hampshire; White Mountains; polar exploration; papers of literary, political, scientific, artistic figures. **Published Guides:** *Brief Guide to the Principal Collections of the Rare Books Department* (1964, op); *Illuminated Manuscripts . . .; Incunabula in the Dartmouth College Library.* **Subjects:** Americana; Illustrated Books; Literature 1900 to present; Press Books; Regional—New Hampshire & White Mountains; Travel & Exploration (especially Arctic). **Access Policy:** Open to public.

NEW JERSEY, Madison

DREW UNIVERSITY. Library, Rare Book Division. Madison 07940. Tel: 201-

377-3000 ext 469. Arthur E. Jones, *Director*.

Holdings: Bks 4600; Mss 311 ln ft. **Scope:** Six Greek Gospel manuscripts; 22 incunabula; 3000 16th- & 17th-century history & religion titles; US presidents & cabinet members; Book of Common Prayer collection; major emphasis in Wesleyana & Methodism. **Subjects:** Books about Books; History; Literature 1640 to present; Religion; Georges Simenon; Joanna Southcott; Methodism & Wesleyana; Hymnology. **Budget:** $16,000 per year. **Access Policy:** Appointment required.

FAIRLEIGH DICKINSON UNIVERSITY LIBRARY. Department of Special Collections. 285 Madison Ave, Madison 07940. Tel: 201-377-4700 ext 516. James Fraser, *Library Director*. **Staff:** Renée Weber, *Curator of Special Collections*.

Holdings: Bks 5000; Mss 150,000 items; 5000 photographs; 5000 phonorecordings; 6000 pieces of original art. **Scope:** Emphasis is on printing history, including press books & books on the mechanical aspects of printing; books on the development of the poster in the United States & abroad; original comic art & illustrations. Deposit library for the Outdoor Advertising Association. **Subjects:** Books about Books; Ephemera; Press Books; Theater & Performing Arts; Books on Satire & Caricature; Anthropology; Psychology. **Access Policy:** Open to public by appointment for research.

NEW JERSEY, Newark

THE NEW JERSEY HISTORICAL SOCIETY. Library. 230 Broadway, Newark 07104. Tel: 201-483-3939. Barbara S. Irwin, *Library Director*. **Staff:** Carl Lane, *Keeper of Manuscripts;* Kathleen Stavec, *Reference Librarian*.

Holdings: Bks 62,000; Mss 1350 ln ft. **Scope:** Rare books: New Jersey pre-1850 imprints; Revolutionary War materials. Manuscripts: primarily collections relating to New Jersey history.

Published Guides: Morris & Skemer, *Guide to the Manuscript Collections of the New Jersey Historical Society* (1979). **Subjects:** Americana; Regional — New Jersey; Genealogy & Family History (primarily New Jersey but also New York, Pennsylvania & other northeastern states). **Budget:** $100,000 per year. **Access Policy:** Open to public.

NEW JERSEY, Princeton

PRINCETON UNIVERSITY LIBRARY. Rare Books & Special Collections. Princeton 08544. Tel: 609-452-3184. Richard M. Ludwig, *Assistant University Librarian*. **Staff:** Nancy Bressler, *Curator of Public Affairs Papers;* Karl Buchberg, *Rare Books & Manuscripts Conservator;* Alfred L. Bush, *Curator of the Princeton Collections of Western Americana;* Stephen Ferguson, *Curator of Rare Books;* Mary Ann Jensen, *Curator of Theater Collection;* Jean F. Preston, *Curator of Manuscripts;* Dale Roylance, *Curator of Graphic Arts;* Lawrence E. Spellman, *Curator of Maps;* Brooks Levy, *Numismatist;* Ann Hanson, *Papyrologist*.

Holdings: Bks 200,000; Mss 7000 ln ft; 150,000 maps; 40,000 prints & photographs. **Scope:** Rare books: English & American literature & history; theater; graphic arts; early printed Continental books. Manuscripts: English & American literature & history; history of science; modern Latin American literature. **Published Guides:** *Guide to Selected Special Collections of Printed Books & Other Materials in the Princeton University Library* (1983); *The Manuscript Collections of the Princeton University Library. An Introductory Survey* by Alexander P. Clark (1960); *LITMSS: An Indexed Catalogue of Literary & Historical Manuscripts in Selected Manuscript Collections of Firestone Library* (1983). **Subjects:** Americana; Economics; Fine & Applied Arts; History; History of Science; Illustrated Books; Incunabula; Literature pre–1640 to present; Press Books; Regional—Western Americana; Theater & Performing Arts; Travel & Exploration. **Access Policy:** Open to public.

NEW MEXICO, Albuquerque

UNIVERSITY OF NEW MEXICO. General Library, Special Collections Department. Albuquerque 87131. Tel: 505-277-6451. James Wright, *Acting Head.* **Staff:** Tim Wehrkamp, *Assistant Head.*

Holdings: Bks 29,500; Mss 2200 ln ft. **Scope:** Rare & special access books; New Mexicana; Western Americana; archives; photographs; university theses & dissertations; oral history; John Gaw Meem Architectural Records Collections; pamphlet collections. The New Mexicana & Western Americana collections include monographs, serials & microfilm. **Printed Guides:** *Guide to the Collections* (1957). **Subjects:** Americana; History; Regional—Western Americana, New Mexicana; Legislative Archives; Native American Oral History; Commissioners of BIA Papers; New Mexican Pioneers Oral History. **Budget:** $17,000 per year. **Access Policy:** Apply to library.

NEW MEXICO, Portales

EASTERN NEW MEXICO UNIVERSITY. Golden Library, Special Collections Department. Portales 88130. Tel: 505-562-2624. Mary Jo Walker, *Librarian.* **Staff:** Leone Reynolds, *Assistant.*

Holdings: Bks 11,947; Mss 524.5 cu ft; 700 periodicals titles; 10,318 issues. **Scope:** Rare, out-of-print & some current materials (including some 700 oral history interviews) in both published & unpublished form pertaining to the Southwest, with primary emphasis on New Mexico & Roosevelt County (also includes scattered holdings of some old New Mexico newspaper titles); the Jack Williamson Science Fiction Library, spanning a period of 70 years or more, with approximately 9000 books & many thousands of specialty magazines, manuscripts, etc,

from established science fiction writers. **Subjects:** Regional—New Mexico & Roosevelt County; Theater & Performing Arts; Science Fiction. **Access Policy:** Circulation & ILL for research only; otherwise in-house use only.

NEW YORK, Albany

STATE UNIVERSITY OF NEW YORK AT ALBANY. University Libraries, Special Collections. 1400 Washington Ave, Albany 12222. Tel: 518-457-7529. Marion P. Munzer, *Coordinator.* **Staff:** Mary Osielski, *Assistant Coordinator.*

Holdings: Bks 17,643; Mss 300 ln ft; 92 maps; 254 broadsides & posters; 69 prints, photos & drawings. **Scope:** Personal papers of German-speaking exiles (after 1933); papers of local individuals; materials on the history of the university. **Published Guides:** "The German Exile Collection" (leaflet). **Subjects:** Economics; Fine & Applied Arts; History; Regional—Albany; Theater & Performing Arts; History of State University of New York (formerly New York State College for Teachers) & History of Teacher Education; Political Science; German-Speaking Emigres to the United States (after 1933). **Access Policy:** Open to public.

NEW YORK, Alfred

ALFRED UNIVERSITY. Herrick Memorial Library, Special Collections. Alfred 14802. Tel: 607-871-2184. June E. Brown, *University Librarian.* **Staff:** Norma B. Higgins, *Library Assistant.*

Holdings: Bks 9200; Mss 410 ln ft; 9400 photos & ephemera. **Scope:** Rare books, 1502–present, mixed subjects, mostly history, religion, literature & art; German & Nazi literature, 1900–1945; modern British literature & social history, Victorian era to present; many rare, first, limited & special editions & literary ephemera. **Subjects:** History (19th century); Literature 1900 to present; Regional—Alfred, New York Area & Southern Tier Region; Religion (Seventh Day Baptist); Old Testament Collection; Travel & Exploration (19th century). **Budget:** $2000 per year. **Access Policy:** Open to qualified scholars.

NEW YORK, Brooklyn

LONG ISLAND HISTORICAL SOCIETY. Emma Toedteberg Manuscripts Room. 128 Pierrepont St, Brooklyn 11201. Tel: 212-624-0890. Lucinda Manning, *Head Librarian.*

Holdings: Bks 125,000; Mss 1328 ln ft; 10,000 photographs. **Scope:** Brooklyn, Long Island & some New York State history; American Revolution; abolitionism/slavery; genealogy; art & architecture; 19th-century paintings & prints; biographies. **Published Guides:** *Calendar of Manuscripts: 1763–1783* (Long Island Historical Society, 1980); *A Guide to Brooklyn Manuscripts in the Long Island Historical Society,* prepared by Brooklyn Rediscovery, a program of BECA (1980). **Subjects:** Americana; Ephemera; Fine & Applied Arts; History; Regional — Long Island; Theater & Performing Arts; Genealogy. **Access Policy:** Apply to head librarian.

NEW YORK, Buffalo

BUFFALO & ERIE COUNTY PUBLIC LIBRARY. Rare Book Room. Lafayette Sq, Buffalo 14203. Tel: 716-856-7525. William H. Loos, *Curator.*

Holdings: Bks 30,000; Mss 4000 items; 3000 posters; 450 prints & maps. **Scope:** Nucleus of collection is some 3000 volumes of early printed books, including examples by nearly all the great printers from the 15th–20th centuries. The development of modern fine printing is represented in a collection of works from the private press movement. The largest single collection is devoted to Americana, from the 16th century on, including some 3000 early American imprints. Collection also includes American literary works, 18th–20th centuries & English literature, including four Shakespeare folios.

Published Guides: *Pollard & Redgrave Titles . . . in the Rare Book Room . . .* (1968); *Wing Titles . . . in the Rare Book Room . . .* (1968); *Evans Titles in the Rare Book Room . . .* (1969). **Subjects:** Americana; Books about Books; Children's Literature; Fine & Applied Arts; History; History of Medicine & Science; Illustrated Books; Incunabula; Literature 1640 to present; Natural History; Press Books; Regional — Western New York; Theater & Performing Arts; Travel & Exploration; Slavery & Antislavery; Shakers; Roycroft Press; Pre-1900 Books with Mounted Photographs; Minstrel Songsters; Bibles; Miniature Books; Special Collection of English & Foreign Language Editions of Huck Finn; World War I & II Posters; Major Works of Dard Hunter. **Budget:** $4000 per year. **Access Policy:** Open to public by appointment.

STATE UNIVERSITY OF NEW YORK AT BUFFALO. University Libraries, Poetry/Rare Books Collection. 420 Capen Hall, Buffalo 14260. Tel: 716-636-2917. Robert J. Bertholf, *Curator.*

Holdings: Bks 100,000; Mss 250 ln ft; paintings; drawings; photographs; tapes; records. **Scope:** Poetry in English in the 20th century; 18th- & 19th-century British & American literature; history of science. **Published Guides:** Steven L. Meyer, *The Manuscripts & Letters of William Carlos Williams in the Poetry Collection . . .* (Hall, 1978); Robert J. Bertholf, *A Descriptive Catalogue of the Private Library of Thomas B. Lockwood* (University Libraries, 1983). **Subjects:** History of Medicine & Science; Literature 1640 to present; Press Books. **Access Policy:** Open to public.

NEW YORK, Garden City

ADELPHI UNIVERSITY LIBRARIES. Special Collections. Garden City 11530. Tel: 516-663-1042. Erica Doctorow, *Fine Arts Librarian.*

Holdings: Bks 9000; Mss 100 ln ft.

Scope: Americana source material illustrative of life in the United States from the Revolutionary War to late 19th century; William Blake-Trianon Press facsimiles; William Cobbett (including Cobbett-Hunt correspondence); expatriate writers; Cuala Press; Sandor Voros papers on Spanish Civil War; Christopher Morley; Walt Whitman; Gerhart Hauptmann. **Published Guides:** Donald V. L. Kelly, *The William Cobbett Collection at Adelphi University* (Adelphi Libraries, 1982). **Subjects:** Americana. **Budget:** $4000. **Access Policy:** Open to public, valid identification required.

NEW YORK, Hempstead

HOFSTRA UNIVERSITY. Library, Special Collections Department. Hempstead 11550. Tel: 516-560-5974. Charles Andrews, *Dean of Library Services.* **Staff:** Marguerite Regan, *Curator & Assistant;* Nancy Herb, *Assistant.*
Holdings: Bks 20,000; Mss 20 boxes. **Scope:** Collections include 50 author collections with manuscript holdings, including Bloomsbury group, H. G. Wells, Shaw, Conrad, Belloc, Chesterton, etc.; Nila Banton Smith collection of the history of the methodology of teaching reading; Howard & Muriel Weingrow collection of avant-garde literature & art; Utopian Communities collections; New York State/Long Island history collection. **Subjects:** Americana (New York State/Long Island history); Books about Books; Children's Reading Books; Fine & Applied Arts; Illustrated Books; Incunabula; Literature 1900 to present; Press Books. **Budget:** $4000–$6000 per year. **Access Policy:** Open to public for research.

NEW YORK, Jamaica

ST. JOHN'S UNIVERSITY LIBRARY. Special Collections. Grand Central & Utopia Pkwys, Jamaica 11439. Tel: 212-990-6161 ext 6737. Szilvia E. Szmuk, *Librarian.*

Holdings: Bks 4700. **Published Guides:** In-house pamphlet. **Subjects:** Children's Literature; Economics (bookkeeping/accounting); Literature 1900 to present (Aldrich Howell, Van Dyke, Wharton); William M. Fischer Lawn Tennis Collection; History of Lawn Tennis (1870s–1950s). **Access Policy:** Open to public by appointment.

NEW YORK, New York

AMERICAN MUSEUM OF NATURAL HISTORY. Rare Book Room & Archives. 79 St & Central Park W, New York 10024. Tel: 212-873-1300. Nina Root, *Chair, Library Services, Rare Books;* Mary Genett, *Assistant Librarian, Manuscripts.* **Staff:** Lynn Wiley, Carol Tucher, *Reference Librarians.*
Holdings: Bks & mss 12,000; 800,000 historical photos; 100 original illustrations of natural history artists. **Scope:** Rare natural history treatises beginning with 1590; fine illustrated natural history books; manuscripts of expeditionary field journals; archives of museum constitute one of the most complete archives tracing development of an American museum & the history of American zoology & anthropology; photographic collection parallels archives. **Published Guides:** *Research Catalog of the American Museum of Natural History Library* (G. K. Hall, 1977). **Subjects:** History of Science; Illustrated Books; Natural History; Travel & Exploration; Serials Collection; Bibliography of Natural History; Museology. **Access Policy:** Open to qualified researchers upon written request.

CITY COLLEGE OF THE CITY UNIVERSITY OF NEW YORK. Morris Raphael Cohen Library, Archives & Special Collections Division. North Academic Center, 5th fl, 137 St & Convent Ave, New York 10031. Tel: 212-690-5367. Barbara J. Dunlap, *Chief.*
Holdings: Bks 7000. **Scope:** The collection contains historical & fine

printing examples from the incunabula period to the present. Strength is in Western European materials, with special emphasis on British literature, 1660–1800. Also an exceptionally strong collection of 18th-century plays. **Subjects:** Literature 1640–1800; Pamphlets relating to the English Civil War (published between 1630 & 1660); Collection of books on costume (many profusely illustrated, often with hand-colored plates; imprints range from the 1700s up to modern times); William Butler Yeats (printed editions only). **Access Policy:** Open to public.

COLUMBIA UNIVERSITY. Rare Book & Manuscript Library. 654 Butler Library, Columbia University, New York 10027. Tel: 212-280-2231, 2232. Kenneth A. Lohf, *Librarian.* **Staff:** Rudolph Ellenbogen, *Assistant Librarian, Rare Books;* Bernard R. Crystal, *Assistant Librarian, Manuscripts;* Hugh Wilburn, *Reference Librarian/Bibliographer, Rare Books;* Alison M. Scott, *Reference Librarian/Bibliographer, Rare Books;* Paul R. Palmer, *Curator, Columbiana;* Mary B. Bowling, *Reference Librarian/Bibliographer, Manuscripts/Curator of Lehman Papers.*
Holdings: Bks 500,000; Mss 22,000,000 items. **Scope:** Covers all areas of the humanities, social sciences & sciences, with the exceptions of law, medicine, architecture, religion & east Asian languages & literature. **Subjects:** Americana; Books about Books; Children's Literature; Economics; Ephemera; History; History of Mathematics; History of Science; Illustrated Books; Incunabula; Literature pre-1640 to present; Press Books; Regional—New York City; Theater & Performing Arts; Travel & Exploration; American Publishing; Literary Agents; International Affairs Organizations; Social Work; Library Science; Russian Culture. **Access Policy:** Open to qualified researchers & scholars.

ENGINEERING SOCIETIES LIBRARY. Wheeler Collection. 345 E 47 St, New York 10017. Tel: 212-705-7611. S. K. Cabeen, *Director.*
Holdings: Bks 2000. **Scope:** Virtually every printed reference prior to 1883 in the fields of magnetism, lodestone, mariner's compass & early electricity. **Published Guides:** *Catalogue of the Wheeler Gift of Books, Pamphlets & Periodicals in the Library of the American Institute of Electrical Engineers* (AIEE, 1909). **Subjects:** History of Science. **Access Policy:** Open to public.

GRAND LODGE OF NEW YORK F & AM. Livingston Library. 71 W 23 St, New York 10010. Tel: 212-741-4506. Allan Boudreau, *Director.* **Staff:** Alan Zwiebach, *Librarian.*
Holdings: Bks 60,000; Mss 1000 ln ft; 250,000 items. **Scope:** New York State & City history; freemasonry. **Published Guides:** Various presentation pamphlets; W. K. Walker, *Masonic Treasures of New York.* **Subjects:** Americana; Fine & Applied Arts; History; Local History (various communities in New York State); Biography (prominent New York State Freemasons). **Access Policy:** Open to qualified scholars by appointment.

GROLIER CLUB OF NEW YORK LIBRARY. 47 E 60 St, New York. Tel: 212-838-6690. Robert Nikirk, *Librarian.* **Staff:** Allen Asaf, *Curator.*
Holdings: Bks 70,000. **Scope:** Research collection dealing with bibliography, book collecting & the book arts. **Published Guides:** *The Grolier Club 1884–1984: Its Library, Exhibitions & Publications* (Grolier Club, 1984). **Subjects:** Books about Books; Ephemera; Incunabula; Press Books. **Budget:** $15,000 per year. **Access Policy:** Open to scholars by appointment.

THE HISPANIC SOCIETY OF AMERICA. Manuscript & Rare Book Department. 613 W 155 St, New York 10032. Tel: 212-926-2234 ext 51. Martha M. de Narváez, *Curator of Manuscripts.*
Holdings: Bks 15,000 (including 250 incunabula); Mss 100,000 items.

Scope: Culture of Spain, Portugal & Hispanic America to 1700. **Published Guides:** *Printed Books 1468–1700 in The Hispanic Society of America* (The Society, 1965); *Nuevo ensayo de una Biblioteca Española de libros raros y curiosos . . . de The Hispanic Society of America* (The Society, 1964); *The Hispanic Society of America. Catalogue of the Library* (G. K. Hall, 1962, supplement 1970); *Medieval Manuscripts in the Library of The Hispanic Society of America* (The Society, 1983); *Los manuscritos juridicos medievales de la Hispanic Society of America* (The Society, 1964); *Catálogo de los manuscritos poéticos castellanos . . . en . . . The Hispanic Society of America* (The Society, 1966). **Subjects:** Books about Books; History; Illustrated Books; Incunabula; Law; Literature to 1640; Natural History; Religion; Theater & Performing Arts. **Access Policy:** Apply to curator.

THE PIERPONT MORGAN LIBRARY. 29 East 36th St, New York 10016. Tel: 212-685-0008. Charles Ryskamp, *Director.* **Staff:** Paul Needham, *Curator of Printed Books & Manuscripts;* Anna Lou Ashby, *Associate Curator of Printed Books & Head of Reference & Library Services;* Herbert Cahoon, *Curator of Autograph Manuscripts;* Pamela White, *Assistant Curator of Autograph Manuscripts;* William M. Voelkle, *Curator of Mediaeval & Renaissance Manuscripts;* J. Rigbie Turner, *Curator of Music Manuscripts;* Gerald Gottlieb, *Curator of Early Children's Books.*

Holdings: Bks 44,500; Mss, Letters, etc 111,590 items; Mediaeval Mss 1398; Music Mss 4178. **Scope:** Incunabula; Caxton; fine bindings; French & Italian illustrated books; William Blake; English literature; William Morris; French literature (Heinemann Collection); 16th- to 18th-century Italian printing; Egyptian papyri; Mediaeval & Renaissance manuscripts; American historical documents; English, American & Continental literary

manuscripts; artists' and theater papers; Italian humanist letters; papers relating to the Reformation in Germany; 18th- to 20th-century musical manuscripts; Gilbert & Sullivan collection; English & Continental children's books to 1850. **Published Guides:** Complete acquisitions published every three years in the *Report to the Fellows of the Pierpont Morgan Library* (1969–); many catalogues of individual collections or exhibitions. **Access Policy:** Open to qualified scholars with letters of introduction.

MUSEUM OF THE CITY OF NEW YORK. Theater Collection. Fifth Ave & 103 St, New York 10029. Tel: 212-534-1672. Mary C. Henderson, *Curator.* **Staff:** Wendy Warnken, MaryAnn Smith, *Associate Curators;*. Bob Taylor, *Curatorial Assistant.*

Scope: Many autographed first editions of American plays & biographies. Play manuscripts & typescripts of plays by Eugene O'Neill & George M. Cohan. **Published Guides:** Various volumes of *Performing Arts Resources* (Theatre Library Association). **Subjects:** Theater & Performing Arts. **Access Policy:** Open to public by appointment.

NEW YORK ACADEMY OF MEDICINE. Malloch Rare Book Room. 2 E 103rd St, New York 10029. Tel: 212-876-8200 ext 310. Sallie Morgenstern, *Curator.* **Staff:** Inge Dupont, *Rare Book Curator.*

Holdings: Bks 50,000; Mss 432 ln ft. **Scope:** Primary & secondary sources of medicine & allied sciences, intended primarily for medical researchers & scholars of other disciplines, ranging from the 17th century BC (The Edwin Smith Surgical Papyrus) to the 20th century. **Published Guides:** *The New York Academy of Medicine: Author Catalog of the Library* (1969, 1974); *Subject Catalog of the Library* (G. K. Hall, 1969, 1974); *Catalog of Biographies in the Library of the New York Academy of Medicine* (G. K.

Hall, 1960); *Illustration Catalog of the Library of the New York Academy of Medicine* (G. K. Hall, 1976); *Portrait Catalog of the Library of the New York Academy of Medicine* (G. K. Hall, 1960, 1965, 1971, 1976). **Subjects:** Americana; Books about Books; History of Medicine & Science; Incunabula; Natural History; Regional—New York City & State; Travel & Exploration; Classics; 16th-Century Medical Books; Infectious Diseases; Pictorial Material; Portraits of Physicians; Letters; Archives of NYAM & Other New York Medical Societies; Diplomas; Broadsides; Medals; Stamps; Instruments. **Budget:** $15,000. **Access Policy:** Open to public by appointment.

THE NEW-YORK HISTORICAL SOCIETY. 170 Central Park W, New York 10024. Tel: 212-873-3400. Larry E. Sullivan, *Librarian.* **Staff:** Katherine Richards, *Associate Librarian;* Claire de Mandy, *Assistant Librarian.*

Holdings: Bks 630,000; Mss 2,000,000 items; 1,000,000 prints & photographs; 30,000 maps. **Scope:** American art; history of the United States & New York City & State; naval history; New York genealogy. **Published Guides:** Arthur Breton, *Guide to the Manuscript Collections of the New-York Historical Society* (1972); Larry E. Sullivan, "The Cartographic Resources of the New-York Historical Society," *The Map Collector* (forthcoming). **Subjects:** Americana; Ephemera; Fine & Applied Arts; History; Regional—New York; Travel & Exploration; American Almanacs; American Genealogy; Early American Imprints; Military & Naval History. **Budget:** $100,000 per year. **Access Policy:** Free to members; $1 charge to nonmembers or Research Libraries Group.

NEW YORK PUBLIC LIBRARY. Art, Prints, and Photographs Division. Spencer Collection. Fifth Ave & 42nd St, New York 10018. Tel: 212-930-0801.

Holdings: Bks 8000. **Scope:** Rare illustrated & illuminated manuscripts &

books in fine bindings, in all languages, of all countries & of all periods, documenting the development of book illustration & the book arts of the world. **Published Guides:** *Dictionary Catalog . . . of the Spencer Collection . . .* (G. K. Hall, 1971, 2 vols.); Sam P. Williams, *Guide to the Research Collections of the New York Public Library* (ALA, 1975). **Subjects:** Fine & Applied Arts. **Access Policy:** Open to qualified researchers and students on graduate level.

NEW YORK PUBLIC LIBRARY. Henry W. and Albert A. Berg Collection of English and American Literature. Fifth Ave and 42nd St, New York 10018. Tel: 212-930-0802. Dr. Lola L. Szladits, *Curator.*

Scope: English and American literature—books and authors' manuscripts—15th to 20th centuries. **Published Guides:** *Dictionary Catalog of the Henry W. and Albert A. Berg Collection of English and American Literature* (G. K. Hall, 1969. Supp. 1975, 1984). **Access Policy:** Open to qualified researchers and students on graduate level.

NEW YORK PUBLIC LIBRARY. Rare Books and Manuscripts Division. Arents Collections. Fifth Ave & 42nd St, New York 10018. Tel: 212-930-0820. William L. Joyce, *Assistant Director for Rare Books and Manuscripts;* Bernard McTigue, *Curator.*

Holdings: 9000 items. **Scope:** Autographs, books, manuscripts, original drawings, pamphlets, prints & music relating to tobacco; rare works in English, French, German, Italian & Spanish; 16th-century herbals; books in parts. **Published Guides:** *Tobacco: Its History . . . in the Library of George Arents, Jr.* (1937–1952; Suppl. 1958–1969); Sam P. Williams, *Guide to the Research Collections of the New York Public Library* (ALA, 1975). **Access Policy:** Open to qualified researchers.

NEW YORK PUBLIC LIBRARY. Rare Books and Manuscripts Division.

Manuscripts and Archives Section. Fifth Ave and 42nd St, New York 10018. Tel: 212-930-0804. William L. Joyce, *Assistant Director for Rare Books and Manuscripts;* Susan E. Davis, *Curator.* **Staff:** Robert E. Sink, John O. Stinson, Melanie Yolles.

Holdings: Mss 20,000 ln ft. **Scope:** The collection ranges from Sumerian and Babylonian clay and stone tablets to 20th-century publishers' archives, and includes personal narratives and diaries, literary manuscripts, and institutional records. **Published Guides:** *Dictionary Catalog of the Manuscript Division of the New York Public Library* (G. K. Hall, 1967, 2 vols); Sam P. Williams, *Guide to the Research Collections of the New York Public Library* (ALA, 1975). **Subjects:** American Revolutionary period; history of New York; literary and publishing history. **Access Policy:** Open to qualified researchers and students on graduate level.

NEW YORK PUBLIC LIBRARY. Rare Books and Manuscripts Division. Rare Books Section. Fifth Ave & 42nd St, New York 10018. Tel: 212-930-0819. William L. Joyce, *Assistant Director for Rare Books and Manuscripts;* Francis O. Mattson, *Curator.* **Staff:** Miriam Mandelbaum, John F. Rathé.

Holdings: Bks 125,000. **Scope:** Books, pamphlets, newspapers, broadsides and ephemera, ranging from over 700 incunables including the first Gutenberg Bible to come to this country, to modern fine printing. The collections are particularly strong in works relating to the European discovery of America; the development of the English colonies in North America; and the growth of American society and culture until 1850. **Published Guides:** *Catalog of Special and Private Presses in the Rare Book Division* (G. K. Hall, 1978, 2 vols); *The Dictionary Catalog of the Rare Book Division* (G. K. Hall, 1971, 21 vols; Supp, 1973); *The Imprint Catalog in the Rare Book Division* (G. K. Hall, 1979, 21 vols); Sam P.

Williams, *Guide to the Research Collections of the New York Public Library* (ALA, 1975). **Subjects:** Americana; Books about Books; Economics; History; Illustrated Books; Incunabula; Literature 1640 to 1800; Natural History; Press Books; Regional—Metropolitan New York Area; Travel and Exploration. **Access Policy:** Open to qualified researchers and students on graduate level.

NEW YORK PUBLIC LIBRARY. Schomburg Center for Research in Black Culture. Rare Books, Manuscripts and Archives Section. 515 Lenox Ave, New York 10037. Tel: 212-283-4915. Dr. Robert C. Morris, *Head.* **Staff:** Diana Lachatanere, *Assistant Archivist.*

Holdings: Bks 1600; Mss 3000 ln ft; literary and scholarly typescripts, sheet music, programs, playbills, broadsides. **Scope:** Black history and culture of all countries and all periods. **Published Guides:** Guide to manuscripts collections in process. **Subjects:** United States, African, and Caribbean history. **Access Policy:** Open to qualified researchers.

NEW YORK UNIVERSITY. Elmer Holmes Bobst Library, Fales Collection. 70 Washington Sq S, New York 10012. Tel: 212-598-3756. Frank Walker, *Curator, Special Collections.*

Holdings: Bks 120,000; Mss 500 ln ft. **Scope:** Major strengths are in the 19th- & 20th-century British novel. Special collections include Elizabeth Robins Archives (theater & the women's movement); Geoffrey Hellman Archives (New York cultural history); Erich Maria Remarque Archives; Hammond Filmscript Collection (French & Spanish films); American Literature Collection. **Published Guides:** *New York University Libraries. Fales Library Checklist* (Arno Press, 1970). **Subjects:** Literature 1640 to present. **Budget:** $20,000 per year. **Access Policy:** Open to qualified researchers.

THE CARL H. PFORZHEIMER LIBRARY (Administered and maintained by The

Carl and Lily Pforzheimer Foundation, Inc.). Rm 815, 41 E 42nd St, New York 10017. Tel: 212-697-7217. **Staff:** Mihai H. Handrea, *Librarian.* Donald H. Reiman, *Editor, Shelly & His Circle;* Robert Yampolsky, *Bibliographer.*

Scope: English literature 1475–1700; first editions of 18th & 19th centuries, including manuscript material on Shelley & his circle; fine presses (Bruce Rogers); George Gissing; women writers 1790–1840 (Mary Wollstonecraft, Mary Hays, Lady Blessington. **Published Guides:** *English Literature, 1475 to 1700; Shelley & His Circle 1773–1822* (in progress). **Access Policy:** Open to qualified scholars upon approval of application.

RACQUET & TENNIS CLUB LIBRARY. 370 Park Ave, New York 10022. Tel: 212-753-9700. Gerard J. Belliveau, Jr, *Librarian.*

Holdings: Bks 17,200. **Scope:** Rare & old books on the history of sport & sports in general. **Published Guides:** *A Dictionary Catalogue of the Library of Sports in the Racquet & Tennis Club, with Special Collections on Tennis, Lawn Tennis & Early American Sport* (G. K. Hall, 1970); Robert W. Henderson, *Early American Sport: A Checklist of Books by American & Foreign Authors Published in America Prior to 1860 Including Sporting Songs* (Fairleigh Dickinson University Press, 1977). **Subjects:** Americana (sport); Books about Books (bibliographies of sport); History of Sport; Incunabula; Archery; Athletics; Badminton; Baseball; Basketball; Bibliography of Sport; Billiards; Birds; Boxing; Bullfighting; Carriages & Coaching; Chess; Cricket; Croquet; Dogs; Falconry; Fencing; Fishing; Football; Golf; Hockey (ice); Horse; Hunting; Indoor Games; Lawn Tennis; Lacrosse; Motoring; Mountaineering; Polo; Racquets; Rowing; Sailing; Sea; Skating; Skiing; Soccer; Squash; Tennis (jeu de paume); Walking; Wild Fowling; Yachting. **Budget:** $6000 per year. **Access Policy:** Written application required.

UNION THEOLOGICAL SEMINARY. Burke Library. 3041 Broadway at Reinhold Niebuhr Place, New York 10027. Tel: 212-662-7100. Seth Kasten, *Head of User Services.* **Staff:** Paul A. Byrnes, *Archivist.*

Holdings: Bks 35,000. **Scope:** Religion & theology with special strengths in incunabula (Van Ess collection), 16th- & 17th-century British imprints (McAlpin collection). **Published Guides:** *Union Theological Seminary, New York (City) Library. Alphabetical Arrangement of Main Entries from the Shelf List* (G. K. Hall, 1960); *Union Theological Seminary, New York (City). Catalogue of the McAlpin Collection of British History & Theology* (Union Theological Seminary, 1927–1929) (G. K. Hall, 1979). **Subjects:** Literature 1640–1800; Religion. **Access Policy:** Open to qualified scholars with letter of reference.

NEW YORK, Old Chatham

SHAKER MUSEUM. Emma B. King Library. Shaker Museum Rd, Old Chatham 12136. Tel: 518-794-9100. Ann Kelly, *Archivist/Librarian.*

Holdings: Bks 2000; Mss 3000 items; 2300 photographs; 500 maps, art, etc; slides; microfilm. **Scope:** Books written & printed by Shakers; books owned by Shakers; diaries, account books, journals, deeds, correspondence from 1790 representing all 19 Shaker communities. **Budget:** $11,218 per year. **Access Policy:** Open to public by appointment.

NEW YORK, Oswego

STATE UNIVERSITY OF NEW YORK, COLLEGE OF ARTS & SCIENCES AT OSWEGO. Penfield Library, Special Collections. Oswego 13126. Tel: 315-341-3110. Nancy Osborne, *Senior Assistant Librarian.* **Staff:** Vaughan Stanley, Thomas Hill.

Holdings: Bks 6398; Mss 558 ln ft; 3493 photographs. **Scope:** Rare book collection includes 19th-century American & English literature (adult & children's), much in fine binding; 19th- & early 20th-century textbook collection (elementary & higher education). Manuscripts collection includes papers of local personalities notable in creating local history & papers of college professors. **Published Guides:** *Guides to the Marshall Family Papers (1762–1908); Guide to the Microfilm Edition of the Millard Fillmore Papers.* **Access Policy:** Open to public.

NEW YORK, Poughkeepsie

VASSAR COLLEGE. Library, Special Collection Department. PO Box 20, Poughkeepsie 12601. Tel: 914-452-7000 ext 2135. Lisa Browar, *Curator of Rare Books & Manuscripts.* **Staff:** Nancy MacKechnie, *Assistant Curator of Rare Books & Manuscripts.*

Holdings: Bks 3500; Mss 900 ln ft. **Scope:** Early atlases, 19th- & 20th-century American literary & historical papers, women's suffrage movement, printing history, college history & archives. **Published Guides:** *Manuscript Collections of Value for Women's Studies in the Vassar College Library* (1981); *A Checklist of Western Mediaeval Manuscripts & Incunabula in the Vassar College Library* (1977). **Subjects:** Children's Literature: Fine & Applied Arts; Incunabula; Literature 1640 to present; Press Books; Regional—Hudson River Valley; Theater & Performing Arts; Travel & Exploration; History of Vassar College; Etiquette, Courtesy, Household Books; Village Press; Ruth Benedict Papers; Robert Owens Collection; Mark Twain Collection. **Budget:** $5000 per year. **Access Policy:** Open to public.

NEW YORK, Purchase

MANHATTANVILLE COLLEGE. Library, Elizabeth C. O'Connor, RSCJ, Rare Book Room. Purchase 10577. Tel: 914-694-2200. Donna L. Nickerson, *Special Collections Librarian.*

Holdings: Bks 2400; Mss 50 ln ft.

Scope: Books range from incunabula & early printing (1500–1799) to publications of 19th & 20th centuries. The collection also contains a number of artifacts, manuscripts (literary & music holographs), letters, diaries, autographs & maps. The subject areas of special interest are Civil War, early American textbooks, Catholic church history in the United States, liturgical music, English & American literature, New York City & Westchester County. **Subjects:** Correspondence of Historical Figures of the Civil War Period. **Access Policy:** Open to public by appointment.

NEW YORK, Riverdale

MANHATTAN COLLEGE. Cardinal Hayes Library, Christian A. Zabriskie Rare Book Room. Riverdale 10471. Tel: 212-920-0131. Philip M. Dowd, *Curator.*

Holdings: Bks 4275; Mss 10 ln ft; 11 manuscript books. **Scope:** Half of the collection is the Bishop Loughlin collection of 18th- & 19th-century editions of books in mathematics & science, with 91 incunabula. Remainder of the collection is in history, literature, religion. **Published Guides:** *A Short Title Catalogue of Rare Books & Manuscripts in the Cardinal Hayes Library; A Descriptive Catalogue of Incunabula in the Cardinal Hayes Library.* **Subjects:** History; History of Mathematics; Incunabula; Literature pre-1640–1800; Religion. **Budget:** $5000 per year. **Access Policy:** Open to qualified scholars by appointment.

NEW YORK, Rochester

THE LANDMARK SOCIETY OF WESTERN NEW YORK, INC. John Wenrich Memorial Library. 130 Spring St, Rochester 14608. Tel: 716-546-7029. Ann B. Parks, *Director of Education & Museum Properties.*

Holdings: Bks 2600. **Scope:** Collection of books on architecture, decorative arts & local history. Rare books focus on 19th-century histories of Rochester & Monroe County & original editions of 19th-century architecture books by noted US architects. **Subjects:** Fine & Applied Arts (architecture); Regional — Architecture of New York State. **Access Policy:** Open to public.

ROCHESTER INSTITUTE OF TECHNOLOGY. Melbert B. Cary Jr. Graphic Arts Collection. School of Printing, One Lomb Memorial Dr, Rochester 14623. Tel: 716-475-2408. David Pankow, *Librarian.*
Holdings: Bks 12,000; 30 ft of vertical file material. **Scope:** Books about the history of printing; representative collection of specimens of printing from 15th century to present; books on the book & graphic arts. **Subjects:** Books about Books; Ephemera; Illustrated Books; Press Books; Books on Bookbinding; Type Specimen Books; Punch & Matrix Collection. **Access Policy:** Open to public.

UNIVERSITY OF ROCHESTER. Eastman School of Music, Sibley Music Library, Rare Books Department. 44 Swan St, Rochester 14604. Tel: 716-275-8210. Mary Wallace Davidson, *Librarian.* **Staff:** Louis Goldberg, *Rare Books Librarian.*
Holdings: Bks 30,000 (including Mss); 10,000 pieces of pre-1850 sheet music. **Scope:** Major collection of primary sources & research materials in music. Printed materials — early theoretical & historical treatises, Renaissance & early Baroque partbooks; incunabula; early opera orchestral & vocal scores & libretti; collection of almanacs (mostly 18th- & 19th-century French); 18th- & 19th-century chamber music; pre-1825 American tunebooks (sacred & secular, some manuscripts) & sheet music. Manuscripts — early manuscript materials including the 11th-century Rochester (Reichenau) Codex, the 12th-century Admont-Rochester Codex & Oskar Fleischer collection of notebooks and manuscript fragments relating to his

notation studies; manuscripts of Beethoven, Brahms, Debussy, Fauré, Haydn, Krenek, Liszt, Mendelssohn, Mozart, Anton Rubinstein, Saint-Saëns, Schubert; manuscripts of 19th- & 20th-century American composers, including Chadwick, Copland, Hanson, MacDowell, Burrill Phillips, Gardner Read, Sowerby, Thompson; manuscript letters, including Berlioz, Brahms, Handel, Liszt, Mendelssohn, Verdi, Wagner; collections of letters to Arthur Hartmann & John Rowe Parker. **Published Guides:** Barbara Duncan, "The Sibley Musical Library," in *University of Rochester Library Bulletin* 1 (1962); Ruth Watanabe, "Historical Introduction to the Sibley Music Library," *University of Rochester Library Bulletin* 17 (1962). **Access Policy:** Open to public, identification required.

UNIVERSITY OF ROCHESTER. Library, Department of Rare Books & Special Collections. Rochester 14627. Tel: 716-275-4477. Peter Dzwonkoski, *Head.* **Staff:** Mary M. Huth, *Assistant Head;* Karl Sanford Kabelac, *Manuscripts Librarian/University Archivist;* Evelyn Walker Cilveti, *Rare Book Librarian;* Alma Burner Creek, *Library Assistant.*
Holdings: Bks 75,000; Mss 10,000 ln ft. **Scope:** 19th- & 20th-century public affairs; social & natural science; 19th-century botany & horticulture; English history & literature; American literature; regional history. **Published Guides:** *University of Rochester Library Bulletin* (each issue provides update on collection). **Subjects:** Americana; Children's Literature; Ephemera; History; Illustrated Books; Incunabula; Law; Literature pre-1640 to present; Natural History; Regional — Upstate New York; Theater & Performing Arts; Travel & Exploration; Victorian Editions-Bindings; Books Illustrated with Original Photographs; Tauchnitz Collection; Papers of William Henry Seward, Susan B. Anthony, Thomas E. Dewey, etc.; Claude

Bragdon Architectural Drawings & Papers. **Access Policy:** Open to qualified scholars.

UNIVERSITY OF ROCHESTER SCHOOL OF MEDICINE & DENTISTRY. Edward G. Miner Library, George W. Corner History of Medicine Room. 601 Elmwood Ave, Rochester 14642. Tel: 716-275-2979. Janet Brady Berk, *Librarian.*
Holdings: Bks 10,000; Mss 30 ln ft; 500 photographs. **Scope:** Primary works in medicine & preclinical sciences, 15th–20th centuries; personal & professional manuscripts of physicians & scientists, 19th & 20th centuries. **Published Guides:** *The History of Medicine Collections of the Edward G. Miner Library,* available from the library. **Access Policy:** Open to public by appointment; identification required.

NEW YORK, Staten Island

STATEN ISLAND HISTORICAL SOCIETY. Curatorial Department. 441 Clarke Ave, Staten Island 10306. Tel: 212-351-1611, ext 209. Charles Sachs, *Chief Curator.* **Staff:** Stephen Barto, *Archivist/Librarian.*
Holdings: Bks 5000; Mss 200 ln ft. **Subjects:** Americana; Children's Literature; Ephemera; History; History of Medicine; Illustrated Books; Law; Literature 1800–1900; Regional—Staten Island, New York City, New York State; Religion. **Access Policy:** Open to public by appointment.

NEW YORK, Stony Brook

STATE UNIVERSITY OF NEW YORK AT STONY BROOK. Frank Melville Jr. Memorial Library, Department of Special Collections. Stony Brook 11794. Tel: 516-246-3615. Evert Volkersz, *Head.* **Staff:** Rose C. Brown, *Assistant.*
Holdings: Bks 20,000; Mss 2500 cu ft. **Subjects:** Books about Books; Children's Literature; Ephemera; Literature 1900 to present; Press Books; Regional—Long Island; Theater & Performing Arts; Latin American Liter-

ature; Environment & Conservation. **Access Policy:** Open to the public by appointment.

NEW YORK, Troy

RENSSELAER POLYTECHNIC INSTITUTE. Folsom Library, Institute Archives & Department of Special Collections. Troy 12181. Tel: 518-266-8340. Elizabeth C. Stewart, *Archivist & Head.* **Staff:** Kristine Waldron, *Library Assistant.*
Holdings: Bks 7000; Mss 150 ln ft; 1200 ln ft archives. **Scope:** History of American science & technology. **Published Guides:** *Guide to the Roebling Collections* (RPI, 1983). **Subjects:** History of Mathematics & Science: Natural History; History of Technology (especially civil engineering). **Budget:** $50,000 per year. **Access Policy:** Open to public.

NEW YORK, West Point

U.S. MILITARY ACADEMY. Library, Special Collections Division. West Point 10996. Tel: 914-938-2954. Robert E. Schnare, *Assistant Librarian.* **Staff:** Marie Capps, *Map & Manuscript Librarian;* Elaine Eatroff, *Rare Book Curator & Cataloguer;* Angela Kao, *Orientalia Librarian.*
Holdings: Bks 50,000; Mss 900 ln ft; 5000 maps; 50,000 photographs. **Scope:** Monographs focusing on the history of West Point, military engineering & fortification; manuscripts concerning military training & cadet life at West Point, personal narratives of war experiences; Revolutionary War orderly books & waste books. **Subjects:** Americana; Military History (US); Military Art & Science; Fortifications; Military Manuals (US, Great Britain); US Military Academy; US History; Revolutionary War; Hudson Highlands. **Budget:** $20,000 per year. **Access Policy:** Open to public by appointment.

NORTH CAROLINA, Boone

APPALACHIAN STATE UNIVERSITY. Belk Library, W. L. Eury Appalachian Collection. Boone 28608. Tel: 704-262-2186. Eric J. Olson, *Librarian.* **Staff:** Judy Ball, *Assistant Librarian.*

Holdings: Bks 12,000; Mss 123 ln ft; 900 phono-records; 1000 slides; 300 photoprints; 250 maps. **Scope:** Materials in all media relating to the southern Appalachian region. **Strengths:** Regional — Southern Appalachian. **Budget:** $5000 per year. **Access Policy:** Open to public.

NORTH CAROLINA, Chapel Hill

UNIVERSITY OF NORTH CAROLINA AT CHAPEL HILL. Wilson Library, Rare Book Collection. Chapel Hill 27514. Tel: 919-962-1143. Paul S. Koda, *Curator.* **Staff:** Roberta Engleman, *Associate Curator;* Elizabeth Lansing, *Cataloguer;* Elizabeth A. Chenault, *Gray Collection Cataloguer.*

Holdings: Bks 65,000; Mss 1550 items; 24,000 graphics (posters & prints). **Scope:** Printed books exclusive of North Caroliniana & manuscripts prior to 1700. Special strengths are the origin & development of the book, incunabula & British literature. **Published Guides:** *Incunabula in the Hanes Collection* (1960). **Subjects:** Books about Books; History; Illustrated Books; Incunabula; Literature pre-1640 to present; Theater & Performing Arts; Charles Dickens; Johnson & Boswell; George Bernard Shaw; French Revolution & Napoleon; Estienne Family. **Access Policy:** Open to public.

NORTH CAROLINA, Cullowhee

WESTERN CAROLINA UNIVERSITY. Hunter Library, Special Collections. Cullowhee 28723. Tel: 704-227-7474. James B. Lloyd, *Curator.* **Staff:** George E. Frizzell, *Manuscripts Processor.*

Holdings: Bks 1150; Mss 800 ln ft; University Archives 200 ln ft. **Scope:** Collection focuses on the Appalachian Region, both social & natural history; Cherokee studies; spider behavior; history of Western Carolina University. Rare book collection also contains the library of Horace Kephard, dean of American campers. **Subjects:** History; Natural History; Regional — Appalachia. **Access Policy:** Open to public.

NORTH CAROLINA, Durham

DUKE UNIVERSITY. William R. Perkins Library. Durham 27706. Tel: 919-684-4134 (Rare Books), 3372 (Manuscripts). John L. Sharpe III, *Curator of Rare Books;* Mattie U. Russell, *Curator of Manuscripts.*

Holdings: Bks 100,000; Mss 6,000,000 items. **Scope:** Theology; southern history; Confederate imprints; 18th-century English literature, political tracts & sermons; 18th-century French political pamphlets; plays; Walt Whitman & 19th-century Americana; emblems. **Subjects:** Americana; Economics; History; Literature 1640–1800; Regional — Southern History, Confederacy; Religion. **Access Policy:** Apply to curator.

NORTH CAROLINA, Greensboro

UNIVERSITY OF NORTH CAROLINA AT GREENSBORO. Walter Clinton Jackson Library, Special Collections. Greensboro 27412. Tel: 919-379-5246. Emilie W. Mills, *Librarian.* **Staff:** Blanche Jantzen, *Assistant Archivist;* James A. Rogerson, *Library Technical Assistant.*

Holdings: Bks 20,000; Mss 750 ln ft. **Scope:** Book collection: history of books/printing, 15th to 20th centuries, emphasis on 19th & 20th centuries; books by & about women to 19th century. Manuscript collection: miscellaneous historical/literary manuscripts; some emphasis on southern women. **Published Guides:** *Woman's Collection — A Checklist* (1975); *Cello Music Collections — Luigi Silva Collection* (1978). **Subjects:** Books about Books; Children's Literature; Ephemera; Illustrated Books; Press Books; Randall Jarrell (books & manuscripts); Imprints of Chicago Firm of Way & Williams, 1895–1898; Lois Lenski (books & manuscripts, manuscript-related research materials, original drawings, etc. of author/illustrator). **Budget:** $10,000 per year. **Access Policy:** Open to public for serious research; photocopying restricted.

OHIO, Athens

OHIO UNIVERSITY LIBRARIES. Department of Archives & Special Collections. 29 Park Place, Athens 45701. Tel: 614-594-5755, 5728. Gary A. Hunt, *Assistant Director.* **Staff:** Michel S. Perdreau, *Archives Librarian;* Richard Lin Coleman, *Records Management Officer;* George Bain, *Local Government Records Specialist.*

Holdings: Bks 40,914; Mss 5911 ln ft; 30,852 photographs; 1044 maps. **Scope:** Local history (Southeastern Ohio); English literature, 1780–1830 & 1880–1930; history of chemistry; history of osteopathic medicine; 19th- & early 20th-century children's literature; World War II history & journalism. **Published Guides:** *The Morgan Collection in the History of Chemistry: A Checklist; A Catalogue of the Library of Edmund Blunden; Guide to Local Government Records at the Ohio University Library.* **Subjects:** Americana; Books about Books; Children's Literature; History of Medicine (osteopathy); History of Science (chemistry); Literature 1640 to present; Regional—Southeastern Ohio; Theater & Performing Arts. **Access Policy:** Open to public.

OHIO, Bowling Green

BOWLING GREEN STATE UNIVERSITY. Jerome Library, Center for Archival Collections, Rare Books Division. Bowling Green 43403. Tel: 419-372-2411. Nancy Steen, *Librarian.*

Holdings: Bks 13,000; Mss 85 ln ft; 1000 bound periodicals. **Scope:** In-

cludes rare books from 1497 to present with large special collections on William Dean Howells, Franklin D. Roosevelt, modern poetry, Walt Whitman, Ray Bradbury, Jan Wahl, detective fiction, private press books & a heavy emphasis on 19th- & 20th-century literature & theater. **Published Guides:** *The Robert Rogers Hubach Collection of Walt Whitman* (Popular Press, 1982). **Subjects:** History; Literature 1800 to present; Theater & Performing Arts; Science Fiction & Fantasy. **Budget:** $6000 per year. **Access Policy:** Open to public.

OHIO, Cincinnati

CINCINNATI HISTORICAL SOCIETY. Manuscripts Department. Eden Park, Cincinnati 45202. Tel: 513-241-4622. Alden N. Monroe, *Manuscript Supervisor.* **Staff;** Mary Jane Neely, Anne Shepherd, *Manuscript Curators.*

Holdings: Mss 5000 ln ft. **Scope:** The collections document the political, social, cultural & economic history of the greater Cincinnati area, Ohio & the Old Northwest from the late 18th century to the present. **Subjects:** Economics; Fine & Applied Arts; History; Religion; Theater & Performing Arts. **Budget:** $2500 per year. **Access Policy:** Open to public.

CINCINNATI HISTORICAL SOCIETY. Rare Books Department. Eden Park, Cincinnati 45202. Tel: 513-241-4622. Laura L. Chace, *Librarian.* **Staff:** Frances M. Forman, Mary M. Rider, *Reference Librarians.*

Holdings: Bks 2340. **Scope:** History of Cincinnati, Ohio & Old Northwest Territory. **Budget:** $2500 per year. **Access Policy:** Open to public.

HEBREW UNION COLLEGE-JEWISH INSTITUTE OF RELIGION. Klau Library, Special Collections. 3101 Clifton Ave, Cincinnati 45220. Tel: 513-221-1875. Arnona Rudavsky, *Coordinator.*

Holdings: Bks 10,000; Mss 150 ln ft; 135 cu ft of boxes. **Scope:** Incunabula; 16th-century Hebrew printed books; maps; broadsides; bookplates; stamps; Jewish community records from Berlin, Alsace-Lorraine, Amsterdam, France. Israel Samuel Reggio, Laudadio Sacerdote, Israel Solomons, Salli Kirschstein, Eduard Birnbaum collections. **Subjects:** Incunabula; Religion; Jewish Music; Jewish Americana; Bible; Responsa; Yiddish Theater Collection; Josephus Collection; Spinoza Collection; Inquisition Collection; Judezmo Collection; Yiddish Collection. **Access Policy:** Open to public for serious research.

PUBLIC LIBRARY OF CINCINNATI & HAMILTON COUNTY. Department of Rare Books & Special Collections. 800 Vine St, Library Sq, Cincinnati 45202. Tel: 513-369-6957. Yeatman Anderson III, *Curator.* **Staff:** Jean Hamer, *First Assistant/Cataloguer.*

Holdings: Bks 34,000; Mss 80 ln ft; 20,000 photographs. **Scope:** Cincinnatiana; Americana; inland rivers; English-language dictionaries; bibles; fine printing; first editions. **Published Guides:** *Catalogue of the Inland Rivers Library* (1968); *Catalogue of Dictionairies . . . The Louis E. Kahn Collection* (1972). **Subjects:** Americana; Books about Books; Illustrated Books; Press Books; Regional—Ohio Valley; Travel & Exploration; Inland Rivers Library—Commercial Navigational Use of the Ohio-Mississippi River System; English-Language Dictionaries to 1801; Cincinnati 19th-Century Imprints; Bibles (important editions & translations). **Budget:** $15,000 per year. **Access Policy:** Open to public.

OHIO, Cleveland

CLEVELAND PUBLIC LIBRARY. Fine Arts & Special Collections Department. 325 Superior Ave, Cleveland 44114. Tel: 216-623-2818. Alice N. Loranth, *Head.* **Staff:** Russell A. Hehr, *Assistant Head.*

Holdings: Bks 26,000; Mss 507 ln ft; 2000 microfilms. **Scope:** Rare books & the John G. White Collection of Folklore, Orientalia & Chess are the "Special Collections" section of the Fine Arts & Special Collections Department. Rare holdings, which include all subject areas, are strong in chess & checkers; early descriptions of travel in Europe, in the Americas & in the Orient; material related to folklore, such as medieval romance literature, chapbooks, customs related to tobacco; classic Oriental literary & religious texts in Western & Oriental languages; European & Oriental manuscripts; East India Company manuscript collection, 1741–1859; 16th-century imprints; & the Newbell Niles Puckett Archives of American Folklore & the May Augusta Klipple Archives of African Folktales. **Published Guides:** *Catalog of the Chess Collection (Including Checkers)* (G. K. Hall, 1965); *Catalog of Folklore, Folklife & Folk Songs* (G. K. Hall, 1978). **Subjects:** Children's Literature (19th & early 20th century); History; Incunabula; Literature pre-1640 to 1800; Press Books; Regional—Cleveland Authors, Early Cleveland Imprints; Religion; Travel & Exploration; Oriental Studies; Folklore; Chess. **Access Policy:** Open to public; identification required.

OHIO, Columbus

THE OHIO HISTORICAL SOCIETY. Archives-Library. 1982 Velma Ave, Columbus 43211. Tel: 614-466-1500 ext 209. Dennis East, *Chief.* **Staff:** William Myers, *Head of Manuscripts-AV;* David Levine, *State Archives-Local Records;* Robert Jones, *Microfilming Supervisor;* Vernon Will, *Conservation;* James B. Casey, *Head Librarian.*

Holdings: Bks 125,000; Mss 22,000 cu ft; 20,000 newspaper volumes; 500,000 photographs. **Scope:** Ohio history, archeology, natural history, religion, agriculture, government (state archives & local records), transportation, labor, education, genealogy, temperance & prohibition. **Published Guides:** Patricia Swanson, *Union Bibliography of Ohio Printed State Docu-*

ments 1803-1970 (Oberlin Printing Co, 1973). Guides to other collections available from the society. **Subjects:** Americana; Books about Books; Children's Literature; Economics; Ephemera; Fine & Applied Arts; History; History of Mathematics, Medicine & Science; Natural History; Regional– Ohio, Northwest Territory; Religion; Travel & Exploration; Temperance; Genealogy; Civil War; Labor; American Indians. **Budget:** $37,500 per year. **Access Policy:** Open to public for serious research; identification required.

OHIO STATE UNIVERSITY LIBRARIES. Division of Special Collections. 1858 Neil Ave Mall, Columbus 43210. Tel: 614-422-5938. Robert A. Tibbetts, *Head.*

Holdings: Bks 45,000; Mss 250,000 items. **Scope:** General collection with strengths in English & American literature 18th–20th centuries; English history, 17th & 18th centuries; continental history, 16th & 17th centuries. **Subjects:** Americana; History; History of Science; Literature 1640 to present; Natural History; Press Books; Theater & Performing Arts; Travel & Exploration; Overland Narratives; Civil War; Reformation; James Thurber, Nelson Algren, Samuel Beckett (books & manuscripts). **Access Policy:** Open to the public.

OHIO, Dayton

WRIGHT STATE UNIVERSITY. Library, Archives & Special Collections. Colonel Glenn Hwy, Dayton 45435. Tel: 513-873-2092. Patrick B. Nolan, *Head.* **Staff:** Robert H. Smith, Jr, *Supervisor of Micrographics & Archives;* Dorothy Smith, *Reference & Processing Specialist;* Phyllis Steele, *Local Government Records Specialist.*

Holdings: Bks 5000; Mss 1900 ln ft. **Scope:** Books, manuscripts, etc, relating to the life & work of the Wright brothers, on early flight & aeronautics prior to World War I, on the history of Southwest Ohio & the Miami Valley.

Published Guides: Patrick Nolan & John Zamonski, *The Wright Brothers Collection* (Garland, 1977). **Subjects:** History; History of Science; Regional— Southwest Ohio. **Budget:** $10,000 per year. **Access Policy:** Open to public.

OHIO, Kent

KENT STATE UNIVERSITY. Library, Department of Special Collections. Kent 44242. Tel: 216-672-2270. Dean H. Keller, *Head.* **Staff:** Nancy Birk, Alex Gildzen, *Associate Curators;* Stephen Morton, *University Archivist.*

Holdings: Bks 21,000; Mss 5000 ln ft. **Scope:** 19th-century English & American literature; drama; motion pictures; midwestern Americana; history of books & printing; university archives. **Subjects:** Americana; Books about Books; Children's Literature; Literature 1900 to present; Regional— Midwest; Theater & Performing Arts. **Budget:** $5000 per year. **Access Policy:** Open to public.

OHIO, Marietta

MARIETTA COLLEGE. Dawes Library, Special Collections. Marietta 45750. Tel: 614-374-4757. Robert F. Cayton, *Librarian.* **Staff:** Sandra B. Neyman, *Head, Readers' Services.*

Holdings: Bks 35,000; Mss 27,090 items. **Scope:** Americana; Northwest Territory & early Ohio; notable personages' autographs; Ohio history & scientific collection; rare books (16th–19th centuries). **Subjects:** Americana; History; History of Science; Literature pre-1640 to present; Natural History; Regional—Ohio; Religion; Travel & Exploration. **Budget:** $4000 per year. **Access Policy:** Open to public by appointment.

OHIO, Oberlin

OBERLIN COLLEGE. Library. Oberlin 44074. Dina Schoonmaker, *Curator of Special Collections.*

Holdings: Bks 40,000. **Scope:** Antislavery materials (pre-1863); Spanish drama; book arts & history of printing; early printed books; Oberliniana; women's history; voyages of discovery; architecture; literature 1640–1800; religion; music; dime novels. **Subjects:** Fine & Applied Arts; Religion; Theater & Performing Arts (music). **Budget:** $80,000 FY 1983. **Access Policy:** Open to public.

OHIO, Oxford

MIAMI UNIVERSITY. King Library, Walter Havighurst Special Collections Library. Oxford 45056. Tel: 513-529-2537. Helen C. Ball, *Curator.*

Holdings: Bks 44,165; Mss 133 ln ft. **Scope:** Old Northwest (includes manuscripts); McGuffey readers & other 19th-century textbooks; early children's books. **Subjects:** Americana; Children's Literature; Literature 1640 to present; Natural History; Press Books; Regional—Old Northwest; Travel & Exploration; Jefferson Davis Letters; William H. McGuffey Letters; Robert C. Schenck Papers; John H. James Papers; Burton French Papers; Russian Military History; William D. Howells; 19th-Century Textbooks; 19th-Century Botanical Medicine. **Budget:** $50,000 per year. **Access Policy:** Open to public for serious research; identification required.

OHIO, Springfield

WITTENBERG UNIVERSITY. Thomas Library. PO Box 720, Springfield 45502. Tel: 513-327-7016. Betty Beatty, *Acting Director.*

Holdings: Bks 7500. **Scope:** Original Luther/Reformation materials, hymn book collection, the Cyril dos Passos Lepidoptera collection & the Walter Tittle diaries. **Access Policy:** Open to public by appointment.

OHIO, Toledo

UNIVERSITY OF TOLEDO LIBRARIES. Ward M. Canaday Center. 2801 W Bancroft St, Toledo 43606. Tel: 419-537-2443. David J. Martz, Jr, *Director.*

Holdings: Bks 40,000; Mss 50 ln ft. **Scope:** 20th-century Anglo-American literature: Pound & the Imagists (Eliot, Williams, Moore, H.D., Lowell, etc), William Faulkner, K. A. Porter, McCullers, F. O'Connor, William Dean Howells, Leigh Hunt. Manuscript collections of Etheridge Knight, Herbert W. Martin, Jean Gould & Noel Stock. **Subjects:** Books about Books; Literature 1900 to present; Regional—Toledo History/Faculty Authors; 20th-Century Black American Poetry. **Budget:** $22,000 per year. **Access Policy:** Open to public.

OKLAHOMA, Lawton

MUSEUM OF THE GREAT PLAINS. Special Collections. PO Box 68, 601 Ferris, Lawton 73502. Tel: 405-353-5675. Steve Wilson, *Director.* **Staff:** Paula Williams, *Curator.*

Holdings: Bks 20,000; Mss 200,000 items; 22,000 photographs. **Scope:** Manuscript collections pertain mainly to business papers of early Lawton & southwest Oklahoma; book collection relates to American West. **Subjects:** History; History of Science; Natural History; Regional—Great Plains & Southwest; Travel & Exploration; History of Agriculture. **Access Policy:** Open to public.

OKLAHOMA, Norman

UNIVERSITY OF OKLAHOMA LIBRARIES. The History of Science Collection. 401 W Brooks, Norman 73019. Tel: 405-325-2741. Duane H. D. Roller, *Curator.* **Staff:** Marcia M. Goodman, *Librarian.*

Holdings: Bks 61,000; Mss 17.7 cu ft. **Scope:** Research & teaching collection in the history of science. **Published Guides:** *The Catalogue of the History of Science Collections of the University of Oklahoma Libraries* (Mansell, 1976). **Subjects:** History of Science; Illustrated Books; Incunabula; Natural

History; Press Books. **Access Policy:** Open to qualified scholars by appointment.

OKLAHOMA, Tulsa

UNIVERSITY OF TULSA. McFarlin Library, Rare Books & Special Collections Division. 600 S College Ave, Tulsa 74104. Tel: 918-592-6000 ext 2496. David Farmer, *Head.* **Staff:** Toby Murray, *Archivist/Preservation Officer;* Caroline S. Swinson, *Curator of Literary Manuscripts & Art.*

Holdings: Bks 80,000; Mss 300 ln ft; 3000 photographs; American Indian art. **Scope:** English & American literature of the 20th century, including first editions, translations, contributions to periodicals, manuscripts; westward expansion & American Indian history, especially the Five Civilized Tribes; history & literature of WWI (mainly English). Special collections include Proletarian Collection (items based on Walter Rideout's *Radical Novel in America*); Cyril Connolly's working library; Edmund Wilson's working library; Indian Claims Commission file; John Shleppey American Indian Collection; individual author collections, in-depth for D. H. Lawrence, James Joyce, Siegfried Sassoon, Robert Graves, Robert Frost, Ruth Prawer Jhabvala, Anna Kavan, Stevie Smith (including her library) & Jean Rhys; literary manuscript holdings include works by these figures & others. **Published Guides:** *A Guide to Literary & Related Materials; Joyce at 101* (McFarlin Library, Univ. of Tulsa, 1983). **Subjects:** Americana; Literature 1900 to present; Press Books; Regional — Southeastern Indians, Plains, Oklahoma/Texas. **Budget:** $20,000 per year. **Access Policy:** Researchers must describe needs & apply for permission.

OREGON, Ashland

SOUTHERN OREGON STATE COLLEGE. Library, Margery Bailey Renaissance Collection. Ashland 97520. Tel: 503-482-6445. Harold M. Otness, *Acquisitions Librarian.*

Holdings: Bks 5000. **Scope:** Shakespeare & his times; his plays in their important editions & the plays of his contemporaries; criticism & interpretation to the present. **Published Guides:** Cecil L. Chase, *Early Printed Books in the Margery Bailey Renaissance Collection at Southern Oregon State College* (Friends of the Library at Southern Oregon State College, 1979). **Subjects:** Literature to 1640; Theater & Performing Arts. **Access Policy:** Open to public.

OREGON, Eugene

UNIVERSITY OF OREGON LIBRARY. Department of Special Collections. Eugene 97403. Tel: 503-686-3068. Kenneth W. Duckett, *Curator.* Hilary Cummings, *Curator of Manuscripts;* Martin Antonetti, *Rare Books/Special Collections Librarian.*

Holdings: Bks 38,000; Mss 18,000 ln ft; Oregon Collection 35,000 items; sheet music 20,000 items; broadsides 3000; photography 125,000 items. **Scope:** Rare books collection includes works from all periods from most European countries & the US, chiefly 18th century to present. Manuscripts collections emphasize political, social, economic & literary history of the US in the 20th century & also have strengths in political conservatism & missionary movements in the Far East. **Published Guides:** Martin Schmitt, *Catalogue of Manuscripts in the University of Oregon Library* (UO Books, 1971). **Subjects:** Americana; Children's Literature; History (20th century); Illustrated Books (children's); Literature 1900 to present (popular); Natural History (herbal); Regional — Oregon; Travel & Exploration; Esperanto; Oriental Art; Sanford Burgess Collection of Early Printed Books. **Access Policy:** Open for scholarly use.

OREGON, Portland

OREGON HISTORICAL SOCIETY. Library. 1230 SW Park Ave, Portland

97205. Tel: 503-222-1741. Louis Flannery, *Chief Librarian.* **Staff:** Layne Woolschlager, *Manuscripts Librarian;* Peggy Haines, *Assistant Manuscripts Librarian.*

Holdings: Bks 16,000; Mss 8200 ln ft; 1500 sets of architectural plans. **Scope:** Materials documenting the history of the Oregon Country, defined as including northern California, Oregon, Washington, Idaho, Montana, Alaska & the northern Pacific basin. **Published Guides:** *Guide to the Manuscripts Collection, Research & Bibliography Series* (1971, 1974–1975). **Subjects:** Americana (Western); Regional — Pacific Northwest History (including Siberia); Travel & Exploration; Early Coastal Exploration by British, Spanish & Russians; Fur Trading Period (including documents of the Hudson's Bay Company and its factors); Protestant & Catholic Missionaries; Overland Journeys to the Pacific; Oregon Provisional & Territorial Government Records; Regional Church, Business & Association Records (1860 to present); Personal Papers (of state & local politicians, business leaders, suffragettes, authors & educators); Records Documenting Lumber & Fishing Industries in the Northwest; Architectural Plans, Renderings, Specifications for Buildings & Homes in Oregon; Materials on Performing Arts. **Budget:** $20,000 per year. **Access Policy:** Open to public.

PENNSYLVANIA, Bryn Mawr

BRYN MAWR COLLEGE. Library, Special Collections. Bryn Mawr 19010. Tel: 215-645-5285. James Tanis, *Director of Libraries & Head.* **Staff:** Lucy Fisher West, *Archivist;* John Dooley, *Bibliographer;* Leo Dolenski, *Manuscripts Librarian;* Carol Campbell, *Prints & Drawings;* M. Winslow Lundy, *Rare Books Cataloguer;* Mary Leahy, *Rare Books Librarian.*

Holdings: Bks 22,137; Mss 720 ln ft; 900 ln ft prints, drawings, photographs & memorabilia. **Scope:** Collections created to support undergraduate & graduate teaching programs; manuscripts range from Assyrian clay tablets to contemporary literary manuscripts; rare books from 15th-century strength to 20th-century subject collections. **Published Guides:** Guides to the M. Carey Thomas Papers, the Adelman Collection, and the Maser Collection of American Bindings. **Subjects:** Americana; Books about Books; Fine & Applied Arts; History; History of Science; Illustrated Books; Incunabula; Literature pre-1640 to present; Natural History; Press Books; Religion; Theater & Performing Arts; Travel & Exploration; History of & Writings by Women; History of Higher Education; Latin American, Southeast Asian, English & Dutch History, Travel & Exploration; Urban History with Emphasis on New York, London & Paris; Author Collections (particularly A. E. Housman, Marianne Moore, Keats Circle; Graphic Arts (depth in C. Lovat Fraser & 20th-century lithography); Botany & Herbals. **Budget:** $12,000 per year. **Access Policy:** Open to public.

PENNSYLVANIA, Gettysburg

GETTYSBURG COLLEGE. Musselman Library, Special Collections. Gettysburg 17325. Tel: 717-334-3131 ext 363. Nancy C. Scott, *Librarian.*

Holdings: Bks 5000; Mss 1000 ln ft. **Scope:** Civil War books & manuscripts; organ music scores; rare maps; Gettysburgiana. **Budget:** $1500 per year. **Access Policy:** Apply to librarian.

PENNSYLVANIA, Haverford

HAVERFORD COLLEGE. James P. Magill Library, Treasure Room. Haverford 19041. Tel: 215-896-1161. Edwin B. Bronner, *Curator.* **Staff:** Diana F. Alten, *Manuscripts Cataloguer;* Elisabeth Potts Brown, *Quaker Bibliographer;* Donald N. Rash, *Library Conservator;* Shirley Stowe, *Humanities Bibliographer.*

Holdings: Bks 10,500; Mss 250,000 items. **Scope:** Quaker Collection: printed & manuscript material about the Society of Friends from inception (1650) reflecting interests in social reforms & theological concerns. Philips Collection: rare books & manuscripts mostly of the Renaissance period. Lockwood Collection: works by & about Italian humanists. Roberts Collection: manuscript items of religious, political & military historical significance. **Published Guides:** *The Quaker Collection of the Haverford College Library* (1971); *William Pyle Philips . . . Catalogue to His Rare Book Collection* (1952). **Subjects:** History; Literature to 1640; Regional — Delaware Valley; Society of Friends; Social Reforms; American Indians; Women; Minorities. **Budget:** $6500 per year. **Access Policy:** Apply to curator.

PENNSYLVANIA, Latrobe

SAINT VINCENT COLLEGE & ARCHABBEY LIBRARIES. Special Collections. Latrobe 15650. Tel: 412-539-9761 ext 312, 307. Fintan R. Shoniker, *Librarian.*

Scope: Incunabula; 16th- to 18th-century theological imprints; Benedictina; small collection of fore-edge paintings; small collection of medieval manuscripts. **Published Guides:** Virginia Louis Cassady, *A Descriptive Catalog of the Incunabula in St. Vincent College & Archabbey Library* (University of Pittsburgh, 1976). **Subjects:** Incunabula; Religion; Roman Catholic Theology; Church History; Benedictine Order; Patrology. **Access Policy:** Open to public; advance notice required.

PENNSYLVANIA, Lewisburg

BUCKNELL UNIVERSITY. Bertrand Library, Special Collections. Lewisburg 17837. Tel: 717-524-1471. George M. Jenks, *Librarian.*

Holdings: Bks 5400; Mss 2 ln ft; 40 ln ft letters. **Scope:** General collection of rare books, with local imprints. Collection of books, letters & manuscripts

of D. H. Lawrence, G. B. Shaw, Oliver D. Gogarty, W. B. Yeats & book collection of other Irish writers. **Published Guides:** *Information for Prospective Readers.* **Access Policy:** Open to public.

PENNSYLVANIA, Millersville

MILLERSVILLE UNIVERSITY. Ganser Library, Special Collections. Millersville 17551. Tel: 717-872-3624. Robert E. Coley, *University Archivist & Librarian.* **Staff:** Marjorie A. Markoff, *Cataloguer;* Dorothea Zimmermann, *Assistant to the Archivist.*

Holdings: Bks 20,000; Mss 805 ln ft. **Scope:** Pennsylvania imprints, 1700–1865; university archives. **Published Guides:** Selected bibliographies. **Subjects:** History; Regional — Pennsylvania & Local; Pennsylvania Germans; 18th- & 19th-Century Education; Published Works by & about William Penn & Benjamin Franklin; Operetta Music. **Budget:** $15,000 per year. **Access Policy:** Open to public.

PENNSYLVANIA, Philadelphia

AMERICAN PHILOSOPHICAL SOCIETY LIBRARY. 105 S Fifth St, Philadelphia 19016. Tel: 215-627-0706. Edward C. Carter II, *Librarian.* **Staff:** Murphy D. Smith, *Associate Librarian;* Hildegard Stephans, *Assistant Librarian & Cataloguer;* Willman Spawn, *Conservator.*

Holdings: Bks 162,430; Mss 5296 ln ft. **Scope:** American history to 1840; Darwin & evolution; electricity; genetics; history of science in America & its European background; Lewis & Clark Expedition; quantum & modern physics; Thomas Paine. Special collections include American Indian linguistics (Frank Boas et al); Benjamin Franklin & his circle; Stephen Girard papers (on film); medical research (Simon Flexner et al). **Published Guides:** *Guide to Archives & Manuscripts Collection; Guide to Manuscripts Relating to the American Indian; Sources for the History of Quantum Physics; Calendar of* the Papers of Benjamin Franklin; The Thomas Paine Collection of Richard Gimbel; Electricity, Magnetism & Animal Magnetism: A Checklist; An Annotated Calendar of the Letters of Charles Darwin in the Library; Catalogue of Portraits; Catalogue of Instruments & Models. **Subjects:** History of Medicine; History of Science; Natural History; Travel & Exploration. **Access Policy:** Open to public.

THE ATHENAEUM OF PHILADELPHIA. Research Department. 219 S Sixth St, Philadelphia 19106. Tel: 215-925-2688. Roger W. Moss, Jr, *Director.* **Staff:** Keith A. Kamm, *Bibliographer;* Sandra Tatman, *Architectural Librarian.*

Holdings: Bks 100,000; Mss 100 ln ft; 20,000 architectural drawings. **Subjects:** Americana; Fine & Applied Arts; History; Literature 1640 to present; Regional—Philadelphia Area; Travel & Exploration; 19th-Century Social & Cultural History; US Architecture & Decorative Arts to 1930; Architectural Drawings & Records; Special Collections in Railroading, Fox Hunting, Poetry, S. Holmes. **Budget:** $12,000 per year. **Access Policy:** Open to public by appointment.

COLLEGE OF PHYSICIANS OF PHILADELPHIA. Library, Historical Collections. 19 S 22nd St, Philadelphia 19103. Tel: 215-561-6050. Christine Ruggere, *Curator.*

Holdings: Bks 15,000 (pre-1801); 1200 Ms groups; 10,000 prints & photographs; 3000 pamphlets. **Scope:** Collections cover all aspects of medicine. Books range from 15th to 20th century and include 423 incunables. Manuscript collections range from 13th to 20th century and are especially strong in 18th- & 19th-century American medical manuscripts, including physicians' correspondence, archives of medical societies & institutions & student lecture notes. **Published Guides:** *Catalogue of the Manuscripts & Archives of the Library of the College of Physicians*

of Philadelphia (Univ. of Penn. Press, 1983). **Subjects:** Medicine; History of Medicine & Science; Illustrated Books; Incunabula; Natural History. **Access Policy:** Open to public Tuesday through Friday, 9–5.

FREE LIBRARY OF PHILADELPHIA. Rare Book Department. Logan Sq, Philadelphia 19103. Tel: 215-686-5416. Marie E. Korey, *Head.* **Staff:** Frank M. Halpern, *Bibliographer;* David King, *Reference Librarian.*

Holdings: Bks 50,000; Mss 20,000; 21,000 prints & broadsides. **Scope:** Illuminated Manuscripts (Medieval & Oriental); incunabula; common law; early American children's books (including the American Sunday School Union Collection); literature—Horace, Oliver Goldsmith, Charles Dickens (letters & printed books), Edgar Allan Poe (manuscripts & printed books), James Branch Cabell; Americana (discovery & exploration); Pennsylvania German Fraktur & imprints (to 1850); illustrated books (including original drawings) of Beatrix Potter, Arthur Rackham, Kate Greenaway, Robert Lawson, A. B. Frost & Howard Pyle. **Published Guides:** *Catalog of the Hampton L. Carson Collection Illustrative of the Growth of the Common Law* (1962); *A Descriptive Catalogue of the John Frederick Lewis Collection of European Manuscripts in the Free Library of Philadelphia* (1937); *Oriental Manuscripts of the John Frederick Lewis Collection in the Free Library of Philadelphia* (1937); A. S. W. Rosenbach, *Early American Children's Books* (1933); *The Pennsylvania German Fraktur of the Free Library of Philadelphia* (1976); "Portrait of a Philadelphia Collector William McIntire Elkins (1882–1947). With a Checklist of the Elkins Americana," *PBSA* 50 (1956). **Subjects:** Americana; Children's Books; Illustrated Books; Incunabula; Law; Literature 1640 to present; Travel & Exploration. **Budget:** $51,000 FY 1983–1984. **Access Policy:** Open to public.

HISTORICAL SOCIETY OF PENNSYLVANIA. Manuscript Department. 1300 Locust St, Philadelphia 19107. Tel: 215-732-6200. Peter J. Parker, *Administrator.*

Holdings: Bks 500,000; Mss 14,000,000 items. **Published Guides:** *Guide to the Manuscripts Collection of the Historical Society of Pennsylvania,* 2nd ed (1949), currently being revised & enlarged. **Subjects:** Americana; History; History of Medicine & Science; Illustrated Books; Literature 1900 to present (Pennsylvania); Regional — Pennsylvania; Religion; Theater & Performing Arts; Travel & Exploration; 18,000 Bound Newspapers (18th & 19th centuries). **Access Policy:** Apply to administrator.

LIBRARY COMPANY OF PHILADELPHIA. 1314 Locust St, Philadelphia 19107. Tel: 215-546-3181. Edwin Wolf 2nd, *Librarian.* **Staff:** Gordon Marshall, *Assistant Librarian;* James Green, *Curator of Printed Books;* Kenneth Finkel, *Curator of Prints;* Phillip Lapsansky, *Chief of Reference;* Jennifer Woods, *Chief of Conservation;* Sarah Whitley Ferguson, *Rare Book Cataloguer.*

Holdings: Bks 450,000; Mss 280 ln ft; 50,000 prints, photographs, maps, drawings. **Scope:** History & background of American civilization to 1880. **Published Guides:** *The Library of James Logan* (1974); *Catalogue of the Books Belonging to the Library Company of Philadelphia,* 3 vols (1835–1856); *Afro-Americana, 1553–1906* (1973); *Quarter of a Millennium* (1981); *American Song Sheets, Slip Ballads & Poetical Broadsides, 1850–1870* (1963) — all published by the Library Company; also annual report & various exhibition catalogues; *American Philanthropy, 1731–1860* (Garland, 1984); *Agriculture in America, 1622–1860* (Garland, 1984). **Subjects:** Americana; Fine & Applied Arts; History; History of Medicine & Science; Natural History; Regional — Philadelphia; Travel & Exploration; Afro-Americana to 1906; German Americana to 1830; American Judaica; Women's History to 1880; Philadelphia Area Prints & Photographs; Early American Agriculture; Early American Education & Philanthrophy; Philadelphia Printing & Book Collecting. **Budget:** $35,000 per year. **Access Policy:** Open to public.

PENNSYLVANIA HOSPITAL. Historic Library. Eighth & Spruce St, Philadelphia 19107. Tel: 215-829-3998. Caroline Morris, *Librarian/Archivist.*

Holdings: Bks 12,500; Mss 10 ln ft. **Scope:** The first medical library in the United States, established 1762. **Subjects:** History of Medicine; Natural History. **Access Policy:** Apply to librarian/archivist.

THE ROSENBACH MUSEUM & LIBRARY. 2010 DeLancey Place, Philadelphia 19103. Tel: 215-732-1600. Ellen S. Dunlap, *Director.* **Staff:** Patricia C. Willis, *Curator of Literature;* Clive E. Driver, *Lessing J. Rosenwald Research Associate.*

Holdings: Bks 30,000; Mss 130,000 sheets; 2000 drawings (primarily Sendak). **Scope:** English & American literature; North & South Americana; book illustration; Maurice Sendak Collection; Marianne Moore Archive; Rosenbach Company Archives. **Published Guides:** *A Selection from Our Shelves* (1973); *Early American Maps & Views* (1972); *A Calendar of Peruvian & Other South American Manuscripts . . . 1536–1914* (1972); *The Viceroyalty of New Spain & Early Independent Mexico: A Guide to Original Manuscripts* (1981). **Subjects:** Americana; Books about Books; Children's Literature; Illustrated Books; Incunabula; Literature 1640 to present; Religion; Travel & Exploration; Bookselling; Judaica. **Access Policy:** By appointment only.

TEMPLE UNIVERSITY LIBRARIES. Special Collections Department. Philadelphia 19122. Tel: 215-787-8230. Thomas M. Whitehead, *Head & Curator.* **Staff:** Cornelia King, *Rare Book*

Bibliographer; Fredric Miller, *Curator, Urban Archives Center;* Miriam Crawford, *Curator, Conwellana-Templana Collection;* Stephanie Morris, *Curator, National Immigration Archives;* George Brightbill, *Librarian for the* Inquirer/Bulletin *Newspaper Archives;* Patricia Case, *Curator, Contemporary Culture Collection.*

Holdings: Bks 50,000; Mss 100,000; 13,000,000 photographs. **Scope:** All fields, 19th–20th centuries: history of printing & publishing, archives of the contemporary alternative press, archives of Philadelphia housing, social service, political & educational history; black history; Temple history. **Subjects:** Books about Books; Economics; History of Mathematics; Illustrated Books; Literature 1900 to present; Press Books; Regional—Philadelphia; Religion; Lithography; Business History. **Budget:** Under $50,000 per year. **Access Policy:** Open to public.

UNIVERSITY OF PENNSYLVANIA. Van Pelt Library, Special Collections. Philadelphia 19104. Tel: 215-898-7088. Daniel H. Traister, *Curator.* **Staff:** Neda M. Westlake, *Rare Books Librarian;* Georgianna Ziegler, *Curator, Furness Memorial Library & Assistant Curator.*

Holdings: Bks 140,000; Mss 2500 ln ft. **Scope:** A general collection covering much the same areas of interest as those of the larger university library of which it is a part. **Published Guides:** M. A. Shaaber, *Sixteenth-Century Imprints in the Libraries of the University of Pennsylvania* (University of Pennsylvania Press, 1976); M. A. Shaaber, *English Seventeenth-Century Imprints in the Libraries of the University of Pennsylvania* (KTO Press, 1978); *Catalogue of Manuscripts in the Libraries of the University of Pennsylvania* (University of Pennsylvania Press, 1965), with periodic supplements in *The Library Chronicle of the University of Pennsylvania;* Lyman W. Riley, *Aristotle Texts & Commentaries to 1700 in the University of Pennsylvania Library* (University of Pennsylvania Press, 1961); many additional guides also exist. **Subjects:** Americana; Economics; History; History of Science; Illustrated Books; Incunabula; Literature pre-1640 to present; Natural History; Theater & Performing Arts; American Literature (19th-century novel & drama); English Literature (18th–19th century fiction); Spanish Literature (17th-century drama); Italian Literature (Tasso, Boccaccio, etc); German Literature (16th-century literature & religious controversy); History of Chemistry (E. F. Smith collection); Shakespeare & His Contemporaries (Furness Memorial Library); Medieval & Renaissance History (Henry Charles Lea Library); Aristotle in Early Printed & Manuscript Texts & Commentaries; Theodore Dreiser; James T. Farrell, Van Wyck Brooks, etc (literary & personal manuscripts). **Access Policy:** Open to public; identification required.

PENNSYLVANIA, Pittsburgh

CARNEGIE-MELLON UNIVERSITY LIBRARIES. Hunt Institute for Botanical Documentation, Department of Archives. Pittsburgh 15213. Tel: 412-578-2437. Michael T. Stieber, *Archivist.* **Staff:** Anita Karg, *Assistant Archivist.*

Holdings: Mss 246 collections; 20,000 portraits of botanists. **Scope:** Papers of botanists, horticulturists & some botanical artists. **Published Guides:** *Guide to the Botanical Records & Papers in the Archives of Hunt Institute* (Part 1, 1981; Parts 2 & 3, in progress). **Access Policy:** Open to the public.

CARNEGIE-MELLON UNIVERSITY LIBRARIES. Hunt Institute for Botanical Documentation, Hunt Botanical Library. Pittsburgh 15213. Tel: 412-578-2434. Bernadette G. Callery, *Librarian.* **Staff:** Elizabeth E. Mosimann, *Assistant Librarian.*

Holdings: Bks 25,000. **Scope:** Botany, particularly systematic botany;

history of botany; botanical bibliography; botanical illustration. **Access Policy:** Open to the public by appointment.

CARNEGIE-MELLON UNIVERSITY LIBRARIES. Special Collections. Schenley Parks, Pittsburgh 15213. Tel: 412-578-6622. Mary Catharine Schall, *Librarian.*
Holdings: Bks 8000; Mss 80 ln ft. **Scope:** Books about books & fine printing; landmark works of English & American literature & the history of science; small collection of architectural drawings; Herbert Simon papers, W. Van Dyke Bingham papers. **Budget:** $3000 per year plus gift funds. **Access Policy:** Open to the public.

PENNSYLVANIA, Swarthmore

SWARTHMORE COLLEGE. Friends Historical Library. Swarthmore 19081. Tel: 215-447-7496. J. William Frost, *Director.* **Staff:** Albert W. Fowler, *Associate Director;* Jean R. Soderlund, *Curator, Swarthmore College Peace Collection.*
Holdings: Bks 43,190; Mss 3000 ln ft; 3255 microfilm reels; pictures & posters. **Scope:** History & doctrine of the Society of Friends from the 1650s to the present — includes reforms sponsored by Quakers & other activities. Also part of Friends Historical Library is the Swarthmore College Peace Collection, which includes papers of individuals & records of organizations committed to establishment of world peace through disarmament, pacifism, conscientious objection & nonviolent social change. **Published Guides:** *Catalog of the Book & Serials Collection of Friends Historical Library* (Hall, 1982); *Guide to the Swarthmore College Peace Collection,* 2nd ed (Swarthmore College, 1981); *Guide to the Manuscript Collections of Friends Historical Library of Swarthmore College* (Swarthmore College, 1982). **Subjects:** Americana; History; Religion; Swarthmore College Peace Collection.

Budget: $2000 per year. **Access Policy:** Open to public.

SWARTHMORE COLLEGE. Library, Special Collections. Swarthmore 19081. Tel: 215-447-7495. Edward Fuller, *Librarian.*
Holdings: Bks 25,000; Mss 6 ln ft. **Scope:** Auden printed materials; British-Americana (accounts by Britons of their travels in America); private press; history of science & technology; travel & exploration.

PENNSYLVANIA, University Park

PENNSYLVANIA STATE UNIVERSITY LIBRARY. Rare Books & Special Collections Department. Rm W342 Pattee Library, University Park 16802. Tel: 814-865-1793. Charles Mann, *Chief.* **Staff:** Peter Gottlieb, *Head, Historical Manuscripts Collections;* Leon J. Stout, *Head, Pennsylvania State Collections.*
Holdings: Bks 90,000; Mss 7000 ln ft. **Scope:** English & European languages, historical documents & books 1425 to present. **Subjects:** Children's Literature; Fine & Applied Arts; History; Illustrated Books; Literature 1640 to present; Press Books; Regional — Pennsylvania; Religion; Theater & Performing Arts; Travel & Exploration; Anglo-German Literary & Cultural Relations (16th century to present); 20th Century Literature, Society & Politics. **Access Policy:** Open to public.

PENNSYLVANIA, West Chester

WEST CHESTER UNIVERSITY. Francis Harvey Green Library, Special Collections. West Chester 19383. R. Gerald Schoelkopf, *Librarian.*
Holdings: Bks 6088; Mss 8 ln ft. **Scope:** The basis of the collection is the library of William Darlington (botanist); the library of the Chester County Cabinet of Natural Sciences; books written about Chester County or by Chester County authors; the *Biogra-*

phies of the Signers of the Declaration of Independence by John Sanderson; the Shakespeare Folios; letters of Anthony Wayne & the Philips Autograph Library. **Subjects:** Children's Literature; History; History of Science; Literature 1640 to present (mostly 1800s); Regional — Chester County, Pennsylvania. **Access Policy:** Open to public, restricted hours.

RHODE ISLAND, Kingston

UNIVERSITY OF RHODE ISLAND. Library, Special Collections. Kingston 02881. Tel: 401-792-2594. David C. Maslyn, *Head.*

Holdings: Bks: 7500; Mss 3000 ln ft; 11,500 maps. **Scope:** Books: 1400 to present, general rare books with emphasis on historic botany & zoology, American poetry, fine presses. Manuscripts: Rhode Island history, political papers. **Subjects:** Books about Books; Literature 1900 to present; Natural History; Press Books; Regional — Rhode Island; Walt Whitman; Ezra Pound; Edna St. Vincent Millay; E. A. Robinson; Herbals; Defense Mapping Agency Repository; Senator Pell Papers; Governors of Rhode Island Papers (Licht & Noel). **Budget:** $3000 per year. **Access Policy:** Open to public.

RHODE ISLAND, Providence

BROWN UNIVERSITY. John Hay Library, Special Collections. PO Box A, 20 Prospect St, Providence 02912. Tel: 401-863-2146. Samuel Allen Streit, *Assistant University Librarian.* **Staff;** John H. Stanley, *Head;* Mark N. Brown, *Curator of Manuscripts;* Rosemary L. Cullen, *Curator of Harris Collection;* Catherine Denning, *Curator of the Annmary Brown Memorial Library;* Richard B. Harrington, *Curator of the Anne S. K. Brown Military Collection;* Peter Harrington, *Assistant Curator of the Anne S. K. Brown Military Collection;* Jennifer B. Lee, *Readers' Services Librarian;* Martha L. Mitchell, *University Archivist;* Mary T. Russo, *Curator of Broadsides.*

Holdings: Bks: 350,000; Mss 2600 ln ft; 40,000 broadsides; 500,000 pieces of sheet music; 3000 museum objects. **Scope:** 170 book collections, 150 discrete manuscript collections, as well as important holdings of broadsides, museum objects & institutional archives. Chronology spans ancient Egypt & Babylon to present. Subject areas widely diverse but especially strong in humanities. **Published Guides:** *Books at Brown* (Brown Library, annual); *Dictionary Catalogue of the Harris Collection of American Poetry & Plays* (Hall); David Godine, *Renaissance Books of Science from the Collection of Albert E. Lownes* (Dartmouth College, 1970). **Subjects:** Americana; Books about Books; Ephemera; Fine & Applied Arts; History; History of Mathematics, Medicine & Science; Illustrated Books; Incunabula (Annmary Brown Memorial); Literature pre-1640 to present; Natural History; Press Books; Regional — New England; Religion; Travel & Exploration; Classics; Music (songsters, song sheets & sheet music); Military History & Iconography; American & Canadian Poetry & Plays; American Fantasy Literature (Lovecraft & Clark Ashton Smith). **Budget:** $200,000 per year. **Access Policy:** Open to public.

JOHN CARTER BROWN LIBRARY. Brown University, Box 1894, Providence 02912. Tel: 401-863-2725. Norman Fiering, *Director.* **Staff:** Everett C. Wilkie, Jr, *Bibliographer;* Susan Danforth, *Curator, Maps & Prints;* Earl Taylor, *Head of Cataloguing.*

Holdings: Bks 50,000; Mss 600 ln ft plus 300 bound mss; 1200 maps; 500 engraved prints. **Scope:** Printed documents and manuscripts about the Americas during the Colonial period. **Published Guides:** *Opportunities for Research in the John Carter Brown Library* (The Library, 1968); *Catalogue* (of the John Carter Brown Library) (1865–1871; 1875–1882; 1919–1931; Supp. 1973). **Subjects:** Americana; Books about Books; Economics; History; History of Medicine; History of Science; Illustrated Books; Law; Literature pre-1640 to 1830; Natural History; Religion; Travel and Exploration; Architecture; Linguistics of native American peoples, particularly Mexico and South America; Maritime History, particularly ship building. **Access Policy:** Open to the public.

PROVIDENCE PUBLIC LIBRARY. Special Collections. 150 Empire St, Providence 02903. Tel: 401-521-7722 ext 231. Lance J. Bauer, *Librarian.*
Holdings: Bks 15,000; Mss 20 ln ft. **Subjects:** Americana; Books about Books; Children's Literature; Ephemera; Illustrated Books; Press Books; Regional — Rhode Island; Whaling; Civil War; Irish Culture; Magic; American Band Music; Checkers; Supreme Court Collection; Kennedy Collection; Marine & Naval Architecture; Printing History. **Access Policy:** Open to public.

RHODE ISLAND HISTORICAL SOCIETY. Manuscripts Division. 121 Hope St, Providence 02906. Tel: 401-331-8575. Harold Kemble, *Administrator for Manuscripts;* Paul R. Campbell, *Library Director.*
Holdings: Mss 3000 ln ft. **Scope:** Collection deals principally with materials relating to Rhode Island. **Subjects:** Americana; Maritime, Economic, Political, Social & Religious History; Personal Correspondence. **Access Policy:** Open to adults with valid identification.

SOUTH CAROLINA, Charleston

CHARLESTON LIBRARY SOCIETY. 164 King St, Charleston 29401. Tel: 803-723-9912. Catherine Sadler, *Librarian.* **Staff:** Theresa E. Wilson, *Assistant Librarian.*
Holdings: Bks 150,000; Mss 2000 ln ft. **Scope:** Books, periodicals & clippings all pertaining to the Revolutionary & Civil Wars & South Caroliniana. **Subjects:** Americana; Books about Books; Children's Literature; History; History of Medicine; Illustrated Books; Literature pre-1640 to present; Natural History.

SOUTH CAROLINA, Columbia

UNIVERSITY OF SOUTH CAROLINA. Thomas Cooper Library, Special Collections. Columbia 29208. Tel: 803-777-8154. Roger Mortimer, *Head.*
Holdings: Bks 30,000. **Subjects:** Americana; Books about Books; Children's Literature; History; History of Science; Illustrated Books; Incunabula; Literature 1640 to present (English & American); Natural History; Press Books; Travel & Exploration; Civil War 1860–1865; Ornithology; History of Bookmaking. **Access Policy:** Open to public.

UNIVERSITY OF SOUTH CAROLINA. South Caroliniana Library, Manuscript & Book Divisions. Columbia 29208. Tel: 803-777-3131. Herbert Hartsook, *Manuscripts Curator.* **Staff:** Eleanor Richardson, *Reference Librarian.*
Holdings: Bks 75,000; Mss 2,500,000; large collection of early maps of South Carolina & Southeastern United States. **Scope:** Manuscript & book collections relate to literature, history & culture of South Carolina & span the period from the 17th to the 20th centuries. **Published Guides:** *A Guide to the Manuscript Collection of the South Caroliniana Library* (1982). **Access Policy:** Open to public.

TEXAS, Austin

THE UNIVERSITY OF TEXAS. Harry Ransom Humanities Research Center. PO Box 7912, Austin 78712. Tel: 512-471-9119. Decherd Turner, *Director.* **Staff:** John P. Chalmers, *Librarian;* Carlton Lake, *Curator, Lake Collection;* Roy Flukinger, *Curator, Photography Collection;* William H. Crain, *Curator, Theater Arts Collection;* Kathleen Gee, *Curator, Iconography Collection;* L. Cathy Henderson, *Research Librarian.*
Holdings: Bks 1,000,000; Mss 9,000,000 items; 5,000,000 photographs. **Scope:** Comprehensive general holdings of rare books of all periods with emphasis on architecture; history of books & printing; private press; fine

binding; history of photography; theater arts; film; English, American & French 19th- & 20th-century literature; 17th- & 18th-century English literature; T. J. Wise. **Subjects:** Books about Books; Fine & Applied Arts; History; History of Mathematics, Medicine & Science; Illustrated Books; Law; Religion; Travel & Exploration; Livres d'Artiste. **Access Policy:** Open to public, valid identification required.

UNIVERSITY OF TEXAS AT AUSTIN. General Libraries, Eugene C. Barker Texas History Center, Texas Collection Library & Archives & Manuscripts Unit. Sid Richardson Hall, Unit 2, Austin 78712. Tel: 512-471-1741. Don E. Carleton, *Director.* **Staff:** Katherine Adams, *Assistant Director & Head, Texas Collection Library;* Alison Beck, *Head, Archives & Manuscripts Unit.*

Holdings: Bks 125,000; Mss 22,000 ln ft; 8000 mss & printed maps; 2000 historic Texas newspaper titles; sound recordings. **Scope:** Documenting the history & development of Texas & the Southwest. **Published Guides:** *The University of Texas Archives: A Guide to the Historical Manuscripts Collections in the University of Texas Library* (Univ. of Texas Press, 1967); *Catalog of the Texas Collection: Eugene C. Barker Texas History Center. University of Texas at Austin* (G. K. Hall, 1979). **Subjects:** Americana; Regional—Texas & Southwest, West; Religion; Travel & Exploration. **Budget:** $43,000 per year. **Access Policy:** Photo identification required.

TEXAS, Canyon

PANHANDLE-PLAINS HISTORICAL MUSEUM. Research Center. PO Box 967, W. T. Sta, Canyon 79016. Tel: 806-655-7191. Claire R. Kuehn, *Archivist/Librarian.* **Staff:** Lynette Guy, *Assistant Archivist.*

Holdings: Bks 11,500; Mss 11,000 ln ft; 1560 microfilm reels. **Subjects:** Americana; Fine & Applied Arts; History; Regional—Texas & the Southwest; Texas Panhandle; Ranching;

Indians of the Great Plains; Archaeology of Texas Panhandle; Ethnology; Clothing & Textiles; Antiques; Interviews with Early Settlers; Popular Music Archives; 16th- & 17th-Century Books Printed in Europe by Aldus Manutius (Aldine Press); Elsevier Press of the Netherlands; John Baskerville & Charles & Robert Stephenus; The Classics in Greek & Latin. **Budget:** $5000 per year. **Access Policy:** Open to public.

TEXAS, College Station

TEXAS A&M UNIVERSITY LIBRARY. Special Collections. College Station 77843. Tel: 409-845-1951. Donald H. Dyal, *Head.*

Holdings: Bks 60,000. Mss 40 ln ft. **Published Guides:** *Loran L. Laughlin Collection of Rare, Antiquarian Books* (1979). **Subjects:** Americana; History; Illustrated Books; Incunabula; Literature 1900 to present; Matthew Arnold; W. Somerset Maugham; P. G. Wodehouse; C. S. Forester; Science Fiction & Fantasy; Range Livestock Industry. **Budget:** $40,000–$60,000 per year. **Access Policy:** Open to public.

TEXAS, Denton

NORTH TEXAS STATE UNIVERSITY. Willis Library, Rare Book & Texana Collections. NT Sta Box 5188, Denton 76203. Tel: 817-565-2769. Kenneth Lavender, *University Bibliographer.*

Holdings: Bks 5100. **Scope:** General rare book collection with strengths in 18th-century English literature, children's literature, Mary Webb, Willa Cather. General Texana collection with strengths in Texas county history, Civil War, Anson Jones, Larry McMurtry. **Subjects:** Children's Literature; Literature 1640–1800; Regional—Texana. **Budget:** $5000 per year. **Access Policy:** Open to public.

TEXAS, El Paso

EL PASO PUBLIC LIBRARY. Southwest Collection. 501 N Oregon, El Paso

79901. Tel: 915-541-4869. Mary A. Sarber, *Head.*

Holdings: Bks 15,000; Mss 200 ln ft; 20,000 photographs; 900 map sheets; 400 sets of architectural plans; 60 drawers of vertical files. **Scope:** All aspects of region including west Texas, New Mexico, Arizona, northern Sonora & Chihuahua, with emphasis on El Paso County. Significant book & photograph collection on Mexican Revolution in Chihuahua. **Subjects:** Regional—American Southwest. **Budget:** FY 1983–1984 $5000. **Access Policy:** Open to public.

TEXAS, Fort Worth

AMON CARTER MUSEUM. Library. PO Box 2365, Fort Worth 76113. Tel: 817-738-1933. Nancy G. Wynne, *Librarian.* **Staff:** Milan R. Hughston, *Associate Librarian.*

Holdings: Bks 20,000. **Scope:** 19th-& early 20th-century American art, history, photography with strengths in 19th-century travel & exploration books on the American West (color-plate illustrations). **Subjects:** Americana; Fine & Applied Arts; History; Illustrated Books; Travel & Exploration; History of Photography; Mexican War. **Access Policy:** Open to public by appointment only.

FORT WORTH PUBLIC LIBRARY. 300 Taylor, Fort Worth 76102. Tel: 817-870-7700. Linda Allmand, *Director.*

Holdings: Bks 2800. **Scope:** A collection of old & rare children's books representing authors, illustrators, publishers & printers whose works had significant impact on the field of children's literature. Majority of collection published during 1800s & early 1900s. **Published Guides:** *Little Truths Better Than Fables: A Collection of Old & Rare Books for Children in the Fort Worth Public Library* (Branch-Smith Inc, 1976). **Subjects:** Children's Literature; Regional—Tarrant County, Texas. **Access Policy:** Special requests under supervision of library staff.

TEXAS CHRISTIAN UNIVERSITY. Mary Couts Burnett Library, Special Collections. PO Box 32904, Fort Worth 76129. Tel: 817-921-7108. Roger L. Rainwater, *Librarian.*

Holdings: Bks 5000; Mss 500 ln ft; 1500 photographs. **Scope:** Rare book collection includes British & American literature, Texas & Texas history & regional poetry. Manuscript collection includes papers of local business leaders, TCU faculty & regional poets. **Published Guides:** Lyle H. Kendall Jr, *A Descriptive Catalogue of the W. L. Lewis Collection, Part I, Manuscripts, Inscriptions, Art* (TCU Press, 1970). **Subjects:** Literature pre-1640 to 1800. **Access Policy:** Open to public.

TEXAS, Houston

RICE UNIVERSITY. Fondren Library, Woodson Research Center. Houston 77251. Tel: 713-527-8101 ext 2586. Nancy Boothe Parker, *Director.* **Staff:** Lauren Brown, *Librarian.*

Holdings: Bks 16,000; Mss 1650 ln ft; 1300 ln ft Rice University archives. **Scope:** Special collections include Masterson Texana, Axson 18th-century British drama, Bartlett Beethoven, Confederate imprints, Julian Huxley natural history collection. **Published Guides:** Nancy Boothe Parker, *A Bibliography of Catalogued Archival Publications in the Fondren Library* (1980) and many guides published by the Center. **Subjects:** History; History of Science; Literature 1640 to present (18th-century British drama); Press Books; Regional—Houston & Texas generally; Texas History & Entrepreneurship; Civil War; Rice University History; 20th-Century American Literature; British Naval History; US Manned Space Effort (1959–1975). **Budget:** $11,000 per year. **Access Policy:** Open to public.

UNIVERSITY OF HOUSTON LIBRARIES. Special Collections. University Park, Houston 77004. Tel: 713-749-2726. **Staff:** Gene Jackson, *Acting Head.* Wendy Sterby, *Library Assistant.*

Holdings: Bks 20,000; Mss 120 ln ft. **Scope:** Early English & American literature; modern creative arts; history of Texas & Southwest; history of Houston; bibles; modern fiction writers; modern poets. Manuscripts of modern fiction writers, including Larry McMurtry manuscripts, drafts, publishers working copies, proof copies, signed copies. **Published Guides:** *William B. Bates Collection of Texana & Western Americana, 1965 and 1971.* **Subjects:** Americana; History; Incunabula; Literature pre-1640 to present; Regional—Texas & Houston; Theater & Performing Arts. **Access Policy:** Open to public.

TEXAS, Lubbock

TEXAS TECH UNIVERSITY LIBRARY. Rare Books/Special Collections. Lubbock 79409. Tel: 806-742-3749. David Murray, *Associate Director.* **Staff:** Ray Janeway, *Rare Books Librarian;* Kathryn Lewis, *Librarian.*
Holdings: Bks 50,000; Mss 40 ln ft. **Scope:** English & American literary works, including those of Rudyard Kipling, William Faulkner, Joseph Conrad & John Donne; large collection of books & manuscripts on West Africa. **Subjects:** History of Science; Literature 1640 to present; Religion; Selig Heller Collection of Hebraica & Judaica; African Collection; Turkish Folklore; Pragmatism. **Budget:** $18,000. **Access Policy:** Open to public.

TEXAS TECH UNIVERSITY LIBRARY. Southwest Collection. PO Box 4090, Lubbock 79409. Tel: 806-742-3749. David Murrah, *Director.* **Staff:** Michael Q. Hooks, Doris A. Blaisdell, *Associate Archivists;* Janet Neugebauer, Jan Blodgett, Rebecca Herring, *Assistant Archivists.*
Holdings: Bks 30,000; Mss 7500 ln ft; 8195 reels microfilm. **Scope:** Collection pertains to the American Southwest & its indigenous institutions. **Published Guides:** "Music & Enter-

tainment" (1983); "Plains Indians" (1982); "Railheads in the Southwest" (1982); "Women on the Southwestern Frontier" (1982). **Subjects:** Americana; History; Literature 1900 to present; Regional—American Southwest; Religion; Travel & Exploration; Agriculture; Ranching; Land Colonization; Politics; Water Development; Ethnic Groups. **Budget:** $49,000. **Access Policy:** Open to public.

TEXAS, Richardson

THE UNIVERSITY OF TEXAS AT DALLAS. McDermott Library, Special Collections Department. PO Box 830643, Richardson 75083. Tel: 214-690-2570. Larry D. Sall, *Assistant Director.*
Holdings: Bks 4000; Mss 1500. **Scope:** Collection consists of early editions of Carl Linneaus's work in botany as well as other botany-related works and rare books on aviation history, philately, Latin America, art & photography. **Subjects:** Fine & Applied Arts; History; Illustrated Books; Natural History. **Budget:** $20,000 per year. **Access Policy:** Open to public.

UTAH, Provo

BRIGHAM YOUNG UNIVERSITY. Harold B. Lee Library. Special Collections. Provo 84602. Tel: 801-378-2932. Chad J. Flake, *Curator.* **Staff:** Dennis Rowley, *Curator of Manuscripts and Archives.*
Holdings: Bks 70,000; Mss, Maps, Photographs, Theater Broadsides. **Scope:** Collections strengths are in 19th- and 20th-century English and American literature; Renaissance and Reformation; European diplomatics; Western Americana; Printing history. **Subjects:** Americana; Books about Books; Children's Literature (Victorian); Fine and Applied Arts; History; History of Mathematics; Incunabula; Literature 1800 to present; Press Books; Regional—Western Americana, The Great Basin; Religion; Theater and Performing Arts; Travel and Ex-

ploration, particularly the South Seas; Astronomy. **Access Policy:** Open to qualified researchers.

UTAH, Salt Lake City

UTAH STATE HISTORICAL SOCIETY. Library. 300 Rio Grande Ave, Salt Lake City 84101. Tel: 801-533-5808. Gary Topping, *Manuscripts Curator.* **Staff:** Linda Thatcher, *Librarian.*

Holdings: Bks 21,000; Mss 5500 ln ft; 20,000 pamphlets; 6000 microfilm reels; 450 active & inactive periodicals. **Scope:** Collection built around Utah history, Mormon history & Western history. Most rare materials are early Mormon or Utah monographs (19th century) or manuscripts relating to Mormon doctrinal & local Utah history materials. **Published Guides:** *Guide to Unpublished Materials.* **Subjects:** History; Regional—Utah, Western US; Religion (Mormon); Travel & Exploration. **Budget:** $30,000 per year. **Access Policy:** Open to public.

VERMONT, Burlington

UNIVERSITY OF VERMONT. Bailey/Howe Library, Department of Special Collections. Burlington 05405. Tel: 802-656-2138. John Buechler, *Assistant Director.* **Staff:** Connell Gallagher, *University Archivist & Curator of Manuscripts;* J. Kevin Graffagnino, *Curator of the Wilbur Collection of Vermont;* Nadia Halpern, *Reference Specialist.*

Holdings: Bks & pamphlets 70,000; Mss 3200 ln ft (excluding university archives); 100,000 photographs; 450 Vermont maps. **Scope:** Vermontiana: printed & manuscripts; maps & broadsides: illustrated editions of Ovid's *Metamorphoses;* collection of John Masefield & Diane Wakoski; collection of Chiswick Press & Charles Whittingham imprints; collection of scarce works on printing history & bookmaking. **Published Guides:** *Folklore & Oral History Catalogue. University of Vermont Bailey/*

Howe Library (Center for Research on Vermont, 1981); "Sources for the Study of Vermont at the Bailey/Howe Library. Special Collections," in *Basic Sources for Vermont Historical Research* (Secretary of State, 1981). **Subjects:** Regional—all aspects of Vermont; Classical Literature (especially Ovid). **Budget:** $22,000 per year. **Access Policy:** Open to public for research.

VERMONT, Montpelier

VERMONT DEPARTMENT OF LIBRARIES. Law & Document Unit. c/o State Office Bldg, Montpelier 05602. Tel: 802-828-3268. Vivian Bryan, *Director.*

Scope: Early Vermont imprints & Vermontiana plus a scattering of items culled from the general collection. **Published Guides:** Vivian Bryan, "Materials Related to Vermont at the Vermont Department of Libraries Law & Documents Unit" (1981). **Subjects:** Americana; Law; Regional—Vermont, New England. **Access Policy:** Open to public.

VERMONT HISTORICAL SOCIETY LIBRARY. Pavilion Office Bldg, Montpelier 05602. Tel: 802-828-2291. Reidun D. Nuquist, *Librarian.*

Scope: Vermontiana from the founding of the state to the present. **Access Policy:** Open to public.

VIRGINIA, Charlottesville

UNIVERSITY OF VIRGINIA LIBRARY. Manuscripts Department. Charlottesville 22901. Tel: 804-924-3025. Edmund Berkeley, Jr, *Curator.* **Staff:** Michael F. Plunkett, Anne Freudenberg, *Assistant Curators;* Ann Southwell, *Manuscripts Cataloguer;* Janet Linde, *Assistant Archivist for University Archives;* Ervin Jordan, *Technical Services Archivist.*

Holdings: Mss & university archives 15,000 ln ft. **Scope:** Virginia & southeastern historical manuscripts including family, business, political, organizational & other papers; literary papers including the entire field of American literature; Virginia literature; specific figures in English literature; Thomas Jefferson, James Madison & James Monroe as private citizens. **Published Guides:** *Annual Report on Historical Collections, University of Virginia Library* (1930–1950); *The Thomas Jefferson Papers of the University of Virginia.* **Subjects:** Americana; History; Literature pre-1640 to present; Regional — Virginia. **Access Policy:** Open to public.

UNIVERSITY OF VIRGINIA LIBRARY. Rare Book Department. Charlottesville 22901. Tel: 804-924-3366. Julius P. Barclay, *Curator.* **Staff:** William H. Runge, *Curator, Tracy W. McGregor Library of American History;* Joan St. C. Crane, *Curator of American Literature Collections;* C. Clinton Sisson, *Assistant to Curator;* Mildred K. Abraham, *Librarian for Readers' Services.*

Holdings: Bks 200,000; 7500 broadsides; 2156 posters; 5000 maps; 470 boxes of newspapers. **Scope:** Strongest collections are in the fields of American History (McGregor Library) & American Literature (Barrett Library). Also Virginiana; 18th- & 19th-century British literature; typography & the book arts; 18th-century music; Sadleir-Black Gothic Novel Collection; William Faulkner Collection. **Subjects:** Americana; Books about Books; History; History of Science (optics, evolution); Literature 1801 to present; Press Books; Regional — Virginia & Southeast. **Access Policy:** Open to public.

VIRGINIA, Lexington

WASHINGTON & LEE UNIVERSITY. The University Library, Special Collections. Lexington 24450. Tel: 703-463-9111 ext 438. Richard Oram, *Librarian.*

Holdings: Bks 30,000; Mss 588 ln ft; 50 glass negatives. **Scope:** Confederacy (Lee); classical literature; depository for Rockbridge Historical Society manuscript collection; Valley of Vir-

ginia manuscripts (colonial to present). **Published Guides:** *Guide to the Manuscripts Collection,* no 11. **Subjects:** Regional — Virginia. **Access Policy:** Open to public.

VIRGINIA, Lorton

GUNSTON HALL LIBRARY. Gunston Hall, Lorton 22079. Tel: 703-550-9220. Bennie Brown Jr, *Librarian/Archivist.*

Holdings: Bks 3000; Mss 50 ln ft. **Scope:** 15th- to early 19th-century collections emphasizing colonial America, early Virginia, George Mason family & social history. **Subjects:** Americana; Fine & Applied Arts; History; Law; Literature pre-1640–1800; Natural History; Travel & Exploration; Gardening & Farming; Domestic Arts; Medicine. **Access Policy:** Open to public by appointment only.

VIRGINIA, Richmond

VIRGINIA HISTORICAL SOCIETY. PO Box 7311, 428 North Blvd, Richmond 23221. Tel: 804-358-4901. Virginius C. Hall Jr, *Associate Director.* **Staff:** Robert F. Strohm, *Librarian, Books & Serials;* Barbara M. Smith, *Associate Librarian, Books & Serials;* E. Lee Shepard, *Librarian, Manuscript Acquisitions & Archives;* Alan L. Golden, *Associate Librarian, Manuscript Acquisitions & Archives;* Howson W. Cole, *Senior Librarian, Manuscript Cataloguing;* Waverly K. Winfree, *Librarian, Manuscript Cataloguing.*

Holdings: Bks 250,000; Mss 3,000,000; 10,000 maps; 2000 pieces sheet music; numerous early prints & photographs. **Scope:** Books include all aspects of Virginia history from 16th century to present, with particular strengths in Virginia imprints, English history, colonial America, Revolutionary War, Civil War. Manuscripts feature family & personal papers dating from 17th century to present, including some of the most illustrious names in Virginia & American history. **Subjects:**

Americana; Books about Books; Fine & Applied Arts; History; Law; Travel & Exploration. **Access Policy:** Open to public.

VIRGINIA, Roanoke

ROANOKE PUBLIC LIBRARY. Virginia Room. 706 S Jefferson St, Roanoke 24013. Tel: 703-981-2475. A. Carol Tuckwiller, *Administrator.* **Staff:** Daniel E. Jones, *Head, Technical Services.*

Holdings: Bks 11,000; pamphlets 2500; Mss 8–10 ln ft; photographs; scrapbooks; maps. **Scope:** Anything about Virginia, especially southwest Virginia; strong in Virginia history & genealogy; areas people left to come to Virginia & areas people went to from Virginia, ie, Pennsylvania, Maryland, North Carolina, Kentucky, Tennessee. **Subjects:** History, Literature 1900 to present; Natural History; Regional— Virginia; Religion; Travel & Exploration. **Budget:** $6500 per year. **Access Policy:** Open to public.

VIRGINIA, Sweet Briar

SWEET BRIAR COLLEGE. Library, Rare Books/Archives Department. Sweet Briar 24595. Tel: 804-381-6139. John G. Jaffee, *Librarian/Archivist.*

Holdings: Bks 10,000; Mss 2 ln ft. **Scope:** W. H. Auden Collection (books, periodicals, articles, manuscripts); Virginia Woolf Collection (books, manuscripts); George Meredith Collection (books, periodicals, manuscripts); college archives. **Budget:** $1000 per year. **Access Policy:** Require letter from institutional library stating purpose of research.

VIRGINIA, Williamsburg

THE COLLEGE OF WILLIAM & MARY. Earl Gregg Swem Library, Manuscripts & Rare Books Department. Williamsburg 23185. Tel: 804-253-4550. Margaret Cook, *Curator.* **Staff:** Cynthia B. Brown, *Assistant to Department Head;*

Marylee McGregor, *Manuscripts Cataloguer.*

Holdings: Bks 30,000; Mss 2000 ln ft. **Scope:** Manuscript collection focuses on American & Virginia history, 17th century to present. Rare book collection focuses on same with additional strengths in US travel accounts, printing, papermaking & dogs. **Subjects:** Americana; History; Regional— Virginia; Travel & Exploration; Printing. **Budget:** $23,000 per year. **Access Policy:** Open to public.

WASHINGTON, Olympia

WASHINGTON STATE LIBRARY. Washington/Northwest Room. Olympia 98504. Tel: 206-753-4024. Nancy Pryor, *Librarian.* **Staff:** Kathryn Hamilton, Assistant Librarian.

Holdings: Bks 2500; Mss 432 ln ft. **Scope:** Contains original territorial library, first in state, purchased by Governor Isaac Stevens in 1853. General collection with emphasis on exploration & discovery. Many books date from 16th century. First editions, etc, of material pertaining to history & description of Washington state. **Published Guides:** Hazel E. Mills, "Governor Isaac I. Stevens & the Washington Territorial Library," *Pacific Northwest Quarterly,* vol 53, no 1; *Historical Records of Washington State: Records & Papers Held at Repositories.* **Subjects:** Americana; Regional— Pacific Northwest; Travel & Exploration. **Access Policy:** Open to public.

WASHINGTON, Pullman

WASHINGTON STATE UNIVERSITY LIBRARIES. Manuscripts, Archives & Special Collections. Pullman 99164. Tel: 509-335-6691. John F. Guido, *Head.* **Staff:** Terry Abraham, *Manuscript-Archives Librarian;* Edward R. Kukla, *Rare Books Librarian;* Leila Luedeking, *Library Specialist, Modern Literary Collections.*

Holdings: Bks 15,000; Mss 5000 ln

ft; 250,000 historical photographs; 1000 ln ft university archives. **Scope:** Printed materials include incunabula to modern first editions, private press books & rare Pacific Northwest Americana; personal library of Leonard & Virginia Woolf (modern British literary collections); contemporary American literature (books & broadsides from small, fine regional presses); Wildlife & Outdoor Recreation Collection (angling books); Veterinary History Collection; Germans from Russia Collection. Manuscripts cover exploration, settlement & development of the Palouse Country, the Inland Empire, the Columbia Basin & Pacific Northwest; history of agriculture; Mexican history; modern European & American composers. **Published Guides:** *Selected Manuscript Resources in the Washington State University Libraries* (1974). **Subjects:** History; Literature 1900 to present; Regional—Inland Pacific Northwest; Theater & Performing Arts. **Budget:** $12,000–$17,000 per year. **Access Policy:** Open to public.

WASHINGTON, Tacoma

WASHINGTON STATE HISTORICAL SOCIETY. Hewitt Reference Library. 315 N Stadium Way, Tacoma 98403. Tel: 206-593-2830. Frank L. Green, *Librarian.* **Staff:** Jeanne Engerman, *Assistant Librarian.*

Holdings: Bks 10,000; Mss 1000 ln ft; photographs; maps; magazine clippings; newspapers; microfilm. **Scope:** History of the Pacific Northwest with emphasis on early pioneer life, missions, Indians & the major industries of the area. **Published Guides:** *Historical Records of Washington State* (Washington State Historical Records Advisory Board, 1981). **Subjects:** Americana; History; Regional—Pacific Northwest; Travel & Exploration. **Access Policy:** Open to public.

WISCONSIN, Madison

STATE HISTORICAL SOCIETY OF WISCONSIN. 816 State St, Madison 53706.

Tel: 608-262-5867. Michael Edmonds, *Librarian.* **Staff:** F. Gerald Ham, *Manuscripts & Archives.*

Holdings: Bks 5000; Mss 78,000; 25,000 maps & atlases. **Scope:** Books—Americana, especially early travels, political pamphlets, rare newspapers, slave & Indian narratives, almanacs & pamphlets. Manuscripts—archives of the state of Wisconsin, Draper Collection (manuscripts documenting western frontier to 1830), social & political action, theater & mass communication. **Published Guides:** Alice E. Smith, *Guide to the Manuscripts of the Wisconsin Historical Society* (1944, supplements 1957 & 1966); the library also publishes finding aids to many of its special collections. **Subjects:** Americana; Ephemera; History; Regional—North Central States; Theater; Travel & Exploration. **Access Policy:** Open to public.

UNIVERSITY OF WISCONSIN—MADISON. Memorial Library, Department of Rare Books & Special Collections. 728 State St, Madison 53706. Tel: 608-262-3243. John New, *Acting Curator.* **Staff:** Deborah Reilly, *Assistant Curator.*

Holdings: Bks 81,000; Mss 100 ln ft. **Scope:** 35 collections with specialization in history of science & 20th-century literature; Russian underground; private press; Dutch & French pamphlets; American women writers; large collection of little magazines. **Budget:** $6000 per year (for little magazines). **Access Policy:** Open to public.

WISCONSIN, Milwaukee

MARQUETTE UNIVERSITY. Memorial Library, Department of Special Collections & University Archives. 1415 W Wisconsin Ave, Milwaukee 53233. Tel: 414-224-7256. Charles B. Elston, *Head.* **Staff:** Philip C. Bantin, *Associate Archivist.*

Holdings: Bks 6330; Literary Mss 50 cu ft; 5000 cu ft nonliterary archives & manuscripts. **Scope:** Rare books subject strengths in theology, philosophy, literature, history of printing, Jesuitica (1482 to present). Literary manuscripts include J. R. R. Tolkien Collection; Joyce Kilmer/Campion College collection; Elizabeth Whitcomb Houghton collection; Karl J. Priebe papers, Milwaukee artist; Dorothy Day papers. **Published Guides:** *Guide to Historical Resources*

in Milwaukee Area Archives (1976); Robert V. Callen, SJ, *The Marquette Archives: Focus on Social Change* (1981); *Guide to J. R. R. Tolkien Collection* (1983). **Subjects:** Americana; Books about Books; Fine & Applied Arts: History; Literature 1900 to present; Religion. **Access Policy:** Open to public.

CANADA

BRITISH COLUMBIA, Vancouver

UNIVERSITY OF BRITISH COLUMBIA LIBRARY. Special Collections Division. 1965 Main Mall, Vancouver V6T 1Y3. Tel: 604-228-4879. Anne Yandle, *Head.* **Staff:** Joan Selby, *Colbeck Librarian;* Frances Woodward, *Reference Librarian;* Laurenda Daniells, *University Archivist;* George Brandak, *Curator of Manuscripts.*
   Holdings: Bks 60,000; Mss 4706 ln ft; 25,000 maps. **Scope:** Books, manuscripts, maps, photographs & other ephemera relating to the history of Canada & British Columbia in particular, plus other collections, notably 19th-century English literature, early children's books & history of printing. **Subjects:** Books about Books; Children's Literature; Ephemera; History; Press Books; Regional—Canada; Travel & Exploration. **Budget:** $20,000 per year. **Access Policy:** Open to public for research.

BRITISH COLUMBIA, Victoria

UNIVERSITY OF VICTORIA. McPherson Library, Special Collections. PO Box 1800, Victoria V8W 3H5. Tel: 604-721-8257, 8258. Howard B. Gerwing, *Librarian.* **Staff:** Christopher G. Petter, *Archivist Librarian.*
   Holdings: Bks 35,000; Mss 240 ln ft; 10,000 photographs; 400 oral history tapes; 85 recordings of poets. **Scope:** Modern British literature collection centered on the Dolmen Press (Dublin) & the writers Sir Herbert Read, Sir John Betjeman, Robert

Graves & Aidan Higgins. Collections of British Columbia writers, military history, local politics. **Published Guides:** *Union List of Manuscripts in Canadian Repositories; Checklist of the Herbert Read Archive* (University of Victoria, 1969); *Special Collections Manuscript Holdings* (1977). **Subjects:** Children's Literature; Fine & Applied Arts; Literature 1900 to present; Regional—Western Canadiana; Theater & Performing Arts; Travel & Exploration; North American Indians (Northwest); Canadian Literature (British Columbia); Anglo-Irish Literature; Military History (Western Canada); Political History (British Columbia). **Budget:** $20,000 per year. **Access Policy:** Open to public for reference use.

NOVA SCOTIA, Halifax

MOUNT SAINT VINCENT UNIVERSITY LIBRARY. 166 Bedford Hwy, Halifax B3M 2J6. Tel: 902-443-4450 ext 120. Kathleen Currie, *Special Collections Librarian.*
   Holdings: Bks 12,000. **Scope:** Fine bindings, first editions, autographs, illustrations, private presses, limited editions. **Subjects:** Children's Literature; Illustrated Books; Literature 1900 to present. **Access Policy:** Open to public for reference use.

ONTARIO, Hamilton

McMASTER UNIVERSITY LIBRARY. Division of Archives & Research Collections. 1280 Main St W, Hamilton L8S

4L6. Tel: 416-525-9140 ext 4737, 2079. Charlotte A. Stewart, *Director.* **Staff:** Bruce Whiteman, *Research Collections Librarian;* Kenneth Blackwell, *Russell Archivist;* Carl Spadoni, *Assistant Russell Archivist.*

Holdings: Bks 56,000; Mss 4797 ln ft. **Scope:** Rare Books—18th-century British literature, modern first editions, modern Canadian Poetry (1945–1960). Archives—Bertrand Russell Archives, war & peace, Canadian social history, business & labor & literature. **Published Guides:** "A Guide to Archives & Research Collections," *McMaster University Library Research News,* vol 5, no 1 (May 1981); *Russell* (journal of the Bertrand Russell Archives). **Subjects:** History (18th century); Literature 1640 to present; Theater & Performing Arts (18th century); Travel & Exploration (18th century); Canadian Literature (papers of Farley Mowat, Pierre Berton, Marian Engel, Peter C. Newman, Matt Cohen, Susan Musgrave). **Budget:** $50,000 per year. **Access Policy:** Open to public.

ONTARIO, Sudbury

LAURENTIAN UNIVERSITY LIBRARY. Special Collections. Sudbury P3E 2C6. Tel: 705-675-1151. Andrzej H. Mrozewski, *Chief Librarian.* **Staff:** Ashley Thomson, *Head, Reference & Circulation.*

Holdings: Bks 2500. **Scope:** Canadiana—18th- & 19th-century books, mainly history, religion, dictionaries & encyclopedias—mainly in French & English. **Subjects:** History; Literature 1640 to present; Natural History; Regional—Eastern Canada; Religion; Travel & Exploration. **Access Policy:** Open to researchers.

ONTARIO, Toronto

TORONTO PUBLIC LIBRARY. Osborne Collection of Early Children's Books. 40 Saint George St, Toronto M5S 2E4. Tel: 416-593-5350. Margaret Crawford Maloney, *Curator.* **Staff:** Jill Shefrin, *Librarian;* Dana Tenny, *Bibliographer.*

Holdings: Bks & Mss 21,500. **Scope:** The Osborne Collection of Early Children's Books includes a 14th-century manuscript of Aesop's Fables, a 15th-century printing of a Venetian fairy tale, 16th-century school texts & courtesy books, godly Puritan works, 18th-century chapbooks & moral tales, Victorian classics of fantasy & adventure up to 1910. The Lillian H. Smith Collection is comprised of 3500 distinguished children's books in English published since 1910. The Canadiana Collection consists of 3500 children's books in English by Canadian authors, about Canada or published in Canada. All three collections include manuscripts, letters & original artwork. **Published Guides:** *The Osborne Collection of Early Children's Books 1566–1910, a Catalogue* (1958); *The Osborne Collection of Early Children's Books 1476–1910, a Catalogue* (1975); *A Token for Friends* (1979). **Subjects:** Children's Literature. **Access Policy:** Open to public.

UNIVERSITY OF TORONTO. Thomas Fisher Rare Book Library, Rare Books & Special Collections. 120 Saint George St, Toronto M5S 1A5. Tel: 416-978-5285. Richard Landon, *Head.* **Staff:** Katharine Martyn, *Assistant Head;* Anne Jocz, *Chief Cataloguer;* Rachel Grover, *Manuscript Librarian;* Emrys Evans, *Conservator & Rare Book Binder;* Mary Garvie-Yohn, Verneice Webber, Luba Hussel, Margery Pearson, Philip Oldfield, *Cataloguing;* Elizabeth Hulse, Edna Hajnal, *Public Service;* Graham Bradshaw, *Special Project.*

Holdings: Bks 200,000; Mss 5000 ln ft. **Scope:** Wide-ranging, excluding East Asian materials. Concentration on Canadiana (manuscripts, maps, serials, books), British & European history, English & European Literature. Manuscripts include Canadian historical documents, papers of Canadian authors & public figures & material documenting Canadian social & political movements; manuscripts of works by English, Italian & French authors. **Published Guides:** *A Brief Guide to the Collections* (1982); Peter Heyworth, *Forbes Collection* (1968); R. G. Landon, *Species of 'Origin'* (1971); E. Evans & R. Grover, *The Birdsall Collection of Bookbinders' Finishing Tools* (1972). **Subjects:** Books about Books; Economics; Fine & Applied Arts; History; History of Mathematics, Medicine & Science; Illustrated Books; Incunabula; Literature pre-1640 to present; Natural History; Press Books; Regional—Canada/Toronto; Religion; Theater & Performing Arts; Travel & Exploration; English Typography & Antiquities; Etchings of Wenceslaus Hollar (17th-century English & European views); English Philosophy (Bacon, Hobbes, Locke); Military Science; Italian & Spanish Literature (1500–1800); French Literature (Rousseau, Voltaire); Czechoslovakian Petlice (also historical materials relating to 1968); Bookbinding Finishing Tools. **Access Policy:** Open to public.

VICTORIA UNIVERSITY LIBRARY. 71 Queen's Park Crescent E, Toronto M5S 1K7. Tel: 416-978-3821. R. C. Brandeis, *Chief Librarian.* **Staff:** Konrad Eisenbichler, *Curator, Centre for Reformation & Renaissance Studies;* Lila Laakso, *Head, Reader Services Department;* Anne Schultz, *Librarian.* **Holdings:** Bks 10,000; Mss 60 ln ft. **Published Guides:** H. O. Dendurent, *The Coleridge Collection in Victoria University Library; The Wordsworth Circle* (Temple University, 1974); Lila & Raymond Laakso, "E. J. Pratt: An Annotated Bibliography," in *An Annotated Bibliography of Canada's Major Authors; Humanist Editions of the Classics at the Centre for Reformation & Renaissance Studies* (Victoria University, 1979); *Humanist Editions of Statutes & Histories at the Centre for Reformation & Renaissance Studies* (Victoria University, 1980); *Bibles, Theological Treatises & Other Religious Literature 1491–1700 at the Centre for Reformation & Renaissance*

Studies (Victoria University, 1981). **Subjects:** Religion; Wesley & Wesleyana; Erasmus; Canadian Literature (19th- & 20th-century poetry); English Literature (S. T. Coleridge, Virginia Woolf, Hogarth Press, Bloomsbury); Reformation & Renaissance Studies; Canadian Church History; Hymnology. **Access Policy:** Open to researchers & students with identification.

ONTARIO, Waterloo

UNIVERSITY OF WATERLOO LIBRARY. Doris Lewis Rare Book Room. Waterloo N2L 3G1. Tel: 519-885-1211 ext 3122. Susan Bellingham, *Head Librarian.* **Staff:** Joan Eadie, *Librarian, Special Collections;* Jane Britton, *Library Assistant, Special Collections.* **Holdings:** Bks 17,000; Mss 154 ln ft. **Scope:** Materials are acquired to support the teaching & research of the students & faculty at the University of Waterloo. **Published Guides:** *A Catalogue of the Dance Collection in the Doris Lewis Rare Book Room* (Univ. of Waterloo, 1979); *A Catalogue of the Library of George Santayana* (Univ. of Waterloo, 1980); *A Catalogue of the Lady Aberdeen Library on the History of Women* (Univ. of Waterloo, 1982); *Twenty-five Fine Books* (1982). **Subjects:** History of Mathematics; Press Books; Regional—Waterloo County; Theater & Performing Arts; Women's Studies (Canadian, books & archives); Library of George Santayana; Eric Gill; Robert Southey (& lesser romantic poets); William Blake. **Budget:** $25,000 per year. **Access Policy:** Open to public.

QUEBEC, Montreal

PRESBYTERIAN COLLEGE LIBRARY. 3495 University St, Montreal H3A 2A8. Tel: 514-288-5256. Daniel Shute, *Librarian.* **Holdings:** Bks 1700. **Scope:** A few incunabula, a few genuinely rare books (including Canada's only copy of the Complutensian Polyglot Bible), early printed Italian literature, many British

Puritan works, some exotic language theological literature, early printed Greek & Roman classics, many bibles from all stages of early printing. **Subjects:** Religion; Monographs & Early

Periodicals (Canadian Presbyterian churches, from 1835 on). **Access Policy:** Open for research in restricted areas only.

NAME INDEX

Independent research libraries whose names do not reflect their locations, and other rare book collections whose names differ from those of their parent institutions, are listed below.

26

Dealers in

Antiquarian Books

and Manuscripts

Antiquarian booksellers in the United States and Canada are grouped geographically by state or province and then city. Most cities are followed by current population numbers. Abbreviations used in the entries are listed below. In the entries a dagger (†) following the store name indicates membership in the Antiquarian Booksellers Association of America. Two indexes complete the chapter: an index of specialties (arranged alphabetically by specialty heading, then geographically), and an index by store name.

ABBREVIATIONS

acad–academic, academy
acctg–accounting
accts–accounts
adv–advertising
Afr–Africa(n)
agr–agriculture
Alb–Albania(n)
alt–alternative
Am–America(n)
Amer–Americana
ann–annual(ly)
anthrop–anthropology
antq–antiques
appr libr collec–appraises
  library collections
archaeol–archaeology
archit–architecture
astrol–astrology
astron–astronomy
autg–autographs
auth–author(s)
av mat–audiovisual mate-
  rial

bibliog–bibliography
biog–biography
biol–biology
biper–back issue periodicals
bkst–bookstore(s)
bldg–building
bnd–binding(s)
bot–botany
br–branch(es)
Bulg–Bulgaria(n)
bus–business
Can–Canada, Canadian
cat 3x ann–catalog 3 times
  annually
cds–cards
Celt–Celtic
ch–church
chem–chemistry
chts–charts
class–classical
col–college
Czech–Czechoslovakia(n)
Den–Denmark

dent–dentistry
Dept–Department
dict–dictionaries
doc–document
econ–economics
educ–education
EEur–East Europe
EGer–East Germany
encycl–encyclopedia
eng–engineering
Eng–England, English
Eur–Europe(an)
exp–export(s)
ext–extension
fac ed–facsimile edition
fict–fiction
for lang–foreign language(s)
Fr–France, French
geneal–genealogy
geol–geology
Ger–Germany
Gr–Greece, Greek
gr cds–greeting cards

287

hb–hardbound
Hebr–Hebrew
hist–history
hort–horticulture
hp–higher priced
hydrol–hydrology
ichthyol–ichthyology
illus–illustration(s)
imp–import(s)
incunab–incunabula
indep–independent(ly)
indust–industrial, industry
ins–insurance
int–international
Isr–Israel
Ital–Italian, Italy
Jap–Japan(ese)
juv–juvenile
Kor–Korea(n)
lang–language(s)
LDS–Church of Jesus Christ
  of Latter Day Saints
  (Mormon)
libr–libraries, library
lit–literary, literature
Lith–Lithuania(n)
ltd ed–limited edition
mag–magazines
mat–material
mech–mechanic(s, al)
med–medical, medicine
merch–merchandise
metaphys–metaphysical,
  metaphysics
Mex–Mexico
mgt–management
mil–military
mm–mass market
mod–modern
mss–manuscripts
mus–music(al)

musicol–musicology
nat hist–natural history
Neth–Netherlands
newspr–newspapers
nonfict–nonfiction
numis–numismatic(s)
nutrit–nutrition
o&r–old & rare
oceanog–oceanography
off equip–office furniture &
  equipment
off sup–office supplies
op–out of print
oper–operated, operates
orig–original
ornith–ornithology
ov tr–overhead transparen-
  cies
papbk–paperback(s)
per–periodicals
Pers–Persia(n)
pharm–pharmacy
pharmaceut–pharmaceuti-
  cal
Phil–Philippines
philat–philately
philos–philosophy
photog–photography
Pl–Place
Pol–Poland, Polish
polit–political, politics
Port–Portugal, Portuguese
prbnd–prebind(s)
psychiat–psychiatry
psychol–psychology
pub–public
publ–publish(er) (ing),
  publication(s)
pvt–private
rec–records
ref–reference

rel–religion, religious
  (C-Catholic, J-Jewish,
  P-Protestant)
remd–remainder(s)
reprod–reproductions
restr–restricted
Rom–Romanian
Russ–Russia(n)
s/s–sidelines & services
SAfr–South Africa
SAm–South America
SAN–Standard Address
  Number
sch–school
sci–science
sci-tech–science-technology
S/Ctr–Shopping Center
sec–secondary
sem–seminary
serv–service(s)
sh mus–sheet music
soc–social
sociol–sociology
Sp–Spain, Spanish
spec–special
subj–subject(s)
subs–subscription, subsidi-
  ary
sup–supplies
tech–technical
theol–theology
Tib–Tibet(an)
transp–transportation
Turk–Turkey, Turkish
tv–television
vet med–veterinary medi-
  cine
WGer–West Germany
Yugo–Yugoslavia(n)
zool–zoology

ALABAMA

Geneva

ALLENSON-BRECKINRIDGE
  BOOKS†
PO Box 447, 36340
Owner, Robert D Allenson
Subj: Theol

ARIZONA

Phoenix—764,911

FRANK LA MONT
856 E Edgemont Ave, 85006.
  Tel 602-274-6456
SAN 170-3277
Owner, Frank La Mont
Estab 1962. 20,000 Vols. 1500 sq ft.
  Cat 2x ann
Types: O&r, op, remd, used
Subj: Southwestern Amer
S/S: Art sup, search serv

HAROLD J MASON INC
PO Box 32363, 85064.
  Tel 602-956-6269.
  Telex 910-950-1113
SAN 161-651X
Pres, Dr Harold J Mason
Present Owner 1972. 250,000 Vols. Cat
  ann
Subj: Bus & mgt, econ, reference, soc
  sci, govt doc
S/S: Appr libr collec, biper, deal libr
  only, export
See Also: Norwalk, CT

BONITA PORTER BOOKS
2011 W Bethany Home Rd (Mail add:
  PO Box 1765, Litchfield Park,
  85340). Tel 602-242-9442
SAN 157-8839
Owners, Bonita Porter & Paul Porter
Estab 1965. 4500 Vols. 960 sq ft. Cat
Types: Fine bnd, 1st ed, hb, illus bk, ltd
  ed, new, o&r, op
Subj: Western Amer, cowboy art bk
S/S: Appr libr collec, prints

RUSS TODD BOOK SCOUT
4201 E Beryl La, 85028.
  Tel 602-996-7277

SAN 158-2674
5000 Vols. Cat 2x ann
Types: 1st ed, o&r, op
Subj: Am Indian studies, Arizonana,
  New Mexicana, Western Amer
S/S: Appr libr collec

Scottsdale—88,364

ANTIQUARIAN SHOP
4246 N Scottsdale Rd, 85251.
  Tel 602-947-0535
SAN 170-4559
Owner, George Chamberlain
Estab 1963
Types: 1st ed, illus bk, juv, o&r, op
S/S: Appr libr collec

VAN ALLEN BRADLEY INC†
PO Box 4130, Hopi Station, 85261.
  Tel 602-991-8633
SAN 160-2225
Owner, Van Allen Bradley
Estab 1964. Cat 4x ann
Types: 1st ed, hb
Subj: Amer, Am hist & lit
S/S: Appr libr collec, search serv

GUIDON BOOKS
7117 Main St, 85251.
  Tel 602-945-8811
SAN 121-5531
Owners, Aaron L Cohen & Ruth K
  Cohen
Estab 1964. Cat ann
Types: 1st ed, hb, imp, new, op, papbk,
  remd, o&r
Subj: Civil War, Western Amer
S/S: Appr libr collec, autg, biper, maps,
  orig art, search serv

WILLIAM R HECHT
Box 67, 85252. Tel 602-948-2536
SAN 160-225X
Owner, William R Hecht
Estab 1950. 3000 Vols. Cat 4x ann
Types: Imp, new & used, op, o&r
Subj: Amer, natural hist, falconry
S/S: Orig art

Tempe— 106,743

RUBY D KAUFMAN
518 E Loma Vista Dr, 85282.
Tel 602-968-9517 (by appt only)
SAN 170-2491
Owner, Ruby D Kaufman
Estab 1980. 2000 Vols
Types: Juv, papbk, op, remd, fac ed,
1st ed, illus bk, ltd ed, new
Subj: Illus, art, psychol
S/S: Search serv

THOSE WERE THE DAYS
516 S Mill Ave, 85281.
Tel 602-967-4729
SAN 128-2743
Owners & Mgrs, Victor & Vicky Linoff
Estab 1973
Types: Hb, new, op, o&r, papbk,
remd, used
Subj: Antq, collecting, furniture
S/S: Biper, gr cds, posters, rec & tapes,
sh mus, spec order, furniture

Tombstone— 1632

ROSE TREE INN BOOKSHOP
116 S 4th (Mail add: PO Box 7, 85638).
Tel 602-457-3326
SAN 160-2470
Owner, Burton Devere
Estab 1965. 5000 Vols. 450 sq ft. Cat
3x ann
Types: Fac ed, 1st ed, new & used, o&r
Subj: Western Amer
S/S: Search serv

Tucson— 330,537

JANUS BOOKS LTD
PO Box 35040, 85740.
Tel 602-297-2212
SAN 160-2675
Owner, Michael S Greenbaum
Estab 1978. Cat 3x ann
Types: 1st ed, ltd ed
Subj: Mystery, detective & suspense
fiction, related bibliog, criticism

J & T NIE BOOKSELLERS
5828 E Linden, 85712.
Tel 602-885-8164
SAN 160-2500

Owner, Joseph Nie
Estab 1959. 25,000 Vols. 1800 sq ft.
Cat 12x ann
Subj: Western Amer

BEN SACKHEIM— RARE BOOKS &
FINE ART
5425 E Fort Lowell Rd, 85712. Tel
602-327-4285
SAN 160-2748
Owner, Ben Sackheim; Assoc, P J Lynch
Estab 1969. 5000 Vols. Cat
Types: Fine bnd, 1st ed, illus bk, ltd ed
S/S: Autg, mss, orig art, prints

R M SCHRAMM
7101 E 34th St, 85710.
Tel 602-885-4839
SAN 158-4952
Owner, R M Schramm
Types: Hb, op, remd
Subj: Ornithology
S/S: Search serv

Yuma— 42,433

THE RAVENSTREE CO
1472 Gateway Dr, PO Box 10552,
85364. Tel 602-785-4003
SAN 160-2853
Owner, G William Stuart Jr
Estab 1964. 4000 Vols. Cat 14x ann
Types: 1st ed, fine bnd, hb, illus bk,
imp, incunab, juv, ltd ed, o&r, op,
used
Subj: Amer, bibliog, drama, Eng hist &
lit, classical lit
S/S: Appr libr collec, mss

ARKANSAS

Eureka Springs— 1989

JACK BAILES— BOOKS
66 Mountain St (Mail add: PO Box 150,
72632). Tel 501-253-9131
SAN 160-2977
Owner, Jack Bailes
Estab 1937. 10,000 Vols. Cat
Types: Illus bk, op
Subj: Arkansiana, hunting & fishing,
caves, Harrison Fisher, Maud Hum-
phrey, Kay Nielsen, Maxfield Par-
rish, A Rackham
S/S: Prints, search serv, staty

Fayetteville— 36,604

DICKSON STREET BOOKSHOP
318 W Dickson, 72701. Tel 501-442-
8182
SAN 160-3000
Owners, Don Choffel & Charles
O'Donnell
Estab 1978. 25,000 Vols. 2500 sq ft
Types: 1st ed, fac ed, hb, illus bk, o&r,
op, papbk, used
Subj: Literary criticism, poetry, Ozarks
S/S: Search serv

Forrest City— 13,803

MARSHALL VANCE PUBLISHER—
BOOKSELLER
1102 N Division (Mail add: PO Box 27,
72335). Tel 501-633-1980
SAN 160-3051
Owner & Mgr, Marshall Vance
Estab 1964
Types: Fac ed, fine bnd, 1st ed, imp,
new, op, o&r, private presses
Subj: Archit, Arkansiana, art, bks on
bks, cooking & nutrit, gardening,
hort, humor, Amer juv, miniature
bks, Ozark Mountains, printing hist
& tech, Southern folklore & hist
S/S: Appr libr collec, biper, orig art,
prints, search serv

Hot Springs— 36,166

YESTERDAY'S BOOKS ETC
PO Box 1728, 71901.
Tel 501-623-6082
SAN 160-3159
Owner, Rose Lee Edwards
Estab 1974. Cat
Types: Hb, o&r, op, used
Subj: Amer, Arkansiana
S/S: Search serv

Williford— 169

APPLETREE BOOKS
Rte 1, Box 361, 72482. Tel 501-966-
4666
SAN 160-354X
Owner, Margaret M Hudspith
Estab 1970. 1000 Vols. Cat ann
Types: Hb, imp, op, used, 1st ed

Subj: Gardening, cooking
S/S: Prints, search serv

CALIFORNIA

Albany

SAND DOLLAR BOOKS†
1222 Solano Ave, 94706.
Tel 415-527-1931
Owner, Jack Shoemaker
Types: Mod 1st ed, lit mag, letters, mss

Altadena— 42,380

ROBERT ALLEN BOOKS
PO Box 582, 91001. Tel 213-794-4210
SAN 170-4370
Owner, Robert Allen
5000 Vols. Cat 12x ann
Types: Fine bnd, 1st ed, hb, illus bk,
imp, o&r
Subj: Classical authors of Greece &
Rome, Eng & Am works
S/S: Search serv

Anaheim— 221,847

THE BOOK BARON
1236 S Magnolia Ave, 92804.
Tel 714-527-7022
SAN 157-2067
Owner, Robert Weinstein
Estab 1980. 150,000 Vols. 8600 sq ft.
Cat 2x ann
Types: 1st ed, fac ed, fine bnd, hb, illus
bk, juv, ltd ed, new, o&r, op, papbk,
remd, used
Subj: Fiction, mystery & detective, sci
fiction & fantasy
S/S: Appr libr collec, orig art, search
serv

HOUSE OF BOOKS
1758 Gardenaire Ln, 92804.
Tel 619-778-6406
SAN 158-7676
Owner, Marilyn L Bennett
Estab 1973. 200 Vols. Cat
Types: Imp UK, new & used
Subj: Scottish, Irish & Welsh
S/S: Search serv

Aptos—8704

JERROLD G STANOFF RARE ORI-
ENTAL BOOK CO
PO Box 1599, 95003.
   Tel 408-724-4911
SAN 160-7804
Owner, Jerrold Stanoff
Estab 1966. 5000 Titles. Cat 6-8x ann
Types: 1st ed, illus bk, o&r
Subj: Rel-Buddhist, Lafcadio Hearn, Jap
   & Chinese art ref, Jap & Chinese in
   Am, Jap lit in Eng translation, Jap
   woodblock prints, bks & maps,
   Korea, missionaries in Far East, Jap
   & Chinese nat sci & sci
S/S: Appr libr collec, maps, mss, orig
   art, prints, search serv

Arcadia—45,994

LIVE OAK BOOKSELLERS
11109 Daines Dr (Mail add: PO Box
   853, Temple City, 91780).
   Tel 213-442-1151
SAN 159-0510
Owners, Paul DiBiase & Linda DiBiase
Estab 1979. 3000 Vols. 2000 sq ft. Cat
   4x ann
Types: Fine bnd, 1st ed, hb, ltd ed,
   o&r, op
Subj: Bibliog, mountains, Western
   Amer, travel logs
S/S: Biper

Auburn—7540

RICHARD HANSEN
11245 Dry Creek Rd, 95603.
   Tel 916-885-4878
SAN 121-5809
Owner, Richard Hansen
Estab 1966. 8000 Vols. 800 sq ft. Cat
   4x ann
Types: Fac ed, 1st ed, hb, o&r, op, used
Subj: Californiana, Western Amer
S/S: Maps, ephemera

Bakersfield—105,611

UNUSUAL BOOKS
5908 Sunny Palms Ave, 93309.
   Tel 805-832-1757

SAN 160-3779
Owner, R M Mowry
Estab 1976. 300 sq ft
Types: Hb, new & used
Subj: Astrol, health & phys educ,
   metaphys & occult

Balboa

PENINSULA ANTIQUARIAN BOOK-
SELLERS
506 1/2 W Balboa Blvd, 92661.
   Tel 714-675-1990
SAN 160-3795
Owners, Dorothy Beek & Joan Spangler
Estab 1977. 2000 Vols. 400 sq ft
Types: Fine bnd, 1st ed, hb, illus bk,
   imp, juv, ltd ed, o&r, op, used
Subj: Californiana, illus
S/S: Appr libr collec, search serv

Bellflower—53,441

GREEN DOOR BOOKS &
ANTIQUES
17824 S Clark Ave, 90706.
   Tel 213-925-0630
SAN 160-3817
Owner, Blanche M Pryor
Estab 1959
Types: Op, used
Subj: Amer, antq
S/S: Ephemera

OSTBY'S AMERICANA
8758 Park Ave (Mail add: Box 89,
   90706). Tel 213-925-7767
SAN 160-3825
Owner, Duane C Ostby; Mgr, Anthony
   Wiley
Estab 1950. 12,000 Vols. Cat ann
Types: Fac ed, 1st ed, hb, o&r, new &
   used, op, papbk, remd
Subj: Amer, Civil War, genealogy,
   federal & state rosters, registers,
   reports
S/S: Appr libr collec, biper, maps, mss,
   search serv
Military research on microfilm, discs
   and cassettes

Berkeley—103,328

ADAMS ANGLING BOOKS & PARA-
PHERNALIA
1170 Keeler Ave, 94708.
Tel 415-849-1324
SAN 158-6904
Owner, James R Adams
Estab 1978. 3000 Vols. 250 sq ft. Cat
2x ann
Types: Fac ed, fine bnd, 1st ed, hb, illus
bk, imp, ltd ed, o&r, op, used
Subj: Hunting & fishing, natural hist,
nature & environ, fishing
S/S: Appr libr collec, fishing sup

ALBION FINE PRINTS†
1751 San Lorenzo Ave, 94707.
Tel 415-527-0103
SAN 158-121X
Owners, Albert M Shapiro & Betsy
Cohen
Estab 1975. 4000 Vols. Cat 2x ann
Types: Fac ed, 1st ed, illus bk, o&r, op
Subj: Art, graphic arts, hist, psychol
S/S: Orig art, prints, search serv

ANACAPA BOOKS
3090 Claremont Ave, 94705.
Tel 415-654-3517
SAN 158-2615
Owner, David S Wirshup
Estab 1975. 15,000 Vols. Cat 8x ann
Types: 1st ed, o&r

ARK BOOKSHOP
1703 University Ave, 94703.
Tel 415-841-2853
SAN 160-3841
Owner, Louis Laub
Estab 1965. 20,000 Vols. Cat 2x ann
Types: 1st ed, hb, juv, ltd ed, o&r, op,
used
Subj: Californiana, humanities, schol-
arly lit, sci-tech, 17th & 18th century
lit
S/S: Appr libr collec, biper

BIBLIOMANIA
2556 Telegraph Ave, 94704.
Tel 415-848-1178
SAN 160-3876
Owner, Daryl B VanFleet
Estab 1974

Types: Used, op, 1st ed
Subj: Black studies, feminism, indust &
labor, mystery & detective, socialism, Sp hist & lit
S/S: Search serv

ROY BLEIWEISS FINE BOOKS†
92 Northgate Ave, 90064.
Tel 415-548-1624
SAN 160-6751
Owner, Roy Bleiweiss
Estab 1972. 3500 Vols. 800 sq ft. Cat
4x ann
Types: Fine bnd, 1st ed, hb, illus bk, ltd
ed, o&r, op, fine press
Subj: Amer, law, scholarly lit, tobacco
& pipe bks
S/S: Appr libr collec, autg, mss, orig
art, search serv
By appt only

CAROL DOCHEFF—BOOKSELLER
1605 Spruce St, 94709.
Tel 415-841-0770
SAN 158-0353
Owner, Carol Docheff
Estab 1979. 7500 Vols. 1000 sq ft. Cat
4x ann
Types: 1st ed, illus bk, juv, op
Subj: Folklore, mythology, sci fiction &
fantasy, Newberry & Caldecott
authors, animal titles
S/S: Orig art

THE INVISIBLE BOOKMAN
97 Franciscan Way, 94707.
Tel 415-524-7823
SAN 160-3949
Owner, Allan Covici
Estab 1963. 7500 Vols
Types: 1st ed, op, o&r, used
Subj: Drama, fiction, humanities, liter-
ary criticism, poetry
S/S: Appr libr collec, search serv

J B MUNS, BOOKS
1162 Shattuck Ave, 94707.
Tel 415-525-2420
SAN 160-3981
Owner, J B Muns
Estab 1964. 2500 Vols. Cat ann
Types: Hb, imp, o&r, op, remd, used
Subj: Art, music, archit, photog, city
planning

S/S: Appr libr collec, search serv
Appt only

GEORGE K OPPENHEIM†
51 Vallejo St, 94707. Tel 415-527-5169
Subj: Fine arts, illus bks, for lang, decorative prints
By appt only

REGENT STREET BOOKS
2747 Regent St, 94705. Tel 415-548-8459
SAN 158-1236
Owner, Mark Weiman
Estab 1978. 1000 Vols. 140 sq ft. Cat ann
Types: O&r, op
Subj: Design, graphic arts, psychol, yoga
S/S: Appr libr collec

SCATTERGOOD BOOKS
PO Box 7043, Landscape Sta, 94707
SAN 160-404X
Owner, I M Scattergood
Estab 1968. 4200 Vols. Cat
Types: O&r, op
Subj: Communism, socialism, radical polit, Jewish question, Russia
S/S: Search serv

SERENDIPITY BOOKS INC†
1790 Shattuck Ave, 94709.
   Tel 415-841-7455
SAN 160-4058
Owner, Peter B Howard; Mgr, Thomas A Goldwasser; Buyer, Nancy Kosenka
Estab 1962. 60,000 Vols. 10,000 sq ft. Cat ann
Types: 1st ed, ltd ed, new, o&r
Subj: Am hist & lit, Eng hist & lit, mod lit
S/S: Appr libr collec, autg, mss, orig art, per

SARKIS SHMAVONIAN BOOKS & PRINTS
1796 Shattuck Ave, 94709.
   Tel 415-843-5910
SAN 160-4066
Owner, Sarkis Shmavonian; Mgr, Laurel Lobovits
Estab 1976. 6000 Vols. 1500 sq ft. Cat 2x ann

Types: 1st ed, hb, illus bk, imp, o&r, op
Subj: Discovery & explor, graphic arts, oceanog, photog, travel, Western Amer, 19th century fiction
S/S: Appr libr collec, maps, orig art, prints, sh mus

WHALING RESEARCH
PO Box 5034, 94715
SAN 160-4120
Owner, E M McDermott
Estab 1963. 3000 Vols
Types: 1st ed, hb, imp, op, o&r, used
Subj: Whales & whaling
S/S: Biper, maps, mss, search serv

Beverly Hills — 32,367

HARRY A FRANKLIN GALLERY
9601 Wilshire Blvd, Sta 728, 90210.
   Tel 213-271-9171
SAN 128-7419
Owner, Valerie Franklin
Estab 1955. Present Owner 1980
Subj: African, Oceanic, primitive & ancient art
S/S: Orig art

HARRY A LEVINSON RARE BOOKS†
PO Box 534, 90213. Tel 213-276-9311
SAN 160-4163
By appointment only
Owner, Harry A Levinson
Estab 1929. 6000 Vols
Types: 1st ed, incunab, o&r
Subj: Eng & Continental hist, lit, sci & scholarship to 19th century
S/S: Appr libr collec, autg, mss

THE SCRIPTORIUM†
427 N Canon Dr, 90210.
   Tel 213-275-6060
Owner, Charles W Sachs
Subj: Autg, mss, motion picture memorabilia
S/S: Appr

Bishop — 3333

JOHN ALAN WALKER
PO Box 516, 93514
SAN 160-4201

Owner, John Alan Walker
Estab 1970. 4000 Titles. 1000 sq ft. Cat
3x ann
Types: 1st ed, fine bnd, ltd ed, new, op
Subj: Amer, art, European art

Burbank — 84,625

BOOK CITY OF BURBANK
308 N Golden Mall, 91502. Tel 213-
848-4417
SAN 156-6652
Mgr, Teri Langwald
Estab 1981. 50,000 Vols. 10,000 sq ft
Branch
Types: Hb, op, papbk
Subj: Art, biog, films & filmmaking,
metaphys & occult, photog
Hq: Hollywood Book City, Los Angeles

HAROLD B DIAMOND — BOOK-
SELLER
Box 1193, 91507. Tel 213-846-0342
SAN 160-4309
Owner, Harold B Diamond
Estab 1964. Cat 6x ann
Types: 1st ed, illus bk, ltd ed, op, o&r
Subj: Art, bks on bks, econ, Latin Am,
polit sci, reference, sci-tech, scholarly
lit, soc sci, archit, performing arts, sci
fiction & fantasy, class studies, Juda-
ica, Am, Eng, Fr, Ger & Sp hist & lit,
Dickensiana, E Eur, Mark Twain,
World War I

Burlingame — 26,173

VERNON HOWARD BOOKS
723 California Dr, 94010.
Tel 415-347-5620
SAN 160-4368
Owner, Vernon Howard
Present Owner 1940. 50,000 Vols.
1000 sq ft
Types: Hb, imp, op, o&r, used
Subj: Drama, hist, music, travel, West-
ern Amer, mountaineering

PENINSULA BOOKSEARCH
PO Box 1305, 94010
SAN 160-4376
Owner, James C Nagel; Mgr, Terry
Nagel
Estab 1978

Types: 1st ed, illus bk, ltd ed, op, pvt
presses
Subj: Fiction, mod lit, Oz bks
S/S: Search serv

KEN PRAG PAPER AMERICANA
Box 531, 94010. Tel 415-566-6400
SAN 157-2083
Owner, Ken Prag
Estab 1972. Cat 4x ann
Subj: Californiana, mining, Nevadiana,
railroadiana, shipping, Western states
S/S: Stock certificates & bonds, western
railroad ephemera, old post cards &
photographs

Cambria — 1716

TAYLOR COFFMAN BOOKSELLER
1441 Astor Ave, 93428.
Tel 805-927-4343
SAN 128-4312
Owner, Taylor Coffman
Estab 1980. 500 Vols. Cat
Types: Hb, op, remd
Subj: Archit, art, hist, humanities
S/S: Search serv

Cardiff — 5724

AIDE
PO Box 666, 92007. Tel 619-753-3392
SAN 160-4449
Owner, Ted Rogers
Estab 1954.
Types: Hb, new & used, op
Subj: Hypnosis, metaphys & occult,
psychol, bot med, consciousness
expansion, death & dying, psychic &
spiritual healing
S/S: Search serv

BOOKPOST
962 Greenlake Ct, 92007.
Tel 619-753-3392
SAN 160-4457
Owner, T Rogers
Estab 1954. 1200 Vols. 360 sq ft
Types: Hb, new & used, op
Subj: Hypnosis, metaphysics, metaphys
& occult, parapsychol, bot med, new
age philos, unorthodox healing
S/S: Search serv, collector counseling,
lectures

Carlsbad—35,490

JAMES HANSEN BOOKS
3514 Highland, 92008. Tel 619-729-
3383
SAN 157-2105
Owner, James Hansen
Estab 1979. 10,000 Vols. 800 sq ft. Cat
ann
Types: 1st ed, fine bnd, hb, illus bk, juv,
ltd ed, o&r, op, papbk, remd, used
Subj: Californiana, Southwestern Amer,
Amer & British literary 1st editions
S/S: Appr libr collec, autg, biper, mss,
deal with libraries

MEMORABILIA LTD†
7624 El Camino Real, 92008. Tel 619-
436-2321
SAN 160-4465
Owner, Leon H Becker
Estab 1973

Carmel—4707

J S EDGREN†
Mission & 8th Ave (Mail add: PO Box
326, 93921). Tel 408-625-2575,
624-3611
SAN 160-4481
Owner, Soren Edgren; Mgr, Paul
Lejeune
Estab 1977. 15,000 Vols. Cat
Types: O&r
Subj: Antq, lang arts, Far East
S/S: Appr libr collec
Hq: Los Angeles

IRVING KEATS
280 Del Mesa Carmel, 93921. Tel 408-
624-5428
SAN 160-4503
Owner, Irving Keats
Estab 1930. 2000 Vols
Types: Fine bnd, 1st ed, color plate bks,
press bks
S/S: Autg

Carmel Valley—4725

KESTREL BOOKS
1 W Carmel Valley Rd (Mail add: PO
Box Q, 93924). Tel 408-659-4534
SAN 160-452X

Owner, Michael E Clark
Estab 1976. 9000 Vols. 950 sq ft. Cat 1-
3x ann
Types: O&r, op
Subj: Western Amer
S/S: Appr libr collec

Carpenteria—10,835

RICHARD GILBO—BOOKS
1328 Vallecito Rd (Mail add: PO Box
12, 93013). Tel 805-684-2892
SAN 158-7897
Owner, Richard Gilbo
Estab 1978. 20,000 Vols. Cat 6x ann
Types: Fine bnd, 1st ed, hb, illus bk,
juv, ltd ed, o&r, op, used
Subj: Art, black studies, mod lit, natural
hist, philos

Chico—26,601

BOOKS ET CETERA
PO Box 3507, 95927.
Tel 916-343-8788
SAN 157-2121
Owner, E J Schonleber
Estab 1979. 7500 Vols
Types: Fine bnd, 1st ed, hb, illus bk, ltd
ed, o&r, op, used
Subj: Bks on bks, Californiana
S/S: Search serv

McLAUGHLIN'S BOOKS
932 W 8th Ave (Mail add: PO Box
3083, 95927). Tel 916-345-2626
SAN 157-8855
Owner, Robert F McLaughlin
Estab 1946. 1000 Vols. 350 sq ft. Cat
2x ann
Types: Hb, o&r, op
Subj: Alaskana, Arctic, Can, local hist,
big game & hunting
S/S: Search serv

Chula Vista—83,927

CHULA VISTA BOOKSTORE
265 1/2 3rd Ave, 92010.
Tel 619-427-9518
SAN 160-466X
Owner, Lew Moats

Types: Hb, juv, new & used, o&r,
   papbk
S/S: Sh mus, Old sh mus

Compton—81,286

AVIATION BOOKMOBILE — MIL-
   AIR PHOTOS & BOOKS
901 W Alondra Hangar Q5, 90220.
   Tel 213-632-8081
SAN 160-4767
Owners, Harold N Miller & Phyllis
   Miller
Estab 1960. 10,000 Vols
Branch. Buys indep & through hq
Types: 1st ed, hb, imp, new & used,
   o&r, op, papbk, remd
Subj: Aviation, hunting & fishing,
   military, nature & environ, photog,
   radio, sci-tech, tv, Western Amer,
   guns, lighter-than-air flight technol-
   ogy
S/S: Research, consulting
Hq: Norwalk, CA

Corona Del Mar

THE MEMORY BOX
519 Jasmine Ave, 92625.
   Tel 714-644-1053
SAN 157-2156
Owners, Sandy Freeman & Barbara
   Freeman
Estab 1973
Types: Hb, illus bk, imp, juv, o&r
Subj: Bks with colored lithographs
S/S: Orig art, posters, prints, sh mus

Costa Mesa—82,291

APOLLO BOOK SHOP
545 W 18th St, 92627.
   Tel 714-646-7045
SAN 160-483X
Owner, James L Currie
Estab 1961. 25,000 Vols
Types: Op, used
Subj: Alaskana, Arctic, humor, nautical,
   South Seas, Western Amer
S/S: Biper, search serv

Crestline—3509

GEORGE FREDERICK KOLBE FINE
   NUMISMATIC BOOKS
PO Box Drawer 1610 A, 92702. Tel
   714-768-6854
SAN 157-2652
Owner, G F Kolbe
Estab 1978. Present Owner 1967.
   25,000 Vols. 1100 sq ft. Cat 3x ann
Types: New, o&r, op, Fr & Ger lang,
   Austria, Eng & Ger imp
S/S: Appr libr collec

Cupertino—25,720

SAL NOTO—BOOKS
21995 McClellan Rd, 95014.
   Tel 408-253-7864
SAN 160-4929
Owner, Sal Noto
Estab 1977. 250 sq ft
Types: 1st ed, hb, o&r, op, used
Subj: Californiana, Jack London, John
   Muir, John Steinbeck, Stephen
   Crane, Frank Norris

Daly City—78,519

BEAVER BOOKS
Box 974, 94017. Tel 415-584-1302
SAN 157-2164
Owner, Edgar L Weber
2500 Vols. Cat 1-2x ann
Types: Fac ed, 1st ed, hb, ltd ed, new &
   used, o&r, op, imp Can & Eng
Subj: N Amer fur trade & related explo-
   ration, Lewis & Clark, Hudson's Bay
   Co
S/S: Search serv

Danville

DANVILLE BOOKS
176 S Hartz Ave, 94526.
   Tel 415-837-4200
SAN 160-4953
Owners, Mr & Mrs James E Sherriff
Estab 1977. 5000 Vols. 350 sq ft
Types: Fine bnd, 1st ed, hb, illus bk,
   juv, ltd ed, o&r, op, used
Subj: Belles lettres, Chinese-Am studies,
   Civil War, hist, Calif auth, Eugene

O'Neill, Mark Twain, J Muir, Steinbeck
S/S: Appr libr collec, search serv, sh
mus

Dutch Flat

TOWN & GOWN BOOK CO
PO Box 190, 95714. Tel 916-389-2363
(by appt)
SAN 160-3701
Owner, Nicolaas Pansegrouw
Estab 1960. 100,000 Vols. 2000 sq ft.
Cat 4x ann
Types: O&r, op, used
Subj: Law, soc sci, hist, Africa, crimi-
nology
S/S: Appr libr collec

El Cerrito — 22,731

GRAEME VANDERSTOEL
Box 599, 94530. Tel 415-527-2882
SAN 157-2180
Owners, Graeme Vanderstoel & Eve
Vanderstoel
Estab 1962. 3500 Vols. Cat 6x ann
Types: New, o&r, op
Subj: Africa, art, Asian studies, Austra-
lia, Orientalia, Pacific, performing
arts, jazz
S/S: Appr libr collec, search serv

Elkgrove — 17,327

SHUEY BOOK SEARCH
8886 Sharkey Ave, 95624.
Tel 916-685-3044
SAN 157-7182
Owner, Claudine Shuey
1000 Vols
Types: Hb

TEN O'CLOCK BOOKS
8786 Cling Court, 95624
SAN 160-7847
Owner, J A Grenzeback
Estab 1973
Types: Imp UK, op
Subj: Humanities
Functions as a search service for college
& university libraries

Encinitas — 5375

P F MULLINS BOOKS
109 Beechtree Dr, 92024.
Tel 619-436-7810
SAN 159-0995
Owners, Paul Mullins & Roslyn Mul-
lins; Mgr, Paul Mullins
Estab 1979. 10,000 Vols. 500 sq ft. Cat
2x ann
Types: 1st ed, ltd ed
Subj: James Michener, John Steinbeck

RAIR LITERATURE
PO Box 2488, Leucadia, 92024
SAN 158-2046
Owner, Bettie Hummel; Mgr, Burton
Gerard
Estab 1960. 3000 Vols
Types: Hb, papbk, o&r, op, used
Subj: Aviation hist, World War I, Korea
& Vietnam
S/S: Per, prints, aviation hist & combat
aviation

Encino

ALPHA BOOKS
18046 Ventura Blvd, 91426.
Tel 213-344-6365
SAN 120-0550
Owners, Ray Vasin & Betty Vasin
Estab 1965. 40,000 Vols. 880 sq ft
Types: 1st ed, fac ed, fine bnd, hb, illus
bk, incunab, juv, ltd ed, op, o&r,
papbk, used
Subj: Art, arts & crafts, how-to,
metaphys & occult
S/S: Biper, prints, search serv, sh mus

BOOKS & THE COLLECTOR ARTS
PO Box 589, 91316. Tel 213-981-6453
SAN 125-5010
Owner, Alexander A Dzilvelis
Estab 1971. 5000 Vols. 1000 sq ft. Cat
Types: Fac ed, fine bnd, 1st ed, hb, imp,
incunab, ltd ed, new & used, op,
o&r, remd
Subj: Art, printing & bookmaking
S/S: Orig art, prints, graphics

TROPHY ROOM BOOKS — BIG
GAME HUNTING BOOKS†
4858 Dempsey Ave, 91436.
Tel 213-784-3801

SAN 157-2202
Owner, Ellen R Enzler
Estab 1976. 3000 Vols. Cat 3-4x ann
Types: Ltd ed, op, o&r, used, color
plate bks
Subj: Africa, Asia & NAmer big game
explor, hunting & studies
S/S: Appr libr collec, search serv

Fairfax—7391

NEW ALBION BOOKSHOP
1820 Sir Francis Drake Blvd (Mail add:
PO Box 521, 94930).
Tel 415-456-1464
SAN 144-865X
Owner, Harold Bertram; Mgr, William
Bertram
Estab 1965. 20,000 Vols. 1500 sq ft
Types: Hb, juv, op, papbk, used
Subj: Drama, fiction, military, mystery
& detective, soc sci, sci fiction &
fantasy, Western Amer
Branches:
—NEW ALBION RARE BOOKS
765 Center Rd (Mail add: PO Box
521, 94930). Tel 415-456-6199
SAN 144-8668
Mgr, Gwendolyn Scott
Estab 1979. 35,000 Vols. 1500 sq ft.
Cat
Types: 1st ed, o&r, op
Subj: Art, Californiana, discovery &
explor, mystery & detective, sci
fiction & fantasy, travel, Western
Amer
S/S: Appr libr collec
See Also: Mandrake Bookshop, San
Rafael

Fair Oaks—11,256

J C BONNETTE BOOKSELLER
5525 Dewey Dr, Suite 104, 95628.
Tel 916-966-5780
SAN 157-2210
Owners, J C Bonnette et al
Estab 1979. 600 Vols. Cat ann
Types: O&r, remd, op
*Subj:*Californiana, Western Amer, J C
Fremont
S/S: Maps, print

Farmersville—5544

PACIFIC BOOK SUPPLY CO
1238 N Rose Ave (Mail add: PO Box
337, 93223). Tel 209-594-4155
SAN 160-533X
Owner, Anna S Tornow
Estab 1952. 65,000 Vols. 1500 sq ft.
Cat 6x ann
Types: Hb, new & used, op, remd
Subj: Bus & mgt, econ, educ, hist, polit
sci, psychol, sci-tech, sociol
S/S: Search serv, univ-col libr placement

Ferndale—1367

FERNDALE BOOKS
405 Main St, PO Box 1034, 95536.
Tel 707-786-9135
SAN 129-6639
Owners, Carlos E Benemann & Marilyn
F Benemann
Estab 1980. 45,000 Vols. 4600 sq ft.
Cat 4x ann
Types: 1st ed, o&r, op, used, imp Latin
Am
S/S: Appr libr collec, maps, mss, prints,
search serv

Fremont—131,945

ROBERT MITCHELL—BOOKS
PO Box 3121, 94539
SAN 157-5589
Owner, Robert J Mitchell
Estab 1979. 2000 Vols. 400 sq ft. Cat
Types: Hb, op, used
Subj: Californiana, Western Amer
S/S: Appr libr collec, search serv

Fresno—218,202

AMERICAN BOOKSTORE
608 E Olive, 93728. Tel 209-264-2648
SAN 143-7631
Owner, Marilyn Affeldt
Estab 1972. 25,000 Vols. 1600 sq ft
Types: Rare
Subj: Amer, fiction, nonfiction, rel
S/S: Search serv, flags

MONROE BOOKS
809 E Olive, 93728. Tel 209-441-1282
SAN 122-2023

Owner, John M Perz Jr; Mgr, Jack M Perz
Present Owner 1979. 50,000 Vols. Cat ann
Types: Fac ed, 1st ed, hb, juv, new & used, op, remd
Subj: Adv, archaeol, art, mystery & detective, fiction, metaphys & occult, sci fiction & fantasy, travel, Western Amer
S/S: Appr libr collec, autg, deal libr only, search serv

Fullerton—102,034

ALADDIN BOOKS & MEMORA-BILIA
122 W Commonwealth Ave, PO Box 152, 92632. Tel 714-738-6115
SAN 159-3811
Owner, John T Cannon
Estab 1982. 8000 Vols. 1300 sq ft
Types: 1st ed, hb, juv, new, op, papbk, used
Subj: Magic & conjuring, art, cinema & tv
S/S: Posters, search serv

THE BOOK CELLAR†
124 Orangefair Mall, 92632. Tel 714-879-9420
SAN 160-5534
Owner, David Cormany; Mgr, Ron Smith
Estab 1975. 28,000 Vols. 2500 sq ft. Cat 2x ann
Types: Bibles, fac ed, fine bnd, 1st ed, hb, illus bk, ltd ed, o&r, op, used
Subj: Ancient hist & lit, archaeol, architect, art, biog, bks on bks, diaries, Egyptology, folklore, literary criticism, mythology, philos, scholarly works, women, cookery & wine, erotica, collected letters & journals, Mormonism, voyages & exploration
S/S: Appr libr collec, search serv

THE BOOK HARBOR
201 N Harbor Blvd, 92632. Tel 714-738-1941
SAN 160-5542
Owners, Al Ralston & Jerome Joseph
Estab 1978. 65,000 Vols. 3000 sq ft
Types: Fac ed, fine bnd, 1st ed, hb, illus

bk, imp, juv, ltd ed, new & used, o&r, op, papbk, remd
Subj: Art, cooking & nutrit, fiction, metaphys & occult, philos, photog, transp, Eastern philos, military, literature in translation
S/S: Appr libr collec, search serv

ROY V BOSWELL—ANTIQUARIAN BOOKS & MAPS
1840 West Orangethorpe Ave, PO Box 2034, 92633. Tel 714-738-1340
SAN 120-7482
Owner, Roy V Boswell
Estab 1952. Cat ann
Types: Fac ed, 1st ed, hb, imp, incunab, new & used, op, o&r, remd
Subj: Hist of cartography
S/S: Maps

LORSON'S BOOKS & PRINTS
305 N Harbor Blvd, 92632. Tel 714-526-2523
SAN 160-5577
Owner, James Lorson
Present Owner 1977. 7500 Vols. 700 sq ft. Cat 10x ann
Types: 1st ed, fine bnd, hb, illus bk, ltd ed, o&r, miniature bks
Subj: T E Lawrence
S/S: Autg, search serv

RALSTON POPULAR FICTION
PO Box 4174, 92634. Tel 714-990-0432
SAN 160-5585
Owner, Al Ralston
Estab 1976. 5000 Vols
Types: 1st ed, hb, imp, juv, o&r, op, used
Subj: Drama, fiction, mystery & detective, poetry, sci fiction & fantasy, westerns
S/S: Appr libr collec

Garden Grove—123,351

FANTASY ILLUSTRATED
12531 Harbor Blvd, 92640. Tel 714-537-0087
SAN 157-2245
Owner, David W Smith
Estab 1979. 70,000 Vols. 900 sq ft. Cat 2x ann

Types: Hb, illus bk, rare comic bks &
paperback bks
Subj: Sci fiction & fantasy
S/S: Biper, orig art

Georgetown

TALISMAN PRESS, BOOKSELLERS
& PUBLISHERS
Box 455, 95634. Tel 916-333-4486
SAN 160-5658
Owners, Robert Greenwood & Newton
Baird
Estab 1954. 12,000 Vols. Cat 5x ann
Types: 1st ed, hb, new & used, op,
o&r, remd
Subj: Amer, bibliog, reference, photo-
graphica
S/S: Autg, deal libr only, maps, mss,
prints, search serv

Glendale — 139,060

ARTHUR H CLARK CO
1264 S Central Ave (Mail add: PO Box
230, 91209). Tel 213-245-9119
SAN 160-5712
Owners, Arthur H Clark & Paul W
Galleher; Mgr & Buyer, Robert A
Clark
Estab 1902. 50,000 Vols. 7300 sq ft.
Cat 9x ann
Types: 1st ed, hb, new & used, op,
o&r, fine print
Subj: Amer, Western Amer
S/S: Appr libr collec, mss, search serv,
wholesale

XANADU GALLERIES CO
212 N Orange, 91203.
Tel 213-244-0828, 243-0068
SAN 160-5763
Owner, Eric Schneirsohn
Estab 1950. 250,000 Vols. Cat
Types: 1st ed, hb, imp, new & used, op,
o&r, remd
Subj: Civil War, drama, hist, natural
hist, Western Amer, 19th & 20th
Century Am art
S/S: Autg, biper, mss, prints, sh mus,
appr antq, art, bks & mss

Glendora — 38,654

WAYNE G KOSTMAN BOOKS
Box 393, 91740. Tel 213-963-1755
SAN 157-2253
Owner & Mgr, Wayne G Kostman
Estab 1975. 5000 Vols. 1000 sq ft. Cat
1x ann
Types: Hb, o&r, op
Subj: Travel, ref & facsimiles on mss
illumination, A C Black travel guides
& color imprints, Murray & Baede-
ker guides
S/S: Maps, prints, search serv

Glen Ellen

JACK LONDON BOOKSTORE
14300 Arnold Dr (Mail add: PO Box
337, 95442). Tel 707-996-2888
SAN 160-5674
Owner, Winifred Kingman; Assoc, Russ
Kingman
Estab 1971. 12,000 Vols. 4000 sq ft
Types: Fine bnd, 1st ed, hb, illus bk,
juv, ltd ed, new, o&r, op, remd, used
Subj: Alaskana, Californiana, Hawaii-
ana, Western Amer, Jack London
S/S: Appr libr collec, autg, biper, prints

Goleta — 14,029

AMERICAN FRAGMENTS
7127 Hollister (Mail add: 93117).
Tel 805-964-8196
SAN 157-227X
Owner, Jim Lance
Estab 1976. 3000 Vols. 600 sq ft. Cat
2x ann
Types: Fine bnd, 1st ed, hb, illus bk,
imp, juv, ltd ed, new & used, o&r,
op
S/S: Appr libr collec, biper, maps,
prints

Hayward — 94,167

BRYAN BARRETT BOOKS
27946 Pueblo Calle, PO Box 6202,
94540-6202. Tel 415-657-1919
SAN 130-5328
Owner, Bryan Barrett
Estab 1981. 6000 Vols. 350 sq ft. Cat
4x ann

Types: 1st ed, hb, illus bk, ltd ed, new, imp, op, papbk, remd, used
Subj: Sci fiction & fantasy, mystery & detective, illus
S/S: Search serv

MOUNT EDEN BOOKS & BINDERY
2315 Bermuda Lane (Mail add: PO Box 421, Mount Eden, 94557). Tel 415-782-7723
SAN 156-9562
Owner, Jerome Pressler
Estab 1980. 2500 Vols. Cat 3x ann
Types: O&r, op, used
Subj: Anthrop, geol, geography
S/S: Maps, search serv, book restoration

Hermosa Beach— 18,070

THE SILVER DOOR
901 Hermosa Ave (Mail add: PO Box 3208, Redondo Beach, 90277). Tel 213-379-6005
SAN 158-6076
Owner, Karen La Porte
Estab 1980. Present Owner 1977. 9000 Vols. 100 sq ft. Cat 2x ann
Types: 1st ed, hb, illus bk, imp, o&r, op, papbk, used
Subj: Suspense & thrillers
S/S: Appr libr collec, search serv

Hollywood

LOUIS EPSTEIN
7140 Senalda Rd, 90068. Tel 213-851-2329
SAN 125-3786
Owner, Louis Epstein

Huntington Park — 46,223

JAX USED BOOKSTORE
2670 E Florence Ave, 90255. Tel 213-589-4500
SAN 121-7585
Types: Imp, new & used, op, papbk, remd
S/S: Biper, maps

Isla Vista— 13,441

MERLIN'S BOOKSHOP
6543 Pardall Rd, 93117. Tel 805-968-7946

SAN 160-578X
Owners, Merlin Schwegman & Flora Schwegman
Estab 1975. 25,000 Vols. 800 sq ft. Cat 2x ann
Types: 1st ed, hb, juv, ltd ed, o&r, op, used
Subj: Am Indian studies, art, biog, comedy, cooking & nutrit, engineering, films & filmmaking, hist, math, philos, psychol, sci fiction & fantasy, autobiog, sci
S/S: Biper, seach serv, sh mu, book bnd repair, gold stamping

Kensington— 4823

WILLIAM RILEY— BOOKS
86 Arlington, 94707. Tel 415-526-2300
SAN 157-8316
Owner, William Riley
Estab 1972. 5500 Vols. Cat 4x ann
Types: 1st ed, ltd ed, op
Subj: Fiction, poetry, 20th century lit

La Canada— 20,153

CELESTIAL BOOKS
Box 1066, 91011. Tel 213-790-4984
SAN 157-230X
Owner, Donald K Yeomans
Present Owner 1975. Cat 2x ann
Types: O&r
Subj: Astron, physics, optics
S/S: Appr libr collec, search serv

Laguna Beach— 17,860

ALTA CALIFORNIA BOOKSTORE†
428 Glnneyre, PO Box 296, 92652. Tel 714-494-5252 (by appt)
SAN 160-6212
Owners, John Swingle & Mary Bell Swingle
Estab 1959. 100,000 Vols. Cat
Types: O&r
S/S: Ephemera

La Jolla

LAURENCE McGILVERY†
PO Box 852, 92038. Tel 619-454-4443
SAN 160-6131
Owners, Laurence McGilvery &

Geraldine McGilvery
Estab 1960. 50,000 Vols. Cat 2x ann
Types: O&r, op
Subj: Art
S/S: Appr libr collec, biper

La Mesa— 50,342

LA MESA BOOKSTORE
8209 Broadway, 92041.
   Tel 619-464-3802
SAN 157-2318
Owner, Alverda Williams
Estab 1976. 20,000 Vols. 1000 sq ft
Types: Fine bnd, 1st ed, hb, illus bk,
   juv, ltd ed, o&r, op, papbk, used
S/S: Appr libr collec, autg

Long Beach— 361,334

SYMPOSIUM BOOKSELLER
4458 Myrtle Ave, 90807. Tel 213-424-
   9607
SAN 158-524X
Owner & Mgr, Jerry Vanley
Estab 1977. 1500 Vols. 300 sq ft. Cat
   ann
Types: Illus bk, op
Subj: Travel
S/S: Orig art, prints

Los Altos— 25,769

THE BOOK NEST
366 Second St, 94022.
   Tel 415-948-4724
SAN 160-6581
Owner, Edwin F Schmitz
Estab 1978. 10,000 Vols. 1200 sq ft
Types: Fine bnd, 1st ed, hb, juv, ltd ed,
   o&r, op, used
Subj: John Steinbeck
S/S: Appr libr collec, search serv

Los Angeles— 2,966,763

ABBEY BOOKSHOP
Box 64384, 90064. Tel 213-470-2296
SAN 157-2342
Owner, Gideon Berman
Estab 1937. Present Owner 1952.
   10,000 Vols. Cat 6x ann
Types: Hb, o&r, op, remd, used
Subj: Hist, polit sci, econ, bus & mgt,

Amer, Mex, Latin Am, travel, Asian
   studies, Africa
S/S: Search serv

BENNETT & MARSHALL†
8205 Melrose Ave, 90046. Tel 213-653-
   7040
SAN 160-6727
Owners, George Allen, et al
Estab 1941. Present Owner 1973.
   20,000 Vols. 1250 sq ft. Cat 3x ann
Types: 1st ed, incunab, imp, o&r, pvt
   presses
Subj: Amer, med, Orientalia, sci-tech,
   travel, econ
S/S: Appr libr collec, autg, maps, mss,
   orig art, prints

CALIFORNIA BOOK AUCTION
   GALLERIES†
1749 N LaBrea Ave, 90046.
   Tel 213-850-0424
SAN 160-6859
Owners, Maurice F Powers & David E
   Belch
Estab 1979. 2000 sq ft. Cat 6-8x ann
Branch. Buys indep & through hq
Types: 1st ed, fine bnd, hb, incunab,
   illus bk, juv, o&r
Subj: Art, bks on bks, Californiana,
   cooking & nutrit, graphic arts, hist,
   photog, wines, Western Amer
S/S: Appr libr collec, autg, mss, orig art
Hq: San Francisco

CANTERBURY BOOKSHOP
8344 Melrose Ave, 90069.
   Tel 213-653-9467
SAN 160-6867
Owner, Charles A Salzman
Estab 1949. 8000 Vols. Cat
Types: 1st ed, hb, op
Subj: Anthrop, archaeol, Eur studies,
   evolution, philos
S/S: Appr libr collec

CARAVAN BOOKSTORE†
550 S Grand Ave, 90071.
   Tel 213-626-9944
SAN 160-6875
Owner, Lillian Bernstein; Mgr, Leonard
   Bernstein
Estab 1954. 45,000 Vols. 1700 sq ft
Types: 1st ed, hb, imp, incunab, new &
   used, o&r, op
Subj: Art, discovery & explor, nautical,

railroadiana, Western Amer, cooking
S/S: Appr libr collec, autg, maps, prints, search serv, sh mus

CHAPMAN & BERRYMAN BOOKSELLERS
2377 Teviot St, 90039.
  Tel 213-667-2430
SAN 157-2350
Owners, David Chapman & David Berryman
Estab 1977. 3000 Vols. Cat 6x ann
Types: Hb, o&r, op, used
Subj: Hawaiiana, South Pacific islands
S/S: Maps, prints, photographs, ephemera

CHEROKEE BOOKSHOP INC†
6607 Hollywood Blvd (Mail add: PO Box 3427, 90028).
  Tel 213-463-6090, 463-5848
SAN 160-6883
Cat 6x ann
Types: Illus bk, fine bnd, op, o&r, used, color plated
Subj: Amer, art, hist, metaphys & occult, military
S/S: Biper

PEGGY CHRISTIAN BOOKSELLER
110 S La Brea Ave, 90036.
  Tel 213-939-5636
SAN 160-6921
Owner, Peggy Christian
Estab 1948. Cat
Types: Op

WILLIAM & VICTORIA DAILEY†
8216 Melrose Ave (Mail add: PO Box 69812, 90069). Tel 213-658-8515
SAN 160-6980
Estab 1974. Present Owner 1976. 5000 Vols. 1250 sq ft. Cat 6x ann
Types: Illus bk, incunab, ltd ed, o&r
Subj: Sci-tech, art ref
S/S: Appr libr collec, orig art, prints

DAVIS & SCHORR ART BOOKS†
1547 Westwood Blvd, 90024.
  Tel 213-477-6636
SAN 123-7195
Owners, L Clarice Davis & Elissa Schorr
Estab 1971. Present Owner 1979. 7000 Vols. 800 sq ft. Cat 3x ann
Types: Fac ed, hb, illus bk, imp, ltd ed,

new, o&r, op, papbk, remd, used
Subj: Archit, art, photog
S/S: Appr libr collec, orig art, prints, search serv

DAWSON'S BOOKSHOP†
535 N Larchmont Blvd, 90004.
  Tel 213-469-2186
SAN 121-1560
Owners, Glen Dawson & Muir Dawson
Estab 1905. Present Owner 1941.
  25,000 Vols. 3233 sq ft. Cat 6x ann
Types: 1st ed, new, o&r, op, ltd ed, miniature
Subj: Hist, Western Amer, hist of bks & printing, mountaineering, Oriental art
S/S: Appr libr collec

J S EDGREN
8214 Melrose Ave, 90046.
  Tel 213-653-2665
SAN 170-3536
Owner, Soren Edgren; Mgr, A von Harringa
See Also: Carmel

THE GLOBE BOOKSTORE†
2509 Thames St, 90046.
  Tel 213-654-8615
SAN 124-0501
Owner, Michael R Goth
Estab 1971. 3000 Vols. Cat ann
Types: O&r
Subj: Military

HERITAGE BOOKSHOP INC†
847 N La Cienega Blvd, 90069.
  Tel 213-659-3674
SAN 160-7170
Owners, Benjamin Weinstein & Louis Weinstein
Estab 1963. 5000 Vols. 1600 sq ft. Cat 4-5x ann
Types: 1st ed, fac ed, fine bnd, illus bk, incunab, o&r
Subj: Californiana, travel
S/S: Appr libr collec, autg, mss, orig art, press bks

HOLLYWOOD BOOK CITY
6625-31 Hollywood Blvd, Hollywood, 90028. Tel 213-466-2525, 466-1049
SAN 157-7166
Owners, Alan & Frances Siegel

Present Owner 1974. 250,000 Vols. 10,000 sq ft

Types: Fac ed, fine bnd, 1st ed, hb, imp, illus bk, juv, ltd ed, mm papbk, o&r, op, used

Subj: Art, aviation, biog, films & film-making, metaphys & occult, photog, World Wars I & II

S/S: Appr libr collec, autg, maps, mss, prints, search serv

See Also: Book City of Burbank, Burbank

HOLLYWOOD BOOK SERVICE
1654 Cherokee Ave, 90028. Tel 213-464-4164
SAN 160-7200
Owner, Helen Hall
Estab 1965. 40,000 Vols
Types: 1st ed, hb, op, used
Subj: Biog, polit sci, reference, scholarly lit, stage & screen
S/S: Search serv, sh mus, portraits & stills of film stars

HOLLYWOOD BOOKSHOP†
6613 Hollywood Blvd, 90028. Tel 213-469-7409
SAN 160-7219
Owner, Jack Garvin
Estab 1966. 15,000 Vols. 1000 sq ft
Types: Fac ed, fine bnd, 1st ed, hb, illus bk, o&r, op, used
Subj: Amer, gemology, geol, mineralogy, paleontology
S/S: Biper

GEORGE HOULE — RARE BOOKS & AUTOGRAPHS†
2277 Westwood Blvd, 90064.
Tel 213-474-1539, 474-1530
SAN 126-0146
Owner, George Houle
Estab 1976. 7000 Vols. Cat 8x ann
Types: 1st ed, fac ed, fine bnd, hb, illus bk, imp, ltd ed, o&r, op, remd, used
Subj: Antq, art
S/S: Autg, mss, orig art, prints, antq

PAUL HUNT
PO Box 2713, 90051.
Tel 213-845-1563
SAN 157-2377
Owner, Paul Hunt
Estab 1979. 10,000 Vols. Cat 2x ann

Types: Hb, illus bk, new & used, o&r, op, papbk, remd
Subj: Military, cinema & movie stars
S/S: Appr libr collec, autg, biper, posters, search serv, sh mus

HYMAN & SONS RARE BOOKS
2341 Westwood Blvd, Suite #3, 90064.
Tel 213-474-8023
SAN 160-7235
Dirs, Paul S Hyman & V Lee Blackburn
Estab 1978. 6000 Vols. 1500 sq ft. Cat
Types: Fac ed, fine bnd, 1st ed, for lang, hb, incunab, illus bk, imp, o&r, op
Subj: Egyptology, Middle East, archaeol, for lang
S/S: Maps, search serv

KENNETH KARMIOLE, BOOK-SELLER INC†
2255 Westwood Blvd, 90064.
Tel 213-474-7305
SAN 160-7308
Owner, Kenneth Karmiole; Mgr, Andrea Braver
Estab 1976. 15,000 Vols. 1000 sq ft. Cat 15x ann
Types: 1st ed, incunab, illus bk, ltd ed, o&r, op
Subj: Art, bks on bks, history of printing
S/S: Appr libr collec, autg, mss, orig art, prints, search serv

SAMUEL W KATZ†
10845 Lindbrook Dr, 6, 90024.
Tel 213-474-6910 (by appt only)
SAN 160-7324
Owner, Samuel W Katz
Estab 1976. Cat
Types: Incunab, illus bk, o&r
Subj: Calligraphy, for lang, Latin Am, med, Mex, sci-tech, women's studies
S/S: Appr libr collec, mss, prints

JAY KIEFFER BOOKS
430 S Burnside, 90036.
Tel 213-938-4627
SAN 158-5258
Owner & Mgr, Jay Kieffer
Estab 1940. 10,000 Vols
Types: Hb, op, o&r
S/S: Search serv

ALFRED KRONFELD BOOKSELLER
1621 Golden Gate Ave, 90026.
Tel 213-661-3658

SAN 130-5581
Owner, Alfred Kronfeld
Estab 1980
Types: 1st ed, hb, juv, ltd ed, o&r, op
Subj: Soc sci, Amer, Western Amer,
Californiana
S/S: Search serv

KROWN & SPELLMAN, BOOK-
SELLERS
2283 (Rear) Westwood Blvd, 90064.
Tel 213-474-1745
SAN 160-7367
Owners, Franklin V Spellman & Eliza-
beth Krown Spellman
Estab 1977. 10,000 Vols. Cat 3x ann
Types: Fac ed, 1st ed, hb, imp, incunab,
op, o&r, remd
Subj: Ancient hist & lit, Egyptology,
medieval studies, Renaissance hist &
lit, theol, class lang
S/S: Appr libr collec, autg, biper, maps,
mss

BARRY R LEVIN SCIENCE FICTION
& FANTASY LITERATURE†
2253 Westwood Blvd, 90064.
Tel 213-474-5611
SAN 125-0019
Owner, Barry R Levin
Estab 1973. 20,000 Vols. 800 sq ft.
Cat 2x ann
Types: Fine bnd, 1st ed, hb, imp, ltd ed,
new & used, o&r, op, pvt presses
Subj: Sci fiction & fantasy 17th-20th
centuries, imaginary voyages, future
war, horror, utopias
S/S: Appr libr collec, autg, biper, mss,
search serv, consultants, science
fiction film consultants

NEEDHAM BOOK FINDERS†
12021 Wilshire Blvd, #13, 90025.
Tel 213-475-9553
SAN 122-2910
Pres, Stanley Kurman
Estab 1954. 5000 Vols
Types: Op, used
S/S: Search serv

JOHN B NOMLAND BOOKSELLERS
404 S Benton Way, 90057.
Tel 213-389-9745
SAN 160-757X
Owner, John B Nomland

Estab 1963. 15,000 Vols. 3000 sq ft.
Cat ann
Types: 1st ed, hb, op, o&r
Subj: Mex & Spanish poetry

JAMES NORMILE—BOOKS
6888 Alta Loma Terrace, 90068.
Tel 213-874-8434
SAN 160-7588
Owner, James Normile
Estab 1970. 5000 Vols. Cat
Types: 1st ed, o&r, op
Subj: Ethnography, oriental arts, primi-
tive arts
S/S: Search serv

PETTLER & LIEBERMAN, BOOK-
SELLERS
7970 Melrose Ave, 90046.
Tel 213-651-1568
SAN 160-7669
Owners, Robert J Pettler & Victor S
Lieberman
Estab 1978. 8000 Vols. 800 sq ft. Cat
Types: 1st ed, hb, imp, ltd ed, o&r, op,
papbk, used
Subj: Biog, drama, fiction, films &
filmmaking, humor, mystery &
detective, nonfiction, poetry
S/S: Appr libr collec, mss, search serv,
sh mus, screenplays

O P REED JR
521 N La Clenega (Mail add: 21536
Rambla Vista, Malibu, 90265).
Tel 213-456-6160, 652-5500
SAN 158-1589
Owner, Orrel P Reed Jr
Estab 1959
Types: 1st ed, incunab, illus bk, imp
Ger, o&r
Subj: Art, mod lit, Ger expressionism
S/S: Appr libr collec, orig art, prints

THE SCHOLARLY BOOKFINDERS
415 W Ave 42, 90065.
Tel 213-223-8257
SAN 170-5326
Owner, Norma Almquist
Estab 1981. Cat 2x ann
Types: Hb, o&r, op, used
Subj: World Wars I & II, travel, mod
foreign fict

KURT L SCHWARZ†
738 S Bristol Ave, 90049.

Tel 213-828-7927
SAN 122-803X
Owners, Kurt L Schwarz & Martha M
Schwarz
Estab 1947. Cat 6x ann
Types: Incunab, op, o&r, imp Fr, Ger,
Ital & Sp
Subj: Fine arts, Ger hist & lit, Orientalia, sociol

SUN DANCE BOOKS†
1520 N Crescent Heights, Hollywood,
90046. Tel 213-654-2383
SAN 160-7820
Owner, Allan Adrian
Estab 1967. 6000 Vols. Cat 3x ann
Types: Hb, op, o&r, used
Subj: Am Indian studies, anthrop, Californiana, ethnic studies, Latin Am,
Mex, Southwestern Amer, Pacific
Ocean voyages, western art
S/S: Appr libr collec, maps, mss, orig
art, prints

SYLVESTER & ORPHANOS
2484 Cheremoya Ave (Mail add: Box
2567, 90028). Tel 213-461-1194
SAN 157-2393
Owners, Ralph Sylvester & Stathis
Orphanos
Estab 1973. 20,000 Vols. 770 ft. Cat
4x ann
Types: Hb, 1st ed, ltd ed, o&r, op, ltd-
signed publications
Subj: Contemporary literature

THIRD WORLD ETHNIC BOOKS
3617 Montclair St (Mail add: PO Box
38237, 90038). Tel 213-737-3292
SAN 160-7871
Owners, Mayme A Clayton & Avery
Clayton
Estab 1972. 8000 Vols
Types: New & used, op, o&r
Subj: Black studies, Mex, Asian Am,
Black cinema
S/S: Biper, sh mus, search serv, W
States Black Research Ctr

TOLLIVER'S BOOKS
1634 Stearns Dr, 90035.
Tel 213-939-6054
SAN 123-0557
Owner, James D Tolliver Jr; Buyer,
Evelyn Tolliver

Estab 1969. 12,000 Vols. 5000 sq ft.
Cat 6x ann
Types: 1st ed, hb, new & used, op,
papbk, o&r, remd, for lang
Subj: Anthrop, archaeol, biol, geol,
ichthyol, math, natural hist, oceanog,
ornith, physics, elec engineering,
Mesoamer, Mexico, Baja Calif
S/S: Appr libr collec, biper, mss, orig
art, search serv, bnd

MANUEL URRIZOLA OLD & RARE
MAPS & ATLASES
136 S Virgil Ave, Suite 139, 90004.
Tel 213-487-3238
SAN 158-1562
Owner & Buyer, Manuel Urrizola;
Mgr, Ernest Howard; Merch Mgr,
Charles J Smith
Present Owner 1981. Cat 3x ann
Types: O&r
Subj: Cartography, geosci, travel

VAGABOND BOOKS
2076 Westwood Blvd, 90025.
Tel 213-475-2700
SAN 157-2407
Owners, Patricia Graham & Craig
Graham
Estab 1978. 30,000 Vols. 1000 sq ft.
Cat
Types: 1st ed, fac ed, fine bnd, hb, illus
bk, juv, ltd ed, o&r, op, used
Subj: Art, mystery & detective, cinema,
theater
S/S: Appr libr collec, mss, prints, search
serv, sh mus

WEST LOS ANGELES BOOK
CENTER
1650 Sawtelle Blvd, 90025.
Tel 213-473-4442
SAN 160-7995
Onwer, K M Hyre
Estab 1959. 50,000 Vols. 1000 sq ft.
Cat 2x ann
Types: Fac ed, fine bnd, 1st ed, hb, illus
bk, juv, ltd ed, o&r, op, papbk,
remd, used
Subj: Art, drama, Eng hist & lit, Eur
studies, films & filmmaking, humor,
military, mystery & detective, poetry,
sci fiction & fantasy

STEPHEN WHITE'S GALLERY OF
  PHOTOGRAPHY
752 N La Cienega Blvd, 90069.
  Tel 213-657-6995
SAN 160-8010
Owner, Stephen L White; Asst Dir,
  Theresa Chavez
Estab 1975. 1000 Vols. 2000 sq ft. Cat
  ann
Types: Illus bk, op, o&r
Subj: Photog
S/S: Appr libr collec, search serv, origi-
  nal vintage photog

ZEITLIN & VER BRUGGE BOOK-
  SELLERS†
815 N La Cienega Blvd, 90069.
  Tel 213-652-0784
SAN 160-807X
Owners, Jacob Zeitlin & Josephine
  Ver Brugge Zeitlin
Estab 1927. 15,000 Vols. Cat 4x ann
Types: Fine bnd, 1st ed, new & used
Subj: Amer, art, Californiana, bks on
  bks, photog, hist of sci & med
S/S: Appr libr collec, autg, mss, orig
  art, per, prints

Los Gatos—26,593

CURIOUS BOOK SHOPPE
198 W Main St, 95030.
  Tel 408-354-5560
SAN 160-810X
Owner, Richard Price Balch
Estab 1973. 70,000 Vols
Types: Fine bnd, 1st ed, hb, illus bk,
  juv, ltd ed, op, remd, used
S/S: Spec order

Los Osos

DONALD LA CHANCE†
1032 Bay Oaks Dr, 93402.
  Tel 805-528-7363
By appt only
S/S: Search serv

Manhattan Beach—31,542

G F HOLLLINGSWORTH BOOKS
PO Box 3725, 90266.
  Tel 213-374-1641
SAN 160-8150

Owner, G F Hollingsworth
Estab 1953. 30,000 vols. Cat 8x ann
Types: 1st ed, fac ed, op, o&r, remd,
  used
Subj: Western Amer

Martinez—22,582

JOYCE BOOK SHOPS OFFICES†
Box 310, 94553. Tel 415-228-4462
SAN 144-9959
Owner, Everett V Cunningham
Estab 1935. 600,000 Vols. Cat
Types: 1st ed, hb, illus bk, juv, ltd ed,
  o&r, op, papbk, used, for lang
S/S: Appr libr collec
See Also: Gull Book Shop, Oakland

Menlo Park—25,673

JAMES G LEISHMAN—BOOK-
  SELLER
PO Box A, 94025. Tel 415-322-7034
SAN 124-2563
Owner, James G Leishman; Mgr, Mary
  W Becker
Estab 1972. 10,000 Vols. 500 sq ft. Cat
  12x ann
Types: Fine bnd, 1st ed, hb, incunab,
  illus bk, juv, ltd ed, o&r, op, pvt
  presses
Subj: Californiana, geol, paleontology
S/S: Appr libr collec, maps, mss, prints,
  search serv

Mill Valley—12,967

DIANCO INTERNATIONAL
390 Tennessee Ave, 94941.
  Tel 415-383-4071
SAN 160-8290
Owner & Buyer, Donald C Shearer II
Estab 1962. 50,000 Vols. 950 sq ft. Cat
  5x ann
Types: Imp, o&r, op
Subj: Med, sci-tech, humanities, mili-
  tary
S/S: Appr libr collec, biper, maps, per

THE ECLECTIC GALLERY
1031 Trillium (Mail add: PO Box 1581,
  Sausalito, 94965). Tel 415-383-1125
SAN 161-2727
Owners, Dick Rykken & Robert Scull

Estab 1974. 900 Vols
Types: Illus bk, ltd ed, fine press
Subj: Art

Milpitas — 37,820

RIK THOMPSON — BOOKS
PO Box 69, 95035. Tel 408-946-0698
SAN 160-8320
Owner, Rik Thompson
Estab 1972. 3500 Vols. Cat 1-4x ann
Types: 1st ed, hb, juv, ltd ed, new, o&r,
op, papbk, remd, used
Subj: Mystery & detective, nonfiction,
sci fiction & fantasy
S/S: Mss, orig art, per, ephemera

Mission Viejo — 48,384

GEORGE FREDERICK KOLBE FINE
NUMISMATIC BOOKS†
23881 Via Fabricante #511, 92691.
Tel 714-768-6854
Subj: Numismatics, books, sale catalogues, scholarly periodicals (all
languages & periods)

Monterey — 27,558

THE BOOK END
245 Pearl St, 93940. Tel 408-373-4046
SAN 160-8452
Owner, Sylvia Anderson
Estab 1976. 15,000 Vols
Types: Hb, papbk, used, 1st ed, op
S/S: Search serv

North Hollywood

SHARP'S BOOKSTORE
5041 Lankershim Blvd, 91601.
Tel 213-980-6980, 762-7595
SAN 124-7905
Owner, Elisabeth Sharp
Estab 1973. 16,000 Vols
Types: Hb, papbk, o&r, op, used
Subj: Genealogy, metaphys & occult,
rel studies
S/S: Bnd, gold stamping, laminating

VALLEY BOOK CITY
5249 Lankershim Blvd, 91601.
Tel 213-985-6911
SAN 160-8754

Owner & Mgr, Mark Marlow
Estab 1975. Present Owner 1979.
100,000 Vols. 4500 sq ft. Cat 4x ann
Types: Fine bnd, 1st ed, hb, illus bk,
juv, ltd ed, new & used, o&r, op
Subj: Art, circus, drama, hunting &
fishing, magic & conjuring, photog,
sci fiction & fantasy, Western Amer,
guns
S/S: Appr libr collec, search serv

Norwalk — 85,232

AVIATION BOOKMOBILE — MIL-
AIR PHOTOS & BOOKS
11809 S Alburtis Ave (Mail add: PO
Box U, 90650). Tel 213-863-5028
SAN 160-8851
Owner, Harold N Miller
Estab 1960. 18,000 Vols. Cat
Types: 1st ed, hb, imp, new & used,
o&r, op, papbk, remd
Subj: Aviation, military, photog, radio,
sci-tech, tv, Naval, Marine Corps,
Guns
S/S: Appr libr collec, biper, maps, mss,
orig art, wholesale
See Also: Compton

Oakland — 339,288

J & J BERGER BOOKSELLERS
3905 MacArthur Blvd, 94619.
Tel 415-530-8252
SAN 128-9012
Owners, John Berger & Jocelyn Berger
Estab 1980. 5000 Vols. 500 sq ft
Types: 1st ed, hb, illus bk, juv, new &
used, op, papbk
Subj: Mystery & detective
S/S: Search serv

GULL BOOK SHOP†
1547 San Pablo Ave, 94612.
Tel 415-834-8108
SAN 144-9966
Owner, Everett V Cunningham
Estab 1962. 30,000 Vols. Cat
Branch. Buys indep & through hq
Types: 1st ed, hb, illus bk, juv, ltd ed,
o&r, op, papbk, used, for lang
Subj: Appr libr collec, biper, maps, orig
art, prints
Hq: Joyce Book Shops Offices, Martinez

EDWARD M HERNY BOOKSELLER
1409 Fifth St, 94607. Tel 415-547-0469
SAN 160-3930
Owner, Edward M Herny
Estab 1974
Types: 1st ed, hb, illus bk, juv, ltd ed,
o&r
Subj: Californiana, 19th century west-
ern photogs, 19th century travel &
exploration, pre-1920 postcards
S/S: Maps, mss, orig art, prints, sh mus

NORTHWEST BOOKS†
3814 Lyon Ave, 94601.
Tel 415-532-5227
Owner, Donald McKinney
Subj: Western Americana, fine arts

ROBERT PERATA BOOKS†
3170 Robinson Dr, 94602.
Tel 415-482-0101
SAN 156-9899
Estab 1969. 700 Vols. Cat 4x ann
Types: Fine bnd, 1st ed, illus bk, ltd ed
Subj: Bks on bks, Western Amer
S/S: Appr libr collec, search serv

MARVIN STANLEY BOOKSELLERS
3007 E 12th St, 94601.
Tel 415-533-8800
SAN 159-012X
Estab 1975. 15,000 Vols. 650 sq ft
Types: Fine bnd, 1st ed, hb, illus bk,
juv, o&r, op, used
Subj: Rel studies, theol

Orange—91,788

BOOK CARNIVAL
840 N Tustin, 92667. Tel 714-538-
3210
SAN 156-9651
Owner, What Books Inc; Mgr, Ed
Thomas; Papbk Buyer & Juv Buyer,
Pat Thomas
Estab 1981. 20,000 Vols. 2500 sq ft
Types: Fine bnd, 1st ed, hb, illus bk,
imp, juv, ltd ed, new & used, op,
papbk, remd
Subj: Mod lit, mystery & detective, sci
fiction & fantasy
S/S: Orig art

BOOK SAIL†
1186 N Tustin, 92667.
Tel 714-997-9511
SAN 160-9149
Owner, John K McLaughlin
Estab 1966. 40,000 Vols. 1705 sq ft.
Cat ann
Types: Hb, op, fine bnd, illus bk, 1st ed,
ltd ed, o&r, comics, early printed bks
& mss, pulps
Subj: Art, sci fiction & fantasy, transp,
Western Amer, mystery & detective
S/S: Per, search serv

Pacific Palisades

FAIN'S FIRST EDITIONS
693 Amalfi Dr, 90272.
Tel 213-454-2341
SAN 158-6939
Owner, John Fain Lawrence
Estab 1979. 3000 Vols. Cat 4x ann
Types: 1st ed, hb, o&r
Subj: Art, dance, fiction, 20th century
Am & Eng
S/S: Prints

INTERNATIONAL BOOKFINDERS
INC†
PO Box 1, 90272
SAN 160-9254
Pres, Richard Mohr
Estab 1950
Types: 1st ed, ltd ed, op, o&r
S/S: Search serv

Palo Alto—55,255

BUCKABEST BOOKS & BINDERY
247 Fulton St, 94301.
Tel 415-325-2965
SAN 160-8231
Owner, Margaret Simmons
Estab 1973. 2000 Vols. 110 sq ft. Cat
Types: Fine bnd, 1st ed, hb, imp, o&r,
op, used
Subj: Biog, drama, ballet, Wales, uni-
corns
S/S: Bnd, prints, search serv

JOHN SLATTERY BOOKS & PRINTS
352 Stanford Ave, 94306.
Tel 415-323-9775

SAN 157-2431
Owner, John P Slattery
Estab 1970. 5000 Vols. 1200 sq ft. Cat
4x ann
Types: Illus bk, o&r, op
Subj: Printing, early Russia, Baedeker
travel guides
S/S: Autg, biper, maps, prints

WILLIAM P WREDEN, BOOKS &
MANUSCRIPTS†
200 Hamilton Ave, PO Box 56, 94302.
Tel 415-325-6851
SAN 123-4048
Mgr, William P Wreden Jr
Estab 1937. 15,000 Vols. 4000 sq ft.
Cat ann
Types: 1st ed, hb, incunab, ltd ed, op,
o&r
Subj: Western Amer, Eng & Am lit,
printing
S/S: Appr libr collec, autg, maps,
prints, mss, ephemera

Pasadena—119,374

BOOK CASE BOOKS
461 N Lake Ave, 91101.
Tel 213-793-6527
SAN 158-264X
Owner, Alice S Lee
Estab 1979. 30,000 Vols
Types: Fac ed, fine bnd, 1st ed, hb, juv,
ltd ed, o&r, op, papbk, used, illus bk
Subj: Cooking & nutrit, fiction, mystery
& detective
S/S: Search serv

BOOK COMPANY
1328 N Lake Ave, 91104.
Tel 213-798-4630
SAN 159-575X
Owner, Mark W Sailor
Estab 1983. 6000 Vols. 900 sq ft. Cat
17x ann
Types: Fine bnd, hb, op, papbk, remd,
used, 1st ed, o&r
S/S: Appr libr collec, prints, search serv

DIRK CABLE BOOKSELLER
350 S Lake Ave, 91101.
Tel 213-449-7001
SAN 170-4133

DANIEL H DEUTSCH PHD—BOOKS
141 Kenworthy Dr, 91105.
Tel 213-681-9638
SAN 160-9491
Owner & Mgr, Daniel H Deutsch
Types: Hb, o&r, papbk, used
Subj: Astron, chem, physics, thermo-
dynamics

G F GUSTIN JR BOOKS
56 E Colorado Blvd, 91105.
Tel 213-795-8528
SAN 157-2458
Owner & Mgr, G F Gustin Jr
Estab 1974. 10,000 Vols
Types: Fac ed, fine bnd, 1st ed, hb, juv,
ltd ed, o&r, op, used
Subj: Literary criticism, local hist,
Western Amer
S/S: Search serv, rec

MAXWELL HUNLEY
634 Mission, 91030. Tel 213-799-8195
Types: Am & Eng 1st ed
Subj: Western Americana, early Am
plays & poetry

Pomona—92,742

ROCHELLE R RONKETTY BOOK-
SELLER
PO Box 2776, 91769
SAN 158-2267
5000 Vols. Cat 2x ann
Types: Hb, illus bk, op, papbk, used
Subj: Art, cooking & nutrit, aesthetics
S/S: Search serv

Rancho Cordova—30,451

JOANNA TAYLOR BOOKS
2461 El Pavo Way, 95670
SAN 157-9983
Mgr, Joanna Taylor
Estab 1976. 4600 Vols. Cat 6x ann

Rancho Santa Fe

FIVE QUAIL BOOKS
5491 Calzada del Bosque (Mail add: PO
Box 91, 92067). Tel 619-756-1509
SAN 158-7404
Owner & Mgr, Clement David Hellyer

Estab 1978. 2000 Vols. Cat
Types: 1st ed, fac ed, fine bnd, hb, illus
bk, imp, ltd ed, op, o&r, used
Subj: Californiana, angling, Colorado
River, Grand Canyon, Am deserts,
Baja California, US govt publn pre
1900, San Diego
S/S: Search serv

Redding—41,995

ROBERT LARKIN LINK BOOK-
SELLER
1855 Wisconsin Ave, 96001.
Tel 916-243-2125
SAN 160-8924
Owners, Robert L Link & Charles
Renteria
Estab 1970. 30,000 Vols. Cat 2-3x ann
Types: 1st ed
Subj: Drama, fiction, poetry, Brit & Am
lit, press books

Redlands—43,619

LIBROS LATINOS†
PO Box 1103, 92373.
Tel 714-793-8423
SAN 160-9750
Owner, George Elmendorf
Estab 1974. 60,000 Vols. 6000 sq ft.
Cat 10x ann
Types: Hb, imp, new & used, papbk
Subj: Latin Am, Fr lang, Iberian Penin-
sula
S/S: Search serv

Redondo Beach—57,102

BAILEY SEARCH SERVICE
PO Box 326, 90277
SAN 160-9769
Owner, Bill Bailey
Estab 1959. 5000 Vols
Types: Hb, imp, new & used, op, o&r
Subj: Metaphys & occult, sci fiction &
fantasy, Edgar Rice Burroughs, Aleis-
ter Crowley, pulps of the 1930's &
1940's
S/S: Biper, search serv

THE BEAUTIFUL & THE UNUSUAL
290 N Harbor Dr, Suite 32 (Mail add:

PO Box 15676, Long Beach, 90815).
Tel 213-421-1382
SAN 127-8800
Owners, Stanley Katz & Sylvia Katz
Estab 1977
Types: 1st ed, hb, illus bk, juv, new,
o&r, op, used
Subj: Cooking & nutrit, law, med,
erotica
S/S: Orig art, search serv, sh mus

Redwood City—54,965

GRADY'S BOOKS
142 Rutherford Ave, 94061. Tel 415-
364-9636, 364-9808
SAN 157-7220
Owner, Agnes Grady
Estab 1975. Present Owner 1980. Cat
2x ann
Types: Hb, juv, op, used
Subj: Western Amer, Indians
S/S: Search serv

Reseda

THE BOOKIE JOINT
7246 Reseda, 91335.
Tel 213-343-1055, 345-2083
SAN 160-9858
Owner, Jerry Blaz; Mgr, Shush Blaz
Estab 1975. 75,000 Vols. 2200 sq ft
Types: Fac ed, fine bnd, 1st ed, hb, illus
bk, juv, ltd ed, o&r, op, papbk, used
Subj: Anthrop, archaeol, comedy, cook-
ing & nutrit, Judaica, Middle East,
sci fiction & fantasy, sociol, Bible
Research, Islamic
S/S: Appr libr collec, biper, maps,
search serv, per

LIBRA BOOKS
18563 Sherman Way, 91335.
Tel 213-344-5400
SAN 160-9866
Owner, CLF Inc; Pres, Leon Frumkin;
Mgr & Buyer, Martha Frumkin
Estab 1972. 20,000 Vols. 1200 sq ft
Types: 1st ed, hb, illus bk, juv, o&r,
op, papbk, remd, used
Subj: Class studies, mod lit, performing
arts, sci fiction & fantasy, mystery &
detective
S/S: Search serv

PERSONAL BOOKSHOP
18523 Sherman Way, 91335.
　Tel 213-343-5951
SAN 122-4980
Owner, Blanche Spindel
Estab 1962. 50,000 Vols
Types: 1st ed, hb, op, papbk, o&r, used
S/S: Search serv

Richmond—74,676

THE MERMAID—BOOKS
433 44th St, 94805. Tel 415-232-4447
　(by appt only)
SAN 159-5733
Owner, Martin N Israel
Estab 1980. 1500 Vols. Cat 2x ann
Types: 1st ed, hb, o&r, op, used
Subj: Mystery & detective
S/S: Search serv, rare jazz rec

Sacramento—275,471

ARGUS BOOKS & GRAPHICS†
1714 Capitol Ave, 95814.
　Tel 916-443-2233
SAN 160-9955
Owner, Herb Caplan
Estab 1971. 30,000 Vols. Cat
Types: 1st ed, hb, fac ed, fine bnd, illus
　bk, ltd ed, new & used, op, o&r
Subj: Californiana, popular cultural
　ephemera
S/S: Appr libr collec, mss, prints, search
　serv

BLACK SWAN BOOKS
PO Box 22028, 95822.
　Tel 916-441-2156
SAN 170-3250
Owner, Charles L Vercoutere
Estab 1979. 2500 Vols. Cat 3x ann
Types: O&r, op
Subj: Natural hist, gardening, archit
S/S: Search serv

BARRY CASSIDY RARE BOOKS
2003 T St, 95814. Tel 916-456-6307
SAN 161-0007
Owner, Barry Cassidy
Estab 1975. 4500 Vols. 750 sq ft. Cat
　6x ann
Types: 1st ed, ltd ed, o&r
Subj: Fiction, Western Amer
S/S: Autg

CHLOE'S BOOKSTORE
PO Box 255673, 95865
SAN 161-0015
Owners, P Ciapponi & G Whitney
Estab 1973. Cat 6x ann
Types: 1st ed, ltd ed, op, used
Subj: Mod lit, poetry
S/S: Search serv

GAMMAGE CUP BOOKS
Box 19358, 95819
SAN 157-2512
Estab 1974. Present Owner 1974. 500
　Vols. Cat
Types: Illus bk, juv, op
Subj: Compuer sci, weaving, puppetry

HAMMON'S ARCHIVES & ARTI-
　FACTS
1115 Front St, 95814.
　Tel 916-446-1782
SAN 161-0082
Owner & Mgr, Wendell P Hammon
Estab 1958. 2750 Vols. 542 sq ft. Cat
Types: Hb, papbk, op, o&r, used
Subj: Amer, Californiana, geol, mining.
　Nevadiana, railroadiana, Japan
S/S: Appr libr collec, maps, mss, prints,
　search serv, sh mus

JUST BOOKS AND . . .
3630 La Habra Way, 95825.
　Tel 916-482-7493
SAN 161-0112
Owner & Mgr, Frank Just
Estab 1977. 2500 Vols
Types: Hb, op, o&r, used
Subj: Arts & crafts, aviation, guns,
　hunting & fishing, military, Western
　Amer
S/S: Search serv

RICHARD L PRESS FINE & SCHOL-
　ARLY BOOKS
1228 N St, Suite 2, 95814.
　Tel 916-447-3413
SAN 129-8453
Owner, Richard L Press
Estab 1980. 4500 Vols. 800 sq ft. Cat
　2x ann
Types: Fine bnd, 1st ed, hb, illus bk,
　juv, ltd ed, new, op, o&r, remd
Subj: Archit, art, fine arts, graphic arts,
　Middle East

San Bernardino—118,057

D-J BOOK SEARCH SERVICE
PO Box 3352, 92413
SAN 121-1951
Owners, Dorothy A Bright & John
  Bright; Mgr, John Bright
Estab 1956. 25,000 Vols
Types: Hb, op, used
Subj: Californiana, Western Amer
S/S: Search serv, spec order

HAPPY BOOKER
4645 N Sierra Way, 92407.
  Tel 714-883-6110
SAN 159-0839
Owners, Breck J Petersen & Ruth Peter-
sen
Estab 1973. 40,000 Vols. 2000 sq ft
Types: Fine bnd, 1st ed, hb, juv, new &
  used, o&r, op
S/S: Appr libr collec, search serv

San Carlos—24,710

WILLIAM BLEDSOE, BOOK-
  SELLER†
PO Box 763, 94070. Tel 415-593-6878
SAN 161-0384
Owner, Lela Bledsoe
Cat ann
Types: Op
Subj: Bus & mgt, econ, indust & labor,
  polit sci, govt docs, soc hist & allied
  soc sci
S/S: Exp

CARLOS CANTERBURY BOOK-
  STORE†
1107-1117 San Carlos Ave, 94070.
  Tel 415-593-7466, 593-3392
SAN 120-8578
Owner, Donna Houtchens
Estab 1951. 1000 Vols
Types: Fac ed, fine bnd, 1st ed, hb, illus
  bk, imp, juv, ltd ed, o&r, op, papbk,
  used
Subj: Californiana, Western Amer
S/S: Gifts, search serv

San Clemente—27,325

OUT-OF-STATE BOOK SERVICE
PO Box 3253 D, 92672.
  Tel 714-492-2976

SAN 161-0422
Owner, Ann Spigler
Estab 1958. 5000 Vols
Types: Op
Subj: Aviation, fiction, Hawaiiana,
  horses
S/S: Search serv, spec order

San Diego—875,504

ADAMS AVENUE BOOKSTORE
3502 Adams, 92116. Tel 619-281-3330
SAN 161-0430
Estab 1965. 70,000 Vols
Types: Hb, papbk, op
Subj: Amer, mystery & detective
S/S: Search serv, bk fairs

ATTICUS BOOKS†
PO Box 26668, 92126.
  Tel 619-566-8208
By appointment only
Owner, Deborah Cook
Types: 1st ed
Subj: Beat lit, mod fict, mod poetry

CORN MILL BOOKS
5505 Lindo Paseo, 92115.
  Tel 619-287-0041
SAN 161-0600
Owner, John R Sievers
Estab 1971. 6000 Vols. 1200 sq ft
Types: Used, op, o&r, 1st ed
Subj: Amer, astron
S/S: Search serv

GOLDEN HILL ANTIQUARIAN
  BOOKS & ANTIQUES
2456 Broadway, 92102.
  Tel 619-236-9883
SAN 161-0651
Owners, Robert L Summers & Marga-
  ret Summers
Estab 1977. 15,000 Vols. 1500 sq ft
Types: 1st ed, fine bnd, hb, illus bk, juv,
  o&r, op, juv
Subj: Amer, Californiana
S/S: Appr libr collec, biper, maps,
  prints, search serv

J & J HOUSE BOOKSELLERS
PO Box 20734, 92120.
  Tel 619-265-1113
SAN 161-0694
Owners, J G House & J B House
Estab 1978. 5000 Vols. Cat 12-18x ann

Types: 1st ed, fac ed, fine bnd, illus bk, ltd ed, o&r, op, pvt presses, 17th-19th Century pamphlets
Subj: Am Indian studies, Californiana, discovery & explor, NAmer, Orientalia, philos, natural hist, Western Amer, 17th & 18th Century Drama
S/S: Appr libr collec, maps

ROBERT W MANN RARE BOOKS
743 E St, 92101. Tel 619-233-8568
SAN 158-1279
Owner, Robert W Mann
Estab 1978. 230 Vols. 450 sq ft
Types: O&r
S/S: Appr libr collec, autg, mss, prints

OLINGHOUSE & TYSON BOOK-SELLERS & LA QUERENCIA PRESS
Box 3120, 92103. Tel 619-233-4881
SAN 159-2068
Owner, W B Tyson
Cat
Types: O&r, op, used
Subj: Amer, anthrop, natural hist

"OTENTO" BOOKS†
3817 5th Ave, 92103. Tel 619-296-1424
SAN 161-0791
Owner, Robert J Gelink
Estab 1963. 40,000 Vols. 1500 sq ft
Types: For lang, o&r, op, old leather bnd
Subj: Drama, hist, nautical, sci fiction & fantasy, travel
S/S: Appr libr collec, sh mus

PERI LITHON BOOKS†
PO Box 9996, 92109.
Owner, John Sinkankas
Subj: Geology, mineralogy, paleontology, gemology, jewelry

JOHN ROBY
3703 Nassau Dr, 92115.
Tel 619-583-4264
SAN 161-0864
Owner, Frances B Roby; Mgr, John Roby
Estab 1960. Present Owner 1980. 17,000 Vols. Cat
Types: Fac ed, 1st ed, hb, imp, incunab, new & used, papbk, remd, op

Subj: Aviation, energy, nautical, sci-tech
S/S: Appr libr collec, biper, search serv

WAHRENBROCK'S BOOK HOUSE†
726-28 Broadway, 92101.
Tel 619-232-0132
Owner, C A Valverde
Types: 1st ed
Subj: Mod fict, voyages & travel, Mormon hist, So Cal hist, Baja Cal

San Dimas—24,014

PEG & DON KENYON BOOKS
408 DeAnza Heights Dr, 91773.
Tel 714-599-1651
SAN 157-0021
Owners, Peg Kenyon & Don Kenyon
Estab 1972. 4500 Vols. 250 sq ft
Types: Hb, op
S/S: Appr libr collec, search serv

San Francisco—678,974

ACORN BOOKS
510 O'Farrell St, 94102.
Tel 415-563-1736
SAN 158-0361
Owner, Joel M Chapman
Estab 1980. 20,000 Vols. 600 sq ft
Types: Fac ed, fine bnd, 1st ed, Fr lang, hb, illus bk, juv, ltd ed, o&r, op, papbk, used
S/S: Search serv

THE ALBATROSS BOOK STORE†
166 Eddy St, 94102. Tel 415-885-6501
SAN 161-1011
Owners, Donald W Sharp & Rose H Sharp
Estab 1961. Present Owner 1963. 400,000 Vols. 3300 sq ft
Types: 1st ed, illus bk, juv, ltd ed, op, papbk, remd, used, o&r, hb
Subj: Art, aviation, biog, metaphys & occult, mystery & detective, sci fiction & fantasy, Western Amer, maritime
S/S: Appr libr collec, biper, prints, search serv

ANTIQUUS BIBLIOPOLE†
4147 24th St, 94114. Tel 415-285-2322
SAN 125-6637
Owner, Pauline A Grosch

Estab 1973. 20,000 Vols. 3000 sq ft
Types: 1st ed, illus bk, juv, op, o&r
Subj: Bibliog, biog, philos, scholarly lit,
Western Amer
S/S: Search serv

ARGONAUT BOOKSHOP†
786-792 Sutter St, 94109.
Tel 415-474-9067
SAN 161-1046
Owner, Robert D Haines Jr
Estab 1941. 1500 sq ft. Cat 3x ann
Types: 1st ed, hb, illus bk, ltd ed, o&r,
op, used
Subj: Californiana, Western Amer,
cartography
S/S: Appr libr collec, autg, maps, mss,
orig art, prints

ARKADYAN BOOKS & PRINTS†
926 Irving St, 94122. Tel 415-664-6212
SAN 161-1054
Owners, Gerald Webb & Diane Vasica
Estab 1976. 4000 Vols. 500 sq ft. Cat
2-3x ann
Types: Illus bk, juv
Subj: Victorian-Edwardian lit
S/S: Appr libr collec, maps, prints,
search serv

BOLERIEM BOOKS
931 Judah, 94122. Tel 415-665-6110
SAN 158-7900
Owners, Nancy Elnor & John Durham,
et al
Estab 1981. 10,000 Vols. 1500 sq ft.
Cat 6x ann
Types: 1st ed, hb, imp, new & used,
o&r, remd
Subj: Art, class studies, econ, indust &
labor, women's studies, hist of law
S/S: Appr libr collec, biper, search serv,
consult in collection building

THE BOOKSTALL†
708 Sutter St, 94109. Tel 415-673-5446
SAN 160-8886
Owners, Henry Moises & Louise
Moises
Estab 1975. 8000 Vols. 900 sq ft. Cat
4x ann
Types: Fine bnd, 1st ed, hb, juv, ltd ed,
op, o&r, used
Subj: Californiana, gardening, math,
physics, children's collectables, cook-

ing, hist of science, mountaineering
S/S: Search serv

MEYER BOSWELL BOOKS
982 Hayes St, 94117.
Tel 415-346-1839
SAN 157-2598
Owner, Jordan D Luttrell
Estab 1976. 3000 Vols. 500 sq ft. Cat
2x ann
Types: Fac ed, fine bnd, hb, incunab,
imp, new, o&r, op, used
Subj: Law, legal & constitutional hist
S/S: Appr libr collec, autg, mss, prints,
search serv

THE BRICK ROW BOOK SHOP
Suite 303, 278 Post St, 94108.
Tel 415-398-0414
SAN 161-1070
Owners, Matt P Lowman & John
Crichton
Estab 1915. Present Owner 1983.
10,000 Vols. 1200 sq ft. Cat
Types: 1st ed, o&r, op, imp
Subj: Am hist & lit, bibliog, Eng hist &
lit, Latin Am, Mex, Texana, fine
printing
S/S: Appr libr collec, autg, mss, prints

CALIFORNIA BOOK AUCTION
GALLERIES†
358 Golden Gate Ave, 94102.
Tel 415-775-0424
SAN 161-1097
Owners, Maurice F Powers & David E
Belch
Estab 1956. 8000 sq ft. Cat 10-12x ann
Types: Fine bnd, 1st ed, hb, incunab,
illus bk, juv, ltd ed, o&r, press bks
Subj: Art, bks on bks, Californiana,
cooking & nutrit, graphic arts, hist,
photog, wines, Western Amer
S/S: Appr libr collec, autg, mss, orig
art, prints, sh mus
See Also: Los Angeles

LOUIS COLLINS BOOKS†
1083 Mission St, 94103.
Tel 415-431-5134
SAN 161-116X
Owner, Louis B Collins Jr
Estab 1970. 10,000 Vols. 700 sq ft. Cat
3x ann
Types: 1st ed, hb, o&r, op

Subj: Am Indian studies, anthrop
S/S: Appr libr collec, autg, biper, search
serv, collection development

THE COMPASS BOOKSTORE
689 Clay St, 94111. Tel 415-397-0663
SAN 161-1186
Owner, Martin Jackson
Types: Op, used
Subj: Discovery & explor, Orientalia
S/S: Search serv

JOHN PARKE CUSTIS BOOK-
SELLERS
PO Box 2153, 94126.
Tel 415-433-2335
SAN 160-4791
Owner, J Custis
Estab 1968. 10,000 Vols. Cat 6x ann
Types: 1st ed, hb, op, o&r
Subj: British lit, Oliver Oriole Collec of
19th century Am lit

ELDORADO BOOKS
PO Box 14-036, 94114. Tel 415-552-
8122
SAN 161-1275
Owner, Irving Eidenberg
Estab 1962. 3000 Vols. Cat
Types: Hb, op, o&r, used
Subj: Am hist & lit, Californiana, Eng
hist & lit, fine arts
S/S: Appr libr collec, autg, mss

HAIGHT STREET BOOKSHOP
1682 Haight St, 94117.
Tel 415-864-9636
SAN 159-2718
Owners, David Eshner & John Quinn;
Mgr, Pablo Heising
Estab 1980. 20,000 Vols. 1250 sq ft
Subj: Ethnic studies, Latin Am, per-
forming arts
S/S: Appr libr collec

THE HOLMES BOOK COMPANY†
22 Third St, 94103. Tel 415-362-3283
Owner, Craig H Keyston
Types: O&r, scholarly, op
Subj: Amer, Western Amer

JOHN HOWELL—BOOKS†
434 Post St, 94102. Tel 415-781-7795
SAN 121-6996
Pres, Warren R Howell
Estab 1912. Present Owner 1972.
60,000 Vols. 3500 sq ft

Types: 1st ed, hb, imp, incunab, new &
used, op, o&r
Subj: Art, Californiana, med, medieval
studies, natural hist, sci-tech, travel,
Western Amer
S/S: Appr libr collec, autg, maps, mss,
orig art, prints

FRANK L KOVACS ARCHAEOLOGY
BOOKS†
442 Post St, 94102. Tel 415-982-4072
SAN 157-258X
Owner, Frank L Kovacs; Mgr, Arthur S
Richter
Estab 1978. 2500 Vols. 1100 sq ft. Cat
4x ann
Types: Incunab, ltd ed, o&r, op, used
Subj: Archaeol, anthrop, early travel to
ancient lands
S/S: Autg, orig art, prints, search serv

ROBERT KUHN ANTIQUES—
AUTOGRAPHS
720 Geary St, 94109. Tel 415-474-6981
SAN 161-1380
Owner, Robert S Kuhn
Estab 1963. 850 Vols
Types: Hb, op, o&r
Subj: Antq, autg, circus, performing
arts, boxing
S/S: Appr libr collec, autg

LION BOOKSHOP
3427 Balboa, 94121.
Tel 415-221-5522, 221-5529
SAN 125-6122
Owner, Marion Pietsch
Estab 1940. Present Owner 1960.
20,000 Vols. 1200 sq ft
Types: Hb, op, used
Subj: Biog, hist, local hist, performing
arts
S/S: Appr libr collec, search serv

ERNEST LUBBE, BOOKS†
280 Golden Gate Ave, 94102.
Tel 415-441-5682
SAN 161-1453
Owner, Ernest Lubbe
Estab 1971. 25,000 Vols. 1600 sq ft
Types: Hb, op, papbk, used
S/S: Biper

MAELSTROM
572 Valencia, 94110. Tel 415-863-
9933

SAN 157-7255
Owner, Chris Bogosian
Present Owner 1979. 12,000 Vols.
1000 sq ft
Types: 1st ed, hb, illus bk, imp, juv, ltd
ed, new & used, o&r, papbk, remd
Subj: Art, metaphys & occult, soc sci,
sci-tech
S/S: Search serv

MANNING'S BOOKS†
1255 Post St, Suite 625, 94109.
Tel 415-673-1900 (by appt only)
SAN 157-5384
Owner, Kathleen Manning: Exec Asst,
Kathy Smith; Art Dir, John Hurtado;
Operations Dir, Caroline Yu
Estab 1972. Cat
Types: Illus bk
Subj: Amer, antq
S/S: Maps, per, prints

McDONALD'S BOOKSHOP
48 Turk St, 94102. Tel 415-673-2235
SAN 161-1461
Mgr, Liza Volansky
Estab 1926. 100,000 Vols
Types: Op, used
S/S: Per, rec

JEREMY NORMAN & CO INC†
442 Post St, 94102. Tel 415-781-6402
SAN 122-3380
Pres, Jeremy M Norman
Estab 1970. 5000 Vols. Cat 2x ann
Types: Fac ed, 1st ed, illus bk, incunab,
o&r, op
Subj: Hist of ideas, sci-tech, travel, hist
of med, voyages
S/S: Appr libr collec, autg, maps, mss,
orig art, prints

THE OLD BOOKSHOP
1104 Sutter St, 94109.
Tel 415-776-3417
SAN 161-1534
Types: 1st ed, imp, op, o&r, used
S/S: Maps, prints, search serv

RANDALL HOUSE†
185 Post St, Suite 301, 94108.
Tel 415-781-2218
SAN 161-1577
Pres, Ronald R Randall
Estab 1975. 16,000 Vols. 1600 sq ft.
Cat 2-3x ann

Types: Fac ed, fine bnd, 1st ed, incunab,
illus bk, ltd ed, o&r
S/S: Appr libr collec, autg, maps, mss,
orig art, prints

BERNARD M ROSENTHAL INC
251 Post St, 94108. Tel 415-982-2219
SAN 161-1593
Owner, Bernard M Rosenthal; Vpres,
Ruth Rosenthal
Estab 1953. Cat 3x ann
Types: Fac ed, incunab, op, o&r, 16th
century fine bnd
Subj: Bibliog, medieval studies, Renais-
sance hist & lit, paleography
S/S: Appr libr collec

SAN FRANCISCIANA SHOP†
Cliff House, 1090 Point Lobos Ave,
94121. Tel 415-751-7222
SAN 161-1607
Owner, Marilyn Blaisdell
Estab 1973. 200 Vols
Subj: Californiana, San Francisciana
S/S: Maps, posters, prints, photos,
postcards

JOHN SCOPAZZI BOOKS†
Union Sq, 278 Post St, Suite 305,
94108. Tel 415-362-5708
SAN 161-1615
Owner, John Scopazzi
Types: Fine bnd, illus bk, o&r, pvt
presses

SERGIO OLD PRINTS†
50 Maiden Lane, 94108.
Tel 415-434-3312
SAN 161-1631
Owner, Sergio Domeyko
Estab 1977
Subj: Travel, old prints prior 1880
S/S: Audubon, Amer & Hawaiiana
prints

KENNETH STAROSCIAK†
117 Wilmot Pl, 94115.
Tel 415-346-0650
SAN 157-5562
8000 Vols. Cat 10-15x ann
Types: 1st ed, illus bk, ltd ed, o&r, op
Subj: Archit, art
Branches:
ARTS & LETTERS BOOKSHOP
555 Sutter St, 94102
SAN 157-5570

CHRISTOPHE STICKEL, FINE BOOKS & AUTOGRAPHS
5 Surrey St, 94131. Tel 415-334-0636 (by appt)
SAN 159-5555
Owner, Christophe Stickel
Estab 1980. 3000 Vols. Cat 3x ann
Types: 1st ed, hb, ltd ed, o&r
Subj: Western Amer, bks on bks, autg of Am writers
S/S: Appr libr collec, autg, mss, prints

JEFFREY THOMAS FINE & RARE BOOKS
49 Geary St, Suite 215, 94102.
Tel 415-956-3272
SAN 170-3234
Owner, Jeffrey Thomas
Estab 1982. 3500 Vols. 1300 sq ft. Cat 2-3x ann
Types: 1st ed, illus bk, ltd ed, o&r
S/S: Appr libr collec

TRANSITION BOOKS
445 Stockton St, 94114.
Tel 415-391-5161
SAN 124-2180
Owner, Richard Praeger
Estab 1979. 3000 Vols. 1000 sq ft. Cat 2x ann
Types: 1st ed, imp Fr, illus bk, ltd ed, o&r, op, fine press
Subj: Am hist & lit, Eng hist & lit, illus, literary criticism, mod lit
S/S: Appr libr collec, prints, search serv, orig graphics & posters by mod artists

ALAN WOFSY FINE ARTS
401 China Basin St (Mail add: PO Box 2210, 94126). Tel 415-986-3030
SAN 123-3750
Estab 1969. Cat 3x ann
Types: Imp, op, o&r
Subj: Art, bibliog, 15th-20th century illus
S/S: Prints, wholesale

San Gabriel — 30,072

MARIAN L GORE BOOKSELLER†
PO Box 433, 91778. Tel 213-287-2946
SAN 161-1712
Owner, Marian L Gore
Estab 1965. 5000 Vols. Cat ann

Types: Op, o&r, for lang
Subj: Food, wines, beverages, cookery, hotels & inns, history of food
By appointment only

San Jose — 636,550

A S FISCHLER — RARE BOOKS
604 S 15th St, 95112. Tel 408-297-7090
SAN 157-2628
Owner, A S Fischler
Estab 1975. 2000 Vols. 1000 sq ft. Cat 2-3x ann
Types: Fac ed, fine bnd, 1st ed, hb, illus bk, imp, ltd ed, o&r, pvt presses
Subj: Western Amer, British lit
S/S: Appr libr collec, fine printing

HARMON BOOKS
964 Chapel Hill Way, 95122.
Tel 408-297-2810
SAN 157-9428
Owner, Robert B Harmon
Estab 1970. 100 Vols. Cat
Types: 1st ed, hb
Subj: Bibliog, polit sci, John Steinbeck, Ernest Hemingway
S/S: Appr libr collec, search serv

PERRY'S ANTIQUES & BOOKS
1863 W San Carlos, 95128.
Tel 408-286-0426
SAN 161-1801
Owner, Frank D Perry
Estab 1949. 100,000 Vols
Types: 1st ed, hb, juv, ltd ed, op, o&r
Subj: Western Amer, Edgar Rice Burroughs, Jack London, 20th century lit
S/S: Appr libr collec, autg, biper, orig art, search serv, sh mus

San Leandro — 63,952

ROSKIE & WALLACE BOOKSTORE
14595 E 14th St, 94578.
Tel 415-483-4163
SAN 160-905X
Owner, Philip M Roskie
Estab 1940
Types: Op, used
Stock includes 100,000 book vols & 100,000 magazines

San Luis Obispo — 34,252

THE NOVEL EXPERIENCE
778 Marsh St (Mail add: 880 Buchon St,
93401). Tel 805-544-1549
SAN 161-1925
Owner, Margaret Nybak
Estab 1976. 6000 Vols. 300 sq ft. Cat
ann
Types: Fine bnd, 1st ed, hb, illus bk,
juv, o&r, op, used
Subj: Belles lettres
S/S: Appr libr collec, search serv

San Marcos — 17,479

THE BOOK HABIT
PO Box 941, 92069. Tel 619-480-1200
SAN 159-1010
Owners, Charles Annegan & Bobbie
Annegan
Cat 8x ann
Types: Hb, o&r, op
Subj: Civil War, genealogy, local hist,
military, Western Amer
S/S: Autg, prints

San Mateo — 77,561

GRAPEVINE ANTIQUES & BOOKS
PO Box 1134, 94403.
Tel 415-341-7009
SAN 161-1992
Owner, Sharalyn Spiteri
Estab 1972. 4000 Vols
Types: Fine bnd, 1st ed, hb, illus bk,
juv, ltd ed, op, used
Subj: Children's illus bk

San Pedro

GEORGE DEEDS BOOK FINDER
1025 S Goodhope Ave, 90732.
Tel 213-831-3700
SAN 121-1625
Owner, George Deeds
Present Owner 1971. 2000 Vols. 150 sq
ft
Types: 1st ed, hb, illus bk, juv, ltd ed,
new & used, o&r, op
S/S: Search serv

San Rafael — 44,700

CARL BLOMGREN BOOKS
51 Gold Hill Grade (Mail add: PO Box
3597, 94912). Tel 415-456-7610
SAN 158-6327
Owner, Carl Blomgren
Types: 1st ed, hb, illus bk, juv, op, o&r
Subj: Californiana, photog
S/S: Biper

MICHAEL S HOLLANDER RARE
BOOKS†
PO Box 3678, 94902.
Tel 415-924-7201
SAN 161-2026
Owner, M S Hollander
Present Owner 1973. 5000 Vols. Cat
Types: 1st ed, o&r, illus bk, illuminated
mss, color plate
Subj: 19th cent tech & art
S/S: Mss, prints, search serv

HORIZON BOOKSHOP
832 B St, 94901. Tel 415-453-6830
SAN 161-2034
Owners, Roy Brown & Peggy Brown
Types: Hb, juv, papbk, remd
Subj: Western Amer

R E LEWIS INC†
PO Box 1108, 94902. Tel 415-461-
4161
SAN 161-2042
Buyer, Raymond E Lewis
Cat 4x ann
Types: Illus bk, o&r, imp Eng, Fr, Ger,
India, Italy & Jap
S/S: Appr libr collec, Indian miniature
paintings & mss, orig prints from
1500 to 1950, Japanese prints

MANDRAKE BOOKSHOP
817 4th St, 94901. Tel 415-453-3484
SAN 144-8676
Owner, Harold Bertram; Mgr, Jean
Birdsall
Estab 1968. 50,000 Vols. 2000 sq ft
Branch. Buys indep & through hq
Types: Hb, juv, new & used, op, papbk
Subj: Bus & mgt, soc sci, fiction, sci-
tech
S/S: Prints
Hq: New Albion Bookshop, Fairfax, CA

Santa Ana—203,713

BOOK CENTER—DAVE HENSON, BOOKS
PO Box 11402, 92711.
Tel 714-542-8839
SAN 161-2085
Owner, David L Henson
Estab 1959. Cat 10x ann
Types: Hb, op, o&r, remd, used
Subj: Californiana, the West

BOOK VAULT
3682-A S Bristol St (Mail add: PO Box 1618, Costa Mesa, 92626).
Tel 714-549-9548
SAN 161-2093
Owner, Ron Greenwood
Estab 1976. 13,000 Vols. 1050 sq ft
Types: Fine bnd, 1st ed, hb, illus bk, juv, o&r, op, papbk, used
Subj: Metaphys & occult, military, sci-tech, Thomas Paine
S/S: Search serv

WADE LILLYWHITE BOOKS
2521-F No Grand Ave, 92701.
Tel 714-997-1384 (by appt only)
SAN 128-9829
Estab 1981. Present Owner 1983. 3000 Vols. 500 sq ft. Cat 8x ann
Types: Op
Subj: Western Amer, bks on bks, scholarly lit
S/S: Appr libr collec, autg, biper, mss, search serv

Santa Barbara—74,542

DREW'S BOOKSHOP†
31 E Canon Perdido (Mail add: PO Box 163, 93102). Tel 805-966-3311
SAN 161-228X
Owner, Warren E Drew
Estab 1957. 15,000 Vols. 1100 sq ft. Cat 3-4x ann
Types: Fine bnd, 1st ed, hb, illus bk, juv, o&r, op
Subj: Amer, Am hist & lit, Eng hist & lit, literary criticism
S/S: Appr libr collec, autg, maps, prints, mss, search serv

HELAN HALBACH—BOOKSELLER
Studio 3, Meridian Studios, 116 E De La Guerra St, 93101. Tel 805-965-6432
SAN 157-2687
Owner & Mgr, Helan Halbach
Estab 1969. 2500 Vols. 500 sq ft. Cat
Types: 1st ed, fac ed, fine bnd, hb, illus bk, juv, ltd ed, new, o&r, op, papbk, remd, used
Subj: Mystery & detective, fiction, vintage travel guides, Rubaiyat of Omar Khayyam, Sherlock Holmes, theatre
S/S: Biper, maps, orig art, prints, search serv

MILTON HAMMER BOOKS†
Suite 125, El Paseo, 93101.
Tel 805-965-8901
SAN 161-2301
Owner, Milton Hammer
Estab 1969. 10,000 Vols. 860 sq ft
Types: Hb, papbk, o&r, illus bk
Subj: Amer
S/S: Maps, prints

JOSEPH THE PROVIDER BOOKS†
903 State St, 93101. Tel 805-962-6862
SAN 161-2336
Pres, Ralph B Sipper
Estab 1970. 10,000 Vols. Cat 3x ann
Types: 1st ed, o&r
Subj: Mod lit
S/S: Appr libr collec, autg, mss

MAURICE F NEVILLE RARE BOOKS†
835 Laguna St, 93101. Tel 805-963-1908
SAN 161-2360
Owner, Maurice F Neville
Estab 1977. 8000 Vols. Cat 3x ann
Types: 1st ed, ltd ed, o&r, inscribing
Subj: Eng hist & lit, mod lit
S/S: Appr libr collec, autg, mss

PEPPER & STERN—RARE BOOKS INC†
PO Box 2711, 93120.
Tel 805-569-0735
Owners, James Pepper & Peter L Stern
Types: 1st ed, o&r, op, inscribed bks
Subj: Eng & Am lit, mystery & detective fiction, sci fiction
By appt only
See Also Sharon, Mass.

MARTIN A SILVER MUSICAL LIT-
ERATURE
643 Willowglen Rd, 93105. Tel 805-
687-4198
SAN 122-8676
Owner, Martin A Silver
Estab 1970. 5000 Vols. Cat
Types: Fac ed, 1st ed, hb, imp, o&r, op,
papbk, remd, used
S/S: Appr libr collec, search serv, sh
mus

VOLKOFF & VON HOHENLOHE†
1514 La Coronilla Dr, 93109.
Tel 805-966-2100
Owners, Ivan Volkoff & Adelheid A
Von Hohenlohe
Types: O&r books & mss
Subj: Polit sci, philos, European hist,
Polonica & Slavica

Santa Clara—87,746

TIGER'S TALE BOOKSHOP
3435 Forest Ave, 95050.
Tel 408-241-8532
SAN 158-0388
Owner, Art Kompolt
Estab 1979. 1000 sq ft. Cat 2x ann
Types: Hb, o&r, op, used, imp Scot-
land
Subj: Archaeol, bks on bks, metaphys &
occult

Santa Cruz—41,483

GEORGE ROBERT KANE BOOKS†
252 3rd Ave, 95062. Tel 408-426-4133
(by appt)
SAN 170-2998
Owner, George Robert Kane
Estab 1978. 4000 Vols. 750 sq ft. Cat
3x ann
Types: Fine bnd, 1st ed, illus bk, imp
Eng, Jap, Fr, juv, ltd ed, o&r
Subj: Typography, illus
S/S: Appr libr collec, maps, prints

Santa Monica—88,314

F & I BOOKS†
PO Box 1900, 90406.
Tel 213-393-2116

SAN 158-2089
Owner, Isidoor Berkelouw
Estab 1977. 3000 Vols
Types: O&r, op
Subj: Africa, Australia, South Seas,
Antarctic
S/S: Maps, mss, prints, search serv

HOWARD KARNO BOOKS, INC
PO Box 431, 90406. Tel 213-458-1619
SAN 160-7316
Owner, Howard L Karno; Mgr, Con-
suelo Potdevin
Estab 1978. 15,000 Vols. Cat 20x ann
Types: Fac ed, 1st ed, hb, illus bk, imp,
o&r, op, papbk, remd, used
Subj: Genealogy, hist, Latin Am, med,
music, natural hist, opera, perform-
ing arts, scholarly lit, Arctic art
S/S: Appr libr collec, mss, search serv
By appointment only

NILES & SILVER
1213 Pine St, 90405. Tel 213-392-9791
SAN 128-4908
Owners, William Niles & Joel Silver
3000 Vols
Branch
Types: 1st ed, ltd ed, op, o&r
S/S: Appr libr collec, mss, search serv,
spec order, legal referencing, docu-
ments

SANTA MONICA BOOK BAZAAR
131 Broadway, 90401.
Tel 213-451-2710
SAN 161-2611
Types: Op, used

Santa Rosa—83,205

VIRGINIA BURGMAN
3198 Hidden Valley Dr, 95404.
Tel 707-526-2482
SAN 161-2654
Owner & Mgr, Virginia Burgman
Estab 1959. 3000 Vols. Cat 2x ann
Types: 1st ed, hb, juv, o&r, op
Subj: Art, Californiana, mystery &
detective, photog, rel
S/S: Search serv

Saratoga—29,261

ESTAMPE ORIGINALE†
PO Box 3117, 95070.

Tel 408-867-0833
Owner, Sandra A Sofris
Types: Illus bks, 19th & 20th cent
prints, old master prints, posters
Subj: Art

Sausalito—7090

THE ECLECTIC GALLERY†
PO Box 1581, 94965. Tel 415-383-
1125
By appointment only
Owner, Dick Rykken
Types: Illus bks, press bks
Subj: Baumiana, Edward S Curtis pho-
togravures, art

EDWIN V GLASER RARE BOOKS†
25 Rodeo Ave, PO Box 1765, 94965.
Tel 415-332-1194
SAN 164-8748
Owner, Edwin V Glaser
Estab 1964. 3000 Vols. 1200 sq ft. Cat
4x ann
Types: O&r
Subj: Med, sci-tech
S/S: Appr libr collec

Scotts Valley—6891

CHIMNEY SWEEP BOOKS
220-A Mt Hermon Rd, 95066.
Tel 408-438-1379
SAN 127-4376
Owner, Lillian Smith-Kaiser; Mgr,
Jennifer Kaiser
Estab 1972. 25,000 Vols. 1200 sq ft.
Cat 3x ann
Types: Hb, used, Ireland, pre-1940 juv
Subj: Californiana, rel studies
S/S: Appr libr collec, prints, search serv

L S KAISER BOOKS—CHIMNEY
SWEEP BOOKS
220-A Mount Hermon Rd, 95066.
Tel 408-438-1379
SAN 159-6322
Estab 1975. 1200 sq ft. Cat 4x ann
Types: Fine bnd, 1st ed, hb, incunab,
illus bk, juv, ltd ed, new, o&r, op,
papbk, remd, used
Subj: Gardening, rel
S/S: Appr libr collec, search serv

Sebastopol—5500

SEBASTOPOL BOOK SHOP†
133 N Main St, 95472
Owner, William L McDonnell
Types: Op & fine bks
Subj: Modern lit, metaphys, post-1850
physical sci, East Asia

Sepulveda

LOIS GEREGHTY BOOKS
9521 Orion Ave, 91343.
Tel 213-892-1053
SAN 157-2725
Owner, Lois Gereghty
Estab 1969. 9000 Vols
Types: Used
S/S: Search serv
By appointment only

Sherman Oaks

MAINLY MYSTERIES
4752 Ventura Canyon Ave, 91413.
Tel 213-995-1202
SAN 156-9244
Owners, Sol Grossman & Patty Gross-
man
Estab 1981. 3500 Vols. Cat 3x ann
Types: 1st ed, hb, o&r, used
Subj: Mystery & detective

OUT-OF-PRINT BOOKS
5038 Hazeltine Ave, Suite 305, 91423.
Tel 213-789-6431
SAN 161-2786
Owner, Arnold Jacobs
Estab 1955. 2000 Vols. Cat 4x ann
Types: 1st ed, hb, op, used
Subj: Western Amer, World War II
S/S: Search serv

B & L ROOTENBERG FINE & RARE
BOOKS†
15422 Sutton St (Mail add: PO Box
5049, 91403). Tel 213-788-7765
SAN 161-2808
Owner, Barbara Rootenberg
Estab 1970. 4000 Vols. Cat ann
Types: O&r, op
Subj: Econ, hist of ideas, med, sci-tech,
early sci
S/S: Appr libr collec, biper, mss, prints

Solana Beach— 5023

BOOK SWAP
129 N Hwy 101, 92075.
 Tel 714-755-7323
SAN 161-2840
Owner, Ken Esserman
Estab 1975. 20,000 Vols
Types: Fac ed, fine bnd, 1st ed, hb, illus
 bk, juv, ltd ed, new, o&r, op, papbk,
 remd, used
Subj: Civil War, sci fiction & fantasy,
 biog

Soquel— 5795

BAY SIDE BOOKS
PO Box 57, 95073
SAN 158-1058
Owner, M P Beckham
Estab 1971. Cat 4x ann
Subj: Anthrop, mod lit, poetry, British
 & American poetry
S/S: Search serv

Stockton— 149,779

BONNIE DENVER BOOKS
2513 Alexa Way, 95209.
 Tel 209-952-8364
SAN 158-7293
Owner, Bonnie Denver Ruttan
Types: 1st ed, hb, illus bk, juv, o&r,
 used
Subj: Aviation
S/S: Search serv

Studio City

FRED A BERK
PO Box 1367, 91604.
 Tel 213-789-4372
SAN 161-3030
Owner, Fred A Berk
2000 Vols. Cat
Types: O&r
Subj: Amer, Californiana, world travel
S/S: Travel ephemera

Torrance— 131,497

BOB FINCH, BOOKS†
PO Box 1362, 90505.
 Tel 213-378-2771

SAN 161-326X
Owner, Bob Finch
3000 Vols. Cat 3x ann
Types: O&r, used
Subj: Arctic, discovery & explor, nauti-
 cal, Polar, Antarctic
S/S: Biper, maps

Turlock— 26,291

BOOKS IN TRANSIT
2830 Case Way, 85380.
 Tel 209-632-6984
SAN 158-6068
Owner, Mary T Peterson
Estab 1975. 1500 Titles. Cat 3x ann
Types: Used
Subj: Arts & crafts
Open by appt only

GARCIA-GARST, BOOKSELLER
334 North Center, 95380.
 Tel 209-632-5054
SAN 161-3375
Owners, Kenneth M Garst & Beverly A
 Garst
Estab 1978. 50,000 Vols. 950 sq ft
Types: 1st ed, hb, juv, o&r, op, papbk,
 used
Subj: Amer, Californiana
S/S: Orig art, prints, search serv

Van Nuys

JOHN MAKAREWICH, BOOKS
PO Box 7032, 91409
SAN 161-3502
Owner, John Makarewich
Present Owner 1946. 30,000 Vols. Cat
 6x ann
Types: Ltd ed, 1st ed, hb, op, used, fine
 press
Subj: Martial arts, performing arts,
 psychol, scholarly lit, sci-tech, sociol,
 Western Amer, art ref
S/S: Appr libr collec

LOIS ST CLAIR
PO Box 247, 91408. Tel 213-781-5376
SAN 161-3499
Owner, Lois St-Clair
Estab 1969. 1000 Vols
Types: O&r, op, used

Subj: Embroidery, related needle-crafts, fiction of 1920's & 1930's
S/S: Search serv

Ventura — 55,797

CALICO CAT BOOKSHOP
495 E Main St, 93001.
 Tel 805-643-7849
SAN 159-6101
Owner, Elaine Hansen
Estab 1975. 25,000 Vols. 1500 sq ft
Types: Fac ed, fine bnd, 1st ed, hb, illus bk, juv, ltd ed, new, o&r, op, papbk, remd, used
Subj: Art, cooking & nutrit, gardening
S/S: Search serv

Walnut Creek — 53,643

JAMES M DOURGARIAN, BOOK-
 MAN
1299 Las Juntas Way, 94596.
 Tel 415-939-7102
SAN 158-8966
Owner, James M Dourgarian
Estab 1981. 1000 Vols. 1000 sq ft. Cat 4x ann
Types: Fac ed, fine bnd, 1st ed, hb, illus bk, ltd ed, o&r, papbk
Subj: Mod lit, John Steinbeck

Weaverville — 5950

BLITZ BOOKS
PO Box 1076, 96093.
 Tel 916-623-5430
SAN 161-3685
Owner, R Krieg
Estab 1957. 5000 Vols. Cat 8x ann
Types: O&r, op
Subj: Californiana, Western Amer
S/S: Appr libr collec, search serv

Westlake Village

221 BOOKS
760 Carlisle Canyon Rd, 91361.
 Tel 213-889-2640
SAN 157-2792
Owners, Phillip Gold & Mary Lou Gold
Estab 1978. 4500 Vols. 250 sq ft. Cat
Types: 1st ed, o&r, op, used

Subj: Literary criticism, A Conan Doyle, H Rider Haggard, Sherlock Holmes, H G Wells
S/S: Search serv

Whittier — 68,872

FAMILY BOOKSTORE
6725 Comstock Ave, 90601.
 Tel 213-696-2683
SAN 161-3790
Owner, Don Wigren
Estab 1956. 65,000 Vols
Types: Fac ed, hb, imp, op, papbk, o&r, used
Subj: Alaskana, Arctic, Can, hunting & fishing, stock market
S/S: Appr libr collec, autg, biper, search serv

Willits — 4008

J E REYNOLDS, BOOKSELLER
3801 Ridgewood Rd, 95490.
 Tel 707-459-4321
SAN 161-3820
Owner, J E Reynolds
Estab 1948. Cat 2x ann
Types: Hb, new & used, o&r, op, remd, fine press
Subj: Californiana, Western Amer

Woodland Hills

OKMAN'S HAPPY ENDINGS
20418 Califa St, 91367.
 Tel 213-346-8934
SAN 157-2814
Owner, Louella Okman
Estab 1970. 5000 Vols
Types: 1st ed, hb, illus bk, juv, new, o&r, op, papbk, remd, used
Subj: Performing arts, cooking & nutrit, biog, arts & crafts
S/S: Autg, gifts, search serv

ROBERT ROSS & CO
6101 El Escorpion Rd, 91367.
 Tel 213-346-6152
SAN 159-1789
Owners, Robert Ross & Marilyn Ross
Present Owner 1980. Cat
Types: Illus bk, o&r, op, used
Subj: Hist, travel, cartography, geography

S/S: Maps, prints
Stock consists of 1000 old maps &
prints

RUDOLPH WILLIAM SABBOT—
NATURAL HISTORY BOOKS†
5239 Tendilla Ave, 91364.
Tel 213-346-7164
SAN 122-7246
Owners, Rudolph W Sabbot & Irene M
Sabbot
Estab 1965. 5000 Vols. Cat 3x ann
Types: 1st ed, hb, incunab, o&r, op,
used, imp
Subj: Natural hist, zool
S/S: Appr libr collec, prints, search serv
North American Agent and Stockist for
the publications of the British Mu-
seum of Natural History.

COLORADO

Boulder—76,685

THE KING'S MARKET—BOOKS &
PRINTS
1021 Pearl St, Suite D (Mail add: PO
Box 709, 80306). Tel 303-444-8484
SAN 159-0596
Owner, Robert C Wayne
Estab 1981. Present Owner 1982. 1000
sq ft. Cat
Types: Fine bnd, 1st ed, hb, o&r, op,
used
Subj: Coloradiana, geol, mountains,
natural hist, psychol, sci-tech, West-
ern Amer
S/S: Appr libr collec, prints, search serv

STAGE HOUSE NEW II
1039 Pearl St, 80302. Tel 303-447-
1433
SAN 161-4061
Owners, Richard Schwarz & George
Coffer
Types: 1st ed, o&r, papbk, used
S/S: Prints, fine art

Colorado Springs—215,150

HENRY A CLAUSEN BOOKSHOP
224 1/2 N Tejon St, 80903.
Tel 303-634-1193
SAN 161-4150

Estab 1931. 24,000 Vols. Cat
Types: Fac ed, 1st ed, hb, op, o&r,
remd, used
Subj: Class studies, Coloradiana, hist,
theol
S/S: Appr libr collec, autg, biper, mss,
search serv

Denver—491,396

AARDVARK BOOKS
900 Delta, 80221. Tel 303-428-5420
SAN 125-3107
Owner, James D Fredlund
Estab 1972. 1000 Vols
Types: 1st ed, hb, op, papbk, o&r, used
Subj: Coloradiana, Western Amer
S/S: Search serv, paper collectibles

ABACO BOOKS
5924 E Colfax Ave, 80220.
Tel 303-333-1269
SAN 157-2857
Owners, Steve Wilson & Linda K
Wilson; Mgr, Hanna K Margan
Estab 1979. 10,000 Vols. 1000 sq ft
Types: Op, used, modern 1st ed
Subj: Western Amer
S/S: Appr libr collec

BOOK FORUM
709 E 6th, 80203. Tel 303-837-9069
SAN 159-0642
Owner, Edgar Jepson
Estab 1980. 12,000 Vols. 750 sq ft
Types: Hb, o&r, op

W J BOOKUNTER
PO Box 2795, 80201.
Tel 303-757-0160
SAN 161-4312
Owner, Barrie D Watson
Estab 1969. 20,000 Vols. Cat 4x ann
Types: Fac ed, 1st ed, hb, incunab, op,
o&r, used
Subj: Am hist & lit, law, natural hist,
falconry
S/S: Appr libr collec, biper, search serv

COLLECTORS' CENTER, RARE
BOOKS
609 Corona St, 80218.
Tel 303-831-7237
SAN 161-4320
Owner, Don Bloch

Estab 1952. 10,000 Vols
Types: 1st ed, hb, juv, new & used, op,
 o&r, press bound, rare papbk
Subj: Amer, anthrop, arts & crafts,
 auto, aviation, biog, hist, metaphys
 & occult, sports, railroadiana
S/S: Appr libr collec, search serv, rare
 per & sheet mus

THE COURT PLACE ANTIQUAR-
IAN BOOKSHOP
3827 W 32nd Ave, 80211.
 Tel 303-455-0317
SAN 161-4576
Owner, Alan Culpin
Estab 1977. 75,000 Vols. 4500 sq ft.
 Cat
Types: Fac ed, fine bnd, 1st ed, hb, illus
 bk, ltd ed, new, op, o&r
Subj: Amer, archit, aviation, fiction,
 geol, interior design, med, military,
 mystery & detective, nautical, schol-
 arly lit, travel, Western Amer
S/S: Appr libr collec, maps, prints,
 search serv

THE HERMITAGE ANTIQUARIAN
BOOKSHOP†
2817 E 3rd Ave, 80206.
 Tel 303-388-6811
SAN 161-4444
Owner, Robert W Topp
Present Owner 1973. 20,000 Vols. Cat
Types: 1st ed, hb, op, o&r
Subj: Hist, philos, scholarly lit, Western
 Amer, western history
S/S: Appr libr collec, prints, search serv

FRED A ROSENSTOCK—BOOKS &
ARTS
1228 E Colfax Ave, 80218.
 Tel 303-832-7190
SAN 161-4517
Owner, Fred A Rosenstock; Mgr,
 Stephen L Good
Estab 1928. 10,000 Vols
Types: New, op
Subj: Amer, art
S/S: Orig paintings by Western artists

Fort Collins — 64,632

OLD CORNER BOOKSHOP
216 Linden St, 80524.

Tel 303-484-6186
SAN 161-4681
Owner, Jane Tester
Estab 1970. 50,000 Vols. Cat
Types: Hb, juv, for lang, 1st ed, o&r,
 op, papbk, new & used, fine bnd
Subj: Coloradiana, Western Amer
S/S: Biper, per, search serv

Johnstown — 1535

ARTHUR M GRIFFITHS
PO Box 38, 80534. Tel 303-587-4702
SAN 159-1908
Owner, Arthur M Griffiths
Estab 1976. 1750 Vols
Types: 1st ed, o&r, op, used
Subj: Sports, Western Amer
S/S: Prints

Littleton — 28,631

THE PROSPECTOR
2505 W Alamo Ave, 80120.
 Tel 303-798-5552, 798-5882
SAN 161-4924
Owner, Melville L Moore
Estab 1972. Present Owner 1980.
 10,000 Vols. 500 sq ft
Types: 1st ed, hb, illus bk, juv, ltd ed,
 op, o&r, Fr & Ger lang
Subj: Camping & hiking, geosci, hunt-
 ing & fishing, mining, natural hist,
 poetry, railroadiana, Western Amer
S/S: Biper, sh mus, antq

FRED B ROTHMAN & CO
10368 West Centennial Rd, 80127.
 Tel 303-979-5657
SAN 122-7106
Owners, Fred B Rothman & Paul A
 Rothman; Buyer, Richard J Spinelli
Estab 1945. Cat ann
Types: Domestic & imp, journals,
 monographs
Subj: Law, related fields
S/S: Wholesale

Loveland — 30,244

THE CACHE
7157 W US 34, 80537.
 Tel 303-667-1081

SAN 158-488X
Owner, Martha P Anderson
Estab 1973. 20,000 Vols. 400 sq ft
Types: 1st ed, hb, juv, new, op, o&r,
  papbk, used
S/S: Appr libr collec, search serv

Norwood—478

COLORADO BOOKMAN
PO Box 156, 81423. Tel 303-327-4417
SAN 159-6365
Estab 1974. 900 Vols
Types: Op
S/S: Search serv

Pueblo—101,686

THE COLLECTIVE—MILLET &
  SIMPSON ANTIQUARIAN BOOK-
  SELLERS
130 S Union, 81003. Tel 303-542-4462
SAN 158-1473
Owners, Leland A Millet & Ronald C
  Simpson
Estab 1975. 6500 Vols. Cat 3x ann
Types: 1st ed, hb, illus bk, juv, ltd ed,
  op, o&r
Subj: Genealogy, Western Amer
S/S: Appr libr collec, prints, rec, search
  serv, sh mus

CONNECTICUT

Bethany—4330

THE ANTIQUARIUM
66 Humiston Dr, 06525.
  Tel 203-393-2723
SAN 161-5262
Owners, Lee & Marian Ash
Estab 1958. 25,000 Vols. Cat ann
Types: Fac ed, 1st ed, imp, incunab,
  o&r, used
Subj: Bibliog, bks on bks, med, natural
  hist, Renaissance hist & lit, Icelan-
  dica, witchcraft
S/S: Appr libr collec, autg, maps, mss,
  prints, search serv

WHITLOCK FARM BOOKSELLERS†
20 Sperry Rd, 06525. Tel 203-393-1240
SAN 161-6005

Owner, Gilbert Whitlock; Mgr, Maria
  Lull; Merch Mgr, Everett Whitlock
Estab 1940. 100,000 Vols. 6500 sq ft.
  Cat 24x ann
Types: Fac ed, fine bnd, 1st ed, hb, illus
  bk, incunab, imp, juv, ltd ed, new &
  used, o&r, op, papbk, remd
Subj: Agr, Amer, archit, art, natural hist
S/S: Appr libr collec, autg, biper, mss,
  orig art, prints

Bethel—16,004

ALFRED W PAINE—BOOKS
Wolfpits Rd, 06801. Tel 203-748-4125
By appointment only
Owner, Carola Paine Wormser
Subj: Whaling, voyages, naval hist,
  nautical sci, West Indies

Branford—23,363

BRANFORD RARE BOOK & ART
  GALLERY
221 Montowese St, Box 56, 06405.
  Tel 203-488-5882
SAN 161-5319
Owner, John R Elliot
Estab 1978. 2000 Vols. 600 sq ft. Cat
  2x ann
Types: 1st ed, illus bk, o&r
Subj: Amer, discovery & explor, travel,
  cartography
S/S: Appr libr collec, maps, mss, orig
  art, prints

Colebrook—1221

COLEBROOK BOOK BARN†
Rt 183, Box 108, 06021.
  Tel 203-379-3185
SAN 161-5408
Owner, Robert Seymour
Estab 1955. 10,000 Vols. Cat
Types: 1st ed, hb, op, o&r, used
S/S: Appr libr collec

Collinsville—2897

COUNTRY LANE BOOKS†
38 Country Lane, 06022.
  Tel 203-693-2245
SAN 161-5424

Owners, Edward Meyers & Judith
Meyers
5000 Vols. Cat 3x ann
Types: Fine bnd, hb, juv, 1st ed Am &
Brit
Subj: Arctic, Can, fiction, Amer
S/S: Appr libr collec, autg, mss, prints,
sh mus

LAWRENCE F GOLDER RARE
BOOKS
14 Country Lane (Mail add: PO Box
144, 06022). Tel 203-693-8110,
693-8631
SAN 161-5416
Owner, Lawrence F Golder
Estab 1969. 550 Vols. Cat ann
Types: 1st ed, ltd ed, o&r
Subj: Am Indian studies, Amer, Arctic,
Can, med, travel, warfare, Western
Amer, early voyages & travel
S/S: Appr libr collec, maps

Cos Cob

THE BOOK BLOCK†
8 Loughlin Ave, 06807.
Tel 203-629-2990 (by appt)
SAN 157-292X
Owner, David M Block
Estab 1979. 3000 Vols. 350 sq ft. Cat
6x ann
Types: Fine bnd, 1st ed, incunab, illus
bk, ltd ed, o&r, pvt presses
Subj: Amer, travel, bks on bks
S/S: Appr libr collec, autg, mss, prints

HARRINGTON'S
333 Cognewaug Rd, 06807.
Tel 203-869-1070
SAN 158-7919
Owner & Mgr, Alton Ketchum
Cat
Types: Am & British newsprs, mags for
past 3 centuries

Coventry—8895

ALLISON GALLERY INC
46 Fieldstone Lane, 06238.
Tel 203-742-8990
SAN 157-5597
Owner & Mgr, Jane Allinson, PhD
Estab 1977. 300 Vols. Cat 2x ann

Types: Op
Subj: Fine prints & drawings
S/S: Orig art, prints, fine arts appr

BOOKS & BIRDS
Mason St (Mail add: 107 B Jan Dr,
Hebron, 06248). Tel 203-742-8976
SAN 159-5725
Owner, Gil Salk
Estab 1980. 10,000 Vols. 1000 sq ft
Types: Hb, juv, op, papbk, used, o&r
S/S: Search serv
Open Sat 12-4 & by appt

JOHN WOODS BOOKS—(OUT OF
PRINT)
1117 Main St, 06238.
Tel 203-742-7457
SAN 158-2682
Owner, John A Woods
Estab 1976. 8000 Vols
Types: Fine bnd, 1st ed, hb, illus bk,
juv, ltd ed, o&r, op
Subj: Connecticutana, med
S/S: Appr libr collec, search serv

Danielson—4553

EXTENSIVE SEARCH SERVICE
Squaw Rock Rd, 06239.
Tel 203-774-1203
SAN 158-605X
Owner, David Haveles
Estab 1981. Cat 3x ann
Types: Juv, op, hp papbk, used
Subj: Connecticutana, local hist, mys-
tery & detective, sci fiction & fan-
tasy, Walt Disney titles, comics &
comic-related bks
S/S: Games, orig art, posters, search
serv, toys, ephemera

Darien—18,892

GILANN BOOKS
PO Box 67, 06820. Tel 203-655-4532
SAN 161-5491
Owner, Gil Rodriquez
5000 Vols
Types: Fine bnd, hb, illus bk, juv
Subj: Mod lit

Fairfield— 54,849

WARREN BLAKE BOOKSELLER
131 Sigwin Dr, 06430.
  Tel 203-259-3278
SAN 158-7617
Owner, Warren Blake
Estab 1972. 1000 Vols. 300 sq ft
Types: O&r, op
Subj: Amer

JOHN M SKUTEL RARE BOOKS
251 Carroll Rd, 06430.
  Tel 203-259-1997
SAN 161-5580
Cat 4x ann
Types: Op, o&r
Subj: Am Indian studies, Amer, avia-
  tion, illus, med
S/S: Autg, maps, mss, prints, sh mus
Branches:
  CONNECTICUT BOOK AUCTION
  GALLERY
  251 Carroll Rd, 06430. Tel 203-259-
  1997
  SAN 161-5599
  Cat 8x ann

Falls Village

R & D EMERSON†
The Old Church, Main St, 06031.
  Tel 203-824-0442
SAN 156-9759
Owners, Robert Emerson & Dorothy
  Emerson
Estab 1948. 50,000 Vols. 3000 sq ft
Types: Fac ed, fine bnd, 1st ed, hb, illus
  bk, incunab, imp, juv, ltd ed, o&r

GEOLOGICAL BOOK CENTER
Box 235, 06031. Tel 203-824-0442
SAN 159-1851
Owners, Robert Emerson & Dorothy
  Emerson
Types: O&r, op
Subj: Geol, mining, petroleum
S/S: Biper, maps

Georgetown

WOLFGANG SCHIEFER BOOKS
  ABOUT BRAZIL
23 Church St, 06829. Tel 203-544-9046
SAN 157-2946

Owner, Wolfgang Schiefer
Estab 1979. 3000 Vols. 400 sq ft. Cat
  2x ann
Types: Op, o&r, imp Brazil

Goshen— 1706

ANGLER'S & SHOOTER'S BOOK-
  SHELF†
06756. Tel 203-491-2500
SAN 161-5637
Owner, Col Henry A Siegel
Estab 1967. 75,000 Vols. Cat 2x ann
Types: Fac ed, 1st ed, hb, imp, incunab,
  new & used, op, o&r
Subj: Hunting & fishing
S/S: Appr libr collec, biper, orig art,
  prints

Granby— 7956

WILLIAM & LOIS PINKNEY ANTI-
  QUARIAN BOOKS†
240 N Granby Rd, 06035.
  Tel 203-653-7710
SAN 161-5645
Owners, William Pinkey & Lois
  Pinkney
Estab 1960. 12,000 Vols
Types: 1st ed, illus bk, juv, op, o&r
Subj: Amer, New Yorkiana, Western
  Amer
S/S: Prints, sh mus

Hamden— 51,071

ANTIQUE BOOKS
3651 Whitney Ave, 06518. Tel 203-281-
  6606
SAN 158-9695
Owner, Willis O Underwood
Estab 1972. 20,000 Vols. 1950 sq ft.
  Cat 6x ann
Types: 1st ed, hb, juv, o&r, op, used
Subj: Agr, hist, sci-tech, 19th century lit
S/S: Appr libr collec, maps

DAVID LADNER BOOKS
34 Wakefield St (Mail add: PO Box
  6179, Whitneyville, 06517).
  Tel 203-288-6575
SAN 158-2720
7000 Vols

Types: Fac ed, fine bnd, 1st ed, hb, illus
bk, imp, ltd ed, o&r, op, remd, used
Subj: Art, bibliog, literary criticism,
whales & whaling, Latin Am, Hebr,
Gr, Slavic langs
S/S: Appr libr collec, biper, maps

Hartford — 136,392

WALTER E HALLBERG — BOOK-
SELLER
16 Hawthorn St, 06105.
Tel 203-524-1618
SAN 158-8702
Owner, Walter E Hallberg
Estab 1935. 5000 Vols
Types: O&r, op
Subj: Connecticutana
S/S: Maps, prints

McBRIDE FIRST EDITIONS
157 Sisson Ave, 06105.
Tel 203-523-7707
SAN 158-2690
Owner, William M McBride
Estab 1978. 3000 Vols
Types: 1st ed, hb, o&r, op, used
Subj: Drama, fiction, humor, poetry
S/S: Appr libr collec, automobile adv
from 1900 to present
Branches:
JUMPING FROG
161 S Whitney St, 06105. Tel 203-
523-7707
SAN 170-2599
Dir, Deidre K Whitlock
Estab 1983
Types: 1st ed, hb, op, o&r, used, juv
Subj: Fiction, drama, humor, poetry,
literary firsts
S/S: Auto advertising 1895-present

Morris — 1899

ROBERT SHUHI — BOOKS
Rte 63 (Mail add: PO Box 268, 06763).
Tel 203-567-5231
SAN 161-5831
Owner, Robert Shuhi
Estab 1970. 30,000 Vols. Cat
Types: 1st ed, illus bk, ltd ed, o&r, used
Subj: Amer, biog, gardening, natural
hist, sports, military

New Canaan — 17,931

JAN & LARRY MALIS†
PO Box 211, 06840. Tel 203-966-8510
SAN 161-5890
Owner, Larry Malis; Mgr, Jan Malis
Estab 1971. 3000 Vols
Types: 1st ed, hb, illus bk, juv, ltd ed,
o&r, op, used
Subj: Amer, aviation, hist, soc sci
S/S: Autg, maps, mss, sh mus, paper
ephemera

New Haven — 126,109

HUGH MILLER, BOOKSELLER
216 Crown St, Rm 506, 06510.
Tel 203-481-6309
SAN 161-5939
Owner, Hugh Miller
Estab 1976. 33,000 Vols. 1250 sq ft.
Cat 3-6x ann
Types: 1st ed, ltd ed, new, o&r, op
Subj: Twentieth century poetry in Eng
S/S: Appr libr collec, spec order

OLD BOOK & PHOTO — RUSSELL
NORTON
PO Box 1070, 06504. Tel 203-562
7800
SAN 158-8206
Owner, Russell Norton
Estab 1974
Types: New, o&r, op
Subj: Hist of photog
S/S: Appr libr collec, original photo-
graphs, 19th cent photos

PHAROS BOOKS — FINE FIRST EDI-
TIONS
PO Box 17, 06513. Tel 203-562-0085,
by appt only
SAN 161-5963
Owners, Matthew Jennett & Sheila
Jennett
Estab 1977. 40,000 Vols. Cat 20x ann
Types: 1st ed, fine bnd, imp Gr, illus bk,
juv, ltd ed, o&r
Subj: Ezra Pound: contemporary poetry,
modern lit-Am, British & European
in translation
S/S: Appr libr collec, autg, mss

WILLIAM REESE CO†
409 Temple St, 06511.
Tel 203-789-8081

SAN 158-2704
Mgr, Terry Halladay
Estab 1979. 10,000 Vols. Cat 8x ann
Types: 1st ed, illus bk, o&r
Subj: Am hist & lit, Amer, Eng hist &
   lit, natural hist
S/S: Appr libr collec, maps, mss, orig
   art

R W SMITH—BOOKSELLER
51 Trumbull St, 06510.
   Tel 203-776-5564
SAN 129-5187
Owner, Raymond W Smith
Estab 1975. 15,000 Vols. 200 sq ft. Cat
   3x ann
Types: Op
Subj: Antq, archit, art, photog
S/S: Biper, search serv

C A STONEHILL INC†
282 York St, 06511. Tel 203-865-5141
Owner, Robert J Barry, Jr
Types: O&r, incunabula, mss
Subj: Eng lit & hist
S/S: Appraisals

WHITLOCK'S INC
17 Broadway, 06511. Tel 203-562-9841
SAN 161-6013
Owner, Reverdy Whitlock
Estab 1900
Types: Hb, imp UK, o&r, op, papbk
Subj: Connecticutana
S/S: Appr libr collec, maps, search serv

New Milford—19,420

N FLAYDERMAN & CO, INC
Squash Hollow, 06776.
   Tel 203-354-5567
SAN 161-6056
Admin Asst, Linda Kuhne
Estab 1954. Cat ann
Types: 1st ed, op, o&r
Subj: Military, weapons

SCARLET LETTER BOOKS &
   PRINTS
Candlewood Mountain Rd, 06776.
   Tel 203-354-4181
SAN 161-6072
Owner, Kathleen A Lazare
Estab 1971. 3000 Vols. 200 sq ft. Cat
   ann

Types: 1st ed, illus bk, o&r, op, hb
Subj: Antq
S/S: Appr libr collec, biper, maps, orig
   art, prints, search serv, 20th century
   wood engravings

Norfolk—2156

JOHN S CRAIG PHOTOGRAPHIC
   HISTORIAN
PO Box 656, 06058. Tel 203-542-5479
SAN 157-5627
Owner, John S Craig
Estab 1970. 5000 Vols. 1600 sq ft
Types: Fac ed, 1st ed, illus bk, o&r, op,
   remd, new & used
Subj: Photog
S/S: Appr libr collec, biper, prints,
   photog equip

Northford

ELLIOT'S BOOKS, OUT OF PRINT
   SPECIALISTS
Forest Rd, Box 6, 06472.
   Tel 203-484-2184
SAN 158-4774
Owner, E Ephraim
Estab 1957. 500,000 Vols. 10,000 sq ft
Types: 1st ed, illus bk, incunab, imp, ltd
   ed, o&r, op, papbk
Subj: Art, humanities, soc sci, scholarly
   lit, sci-tech
S/S: Appr libr collec, autg, mss, per,
   search serv, sh mus

North Stonington—4219

CARTOGRAPHICS
PO Box 67, 06359. Tel 203-535-3152
SAN 159-0162
Owner, Jon K Rosenthal
Estab 1978. 400 sq ft. Cat 2x ann
Subj: Reference, antq maps & atlases,
   prints
S/S: Appr libr collec

Norwalk—77,767

HAROLD J MASON INC
25 Van Zant St, 06855. Tel 203-838-
   6809
SAN 159-3919

Mgr, Robert Edwards
Hq: Phoenix, AZ

Old Mystic

OLD MYSTIC BOOKSHOP†
58 Main St, 06372. Tel 203-536-6932
SAN 161-6153
Owner, Charles B Vincent
Cat ann
Types: 1st ed, o&r, op, used
Subj: Amer, genealogy, local hist, Can, marine
S/S: Maps, prints, search serv

Orange—13,237

I-AM-I BOOKS
474 Orange Center Rd, 06477.
Tel 203-795-5382
SAN 161-617X
Owner, Suzanne Kaftal
Estab 1973. 60,000 Vols
Types: 1st ed, hb, illus bk, juv, op, papbk, used
Subj: Amer, art, biog, hist
S/S: Biper

Pawcatuck—5255

THE RAVEN BOOKSHOP
40 W Broad St, 06379.
Tel 203-599-3535
SAN 157-2954
Owner, James A Faiella
Estab 1973. 3000 Vols
Types: Fine bnd, 1st ed, hb, illus bk, juv, o&r, op, used
S/S: Appr libr collec, prints, search serv

Pomfret—2775

ROGER BLACK
Route 44 (Mail add: PO Box 214, 06259). Tel 203-928-2862
SAN 161-6188
Mgr, Judith A Black
Estab 1975. 6000 Vols. Cat 2x ann
Types: O&r, op, used
Subj: Connecticutana
S/S: Search serv

Putnam—6855

BLUE STAR BOOKSTORE
355½ Kennedy Dr (Mail add: Box 161, 06260). Tel 203-928-4832
SAN 157-2962
Owners & Mgrs, David Bates & Susannah Bates
Estab 1976. 24,000 Vols. Cat 6x ann
Types: 1st ed, hb, illus bk, imp, juv, ltd ed, new, op, o&r, papbk, used
Subj: Mystery & detective, sci fiction & fantasy, Western Amer
S/S: Biper, per, prints, search serv, staty

Sandy Hook

CHISWICK BOOKSHOP INC†
Walnut Tree Hill Rd, 06482.
Tel 203-426-3220
SAN 161-6234
Owners, Herman Cohen & Aveve Cohen
Estab 1935, Cat
Types: 1st ed, hb, illus bk, ltd ed, o&r
Subj: Bibliog, calligraphy, typography

Sherman—2281

KATHLEEN & MICHAEL LAZARE
PO Box 117, 06784. Tel 203-354-4181
SAN 156-8558
Owners & Mgrs, Kathleen Lazare & Michael Lazare
Estab 1970. Present Owner 1975.
10,000 vols. Cat 2-4x ann
Types: 1st ed, hb, illus bk, juv, o&r, op
S/S: Appr libr collec, maps, orig art, posters, search serv, spec order

Southport

THE MUSEUM GALLERY BOOK-SHOP
363 Pequot, 06490. Tel 203-259-7114
SAN 122-235X
Owner, Henry B Caldwell
Estab 1976. 10,000 Vols. 610 sq ft. Cat
Types: Op, o&r
Subj: Archaeol, archit, art, prints & dec arts
S/S: Search serv

LAURENCE WITTEN RARE BOOKS
181 Old Post Rd (Mail add: PO Box
490, 06490). Tel 203-255-3474
SAN 161-6285
Owner, Laurence C Witten II; Assoc,
Kenneth M Nesheim
Estab 1951. 2000 Vols. 3000 sq ft. Cat
2x ann
Types: Incunab, illus bk, o&r
Subj: Medieval & Renaissance
S/S: Appr libr collec, autg, maps, mss,
orig art

South Woodstock

CHARLES B WOOD III INC, ANTI-
QUARIAN BOOKSELLERS†
06267. Tel 203-928-4041 (by appt only)
SAN 161-6269
Cat 4x ann
Types: Op, o&r
Subj: Archit, art, sci-tech, photog

Stamford—102,453

JOHN BRIDGE
26 Lanark Rd. Tel 203-324-0541
SAN 161-6307
Owner, John Bridge
Types: Op, used, o&r
Subj: Ancient hist & lit, Greek & Ro-
man antiquity

AVIS & ROCKWELL GARDINER†
60 Mill Rd, 06903. Tel 203-322-1129
SAN 161-6315
Owners, Avis Gardiner & Rockwell
Gardiner
Estab 1946. 6000 Vols
Types: Illus bk, o&r
Subj: Am hist & lit, travel, early maps
& atlases
S/S: Appr libr collec, autg, orig art,
prints, early Am newspr, wholesales
to dealers & museums

Stonington—16,220

BARRY SCOTT†
PO Box 207, 06378. Tel 203-535-2643
SAN 165-1188
Owner, B Scott
Estab 1970. 2000 Vols. Cat
Types: 1st ed, ltd ed, illus bk

Subj: Eng hist & lit, Am hist & lit,
typography, fine print
S/S: Appr libr collec, autg, mss, orig
art, letters

Stratford—50,541

PRESTON C BEYER FINE LITER-
ARY PROPERTY
752A Pontiac Lane, 06497.
Tel 203-375-9073
SAN 161-634X
Owner, Preston Beyer
Estab 1975. 3000 Vols. Cat 4-5x ann
Types: Fac ed, fine bnd, 1st ed, hb, illus
bk, ltd ed, o&r, op, used
Subj: Bks on bks
S/S: Appr libr collec

Watertown—19,489

A CABINET OF BOOKS
PO Box 195, 06795. Tel 203-274-4825
SAN 157-7301
Owners, Lee & Sue Kirk
Estab 1975. 5000 Vols. Cat ann
Types: 1st ed, hb, illus bk, ltd ed, o&r,
op, used
Subj: Hunting & fishing, sci-tech, natu-
ral hist, skating

West Cornwall

DEBORAH BENSON BOOKSELLER
River Rd, 06796. Tel 203-672-6614
SAN 157-2970
Owner, Deborah Benson
Estab 1956. 9000 Vols. Cat 3-4x ann
Types: Fac ed, fine bnd, 1st ed, hb, illus
bk, ltd ed, o&r, op, used
Subj: 18th-20th century lit, for-edge
paintings, bks on diabetes-pre 1920,
Alice in Wonderland variants
S/S: Appr libr collec, mss, search serv

BARBARA FARNSWORTH BOOK-
SELLER
Route 128, 06796. Tel 203-672-6333,
672-6571
SAN 161-6447
Owner, Barbara Farnsworth
Estab 1968. 45,000 Vols. 3600 sq ft.
Cat
Types: 1st ed, fine bnd, hb, illus bk, juv,

ltd ed, o&r, op, used
Subj: Amer, Am hist & lit, Eng hist &
   lit, hort
S/S: Appr libr collec, biper, autg, orig
   art, search serv, sh mus

West Hartford — 61,301

PARK ROAD BOOKSHOP
258 Park Rd, 06119. Tel 203-232-3001
SAN 161-648X
Owner, Ivan S Daugherty Jr
Estab 1976. 10,000 Vols. 950 sq ft. Cat
   2-3x ann
Types: 1st ed, hb, juv, o&r, fine bnd, op
Subj: Amer, hist, biog, scholarly lit
S/S: Appr libr collec, autg, maps, search
   serv

West Haven — 53,184

FULLER'S BOOKS
12 Holcomb St, 06516. Tel 203-933-
   9569
SAN 170-3013
Owner, Paul H Fuller
Estab 1940. 6000 Vols. Cat 4x ann
Types: 1st ed, hb, illus bk, o&r, op,
   used

Westport — 25,290

GUTHMAN AMERICANA†
PO Box 392, 06881. Tel 203-259-9763
Owner, William H Guthman
Subj: Am Revolution, Fr & Indian War,
   Colonial Indian warfare

TURKEY HILL BOOKS
46 Turkey Hill Rd S, 06880.
   Tel 203-255-0041
SAN 158-2712
Owners, Jack L Grogins & Marilyn
   Grogins; Mgr, Jack L Grogins
Estab 1977. 8000 Vols. Cat ann
Types: Fine bnd, 1st ed, hb, illus bk,
   juv, ltd ed, o&r, op, used
Subj: Amer, fiction, poetry
S/S: Orig art, prints, search serv, bk
   fairs

West Redding

PAULA STERNE — BOOKS
Huckleberry Rd, RFD 2, 06896.

Tel 203-938-2756
SAN 161-6498
Owners, George Burgeson & Janice
   Burgeson
Types: O&r, op
Subj: Amer, dogs, guns, sports

Wethersfield — 26,013

E TATRO — BOOKSELLER
60 Goff Rd, 06109. Tel 203-563-7884
SAN 161-6587
Owner, E Tatro
Cat 10x ann
Types: Op, o&r, used
Subj: Health & phys educ, sports, olym-
   pics

Wilton — 15,351

STEPHEN AUSLENDER
PO Box 122, 06897. Tel 203-834-1674
SAN 170-3021
5000 Vols. Cat ann
Types: Hb, illus bk, imp, papbk
Subj: Military, tech

Windsor — 25,204

CEDRIC L ROBINSON, BOOK-
   SELLER
597 Palisado Ave, 06095.
   Tel 203-688-2582
SAN 161-6617
Owners, Cedric L Robinson & Regina
   M Robinson
20,000 Vols. Cat 3x ann
Types: Op, hb
Subj: Art, archit, Am hist & lit, Am
   Indian studies, oceanog, Western
   Amer
S/S: Appr libr collec, autg, maps, mss,
   prints, appraisals

DELAWARE

Hockessin

DALE A BRANDRETH, BOOKS
White Briar, 19707. Tel 302-239-4608
SAN 158-281X
Present Owner 1969. 25,000 Vols. 800
   sq ft. Cat 14x ann
Types: Fac ed, fine bnd, for lang, imp,

ltd ed, new & used, o&r
Subj: Chess, checkers
S/S: Appr libr collec, autg, biper, mss

Milford — 5356

KEN BESSINGER
916 S Dupont Blvd, 19963.
Tel 302-422-5483
SAN 161-6676
Estab 1966. 2500 Vols
Types: Hb, juv, op, used
Subj: Discovery & explor, mystery &
detective
S/S: Biper, search serv

Newark — 25,247

ATTIC BOOKS
1175 Pleasant Hill Rd, 19711.
Tel 302-738-7477
SAN 161-6706
Owner, C W Mortenson
Estab 1947. 20,000 Vols
Types: 1st ed, hb, imp, incunab, op,
o&r, used
S/S: Appr libr collec, autg, orig art,
prints, search serv

HORSEHOE LANE BOOKS
436 New London Rd, 19711.
Tel 302-731-9445
SAN 161-6714
Owners, Rob Eisenberg & Lynne Eisen-
berg
Estab 1975. Present Owner 1976. 3500
Vols. 500 sq ft. Cat
Types: O&r, op
Subj: Delawariana, hort, illus, mystery
& detective, natural hist
S/S: Prints

New Castle — 4907

OAK KNOLL BOOKS†
414 Delaware St, 19720.
Tel 302-328-7232
SAN 161-6722
Owner, Cedar Lane Inc; Mgrs, Robert D
Fleck, et al
Estab 1976. 20,000 Vols. 1500 sq ft.
Cat 8x ann
Types: Fac ed, 1st ed, hb, imp, o&r, op
Subj: Bibliog, bks on bks
S/S: Appr libr collec

Oceanview — 495

ANTIQUE PRINTS
Central Ave, PO Box 48, 19970.
Tel 302-539-6702
SAN 158-5533
Owner, Martha Seamans; Mgr & Buyer,
Robert Seamans
Estab 1972. 6000 Vols
Types: Illus bk, o&r
Subj: Bks prior to 1880
S/S: Autg, orig art, prints, sh mus,
engravings

Wilmington — 70,195

HOLLYOAK BOOK SHOP
300 E Delaware Ave, 19809.
Tel 302-798-2708
SAN 158-9725
Owner, Morton Rosenblatt
Estab 1970. 40,000 Vols. 1000 sq ft
Types: Fine bnd, hb, illus bk, juv,
papbk, remd, used
Subj: Military, travel
S/S: Appr libr collec, biper, orig art,
prints

PALMA BOOK SERVICE
120 W 19th St, PO Box 602, 19899
SAN 159-1576
Mgr, Harry M Stuart
4000 Vols
Types: Hb, op, used
Subj: Amer, biog, hist

DISTRICT OF COLUMBIA

Washington — 637,651

BICKERSTAFF & BARCLAY
PO Box 28452, 20005
SAN 158-6947
Estab 1979. Cat 1-2x ann
Types: Used, op, o&r
Subj: Photog
S/S: Search serv

BOOKED UP INC†
1209 31st St NW, 20007.
Tel 202-965-3244
SAN 161-6846
Owners, Larry McMurty & Marcia
McGhee Carter
Types: 1st eds
Subj: Lit, travel

Q M DABNEY & CO, INC†
PO Box 42026, 20015.
  Tel 301-881-1470
Owner, Michael E Schnitter
Subj: Mil, hist, Amer, law

ESTATE BOOK SALES
2824 Pennsylvania Ave NW, 20007.
  Tel 202-965-4274
SAN 161-6919
Owners, Howard Wilcox & Chris
  Cooper
Estab 1948. 25,000 Vols. Cat
S/S: Prints, bookbinding

WILLIAM F HALE — BOOKS†
1222 31st St NW, 20007.
  Tel 202-338-8272
Types: General antiquarian
Subj: Visual & performing arts, travel

LLOYD BOOKS
1346 Connecticut Ave NW, Suite 719,
  20036. Tel 202-785-3826
SAN 129-5098
Owner, Stacy B. Lloyd; Merch Mgr,
  Margaret Davis
Estab 1980. 500 Vols. 525 sq ft. Cat
  ann
Types: Fine bnd, 1st ed, hb, illus bk, ltd
  ed, o&r
Subj: Amer, hist, sports, travel, mari-
  time
S/S: Appr libr collec, search serv

THE OLD PRINT GALLERY†
1220 31st St NW. Tel 202-965-1818
Owner, James C Blakely
Types: 18th & 19th cent Am prints,
  maps, paper, conservation, plate bks,
  atlases

SECOND STORY BOOKS†
3236 P St NW, 20007.
  Tel 202-338-6860
SAN 145-3106
Owner, Allen Stypeck; Mgr, Alan Fuller
Estab 1974. 500,000 Vols. 15,000 sq ft.
  Cat
Types: Fac ed, fine bnd, 1st ed, hb, illus
  bk, incunabula, ltd ed, o&r, op,
  papbk, remd, used
S/S: Appr libr collec, autg, search serv

OSCAR SHAPIRO†
3726 Connecticut Ave NW, 20008.
  Tel 202-244-4446
SAN 161-7222

Estab 1961. 5000 Vols. Cat
Types: Op, o&r
Subj: Chess, mus, violin

WAYWARD BOOKS
1002-B Pennsylvania Ave SE, 20002.
  Tel 202-546-2719
SAN 161-7419
Owners, Sybil Pike & Doris Grumbach
Present Owner 1976. 8000 Vols. 750 sq
  ft. Cat
Types: 1st ed, illus bk, op, pvt presses
Subj: Mod lit, Afro-Amer fict
S/S: Search serv

FLORIDA

Atlantic Beach — 7847

TAPPIN BOOK MINE
705 Atlantic Blvd, 32233.
  Tel 904-246-1388
SAN 161-746X
Owner, F Donald Tappin
Estab 1975. 30,000 Vols. 1600 sq ft
Types: 1st ed, hb, illus bk, juv, o&r, op,
  papbk, used
Subj: Military, nautical
S/S: Appr libr collec, search serv

Bonita Springs — 1932

JEAN COHEN BOOKS
PO Box 654, 33923. Tel 813-992-1262
SAN 161-7540
Owner, Jean Cohen
Estab 1968. 30,000 Vols. Cat 25x ann
Types: Hb, op, used

Boynton Beach — 35,624

GILBERT K WESTGARD II
703 S W 18th St, 33435.
  Tel 305-737-4294
SAN 157-566X
Owner, Gilbert K Westgard II
Types: Fac ed, 1st ed, hb, juv, ltd ed,
  new & used, o&r, op
Subj: By & about Horatio Alger Jr

Clearwater — 85,450

A BLUE MOON BOOKS &
  RECORDS
1415 Cleveland St, 33515.

Tel 813-443-7444
SAN 158-1570
Owner, Lowell Kelly
Estab 1979. 25,000 Vols. 1500 sq ft
Types: 1st ed, fine bnd, hb, illus bk, ltd
ed, o&r, op, papbk, used
Subj: Art, Civil War, comedy, fiction,
Floridiana, metaphys & occult, pho-
tog, rel, Southern Amer
S/S: Rec
Branches:
AVATAR BOOKS & RECORDS
1415 Cleveland St, 33515. Tel 813-443-
7444
SAN 158-1597

THE MIDNIGHT BOOKMAN
1908 Seagull Dr, Largo, 33546.
Tel 813-536-4029 (by appt)
SAN 170-3005
Owner, Lee Harrer
Estab 1981. 1000 Vols.
Types: O&r, op
S/S: Search serv

Coral Gables—43,241

BOOK WAREHOUSE INC
2010 Ponce De Leon, 33134.
Tel 305-448-3223
SAN 124-471X
Owners, Arthur S Rosichan & Florence
Rosichan
Estab 1977. 18,000 Vols.
Types: Fine bnd, 1st ed, hb, illus bk,
imp, juv, op, o&r
Subj: Amer, antq, archit, art, dance,
drama, hist, metaphys & occult,
nature & environ, photog, psychol,
rel, sci-tech, sports
S/S: Appr libr collec, search serv

Daytona Beach—54,176

MANDALA BOOKS
224 S Beach St, 32014.
Tel 904-255-6728
SAN 158-2844
Estab 1981. 35,000 Vols. 2000 sq ft.
Cat 2x ann
Types: Fine bnd, 1st ed, hb, illus bk,
o&r, op, papbk, remd, used
Subj: Art, biog, fiction, metaphys &
occult, oceanog, rel studies, travel
S/S: Rec

Fernandina Beach—7224

GUIDEWAYS INC
95 Sea Marsh Rd, Amelia Island,
32034. Tel 904-261-8711
SAN 161-7931
Owner, I E Deibert
Estab 1976. Cat ann
Types: Hb, o&r, op, papbk, used
Subj: Amer, nature & environ, oceanog

Fort Lauderdale—153,256

ROBERT A HITTEL—BOOKSELLER
3020 N Federal Hwy, Bldg 6, 33306.
Tel 305-563-1752
SAN 126-6373
Owner, Robert A Hittel
Estab 1974. 80,000 Vols. 2600 sq ft
Types: Fine bnd, 1st ed, hb, illus bk,
juv, ltd ed, new & used, o&r, op,
mm papbk, remd
Subj: Am Indian studies, Amer
S/S: Appr libr collec, autg, biper, mss,
search serv

WAKE-BROOK HOUSE BOOKS
PO Box 11072, 33339.
Tel 305-563-9301
SAN 161-7966
Owner, Edwin P Geauque
Estab 1947. 2000 Vols. Cat
Types: 1st ed, hb, op, papbk, o&r
Subj: Boats, rum running, Seminole
Indians, S Fla hist
S/S: Gold stamping
See Also: Hyannis, MA

Gainesville—81,371

VIVIAN KANTOR, BOOKSELLER
3621 NW 7th Ave, 32607.
Tel 904-373-6843
SAN 161-8180
Owner & Mgr, Vivian Kantor
Estab 1960. 5000 Vols
Types: Op, o&r, used
Subj: Soc sci, Latin Am

Hollywood—117,188

OMNI GRAPHIC MEDIA CO
2231 Washington St, Suite 206, 33020.
Tel 305-922-4881

SAN 129-055X
Owner, Michael Weinstock; Mgr, Steven
Olit
Estab 1979. 2000 Vols
Types: Op, remd, used
Subj: Art, music
S/S: Orig art, prints, sh mus

Jacksonville— 540,898

DOWNTOWN BOOKSHOP
100 E Adam St, 32202.
Tel 904-356-9271
SAN 161-8385
Owner, Mike Pivko; Mgrs, Guy Har-
wood & Helen Flank
Types: New & used, o&r, remd
S/S: Appr libr collec

EUGENE F KRAMER
2804 Downing St, 32205.
Tel 904-388-1123
By appointment only
Subj: Amer, US mil, bk restoration &
preservation

THE OLD BOOKSHOP
3142 Beach Blvd, 32207.
Tel 904-398-6163
SAN 161-8466
Owner, Bob L Gavilan
Estab 1970. 100,000 Vols. 4000 sq ft
Types: 1st ed, hb, op, papbk, used,
comics
S/S: Appr libr collec, search serv, com-
ics

Lake Worth— 27,048

ALLA T FORD RARE BOOKS
114 S Palmway Ave, 33460.
Tel 305-585-1442
SAN 161-8644
Owner, Alla T Ford
Estab 1956. 10,000 Vols. Cat
Types: 1st ed, hb, juv, op, o&r, minia-
tures
Subj: Sci fiction & fantasy, Edgar Bur-
roughs, L Frank Baum, Sherlock
Holmes
S/S: Appr libr collec

Lantana— 8048

RICHARD G UHL
6319 Pine Dr, 33462. Tel 305-582-4029
SAN 161-8709
Types: 1st ed
Subj: Anthrop, art, sci-tech
S/S: Biper

Largo— 58,977

GEPPI'S COMIC WORLD
2226 East Bay Dr, 33541.
Tel 813-585-0226
SAN 156-8175
Owner, Steve Geppi; Mgr, Jay Warmke
Hq: Baltimore, MD

Lauderhill— 37,271

RENREL BOOKS
1843 NW 58th Ave, 33313
SAN 161-8733
Owners, Richard V Lerner
Estab 1979. 4000 Vols
Types: 1st ed, hb, illus bk, ltd ed, o&r,
op, used
S/S: Search serv

Longboat Key— 4843

FLEURON BOOKS
541 Chipping Lane, 33548.
Tel 813-383-5969
SAN 161-8784
Owner, Weber deVore
Estab 1955. Cat
Types: Hb, imp, new & used, o&r, op
Subj: Sports, angling

Margate— 36,044

AMERICAN LIBRARY SERVICE
SOUTH
6420 Brandywine, 33063.
Tel 305-972-1987
SAN 161-8814
Owner, Raphael Gould; Associate,
Eleanor Forte
Estab 1975
Branch. Buys indep & through hg
Types: Op
S/S: Search serv
Hq: New City, NY

Miami—346,931

BOOKS & ART PRINTS STORE
4329 SW 8th St, 33134.
  Tel 305-444-5001
SAN 161-8938
Owner, Al Ledoux
Estab 1949. 100,000 Vols. 1200 sq ft
Types: 1st ed, papbk, used
Subj: Art, fiction, hist, metaphys &
  occult, nonfiction, poetry, rel studies,
  comics
S/S: Gr cds, maps, per, prints, search
  serv, sh mus

DEMERARA BOOK SERVICE
13018 SW 85 Rd, 33156.
  Tel 305-238-8761
SAN 161-9004
Owner, Robert M Hamer; Mgr, John
  Eckhoff
Estab 1975. 40,000 Vols. 1500 sq ft.
  Cat 2x ann
Types: Fine bnd, 1st ed, hb, illus bk,
  imp, juv, ltd ed, o&r, op, remd, used
Subj: Art, Floridiana, Latin Am, mod
  lit, natural hist
S/S: Appr libr collec, maps, prints,
  search serv, sh mus

Miami Beach—96,298

THE BOOKFINDERS INC
PO Box 2021, Ocean View Beach,
  33140. Tel 305-538-4795
SAN 161-9160
Pres, Leon Cooke
Estab 1935. 65,000 Vols
Types: Col text, hb, new & used, op,
  papbk, remd, imp
Subj: Art, Eng hist & lit, music
S/S: Rec, search serv, sh mus

Micanopy—737

LEWIS ANTIQUES
PO Box 410, 32667. Tel 904-466-3061
SAN 161-9217
Owners, Sylvia Lewis & Jerry Lewis
Estab 1972. 10,000 Vols. 4000 sq ft
Types: Fine bnd, 1st ed, hb, juv, ltd ed,
  o&r, op, used
S/S: Autg, biper, maps, orig art, sh mus

Naples—17,581

ROBERT C DEMAREST BOOK-
  SELLER
1166 Royal Palm Dr, 33940.
  Tel 813-262-3363
SAN 157-7360
Owner, Robert C Demarest
Present Owner 1978. 1000 Vols. Cat 2x
  ann
Types: Op, o&r, new
Subj: Med, pharmacy, drug culture
S/S: Search serv
Branches:
  MYCOPHILE BOOKS
  PO Box 93, 33939
  SAN 157-0919

Newberry—1826

SAMADHI—METAPHYSICAL LIT-
  ERATURE
SW 8th St & W Central Ave, PO Box
  729, 32669. Tel 904-472-3451
SAN 159-2181
Owner, D E Whelan
Estab 1970. 2000 Vols. Cat 2x ann
Types: 1st ed, hb, o&r, op, used
Subj: Astrol, magic & conjuring,
  metaphysics, yoga, alchemy, Atlantis,
  herbology, hermetics, homeopathy,
  UFOs
S/S: Gifts, maps, orig art, posters,
  prints, search serv

North Miami—42,566

LUCILE COLEMAN, BOOKS,
  A-TO-Z BOOK SERVICE†
PO Box 610813, 33261
SAN 161-9306
Owner, Lucile Coleman
Estab 1961. Cat
Types: 1st ed, hb, illus bk, juv, o&r, op,
  papbk, used, op only
Subj: Amer, biog, fiction, poetry, 19th
  & 20th century lit, sci fiction
S/S: Biper, search serv

Palm Beach—9729

THE OLD BOOKSHOP
113 N County Rd, 33480.

Tel 305-833-3920, 585-0395
SAN 157-5643
Owner, Jack M D Owen
Estab 1965. Present Owner 1977.
12,000 Vols. 400 sq ft. Cat
Types: Fac ed, fine bnd, 1st ed, hb, ltd
ed, illus bk, imp, juv, o&r, op,
papbk, used
Subj: Biog, Amer, Floridiana, nautical,
travel
S/S: Appr libr collec, search serv

CARROLL MINER ROBINSON OLD
BOOKS
251 Park Ave (Mail add: PO Box 501,
33480). Tel 305-833-2028
SAN 161-9551
Owner, Carroll M Robinson
Estab 1966. 5000 Vols.
Types: Fine bnd, hb, papbk
Subj: Auto, Floridiana, gardening, golf,
hist, hunting & fishing, Eng, Fr &
Ger lang, theatrical personalities

Pensacola—57,619

FARLEY'S OLD & RARE BOOKS
5855 Tippen Ave, 32504.
Tel 904-477-8282
SAN 157-7379
Owners, Owen Farley & Moonean
Farley
Present Owner 1975. 6000 Vols. 700 sq
ft
Types: Fine bnd, 1st ed, hb, illus bk,
imp UK, juv, ltd ed, o&r, op, used
Subj: Hist, military, theol
S/S: Appr libr collec, search serv, sh
mus

GALVEZ BOOKS & SILVER INC
208 S Florida Blanca St, 32501.
Tel 904-432-2874
SAN 158-2852
Mgr, Lana Servies
Estab 1979. 11,000 Vols. 820 sq ft
Types: Hb, o&r, op, used
S/S: Maps, prints, search serv

Plantation—48,501

HISTORICAL BOOKSHELF LTD
4210 SW 3rd St, 33317.
Tel 305-583-2378

SAN 159-009X
Owner, Jim Wilkinson; Mgr, Pat
Wilkinson
Estab 1978. 6000 Vols. 733 sq ft
Types: 1st ed, hb, imp, o&r, op, used
Subj: Aviation, military, political
thought
S/S: Appr libr collec, prints, search serv

Saint Augustine—11,985

GLOBE & ANCHOR BOOK CO
3 Arenta (Mail add: PO Box 1173,
32084). Tel 904-824-4617
SAN 161-9802
Types: Hb, Am imprints
See Also: C R Sanders, Jr

RARE BOOKS, MAPS & PRINTS
PO Box 3005, 32084.
Tel 904-829-9782
SAN 158-9989
Owner, A Mueller
Estab 1962. Present Owner 1982. 5000
Vols. 500 sq ft
Types: Fine bnd, 1st ed, hb, illus bk,
incunab, imp, o&r, op, used
Subj: Floridiana
S/S: Maps, orig art, prints, sh mus

C R SANDERS JR
172 Avenida Menendez (Mail add:
9 Seapark Dr, 32084).
Tel 904-471-2832
SAN 161-9810
Subj: Amer, Civil War, military
See Also: Globe & Anchor Book Co

Saint Petersburg—236,893

JOHN C DAUB
316-4th Ave N, Apt 308-L, 88701.
Tel 813-896-4171
SAN 161-9853
Types: Imp, o&r
Subj: Amer, Western Pennsylvania

LIGHTHOUSE BOOKS†
148 Central Ave, 33701.
Tel 813-822-3278
SAN 161-9888
Owner, Michael F Slicker
Estab 1977. 10,000 Vols. 1000 sq ft.
Cat 3x ann

Types: Fac ed, fine bnd, 1st ed, hb, illus
bk, incunab, ltd ed, o&r, op, remd
Subj: Floridiana, Southern Amer
S/S: Appr libr collec, orig art, prints,
search serv, sh mus

WALLACE A ROBINSON
461 12th Ave N, 33701.
    Tel 813-823-3280 (by appt)
SAN 170-1975
Owner, Wallace A Robinson
Estab 1981. 40,000 Vols. Cat 2x ann
Types: Fac ed, fine bnd, 1st ed, hb, illus
bk, juv, o&r, papbk
Subj: Humor
S/S: Appr libr collec, biper, maps, mss,
orig art, prints, search serv, sh mus

Sarasota—48,868

ACETO BOOKMEN
5721 Antietam Dr, 33581.
    Tel 813-924-9170
SAN 161-9942
Owner, Charles D Townsend
Estab 1961
Types: Hb, o&r, used
Subj: Amer, biog, genealogy, hist
S/S: Appr libr collec

J W HARMAND & SONS, LTD
1468 Main St, 33577.
    Tel 813-955-4900
SAN 157-9606
Owner & Mgr, John Harmand
15,000 Vols
Types: 1st ed, hb, juv, o&r, op, used
Subj: Amer
S/S: Prints, search serv, antq

Tampa—271,523

FINE PRINT
509 Franklin St, 33602.
    Tel 813-228-0871
SAN 128-732X
Owners, Janet Swarnf & Charles
Swarnf; Mgr, Judith L McAfee
Types: Hb, juv, papbk, remd
S/S: Gifts, gr cds, spec order

McFARLAND BOOKS
112 N Gilchrist Ave, 33606.
    Tel 813-251-4858
SAN 162-0193

Owner & Mgr, O S McFarland
5000 Vols. Cat ann
Types: Hb
Subj: Mystery & detective, sci fiction &
fantasy

RED HORSE AT YBOR SQUARE
1901 N 13th St, 33605.
    Tel 813-248-8859
SAN 162-0223
Owner, Lucy O'Brien
Estab 1965. 2000 Vols
Types: Hb, op
Subj: Amer, archit, art, fiction, Floridi-
ana, for lang, hist, military, trades
S/S: Biper, gr cds, sh mus, maps, per

GEORGIA

Athens—42,549

HORSE TRADER ANTIQUE MALL
1855 W Broad St, 30606.
    Tel 404-548-5010
SAN 158-8230
Owner, C A Rowland
Estab 1980. 3000 Vols
Types: 1st ed, hb, illus bk, juv, o&r, op,
used

Atlanta—425,022

AABS-ATLANTA ANTIQUARIAN
BOOKSELLERS
1387 Oxford Rd NE, 30326.
SAN 162-0576
Owner, James F Kirsch
Estab 1979. 10,000 Titles. Cat 1-3x
ann
Types: Op, used
Subj: Arts & crafts, bks on bks, hist,
linguistics, music, philos, psychol,
scholarly lit, fine & applied arts, hist
of sci, tech
S/S: Search serv, collections built

HARVEY DAN ABRAMS—BOOK-
SELLER†
30703 Peachtree Rd, 30341.
    Tel 404-233-6763
SAN 162-0584
Owner, Harvey Dan Abrams
Estab 1960

Types: 1st ed, incunab, o&r, remd
Subj: Southern Amer, Georgiana, black studies, Am Indian studies, Amer
S/S: Appr libr collec, autg, maps, mss, prints

JULIAN BURNETT BOOKS
PO Box 229, 30301. Tel 404-252-5812
SAN 158-4359
Owner, John Burnett Morris
Present Owner 1980. 3000 Vols. Cat 2x ann
Types: 1st ed, fac ed, fine bnd, hb, illus bk, incunab, imp, ltd ed, op, o&r
Subj: Maritime, naval, Panama canal, nautical documents & autographs
S/S: Appr libr collec, maps, mss, search serv

COLLECTOR'S WORLD
5351-1 Buford Hwy, 30340.
  Tel 404-452-7102
SAN 158-1724
Owner, Steve Folio
Estab 1980. 7500 Vols. 1400 sq ft
Types: Hb, illus bk, op, o&r, papbk, used
Subj: Class studies, Ger hist & lit, military, nonfiction
S/S: Autg, biper, prints, sh mus, vintage photog

CONCORD BOOK SERVICE
Box 13672, 30324
SAN 129-5578
Owner, Ross Cockrell
Estab 1962. Present Owner 1980
Types: O&r, op
S/S: Appr libr collec, search serv, spec order

DAVID McCORD BOOKS
1069 Juniper St NE, 30309.
  Tel 404-874-7761
SAN 159-1916
Owner, David McCord
Estab 1978. 5000 Vols. 250 sq ft. Cat 4x ann
Types: Fac ed, fine bnd, 1st ed, hb, illus bk, juv, ltd ed, o&r, op, used
Subj: Amer, black studies, Latin Am, photog, West Indies, Am Indian
S/S: Appr libr collec, autg, biper, prints, search serv

THE OLD BOOK SCOUT—JIM McMEANS
4175 Roswell Rd, 30342.
  Tel 404-257-1012
SAN 157-5651
Owner, James O McMeans Jr
Present Owner 1980. 4000 Vols. Cat 4x ann
Types: 1st ed, hb, o&r, op, used
Subj: Fiction, Georgiana, hist, natural hist, polit sci, Southern Amer
S/S: Appr libr collec, search serv

OLD NEW YORK BOOKSHOP
1069 Juniper St NE, 30309.
  Tel 404-881-1285
SAN 162-0711
Owner, Cliff Graubart
Estab 1971. 30,000 Vols. Cat
Types: 1st ed, ltd ed, op, used, hb, signed ed
S/S: Appr libr collec, maps, prints

PEACHTREE BOOKSTORE INC
5091 C Buford Hwy, 30340.
  Tel 404-452-1676
SAN 170-8147
Mgr, John Albers
100,000 Vols

YESTERYEAR BOOKSHOP INC†
256 E Paces Ferry Rd NE, 30305.
  Tel 404-237-0163
SAN 162-0843
Owner, Frank Ogden Walsh III
Estab 1971. 22,000 Vols. 1700 sq ft. Cat ann
Types: 1st ed, hb, juv, op, o&r, used
Subj: Am hist & lit, archit, biog, Eur studies, gardening, Georgiana, military, Southern Amer, guns
S/S: Appr libr collec, maps, prints, search serv

Avondale Estates—1313

BOOK SEARCH SERVICE
36 Kensington Rd, 30002.
  Tel 404-294-5398
SAN 157-8340
Owner & Mgr, Edmond D Keith
Estab 1953. 500 Vols. Cat 2x ann
Types: Fac ed, fine bnd, 1st ed, hb, new, o&r, op

Subj: Ch music & hymnology
S/S: Appr libr collec, search serv

Decatur—18,404

COOPER'S BOOKS
2403 Lawrenceville Hwy, 30033.
  Tel 404-636-1690
SAN 157-3101
Owner & Buyer, Emily Cooper; Mgr,
  Wayne Cooper
Estab 1979. 40,000 Vols. 1200 sq ft
Types: 1st ed, hb, for lang, juv, new &
  used, o&r, op, papbk
S/S: Gr cds, prints, appraise stamp
  collec

HOUND DOG PRESS BOOK SHOP
4285 Memorial Dr, Suite A, 30032.
  Tel 404-292-2093
SAN 162-119X
Owner & Mgr, Fred C Bose
Estab 1973, 18,000 Vols. 800 sq ft. Cat
  3x ann
Types: 1st ed, hb, o&r, op
Subj: Appalachia, Georgiana, Southern
  Amer
S/S: Maps, prints, search serv

Marietta—30,805

JUDITH R LONG
2710 Harvest Way, 30062.
  Tel 404-977-0794
SAN 158-4944
Owner, Judith R Long
Estab 1970. 5000 Vols
Types: Op
Subj: Indianiana, local hist

Powersville

O G LANSFORD
31074. Tel 912-956-3484
SAN 162-1580
Mgr, O G Lansford
Estab 1924. 10,000 Vols
Types: Bibles, 1st ed, hb, op, papbk,
  used
Subj: Reference, Ben A Williams, Vardi
  Fisher, Napoleon, Robert E Lee, Sir
  Walter Scott, John Buchan
S/S: Rec, Edison phonographs

Rome—29,654

G S HERRON BOOKS
14 Crosscreek Dr, 30161.
  Tel 404-232-1441
SAN 159-1967
Owner, G S Herron
Estab 1972. 40,000 Vols. 1000 sq ft.
  Cat ann
Types: Hb, juv, o&r, used
Subj: Amer, fiction, genealogy
S/S: Search serv

Rossville—3749

WHISTLES IN THE WOODS
Rte 1, Box 265-A, 30741.
  Tel 404-375-4326
SAN 162-1637
Owners, Robert L Johnson & Mary
  Ellen Johnson
Estab 1954. 4500 Vols. 1200 sq ft. Cat
  3-4x ann
Types: Hb, imp, new & used, op,
  papbk, o&r, remd
Subj: Antq, collecting, natural hist,
  railroadiana, steam engines, water
  wheels, machinery of 19th century,
  indust archaeol, hist of tech, goats
S/S: Appr libr collec, biper, maps, per,
  search serv, broadsides

Savannah—141,634

THE BOOK LADY
414 Bull St, 31401. Tel 912-233-3628
SAN 157-311X
Owner, Anita L Raskin
Estab 1979. 4000 Vols. 1000 sq ft
Types: 1st ed, papbk, hb, illus bk, o&r,
  op, used
S/S: Search serv

LONNIE E EVANS—BOOKS
8 Burbank Blvd, 31406.
  Tel 912-925-5455
SAN 158-2879
Cat 2x ann
Types: 1st ed, hb, illus bk, juv, o&r, op,
  used
Subj: Georgiana, mystery & detective,
  Kay Boyle, Paris in the 1920s, Ger-
  trude Stein, Boys & Girls Series
S/S: Autg, search serv

JACQUELINE LEVINE BOOKS†
107 E Oglethorpe Ave, 31401.
Tel 912-233-8519
SAN 161-6293
Owner, Stanley H Levine; Mgr, Jacqueline Levine
Estab 1938. 10,000 Vols. Cat 2x ann
Types: Ltd ed, op
Subj: Bks on bks, Amer, nautical
S/S: Appr libr collec

Stone Mountain— 4867

MEMORABLE BOOKS
5380 Manor Dr, 30083.
Tel 404-469-5911
SAN 156-9171
Owner, George M Hoak: Mgr, Ella J Hoak
Estab 1979. 12,000 Vols. 1000 sq ft
Types: Fine bnd, 1st ed, hb, illus bk, juv, o&r, op, used
Subj: Anthrop, archaeol, arts & crafts, biog, hist, mod lit, polit sci, psychol, social
S/S: Search serv

Thomasville— 18,463

P R RIEBER
429 S Hansell St, Box 2202, 31792.
Tel 912-226-7415
SAN 157-9002
Owner, P R Rieber
Estab 1976. 6000 Vols. 400 sq ft
Types: 1st ed, hb, juv, op, used
Subj: Black studies, natural hist, hunting & fishing
S/S: Prints, search serv

HAWAII

Hilo— 26,353

BOOKFINDERS OF HAWAII
150 Haili St, 96720. Tel 808-961-5055
SAN 162-1947
Owner, Frances Reed
Estab 1970. 200 Vols. Cat 2x ann
Types: Op
Subj: Hawaiiana, whales & whaling, tropical flora & fauna, volcanoes

Honolulu— 324,871

PACIFIC BOOK HOUSE†
Kilohana Square, 1016 Kapahulu Ave, 96816. Tel 808-737-3475
SAN 162-2102
Owner, Gay N Slavsky
Estab 1963. 6000 Vols. Cat
Types: 1st ed, juv, op, o&r, used
Subj: Hawaiiana, Pacific, Eng & Am lit
S/S: Appr libr collec, autg, maps, mss, prints, sh mus

Kailua— 33,783

TUSITALA BOOKSHOP
116 Hekili St, 96734. Tel 808-262-6343
SAN 162-220X
Owner, Lee Reeve
Estab 1976. 40,000 Vols. 1750 sq ft. Cat
Types: Fine bnd, 1st ed, hb, illus bk, juv, ltd ed, op, o&r, papbk, used
Subj: Hawaiiana, Pacific, Robert Louis Stevenson
S/S: Appr libr collec, autg

Kaneohe— 29,903

ALOHA BOOK CORNER
PO Box 1430, 96744.
Tel 808-235-1562
SAN 158-1481
Owner, Patrick Boland
Estab 1975. 4000 Vols. Cat
Types: O&r, op, used
Subj: Hawaiiana, Pacific

Wailuku— 7979

PRINTS PACIFIC
RR 1, PO Box 276, 96793. Tel 808-244-9787 (by appt)
SAN 159-5946
Owner, Susan Halas
Estab 1979. Cat 2-4x ann
Types: O&r
Subj: Hawaii & the Pacific
S/S: Appr libr collec, maps, orig art, prints, search serv

IDAHO

Boise—102,451

BOISE BOOK MART
1810 W State St, 83702.
  Tel 208-342-3161
SAN 162-2323
Owner, Ted Spangler
Estab 1978. 40,000 Vols
Types: 1st ed, hb, new & used, op,
  papbk
Subj: Idahoana, Western Amer
S/S: Search serv

Lewiston—27,986

OPPORTUNITY BOOKS
659 Thain Rd, 83501.
  Tel 208-746-1538
SAN 162-248X
Owners, Frank Ryset & Lorn Ryset
Estab 1966. 45,000 Vols
Types: Hb, new & used, o&r, papbk
Subj: Rel studies, Western Amer
S/S: Search serv

Nampa—25,112

THE YESTERYEAR SHOPPE†
1221 1st St S, 83651. Tel 208-467-3581
SAN 162-2544
Owner, Dave C Gonzales
Estab 1974. 20,000 Vols. 1650 sq ft
Types: Illus bk, juv, ltd ed, o&r, op,
  papbk
Subj: Amer, Idahoana
S/S: Biper, prints, sh mus, old postcards

ILLINOIS

Barrington—9029

BARRINGTON OLD BOOKSHOP
310 W Northwest Hwy, 60010.
  Tel 312-381-6698
SAN 163-4305
Owner, Juanita Shearer
Estab 1980. Present Owner 1981. 5000
  Vols. 200 sq ft. Cat 12x ann
Types: Fac ed, 1st ed, hb, illus bk, juv,
  ltd ed, o&r, used, op
Subj: Antq, metaphysics, rel, philos
S/S: Appr libr collec, search serv

Berkeley—5467

ESTATE BOOKS
5827 Burr Oak, 60163.
  Tel 312-547-6239
SAN 158-4766
Owner, Rose Lasley
Present Owner 1974. 2000 Vols
Types: 1st ed, hb, illus bk, juv, o&r, op,
  used
Subj: Abraham Lincoln, Chicago
S/S: Search serv

Berwyn—46,849

H POPINSKI BOOKS
4225 East Ave, 60402
SAN 159-1177
Owner, H J Popinski
Types: Fac ed, fine bnd, 1st ed, hb, illus
  bk, incunab, juv, new & used, o&r,
  op, papbk, Czech, Ger, Pol & Sp lang
Subj: World Wars I & II, mil hist &
  related subj
S/S: Biper, search serv

Champaign—58,133

STONEHILL'S ANTIQUARIAN
  BOOKS
806 Richard Lane (Mail add: PO Box
  5015 Sta A, 61820).
  Tel 217-359-2607
SAN 162-2838
Owners, Cecile Steinberg & Allan Stein-
  berg
Estab 1976. 15,000 Vols. 1000 sq ft.
  Cat
Types: Find bnd, 1st ed, hb, illus bk, ltd
  ed, o&r, op, used
Subj: Amer, graphic arts, Illinoisiana,
  scholarly lit
S/S: Appr libr collec, maps, prints,
  search serv, sh mus

Chicago—3,005,072

RICHARD ADAMIAK
1545 E 60th St, 60637.
  Tel 312-955-4571
SAN 158-6157
Owner, Richard Adamiak
Estab 1971. 1000 Vols. Cat ann
Types: Hb, 1st ed, fine bnd, op, o&r

Subj: Econ, law, philos, polit sci
S/S: Appr libr collec, prints, search serv

MARY BETH BEAL
3919 N Claremont Ave, 60618.
Tel 312-539-0105
SAN 159-2734
Owner, Mary Beth Beal
Estab 1974
Appraisals of library collections, autographs, back issue periodicals, maps, mss, prints & photographs

BEASLEY BOOKS
1533 W Oakdale, 60657.
Tel 312-472-4528
SAN 159-0634
Owners, Paul Garon & Elizabeth Garon
Estab 1979. 2000 Vols. Cat 4-6x ann
Types: Modern 1st ed
Subj: Fiction, mystery & detective, radical lit

HERBERT BIBLO BOOKSELLER
5225 Blackstone Ave, 60615.
Tel 312-643-2363
SAN 162-2943
Owner, Herbert Biblo
5000 Vols. Cat
Types: Op
Subj: Africa, black studies, presidents & presidency
S/S: Appr libr collec, search serv

BOOKLEGGER'S
6743 N Sheridan Rd, 60626.
Tel 312-743-4195
SAN 158-2410
Owners, Lawrence VanDeCarr & Janet VanDeCarr
Estab 1980. 7000 Vols. 600 sq ft
Types: 1st ed, hb, illus bk, juv, ltd ed, o&r, op, papbk, used
Subj: Amer

BOOKSELLERS ROW
2445 N Lincoln, 60614.
Tel 312-348-1170
SAN 158-8265
Owner, Howard Lee Cohen
Estab 1978. 30,000 Vols. 2200 sq ft
Types: 1st ed, hb, o&r, op, papbk, used

JAMES M W BORG INC†
8 S Michigan, 60603. Tel 312-236-5911
SAN 156-9821
Estab 1976. 5000 Vols. Cat 6x ann

Types: Fine bnd, 1st ed, hb, illus bk, ltd ed, o&r
Subj: Class studies, Eng hist & lit
S/S: Appr libr collec, autg, mss, orig art

CREEDMOOR BOOKSTORE
2323 W. Foster, 60625.
Tel 312-769-4232
SAN 121-1072
Owners, Chester Slome & H J Morris
Estab 1974. 12,000 Vols
Types: Hb, new & used, op, papbk, remd
Subj: Hunting & fishing, natural hist, Chicago hist, guns

N FAGIN BOOKS
17 N State St, Room 1326, 60602.
Tel 312-236-6540
SAN 128-7796
Owner, Nancy L Fagin
Estab 1980. 2500 Vols. 244 sq ft. Cat 2x ann
Types: Hb, op, hp papbk, used
Subj: Anthrop, bot, nature & environ, zool
S/S: Posters, prints, search serv

THE GLOBE†
Box A3398, 60690. Tel 312-528-6228
SAN 157-3144
Owner & Buyer, George Ritzlin; Mgr, Mary McMichael
Estab 1977. 1200 Vols. Cat
Types: O&r, op, used
Subj: Antq, cartographic reference

HAMILL & BARKER†
400 N Michigan Ave, 60611. Tel 312-644-5933
SAN 162-329X
Owners, Francis Hamill & Terence Tanner
Types: 1st ed, incunab, o&r
S/S: Autg. mss

LARRY LAWS BOOKSTORE
831 Cornelia, 60657. Tel 312-477-9247
SAN 158-152X
Owner & Mgr, Larry Laws
Estab 1975. 100,000 Vols. 5000 sq ft. Cat 4x ann
Types: Op, used
Subj: Dance, performing arts, fairs & exhibitions, nudist mags, Victorian mags, Naval Institute proceedings
S/S: Per, search serv

THE LONDON BOOKSHOP
PO Box 10115, Fort Dearborn Sta,
  60610. Tel 312-642-8417
SAN 162-3443
Owner & Mgr, Glen Norman Wiche
Estab 1974. 5000 Vols. Cat
Types: 1st ed, fine bnd, illus bk, o&r,
  op
Subj: Eng hist & lit
S/S: Autg, maps, orig art, prints

G B MANASEK INC
5805 S Dorchester Ave, 46304.
  Tel 312-684-5122
SAN 158-3743
Director, F J Manasek
Cat ann
Types: O&r
Subj: Astron
S/S: Prints

MARSHALL FIELD & CO†
111 N State St, 60690.
  Tel 312-781-3339
Types: 1st ed, fine bindings, prints, old
  maps, lit & hist, autg

DOUGLAS D MARTIN
1460 N Sandburg Terrace, 305A,
  60610. Tel 312-664-3662
Types: 1st ed
Subj: Lit, mystery & detective fict

KENNETH NEBENZAHL INC†
333 N Michigan Ave, 60601.
  Tel 312-641-2711
SAN 162-3567
Pres, Kenneth Nebenzahl
Estab 1957. 15,000 Vols. Cat 3-4x ann
Types: Imp, 1st ed, incunab, o&r,
  atlases, collected works
Subj: Amer, econ, natural hist, polit sci,
  sci-tech, travel, voyages, exploration,
  soc hist, geog
S/S: Autg, maps, mss, prints

JOSEPH O'GARA BOOKSELLER†
1311 E 57th St, 60637.
  Tel 312-363-0993
SAN 162-3613
Owner, Joseph O'Gara
Estab 1882. 200,000 Vols
Types: Fac ed, 1st ed, hb, op, papbk,
  remd, used
S/S: Humanities, rel

OLD PRINT STORE
1407 N Wells, 60610.
  Tel 312-266-8631
SAN 170-5156
Owner, Jim Nowik
Estab 1977. 300 Vols
Types: Hb, juv, imp
Subj: Illus, antq

ELSIE M PHALEN — OUT-OF-PRINT
  BOOKS
4510 N Troy, 60625. Tel 312-583-0513
SAN 162-3648
Owner, Elsie M Phalen
2000 Vols
Types: 1st ed, op, o&r
Subj: Fiction, nonfiction
S/S: Search serv

A & A PROSSER
3118 N Keating Ave, 60641.
  Tel 312-685-7680
SAN 162-3699
Owners, Antoinette Prosser & Andrew
  Prosser
Estab 1936. 15,000 Vols. Cat ann
Types: Op
Subj: Chesterton & Belloc, pre-Vatican
  II Catholic authors

ROGERS PARK USED BOOKSTORE
1422 W Morse, 60626.
  Tel 312-262-3765
SAN 162-3745
Owner, Jeffrey Ennis
Estab 1975. 23,000 Vols. 1200 sq ft
Types: Fac ed, fine bnd, 1st ed, hb, illus
  bk, ltd ed, op, used, remd

PAUL ROMAINE — BOOKS
635 W Grace, Suite 1104, 60613.
  Tel 312-348-7551
SAN 162-3753
Owner, Paul Romaine
Estab 1927. 2000 Vols
Types: 1st ed, hb, imp, op, o&r, used
Subj: Films & filmmaking, polit sci, jazz
S/S: Appr libr collec

JOHN RYBSKI BOOKSELLER
2319 W 47th Pl, 60609.
  Tel 312-847-5082
SAN 162-3761
Owner, John Rybski
Estab 1968. 20,000 Vols. Cat 3x ann

Types: Hb, imp, op
Subj: Alaskana, Am hist & lit, Arctic, Civil War, Am Indian studies, Latin Am, Revolutionary War, Western Amer, Am bus hist, midwest

HARRY L STERN LTD†
620 N Michigan Ave, 60611.
Tel 312-787-4433
SAN 158-6998
Owner, Harry L Stern
Estab 1976. 1000 Vols. 500 sq ft
Types: Fine bnd, incunab, o&r
Subj: Amer, antq, travel
S/S: Appr libr collec, maps, prints

SULLIVAN SPORTING BOOKS
3748 N Damen Ave, 60618.
Tel 312-472-2638
SAN 162-3826
Owner, John Sullivan
Estab 1969. 2000 Vols
Types: Hb, o&r, op
Subj: Sports

ROBERT W THOMPSON—BOOKS
PO Box 2978, 60690
SAN 162-3877
Cat
Types: O&r, atlases
Subj: Discovery & explor, travel
S/S: Maps, search serv

YESTERDAY
1143 W Addison St (Mail add: 1771 W Cullom Ave, 60613).
Tel 312-248-8087
SAN 157-9843
Owner, Tom Boyle
Estab 1976. 750 Vols. 400 sq ft
Types: 1st ed, hb, illus bk, juv, op, o&r, papbk, used
Subj: Biog
S/S: Autg, biper, posters, prints, sh mus, toys

Cicero—61,232

JOAN MARIE BRUNA
1215 S Lombard Ave, 60650.
Tel 312-652-3459
SAN 162-4016
1000 Vols. Cat
Types: Hb, new & used, op, o&r
Subj: Metaphys & occult, parapsychol

Decatur—94,081

DOROTHY V KECK—OUT-OF-PRINT BOOKS
1360 W Riverview, 62522.
Tel 217-428-5100
SAN 162-4148
Owner, Dorothy V Keck
Estab 1968. 7500 Vols
S/S: Search serv

Deerfield—17,430

NORMA K ADLER BOOKS
59 Eastwood Dr, 60015.
Tel 312-945-8575
SAN 159-608X
Owner, Norma K Adler
Estab 1977
Types: Fine bnd, 1st ed, hb, ltd ed, o&r, op, remd
S/S: Appr libr collec, autg, search serv

Downers Grove—39,274

THOMAS W BURROWS, BOOK-SELLER
PO Box 400, 60515. Tel 312-960-1028
SAN 162-4202
Owner, Thomas W Burrows
Estab 1971. 10,000 Vols. Cat
Types: Fine bnd, 1st ed, hb, illus bk, ltd ed, new & used, o&r, op
Subj: Amer, bks on bks, bibliog, class studies, hist, humanities, scholarly lit
S/S: Search serv

Evanston—73,706

ABRAHAM'S BOOKS
805 Chicago Ave, 60202.
Tel 312-475-1777
SAN 162-2870
Owners, Arnold J Glass & Madelon Glass
Estab 1979. 5000 Vols. 475 sq ft. Cat
Types: Fac ed, fine bnd, 1st ed, hb, op, o&r, remd, used
Subj: Art, hist, philos, psychol, scholarly lit, sociol
S/S: Autg, maps, prints

THE ATHENAEUM
1814 Central St, 60201.
  Tel 312-475-0990
SAN 162-4288
Owner, Morton Robbins; Mgr, Sylvia
  Robbins
Estab 1970. 2000 Vols. 600 sq ft. Cat
Types: Hb, illus bk, imp, op, o&r,
  remd, used
Subj: Amer, art, class studies, drama,
  films & filmmaking, fine arts, music,
  photog, travel
S/S: Appr libr collec, prints

RICHARD S BARNES & CO,
  BOOKS†
821 Foster St, 60201. Tel 312-869-2272
SAN 162-4296
Owner, Patricia N Barnes; Mgr, Sandra
  B Brown
Estab 1951. 15,000 Vols
Types: Fine bnd, 1st ed, hb, juv, op,
  o&r, used
Subj: Biog, hist, mod lit, mystery &
  detective, travel
S/S: Appr libr collec, libr sup

BOOKMAN'S ALLEY
1712 Rear Sherman Ave, 60201.
  Tel 312-869-6999
SAN 158-6033
Owner, Roger Carlson
Estab 1980. 15,000 Vols. 2500 sq ft
Types: 1st ed, hb, illus bk, juv, ltd ed,
  o&r, op, used
Subj: Amer, drama, humor, mod lit,
  poetry, Chicago
S/S: Appr libr collec, prints, search serv,
  sh mus

KENNEDY'S BOOKSHOP†
1911 Central St (Mail add: PO Box 191,
  60204). Tel 312-864-4449, 475-2481
SAN 162-4342
Owner, Ashley Kennedy III
Estab 1962. 20,000 Vols. 1000 sq ft
Types: 1st ed, hb, juv, op, papbk, o&r,
  used
Subj: Amer, biog, hist, military, polit sci,
  sci-tech, transp

Galena—3876

VALLEY BOOKSHOP
304 S Main St (Mail add: PO Box 37,
  61036). Tel 815-777-2506

SAN 162-4466
Estab 1969. 20,000 Vols
Types: O&r, op
Subj: Amer, Illinoisiana, railroadiana,
  Western Amer, Catholic Amer

Galesburg—35,305

VAN NORMAN BOOK CO†
422-424 Bank of Galesburg Bldg,
  61401. Tel 309-343-4516
SAN 162-4423
Owner, C E VanNorman Sr
Estab 1928. 10,000 Vols. Cat 2x ann
Types: O&r
Subj: Amer, Eng hist & lit

Geneva—9881

THOMAS J JOYCE & CO†
8 & 12 S Third St, PO Box 561, 60134.
  Tel 312-232-6383, 232-6388
SAN 162-4458
Owner, Thomas J Joyce
Estab 1975. 6500 Vols. 1100 sq ft. Cat
  2x ann
Types: Fac ed, fine bnd, 1st ed, hb, illus
  bk, juv, ltd ed, o&r, op, pvt presses,
  used
Subj: Amer mod lit, sci fiction & fan-
  tasy, Western Amer, Chicago
S/S: Appr libr collec, autg, maps, mss,
  prints, search serv

Glenview—30,842

HERBERT FURSE—BOOKMAN
1461 Baffin Rd, 60025.
  Tel 312-724-4594
SAN 158-0191
14,000 Titles

Highland Park—30,611

TITLES INC†
1931 Sheridan Road, 60035.
  Tel 312-432-3690
SAN 162-4547
Pres, Florence Shay
Estab 1977. 6000 Vols
Types: Fine bnd, 1st ed, illus bk, juv, ltd
  ed, o&r
Subj: Amer, art, photog, Chicagoana,
  20th century authors
S/S: Appr libr collec, autg, mss, search
  serv

Kankakee—30,141

MAX GATE BOOKS
641 S Chicago, 60901.
  Tel 815-939-0422
SAN 162-4628
Mgr, T Trafton
70,000 Vols. Cat 2x ann
Types: Hb, o&r, used, 1st ed, holographs
Subj: Thomas Hardy
S/S: Bnd

La Grange—15,681

JOHN WILLIAM MARTIN—BOOKSELLER
436 S 7th Ave, 60525.
  Tel 312-352-8115
SAN 157-3179
Owner & Mgr, John W Martin
Estab 1973. 5000 Vols. 800 sq ft. Cat 5x ann
Types: Fac ed, fine bnd, 1st ed, hb, o&r, op
Subj: Bks on bks, Am & Brit lit & criticism 1700-1930
S/S: Appr libr collec, search serv

Lake Bluff—4434

E F KEENAN BOOKS
506 North Ave, 60044.
  Tel 312-234-5054
SAN 157-3187
Owner, Edward F Keenan
Estab 1969. 4000 Vols. Cat 2x ann
Types: 1st ed, illus bk, ltd ed, o&r
Subj: Amer, art, photog, Western Amer, Chicago, Midwest states, 19th century artists monographs
S/S: Appr libr collec, orig art, prints, sh mus

Lansing—29,039

FUR FIN FEATHER BOOKS
17536 Shirley Dr (Mail add: Box 272, South Holland, 60473).
  Tel 312-474-3625
SAN 157-3209
Owners, D Miller & J Miller
Estab 1978. 1800 Vols. 400 sq ft. Cat 4x ann
Types: Fine bnd, 1st ed, hb, illus bk, imp, ltd ed, new & used, o&r, op, papbk, remd
Subj: Dogs, hunting & fishing, sports, birds, decoys
S/S: Prints, search serv

Libertyville—16,520

COGITATOR BOOKS†
PO Box 405, 60048. Tel 312-566-5621
  (open by appointment only)
SAN 162-5705
Owner, Donald V Vento
Estab 1963. 25,000 Vols. Cat
Types: 1st ed, juv, illus bk, op, o&r, pvt presses
Subj: Class studies, literary criticism

Martinton—363

LEONARD HOFFNUNG BOOKS
RR1 Box 148A, 60951.
  Tel 815-486-7281
SAN 162-332X
Owner, Leonard Hoffnung
Estab 1977. 10,000 Vols. Cat 4x ann
Types: Col text, 1st ed, o&r, op, used
Subj: Bibliog, bks on bks, scholarly lit

Moline—45,709

AVATAR BOOKS
423 15th St, 61265. Tel 309-764-7271
SAN 170-4788
Owner, Phyllis Erickson
Estab 1982. 45,000 Vols. 1800 sq ft
Types: Op
Subj: Amer, Civil War
S/S: Search serv

Northbrook—30,735

LEIDEN GALLERY
1045 Morrison Lane, 60062.
  Tel 312-291-0919
SAN 157-5678
Owners, Irving Leiden & Barbara Leiden
Present Owner 1978. 2000 Vols. 800 sq ft
Types: Hb, imp, op, papbk, remd, new & used, fac ed, 1st ed, illus bk, ltd ed, o&r, papbk
S/S: Appr libr collec, biper, orig art, prints, search serv

Oak Park—54,887

JOYCE KLEIN BOOKSELLER
177 S Oak Park Ave, 60302.
  Tel 312-386-6564
SAN 162-5020
Owner, Joyce Klein
Estab 1973. 8000 Vols. 1200 sq ft
Types: 1st ed, illus bk, juv, o&r, used
Subj: Cooking & nutrit, rel-c
S/S: Jewelry, search serv, antq

BERN WHEEL, BOOKS
834 Wenonah Ave, 60304.
  Tel 312-386-4974
SAN 162-5047
Owner, Bernard F Wheel
Estab 1972. 5000 Vols. Cat
Types: Hb, papbk
Subj: For lang, Esperanto (only)
S/S: Per

Paris—9885

T T & JEAN FOLEY—ANTIQUES
PO Box 60, 61944-0060. Tel 217-466-
  8585
SAN 161-2859
Owner, T T Foley
1000 Vols
Types: New, op, remd, used
Subj: Antq, art
S/S: Antiques

T A SWINFORD BOOKSELLER
235 W Wood, PO Box 93, 61944.
  Tel 217-465-5182
SAN 158-8710
1500 Vols. 485 sq ft. Cat 3-4x ann
Subj: Western Amer

Prospect Heights—11,808

VALERIE KRAFT, FINE BOOKS
309 N Elmhurst Rd, 60070.
  Tel 312-253-1419
SAN 162-5187
Owner, Valerie Kraft
Estab 1970. 10,000 Vols
Types: Illus bk, juv, colorplate
Subj: Art, sports, artist illus, decorative
  archit, early Chicago & Illinois, 19th
  century view bks
S/S: Search serv

Richmond—1068

MOON MARINE
1905 Emporium, 60071
SAN 156-5435
Pres, Martin M Cassidy; Mgr, Judy
  Scott
Estab 1977. 3000 Vols. Cat 4x ann
S/S: Search serv

Rockford—139,712

BOOKSTALL OF ROCKFORD
606 Gregory St, 61108.
  Tel 815-963-1671
SAN 158-6874
Owners, Karl Moehling & John Peter-
  son
Estab 1980. 10,000 Vols. 1000 sq ft
Types: 1st ed, hb, illus bk, juv, o&r, op,
  used
Subj: Amer, military, sci-tech
S/S: Biper

Rolling Meadows—20,167

CAROL HACKER—BOOKS
5 Shagbark Rd, 60008.
  Tel 312-397-3896
SAN 159-5687
Owner, Carol Hacker
Types: Hb, o&r, op, used
S/S: Search serv

Saint Charles—17,492

JAMES DOWD—BOOKSELLER
38 W 281 Toms Trail Dr, 60174.
  Tel 312-584-1930
SAN 162-5349
Owners, James Dowd & Frances Dowd
Estab 1980. 5000 Vols. Cat
Types: 1st ed, fac ed, fine bnd, hb, juv,
  ltd ed, new & used, o&r, op
Subj: Civil War, Illinoisiana, local hist,
  Wester Amer
S/S: Appr libr collec, search serv, sh
  mus

Skokie—60,278

HISTORICAL NEWSPAPERS &
JOURNALS
9850 Kedvale, 60076.
Tel 312-676-9850
SAN 157-3225
Owners, Steve Alsberg & Linda Alsberg
Present Owner 1976. Cat 3x ann
Types: Illus bk, o&r, bd per
Subj: Civil War, hist, Illinoisiana, Revo-
lutionary War, Chicago, Lincoln,
Washington
S/S: Autg, biper, maps, mss, per, prints,
search serv, hist maps

Springfield—99,637

FAMILY BOOK EXCHANGE
3129 S Dirkson Pkwy, 62703.
Tel 217-529-1709
SAN 158-1651
Owner & Mgr, Sharon Farnam; Asst
Mgr, Russell Farnam
Estab 1979. Cat 3x ann
Types: Juv, ltd ed, papbk, used
S/S: Games, gr cds, per, posters, ap-
praise comic collections, comics,
minatures, model kits

PRAIRIE ARCHIVES
641 W Monroe, 62704.
Tel 217-522-9742
SAN 162-5446
Owner, John R Paul
Estab 1970. 40,000 Vols. 1200 sq ft.
Cat 3x ann
Types: Fac ed, hb, op, papbk
Subj: Amer, Illinoisiana, World Wars I
& II, Lincoln
S/S: Biper, maps, prints

Sycamore—9219

STOREYBOOK ANTIQUES &
BOOKS
1325 E State St, 60178.
Tel 815-895-5910
SAN 158-5371
Owner & Mgr, Jean A Larkin
Estab 1972. 3500 Vols
Types: 1st ed, fine bnd, hb, illus bk, juv,
ltd ed, op, o&r, used

Subj: Biog, psychol
S/S: Prints, search serv, sh mus, antq,
ephemera

Urbana—35,798

BURKWOOD BOOKS
PO Box 172, 61801. Tel 217-344-1419
SAN 162-5543
Owner, Robert L Hodges
Estab 1973. 6000 Vols. 1500 sq ft. Cat
Types: Fine bnd, 1st ed, hb, illus bk, ltd
ed, o&r, op
Subj: Am hist & lit, Amer, Western
Amer
S/S: Prints, search serv

Villa Park—23,185

YELLOWSTONE BOOKS
PO Box 69, 60181
SAN 167-1685
Owner, Dave Turner
Estab 1971. Cat 2x ann
Types: 1st ed, hb, op, o&r
Subj: Western Amer, mystery
S/S: Search serv

Walnut—1513

BOOK BARN
RR1, 61376. Tel 815-379-2581
SAN 159-2076
Owners, Nancy Gillfillan & Richard
Gillfillan
Estab 1980. 13,000 Vols. 400 sq ft
Types: Fac ed, 1st ed, hb, ltd ed, o&r,
op, used
Subj: Civil War, fiction, local hist, rel
S/S: Appr libr collec, search serv

Wheaton—43,043

RICHARD OWEN ROBERTS BOOK-
SELLERS
205 E Kehoe Blvd, 60187.
Tel 312-668-1025
SAN 157-3233
Owners, Richard Owen Roberts &
Margaret J Roberts; Mgr, Richard
Owen Roberts

Estab 1961. 150,000 Vols. 6630 sq ft.
Cat 4x ann
Types: Fac ed, fine bnd, 1st ed, hb,
incunab, illus bk, bibles, imp, ltd ed,
new & used, o&r, op, papbk
Subj: Biog, hist, philos, psychol, rel
studies, theol
S/S: Appr libr collec, autg, biper, mss,
prints, search serv

White Hall— 2935

MARY F WENDELL BOOKS
135 E Lincoln, 62092.
Tel 217-374-2091
SAN 162-5683
Owner, Mary F Wendell; Mgr, Ray
Wendell
Estab 1960. 3000 Vols. 600 sq ft
Types: 1st ed, hb, illus bk, juv, ltd ed,
o&r, op
S/S: Appr libr collec

Winnetka— 12,772

BUNTER BOOKS
PO Box 153, 60093. Tel 312-441-7876
SAN 157-9436
Owner, Mark Kulieke
Estab 1979. 200 Vols
Types: 1st ed, hb, new & used, op, o&r
S/S: Search serv

Winthrop Harbor— 5438

LEEKLEY BOOK SEARCH†
711 Sheridan Rd (Mail add: PO Box
337, 60096). Tel 312-872-2311
SAN 162-573X
Owner, Brian Leekley
Estab 1964. 20,000 Vols
Types: 1st ed, hb, op, o&r, used
Subj: Humanities, mod lit, radical
polit, scholarly lit, Midwest Amer
S/S: Search serv

INDIANA

Bloomington— 51,646

BETWEEN THE LINES
1400 E 3rd St, 47401.
Tel 812-332-4440

SAN 158-913X
Owner, Danna D'Esopo Jackson
Estab 1981. 10,000 Vols. 500 sq ft. Cat
3x ann
Types: Hb, op, papbk, used
S/S: Appr libr collec, search serv

CAVEAT EMPTOR
208 S Dunn St, 47401.
Tel 812-332-9995
SAN 162-5861
Owner, Free Market Inc
Estab 1971. 40,000 Vols. 1300 sq ft.
Cat
Types: Hb, juv, op, papbk, used
Subj: Sci fiction & fantasy, soc sci
S/S: Appr libr collec, search serv, used
comics & rec

CHRISTOPHER'S BOOK ROOM
105½ N Dunn St (Mail add: PO Box
1061, 47402). Tel 812-333-5774
SAN 156-952X
Owner, Christopher Crockett
Estab 1978. 10,000 Vols. 600 sq ft
Types: 1st ed, hb, illus bk, o&r, op,
papbk, remd, used
Subj: Eur studies, fine arts, philos
S/S: Appr libr collec

KATHLEEN RAIS BOOKS
612 N Dunn, 47401. Tel 812-336-7687
SAN 166-1833
Owner, Kathleen Rais
Estab 1978. Cat 4x ann
Types: 1st ed, hb, illus bk, ltd ed, o&r,
op
Subj: Amer, dogs, Indianiana, sports,
Albert Payson Terhune, field sports
S/S: Prints, search serv

GARY L STEIGERWALD BOOK-
SELLER†
1500 Maxwell Lane, PO Box 1951,
47402. Tel 812-339-8220
SAN 160-7812
Owner, Gary Lee Steigerwald
Estab 1978. 2000 Vols. 300 sq ft. Cat
2x ann
Types: Fac ed, fine bnd, 1st ed, hb,
incunab, illus bk, ltd ed, new, imp,
o&r, op, remd
Subj: Art, bibliog, bks on bks, book
arts, hist of the book
S/S: Appr libr collec, search serv

Clayton—703

SYCAMORE BOOKS
311 Iowa, 46118. Tel 317-539-4993
SAN 159-5938
Estab 1961. 1000 Vols. 300 sq ft
Types: 1st ed, hb, illus bk, juv, o&r
S/S: Appr libr collec, search serv

Elkhart—41,305

THE BOOKSTACK
112 W Lexington Ave, 46516.
   Tel 219-293-3815
SAN 162-6140
Owners, George A Foster Jr & Charles
   E Brothers; Mgr, George A Foster Jr
Estab 1975. 25,000 Vols. 1000 sq ft.
   Cat 2x ann
Types: Fac ed, 1st ed, hb, illus bk, juv,
   o&r, op, papbk, remd, used
Subj: Amer, hist, hunting & fishing,
   nature & environ
S/S: Appr libr collec, search serv

Fort Wayne—172,196

A & OP FORT WAYNE BOOKSHOP
1412 Delaware Ave, 46805.
   Tel 219-424-1058
SAN 157-325X
Mgr, J W Morris
Estab 1979. 1000 Vols
Types: Op, o&r
S/S: Appr libr collec, search serv

FOREST PARK BOOKSHOP
1412 Delaware Ave, 46805.
   Tel 219-424-1058
SAN 162-640X
Owner, Lois Morris; Buyer, J W Morris
Estab 1970. 8000 Vols. 800 sq ft
Types: 1st ed, hb, illus bk, juv, o&r, op,
   papbk, remd, used
Subj: Mystery & detective, Am Indian
   studies
S/S: Appr libr collec, maps, search serv,
   genealogy sup

Indianapolis—700,807

BACK TRACTS INC
PO Box 30008, 46220.
   Tel 317-257-3686

SAN 162-6612
Owner, Joan H Morris
Estab 1975. 1500 Vols. 400 sq ft. Cat
Types: Fine bnd, 1st ed, hb, illus bk,
   juv, ltd ed, o&r, op, used
Subj: Am hist & lit, Indianiana
S/S: Appr libr collec, maps, mss, search
   serv

HOOSIER BOOKSHOP
3820 E 61st St, 46220.
   Tel 317-257-0888
SAN 162-6744
Owner, Robert R Russo
Cat 4x ann
Types: 1st ed, op, o&r
Subj: Indianiana, Midwest Amer
S/S: Appr libr collec, mss, search serv

WILLIAM S JOHNSON BOOKS
829 E Drive, Woodruff Pl, 46201.
   Tel 317-639-1256
SAN 162-6779
5000 Vols
Types: Hb, op
Subj: Literary criticism, Russ lang,
   World Wars I & II, Chinese art
S/S: Search serv

Lapel—1881

CARMEL BOOKSHOP
PO Box 866, 46051. Tel 317-534-4862
SAN 162-5977
Owner, Thomas R Russo
Cat 4x ann
Types: O&r
Subj: Bus & mgt, co & indus hist
S/S: Search serv

South Bend—109,727

BARNETTE'S BOOKS
22727 Adams Rd, 46628.
   Tel 219-272-9880
SAN 162-7376
Owner, Harriette A Barnette
Estab 1961. 6000 Vols. 600 sq ft
Types: 1st ed, hb, incunab, op, o&r,
   used
S/S: Appr libr collec, Am hist pamphlets

ERASMUS BOOKS
1027 E Wayne, 46617.
   Tel 219-232-8444

SAN 159-5679
Owners, Philip Schatz & William Storey
Estab 1980. Present Owner 1983.
  30,000 Vols. 1800 sq ft
Types: Fine bnd, 1st ed, hb, illus bk,
  imp, juv, ltd ed, o&r, op, papbk,
  remd, used
S/S: Appr libr collec, search serv

Tennyson— 331

RICHARD'S READERS
RR 1, Box 260A, 47637.
  Tel 812-362-8462
SAN 170-1738
Owner, Richard R Smith
Estab 1982. 16,000 Vols. Cat 4x ann
Types: 1st ed, hb, o&r, op
Subj: Amer, calligraphy, treasure hunt-
  ing
S/S: Appr libr collec, maps, search serv

Wabash— 12,985

MASON'S RARE & USED BOOKS
264 S Wabash St, 46992.
  Tel 219-563-6421
SAN 157-3268
Owner, Jon D Mason
Estab 1974. Present Owner 1975.
  110,000 Vols. 3600 sq ft. Cat
Types: 1st ed, fine bnd, hb, juv, ltd ed,
  o&r, op, papbk, used
Subj: Natural hist, Indianiana, military,
  theol
S/S: Appr libr collec, autg, search serv

West Lafayette— 21,247

MIDNIGHT BOOKMAN
237 Schilling, 47906. Tel 317-743-1790
SAN 158-3980
Owner, Edwin D Posey
Estab 1970. 5000 Vols. 450 sq ft
Types: 1st ed, fine bnd, hb, illus bk, ltd
  ed, o&r, op, used
Subj: Bks on bks, calligraphy, collecting,
  illus, typography, papermaking,
  printing, publ hist

IOWA

Akron— 1517

BROKEN KETTLE BOOKS
RR 1, 51001. Tel 712-568-2114
SAN 162-7562
Owner, Eldon J Bryant
50,000 Vols
Types: Op, o&r, used
Subj: Farm machinery
S/S: Trade catalogs

Cedar Rapids— 110,243

MIKE MADDIGAN
279 Johnson Ave NW (Mail add: Box
  824, 52406). Tel 319-363-4821
SAN 158-5509
Owner & Buyer, Mike Maddigan
Estab 1974. 1500 Vols
Types: O&r
S/S: Search serv

Davenport— 103,264

PETERSEN BOOK CO
235 McClellan Blvd (Mail add: PO Box
  966, 52805). Tel 319-355-7051
SAN 157-5694
Owners & Mgrs, Peter C Petersen &
  Mary Lou Petersen
Estab 1944. Present Owner 1980. 1500
  Vols. 450 sq ft. Cat 2x ann
Types: Col text, hb, op, papbk, used,
  imp Central & South Amer, UK
Subj: Natural hist, ornith
S/S: Search serv

THE SOURCE BOOKSTORE
232 W 3rd St, 52801. Tel 319-324-8941
SAN 162-7732
Owner, Robert Pekios
Estab 1939. 200,000 Vols
Types: 1st ed, hb, new & used, o&r,
  op, papbk, remd
Subj: Amer, biog, chiropractic, class
  studies, Iowiana, travel, jazz mus,
  Lincoln
S/S: Appr libr collec, biper, maps,
  search serv

Des Moines—191,003

McBLAIN BOOKS†
PO Box 971, 50304. Tel 515-274-3033
SAN 162-7848
Owners, Philip A & Sharon L McBlain
Estab 1970. 20,000 Vols. Cat 10-12x
  ann
Types: O&r, op
Subj: Africa, Asian studies, black stud-
  ies, Latin Am, Middle East, Pacific,
  West Indies, East Eur studies

PAULINE C MILLEN—BOOKS
3325 Crescent Dr, 50312.
  Tel 515-255-1588
SAN 162-7856
Owner & Mgr, Pauline Millen
Estab 1965. 7500 Vols. Cat
Types: 1st ed, hb, o&r, op, pvt presses
Subj: Iowiana, Western Amer, early Am
  fict, local hist, Midwest
S/S: Maps, prints, search serv

GIL O'GARA
2019 SE 8th St, 50315.
  Tel 515-280-6756
SAN 170-7221
Cat 6x ann
Types: Juv
S/S: Search serv

Iowa City—50,508

THE HAUNTED BOOKSHOP
227 S Johnson St, 52240.
  Tel 319-337-2996
SAN 162-8100
Owner & Mgr, J A Williams
Estab 1978. 12,000 Vols
Types: Fine bnd, 1st ed, hb, illus bk,
  imp, juv, o&r, op, papbk, used
Subj: For lang, med, mod lit, psychol,
  sci-tech, philos, cooking & nutrit
S/S: Orig art, classical & jazz lp's and
  78's

Maquoketa—6313

ANDROMEDA BOOKSHOP
E Platte Rd, 52060. Tel 319-652-6455
SAN 162-8216
Owner, David L Rosheim

Estab 1976. 10,000 Vols. 200 sq ft
Types: 1st ed, fac ed, fine bnd, hb, illus
  bk, juv, new & used, op, o&r, papbk
S/S: Biper, search serv, old cameras &
  rec, original photos

Marion—19,474

O G WAFFLE BOOK CO
956 13th St (Mail add: PO Box 369,
  53202). Tel 319-377-0489
SAN 123-2576
Owner, Norman J Waffle
18,000 Vols
Types: Hb, papbk, remd, op, juv

Marshalltown—26,938

GALE BOOKS
RR One Box 61, 50158.
  Tel 515-366-2474
SAN 158-6882
Owner, Ruth A Gale
Estab 1967
Types: 1st ed, juv, op, used
Subj: Biog, educ, fiction, Iowiana, rel
  studies

Wilton—2502

DONALD R DOERRES
503 E 3rd St (Mail add: PO Box 676,
  52778). Tel 319-732-2874
SAN 162-850X
Owner, Donald R Doerres
Present Owner 1956. 1000 Vols
Types: 1st ed, new & used, op
Subj: Iowiana, radio, railroadiana,
  locks & locksmithing, Mississippi
  River hist, steamboat & engines
  zeppelin, mercenaries, weapons &
  armored vehicle manuals

KANSAS

Lawrence—52,738

DAVID DARY WESTERN BOOKS
1101 W 27th St, 66044.
  Tel 913-843-5268
SAN 170-1673
Owners, David & Sue Dary
Estab 1981. 5000 Vols. Cat 4x ann

Types: Fac ed, 1st ed, ltd ed, new, o&r,
op, used
Subj: Nonfiction West Amer
S/S: Appr libr collec

J HOOD BOOKSELLER
1401 Massachusetts, 66044.
Tel 913-841-4644
SAN 162-8798
Owner, John J Hood
Estab 1974. 75,000 Vols. 2500 sq ft
Types: Op, used
Subj: Art, psychol
S/S: Search serv

Shawnee Mission

T N LUTHER BOOKS
8820 Delmar (Mail add: Box 6083,
66207). Tel 913-381-9619
SAN 162-9107
Owner, T N Luther
8000 Vols. Cat 5-6x ann
Types: O&r, op, 1st ed, hb, juv, papbk,
remd
Subj: Western Amer, archaeol, ethnic
studies, Am Indian studies, Indian
artifacts
S/S: Appr libr collec, maps, orig art,
Am Indian art

Wichita—279,272

AL'S OLD & NEW BOOKSTORE
1710 W Douglas (Mail add: PO Box
11244, 67211). Tel 316-264-8763
SAN 162-9204
Owner, Helen Woodward
100,000 Vols
Types: O&r, op, used
Subj: Western Amer, Kansasana
S/S: Search serv, spec order

DICKEY BOOKS
107 N Clifton, 67208. Tel 316-686-
5817 (by appt)
SAN 170-0707
Owner, Paul E Dickey
Estab 1981. 10,000 Vols. 900 sq ft. Cat
2x ann
Types: 1st ed, hb, op, o&r, remd, used
Subj: Philos, genealogy, 20th century
Amer poetry & fiction
S/S: Search serv

GREEN DRAGON BOOKSTORE
2730 Boulevard Plaza, PO Box 17338,
67217. Tel 316-681-0746
SAN 123-9252
Owners, Larue Basom & Charles Ba-
som
Estab 1975. 20,000 Vols. 4500 sq ft
Types: Fac ed, fine bnd, 1st ed, hb, illus
bk, op, remd, used
Subj: Aviation, biog, Southwestern
Amer

PIED PIPER BOOKSTORE
3928 E 13th, 67208. Tel 316-686-0401
SAN 162-9263
Mgr, Irvin Lesser
Estab 1960. 15,000 Vols
Types: Hb, juv, op, papbk
Subj: Amer, Kansasana, humor, sci-tech

KENTUCKY

Berea—8226

GEORGE BROSI BOOKSELLER
123 Walnut St, 40403. Tel 606-986-
3262
SAN 130-3279
Owner, George Brosi
Estab 1983. 5000 Vols. Cat 12x ann
Types: 1st ed, hb, illus bk, juv, ltd ed,
new, o&r, op, papbk, remd, used
Subj: Southern Appalachian Mountains
S/S: Search serv

Harrodsburg—7265

ERNEST DAVIS
586 Ross Ave, 40330.
Tel 606-734-3165
SAN 162-9484
Types: Hb, op, o&r
Subj: Amer

Lexington—204,165

ALBERT BOOKS
510 N 3rd St, 40508. Tel 606-233-9673
SAN 158-3182
Owner, Stephen Albert
Estab 1981
Types: Hb, o&r, op, used, trade cata-
logs
S/S: Search serv

GLOVER'S BOOKS
397 Virginia Ave, 40504. Tel 606-253-0614
SAN 158-5886
Owner, John T Glover
Estab 1978. 30,000 Vols. 2000 sq ft. Cat
Types: Fine bnd, 1st ed, hb, illus bk, o&r, op, used
Subj: Amer, horses, Kentuckiana
S/S: Appr libr collec, maps, prints, sh mus, picture framing

SHAWK'S GREEN DOME ANTIQUES
3288 Georgetown Rd, PO Box 11253, 40574. Tel 606-255-9716
SAN 159-0901
Owner, G Malcolm Shawk
Estab 1970. 500 Vols. 5000 sq ft
Types: 1st ed, illus bk, juv, o&r, op
Subj: Amer, local hist
S/S: Appr libr collec, auction serv

Louisville—298,451

DONALD S MULL
1706 Girard Dr, 40222.
   Tel 502-426-2947
SAN 159-222X
Cat
Types: Op, used
Subj: Civil War, Kentuckiana, Western Amer, George Custer

OLD LOUISVILLE BOOKS
426 W Oak St, 40203. Tel 502-637-6411
SAN 162-9735
Owner, Don Grayson
Estab 1976. 7000 Vols
Types: 1st ed, hb, illus bk, juv, o&r, op, used
Subj: Amer, Kentuckiana, rel, Jesse Stuart
S/S: Search serv

PHILATELIC BIBLIOPOLE
1819 Gresham Rd (Mail add: PO Box 36006, 40233). Tel 502-451-0317
SAN 159-0111
Owner, Leonard H Hartmann; Mgr, Mary Jule Hartmann
Estab 1965. 3000 sq ft. Cat 2x ann

Types: Fac ed, fine bnd, 1st ed, hb, incunab, imp, ltd ed, o&r, op, used
Subj: Philately, postal history
S/S: Appr libr collec, biper

S-T ASSOCIATES
1317 Cherokee Rd, 40204
SAN 159-2505
Owner, Norwin E Green III
Estab 1975. 8000 Vols. Cat ann
Types: 1st ed, hb, illus bk, ltd ed, new, o&r, op
Subj: Amer, fiction, sci fiction & fantasy, modern firsts, Lyle Wright
S/S: Appr libr collec, search serv

Mount Sterling—5820

THE MOUNT STERLING REBEL
402 N Maysville St, PO Box 481, 40353. Tel 606-498-5821
SAN 159-1991
Estab 1979. 1000 Vols. Cat 10x ann
Types: 1st ed, o&r, op
Subj: Civil War, Virginiana
S/S: Appr libr collec, biper, search serv

LOUISIANA

Baton Rouge—219,486

COTTONWOOD BOOKS
3054 Perkins Rd, 70808.
   Tel 504-343-1266
SAN 126-6888
Pres, Claire Blondeau
Estab 1978. 10,000 Vols. 1400 sq ft
Types: Juv, op, papbk, used
Subj: Liberal arts
S/S: Bkplates & bkmarks, search serv, staty

TAYLOR CLARK'S INC†
2623 Government St, 70806.
   Tel 504-383-4929
SAN 163-0237
Owner, Taylor Clark
Estab 1969. Cat ann
Types: Imp, o&r, colored plate
Subj: Natural hist
S/S: Appr libr collec, maps, orig art, prints

Gretna—20,615

BAYOU BOOKS INC
1005 Monroe St, 70053.
 Tel 504-368-1171
SAN 120-1913
Mgr & Buyer, Phoebe Murrell
Estab 1961. 20,000 Vols
Types: Hb, juv, op, new & used,
 papbk, remd
Subj: Louisianiana
S/S: Maps, search serv, sculpture re-
 prod

Lafayette—81,961

G & C ENTERPRISES
612 Alonda Dr, 70503.
 Tel 302-984-9305
SAN 159-1592
Owner, Charles F Hamsa
Estab 1980. 1000 Vols
Types: Op
Subj: Photog, recreation, wines, viticul-
 ture
S/S: Autg

New Orleans—557,482

A COLLECTOR'S BOOK SHOP†
3119 Magazine St, 70115.
 Tel 504-899-7016
Owner, Jeanne L Weiss
Types: 19th & 20th cent, 1st ed, early
 children's bks
Subj: Arthur Conan Doyle & Sherlock
 Holmes, detective and mystery fict,
 Louisianiana, Civil War

LIBRAIRIE BOOKSHOP
829 Royal St, 70116. Tel 504-525-4837
SAN 121-9324
Owner, Carey C Beckham
Estab 1967. 25,000 Vols
Types: Hb, op, o&r
Subj: Louisianiana
Branches:
 BECKHAM'S BOOKSHOP
 228 Decatur St, 70130.
  Tel 504-522-9875
 SAN 163-058X
 Owners, Carey C Beckham & Alton L
  Cook
 Estab 1972. 35,000 Vols. 3500 sq ft

Types: Hb, o&r, op, used
S/S: Prints
OLD BOOKS
811 Royal St, 70116.
 Tel 504-522-9875
SAN 163-0598
12,000 Vols

Shreveport—205,815

ARK-LA-TEX BOOK CO
Box 564, 71162. Tel 318-221-6820
SAN 157-3322
Owner, L S Hooper
Estab 1950. 2500 Vols
Types: Fac ed, hb, o&r, op, used
Subj: Amer, Arkansiana, Civil War,
 Louisianiana, Texana
S/S: Maps, search serv, ephemera Amer

RED RIVER BOOKS
6226 Border Lane (Mail add: PO Box
 3606, 71103). Tel 318-636-4755
SAN 157-5716
Owner, Eugene Spruell
Estab 1979. 10,000 Vols. 500 sq ft. Cat
 2x ann
Types: New & used, op
Subj: Petroleum, Louisianiana, guns

MAINE

Augusta—21,819

THE MATHOM BOOKSHOP &
 BINDERY
Blinn Hill Rd off Rte 27, PO Box 161,
 04342. Tel 207-737-8806
SAN 170-2777
Owner, Wesli Court
Estab 1979. 5000 Vols. 375 sq ft
Types: Fac ed, fine bnd, 1st ed, hb, illus
 bk, juv, ltd ed, new, o&r, op, remd,
 used
Subj: Amer, poetry, scholarly lit
S/S: Appr libr collec, autg, maps, orig
 art, prints
Open July-Aug only by chance or appt

Bath—10,246

CROSS HILL BOOKS
866 Washington St (Mail add: PO Box
 798, 04530). Tel 207-443-5652

SAN 163-0954
Owner, William W Hill
Estab 1977. Cat
Types: Fine bnd, 1st ed, hb, o&r, op,
   used
Subj: Nautical
S/S: Appr libr collec, maps, nautical
   charts & prints

Brunswick — 17,366

BOOK PEDLARS
Holbrook St, RD 2 Cundy's Harbor,
   04011. Tel 207-729-0087
SAN 159-0138
Owners, Walter A O'Brien Jr & Laura
   M O'Brien
Estab 1980. 5000 Vols. 400 sq ft
Types: Hb, illus bk, juv, o&r, op, remd,
   used
Subj: Amer, Maineana, nonfiction
S/S: Orig art, search serv, deals with
   some librs

OLD BOOKS
136 Maine St, 04011. Tel 207-725-4524
SAN 163-1047
Owner, Clare C Howell
Estab 1977. 12,000 Vols. 750 sq ft
Types: Hb, juv, op, used
Subj: Bks by & about women
S/S: Search serv

Buckfield — 1333

PATRICIA LEDLIE — BOOKSELLER†
Box 46, 04220. Tel 207-336-2969
SAN 163-1055
Owner, Patricia Ledlie
Cat 3x ann
Types: New, op, o&r
Subj: Natural hist

Camden — 4584

LILLIAN BERLIAWSKY — BOOKS†
23 Bay View St, 04843. Tel 207-236-
   3903
SAN 163-1063
Owner, Lillian Berliawsky
50,000 Vols
Types: Hb, juv, op, o&r, papbk
Subj: Biog, Amer, hist
S/S: Antiques, paintings

DOLPHIN BOOKSTORE
78 Elm St, PO Box 582, 04843
SAN 170-2963
Owner, Leon H Ballou Jr
Estab 1976. Present Owner 1982.
   10,000 Vols. 400 sq ft
Types: Juv, hb, imp, for lang, 1st ed,
   illus bk, ltd ed, o&r, op, used
Subj: Fiction, Maineana, music, drama,
   art, illus
S/S: Biper, orig art, prints, sh mus

Dexter — 4286

FREDERICA DE BEURS BOOKS
Upper Garland Rd, RFD 1, Box 2880,
   04930. Tel 207-924-7474 (by appt)
SAN 170-2971
Owner, Frederica de Beurs
Estab 1980. 4000 Vols. 400 sq ft
Types: 1st ed, hb, illus bk, juv, o&r, op,
   papbk, used
Subj: Maineana, sci-tech
S/S: Search serv

Dover-Foxcroft — 4323

COLLECTABLES BOOKSHOP
Dover-Dexter Rd, Box 160, Rte 1,
   04426. Tel 207-564-2670
SAN 163-111X
Owner, Orrin F Coombs
Estab 1973. 8000 Vols
Types: Hb, juv, papbk
Subj: Nonfiction
S/S: Sh mus, wholesale, per

Ellsworth — 5179

BEDFORD'S USED BOOKS
54 High St, 04605. Tel 207-667-7308
SAN 157-3349
Owner & Mgr, Bedford Riggs
Estab 1978. Present Owner 1980.
   35,000 Vols
Types: 1st ed, hb, illus bk, juv, ltd ed,
   op, o&r, papbk, used
Subj: Hunting & fishing, Maineana,
   natural hist, marine
S/S: Search serv, sh mus

Freeport — 5863

BOOK CELLAR
36 Main St, 04032. Tel 207-865-3157

SAN 170-303X
Estab 1970. 40,000 Vols
Types: Hb, used, juv
S/S: Appr libr collec, search serv

Gardiner — 6485

BUNKHOUSE BOOKS
Lewiston Rd-126, Rte 5A, 04345.
 Tel 207-582-2808
SAN 163-1160
Owner, Isaac Davis Jr
Estab 1975. 15,000 Vols. Cat 2x ann
Types: 1st ed, o&r, used
Subj: Hunting & fishing, local hist,
 Maineana
S/S: Search serv

Manchester — 1949

CHARLES L ROBINSON RARE
 BOOKS
The Pond Rd, 04351. Tel 207-622-1885
SAN 163-0873
Owner, Charles L Robinson
Estab 1975. 5000 Vols. 1100 sq ft. Cat
Types: Fine bnd, 1st ed, hb, illus bk,
 juv, ltd ed, o&r, op, used
Subj: Natural hist, travel
S/S: Appr libr collec, maps, orig art,
 prints

Ogunquit — 1492

FRANK MICHELLI BOOKS
PO Box 627 (Mail add: 03907).
 Tel 207-646-3275
SAN 163-1292
Owners, Frank Michelli & Paul Grippo
Estab 1962. 15,000 Vols
Types: Op, used
S/S: Search serv

Paris — 4168

HAUNTED BOOKSHOP
Main St, 04271. Tel 207-743-6216
SAN 170-8155
Owner, Winnie Mott

Pittsfield — 4125

WINTER FARM BOOKS
RFD 2, Box 540, 04967.

 Tel 207-938-4141
SAN 170-2955
Owner, Robert K Foote
Cat ann
Types: 1st ed, incunab, o&r, op, used
S/S: Maps, mss

Portland — 61,572

CARLSON & TURNER BOOKS
241 Congress St, 04101.
 Tel 207-773-4200
SAN 163-1314
Owners, David John Turner & Norma
 C Carlson
Estab 1972. 35,000 Vols. 2500 sq ft.
 Cat
Types: O&r, op
Subj: Graphic arts
S/S: Appr libr collec, search serv, resto-
 ration consulting

NATHAN COPELAND BOOK-
 SELLER
72 Groveside Rd, 04102.
 Tel 207-773-3647
SAN 157-3365
Owner, Nathan Copeland
Estab 1962. 5000 Vols
Types: 1st ed, hb, o&r, op, used
Subj: Maineana, travel, maritime com-
 munications
S/S: Appr libr collec, search serv

CUNNINGHAM BOOKS
762 Congress St (Mail add: PO Box
 3756, 04104). Tel 207-775-2246
SAN 157-7530
Owners, J M Cunningham & J E Pick-
 ard
Estab 1980. 12,000 Vols. 1000 sq ft.
 Cat 3x ann
Types: 1st ed, hb, new & used, op,
 papbk, remd
S/S: Search serv

F M O'BRIEN OLD BOOK SHOP†
38 High St, 04101. Tel 207-774-0931
SAN 163-1357
Owner, F M O'Brien
Estab 1934. 100,000 Vols. Cat
Types: Used, op, o&r, remd
Subj: Amer, Maineana, Am hist & lit
S/S: Appr libr collec, autg, maps, mss,
 search serv

Southwest Harbor — 1855

SOUTHWEST HARBOR ANTIQUES
GALLERY
Clark Point Rd (Mail add: Box 732,
04679). Tel 207-244-3162
SAN 163-1470
Owner & Mgr, Lee Freedman
Estab 1965. 4000 Vols. 1000 sq ft
Types: Fine bnd, 1st ed, hb, illus bk,
o&r, op, used
S/S: Appr libr collec, autg, maps, mss,
orig art, photog sup

Springvale — 2914

HARLAND H EASTMAN BOOKS &
PRINTS
66 Main St, PO Box 276, 04083.
Tel 207-324-2797
SAN 170-3781
Owner, Harland H Eastman
Estab 1979. 6000 Vols. 1125 sq ft
Types: Fac ed, fine bnd, 1st ed, hb, illus
bk, juv, o&r, op, used
Subj: Local hist
S/S: Appr libr collec, maps, prints

F P WOOD BOOKS
256 Main St (Mail add: Box 365,
04083). Tel 207-324-8319
SAN 158-9946
Estab 1979. 2000 Vols. Cat 4x ann
Types: 1st ed, hb, illus bk, juv, o&r, op,
remd, used
Subj: Amer, Maineana, utopias
S/S: Appr libr collec, autg, biper, mss,
search serv, sh mus

Stockton Springs — 1230

ANDREW B W MacEWEN AND
AIMEE B MacEWEN
E Main St (Mail add: PO Box 97,
04981). Tel 207-567-3351
SAN 163-1500
Owner, Andrew B W MacEwen
Estab 1961. 30,000 Vols. 3200 sq ft
Types: 1st ed, hb, op, o&r, used
Subj: Amer, Maine, mystery & detective
S/S: Search serv
Branches:
   BOOK BARN — VICTORIAN
   HOUSE

E Main St, 04981. Tel 207-567-3351
SAN 156-4358

Wells — 8211

EAST COAST BOOKS
PO Box 849, 04090. Tel 207-646-3584
SAN 163-1519
Owners, Merv Slotnick & Kaye Slotnick
Estab 1976. 20,000 Vols. Cat
Types: 1st ed, illus bk, o&r, hb, juv,
papbk, remd
Subj: Antq, art, autg
S/S: Autg, prints, 17th-20th century
art, paper Amer

DOUGLAS N HARDING†
Box 184, Rte 1, Webhannet Farm,
04090. Tel 207-646-8785
SAN 164-2820
Owner, Douglas N Harding
Estab 1962. 4500 Vols. Cat 4x ann
Types: Fine bnd, 1st ed, imp, juv, o&r,
color plate bks
Subj: Can, Arctic, Antarctic, Amer &
Eng atlases
S/S: Appr libr collec

Windham — 11,282

COUNTRY BOOK ROOM
Rte 302 & Pope Rd, 1 Pope Rd, West-
brook, 04092. Tel 207-892-6518
SAN 163-1535
Owners, Larry & Peg Geraghty
Estab 1963. 25,000 Vols
Types: Hb, juv, op, used, fine bnd, 1st
ed, illus bk, ltd ed, o&r
Subj: Amer, Maineana
S/S: Maps, posters, sh mus, prints, appr
libr collec

MARYLAND

Annapolis — 31,740

DRAGOMAN BOOKS
680 Americana Dr - 38, 21403.
Tel 301-263-2757
SAN 159-1568
Owner, Fred Drake
Estab 1977. 5000 Vols. 2600 sq ft
Types: Fac ed, fine bnd, 1st ed, hb, illus

bk, juv, ltd ed, o&r, op, used
Subj: Archaeol, for lang, poetry
S/S: Search serv

MAIN STREET BOOKS
185 Main St, 21401. Tel 301-268-3321
SAN 156-7837
Owners, Cecelia Clark, et al
Estab 1981. 30,000 Vols. 3000 sq ft
Types: O&r, op
S/S: Appr libr collec, bnd, search serv
See Also: Firstborn Books, Galesville

Baltimore—736,775

MARILYN BRAITERMAN†
20 Whitfield Rd, 21210.
   Tel 301-235-4848
SAN 158-9784
2000 Vols. Cat
Types: Fine bnd, 1st ed, hb, illus bk,
   juv, ltd ed, o&r
Subj: Archit, art, travel
S/S: Appr libr collec, search serv

CHIRURGICAL BOOKSHOP
1211 Cathedral St, 21201.
   Tel 301-539-0872, Ext 235
SAN 159-219X
Owner, Maryland Medical & Chirurgi-
   cal Faculty; Mgr, Deborah K
   Woolverton
Estab 1980. 1000 Vols. Cat 2x ann
Types: Fac ed, fine bnd, 1st ed, hb, illus
   bk, incunab, imp, ltd ed, o&r, op,
   used
Subj: Med
S/S: Appr libr collec

GEPPI'S COMIC WORLD
Hechinger's in Security Sq, 21207.
   Tel 301-788-8222
SAN 163-1748
Owner, Steve Geppi; Mgr, Charles D
   Zepp
Estab 1974. 100,000 Vols. 1000 sq ft
Subj: Walt Disney, super heroes
S/S: Wholesale, appraise comic books
   & pulp collections
Branches:
   Harbor Place, Upper Level Light St
      Pavilion, 21202.
   Tel 301-547-0910
   SAN 156-5893
   Mgr, Steve Swink

See Also: Silver Spring; Alexandria,
   Arlington, VA; Largo, FL

HARDFORD COINS
2160 E Joppa Rd, 21234.
   Tel 301-665-1814
SAN 163-1764
Owner & Merch Mgr, Milton O Lynn
Estab 1961. Present Owner 1963. 1600
   Vols. 1200 sq ft. Cat ann
Types: For lang, hb, imp, o&r, op,
   remd, used
Subj: Numismatics, banking, medals
S/S: Autg

KELMSCOTT BOOKSHOP
32 W 25th St, 21218. Tel 301-235-6810
SAN 157-3403
Owners, Donald Johanson & Teresa
   Johanson
Estab 1978. 25,000 Vols. 1500 sq ft
Types: Fine bnd, 1st ed, hb, illus bk,
   juv, ltd ed, o&r, op
Subj: Eng hist & lit, Marylandiana,
   travel
S/S: Appr libr collec, maps

KEY BOOKS
2 West Montgomery St, 21230.
   Tel 301-539-5020 (by appt)
SAN 170-3390
Owner, Raymond D Cooper; Mgr,
   Carolyn L Cooper
Estab 1982. 5000 Vols. Cat 5x ann
Types: 1st ed, o&r
Subj: Mystery & detective, hist of sci &
   tech
S/S: Autg, maps

CECIL ARCHER RUSH
1410 Northgate Rd, 21218.
   Tel 301-323-7767
SAN 163-1845
Owner, Cecil A Rush; Vpres, Gordon D
   Rush
Estab 1942. 3000 Vols. Cat ann
Types: Fac ed, hb, imp, incunab, new &
   used, op, o&r
Subj: Orientalia, China, erotic art,
   India, Japan, Tibet
S/S: Search serv, oriental art

SECOND STORY BOOKS†
3322 Greenmount Ave, 21218.
   Tel 301-467-4344
SAN 129-7953

Owner, Allen Stypeck; Mgr, Norman
Yeia
35,000 Vols. 1500 sq ft
Branch
Hq: Washington, DC

SHERLOCK BOOK DETECTIVE
PO Box 1174, 21203.
Tel 301-235-2326
SAN 163-1888
Owner, William S Forshaw
Types: Op, used
S/S: Rec

Bethesda—71,621

FOLKWAYS SCHOLARLY BOOKS
5309 Tuscarawas Rd, 20816.
Tel 301-320-5672
SAN 163-2027
Owner, Bradford N Gray
Estab 1978. 2500 Vols. Cat 1-2x ann
Types: Hb, o&r, op, used
Subj: Soc sci, psychol, med

QUILL & BRUSH BOOKSTORE
7649 Old Georgetown Rd, 20014.
Tel 301-951-0919
SAN 123-9422
Owners, Allen Ahearn & Patricia
Ahearn
Estab 1976. 10,000 Vols. 1700 sq ft.
Cat 12x ann
Types: 1st ed, illus bk, ltd ed, o&r, op
Subj: Art, travel, 20th century authors
S/S: Appr libr collec, autg, orig art,
prints, search serv

SECOND STORY BOOKS†
7730 Old Georgetown Rd, 20014.
Tel 301-656-0170
SAN 145-3149
Owner, Allen Stypeck
Estab 1981. 500,000 Vols. Cat
Branch
Types: Fac ed, fine bnd, 1st ed, hb, illus
bk, incunab, ltd ed, o&r, papbk,
remd, used
S/S: Appr libr collec, autg, biper, mss,
search serv
Hq: Washington DC

Brinklow

OLD HICKORY BOOKSHOP LTD
20225 New Hampshire Ave, 20862.

Tel 301-924-2225
SAN 163-2051
Owners, Ralph Grimes & Johanna
Grimes
Estab 1940. 20,000 Vols. Cat 4x ann
Types: O&r, op
Subj: Dent, med, sci-tech

Camp Springs—22,776

STEWART'S STAMP & BOOKSTORE
6504 Old Branch Ave, 20031.
Tel 301-449-6766
SAN 163-2094
Owner, William F Stewart
Estab 1975. 15,000 Vols. 800 sq ft
Types: Hb, op, used
S/S: Sh mus, postcards, stamps

College Park—23,614

MARY CHAPMAN BOOKSELLER
PO Box 304, 20740. Tel 301-490-5432
SAN 157-7565
Owner, Mary Chapman; Buyer, David
Kueker
Estab 1975. 2500 Vols. Cat ann
Types: O&r, op
Subj: Needlecrafts, textiles, weaving,
lace
S/S: Biper, search serv

DYKES, JEFF—WESTERN BOOKS†
Box 38, 20740. Tel 301-864-0666
Subj: Western Amer, Western illustrators

Columbia—8815

JOHN GACH BOOKS INC†
5620 Waterloo Rd, 21045.
Tel 301-465-9023
SAN 140-6078
Owners, John Gach & Frank Gach
Estab 1973. 20,000 Vols. Cat 4x ann
Types: 1st ed, hb, imp, o&r, used
Subj: Hist of ideas, philos, psychiat,
psychol
S/S: Appr libr collec, autg, maps, mss,
orig art

Cumberland—25,933

PAUL A RUDDELL BOOKS—HOBBY
HOUSE PRESS, INC
900 Frederick St, 21502.

Tel 301-759-3770
SAN 121-6600
Pres, Gary R Ruddell
Estab 1939. 2300 Vols. Cat 4x ann
Types: Hb, imp UK, papbk, remd
Subj: Dolls, doll houses, miniatures, teddy bears

Ellicott City—9506

DEEDS BOOKSHOP
8012 Main St, PO Box 85, 21043. Tel 301-465-9419
SAN 170-4087
Estab 1981. 9000 Vols
Types: Op, used, juv, hb, o&r, remd, illus bk, 1st ed
Subj: Poetry
S/S: Search serv, appr libr collec

GAIL KLEMM—BOOKS†
PO Box 551, 21043. Tel 301-465-7414
SAN 159-0375
Owner, Gail E Klemm; Mgr, Waldemar Klemm
Estab 1967. Cat
Types: 1st ed, illus bk, for lang, imp, juv, ltd ed, o&r, op
Subj: Amer, typography, papermaking, printing, Randolph Caldecott
S/S: Autg, maps, orig art, prints, search serv, sh mus, collection development, individual or libr

Gaithersburg—26,424

DORIS FROHNSDORFF†
PO Box 2306, 20879. Tel 301-869-1256
Owner, Dr Geoffrey Frohnsdorff
Types: Miniature bks, illus bks, early & modern rare children's bks, fine bindings

Galesville

FIRSTBORN BOOKS
1007 E Benning Rd, 20765. Tel 301-867-7050
SAN 163-2329
Owners, Cecelia P Clark & James W Clark
Estab 1976. 7000 Vols. 900 sq ft. Cat
Types: O&r, op, used

Subj: Mod lit, Western Amer, country & western music
S/S: Appr libr collec, bnd, search serv
See Also: Main Street Books, Annapolis

Greenbelt—16,000

E DONBULLIAN BACK NUMBER MAGAZINE COMPANY
7-D Ridge Rd, 20770. Tel 301-345-7430
SAN 159-1169
Owner, E DonBullian
Estab 1927. Present Owner 1964. 2500 sq ft
Subj: Med, sci-tech
S/S: Biper
Stock contains one million magazines

Kensington—1822

THE OLD PRINTED WORD
3746 Howard Ave, 20895. Tel 301-949-7350
SAN 163-2442
Owner, Doc Des Roches
Estab 1969. 200,000 Vols. 1100 sq ft. Cat 6x ann
Types: Fac ed, fine bnd, 1st ed, hb, incunab, illus bk, juv, ltd ed, o&r, op, used
S/S: Appr libr collec, autg, biper, maps, mss, posters, search serv, sh mus

Lutherville—24,055

DRUSILLA'S BOOKS
202 W Seminary Ave (Mail add: PO Box 16, 20193). Tel 301-321-6687
SAN 163-2574
Owner, Drusilla P Jones
Estab 1977. 3000 Vols. Cat ann
Types: 1st ed, hb, illus bk, juv, o&r, op, used
S/S: Search serv, sh mus, antq relating to children's bks

Monkton

CHARLOTTE'S WEB ANTIQUES
1901 Monkton Rd (Mail add: c/o Eleanor C Weller, 16135 Old York Rd, 21111). Tel 301-771-4239, 771-4753

SAN 129-9042
Owners, Eleanor Weller, et al; Mgr,
Judy Compton
Estab 1981. 1000 Vols
Types: Fac ed, fine bnd, 1st ed, hb, illus
bk, imp, new & used, o&r, op, remd
Subj: Antq, archit, art, gardening,
sports, travel, flower arranging,
landscaping
S/S: Gifts, gr cds

Mount Airy—2450

B & B SMITH—BOOKSELLERS
710 Park Ave, 21771. Tel 301-549-1227
SAN 129-8631
Owner & Mgr, Barbara L Smith; Buyer,
W P Smith
Estab 1980. 5000 Vols. 600 sq ft. Cat
3x ann
Types: Hb, ltd ed, new & used, o&r,
op, papbk, remd
Subj: Archaeol, class studies, hist, an-
cient hist & lit
S/S: Search serv

Pikesville—25,395

SHIRLEY BALSER 16TH-20TH
CENTURY PAINTINGS, PRINTS,
& BOOKS
PO Box 5803, 21208.
Tel 301-484-0880
SAN 163-2639
Owner, Shirley L Balser
Estab 1961. 25,000 Vols. 1500 sq ft
Types: 1st ed, fine bnd, illus bk, ltd ed,
op, o&r
Subj: Amer, art, Marylandiana, hist, sci-
tech
S/S: Autg, maps, mss, 16th-20th
century paintings, prints & books
bought, sold & appraised

Poolesville—3428

OLDE SOLDIER BOOK
19932 Westerley Ave, 20837.
Tel 301-349-5209
SAN 157-8383
Owners, Dave Zullo & Chris Zullo
Estab 1976. 2500 Vols. Cat 3-4x ann
Types: New & used, o&r, op, remd

WILLIS VAN DEVANTER BOOKS
19558 Fisher Ave, PO Box 277, 20837.
Tel 301-972-7298 (by appt)
SAN 159-6616
Owner, Willis VanDevanter
Estab 1973
Types: O&r, op
Subj: Cooking & nutrit, black studies,
biking
S/S: Appr libr collec

Port Tobacco

OLD QUENZEL STORE
Town Square, PO Box 326, 20677. Tel
301-934-8045
SAN 158-538X
Owner, James L Barbour
Estab 1973. 5000 Vols. 900 sq ft. Cat
7x ann
Types: Fac ed, hb, op, o&r
Subj: Civil War, hist, Lincoln
S/S: Autg, prints, search serv

Rockville—43,811

STEVEN C BERNARD FIRST
EDITIONS
138 New Mark Esplanade, 20850.
Tel 301-340-8623
SAN 157-342X
Owner, Steven C Bernard
Estab 1974. 4000 Vols. Cat 3x ann
Types: 1st ed, hb, illus bk, ltd ed, o&r,
op, used
Subj: Mod lit, sci fiction & fantasy
S/S: Search serv

Q M DABNEY & CO
11910 Parklawn Dr (Mail add: PO Box
42026, Washington, DC, 20015).
Tel 301-881-1470
SAN 163-2744
Cat 20x ann
Types: Fac ed, 1st ed, hb, illus bk, ltd
ed, o&r, op, remd, used
Subj: Govt publn, humanities, law,
military, soc sci
S/S: Appr libr collec, search serv

Salisbury—16,429

HENRIETTA'S ATTIC
205B Maryland Ave, 21801.
Tel 301-546-3700

SAN 158-4960
Owner & Mgr, Henrietta J Moore
Estab 1980. 10,000 Vols. 1500 sq ft.
Cat 12x ann
Types: 1st ed, hb, illus bk, juv, op, o&r,
papbk, used
Subj: Amer, fiction, rel
S/S: Per, prints, search serv, antq

Silver Spring—77,496

GEPPI'S COMIC WORLD
8317 Fenton St, 20910.
Tel 301-588-2545, 792-2754
SAN 163-285X
Owner, Steve Geppi; Mgr, Tom Fielding
Estab 1978. 100,000 Vols
Branch. Buys through hq
Subj: Walt Disney, super heroes
S/S: Wholesale
Hq: Baltimore

HIRSCHTRITT'S "1712"
1712 Republic Rd, 20902.
Tel 301-649-5393
SAN 158-5630
Owner, Anita Hirschtritt; Mgr, Ralph
Hirschtritt
Estab 1970. 2000 Vols
Types: 1st ed, hb, illus bk, ltd ed, o&r,
op
Subj: Amer, Orientalia
S/S: Appr libr collec, search serv

IMAGINATION BOOKS
946 Sligo Ave, 20910.
Tel 301-589-2223
SAN 157-3446
Owners, James Gscheidle, et al
Estab 1973. 75,000 Vols. 2000 sq ft
Types: 1st ed, hb, illus bk, imp, juv, ltd
ed, o&r, op, papbk, used
Subj: Class studies, metaphys & occult,
music, mystery & detective, philos,
sci fiction & fantasy, World Wars I &
II
S/S: Appr libr collec, autg, prints,
search serv

Westminster—8804

CHRISTIAN CLASSICS INC
PO Box 30, 21157. Tel 301-848-3065
SAN 163-2949
Dir, John J McHale

Estab 1968. 100,000 Vols. Cat 4x ann
Types: Hb, imp, new & used, op,
papbk, o&r, remd
Subj: Rel-c

Wheaton—66,247

ATTIC BOOKS
2442 Ennalls Ave, 20902.
Tel 301-949-1007
SAN 163-2965
Owner, Richard Cook
Estab 1970. 20,000 Vols
Types: Op, o&r, used
Subj: Military, mystery & detective, sci
fiction & fantasy

BOOKS OF COLONIAL AMERICA
3611 Janet Rd, 20906.
Tel 301-946-6490
SAN 158-6866
Owner, George A Young
Estab 1981. 1000 Vols. 200 sq ft
Types: Hb, o&r, op, used
Subj: Amer, hist, Marylandiana, New
Yorkiana, Pennsylvaniana
S/S: Search serv

MASSACHUSETTS

Adams—10,381

SECOND LIFE BOOKS†
Upper E Hoosac St, 01220.
Tel 413-743-4561
SAN 157-3454
Owners, Russell Freedman & Martha
Freedman
Estab 1972. 30,000 Vols. 1500 sq ft.
Cat 4x ann
Types: 1st ed, fine bnd, hb, illus bk,
imp, juv, ltd ed, o&r, op, used
Subj: Polit sci, hist, agr, hort, women's
studies
S/S: Appr libr collec, autg, mss, search
serv

Allston

ALLSTON BOOKSHOP
169 Brighton Ave, 02134.
Tel 617-254-7210
SAN 163-3058
Owner, Robert Franklin

Estab 1978. 5000 Vols. 500 sq ft
Types: 1st ed, ltd ed, papbk, used
Subj: Mod lit, boxing
S/S: Per, search serv, magazines pre
1940

Amesbury—13,971

THE ANTIQUARIAN SCIENTIST
PO Box 602, 01913. Tel 617-388-2314
SAN 166-9834
Owner, Raymond V Giordano
Present Owner 1976. 1000 Vols. Cat 2x
ann
Types: O&r
Subj: Hist of sci & med
S/S: Appr libr collec, mss, antq scientific instruments

Amherst—33,229

VALLEY BOOKSHOP
5 E Pleasant St, 01002.
Tel 413-549-6052
SAN 163-3104
Owner, Lawrence Pruner
Estab 1975. 25,000 Vols. 1500 sq ft
Types: 1st ed, used, hb, papbk, remd
S/S: Biper

Arlington—48,219

THE COLLECTOR'S LIBRARY
11 Bartlett Ave, 02174. Tel 617-643-4039
SAN 163-3112
Owner, Benjamin D Scharneck
Estab 1977. Cat 3x ann
Types: Fac ed, fine bnd, illus bk, imp, ltd ed
Subj: Hist of art, med & natural sci
S/S: Prints, gilded miniatures

ECHO BOOKS
1173 A Mass Ave, 02174.
Tel 617-643-3369
SAN 159-1258
Owner, Eva Arond
Estab 1981. 7500 Vols. 375 sq ft
Types: Juv, op, used
S/S: Search serv, toys

MARK A KALUSTIAN
259 Pleasant St, 02174.
Tel 617-648-3437

SAN 163-3120
Types: Op, used
Subj: Armenia, Asia Minor, Near East,
Ottoman Empire, Persia, Turkey

THE PRINTERS' DEVIL†
One Claremont Court, 02174.
Tel 617-646-6762
SAN 163-3155
Owner, Barry Wiedenkeller; Mgr, Anne
Wiedenkeller
Estab 1973. 2500 Vols. Cat 4x ann
Types: O&r
Subj: Hunting & fishing, trades, hist of
med
S/S: Appr libr collec, medical antiques

Assonet

OSEE H BRADY BOOKS
12 Elm St, 02702. Tel 617-644-5073
SAN 158-1929
Owner, Osee H Brady
Estab 1975. 8000 Vols
Types: Juv, o&r, used
Subj: Biog, fiction, New England
S/S: Appr libr collec

Auburn—14,845

KENNETH ANDERSEN—BOOKS
38 Silver St, 01501. Tel 617-832-3524
SAN 158-7269
Owner, Kenneth Andersen
Cat 3x ann
Types: 1st ed, hb, illus bk, o&r, op,
used
Subj: Golf, hunting & fishing, mountains, mountaineering
S/S: Appr libr collec

Auburndale

ROBIN WILKERSON BOOKS
24 Groveland St, 02166.
Tel 617-969-2678
SAN 165-1633
Present Owner 1978. 2000 Vols. Cat
Types: 1st ed, o&r, used
Subj: Hort, landscape design
S/S: Search serv

Bellingham—14,300

THE CATHOLIC BOOK COL-
LECTOR
381 Wrentham Rd, 02019.
Tel 617-883-4344
SAN 163-3201
Owner, Edward J Fontenarosa
Estab 1974. 19,000 Vols. 1000 sq ft
Types: 1st ed, hb, op, o&r, papbk, used
Subj: Theol, rel-c

Belmont—26,100

PAYSON HALL BOOKSHOP
80 Trapelo Rd, 02178.
Tel 617-484-2020
SAN 124-3292
Owner, Clare Murphy
Estab 1978. 5000 Vols
Types: O&r, used
Subj: Art
S/S: Search serv

Beverly—37,655

JEAN S McKENNA OLD, SCARCE,
OUT-OF-PRINT BOOKS
131 Dodge St, PO Box 397, 01915.
Tel 617-927-3067
SAN 163-3236
Owner, Jean S McKenna
Estab 1977. 5000 Vols. 700 sq ft
Types: 1st ed, hb, illus bk, juv, o&r, op,
used
Subj: Local hist
S/S: Search serv

Blandford—1038

ROBERT F LUCAS†
Main St (Mail add: PO Box 63, 01008).
Tel 413-848-2061
SAN 163-3244
Owner, Robert F Lucas
Estab 1977. 2000 Vols. 400 sq ft. Cat
Types: Op
Subj: Amer, whales & whaling, Am
diaries & narratives
S/S: Appr libr collec

Boston—562,994

ARS LIBRI LTD†
286 Summer St, 02210.
Tel 617-357-5212
SAN 163-3260
Owner, Elmar W Seibel
Estab 1976. 50,000 Vols. 7500 sq ft.
Cat 12x ann
Types: Fine bnd, 1st ed, hb, imp Fr, imp
Sp, illus bk, incunab, ltd ed, op, o&r
Subj: Archit, art, photog, reference,
scholarly lit
S/S: Appr libr collec, biper, orig art,
photog sup, prints

ARTISTIC ENDEAVORS†
24 Emerson Pl, 02114.
Tel 617-227-1967
SAN 163-3287
Owner, B R Gantshar
Estab 1975. 1500 Vols. Cat 2x ann
Types: 1st ed
Subj: Fine arts, performing arts
S/S: Appr libr collec, autg, maps, mss,
orig art, photog sup, prints, search
serv, ephemera

ATLANTIC BOOK SERVICE
10 Cedar-Charlestown, 02129.
Tel 617-242-0188
SAN 163-3295
Owner, Paul Dembicki
Cat
Types: 1st ed, hb, incunab, new &
used, op, o&r
Subj: Oceanog
S/S: Search serv

BOSTON BOOK ANNEX
906 Beacon St, 02215.
Tel 617-266-1090
SAN 158-8745
Owners, Helen Kelly & Francine L Ness
30,000 Vols. 2000 sq ft. Cat 5x ann
Types: Fac ed, fine bnd, 1st ed, hb, juv,
ltd ed, op, o&r, papbk, used
Subj: 19th & 20th century literary first
ed
S/S: Appr libr collec, mss, search serv

BRATTLE BOOK STORE†
5 West St, 02111. Tel 617-542-0210
SAN 163-3392
Owner, George J Gloss; Mgr, Kenneth
M Gloss

Estab 1948. 350,000 Vols
Types: Op, o&r, used
S/S: Appr libr collec, autg, biper, maps,
mss

BROMER BOOKSELLERS INC†
607 Boylston St, 02116.
Tel 617-247-2818
SAN 163-531X
Owners, Anne Bromer & David Bromer
Estab 1963. 4000 Vols. 1000 sq ft. Cat
3x ann
Types: Fine bnd, 1st ed, illus bk, in-
cunab, juv, o&r, pvt presses, minia-
ture
S/S: Appr libr collec, autg, maps, mss,
prints, search serv, bookfairs

**MAURY A BROMSEN ASSOCIATES
INC†**
770 Boylston St, 02199.
Tel 617-266-7060 (by appt only)
SAN 163-3406
Dir, Maury A Bromsen
Estab 1955. 30,000 Vols
Types: Incunab, o&r
Subj: Amer, fine arts, Latin Am, bibliog,
travel, discovery & explor
S/S: Appr libr collec, autg, manuscripts
Issues special lists & catalogs to libraries
& collectors only

BUDDENBROOKS BOOKS INC
753 Boylston St, 02116.
Tel 617-536-4433
SAN 126-5288
Owner & Pres, Martin R Weinkle
Estab 1970. Present Owner 1975.
60,000 Titles. 5000 sq ft. Cat
Types: Fr lang, hb, imp, juv, ltd ed,
papbk, remd, illus bk
Subj: Sci fiction & fantasy, mystery &
detective, fiction, bus & mgt, dance,
art, music, travel, psychol, Africa,
Arab studies, Boswell & Johnson
S/S: Bkplates & bkmarks, maps, search
serv, spec order, tapes, software,
prints & drawings

CHILDS GALLERY†
169 Newbury St, 02116.
Tel 617-266-1108
Owner, D Roger Howlett
Types: Fine old master & modern
prints, illus for fine ed bks

CHOREOGRAPHICA
103 B Charles St, 02114.
Tel 617-227-4780
SAN 163-3449
Owner, Ernest J Morrell
Estab 1964. 6000 Vols
Types: 1st ed, fine bnd, hb, illus bk, juv,
ltd ed, o&r, op, used
Subj: Dance, art, illus
S/S: Orig art, search serv

GOODSPEED'S BOOKSHOP INC†
7 Beacon St, 02108. Tel 617-523-5970
SAN 163-3503
Cat
Types: 1st ed, incunab, op, o&r, used
Subj: Amer, genealogy, local hist
S/S: Autg, maps, mss, prints
Branches:
2 Milk St, 02108. Tel 617-523-5970
SAN 156-3599

R H KRISTIANSEN RARE BOOKS
PO Box 524, Kenmore Station, 02215.
Tel 617-424-1527
SAN 157-9568
5000 Vols. Cat
Types: 1st ed, o&r, op
Subj: Sci fiction & fantasy, detective

EDWARD MORRILL & SON INC†
25 Kingston St, 02111. Tel 617-482-
3090
SAN 163-3554
Pres & Buyer, Samuel R Morrill
Estab 1939. Cat 10x ann
Types: Op, o&r
Subj: Amer, arts & crafts
S/S: Autg, maps, mss, prints, sh mus

STARR BOOK CO INC
186 South St, 02111. Tel 617-542-2525
SAN 163-3635
Owners, Ernest & Norman Starr
Estab 1930. 300,000 Vols. 3000 sq ft
Types: Op
Subj: Am hist & lit, drama, Eng hist &
lit, feminism, fiction, mystery &
detective, nautical, nonfiction,
philos, psychol
S/S: Appr libr collec

E WHARTON & CO
36 Hancock St, 02114.
Tel 617-523-1650
Owner, Sarah Baldwin

Types: 1st ed
Subj: Bks by women

Braintree—36,337

XANADU BOOK SEARCH
PO Box 91, 02184. Tel 617-848-8584
SAN 170-3803
Owner, Joseph Manfredonia
Present Owner 1975
Types: O&r, op
S/S: Search serv

Brookline—55,062

BROOKLINE VILLAGE BOOKS &
PRINTS
23 Harvard St, 02146.
Tel 617-734-3519
SAN 158-7781
Owner, James Lawton; Asst Mgr, Jamie
Shaw Lawton
Estab 1981. 20,000 Vols. 1000 sq ft.
Cat 4x ann
Types: 1st ed, hb, incunab, o&r, remd,
used
Subj: Amer, nautical, scholarly lit
S/S: Appr libr collec, autg, mss, orig
art, prints, search serv

HORSE IN THE ATTIC BOOKSHOP
52 Boylston St, 02147.
Tel 617-566-6070
SAN 163-3767
Owner, Margo Lockwood
Estab 1975. 18,000 Vols
Types: 1st ed, hb, juv, op, o&r, remd
Subj: Art, local hist
S/S: Appr libr collec, search serv

Cambridge—95,322

AHAB RARE BOOKS
5 John F Kennedy St, Suite 401, 02138.
Tel 617-547-5602
SAN 158-9180
Owner, James Randall
Estab 1972. 1500 Vols. 350 sq ft. Cat
8x ann
Types: Fine bnd, 1st ed, ltd ed, o&r
Subj: Amer, 19th century Am lit
S/S: Appr libr collec, autg, mss

THE CHARLES DALY COLLEC-
TION†
66 Chilton St, 02138. Tel 617-547-8228
By appointment only
Owner, Howard B Walzer
Subj: Sporting, women's bks

HURST & HURST
53 Mt Auburn St, 02138.
Tel 617-491-6888
SAN 129-0606
Owner, Norman Hurst
750 sq ft. Cat
Types: Fine bnd, 1st ed, hb, o&r, op
Subj: Art, travel, ethnography
S/S: Appr libr collec, maps, mss

IN OUR TIME
PO Box 386, 02139. Tel 617-267-4189
Owner, Eugene O'Neill
Types: 1st eds, press bks & fine printing
Subj: Am & Eng lit, Amer

PANGLOSS BOOKSHOP
1284 Massachusetts Ave, 02138.
Tel 617-354-4003
SAN 163-3910
Owner, Herbert R Hillman
Cat 2x ann
Types: 1st ed, hb, o&r, op, remd, used
Subj: Humanities, soc sci
S/S: Mss, search serv

STARR BOOKSHOP INC
29 Plympton St, 02138.
Tel 617-547-6864
SAN 163-3937
Owner, Marc Starr; Mgr, Matthew Starr
Estab 1930. 150,000 Vols
Types: 1st ed, op, o&r, used
Subj: Am hist & lit, art, Eng hist & lit,
philos

TEMPLE BAR BOOKSHOP†
9 Boylston St, 02138. Tel 617-876-6025
Owner, James O'Neal
Types: 1st ed, new
Subj: Photog (bks & images)

WAITING FOR GODOT BOOKS
137 Magazine St, PO Box 810, 02139.
Tel 617-661-1824
SAN 158-7307
Owner, Gary Oleson
Cat 3x ann

Types: 1st ed, ltd ed, o&r
Subj: Mod lit
S/S: Search serv
By appointment only

Canton—18,182

ISHTAR BOOKS
318 Sherman St, 02021.
 Tel 617-828-2753 (by appt)
SAN 170-141X
Cat ann
Subj: Op & rare Arabian horse books

Charlestown

CYNTHIA ELYCE RUBIN
PO Box 297, 02129. Tel 617-242-2108
SAN 163-397X
Cat 3x ann
Types: 1st ed, o&r, used
Subj: Fine arts, Shaker & American
 utopian material, folk art, decorative
 arts
S/S: Search serv

Chelmsford—31,174

CHELMSFORD
212 North Rd, 01824
SAN 170-0472
Owner, Matthew J Needle; Mgr, Cheryl
 Needle

Chestnut Hill

BOOK & TACKLE SHOP†
29 Old Colony Rd, 02167.
 Tel 617-965-0459
SAN 163-4003
Owner, B L Gordon
Estab 1953. 25,000 Vols. Cat 3x ann
Types: 1st ed, hb, juv, new & used,
 o&r, op, papbk
Subj: Amer, art, cooking & nutrit,
 feminism, hunting & fishing, med,
 nature & environ
S/S: Appr libr collec, orig art, prints,
 search serv

Cohasset—7174

A E MAXTED
PO Box 276, 02025
SAN 163-4011
Owner & Mgr, A E Maxted
25,000 Vols
Types: Op
Subj: Art, econ, fiction, law, philos,
 psychol, rel, sociol
S/S: Rec

Concord—16,293

THE BARROW BOOKSTORE
79 Main St, 01742. Tel 617-369-6084
SAN 163-402X
Owner, Claiborne Dawes
Estab 1971. 4000 Vols. 600 sq ft
Types: 1st ed, hb, illus bk, juv, o&r, op,
 papbk, used
Subj: The Alcotts, Emerson, Thoreau,
 Concord hist & literary traditions
S/S: Search serv

MALCOLM M FERGUSON
1489 Main St, 01742. Tel 617-369-
 2898
SAN 163-4038
Types: Hb, illus bk, o&r, op, used
S/S: Search serv

Conway—1213

ROBERT L MERRIAM
Newhall Rd, 01341. Tel 413-369-4052
SAN 163-4070
Owner, Robert L Merriam
Estab 1960. 10,000 Vols. 900 sq ft. Cat
Types: 1st ed, hb, imp, new & used,
 o&r, remd
Subj: Amer, antq, art, bibliog
S/S: Appr libr collec

Deerfield—4517

M DOUGLAS SACKMAN
PO Box 308, 01342. Tel 413-774-3507
SAN 163-5050
Cat 2x ann
Types: Hb, op, o&r, used
Subj: Amer, genealogy, Massachusettsana
S/S: Mss, search serv

East Bridgewater — 9945

ELMWOOD BOOKSHOP
461 West St, 02333. Tel 617-378-7587
SAN 158-7315
Owner, Michael J Fruzzetti
Estab 1965
Types: Illus bk, o&r
S/S: Autg, maps, orig art, prints

East Longmeadow — 12,905

W D HALL
99 Maple St, 01028. Tel 413-525-3064
SAN 163-4127
Owners, W Douglas Hall & Marjorie Hall
Estab 1965. 8000 Vols. Cat 12x ann
Types: Hb, o&r, op, used
Subj: Amer, art, Civil War, nature &
    environ, nautical, travel
S/S: Prints, ephemera

East Sandwich

TITCOMB'S BOOKSHOP
432 Rte 6-A (Mail add: PO Box 45,
    02537). Tel 617-888-2331
SAN 163-4151
Owners, Ralph Titcomb & Nancy
    Titcomb
Estab 1966. 8000 Vols
Types: 1st ed, hb, new, o&r, op, remd
Subj: Amer, New England, nonfiction

Fairhaven — 15,759

EDWARD J LEFKOWICZ INC†
43 Fort St (Mail add: PO Box 630,
    02719). Tel 617-997-6839
SAN 163-4186
Pres, Edward J Lefkowicz
Estab 1974. Cat 5x ann
Types: O&r
Subj: Arctic, discovery & explor, nauti-
    cal, Pacific, whales & whaling, navi-
    gation, naval archit
S/S: Appr libr collec, maps, mss

Fall River — 92,574

TASTE OF HONEY BOOKSTORE
1749 N Main St, 02720.
    Tel 617-679-8844
SAN 159-0707

Owner, James H McKenna
Estab 1972. 25,000 Vols. 1000 sq ft.
    Cat ann
Types: Fine bnd, 1st ed, hb, illus bk,
    o&r, op, papbk, used
Subj: New England, Rhode Islandana
S/S: Appr libr collec, prints, search serv,
    sh mus

Framingham — 65,113

REBECCA B DESMARAIS RARE
    BOOKS†
One Nixon Rd (Mail add: PO Box
    2286, 01701). Tel 617-877-4564
SAN 163-4216
Owners, Rebecca B Desmarais & Gilles
    M K Desmarais
Estab 1978. 12,000 Vols. Cat 6x ann
Types: 1st ed, ltd ed, o&r, op, press bks
Subj: Amer, autg, bks on bks
S/S: Autg

Gardner — 17,900

IRENE'S BOOKSHOP
49 W Broadway, 01440. Tel 617-632-
    5574
SAN 163-4224
Owner, Irene M Walet
Estab 1967. 30,000 Vols. 1600 sq ft.
    Cat 6x ann
Types: Fine bnd, 1st ed, hb, illus bk,
    juv, ltd ed, op, o&r, used
S/S: Appr libr collec, biper, prints, sh
    mus

Gloucester — 27,768

THE ENGLISH BOOKSHOP
22 Rocky Neck Ave, 01930.
    Tel 617-283-8981
SAN 157-9703
Owner, Peggy Sibley
Estab 1956. 5000 Vols
Types: Juv, illus bk, hb, imp, o&r, op,
    used
Subj: Nautical, theol, women's studies,
    Great Britain
S/S: Search serv
Open afternoons only; closed Mondays

TEN POUND ISLAND BOOK CO
93 Main St, 01930. Tel 617-283-5299
SAN 163-4259
Owner, G Gibson
Estab 1976. 10,000 Vols. 1000 sq ft
Types: Fac ed, 1st ed, hb, illus bk, juv,
ltd ed, o&r, op
Subj: Amer, local hist, nautical, wom-
en's studies

Great Barrington—7405

GEORGE ROBERT MINKOFF INC†
Rowe Rd, RFD 3, Box 147, 01230.
Tel 413-528-4575
SAN 163-4275
Pres, George Robert Minkoff
Estab 1968. 3000 Vols. Cat 10x ann
By appointment only
Types: Fine bnd, 1st ed, illus bk, imp,
ltd ed, o&r
Subj: Am hist & lit, Amer, Eng hist & lit
S/S: Appr libr collec, autg, mss, orig art

Green Harbor—2562

C & M HUTCHINSON
PO Box 89, 02041. Tel 617-834-9509
SAN 163-4283
Owner, Charles Hutchinson
Estab 1954. 30,000 Vols
Types: For lang, imp, op, o&r, used
Subj: Scholarly lit, sci-tech
S/S: Search serv, spec order, scientific
journals

Hamilton—6960

ELMCRESS BOOKS
587 Bay Rd, 01936. Tel 617-468-3261
SAN 157-8391
Owners, Cheever Cressy & Britta K
Cressy
Estab 1978. 4000 Vols. 1000 sq ft. Cat
6x ann
Types: Fac ed, fine bnd, 1st ed, hb, illus
bk, juv, ltd ed, o&r, op, used
Subj: Bibliog, nautical, bks on bks, Mod
British royal family
S/S: Appr libr collec, maps, mss, prints,
search serv

Hingham—20,339

HINGHAM BOOK HOUSE
112 North St, 02043. Tel 617-749-1651
SAN 163-4313
Owner, John P Richardson
Estab 1944. 25,000 Vols
Types: 1st ed, hb, incunab, op, o&r,
used
S/S: Appr libr collec, autg, maps, mss,
orig art, search serv

Hull—9714

UNIVERSITY BOOK RESERVE
75 Main St, 02045. Tel 617-925-0005,
925-0570
SAN 163-4348
Owner, Paul Bassinor
Estab 1941. 100,000 Vols. 4823 sq ft.
Cat
Types: 1st ed, hb, o&r, op, used
Subj: Philos, rel studies, soc sci, class
studies
S/S: Appr libr collec
Branches:
815 Northasket Ave, 02045
SAN 157-1281
1123 sq ft

Huntington—1804

ROBERT & BARBARA PAULSON
BOOKS†
Allen Coit Rd, 01050. Tel 413-667-
3208
SAN 164-3444
Owner, Robert A Paulson
Estab 1964. Present Owner 1981.
25,000 Vols. 1500 sq ft
Types: Fine bnd, 1st ed, hb, illus bk,
juv, ltd ed, o&r, op, used
Subj: Autg, Massachusettsana,
Adirondacks, Rockwell Kent, bus &
indust
S/S: Appr libr collec, autg, maps, mss,
orig art, search serv

Hyannis—6847

WAKE-BROOK HOUSE BOOKS
PO Box 153, 02601. Tel 617-775-5860
SAN 163-4356
Owner, Edwin P Geauque

Estab 1968. 2000 Vols. Cat
Types: 1st ed, hb, op, o&r
Subj: New England, Joseph C Lincoln,
Thornton W Burgess
S/S: Gold stamping
See Also: Fort Lauderdale, FL

Jamaica Plain

HOWLAND & CO
100 Rockwood St, 02130.
Tel 617-522-5281
SAN 158-2801
Owner, Llewellyn Howland III
Estab 1978. 3000 Vols. Cat 2x ann
Types: Fine bnd, 1st ed, hb, illus bk, ltd
ed, o&r
Subj: Maritime, yachting
S/S: Appr libr collec, orig art, prints

Leominster — 34,508

WILLIAM T GAVIN
86 Maple Ave, 01453. Tel 617-534-
4038
SAN 163-4410
Owner, William T Gavin
Estab 1973. Cat
Types: Illus bk, op, o&r
Subj: Amer, photog
S/S: Biper, maps, mss, orig art, prints

Lowell — 92,418

UNIVERSITY BOOK EXCHANGE
181 Dracut St (Mail add: PO Box 28,
01853). Tel 617-454-7108
SAN 125-2232
Owners, Anthony Ziagos & Diane
Ziagos
Estab 1976. 10,000 Vols. 600 sq ft
Branch
Types: Fine bnd, 1st ed, hb, illus bk,
o&r, op, papbk, remd, used
Subj: Local hist, Masonic
S/S: Appr libr collec, globes, mss,
prints, search serv, sh mus
Hq: Anthony G Ziagos Bookseller

ANTHONY G ZIAGOS BOOK-
SELLER
Box 28, 01853. Tel 617-454-7108.
Telex 95-5329
SAN 157-3535

Owners, Anthony G Ziagos & Diane
Ziagos
Types: 1st ed, hb, ltd ed, new & used,
o&r, op, remd
Subj: Local hist, Masonic, Freemasonry,
Scottish Rite
S/S: Appr libr collec, orig art, prints,
search serv, sh mus
See Also: University Book Exchange

Lunenburg — 8405

GORDON TOTTY — SCARCE PAPER
AMERICANA
570 Massachusetts Ave, 01462.
Tel 617-582-7844
SAN 157-3543
Owner, Gordon Totty
Estab 1978. 5000 Vols. Cat 4x ann
Types: Fine bnd, incunab, o&r, used
Subj: Amer, military
S/S: Biper, maps, mss, sh mus, stereo-
view images

Marblehead — 20,126

IRVING GALIS
357 Atlantic Ave, 01945.
Tel 617-631-5351
SAN 158-0256
Owner, Irving Galis
Types: 1st ed, hb, illus bk, ltd ed, o&r,
op, remd, used, imp Eng
Subj: Biog, Eng hist & lit, military, polit
sci, presidents & presidency, World
Wars I & II, JFK assassination,
Richard Nixon, Watergate
S/S: Search serv

NEATH THE ELMS
235 Washington St, 01945.
Tel 617-631-6222
SAN 163-4488
Owners, Robert Allison & Lorraine
Allison; Mgr, Rory Goff
Estab 1977. 8000 Vols. 800 sq ft
Types: 1st ed, hb, o&r, op, used
Subj: Local hist, nautical, New England
S/S: Appr libr collec, maps, search serv

Marshfield — 20,916

LORD RANDALL BOOK & PRINT
SHOP
22 Main St, 02050.

Tel 617-837-1400, 834-8330
SAN 163-450X
Owner, Gail Wills
Estab 1972. 10,000 Vols
Types: Op, o&r
Subj: Amer, art
S/S: Appr libr collec, search serv

Montague — 8011

PETER L MASI — BOOKS†
217 Central (Mail add: PO B, 01351).
   Tel 413-367-2628
By appointment only
Types: Early Am juv, trade catalogs
Subj: Archit, bus & indust

New Bedford — 98,478

D R NELSON & CO BOOKSELLERS
PO Box C-2, 02741. Tel 617-996-6234
SAN 163-416X
Owners, David Nelson & Joyce Nelson
Estab 1972
Types: 1st ed, used, juv, o&r
Subj: Amer, whaling
S/S: Autg, biper, prints, paper Amer

Newburyport — 15,900

GRACE MUNSELL — SCOTTISH
   BOOKS
110 High St, 01950
SAN 163-4909
Owner, Grace Munsell
Types: New, op
Subj: Scottish Bks
S/S: Search serv
Lists on request

NEWBURYPORT RARE BOOKS
32 Oakland St, 01950.
   Tel 617-462-7398 (by appt only)
SAN 159-6861
Owner, Matthew J Needle; Mgr, M G
   Schoene
Estab 1978. 3000 Vols
Types: 1st ed, fine bnd, illus bk, o&r
Subj: Nonfiction, archit, med, travel
S/S: Appr libr collec, autg, maps, mss,
   prints

FRANK E REYNOLDS BOOKSELLER
8 Jefferson Ct, PO Box 805, 01950.
   Tel 617-462-3258

SAN 158-1945
Owner, Frank E Reynolds
Estab 1968. 1000 Vols. 300 sq ft. Cat
   4x ann
Types: Hb, o&r, op, remd, used
Subj: Civil War, Abraham Lincoln

STEPHEN SCHAROUN
33-A State St, 01950. Tel 617-465-0775
SAN 163-4607
Owner, Stephen Scharoun
Estab 1978. 5000 Vols
Types: Hb
Subj: Archaeol, Eng hist & lit, folklore
S/S: Search serv

New Salem — 688

COMMON READER BOOKSHOP
Old Main St (Mail add: Box 32, 01355).
   Tel 617-544-3002
SAN 157-3551
Owners, Dorothy A Johnson & Doris E
   Abramson
Estab 1977. 5000 Vols. 300 sq ft
Types: 1st ed, hb, illus bk, o&r, op
S/S: Autg, prints, search serv, ephemera

Newton — 83,622

THE BOOK COLLECTOR
375 Elliot St, 02164. Tel 617-964-3599
SAN 163-4623
Owner, Theodore Berman
Estab 1972. 30,000 Vols. 1200 sq ft
Types: 1st ed, fac ed, fine bnd, hb, illus
   bk, imp, juv, ltd ed, o&r, op, papbk,
   used
S/S: Appr libr collec, autg, search serv

THE RENDELLS INC†
154 Wells Ave, 02159.
   Tel 617-965-4670
SAN 163-4631
Dirs, Kenneth W Rendell & Diana J
   Rendell
Estab 1961. 70,000 Vols. 3000 sq ft.
   Cat 10x ann
Types: Imp, incunab, o&r
Subj: Medieval studies, ancient hand-
   writing
S/S: Appr libr collec, autg, maps, mss

SUZANNE SCHLOSSBERG†
529 Ward St, 02159. Tel 617-964-0213
SAN 163-464X

Owner, Suzanne Schlossberg
Estab 1975. 1500 Vols.
Types: Fine bnd, 1st ed, hb, illus bk,
  juv, ltd ed, o&r, op, used
S/S: Autg, mss, orig art, prints, search
  serv

North Amherst

MAGNALIA AMERICANA
115 Montague Rd, PO Box M, 01059.
  Tel 413-549-6569
SAN 159-2130
Owner, Hugh F Bell
Estab 1977. 2500 Vols. 350 sq ft. Cat
  ann
Types: Hb, o&r, op
Subj: Am hist & lit, discovery & explor,
  law, travel, maritime
S/S: Maps, prints

Northampton—29,286

DWYER'S BOOKSTORE INC†
44 Main St (Mail add: PO Box 426,
  01060). Tel 413-584-7909
SAN 163-4739
Owner, Jeffrey P Dwyer
Estab 1973. 15,000 Vols. 2500 sq ft.
  Cat 4x ann
Types: Fine bnd, illus bk, ltd ed, used
Subj: Calligraphy, hist of the bk, print-
  ing
S/S: Appr libr collec, autg, orig art

BARBARA L FERET
136 Crescent St, 01060.
  Tel 413-586-6365
SAN 126-575X
Owner, Barbara L Feret
Estab 1978. 6000 Vols. Cat 2x ann
Types: 1st ed, fac ed, fine bnd, hb, imp,
  o&r, op, remd, used
Subj: Cooking & nutrit, wines, bever-
  ages, gastronomy
S/S: Appr libr collec, search serv

OLD BOOKSTORE
32 Masonic St, 01060.
  Tel 413-586-0576
SAN 163-4755
Mgr, Henry Walz
Estab 1958. 25,000 Vols
Types: Hb, papbk, used

OMEGA BOOKS
213 Main St, 01060. Tel 413-586-2271
SAN 163-4763
Owner, Norman Witty
Estab 1972. 10,000 Vols
Types: Illus bk, op, papbk
Subj: Films & filmmaking, comedy, for
  lang comics
S/S: Orig art, movie memorabilia

Onset—1771

JOSEPH A DERMONT FINE BOOKS
13 Arthur St, PO Box 654, 02558.
  Tel 617-295-4760
SAN 157-8405
Owner, James A Dermont
5000 Vols. Cat 6x ann
Types: 1st ed, illus bk, imp, ltd ed
Subj: Mod lit

Palmer—11,389

THE OPEN CREEL
25 Breton St, 01069. Tel 413-283-3960
SAN 157-5732
Owners, Joan Taylor & Dick Taylor
Estab 1975. 500 Vols. Cat 4x ann
Types: Op, used
Subj: Fishing
S/S: Appr libr collec, biper, search serv
Branches:
  FOX HILL BOOKS
  436 Main St, 01069. Tel 413-283-
    7681
  SAN 156-7705
  Owners, Joan & Dick Taylor
  Estab 1979. 8500 Vols
  Types: Op, used
  S/S: Search serv

Provincetown—3536

BRYANT'S
467 Commercial St, 02657.
  Tel 617-487-0134
SAN 157-3578
Owner, Marie-Louise Bryant; Mgr,
  George D Bryant
Estab 1837. Present Owner 1946. 5000
  Vols
Types: Illus bk, new, o&r, op
Subj: Fiction, nonfiction, fishing indust,

marine transp, lifesaving, light-
houses, Provincetown & Cape Cod
S/S: Mss, prints

Salem—38,220

ROBERT MURPHY BOOKSELLER
14 Derby Sq, 01970. Tel 617-745-6406
SAN 163-4925
Owner, Robert A Murphy
Estab 1970. 15,000 Vols. 1000 sq ft
Types: Fine bnd, 1st ed, hb, o&r, op,
papbk, remd, used

SAXIFRAGE BOOKS
13 Central St, 01970. Tel 617-745-7170
SAN 163-4968
Owners, Gerry Williams, et al
Estab 1978. 15,000 Vols. 1000 sq ft.
Cat 2x ann
Types: Fine bnd, 1st ed, hb, illus bk,
juv, ltd ed, o&r, op, used
Subj: Art, natural hist
S/S: Bnd, search serv

Savoy

SAVOY BOOKS†
Chapel Rd, 01256. Tel 413-743-5596
Owner, Robert H Fraker
Subj: Eng & Am lit, hist of agr & hort

Sharon—13,601

MICHAEL GINSBERG BOOKS INC†
PO Box 402, 02067. Tel 617-784-8181
SAN 163-4992
Owner, Michael Ginsberg; Vpres,
Elaine C Brockman
Estab 1974. 15,000 Vols. Cat 9x ann
Types: 1st ed, ltd ed, o&r
Subj: Amer, Can, church hist, scholarly
lit, Western Amer
S/S: Appr libr collec, autg, biper, mss

PEPPER & STERN—RARE BOOKS
INC†
PO Box 160, 02067. Tel 617-784-7618
SAN 163-500X
Owners, James Pepper & Peter L Stern
Estab 1973. 10,000Vols. Cat 6x ann
By appointment only
Types: 1st ed, o&r, op, signed & in-
scribed bks, autg

Subj: Eng & Am lit, mystery & detec-
tive fict, sci fict
S/S: Appr libr collec, autg, mss, orig art
See Also: Santa Barbara, CA

Sheffield—2743

HOWARD S MOTT INC†
S Main St, 01257. Tel 413-229-2019
SAN 163-5018
Owners, Howard S Mott, et al
Estab 1936. Cat
Types: 1st ed, imp, o&r
Subj: Am hist & lit, Eng hist & lit, West
Indies
S/S: Appr libr collec, mss
Holdings 15,000 including autographs,
drawings, & maps

Southbridge—16,665

SECOND FIDDLE BOOKSHOP
62 Elm St, 01550. Tel 617-347-7564,
765-0370
SAN 163-5247
Owner, Roland Boutwell
Estab 1977. 7500 Vols
Types: Fine bnd, 1st ed, hb, illus bk,
juv, ltd ed, o&r, op, papbk, used
Subj: Amer, art, med, travel
S/S: Appr libr collec, maps, orig art,
prints, search serv

South Egremont

BOOKS
Rte 23 (Mail add: Box 404, 01258).
Tel 413-528-2327; 528-9499
(for appts only)
SAN 128-8350
Owners, Bruce Gventer & Susan Gven-
ter; Mgr, Bruce Gventer
Estab 1980. 10,000 Vols. Cat
Types: Papbk, 1st ed, hb, illus bk, juv,
ltd ed, new, o&r, op, papbk, remd,
used
Subj: 19th cent women's fashion
S/S: Search serv

South Lee

J & J LUBRANO
Main St, PO Box 127, 01260.

Tel 413-243-2218
SAN 163-5085
Owners, John & Jude Lubrano
Estab 1977. 6000 Vols. 250 sq ft. Cat
2x ann
Types: Fac ed, hb, illus bk, o&r, op,
used
Subj: Circus, dance, magic & conjuring,
music, theatre
S/S: Appr libr collec, autg, biper, prints,
sh mus

Springfield—152,319

MURRAY'S BOOKFINDING
SERVICE
115 State St, 01103. Tel 203-335-5598
SAN 163-5174
Owner, Murray Novick
Estab 1953. 45,000 Vols
Types: O&r, op, used
Subj: Fiction
S/S: Search serv

TROTTING HILL PARK ANTIQUAR-
IAN BOOKSELLERS
PO Box 1324, 01101.
Tel 413-567-6466
SAN 163-5182
Owners, Rocco Verrilli & Barbara
Verrilli
7000 Vols. Cat 2-4x ann
Types: 1st ed, juv, o&r, op
Subj: Amer, Can, med, photog

Stockbridge—2328

JOHN R SANDERSON PHD—
ANTIQUARIAN BOOKS
W Main St (Mail add: Box 285, 01262).
Tel 413-274-6093
SAN 158-9997
Estab 1976. 3000 Vols. Cat ann
Types: 1st ed, hb, illus bk, juv, ltd ed,
o&r
Subj: Drama
S/S: Appr libr collec, mss

Stoughton—26,710

ROBERT H RUBIN BOOKS†
PO Box 558, 02072. Tel 617-344-0740
SAN 157-9614

Owner, Robert H Rubin
Estab 1978. Cat 4x ann
Types: O&r, op
Subj: Amer, econ, law, philos, soc sci

HENRY J VICKEY
PO Box 268, 02072. Tel 617-344-3649
SAN 163-5220
Owner, David Vickey
Estab 1945
Types: Op, used

WESTERN HEMISPHERE INC†
144 West St (Mail add: PO Box 178,
02072). Tel 617-344-8200
SAN 163-5239
Owners, Eugene L Schwaab & Eugene
L Schwaab Jr
Cat
Types: Op, o&r
Subj: Econ, govt publn, law, soc sci

Templeton—6070

PAUL C RICHARDS—AUTO-
GRAPHS†
High Acres, 01468. Tel 617-939-8981
By appointment only
Types: Autg & letters, signed photos,
signed 1st eds

Turners Falls—5168

STEVE FINER—BOOKS
PO Box 365, 01376. Tel 413-863-2375
SAN 157-7603
Owner, Steven Finer
Estab 1979. 7500 Vols. Cat 4x ann
Types: Fine bnd, 1st ed, hb, illus bk,
o&r, op, used
Subj: Games, horses, magic & conjur-
ing, New England, photog, sci-tech
S/S: Appr libr collec, search serv, auc-
tioning of literary properties & libr
collections

Waltham—58,200

HAROLD M BURSTEIN, ANTI-
QUARIAN
36 Riverside Dr, 02154.
Tel 617-893-7974
SAN 163-5301
Estab 1954. Cat 3x ann

Types: 1st ed, juv, o&r, op
Subj: Am hist & lit, Amer, bibliog
S/S: Biper, deal libr only

Wayland — 12,170

ROGER F CASAVANT
88 Dudley Rd, 01778.
   Tel 617-653-4104
SAN 158-1961
Owner, Roger F Casavant
10,000 Vols
*Types:*Fine bnd, 1st ed, hb, illus bk, juv,
   ltd ed, o&r, op
Subj: Amer, Am & Eng hist & lit
S/S: Appr libr collec, maps, mss

Wellfleet — 2209

TWICE SOLD TALES
W Main St (Mail add: PO Box 725,
   02667). Tel 716-349-9517
SAN 158-6491
Owners, Elaine R McIlory & Stephen L
   Russell
Estab 1978. 5000 Vols. Cat
Types: 1st ed, illus bk, juv, ltd ed, op,
   o&r, new & used, hb, papbk
Subj: Feminism, folklore, women's
   studies
S/S: Appr libr collec, search serv

Westborough — 13,619

LINDA HONAN ART BOOKS
49 Church St, 01581.
   Tel 617-366-0860
SAN 163-5409
Mgr, Linda Honan
Estab 1976. 4000 Vols. 266 sq ft. Cat
   4x ann
Types: O&r, op
Subj: Archaeol, archit, art, art history
   & ref
S/S: Biper, search serv

West Brookfield — 3026

THE BOOK BEAR
West Main St, Box 663, 01585.
   Tel 617-867-8705
SAN 158-9660
Owner, Albert Navitski

Estab 1977. 30,000 Vols. 2000 sq ft.
   Cat 5x ann
Types: Fine bnd, 1st ed, hb, op, papbk,
   remd, used
Subj: Anthrop, metaphys & occult,
   psychol
S/S: Appr libr collec, search serv

Westfield — 36,465

GUSTAVE H SUHM BOOK-TIQUE
81 Llewellyn Dr, 01085.
   Tel 413-568-5627
SAN 158-2291
Estab 1978. 5000 Vols. Cat 4x ann
Types: 1st ed, hb, illus bk, ltd ed, o&r,
   op, used
Subj: Guns, hunting & fishing
Open by appointment

Weston — 11,169

M & S RARE BOOKS INC†
45 Colpitts Rd, PO Box 311, 02193.
   Tel 617-891-5650
SAN 163-545X
Pres, Daniel G Siegel
Estab 1969. 10,000 Vols. 1200 sq ft.
   Cat 2x ann
Types: 1st ed, o&r
Subj: Am hist & lit, econ, Eur studies,
   sci-tech
S/S: Appr libr collec, autg, maps, mss,
   prints, sh mus

Westport — 13,763

PHILIP LOZINSKI SCHOLARLY
   BOOKS
1504 Drift Rd, 02790.
   Tel 617-636-2044
SAN 163-5468
Owner, Philip Lozinski PhD
Estab 1960. 40,000 Vols. Cat 6x ann
Types: Fac ed, hb, imp, o&r, op, reprint
Subj: Amer, for lang, hist, humanities,
   Slavica
S/S: Appr libr collec, biper, deal libr
   only, search serv, subs agency
See Also: St Bruno, PQ, Canada

West Stockbridge— 1280

DOROTHY ELSBERG
Box 178, 01266. Tel 413-232-8560
SAN 158-5150
Cat 4x ann
Types: O&r, op

Whitman— 13,534

ELLIE PANOS BOOKS
402 Bedford St, 02382.
  Tel 617-447-2730
SAN 163-5484
Owner, Ellie Panos
Estab 1955. 50,000 Vols. 1450 sq ft.
  Cat 2x ann
Types: Hb, illus bk, juv, o&r, used
Subj: Amer, biog, fiction, how-to, nee-
  dlecrafts, cookbooks
S/S: Search serv

Wilbraham— 12,053

MURRAY BOOKS†
477 Main St, PO Box 477, 01095.
  Tel 413-596-3801, 596-9372
SAN 163-5492
Owner, Samuel Murray; Mgr, Paul M
  Murray
Estab 1967. 15,000 Vols. 500 sq ft
Types: Fine bnd, illus bk, juv, ltd ed,
  o&r
Subj: Travel
S/S: Appr libr collec, maps, prints,
  wholesale
Dealers only, by appointment

Williamstown— 8741

CARRIAGE-BARN BOOKS AND
  ANTIQUES
Cold Spring Rd, Rte 7, PO Box 366,
  01267. Tel 413-458-9326
SAN 163-5514
Owner, Martha Mercer
Types: Hb, o&r
Subj: Amer, psychol, soc sci

Worcester— 161,799

JEFFREY D MANCEVICE INC
PO Box 413, West Side Sta, 01602.
  Tel 617-755-7421

Types: Early printed bks, Renaissance,
  Reformation
Subj: Sci & med, bibliog

ISAIAH THOMAS BOOKS &
  PRINTS†
980 Main St, 01603. Tel 617-754-0750
SAN 121-7429
Owner, James A Visbeck
Estab 1970. 50,000 Vols. Cat
Types: Fac ed, fine bnd, 1st ed, hb, illus
  bk, incunab, juv, ltd ed, o&r, op,
  remd, used
S/S: Appr libr collec, autg, orig art,
  prints, search serv

MICHIGAN

Algonac— 4412

JAMES M BABCOCK BOOKSELLER
5055 Point Tremble Rd, 48001.
  Tel 313-794-2277
SAN 163-5891
Owner, James M Babcock
Estab 1973. 20,000 Vols. 800 sq ft. Cat
  ann
Types: Fac ed, fine bnd, 1st ed, hb,
  incunab, illus bk, juv, ltd ed, o&r, op
Subj: Am Indian studies, genealogy,
  Michiganiana
S/S: Appr libr collec, autg, maps, mss,
  search serv

Ann Arbor— 107,316

THE DAWN TREADER BOOK SHOP
525 E Liberty, 48104.
  Tel 313-995-1008
SAN 159-5660
Owner, William Gillmore; Mgr, David
  Oyerly
Estab 1978. 35,000 Vols. 2500 sq ft.
  Cat ann
Types: Fine bnd, 1st ed, hb, illus bk, ltd
  ed, o&r, op, papbk, used
Subj: Folklore, natural hist, mystery &
  detective, sci fiction & fantasy, voy-
  ages, 19th-20th century 1st ed
S/S: Appr libr collec, autg, biper, maps,
  mss, prints

HARTFIELD FINE & RARE BOOKS
117 Dixboro Rd, 48105.

Tel 313-662-6035
SAN 157-3608
Owner, Ruth Iglehart
Estab 1970. 10,000 Vols. 1000 sq ft.
Cat 4x ann
Types: Fine bnd, 1st ed, hb, illus bk, ltd
ed, o&r, op, fine press
Subj: Eng hist & lit, 18th & early 19th
century lit
S/S: Appr libr collec, autg, mss, orig
art, search serv

LEAVES OF GRASS
2433 Whitmore Lake Rd, 48103.
Tel 313-995-2300
SAN 163-5751
Owner, Tom Nicely
Estab 1973. 10,000 Vols. Cat 3x ann
Types: Fine bnd, 1st ed, hb, illus bk, ltd
ed, o&r, op, used
Subj: Am hist & lit, Amer, bks on bks,
Eng hist & lit
S/S: Appr libr collec, search serv

THE SCIENCE BOOKSHELF
525 Fourth St, 48103.
Tel 313-665-0537
SAN 163-5778
Owner & Mgr, C A Hough
Present Owner 1977. 4000 Vols. Cat 2x
ann
Types: 1st ed, hb, o&r, op, used
Subj: Med, natural hist, sci fiction &
fantasy, sci-tech
S/S: Search serv

STATE STREET BOOKSHOP
316 S State St, 48104.
Tel 313-994-4041
SAN 163-5786
Owners, Kevin Sheets & Cathy Sheets
Estab 1975. 25,000 Vols. 2000 sq ft.
Cat
Types: 1st ed, hb, illus bk, imp, o&r,
op, used
Subj: Philos, linguistics, anthrop, Fr,
Ger & It lang, Sp lang, nat sci
S/S: Appr libr collec, biper, maps,
search serv

WEST SIDE BOOKSHOP†
113 W Liberty, 48103.
Tel 313-995-1891
SAN 163-5816
Owner, Jay Platt
Estab 1975. 10,000 Vols. 1000 sq ft

Types: Fine bnd, 1st ed, hb, illus bk,
juv, ltd ed, o&r, op
Subj: Nautical, polar exploration
S/S: Appr libr collec, search serv

THE WINE & FOOD LIBRARY
1207 W Madison, 48103.
Tel 313-663-4894
SAN 157-3616
Owner & Mgr, Jan Longone
Estab 1973. 10,000 Vols. 1100 sq ft.
Cat 2x ann
Types: Fac ed, fine bnd, 1st ed, hb,
incunab, illus bk, imp, ltd ed, new &
used, o&r, op
Subj: Cooking & nutrit, food, garden-
ing, hort, wines, beverages, gastron-
omy, decorative arts, herb & spices
S/S: Appr libr collec, search serv,
menus, wine-labels, gastronomic
ephemera

Auburn Heights

GUNNERMAN BOOKS
Box 4292, 48057. Tel 313-879-2779
SAN 157-3624
Owners, Lawrence G Barnes & Carol M
Barnes
Estab 1978. 5000 Vols. Cat
Types: O&r, op, remd, used
Subj: Hunting & fishing, dogs, big
game, bird dogs
S/S: Search serv

MARION THE ANTIQUARIAN
LIBRARIAN
3668 S Shimmons Circle 48057.
Tel 313-373-8414
SAN 163-7576
Owner, Marion E Brodie
Estab 1979. 1500 Vols. 130 sq ft. Cat
Types: 1st ed, hb, illus bk, juv, ltd ed,
o&r, op
Subj: Automobilia
S/S: Search serv

Belding — 5634

GLOBAL BOOK RESEARCH
615 N State Rd, PO Box 153, 48809.
Tel 616-794-3992
SAN 163-5875
Owner, William J Delp

Estab 1978. 10,000 Vols. 1000 sq ft.
Cat ann
Types: 1st ed, hb, o&r, op, remd, used
Subj: Hunting & fishing, Michiganiana,
military, sci-tech, guns
S/S: Appr libr collec, search serv

Dearborn—90,660

BYGONE BOOK HOUSE
12922 Michigan Ave, 48126.
Tel 313-581-1588
SAN 158-3034
Owner, Linda S Noreen; Mgr, Kathy
Kaiser
Estab 1980. 33,000 Vols. 750 sq ft
Types: Fac ed, fine bnd, 1st ed, hb, illus
bk, juv, o&r, op, papbk, remd, used
Subj: Antq, art, auto, cooking & nutrit,
military, railroadiana, ships, guns

Detroit—1,203,339

ANGELESCU BOOK SERVICE
18000 Fairfield, 48221.
Tel 313-861-5342
SAN 163-6073
Owner & Mgr, Victor Angelescu
Estab 1954. 5000 Vols. Cat
Types: Hb, imp, new & used, op, remd,
Fr, Ital, Sp lang
Subj: Am hist & lit, music, philos, rel
studies
S/S: Mss, orig art, prints, search serv

BIG BOOKSTORE
3915 Woodward Ave, 48201.
Tel 313-831-8511
SAN 163-6081
Mgr, Bill Foulkes
Estab 1930. 35,000 Vols
Types: Hb, papbk, used
S/S: Per

THE CELLAR BOOKSHOP†
18090 Wyoming, 48221.
Tel 313-861-1776
SAN 127-0265
Mgr, Petra F Netzorg
Estab 1946. Cat
Types: Imp, op, o&r
Subj: Australia, New Zealand, South-
east Asia, Pacific Islands

JOHN K KING BOOKS
214 Bagley (Mail add: PO Box 363-A,
48232). Tel 313-961-0622
SAN 163-6170
Mgr, Thomas R Schlientz
Estab 1970. 250,000 Vols. Cat 24x ann
Types: Hb, op, o&r, papbk, used
Subj: Autg, Civil War, Michiganiana
S/S: Appr libr collec, autg, biper, maps,
search serv

East Lansing—48,309

CURIOUS BOOKSHOP
307 E Grand River Ave, 48823.
Tel 517-332-0112
SAN 163-6359
Owner, Ray Walsh
Estab 1970. 35,000 Vols. 3700 sq ft.
Cat 3x ann
Types: Fine bnd, 1st ed, hb, illus bk,
juv, ltd ed, new & used, op, o&r,
papbk, remd
Subj: Illus, Michiganiana, nostalgia, sci
fiction & fantasy
S/S: Appr libr collec, autg, biper, mss,
orig art, sh mus

Grand Rapids—181,843

DON'S BOOKSTORE & BLACK
LETTER PRESS
663 Bridge NW, 49504.
Tel 616-454-7300
SAN 163-6626
Owner, Donald D Teets
Estab 1966. 30,000 Vols. 6000 sq ft
Types: 1st ed, juv, new & used, op,
o&r, papbk
Subj: Civil War, Great Lakes, Michi-
ganiana, Abraham Lincoln, 20th
century lit
S/S: Autg, biper, maps, mss, posters,
prints

MEMORY AISLE
1509 Lake Dr, 49506.
Tel 616-456-5908
SAN 170-2424
Owner, Maxine P Hondema
Estab 1983. 15,000 Vols. 2400 sq ft
Types: Fac ed, fine bnd, 1st ed, hb, illus

bk, juv, ltd ed, new, o&r, op, papbk, remd, used
Subj: Western Amer, hunting & fishing, metaphysics, Michigan esp Grand Rapids
S/S: Appr libr collec, autg, biper, maps, orig art, prints, search serv, sh mus

Grosse Pointe Park—13,639

GRUB STREET—A BOOKERY
17194 E Warren, 48230.
  Tel 313-882-7143
SAN 157-8413
Owner & Mgr, Mary C Taylor
Estab 1977. Present Owner 1980.
  30,000 Vols. 2600 sq ft. Cat ann
Types: Fac ed, fine bnd, 1st ed, hb, illus bk, juv, ltd ed, o&r, op, papbk, remd, used
Subj: Art, class studies, photog
S/S: Appr libr collec, autg, maps, prints, search serv

Hastings—6418

J E SHELDON FINE BOOKS
421 E Madison, 49058.
  Tel 616-948-2131
SAN 163-5999
Owner, Julie E Sheldon
Estab 1975. 4000 Vols. 350 sq ft. Cat 3x ann
Types: 1st ed, hb, illus bk, juv, o&r, op, used
Subj: Civil War, Michiganiana, A Conan Doyle
S/S: Appr libr collec

Jackson—39,739

GEORGE TRAMP—BOOKS
709 2nd St, 49203. Tel 517-784-1057 (by appt)
SAN 159-6276
Owner, George Tramp
Estab 1976. 25,000 Vols. 376 sq ft. Cat ann
Types: O&r, op, used
Subj: Hist, natural hist, biog, anthrop, sci fiction & fantasy, rel, class studies, Latin Am, Arctic, black studies, Revolutionary War
S/S: Appr libr collec, search serv

Kalamazoo—79,722

OLD & RARE LITERATURE
211 Woodward Ave, 49007.
  Tel 616-344-8869
SAN 128-3235
Owner, H Vanhamersveld
Estab 1981. 500 Vols
Types: 1st ed, illus bk, ltd ed, o&r, op
S/S: Autg, prints

Lawton—1558

BOHLING BOOK CO†
PO Box 215, 49065. Tel 616-624-6002
SAN 163-6952
Owners, Curt Bohling & Lynn Bohling
Estab 1967. 25,000 Vols. 2400 sq ft.
  Cat 4-6x ann
Types: Hb, o&r, op
Subj: Amer, local hist, Northwest US
S/S: Appr libr collec

Monroe—23,531

BERNARD A MARGOLIS—BOOKS
1565 Arbor Ave, 48161. Tel 313-243-5213
SAN 159-1045
Owner, Bernard A Margolis
Estab 1975. 4000 Vols. Cat
Types: Fine bnd, 1st ed, hb, illus bk, juv, ltd ed, o&r, op, papbk, used
Subj: Art nouveau, Jack Kerouac, The Shakers
S/S: Appr libr collec, autg, biper, search serv

New Troy

WENZEL BOOKS
502 California Rd, PO Box 351, 49119.
  Tel 616-426-4991
SAN 159-2122
Owner, Rupert L Wenzel Jr
Estab 1981. 25,000 Vols. 1200 sq ft.
  Cat 4x ann
Types: 1st ed, hb, illus bk, o&r, op, used
Subj: Amer, photog
S/S: Prints, sh mus

Oak Park—31,537

YESTERDAY'S BOOKS
25222 Greenfield Rd, 48237.
Tel 313-968-1510
SAN 159-1053
Owner & Mgr, Lois Wodika
Estab 1980. 75,000 Vols. 1000 sq ft
Types: Fine bnd, 1st ed, hb, illus bk,
juv, ltd ed, o&r, op, papbk, used

Okemos—7770

EINER NISULA—RARE BOOKS
1931 Osage Dr, 48864.
Tel 517-349-0495
SAN 163-7339
Owner, Einer Nisula
Cat 4x ann
Types: 1st ed, fine bnd, incunab, illus
bk, ltd ed, o&r, op
S/S: Appr libr collec, search serv

Petoskey—6097

BOOK WORLD
207 E Mitchell, PO Box 472, 49770.
Tel 616-347-0480
SAN 157-9312
Owner, M L Amtsbuechler
Estab 1977. 30,000 Vols. 1500 sq ft
Types: 1st ed, hb, o&r, op, papbk, used
S/S: Appr libr collec, search serv

Pleasant Ridge—3217

ENTROPY BOOKS
31 Oakland Park Blvd, 48069.
Tel 313-546-6078 (by appt only)
SAN 159-6969
Owner, Fred E Shearer II
Estab 1982. 2000 Vols. 450 sq ft. Cat
2x ann
Types: Fac ed, fine bnd, 1st ed, hb, imp,
ltd ed, new, o&r, papbk, remd, op
S/S: Appr libr collec, autg

Pontiac—76,715

A G ROBINSON BOOKMAN
670 E Mansfield, 48055. Tel 313-334-
9739
SAN 159-6586

Owner, A G Robinson
Estab 1978. 6000 Vols
Types: 1st ed, hb, op, used
S/S: Search serv, bnd

Rochester—7203

THE FINE BOOKS CO & DAVID
ARONOVITZ—BOOKS
781 E Snell Rd, 48063. Tel 313-651-
5735 (by appt only)
SAN 170-1657
Estab 1982. 3000 Vols. Cat 4-5x ann
Types: 1st ed, hb, ltd ed, o&r
Subj: Sci fiction & fantasy, mystery &
detective, fiction

BARBARA J RULE BOOKS
425 Walnut, 48063. Tel 313-652-3014
SAN 157-762X
Owner, Barbara J Rule
Estab 1979. 2000 Vols
Types: Hb, imp, op, used
Subj: Golf, nonfiction, cookbooks
S/S: Search serv, consignment sales

RAY RUSSELL—BOOKS
111 E 4th St (Mail add: PO Box 1008,
48063). Tel 313-651-2525
SAN 163-7444
Owner, Brian Russell
Estab 1976. 50,000 Vols. 1200 sq ft.
Cat 6x ann
Types: Fine bnd, 1st ed, o&r, op, used
Subj: Alaskana, Arctic, hist, military,
Western Amer, fire arms, fur trade
S/S: Binding & rebinding

TREASURES FROM THE CASTLE
1720 N Livernois, 48063.
Tel 313-651-7317 (by appt)
SAN 159-6578
Owner, Connie Castle
Estab 1981. Cat 2x ann
Types: Juv, op
S/S: Search serv

DALE WEBER BOOKS
5740 Livernois, 48063.
Tel 313-651-3177
SAN 158-8303
Owners, Dale Weber & Phyllis Weber
Estab 1975. 1000 Vols
Types: Fac ed, fine bnd, 1st ed, hb, ltd
ed, op, o&r
Subj: Poe & Roycroft Press

Southfield—75,568

MUCH LOVED BOOKS
PO Box 2005, 48037.
Tel 313-355-2040
SAN 163-7509
Owner, Paul M Branzburg
Estab 1978. 10,000 Vols. Cat
Types: Fine bnd, 1st ed, illus bk, ltd ed,
op, o&r, pvt presses
Subj: Amer, autg, bibliog, Michigan-
iana, New Jerseyana, New Yorkiana
S/S: Appr libr collec, autg, maps,
prints, search serv

Three Oaks—1774

DON ALLEN
208 Chicago, PO Box 3, 49128.
Tel 616-756-9218
SAN 163-7614
Owner, Don Allen
Estab 1960. 100,000 Vols. 1000 sq ft
Types: O&r, op
Subj: Amer, music, travel, 19th century
lit, social hist
S/S: Appr libr collec, autg, maps, mss,
sh mus

Traverse City—15,516

ARNOLD'S OF MICHIGAN†
511 S Union St, 49684.
Tel 616-946-9212
SAN 120-1255
Owner, B Elizabeth Griffin
S/S: Search serv

HIGHWOOD BOOKSHOP
Box 1246, 49684. Tel 616-271-3898
SAN 157-3705
Owner, Lewis L Razek
Estab 1970. 10,000 Vols. 1500 sq ft.
Cat 1-2x ann
Types: Hb, illus bk, ltd ed, o&r, op
Subj: Hunting & fishing, Michiganiana,
dogs, guns
S/S: Orig art, prints, gun & fishing
tackle catalogs

Warren—161,134

EXNOWSKI ENTERPRISES
31512 Reid Dr, 48092.
Tel 313-264-1686

SAN 163-769X
Owner, Eugene Exnowski
Estab 1971
Types: Fac ed, 1st ed, hb, incunab, new
& used, o&r, pvt presses, op, hp
papbk, remd, imp Poland & UK
Subj: Amer, art, arts & crafts, bibliog,
biog, Civil War, ethnic studies, hist,
Michiganiana, reference, World Wars
I & II, erotica
S/S: Appr libr collec, maps, mss, orig
art, prints, search serv, annual collec-
tor plates

Williamston—2981

HOUSE OF TRIVIA
136 E Middle St, 48895.
Tel 517-655-1136
SAN 163-7711
Owners, John McAuliffe & Kathy
McAuliffe
Estab 1976. 37,000 Vols. 400 sq ft
Types: 1st ed, hb, juv, ltd ed, o&r, op,
papbk, used, op comics, scouting bks
Subj: Collecting, philately, coins, col-
lectibles
S/S: Appr libr collec, biper, search serv,
sports cds

MINNESOTA

Anoka—15,634

J & J O'DONOGHUE BOOKS
1926 2nd Ave S, 55303.
Tel 612-427-4320
SAN 163-7762
Owner, Jean O'Donoghue
Estab 1966. 25,000 Vols. 2000 sq ft.
Cat 2x ann
Types: Hb, juv, op, papbk, used
Subj: Fiction, Irish hist & lit, mystery &
detective, nonfiction, sci fiction &
fantasy

Excelsior—2523

MELVIN McCOSH BOOKSELLER
26500 Edgewood Road, 55331.
Tel 612-474-8084
SAN 163-8025
Owner, Melvin McCosh
Estab 1952. Cat

Types: 1st ed, hb, op, remd, used
Subj: Bibliog, hist, literary criticism, philos
S/S: Appr libr collec

Minneapolis—370,951

BIERMAIER'S B H BOOKS
809 SE 4th St. 55414. Tel 612-378-0129
SAN 120-2391
Owner, Biermaier & Hanson; Merch Mgr & Buyer, William Biermaier
Estab 1930. Present Owner 1972. 100,000 Vols
Types: 1st ed, hb, juv, o&r, op, papbk, used
S/S: Appr libr collec, biper, maps, search serv, sh mus, spec order

THE BOOK HOUSE BOOKSELLERS
429 SE 14th Ave, 55414.
Tel 612-439-8944
SAN 163-9099
Owners, James & Kristen Cummings
Estab 1961. 100,000 Vols. Cat 6-10x ann
Types: Hb, op, o&r, used
Subj: Hist, bibliog, bks on bks, mythology, folklore, diaries, humanities
S/S: Appr libr collec

THE BOOKMAILER
2730 W Broadway, 55411.
Tel 612-588-2830
SAN 157-3713
Owner, John T Kelly
Estab 1965. 10,000 Vols. Cat 12x ann
Subj: Med, Celtic hist & lit
S/S: Appr libr collec, prints, search serv, sh mus

CHINA BOOK GALLERY
PO Box 19324, 55419.
Tel 612-926-6887
SAN 159-6047
Owner, Jerome Cavanaugh
Estab 1978. 40,000 Vols. 1400 sq ft. Cat 4x ann
Types: Hb, imp China, new, o&r, op, papbk, remd, used
S/S: Appr libr collec, biper, search serv

THE CURRENT COMPANY
716 N 1st St, 55401. Tel 612-339-5779

SAN 156-8744
Owner, Robert Rulon Miller; Mgr, Robert Rulon Miller Jr
Types: 1st ed, hb, hp papbk, illus bk, incunab, juv, ltd ed, op, used
Subj: Amer, scholarly lit, sci-tech, marine
S/S: Autg, mss, orig art, prints, reprod
Hq: Bristol, RI

DINKYTOWN ANTIQUARIAN BOOKSHOP†
1316 SE 4th St, 55414.
Tel 612-378-1286
SAN 163-8378
Owner, Larry Dingman
Estab 1974. 30,000 Vols. 1800 sq ft. Cat 8x ann
Types: Fac ed, 1st ed, ltd ed, o&r, papbk, remd, used
Subj: Fine arts, belles lettres
S/S: Appr libr collec

LELAND N LIEN BOOKSELLER†
413 S 4th St, 55415. Tel 612-332-7081
SAN 163-8475
Owner, Leland N Lien
Estab 1974. 75,000 Vols
Types: Hb, o&r, op, used
Subj: Am & Eur hist & lit
S/S: Appr libr collec, search serv

ORIGIN BOOKS
821 W 43rd St, 55409.
Tel 612-823-0150
SAN 170-1649
Owner, Steven E Clay
Estab 1982. Present Owner 1983. 10,000 Vols. 325 sq ft. Cat 3x ann
Types: 1st ed, hb, ltd ed, new, o&r, op, papbk, remd, used
By appt

OUDAL BOOKSHOP
315 9th St, 55402. Tel 612-332-7037
SAN 163-8572
Owner, Justin T Oudal
Estab 1901
Types: Fac ed, 1st ed, hb, incunab, op, o&r, used
Subj: Amer, metaphys & occult, theol
S/S: Appr libr collec, autg, biper, maps, mss, prints

SCIENTIA, BOOKS IN SCIENCE &
MEDICINE
121 SE Warwick St, Box 14042, 55414.
Tel 612-379-7463 (by appt)
SAN 158-2984
Owner, Malcolm Kottler
Present Owner 1978. 3000 Vols. Cat 2x
ann
Types: O&r, op
Subj: Evolution, med, sci-tech
S/S: Appr libr collec, search serv

North Saint Paul — 11,921

KEN CRAWFORD BOOKS
2735 E 18 Ave, 55109.
Tel 612-777-6877
SAN 163-8742
10,000 Vols. Cat 3x ann
Subj: Amer, Civil War, local hist, West-
ern Amer, Lincolniana
S/S: Appr libr collec

Saint Paul — 270,230

HAROLD'S BOOKSHOP
186 W 7th St, 55102. Tel 612-222-4524
SAN 163-8920
Owner, Harold H Lensing
Estab 1949. 40,000 Vols. 2500 sq ft
Types: 1st ed, hb, op, o&r, used
Subj: Minnesotiana, Western Amer

JAMES & MARY LAURIE BOOK-
SELLERS
251 S Snelling, 55105.
Tel 612-699-1114
SAN 163-8939
Owners, James Laurie & Mary Laurie
Estab 1978. 20,000 Vols. Cat 4-6x ann
Types: 1st ed, imp, ltd ed, o&r, op,
used
Subj: Bibliog, bks on bks, typography,
lit, criticism, press bks
S/S: Appr libr collec, search serv, maps,
prints

S & S BOOKS
80 N Wilder, 55104. Tel 612-645-5962
SAN 163-9048
Owners, John M Sticha & Pat Sticha
Estab 1971. 15,000 Vols. 600 sq ft. Cat
Types: 1st ed, hb, imp, juv, new &
used, op, papbk, o&r, remd

Subj: Fiction, inspirational, metaphys &
occult, mystery & detective, rel studies, sci fiction & fantasy
S/S: Autg, biper, search serv

A WILLIAMS BOOKS
467 Portland Ave, 55102.
Tel 612-291-1639
SAN 163-870X
Owner, Leon G Williams
Estab 1976. 50,000 Vols. 1000 sq ft
Types: O&r
S/S: Biper, per, search serv

Wayzata — 3621

ROSS & HAINES OLD BOOKS CO
639 E Lake St, 55391.
Tel 612-473-7551
SAN 163-9161
Pres & Mgr, S B Anderson
20,000 Vols. Cat
Types: 1st ed, o&r, used
S/S: Hist, militaria

Winona — 25,075

MARY TWYCE ANTIQUES &
BOOKS
601 E 5th St, 55987. Tel 507-454-4412
SAN 163-9188
Owners, Mary E Pendleton, John C
Pendleton, et al
Estab 1970. 10,000 Vols. 1000 sq ft
Types: 1st ed, hb, juv, illus bk, used
Subj: Amer
S/S: Prints, sh mus, pamphlets, post-
cards

MISSISSIPPI

Jackson — 202,895

NOUVEAU RARE BOOKS
5005 Meadow Oaks Park Dr, PO Box
12471, 39211. Tel 601-956-9950 (by
appt)
SAN 159-5903
Owner, Stephen L Silberman
Estab 1981. 1500 Vols. Cat 3-5x ann
Types: Fine bnd, 1st ed, hb, imp, ltd ed,
op, used
Subj: Poetry, drama
S/S: Appr libr collec, search serv

Ocean Springs—14,504

WILLIAM M HUTTER
Rte 3, Box 123, 39564.
 Tel 601- 875-3150
SAN 158-1813
Owners, William M Hutter & Patricia
 A Hutter
2500 Vols
Types: 1st ed, hb, illus bk, imp, o&r,
 op, used
Subj: Hist, Mississippiana, philos
S/S: Appr libr collec, autg, biper, maps,
 orig art, prints

Pearl—20,778

BOOKS & STUFF
Rankin Sq S/Ctr, 39208.
 Tel 601-939-8827
SAN 163-9412
Owners, Betty Blum & Henry Blum;
 Mgr, Mike Griffin
Present Owner 1979. 14,000 Vols. 1800
 sq ft
Types: 1st ed, hb, illus bk, juv, o&r, op,
 papbk, used
Subj: Comedy, sci fiction & fantasy, rel
S/S: Biper, prints, baseball cds

MISSOURI

Ballwin—12,750

MARVELOUS BOOKS
PO Box 1420, 63011.
 Tel 314-227-7211
SAN 158-3999
Owners, Helmar & Dorothy Kern
Estab 1976. 1000 Vols. 120 sq ft. Cat
 4-6x ann
Types: Fine bnd, illus bk, juv, ltd ed,
 o&r, op, used
S/S: Search serv

Columbia—62,061

THE BOOKSELLER—COLUMBIA
27 N Ninth, 65201. Tel 314-874-4100
SAN 163-9854
Owner, Larry Hamman
Estab 1976. 18,000 Vols. 1000 sq ft.
 Cat

Types: Fac ed, fine bnd, 1st ed, hb,
 incunab, illus bk, imp, juv, ltd ed,
 new & used, o&r, op, remd
Subj: Amer, illus
S/S: Appr libr collec, maps, mss, search
 serv

COLUMBIA BOOKS
111 Strollway, PO Box 27, 65201.
 Tel 314-449-7417
SAN 158-2941
Owners, Charles O'Dell, et al; Mgr,
 Annette Weaver
Estab 1978. 11,000 Vols. 800 sq ft
Types: Fac ed, fine bnd, 1st ed, hb, illus
 bk, juv, ltd ed, o&r, op, used
Subj: Art, mod lit
S/S: Appr libr collec, orig art, prints,
 search serv, sh mus

HARRY B ROBINSON BOOK
 SEARCH SERVICE
915 Texas Ave, 65202.
 Tel 314-449-1611
SAN 163-9889
Owner, Harry B Robinson
Present Owner 1972. 7000 Vols
Types: Hb, op
Subj: Art, Asian studies, biog, commu-
 nism, fiction, natural hist, music,
 philos, rel studies, Western Amer
S/S: Appr libr collec, search serv

Crystal City—3573

HALL'S BOOKSHOP
202 Taylor Ave, 63019
SAN 163-9919
Owner, David Hall
Estab 1968. 20,000 Vols. 1000 sq ft
Types: 1st ed, fine bnd, hb, illus bk, ltd
 ed, o&r, op, used, papbk
Subj: Adv, romance, sci fiction & fan-
 tasy, James Branch Cabell
S/S: Appr libr collec, orig art, search
 serv

Kansas City—448,159

WILLIAM J CASSIDY†
109 E 65th St, 64113.
 Tel 816-361-4271
SAN 164-0240
Owner, William J Cassidy

Estab 1953. 30,000 Vols. 2500 sq ft.
Cat 3x ann
Types: Hb, imp, op, papbk, o&r, used
Subj: Econ, dance
S/S: Search serv

GLENN BOOKS INC†
1227 Baltimore, 64105.
Tel 816-842-9777
SAN 121-4926
Owner, Ardis L Glenn
Estab 1933. Present Owner 1960.
75,000 Vols. 2000 sq ft. Cat
Types: Fine bnd, 1st ed, hb, incunab,
illus bk, imp, ltd ed, o&r, op, used
Subj: Antq, hist, scholarly lit, Western
Amer, printing hist
S/S: Appr libr collec, maps, mss, prints

GRUNEWALD KLAUS — BOOK-
DEALER
807 W 87 Terr, 64114.
Tel 816-333-7799
SAN 158-1821
Cat
Types: Fac ed, fine bnd, 1st ed, hb, illus
bk, juv, ltd ed, o&r, op, remd, used
Subj: Kansasana, Missouriana, philos
S/S: Appr libr collec, search serv

DAVID R SPIVEY FINE BOOKS &
PRINTS
900 Manheim Rd, 64109.
Tel 816-531-6088
SAN 158-9741
Owner, David R Spivey
Estab 1980. 8000 Vols. 200 sq ft
Types: Fine bnd, ltd ed, o&r
Subj: Bks on bks, Western Amer
S/S: Appr libr collec, maps, prints

Saint Louis — 453,085

AMITIN'S BOOKSHOP
711 Washington Ave, 63101.
Tel 314-421-9208, 421-2426
SAN 164-081X
Owner, Samuel Amitin; Mgr, Larry
Amitin
Estab 1936. 3969 sq ft
Types: Used
Subj: Amer, Missouriana
S/S: Appr libr collec, sh mus

MILLARD S COHEN
727 Craig Rd, Suite 101 (Mail add: PO
Box 27479, 63141).
Tel 314-872-8500
SAN 121-0122
Owner, Millard S Cohen
Estab 1970
Types: Hb, papbk, juv, remd
Subj: Wines, food
S/S: Games, gifts, posters, search serv,
subs agency, video cassettes, com-
puter software

R DUNAWAY, BOOKSELLER†
6138 Delmar Blvd, 63112.
Tel 314-725-1581
SAN 164-0925
Owner, Reginald P Dunaway
Estab 1965. 50,000 Vols. 600 sq ft. Cat
10x ann
Types: Hb, remd, fine bnd, 1st ed, illus
bk, ltd ed, new, o&r, op
Subj: Hist
S/S: Appr libr collec, biper, search serv

ELIZABETH F DUNLAP, BOOKS &
MAPS
6063 Westminster Pl, 63112.
Tel 314-863-5068
SAN 164-0933
Owner, Elizabeth F Dunlap
Estab 1955. 3000 Vols. Cat 4x ann
Types: Hb, op, o&r, used
Subj: Western Amer, Missouriana, Illi-
noisiana, Amer, Abraham Lincoln
S/S: Maps, search serv

ANTHONY GARNETT — FINE
BOOKS†
PO Box 4918, 63108.
Tel 314-367-8080
SAN 164-0968
Owner, Anthony Garnett
Estab 1967. 25,000 Vols. Cat
Types: 1st ed, hb, illus bk, ltd ed, o&r,
op
Subj: Art, hist, philos, Eng lit 17th-20th
century
S/S: Appr libr collec

D HALLORAN BOOKS
7629 Wydown Blvd, 63105.
Tel 314-863-1690
SAN 158-0051
Estab 1976

Types: Fine bnd, 1st ed, hb, incunab, illus bk, imp, juv, ltd ed, op, o&r
Subj: Sports
S/S: Appr libr collec, autg, maps, search serv

Springfield — 133,116

ABC THEOLOGICAL INDEX
Box 2786 CSS, 65803.
Tel 417-833-2019
SAN 158-6211
Estab 1961. 92,000 Vols
Types: 1st ed, fine bnd, hb, illus bk, juv, op, o&r, remd, used
Subj: Amer, Civil War, military, nostalgia, rel
S/S: Appr libr collec, autg, search serv

ADDISON'S BOOKSTORE
314 E Commercial, 65803.
Tel 417-862-8460
SAN 164-1174
Owner, Richard Addison
Estab 1952. Present Owner 1975.
20,000 Vols
Types: 1st ed, op, used, hb, o&r, papbk
Subj: Biog, fiction, hist, rel, 1st ed Am & Eng novels & poetry
S/S: Appr libr collec

H L PROSSER BIBLIOPHILE, PROFESSIONAL APPRAISER & COLLECTOR
1313 S Jefferson Ave, 65807.
Tel 417-866-5141
SAN 164-1239
Owner, H L Prosser
1000 Vols
Types: 1st ed, ltd ed, o&r, op
Subj: Mod lit, sci fiction & fantasy
S/S: Appr libr collec, autg, mss

SHIRLEY'S OLD BOOKSHOP
1948-G S Glenstone, 65804.
Tel 417-882-3734
SAN 159-0189
Owner, Sherlu R Walpole; Mgr, Hugh N Walpole
Estab 1979. Present Owner 1981
Types: 1st ed, hb, illus bk, juv, ltd ed, new & used, o&r, papbk, remd
S/S: Search serv, quality landscape photos of the Ozarks

MONTANA

Alberton — 368

MONTANA VALLEY BOOKSTORE
Railroad Ave, 59820. Tel 406-722-4590
SAN 164-1344
Owner, Karen Wales Fredette
Estab 1978. 50,000 Vols. 5000 sq ft
Types: 1st ed, hb, imp, op, papbk, used

Big Fork — 1998

BAY BOOKS & PRINTS
Grand St (Mail add: PO Box 426, 59911). Tel 406-837-4646
SAN 121-3857
Mgr, Terry Jones
Estab 1976. 8000 Vols. 1600 sq ft. Cat
Types: 1st ed, hb, new, op
Subj: Discovery & explor, Montaniana, Western Amer, fur trade
S/S: Appr libr collec, biper, per, prints, search serv

GALLERY OF THE OLD WEST
East Lake Shore (Mail add: PO Box 556, 59911). Tel 406-982-3221
SAN 159-0677
Owner, Robert T Borcherdt
Estab 1972. 2500 Vols. 800 sq ft
Types: 1st ed, hb, ltd ed, new, o&r, op, remd, used
Subj: Guns, hunting & fishing, Montaniana, Western Amer, natural hist of western states
S/S: Maps, prints, search serv

Billings — 66,798

BARJON'S BOOKS & GRAPHICS
2516 1st Ave N, 59101. Tel 406-252-4398
SAN 164-1352
Owner, Barbara E Shenkel
Estab 1977. 7000 Vols. 900 sq ft
Types: New & used, 1st ed, hb, illus bk, juv, o&r, op
Subj: Metaphys & occult, mystery & detective, philos, sci fiction & fantasy, Western Amer, comparative rel
S/S: Appr libr collec, maps, per, prints,

search serv, fantasy & role-playing game sup

THOMAS MINCKLER ART & BOOKS
111 N 30th, 59101. Tel 406-245-2969
SAN 164-1409
Owner, Thomas Minckler
Estab 1977. 5000 Vols
Types: Fine bnd, 1st ed, hb, illus bk, ltd ed, o&r, op, used
Subj: Geol, Montaniana, scholarly lit, Western Amer
S/S: Appr libr collec, autg, biper, maps, mss, search serv

Bozeman—21,645

JANE GRAHAM TREASURED BOOKS FROM THE TREASURE STATE
528 Dell Pl, 59715. Tel 406-587-5001
SAN 164-1441
Owner, Jane Graham
Estab 1975. 1599 Vols. 368 sq ft. Cat
Types: Hb, op, o&r, used
Subj: Montaniana, Western Amer, Western fiction, Yellowstone Park
S/S: Search serv

Great Falls—56,725

H-P (HARDBACK-PAPERBACK) BOOKSTORE
508 2nd Ave N, Box 1445, 59403.
Tel 406-454-1393
SAN 158-9598
Owner, Glenn A Gordon
Estab 1982. 12,000 Vols
Types: 1st ed, hb, illus bk, o&r, papbk, used
S/S: Appr libr collec, sh mus

Missoula—33,388

BIRD'S NEST
136 E Broadway, PO Box 8809, 59807.
Tel 406-721-1125
SAN 164-1670
Owner & Mgr, Betty R Anderson
Estab 1975. 10,000 Vols. 500 sq ft
Types: Hb, op, o&r, used

Subj: Montaniana, Western Amer
S/S: Search serv, rare dolls, doll repair

THE BOOK EXCHANGE
Holiday Village S/Ctr, 59801. Tel 406-728-6342
SAN 157-3829
Owner & Mgr, Rebecca L Haddad
Estab 1979. 26,400 Vols. 1200 sq ft
Types: Fine bnd, 1st ed, hb, illus bk, imp, juv, ltd ed, new & used, o&r, op, papbk, remd
Subj: Montaniana, Northwest hist, Lewis & Clark
S/S: Appr libr collec, biper, maps
See Also: Spokane, WA

NEBRASKA

Lincoln—171,932

BLUESTEM BOOKS
1234 A St, 68502. Tel 402-475-0621
SAN 157-3845
Owners & Mgrs, Scott Wendt & Pat Wendt
Estab 1975. 20,000 Vols
Types: 1st ed, hb, o&r, op, used
Subj: Nebraskana
S/S: Search serv, photographs

Omaha—311,681

THE ANTIQUARIUM
1215 Harney St, 68102.
Tel 402-341-8077
SAN 164-2103
Owners, Thomas Rudloff & Judy Rudloff
Estab 1969. 350,000 Vols. 25,000 sq ft. Cat
Types: 1st ed, hb, illus bk, ltd ed, o&r, op, papbk, used
Subj: Am hist & lit, Amer, med, psychol

D N DUPLEY, BOOK DEALER
9118 Pauline St, 68124.
Tel 402-393-2906
SAN 164-2138
Owner, D N Dupley
Estab 1964. 4000 Vols. Cat ann
Types: Hb, o&r, op, used

Subj: Western Amer, Nebraskana
S/S: Appr libr collec, search serv

RICHARD FLAMER BOOKSELLER
PO Box 3668, 68103.
 Tel 402-553-8201
SAN 158-5479
Mgrs, R Flamer & Meg Flamer
Estab 1976. Present Owner 1975.
 45,000 Vols. 6580 sq ft. Cat 4x ann
Types: Fine bnd, 1st ed, illus bk, ltd ed,
 o&r, pvt presses
S/S: Appr libr collec, maps, prints
Branches:
 1023 BOOKSELLERS
 4811 Leavenworth St, 68103
 SAN 157-8707
 Mgr, Meg Flamer
 Estab 1980. 30,000 Vols
 Types: 1st ed, hb, illus bk, juv, op,
 used
 Subj: Nebraskana
 S/S: Appr libr collec, maps, search
 serv

MOSTLY BOOKS
1025 S 10th St, 68108.
 Tel 402-345-0999
SAN 164-2189
Owner, Mgr & Buyer, Roger O'Connor
Estab 1978. 35,000 Vols. 2740 sq ft.
 Cat 6x ann
Types: Fac ed, fine bnd, 1st ed, hb,
 incunab, illus bk, imp, juv, ltd ed,
 o&r, op, used
Subj: Nebraskana, Western Amer, Nebr
 authors
S/S: Appr libr collec, autg, maps, mss,
 orig art, prints

South Sioux City—9339

BOOK BARN
RR One Box 304-H, 68776.
 Tel 402-494-2936
SAN 164-2251
Owner, Darleen J Volkert
Estab 1977. 60,000 Vols
Types: Illus bk, juv, op, o&r, used
Subj: Art, archit, auto, autg, Civil War,
 music, poetry, travel, Western Amer,
 Indians

S/S: Appr libr collec, autg, biper, per,
 search serv, sh mus

NEVADA

Las Vegas—164,674

BOOK STOP III
3732 E Flamingo Rd, 89121.
 Tel 702-456-4858
SAN 157-3853
Owner, Gini Segedi
Estab 1973. 1000 sq ft
Types: 1st ed, hb, illus bk, juv, ltd ed,
 o&r, op, papbk, used
Subj: Metaphys & occult, psychol, sci
 fiction & fantasy, classical lit
S/S: Appr libr collec, orig art, prints,
 search serv

DONATO'S FINE BOOKS
2202 W Charleston Blvd, Suite 9,
 89102. Tel 702-702-5838
SAN 158-9539
Owner, Lou Donato
Estab 1981. 18,000 Vols. 1200 sq ft
Types: Fac ed, fine bnd, 1st ed, hb, illus
 bk, juv, ltd ed, o&r, op, used
Subj: Nonfiction, sci fiction & fantasy,
 Western Amer
S/S: Appr libr collec, mss, search serv

M F DUFFY—BOOKS
5609 Ridgeline Ave, 89107.
 Tel 702-878-3294
SAN 159-6853
Types: 1st ed, o&r, op
Subj: American biography
S/S: Search serv

Reno—100,756

FIVE DOG BOOKS
Relington Gardens (Mail add: 606 W
 Plumb Ln, 89509). Tel 702-826-0650
SAN 158-9474
Owner, Manuel Simpson
Estab 1980. 5000 Vols. 400 sq ft
Types: Fine bnd, 1st ed, illus bk, o&r
Subj: Nevadiana, reference, Meso-Amer
 studies
S/S: Appr libr collec, mss, orig art,
 posters, search serv

NEW HAMPSHIRE

Ashland—1807

BUMP'S BARN BOOKSHOP
23 Depot St, Box 531, 03217.
  Tel 603-968-3354
SAN 159-2521
Owner, Donald Bump
Estab 1958. 10,000 Vols. 2000 sq ft.
  Cat ann
Types: Hb, mag & newspr, op, papbk,
  used
Subj: Hypnosis, metaphys & occult,
  photog
S/S: Search serv
See Also: Bump's Books, Scarsdale, NY

Contoocook

EMERY'S BOOKS
Rte 2, Duston Rd, 03229.
  Tel 603-746-5787
SAN 157-3888
Owner, Ron Emery
Estab 1975. 3000 Vols. Cat 12-20x ann
Types: Fac ed, fine bnd, 1st ed, hb, illus
  bk, juv, ltd ed, o&r, op, used
Subj: Amer, art, Eng hist & lit, sci-tech,
  travel, bks before 1800
S/S: Maps

WOMEN'S WORDS BOOKS
12 Main St (Mail add: PO Box 295,
  03229). Tel 603-746-4483
SAN 164-2588
Owners, Ann Grossman & Nancy
  Needham
Estab 1977. 15,000 Vols
Types: 1st ed, hb, illus bk, ltd ed, o&r,
  op, papbk, remd, used
Subj: Feminism
S/S: Search serv

Derry—18,875

BERT BABCOCK—BOOKSELLER†
5 E Derry Rd (Mail add: PO Box 1140,
  03038). Tel 603-432-9142
SAN 164-2596
Owner, Bert Babcock
Estab 1976. 4000 Vols. 700 sq ft. Cat
  10x ann

Types: 1st ed, hb, imp, ltd ed, new &
  used, o&r, op
Subj: Fiction, poetry
S/S: Letters by Am & British authors

Dover—20,377

EX LIBRIS ETCETERA
21 1st St, 03820. Tel 603-742-6353
SAN 158-9458
Owner, Mary C Townsend
Estab 1981. 5000 Vols. 1800 sq ft
Types: Hb, imp, juv, op, papbk
Subj: Women's studies, Greek hist & lit
S/S: Orig art, search serv

Epping—3460

COLOPHON BOOKSHOP†
PO Box E, 03042. Tel 312-354-0022
SAN 162-4660
Owners, Robert Liska & Christine
  Liska
Cat 2x ann
Types: 1st ed, o&r
S/S: Autg, mss

JOHN F HENDSEY, BOOKSELLER†
N River Rd (Mail add: Box 60, 03042).
  Tel 603-679-2428
SAN 161-5246
Estab 1960. 4000 Vols. Cat 2x ann
Types: Fine bnd, 1st ed, o&r
Subj: Amer, Eng hist & lit, med, sports,
  printing
S/S: Appr libr collec, autg, maps

Exeter—11,024

LANDSCAPE BOOKS
PO Box 483, 03833. Tel 603-964-6519
SAN 126-4370
Owner, Jane W Robie
Estab 1972. 700 Vols
Types: Hb, imp, new & used, op, o&r,
  remd
Subj: Landscape archit

Franklin—7901

EVELYN CLEMENT—DEALER IN
  OLD BOOKS
45 Central St, 03235. Tel 603-934-5496

SAN 164-2650
Owner, Evelyn S Clement
10,000 Vols
Types: Hb, juv, o&r, used
Subj: Biog, metaphys & occult, New
Hampshireana, sci-tech
S/S: Search serv

Haverhill — 3445

CARRY BACK BOOKS†
Dartmouth Hwy, Rte 10, Box 68,
03765. Tel 603-989-5943
SAN 164-2634
Owners, Don St John & Ruth St John
Estab 1970. 2500 Vols. Cat 4x ann
Types: 1st ed, used
Subj: Amer, photog, Vermontiana,
White Mountains

Henniker — 3246

BOOK FARM
Concord Rd, Box 515, 03242.
Tel 603-428-3429
SAN 164-2642
Owner, W K Robinson
30,000 Vols. Cat 6x ann
Types: 1st ed, hb, op, o&r, remd, used
Subj: Amer, biog, class studies, New
England, poetry
S/S: Appr libr collec, search serv

OLD NUMBER SIX BOOK DEPOT
Depot Hill, Box 525, 03242.
Tel 603-428-3334
SAN 156-9775
Owner, Ian Morrison & Helen Morri-
son
Estab 1975. 55,000 Vols. 2000 sq ft.
Cat 3x ann
Types: Used
Subj: Hist, med, New England, soc sci

Hollis — 4679

ARTHUR STILES
108 Depot Rd, 03049.
Tel 603-465-2543
SAN 170-5946
Owner, Arthur Stiles
Estab 1983. 1000 Vols
Types: Hb
Subj: Hist, natural hist
S/S: Mss

Nashua — 67,865

PAUL HENDERSON BOOKS
50 Berkeley St, 03060.
Tel 603-883-8918
SAN 159-1320
Cat
Types: O&r, op
Subj: Genealogy, local hist
S/S: Maps, prints, sh mus

Peterborough — 4895

DAVID L O'NEAL, ANTIQUARIAN
BOOKSELLERS INC†
263 Elm Hill Rd, 03071.
Tel 603-824-7489
SAN 164-2847
Owner, David L O'Neal
Estab 1971. 6000 Vols. 960 sq ft. Cat
5x ann
Types: Fine bnd, 1st ed, illus bk, o&r
Subj: Am hist & lit, bks on bks, typog-
raphy, 16th century to mod, printing
S/S: Appr libr collec, autg, maps, prints

Portsmouth — 26,254

THE ANTIQUARIAN OLD BOOK
STORE
1070 Lafayette Rd, US Rte 1, 03801.
Tel 603-436-7250
SAN 158-9938
Estab 1973. 135,000 Vols. 2000 sq ft

J & J HANRAHAN
62 Marcy St, 03801. Tel 603-436-6234
SAN 164-2863
Owners, Edward J Hanrahan & Joyce Y
Hanrahan
Estab 1960. 7000 Vols. Cat
Types: 1st ed, op, o&r
Subj: Music, New England, naval
S/S: Appr libr collec, maps, orig art,
prints

Rumney — 1212

STINSON HOUSE BOOKS†
Rumney Villa, 03266.
Tel 603-786-9300
SAN 164-2928
Owners, George N Kent & Ann S Kent
Estab 1963. 20,000 Vols. Cat ann
Types: Hb

Subj: Amer, New Hampshireana, local hist
S/S: Orig art, prints, antq

Salisbury — 781

EDWARD C FALES OLD & RARE BOOKS & MANUSCRIPTS†
Turnpike Rd, Box 56, 03268.
Tel 603-648-2484
SAN 164-2952
Juv Buyer, Hazel B Fales
Estab 1960. 25,000 Vols. Cat 2x ann
Types: 1st ed, imp, juv, o&r
Subj: Amer, arts & crafts, gardening, rel-Shaker
S/S: Appr libr collec, autg, mss

Temple — 692

CALLAHAN & CO BOOKSELLERS
Box 42, 03084. Tel 603-878-3547
SAN 158-5657
Owner, Kenneth Callahan
Cat 6x ann
Types: Op, o&r
Subj: Hunting & fishing, natural hist

Warner — 1963

ROBERT M O'NEILL, RARE BOOKS
Main St, 03278. Tel 603-456-3260
SAN 164-3002
Owner, Robert M O'Neill
Estab 1971. 3500 Vols
Types: Fac ed, fine bnd, 1st ed, hb, illus bk, ltd ed, o&r
Subj: Nautical
S/S: Appr libr collec, mss, orig art, prints, antiques

Weare — 3232

SYKES & FLANDERS OLD & RARE BOOKS†
Rte 77 N, PO Box 86, 03281.
Tel 603-529-7432
SAN 164-2987
Owners, Richard Sykes & Mary Sykes
Estab 1976. 3500 Vols. Cat
Types: Op, o&r
Subj: Amer, discovery & explor, illus, mystery & detective, natural hist, travel

Westmoreland — 1452

HURLEY BOOKS†
Rte 12, RR 1, Box 160, 03467.
Tel 603-399-4342
SAN 164-3010
Owner, Henry Hurley
Estab 1966. 25,000 Vols. Cat 6x ann
Types: 1st ed, op, o&r, used
Subj: Agr, Amer, gardening, theol, typography
S/S: Offset catalog printing
Branches:
  CELTIC CROSS BOOKS
  Box 160, 03467
  SAN 170-2564
  Estab 1976. Present Owner 1982. 10,000 Vols. Cat 2x ann
  Types: 20th cent op
  Subj: Rel-c

NEW JERSEY

Asbury Park — 17,015

WHITE'S GALLERIES INC, BOOK DEPT
607 Lake Ave, 07712.
Tel 201-774-9300
SAN 164-3037
Estab 1967. 85,000 Vols
Types: New & used, o&r
S/S: Orig art, prints, search serv, antq

Atlantic City — 40,199

BAUMAN RARE BOOKS†
14 S La Clede Pl, 08401.
Tel 609-344-0763
SAN 158-3964
Owners, David Bauman & Natalie Bauman
Estab 1974. 5000 Vols. Cat
Types: Fine bnd, 1st ed, illus bk, incunab, o&r
Subj: Amer, black studies, class studies, natural hist
S/S: Appr libr collec, bnd, maps, prints
See Also: Philadelphia, PA

Berkeley Heights — 12,549

PAPER & INK BOOKSHOP
44 Beech Ave, 07922

SAN 164-3096
Owner, R Chris Wolff
1000 Vols. Cat
Types: Hb, o&r, op
Subj: New Jersey hist, Eastern Amer
S/S: Appr libr collec, maps, mss, search
serv

Brick Town

RICHARD W SPELLMAN OLD &
RARE HISTORICAL NEWSPAPERS
610 Monticello Dr, 08723.
Tel 201-477-2413
SAN 159-1673
Owner, Richard W Spellman
100,000 Vols. Cat 10x ann
S/S: Autg, biper, maps, prints

Camden—84,910

RICHARDSON BOOKS
209 Stratford Ave, 08108.
Tel 609-854-3348
SAN 159-284X
Owners, Herbert & Christine Richard-
son
Cat
Types: Op, o&r, used
Subj: Amer, anthrop, archit, hist, travel
S/S: Appr libr collec, sh mus, ephemera

Cherry Hill—64,395

ELDORADO COMICS
1400 N Kings Hwy (Mail add: PO Box
153, Pennsauken Sta, Pennsauken,
08110). Tel 609-795-7557
SAN 158-5215
Owners, David M Braunstein & Neal H
Braunstein; Mgr, David M Braunstein
Estab 1978. 50,000 Vols. 1000 sq ft.
Cat 2x ann
S/S: Biper, orig art, rec

Closter—8164

HARVEY W BREWER†
PO Box 322, 07624. Tel 201-768-4414
SAN 164-324X
Owner, Harvey W Brewer
By appointment only
Types: O&r

Subj: Archit, art, photog, textiles
S/S: Maps, mss, orig art, prints

Cranford—24,573

CRANFORD ANTIQUE EXCHANGE
9 Columbia Ave, 07016.
Tel 201-272-3999
SAN 158-3956
Owner, Harold Cohen
Estab 1965. 8000 Vols. 10,000 sq ft
Types: 1st ed, illus bk, juv, ltd ed, o&r,
op
Subj: Art, biog, drama
S/S: Sh mus

Dover—14,681

LEO LOEWENTHAL
4 N Elk Ave, 07801. Tel 201-328-7196
SAN 158-5665
Present Owner 1975
Types: Hb, illus bk, o&r, op, used
Subj: Archit, art, dance, films & film-
making, performing arts, photog,
poetry
S/S: Search serv

Egg Harbor City—4618

EGG HARBOR BOOKS
612 White Horse Pike, 08215. Tel 609-
965-1708
SAN 164-341X
Mgr, Norman Arrington; Buyer, Wil-
liam Spangler
Estab 1978. 20,000 Vols. 1200 sq ft
Types: 1st ed, hb, illus bk, op, papbk,
used
S/S: Rec & tapes

HEINOLDT BOOKS†
1325 W Central Ave, 08215. Tel 609-
965-2284
SAN 164-3428
Owners, Margaret Heinoldt & Theodore Heinoldt
Estab 1959. 7000 Vols. 800 sq ft. Cat
3x ann
Types: Op, o&r
Subj: Am Indian studies, Amer, discovery & explor, local hist, Revolutionary War, Am hist
S/S: Appr libr collec

Englewood — 23,701

LEONARD BALISH†
124 A Engle St, 07621.
 Tel 201-871-3454
By appointment only
Subj: Amer, printed ephemera, plate
 bks, early printing & lithography

THE BOOKSTORE AT DEPOT
 SQUARE
8 Depot Square, 07631.
 Tel 201-568-6563
SAN 164-4645
Owner, Rita Alexander
Estab 1978. 25,000 Vols
Types: Hb, o&r, op, used
S/S: Appr libr collec, search serv
Open Tues-Sat 10:30-5:30 & by appt

KEN LOPEZ BOOKSELLER
156 E Hamilton Ave, 07631.
 Tel 201-567-0063
SAN 129-9905
Owner, Ken Lopez
Estab 1981. 2000 Vols. Cat 4x ann
Types: 1st ed, hb, ltd ed, new & used,
 o&r, op, remd
Subj: Am Indian studies, Latin Am, mod
 lit, nature & environ
S/S: Autg, biper

Fairfield — 5693

ANTIC HAY BOOKS
104 Pier Lane (Mail add: PO Box 1441,
 West Caldwell, 07006).
 Tel 201-277-0963
SAN 164-3479
Owner, Don Darryl Stine
3000 Vols. Cat
Types: 1st ed
Subj: Autg, 1st editions of Am & Eng lit

Freehold — 10,020

RARE BOOK CO
PO Box 957, 07728. Tel 201-780-1393
SAN 164-3525
Owner, Gerard Lupo
Estab 1920. Present Owner 1980.
 20,000 Vols. 1000 sq ft. Cat ann
Types: Fac ed, 1st ed, hb, imp, new &
 used, op, papbk, o&r
Subj: Rel-Christian Sci
S/S: Appr libr collec, autg, biper

Guttenberg — 7340

BOOKS ON FILE†
701 Park Ave (Mail add: Box 195-Dept
 4, Union City, 07087).
 Tel 201-869-8786
SAN 120-6664
Owner, Mary Snyder
Types: Op
S/S: Search serv; mail order only

Hopewell — 2001

ELISABETH WOODBURN†
Booknoll Farm, 08525.
 Tel 609-466-0522
SAN 164-3681
Owner, Elisabeth Woodburn
Estab 1946. 13,000 Vols. Cat 2x ann
Types: Hb, imp, new & used, op, remd,
 reprints
Subj: Agr, hort
S/S: Appr libr collec, search serv

Kenilworth — 8221

OZ & ENDS BOOK SHOPPE
14 Dorset Dr, 07033. Tel 201-276-8368
SAN 159-5873
Owner, Judy Bieber
Estab 1978. 1000 Vols. 200 sq ft. Cat
 4x ann
Types: 1st ed, juv, o&r, op, used
Subj: Oziana & other bks by Oz auth &
 illustrators
S/S: Biper, orig art, search serv, sh mus

Lakewood — 17,874

MILTON KRONOVET
881-C Balmoral Court, 08701.
 Tel 201-477-7771
SAN 164-3738
Owner, Milton Kronovet
Cat 5x ann
Types: Doc
Subj: Autg, hist
S/S: Autg

Lincroft

PAST HISTORY
136 Parkview Terr, 07738.
 Tel 201-842-4545
SAN 164-3789

Owners, Betty Massey & Michael Massey
Estab 1962. 25,000 Vols. 3000 sq ft.
Cat 6x ann
Types: Fac ed, hb, op, o&r, 1st ed
Subj: Amer, Am hist & lit, New Jersey-ana
S/S: Appr libr collec, maps, search serv

Little Silver — 5548

POLLOCK PUBLICATIONS
178 Pinckney Rd, 07739.
Tel 201-741-5788
SAN 124-7867
Owner, David Pollock
Estab 1955. 400 sq ft
Types: Col text, hb
Subj: Professional
S/S: Lit mags, subs agency

Long Branch — 28,819

KEEN BOOKS
198 Broadway, 07740. Tel 201-229-5060
SAN 164-3835
Owner, Robert D Keen
Types: Hb, op, remd, used
S/S: Dealing with cols & public libr only

Madison — 15,357

THE CHATHAM BOOKSELLER†
8 Green Village Rd, 07940.
Tel 201-882-1361
SAN 120-9477
Owner, Frank Deodene
Present Owner 1970. 70,000 Vols. Cat ann
Types: Hb, imp, op, papbk, used, translations
Subj: Hist of sci, tech & med
S/S: Appr libr collec

Metuchen — 13,762

BEL CANTO BOOKSHOP
PO Box 55, 08840
SAN 164-3398
Owner, Robert Hearn
Estab 1956. Present Owner 1979. 7500

Vols. 300 sq ft. Cat
Types: 1st ed, fac ed, hb, illus bk, imp, new & used, o&r, op, papbk
Subj: Music, musicians
S/S: Search serv

Millville — 24,815

SOUTH JERSEY MAGAZINE
24 Westwood Terrace (Mail add: PO Box 847, 08332). Tel 609-825-1615
SAN 164-3932
Owner, Shirley Bailey
Estab 1972
Types: O&r, op
Subj: Diaries, New Jerseyana, nostalgia, railroadiana
S/S: Old catalogues, restoring photographs

Montclair — 38,321

PATTERSON SMITH†
23 Prospect Terrace, 07042.
Tel 201-744-3291
SAN 122-8889
Estab 1955. 50,000 Vols. 4000 sq ft
Types: Op, o&r, used
Subj: Criminology, sociol, gambling, tech hist
S/S: Appr libr collec, autg, search serv

WANGNER'S BOOKSHOP & BOOK SEARCH
9 Midland Ave, 07042
Tel 201-744-4211
SAN 170-3919
Owners, Victor & Lorraine Wangner
Estab 1977. 25,000 Vols. 1200 sq ft
Types: Fac ed, fine bnd, 1st ed, hb, incunab, illus bk, juv, ltd ed, o&r, op, used
S/S: Appr libr collec, search serv

Morristown — 16,614

THE OLD BOOKSHOP
75 Spring St, 07960. Tel 201-538-1210
SAN 164-4025
Owners, C Wolff & V Faulkner
Estab 1945. 25,000 Vols. Cat
Types: 1st ed, hb, o&r, op, papbk, used
Subj: Amer

S/S: Appr libr collec, biper, maps, antq
   postcards

Norwood — 4413

WALTER J JOHNSON INC†
355 Chestnut St, 07648.
Tel 201-767-1303. Telex 13-5393
SAN 164-422X
Types: Fac ed, imp, new & used, op, o&r
Subj: Humanities, med, sci-tech, soc sci
S/S: Biper, search serv

Plainfield — 45,555

P M BOOKSHOP
321 Park Ave, 07060. Tel 201-754-3900
SAN 164-4351
Owner, Sidney Pinn
Estab 1940. Present Owner 1960.
   100,000 Vols
Types: 1st ed, fac ed, hb, incunab, o&r,
   op, papbk, remd, used
S/S: Biper, prints, sh mus

Plainsboro — 5605

LA SCALA AUTOGRAPHS INC†
PO Box 268, 08536. Tel 609-799-8523
SAN 158-6262
Owner, James Camner
Estab 1975. 1000 Vols. Cat
Types: Fac ed, new & used, o&r, op
Subj: Performing arts
S/S: Appr libr collec, autg, mss, prints

Pleasantville — 13,435

JOSEPH RUBINFINE†
RFD #1, 08232. Tel 609-641-3290
By appointment only
Subj: Amer historical autg

Princeton — 12,035

JOSEPH J FELCONE INC, RARE
   BOOKS
Box 366, 08540. Tel 609-924-0539
SAN 157-3918
Owner, Joseph J Felcone
Estab 1972. 10,000 Vols. Cat
Types: O&r, op, used
Subj: Am hist & lit, sports, bks on bks,

New Jerseyana
S/S: Appr libr collec, mss, collec develop

WITHERSPOON ART & BOOK-
   STORE
12 Nassau St, 08540. Tel 609-924-3582
SAN 164-4432
Owner, Thom P McConahay
Estab 1925. 30,000 Vols. Cat
Types: 1st ed, fac ed, incunab, ltd ed,
   o&r, op, used
S/S: Appr libr collec, orig art, prints

Roosevelt

R & A PETRILLA, BOOKSELLERS
PO Box 306, 08555. Tel 609-448-5510
Subj: Am hist, Eng & Am lit
S/S: Appraisals

Sea Isle City — 2644

BOOKFINDER — WORLD-WIDE
   BOOKSEARCH
3600 Landis Ave, PO Box 623, 08243.
   Tel 609-263-1435
SAN 157-7735
Owners, Robert B Taylor & Rebecca M
   Taylor
Present Owner 1977
Types: 1st ed, hb, illus bk, imp, ltd ed,
   new & used, op, o&r, papbk, remd
Subj: Genealogy, local hist, rel studies
S/S: Prints, search serv

Summit — 21,071

ERNEST S HICKOK†
382 Springfield Ave, 07901. Tel 201-
   277-1427
SAN 164-4610
Estab 1958. 5000 Vols
Types: Hb, op
Subj: Hunting & fishing, Am paintings
   & prints
S/S: Sporting etchings

Tenafly — 13,552

COLLECTORS' CORNER
2 Highwood Ave, 07670
SAN 159-1878

Owner, Veronica K Ronyets
Estab 1963. 3000 Vols. 8500 sq ft
Types: Fine bnd, 1st ed, for lang, hb,
    illus bk, imp, juv, ltd ed, new & used,
    o&r, op, papbk, remd
S/S: Autg, biper, gifts, gr cds, maps,
    orig art, posters, prints, search serv,
    sh mus, toys

JOHN C O'CONNOR
54 Norman Pl, 07670.
    Tel 201-568-0717
SAN 157-3934
Owner, John C O'Connor
Estab 1958. 2500 Vols
Subj: Sci-tech, humanities
S/S: Biper

RENA & MERWIN L ORNER
39 N Browing Ave, 07670.
    Tel 201-568-5796
SAN 158-3328
Owners, Rena Orner & Merwin L
    Orner
Estab 1970. 3000 Vols. Cat
Types: Fac ed, fine bnd, 1st ed, hb, illus
    bk, o&r, op, used
Subj: Polit assassinations, radical polit
S/S: Search serv

Trenton — 92,124

ACRES OF BOOKS
35 E State St, 08608. Tel 609-392-0459
SAN 164-470X
Owner, Dr John A Muscalus
Present Owner 1955. 200,000 Vols
Types: Hb, new & used, op, papbk,
    remd
Subj: Biog, educ, fiction, hist, poetry,
    psychol
S/S: Biper, prints, sh mus

Upper Montclair

WILSEY RARE BOOKS†
80 Watchung Ave, 07043. Tel 201-744-
    8366
Owner, Edward Ripley-Duggan
By appointment only
Subj: Hist of printing & papermaking,
    bks about bks, fine binding, press bks

Verona — 14,166

STEPHEN KOSCHAL AUTOGRAPHS
    & SIGNED BOOKS
159 Woodland Ave, PO Box 201,
    07044. Tel 201-239-7299
SAN 164-4777
Owner, Stephen Koschal; Mgr, Karen
    Koschal
Cat 4-5x ann
Types: Ltd ed, author autg bks, autg 1st
    ed
Subj: Amer, autg, aviation, discovery &
    explor, mod lit, presidents & presi-
    dency
S/S: Orig art, photog sup, staty

Waldwick — 10,802

HAROLD NESTLER†
13 Pennington Ave, 07463.
    Tel 201-444-7413
SAN 164-4807
Pres, Harold Nestler
Estab 1952. 3800 Vols. Cat 8x ann
Types: O&r, op
Subj: Amer, Am Indian studies, New
    England, New Jerseyana, New
    Yorkiana, Revolutionary War, canals,
    Shakers, Early Am indust & tech
S/S: Autg, maps, mss

Westfield — 30,447

HOBBIT RARE BOOKS
305 W South Ave, 07090.
    Tel 201-654-4115
SAN 157-3942
Owner, Arby Rolband
Estab 1969. 5000 Vols. 800 sq ft
Types: Fac ed, fine bnd, 1st ed, hb,
    incunab, illus bk, juv, ltd ed, o&r, op
S/S: Appr libr collec, maps, orig art,
    prints, bk repair

West Orange — 39,510

ALBERT SAIFER
102 Longview St, 07052.
    Tel 201-731-5701
SAN 158-3913
Owner, Albert Saifer
Estab 1932. 20,000 Vols. Cat 12x ann

Types: Fac ed, fine bnd, 1st ed, hb,
incunab, ltd ed, o&r, op, remd, used
S/S: Appr libr collec, search serv

NEW MEXICO

Albuquerque — 331,767

BOOKS-BY-MAIL
1833 Central Ave NW, 87104.
Tel 505-247-3043
SAN 164-5005
Owner, Katharine Ransom
Estab 1959
Types: Fac ed, 1st ed, hb, new & used,
op, papbk
Subj: Archaeol, Southwestern Amer
S/S: Search serv

BOOKSTOP ALBUQUERQUE
3500 Central SE, 87106.
Tel 505-268-8898
SAN 157-3969
Owners, Gerald Lane & Laurie Allen
Estab 1979. 40,000 Vols. 6000 sq ft
Types: 1st ed, hb, illus bk, o&r, op,
papbk, used
S/S: Search serv

CHAFEY'S OLD & RARE BOOKS
111 Cornell Dr SE, 87106.
Tel 505-265-9473
SAN 157-3977
Mgr, John Randall
Estab 1979. 10,000 Vols. Cat 3x ann
Types: Fac ed, fine bnd, 1st ed, hb, illus
bk, imp, juv, ltd ed, o&r, op, remd
Subj: Eng hist & lit, Am hist & lit,
Amer
S/S: Gr cds, rec

TOM DAVIES BOOKSTORE
218 Central SW, 87102.
Tel 505-247-2072
SAN 164-5056
Owner, Eric Holmes Patterson
Present Owner 1975. 7000 Vols. 1500
sq ft
Types: Hb, op, o&r, used, fine press
Subj: Am Indian studies, art, class stud-
ies, Southwestern Amer
S/S: Appr libr collec, biper, orig art,
prints

EL PAISANO BOOKS
1000 Park Ave SW, 87102.
Tel 505-242-9121
SAN 121-3024
Owner, Katherine Stamm
Estab 1965. 6500 Vols
Types: Hb, op, used
Subj: Southwestern Amer
S/S: Search serv

HUMMINGBIRD BOOKS
2400 Hannett NE, 87106.
Tel 505-268-6277 (by appt)
SAN 170-1932
Owner, Gail Baker
Estab 1978. 2000 Vols
Types: 1st ed, hb, new, o&r, op, remd,
used
Subj: Philos, travel
S/S: Search serv

JACK D RITTENHOUSE BOOKS
PO Box 4422, 87196.
Tel 505-255-2479
SAN 124-2652
Owner, Jack D Rittenhouse
Estab 1951. 10,000 Vols. 700 sq ft. Cat
4x ann
Types: Hb, new, op, o&r
Subj: Western Amer

SALT OF THE EARTH BOOKSTORE
LTD
2920 Central SE, 87106.
Tel 505-265-9473
SAN 157-3985
Mgr, John D Randall
Estab 1976
Types: Col text, hb, o&r, papbk, used
Subj: Art, radical polit

JANE ZWISOHN BOOKS
524 Solano Dr NE, 87108.
Tel 505-255-4080
SAN 159-1762
Owner, Jane Zwisohn
Estab 1981. 1000 Vols. Cat 2x ann
Types: 1st ed, o&r, op
Subj: Latin Am, travel, Western Amer
S/S: Prints

Corrales — 2791

PEGGY & HAROLD SAMUELS
Star Rte, Box 1281, 87048.

Tel 505-898-7258
SAN 164-5307
Owner, Peggy Samuels
Types: O&r, op
Subj: Art, Frederic Remington, Rough
    Riders
S/S: Orig art

Placitas—150

WOODSTOCK INK
PO Box 492, 87043
SAN 122-4026
Owner & Buyer, Stan Orrell
Estab 1969. 16,000 Vols. 600 sq ft. Cat
    ann
Types: Hb, imp, new & used, op
Subj: Hort, natural hist, sci-tech
S/S: Appr libr collec, maps, search serv

Santa Fe—48,899

ABACUS BOOKS
Timberwick Rd, PO Box 5555, 87502.
    Tel 505-983-6434
SAN 157-4000
Owner, Robert F Kadlec
Estab 1970. 5000 Vols. 600 sq ft
Types: 1st ed, op, o&r
Subj: Bks on bks, Southwestern Amer
S/S: Appr libr collec

ANCIENT CITY BOOKSHOP
109 East Palace Ave, PO Box 1986,
    87501. Tel 505-982-8855
SAN 120-078X
Owner, N Romanov
Estab 1959. 2500 Vols. Cat
Types: Hb, o&r, used
Subj: Bks on bks, class studies, South-
    western Amer
S/S: Search serv

CHAPARRAL BOOKS OF SANTA FE
535 Cordova Rd, Suite 470, 87501.
    Tel 505-988-1076
SAN 158-3905
Owners, Riley Parker & Betty Parker
Estab 1980. 2500 Vols. 250 sq ft. Cat
Types: Hb, o&r, op, used
Subj: Am hist & lit, Western Amer

DE LA PENA BOOKS
322¹/₂ Camino Cerrito, 87501.
    Tel 505-982-1299

SAN 164-5587
Owner, Hobart N Durham Jr
Estab 1974. 5000 Vols. 2000 sq ft
Types: 1st ed, hb, illus bk, imp, ltd ed,
    o&r
Subj: Am Indian studies, Latin Am,
    Mex, New Mexicana, photog, South-
    western Amer, Am hist
S/S: Appr libr collec, maps, mss, orig
    art, prints

RICHARD FITCH OLD MAPS &
    PRINTS & BOOKS
2324 Calle Halcon, 87501.
    Tel 505-982-2939
SAN 157-4019
Owner, Richard Fitch
Estab 1973. 6000 Vols. 1000 sq ft. Cat
    2x ann
Types: Hb, illus bk, o&r
Subj: Can, Southwestern Amer, cartog-
    raphy
S/S: Appr libr collec, maps, prints,
    search serv

GREAT SOUTHWEST BOOKS
960 Camino Santander, 87501.
    Tel 505-983-1680
SAN 158-1872
Owner, Clark Kimball
Estab 1976. 5000 Vols. 1000 sq ft
Types: Fine bnd, 1st ed, hb, illus bk,
    juv, ltd ed, o&r, op, used
Subj: New Mexicana, Southwestern
    Amer, Rydal Press
S/S: Appr libr collec, autg, mss

MARGOLIS & MOSS
410 Old Santa Fe Trail (Mail add: PO
    Box 2042, 87501). Tel 505-982-1028
SAN 159-0103
Owners, David Margolis & Jean Moss
Estab 1979. 3000 Vols. 900 sq ft. Cat
Types: Fine bnd, 1st ed, illus bk, juv, ltd
    ed, o&r
S/S: Appr libr collec, autg, maps, mss,
    photog sup, prints, sh mus, ephemera

NICHOLAS POTTER, BOOK-
    SELLER†
203 E Palace Ave, 87501.
    Tel 505-983-5434
SAN 164-5641
Owner, Nicholas Potter
Estab 1969. Present Owner 1975. 6000
    Vols. 1000 sq ft

Types: Fac ed, fine bnd, 1st ed, hb, illus bk, juv, ltd ed, o&r, op, used
Subj: Photog, Southwestern Amer, mod lit
S/S: Appr libr collec, rec

NEW YORK

Albany — 101,727

FAR COUNTRY BOOKSTORE
79 Central Ave, 12206.
  Tel 518-465-2755
SAN 164-5765
Owner, M Pickands
Estab 1982. 10,000 Vols. 3500 sq ft
Types: Fine bnd, 1st ed, hb, illus bk, incunab, ltd ed, o&r, op, used, new
Subj: Illus, photog, martial arts, sci fiction & fantasy
S/S: Appr libr collec, autg, biper, maps, mss, orig art, martial arts equipment

THE LONDON BOOKSHOP
456 Madison Ave, 12208.
  Tel 518-436-1425
SAN 157-4035
Owners, Irene Carr & Joseph Lynch
Estab 1979. 5000 Vols. 1000 sq ft
Types: 1st ed, o&r
Subj: Am hist & lit, Eng hist & lit, hist, New Yorkiana
S/S: Appr libr collec, prints, search serv

PAGE ONE BOOKS
114 Central Ave, 12206.
  Tel 518-434-3860
SAN 164-5803
Owner, Mary E Williams
Present Owner 1978. 12,500 Vols. 1300 sq ft
Types: Fine bnd, 1st ed, hb, illus bk, juv, ltd ed, new & used
Subj: Agr
S/S: Biper, maps, mss, per, prints

THE QUESTION MARK
PO Box 9107, 12209.
  Tel 518-465-8135
SAN 159-1894
Owner, Michael Linehan
Estab 1979. 5000 Vols. 1000 sq ft
Types: Hb, o&r
Subj: Amer, hunting & fishing, photog, cooking
S/S: Appr libr collec, autg, mss

Amsterdam — 21,872

RESTON'S BOOKNOOK
59 Rockton St, 12010.
  Tel 518-843-1601
SAN 158-1880
Owner, Donna Reston
Estab 1965. Present Owner 1971. 1200 Vols
Types: 1st ed, incunab, juv, o&r, op, used
Subj: New Yorkiana, sci fiction & fantasy
S/S: Maps, orig art, prints, antiques

Ancramdale

JOHN F SCHULTZ ANCRAMDALE BOOK BARN
Woods Dr, 12503. Tel 518-329-0193
SAN 164-5870
Owner, John F Schultz
Estab 1965. 10,000 Vols
Types: Op
See Also: Country Book Centre, New York, NY

Bayside

CHARLES E GARDINER
39-20 220th St, 11361.
  Tel 212-229-3260
SAN 164-5935
Owner, Charles E Gardiner
Estab 1965. 300 Vols. Cat 12x ann
Types: 1st ed, hb, imp, o&r, op, used
Subj: Railroadiana, engineering, engines & machines, nautical, steam

Boiceville

EDITIONS
Rte 28A, 12412. Tel 914-657-7000
SAN 164-6001
Owner, Norman Levine
Estab 1948. 100,000 Vols. Cat 12x ann
Types: Hb, op, o&r, used
Subj: Art, fiction, hist, philos, soc sci
S/S: Appr libr collec

Brewster — 1650

OLANA GALLERY
Drawer 9, 10509. Tel 914-279-8077

SAN 164-6125
Owner, Bernard Rosenberg
Estab 1971. 5000 Vols. 3500 sq ft. Cat
   4x ann
Types: Fac ed, ltd ed, new, o&r, op,
   used
Subj: Am art
S/S: Appr libr collec, autg, biper, orig
   art, search serv

Bronx—1,169,115

CHARLES BARON
55 Knolls Crescent, 10463.
   Tel 212-548-3951
SAN 164-6052
Owner, Charles Baron
Estab 1936. 1200 Vols
Types: 1st ed, op, used
Subj: Amer
S/S: Search serv

DENBRY BOOKS
3555 Rochambeau Ave, 10467.
   Tel 212-881-7459
SAN 158-3883
Owner, Roman Myroniuk
Types: 1st ed, hb, illus bk, juv, ltd ed,
   o&r, op, used

PAUL J DRABECK
2886 Roosevelt Ave, 10465.
   Tel 212-822-0183
SAN 164-6095
Owner, Paul J Drabeck
Estab 1957. Cat 4x ann
Types: Op, o&r, remd, used, Derrydale
   press
Subj: Hunting & fishing, archery, fire-
   arms, falconry
S/S: Prints, original art

WILLIAM B LIEBMANN
5700 Arlington Ave, Riverdale, 10471.
   Tel 212-548-6014
SAN 164-0386
Associate, James E Liebmann
Estab 1934
Types: O&r
S/S: Appr libr collec, autg, mss, ap-
   praisals & consulting

NATHAN SIMONS
1816 Seminole Ave, 10461.
   Tel 212-863-4328

SAN 164-615X
Estab 1950. 10,000 Vols
Types: Hb, imp, used
Subj: Atheism, freethought
S/S: Appr libr collec, search serv

Bronxville—6267

NICHOLAS T SMITH, BOOKSELLER
PO Box 66, 10708. Tel 914-337-2794
SAN 164-6192
Types: Fine bnd, press bks
Subj: Bks about bks, papermaking &
   marbling

Brooklyn—2,230,936

GEORGE A BERNSTEIN
c/o Boro Bookstore, 146 Lawrence St,
   11201. Tel 212-875-7582
SAN 157-406X
Owner, George A Bernstein
10,000 Vols. Cat
Types: Op, o&r
Subj: Anthrop, archaeol, discovery &
   explor, Judaica, sci-tech, travel,
   Islamica
S/S: Orig art

BINKIN'S BOOK CENTER
54 Willoughby St, 11201.
   Tel 212-855-7813
SAN 164-6281
Owner, Irving Binkin
Estab 1935
Types: O&r, op, used

BORO BOOK STORE
146 Lawrence St, 11201.
   Tel 212-522-5278
SAN 164-6311
Owner, R Colton
Estab 1952. 25,000 Vols. Cat
Types: 1st ed, hb, papbk, used
S/S: Search serv, per

CHARLIE BROWN'S
   BOOK-GALLERIE
34 Middagh St, 11201.
   Tel 212-624-1373
SAN 124-146X
Owner, Charles C Brown
Estab 1974. 20,000 Vols. Cat
Types: Hb, op, o&r, used
Subj: Archaeol, folklore, metaphys &
   occult, mythology

LAWRENCE FEINBERG RARE
 BOOKS & MANUSCRIPTS
68 Ashford St, 11207.
 Tel 212-235-7106
SAN 157-4094
Owner, Lawrence Feinberg
Estab 1977. Cat 2x ann
Types: Incunab, illus bk, o&r
Subj: Renaissance hist & lit, early Amer
 & Latin Amer, early sci & med
S/S: Appr libr collec, mss

FRANCES KLENETT
13 Cranberry St, 11201.
 Tel 212-852-2424
SAN 164-6478
Estab 1955
Types: Op, used
S/S: Search serv

MAIN STREET BOOKSELLERS
Box 103, Vanderveer Sta, 11210.
 Tel 212-381-8084
SAN 164-6494
Owner & Buyer, Arnold Cohen; Mgr,
 Sharon Cohen
Estab 1968. 25,000 Vols. 1500 sq ft.
 Cat 4x ann
Types: 1st ed, hb, ltd ed, o&r, op
Subj: Biog, fiction, literary criticism,
 short stories

S MILLMAN
Box 23, New Lots Sta, 11208.
 Tel 212-649-0111
SAN 164-6516
Owner, Sidney Millman
Estab 1958. Cat 4x ann
Types: Op, o&r
Subj: Econ, soc sci
S/S: Appr libr collec, search serv

NATIONWIDE BOOK SERVICE
150 Manhattan Ave (Mail add: PO
 Box 211, Williamsburg Sta, 11211).
 Tel 212-782-4328
SAN 164-6524
Owner, Isidor Suarez
Estab 1976. 150,000 Vols. 4000 sq ft.
 Cat 6x ann
Branch. Buys through hq
Types: Hb, new, o&r, op, used
Subj: Amer, biog, drama, mystery &
 detective, sci fiction & fantasy, op
 fiction
S/S: Deal libr only

Hq: Pioneer Book Service, Brooklyn,
 NY

PIONEER BOOK SERVICE
150 Manhattan Ave, 11206
SAN 164-6559
Owner, Robert Chalfin; Mgr, Isidor
 Suarez
100,000 Vols. 3000 sq ft
Types: Hb, juv, o&r, op, used
Subj: Amer, biog, fiction, nonfiction
S/S: Deal libr only, per, search serv
See Also: Nationwide Book Service,
 Brooklyn, NY

H C ROSEMAN BOOKSELLER
85 Livingston St, 11201.
 Tel 212-834-8928
SAN 164-6575
Cat 2x ann
Types: Imp, new, op, papbk, o&r
Subj: Amer, biog, Brazil, dance, films &
 filmmaking, econ, Caribbean

C J SCHEINER BOOKS
275 Linden Blvd, 11226. Tel 212-469-
 1089
SAN 157-5821
Owner & Buyer, C J Scheiner
Estab 1977. 4000 Vols. 500 sq ft. Cat
 2x ann
Types: Fac ed, fine bnd, 1st ed, hb, illus
 bk, ltd ed, o&r, op, papbk, imp Eur
Subj: Curiosa, erotica, sexology
S/S: Search serv

Buffalo — 357,870

CLAUDE HELD
PO Box 140, 14225
SAN 164-680X
Owner, Claude Held
Estab 1942. Cat 4x ann
Types: Imp, op, o&r, comics
Subj: Sci fiction & fantasy, mystery &
 detective, E R Burroughs, G A Henty
S/S: Biper
Stock includes 8000 bk vols & 40,000
 mags

MAHONEY & WEEKLY, BOOK-
 SELLERS
513 Virginia St, 14202. Tel 716-856-
 6024
SAN 159-0480

Owners, Thomas D Mahoney & Jon W
  Weekly
Estab 1972. 25,000 Vols. Cat 3-4x ann
Types: 1st ed, hb, incunab, illus bk, juv,
  ltd ed, o&r
Subj: Amer
S/S: Appr libr collec, autg, maps, mss,
  orig art, prints

MORE'S OLD-RARE BOOKS
169 Allen St, 14201. Tel 716-886-5800
SAN 164-6826
Types: 1st ed, imp, incunab

OLD EDITIONS BOOKSHOP
23 Allen St, 14202. Tel 716-885-6473
SAN 164-6834
Owner, Ronald L Cozzi
Estab 1976. 12,000 Vols. 800 sq ft
Types: Fine bnd, 1st ed, hb, illus bk, op,
  used
Subj: Art, chess, hist
S/S: Prints

PAGE ONE BOOKS
PO Box B, Main PO, 14240
SAN 158-8311
Mgr, M Sommer
Estab 1976. 40,000 Vols. 3000 sq ft.
  Cat 3x ann
Types: Ltd ed, o&r, op, remd, used
Subj: Food, military
S/S: Appr libr collec, search serv

Canaan — 1654

SYDNEY R SMITH SPORTING
  BOOKS†
12029. Tel 518-794-8998
SAN 164-6915
Owner, Camilla P Smith
Estab 1940
Types: Hb, imp, new & used, op, o&r
Subj: Dogs, horses, hunting & fishing
S/S: Appr libr collec, prints, search serv

Canandaigua — 10,419

THE BOOK BARN
237 S Main St, 14424
SAN 159-1754
Owners, Paul & Bonnie Stillman;
  Merch Mgr, Janet Snyder; Papbk
  Buyer, Sylvia Ramon; Text Buyer,

Rosarie Hallinan; Juv Buyer, James
  Osterchout
Estab 1975. 28,000 Vols. 4000 sq ft
Types: Col & el-hi text, fac ed, fine
  bnd, 1st ed, for lang, hb, illus bk,
  imp, juv, new & used, o&r, op,
  papbk, remd
S/S: Appr libr collec, posters, rental,
  search serv, 18th century clothing,
  lock muskets, rifles & pistols

Catskill — 4718

PAN BOOKS & GRAPHICS
401 Main St, 12414. Tel 518-943-4771
SAN 157-7751
Owners, Gordon Usticke & Ric Zank
Present Owner 1978. 6000 Vols. 975
  sq ft
Types: Hb, juv, op, papbk, remd, used
Subj: Graphic arts, photog
S/S: Av mat, gr cds, maps, reprod,
  rental, search serv

Cattaraugus — 1200

ROCKLAND BOOKMAN
Washington St, 14719.
  Tel 716-257-9504
SAN 166-235X
Owner, T Cullen
Estab 1970. 15,000 Vols. Cat 3x ann
Types: 1st ed, hb, illus bk, op, o&r,
  used
Subj: Amer, archaeol, art
S/S: Appr libr collec, autg, mss, orig
  art, prints, search serv

Cazenovia — 2599

JOHN C HUCKANS RARE BOOKS —
  PAN AMERICAN BOOKS
16 Farnham St (Mail add: PO Box 270,
  13035). Tel 315-655-8499, 655-9654
SAN 164-6931
Owners, John C Huckans & Raquel G
  Huckans
Estab 1967. 8000 Vols. Cat
Types: Fine bnd, 1st ed, incunab, illus
  bk, ltd ed, o&r
Subj: Amer, travel
S/S: Appr libr collec, autg, mss, sh mus
By appt only; not open to general public

PAN AMERICAN BOOKS
Box 270, 13035
SAN 156-5761
Cat
Subj: Latin Am
S/S: Appr libr collec, mss
Not open to general public
See Also: John C Huckans Rare Books,
Cazenovia, NY

Chester—1910

CARL SANDLER BERKOWITZ
PO Box 573, 10918. Tel 914-469-4231
SAN 159-1770
Owner, Carl Sandler Berkowitz
Estab 1975. 5000 Vols. Cat 5x ann
Types: O&r
Subj: Art, old world archaeology, civilizations
S/S: Appr libr collec, search serv

Clarence—18,146

VI & SI'S ANTIQUES
8970 Main St, 14031.
Tel 716-634-4488
SAN 158-3298
Owner, Violet Altman
Estab 1951. 100 Vols. Cat 6x ann
Subj: Music, mechanical
S/S: Per, mechanical & automatic music
items, antiques

Cobleskill—5272

C G FISHER—BOOKS
62 E Main St, 12043. Tel 518-234-3374
SAN 164-7024
Owner, Clifford G Fisher
Estab 1960
Types: O&r, op
Subj: New Yorkiana, Amer
S/S: Maps, prints, search serv

Cold Spring Harbor—5498

LORRAINE GALINSKY
46 Glen Way, 11724. Tel 516-692-4315
SAN 157-5856
Owner, Lorraine Galinsky
Estab 1978. 6000 Vols. 500 sq ft

Types: 1st ed, hb, illus bk, juv, o&r, op,
used
Subj: Antq, art, biog, humor, literary
criticism, poetry, travel, plays
S/S: Appr libr collec, biper, prints, antq
appr & research

Cooperstown—2342

WILLIS MONIE BOOKS†
RD 1, Box 336, 13326.
Tel 607-547-8363
SAN 157-4108
Owner, Willis Monie
Estab 1979. 20,000 Vols. Cat 12x ann
Types: 1st ed, o&r, op
Subj: Amer, class studies, New Yorkiana
S/S: Appr libr collec, maps, mss, prints

Corning—12,953

THE BOOKWORM
18 W Market, PO Box 263, 14830.
Tel 607-962-6778
SAN 157-4116
Owner, Billie Weetall
Estab 1976. 20,000 Vols. 1400 sq ft
Subj: Amer, archit, Civil War
S/S: Appr libr collec, search serv, autg,
mss, maps

Croton-on-Hudson—6889

BEV CHANEY JR, BOOKS
60 Radnor Ave, 10520.
Tel 914-271-8153, 941-1002
SAN 164-7105
Estab 1973. 15,000 Vols. Cat
Types: 1st ed, ltd ed, op
Subj: Bks on bks, mod lit, proofs

CROTON BOOK SERVICE—
SPORTSMAN'S BOOK SERVICE
PO Box 131, 10520. Tel 914-271-6575
SAN 164-7113
Mgr, Robert F Scott
Estab 1966
Types: Hb, juv, papbk, o&r, op
Subj: Military, Hudson River, Croton
Dam & Aqueduct, West Point & US
Military Academy
S/S: Search serv

Branches:
SPORTSMAN'S BOOK SERVICE
PO Box 131, 10520. Tel 914-271-
6575
SAN 126-6144
Estab 1974
Types: New, o&r, op

Deansboro

BERRY HILL BOOKSHOP
Rte 12-B, RD Box 118, 13328.
Tel 315-821-6188
SAN 164-7148
Owner, D L Swarthout
Estab 1966. 60,000 Vols. 1500 sq ft.
Cat
Types: 1st ed, hb, illus bk, juv, ltd ed,
o&r, op, used
Subj: Amer, New Yorkiana
S/S: Appr libr collec, biper, prints,
search serv, sh mus

Depew — 19,819

J NORMAN BOOKS 'N TOBACCO
Towne Edge Sq S/Ctr, 4845 Transit Rd,
14043. Tel 716-668-8448
SAN 158-6645
Estab 1978. 6000 Vols. 800 sq ft
Types: 1st ed, hb, juv, o&r, op, used
Subj: Scouting, Western Amer
S/S: Biper, search serv

Dobbs Ferry — 10,053

FREDERICK ARONE RAILROAD
ITEMS
377 Ashford Ave, 10522.
Tel 914-693-5858
SAN 158-3611
Owner & Mgr, Frederick Arone
Estab 1956. 20,000 Vols. 1600 sq ft.
Cat 8x ann
Types: 1st ed, fac ed, hb, illus bk, new,
op, o&r, used
Subj: Railroadiana
S/S: Appr libr collec, maps, per, prints,
search serv, railroad memorabilia

OCEANA PUBLICATIONS INC
75 Main St, 10522. Tel 914-693-1320
SAN 164-7164

Types: Fac ed, imp
Subj: Foreign & int law
S/S: Biper

N & N PAVLOV†
84 Main St (Mail add: 37 Oakdale Dr,
10522). Tel 914-693-1776
SAN 164-7172
Owners, Nicolai Pavlov & Nina Pavlov
Estab 1971. 2000 Vols. 400 sq ft
Types: Incunab, illus bk, juv, op, o&r
S/S: Appr libr collec, autg, biper, maps,
prints

ROY YOUNG BOOKSELLER
145 Palisade St, 10522.
Tel 914-693-6116
SAN 158-5975
Owner, Roy Young
Estab 1980. 10,000 Vols. 2000 sq ft.
Cat 3x ann
Types: 1st ed, o&r
Subj: Archit, art, mod lit, Western Amer
S/S: Appr libr collec, per

Douglaston

INTERNATIONAL BOOKS &
PERIODICALS
46-41 Overbrook St, 11362.
Tel 212-729-5655, 224-4567
SAN 158-2313
Owner, V Hatenesian
Estab 1969
S/S: Appr libr collec, biper, search serv

Eastchester — 32,648

JERRY ALPER INC
274 White Plains Rd, PO Box 218,
10707. Tel 914-793-2100.
TWX 710-562-0119
SAN 170-1371
Owner, Jerry Alper; Mgr, Ken Hoch
Estab 1981. Cat ann
Types: Hb, imp, o&r, op, used
S/S: Appr libr collec, biper

HECTOR'S
195 Park Dr, 10707. Tel 914-337-8854
SAN 130-1187
Owners, Helen Lynch & Lucia Ferrero
Estab 1981. 10,000 Vols. Cat 2x ann
Subj: Antq, arts & crafts, cats, cooking

& nutrit, med, cookbooks
S/S: Search serv

BERNICE WEISS — RARE BOOKS†
36 Tuckahoe Ave, 10707.
Tel 914-793-6200
SAN 164-7229
Owner, Bernice Weiss
Estab 1963. Cat 4x ann
Types: 1st ed, fine bnd, ltd ed, hb, juv,
illus bk, o&r, pvt presses, small
presses, signed
Subj: Drama, mod lit, poetry
S/S: Appr libr collec, autg, biper, mss,
orig art

Edmeston — 1732

INGEBORG QUITZAU THE EDMES-
TON TRADER
Rt 80, PO Box 5160, 13335.
Tel 607-965-8605
SAN 157-4124
Owner, Ingeborg Quitzau
Estab 1971. 10,000 Vols
Types: Fine bnd, 1st ed, hb, illus bk,
imp Ger, juv, ltd ed, o&r, op, used

Elizabethtown — 659

L W CURREY RARE BOOKS, INC†
Church St, PO Box 187, 12932.
Tel 518-873-6477 (by appt only)
SAN 164-7237
Owners, L W Currey & Alida Currey
Estab 1967. 30,000 Vols. Cat 8x ann
Types: Hb, imp, new & used, o&r, op,
fine printing, modern 1st ed
Subj: Am hist & lit, mod lit, sci fiction
& fantasy
S/S: Appr libr collec, autg, mss

Elma — 10,574

AS YOU LIKE IT BOOKSHOP
Bullis Rd, 14059. Tel 716-652-0060
SAN 164-7245
Owner, James A Kraynik
Estab 1976. 5000 Vols. 450 sq ft
Types: Hb, fine bnd, 1st ed, illus bk,
juv, o&r, op, papbk, used
Subj: Art, nature & environ, sci fiction
& fantasy, sci-tech, travel, polit hist

S/S: Orig art, prints, search serv, sh
mus, house portraits

Elmhurst

ELYSIAN FIELDS BOOKSELLERS
80-50 Baxter Ave, Suite 339, 11373. Tel
212-424-2789
SAN 157-4132
Owner & Mgr, Ed Drucker
Estab 1973. 10,000 Vols. Cat 3x ann
Types: 1st ed, hb, ltd ed, new & used,
op, papbk
Subj: Homosexuality
S/S: Biper, mss, orig art, per, prints,
search serv

ANTON GUD
41-22 Judge St, 11373
SAN 164-7253
Owner, Anton Gud
Estab 1935. 10,000 Vols. Cat
Types: Fac ed, 1st ed, hb, illus bk, imp,
new & used, op, papbk, o&r, remd,
fine press
Subj: Amer, sci fiction & fantasy
S/S: Appr libr collec, autg, mss, orig
art, search serv

V JANTA†
88-28 43rd Ave, 11373.
Tel 212-898-6917
Subj: Pol & EEur, general Slavica,
Balkan countries
By appointment only

Endicott — 14,457

RICHARD E DONOVAN
305 Massachusetts Ave, 13760.
Tel 607-785-5874
SAN 158-362X
Owner, Richard E Donovan
Cat 4x ann
Types: 1st ed, illus bk, new, op, o&r,
used
Subj: Golf, interior design, mod lit
S/S: Appr libr collec

Flushing

M & M HALPERN BOOKDEALERS
67-32 136th St, 11367.
Tel 212-544-3885

SAN 157-5848
Owners, Michael Halpern & Mildred
   Halpern
Present Owner 1979
Types: Op, 1st ed, illus bk, juv, o&r
Subj: Fiction, communism, photog,
   cinema
S/S: Prints, sh mus, bk fairs

RICHARD T JORDAN ANTI-
   QUARIAT
PO Box 43, Woodside, 11377.
   Tel 212-339-8758
SAN 165-022X
Owner, Richard T Jordan
Estab 1977. 20,000 Vols. 2000 sq ft.
   Cat ann
Types: 1st ed, hb, new & used, op,
   o&r, papbk, remd
Subj: Archit, art, feminism, films &
   filmmaking, performing arts, refer-
   ence, sociol, theol, Vietnam, Negro
   history, op, museum publications,
   physics conference & tech reports
S/S: Biper, gr cds, search serv, off sup,
   per, op records, theatre & music
   programs

Fly Creek — 910

FLY CREEK BOOKSTALL
RD Box 114, 13337. Tel 607-547-2036
SAN 157-907X
Owner, Ruth Yule
Estab 1979. Present Owner 1980. 3000
   Vols. 400 sq ft. Cat ann
Types: 1st ed, fine bnd, hb, incunab,
   illus bk, ltd ed, o&r, op, used, small
   presses
Subj: Poetry
S/S: Miniatures

Forest Hills

BIBLION INC
PO Box 9, 11375. Tel 212-263-3910
SAN 164-7482
Mgr, Ludwig Gottschalk
Estab 1948. 15,000 Vols. Cat
Types: Incunab, o&r
Subj: Med, sci-tech
S/S: Mss, per op

THEORIA SCHOLARLY BOOKS
PO Box 369, 11375. Tel 201-432-8009
SAN 157-4140
Owner & Buyer, Marvin Lipper; Mgr,
   Susan Lipper
Present Owner 1976. 50,000 Vols. Cat
   50x ann
Types: Fac ed, fine bnd, 1st ed, hb,
   incunab, illus bk, imp, ltd ed, new,
   o&r, op, remd
Subj: Linguistics, philos, soc sci, rel,
   philos & hist of sci, scientific &
   research methodologies
S/S: Autg, biper, mss, search serv

Geneseo — 6746

LESLIE POSTE
Lakeville Rd (Mail add: PO Box 68,
   14454). Tel 716-243-3246
SAN 124-2954
Owner, Leslie Poste
Estab 1971. 10,000 Vols. 600 sq ft
Types: 1st ed, op, o&r
Subj: Scholarly lit
S/S: Search serv

Getzville

ROY W CLARE†
47 Woodshire S, PO Box 136, 14068.
   Tel 716-688-8723
SAN 164-7601
Owner, Roy W Clare
Estab 1970. 400 Vols. Cat ann
Types: Incunab
Subj: Early sci & med, early wood cut,
   16th & 17th century Eng, witchcraft

Glen Cove — 24,618

HARRY A CUTTLER
48 Harwood Dr E, 11542.
   Tel 516-676-7066
SAN 164-761X
10,000 Vols
Types: Hb, op, o&r
Subj: Cosmetics, Amer, perfumery,
   Allen Ginsberg, Sam Johnson

Glen Head — 4000

CHARLES DVORAK — BOOK
 DEALER
Bowden Lane, 11545.
 Tel 516-671-6551
SAN 157-843X
Owner, Charles Dvorak
Types: Fine bnd, 1st ed, incunab, illus
 bk, o&r
Subj: Discovery & explor, travel
S/S: Mss

XERXES BOOKS
PO Box 428, 11545. Tel 516-671-6235
SAN 158-3646
Owners, Carol & Dennis Travis
Estab 1980. 10,000 Vols. Cat
Types: 1st ed, fac ed, fine bnd, hb, illus
 bk, incunab, juv, ltd ed, op, o&r,
 used
Subj: Orientalia, travel, hist doc
S/S: Appr libr collec, per

Glens Falls — 15,897

BLANCHE E TURNER, BOOKS
8 Glendale Dr, 12801.
 Tel 518-792-5454
SAN 164-7628
Types: Op, used, color print bks
Subj: New Yorkiana, Adirondacks

Greenwich — 1955

OWL PEN — BOOKS
12834. Tel 518-692-7039
SAN 164-7679
Owners, Edith P Brown & H H
 Howard
Estab 1960. 40,000 Vols. Cat
Types: Op, used, hb, juv
Subj: Natural hist
S/S: Search serv

Harriman — 796

ALAN C HUNTER BOOKS
Harriman Hts Rd, 10926.
 Tel 914-783-1930
SAN 157-4159
Owner, Alan C Hunter
Estab 1970. 10,000 Vols

Types: O&r, op
Subj: New Jerseyana, New Yorkiana,
 Hudson River
S/S: Maps, mss, search serv
By appt only

Hartsdale — 12,226

KARL SCHICK
180 E Hartsdale Ave, 10530.
 Tel 914-725-0408
SAN 159-1983
2000 Vols. Cat
Types: O&r
Subj: Med, philos, psychol, sci

Hastings-on-Hudson — 8573

RIVERRUN
7 Washington Ave, 10706.
 Tel 914-478-4307
SAN 159-1193
Mgr, Louisa Stephens
Estab 1977. 130,000 Vols. 5000 sq ft
Types: 1st ed, hb, op, used
Subj: Fiction, mod lit
S/S: Appr libr collec, search serv

7 TERRACE DRIVE
7 Terrace Dr, 10706. Tel 914-478-2522
 (by appt)
SAN 165-1323
Owner, Christopher P Stephens
Estab 1973. 30,000 Vols. 1000 sq ft.
 Cat 8x ann
Types: 1st ed, op, illus bk, ltd ed, o&r,
 fine presses
Subj: Fiction, mystery & detective,
 poetry, sci fiction & fantasy, author
 collec, translations, letters, scholarly
 symposia & scientific conferences
S/S: Appr libr collec, mss, search serv

Hauppauge — 13,957

H & R SALERNO
1 Given Ct, 11788. Tel 516-724-8795,
 265-3008
SAN 157-4167
Owner, Henry Salerno
Estab 1977. Cat
Types: 1st ed, hb, illus bk, juv, ltd ed,
 o&r, op, used

Subj: Art, mystery & detective, photog,
sci fiction & fantasy, Long Island hist
S/S: Autg, orig art, prints

Hempstead—40,404

LONG ISLAND BOOK CENTER
191 Front St, 11550. Tel 516-483-6527
SAN 164-7741
Owner & Buyer, Ben Gottliev
Types: New & used, op, fine bnd, o&r

Hewlett—6796

JERRY GRANAT MANUSCRIPTS
1481 Stevenson Rd (Mail add: PO Box
92, Woodmere, 11598).
Tel 516-374-7809
SAN 164-7768
Pres, Jerry Granat; Mgr, Ellen Granat
Estab 1977. Cat 5-6x ann
Types: 1st ed, ltd ed, o&r, papbk
Subj: Class studies, drama, presidents &
presidency
S/S: Autg, mss

Hilton—4151

A COLLECTOR'S LIBRARY
520 N Greece Rd, 14468.
Tel 716-392-7720
SAN 157-7786
Owner, Carmen Pitman
Estab 1973
Types: O&r, op, used
Subj: Cooking & nutrit, fishing
S/S: Search serv

Hopewell Junction—2055

DANIEL HIRSCH†
PO Box 315, 12533. Tel 914-462-7404
(by appt)
SAN 164-7814
Estab 1972. 300 Vols. Cat 6x ann
Types: 1st ed, hb, illus bk, juv, ltd ed,
o&r
Subj: Illus, reference, 18th-20th cent lit
S/S: Appr libr collec, mss, orig art

Hudson Falls—7419

THE VILLAGE BOOKSMITH
223 Main St, 12839. Tel 518-747-3261
SAN 124-9789

Owner, Clifford E Bruce
Estab 1976. 30,000 Vols. 1000 sq ft
Types: Op, used
Subj: Magic & conjuring
S/S: Search serv

Hunter—511

WALTER R BENJAMIN AUTO-
GRAPHS INC†
Scribner Hollow Rd (Mail add: PO Box
255, 12442). Tel 518-263-4133
SAN 164-7857
Pres, Mary A Benjamin; Vpres, Chris-
topher C Jaeckel
Estab 1887. Cat 8x ann
S/S: Autg, mss

Huntington—201,512

NORTH SHORE BOOKS LTD
8 Green St (Mail add: PO Box 334,
11743). Tel 516-271-5558
SAN 158-5681
Owner, Phyllis Ruth Nottman
Estab 1975. 25,000 Vols. Cat 3x ann
Types: Fac ed, fine bnd, 1st ed, hb, illus
bk, juv, ltd ed, o&r, op, papbk, used
S/S: Appr libr collec, autg, biper, mss

Huntington Station—28,817

JANUS BOOKS
36 Wyoming Dr, 11746.
Tel 516-271-6454
SAN 164-789X
Owners, Sylvia Levin & Joan Bossi
Estab 1978. 15,000 Vols.
Types: 1st ed, hb, illus bk, juv, new &
used, op
Subj: Cooking & nutrit, natural hist,
ornith, sci fiction & fantasy, travel,
World Wars I & II
S/S: Appr libr collec, search serv

Ithaca—28,732

CHARLES GARVIN RARE BOOKS
203 Dey St, 14851. Tel 607-277-4225
SAN 159-5865
Owner, Charles Garvin
Estab 1973. 60,000 Vols. 3100 sq ft
Types: 1st ed, hb, ltd ed, op, papbk,
used

Subj: Sci fiction & fantasy, mystery & detective, Eng hist & lit
S/S: Biper, mss, orig art, search serv
Open Wed-Sun 11-5; Fri 11-9

Jamaica — 100,000

CARAVAN-MARITIME BOOKS†
87-06 168th Pl, 11432.
Tel 212-526-1380
SAN 120-8683
Owner, Anne Klein
Estab 1947. 30,000 Vols. Cat 4x ann
Types: Fac ed, hb, illus bk, imp, ltd ed, o&r, used
Subj: Maritime subjects only
S/S: Appr libr collec, maps, mss, search serv, maritime prints only

Kew Gardens

EMILY OFFENBACHER†
84-50 Austin St, Box 96, 11415. Tel 212-849-5834
SAN 164-8187
Owner, Emil Offenbacher
Estab 1945. Cat ann
Types: 1st ed, imp, o&r
Subj: Med, sci-tech
S/S: Appr libr collec, autg, mss

Kirkwood — 5834

CARRIAGE HOUSE BOOKS
Kirkwood Rd, Box 670, Service Rd, 13795. Tel 607-775-2328
SAN 164-8225
Owner, David Klenotiz
Present Owner 1975. 8500 Vols. Cat 10x ann
Types: 1st ed, hb, op, papbk, o&r, used
Subj: Alaskana, Amer, Civil War, hunting & fishing, military, photog
S/S: Biper, maps, prints, search serv, wholesale

Lake Placid — 2490

WITH PIPE & BOOK
117 Main St, 12946. Tel 518-523-9096
SAN 164-8268
Owner, Breck Turner
Estab 1977. 4000 Vols. 750 sq ft. Cat
Types: 1st ed, hb, illus bk, juv, o&r, op, used

Subj: Adirondacks, winter sports
S/S: Biper, maps, prints, search serv

Larchmont — 6308

F A BERNETT INC†
2001 Palmer Ave (Mail add: PO Box 948, 10538). Tel 914-834-3026
SAN 164-8284
Owners, Frederick A Bernett, et al
Estab 1944. 6000 Vols. Cat 6x ann
Types: Op, o&r
Subj: Archaeol, art, archit
S/S: Appr libr collec, search serv

Lewiston — 3326

BROADWATER BOOKS
PO Box 278, 14092. Tel 716-754-8145
SAN 164-3509
Owner, Lyman W Newlin
Estab 1948. 7500 Vols. Cat ann
Types: Op, used
Subj: Natural hist
S/S: Search serv

Liverpool

JOHNSON & O'DONNELL, RARE BOOKS†
84 Bayberry Circle, 13088.
Tel 315-476-5312
Owner, Bruce Johnson
Subj: 19th & 20th cent Am & Eng lit

Livingston — 3087

HOWARD FRISCH†
PO Box 75, 12541. Tel 518-851-7493
SAN 164-8357
Owners, Howard Frisch & Fred Harris
Estab 1954. 10,000 Vols. Cat 2x ann
Types: Hb, juv, op, used
Subj: Amer

Mahopac — 5265

RICHARD A LOWENSTEIN
Geymer Dr, Rd 7, 10541.
Tel 914-628-3325
SAN 164-8438
Estab 1966. Cat
Types: 1st ed, hb, ltd ed, new & used, op, o&r, remd

Subj: World Wars I & II, Lincoln Steffens, Mark Twain, John Sloan, Normandie, ocean liners, battlefield art
S/S: Orig art, prints, search serv, subs agency

Mamaroneck — 17,616

JENS J CHRISTOFFERSEN RARE
BOOKS†
221 S Barry Ave, 10543.
Tel 914-698-3495
SAN 157-7816
Pres, Jens J Christoffersen
Estab 1978. 2000 Vols. Cat 2-3x ann
Types: Fine bnd, 1st ed, illus bk, ltd ed, o&r
Subj: Amer, New Yorkiana
S/S: Maps

LITTWIN & FEIDEN†
124 E Prospect Ave, 10543.
Tel 914-698-6504
SAN 157-4221
Owner, Elaine Feiden & Suzanne
Littwin
Estab 1975. 4000 Vols. Cat 1-2x ann
Types: 1st ed, fine bnd, illus bk, juv, ltd ed, o&r, op
Subj: Art, lit
S/S: Appr libr collec, mss, maps, search serv, prints

VICTOR TAMERLIS†
911 Stuart Ave, 10543.
Tel 914-698-8950
SAN 164-8462
Owner, Victor Tamerlis
Estab 1959
Types: Illus bk, imp, op, o&r, used
Subj: Art, bibliog, early ptg
S/S: Appr libr collec, prints

Manhasset — 8541

MARGARET ZERVAS RARE BOOKS
PO Box 562, 11030. Tel 516-767-0907
SAN 164-8500
Owner, Margaret Zervas
Types: Op, o&r
Subj: Amer, antq, scientific instruments
By appt only

Middletown — 21,454

QUALITY BOOK SERVICE —
T EMMETT HENDERSON
130 W Main St, 10940.
Tel 914-343-1038
SAN 164-8586
Owner & Mgr, T Henderson; Asst Mgr, Barbara Lynn
Estab 1954. 7000 Vols. Cat ann
Types: 1st ed, hb, new & used, op, papbk, o&r, remd
Subj: Amer, early sci
S/S: Appr libr collec, maps, mss, search serv

Millwood

KRAUS PERIODICALS CO†
Rt 100, 10546. Tel 914-762-2200
Types: Scholarly periodicals, bibliog, ref works

Monroe — 5996

MISSION BOOKSTORE
Seven Springs, PO Box 205, 10950
SAN 164-8624
Owner, Gonzaga-Seven Springs; Mgr, John F Treubig
Types: Col text, hb, hp papbk, op
S/S: Av mat, microfilm

Monticello — 6306

LUBRECHT & CRAMER†
RFD 1, Box 227. Tel 914-794-8539
Owner, Harry D Lubrecht
Subj: Bot & biol

Mount Kisco — 8025

PAGES
16 Dakin Ave, 10549.
Tel 914-666-8281
SAN 158-751X
Owners, Bruce H Heckman, Lewis S Goldmann & Trudie Goldmann
Estab 1981. 6000 Vols. 205 sq ft
Types: 1st ed, hb, illus bk, juv, ltd ed, op, o&r, used
Subj: Art, Hudson River, Westchester
S/S: Mss, prints, search serv, ephemera

Mount Vernon — 66,713

PAUL P APPEL†
216 Washington St, 10553.
 Tel 914-667-7365
SAN 164-8446
Owner, Paul P Appel
Estab 1946. 5000 Vols
Types: 1st ed, o&r
Subj: Mod art, 19th & 20th century
 Am & British lit

Neversink

WANTAGH RARE BOOK CO
Myers Rd, PO Box 605, 12765.
 Tel 914-985-7482
SAN 164-7520
Owner, Clare Van Norman
Cat 6x ann
Types: Hb, op, o&r, used, juv
Subj: Am hist & lit, Amer

New City — 27,344

AMERICAN LIBRARY SERVICE
PO Drawer A, 10956.
 Tel 914-634-5229
SAN 164-8683
Owner, Raphael Gould; Associate,
 Eleanor Forte
Estab 1921. 75,000 Vols
Types: Op, o&r, newspr, doc
Subj: Amer, autg, black studies, hist,
 Pacific, sports, perfumes, polo, shoes,
 Walt Whitman
S/S: Appr libr collec, maps, mss, per,
 search serv
See Also: Margate, FL

New York — 7,071,030

ABRAHAMS MAGAZINE SERVICE
56 E 13th St, 10003. Tel 212-777-4700
SAN 164-8772
Mgr, Teresa Spada
Estab 1889. Cat
Types: Fac ed, imp, new & used, op,
 o&r
S/S: Appr libr collec, biper, deal libr
 only, search serv, wholesale

ACADEMY BOOKSTORE
10 W 18th St, 10011. Tel 212-242-4848
SAN 164-8780

Owner, Alan Weiner
Estab 1973. Present Owner 1976.
 75,000 Vols. 3500 sq ft
Types: Fine bnd, 1st ed, illus bk, op,
 o&r, remd
Subj: Amer, art, music, performing arts,
 philos, photog, poetry, psychol,
 scholarly lit
S/S: Appr libr collec, autg, rec

ACANTHUS BOOKS
46 W 87th St 4B, 10024.
 Tel 212-787-1753 (by appt)
SAN 170-1258
Owner, Barry Cenower
Estab 1982. 1000 Vols. Cat 5x ann
Types: O&r, op
Subj: Archit
S/S: Appr libr collec

NOAH ALBAY COMPANY
245 W 29th St, 10001.
 Tel 212-675-4188
SAN 158-9881
Owner, Arlene McDonald; Mgr, Noah
 Albay
Estab 1965. Present Owner 1981.
 35,000 Vols. 1400 sq ft. Cat 4x ann
Types: Hb, imp, new & used, op, o&r,
 papbk
Subj: Africa, econ, hist, Middle East,
 philos, polit sci, Turkey & Ottoman
 Empire, Chinese & Jap studies
S/S: Search serv

AMPERSAND BOOKS
PO Box 674, Cooper Sta, 10276.
 Tel 212-674-6795
SAN 164-8810
Owner, George Bixby
Estab 1968. 2500 Vols. Cat 3-4x ann
Types: 1st ed, ltd ed, new
Subj: Mod lit
S/S: Appr libr collec

ANTIQUARIAN BOOKSELLERS'
 CENTER
50 Rockefeller Plaza, 10020.
 Tel 212-246-2564
SAN 164-8845
Co-operative Rare Book Shop limited to
 members of Antiquarian Booksellers
 Association of America; Exec. Secy,
 Edith M Wells
Estab 1965. 1200 Vols

Types: 1st ed, incunab, o&r
S/S: Autg, maps, mss, prints

APPELFELD GALLERY†
1372 York Ave, 10021.
Tel 212-988-7835
SAN 164-8853
Owner, Louis Appelfeld
Estab 1960. 25,000 Vols. Cat
Types: Fine bnd, illus bk, juv, ltd ed,
o&r
Subj: Am & Eng hist & lit
S/S: Appr libr collec, autg, mss

W GRAHAM ARADER III
23 E 74th St, Suite 5A, 10021.
Tel 212-628-3668
SAN 156-8027
Owner, W Graham Arader III; Mgr,
Sharon McIntosh
Subj: Amer, bibliog, reference, travel,
cartography
S/S: Appr libr collec, prints, paper
restoration, rare maps
Hq: King of Prussia, PA

ARGOSY BOOKSTORE INC†
116 E 59th St, 10022.
Tel 212-753-4455
SAN 164-8861
Owner, Louis Cohen
Estab 1924. 500,000 Vols. Cat 10x ann
Types: 1st ed, op, used
Subj: Amer, art, biog, med
S/S: Appr libr collec, maps, prints

RICHARD B ARKWAY INC†
131 5th Ave, 1003. Tel 212-475-6777
SAN 164-8888
Types: Illus bk, o&r
Subj: Discovery & explor, travel, voy-
ages
S/S: Maps

ASIAN RARE BOOKS INC
234 5th Ave (3/F), 10001.
Tel 212-259-3732. Cable: Asianrare
SAN 164-8896
Assoc Dir, Stephen Feldman
Estab 1976. Cat 10x ann
Types: Op, o&r
Subj: Asian studies, Middle East

BART AUERBACH LTD
411 West End Ave, 10024. Tel 212-724-
4054

Estab 1976
Types: 1st ed, mss
Subj: 19th & 20th cent lit
S/S: Appr libr collec
By appointment only

C VIRGINIA BARNES—
BOOKSELLER
PO Box 112, Cathedral Sta, 10025
SAN 164-8934
Owner, C Virginia Barnes
Estab 1954. Cat
Types: Fac ed, 1st ed, hb, imp, incunab,
juv, new & used, op, o&r, papbk,
remd
Subj: Genealogy, magic & conjuring,
Pennsylvaniana, Southern Amer,
memory, mnemonics
S/S: Appr libr collec, autg, mss, prints,
sh mus

BARNSTABLE BOOKS INC
Rm 506A, 799 Broadway, 10003.
Tel 212-473-8681
SAN 164-8942
Mgr, E Krastin
Estab 1960. 15,000 Vols. Cat 3x ann
Types: 1st ed, ltd ed, o&r, op, remd
Subj: Belles lettres, bibliog, urban stud-
ies, nature & environ, feminism,
scholarly lit
S/S: Appr libr collec, art sup, appraisal

J N BARTFIELD BOOKS, INC†
45 W 57th St, 10019. Tel 212-753-1830
SAN 164-8950
Mgr, George Murray
Estab 1937. 375,000 Vols. 15,000 sq ft
Types: Fine bnd, 1st ed, incunab, illus
bk, ltd ed, o&r, atlases, color plate
bks
Subj: Amer, art, Can, discovery &
explor, natural hist, sports, travel
S/S: Appr libr collec, autg, maps, mss,
orig art, prints

BELANSKE & LEVINGER INC
43 W 54 St, 10708. Tel 212-697-3091
SAN 164-6184
Owners, Ron Belanske & Sonja
Levinger
Estab 1979. 4000 Vols. 400 sq ft. Cat
3x ann
Types: 1st ed, fine bnd, illus bk, ltd ed,
o&r

Subj: Amer, Eng hist & lit
S/S: Autg

BLACK SUN BOOKS†
667 Madison Ave, 10021.
Tel 212-688-6622
SAN 164-9000
Owners, Harvey Tucker & Linda
Tucker
Estab 1969. Cat ann
Types: 1st ed, illus bk, o&r, fine press,
literary mss
S/S: Appr libr collec, orig art for books

BOOKFINDER'S GENERAL INC
145 E 27th St, 10016.
Tel 212-689-0772
SAN 164-906X
Cat
Types: Op, o&r
Subj: Bus & mgt, fiction, hist, horses,
law, linguistics, math, med, military,
nautical, poetry, polit sci, rel studies,
scholarly lit, sci-tech
S/S: Biper, deal libr only, search serv

BOOK RANGER
105 Charles, 10014. Tel 212-924-4957
SAN 164-9051
Owner, Shepard Rifkin
Estab 1973. 9500 Vols. 550 sq ft
Types: 1st ed, hb, illus bk, ltd ed, op
Subj: Amer, scholarly lit, travel
S/S: Search serv

BOOKS 'N THINGS
34 E 7th St, 10003. Tel 212-533-2320
SAN 164-9094
Owner, Gertrude Briggs
Estab 1941. 10,000 Vols
Types: 1st ed, hb, juv, op, papbk, used
Subj: Dance, literary criticism, music,
poetry, theater
S/S: Per, search serv, sh mus, old post
cds, programs

BOOKS OF WONDER
464 Hudson St, 10014.
Tel 212-989-3270
SAN 128-2425
Owner, Peter Glassman
Estab 1980. 3000 Vols. Cat
Types: Hb, juv, o&r, papbk
Subj: Sci fiction & fantasy, juv fantasy,
Oz & Baumania
S/S: Orig illustrations

WILLIAM G BOYER
Box 70, Planetarium Sta, 10024
SAN 158-3603
5000 Vols
Types: 1st ed, hb, illus bk, juv, ltd ed,
op, o&r, used
Subj: Am auth, Amer, archit, opera
S/S: Appr libr collec, autg, maps, mss,
orig art, prints

MARTIN BRESLAUER INC†
PO Box 607, 10028. Tel 212-794-2995
Owner, B H Breslauer
Types: Autg, early illus bks, fine bnd,
incunab, mss

BROUDE BROTHERS LIMITED†
170 Varick St, 10013. Tel 212-242-7001
Owner, Dr Ronald Broude
Subj: Early bks on mus, art & theater
By appointment only

ROBERT K BROWN
120 E 86th St, 10028. Tel 212-410-4223
SAN 164-9159
Cat 3x ann
Types: Hb, imp, o&r, op
Subj: Archit, art, design
S/S: Appr libr collec, per, posters,
prints, exhibit cat

BUCEPHALUS BOOKS
332 W 22nd St, 10011.
Tel 212-242-7768
SAN 158-6203
Owner, Patricia Randazzo
Estab 1980. 400 Vols. 1200 sq ft
Types: 1st ed, illus bk
Subj: Rare horse bks, 16th-20th century

CARNEGIE BOOKSHOP INC
30 E 60th St, 10022. Tel 212-755-4861
SAN 164-9221
Owner, David Kirschenbaum
Estab 1914. Present Owner 1978.
50,000 Vols. Cat 6-8x ann
Types: Fine bnd, 1st ed, hb, incunab,
illus bk, ltd ed, o&r
Subj: American hist & lit autg letters,
docs & mss
S/S: Appr libr collec, autg

CHIP'S BOOKSHOP INC
Box 639-Cooper Sta, 10003
SAN 164-9329
Pres, Emily Pearlman
5000 Vols. Cat 2x ann

Types: 1st ed, hb, imp, op, used
Subj: Art, humanities, literary criticism
S/S: Search serv, collec consult

COUNTRY BOOK CENTRE
Rte 82, W Taghkanic, 12534
SAN 156-8590
Owner, John F Schultz
Estab 1975. 10,000 Vols
Branch
Types: Op
S/S: Prints
Open by appointment only
Hq: John F Schultz, Ancramdale, NY

JAMES CUMMINS BOOKSELLER, INC†
667 Madison Ave, Suite 1005, 10021.
    Tel 212-371-4151
SAN 158-3662
Owner, James B Cummins Jr
Estab 1978. 50,000 Vols. 2000 sq ft.
    Cat 4x ann
Types: 1st ed, fine bnd, illus bk, incunab, juv, ltd ed, o&r
Subj: Horses, hunting & fishing, sports, travel, bks of the 1890's
S/S: Appr libr collec, autg, mss, orig art, prints

MITCHELL CUTLER CO
61 W 37th St, 10018. Tel 212-921-9234
SAN 127-0591
Owner, Mitchell Cutler
Estab 1977. 3500 Vols
Subj: 19th & 20th century Am & Eur art, 20th century & 50's design

HOWARD C DAITZ—PHOTO-GRAPHICA
446 W 20th St (Mail add: Box 530, Old Chelsea Station, 10113).
    Tel 212-929-8987
SAN 157-4264
Owner, Howard C Daitz
Present Owner 1972. 3000 Vols
Types: O&r, op
Subj: 19th or 20th century bks or photographs
S/S: Appr libr collec, autg, biper, orig art, sh mus

DE SIMON COMPANY†
793 Lexington Ave, 10021. Tel 212-319-0577
Owner, Daniel DeSimon

Subj: Bibliog, hist of printing, bk binding and bk collecting, libr, auction & bksellers catalogues

BEVAN DAVIES BOOKS
431 W Broadway, 10012. Tel 212-925-9132
SAN 158-9733
Owner, B Davies
Estab 1981. 5000 Vols. 1000 sq ft. Cat 4x ann
Types: New, o&r, op
Subj: Photog, Amer art, 20th century art

JORDAN DAVIES, BOOKS
356 Bowery, 10012. Tel 212-477-3891
Estab 1981. 25,000 Vols. Cat 6x ann
Types: 1st ed, press bks
Subj: Mod poetry & fiction

DOLPHIN BOOKSHOP
2743 Broadway, 10025. Tel 212-866-8454
SAN 125-1678
Owner, Linda K Montemaggi
Estab 1976. 680 sq ft. Cat
Types: 1st ed, hb, ltd ed, o&r, op, papbk, used
Subj: Archit, art, bks on bks, hist, scholarly lit
S/S: Search serv

PHILIP C DUSCHNES INC†
699 Madison Ave, 10021.
    Tel 212-838-2635
SAN 164-9523
Pres, Fanny Duschnes
Estab 1931. Cat 4x ann
Types: 1st ed, illus bk, ltd ed, pvt presses, illuminated mss & leaves

EL CASCAJERO, THE OLD SPANISH BOOK MINE
506 La Guardia Pl, 10012.
    Tel 212-254-0905
SAN 164-9566
Owner, A Gran
Estab 1956. 10,000 Vols. Cat
Types: 1st ed, hb, imp, o&r, op
Subj: Hispanica
S/S: Appr libr collec, autg, biper, maps, search serv, spec order

EX LIBRIS†
160A E 70th St, 10021.
    Tel 212-249-2618
SAN 164-9647

Owner, Arthur A Cohen; Mgr, W
Michael Sheehe; Mgr Serials Dept,
Everett Potter
Estab 1974. 5000 Vols. Cat 6-8x ann
Types: 1st ed, hb, illus bk, for lang, ltd
ed, new, o&r, op, doc ephemera
Subj: Graphic arts, photog, 20th cen-
tury archit, Russ avant-garde, sur-
realism, Vienna secession
S/S: Appr libr collec, autg, mss, orig
art, prints, rare art per

PETER THOMAS FISHER—
BOOKSELLER
41 Union Square W, 10003.
Tel 212-255-6789
SAN 124-7174
Owner, Peter Thomas Fisher
Estab 1976. 10,000 Vols. Cat 4x ann
Types: For lang, hb, fine bnd, 1st ed,
incunab, illus bk, imp, juv, o&r, op,
used
S/S: Ger lang

JOHN F FLEMING INC†
322 E 57th St, 10022. Tel 212-755-
3242
Types: 1st eds, o&r, mss

LEONARD FOX LTD†
667 Madison Ave, 10021. Tel 212-888-
5480
SAN 164-9760
Owner, Leonard Fox Ltd; Pres, Leonard
Fox
Estab 1976. 500 Vols. 400 sq ft. Cat
ann
Types: Illus bk, imp Fr, imp Ger, o&r,
used, chromo-litho
Subj: Photog, reference, art nouveau &
art deco
S/S: Appr libr collec, orig art, prints

RALPH D GARDNER
135 Central Park W, 10023.
Tel 212-877-6820
SAN 164-9817
Owner, Ralph D Gardner
Types: 1st ed, hb, juv, new & used, op,
o&r, papbk
S/S: Appr libr collec, autg, mss, orig art

GEM ANTIQUES
1088 Madison Ave, 10028.
Tel 212-535-7399
SAN 158-510X

Owner, Jack Feingold; Mgr, Bruce Al-
dini
Estab 1967. 500 Vols
Types: O&r

V F GERMACK, PROFESSIONAL
PHOTOGRAPHY COLLECTORS
1199 Park Ave, 10028.
Tel 212-289-8411
SAN 156-9643
Owner, Victor F Germack
Estab 1978
Types: O&r, op
By appointment only

STANLEY GILMAN†
Box 131, Cooper Sta, 10276
SAN 164-9876
Types: Op
Subj: Newspaper hist, lit, Am hist

GOLDEN GRIFFIN BOOKSHOP
PO Box 748 FDR Sta, 10150-0748.
Tel 212-355-3353
SAN 164-9892
Owner, Arts Inc; Mgr, J Vanos
Estab 1952. 6000 Vols
Types: Hb, Fr lang, Gr lang, juv, op,
papbk
Subj: Art
S/S: Posters, prints, spec order, gifts, gr
cds, search serv, lithographs
By appointment only

LUCIEN GOLDSCHMIDT INC†
1117 Madison Ave, 10028.
Tel 212-879-0070
SAN 164-9906
Pres, Lucien Goldschmidt
Estab 1953. Cat 2x ann
Types: Illus bk, o&r
Subj: Archit, Fr hist & lit, fine arts
S/S: Prints, drawings

GOTHAM BOOK MART & GAL-
LERY INC†
41 W 47th St, 10036. Tel 212-719-4448
Owner, Andreas Brown
Types: Lit archives, lit mss & letters,
mod 1st eds, used
S/S: Appraisals, collection development

GRAMMERCY BOOK SHOP
22 E 17th St , 10003. Tel. 212-255-5568
SAN 164-9949
Owner, L Wilbur; Mgr, R Wilbur

Estab 1940. 8500 Vols. Cat 3-4x ann
Types: 1st ed, hb, op, o&r, remd, used
Subj: Poetry, drama, biog, literary criticism, Eng lit, Amer lit
S/S: Autg, mss

GREENWICH BOOKS LTD
127 Greenwich Ave, 10012. Tel 212-242-3095
SAN 164-9957
Owner, Brian Bailey
Estab 1976. 7500 Vols. Cat 2x ann
Types: Fac ed, fine bnd, 1st ed, hb, illus bk, ltd ed, new, o&r, pvt presses
Subj: Art, letters, autg photos
S/S: Appr libr collec, autg, mss, orig art

K GREGORY
222 E 71st St, 10021. Tel 212-288-2119
SAN 164-9965
Owner, K Gregory
Estab 1931. Cat ann
Types: Illus bk, color plate, miniatures
Subj: Bot, natural hist, valentines

GRYPHON BOOKSHOP
216 W 89th St, 10024. Tel 212-362-0706
SAN 124-5163
Owners, Marc Lewis & Henry Holman
Estab 1974. 10,000 Vols
Types: Fine bnd, 1st ed, illus bk, juv, ltd ed, o&r, op
S/S: Appr libr collec, search serv, rec

ALBERT GUTKIN
1133 Broadway, 10010. Tel 212-243-3600
SAN 165-0025
Owner, Albert Gutkin
Types: O&r, atlases, color plate bks
Subj: Costuming, hort, natural hist, ornith, sports, travel, topography
S/S: Maps, prints, engravings

RENATE HALPERN GALLERIES INC
325 E 79th St, 10021. Tel 212-988-9316
SAN 157-4337
Owners, Renate Halpern & Arthur Halpern; Mgr & Merch Mgr, Arthur Halpern
Estab 1974. Present Owner 1979. 1000 Vols. 500 sq ft. Cat
Types: 1st ed, hb, illus bk, imp, juv, ltd ed, new & used, o&r, op

Subj: Am Indian studies, art, textiles, travel, ethnic studies, Oriental rugs, tapestries
S/S: Appr libr collec, orig art, prints, search serv

LATHROP C HARPER INC†
300 Madison Ave, 10017. Tel 212-490-3412
SAN 165-005X
Owners, Felix Oyens, et al
Estab 1881. 1000 Vols. Cat
Types: 1st ed, illus bk, imp, incunab, o&r
Subj: Amer, hist of med & sci
S/S: Maps, mss

W S HEINMAN†
PO Box 602, Ansonia Sta, 1966 Broadway, 10023. Tel 212-787-3154
Subj: Africana, dict, ref, tech, spec imp

J N HERLIN INC
68 Thompson St, 10012. Tel 212-431-8732
SAN 165-0092
Owner, Jean-Noel Herlin
Estab 1972. 10,000 Vols. 350 sq ft. Cat 2x ann
Types: Op
Subj: Films & filmmaking, 20th century art
S/S: Appr libr collec, biper, autg, per, exhibition cat

JONATHAN A HILL, BOOKSELLER†
470 West End Ave, 10024. Tel 212-496-7856
Subj: Sci, med, bibl, fine & early printing, lit, travel
By appointment only

PETER HLINKA HISTORICAL AMERICANA
226 E 89th St, PO Box 310, 10028. Tel 212-369-1660
SAN 165-0106
Owner, Peter Hlinka
Estab 1963. 200 Vols. 300 sq ft. Cat 2x ann
Types: Hb, o&r, remd, used
Subj: Military
S/S: Military medals, war relics

GLENN HOROWITZ BOOKSELLER
INC
141 E 44th St, Suite 712, 10017.
Tel 212-557-1381
Estab 1980. 5,000 Vols. 1,500 autg,
letters & mss
Types: 1st ed
Subj: 19th & 20th cent Eng & Am lit,
poetry & drama

HOUSE OF BOOKS LTD†
667 Madison Ave, 10021.
Tel 212-755-5998
SAN 165-0114
Owner, Mrs Louis Henry Cohn
Estab 1930. Cat
Types: 1st ed, imp
Subj: 20th century Am & Eng
S/S: Appr libr collec, autg, mss

HUCKLEBERRY DESIGNS
235 W 76th St, 10023.
Tel 212-874-3631
SAN 157-4280
Pres, John Taylor Gatto
Estab 1969. 53,000 Vols. 1300 sq ft
Types: 1st ed, illus bk, o&r, papbk
Subj: Radio, tv, photog, sci fiction &
fantasy, fiction, hist radio broadcasts
S/S: Autg, biper, search serv, sh mus,
Hogarth & other 18th century prints

IDEAL BOOKSTORE
1125 Amsterdam Ave, 10025.
Tel 212-662-1909
SAN 165-0149
Owner, Milton Epstein
Estab 1931. 20,000 Vols. 1500 sq ft.
Cat 6x ann
Types: Imp, new & used, op, remd
Subj: Humanities, soc sci

INTERNATIONAL UNIVERSITY
BOOKSELLERS INC†
30 Irving Place, 10003. Tel 212-254-
4100. Telex 23-6845
SAN 165-0181
Pres, Max J Holmes
Types: Imp
Subj: Humanities, med, sci-tech, sociol
S/S: Appr libr collec, biper, per, subs
agency

HARMER JOHNSON BOOKS LTD
667 Madison Ave, Suite 906, 10021.
Tel 212-752-1189

SAN 165-0211
Mgr, Nancy Scheck
Estab 1977. 10,000 Vols. Cat 12x ann
Types: Fac ed, 1st ed, hb, illus bk, imp,
ltd ed, o&r, op
Subj: Art reference, colorplate bks
(Egyptian, Roman, & Gr antq, eth-
nographic art)
S/S: Appr libr collec prints

JOLLY ROGER RECORDS & MUSIC
BOOKS
133 W 72nd St, Suite 404, 10023.
Tel 212-877-1836 (open by appt)
SAN 157-4299
Owner & Mgr, Joslyn Tascher
Estab 1977. Present Owner 1982
Types: Op, papbk, used
Subj: Music, theatre
S/S: Mail order, op records

KIM KAUFMAN BOOKSELLER
1370 Lexington Ave, Suite 2F, 10028.
Tel 212-369-3384
SAN 170-2246
Owner, Kim Kaufman
Estab 1982. 1000 Vols. Cat 4x ann
Types: 1st ed, hb, illus bk, juv, new,
o&r
Subj: Fiction, illus, reference
S/S: Appr libr collec, autg, mss, orig
art, prints

ELLIOT KLEIN LTD
19 W 44th St, 10036. Tel 212-840-6885
SAN 159-0413
Owner, Elliot Klein
Estab 1975. 15,000 Vols. 800 sq ft. Cat
3-5x ann
Types: Imp, juv, o&r, op
Subj: Anthrop, folklore, comparative rel
& cultural hist

H P KRAUS BOOKS†
16 E 46th St, 10017. Tel 212-687-4808
SAN 165-2070
Cat
Types: 1st ed, imp, incunab, o&r
Subj: Amer, cartography, bibliog, early
sci
S/S: Autg, globes, mss, maps, prints

LEE & LEE BOOKSELLERS INC
424 Broome St, 10013.
Tel 212-226-3460
SAN 157-5899

Owners, Virginia Lee Green & David
Cronin
Estab 1971. 3000 Vols. 1200 sq ft. Cat
6x ann
Types: 1st ed, hb, illus bk, ltd ed, o&r,
op, used
Subj: Archaeol, archit, Egyptology,
photog, art hist & ref works
S/S: Appr libr collec, biper, search serv

JANET LEHR INC†
1411 3rd Ave, PO Box 617, Gracie Sq
Sta, 10028. Tel 212-288-1802
SAN 165-0327
Dir, Janel Lehr; Asst Dir, Lewis Lehr
Present Owner 1966. 5000 Vols. 2000
sq ft. Cat ann
Types: Op, photog illus bks
Subj: Asian studies, Western Amer, 19th
& 20th cent travel
S/S: Autg, mss, search serv, photo-
graphs

BARBARA LEIBOWITS, GRAPHICS
LTD†
80 Central Park West, 10023.
Tel 212-799-0570
Types: 19th cent Eur & Am drawings,
illus bks & posters
By appointment only

LE VALOIS RARE BOOKS
PO Box 386, Gracie Sta, 10028.
Tel 212-722-1877
SAN 165-0300
Owner, H K Fried
Estab 1975. 3000 Vols. Cat 3x ann
Types: Fine bnd, imp Fr, o&r
Subj: Fr hist & lit, 18th century Fr bks,
Fr Revolution ref mat
S/S: Autg, mss prints

WILLIAM B LIEBMANN†
211 E 70th St, 10021. Tel 212-879-0669
Owner, James E Liebmann
Types: Autg, mss, press bks, o&r
S/S: Appraisals
By appointment only

LION HEART AUTOGRAPHS INC
12 W 37th St, Suite 1212, 10018.
Tel 212-695-1310
SAN 157-4310
Owner, David H Lowenherz
Estab 1978. Cat 2x ann
Subj: Art, hist, music, sci-tech
S/S: Autg documents, photos & bks

JAMES LOWE AUTOGRAPHS, LTD†
30 E 60th St, Suite 907, 10022.
Tel 212-759-0775
SAN 165-0432
Pres, James Lowe; Vpres, Sal Alberti
Estab 1980. Cat 4x ann
Types: 1st ed, illus bk, ltd ed, o&r,
signed bks
Subj: Amer, art, hist, music, New
Yorkiana, photog, poetry, World's
Fairs
S/S: Autg, mss, prints, search serv, sh
mus, appr autg & mss, photographs

MAIDEN VOYAGE BOOKS
1 5th Ave, 10003. Tel 212-260-5131
SAN 159-1843
Owner, Gordon R Robotham
Estab 1980. 5000 Vols. Cat 5x ann
Types: Fine bnd, 1st ed, hb, ltd ed, o&r
Subj: Black studies, mod lit, natural hist
S/S: Appr libr collec, mss, search serv

TIMOTHY MAWSON
134 W 92nd St, 10025.
Tel 212-874-6839
SAN 158-6238
Estab 1979. 5000 Vols. Cat 4x ann
Types: Illus bk, op, o&r, imp Eng
Subj: Gardening, illus, decorative arts,
Eng life

M M EINHORN MAXWELL
BOOKS — AT THE SIGN OF THE
DANCING BEAR
80 E 11th St, 10003. Tel 212-228-6767
SAN 165-0505
Owner, Marilyn M Einhorn
Estab 1977. 10,000 Vols. Cat 4x ann
Types: Hb, imp, new & used, op, o&r,
remd
Subj: Dance, food, puppetry, Shake-
speareana, theatre

ISAAC MENDOZA BOOK CO†
15 Ann St, 10038. Tel 212-227-8777
Owner, Walter L Caron
Types: 1st ed
Subj: Sci fict, detective fict

THE MILITARY BOOKMAN
29 E 93rd St, 10028. Tel 212-348-1280
SAN 165-053X
Owners, Margaretta Colt, et al
Estab 1976. 8000 Vols. 750 sq ft. Cat
2-3x ann
Types: O&r, op

Subj: Aviation, military, naval, military
subjects only
S/S: Appr libr collec, prints, WWI & II
posters

ARTHUR H MINTERS INC†
84 University Pl, 10003.
Tel 212-989-0593
SAN 165-0556
Pres, Arthur Minters
Estab 1957. 10,000 Vols. 2200 sq ft.
Cat 6x ann
Types: Fac ed, 1st ed, hb, illus bk, o&r,
op, used
Subj: Archit, art, films & filmmaking,
graphic arts, mod lit, photog
S/S: Appr libr collec, biper, mss, orig
art, prints, search serv

JAMES C MOREL FINE BOOKS
241 Central Park W, 10024.
Tel 212-580-9140
SAN 165-0572
Owner, James C Morel
Estab 1974. Cat ann
Types: 1st ed, illus bk, op
Subj: Mod lit, British & Am poetry

BRADFORD MORROW BOOK-
SELLER
33 W 9th St, 10011. Tel 212-477-1136
SAN 159-1029
Owner, Bradford Morrow
Estab 1977. 5000 Vols. Cat 2x ann
Types: 1st ed, ltd ed
Subj: Mod lit
S/S: Appr libr collec, mss

NEW YORK BOUND BOOKSHOP†
43 W 54th St, 10019. Tel 212-245-8503
SAN 165-067X
Owner, Barbara L Cohen
Estab 1976. 3000 Vols. Cat 4x ann
Types: Op, o&r
Subj: New Yorkiana
S/S: Search serv

NUDEL BOOKS
135 Spring St, 10012.
Tel 212-966-5624 (by appt only)
SAN 170-3153
Owner, Harry Nudel
Estab 1981. 7500 Vols. 1000 sq ft. Cat
4x ann
Types: 1st ed, illus bk, ltd ed, o&r, op
Subj: Photog, black lit
S/S: Appr libr collec, orig art

THE OLD PRINT SHOP INC†
150 Lexington Ave, 10016.
Tel 212-683-3950
SAN 165-0750
Owner, Kenneth M Newman
Types: Maps, old prints
Subj: Amer
S/S: Maps

ORSAY BOOKS
86-32 Eliot Ave, Rego Park, 11374.
Tel 212-651-6177
SAN 158-4138
Estab 1960
Types: 1st ed, hb, illus bk, new & used,
o&r, op
S/S: Search serv

PAGEANT BOOK AND PRINT
SHOP†
109 E 9th St, 10003. Tel 212-674-5296
SAN 165-0807
Owners, Sidney B Solomon, et al
Estab 1945. 250,000 Vols. Cat
Types: 1st ed, o&r, op
Subj: Art, fiction, psychol
S/S: Maps, prints

PHILLIPS AUCTIONEERS, NEW
YORK
406 E 79th St, 10021.
Tel 212-570-4830
SAN 165-0866
Specialist, Michael F Robinson
Estab 1796. Cat 6x ann
Types: O&r
S/S: Appr libr collec, maps, mss, orig
art, sh mus

PHOENIX BOOKSHOP
22 Jones St, 10014. Tel 212-675-2795
SAN 165-0874
Owner, R A Wilson
Estab 1936. Present Owner 1962.
14,000 Vols. Cat 4x ann
Types: 1st ed, hb, imp, new, o&r
Subj: Drama, fiction, poetry
S/S: Appr libr collec, autg, biper, mss

RICHARD C RAMER OLD & RARE
BOOKS†
225 E 70th St, 10021.
Tel 212-737-0222, 737-0223
SAN 165-0955
Owner, Richard C Ramer
Estab 1969. 10,000 Vols. Cat
Types: Op, o&r

Subj: Amer, Asian studies, Brazil, Latin Am, Port lang, nautical, Sp lang, travel, cartography
S/S: Appr libr collec, mss, search serv, auction rep

RIVENDELL BOOKSHOP LTD
149 1st Ave, 10003. Tel 212-533-2501
SAN 165-1005
Owner, Mgr & Buyer, Eileen Campbell Gordon
Estab 1978. 10,000 Vols
Types: 1st ed, illus bk, imp UK, juv, new & used, o&r, op
Subj: Folklore, mythology, sci fiction & fantasy, Celt studies
S/S: Maps, prints, search serv, Celtic rec

PAULETTE ROSE LTD
360 E 72nd St, 10021
SAN 159-110X
Owner, Paulette Rose
Present Owner 1978. 1000 Vols. Cat 2x ann
Types: 1st ed, illus bk, imp Fr, ltd ed, o&r, op
Subj: Class studies, feminism, women's studies, Fr lit

MARY S ROSENBERG†
17 W 60th St, 10023. Tel 212-362-4873
Subj: German & Fr, linguistics, lit, psychoanalysis, Judaica, children's bks

LEONA ROSTENBERG & MADE-LEINE B STERN — RARE BOOKS†
40 E 88 St (Mail add: Box 188, Gracie Sta, 10028). Tel 212-831-6628
SAN 165-1048
Owners, Leona Rostenberg & Madeleine B Stern
Estab 1944. 3000 Vols. Cat 3x ann
Types: Imp, o&r, imprints
Subj: Eur studies, hist, political thought, Renaissance hist & lit
S/S: Appr libr collec
By appt

J B RUND
PO Box BB, Old Chelsea Sta, 10113
SAN 165-1064
Owner, J B Rund
Estab 1967
Types: Fac ed, 1st ed, op, o&r, used

Subj: Erotica
S/S: Appr libr collec, autg, mss, orig art, search serv

CHARLOTTE F SAFIR BOOKS
1349 Lexington Ave, 10028. Tel 212-534-7933
SAN 158-3700
1000 Vols
Types: Juv, o&r, op, used
Subj: Art, cooking & nutrit, for lang, hist

WILLIAM H SCHAB GALLERY, INC†
11 E 57th St, 10019. Tel 212-758-0327
SAN 165-1129
Owner, Frederick G Schab
Estab 1940. Cat ann
Types: 1st ed, imp, incunab, o&r, illus 15th-18th century
Subj: Ancient hist & lit, humanities, hist of art, hist of sci
S/S: Mss, prints

JUSTIN G SCHILLER LTD†
PO Box 1667, FDR Sta, 10150. Tel 212-832-8231
SAN 165-1137
Owners, Justin G Schiller & Raymond M Wapner
Estab 1959. Present Owner 1969. 3500 Vols. Cat 2-3x ann
Types: 1st ed, illus bk, incunab, juv, o&r
Subj: Historical children's lit
S/S: Appr libr collec, autg, mss, orig art, prints, graphics

E K SCHREIBER
135 E 65th St, 10021. Tel 212-772-3150
SAN 164-6141
Owner, Ellen Schreiber; Mgr, Fred Schreiber
Estab 1971. 500 Vols. Cat 2x ann
Types: Fine bnd, incunab, illus bk, o&r
Subj: Humanism, Renaissance hist & lit, classical antiquity
S/S: Appr libr collec, mss

OSCAR SCHREYER BOOKS
230 E 79th St, 10021. Tel 212-628-6227
SAN 157-4345
Owner, Oscar Schreyer
Estab 1969

Types: O&r
Subj: Med, Brazil, Fiji, Morocco, Near East, Portugal, earthquakes, electricity, glass, sugar
S/S: Mss

S R SHAPIRO CO, BOOKS FOR LIBRARIES
29 E 10th St, 10003. Tel 212-673-0610
SAN 165-1234
Mgr, A M Robinson
Estab 1935. 100,000 Vols. Cat 12x ann
Types: Fac ed, 1st ed, imp, incunab, new, op, o&r
Subj: Africa, bibliog, fine arts, Latin Am, hist, Far, Near & Middle East, Slavic lands
S/S: Biper, deal libr only

ROSEJEANNE SLIFER†
30 Park Ave, 10016.
    Tel 212-685-2040 (by appt only)
SAN 165-1269
Estab 1967
Subj: Autg
S/S: Maps

ANNA SOSENKO INC†
76 West 82 St, 10024.
    Tel 212-247-4816
Subj: Classical & Am popular composers, performing arts, lit

PETER SPERLING — BOOKS
207 E 21, Box 300, Old Chelsea Sta, 10113. Tel 212-242-5167
SAN 157-9096
Owners, Peter Sperling & Lucy Kolk
Estab 1977. 20,000 Vols
Types: 1st ed, fine bnd, illus bk, o&r, op, used, imp UK
S/S: Search serv, antq

STEVENS & CO BOOKS INC
200 Park Ave South, Rm 914, 10003.
    Tel 212-477-2930
SAN 165-1331
Estab 1951. 35,000 Vols. Cat
Types: New, used, op
Subj: Chem, engineering, math, physics, sci-tech, sci hist
S/S: Search serv

RICHARD STODDARD PERFORM-ING ARTS BOOKS
90 E 10th St, 10003. Tel 212-982-9440

SAN 165-134X
Owner, Richard Stoddard
Estab 1975. 8000 Vols. 500 sq ft. Cat 6x ann
Types: 1st ed, hb, ltd ed, new & used, o&r, op, papbk
Subj: Circus, dance, films & filmmaking, magic & conjuring, performing arts
S/S: Appr libr collec, autg, biper, mss, orig art, search serv

DANIEL STOKES
186 Norfolk St, 10002.
    Tel 212-477-4137
Types: O&r, 1st ed
Subj: Lit, poetry

STRAND BOOKSTORE†
828 Broadway, 10003.
    Tel 212-473-1452
SAN 165-1358
Owner, Fred Bass; Buyer, Marvin Mondlin
Estab 1949. 2,000,000 Vols. 32,000 sq ft. Cat 2-3x ann
Types: 1st ed, fac ed, hb, imp, new & used, op, o&r, remd
Subj: Amer, art, hist, nature & environ, performing arts, soc sci

JOHN H STUBBS RARE BOOKS & PRINTS
28 E 18th St, 10003. Tel 212-982-8368
SAN 159-2688
Owner, John H Stubbs; Mgr, Jane E Kelley
Estab 1981. 6000 Vols. 1500 sq ft. Cat 2x ann
Types: Fine bnd, 1st ed, hb, illus bk, imp, op, o&r
Subj: Archit, Egyptology, archaeol, landscape archit
S/S: Orig art, prints

TREBIZOND RARE BOOKS†
667 Madison Ave, 10021.
    Tel 212-371-1980
SAN 165-1447
Owner, Williston R Benedict
Estab 1975. 1500 Vols. 720 sq ft. Cat 3x ann
Types: 1st ed, o&r
Subj: Am hist & lit, Eng hist & lit, travel

PETER TUMARKIN FINE BOOKS
INC
310 E 70th St, 10028.
Tel 212-348-8187
SAN 163-3953
Owner, Peter Tumarkin
Estab 1973. 5000 Vols. Cat 3x ann
Types: Fine bnd, 1st ed, illus bk, in-
cunab, imp Ger, juv, o&r
Subj: Ger hist & lit
S/S: Appr libr collec

DAVID TUNICK INC†
12 E 81st St, 10028. Tel 212-570-0090
SAN 165-1463
Pres, David Tunick
Cat
Types: Illus bk, imp, o&r
S/S: Orig prints — 1450–1950

U S GAMES SYSTEMS INC
38 E 32nd St, 10016.
Tel 212-685-4300. Telex 23-5456
SAN 158-6483
Pres, Stuart R Kaplan
Cat 2x ann
Types: 1st ed, illus bk, imp, o&r, op,
used
Subj: Metaphys & occult
S/S: Appr libr collec, search serv, occult
sup

UNIVERSITY PLACE BOOKSHOP†
821 Broadway, 10003.
Tel 212-254-5998
SAN 165-151X
Owner, Walter Goldwater; Mgr, Wil-
liam P French
Estab 1932. 30,000 Vols. 3000 sq ft.
Cat 4x ann
Types: Hb, imp, incunab, op, o&r,
used, for lang
Subj: Africa, black studies, West Indies,
chess
S/S: Appr libr collec

URSUS BOOKS LTD†
1011 Madison Ave, 10021.
Tel 212-772-8787
SAN 165-1528
Owner, T Peter Kraus
Estab 1972. Cat 5x ann
Types: Illus bk, op, o&r
Subj: Art, reference, fine painting
S/S: Appr libr collec

VICTORIA BOOKSHOP†
303 5th Ave, Rm 809, 10016.
Tel 212-683-7849
SAN 165-1552
Owner, Milton Reissman
Estab 1967. 4000 Vols. Cat 3x ann
Types: Illus bk, juv from 16th to 20th
century
S/S: Appr libr collec, autg, mss, orig
art, prints

SAMUEL WEISER INC†
740 Broadway, 10003.
Tel 212-777-6363
Owner, Daniel Weiser
Subj: Occult, theol, Egyptology, astrol,
Orientalia

LEO WEITZ — HERBERT E WEITZ
1377 Lexington Ave, 10028. Tel 212-
831-2213
SAN 165-1609
Owner, Herbert Weitz
Estab 1909. 15,000 Vols. Cat ann
Types: Imp, op, hb, juv, o&r, used
Subj: Amer, art, bks on bks, hist
S/S: Bnd

WEYHE ART BOOKS INC†
794 Lexington Ave, 10021.
Tel 212-838-5466
SAN 123-319X
Owner, Deborah Weyhe Dennis; Vpres,
Gertrude W Dennis
Estab 1916
Types: Fac ed, 1st ed, hb, illus bk, in-
cunab, new & used, op, papbk, o&r,
remd, Dutch, Fr, Ger, It & Sp lang
Subj: Archit, fine arts, interior design
S/S: Biper, maps, orig art, prints, search
serv

FRED WILSON — BOOKS
80 E 11th St, Suite 334, 10003.
Tel 212-533-6381
SAN 165-1641
Owner, Fred Wilson
Estab 1973. 3000 Vols. 130 sq ft. Cat
3x ann
Types: O&r, op
Subj: Chess
S/S: Appraisals of chess collections,
foreign lang per

THE WITKIN GALLERY†
41 E 57th St, 10022. Tel 212-355-1461
SAN 157-4361
Owner, Lee D Witkin
Estab 1969
Types: O&r, op, used
Subj: Photographic lit & prints

WURLITZER-BRUCK†
60 Riverside Dr, 10024
Owners, Marianne Wurlitzer & Gene
Bruck
Subj: Mus, bks on mus

XIMENES: RARE BOOKS INC†
19 E 69th St, 10028. Tel 212-744-0226
SAN 165-1706
Owner, Stephen Weissman
Estab 1963. Cat 4x ann
Types: 1st ed, imp, o&r
Subj: Amer, travel, Eng & Am lit pre-
1900
S/S: Appr libr collec, autg, mss

ALFRED F ZAMBELLI†
156 Fifth Ave, 10010.
Tel 212-734-2141
SAN 165-1714
Owner, Alfred F Zambelli
Estab 1949. Cat 6x ann
Types: O&r, op, imp Ital, Fr, Ger & Sp
Subj: Bibliog, Ger lang, Sp lang, medie-
val studies, philos, rel studies, Renais-
sance & Reformation hist & lit, hist
of ptg
S/S: Deal libr only

IRVING ZUCKER ART BOOKS†
265 5th Ave, 10001. Tel 212-679-6332
SAN 165-1730
Estab 1940. 7000 Vols. 2500 sq ft
Types: Illus bk, imp, op, o&r, color
plates
Subj: Art, archit, natural hist, travel,
fine arts, applied arts
S/S: Appr libr collec, prints, etchings &
engravings

Northport — 7651

BAYVIEW BOOKS & BINDERY
PO Box 208, 11768. Tel 516-757-3563
SAN 158-3077
Owners, Mary G Bond, et al
1000 Vols. Cat 1-2x ann

Types: Fine bnd, 1st ed, hb, illus bk,
o&r, op
Subj: Discovery & explor, nautical,
travel
S/S: Appr libr collec, search serv

Nyack — 6428

DEECEE BOOKS
32 Washington St, PO Box 506, 10960.
Tel 914-358-3989
SAN 165-1811
Owner, David Carpenter
Estab 1954. 35,000 Vols
Types: 1st ed, op, o&r, used
Subj: Soc sci, political thought, China,
19th & 20th century lit, Soviet Union

FREDERIC L ROSSELOT
586 Route 9 W, Grandview, 10960.
Tel 914-358-0254
SAN 158-9903
Estab 1977. 25,000 Vols
Types: Hb, op, papbk, used
Subj: Fiction

Oceanside — 35,028

OCEANSIDE BOOKS UNLIMITED
2856 St John Rd, 11572.
Tel 516-764-3378
SAN 158-7366
Owner, Adrienne Williams
Estab 1973. 10,000 Vols. Cat 6-7x ann
Types: 1st ed, hb, op, o&r
Subj: Mystery & detective, bibliog,
1850 to present
S/S: Search serv

Old Forge

WILDWOOD ENTERPRISES
Main St (Mail add: Box 560, 13420).
Tel 315-369-3397
SAN 157-7905
Owners, Ted Comstock & Sarah Com-
stock
Estab 1979. 3500 Vols. 1000 sq ft. Cat
2x ann
Types: 1st ed, hb, illus bk, new & used,
o&r, op
Subj: Camping & hiking, hunting &
fishing, New Yorkiana, canoeing,
Adirondackiana

S/S: Maps, mss, orig art, prints, search serv, antiques

Oneonta — 14,933

CARNEY BOOKS
44 Elm St, 13820. Tel 607-432-5360
SAN 157-5910
Owners, Margaret Carney & John J Carney Jr
Estab 1978. 20,000 Vols. 1200 sq ft
Types: 1st ed, hb, illus bk, papbk, o&r, op, papbk, remd, used
S/S: Appr libr collec, autg, search serv

SERPENT & EAGLE BOOKS
1 Dietz St, 13820. Tel 607-432-5604
SAN 157-910X
Owner, Joseph Mish
Estab 1979. 1500 Vols. Cat
Types: O&r, op, used
Subj: Folklore

Ossining — 20,196

HERBERT B LAZARUS
56 Grace Lane, 10562.
Tel 914-941-6066
SAN 158-3085
Types: Signed bks
Subj: Presidents & presidency, hist persons

WILLIAM SALLOCH†
Pines Bridge Rd, 10562.
Tel 914-941-8363 (by appointment only)
SAN 165-1897
Owners, William Salloch & Marianne Salloch
Estab 1939. 20,000 Vols. Cat 10x ann
Types: 1st ed, imp, incunab, o&r
Subj: Class studies, humanities, Renaissance hist & lit, Middle Ages
S/S: Appr libr collec, mss, prints

Owego — 4364

MRS KENNETH F COOPER
Rte 17C West (Mail add: Box 343, 13827). Tel 607-687-1422
SAN 158-3093
Vpres, Marilyn J Cooper
Types: Op, used

RIVEROW BOOKSHOP†
204 Front St, 13827. Tel 607-687-4094
SAN 125-2550
Owner, John D Spencer
Estab 1976. Present Owner 1979.
12,000 Vols. 700 sq ft. Cat 2x ann
Types: Fine bnd, 1st ed, hb, illus bk, juv, ltd ed, new & used, o&r, op
Subj: Archit, art, cooking & nutrit, hist, illus, nature & environ, New Yorkiana, aesthetic movement
S/S: Appr libr collec, maps, mss, search serv, sh mus

Peekskill — 18,236

CHANG TANG BOOKS
35 Di Rubbo Dr (Mail add: Box 42, Hawthorne, 10532).
Tel 914-739-8167
SAN 159-1266
Owner, Donald E Roy
Estab 1979. Present Owner 1982. 1000 Vols. Cat
Types: Fac ed, 1st ed, illus bk, imp, o&r, op, used
Subj: Dogs, dogs of Tibet and East Asia
S/S: Biper, prints, search serv

TIMOTHY TRACE†
Red Mill Rd, 10566. Tel 914-528-4074
SAN 165-1978
Owner, Timothy Trace & Elizabeth Trace
7000 Vols. Cat
Types: Hb, imp, op, o&r
Subj: Antq, archit, arts & crafts, trades

Pittsford — 1568

THE ACORN ANTIQUES
117 Crescent Hill Rd, 14534.
Tel 716-586-4494
SAN 123-7802
Owners, Louis M Clark Jr & Joan F Clark
Estab 1974. 5000 Vols. 1000 sq ft. Cat 4x ann
Types: 1st ed, hb, illus bk, imp, ltd ed, new, o&r, op, papbk, used
S/S: Antq, archit, art, local hist

Plainview—10,759

BENGTA WOO
1 Sorgi Ct, 11803. Tel 516-692-4426
SAN 157-4388
Owner, Bengta Woo
Estab 1970. 9000 Vols. Cat 12x ann
Types: 1st ed, hb, op, papbk, used
Subj: Mystery & detective
S/S: Search serv
See Also: The Bookswappers, Wantagh, NY

Plandome—1503

TEMARES FAMILY BOOKS
50 Heights Rd, 11030.
Tel 516-627-8688
SAN 157-8456
Owner, Lee Barnett-Temares; Merch Mgr, Myron Temares
Estab 1972. 20,000 Vols. 700 sq ft. Cat 2x ann
Types: 1st ed, hb, illus bk, juv, ltd ed, o&r, op, used
Subj: Biog, fiction, art, Heritage Press, Limited Editions Club, childrens series
S/S: Appr libr collec, search serv, small antq

Pleasant Valley—1372

FIDDLER'S FOLLY
Rte 44, 12569. Tel 914-635-8376
SAN 159-2114
Owner, Rosemary Geiger
Estab 1973. 10,000 Vols. 900 sq ft
Types: 1st ed, hb, illus bk, juv, ltd ed, o&r, op, used
Subj: Local hist
S/S: Mss, orig art, prints

Pleasantville—6749

COLONIAL OUT-OF-PRINT BOOK SERVICE
PO Box 451, 10570
SAN 164-937X
Owner, Al Scheinbaum
Estab 1934. 5000 Vols
Types: Op

Subj: Art, hist, music, philos, psychol, theol
S/S: Search serv

ANDREW WITTENBORN
152 Mountain Rd, 10570.
Tel 914-769-9018
SAN 157-4396
Owner, Andrew Wittenborn
Types: Used

Port Chester—23,565

RICHARD CADY RARE BOOKS
37 Greenway Lane, Rye Brook (Mail add: PO Box 12, Glenville Sta, Greenwich, CT, 06830).
Tel 914-937-6606
SAN 156-9872
Owner, Richard Cady
Estab 1980. 2000 Vols. Cat 5x ann
Types: Fine bnd, 1st ed, illus bk, ltd ed, o&r, pvt presses
Subj: Bibliog, bks on bks, class studies, 1890's in England
S/S: Appr libr collec, autg, mss, orig art, prints

Port Jefferson—6731

THE GOOD TIMES BOOKSHOP
150 E Main St, 11777.
Tel 516-928-2664
SAN 165-2079
Owners, Mary J Mart & Michael A Mart
Estab 1972. 30,000 Vols
Types: 1st ed, hb, ltd ed, o&r, op, papbk, used
Subj: Scholarly lit, humanities

Port Washington—15,923

COLLECTOR'S ANTIQUES INC
286 A Main St, 11050.
Tel 516-883-2098
SAN 156-9848
Owner, Jean Feigenbaum
Estab 1964. 2000 Vols. 150 sq ft
Types: Fine bnd, 1st ed, hb, illus bk, incunab, juv, o&r, op
Subj: Antq, hist

S/S: Appr libr collec, autg, maps, mss, orig art, sh mus

Poughkeepsie — 29,757

ROBERT E UNDERHILL
85 Underhill Rd, 12603.
Tel 914-452-5986
SAN 165-2109
Owner, Robert E Underhill
Types: 1st ed, hb, imp, new & used, op, papbk, o&r, remd
Subj: Natural hist, hort, agr
S/S: Search serv

Pultneyville

YANKEE PEDDLER BOOKSHOP†
East Lake Rd, 14538. Tel 315-589-2063
SAN 165-2133
Owners, John Westerberg & Janet Westerberg
Estab 1970. 30,000 Vols. 678 sq ft. Cat ann
Types: Fac ed, fine bnd, 1st ed, hb, illus bk, juv, ltd ed, new & used, o&r, op, remd
Subj: World Wars I & II, Amer, Can, Civil War, New Yorkiana, Western Amer, photog, aeronautics
S/S: Appr libr collec, autg, prints, search serv, bk repair, hand-colored engravings & lithos, paintings
Hours Thurs & Sun 1:00-5:00 or by appointment

Rochester — 241,741

VERKUILEN AGER
PO Box 23432, 14692
SAN 170-186X
Owner, V K Ager
Cat 6x ann
Types: Fine bnd, 1st ed, hb, incunab, illus bk, imp, ltd ed, new, o&r, op, papbk, used
Subj: Military
S/S: Autg, biper, maps, search serv

ANG & LIL'S COLLECTOR'S CORNER
149 Stone Rd, 14616. Tel 716-621-8930

SAN 165-2168
Owners, Angela Schiffhauer & Lillian Guthiel
Estab 1971
Types: Fac ed, fine bnd, 1st ed, hb, illus bk, juv, ltd ed, o&r, op, used
S/S: Maps, mss, prints, sh mus

GENESEE BOOKSHOP
2420 Monroe Ave, 14618.
Tel 716-442-3620
SAN 165-222
Owner, Rose S Weiss
Types: 1st ed, hb, o&r, op, papbk, used
S/S: Appr libr collec
Branches:
1966 Monroe Ave, 14618
SAN 165-2230

C F HEINDL BOOKS
PO Box 8345, 14618.
Tel 716-271-1423
SAN 159-5407
Owner, Charles F Heindl
Estab 1975. 10,000 Vols. 800 sq ft
Types: 1st ed, o&r, op
S/S: Appr libr collec
Open Tues & Thurs 11-4

FRANK OPPERMAN
326 Barrington St, 14607.
Tel 716-271-2561
SAN 165-2281
Estab 1950. 10,000 Vols
Types: Op, used
Subj: Amer
S/S: Search serv

Rockville Centre — 25,405

A COLLECTOR'S LIST
68 N Village Ave, 11570.
Tel 516-536-3757
SAN 165-2370
Pres, Herman Abromsom
Estab 1977. 5000 Vols. Cat 2x ann
Types: Used, illus bk, 1st ed, imp, ltd ed, o&r, op
Subj: Art, bks on bks, drama, poetry
S/S: Mss, prints

THE BOOK CHEST INC†
19 Oxford Pl, 11570. Tel 516-766-6105
SAN 120-3150
Owner, Estelle Chessid
Estab 1972. 4000 Vols. Cat 1-2x ann

Types: 1st ed, fac ed, hb, imp, o&r, op, remd
Subj: Natural hist
S/S: Appr libr collec, biper, mss, orig art, prints, search serv

HERMAN M DARVICK AUTO-
   GRAPHS INC
Box 467, 11571. Tel 516-766-0093
SAN 157-4442
Owner, Herman M Darvick
Estab 1970. Cat 6x ann
Types: 1st ed, ltd ed, o&r
S/S: Autg, mss

ELGEN BOOKS
336 DeMott Ave, 11570.
   Tel 516-536-6276
SAN 165-2389
Owners, Esther Geller & Leonard Gel-
   ler
Estab 1977. 5000 Vols. Cat 1-2x ann
Types: Fine bnd, 1st ed, hb, o&r, op, used
Subj: Math, med, natural hist, sci-tech
S/S: Appr libr collec

PAULETTE GREENE†
140 Princeton Rd, 11570.
   Tel 516-766-8602
SAN 165-2397
Owner, Paulette Greene
Estab 1970. 5000 Vols. Cat ann
Types: 1st ed
Subj: Bibliog, mystery & detective, sci fiction & fantasy, reference, 19th cent Am & Eng lit
S/S: Appr libr collec

Roslyn Heights — 7140

ONCE UPON A TIME BOOKS
28 Lincoln Ave, 11577.
   Tel 516-621-4637
SAN 157-5864
Owners, James Dore & Harvey Stanson
Estab 1979. 12,000 Vols. Cat 4x ann
Types: Fine bnd, 1st ed, hb, illus bk, ltd ed, op, o&r, papbk
S/S: Appr libr collec, search serv, base-ball memorabilia

Rye — 15,083

HIGH RIDGE CORNER†
PO Box 286, 10580. Tel 914-967-3332

Owner, Howard S Baron
Subj: Angling, color plates, maps & atlases, numismatics, Amer, travel

Salisbury Mills

DENNING HOUSE
Orrs Mills Rd, Box 42, 12577.
   Tel 914-496-6771
SAN 165-2435
Owner, P R McTague
Cat 15x ann
Types: Op, o&r
S/S: Appr libr collec, autg, biper, mss, orig art

Saranac Lake — 5578

ADIRONDACK YESTERYEARS INC
Lake St Extension, PO Drawer 209, 12983. Tel 518-891-3206
SAN 165-2443
Owner, Maitland C DeSormo
Estab 1967. 10,000 Vols
Types: New, o&r, op
Subj: Adirondacks
S/S: Appr libr collec, orig art, prints

Saratoga Springs — 23,906

HENNESSEY'S BOOKSTORE†
4th & Woodlawn, 12866.
   Tel 518-584-4921
SAN 165-2478
Owners, Joseph Hennessey & Helen Hennessey
Estab 1961
Types: 1st ed, o&r, op, used, sporting
S/S: Appr libr collec, prints, search serv

LYRICAL BALLAD BOOKSTORE†
7 Philadelphia St, 12866.
   Tel 518-584-8779
SAN 165-2486
Owner, John DeMarco & Carolyn DeMarco
Estab 1971. 20,000 Vols. 1000 sq ft
Types: Fine bnd, 1st ed, hb, illus bk, juv, o&r, op, used
Subj: Amer, dance, folklore, horses, local hist, mythology, New Yorkiana, Adirondacks & Saratoga Springs, thoroughbred racing
S/S: Appr libr collec, biper, prints, search serv, sh mus

Scarsdale—17,650

BUMP'S BOOKS
Box 8, 10583. Tel 914-669-5791
SAN 159-2513
Owner, Donald Bump; Mgr, Rodger
Bump
Types: Hb, mag & newspr, op, papbk,
used
Subj: Hypnosis, metaphys & occult,
photog
S/S: Search serv
Hq: Bump's Barn Bookshop, Ashland,
NH

ANNEMARIE SCHNASE ANTI-
QUARIAN BOOKSELLER & PUB-
LISHER†
120 Brown Rd (Mail add: PO Box 119,
10583). Tel 914-725-1284,
603-253-6583
SAN 165-2508
Owner, Annemarie Schnase
Estab 1950. 50,000 Vols. Cat
Subj: Humanities, music, sci-tech
S/S: Biper, per, reprod, academy publn,
secondhand

Schenectady—67,972

BIBLIOMANIA
129 Jay St, 12305. Tel 518-393-8069
SAN 159-1622
Owner, William M Healy
Estab 1981. 8000 Vols. 700 sq ft. Cat
ann
Types: Fac ed, fine bnd, 1st ed, hb, illus
bk, ltd ed, new & used, o&r, op,
remd
Subj: Amer, art, local hist, mod lit,
mystery & detective, photog
S/S: Search serv

HAMMER MOUNTAIN BOOK
HALLS†
841 Union St, 12308. Tel 518-393-5266
SAN 121-5728
Owners, Wayne Somers & Jane Somers
Estab 1971. 10,000 Vols. Cat 4x ann
Types: Op, o&r, remd, used
Subj: Humanities, soc sci
S/S: Appr libr collec, search serv, exp
libr serv

Sea Cliff—5364

JOHN CASHMAN BOOKS
327 Sea Cliff Ave, 11579.
Tel 516-676-6088
SAN 159-1347
Owner, John Cashman
Estab 1981. 25,000 Vols. 1000 sq ft
Types: Fine bnd, 1st ed, hb, illus bk, ltd
ed, o&r, op, used
Subj: Fiction, performing arts, drugs,
media, temperance
S/S: Appr libr collec, autg, prints,
search serv, steel & wood carvings

Sloatsburg—3154

LIBERTY ROCK BOOK SHOPPE
55 Orange Turnpike, 10974.
Tel 914-753-2012
SAN 165-2621
Owners, James Mahoney & Virginia
Mahoney
Estab 1976. 10,000 Vols. Cat
Types: 1st ed, hb, illus bk, juv, op, o&r,
papbk, used
Subj: Music, performing arts, rel, Am,
Eng, Fr & Irish lit
S/S: Search serv

Smithtown—116,663

CADENZA BOOKSELLERS
8 Brilner Dr, 11787. Tel 516-265-0122
SAN 157-7913
Owners, Howard Taube & Mimi Taube
Present Owner 1979. 750 Vols. Cat ann
Types: Hb, new & used, op, papbk
S/S: Search serv

Snyder

KEVIN T RANSOM—BOOKSELLER
116 Audubon Dr (Mail add: PO Box
176, Amherst, 14226).
Tel 716-839-1510
SAN 157-9681
Owner, Kevin Ransom
Estab 1978. 3000 Vols. Cat 3x ann
Types: Fac ed, fine bnd, 1st ed, hb, illus
bk, juv, ltd ed, o&r, op
Subj: Mystery & detective, mod lit

S/S: Appr libr collec, autg, biper, maps, orig art, search serv

Somers — 13,133

TALBOTHAYS BOOKS
316 Horton Dr (Mail add: PO Box 276, Lincolndale, NY, 10540).
  Tel 315-343-0774
SAN 159-0146
Owner, Paul C Mitchell
Present Owner 1977. 7000 Vols. Cat 3-5x ann
Types: 1st ed, hb, op, o&r
Subj: Amer, military
S/S: Search serv

Southampton — 42,849

SOUTHAMPTON BOOK CO
S Main St, PO Drawer 0, 11968.
  Tel 516-283-1612
SAN 122-9028
Owner, Robert Keene
Estab 1950. 25,000 Vols. 100 sq ft
Types: Fac ed, fine bnd, 1st ed, hb, illus bk, incunab, imp, juv, ltd ed, o&r, op, remd, used
Subj: Oceanog, T Capote, K Roberts, L I History
S/S: Appr libr collec, mss, search serv

SOUTH SHORE BOOK RESERVE
Box 768, 11968. Tel 516-283-5347
SAN 165-0726
Owner, Philip Tulchin
2000 Vols. Cat ann
Types: Hb, new, o&r, op
Subj: Archit, art
S/S: Appr libr collec, prints, search serv

Springwater — 2143

SPRINGWATER BOOKS & ANTIQUES
Main St at East Ave (Mail add: PO Box 8, 14560). Tel 716-669-2450
SAN 165-2702
Owner, Mrs Reid Carlson
Estab 1946. Present Owner 1975. 150,000 Vols. 4000 sq ft. Cat 2x ann
Types: Fac ed, fine bnd, 1st ed, hb, incunab, o&r

Subj: Agr, Am Indian studies, Amer, Can, Eur studies
S/S: Appr libr collec, autg, biper, orig art, search serv

Staten Island — 352,121

JACQUES NOEL JACOBSEN JR, COLLECTORS — ANTIQUITIES INC
60 Manor Rd, 10310. Tel 212-981-0973
SAN 157-4477
Mgrs, Jacques Noel Jacobsen Jr & Marion Jacobsen
Estab 1950. 2000 Vols. Cat 4x ann
Types: O&r
Subj: Military, firefighting, Alaskana, Canadian Arctic, police
S/S: Prints

Stone Ridge

RIDGE BOOKS
Box 58, 12484. Tel 914-687-0252
SAN 157-4485
Owner, Peter E Scott
Estab 1963. 3000 Vols. Cat 6x ann
Types: 1st ed, ltd ed, op
Subj: Fitzgerald, Hemingway
S/S: Biper, search serv

Stony Brook — 6391

KOLYER PUBLICATIONS
208 Christian Ave (Mail add: PO Box 235, 11790). Tel 516-751-8888
SAN 157-5937
Owner, Helen Kolyer
Estab 1977. 5000 Vols. 900 sq ft. Cat 2x ann
Types: Fac ed, 1st ed, hb, illus bk, papbk, o&r, op, used
Subj: Auto, aviation, mystery & detective, horology
S/S: Search serv

Swan Lake

MORRIS HELLER
RD 1 Box 87, 12783. Tel 914-583-5879
SAN 165-277X

Owner, Morris Heller
Estab 1963. 4000 Vols. 800 sq ft. Cat
  2x ann
Types: Hb, op, o&r
Subj: Hunting & fishing, natural hist
S/S: Appr libr collec, prints

Syracuse — 170,105

JIM HODGSON BOOKS
3600 E Genesee St, 13214.
  Tel 315-478-1710
SAN 157-9118
Owner, James W Hodgson
Estab 1979. 10,000 Vols
Types: 1st ed, hb, illus bk, juv, op, used
S/S: Biper

JOHNSON & O'DONNELL RARE
  BOOKS LTD
1015 State Tower Bldg, 13202.
  Tel 315-652-3118
SAN 157-4213
Owners, Bruce N Johnson & Ed
  O'Donnell
Cat 4x ann
Types: 1st ed, o&r
Subj: Amer & Eng lit, 19th & 20th
  century
S/S: Autg, mss, orig art, prints

EDWARD J MONARSKI ANTIQUAR-
  IAN BOOKS
1050 Wadsworth St, 13208.
  Tel 315-455-1716
SAN 165-2834
Owner, Edward J Monarski
Estab 1966. 16,000 Vols. Cat 4-7x ann
Types: Fine bnd, 1st ed, hb, ltd ed, o&r,
  papbk, used
Subj: New Yorkiana
S/S: Appr libr collec, autg, mss, orig
  art, prints, search serv, sh mus, World
  War II military

STERLING VALLEY ANTIQUITIES
  AT HOMESTEAD ANTIQUES
Rte 57, 13203. Tel 315-652-5477
SAN 157-7093
Owner, Richard R Loder
Estab 1980. 4000 Vols
Types: 1st ed, fac ed, fine bnd
Subj: Am Indian studies, law, med, New

Yorkiana, Western Amer
S/S: Appr libr collec, search serv

Theresa — 827

CHRIS FESSLER BOOKSELLER
Rd One, PO Box 112 Poole Rd, 13691.
  Tel 315-628-5560
SAN 128-3499
Owner, Christopher Fessler
Types: Fac ed, 1st ed, hb, ltd ed, o&r,
  op, remd, used, imp Asia
Subj: Ancient hist & lit, anthrop, ar-
  chaeol, class studies, Orientalia,
  philos, rel studies, travel
S/S: Search serv

Troy — 56,638

HOFFMAN LANE BOOKS
31 2nd St, PO Box 1045, 12180.
  Tel 518-273-4826
SAN 164-7059
Owner, Earle Nicklas
Estab 1981. 10,000 Vols. 850 sq ft. Cat
Types: Fine bnd, 1st ed, for lang, hb,
  illus bk, imp, juv, ltd ed, o&r, op,
  papbk, used
Subj: Art, mod lit, New Yorkiana, sci-
  tech, sports
S/S: Maps, prints

LA TIENDA EL QUETZAL
PO Box 246, 12181. Tel 518-271-7629
SAN 158-975X
Owner, James C Andrews
Estab 1977. 400 Vols. 100 sq ft. Cat
  ann
Types: Fac ed, 1st ed, hb, illus bk, imp,
  new, o&r, op, papbk, used
Subj: Central Amer & Guatemala
S/S: Appr libr collec, stamps

TROJAN BOOKS
186 River St, 12180. Tel 518-271-6925
SAN 165-2915
Owner, Donald E Murray
Estab 1972. 20,000 Vols. 2000 sq ft.
  Cat 3x ann
Types: Fac ed, fine bnd, ltd ed, hb,
  incunab, illus bk, juv, 1st ed, o&r,
  op, papbk, used
S/S: Appr libr collec, autg, biper, mss,
  prints, search serv

Upper Nyack — 1906

BEN FRANKLIN BOOKSHOP &
PRINTERY
318 N Broadway, 10960.
Tel 914-358-0440
SAN 158-1902
Owner, Stephen Schwartz; Mgr, Donna
Schwartz
Estab 1980. 10,000 Vols. 900 sq ft
Types: Fac ed, 1st ed, hb, illus bk, juv,
ltd ed, o&r, papbk, used
Subj: Art, fiction, metaphys & occult,
philos, rel studies, sci fiction & fan-
tasy
S/S: Custom printing

Valhalla

EDUCO SERVICES INTERNA-
TIONAL LTD†
75 N Kensico Ave, 10595. Tel 914-997-
7044
Owner, Charles Cecere
Types: Gen antiquarian

Valley Cottage — 6007

ALEPH-BET BOOKS
670 Waters Edge, 10989.
Tel 914-268-7410
SAN 158-3107
Owner, Helen Younger
Estab 1978. 4000 Vols. Cat 2x ann
Types: Hb, illus bk, juv, o&r, op, used

Wading River — 900

JO ANN & RICHARD CASTEN AN-
TIQUE MAPS†
RR 2 Little Bay Rd, 11792.
Tel 516-929-6820
SAN 165-2982
Owners, Jo Ann Casten & Richard
Casten
Estab 1974. 1500 Vols. Cat ann
Types: O&r
Subj: Antq maps & atlases, 15th &
18th century maps, world, American
& Holy Land maps
S/S: Maps

Wantagh — 21,873

THE BOOK SWAPPERS
1400 Wantagh Ave, 11793.

Tel 516-785-9029
SAN 156-6741
Owner, Bengta Woo
Present Owner 1980. 20,000 Vols. Cat
12x ann
Types: Papbk, used
Subj: Mystery & detective, romance, sci
fiction & fantasy
S/S: Search serv
See Also: Bengta Woo, Plainview, NY

Wappingers Falls — 5110

LION HARVEY BOOKS
17 E Main, PO Box 331, 12590.
Tel 914-297-7907
SAN 165-3008
Owner & Mgr, Lion Harvey
Estab 1967. 26,000 Vols. Cat ann
Types: 1st ed, hb, illus bk, imp, new &
used, o&r, op, remd
Subj: Art, military, music, photog

Warwick — 4320

BOOK LOOK
51 Maple Ave, 10990. Tel 914-986-
1981
SAN 158-3115
Owner, Jerry Dodd
Estab 1964. 60,000 Vols. 20,000 sq ft.
Cat
Types: Fac ed, fine bnd, 1st ed, hb, illus
bk, ltd ed, o&r, op, papbk, remd,
used
S/S: Biper, search serv

Webster — 5499

THE BACKROOM BOOKSTORE
PO Box 223, 14580. Tel 716-671-0437
SAN 125-118X
Owner, Ronald D Hein
Estab 1976. 10,000 Vols. Cat 4x ann
Types: Fine bnd, hb, juv, new & used,
o&r, op, col text
Subj: Class studies, educ, philos, poetry,
psychol
S/S: Biper, search serv, tech consulting

West Shokan

THE SCRIBBLING BOOKMONGER
Rte 28A, Box 40, 12494. Tel 914-657-
2466

SAN 157-3217
Owner & Buyer, Antoinette G Gersdorf
Estab 1978. 2000 Vols. 300 sq ft. Cat
  2x ann
Types: 1st ed, hb, ltd ed
Subj: Romance, bks for writers, 19th
  century fiction
S/S: Autg, prints, search serv

White Plains — 46,999

AVONLEA BOOKS
Box 74, Main Sta, 10602.
  Tel 914-946-5923
SAN 158-3123
Owner, Leone E Bushkin
Estab 1979
Types: 1st ed, hb, illus bk, juv, o&r, op,
  used
S/S: Search serv

THE BOOK GALLERY†
15 Overlook Road (Mail add: Box 26
  Gedney Station, 10605).
  Tel 914-949-5406
SAN 165-3105
Owner, Ruth Berman
Estab 1960. 8000 Vols. Cat 2x ann
Types: Op
Subj: Archit, art, photog
S/S: Appr libr collec, search serv
By appt only

ALBERT J PHIEBIG, INC†
PO Box 352, 10602. Tel 914-948-0138
Owner, Marianne J Phiebig
Types: Foreign bks & per, int con-
  gresses, irregular serials
S/S: Search serv, collection development

Woodstock — 6804

NATHANIEL COWEN
16 Schoonmaker Lane, 12498. Tel 914-
  679-6475
SAN 165-2494
Owner, Nathaniel Cowen; Associate,
  Florence M Cowen
Types: Hb, op, used
Subj: Am hist & lit, art, Eng hist & lit

Wynantskill

A'GATHERIN'†
PO Box 175, 12198. Tel 518-674-2979

Owner, Robert Dalton Harris
Subj: Postal hist, telegraph hist, drug
  trade

Yonkers — 195, 351

ALICAT GALLERY
64 Ludlow St, 10705. Tel 914-963-4794
SAN 165-3172
Owner, Florenz Baron
Types: Hb, o&r, op, used
S/S: Appr libr collec, autg, orig art,
  prints, search serv

NORTH CAROLINA

Asheville — 53,281

THE ANCIENT PAGE
64 Haywood St, 28803.
  Tel 704-254-1177
SAN 158-7048
Owners, John P McAfee & Elizabeth P
  McAfee
Estab 1981. 11,000 Vols. 3000 sq ft.
  Cat 2x ann
Subj: Biog, Civil War, Eur studies,
  North Carolinana, rel studies, travel,
  Western Amer, Europe & Amer fic-
  tion & hist
S/S: Appr libr collec, search serv

THE BOOK MART
7 Biltmore Plaza, Box 5094, 28803.
  Tel 704-274-2241
SAN 165-3253
Owner, Nancy Brown
Estab 1947. 20,000 Vols. 1044 sq ft
Types: Hb, juv, op, o&r
Subj: Appalachia, North Carolinana,
  rel-p, South Carolinana
S/S: Gr cds, search serv, staty

Carrboro — 7517

CHAPEL HILL RARE BOOKS
PO Box 456, 27510. Tel 919-929-8351
Types: 1st ed
Subj: Lit

Carthage — 925

PERRY'S BOOKS
RD 2 Box 348 A, 28327. Tel 919-947-
  2209

SAN 159-0049
Owner, Perrell F Payne Jr
Estab 1981. 10,000 Vols. 750 sq ft. Cat
Types: Fac ed, fine bnd, hb, illus bk,
juv, ltd ed, o&r, op, papbk, used
S/S: Prints, search serv

Charlotte — 314,447

CAROLINA BOOKSHOP
1601 East Independence Blvd, 28205.
Tel 704-375-7305
SAN 165-3423
Owner, Gordon Briscoe Jr
Estab 1975. 10,000 Vols. 2000 sq ft.
Cat 8x ann
Types: Fine bnd, 1st ed, hb, juv, ltd ed,
o&r, op, papbk, used
Subj: Amer, Civil War, North Caro-
linana, Southern Amer, freemasonry
S/S: Appr libr collec, biper, prints,
search serv, rec

LITTLE HUNDRED GALLERY
6028 Bentway Dr, 28211.
Tel 704-542-3184
SAN 158-6084
Owner, Paul L Whitfield
Estab 1975. 1000 Vols. Cat 8x ann
S/S: Maps, mss, orig art, prints, Am &
Eur documents

B L MEANS — RARE BOOKS & FIRST
EDITIONS†
5935 Creola Rd, 28211.
Tel 704-364-3117
SAN 165-3466
Owner, B L Means
Cat
Types: 1st ed, illus bk, juv, o&r
Subj: Bot, geol
By appointment only

Durham — 100,831

CHELSEA ANTIQUES
905 W Main, 27701. Tel 919-683-1865
SAN 170-7493
Owner, Laura Kotchmar
Estab 1982. 2000 Vols
Types: Op, o&r, juv, fine bnd, 1st ed,
hb, illus bk, ltd ed, imp
Subj: Class studies, North Carolinana,
med
S/S: Orig art, prints, search serv

CROWS NEST ANTIQUE MALL
Lakewood S/Ctr, 2000 Chapel Hill Rd,
27707. Tel 919-493-7494
SAN 170-7485
Owner, Betty Fields
Estab 1981. 3000 Vols
Types: 1st ed, hb, illus bk, juv, ltd ed,
o&r, op
Subj: Fiction, nonfiction
S/S: Orig art, prints

THE HAUNTED BOOKSHOP
231 N Gregson St, 27701.
Tel 919-683-3004
SAN 170-5288
Owner, Virginia L Pigott
Estab 1982. 500 sq ft
Types: Fine bnd, 1st ed, hb, illus bk, juv
Subj: Amer, sci-tech
S/S: Prints, search serv

OLD GALEN'S BOOKS
Box 3044, 27705. Tel 919-489-6246
SAN 158-314X
Mgr, G S T Cavanagh
Estab 1971. 6000 Vols. Cat 5x ann
Types: O&r
Subj: Med, sci-tech
S/S: Appr libr collec

WENTWORTH & LEGGETT RARE
BOOKS
Brightleaf Sq, 905 W Main St, 27701.
Tel 919-688-5311
SAN 170-3889
Owners, David & Barbara Wentworth
Estab 1982. Present Owner 1983
Types: Fine bnd, 1st ed, illus bk, juv, ltd
ed, o&r, op
Subj: Antq, gardening, arts & crafts,
natural hist, med, hist, soc sci, rel,
Civil War, golf, cooking & nutrit
S/S: Biper, maps, prints

Elizabeth City — 13,784

AUTOS & AUTOS — BOOK DEPT
105 Pine Lake Dr, PO Box 280, 27909.
Tel 919-335-1117
SAN 165-3636
Owner, B C West Jr
Estab 1974. Cat 4x ann
Types: 1st ed, hb, ltd ed
Subj: Autg, aviation, med, sci-tech
S/S: Mss

Greensboro—155,642

THE BROWSERY
547 S Mendenhall St, 27403.
  Tel 919-273-7259
SAN 165-3784
Owners, Ben Mathews & Chas Gibson
Estab 1976. 31,000 Vols. 1250 sq ft
Types: 1st ed, hb, illus bk, juv, o&r, op,
  papbk, used
Subj: Biog, drama, fiction, hist, philos,
  poetry
S/S: Search serv, rec
Branches:
  516 South Elm St, 27406.
    Tel 919-274-3231
  SAN 170-0820

Hillsborough—3019

MICHAEL E BERNHOLZ
  ANTIQUES & BOOKS
118 S Churton St (Mail add: 1 Sycamore
  Dr, Chapel Hill, 27514).
  Tel 919-929-3533
SAN 159-1142
Owner, Michael E Bernholz
Estab 1970. 2500 Vols. 1500 sq ft
Types: Fac ed, fine bnd, 1st ed, hb, illus
  bk, incunab, imp, juv, ltd ed, o&r, op
Subj: Fiction, Southern Amer
S/S: Appr libr collec, autg, biper, maps,
  mss, orig art, prints, search serv, sh
  mus

Jamestown—2148

PACIFICANA
PO Box 398, 27282.
  Tel 919-454-4938, 454-3534
SAN 165-3997
Owner, Mary A Browning
Estab 1971. 4000 Vols. Cat 4x ann
Types: Fac ed, 1st ed, hb, illus bk, imp,
  juv, ltd ed, new, o&r, op, papbk,
  remd, used
Subj: Pacific Islands
S/S: Biper, maps, mss, orig art, prints,
  search serv

Pittsboro—1332

H E TURLINGTON BOOKS
Rte 4, Box 131B, 27312.

  Tel 919-542-3403
SAN 158-9520
Owners, H E Turlington Jr & Patricia
  Turlington; Mgr, H E Turlington
Estab 1979. 2500 Vols. 800 sq ft. Cat
  6x ann
Types: 1st ed, hb, ltd ed, op, used
Subj: North Carolinana, 20th century
  lit, Southern fict & poetry

Raleigh—149,771

OCTOBER FARM
Rte 2, Box 183-C, 27610.
  Tel 919-772-0482
SAN 158-6270
Owner, Barbara Beaumont Cole
Estab 1973. Cat 2-3x ann
Types: 1st ed, hb, illus bk, juv, o&r, op,
  used
Subj: Horses
S/S: Biper, orig art, prints, search serv,
  ephemera
Open by appointment only

Troy—2702

GRANDPA'S HOUSE
Rt 1, Box 208, 27371.
  Tel 919-572-3484
SAN 165-4497
Owner, Mary R Parks
Estab 1963. 1500 sq ft
Types: 1st ed, hb, illus bk, juv, op, o&r,
  used
S/S: Biper, prints, search serv, sh mus

Wendell—2222

BROADFOOT'S BOOKMARK†
Rte 3 Box 318, 27591.
  Tel 919-365-6963
SAN 164-4543
Owner, Thomas W Broadfoot; Mgr,
  Marianne J Pair
Estab 1970. 50,000 Vols. Cat 15x ann
Types: 1st ed, op, o&r
Subj: Civil War
S/S: Appr libr collec, maps, mss, orig
  art, prints

NORTH DAKOTA

Bismarck — 44,485

DACOTAH BOOK CO
3107 Winnipeg Dr, Box 512, 58501.
 Tel 701-223-7315
SAN 129-7627
Owner, Douglas R Parks
Estab 1981. 10,000 Vols. Cat 4x ann
Types: 1st ed, hb, illus bk, op, o&r,
 used
Subj: Am Indian studies, anthrop, West-
 ern Amer
S/S: Appr libr collec, biper, search serv

Devils Lake — 7442

HOWARD O BERG
317 7th St, 58301. Tel 701-662-2343
SAN 165-4756
Owner, Howard O Berg
Estab 1951. 22,000 Vols
Types: 1st ed, o&r, used
Subj: Amer, bks on bks, humanities,
 North Dakotana
S/S: Search serv

Velva — 1101

ESTHER ISAACSON
PO Box 154, 58790
SAN 164-4918
Owner, Esther Isaacson
Estab 1931. Present Owner 1975. 8500
 Vols
Types: Op, used
Subj: Auto, fiction, hist, mystery &
 detective, sci fiction & fantasy
S/S: Biper

OHIO

Akron — 237,177

AKRON BOOKS
571 Malvern Rd, 44303.
 Tel 216-867-8784
SAN 170-2408
Owner, William C Chrisant
Estab 1976. 9500 Vols. 800 sq ft
Types: Fac ed, fine bnd, 1st ed, hb,
 incunab, illus bk, imp Fr, imp Ger,
 juv, new, o&r, op, papbk, used

Subj: Egyptology, archaeol, ancient hist
 & lit
S/S: Appr libr collec, biper, prints,
 search serv

THE BOOKSELLER INC
521 W Exchange St, 44302.
 Tel 216-762-3101
SAN 120-6842
Owners, Frank Klein & Patricia Klein;
 Mgr, Frank S Klein; Buyer, Andrea
 Klein; Papbk Buyer, B Alan Fee;
 Cataloguer, H K Hammarstrom
Estab 1948. 30,000 Vols. 2600 sq ft.
 Cat 12x ann
Types: Fine bnd, 1st ed, hb, illus bk,
 juv, ltd ed, o&r, op, papbk, remd,
 used, comics
Subj: Aviation, films & filmmaking,
 military, Ohioana
S/S: Appr libr collec, bnd, biper, search
 serv, sh mus

BRUCE P FERRINI, RARE BOOKS†
933 W Exchange St, 44302.
Tel 216-867-2665
Types: O&r, mss, prints, drawings

OLD BOOKSTORE
210 E Cuyahoga Falls Ave, 44310. Tel 21
SAN 165-5000
Owner, Ronald J Antonucci
Estab 1967. 150,000 Vols. 3600 sq ft.
 Cat 6x ann
Types: 1st ed, hb, juv, op, o&r, papbk,
 used, comics
Subj: Amer, Ohioana, sci fiction &
 fantasy
S/S: Search serv, paper collectibles

STAGECOACH ANTIQUES
439 W Market St, 44303.
 Tel 216-762-5422
SAN 158-9121
Owner, Leo Walter
Estab 1950. 10,000 Vols. 500 sq ft
Types: Fac ed, fine bnd, 1st ed, hb, imp,
 incunab, illus bk, juv, papbk, remd,
 used
S/S: Biper, prints

Bowling Green — 25,728

DE ANIMA: BOOKS IN PSYCHOL-
 OGY
122 E Evers, 43402. Tel 419-352-8533

SAN 157-4558
Owner, Ryan D Tweney
Estab 1973. 2000 Vols. Cat 3x ann
Types: 1st ed, hb, o&r, op, used
Subj: Philos, psychiat, psychol, neuro-
science
S/S: Appr libr collec

JERRY RAY BOOKS
1306 N Orleans, 43402.
Tel 419-352-5321
SAN 158-4421
Owner, Gerald Bergman
Estab 1973. 10,000 Vols. Cat 4x ann
Types: Hb, o&r, op, used
Subj: Anthrop, evolution, psychol, sci-
tech, sociol
S/S: Appr libr collec, biper, search serv

Burton—1401

THE ASPHODEL BOOKSHOP
17192 Ravenna Rd, Rte 44, 44021.
Tel 216-834-4775
SAN 165-5175
Owner, James R Lowell
Estab 1963. 6000 Vols. Cat 6x ann
Types: 1st ed, imp, new, op, o&r
Subj: 20th century lit
S/S: Autg, biper

Canton—94,730

TALLY HO STUDIO
639 Park Ave, SW, 44706.
Tel 216-452-4488
SAN 165-5213
Owner, Darlene Parsons
Estab 1964. 5500 Vols. 800 sq ft. Cat
Types: Hb, juv, papbk, remd, comics
Subj: Amer, antq, films & filmmaking,
horses, sci fiction & fantasy
S/S: Per, staty, toys, collectors items

Carey—3674

ROBERT G HAYMAN ANTIQUAR-
IAN BOOKS†
575 West St, 43316. Tel 419-396-6933
SAN 165-523X
Cat 5x ann
Types: Op, o&r
Subj: Amer, local hist
S/S: Maps, mss

Cincinnati—385,457

ACRES OF BOOKS INC†
633 Main St, 45202. Tel 513-721-4214
SAN 120-0135
Owner, Alex Zoretsky
500,000 Vols
Types: Hb, juv, papbk
Subj: Sci & tech, travel, hist, fict

BARBARA AGRANOFF BOOKS
4025 Paddock Rd, Apt 501 (Mail add:
PO Box 6501, 45206). Tel 513-281-
5095
SAN 165-5264
Owner, Barbara Agranoff
Estab 1972. 4000 Vols
Types: Fine bnd, 1st ed, hb, incunab,
illus bk, juv, ltd ed, o&r, op, used
Subj: Collectible books—all fields, early
trades
S/S: Maps, prints, search serv, sh mus,
paper ephemera, postcards

ALRICH CO
900 Vine St, 45202. Tel 513-621-1314
SAN 165-5272
Vpres & Mgr, Robert Richshafer
Types: O&r
Subj: Amer, discovery & explor,
Ohioana, photog
S/S: Autg, biper, orig art, search serv,
broadsides, doc
Branches:
900 E McMillan
SAN 165-5280

BOOK STALL
1424 Springfield Pk, 45215.
Tel 513-761-8224
SAN 165-5329
Owners, Gordon Nickol & Kitty Nickol
Present Owner 1978. 25,000 Vols
Types: Hb, papbk, op
Subj: Antq
S/S: Search serv

DUTTENHOFER'S BOOK TREA-
SURES
214 W McMillan, 45219.
Tel 513-381-1340
SAN 165-5353
Owner, Stanley A Duttenhofer; Merch
Mgr, Stephen Miles
Estab 1975. 40,000 Vols. 5000 sq ft
Types: 1st ed, for lang, hb, illus bk, ltd

ed, o&r, op, papbk, used
Subj: Biog, metaphys & occult, philos,
poetry, sci fiction & fantasy
S/S: Appr libr collec, bnd, maps, search
serv, sh mus

MRS TROLLOPE'S BAZAAR
6428 Westover Circle (Mail add: PO
Box 1302, 45201). Tel 513-891-7823
SAN 158-4286
Owner, John A Taylor
Estab 1975. 1000 Vols. Cat ann
Types: Fac ed, fine bnd, 1st ed, hb, illus
bk, imp, ltd ed, new & used, o&r,
op, papbk, remd
Subj: Anthony, Thomas Adolphus &
Frances Trollope

OHIO BOOKSTORE
726 Main St, 45202. Tel 513-621-5142
SAN 165-5469
Owner, Jim Fallon; Mgr, Dick
Baringhaus
Estab 1941. Cat 12x ann
Types: 1st ed, new & used, o&r, op,
papbk, remd
Subj: Amer, law, local hist
S/S: Biper, search serv

ROBERT RICHSHAFER
900-902 Vine St, 45202
SAN 158-9822
Types: Fine bnd, 1st ed, incunab, illus
bk, o&r, op
Subj: Amer, discovery & explor,
Ohioana, photog
S/S: Autg, maps, mss, orig art, per,
prints, search serv, sh mus

Cleveland — 573,822

ATTENSON ANTIQUES & BOOKS
2219 Noble Rd, 44112.
Tel 216-381-8788
SAN 170-124X
Owner, Stuart M Attenson
Estab 1981. 7500 Vols. 1500 sq ft
Types: Fine bnd, 1st ed, hb, illus bk,
juv, o&r, op, used
Subj: Amer, illus
S/S: Appr libr collec, prints, sh mus

SUSAN HELLER BOOKS
22611 Halburton Rd (Mail add: Box
22723, 44122). Tel 216-283-2665

SAN 157-454X
Owner & Mgr, Susan Heller
Estab 1974. 30,000 Vols. 1000 sq ft.
By appt only
Types: Fine bnd, 1st ed, illus bk, juv, ltd
ed, o&r, op, signed bks
Subj: Eng hist & lit, fine arts, natural
hist, nautical, photog, sports, art,
Amer
S/S: Appr libr collec, autg, search serv

PETER KEISOGLOFF BOOKS
53 The Arcade, 44114. Tel 216-621-
3094
SAN 123-9937
Owner, Peter Keisogloff
10,000 Vols
Types: Hb, juv, o&r
S/S: Search serv, bnd

PUBLIX BOOK MART
1310 Huron Rd, 44115. Tel 216-621-
6624
SAN 122-5871
Owners & Mgrs, Janet S Williams &
Wesley C Williams; Juv Buyer, Olga
McMahon
Estab 1937. 100,000 Vols. 10,000 sq ft.
Cat
Types: Hb, juv, op, papbk, remd
Subj: Antq, art, biog, cooking & nutrit,
performing arts, ref
S/S: Appr libr collec, gr cds, posters,
search serv, staty

Cleveland Heights — 56,438

RADIOGRAPHICS BOOKS
Box 18492, 44118. Tel 216-943-6374
SAN 157-4566
Owner, Robert E Morgan
Estab 1974. 9000 Vols. Cat 8x ann
Types: 1st ed, fine bnd, hb, new &
used, o&r, op, papbk
Subj: Radio, electricity, telegraphy
S/S: Appr libr collec, autg, biper, search
serv

Columbus — 564,871

COMICS & COMPANY
1486 Oakland Park Ave, 43224.
Tel 614-268-4513

SAN 165-6007
Owner, Rita M Jones
Estab 1974. 300,000 Vols. Cat ann
Types: O&r, papbk, used
Subj: Comedy, sci fiction & fantasy
S/S: Gifts, movie ephemera

HERITAGE BOOKSTORE
4415 N High St, 43214.
 Tel 614-262-0615
SAN 156-9783
Owner, Larry Cosner
Estab 1980. 10,000 Vols. Cat 2x ann
Types: Fine bnd, 1st ed, hb, illus bk, ltd
 ed, o&r, op, used
Subj: Amer, military, Ohioana

MIRAN ARTS & BOOKS
2824 Elm Ave, 43209.
 Tel 614-236-0002
SAN 156-9856
Owner, I Gilbert
Estab 1975. 5000 Vols. 2000 sq ft
Types: 1st ed, hb, illus bk, juv, ltd ed,
 o&r, op
Subj: Med, photog
S/S: Appr libr collec, mss, orig art,
 prints, sh mus

PAUL H NORTH JR†
81 Bullitt Park Pl, 43209.
 Tel 614-252-1826
SAN 165-6090
20,000 Vols. Cat
Types: 1st ed, incunab, op, o&r, used
Subj: Amer, art, antq
S/S: Appr libr collec, autg, mss, orig
 art, search serv

L J RYAN — SCHOLARLY BOOKS
PO Box 243, 43216. Tel 614-258-6558
SAN 165-6112
Owner, L J Ryan
Estab 1972. Cat
Types: 1st ed, hb, o&r, op, remd
Subj: Amer, art, communism, folklore,
 hist, soc sci, women's studies, rel, int
 relations, far east
S/S: Appr libr collec, biper

SHAW-BANFILL BOOKS
PO Box 14850, 43214.
 Tel 614-267-9022
SAN 165-6120
Owners, Richard F Shaw & Lois Banfill
 Shaw

Types: 1st ed, fac ed, fine bnd, hb,
 incunab, illus bk, o&r, op
Subj: Sci-tech, women's hist

TRAIL TO YESTERDAY BOOK
 NICHE
5652 I Little Ben Circle, 43229.
 Tel 614-890-5170
SAN 159-1584
Owner, Robert G Pugh
Estab 1979. 2000 Vols. 600 sq ft. Cat
 11x ann
Subj: Arizonana, Western Amer
S/S: Maps

KAREN WICKLIFF BOOKS
2579 N High St, 43202.
 Tel 614-263-2903
SAN 130-6243
Owner, Karen Wickliff
Estab 1976. Present Owner 1979.
 25,000 Vols. 1400 sq ft
Types: 1st ed, hb, juv, o&r, op, papbk,
 used, for lang
Subj: Fine arts, soc sci, rel, scholarly lit
S/S: Art sup, biper, sh mus

Dayton — 203,588

J D S BOOKS
PO Box 67, MCS, 45402.
 Tel 513-299-7118
SAN 158-426X
Owner, John D Squires
Present Owner 1978. 300 Vols
Types: Hb, new & used, o&r, op
Subj: Military, warfare, 1890-1914 hist
 & lit, M P Shiel, Yellow Devil fict
S/S: Wholesale

OUTDOORSMAN BOOKSHELF
PO Box 492, 45401. Tel 513-268-8980
SAN 165-6279
Owner, James L McGuire
Estab 1970. 2000 Vols. Cat ann
Types: Hb, juv
Subj: Great Lakes, mystery & detective,
 sports
S/S: Search serv, spec order

Greensburg

RON-DOT BOOKFINDERS
4700 Massillon Rd (Mail add: PO Box
 44, 44232). Tel 216-896-3482

SAN 165-6589
Owners, Ronald G Clewell & Dorothy
L Clewell
Estab 1976. 40,000 Vols. 1344 sq ft
Types: 1st ed, hb, illus bk, op, o&r,
papbk, used
S/S: Search serv

Harrison — 5855

MARAN ENTERPRISES
10452 Walkingfern Dr, 45030.
Tel 513-367-9631
SAN 126-4958
Estab 1978. 840 sq ft
Types: Hb, juv, mm papbk, remd
Subj: Arts & crafts, cooking & nutrit,
fiction, fine arts, inspirational, nature
& environ, nonfiction, sci fiction &
fantasy, self-develop, sports
S/S: Spec order

Hudson — 4615

DORIS DAVIS BOOKS
271 Streetsboro St, 44236.
Tel 216-653-5780
SAN 158-5959
Owner, Doris Davis
Cat 2x ann
Types: 1st ed, illus bk, juv, o&r, op
Subj: Travel
S/S: Appr libr collec, search serv

Mansfield — 53,927

OHIO BOOKHUNTER†
323 Park Ave W (Mail add: 564 E
Townview Cir, 44907).
Tel 419-526-1249
SAN 158-2356
Owner, John Stark
Estab 1972. 5000 Vols. Cat 4-5x ann
Types: Fine bnd, 1st ed, incunab, illus
bk, juv, ltd ed, o&r, op
Subj: Amer, Ohioana
S/S: Appr libr collec, autg, maps, mss,
orig art, prints
By appointment

Mentor — 42,065

HILO FARM ANTIQUES
9058 Little Mountain Rd, 44060.

Tel 216-255-9530
SAN 165-6899
Owner, Marjorie Wearsch
Estab 1958. 7000 Vols
Types: 1st ed, o&r, op, used
Subj: Amer
S/S: Biper, maps, prints, sh mus

MAGGIE McGIGGLES ANTIQUES
8627 Mentor Ave, 44060.
Tel 216-255-1623
SAN 159-4923
Owner, Carol J Illner
Estab 1978. 510 sq ft
Types: Juv, op, hb, used, for lang, o&r
Subj: Civil War
S/S: Gr cds, sh mus, toys, prints
Open Mon, Wed, Fri & Sat 11-5; Tues
& Thurs 11-7; Sun 12-5

Mentor-on-the-Lake — 7919

RICHARDSON
7632 Manor Rd, 44060.
Tel 216-257-4191
SAN 170-1746
Owner, Larry Richardson
Types: 1st ed, hb, juv, o&r, used
Subj: Edgar Rice Burroughs
S/S: Appr libr collec, search serv

Miamisburg — 15,304

GLENN ARMITAGE
108 Fifth Ave, 45342.
Tel 513-423-9569
SAN 159-1274
Owner, Glenn Armitage
Estab 1960. 5000 Vols
Types: Fine bnd, 1st ed, hb, illus bk,
imp, ltd ed, o&r, op, papbk, remd,
used
Subj: Fine arts, literary criticism, 20th
century lit
S/S: Biper

Mount Vernon — 14,380

OWL CREEK BOOKSHOP
309 W Vine St, 43050.
Tel 614-397-9337
SAN 165-6945
Owner, B K Clinker
Estab 1968. 9000 Vols. 500 sq ft

Types: 1st ed, hb, illus bk, juv, ltd ed, o&r, op, used
S/S: Biper, rec, search serv, sh mus

Norwalk — 14,358

IRVING M ROTH, ANTIQUES
89 Whittlesey Ave, 44857.
  Tel 419-668-2893
SAN 165-7070
Owner, Irving M Roth
Estab 1946. 20,000 Vols
Types: Op, o&r
Subj: Amer, antq, Civil War, numismatics, Ohioana, Am expositions, ephemera, freemasonry, old advertising mat
S/S: Appr libr collec, cat, Am & foreign postcards & trade cards

Reynoldsburg — 20,661

LOIS WARD — BOOKS
PO Box 4, 92714. Tel 614-863-3464
SAN 124-3705
Owner, Lois H Ward
Present Owner 1974. 3000 Vols. 1000 sq ft. Cat 3x ann
Types: 1st ed, hb, new, o&r, op, used
Subj: Mystery & detective, rel
S/S: Search serv

South Euclid — 25,713

PAPER PEDDLERS
4425 Mayfield Rd, 44121. Tel 216-561-1242
SAN 157-8642
Owners, Janet Blakeley & Carole Lazarus
Estab 1974. 7000 Vols. 550 sq ft
Types: 1st ed, hb, illus bk, o&r, op
S/S: Sh mus, paper antq

Toledo — 354,635

GEORGE D BROWN — BOOKS
7001 Bancroft St, 43617.
  Tel 419-841-4979
SAN 120-7946
Owners, George D Brown & Alberta Brown
Estab 1967. 20,000 Vols. Cat ann

Types: Hb, new & used, op, o&r, remd, bibles
Subj: Archaeol, archit, art, aviation, cooking & nutrit, gardening, Great Lakes, how-to, Indianiana, Michiganiana, natural hist, Ohioana, railroadiana, hunting & fishing, glass

KENDALL G GAISSER, BOOKSELLERS
1242 Broadway, 43609.
  Tel 419-243-7631
SAN 165-7429
Owner, Kendall G Gaisser; Mgr, Lynette Gaisser
Estab 1948. 38,000 Vols. 8500 sq ft. Cat 6x ann
Types: 1st ed, imp, op, o&r
Subj: Amer, art, hist, med, military, music, scholarly lit
S/S: Maps, mss, orig art, prints

Warren — 56,629

McCLINTOCK'S BOOKS
522-A High St NE (Mail add: PO Box 3111, 44485). Tel 216-394-3398
SAN 165-7569
Owner, David A McClintock
Estab 1976. Present Owner 1978.
  20,000 Vols. 765 sq ft. Cat 8-10x ann
Types: Fine bnd, 1st ed, hb, illus bk, ltd ed, new & used, op, o&r, op papbk
Subj: Amer, aviation, mystery & detective, scholarly lit, sci fiction & fantasy
S/S: Appr libr collec, search serv

Willard — 5674

RICHARD P GERMANN
PO Box 67, 44890. Tel 419-668-9640
SAN 165-7585
Mgr, Richard P Germann
Estab 1955. 3000 Vols. Cat
Types: New & used, op, papbk
Subj: Astrol, metaphys & occult, palmistry, sci before 1800
S/S: Biper, maps, search serv

Wooster — 19,289

DOUGLAS GUNN — BOOKS
819 Quinby Ave, 44691.

Tel 216-262-8581
SAN 165-7593
Present Owner 1978. 2000 Vols. Cat
Types: Fine bnd, 1st ed, hb
Subj: Biblical studies, humanities, needlecrafts, rel, scholarly lit, soc sci, 19th century per

Worthington—15,016

THE LOOKING GLASS
5584 Morning St, 43085.
Tel 614-885-4800
SAN 157-4620
Owner, H C Strohl
Estab 1975. 10,000 Vols. Cat 2x ann
Types: 1st ed, hb, illus bk, ltd ed, op, o&r, used
Subj: Can, military, poetry
S/S: Search serv

Youngstown—115,436

CAROL BUTCHER
3955 New Road, 44515.
Tel 216-793-2030
SAN 165-7682
Owner, Carol Butcher
Types: Op, o&r, used
Subj: Dogs, hunting
S/S: Prints, search serv

JOSEPH F SCHEETZ—ANTIQUARIAN BOOKS
6236 Foxridge Dr, 44512.
Tel 216-758-0427
SAN 165-7690
Owners, Joseph F Scheetz & Peggy Scheetz
Estab 1968. 5000 Vols. Cat
Types: 1st ed, hb, op, o&r, used, pvt press
Subj: Amer, Ohioana
S/S: Search serv

OKLAHOMA

Ada—15,902

ADA BOOK STALL
301 W 12th, 74820. Tel 405-332-8062
SAN 150-2115
Owner, Oklahoma Bk Traders Ltd, Inc; Mgr, Johann Cartwright

Estab 1974. 15,000 Vols. 900 sq ft
Types: Fac ed, fine bnd, 1st ed, hb, illus bk, juv, ltd ed, o&r, op, papbk, remd, used
Subj: Comedy
S/S: Appr libr collec
Hq: Book Stall, Norman, OK

Edmond—34,637

RON BEVER
Rt 3, Box 243-B, 73034.
Tel 405-478-0125
SAN 157-4639
Owner & Mgr, Ron Bever
Estab 1977. 13,500 Vols. Cat 4x ann
Types: Hb, o&r, op, used
Subj: Oklahomana, rel, stock market & commodity
S/S: Appr libr collec, search serv

Lawton—80,054

LAWTON BOOK STALL
1832 NW 52nd, Regency Sq S/Ctr, 73505. Tel 405-248-3111
SAN 159-0243
Owners, Dale Hall & Mike Myers; Mgr, Denise Deal
Estab 1980. 25,000 Vols. 1250 sq ft
Types: 1st ed, hb, illus bk, imp, juv, ltd ed, o&r, op, papbk, remd, used
S/S: Appr libr collec, biper, per, comics
Hq: Book Stall, Norman, OK

Muskogee—40,011

McGRATH'S BOOK COLLECTOR
1525 Irving St, 74401.
Tel 918-687-4094
SAN 165-8034
Owner, Mrs J P McGrath
Types: O&r, op, used
Subj: Am Indian studies, Oklahomana
S/S: Indian maps

Norman—68,020

BOOK STALL
1110 W Main, 73069. Tel 405-329-6787
SAN 150-2107
Owner, Oklahoma Bk Traders Ltd, Inc; Mgr, Cathy Ball

Estab 1972. 25,000 Vols. 1400 sq ft
Types: Fac ed, fine bnd, 1st ed, hb, illus
  bk, juv, ltd ed, o&r, op, papbk,
  remd, used
Subj: Comedy
S/S: Appr libr collec
See Also: Ada Book Stall, Ada; Lawton
  Book Stall, Lawton; Shawnee Book
  Stall, Shawnee

Oklahoma City—403,213

ALADDIN BOOK SHOPPE
2037 NW 23rd, 73106. Tel 405-528-
  0814
SAN 165-8115
Owner & Buyer, Jerry Nelson
Estab 1930. Present Owner 1959.
  30,000 Vols. 2800 sq ft
Types: Fine bnd, 1st ed, hb, incunab,
  illus bk, juv, ltd ed, o&r, op, papbk,
  remd, used
Subj: Oklahomana, Southwestern Amer
S/S: Appr libr collec, autg, biper, maps,
  mss, search serv

MELVIN MARCHER—BOOK-
  SELLER
6204 N Vermont, 73112. Tel 405-946-
  6270
SAN 157-4655
Owner, Melvin Marcher
5000 Vols. Cat 2x ann
Types: O&r, used
Subj: Hunting & fishing, natural hist,
  weapons & firearms
S/S: Biper, search serv

MICHAEL'S BOOKSTORE
3636 N Western, 73118.
  Tel 405-525-0123, 525-8888
SAN 165-8239
Owner & Buyer, Nguyen Van Le
Estab 1963. Present Owner 1981.
  12,500 Vols. 2200 sq ft
Types: 1st ed, hb, o&r, op, papbk, used
Subj: Southwestern Amer
S/S: Search serv

Shawnee—26,506

SHAWNEE BOOK STALL
702-B W Ayre, 74801. Tel 405-275-
  5714

SAN 150-2131
Owner, Oklahoma Bk Traders Ltd, Inc;
  Mgr, Mike Myers
Types: Fac ed, fine bnd, 1st ed, hb, illus
  bk, juv, ltd ed, o&r, op, papbk,
  remd, used
Subj: Comedy
S/S: Appr libr collec
Hq: Book Stall, Norman, OK

Yukon—17,112

THE OKLAHOMA BOOKMAN
1107 Foreman Rd NE, 73099
SAN 165-7798
Owner, D R Goulden
Estab 1976. 1200 Vols. 1275 sq ft. Cat
  2x ann
Types: 1st ed, hb, ltd ed, new, o&r, op
Subj: Anthrop, zool, bot, ornith
S/S: Appr libr collec, biper

OREGON

Ashland—19,943

BLUE DRAGON BOOK SHOP
36 S 2nd St, PO Box 216, 97520.
  Tel 503-482-2142
SAN 130-612X
Owners, Robert Peterson & Richard
  Miller
Estab 1983, 500 sq ft
Types: Fac ed, fine bnd, 1st ed, hb,
  incunab, illus bk, imp, juv, ltd ed,
  o&r, op, papbk, remd, used
Subj: Metaphysics, Orientalia, martial
  arts
S/S: Art sup, search serv

Dundee—1223

AUTHORS OF THE WEST
191 Dogwood Dr, 97115.
  Tel 503-538-8132
SAN 165-8905
Owners, Lee Nash & Grayce Nash
Estab 1973. Cat
Types: 1st ed, fine bnd, hb, illus bk, ltd
  ed, new, o&r, op, remd, used
Subj: Fiction, poetry, Western Amer
S/S: Appr libr collec, biper, mss, search
  serv

Gold Hill—904

G A BIBBY BOOKS
1225 Sardine Creek Rd, 97525.
 Tel 503-855-1621
SAN 165-9030
Owner, Bethel L Bibby; Buyer, G A
 Bibby
Estab 1967. 3500 Vols. Cat 6x ann
Subj: Gardening, hort, natural hist
S/S: Search serv

Grants Pass—14,997

ERNEST L SACKETT
100 Waverly Dr, 97526.
 Tel 503-476-6404
SAN 158-6416
Owners, Ernest L Sackett & Esther L
 Sackett
Estab 1970. 3000 Vols. Cat 3x ann
Types: 1st ed, hb, illus bk, juv, ltd ed,
 o&r, op, used
Subj: Hunting & fishing, N Amer, rel-c,
 Western Amer
S/S: Appr libr collec, search serv

Medford—39,603

BARTLETT STREET BOOKSTORE
16 S Bartlett St, 97501.
 Tel 503-772-8049
SAN 165-9138
Owner, Kenneth Corliss; Mgrs, Kenneth
 Corliss & Anita Corliss
Present Owner 1972. 14,000 Vols
Types: 1st ed, hb, juv, o&r, papbk,
 used
S/S: Search serv
Branches:
 APPLEGATE BOOKS
 Box 541, 97501. Tel 503-772-5362
 SAN 157-8014

Newberg—10,394

THE KEN-L-QUESTOR
Rt 4, Box 279, 97132.
 Tel 503-538-2051
SAN 126-9402
Owner, Kenneth M Lewis
Estab 1935. 5000 Vols. 400 sq ft. Cat
 ann

Types: Fac ed, fine bnd, 1st ed, hb, illus
 bk, imp, o&r, op, remd, new & used
Subj: Dogs, horses, cacti, lilies, mush-
 rooms
S/S: Appr libr collec, orig art, prints,
 search serv

Noti

ANTIQUES & ARTIFACTS
20457 Hwy 126, 97461.
 Tel 503-935-1619
SAN 157-8472
Owners, Scott Arden & Barrie Arden-
 Gendel
Estab 1971. 3000 Vols. Cat 12x ann
Types: Fac ed, 1st ed, hb, illus bk, ltd
 ed, new & used, o&r, op, papbk,
 remd
Subj: Railroadiana, transp, express
S/S: Appr libr collec, maps, prints,
 artifacts

Portland—366,383

CAMERON'S BOOK STORE†
336 SW Third Ave, 97204. Tel 503-228-
 2391
Owner, Frederick J Goetz
Types: Hb & papbk, vintage mag

GREEN DOLPHIN BOOKSHOP
1300 S W Washington St, 97205.
 Tel 503-224-3060
SAN 165-9405
Owner, Wright Lewis
Estab 1965. 20,000 Vols. 2000 sq ft
Types: 1st ed, op, o&r
Subj: Art, travel, nautical, NW Amer

HOLLAND'S BOOKSTORE
3522 SE Hawthorne, 97214.
 Tel 503-232-3596
SAN 165-9421
Owner, Stephen Holland
Estab 1979. 15,000 Vols. 1200 sq ft
Types: 1st ed, hb, op, o&r, used
Subj: Amer, hist, humanities, metaphys
 & occult, philos, sci-tech, socialism
S/S: Appr libr collec

LILLIAN KENNEDY BOOKSELLER
1138 SW Cheltenham (Mail add: Box
 19071, 97219)

SAN 157-4663
Owner, Lillian Kennedy
Present Owner 1969. 1000 Vols. Cat 4x
ann
Types: Hb, o&r, op
Subj: Hist, missionaries, Western Amer,
women's studies

LONGFELLOW'S BOOK & RECORD
STORE
6229 SE Milwaukee Ave, 97202.
Tel 503-239-5222
SAN 158-9148
Owner, Edwin (Jon) Hagen
Estab 1981. 30,000 Vols. 1000 sq ft.
Cat
Types: Col text, for lang, hb, hp papbk,
imp Russ, juv, op, remd, used
Subj: Art, fiction, hist, mod lit, sci-tech
S/S: Biper, rec, search serv, sh mus

OLD OREGON BOOKSTORE
525 SW 12th, 97205. Tel 503-227-2742
SAN 165-9502
Owners, Preston McMann & Phyllis
McMann
Estab 1949. 100,000 Vols. 3400 sq ft.
Cat 2x ann
Types: Imp, op, o&r, remd, used
Subj: Art, Western Amer, Am, Eng &
Russ hist & lit
S/S: Appr libr collec

OLD WEIRD HERALD'S
5213 N E Sandy, 97213.
Tel 503-281-4942
SAN 165-9510
Owner, Hazel Herald
Estab 1970. 1500 Vols. 1125 sq ft
Types: Illus bk, juv, o&r, comics
Subj: Amer
S/S: Biper, sh mus, autg, videotapes,
post, trade & baseball cds, memora-
bilia

Salem—89,233

DOUG BEARCE
2130 17th St NE (Mail add: PO Box
7081, 97303). Tel 503-363-1715
SAN 157-8030
Owner, Doug Bearce
1000 Vols. Cat 4-5x ann
Types: Fac ed, hb, juv, op
Subj: Scouting
S/S: Search serv

THE MANUSCRIPT
223 High St NE, 97301. Tel 503-370-
8855
SAN 157-4671
Owner, Barbara Haskell
Estab 1979. 10,000 Vols. 550 sq ft. Cat
Types: Fine bnd, 1st ed, hb, illus bk,
juv, ltd ed, op, o&r, used
S/S: Appr libr collec, autg, mss, search
serv

DALE C SCHMIDT BOOKS
610 Howell Prairie Rd SE, 97301.
Tel 503-364-0499
SAN 157-468X
Owner, Dale C Schmidt
Estab 1973
Types: Used
Subj: Aviation, Pacific NW, paper Amer,
sausage making
S/S: Orig art, sh mus

Woodburn—11,196

99-E ANTIQUE-USED
17207 Hwy 99-E, 97071.
Tel 503-981-0200
SAN 158-2208
Owner, Marvin D Stanton
Estab 1978. 10,000 Vols. 9000 sq ft
Types: 1st ed, hb, illus bk, juv, ltd ed,
o&r, op, papbk, used
Subj: Auto, cooking & nutrit, sci fiction
& fantasy, warfare, Western Amer
S/S: Maps, prints, sh mus

PENNSYLVANIA

Allentown—103,758

PHILIP G LE VAN BOOKSELLER
2443 Liberty St, 18104.
Tel 215-432-6147
SAN 157-4701
Owner & Mgr, Philip LeVan
Estab 1971. 4000 Vols. Cat ann
Types: 1st ed, hb, o&r, op
Subj: Golf

Ambler—6628

ROBERT F BATCHELDER†
1 W Butler Ave, 19002.
Tel 215-643-1430
SAN 165-9936

Mgr, Eileen C Keiter
Cat
Subj: Hist, music, presidents & presidency, sci-tech
S/S: Autg, mss

Berwyn

OUT OF THE PAST
704 Lancaster Ave, 19312. Tel 215-296-9674
SAN 159-5377
Owner, Brett D Snyder
Estab 1982. 10,000 Vols. 600 sq ft
Types: 1st ed, hb, illus bk, juv, o&r, op, used
S/S: Search serv, sh mus
Open Tues-Fri 10-4; Sat 1-5

Bethel Park—34,755

C B YOHE—CONJURING BOOKS
4870 Criss Rd, 15102. Tel 412-835-427
SAN 165-9995
Types: Hb, new & used, op, papbk, o&r, remd, cloth
Subj: Magic & conjuring, ventriloquism, gambling
S/S: Biper, mss, prints, search serv, magic apparatus

Bloomsburg—11,717

SAM LAIDACKER
3 E 5th St (Mail add: PO Box 416, 17815). Tel 717-784-4912
SAN 166-0039
Owner, Sam Laidacker
Estab 1928. Cat
Types: New & used, op, o&r, remd
Subj: Am hist & lit, antq, collecting, guns, local hist
S/S: Biper, prints, antq

Boyertown—3979

WHITE HOUSE BOOKS
49 E Philadelphia Ave (Mail add: PO Box 16, 19512)
SAN 166-0055
Owner, Frank Y Dill
Estab 1977. 5000 Vols. 750 sq ft. Cat 4x ann

Types: O&r, op, remd, used
Subj: U S polit biog, Am polit

Bryn Mawr—5737

THE EPISTEMOLOGIST, SCHOLARLY BOOKS
PO Box 63, 19010. Tel 215-527-1065
SAN 163-8394
Owner, N Lynn Wozniak
Estab 1972. 4000 Vols. 200 sq ft. Cat 4x ann
Types: Hb, o&r, op, used
Subj: Philos, psychiat, sci
S/S: Appr libr collec, autg, biper, photog sup, search serv

Chambersburg—16,174

GEORGE HALL JR, BOOKS
1441 Lincoln Way E, 17201. Tel 717-263-4388
SAN 157-471X
Owner, George Hall Jr
Estab 1975. 3000 Vols. Cat ann
Types: O&r, op
Subj: Nonfiction
S/S: Search serv

CESI KELLINGER, BOOKSELLER
735 Philadelphia Ave, 17201. Tel 717-263-4474
SAN 166-0195
Mgr, Cesi Kellinger
Estab 1974. 15,000 Vols. Cat 2x ann
Types: 1st ed, o&r, op
Subj: Amer, fine arts, mod dance

LEONARD SOLOMON
49 W Commerce St, 17201. Tel 717-264-1441
SAN 166-0209
10,000 Vols
Types: Fac ed, 1st ed, hb, imp, o&r, op, used
Subj: Amer
S/S: Search serv
Sell to dealers only

Dalton—1383

LOCK STOCK & BARREL SHOP
Rd One, 18414. Tel 717-945-5123, 344-5561
SAN 158-4537

Owner, Dan Koth
Estab 1960. 15,000 Vols. 1500 sq ft
Types: 1st ed, illus bk, juv, op, used
S/S: Orig art, appr libr collec, antiques
By appt only

Doylestown—8717

MITCHELL'S BOOKSHOP
296 N Main St, 18901.
   Tel 215-348-4875, 348-3319
SAN 166-0349
Owner, John P Mitchell
Estab 1963. 10,000 Vols. 1584 sq ft
Types: 1st ed, incunab, juv, o&r, used
Subj: Amer, foreign hist
S/S: Appr libr collec, maps

East Greenville—2456

BOOKS 'N THINGS
536 Main St, 18041. Tel 215-679-7051
SAN 166-0373
Owner, Harold Beahm
Types: Hb, juv, papbk, used
S/S: Orig art, gifts, gr cds, rec, rental,
   staty

Easton—26,027

HIVE OF INDUSTRY, BOOK-
   SELLERS
505 Alpha Bldg, PO Box 602, 18042.
   Tel 215-258-6663
SAN 157-8049
Owner, Y Mayer; Merch Mgr, K Perkins
Estab 1960. 30,000 Vols. Cat 4x ann
Types: Op, used
Subj: Bus & mgt, soc sci, rel & sci
S/S: Appr libr collec, autg, biper, deal
   libr only, mss, search serv

Ephrata—11,095

AVOCATIONAL
302 S State St, 17522.
   Tel 717-738-2932
SAN 164-3800
Owner, Lee Reese
10,000 Vols
Types: Hb, op, o&r, used
Subj: Amer, fiction, nonfiction, Pennsyl-
   vaniana
S/S: Ephemera

Erie

ERIE BOOK STORE
717 French St, 16501. Tel 814-452-
   3354
Owner, Kathleen Cantrell
Types: Used
Subj: Great Lakes, Western Pennsylvania

Export—1143

WILLIAM H POWERS
RD 3, 15632. Tel 412-327-6886
SAN 166-0527
Estab 1969. 8000 Vols. 800 sq ft. Cat
   4x ann
Types: Hb, new & used, o&r, op
Subj: Civil War, military, Amer, Pennsyl-
   vaniana, hunting & fishing, firearms
S/S: Appr libr collec, maps, search serv

Ferndale—2204

THE GATEWAY
18921. Tel 215-847-5644
SAN 157-8057
Owner, Jeanne Urich Gorham
Estab 1930. 10,000 Vols. 1500 sq ft.
   Cat
Types: 1st ed, hb, new & used, o&r,
   op, papbk
Subj: Metaphys & occult, mysticism,
   Orientalia
S/S: Appr libr collec, search serv

Gettysburg—7194

BATTLEFIELD BOOKSHOP
PO Box 27, 17325
SAN 130-5549
Owner & Mgr, William F Bowling
Estab 1972. 10,000 Vols. 400 sq ft
Types: Fac ed, 1st ed, new, o&r, op,
   papbk, remd, used
Subj: Civil War, military, technology &
   19th century US hist
S/S: Autg, biper, maps, mss, prints,
   search serv

OBSOLESCENCE
24 Chambersburg St, 17325.
   Tel 717-334-8634
SAN 157-6577
Owner & Mgr, Donald R Hinks
Estab 1972. 40,000 Vols. 3400 sq ft

Types: Hb, o&r, op, used
Subj: Civil War, Pennsylvaniana, Brethren Church hist, German imprints
S/S: Maps, search serv

Glen Rock— 1662

THE FAMILY ALBUM†
RD 1, Box 42, 17327.
  Tel 717-235-2134
SAN 124-7166
Owner, Ronald Lieberman
Estab 1969. 15,000 Vols. 2000 sq ft.
  Cat 4x ann
Types: Fine bnd, 1st ed, hb, incunab, illus bk, imp, ltd ed, o&r, op, used, imprints
Subj: Pennsylvaniana, early imprints, rare photographica
S/S: Appr libr collec, bnd, search serv, int libr agents

Gwynedd Valley

GWYNEDD VALLEY BOOKSTORE
Plymouth Rd at Reading RR Sta, 19437. Tel 215-646-0881
SAN 166-073X
Owners, John H & Alicia W Goodolf
Estab 1967. 150,000 Vols. 7000 sq ft
Types: 1st ed, hb, imp, op, papbk, used

Harrisburg— 53,264

DEANNA BEECHING BOOKSELLER
603 N Front St, 17101. Tel 717-236-2656
SAN 157-4736
Owner, Deanna Beeching
Estab 1979. Cat 2x ann
S/S: Appr libr collec, search serv

Hatfield— 2533

JEAN'S BOOKS
School St (Mail add: Box 264, 19440).
  Tel 215-362-0732
SAN 158-5053
Owner, Jean Kulp
Estab 1976. 5,000 Vols
Types: Hb, juv, o&r, op
S/S: Staty, search serv

Haverford— 52,349

JAMES S JAFFE, RARE BOOKS
442 Montgomery Ave, 19041.
  Tel 215-649-4221
Estab 1982. Cat 4x ann
Types: 1st ed, o&r, press bks
Subj: Eng & Am lit
By appointment only

Havertown

TAMERLANE BOOKS†
Box C, 19083. Tel 215-449-4400
Owner, John W Freas
Subj: Sporting bks, art ref, fine bnd, 19th cent color plate & travel bks

Hershey— 7404

R F SELGAS SPORTING BOOKS
444 W Areba Ave (Mail add: PO Box 227-B, 17033). Tel 717-534-1868
SAN 158-4162
200 Vols
Types: 1st ed, ltd ed, o&r, op, used
Subj: Hunting & fishing
S/S: Appr libr collec, per, prints

Huntingdon Valley

MYSTERY MANOR BOOKS
PO Box 135, 19006. Tel 215-824-1476
SAN 126-6020
Owner, Manor House Publications Inc; Pres, Fred A Stutman
Estab 1975. 10,000 Vols. Cat 2x ann
Types: 1st ed
Subj: Mystery & detective
Branches:
  MANOR HOUSE BOOKS
  PO Box 6, 19006
  SAN 156-8213

D SEDENGER GALLERIES
1571 Huntington Pike (Mail add: PO Box 189, 19006). Tel 215-947-2806
SAN 157-8065
Estab 1960. 10,000 Vols. Cat 2-3x ann
Types: Fac ed, fine bnd, 1st ed, hb, illus bk, juv, ltd ed, o&r, op, used
Subj: Amer, art, mod lit, natural hist
S/S: Appr libr collec, maps, orig art, prints, search serv

Jenkintown—4942

HOBSON'S CHOICE
511 Runnymede, 19046.
  Tel 215-884-4853
SAN 157-5961
Owner, Jane Hobson Walker
Estab 1979. 2000 Vols. 1000 sq ft. Cat
Types: Fine bnd, 1st ed, hb, illus bk,
  juv, ltd ed, o&r, op, pvt presses, used
Subj: Fiction, Pennsylvaniana, poetry
S/S: Biper, gr cds, prints, search serv

Kane—4916

STEPHEN SHUART PHOTO-
  GRAPHIC BOOKS
109 S Edgar St (Mail add: PO Box 419,
  16735). Tel 814-837-7786.
  800-458-6092
SAN 157-4744
Owner, Stephen Shuart
Estab 1969. 10,000 Vols. 1000 sq ft
Types: Fac ed, o&r, op, remd, used,
  imp
Subj: Photog, collecting
S/S: Appr libr collec, biper, prints

Kennett Square—4715

THOMAS MACALUSO RARE &
  FINE BOOKS
PO Box 133, 19348. Tel 215-444-1063
SAN 158-5711
Owner, Thomas P Macaluso
Estab 1973. 4000 Vols. Cat 3x ann
Types: Fac ed, fine bnd, 1st ed, hb, illus
  bk, incunab, ltd ed, o&r, op
Subj: Amer, art, Eng hist & lit, geosci
S/S: Appr libr collec, autg, maps, mss,
  orig art, prints

Kimberton

TALLY PADS BY LORETTA
Box 103, 19442. Tel 215-933-9138
SAN 166-1000
Owner & Mgr, Loretta H Thomas
Estab 1967
Types: O&r, used
S/S: Biper, maps, prints

King of Prussia

W GRAHAM ARADER III
1000 Boxwood Court, 19406.
  Tel 215-825-6570, 688-4565
SAN 166-1019
Owner, W Graham Arader III; Mgr,
  Helen Koehler
Estab 1971. 10,000 Vols. 6000 sq ft.
  Cat 8x ann
Types: Fac ed, illus bk, imp, o&r
Subj: Amer, bibliog, reference, travel,
  cartography
S/S: Appr libr collec, prints, paper
  restoration, rare maps
See Also: New York, NY; Houston, TX;
  Charles Sessler Inc, Philadelphia, PA

Lancaster—54,725

BOOK HAVEN
154 N Prince St, 17603.
  Tel 717-393-0920
SAN 166-1035
Owner & Mgr, John Kinsey Baker III;
  Asst, Joan Drake
Estab 1978. 25,000 Vols. 1500 sq ft
Types: Fine bnd, 1st ed, hb, illus bk,
  o&r, op
Subj: Art, hist, Pennsylvaniana, Ger bks
  printed in Pennsylvania
S/S: Orig art, prints, search serv

Langhorne—1697

T J McCAULEY BOOKS
68 Woodstream Dr, 19047.
  Tel 215-757-1132
SAN 158-5428
Owner, Rita McCauley; Mgr, T J
  McCauley
Estab 1966. 70,000 Vols. 3600 sq ft.
  Cat 50x ann
Types: 1st ed, hb, illus bk, o&r, op,
  used, juv, papbk, imp Eng & Ireland
Subj: Biog, drama, literary criticism,
  military, poetry, sports, ships & the
  sea, autobiog
S/S: Sh mus, bookfairs

Lumberville

GEOFFREY STEELE INC†
18933. Tel 215-297-5187

SAN 166-1167
Owner, Geoffrey Steele
Types: Imp, op, o&r
Subj: Design, archit, fine arts
S/S: Appr libr collec, per

Meadow Lands

MOLLY KIRWAN BOOKS
1st & Pike Sts, PO Box 367, 15347.
  Tel 412-228-3045, 225-5971
SAN 130-5077
Owner, Molly Kirwan
Estab 1983. 3000 Vols. 200 sq ft. Cat
  5x ann
Types: Fine bnd, 1st ed, hb, illus bk,
  juv, ltd ed, o&r, op, remd, used
Subj: Hunting & fishing, gardening,
  military, Civil War, fiction, philos,
  parapsychol, metaphysics
S/S: Reprod

Mechanicsburg—9487

WILLIAM THOMAS—BOOKSELLER
Box 331, 17055. Tel 717-766-7778
SAN 157-4752
Owner, William Thomas
Estab 1970. 5000 Vols. Cat 2x ann
Types: O&r, op, used
Subj: Amer, Pennsylvaniana
S/S: Appr libr collec, maps, search serv

Meshoppen—571

BIG JOHN'S BOOKROOM
RD 2, 18630. Tel 717-833-5323
SAN 158-7730
Owner, John B Wiles; Mgr, Aileen Wiles
Estab 1970. 17,000 Vols. 600 sq ft
Types: Hb, o&r, op, papbk, used
Subj: Biog, hist, mystery & detective,
  Pennsylvaniana, Western Amer
S/S: Search serv

Mount Penn—3025

JOHN E DETURCK
210 Penn Terrace, 19606.
  Tel 215-779-6278
SAN 159-1185
100 Vols
Types: Hb, o&r, op, used
Subj: Natural hist, Pennsylvaniana,

Thomas Merton, J Bennett Nolan,
  Pennsylvania Dutch, Agnes Repplier,
  Christopher Morley
S/S: Gr cds

ROBERT C SALATHE
207 Penn Terrace, 19606.
  Tel 215-779-6361
SAN 166-1302
Owner & Mgr, Robert C Salathe
Cat
Types: Op, o&r
Subj: Amer, Civil War, genealogy, local
  hist, Pennsylvania Dutch
S/S: Autg, mss

New Freedom—2205

MISCELLANEOUS MAN
PO Box 1776, 17349.
  Tel 717-235-4766
SAN 166-140X
Owner, George Theofiles
Estab 1971. 5000 Vols. Cat 2x ann
Types: Illus bk
Subj: Art, European & American illus-
  tration
S/S: Appr libr collec, orig art, posters,
  prints, search serv, sh mus

New Hope—1473

GRAEDON BOOKS INC
RD 1, 18938. Tel 215-794-8351
SAN 125-314X
Pres, Helen Graedon
Estab 1939. 85,000 Vols. Cat 3x ann
Types: 1st ed, hb, illus bk, new, op,
  papbk, o&r, remd, ltd ed, private
  presses
Subj: Art, black studies, New Jerseyana,
  Pennsylvaniana, Revolutionary War,
  Western Amer, manufacturing
S/S: Appr libr collec, autg, maps, mss,
  prints, search serv

Newtown Square

S & C NAJARIAN
852 Milmar Rd, 19073
SAN 170-2890
Owners, Steve & Chris Najarian
Present Owner 1973
Types: O&r, op

S/S: Sh mus
By appt only

North East—3846

CANTRELL'S BOOKS†
15 S Pearl St, 16428.
　Tel 814-725-3681 (by appt)
SAN 159-5350
Owners, Glenn W & Sabra Cantrell
Estab 1979. 1000 Vols
Types: O&r
Subj: American inland waterways

Paoli—5835

JOHN E NORRIS
Box 442, 19301. Tel 215-644-5957
SAN 157-4760
Owner, John E Norris
Estab 1972. 1000 Vols. 400 sq ft. Cat
　6-8x ann
Types: O&r, op
Subj: Cockfighting, pigeons & poultry

Philadelphia—1,688,210

WILLIAM H ALLEN, BOOKSELLER†
2031 Walnut St, 19103.
　Tel 215-563-3398
SAN 166-1477
Owner, George R Allen; Mgr, David M
　Szewczyk
Estab 1918. 30,000 Vols. Cat 5x ann
Types: Hb, imp, op, o&r, used
Subj: Africa, Orientalia, philos, Am,
　Eng, Latin, Gr & Medieval hist & lit,
　Mod Eur lang & hist
S/S: Appr libr collec

BAUMAN RARE BOOKS
1807 Chestnut St, 19103.
　Tel 215-564-4274
SAN 157-1435
Mgr, Corinne Weeks
Branch
Hq: Atlantic City, NJ

BOOK MARK
2049 Rittenhouse Sq W, 19103.
　Tel 215-735-5546
SAN 124-6283
Owners, Robert Langmuir & Valerie J
　Polin

Estab 1976. 10,000 Vols. 1000 sq ft
Types: Fine bnd, 1st ed, hb, illus bk,
　juv, ltd ed, o&r, op, used
Subj: Archit
S/S: Prints

ART CARDUNER
5952 Germantown Ave (Mail add: 6228
　Greene St, 19144). Tel 215-843-6071
SAN 170-1010
Owner, Art Carduner
Estab 1950. 50,000 Vols. 3500 sq ft.
　Cat 4x ann
Types: 1st ed, o&r, papbk, used
Subj: Amer, soc sci
S/S: Search serv

BERNARD CONWELL CARLITZ
1901 Chestnut St, 19103.
　Tel 215-563-6608
SAN 166-1566
Owner, B C Carlitz
Estab 1945. 20,000 Vols. 2100 sq ft
Types: Fine bnd, 1st ed, illus bk, in-
　cunab, juv, ltd ed, op
Subj: Amer, dent, hist, med, photog, sci-
　tech, flight
S/S: Appr libr collec, autg, maps, mss,
　orig art, prints

BRUCE McKITTRICK, RARE
　BOOKS†
2240 Fairmont Ave, 19130.
　Tel 215-235-3209
Subj: 16th–18th cent bks on sci & med,
　art, bibliog, pedagogy
By appointment only

GEORGE S MacMANUS CO†
1317 Irving St, 19107.
　Tel 215-735-4456
SAN 166-1752
Owner, Clarence Wolf
Cat 4x ann
Types: 1st ed, op, o&r
Subj: Amer, Delawariana, New Jersey-
　ana, Pennsylvaniana, Am & Eng lit
S/S: Autg, mss, prints

OLYMPIA BOOKS
1807 Chestnut St, 19103.
　Tel 215-561-6422
SAN 157-9479
Owner, John F Warren
Estab 1979. 3000 Vols. 500 sq ft. Cat
　3x ann

Types: Fine bnd, new & used, o&r, op,
remd, imp Ital, imp Eng
Subj: Fine arts, art hist & reference
S/S: Biper, orig art, prints, search serv

PALINURUS ANTIQUARIAN
BOOKS†
PO Box 15923, 19103.
Tel 215-735-2970
SAN 159-5016
Mgr, John Hellebrand
3000 Vols. Cat 3x ann
Types: 1st ed, o&r
Subj: 18th century lit

SCHUYLKILL BOOK & CURIO
SHOP†
873 Belmont Ave, 19104.
Tel 215-473-4769
SAN 166-1884
Owner, Samuel F Kleinman
Estab 1945. Cat
Types: Bibles, 1st ed, illus bk, incunab,
op, o&r
Subj: Med, sci-tech
S/S: Autg, mss, maps, prints, sh mus

CHARLES SESSLER INC
1308-1310 Walnut St, 19107.
Tel 215-735-1086
SAN 122-8331
Mgr, Barbara Belden
Estab 1882. Present Owner 1979. Cat
6x ann
Types: Fac ed, 1st ed, hb, new & used,
o&r
Subj: Art, hist, travel, Philadelphia
S/S: Appr libr collec, maps, mss, orig
art
Hq: W Graham Arader III, King of
Prussia, PA

CARMEN D VALENTINO
2956 Richmond St, 19134.
Tel 215-739-6056
SAN 158-278X
Owner, Carmen D Valentino
Estab 1978. Present Owner 1981. 5000
Vols
Types: Fine bnd, hb, illus bk, op, o&r,
used
Subj: Amer
S/S: Appr libr collec, autg, maps, mss,
orig art

Pittsburgh— 423,938

BOOK SEARCH SERVICE
135 Sewickley-Oakmont Rd, 15237.
Tel 412-364-6440
SAN 166-2015
Owner, Tally McKee
Cat ann
Types: 1st ed, juv, op, o&r, used
Subj: Biog, Amer, metaphys & occult,
scholarly lit, USSR
S/S: Search serv, sh mus

WILLIAM G MAYER ANTIQUES
204 Auburn St, 15206.
Tel 412-661-6600
SAN 166-2074
Owner, William G Mayer Jr
Estab 1961. 300 Vols
Types: O&r, atlases
Subj: Reference, 19th century atlases
S/S: Maps, prints

ARTHUR SCHARF, TRAVEL BOOKS
5040 Carolyn Dr, 15236.
Tel 412-653-4402
SAN 166-2090
Owner, Arthur Scharf
Estab 1970. 11,000 Vols. 500 sq ft. Cat
3x ann
Types: Hb, imp, op
Subj: Travel, WPA Writers' Project,
Central Asia, Central Afr, Latin Am
S/S: Maps

SCHOYER'S BOOKS
1404 S Negley Ave, 15217.
Tel 412-521-8464
SAN 166-2112
Owners, Maxine A Schoyer & William
T Schoyer
Estab 1952. 50,000 Vols. Cat ann
Types: 1st ed, incunab, juv, ltd ed, op,
o&r
S/S: Appr libr collec, autg, biper, mss,
orig art

THE TUCKERS
2236 Murray Ave, 15217.
Tel 412-521-0249
SAN 166-2147
Owner & Mgr, Esther J Tucker
Estab 1972. 10,000 Vols. 750 sq ft. Cat
6-12x ann
Types: Fac ed, fine bnd, 1st ed, hb, illus
bk, juv, o&r, op

Subj: Amer, art, arts & crafts, biog,
literary criticism, rel studies, soc sci,
sci-tech, travel, world hist
S/S: Appr libr collec, search serv, sh
mus, early newspr & per, paper
ephemera, postcards

Point Pleasant

BENJAMIN W TURNER JR, BOOK-
SELLER
PO Box 262, 18950. Tel 609-397-0954
SAN 158-6610
Owner, Benjamin W Turner Jr
Estab 1969. 2500 Vols. 300 sq ft. Cat
2x ann
Types: Fine bnd, 1st ed, hb, o&r, op
Subj: Anthrop, archaeol, US Govern-
ment Bureau of American Ethnology
S/S: Search serv, appr libr collec

Pottstown—22,729

THE AMERICANIST†
1525 Shenkel Rd, 19464.
Tel 215-323-5289
SAN 166-2252
Owner, Norman H Kane; Mgr, Michal
Kane
Estab 1954. 25,000 Vols. Cat 10x ann
Types: 1st ed, hb, juv, op, o&r
Subj: Amer, black studies, sci-tech, Am
& for lit
S/S: Appr libr collec, autg, maps, mss,
orig art

FRANKLIN M ROSHON
378 Buchert Rd, 19464.
Tel 215-323-6047
SAN 166-2287
Types: Op, o&r
Subj: Arms & armor, hunting & fishing
trades, locks & keys

Revere

J HOWARD WOOLMER—RARE
BOOKS†
Marienstein Rd, 18953.
Tel 215-847-5074
SAN 164-5889
Estab 1961. Cat 4x ann
Types: 1st ed, hb, imp, op, o&r, used
Subj: 20th century lit
S/S: Appr libr collec, autg, mss

Ridley Park—7889

WILLIAM L SCHAFER BOOKS &
PRINTS
308 Linsay Ave, 19078.
Tel 215-583-8144
SAN 166-2384
Types: Op, o&r

Rillton

HOFFMAN RESEARCH SERVICES
7 Howell Dam Rd, Box 342, 15678.
Tel 412-446-3374 (appt only)
SAN 166-2392
Owner, Beverly Hoffman
Estab 1965. 25,000 Vols. Cat 6x ann
Types: Fac ed, 1st ed, hb, imp, new &
used, op, papbk, o&r, remd
Subj: Amer, bus & mgt, criminology,
Pennsylvaniana, photog, soc sci,
sports, Western Amer, psychiat, psy-
chol, sociol, Colonial Am, journal-
ism, literary research
S/S: Appr libr collec, biper, search serv

Rouseville—734

TERRY HARPER BOOKSELLER
PO Box 103, 16344. Tel 814-676-6728
SAN 157-8480
Owner, Terry Harper
7000 Vols. Cat 4-6x ann
Types: Fine bnd, 1st ed, hb, illus bk,
juv, ltd ed, o&r, op, used
Subj: Amer, discovery & explor, natural
hist, travel
S/S: Appr libr collec, biper, search serv

Saxton—814

BRANDYWINE BOOKS
715 Spring St, 16678. Tel 814-635-2874
SAN 158-5797
Owner, William T P Shea
Estab 1963. 70,000 Vols. 11,500 sq ft.
Cat 4x ann
Types: Op, used
Subj: Bus & mgt, law, military

Sayre—6951

VALLEY BOOKS
111 S Elmer Ave, 18840.
Tel 717-888-9785

SAN 157-4787
Owner, Lew Dabe
Estab 1979. 10,000 Vols. 1000 sq ft
Types: Illus bk, juv, ltd ed, op, used
Subj: Art & ref
S/S: Autg, mss, prints, orig art

Shippensburg— 5261

DALE W STARRY SR—BOOKSELLER
115 N Washington St, 17257.
   Tel 717-532-2690
SAN 157-4795
Owner & Mgr, Dale W Starry Sr
Estab 1965. 15,000 Vols. 800 sq ft
Types: 1st ed, hb, illus bk, juv, op, used
Subj: Biog, genealogy, nonfiction
S/S: Search serv

State College— 36,130

HARVEY ABRAMS—BOOKS
352 B E College Ave, PO Box 732,
   16801
SAN 158-8788
Owner, Harvey Abrams
Estab 1980. 5000 Vols. 1500 sq ft. Cat
   ann
Types: Hb, imp, incunab, new & used,
   o&r, op, remd
Subj: Health & phys educ, sports,
   Olympic Games
S/S: Search serv

MICHAEL GIBBS BOOKS
PO Box 883,16801
SAN 159-1630
Owner, Michael Gibbs
Estab 1978. 3000 Vols. Cat 4x ann
Types: O&r, op
Subj: Southwestern Amer, Texana,
   Western Amer, J Evetts Haley, oil
   history
S/S: Appr libr collec

R F PEROTTI, RARE BOOKS
Rm 3B, 112 E Beaver Ave (Mail add:
   PO Box 589, 16801). Tel 814-238-
   5756
SAN 166-2619
Owner, R F Perotti
Estab 1970. 1500 Vols. Cat
Types: 1st ed, o&r
Subj: Am hist & lit, Amer
S/S: Antique watches, dealing with
   collectors & univ libr

Swarthmore— 5950

BOOKSOURCE
7 S Chester Rd (Mail add: PO Box 43,
   19081). Tel 215-328-5083
SAN 127-3418
Owners, Patrick Flanigan & Constance
   Jones
Estab 1976. Present Owner 1978. 5000
   Vols. 800 sq ft
Types: Fine bnd, 1st ed, hb, o&r, op,
   used, illus bk
Subj: Nonfiction, Pennsylvaniana
S/S: Autg, search serv

F THOMAS HELLER RARE BOOKS
435 Riverview Rd, PO Box 356, 19081.
   Tel 215-543-6438
SAN 165-0076
Owner, James A Hinz; Mgr, Christopher
   Wolfe
Estab 1943. 2500 Vols. Cat 2x ann
Types: 1st ed, illus bk, incunab, o&r,
   op
Subj: Med, philos, psychiat, sci-tech,
   psychol, occult
S/S: Appr libr collec

Warren— 12,146

ERNEST C MILLER
PO Box 1, 16365. Tel 814-726-8335
SAN 166-283X
Estab 1950. 4000 Vols. Cat
Types: 1st ed, op, o&r, imp
Subj: Amer, Pennsylvaniana, petroleum
S/S: Mss, maps, prints

West Chester— 17,435

BALDWIN'S BOOK BARN
865 Lenape Rd, 19380.
   Tel 215-696-0816
SAN 166-2872
Owner, William C Baldwin
Estab 1935. 50,000 Vols. Cat
Types: Fine bnd, 1st ed, illus bk, ltd ed,
   o&r, op, used
Subj: Amer
S/S: Autg, biper, mss, prints

Williamsport— 33,401

HUGHES'
2410 N Hills Dr, 17701.

Tel 717-326-1045
SAN 158-4154
Owner, Timothy J Hughes
Cat 8x ann
Types: Early, rare & historic newspapers
S/S: Appr libr collec, per, appraise newspaper collections

Wynnewood

EARL MOORE ASSOCIATES, INC†
PO Box 243, 19096. Tel 215-649-1549
SAN 166-3003
Owner, Earl Moore
Estab 1960. Cat
Types: O&r
Subj: Amer
S/S: Appr libr collec, autg, maps, mss, prints

York— 44,619

MARIE FETROW
1777 W Market St, 17404.
    Tel 717-843-0290
SAN 166-3011
Owner, Marie Fetrow
Types: 1st ed, hb, illus bk, imp, juv, o&r, op, remd, used
S/S: Prints, search serv

RHODE ISLAND

Bristol— 20,128

THE CURRENT COMPANY†
12 Howe St (Mail add: PO Box 46, 02809). Tel 401-253-7824
SAN 166-3062
Owner, Robert Rulon Miller; Mgr, Barbara Walzer
Estab 1971. 8000 Vols. 2000 sq ft. Cat 10x ann
Types: 1st ed, hb, hp papbk, illus bk, incunab, juv, ltd ed, o&r, used
Subj: Amer, scholarly lit, sci-tech, marine
S/S: Autg, mss, orig art, reprod, prints
See Also: Minneapolis, MN

Cranston— 71,992

PATRICK T CONLEY— BOOKS
43 Windsor Rd, 02905.
    Tel 401-785-0169
SAN 166-3097
Owner, Patrick T Conley; Mgr, Paul Campbell
Estab 1963. 8000 Vols. 4500 sq ft. Cat 15x ann
Types: Hb, op, o&r, used
Subj: Am hist & lit, Amer, Civil War, law, literary criticism, Rhode Island, theol, Western Amer
S/S: Appr libr collec, biper, search serv

East Greenwich— 10,211

DON E BURNETT
PO Box 178, 02818. Tel 401-884-6181
SAN 166-3100
Owner, Don E Burnett
Estab 1934. 10,000 Vols. 1200 sq ft
Types: 1st ed, hb, juv, op, o&r, used
Subj: Amer
S/S: Appr libr collec, autg, biper, mss, search serv, early Am newspapers, broadsides
Stock includes children's bks, 1790–1880, architecture bks, 1835–1925

Foster— 3370

LINCOLN BOOK SHOPPE INC & LINCOLN OUT-OF-PRINT BOOK SEARCH LTD
Mt Hygeia Rd, Box 47, 02825. Tel 401-647-2825
SAN 166-3283
Owner, Harold S Ephraim
Estab 1931. 75,000 Vols. 2000 sq ft
Types: O&r, op
Subj: Econ, fine arts, hist, literary criticism, soc sci, ephemera
S/S: Search serv

Hope Valley— 1326

FRANK J WILLIAMS, LINCOLNIANA
RFD Hope Valley Rd, 02832
SAN 166-3119

Owner, Frank J Williams
Cat
Types: Fac ed, 1st ed, hb, incunab, new
& used, op, papbk, o&r, remd
Subj: Civil War, Abraham Lincoln
S/S: Appr libr collec, autg, mss, orig
art, prints, search serv

Newport—29,259

ANCHOR & DOLPHIN BOOKS†
20 Franklin St (Mail add: PO Box 823,
02840). Tel 401-846-6890
SAN 157-5996
Owners, Ann Marie Wall & James A
Hinck
Estab 1979. 2000 Vols. 400 sq ft. Cat
Types: Fine bnd, 1st ed, illus bk, ltd ed,
o&r, op
Subj: Gardening, landscape archit

CORNER BOOKSHOP
418 Spring St, 02840. Tel 401-846-8406
SAN 123-3254
Owner, Rita Whitford
Estab 1962. 4000 Vols
Types: 1st ed, new & used, op, o&r
papbk
Subj: Rhode Islandana, Newport

EDWARD J CRAIG
11 Clarke St, PO Box 189, 02840.
Tel 401-847-6498
SAN 158-2399
Owner, Edward J Craig; Asst Mgr,
Marion Craig
Cat 6x ann
Types: O&r
Subj: 17th & 18th century letters &
documents
S/S: Autg, maps, mss, currency

THE NOSTALGIA FACTORY
Brick Market Pl, 221 Goddard Row,
02840. Tel 401-849-3441
SAN 158-2216
Estab 1971. 600 Vols
Types: Illus bk, o&r, op
Subj: Archit, world exhibitions
S/S: Autg, per, prints, sh mus, ephemera

Peace Dale

SIGN OF THE UNICORN BOOKSHOP
604 Kingstown Rd (Mail add: PO Box

297, 02883). Tel 401-789-8912
SAN 157-6003
Owners, Mary Jo Munroe & John
Romano
Estab 1978. 15,000 Vols. Cat
Types: Fine bnd, 1st ed, hb, illus bk,
juv, ltd ed, new & used, o&r, op
S/S: Appr libr collec, search serv

Providence—156,804

WALTER AXELROD
142 Waterman, St, 02906.
Tel 401-274-3216
SAN 166-3194
Owner, Walter Axelrod
Estab 1965. 1000 Vols
Types: 1st ed, fine bnd, incunab, o&r
S/S: Sh mus
Branches:
AXELROD—MUSIC INC
251 Weybosset St, 02903.
Tel 401-421-4833
SAN 166-3186

IRON HORSE COMICS & COL-
LECTIBLES
834 Hope St, 02906. Tel 401-521-9343
SAN 158-4545
Owner, Samuel J Galentree
Estab 1977. 50,000 Vols. 384 sq ft. Cat
Types: 1st ed, illus bk, ltd ed, o&r,
papbk
S/S: Appr libr collec, biper, orig art,
prints, search serv, price guides

S CLYDE KING RARE & OUT-OF-
PRINT BOOKS
Box 2036 Edgewood Sta, 02905.
Tel 401-781-0837
SAN 166-3275
Owner, S Clyde King
Estab 1935. 10,000 Vols
Types: 1st ed, hb, juv, op, papbk, used
Subj: Am hist & lit, mystery & detec-
tive, sci fiction & fantasy, fiction,
whales & whaling, regional mat
S/S: Giftbooks, lit annuals

MERLIN'S CLOSET INC
166 Valley St, Lower Level, 02909.
Tel 401-351-9272
SAN 157-8073
Owners & Mgr, Elliot Kay Shorter, et al

Estab 1979. 6500 Vols. 950 sq ft. Cat
2x ann
Subj: Hist, illus, mod lit, sci fiction &
fantasy
S/S: Games, orig art, per, prints, search
serv

SEWARDS' FOLLY, BOOKS
139 Brook St, 02906.
Tel 401-272-4454
SAN 166-3313
Owners, Schuyler Seward & Peterkin
Seward
Estab 1976. 25,000 Vols
Types: 1st ed, fine bnd, hb, illus bk,
imp, o&r, op, papbk, remd, used
Subj: Scholarly lit
S/S: Search serv

TYSON BOOKS
334 Westminister Mall 2nd Floor,
02903. Tel 401-421-3939
SAN 166-333X
Owner, Mariette Bedard
Estab 1930. Cat
Types: Hb, op, o&r, used
Subj: Amer, Rhode Islandana
S/S: Search serv

Warwick— 87,123

FORTUNATE FINDS BOOKSTORE
16 W Natick Rd, 02886.
Tel 401-737-8160
SAN 166-3356
Owner, Mildred E Santille-Longo
Estab 1955. 10,000 Vols. Cat 4x ann
Types: Op, o&r
Subj: Genealogy, hist
S/S: Appr libr collec, book auctions,
annual yard sale

Westerly— 18,850

THE WAYSIDE BOOKSHOP
Langworthy Rd (Mail add: Box 501,
02891). Tel 401-322-1698
SAN 158-6297
Owners, J L O'Donnell & Bernadine
O'Donnell
Estab 1974. 3500 Vols. Cat 6x ann
Types: Fac ed, fine bnd, 1st ed, hb, illus
bk, juv, ltd ed, o&r, op
Subj: Mystery & detective, nautical, sci

fiction & fantasy, Eng & Amer lit
S/S: Appr libr collec, autg, sh mus

SOUTH CAROLINA

Beaufort— 8634

BEAUFORT BOOK CO
PO Box 1127, 29902.
Tel 803-524-5172
SAN 156-7225
Owners, Martin Hoogenboom & Isabel
Hoogenboom
Types: Hb, o&r, op, remd
Subj: South Carolinana

Charleston— 69,510

HARPAGON ASSOCIATES
369 King St, 29401. Tel 803-723-6419
SAN 130-0210
Owner, Carl J Eklund
Estab 1980. Present Owner 1966.
100,000 Vols. 4500 sq ft
Types: Hb, op, remd, used

OLD MILL BOOKS
PO Box 12353, 29412.
Tel 803-795-7177
SAN 166-3496
Owners, George Loukides & Sam
Tomlin
Cat 6x ann
Types: Op
Subj: South Carolinana, South Pacific
S/S: Appr libr collec, biper, search serv

Columbia— 99,296

DUPRIEST'S BOOKSHOP†
1230 Pendleton St, 29201.
Tel 803-256-2756
SAN 164-9507
Owner, Margaret Dupriest
Estab 1977
Types: Op, o&r
Subj: Scholarly lit
S/S: Prints, search serv

Greenwood— 21,163

NOAH'S ARK BOOK ATTIC
Stony Point, Rte 2, 29646.
Tel 803-374-3013

SAN 156-7179
Owner, Donald Hawthorne
Estab 1954. 85,000 Vols. Cat 8x ann
Types: Bibles, imp, incunab, op, o&r
Subj: Theol
S/S: Appr libr collec
See Also: The Attic Inc, Hodges, SC

Hodges – 154

THE ATTIC INC
PO Box 128, 29653. Tel 803-374-3013
SAN 122-3364
Pres, Donald Hawthorne
Estab 1961. 65,000 Vols. Cat 2x ann
Types: Imp, op, o&r
Subj: Agr, South Carolinana
S/S: Appr libr collec
See Also: Noah's Ark Book Attic,
   Greenwood, SC

Newberry – 9866

HAMPTON BOOKS
Rte 1, Box 202, 29108.
   Tel 803-276-6870
SAN 166-3836
Owner, Ben Hamilton; Mgr, Muriel
   Price Hamilton
Estab 1946. 2400 sq ft. Cat
Types: Fac ed, imp, op, o&r, juv, 1st ed
Subj: Films & filmmaking, hist, photog,
   South Carolinana, tv, aerospace
S/S: Appr libr collec, autg, biper, maps,
   orig art, sh mus

Rock Hill – 35,344

JAMES S PIPKIN OLD & RARE
   BOOKS
2324-A Rosewood Dr, 29730.
   Tel 803-366-3839
SAN 159-2831
Owner, James S Pipkin
Estab 1968. 10,000 Vols
Types: 1st ed, hb, illus bk, juv, op, o&r,
   used
Subj: Amer, Civil War, fiction, mystery
   & detective, rel studies, South Caro-
   linana, World Wars I & II
S/S: Biper, maps, search serv, sh mus,
   paper ephemera

Spartanburg – 43,968

NORM BURLESON BOOKSELLER
104 First Ave, 29302. Tel 803-583-8845
SAN 159-6500
Owner, Norm Burleson
Estab 1979
Types: Hb, imp, o&r, op, used
S/S: Appr libr collec, search serv

KITEMAUG BOOKS
229 Mohawk Dr, 29301.
   Tel 803-576-3338
SAN 166-395X
Owner, Frank J Anderson
Estab 1959. 700 Vols. Cat ann
Types: Fac ed, 1st ed, hb, new & used,
   o&r, op, papbk, pvt presses, remd
Subj: Nautical, Amer, Navy, submarines
S/S: Prints

WOODSPURGE BOOKS
246 Connecticut Ave (Mail add: PO Box
   18404, 29318). Tel 803-585-4210
SAN 156-9597
Owner, Edwin C Epps
Estab 1979. Cat 2x ann
Types: Fac ed, 1st ed, illus bk, o&r
Subj: South Carolinana, 18th & 19th
   century Eng lit
S/S: Appr libr collec, autg, maps, mss,
   search serv

SOUTH DAKOTA

Sioux Falls – 81,343

LESTER'S PAWNSHOP & BOOK-
   STORE
E Rice (Mail add: PO Box 1152,
   57101). Tel 605-332-2121
SAN 166-4190
Owner, Lester L Larson
Estab 1972. 150,000 Vols. Cat ann
Types: Papbk, used, hb, remd
S/S: Biper, per, remd dlr, sh mus, comics
Stock consists of paper memorabilia
   1800s-1950s

TENNESSEE

Cleveland – 26,415

THE BOOK SHELF
3765 Hillsdale Dr NE, 37311.

Tel 615-472-8408
SAN 157-4841
Owner & Buyer, William R Snell
Estab 1974. 2000 Vols. 600 sq ft. Cat
  4x ann
Types: 1st ed, fac ed, hb, new, o&r, op
Subj: Alabamana, genealogy, Southern
  Amer, Tennesseeana
S/S: Appr libr collec, search serv

Dyersburg — 15,856

MURRAY HUDSON — BOOKS &
  MAPS
Rte 1, Box 362, 38024.
  Tel 901-285-0666
SAN 158-4456
Estab 1979. 3000 Vols. 1200 sq ft. Cat
Types: 1st ed, o&r
Subj: Antq, Eng hist & lit, travel, car-
  tography
S/S: Maps

Kingsport — 32,027

F M HILL — BOOKS
1012 Ransome Lane (Mail add: PO Box
  1037, 37662). Tel 615-247-8740
SAN 166-462X
Owner, F M Hill; Merch Mgr, Mrs F M
  Hill
Estab 1959. 20,000 Vols. Cat
Types: 1st ed, hb, op, o&r, used
Subj: Appalachia, Civil War, hunting &
  fishing, Southern Amer, Tennesseeana
S/S: Appr libr collec, autg, biper, prints,
  sh mus

Knoxville — 183,139

R R ALLEN — BOOKS
5300 Bluefield Rd, 37921.
  Tel 615-584-4487 (by appt only)
SAN 166-4654
Owner, R R Allen
Estab 1963. 6000 Vols. Cat
Types: O&r, op
S/S: Maps, prints, ephemera

ANDOVER SQUARE BOOKS
805 Norgate Rd, 37919.
  Tel 615-693-8984
SAN 157-8081
Owner & Mgr, G A Yeomans; Merch

Mgr, M R Yeomans
Estab 1978. 4000 Vols. Cat 3x ann
Types: 1st ed, illus bk, ltd ed, o&r, op
Subj: Amer
S/S: Search serv

Memphis — 646,356

BURKE'S BOOKSTORE INC
634 Poplar Ave, 38105.
  Tel 901-527-7484
SAN 127-3124
Pres, Diana W Crump
Estab 1875. Present Owner 1978.
  20,000 Vols. 3000 sq ft
Types: Op, el-hi text, used, o&r
Subj: Amer, hist, local authors, sci-tech
S/S: Appr libr collec, search serv

MID-AMERICA BOOKS
105 S Court, 38103. Tel 901-527-0482
SAN 159-6012
Owner, David Brown
Estab 1981. 6000 Vols. 900 sq ft
Types: 1st ed, hb, illus bk, juv, o&r, op,
  papbk, used
Subj: Hist, rel, class studies
S/S: Appr libr collec

OLD SOUTH BOOKS
352 Grandview St, 38111.
  Tel 901-323-6585
SAN 158-748X
Owner, D J Canale
Estab 1979. Cat ann
Subj: Med, sci-tech

OLLIE'S BOOKS
3218 Boxdale St, 38118.
  Tel 901-363-1996
SAN 166-509X
Owner, Ollie McGarrh
Estab 1966. 3000 Vols
Types: Hb, new & used, op
Subj: Astrol
S/S: Biper, search serv

Nashville — 455,651

THE BATTERY BOOK SHOP
PO Box 3107, Franklin Rd, 37219.
  Tel 615-298-1401
SAN 166-5197
Owners, Carter G Baker & Richard S
  Gardner

Estab 1976. 5000 Vols. Cat 3x ann
Types: Fac ed, fine bnd, 1st ed, for lang,
   hb, illus bk, ltd ed, new, o&r, op,
   papbk, used
Subj: Military
S/S: Search serv

CUMBERLAND LITERARY AGENCY
Belle Meade Station, Box 50331,
   37205. Tel 615-790-8951
SAN 166-5200
Owner, John Stoll Sanders
Estab 1978. Cat 4x ann
Types: Hb, imp UK, o&r, op, used
Subj: Irish hist & lit, rel, theol
S/S: Biper

OLD BOOKSTORE
337 2nd Ave S, 37201.
   Tel 615-256-3512
SAN 166-5383
Owner, Vivian P Fox
Estab 1965. 10,000 Vols
Types: Hb, papbk, used
Subj: Biog, Civil War, cooking & nutrit,
   fiction, Tennesseeana
S/S: Antq

Oak Ridge — 27,662

TOM SCOTT FIREBOOKS
26 Montclair Rd, 37830.
   Tel 615-482-3157 (by appt)
SAN 159-5849
Owner, T H Scott
Types: 1st ed, hb, illus bk, imp, juv, ltd
   ed, new, o&r, papbk
S/S: Biper

Ripley — 6366

ENTERPRISE BOOKS
PO Box 289, 38063. Tel 901-635-1771
SAN 166-5421
Owners, William A Klutts & Terry R
   Ford
Estab 1965. 15,000 Vols. 4000 sq ft
Types: Hb, op, remd, o&r, used
Subj: Bks on bks
S/S: Col sup, search serv, staty, subs
   agency, xmas cds

TEXAS

Abilene — 98,315

KINGSTON BOOKSTORE
118 Sayles, 79605. Tel 915-672-8261,
   677-5153, 672-8152
SAN 166-5537
Owners, Ben R Ezzell & Mary M Ezzell
Estab 1972. 100,000 Vols. 2000 sq ft
Types: Fine bnd, 1st ed, hb, o&r, op,
   papbk, used
Subj: Amer, fiction, Texana
S/S: Appr libr collec, search serv

Amarillo — 149,230

AMERICAN SOUTHWEST BOOKS
313 W 15th St, PO Box 148, 79101.
   Tel 806-372-3444
SAN 166-557X
Owner, J R Hollingsworth
Cat ann
Types: O&r
Subj: Southwestern Amer

Austin — 345,496

SUSAN FROST
2311 Longview, 78705.
   Tel 512-477-9393
SAN 159-6005
Owner, Susan Frost
Book collector of Austriaca & German
   in translation

THE JENKINS CO, RARE BOOKS†
7111 S Interregional Hwy (Mail add:
   PO Box 2085, 78768).
   Tel 512-444-6616
SAN 121-7682
Owner, John H Jenkins; Mgr & Buyer,
   Michael Parrish
Estab 1963. 1,650,000 Vols. 20,000 sq
   ft. Cat 15x ann
Types: Fac ed, 1st ed, hb, imp, incunab,
   new & used, o&r
Subj: Autg, sci-tech, travel, Western
   Amer
S/S: Appr libr collec, autg, biper, mss,
   orig art, search serv
See Also: Aldredge Bookstore, Dallas

TOM MUNNERLYN BOOKS
2202 Colgate Lane (Mail add: PO
 Drawer 15247, 78761).
 Tel 512-926-5876
SAN 157-9347
Owner, Tom Munnerlyn
Estab 1977. 10,000 Vols. Cat 2x ann
Types: Op, o&r, used
Subj: Military, Texana, Western Amer
S/S: Appr libr collec

PHOTO-EYE
1818 W 11th (Mail add: PO Box 2686,
 78768). Tel 512-480-8409
SAN 128-7109
Owner, Rixon Reed
Estab 1979. 2000 Vols. Cat 4x ann
Types: Hb, imp Fr, imp Gr, op
Subj: Photog
S/S: Orig art

W THOMAS TAYLOR—BOOK-
 SELLER†
708 Colorado, Suite 704, 78701.
 Tel 512-478-7628
SAN 166-588X
Owner, Tom Taylor; Cataloguer, Elaine
 B Smyth
Estab 1971. 1000 Vols. Cat 5x ann
Types: 1st ed, fine bnd, incunab, ltd ed,
 o&r, press books
Subj: Am hist & lit, Eng hist & lit,
 typography
S/S: Autg, mss, orig art, appr libr collec

T W TINGLE RARE & OUT-OF-
 PRINT BOOKS
3012 Headly Dr, 78745.
 Tel 512-433-6690
SAN 158-2232
Owner & Mgr, Tim W Tingle
Estab 1980. 1000 Vols. 550 sq ft. Cat
 2x ann
Types: 1st ed, hb, ltd ed, o&r, op
Subj: Autg, photog, hist of great depres-
 sion, Steinbeckiana
S/S: Appr libr collec, search serv, work-
 shops on collecting bks

RAY S WALTON—RARE BOOKS†
1310 W 42nd St, 78756.
 Tel 512-458-4182
SAN 166-5936
Owner, Ray S Walton; Mgr, William
 Walton

Estab 1969. 8000 Vols. 2000 sq ft. Cat
 4x ann
Types: 1st ed, hb, illus bk, incunab, ltd
 ed, o&r
Subj: Western Amer, overland narratives, Sp Southwest, voyages, fine
 printing
S/S: Appr libr collec, autg, maps, mss,
 orig art

Bryan—44,337

FRONTIER AMERICA CORPORA-
 TION†
PO Box 3698, 77805.
 Tel 713-846-4462
SAN 166-6126
Owner, Fred White Jr
Estab 1967. 75,000 Vols. Cat
Types: Hb, o&r, op, fine press
Subj: Mex, photog, Texana, travel,
 Western Amer
S/S: Appr libr collec

Clute—9577

A B FENNER BOOKS
601 N Hwy 288, 77531.
 Tel 409-265-2216
SAN 166-6193
Types: Fac ed, 1st ed, op, o&r, used
Subj: Texana, local hist
S/S: Maps, search serv

Dallas—904,078

ALDREDGE BOOKSTORE
2909-1A Maple Ave, 75201.
 Tel 214-748-2043
SAN 123-4382
Owner, John Jenkins; Mgr, R Bosse;
 Buyer, Sam Dobro
Estab 1947. 10,000 Vols. Cat 4x ann
Types: Hb, op, used
Subj: Texana
See Also: The Jenkins Co, Rare Books,
 Austin

CONWAY BARKER—AUTOGRAPH
 DEALER
4126 Meadowdale Lane, PO Box

30625, 75320. Tel 214-358-3786
Types: Autg & historical mss

BIG D BOOKS & COMICS
1516 Centerville, 75228. Tel 214-328-
0130
SAN 166-6363
Owners,Kurt Smith & Henry Crenshaw
Estab 1978. 2000 sq ft. Can ann
Types: Illus bk, juv, o&r, op, papbk,
used, collectible comics
Subj: Comedy, sci fiction & fantasy
S/S: Appr libr collec, biper, maps, orig
art, prints, portfolios

DAVID GROSSBLATT BOOKSELLER
6339 Norway, PO Box 30001, 75230.
Tel 214-373-0218, 361-4320
SAN 157-4884
Owner, David Grossblatt
Estab 1973. 30,000 Vols. 3000 sq ft.
Cat 6x ann
Types: Fine bnd, 1st ed, hb, incunab,
illus bk, juv, ltd ed, new, o&r, op,
papbk, remd
Subj: Amer
S/S: Appr libr collec, autg, maps, mss,
orig art, prints, search serv

THE OLE MOON & OTHER TALES
3016 Greenville Ave, 75206.
Tel 214-827-9921
SAN 158-3549
Owner, G W Lovell; Mgr, Gregory
Marcy
Estab 1979. 20,000 Vols. 1640 sq ft
Types: Fac ed, fine bnd, 1st ed, hb, illus
bk, juv, ltd ed, new & used, o&r, op,
papbk, remd
S/S: Gifts, jewelry, orig art, prints,
search serv, staty, antq

THE WILSON BOOKSHOP†
3118 Routh St, 75201.
Tel 214-747-5804
SAN 166-669X
Owners, Robert A Wilson & Jane M
Wilson
Estab 1965. 8000 Vols. 3000 sq ft
Types: 1st ed, fine bnd, hb, illus bk, op,
o&r, pvt presses, small presses, used
Subj: Bks on bks, Latin Am, Southwest-
ern Amer, Texana
S/S: Maps, prints

Dickinson—7505

SCHROEDER'S BOOK HAVEN
Rte 1, Box 820, 77539.
Tel 713-337-1002
SAN 122-7998
Owner, B C Schroeder Jr
Estab 1968. 110,000 Vols. 3000 sq ft
Types: Hb, op, remd, used
Subj: Texana

Fort Worth—385,141

BOOKS ETC
4912 Camp Bowie Blvd, 76107.
Tel 817-731-9162
SAN 158-4006
Owner, Jim Odom
Estab 1979. 750 sq ft
Types: Fac ed, 1st ed, hb, illus bk, juv,
o&r
Subj: Edgar Rice Burroughs
S/S: Appr libr collec, autg, biper, orig
art, sh mus

ALBERT L PETERS BOOKSELLER
6220 Dovenshire, 76112.
Tel 817-451-1887
SAN 158-6319
Owner & Mgr, Albert L Peters
Estab 1979. 3000 Vols. Cat 4x ann
Types: Hb, op, used
Subj: Amer, Western Amer, Texana
S/S: Search serv

Glen Rose—2075

LIMESTONE HILLS BOOKSHOP†
Box 1125, 76403. Tel 817-897-4991
SAN 158-7498
Owners, Aubyn & Lyle Harris Kendall
Jr
Estab 1975. 10,000 Vols. Cat 2x ann
Types: Fac ed, fine bnd, 1st ed, hb,
illus bk, juv, o&r, op, papbk, used
Subj: Mystery & detective, bks on bks,
19th & 20th century Eng & Am lit,
Thomas J Wise
S/S: Prints, search serv, appr collec

Houston—1,594,086

W GRAHAM ARADER III
2800 Virginia Ave, 77098.

Tel 713-527-8055
SAN 156-594X
Owner, W Graham Arader III; Sales
Mgr, Barry Greenlaw; Off Mgr, William Talbot
Estab 1981. 5000 Vols. 4000 sq ft. Cat
8x ann
Types: Fac ed, illus bk, imp, o&r
Subj: Amer, bibliog, reference, travel,
cartography
S/S: Appr libr collec, prints, paper
restoration, rare maps
Hq: King of Prussia, PA

CARTOGRAPHICA
1514½ Vermont St, 77006.
Tel 713-528-1848
SAN 159-1649
Owner, George P Szontagh
Estab 1978. 500 Vols. 600 sq ft. Cat
Types: Fac ed, illus bk, op, used
S/S: Maps, prints, search serv

COLLEEN'S BOOKS & THINGS
6880 Telephone Rd, 77061.
Tel 713-641-1753
SAN 166-7467
Owner, Colleen Urbanek
Estab 1971. 40,000 Vols. 2200 sq ft
Types: Hb, new
Subj: Hist, petroleum, Texana, auto
repair, World War II
S/S: Search serv

DETERING BOOK GALLERY†
2311 Bissonnet, 77005. Tel 713-526-
6974
SAN 127-8517
Owner, Herman E Detering III; Mgr,
Oscar Dale Graham II; Asst Mgr,
Sarah Greene Marcoolier
Estab 1975. 40,000 Vols. 2000 sq ft.
Cat 2x ann
Types: Fine bnd, 1st ed, illus bk, fine
printing
Subj: Humanities
S/S: Autg, mss

KENDRICK BOOKSTORE
2429 Rice Blvd, 77005. Tel 713-528-
3388
SAN 166-770X
40,000 Vols
Types: 1st ed, new & used, op, o&r
Subj: Texana

MONTROSE BOOKSHOP
PO Box 66265, 77006. Tel 713-522-
1713
SAN 157-0226
Owner, Richard C Palmer
Estab 1968. 5000 Vols
Types: 1st ed, ltd ed, o&r, op
Subj: Am hist & lit, cooking & nutrit,
Eng hist & lit

NORUMBEGA BOOKS
PO Box 25246, 77265. Tel 713-667-
7601
SAN 158-0116
Owner, Elizabeth Labanowski
Estab 1977. 2000 Vols
Types: 1st ed, o&r
Subj: Amer, 19th century lit
S/S: Autg, mss, orig art, prints

TRACKSIDE BOOKS
8819 Mobud Dr (Mail add: PO Box
770264, 77215). Tel 713-772-8107,
772-2433
SAN 166-7904
Owner & Mgr, Lawrence E Madole;
Buyer, Kathleen M Madole
Estab 1964. 12,000 Vols. 2400 sq ft.
Cat 4x ann
Types: Fac ed, 1st ed, hb, imp, ltd ed,
new & used, o&r, op, papbk, remd
Subj: Railroadiana, Texana
S/S: Biper, maps, orig art, prints, search
serv

Keene — 3013

ZANE GREY'S WEST
Drawer A, 76059. Tel 817-641-8536
SAN 159-2041
Owner, Dr Joe L Wheeler
20,000 Vols. 1000 sq ft. Cat
Types: Fine bnd, 1st ed, hb, illus bk,
juv, o&r, op, papbk
Subj: Western Amer, Zane Grey, Harold
Bell Wright
S/S: Appr libr collec, search serv

Longview — 62,762

EDDIE WOODS BOOKS
208 N Center (Mail add: Box 6361,
75608). Tel 214-757-6254
SAN 158-2542
Owner, Eddie Woods

Estab 1976. 1000 sq ft
Types: 1st ed, hb, juv, new & used,
o&r, op, used

Salado

FLETCHER'S BOOKS
Main St, Box 65, 76571.
Tel 817-947-5414
SAN 166-8356
Owner & Buyer, T R Fletcher
Estab 1930. Present Owner 1982. 5000
Vols
Types: 1st ed, hb, new & used, op
Subj: Texana
S/S: Appr libr collec, autg, maps, mss

San Antonio — 785,410

ANTIQUARIAN BOOK MART
3127 Broadway, 78209.
Tel 512-828-4885
SAN 166-8587
Owner, Frank Kellel Jr; Mgr, Robert
Kellel
Estab 1970. 200,000 Vols. 4800 sq ft.
Cat
Types: Fac ed, fine bnd, 1st ed, hb, illus
bk, juv, ltd ed, o&r, remd, used
Subj: Military, Southwestern Amer,
Texana
S/S: Appr libr collec, search serv
Branches:
BOOK MART ANNEX
3132 Ave B. Tel 512-828-7433
SAN 157-3981

BOOKETERIA
3323 Fredericksburg Rd, 78201.
Tel 512-734-8760
SAN 170-1827
Owner, Paul K Harwell; Mgr, Carol
Harwell
Estab 1976. Present Owner 1977.
150,000 Vols. 1400 sq ft
Types: Fine bnd, hb, o&r, op, papbk,
used
S/S: Search serv, rec & tapes

BOOKSEARCH
221 Losoya, 78205. Tel 512-226-6049
SAN 157-8146
Owner, M S Lambeth
Estab 1980. 2500 Vols. Cat 2x ann
Types: Op, o&r

Subj: Art, Southwestern Amer, Texana
S/S: Search serv

JOSHUA DAVID BOWEN
1037 S Alamo, 78210.
Tel 512-227-1771
SAN 166-8617
Estab 1959. 5000 Vols. Cat 2-3x ann
Types: Hb, op
Subj: Mex, performing arts
S/S: Appr libr collec

LEONARD DIXON BOOKSTORE
351 Eastley Dr, 78217. Tel 512-824-
9267
SAN 166-8692
Owner, Leonard Dixon
Estab 1916. Present Owner 1954.
25,000 Vols
Types: Hb, papbk
Subj: Art, bus & mgt, family studies,
metaphys & occult, music, parapsychol, sci-tech, self-develop
S/S: Classes, mail order, astrology
readings

GUTENBERG'S FOLLY: RARE &
SCHOLARLY BOOKS
627 E Guenther, 78210. Tel 512-222-
8449
SAN 159-2254
Owner, J Bryce Milligan; Mgr, Mary G
Milligan
Estab 1978. 4000 Vols. 500 sq ft. Cat
ann
Types: 1st ed, juv, ltd ed
Subj: Autg, mod lit
S/S: Appr libr collec, search serv, bib-
liog & lit research

WILLIAM ORBELO
912 Garraty, 78209. Tel 512-828-1873
(by appt only)
SAN 159-1339
Types: O&r
Subj: Aviation, med, military, nautical,
Texana
S/S: Autg, maps, mss

Stephenville — 11,881

FREDRICK W ARMSTRONG BOOK-
SELLER
319 N McIlhaney, 76401.
Tel 817-965-7128
SAN 157-6062

Owner, Fredrick W Armstrong
Estab 1979. 500 Vols. Cat ann
Types: Hb, ltd ed, o&r, op, used
Subj: Amer, Civil War, Western Amer
S/S: Search serv

Taft — 3686

COLLECTOR'S MUSEUM &
  MARKET
113 Green Ave, 78390. Tel 512-528-
  3353
SAN 166-9028
Owner, Mgr & Buyer, Ken Kruse
Estab 1977. 15,000 Vols. 6000 sq ft
Types: 1st ed, hb, juv, ltd ed, new &
  used, o&r, op, papbk, autg bks
Subj: Autg, comedy, fiction, metaphys
  & occult, nonfiction, sci fiction &
  fantasy
S/S: Mail order

Temple — 42,483

BOOK CELLAR
2 S Main, 76501. Tel 817-773-7545
SAN 158-8044
Owner, Patricia Reynolds
Estab 1978. 60,000 Vols. 2200 sq ft
Types: Fine bnd, 1st ed, hb, illus bk,
  juv, o&r, op, papbk, used
Subj: Poetry, Texana
S/S: Search serv, new & collector
  comics

Victoria — 50,695

JOE PETTY — BOOKS
1704 Park, 77901. Tel 512-573-3320
SAN 166-9176
Owner, J W Petty, Jr
Estab 1940. 4000 Vols
Types: 1st ed, hb, imp, op, o&r, used
Subj: Bks on bks, Texana
S/S: Appr libr collec, search serv

Waxahachie — 14,624

CLARK WRIGHT BOOKDEALER
409 Royal St, 75165. Tel 214-937-3300
SAN 157-5007
Owner, Bessie L Wright

Estab 1925. 3000 Vols. 750 sq ft. Cat
  4x ann
Types: 1st ed, o&r, op, remd, used
Subj: Latin Am, Southwestern Amer,
  Texana, Western Amer

UTAH

Provo — 73,907

WALT WEST BOOKS
1355 Riverside Ave, 84604.
  Tel 801-377-1298
SAN 157-9290
Owner & Mgr, Walter R West Jr
Estab 1979. 10,000 Vols. 1100 sq ft
Types: 1st ed, hb, illus bk, o&r, op,
  used
Subj: Western Amer, Mormon
S/S: Appr libr collec, search serv

Salt Lake City — 163,033

THE BOOK SHOPPE
268 S State St, 84111.
  Tel 801-532-9326
SAN 166-9591
Owners, Bonnie Burt & John Burt
Estab 1968. 3000 Vols
Types: O&r, used
Subj: Rel-LDS, Utahiana
S/S: Porcelain jewelry

COSMIC AEROPLANE BOOKS
258 E 1st S, 84111. Tel 801-533-9409
SAN 124-7808
Owner & Mgr, Bruce Roberts; Trade
  Buyer, Bob Ormsby; Papbk Buyer, Joe
  Knighton
Estab 1976. 100,000 Vols. 4500 sq ft.
  Cat
Types: Hb, juv, op, o&r, papbk, remd,
  used, small presses
Subj: Alt life-styles, art, metaphys &
  occult, poetry, rel-LDS, sci fiction &
  fantasy, Utahiana, Western Amer
S/S: Appr libr collec, lit mags, gr cds,
  posters, rec, search serv

SCALLAWAGIANA BOOKS
PO Box 2441, 84110.
  Tel 801-487-7184
SAN 158-8818
Owner, Kent L Walgren

Estab 1980. 1000 Vols. 100 sq ft. Cat
  4x ann
Types: 1st ed, hb, ltd ed, op, o&r
Subj: Utahiana, Western Amer, Mor-
  mons, Vardis Fisher, Wallace Stegner
S/S: Appr libr collec, maps, mss

VERMONT

Bennington—15,815

AISLINN: IRISH BOOKS &
  RESEARCH
PO Box 589, 05201
SAN 170-2157
Owner, J M Hays
Present Owner 1983. 10,000 Vols. Cat
  4x ann
Types: Fine bnd, hb, illus bk, ltd ed,
  o&r, op, papbk, remd, used
Subj: Irish hist & lit
S/S: Search serv
Mail order only

NEW ENGLANDIANA
121 Benmont Ave, PO Box 589, 05201.
  Tel 802-447-1695
SAN 163-4682
Owner, Roger D Harris
Estab 1961. 15,000 Vols. Cat 4x ann
Types: Op, o&r, remd, used

Brattleboro—11,886

KEN LEACH
16 Elm St, Box 78, 05301.
  Tel 802-257-7918
SAN 166-9729
Cat 4-5x ann
Types: 1st ed, o&r
Subj: Am 18-19 century lit
S/S: Appr libr collec, autg, mss

Burlington—37,712

BYGONE BOOKS INC
91 College, 05401. Tel 802-862-4397
SAN 159-0200
Owners, S Soule, et al; Pres, P Welsh
Estab 1978. 10,000 Vols. 1000 sq ft
Types: Fac ed, fine bnd, 1st ed, hb, illus
  bk, imp, juv, ltd ed, new & used,
  o&r, op, papbk, remd

S/S: Appr libr collec, biper, maps,
  prints, search serv, sh mus

JAMES FRASER†
PO Box 494, 05402. Tel 802-658-0322
Subj: Econ, bus hist
By appointment only

Craftsbury Common—844

CRAFTSBURY COMMON ANTI-
  QUARIAN
Box 69, 05827. Tel 802-586-9677
SAN 163-4577
Owners, Ralph Lewis & Nancy Lewis
Types: Illus bk
Subj: Amer, maritime

Cuttingsville

HAUNTED MANSION BOOKSHOP
05738. Tel 802-492-3337, 492-3462
SAN 166-9818
Owner & Buyer, Clint Fiske
Estab 1966. 50,000 Vols. 2400 sq ft
Types: O&r, op
Subj: Amer, Vermontiana
S/S: Appr libr collec, old bottles

Lyndonville—1401

GREEN MOUNTAIN BOOKS &
  PRINTS
100 Broud St (Mail add: PO Box 74,
  Sutton, 05851). Tel 802-626-5051
SAN 158-7196
Owner, Ralph C Secord; Mgr, Ellen
  Doyle
Estab 1977. Present Owner 1980.
  35,000 Vols. Cat 5-6x ann
Types: Fine bnd, 1st ed, hb, o&r, op,
  papbk, remd, new & used
Subj: Amer
S/S: Appr libr collec, prints, search serv,
  wholesale

Morrisville—2074

BRICK HOUSE BOOKSHOP
Morristown Corners, 05661.
  Tel 802-888-4300
SAN 158-4049
Owner, Alexandra Heller
Estab 1976. 6000 Vols. 800 sq ft

Types: Fac ed, fine bnd, hb, illus bk,
juv, ltd ed, o&r, op, papbk, used

Newport—4756

MICHAEL DUNN BOOKS
Rt 2, Eagle Point, Box 436, 05855.
Tel 802-334-2768
SAN 157-5015
Owner, Michael H Dunn
Estab 1978. 5000 Vols. 500 sq ft.
Cat 5-6x ann
Types: O&r, op, used
Subj: Amer, Can, hunting & fishing,
Vermontiana, mountaineering
S/S: Maps, orig art, search serv

North Bennington—1685

JOHN JOHNSON NATURAL HIS-
TORY BOOKS†
RFD 2, 05257. Tel 802-442-6738
SAN 166-9915
Owner, John Johnson; Mgr, Betty J
Johnson
Estab 1949. 15,000 Vols. 2000 sq ft.
Cat 4x ann
Types: Hb, illus bk, o&r, op, used
Subj: Bot, natural hist, zool, birds,
mammals, insects, fish, reptiles,
paleontology, naturalist travels, voy-
ages & exploration
S/S: Publisher

North Pomfret

RICHARD H ADELSON, ANTI-
QUARIAN BOOKSELLER†
Cloudland Rd, 05053.
Tel 802-457-2608
SAN 166-9923
Owners, Richard H Adelson & Jane K
Adelson
Estab 1971. Cat 4x ann
Types: O&r
Subj: Travel
S/S: Appr libr collec, maps, prints

Plainfield—1549

THE COUNTRY BOOKSHOP
RFD 2, 05667. Tel 802-454-8439
SAN 158-4057
Owners, Benjamin & Alexandra Koenig

Estab 1974. 10,000 Vols. 1000 sq ft.
Cat 2x ann
Types: 1st ed, hb, illus bk, juv, o&r, op,
used
Subj: Folklore, anthrop, archaeol
S/S: Appr libr collec, biper, prints,
search serv, sh mus
Open Wed-Sat 10-5

BENJAMIN KOENIG'S COUNTRY
BOOKSHOP
RFD 2, 05667. Tel 802-454-8439
SAN 166-9931
Owners & Mgrs, Benjamin Koenig &
Alexandra Koenig
Estab 1973. 10,000 Vols. 1000 sq ft.
Cat
Types: 1st ed, hb, o&r, op, used
Subj: Folklore, bells
S/S: Appr libr collec, prints, search serv,
ephemera, paper collectibles

Putney—1850

THE UNIQUE ANTIQUE
Main Street, PO Box 485, 05346.
Tel 802-387-4488
SAN 159-5342
Owner, Jonathon Flaccus
Estab 1977. 8000 Vols. 900 sq ft
Types: 1st ed, illus bk, juv, ltd ed, o&r
Subj: Circus, drama

Rutland—18,436

F P ELWERT
Box 254, 05701. Tel 802-773-3417
SAN 166-994X
Owner, Frederic P Elwert
Estab 1965. 3000 Vols. Cat
Types: Illus bk, op, o&r, used
Subj: Archit, indust archaeol
S/S: Appr libr collec, maps, mss, orig
arts, prints

TUTTLE ANTIQUARIAN BOOKS
INC†
28 S Main, PO Box 541, 05701.
Tel 802-773-8930; 773-8229
SAN 166-9966
Owner, Charles E Tuttle
Estab 1832. Present Owner 1937.
200,000 Vols. 1200 sq ft. Cat
Types: 1st ed, imp, new, o&r, op

Subj: Genealogy, local hist, Orientalia, Vermontiana

Woodstock — 3214

THE ALLEGORY BOOKSHOP
20 Central St, PO Box 252, 05091.
 Tel 802-457-3023
SAN 170-1207
Owner, Bruce Hartman
Estab 1981. 3000 Vols. 400 sq ft. Cat 2x ann
Types: 1st ed, hb, illus bk, o&r, op, used
Subj: Music, ancient hist & lit
S/S: Search serv, sh mus
Open Mon-Sat 12-5

VIRGINIA

Alexandria — 103,217

ECONOMY BOOKS
1125 King St, 22314. Tel 703-549-9330
SAN 158-6300
Owner, Samuel Yudkii; Mgr, Carl Spier
Estab 1970. 50,000 Vols. 3000 sq ft
Types: 1st ed, hb, illus bk, juv, ltd ed, o&r, op, papbk, remd, used
S/S: Search serv, ephemera

GEPPI'S COMIC WORLD INC
8330 A Richmond Hwy, 22309.
 Tel 703-360-3896
SAN 159-6888
Owner, Steve Geppi; Mgr, George Hustalen
Hq: Baltimore, MD

JENNIE'S BOOK NOOK
15 W Howell Ave, 22301.
 Tel 703-683-0694
SAN 167-0115
Owner, Virginia I Bruch
Estab 1976. 1500 Vols. Cat ann
Types: Hb, o&r, op
Subj: Biog, fiction, genealogy, hist, poetry, Virginiana
S/S: Search serv, spec order

IRENE ROUSE — BOOKSELLER
Old Town, 905 Duke St, 22314.
 Tel 703-549-8745, 548-1529
SAN 126-1207
Owner, Irene Rouse

Estab 1972. Present Owner 1977.
 36,000 Vols
Types: Hb, op, o&r
Subj: Amer, fiction, folklore, poetry
S/S: Search serv, spec order

SAMUEL YUDKIN & ASSOCIATES
1225 King St, 22314. Tel 703-549-9330
SAN 167-0166
Owner, Samuel Yudkin
Estab 1970. 60,000 Vols. 3000 sq ft.
 Cat 12x ann
Types: 1st ed, hb, juv, new & used, op, papbk, o&r, remd
S/S: Appr libr collec, biper, orig art, search serv, auctions

Arlington — 174,284

BOOK ENDS
2710 Washington Blvd, 22201.
 Tel 703-524-4976
SAN 157-5023
Owner, Janet D Deatherage
Estab 1979. 30,000 Vols. 1200 sq ft
Types: Hb, illus bk, juv, o&r, op, papbk, used

BOOKHOUSE
805 N Emerson St, 22205.
 Tel 703-527-7797
SAN 167-0212
Owners, Natalie Hughes & Edward Hughes
Estab 1969. 20,000 Vols. 1200 sq ft
Types: Fine bnd, illus bk, op
S/S: Amer, art, military, natural hist

GEPPI'S CRYSTAL CITY COMICS
1755 Jefferson Davis Hwy, Crystal City Underground, 22202. Tel 703-521-4618, 532-2330
SAN 156-5907
Owner, Steve Geppi; Mgr, Russell Smith
Hq: Baltimore, MD

QUIZZICUM BOOKSTORE
6860 Lee Hwy, 22213. Tel 703-534-2631
SAN 167-0220
Owner, Aloise M Bell
Estab 1963. Present Owner 1975. 260 sq ft
Types: 1st ed, op, o&r, used
S/S: Search serv

SCHAEFER ASSOCIATION
Box 2111, 22202. Tel 703-920-1457
SAN 158-457X
Mgr, Ed Schaefer
Estab 1979
Subj: Military, polit sci, World Wars I &
II
S/S: Maps, posters

Charlottesville—45,010

DAEDALUS BOOKSHOP
121 4th St, NE, 22901.
Tel 804-293-7595
SAN 167-0328
Owner, Sandy McAdams
Estab 1974. 90,000 Vols
Types: Fine bnd, 1st ed, hb, illus bk, op,
o&r, papbk, remd, used
Subj: Fiction
S/S: Appr libr collec, biper, search serv

FRANKLIN GILLIAM: RARE BOOKS
112 Fourth St, NE, 22901. Tel 804-979-
2512
Owner, Franklin Gilliam
Estab 1983
Types: 1st ed, o&r, op, imp
Subj: Eng & Am lit, Mex, Texana
S/S: Appr libr collec, autg, mss
By appointment only

HEARTWOOD USED BOOKS†
5 & 9 Elliewood Ave, 22903.
Tel 804-295-7083
SAN 167-0344
Owners, Paul Collinge & Sherry L
Joseph; Mgr, Jon Guillot
Estab 1975. 30,000 Vols. Cat
Types: Op, o&r
Subj: Scholarly lit
S/S: Appr libr collec, search serv

MARY HOSMER LUPTON
PO Box 5206, 22905. Tel 804-296-
3824
SAN 167-0352
Merch Mgr, Mary Hosmer Lupton
Estab 1965
Types: Fac ed, 1st ed, hb, new & used,
papbk, o&r, op
Subj: Metaphys & occult, natural hist,
Virginiana
S/S: Search serv
Open by appt only

Chesapeake—114,226

GREAT BRIDGE BOOKS INC
404 Woodford Dr, 23320.
Tel 804-482-1666
SAN 167-0387
Owner & Buyer, Gordon C Jones
Estab 1975. 8000 Vols. 1000 sq ft
Types: Fine bnd, 1st ed, hb, illus bk,
juv, ltd ed, o&r, op, papbk, used
Subj: Ancient hist & lit, rel studies,
Virginiana
S/S: Appr libr collec, biper, search serv

Fairfax—19,390

ALLBOOKS
4341 Majestic Lane, 22033.
Tel 703-968-7396
SAN 157-8162
Owner, Charles Robinove
Estab 1979. Present Owner 1982. 3000
Vols. 150 sq ft
Types: Hb, op, o&r, papbk, used
Subj: Sci fiction & fantasy
S/S: Search serv

Falls Church—9515

THE ASSOCIATES—MODERN
FIRST EDITIONS
3100 S Manchester St, Suite 1028, PO
Box 4214, 22044. Tel 703-578-3810
(by appt only)
SAN 170-3870
Owner, William Selander
Estab 1978. 2500 Vols. Cat 3x ann
Types: 1st ed, ltd ed, o&r
Subj: 20th cent Am & Eng lit
S/S: Autg, mss

HOLE IN THE WALL BOOKS
905 W Broad St, 22046.
Tel 703-536-2511
SAN 170-3064
Owner, Michael Nally; Mgr, Richard
Gray
Estab 1979. 50,000 Vols. 1000 sq ft.
Cat 2x ann
Types: Hb, illus bk, juv, new, op,
papbk, used
Subj: Sci fiction & fantasy, mystery &
detective
S/S: Art sup, subs agency

ALEXANDER LAUBERT'S BOOKS
1073 W Broad, 22046.
Tel 703-533-1699
SAN 170-1215
Present Owner 1974. 50,000 Vols
Types: O&r
Subj: Amer, aviation, World Wars I & II
Open Wed-Sat 12-5

Glasgow — 1259

AULD STONE BOOKSHOP
RFD 1, Box 200, 24555.
Tel 703-258-2582
SAN 120-1484
Owner, & Buyer, James A McAleer
Estab 1975. 7500 Vols. 920 sq ft
Types: Fine bnd, hb, new & used, o&r,
op, remd, imp Ireland & Scotland
Subj: Virginiana, Celtic heritage, coun-
try life & crafts, Scotland & Ireland
S/S: Appr libr collec, bk bnd, repair &
restoration

Lynchburg — 66,743

DR NOSTALGIA
3237 Downing Dr, 24503.
Tel 804-384-8303
SAN 170-2386
Owners, Bob & Leah Belle Gardner
Estab 1974. 3000 Vols. Cat ann
Types: Hb, juv, o&r
S/S: Prints, sh mus

Manassas — 15,438

ZEN AMERICANA
10606 Manor Ct, 22110.
Tel 703-361-3368
SAN 158-4588
Mgr, Otto Kirchner-Dean
Estab 1977. 2000 Vols. 1000 sq ft
Types: 1st ed, fine bnd, hb, o&r, op
Subj: Amer, water sports, rel, Chesa-
peake Bay

Norfolk — 266,979

GHENT BOOKWORM
1407-1409 Colley Ave, 23517.
Tel 804-627-2267
SAN 167-0824

Owner, William R Hudnall
Estab 1980. Present Owner 1977.
15,000 Vols. 600 sq ft. Cat
Types: Fine bnd, 1st ed, hb, illus bk, ltd
ed, papbk
S/S: Appr libr collec, biper, prints,
search serv, sh mus

THE MEMORABILIA CORNER
PO Box 15052, 23511-0052.
Tel 804-467-4256
SAN 170-5334
Owner, Henry C Hensel
Estab 1978. 5000 Vols. Cat 3x ann
Types: Fac ed, fine bnd, 1st ed, hb,
incunab, illus bk, imp, o&r, papbk
Subj: Hist, Civil War, philately, Western
Amer, military
S/S: Appr libr collec, autg, maps, orig
art, prints, search serv

Petersburg — 41,055

LOUIS GINSBERG — BOOKS &
PRINTS
Box 1502, 23805. Tel 804-732-8188
SAN 167-0891
Owner, Louis Ginsberg
Estab 1955. 10,000 Vols. Cat 12x ann
Types: 1st ed, imp, op, o&r, used
Subj: Black studies, bks on bks, Civil
War, Judaica, law, med, military,
photog, rel, SAm, Southern Amer,
Southwestern Amer, travel, weaving,
wines, bees, coal, ephemera, oil, old
cookbooks
S/S: Maps

Reston — 5723

W B O'NEILL — OLD & RARE BOOKS
11609 Hunters Green Court, 22091.
Tel 703-860-0782
SAN 167-0999
Owner, W B O'Neill
Estab 1951. 2000 Vols. 450 sq ft. Cat
1-2x ann
Types: 1st ed, fac ed, for lang, hb, op,
o&r, used
Subj: Arab studies, hist, Middle East,
military, travel, Armenia, Baedeker
Travel Guides, Central Asia, Cyprus,
modern Greece, Turkey
S/S: Appr libr collec, maps

Richmond—219,214

COLLECTORS' OLD BOOKSHOP
707 E Franklin St, 23219. Tel 804-644-
2097
SAN 167-1030
Owner, Mary Clark Roane
Estab 1945. 15,000 Vols. 1400 sq ft
Types: 1st ed, imp, op, o&r, used, hb
Subj: Amer, Civil War, Virginia
S/S: Appr libr collec, biper, search serv

NOSTALGIA PLUS
5610 Patterson Ave, 23226. Tel 804-
282-5532
SAN 157-5066
Owner, R E Winfree, Inc
Estab 1979. Present Owner 1980.
50,000 Vols. 400 sq ft
Types: New & used, o&r, papbk
Subj: Comedy, sci fiction & fantasy
S/S: Biper, orig art

WAVES PRESS & BOOKSHOP
4040 MacArthur Ave, 23227.
Tel 804-264-7276
SAN 167-1170
Owner, Damon E Persiani
Estab 1973. 10,000 Vols. Cat 2-4x ann
Types: 1st ed, ltd ed, o&r, op
Subj: Bks on bks, mystery & detective,
Virginiana

Roanoke—100,427

NELSON BOND†
4724 Easthill Dr, 24018.
Tel 703-774-2674
SAN 167-1189
Owner, Nelson Bond
Estab 1967. 7500 Vols. Cat 8x ann
Types: O&r, op
Subj: Bks by & about James Branch
Cabell

Springfield—11,613

CAMELOT BOOKS
7603 Mulberry Bottom Ln, 22153.
Tel 703-455-9540
SAN 158-5061
Owner, James Kissko
1000 Vols. Cat 2x ann
Types: 1st ed, illus bk, ltd ed, o&r, op,
used

Subj: Art, autg, Amer
S/S: Biper, prints

THE MANUSCRIPT COMPANY OF
SPRINGFIELD
PO Box 1151, 22151. Tel 703-256-
6748
SAN 167-1324
Owners, Terry Alford & Jeannette
Alford
Estab 1974. Cat 5x ann
Types: O&r
Subj: Diaries, autg, 18th & 19th cen-
tury doc, ship logs, travel journals
S/S: Appr libr collec, autg, mss

Vienna—15,469

JO ANN REISLER LTD†
360 Glyndon St NE, 22180.
Tel 703-938-2967 (by appt only)
SAN 167-1375
Owners, Jo Ann Reisler & Donald L
Reisler
Estab 1972. 3500 Vols. Cat 2x ann
Types: Illus bk, juv
Subj: Art
S/S: Orig art

Williamsburg—9870

THE BOOKPRESS LTD†
420 Prince George St, PO Box KP,
23187. Tel 804-229-1260
SAN 167-1502
Owners, John Robert Curtis Jr, John
Ballinger, Emily Ballinger; Mgr,
Elizabeth Rouse
Estab 1973. 4000 Vols. 800 sq ft
Types: Fine bnd, 1st ed, hb, illus bk,
o&r, op
Subj: Amer, bks about bks, printing,
18th & 19th cent travel
S/S: Appr libr collec, maps, search serv

HENRY STEVENS, SON & STILES†
PO Box 1299, 23185.
Tel 804-220-0925
Owner, Thomas P MacDonnell
Subj: Amer, early travel

Winchester—20,217

APPLELAND BOOKS
446 N Braddock St, 22601.

Tel 703-662-1980
SAN 167-1510
Owner, Gene Miller
Estab 1967. 3000 Vols. Cat 4x ann
Types: 1st ed, op
Subj: Civil War, Virginiana, Western
Amer
S/S: Biper, maps, mss, orig art, search
serv

Woodstock—2627

OLIN O EVANS
371 W Spring St, 22664.
Tel 703-459-2914
SAN 157-8502
Owner, Olin O Evans
Estab 1930
Types: Used
Subj: Natural hist, Virginiana, Civil
War, poultry, Shenandoah County
hist
S/S: Search serv, National Geographics

Wytheville—7135

BOOKWORM & SILVERFISH†
PO Box 639, 23482
SAN 167-1251
Owner, Jim Presgraves
Estab 1969. 10,000 Vols. 1000 sq ft.
Cat 10x ann
Types: 1st ed, o&r, op, used
Subj: Appalachia, Civil War
S/S: Appr libr collec

WASHINGTON

Bellevue—73,903

P T MALLAHAN BOOKSELLER
307 130th SE, 98005.
Tel 206-454-1663
SAN 158-4502
5000 Vols
Types: Op
Subj: Imperial Russia, World War I
S/S: Appr libr collec, search serv

Bremerton—36,208

INTERIM BOOKS
615 4th St, 98310. Tel 206-377-4343
SAN 158-9849

Owner, Nancy Filler
Estab 1981. 7500 Vols. 600 sq ft. Cat
2x ann
Types: 1st ed, hb, illus bk, juv, o&r, op,
papbk
Subj: Aviation, military, nautical, sci
fiction & fantasy
S/S: Biper, search serv

Clarkston—6903

PEGGATTY BOOKS INC
609 Maple St, 99403. Tel 509-758-9517
SAN 123-6768
Owner, Margaret H Behrens
Estab 1975. 14,000 Vols
Types: New, o&r, op, papbk, used
S/S: Search serv

Ellensburg—11,752

WESTERN BOOKS
109 W 3rd St (Mail add: 307 N Pearl St,
98926). Tel 509-925-2075
SAN 167-1863
Owner, Clayton C Denman
Estab 1964. 10,000 Vols
Types: New & used
Subj: Antq, collecting, hist preservation
S/S: Maps, prints, staty, antiques

Kennewick—34,397

CIPRIANO'S BOOKS
2109 S Ledbetter, 99336.
Tel 509-582-4971
SAN 161-2670
Owner, Leta B Cipriano
Estab 1961. 1500 Vols
Types: Op, o&r, used
Subj: Art, photog, fine press
S/S: Search serv

Lopez—1406

R L SHEP
Box C-20, 98261. Tel 206-468-2023
SAN 157-518X
Owner, R L Shep
Estab 1964. Cat 2x ann
Types: Hb, illus bk, imp, o&r, op, used
Subj: Arts & crafts, costuming, per-
forming arts, textiles, weaving

Marysville—5080

THE BOOK EXCHANGE
101 State, 98270. Tel 206-659-5626
SAN 157-5104
Owners, Debbie Young & Pete Young
Estab 1978. 30,000 Vols. 1000 sq ft
Types: Hb, papbk, juv, o&r, used
Subj: Fiction, how-to, sci fiction &
fantasy

Monroe—2869

R M WEATHERFORD—BOOKS
10902 Woods Creek Rd, 98272.
Tel 206-794-4318
SAN 126-4206
Owner, R M Weatherford
Estab 1980. Present Owner 1980. 4000
Vols. Cat 4x ann
Types: Fine bnd, 1st ed, hb, illus bk,
o&r, op
Subj: Alaskana, Am Indian studies,
Amer, NAmer, Pacific, sci-tech, Western Amer
S/S: Appr libr collec, maps, mss, specialist in computer tech and applications for book trade

Olympia—27,447

BROWSERS' BOOKSHOP
107 N Capitol Way, 98501.
Tel 206-357-7462
SAN 167-2096
Owner, Ilene Yates Grimes
Estab 1970. 10,000 Vols
Types: Op, used, hb, papbk, juv
S/S: Search serv

Opportunity—21,241

McDUFFIE'S BOOKS†
PO Box 14557, 99214.
Tel 509-928-3623
Owner, McDuffie Owen
Types: O&r
Subj: Med & Sci, Amer
S/S: Appraisals
By appointment only

Seattle—493,846

ANTIQUES & ART ASSOCIATES
2113 3rd Ave, 98121. Tel 624-4378
SAN 167-224X
Owner, George Harder
Estab 1972
Types: 1st ed, hb, juv, illus bk, ltd ed,
op, o&r
Subj: Northwest U.S. hist

BEATTY BOOKSTORE
1925 3rd Ave, 98101.
Tel 206-624-2366
SAN 167-2282
Owner, Mrs H T Beatty
Estab 1963. Present Owner 1968.
100,000 Vols
Types: 1st ed, hb, illus bk, ltd ed, new
& used, remd
S/S: Appr libr collec

BIBELOTS & BOOKS
112 E Lynn St, 98102.
Tel 206-329-6676
SAN 157-5147
Owner, Shirley Schneider
Estab 1977. 7000 Vols. 450 sq ft
Types: Fac ed, fine bnd, 1st ed, hb, illus
bk, imp, juv, o&r, op, papbk, used
Subj: Mystery & detective
S/S: Prints, orig art, search serv

M TAYLOR BOWIE BOOKSELLER†
2613 5th Ave, 98121. Tel 206-682-5363
SAN 167-2576
Owner & Mgr, M Taylor Bowie
Estab 1968. Present Owner 1976.
10,000 Vols. 550 sq ft. Cat 1-2x ann
Types: 1st ed, hb, illus bk, o&r, op,
used
Subj: Discovery & explor, fine arts, mod
lit, travel
S/S: Appr libr collec

ROBERT L BROWN BOOKMONGER
1832 N 52nd St, 98103. Tel 206-632-8507
SAN 157-6119
Owner, Robert L Brown
Estab 1976. 3000 Vols. 100 sq ft. Cat
2x ann
Types: Fine bnd, 1st ed, hb, ltd ed, o&r,
op, papbk, used

Subj: Mod lit, mystery & detective, sci
fiction & fantasy
S/S: Biper

THE COMIC CHARACTER SHOP
114 Alaskan Way S, Box 99142, 98199.
Tel 206-622-8868, 283-0532
SAN 157-5163
Owner, Dennis' Books
Estab 1978. 2500 sq ft. Cat ann
Types: Illus bk, juv, o&r, op, used
Subj: Antq, art, comedy
S/S: Biper, orig art, prints, sh mus, toys,
Victorian prints, paper collectibles

COMSTOCK'S BINDERY & BOOK-
SHOP
7903 Ranier Ave S, 98118.
Tel 206-725-9531
SAN 167-2347
Owners, David G Comstock & Anita
Comstock
Estab 1968. 46,000 Vols. 2100 sq ft
Types: Op, used, remd, juv, spec inter-
est biper
Subj: Alaskana, art, auto, aviation,
food, military, mystery & detective,
natural hist, nautical, photog, rail-
roadiana, reference, rel, sci fiction &
fantasy, sci-tech, Pac Northwest
S/S: Custom bkbnd

CRUCIBLE BOOKSHOP
5525 University Way NE, 98105.
Tel 206-525-3737
SAN 167-2363
Owners, Russ Johanson & John Huston
Estab 1971. 30,000 Vols. 1500 sq ft
Types: Fine bnd, 1st ed, hb, incunab,
illus bk, o&r, op, used
Subj: Art
S/S: Appr libr collec, autg, maps, mss,
orig art

GASOLINE ALLEY ANTIQUES
6501 20th NE, 98115.
Tel 206-524-1606
SAN 167-2398
Owner & Mgr, Keith T Schneider
Estab 1974. Present Owner 1979. 700
sq ft. Cat 4x ann
Types: 1st ed, illus bk, juv, papbk, used
Subj: Comedy, films & filmmaking, tv,

big little bks, 1909 AYP expo, polit
Amer
S/S: Orig art, sh mus, collectibles,
vintage toys, Walt Disney memorabilia

DAVID ISHII BOOKSELLER
212 1st, S, 98107. Tel 206-622-4719
SAN 167-2487
Owner, David Ishii
Estab 1972. 5000 Vols. 800 sq ft. Cat
Types: Fine bnd, 1st ed, hb, illus bk,
juv, ltd ed, o&r, op, used
Subj: Asia-Am, fly fishing
S/S: Appr libr collec, search serv, sh
mus

JOURNEY
211 Pine St, 98101. Tel 206-623-7220
SAN 167-2509
Owner, Mgr & Buyer, William J Shopes
Estab 1977. 20,000 Vols. 1500 sq ft
Types: Fine bnd, 1st ed, hb, incunab,
illus bk, juv, ltd ed, o&r, op, papbk,
used, pvt presses
S/S: Rec

MAGUS' BOOKSTORE
1408 NE 42nd, 98105.
Tel 206-633-1800
SAN 127-449X
Owner, David L Bell
Estab 1974. Present Owner 1979.
60,000 Vols. 1750 sq ft
Types: Fac ed, fine bnd, 1st ed, hb, illus
bk, ltd ed, o&r, op, papbk, remd,
used
S/S: Search serv

W O MOYE — BOOKSELLER
2231 2nd St, 98103. Tel 206-625-1533
SAN 167-2568
Owner, Wayne O Moye
Present Owner 1978. 10,000 Vols. Cat
Types: O&r
Subj: Discovery & explor, natural hist,
travel, antq prints, paper conserva-
tion, framing

EDWARD D NUDELMAN CHIL-
DREN'S & ILLUSTRATED ANTI-
QUARIAN BOOKS
PO Box 20704, Broadway Sta, 98102.
Tel 206-782-2930

SAN 158-2585
Estab 1980. 1500 Vols. Cat 3x ann
Types: Col & el-hi text, illus bk, juv
Subj: Howard Pyle, Jessie Willcox Smith
S/S: Appr libr collec, orig art, search
serv

OLD SEATTLE PAPERWORKS
1501 Pike Pl, Suite 424, 98101.
Tel 206-623-2870
SAN 158-4685
Owners, Lael Hanawalt & John Hana-
walt
Estab 1976. 600 sq ft. Cat ann
Subj: Alaskana, films & filmmaking,
railroadiana, pacific NW, steamships
S/S: Appr libr collec, autg, orig art, per,
prints, sh mus

SIMON OTTENBERG, BOOK-
SELLERS†
PO Box 15509, 98115.
Tel 206-322-5398
SAN 167-2584
Owner & Buyer, Simon Ottenberg
Estab 1968. 3000 Vols. 100 sq ft. Cat
ann
Types: 1st ed, hb, o&r, op, papbk, used
Subj: Africa, primitive art

JOHN L POLLEY — BOOKSELLER
2231 2nd Ave, 98121. Tel 206-625-
1533
SAN 157-8189
Owners, John L Polley & Wayne Moye
Estab 1978. 4000 Vols. Cat 5x ann
Types: 1st ed, hb, o&r, op, papbk, used
Subj: Natural hist, sci fiction & fantasy,
travel
S/S: Appr libr collec, biper, search serv

THE SHOREY BOOKSTORE
110 Union St, 98101. Tel 206-624-0221
SAN 122-8587
Owner, John W Todd Jr
Estab 1890. Present Owner 1933.
1,250,000 Vols. Cat 6x ann
Types: New & used, op, papbk, rare
Subj: Alaskana, Arctic, natural hist,
Western Amer, marine voyages
S/S: Autg, mss, prints, search serv, sh
mus
Branches:
119 S Jackson, 98104.
Tel 206-622-8720
SAN 167-2665

GEORGE H TWENEY, BOOKS†
16660 Marine View Dr SW, 98166.
Tel 206-243-8243
SAN 167-2673
Owners, George H Tweney & Maxine R
Tweney
Estab 1969. 3000 Vols. 2500 sq ft
Types: 1st ed, ltd ed, hb, imp, new &
used, op, o&r
Subj: Alaskana, Am hist & lit, bibliog,
travel, Western Amer
S/S: Appr libr collec, autg, mss, orig
art, search serv, prints

Sequim — 3013

ROBERT H REDDING BOOKS
391 W Spruce, 98382.
Tel 206-683-8202
SAN 159-1304
Owner, Robert H Redding
Estab 1958
Types: 1st ed, hb, imp, juv, o&r, used
Subj: Alaskana, Arctic, Northwest

Spokane — 171,300

THE BOOK EXCHANGE
University City E, E 10812 Sprague
Ave, 99206. Tel 509-928-4073
SAN 156-8833
Mgrs, Richard Allen & Jolene Allen
Types: Fine bnd, 1st ed, hb, illus bk,
imp, juv, ltd ed, new & used, o&r,
op, papbk, remd
S/S: Biper, maps, search serv
Hq: Missoula, MT

HOUSE OF YESTERDAY ANTIQUES
E 11829 Trent, 99206. Tel 509-922-
4558
SAN 159-0499
Owners, Zoe S Paul & Christina
Jooreas
Estab 1975. 5000 Vols
Types: Fine bnd, 1st ed, hb, illus bk,
juv, ltd ed, op, used
Subj: Cooking & nutrit, pre-1950 chil-
dren's bk
S/S: Biper, prints, search serv, sh mus,
antiques, comics, ephemera, post
cards

McDUFFIE'S OLD BOOKS
618 Monroe, PO Box 596, 99210.

Tel 509-325-9022, 928-3623
SAN 167-2126
Owner, McDuffie Owen
Estab 1953. 15,000 Vols. Cat 6x ann
Types: Fine bnd, hb, illus bk, o&r, op, used
Subj: Amer, archit, art, med, photog, sci-tech, ephemera & prints since 1700, med & sci since 1800
S/S: Appr libr collec, mss, orig art, posters, family records

THE OLD BOOK HOME
PO Box 18777, 99208.
  Tel 509-838-6017
SAN 167-2894
Owner, Jerry D Simpson
Estab 1953. 8000 Vols
Types: 1st ed, fac ed, o&r, op, used, fine press
Subj: Bibliog, bks on bks, food, hist, soc sci, Western Amer, wines
S/S: Appr libr collec, maps, mss

Tacoma— 158,501

CULPEPPER & HANSON BOOK-
  SELLER
741 St Helens St, 98402.
  Tel 206-272-8827
SAN 167-2983
Owners, Lera Hanson & Jerry Culpepper
25,000 Vols. Cat ann
Types: 1st ed, hb, imp UK, op, papbk, o&r, remd, used
Subj: Am hist & lit, Civil War, Eng hist & lit, sci fiction, Washingtoniana
S/S: Appr libr collec, biper, search serv

FOX BOOK CO
1140 Broadway, 98402. Tel 206-627-2223
SAN 167-3009
Owner, Barbara Fox
Estab 1935. 250,000 Vols. Cat 3x ann
Types: 1st ed, fine bnd, o&r, op, remd
Subj: Fiction, nonfiction, NW Am
S/S: Appr libr collec

Vancouver— 42,834

GARY L ESTABROOK— BOOKS
PO Box 61453, 98666. Tel 206-699-5454

SAN 167-3106
Estab 1974. 4000 Vols. Cat 4x ann
Types: 1st ed, fine bnd, hb, ltd ed, o&r, op, used
Subj: Hunting & fishing

Vashon— 7377

PEGASUS BOOKS & PRESS
Glen Acres Rd, Rte 5, Box 220 (Mail add: PO Box 1350, 98070).
  Tel 206-567-5224 (by appt only)
SAN 130-4283
Mgr, J R LeFontaine
Estab 1980. 20,000 Vols. Cat 12x ann
Types: Fac ed, fine bnd, 1st ed, hb, incunab, illus bk, imp, juv, ltd ed, new, o&r, op, papbk, remd, used
Subj: Illus, sci fiction, mystery & detective, bks on bks, Western Amer
S/S: Appr libr collec, autg, mss, orig art, prints, search serv

WEST VIRGINIA

Bluefield— 16,060

APPALACHIAN BOOKSHOP
1316 Pen Mar Ave, 24701.
  Tel 304-327-5493
SAN 159-2904
Owner, Arnold Porterfield
Estab 1972. 20,000 Vols. 2000 sq ft
Types: Hb, o&r, op, papbk, remd, used
Subj: Civil War, genealogy, mountain culture
S/S: Biper, search serv

Charleston— 63,968

J B F YOAK, JR
5401 Virginia Ave SE, 25304.
  Tel 304-925-9793
SAN 167-3297
Owner, J B F Yoak, Jr
300 Vols. Cat 10x ann
Types: Op, o&r
Subj: Theol, methodistica

Morgantown— 27,605

RUTH E ROBINSON BOOKS
Rte 7, Box 162 A, 26505.
  Tel 304-594-3140

SAN 159-1940
Owner, Ruth E Robinson
Estab 1977
Types: 1st ed, hb
Subj: Appalachia, West Virginiana

Shepherdstown

EMILY DRISCOLL†
PO Box 834, 25443. Tel 304-876-2202
Types: Autg, mss, drawings

Walker

TRANS ALLEGHENY BOOKS INC
Box 148, Rte 1, 26180. Tel 304-489-
1858
SAN 157-8510
Owners, Joseph M Sakach & Lynne M
Sakach
Estab 1974. 17,000 Vols. Cat 6x ann
Types: O&r, op, used
Subj: Amer, fiction, Ohioana, Penn-
sylvaniana, West Virginiana, Ohio
River & Valley
S/S: Gr cds, search serv, sh mus

Washington—2595

INLAND RIVER BOOKS
PO Box 87, 26181. Tel 304-428-4948
SAN 167-3459
Owner, C R Williams
Estab 1974. 4000 Vols. Cat
Types: 1st ed, o&r
Subj: West Virginiana, Ohio River Val-
ley
S/S: Appr libr collec, autg, search serv

Wheeling—43,010

THE BISHOP OF BOOKS
117 15th St, 26003. Tel 304-232-8801
SAN 158-4510
Owner, Charles Bishop Jr
Estab 1975. 20,000 Vols. Cat 10-12x
ann
Types: Fine bnd, 1st ed, hb, illus bk, ltd
ed, o&r, op, papbk
Subj: Amer, Ohioana, Pennsylvaniana,
West Virginiana, alcoholism
S/S: Appr libr collec, autg, maps,
prints, sh mus

Branches:
BOOKSELLERS LTD
154 12th St
SAN 157-1125

Williamsburg—1409

STROUD THEOLOGICAL BOOK-
SELLERS
Star Rte, Box 94, Pembroke Rd, 24991.
Tel 304-645-7169
SAN 157-8529
Owners, John Nathan Stroud & Linda
Meyer Stroud
5000 Vols. Cat 6-8x ann
Types: O&r, op, used
Subj: Biblical studies, church hist, theol,
missions
S/S: Appr libr collec

WISCONSIN

Appleton—59,032

BOB'S BOOKSHOP
227 E College Ave, 54911.
Tel 414-731-3531
SAN 167-3599
Owner, Robert Rund
Estab 1977. 20,000 Vols
Types: Fine bnd, 1st ed, hb, illus bk,
juv, ltd ed, o&r, op, used
S/S: Appr libr collec, search serv

Big Bend—1345

ARABEST BOOKSHOP
W224 S 6800 Guthrie Rd, 53103.
Tel 414-662-3766
SAN 157-8537
Owner, W J Trapp
Estab 1972. 450 Vols. Cat
Types: Hb, o&r, op, used, imp Eng &
Ger
Subj: Dogs, horses
S/S: Prints, search serv

Elm Grove—6735

WEST'S BOOKING AGENCY
Box 406, 53122. Tel 414-786-7084
SAN 157-5228
Owner & Buyer, Richard P West

Estab 1977. 5000 Vols. Cat
Types: 1st ed, hb, illus bk, imp, juv, ltd
ed, new, op, o&r
Subj: Fiction, mystery & detective

Lake Delton—1158

WISE OWL BOOKSHOP
Burritt St, Box 377, 53940.
Tel 608-254-2092
SAN 158-6599
Owner, Percy H Seamans
Estab 1970. 10,000 Vols. 600 sq ft
Types: 1st ed, hb, illus bk, juv, o&r, op,
papbk, used
Subj: Wisconsinana

Madison—170,616

AVOL'S BOOKSTORE
405 W Gilman St, 53703.
Tel 608-255-4730
SAN 159-0758
Owners, Richard Avol & Carol Avol
Estab 1979. 35,000 Vols. 110 sq ft
Types: Op, used
Subj: Scholarly lit

BOOKS, THEN & NOW
2137 University Ave, 53705.
Tel 608-233-7030
SAN 167-4048
Owner, Carl A Boedecker
Estab 1975. Present Owner 1976.
14,000 Vols. 750 sq ft
Types: Fine bnd, 1st ed, hb, illus bk,
juv, ltd ed, new, o&r, op, papbk,
remd, used
Subj: Amer, art, biog, hist, Wiscon-
sinana
S/S: Biper, search serv

SPAIGHTWOOD GALLERIES
1150 Spaight St, 53703.
Tel 608-225-3043 (by appt)
SAN 170-2130
Owners, Andrew & Sonja Weiner
Estab 1980. 2000 vols. Cat ann
Types: Fac ed, incunab, illus bk, imp Fr,
imp Sp, ltd ed, new, o&r, op, used
Subj: Art
S/S: Appr libr collec, orig art, prints

STONY HILL ANTIQUES
2140 Regent St, 53705.
Tel 608-231-1247
SAN 157-5295
Owner & Mgr, David H Ward
Estab 1978. 5000 Vols. 500 sq ft
Types: Hb, used, fine bnd, 1st ed, o&r
Subj: Amer, Wisconsinana
S/S: Prints, antq

THIRD COAST BOOKS
306 Owens Rd, 53716.
Tel 608-221-0384
SAN 127-3604
Owner, Mark Trine; Mgr, Chester Nys-
trum
Cat 2x ann
Types: Fine bnd, 1st ed, hb, o&r, used

Marshfield—18,290

W BRUCE FYE ANTIQUARIAN
MEDICAL BOOKS
1607 N Wood Ave, 54449.
Tel 715-384-8128
SAN 157-5309
Owners, W Bruce Fye & Lois B Fye;
Mgr & Buyer, W Bruce Fye
Estab 1973. 7500 Vols. 1500 sq ft. Cat
4x ann
Types: Fac ed, fine bnd, 1st ed, hb, illus
bk, ltd ed, o&r, op, remd, used
Subj: Hist of med
S/S: Autg, prints

Menasha—14,728

BECKONING CAT BOOKSHOP
115 Main St (Mail add: PO Box 155,
54952). Tel 414-729-1255
SAN 167-4242
Owner, Daniel K Shenandoah
Estab 1978. 8000 Vols. 600 sq ft
Types: Op, papbk, used
Subj: Mystery & detective, sci fiction &
fantasy
S/S: Biper, search serv

Milwaukee—636,212

CASTALIA BOOKS
839B N Marshall, PO Box 92534,
53202. Tel 414-272-0249
SAN 158-8842

Owner, J R Spencer
Estab 1981. 10,000 Vols
Types: Fac ed, fine bnd, 1st ed, hb, illus
bk, juv, ltd ed, o&r, op, used
Subj: Fiction, metaphysics, mystery &
detective

CONSTANT READER BOOKSHOP
LTD
1627 E Irving Pl (Mail add: 1901 N
Prospect Ave 504, 53202).
Tel 414-291-0452
SAN 157-5317
Mgr, John Esser; Merch Mgr & Buyer,
David Hurlbutt
Estab 1979. 11,000 Vols. 4000 sq ft.
Cat
Types: 1st ed, fac ed, fine bnd, hb, juv,
ltd ed, o&r, op, used
Subj: Art, biog, fiction, literary criti-
cism, military, nautical, philos, rel
studies, Wisconsinana, show business
S/S: Search serv

DANCING BEAR ANTIQUARIAN
BOOKSHOP & PAPERBACK EX-
CHANGE
2864 N Oakland Ave, 53211.
Tel 414-962-2900
SAN 167-4323
Owners, C George Rzezotarski &
Darlene Wesenberg Rzezotarski
Estab 1973. 40,000 Vols. 750 sq ft
Types: 1st ed, hb, illus bk, juv, ltd ed,
o&r, papbk
Subj: Cooking & nutrit, local hist,
military

RAYMOND DWORCZYK, RARE
BOOKS
2114 W Rogers St, 53204.
Tel 414-383-2659
SAN 167-4331
Estab 1962. 100,000 Vols. Cat 4x ann
Types: Fac ed, fine bnd, 1st ed, hb,
incunab, juv, new & used, op, o&r,
remd
Subj: Amer, Africa, Asian studies, schol-
arly lit, warfare, early tools
S/S: Appr libr collec, autg, biper, mss,
search serv

JUST BOOKS
216 N Water St, 53202.
Tel 414-278-8478
SAN 167-4358

Owner, H W Just
Estab 1973. 10,000 Vols. 1500 sq ft
Types: Fine bnd, hb, o&r, op
S/S: Appr libr collec

RENAISSANCE BOOK SHOP INC
834 N Plankinton, 53203.
Tel 414-271-6850
SAN 167-4439
Pres, Mark Lindvall; Vpres, Robert
John
Estab 1960. Present Owner 1973.
250,000 Vols
Types: Fac ed, 1st ed, for lang, hb, juv,
ltd ed, new & used, o&r, op, papbk
Subj: Biog, cooking & nutrit, fiction,
local hist, med, military, nonfiction,
rel-c,j,p, psychol, sci fiction & fan-
tasy, soc sci, sports
S/S: Appr libr collec, biper, sh mus
Branches:
RENAISSANCE BOOK SHOP
INC — GENERAL MITCHELL
FIELD
5300 S Howell Ave, 53207.
Tel 414-747-4526
SAN 156-3882

SPECTRUM BOOKS & RECORDS
21110 W Wells, 53233.
Tel 414-344-5222
SAN 167-4471
Owner & Mgr, Robert Stein
Estab 1972. 10,000 Vols. 800 sq ft
Types: O&r, op, papbk, used
Subj: Fiction, hist, philos, sci fiction &
fantasy
S/S: Comics, old rec

YESTERDAY'S MEMORIES BOOK &
OLD RECORD SHOP
5406 W Center St, 53210.
Tel 414-444-6210
SAN 170-1177
Owner, Michael G Corenthal
Estab 1976. 10,000 Vols. 1000 sq ft
Types: O&r, op
Subj: Judaica, show bus memorabilia &
musical nostalgia
S/S: Appr libr collec, biper, search serv,
sh mus
Branches:
MUSICAL MEMORIES
833 E Kilbourn Ave, 53202
SAN 170-1185

Mount Horeb — 3251

G F GLAEVE ART & BOOKS
122 E Main St, 53572.
 Tel 608-437-8992
SAN 159-5989
Owner, G F Glaeve
5000 Vols. 1000 sq ft
Types: Op, remd, used, hb, o&r
Subj: Antq, art, midwest regional
S/S: Gr cds, maps, posters, reprod, orig
 art, prints
Open Tues-Sat 10-5

New Berlin — 30,529

MEANDAUR BOOKSELLER
17125 W Cleveland, 53151.
 Tel 414-786-6650
SAN 127-7944
Owners, B A Findley & J A Findley;
 Vpres & Mgr, Ann Findley
Estab 1979. Cat 2x ann
Types: 1st ed, juv, op
S/S: Gr cds, Annalee dolls, Scottish
 porcelain

Phillips — 1522

SPECTRUM
Box 246, Rt 2, 54555.
 Tel 715-339-3663
SAN 157-8545
Owner, Denis Jackson
Estab 1978. 1000 Vols. Cat 6x ann
Types: 1st ed, hb, illus bk, juv, ltd ed,
 o&r, op, papbk, used
S/S: Biper, orig art, prints

Racine — 85,725

THE OLD BOOK CORNER
312 6th St (Mail add: 1815 Park Ave,
 53403). Tel 414-632-5195
SAN 158-636X
Owner, Andrew McLean
Estab 1980. 5000 Vols. 144 sq ft

Types: 1st ed, fine bnd, hb, juv, o&r,
 op, used
S/S: Appr libr collec

Stevens Point — 22,970

THE ANTIQUARIAN SHOP
1329 Strongs Ave (Mail add: PO Box L,
 54481). Tel 715-341-3351
SAN 167-4676
Owner, Ellen Specht
Estab 1970. 65,000 Vols
Types: Hb, juv, op, o&r, used, illus bk
Subj: Antq, hist, hunting & fishing,
 geol, Mississippiana, railroadiana,
 mod authors, Indians, geog
S/S: Appr libr collec, gifts, gr cds, orig
 art, posters, search serv, antq, railroad artifacts

Wisconsin Dells — 2521

RAVENSWOOD BOOKS
51 S Bowman Rd, 53965.
 Tel 608-253-7861
SAN 158-5754
Owner, David Lake
Estab 1972. 3000 Vols
Types: 1st ed, hb, illus bk, juv, o&r, op
Subj: Amer
S/S: Per, prints, sh mus, advertising
 items

WYOMING

Dayton — 701

E & S SUMMERHOUSE BOOKS
PO Box 66, 82836. Tel 307-655-2367
SAN 158-0167
Owner & Mgr, Bonnie Switzer
Types: 1st ed, hb, illus bk, incunab, juv,
 op, o&r, used
Subj: Western Amer, Wyomingana
S/S: Search serv, sh mus

PUERTO RICO & VIRGIN ISLANDS

PUERTO RICO

Mayaguez—69,485

POE BOOKSHOP
Buzon Rurales #119, Car #341, El
  Mani, 00708
SAN 158-4316
Mgr, Al Luckton Jr
Estab 1950. 50,000 Vols. 4500 sq ft.
  Cat
Types: New & used, o&r
Subj: Geosci, earth science, gemstones

VIRGIN ISLANDS

Saint Croix

JELTRUPS'—BOOKS†
51 ABC Company St, Christiansted,
  00820. Tel 809-773-1018
Owner, Mrs Dorothy McKenzie Jeltrup
Subj: Virgin Islands bks, West Indian
  bks

CANADA

ALBERTA

Calgary—560,618

HERITAGE BOOKS
3438 6 St SW, T2S 2M4.
  Tel 403-243-8232
SAN 157-616X
Owner, Robert M Stamp
Estab 1978. 10,000 Vols. 1000 sq ft.
  Cat 12x ann
Subj: Arctic, Canadiana, Rocky Moun-
  tains, natives

TOM WILLIAMS BOOKS
Box 4126, Sta C, T2T 5M9.
  Tel 403-264-0184
SAN 167-5672
Owner, Tom Williams
Estab 1958. 20,000 Vols. Cat
Types: Hb, o&r, op
Subj: Can, Arctic, mountaineering
S/S: Appr libr collec, biper, orig art,
  prints, search serv

BRITISH COLUMBIA

Nanaimo—40,336

ANIAN BOOKS
135 Bastion St (Mail add: Box 88,
  Lantzville, V0R 2H0).
  Tel 604-754-1513
SAN 167-711X
Owners, Robert & Silvia Reeves
Cat ann

North Vancouver—63,471

ACADEMIC BOOKS
Box 86-385, 100 E 1st St Postal Sta,
  V7L 4K6. Tel 604-980-1810
SAN 167-7365
Mgr, B Rowell
Estab 1970. 40,000 Vols. Cat 6x ann
Types: O&r, used
Subj: Amer, Arctic, Australia, Can
S/S: Autg, maps, prints, search serv

STEPHEN C LUNSFORD BOOKS
PO Box 86773, V7L 4L3.
  Tel 604-988-1469
SAN 157-6216
Owner, Stephen C Lunsford
Present Owner 1977. 5000 Vols. Cat 4x
  ann
Types: O&r, op
Subj: Can, Western Amer, Indians of
  N Amer
S/S: Appr libr collec, maps

Tofino—612

VENKATESA BOOKS
Box 524, V0R 2Z0
SAN 158-8907
Owner, C J Hinke
Estab 1979. 1200 Vols. Cat 2x ann
Types: Fine bnd, 1st ed, hb, illus bk,
  juv, ltd ed, o&r, op, used
S/S: Appr libr collec, search serv

Vancouver—410,188

BISHOP-WILLIAMS
346 West Pender St, V6B 1T1.
 Tel 604-688-7434
SAN 170-7574
Owners, Lois Bishop & Joyce Williams
Cat
Subj: Can
S/S: Search serv, prints, maps, hand-
 coloring & restoration

BOND'S BOOKSHOP
523 Richards St (Mail add: Box 3166,
 V6B 3X6). Tel 604-688-5227
SAN 167-790X
Owner, E R Bowes
Estab 1932. 5000 Vols. 1000 sq ft. Cat
 4x ann
Types: Op
Subj: Alaskana, Arctic, Can, travel
S/S: Orig art

E R BOWES BOOKS
Box 3166, V6B 3X6. Tel 604-688-5227
SAN 158-8435
Types: O&r

COLOPHON BOOKS
407 W Cordova St, V6B 1E5.
 Tel 604-685-4138
SAN 157-6240
Owner, James McIntosh
Estab 1978. 25,000 Vols. 1600 sq ft.
 Cat 3x ann
Types: Hb, op
Subj: Can art
S/S: Appr libr collec

WILLIAM HOFFER BOOKSELLER
Ste 104-570 Granville St, V6C 1W6.
 Tel 604-683-3022
SAN 167-8132
Owner, William Hoffer; Assoc, Chris-
 tina Burridge
Estab 1969. 25,000 Vols. Cat 6x ann
Types: Op
Subj: Anthrop, humanities, Can lit &
 hist

TERRY RUTHERFORD BOOK-
 SELLER
432 Homer St, V6B 2V5.
 Tel 604-682-8227
SAN 158-202X
Owner, Terry Rutherford

Estab 1979. 5000 Vols. 700 sq ft. Cat
 4x ann
Types: 1st ed, hb, o&r, op, used
Subj: Mystery & detective, sci fiction &
 fantasy, Eng & Am lit

WINDHOVER BOOKS
8491 Cartier St, V6P 4T7.
 Tel 604-266-2929
SAN 159-2173
Owner, R Klarenbach
Estab 1978. Cat 2x ann
Types: Fine bnd, ltd ed, o&r
Subj: Mod lit
S/S: Search serv

Victoria—62,551

JOHNSON & SMALL BOOK-
 SELLERS
Law Chambers, 45 Bastion Sq, V8W
 1J1. Tel 604-382-1144, 383-4366
SAN 167-8701
10,000 Vols. Cat 8x ann
Types: Fine bnd, 1st ed, hb, illus bk, ltd
 ed, o&r
Subj: Archit, Can, discovery & explor,
 hist, sci-tech, travel, Ferrari, T E
 Lawrence, women's suffrage
S/S: Appr libr collec, autg, maps, mss,
 orig art, prints, Canadian art

MANITOBA

Altona—2480

PANDORA'S BOOKS LTD
Box 1298, R0G 0B0. Tel 204-324-8548
SAN 167-8949
Owner, Grant Thiessen
Estab 1973. 40,000 Vols. Cat 12x ann
Types: 1st ed, hb, imp, ltd ed, new &
 used, o&r, op, papbk
Subj: Can, hist, mystery & detective, sci
 fiction & fantasy
S/S: Biper, search serv

Steinbach—5979

PIONEER BOOKS
101 Maplewood St, R0A 2A0.
 Tel 204-326-2452
SAN 170-7590
Owner, Frances E Coe

Subj: Can, hist, Western Amer, mod lit

Winnipeg— 610,000

ANTIQUARIAN BOOKS
31 D'Arcy Dr, R3T 2K4.
  Tel 204-269-6930
SAN 157-6291
Owner, A Taylor
Estab 1972. 40,000 Vols. 1500 sq ft.
  Cat
Types: 1st ed, hb, ltd ed, o&r, op, used
Subj: Can, polar exploration
S/S: Appr libr collec, biper, orig art,
  prints

BURTON LYSECKI BOOKS
527 Osborne St, R3L 2B2.
  Tel 204-284-4546
SAN 167-9368
Owner, Burton J Lysecki
Estab 1971. 30,000 Vols. 900 sq ft
Types: 1st ed, fine bnd, hb, illus bk,
  o&r, op, papbk, used
Subj: Biog, Can
S/S: Biper, search serv

NEW BRUNSWICK

Fredericton— 45,248

ARCTICIAN BOOKS
538 Queen St (Mail add: PO Box 691,
  E3B 5B4). Tel 506-457-0544
SAN 167-9589
Owner, Harry E Bagley
Estab 1978. 3000 Vols. 400 sq ft. Cat
  12x ann
Types: 1st ed, o&r, op, remd, used
Subj: Arctic, Can
S/S: Appr libr collec, maps, prints, sh
  mus

Saint Andrews— 1711

KATHLEEN & MICHAEL LAZARE
59 Carleton St, E0G 2X0.
  Tel 506-529-3834
SAN 156-8566
Owners & Mgrs, Kathleen Lazare &
  Michael Lazare
15,000 Vols
Types: 1st ed, hb, illus bk, juv, o&r, op

S/S: Maps, orig art, posters, search
  serv, spec order
See Also: Sherman, CT

Sussex— 3938

THE CALEDONIAN
22 Court St (Mail add: PO Box 793,
  E0E 1P0)
SAN 157-633X
Owners, Rodney C Mackay & Anne T
  Mackay; Mgr, Anne T Mackay
Estab 1973. Present Owner 1980.
  10,000 Vols. 1000 sq ft. Cat 25x ann
Types: Hb, juv, new & used, o&r, op,
  papbk, remd, small presses
Subj: Can

NOVA SCOTIA

Halifax— 117,882

NAUTICA BOOKSELLERS
1579 Dresden Row, B3J 2K4.
  Tel 902-429-2741
SAN 168-0153
Owner, John Holland
Estab 1975. 10,000 Vols. Cat 3x ann
Types: Op, 1st ed, fac ed, fine bnd, hb,
  incunab, ltd ed
Subj: Exclusively nautical
S/S: Appr libr collec, search serv

SCHOONER BOOKS STORE
5378 Inglis St, B3H 1J5. Tel 902-423-
  8419
SAN 168-0404
Owners, John D Townsend & Mary Lee
  MacDonald
Estab 1975. Present Owner 1978.
  30,000 Vols. 1200 sq ft. Cat 2x ann
Types: Hb, op, o&r, papbk, used
Subj: Can, Canadian Maritime Prov
S/S: Appr libr collec, mss, search serv

Windsor— 3702

L S LOOMER ANTIQUARIAN
  BOOKS
17 Water St (Mail add: PO Box 878,
  B0N 2T0)
SAN 168-0544
Owner, L S Loomer
Estab 1966. Present Owner 1983.

10,000 Vols. Cat
Types: Fine bnd, 1st ed, hb, illus bk, ltd
ed, o&r, op, used
S/S: Appr libr collec, maps, mss, prints,
sh mus

Wolfville — 3073

THE ODD BOOK
8 Front St (Mail add: Box 863, B0P
1X0). Tel 902-542-9491
SAN 157-6348
Owners, Dick Gifford & Jim Tillotson
Estab 1977. 10,000 Vols. 500 sq ft. Cat
Types: O&r, papbk, used
Subj: Maritime provinces hist, N Amer
geog & anthrop

THOTH'S BOOKSHOPS LTD
12 Gaspereau Ave (Mail add: Box 749,
B0P 1X0). Tel 902-542-2640
SAN 157-4413
Owner & Mgr, J B Snelson
Estab 1979. 10,000 Vols. Cat
Types: 1st ed, hb, juv, op, o&r, papbk,
univ presses, used
Subj: Can, metaphys & occult, philos,
sci fiction & fantasy, theol
S/S: Appr libr collec

ONTARIO

Combermere — 214

MADONNA HOUSE BOOKSHOP
K0J 1L0. Tel 613-756-2252
SAN 168-1052
Mgr, Karen Van DeLoop
Estab 1975. 35,000 Vols. Cat 3-4x ann
Types: 1st ed, hb, op, used
Subj: Can, rel-c

Fort Erie — 23,808

WILLIAM MATTHEWS BOOK-
SELLER
46 Gilmore Rd, L2A 2M1.
Tel 416-821-7859
SAN 170-2122
Owners, William Matthews & Ann Hall
Estab 1976. 5000 Vols. 1000 sq ft. Cat
4x ann
Types: 1st ed, hb, ltd ed, o&r, op,
papbk

Subj: Sci fiction & fantasy
S/S: Appr libr collec, mss, orig art,
search serv

Guelph — 71,408

NOSTALGIA BOOKS
Box 1442, N1H 6N9
SAN 168-1435
Owner, William Roberts; Mgr, Peter
Roberts
Estab 1976. Present Owner 1978. 4000
Vols. Cat 2x ann
Types: 1st ed, hb, o&r, op, used
Subj: Can, sci fiction & fantasy
S/S: Search serv
Mail order only

Hamilton — 306,538

JOHN RUSH BOOKS
396 Herkimer St, L8P 2J3.
Tel 416-522-7094
SAN 158-6432
Owner, John Rush
Cat 6x ann
Types: 1st ed, hb, o&r, op, used
Subj: Can

MARVEN SOMER BOOKSELLER
145 James Street N, L8H 2K9
SAN 170-7566
Owner, Marven Somer
Cat 2x ann
Subj: Can, art, military

Hensall — 1005

JOHN W SMITH BOOKS
Rural Rte 1, N0M 1X0.
Tel 519-262-5122
SAN 168-1605
Owner, J W Smith
Estab 1966. 15,000 Vols. 1000 sq ft.
Cat
Types: Hb, o&r, op, used
Subj: Agr, Can, military, Mennonitica

Kingston — 61,088

KUSKA HOUSE
105 Wellington St (Mail add: PO Box
1507, K7L 5C7). Tel 613-546-7666
SAN 168-1796

Owner, Vratislav Kuska; Mgr, John Gibson; Merch Mgr & Buyer, Vratislav Kuska
Estab 1972. Present Owner 1973. 6000 Vols. 300 sq ft. Cat
Types: 1st ed, hb, ltd ed, op, o&r, imp EEur & Russ
Subj: Can, Eur studies, Czechoslovakia, Russ
S/S: Appr libr collec, search serv, sh mus

Kitchener—136,091

C & E BOOKS
Box 2744 Station B, N2H 6N3
SAN 159-0669
Owners, Alain Charest & Lorne Ellaschuk
Estab 1980. Cat 6x ann
Types: Hb, o&r, op, used
Subj: Can

Locust Hill—89

OLD FAVORITES BOOKSHOP
RR 1, Hwy 7, Green River, L0H 1J0.
Tel 416-294-4298
SAN 156-5788
Owner, L Morris; Gen Mgr, Joy Saunder
Estab 1979. 10,000 Vols
Types: Hb
S/S: Search serv, antq furniture
Hq: Old Favorites Bookshop Ltd, Toronto

London—256,789

ATTIC BOOKS
388 Clarence St, N6A 3M7.
Tel 519-432-6636
SAN 168-1974
Owner, Marvin Post
Estab 1976. 40,000 Vols. 3000 sq ft
Types: Fac ed, fine bnd, 1st ed, hb, illus bk, juv, ltd ed, o&r, op, papbk, used
Subj: Can, mystery & detective
S/S: Appr libr collec, search serv

Manotick—1410

SPORTSMAN'S CABINET
Box 15, K0A 2N0. Tel 613-692-3618
SAN 157-8553

Owners, W A McClure & K H McClure
Estab 1973. 5000 Vols. 1000 sq ft. Cat 4x ann
Types: 1st ed, hb, o&r, op, used, illus bk, ltd ed, new, remd
Subj: Hunting & fishing, dogs
S/S: Prints, search serv, appr libr collec

Oshawa—115,197

MORGAN SELF LTD
84 Simcoe St S, L1H 4G6. Tel 416-723-7621
SAN 168-2490
Owners, Morgan G Self & Marguerite Self
Estab 1970. 175,000 Vols. 1700 sq ft. Cat
Types: Hb, op, papbk, remd, used
S/S: Biper, search serv

Ottawa—303,070

MRS A L ASHTON
49 Birch Ave, K1K 3G5. Tel 613-749-1741
SAN 159-2394
10,000 Vols
Types: Fine bnd, 1st ed, hb, illus bk, juv, ltd ed, o&r, op
Subj: Can, mod lit, nonfiction
S/S: Search serv

AVENUE BOOKSHOP
101 4th Ave, K1S 2L1. Tel 613-233-0966
SAN 157-0714
Owner, R R Knott
Estab 1980. 8000 Vols. 700 sq ft. Cat 2x ann
Types: 1st ed, hb, o&r, op, papbk, used
Subj: Class studies, literary criticism, medieval studies
S/S: Appr libr collec, biper

BOOK BAZAAR
755 Bank St, K1S 3V3.
Tel 613-233-4380
SAN 168-2563
Owner, Mrs Beryl McLeod
Estab 1974. 10,000 Vols
Types: Hb, juv, op, o&r, papbk, used
Subj: Can, music
S/S: Search serv

DYMENT BOOKS—SCHOLARS'
BOOKSTORE
1126 Bank St, K1S 3X6.
Tel 613-235-0565
SAN 168-2679
Owners, J Paul Dyment & Margaret S
Dyment
Estab 1967. 25,000 Vols. Cat 8x ann
Types: Fine bnd, 1st ed, hb, juv, new &
used, op, o&r, papbk
Subj: Academic
S/S: Search serv
Branches:
54½ George St, K1S 3X6.
Tel 613-233-5951
SAN 156-7756

J PATRICK McGAHERN—BOOKS
INC
783 Bank St, K1S 3V5.
Tel 613-233-2215
SAN 168-2865
Estab 1969. 25,000 Vols. 1200 sq ft.
Cat 6-8x ann
Types: O&r, op, used
Subj: Can, Irish hist & lit, Arctica (voyages & travel)
S/S: Appr libr collec, autg, maps, prints

Pembroke— 14,249

TERRENCE KOHLS BOKS
193 Victoria, K8A, 4K2.
Tel 613-735-0001
SAN 170-1150
Owner, Terrence Kohls; Mgr, Debra
Lloyd
5000 Vols
Types: 1st ed, hb, illus bk, o&r, op,
papbk
S/S: Appr libr collec, search serv

Peterborough— 59,981

THE BOOKSTORE
228 Charlotte St, K9J 2T8.
Tel 705-748-1230
SAN 168-3144
Owner, Sandy Stewart
Estab 1967. 10,000 Vols. 500 sq ft. Cat
Types: Fine bnd, 1st ed, hb, o&r, op,
papbk, used
Subj: Can, mod soc criticism (from
1960)
S/S: Appr libr collec, search serv

Rockton

POMONA BOOK EXCHANGE
Hwy 52, L0R 1X0. Tel 519-621-8897
SAN 168-3268
Owners, H Fred Janson & Walda Janson
Estab 1972. Present Owner 1977. 2000
Vols. Cat 3x ann
Types: Fac ed, hb, illus bk, ltd ed, new,
op, o&r, remd, used
Subj: Agr, bot, food, hort
S/S: Appr libr collec, biper, prints,
search serv

Saint Catharines— 123,956

HEADLEY HANNELORE OLD &
FINE BOOKS
71 Queen St, L2R 5G9.
Tel 416-684-6145
SAN 168-3314
Owner, Hannelore Headley
Estab 1972. 8500 Vols
Types: 1st ed, hb, illus bk, o&r, op,
used
Subj: Art, Can, local hist, military
S/S: Search serv

Toronto— 642,449

ABOUT BOOKS
280 Queen St W, M5V 2A1.
Tel 416-593-0792
SAN 168-3934
Owner, Laurence A Wallrich
Estab 1957. 30,000 Vols. 1500 sq ft.
Cat 3x ann
Types: 1st ed, hb, imp, ltd ed, op, o&r,
papbk, remd, used
S/S: Appr libr collec, biper, mss
Branches:
355 Queen Street West.
Tel 416-591-9151
SAN 170-7655

BEN ABRAHAM BOOKS
69 Kennedy Park Rd, M6P 3H2.
Tel 416-762-3721
SAN 170-1533
Owner, Dena Bain Taylor; Mgr, Charles
Taylor
Estab 1981. 3000 Vols. 1000 sq ft. Cat
4x ann
Types: Fac ed, fine bnd, 1st ed, hb,

incunab, illus bk, imp, ltd ed, new,
o&r, op, papbk, remd, used
Subj: Metaphys & occult, astrol, rel
studies, alchemy, classical paganism
& antiquities, spiritualism, witchcraft, demonology, kabbalah & William Blake
S/S: Biper, mss, orig art, prints, mss
Open Sun-Thurs 9am-11pm

ACADIA BOOKSTORE
Queen St E, M5A 1S3. Tel 416-364-
7638
SAN 168-3950
Owner, Asher Joram; Mgr, Rochelle
Joram
Estab 1931. 25,000 Vols. 2000 sq ft.
Cat
Subj: Arctic, art, Can, travel

THE ALPHABET BOOKSHOP
656 Spadina Ave, M5S 2H9. Tel 416-
924-4926
SAN 168-3977
Owners, Richard Shuh & Linda Wool-
ley
Estab 1977. 10,000 Vols. 750 sq ft. Cat
Types: 1st ed, hb, op, papbk, used
Subj: Can, mod, classic & scholarly lit

HUGH ANSON-CARTWRIGHT
229 College St, M5T 1R4. Tel 416-979-
2441
SAN 168-3993
Owner, Hugh Anson-Cartwright
Estab 1966. 20,000 Vols. Cat
Types: Used
Subj: Can, hist
S/S: Publ

ATTICUS BOOKS
698 Spadina Ave, M5S 2J2. Tel 416-
922-6045
SAN 168-5449
25,000 Vols. Cat
Subj: Anthrop, linguistics, philos, sci-
tech, class studies, art, classics, criticism, hist of sciences
Branches:
589 Markham St. Tel 416-533-7540
SAN 157-1362

GLYNIS BARNES
43 Canton, M3M 1N1. Tel 416-241-
6060

SAN 158-0175
Types: Juv, illus bk
Subj: Folklore

BATTA BOOKSTORE
710 The Queensway, M8Y 1L3. Tel
416-259-2618
SAN 168-4051
Owners, Mr & Mrs Bela Batta
Estab 1965. 50,000 Vols. 2500 sq ft
Types: 1st ed, hb, op, papbk, remd,
used
Subj: Biog, Can, fiction, hist, mod lit,
mystery & detective, travel

CANADIANA HOUSE
121 Admiral Rd (Mail add: PO Box
306, Postal Sta F, M4Y 2L7). Tel 416-
924-6577
SAN 168-4264
Owner, David B Noxon
Estab 1961. 25,000 Vols. Cat 6-8x ann
Types: Fine bnd, 1st ed, hb, juv, ltd ed,
o&r, op, remd, used
Subj: Amer, Can

GREAT NORTHWEST BOOK CO
338 Jarvis St, M4Y 2G6. Tel 416-964-
2089
SAN 168-4558
Owners, D V Baker & T Antonov
Estab 1977. Present Owner 1979.
20,000 Vols. 500 sq ft. Cat
Types: 1st ed, hb, illus bk, new & used,
op
Subj: Arctic, art, biog, Can, drama,
ethnic studies, local hist, poetry,
transp
S/S: Appr libr collec, search serv

DORA HOOD'S BOOK ROOM LTD
34 Ross St, M5T 1Z9. Tel 416-979-
2129
SAN 168-4612
Pres, Mrs Tommy Tweed; Mgr,
Lawrence R Cooper
Estab 1928. Present Owner 1962.
75,000 Vols. 9500 sq ft. Cat 12x ann
Types: 1st ed, fac ed, fine bnd, papbk,
illus bk, juv, ltd ed, new, op, o&r,
used
Subj: Can
S/S: Appr libr collec, biper, maps, mss,
search serv, sh mus, spec order

HORTULUS
101 Scollard St, M5R 1G4. Tel 416-
960-1775
SAN 158-2364
Owners, Bruce C Marshall & Linda W
Marshall
Estab 1978. 3500 Vols. 600 sq ft. Cat
2x ann
Types: Fac ed, fine bnd, 1st ed, hb,
incunab, illus bk, imp, ltd ed, new &
used, o&r, op, remd
Subj: Archit, gardening, hort, landscape
archit
S/S: Orig art, prints, search serv

D & E LAKE LTD OLD & RARE
BOOKS
106 Berkeley St, Suite 302, M5A 2W7.
Tel 416-863-9930
SAN 157-647X
Owners, Donald Lake & Elaine Lake
Estab 1977. 6000 Vols. 950 sq ft. Cat
12x ann
Types: Fine bnd, 1st ed, o&r
Subj: Amer, Can, Eur studies, law,
philos, soc sci, travel, political econ
S/S: Appr libr collec

LONGHOUSE BOOKSHOP LTD
630 Yonge St, M4Y 1Z8. Tel 416-921-
9995, 921-0389
SAN 168-4825
Owners, Beth Appeldoorn & Susan
Sandler
Estab 1972. 20,000 Titles. 900 sq ft.
Cat 2x ann
Types: 1st ed, juv, ltd ed, o&r
Subj: Can
S/S: Search serv

THE MAP ROOM, EXPLORATION
HOUSE
18 Birch Ave, M4V 1C8. Tel 416-922-
5153
SAN 170-1789
Owner, Neil H Sneyd; Mgr, Liana Sneyd
Estab 1974
Types: Hb, incunab, illus bk, o&r,
remd, used
Subj: Cartography, natural hist, discov-
ery & explor, hist
S/S: Maps, mss, orig art, prints

DAVID MASON BOOKS
638 Church St, M4Y 2G3. Tel 416-922-
1712
SAN 168-4841
Owner, David Mason; Mgr, Anne Hall
Estab 1968. 35,000 Vols. Cat 4x ann
Types: Fine bnd, 1st ed, hb, illus bk,
incunab, juv, ltd ed, op, used
Subj: 19th century Am & English lit
S/S: Appr libr collec, maps, mss, orig
art, prints

MOSTLY MYSTERIES BOOKS
398 Saint Clair Ave E, M4T 1P5. Tel
416-485-4373
SAN 159-169X
Owner, Ann Skene-Melvin
Estab 1979. 11,000 Vols. 3000 sq ft.
Cat
Types: For lang, hb, imp, juv, op,
papbk, used
Subj: Cooking & nutrit, hort, sci fiction
& fantasy, mystery & detective
S/S: Appr libr collec, games, gr cds,
posters, prints, reprod, search sev

WILLIAM NELSON BOOKS
686 Richmond St W, M6J 1C3. Tel 416-
361-0220
SAN 168-4965
Owner, Nelson Ball
Estab 1972. 40,000 Vols. 2500 sq ft.
Cat 12x ann
Types: 1st ed
Subj: Can
S/S: Search serv

NORTH TORONTO COINS LTD
3234 Yonge St, M4N 2L4. Tel 416-489-
5949
SAN 168-4981
Owner & Mgr, Larry Becker
Estab 1965. 6000 Vols. 800 sq ft
Types: 1st ed, hb, incunab, juv, ltd ed,
o&r, op, papbk, used, military hist
Subj: Adv, Can, military, old magazines,
postcards
S/S: Appr libr collec, autg, maps, mss,
sh mus, collectors centre

OLD FAVORITES BOOKSHOP LTD
250 Adelaide St W, M5H 1X8. Tel 416-
977-2944
SAN 168-5015

Pres, Ken Saunders; Gen Mgr, Laura J
Rust
Estab 1954. 300,000 Vols. 10,000 sq ft.
Cat 2x ann
Types: Fine bnd, 1st ed, hb, incunab,
illus bk, juv, ltd ed, o&r, op, papbk,
used
Subj: Auto, aviation, Can, horses
S/S: Appr libr collec, biper, search serv,
book auctions & book rentals
See Also: Old Favorites Bookshop,
Locust Hill

PASSAGES
109 Niagara St, Suite 211, M5V 1C3.
Tel 416-690-1899
SAN 170-1762
Owner, Brian Purdy
Estab 1980. 10,000 Vols. 350 sq ft. Cat
4x ann
Types: 1st ed, hb, ltd ed, o&r, op,
papbk, remd, used
Subj: Mystery & detective, sci fiction &
fantasy
S/S: Biper, search serv, sh mus

JOSEPH PATRICK BOOKS
1600 Bloor St W (Mail add: Box 148,
Postal Sta M, M6P 1A7). Tel 416-
531-1891
SAN 168-5112
Owner, Joseph G P Sherlock
Estab 1975. 15,000 Vols. 1500 sq ft.
Cat 6x ann
Types: Illus bk, op, o&r
Subj: Arctic, Can, discovery & explor,
Can art & artists, fur trade, Yukon

ST NICHOLAS BOOKS
PO Box 863 Sta F, M4Y 2N7. Tel 416-
922-9640
SAN 168-5201
Owner, Yvonne Knight
Estab 1973. 2500 Vols. Cat 2-3x ann
Types: Juv, o&r
Subj: Bibliog, decorative arts
S/S: Ephemera

STEVEN TEMPLE
308 Queen St W, M5T 2W1. Tel 416-
593-0582
SAN 168-5295
Owner, Steven Temple
Estab 1974. 12,000 Vols. Cat 2x ann
Types: 1st ed, hb, o&r, op, used

Subj: Am, British & Can lit, world lit in
translation, sci
S/S: Appr libr collec

VILLAGE BOOKSTORE
239 Queen St W, M5V 1Z4. Tel 416-
598-4097
SAN 168-5414
Owner, Martin Ahvenus
Estab 1961. 20,000 Vols. 3000 sq ft
Types: Fine bnd, 1st ed, illus bk, ltd ed,
op, o&r, papbk, remd, used
Subj: Antq, bks on bks, Canadian art
S/S: Biper, mss

ARTHUR WHARTON BOOKS
308 Queen St W, PO Box 263, Stn B,
M5T 2W1. Tel 416-593-0582
SAN 170-2351
Owner, A Wharton
20,000 Vols. 1800 sq ft. Cat 5x ann
Types: 1st ed, o&r, op
Subj: Am hist & lit, sci fiction & fan-
tasy, soc sci, hist of science & Cana-
dian lit
S/S: Appr libr collec, biper, orig art

GAIL WILSON— BOOKSELLER
198 Queen St W, M5V 1Z2. Tel 416-
598-2024
SAN 168-5473
Owner, Gail Wilson; Assts, Cynthia
Holz & Channa Verbian
Estab 1978. 15,000 Vols. 1000 sq ft
Types: Hb, op, o&r, papbk, used, used
mags
Subj: Agr, bks on bks, fashion, sci-tech,
domestic econ, social hist

Weston

MICHAEL DAVEY BOOKSELLER
Box 541, M2N 3N1. Tel 416-241-8388
SAN 157-6518
Owner, Michael Davey
Estab 1966. 4000 Vols. Cat 3-4x ann
Types: Fac ed, fine bnd, 1st ed, illus bk,
incunab, imp, ltd ed, o&r, op, used
Subj: Bibliog, Can
S/S: Biper, mss, search serv

PETER L JACKSON— MILITARY
BOOKS & PRINTS
23 Castle Green Crescent, M9R 1N5.
Tel 416-249-4796

SAN 168-5643
Owner, Peter L Jackson
Estab 1970. 1500 Vols. Cat 2x ann
Types: Hb, illus bk, o&r, op, used, imp
British & European
Subj: Military
S/S: Prints

Willowdale

KEN MITCHELL BOOKS
710 Conacher Dr, M2M 3N6. Tel 416-
222-5808
SAN 159-2092
Owner, Ken Mitchell
Present Owner 1964. Cat 2x ann
Subj: Big Little Books 1900-1950's
S/S: Comics & movie mags 1930-1967

QUEBEC

Drummondville — 28,300

LIBRAIRIE O VIEUX BOUQUINS
2125 Gagnon, C P 8, J2B 6V6.
Tel 819-477-2993
SAN 157-6542
Owners, Therese-Isabel Thivierge &
Serge-Patrick Duhamel
Estab 1975. 35,000 Vols. 700 sq ft. Cat
12x ann
Types: O&r, used
Subj: Can, Amer, Eur studies, socialism,
hockey
S/S: Biper, search serv

Montreal — 1,069,700

BIBLIOGRAPHY OF THE DOG
4170 Decarie Blvd, H4A 3K2. Tel 514-
488-6279
SAN 157-6550
Owner, Nigel Aubrey-Jones
Estab 1972. 3500 Vols. Cat 2-3x ann
Types: 1st ed, illus bk, juv, o&r, op
Subj: Dogs
S/S: Biper, prints

MICHEL BRISEBOIS LIBRAIRIE
Dorchester W, H3B 3J7. Tel 514-875-
5210
SAN 158-0183
Owner, Michel Brisebois
Estab 1979. 2000 Vols

Types: Fine bnd, 1st ed, hb, illus bk, ltd
ed, o&r
S/S: Appr libr collec, autg, biper, mss,
orig art, prints

I EHRLICH
Box 994, Sta B, H3B 3K5. Tel 514-842-
7000
SAN 168-6879
Estab 1950. Cat 2x ann
Types: O&r
Subj: Can, travel
S/S: Appr libr collec, maps, mss, prints

HELEN R KAHN ANTIQUARIAN
BOOKS
PO Box 323, Victoria Sta, H3Z 2V8.
Tel 514-844-5344
SAN 157-0099
Owner, Helen R Kahn
Cat 3x ann
Types: O&r
Subj: Adv, Amer, Arctic, Can, travel
S/S: Appr libr collec, maps

LIBRAIRIE D'ANTAN
1995 Baile, H2Y 2V8. Tel 514-989-
5124
SAN 168-7166
Owner, Charles Phillips
Estab 1974. Cat
Types: 1st ed, hb, ltd ed, o&r, op
Subj: Can, genealogy, hist
S/S: Appr libr collec, autg, maps, mss,
search serv

LIBRAIRIE ENCYCLOPEDIQUE
1272 est rue Sainte-Catherine, H2L
2H2. Tel 514-521-2398
SAN 168-728X
Owner, Denis Houle
Estab 1970. 25,000 Vols. 800 sq ft. Cat
2x ann
Types: Op, o&r
Subj: Can, Fr hist & lit

LIBRAIRIE FAUBOURG — QUEBEC,
CANADIANA
1377 Ste Catherine est, H2L 2H7. Tel
514-526-4115
SAN 156-9864
Owners, Francois Auger & Dominique
Auger
Estab 1978. 10,000 Vols. 750 sq ft. Cat
4x ann

Types: Fac ed, fine bnd, 1st ed, illus bk, ltd ed, o&r, used
Subj: Art, Can, hist, local hist, Quebec province
S/S: Search serv

LIBRAIRIE QUEBECOISE
1417 Amherst, H2L 3L2. Tel 514-523-3305
SAN 168-7476
Owner, Michel Leduc; Mgr, Claudette Patry Leduc
Estab 1969. 40,000 Vols. Cat ann
Types: Fine bnd, 1st ed, hb, illus bk, ltd ed, o&r, used
Subj: Amer, Can, Eur studies
S/S: Appr libr collec, biper, prints

WESTMOUNT PARNASSUS
320 Victoria Ave, Westmount, H3Z 2M8. Tel 514-935-9581, 484-4401
SAN 159-0979
Owners, Wilfrid M De Freitas, et al
Estab 1980. 2000 Vols. 150 sq ft
Types: 1st ed, hb, illus bk, o&r, used
Subj: Can, performing arts

Pointe-Claire—25,400

WILLIAM P WOLFE INC RARE BOOKS
PO Box 1190, Pointe Claire, H9S 5K7. Tel 514-697-1630
SAN 168-7859
Owners, Patricia Brown & Michael Brown
Estab 1958. 20,000 Vols. 2000 sq ft. Cat 2x ann
Subj: Amer, Arctic, art, bks on bks, Can, travel
S/S: Appr libr collec, autg, mss, orig art, prints

Quebec—177,082

JEAN GAGNON
PO Box 653 HV, G1R 1S2. Tel 418-523-6760
SAN 168-7921
Estab 1955. Cat 5x ann

Types: Op, o&r
Subj: Can

Saint Bruno—2299

PHILIP LOZINSKI, CANADIAN BRANCH REG'D
1175 Wolfe St, J3V 3K7. Tel 514-653-8890
SAN 168-812X
Owner, Helena Zamoyski
Estab 1964. 17,000 Vols. 1800 sq ft. Cat
Types: Op, o&r, used
Subj: Can, for lang, Slavic lang
S/S: Search serv, reprints
Hq: Westport, MA

SASKATCHEWAN

Regina—149,593

VICTORIA BOOK EXCHANGE
922 Victoria, S4N 0R7. Tel 306-352-3067
SAN 158-4553
Owner, M Canter
Types: Hb, illus bk, op, papbk, remd, used
S/S: Appr libr collec, orig art, prints

Saskatoon—133,750

NORTHLAND BOOKS
813 Broadway Ave, S7N 1B5. Tel 306-242-9466
SAN 168-9010
Owners, Garry Shoquist & Janice Shoquist
Estab 1968. 30,000 Vols. 2000 sq ft. Cat 1-2x ann
Types: 1st ed, hb, illus bk, juv, ltd ed, o&r, op, used
Subj: Biog, Can fiction, local hist, reference, soc sci, natural sci, Western Canada, Northern Canada
S/S: Appr libr collec, biper, mss, search serv

INDEX OF SPECIALTIES

Africa

Town & Gown Book Co, Dutch Flat, CA
Graeme Vanderstoel, El Cerrito, CA
Abbey Bookshop, Los Angeles, CA
F & I Books, Santa Monica, CA
Herbert Biblo Bookseller, Chicago, IL
McBlain Books, Des Moines, IA
Buddenbrooks Books Inc, Boston, MA
Noah Albay Company, New York, NY
W S Heinman, New York, NY
S R Shapiro Co, Books for Libraries, New
    York, NY
University Place Bookshop, New York, NY
William H Allen, Bookseller, Philadelphia,
    PA
Arthur Scharf, Travel Books, Pittsburgh, PA
Simon Ottenberg, Booksellers, Seattle, WA
Raymond Dworczyk, Rare Books, Milwau-
    kee, WI

Agriculture

Whitlock Farm Booksellers, Bethany, CT
Antique Books, Hamden, CT
Broken Kettle Books, Akron, IA
Second Life Books, Adams, MA
Savoy Books, Salem, MA
Hurley Books, Westmoreland, NH
Elisabeth Woodburn, Hopewell, NJ
Page One Books, Albany, NY
Robert E Underhill, Poughkeepsie, NY
Springwater Books & Antiques, Springwater,
    NY
The Attic Inc, Hodges, SC
John W Smith Books, Hensall, ON, Canada
Pomona Book Exchange, Rockton, ON,
    Canada
Gail Wilson — Bookseller, Toronto, ON,
    Canada

Alaskana

McLaughlin's Books, Chico, CA
Apollo Book Shop, Costa Mesa, CA
Jack London Bookstore, Glen Ellen, CA
Family Bookstore, Whittier, CA
Ray Russell — Books, Rochester, MI
Carriage House Books, Kirkwood, NY
Jacques Noel Jacobsen Jr Collectors — Antiq-
    uities Inc, Staten Island, NY
R M Weatherford — Books, Monroe, WA
Comstock's Bindery & Bookshop, Seattle,
    WA
Old Seattle Paperworks, Seattle, WA
The Shorey Bookstore, Seattle, WA

George H Tweney, Books, Seattle, WA
Robert H Redding Books, Sequim, WA
Bond's Bookshop, Vancouver, BC, Canada

American Indians

Russ Todd Book Scout, Phoenix, AZ
Merlin's Bookshop, Isla Vista, CA
Sun Dance Books, Los Angeles, CA
Grady's Books, Redwood City, CA
J & J House Booksellers, San Diego, CA
Louis Collins Books, San Francisco, CA
Lawrence F Golder Rare Books, Collinsville,
    CT
John M Skutel Rare Books, Fairfield, CT
Cedric L Robinson, Bookseller, Windsor, CT
Robert A Hittel — Bookseller, Fort Lauder-
    dale, FL
Wake-Brook House Books, Fort Lauderdale,
    FL
Harvey Dan Abrams — Booksellers, Atlanta,
    GA
David McCord Books, Atlanta, GA
John Rybski Bookseller, Chicago, IL
Forest Park Bookshop, Fort Wayne, IN
T N Luther Books, Shawnee Mission, KS
James M Babcock Bookseller, Algonac, MI
Book Barn, South Sioux City, NE
Heinoldt Books, Egg Harbor City, NJ
Ken Lopez Bookseller, Englewood, NJ
Harold Nestler, Waldwick, NJ
Tom Davies Bookstore, Albuquerque, NM
De La Pena Books, Santa Fe, NM
Renate Halpern Galleries Inc, New York, NY
Springwater Books & Antiques, Springwater,
    NY
Sterling Valley Antiquities at Homestead
    Antiques, Syracuse, NY
Decotah Book Co, Bismarck, ND
McGrath's Book Collector, Muskogee, OK
R M Weatherford — Books, Monroe, WA
The Antiquarian Shop, Stevens Point, WI
Stephen C Lunsford Books, North Vancou-
    ver, BC, Canada

Americana

Van Allen Bradley Inc, Scottsdale, AZ
William R Hecht, Scottsdale, AZ
The Ravenstree Co, Yuma, AZ
Yesterday's Books Etc, Hot Springs, AR
Green Door Books & Antiques, Bellflower,
    CA
Ostby's Americana, Bellflower, CA
Roy Bleiweiss Fine Books, Berkeley, CA
John Alan Walker, Bishop, CA

Americana (cont.)

American Bookstore, Fresno, CA
Talisman Press, Booksellers & Publishers, Georgetown, CA
Arthur H Clark Co, Glendale, CA
Abbey Bookshop, Los Angeles, CA
Bennett & Marshall, Los Angeles, CA
Cherokee Bookshop Inc, Los Angeles, CA
Hollywood Bookshop, Los Angeles, CA
Alfred Kronfeld Bookseller, Los Angeles, CA
Sun Dance Books, Los Angeles, CA
Zeitlin & Ver Brugge Booksellers, Los Angeles, CA
Hammon's Archives & Artifacts, Sacramento, CA
Adams Avenue Bookstore, San Diego, CA
Corn Mill Books, San Diego, CA
Golden Hill Antiquarian Books & Antiques, San Diego, CA
Olinghouse & Tyson Booksellers & La Querencia Press, San Diego, CA
The Holmes Book Company, San Fransisco, CA
Manning's Books, San Francisco, CA
Fred A Berk, Studio City, CA
Garcia-Garst, Bookseller, Turlock, CA
Collectors' Center, Rare Books, Denver, CO
The Court Place Antiquarian Bookshop, Denver, CO
Fred A Rosenstock—Books & Arts, Denver, CO
Whitlock Farm Booksellers, Bethany, CT
Branford Rare Book & Art Gallery, Branford, CT
Country Lane Books, Collinsville, CT
Lawrence F Golder Rare Books, Collinsville, CT
The Book Block, Cos Cob, CT
Warren Blake Bookseller, Fairfield, CT
John M Skutel Rare Books, Fairfield, CT
William & Lois Pinkney Antiquarian Books, Granby, CT
Robert Shuhi—Books, Morris, CT
Jan & Larry Malis, New Canaan, CT
William Reese Co, New Haven, CT
Old Mystic Bookshop, Old Mystic, CT
I-Am-I-Books, Orange, CT
Barbara Farnsworth Bookseller, West Cornwall, CT
Park Road Bookshop, West Hartford, CT
Paula Sterne—Books, West Redding, CT
Turkey Hill Books, Westport, CT
Q M Dabney & Co Inc, Washington, DC
Book Warehouse Inc, Coral Gables, FL
Guideways Inc, Fernandina Beach, FL
Robert A Hittel—Bookseller, Fort Lauderdale, FL
Eugene F Kramer, Jacksonville, FL

Lucile Coleman, Books, A-to-Z Service, North Miami, FL
The Old Bookshop, Palm Beach, FL
C R Sanders Jr, Saint Augustine, FL
Aceto Bookmen, Sarasota, FL
J W Harmand & Sons Ltd, Sarasota, FL
Red Horse at Ybor Square, Tampa, FL
Harvey Dan Abrams—Booksellers, Atlanta, GA
David McCord Books, Atlanta, GA
G S Herron Books, Rome, GA
Jacqueline Levine Books, Savannah, GA
The Yesteryear Shoppe, Nampa, ID
Stonehill's Antiquarian Books, Champaign, IL
Booklegger's, Chicago, IL
Kenneth Nebenzahl Inc, Chicago, IL
Harry L Stern Ltd, Chicago, IL
Thomas W Burrows, Bookseller, Downers Grove, IL
The Athenaeum, Evanston, IL
Bookman's Alley, Evanston, IL
Kennedy's Bookshop, Evanston, IL
Valley Bookshop, Galena, IL
Van Norman Book Co, Galesburg, IL
Thomas J Joyce & Co, Geneva, IL
Titles Inc, Highland Park, IL
E F Keenan Books, Lake Bluff, IL
Avatar Books, Moline, IL
Bookstall of Rockford, Rockford, IL
Prairie Archives, Springfield, IL
Kathleen Rais Books, Bloomington, IN
The Bookstack, Elkhart, IN
Richard's Readers, Tennyson, IN
The Source Bookstore, Davenport, IA
Pied Piper Bookstore, Wichita, KS
Ernest Davis, Harrodsburg, KY
Glover's Books, Lexington, KY
Shawk's Green Dome Antiques, Lexington, KY
Old Louisville Books, Louisville, KY
S-T Associates, Louisville, KY
Ark-La-Tex Book Co, Shreveport, LA
The Mathom Bookshop & Bindery, Augusta, ME
Book Pedlars, Brunswick, ME
Lillian Berliawsky—Books, Camden, ME
F M O'Brien Old Book Shop, Portland, ME
F P Wood Books, Springvale, ME
Andrew B W MacEwen and Aimee B MacEwen, Stockton Springs, ME
Country Book Room, Windham, ME
Gail Klemm—Books, Ellicott City, MD
Shirley Balser 16th-20th Century Paintings, Prints & Books, Pikesville, MD
Henrietta's Attic, Salisbury, MD
Hirschtritt's "1712," Silver Springs, MD
Books of Colonial America, Wheaton, MD
Robert F Lucas, Blandford, MA

Maury A Bromsen Associates Inc, Boston, MA

Goodspeed's Bookshop Inc, Boston, MA

Edward Morrill & Son Inc, Boston, MA

Brookline Village Books & Prints, Brookline, MA

Ahab Rare Books, Cambridge, MA

In Our Time, Cambridge, MA

Book & Tackle Shop, Chestnut Hill, MA

Robert L Merriam, Conway, MA

M Douglas Sackman, Deerfield, MA

W D Hall, East Longmeadow, MA

Titcomb's Bookshop, East Sandwich, MA

Rebecca B Desmarais Rare Books, Framingham, MA

Ten Pound Island Book Co, Gloucester, MA

George Robert Minkoff Inc, Great Barrington, MA

William T Gavin, Leominster, MA

Gordon Totty—Scarce Paper Americana, Lunenburg, MA

D R Nelson & Co, Booksellers, New Bedford, MA

Michael Ginsberg Books Inc, Sharon, MA

Second Fiddle Bookshop, Southbridge, MA

Trotting Hill Park Antiquarian Booksellers, Springfield, MA

Robert H Rubin Books, Stoughton, MA

Harold M Burstein, Antiquarian, Waltham, MA

Roger F Casavant, Wayland, MA

Philip Lozinski Scholarly Books, Westport, MA

Ellie Panos Books, Whitman, MA

Carriage-Barn Books and Antiques, Williamstown, MA

Memory Aisle, Grand Rapids, MI

Bohling Book Co, Lawton, MI

Wenzel Books, New Troy, MI

Ray Russell—Books, Rochester, MI

Much Loved Books, Southfield, MI

Don Allen, Three Oaks, MI

Exnowski Enterprises, Warren, MI

The Current Company, Minneapolis, MN

Oudal Bookshop, Minneapolis, MN

Ken Crawford Books, North Saint Paul, MN

Mary Twyce Antiques & Books, Winona, MN

The Bookseller—Columbia, Columbia, MO

Amitin's Bookshop, Saint Louis, MO

Elizabeth F Dunlap, Books & Maps, Saint Louis, MO

D Halloran Books, Saint Louis, MO

ABC Theological Index, Springfield, MO

The Antiquarium, Omaha, NE

Emery's Books, Contoocook, NH

John F Hendsey, Bookseller, Epping, NH

Carry Back Books, Haverhill, NH

Book Farm, Henniker, NH

Stinson House Books, Rumney, NH

Edward C Fales Old & Rare Books & Manuscripts, Salisbury, NH

Sykes & Flanders Old & Rare Books, Weare, NH

Hurley Books, Westmoreland, NH

Bauman Rare Books, Atlantic City, NJ

Richardson Books, Camden, NJ

Heinoldt Books, Egg Harbor City, NJ

Leonard Balish, Englewood, NJ

Past History, Lincroft, NJ

The Old Bookshop, Morristown, NJ

Stephen Koschal Autographs & Signed Books, Verona, NJ

Harold Nestler, Waldwick, NJ

Chafey's Old & Rare Books, Albuquerque, NM

The Question Mark, Albany, NY

Charles Baron, Bronx, NY

Lawrence Feinberg Rare Books & Manuscripts, Brooklyn, NY

Nationwide Book Service, Brooklyn, NY

Pioneer Book Service, Brooklyn, NY

H C Roseman Bookseller, Brooklyn, NY

Mahoney & Weekly, Booksellers, Buffalo, NY

Rockland Bookman, Cattaraugus, NY

John C Huckans Rare Books—Pan American Books, Cazenovia, NY

C G Fisher—Books, Cobleskill, NY

Willis Monie Books, Cooperstown, NY

The Bookworm, Corning, NY

Berry Hill Bookshop, Deansboro, NY

Anton Gud, Elmhurst, NY

Harry A Cuttler, Glen Cove, NY

Carriage House Books, Kirkwood, NY

Howard Frisch, Livingston, NY

Jens J Christoffersen Rare Books, Mamaroneck, NY

Margaret Zervas Rare Books, Manhasset, NY

Quality Book Service—T Emmett Henderson, Middletown, NY

Wantagh Rare Book Co, Neversink, NY

American Library Service, New City, NY

Academy Bookstore, New York, NY

W Graham Arader III, New York, NY

Argosy Bookstore Inc, New York, NY

J N Bartfield Books Inc, New York, NY

Belanske & Levinger Inc, New York, NY

Book Ranger, New York, NY

William G Boyer, New York, NY

Lathrop C Harper Inc, New York, NY

H P Kraus Books, New York, NY

James Lowe Autographs Ltd, New York, NY

The Old Print Shop Inc, New York, NY

Richard C Ramer Old & Rare Books, New York, NY

Strand Bookstore, New York, NY

Americana (cont.)

Leo Weitz—Herbert E Weitz, New York, NY
Ximenes: Rare Books Inc, New York, NY
Yankee Peddler Bookshop, Pultneyville, NY
Frank Opperman, Rochester, NY
High Ridge Corner, Rye, NY
Lyrical Ballad Bookstore, Saratoga Springs, NY
Bibliomania, Schenectady, NY
Talbothays Books, Somers, NY
Springwater Books & Antiques, Springwater, NY
Carolina Bookshop, Charlotte, NC
The Haunted Bookshop, Durham, NC
Howard O Berg, Devils Lake, ND
Old Bookstore, Akron, OH
Tally Ho Studio, Canton, OH
Robert G Hayman Antiquarian Books, Carey, OH
Alrich Co, Cincinnati, OH
Ohio Bookstore, Cincinnati, OH
Robert Richshafer, Cincinnati, OH
Attenson Antiques & Books, Cleveland, OH
Susan Heller Books, Cleveland, OH
Heritage Bookstore, Columbus, OH
Paul H North Jr, Columbus, OH
L J Ryan—Scholarly Books, Columbus, OH
Ohio Bookhunter, Mansfield, OH
Hilo Farm Antiques, Mentor, OH
Irving M Roth, Antiques, Norwalk, OH
Kendall G Gaisser, Booksellers, Toledo, OH
McClintock's Books, Warren, OH
Joseph F. Scheetz, Youngstown, OH
Holland's Bookstore, Portland, OR
Old Weird Herald's, Portland, OR
Dale C Schmidt Books, Salem, OR
Cesi Kellinger, Bookseller, Chambersburg, PA
Leonard Solomon, Chambersburg, PA
Mitchell's Bookshop, Doylestown, PA
Avocational, Ephrata, PA
William H Powers, Export, PA
D Sedenger Galleries, Huntingdon Valley, PA
Thomas Macaluso Rare & Fine Books, Kennett Square, PA
W Graham Arader III, King of Prussia, PA
William Thomas—Bookseller, Mechanicsburg, PA
Robert C Salathe, Mount Penn, PA
Art Carduner, Philadelphia, PA
Bernard Conwell Carlitz, Philadelphia, PA
George S MacManus Co, Philadelphia, PA
Carmen D Valentino, Philadelphia, PA
The Tuckers, Pittsburgh, PA
The Americanist, Pottstown, PA
Hoffman Research Services, Rillton, PA
Terry Harper Bookseller, Rouseville, PA
R F Perotti, Rare Books, State College, PA

Ernest C Miller, Warren, PA
Baldwin's Book Barn, West Chester, PA
Earl Moore Associates Inc, Wynnewood, PA
The Current Company, Bristol, RI
Patrick T Conley—Books, Cranston, RI
Don E Burnett, East Greenwich, RI
Tyson Books, Providence, RI
James S Pipkin Old & Rare Books, Rock Hill, SC
Kitemaug Books, Spartanburg, SC
Andover Square Books, Knoxville, TN
Burke's Bookstore Inc, Memphis, TN
Kingston Bookstore, Abilene, TX
David Grossblatt Bookseller, Dallas, TX
Albert L Peters Bookseller, Fort Worth, TX
W Graham Arader III, Houston, TX
Norumbega Books, Houston, TX
Frederick W Armstrong Bookseller, Stephenville, TX
Clark Wright Bookdealer, Waxahachie, TX
Ken Leach, Brattleboro, VT
Craftsbury Common Antiquarian, Craftsbury Common, VT
Haunted Mansion Bookshop, Cuttingsville, VT
Green Mountain Books & Prints, Lyndonville, VT
Michael Dunn Books, Newport, VT
Irene Rouse—Bookseller, Alexandria, VA
Bookhouse, Arlington, VA
Alexander Laubert's Books, Falls Church, VA
Zen Americana, Manassas, VA
Collectors' Old Bookshop, Richmond, VA
Camelot Books, Springfield, VA
The Bookpress Ltd, Williamsburg, VA
Henry Stevens, Son & Stiles, Williamsburg, VA
R M Weatherford—Books, Monroe, WA
McDuffie's Books, Opportunity, WA
McDuffie's Old Books, Spokane, WA
Trans Allegheny Books Inc, Walker, WV
The Bishop of Books, Wheeling, WV
Books, Then & Now, Madison, WI
Stony Hill Antiques, Madison, WI
Raymond Dworczyk, Milwaukee, WI
Ravenswood Books, Wisconsin Dells, WI
Academic Books, North Vancouver, BC, Canada
Canadiana House, Toronto, ON, Canada
D & E Lake Ltd Old & Rare Books, Toronto, ON, Canada
Librairie O Vieux Bouquins, Drummondville, PQ, Canada
Helen R Kahn Antiquarian Books, Montreal, PQ, Canada
Librairie Quebecoise, Montreal, PQ, Canada
William P Wolfe Inc Rare Books, Pointe-Claire, PQ, Canada

Americana: Central

Leekley Book Search, Winthrop Harbor, IL
Hoosier Bookshop, Indianapolis, IN
Pauline C Millen—Books, Des Moines, IA
Don's Bookstore & Black Letter Press, Grand Rapids, MI
Grunewald Klaus—Bookdealer, Kansas City, MO
Elizabeth F Dunlap, Books & Maps, Saint Louis, MO
George D Brown—Books, Toledo, OH
G F Glaeve Art & Books, Mount Horeb, WI

Americana: New England

Taste of Honey Bookstore, Fall River, MA
Wake-Brook House Books, Hyannis, MA
Neath the Elms, Marblehead, MA
J & J Hanrahan, Portsmouth, NH
Paper & Ink Bookshop, Berkeley Heights, NJ
Harold Nestler, Waldwick, NJ

Americana: Northwest

Ernest L Sackett, Grants Pass, OR
Green Dolphin Bookshop, Portland, OR
Antiques & Art Associates, Seattle, WA
Robert H Redding Books, Sequim, WA
Fox Book Co, Tacoma, WA

Americana: South

Frank La Mont, Phoenix, AZ
James Hansen Books, Carlsbad, CA
Green Dragon Bookstore, Wichita, KS
Books-by-Mail, Albuquerque, NM
Tom Davies Bookstore, Albuquerque, NM
El Paisano Books, Albuquerque, NM
Abacus Books, Santa Fe, NM
Ancient City Bookshop, Santa Fe, NM
De La Pena Books, Santa Fe, NM
Richard Fitch Old Maps & Prints & Books, Santa Fe, NM
Great Southwest Books, Santa Fe, NM
Nicholas Potter, Bookseller, Santa Fe, NM
Aladdin Book Shoppe, Oklahoma City, OK
Michael's Bookstore, Oklahoma City, OK
Michael Gibbs Books, State College, PA
American Southwest Books, Amarillo, TX
The Wilson Bookshop, Dallas, TX
Antiquarian Book Mart, San Antonio, TX
Booksearch, San Antonio, TX
Clark Wright Bookdealer, Waxahachie, TX

Louis Ginsberg—Books & Prints, Petersburg, VA

Americana: Southwest

Harvey Dan Abrams—Booksellers, Atlanta, GA
The Old Book Scout—Jim McMeans, Atlanta, GA
Yesteryear Bookshop Inc, Atlanta, GA
Hound Dog Press Book Shop, Decatur, GA
C Virgina Barnes—Bookseller, New York NY
The Book Mart, Asheville, NC
Carolina Bookshop, Charlotte, NC
Michael E Bernholz Antiques & Books, Hillsborough, NC
The Book Shelf, Cleveland, TN
F M Hill—Books, Kingsport, TN
Louis Ginsberg—Books & Prints, Petersburg, VA

Americana: West

Bonita Porter Books, Phoenix, AZ
Russ Todd Book Scout, Phoenix, AZ
Guidon Books, Scottsdale, AZ
Rose Tree Inn Bookshop, Tombstone, AZ
J & T Nie Booksellers, Tucson, AZ
Live Oak Booksellers, Arcadia, CA
Richard Hansen, Auburn, CA
Sarkis Shmavonian Books & Prints, Berkeley, CA
Vernon Howard Books, Burlingame, CA
Ken Prag Paper Americana, Burlingame, CA
Kestrel Books, Carmel Valley, CA
Aviation Bookmobile—Mil-Air Photos & Books, Compton, CA
J C Bonnette Bookseller, Fair Oaks, CA
New Albion Bookshop, Fairfax, CA
New Albion Rare Books, Fairfax, CA
Robert Mitchell—Books, Fremont, CA
Monroe Books, Fresno, CA
Jack London Bookstore, Glen Ellen, CA
Arthur H Clark Co, Glendale, CA
Xanadu Galleries Co, Glendale, CA
California Book Auction Galleries, Los Angeles, CA
Caravan Bookstore, Los Angeles, CA
Dawson's Bookshop, Los Angeles, CA
Alfred Kronfeld Bookseller, Los Angeles, CA
G F Hollingsworth Books, Manhattan Beach, CA
Valley Book City, North Hollywood, CA
Edward M Herny, Bookseller, Oakland, CA
Northwest Books, Oakland, CA
Robert Perata Books, Oakland, CA
William P Wreden, Books & Manuscripts, Palo Alto, CA

Americana: West (cont.)

G F Gustin Jr Books, Pasadena, CA
Maxwell Hunley, Pasadena, CA
Five Quail Books, Rancho Santa Fe, CA
Grady's Books, Redwood City, CA
Barry Cassidy Rare Books, Sacramento, CA
Just Books and . . . , Sacramento, CA
D-J Book Search Service, San Bernardino, CA
Carlos Canterbury Bookstore, San Carlos,
    CA
J & J House Booksellers, San Diego, CA
The Albatross Book Store, San Francisco, CA
Antiquus Bibliopole, San Francisco, CA
Argonaut Bookshop, San Francisco, CA
The Holmes Book Company, San Francisco,
    CA
John Howell—Books, San Francisco, CA
Christophe Stickel Fine Books & Auto-
    graphs, San Francisco, CA
A S Fischler—Rare Books, San Jose, CA
Perry's Antiques & Books, San Jose, CA
The Book Habit, San Marcos, CA
Horizon Books, San Rafael, CA
Wade Lillywhite Books, Santa Ana, CA
Milton Hammer Books, Santa Barbara, CA
Out-of-Print Books, Sherman Oaks, CA
John Makarewich, Books, Van Nuys, CA
Blitz Books, Weaverville, CA
J E Reynolds, Bookseller, Willits, CA
The King's Market—Books & Prints, Boul-
    der, CO
Aardvark Books, Denver, CO
Abaco Books, Denver, CO
The Court Place Antiquarian Bookshop,
    Denver, CO
The Hermitage Antiquarian Bookshop,
    Denver, CO
Old Corner Bookshop, Fort Collins, CO
Arthur M Griffiths, Johnstown, CO
The Prospector, Littleton, CO
The Collective—Millet & Simpson Antiquar-
    ian Booksellers, Pueblo, CO
Lawrence F Golder Rare Books, Collinsville,
    CT
William & Lois Pinkney Antiquarian Books,
    Granby, CT
Blue Star Bookstore, Putnam, CT
Cedric L Robinson, Bookseller, Windsor, CT
Boise Book Mart, Boise, ID
Opportunity Books, Lewiston, ID
John Rybski Bookseller, Chicago, IL
Valley Bookshop, Galena, IL
Thomas J Joyce & Co, Geneva, IL
E F Keenan Books, Lake Bluff, IL
T A Swinford Bookseller, Paris, IL
James Dowd—Bookseller, Saint Charles, IL
Burkwood Books, Urbana, IL
Yellowstone Books, Villa Park, IL

Pauline C Millen—Books, Des Moines, IA
David Dary Western Books, Lawrence, KS
T N Luther Books, Shawnee Mission, KS
Al's Old & New Bookstore, Wichita, KS
E & S Summerhouse Books, Dayton, KY
Donald S Mull, Louisville, KY
Dykes, Jeff—Western Books, College Park,
    MD
Firstborn Books, Galesville, MD
Lord Randall Book & Print Shop,
    Marshfield, MA
Michael Ginsberg Books Inc, Sharon, MA
Ken Crawford Books, North Saint Paul, MN
Harold's Bookshop, Saint Paul, MN
Harry B Robinson Book Search Service,
    Columbia, MO
Glenn Books Inc, Kansas City, MO
David R Spivey Fine Books & Prints, Kansas
    City, MO
Elizabeth F Dunlap, Books & Maps, Saint
    Louis, MO
Bay Books & Prints, Big Fork, MT
Gallery of the Old West, Big Fork, MT
Barjon's Books & Graphics, Billings, MT
Thomas Minckler Art & Books, Billings, MT
Jane Graham Treasured Books from the
    Treasure State, Bozeman, MT
Bird's Nest, Missoula, MT
The Book Exchange, Missoula, MT
D N Dupley, Book Dealer, Omaha, NE
Mostly Books, Omaha, NE
Book Barn, South Sioux City, NE
Donato's Fine Books, Las Vegas, NV
Jack D Rittenhouse, Books, Albuquerque,
    NM
Jane Zwisohn Books, Albuquerque, NM
Chaparral Books of Santa Fe, Santa Fe, NM
J Norman Books 'n Tobacco, Depew, NY
Roy Young Bookseller, Dobbs Ferry, NY
Janet Lehr Inc, New York, NY
Yankee Peddler Bookshop, Pultneyville, NY
Sterling Valley Antiquities at Homestead
    Antiques, Syracuse, NY
The Ancient Page, Asheville, NC
Dacotah Book Co, Bismarck, ND
Authors of the West, Dundee, OR
Ernest L Sackett, Grants Pass, OR
Lillian Kennedy Bookseller, Portland, OR
Old Oregon Bookstore, Portland, OR
99-E Antique-Used, Woodburn, OR
Big John's Bookroom, Meshoppen, PA
Graedon Books Inc, New Hope, PA
Hoffman Research Services, Rillton, PA
Michael Gibbs Books, State College, PA
The Jenkins Co, Rare Books, Austin, TX
Tom Munnerlyn Books, Austin, TX
Ray S Walton—Rare Books, Austin, TX
Frontier America Corporation, Bryan, TX
Albert L Peters Bookseller, Fort Worth, TX

Zane Grey's West, Keene, TX
Frederick W Armstrong Bookseller, Stephenville, TX
Clark Wright Bookdealer, Waxahachie, TX
Walt West Books, Provo, UT
Cosmic Aeroplane Books, Salt Lake City, UT
Scallawagiana Books, Salt Lake City, UT
The Memorabilia Corner, Norfolk, VA
Appleland Books, Winchester, VA
R M Weatherford — Books, Monroe, WA
The Shorey Bookstore, Seattle, WA
George H Tweney, Books, Seattle, WA
The Old Book Home, Spokane, WA
Pegasus Books & Press, Vashon, WA
Stephen C Lunsford Books, North Vancouver, BC, Canada
Pioneer Books, Steinbach, MB, Canada

Angling. *See* **Hunting, Fishing & Angling**

Anthropology

Mount Eden Books & Bindery, Hayward, CA
Canterbury Bookshop, Los Angeles, CA
Sun Dance Books, Los Angeles, CA
Tolliver's Books, Los Angeles, CA
The Bookie Joint, Reseda, CA
Olinghouse & Tyson Booksellers & La Querencia Press, San Diego, CA
Louis Collins Books, San Francisco, CA
Frank L Kovacs Archaeology Books, San Francisco, CA
Bay Side Books, Soquel, CA
Collectors' Center, Rare Books, Denver, CO
Richard G Uhl, Lantana, FL
Memorable Books, Stone Mountain, GA
N Fagin Books, Chicago, IL
The Book Bear, West Brookfield, MA
State Street Bookshop, Ann Arbor, MI
George Tramp — Books, Jackson, MI
Richardson Books, Camden NJ
George A Bernstein, Brooklyn, NY
Elliot Klein Ltd, New York, NY
Chris Fessler Bookseller, Theresa, NY
Dacotah Book Co, Bismarck, ND
Jerry Ray Books, Bowling Green, OH
Wentworth & Leggett Rare Books, Durham, NC
The Oklahoma Bookman, Yukon, OK
Benjamin W Turner Jr, Bookseller, Point Pleasant, PA
The Country Bookshop, Plainfield, VT
William Hoffer Bookseller, Vancouver, BC, Canada
The Odd Book, Wolfville, NS, Canada
Atticus Books, Toronto, ON, Canada

Antiques

Those Were the Days, Tempe, AZ
Green Door Books & Antiques, Bellflower, CA
J S Edgren, Carmel, CA
George Houle — Rare Books & Autographs, Los Angeles, CA
Robert Kuhn Antiques — Autographs, San Francisco, CA
Manning's Books, San Francisco, CA
R W Smith — Bookseller, New Haven, CT
Scarlet Letter Books & Prints, New Milford, CT
Book Warehouse Inc, Coral Gables, FL
Whistles in the Woods, Rossville, GA
Barrington Old Bookshop, Barrington, IL
The Globe, Chicago, IL
Old Print Store, Chicago, IL
Harry L Stern Ltd, Chicago, IL
T T & Jean Foley — Antiques, Paris, IL
East Coast Books, Wells, ME
Charlotte's Web Antiques, Monkton, MD
Robert L Merriam, Conway, MA
Bygone Book House, Dearborn, MI
Glenn Books Inc, Kansas City, MO
Lorraine Galinsky, Cold Spring Harbor, NY
Hector's, Eastchester, NY
Margaret Zervas Rare Books, Manhasset, NY
Timothy Trace, Peekskill, NY
The Acorn Antiques, Pittsford, NY
Collector's Antiques Inc, Port Washington, NY
Tally Ho Studio, Canton, OH
Book Stall, Cincinnati, OH
Publix Book Mart, Cleveland, OH
Paul H North Jr, Columbus, OH
Irving M Roth, Antiques, Norwalk, OH
Sam Laidacker, Bloomsburg, PA
Murray Hudson — Books & Maps, Dyersburg, TN
Western Books, Ellensburg, WA
The Comic Character Shop, Seattle, WA
G F Glaeve Art & Books, Mount Horeb, WI
The Antiquarian Shop, Stevens Point, WI
Village Bookstore, Toronto, ON, Canada

Archaeology

Monroe Books, Fresno, CA
The Book Cellar, Fullerton, CA
Hyman & Sons Rare Books, Los Angeles, CA
Tolliver's Books, Los Angeles, CA
The Bookie Joint, Reseda, CA
Frank L Kovacs Archaeology Books, San Francisco, CA
Tiger's Tale Bookshop, Santa Clara, CA

Archaeology (cont.)

The Museum Gallery Bookshop, Southport, CT
Memorable Books, Stone Mountain, GA
T N Luther Books, Shawnee Mission, KS
Dragoman Books, Annapolis, MD
B & B Smith—Booksellers, Mount Airy, MD
Stephen Scharoun, Newburyport, MA
Linda Honan Art Books, Westborough, MA
Books-by-Mail, Albuquerque, NM
George A Bernstein, Brooklyn, NY
Charlie Brown's Book-Gallerie, Brooklyn, NY
Rockland Bookman, Cattaraugus, NY
Carl Sandler Berkowitz, Chester, NY
F A Bernett Inc, Larchmont, NY
Lee & Lee Booksellers Inc, New York, NY
John H Stubbs Rare Books & Prints, New York, NY
Chris Fessler Bookseller, Theresa, NY
Akron Books, Akron, OH
George D Brown—Books, Toledo, OH
Benjamin W Turner Jr, Bookseller, Point Pleasant, PA
The Country Bookshop, Plainfield, VT
F P Elwert, Rutland, VT

Architecture

Marshall Vance Publisher-Bookseller, Forrest City, AR
J B Muns, Books, Berkeley, CA
Harold B Diamond—Bookseller, Burbank, CA
Taylor Coffman Bookseller, Cambria, CA
The Book Cellar, Fullerton, CA
Davis & Schorr Art Books, Los Angeles, CA
Black Swan Books, Sacramento, CA
Richard L Press Fine & Scholarly Books, Sacramento, CA
Kenneth Starosciak, San Francisco, CA
The Court Place Antiquarian Bookshop, Denver, CO
Whitlock Farm Booksellers, Bethany, CT
R W Smith—Bookseller, New Haven, CT
Charles B Wood III, Inc, Antiquarian Booksellers, South Woodstock, CT
The Museum Gallery Bookshop, Southport, CT
Book Warehouse Inc, Coral Gables, FL
Red Horse at Ybor Square, Tampa, FL
Yesteryear Bookshop Inc, Atlanta, GA
Valerie Kraft, Fine Books, Prospect Heights, IL
Marilyn Braiterman, Baltimore, MD
Charlotte's Web Antiques, Monkton, MD
Ars Libri Ltd, Boston, MA

Peter L Masi—Books, Montague, MA
Newburyport Rare Books, Newburyport, MA
Linda Honan Art Books, Westborough, MA
Book Barn, South Sioux City, NE
Richardson Books, Camden, NJ
Harvey W Brewer, Closter, NJ
Leo Loewenthal, Dover, NJ
The Bookworm, Corning, NY
Roy Young Bookseller, Dobbs Ferry, NY
Richard T Jordan Antiquariat, Flushing, NY
F A Bernett Inc, Larchmont, NY
William G Boyer, New York, NY
Robert K Brown, New York, NY
Ex Libris, New York, NY
Lucien Goldschmidt Inc, New York, NY
Lee & Lee Booksellers Inc, New York, NY
Arthur H Minters Inc, New York, NY
John H Stubbs Rare Books & Prints, New York, NY
Weyhe Art Books Inc, New York, NY
Irving Zucker Art Books, New York, NY
Riverow Bookshop, Owego, NY
Timothy Trace, Peekskill, NY
The Acorn Antiques, Pittsford, NY
South Shore Book Reserve, Southampton, NY
The Book Gallery, White Plains, NY
George D Brown—Books, Toledo, OH
Geoffrey Steele Inc, Lumberville, PA
Book Mark, Philadelphia, PA
The Nostalgia Factory, Newport, RI
F P Elwert, Rutland, VT
McDuffie's Old Books, Spokane, WA
Johnson & Small Booksellers, Victoria, BC, Canada
Hortulus, Toronto, ON, Canada

Arctica & Antarctica

McLaughlin's Books, Chico, CA
Apollo Book Shop, Costa Mesa, CA
F & I Books, Santa Monica, CA
Bob Finch, Books, Torrance, CA
Family Bookstore, Whittier, CA
Country Lane Books, Collinsville, CT
Lawrence F Golder Rare Books, Collinsville, CT
John Rybski Bookseller, Chicago, IL
Douglas N Harding, Wells, ME
Edward J Lefkowicz Inc, Fairhaven, MA
George Tramp—Books, Jackson, MI
Ray Russell—Books, Rochester, MI
Jacques Noel Jacobsen Jr Collectors—Antiquities Inc, Staten Island, NY
The Shorey Bookstore, Seattle, WA
Robert H Redding Books, Sequim, WA
Heritage Books, Calgary, AB, Canada

Tom Williams Books, Calgary, AB, Canada
Academic Books, North Vancouver, BC, Canada
Bond's Bookshop, Vancouver, BC, Canada
Antiquarian Books, Winnipeg, MB, Canada
Arctician Books, Fredericton, NB, Canada
J Patrick McGahern—Books Inc, Ottawa, ON, Canada
Acadia Bookstore, Toronto, ON, Canada
Great Northwest Book Co, Toronto, ON, Canada
Joseph Patrick Books, Toronto, ON, Canada
Helen R Kahn Antiquarian Books, Montreal, PQ, Canada
William P Wolfe Inc Rare Books, Montreal, PQ, Canada

Art

Ruby D Kaufman, Tempe, AZ
Marshall Vance Publisher-Bookseller, Forrest City, AR
Albion Fine Prints, Berkeley, CA
J B Muns, Books, Berkeley, CA
Harry A Franklin Gallery, Beverly Hills, CA
John Alan Walker, Bishop, CA
Book City of Burbank, Burbank, CA
Harold B Diamond—Bookseller, Burbank, CA
Taylor Coffman Bookseller, Cambria, CA
Richard Gilbo—Books, Carpenteria, CA
Graeme Vanderstoel, El Cerrito, CA
Books & The Collector Arts, Encino, CA
New Albion Rare Books, Fairfax, CA
Monroe Books, Fresno, CA
Aladdin Books & Memorabilia, Fullerton, CA
The Book Cellar, Fullerton, CA
The Book Harbor, Fullerton, CA
Xanadu Galleries Co, Glendale, CA
Merlin's Bookshop, Isla Vista, CA
Laurence McGilvery, La Jolla, CA
California Book Auction Galleries, Los Angeles, CA
Caravan Bookstore, Los Angeles, CA
Cherokee Bookshop Inc, Los Angeles, CA
William & Victoria Dailey, Los Angeles, CA
Davis & Schorr Art Books, Los Angeles, CA
Hollywood Book City, Los Angeles, CA
George Houle—Rare Books & Autographs, Los Angeles, CA
Kenneth Karmiole, Bookseller Inc, Los Angeles, CA
Vagabond Books, Los Angeles, CA
West Los Angeles Book Center, Los Angeles, CA
Zeitlin & Ver Brugge Booksellers, Los Angeles, CA

The Eclectic Gallery, Mill Valley, CA
Valley Book City, North Hollywood, CA
Fain's First Editions, Pacific Palisades, CA
Rochelle R Ronketty Bookseller, Pasadena, CA
Richard L Press Fine & Scholarly Books, Sacramento, CA
The Albatross Book Store, San Francisco, CA
Boleriem Books, San Francisco, CA
John Howell—Books, San Francisco, CA
Maelstrom, San Francisco, CA
Kenneth Starosciak, San Francisco, CA
Alan Wofsy Fine Arts, San Francisco, CA
Michael S Hollander Rare Books, San Rafael, CA
Virginia Burgman, Santa Rosa, CA
Estampe Originale, Saratoga, CA
The Eclectic Gallery, Sausalito, CA
Calico Cat Bookshop, Ventura, CA
Fred A Rosenstock—Books & Arts, Denver, CO
Whitlock Farm Booksellers, Bethany, CT
David Ladner Books, Hamden, CT
R W Smith—Bookseller, New Haven, CT
Elliot's Books, Out of Print Specialists, Northford, CT
I-Am-I-Books, Orange, CT
Charles B Wood III Inc, Antiquarian Booksellers, South Woodstock, CT
The Museum Gallery Bookshop, Southport, CT
Cedric L Robinson, Bookseller, Windsor, CT
A Blue Moon Books & Records, Clearwater, FL
Book Warehouse Inc, Coral Gables, FL
Mandala Books, Daytona Beach, FL
Omni Graphic Media Co, Hollywood, FL
Richard G Uhl, Lantana, FL
Books & Art Prints Store, Miami, FL
Demerara Book Service, Miami, FL
The Bookfinders Inc, Miami Beach, FL
Red Horse at Ybor Square, Tampa, FL
Abraham's Books, Evanston, IL
The Athenaeum, Evanston, IL
Titles Inc, Highland Park, IL
E F Keenan Books, Lake Bluff, IL
T T & Jean Foley—Antiques, Paris, IL
Valerie Kraft, Fine Books, Prospect Heights, IL
Gary L Steigerwald Bookseller, Bloomington, IN
J Hood Bookseller, Lawrence, KS
Dolphin Bookstore, Camden, ME
Marilyn Braiterman, Baltimore, MD
Quill & Brush Bookstore, Bethesda, MD
Charlotte's Web Antiques, Monkton, MD
Shirley Balser 16th-20th Century Paintings, Prints & Books, Pikesville, MD
The Collector's Library, Arlington, MA

Art (cont.)

Payson Hall Bookshop, Belmont, MA
Ars Libri Ltd, Boston, MA
Buddenbrooks Books Inc, Boston, MA
Choreographica, Boston, MA
Horse in the Attic Bookshop, Brookline, MA
Hurst & Hurst, Cambridge, MA
Starr Bookshop Inc, Cambridge, MA
A E Maxted, Cohasset, MA
Robert L Merriam, Conway, MA
W D Hall, East Longmeadow, MA
Lord Randall Book & Print Shop,
  Marshfield, MA
Saxifrage Books, Salem, MA
Second Fiddle Bookshop, Southbridge, MA
Linda Honan Art Books, Westborough, MA
Bygone Book House, Dearborn, MI
Grub Street, Grosse Point Park, MI
Bernard A Margolis—Books, Monroe, MI
Exnowski Enterprises, Warren, MI
Columbia Books, Columbia, MO
Harry B Robinson Book Search Service,
  Columbia, MO
Anthony Garnett—Fine Books, Saint Louis,
  MO
Book Barn, South Sioux City, NE
Emery's Books, Contoocook, NH
Harvey W Brewer, Closter, NJ
Cranford Antique Exchange, Cranford, NJ
Leo Loewenthal, Dover, NJ
Tom Davies Bookstore, Albuquerque, NM
Salt of the Earth Bookstore Ltd, Albu-
  querque, NM
Peggy & Harold Samuels, Corrales, NM
Editions, Boiceville, NY
Olana Gallery, Brewster, NY
Old Editions Bookshop, Buffalo, NY
Rockland Bookman, Cattaraugus, NY
Carl Sandler Berkowitz, Chester, NY
Lorraine Gallinsky, Cold Spring Harbor, NY
Roy Young Bookseller, Dobbs Ferry, NY
As You Like It Bookshop, Elma, NY
Richard T Jordan Antiquariat, Flushing, NY
H & R Salerno, Hauppauge, NY
F A Bernett Inc, Larchmont, NY
Littwin & Fieden, Mamaroneck, NY
Victor Tamerlis, Mamaroneck, NY
Pages, Mount Kisco, NY
Paul P Appel, Mount Vernon, NY
Academy Bookstore, New York, NY
Argosy Bookstore Inc, New York, NY
J N Bartfield Books Inc, New York, NY
Broude Brothers Limited, New York, NY
Robert K Brown, New York, NY
Chip's Bookshop Inc, New York, NY
Mitchell Cutler Co, New York, NY
Bevan Davies Books, New York, NY
Leonard Fox Ltd, New York, NY

Golden Griffin Bookshop, New York, NY
Greenwich Books Ltd, New York, NY
Renate Halpern Galleries Inc, New York, NY
J N Herlin Inc, New York, NY
Harmer Johnson Books Ltd, New York, NY
Lee & Lee Booksellers Inc, New York, NY
Lion Heart Autographs Inc, New York, NY
James Lowe Autographs Ltd, New York, NY
Arthur H Minters Inc, New York, NY
Pageant Book and Print Shop, New York,
  NY
Charlotte F Safir Books, New York, NY
William H Schab Gallery Inc, New Yorᴸ, NY
Strand Bookstore, New York, NY
Ursus Books Ltd, New York, NY
Leo Weitz—Herbert E Weitz, New York, NY
Irving Zucker Art Books, New York, NY
Riverow Bookshop, Owego, NY
The Acorn Antiques, Pittsford, NY
Temares Family Books, Plandome, NY
Colonial Out-of-Print Book Service, Pleasant-
  ville, NY
A Collector's List, Rockville Centre, NY
Bilbiomania, Schenectady, NY
South Shore Book Reserve, Southampton,
  NY
Hoffman Lane Books, Troy, NY
Ben Franklin Bookshop & Printery, Upper
  Nyack, NY
Lion Harvey Books, Wappingers Falls, NY
The Book Gallery, White Plains, NY
Susan Heller Books, Cleveland, OH
Publix Book Mart, Cleveland, OH
Paul H North Jr, Columbus, OH
L J Ryan—Scholarly Books, Columbus, OH
George D Brown—Books, Toledo, OH
Kendall G Gaisser, Booksellers, Toledo, OH
Green Dolphin Bookshop, Portland, OR
Longfellow's Book & Record Store, Port-
  land, OR
Old Oregon Bookstore, Portland, OR
Tamerlane Books, Havertown, PA
D Sedenger Galleries, Huntingdon Valley, PA
Thomas Macaluso Rare & Fine Books,
  Kennett Square, PA
Book Haven, Lancaster, PA
Miscellaneous Man, New Freedom, PA
Graedon Books Inc, New Hope, PA
Bruce McKittrick, Rare Books, Philadelphia,
  PA
Olympia Books, Philadelphia, PA
Charles Sessler Inc, Philadelphia, PA
The Tuckers, Pittsburgh, PA
Valley Books, Sayre, PA
Booksearch, San Antonio, TX
Leonard Dixon Bookstore, San Antonio, TX
Cosmic Aeroplane Books, Salt Lake City, UT
Bookhouse, Arlington, VA
Camelot Books, Springfield, VA

Jo Ann Reisler Ltd, Vienna, VA
Cipriano's Books, Kennewick, WA
The Comic Character Shop, Seattle, WA
Comstock's Bindery & Bookshop, Seattle, WA
Crucible Bookshop, Seattle, WA
McDuffie's Old Books, Spokane, WA
Books, Then & Now, Madison, WI
Spaightwood Galleries, Madison, WI
Constant Reader Bookshop Ltd, Milwaukee, WI
G F Glaeve Art & Books, Mount Horeb, WI
Colophon Books, Vancouver, BC, Canada
Marven Somer Bookseller, Hamilton, ON, Canada
Headley Hannelore Old & Fine Books, Saint Catharines, ON, Canada
Acadia Bookstore, Toronto, ON, Canada
Great Northwest Book Co, Toronto, ON, Canada
Village Bookstore, Toronto, ON, Canada
Librairie Faubourg — Quebec, Canadiana, Montreal, PQ, Canada
William P Wolfe Inc Rare Books, Montreal, PQ, Canada

Arts & Crafts. *See* Crafts

Asia

Graeme Vanderstoel, El Cerrito, CA
Abbey Bookshop, Los Angeles, CA
Sebastopol Book Shop, Sebastopol, CA
McBlain Books, Des Moines, IA
The Cellar Bookshop, Detroit, MI
Harry B Robinson Book Search Service, Columbia, MO
Asian Rare Books Inc, New York, NY
Janet Lehr Inc, New York, NY
Richard C Ramer Old & Rare Books, New York, NY
Arthur Scharf, Travel Books, Pittsburgh, PA
W B O'Neill — Old & Rare Books, Reston, VA
Raymond Dworczyk, Rare Books, Milwaukee, WI

Astrology

Samadhi — Metaphysical Literature, Newberry, FL
Samuel Weiser Inc, New York, NY
Richard P Germann, Willard, OH
Ollie's Books, Memphis, TN
Ben Abraham Books, Toronto, ON, Canada

Astronomy

Celestial Books, La Canada, CA
Daniel H Deutsch PhD — Books, Pasadena, CA
Corn Mill Books, San Diego, CA
G B Manasek Inc, Chicago, IL

Atlases. *See* Maps, Atlases & Cartography

Australia, New Zealand & Pacific Islands

Graeme Vanderstoel, El Cerrito, CA
The Cellar Bookshop, Detroit, MI
Pacificana, Jamestown, NC
Academic Books, North Vancouver, BC, Canada

Autographed Material

Janus Books Ltd, Tucson, AZ
Ben Sackheim — Rare Books & Fine Art, Tucson, AZ
Sand Dollar Books, Albany, CA
The Scriptorium, Beverly Hills, CA
Robert Kuhn Antiques — Autographs, San Francisco, CA
Christophe Stickel Fine Books & Autographs, San Francisco, CA
East Coast Books, Wells, ME
Rebecca B Desmarais Rare Books, Framingham, MA
Robert & Barbara Paulson Books, Huntington, MA
The Rendells Inc, Newton, MA
Pepper & Stern — Rare Books, Inc, Sharon, MA
Paul C Richards, Templeton, MA
John K King Books, Detroit, MI
Much Loved Books, Southfield, MI
Book Barn, South Sioux City, NE
Antic Hay Books, Fairfield, NJ
Milton Kronovet, Lakewood, NJ
Joseph Rubinfine, Pleasantville, NJ
Stephen Koschal Autographs & Signed Books, Verona, NJ
Bernice Weiss — Rare Books, Eastchester, NY
Walter R Benjamin Autographs Inc, Hunter, NY
American Library Service, New City, NY
Martin Breslauer Inc, New York, NY
Carnegie Bookshop Inc, New York, NY
Greenwich Books Ltd, New York, NY
William B Liebmann, New York, NY
Rosejeanne Slifer, New York, NY

Autographed Material (cont.)

Autos & Autos—Book Dept, Elizabeth City, NC
The Jenkins Co, Rare Books, Austin, TX
T W Tingle Rare & Out-of-Print Books, Austin, TX
Conway Barker—Autograph Dealer, Dallas, TX
Gutenberg's Folly: Rare & Scholarly Books, San Antonio, TX
Collector's Museum & Market, Taft, TX
Camelot Books, Springfield, VA

Aviation & Aeronautics

Aviation Bookmobile—Mil-Air Photos & Books, Compton, CA
Rair Literature, Encinitas, CA
Hollywood Book City, Los Angeles, CA
Aviation Bookmobile—Mil-Air Photos & Books, Norwalk, CA
Just Books and . . . , Sacramento, CA
Out-of-State Book Service, San Clemente, CA
John Roby, San Diego, CA
The Albatross Book Store, San Francisco, CA
Bonnie Denver Books, Stockton, CA
Collectors' Center, Rare Books, Denver, CO
The Court Place Antiquarian Bookshop, Denver, CO
John M Skutel Rare Books, Fairfield, CT
Jan & Larry Malis, New Canaan, CT
Historical Bookshelf Ltd, Plantation, FL
Green Dragon Bookstore, Wichita, KS
The Military Bookman, New York, NY
Yankee Peddler Bookshop, Pultneyville, NY
Kolyer Publications, Stony Brook, NY
Autos & Autos—Book Dept, Elizabeth City, NC
The Bookseller Inc, Akron, OH
George D Brown—Books, Toledo, OH
McClintock's Books, Warren, OH
Dale C Schmidt Books, Salem, OR
Hampton Books, Newberry, SC
William Orbelo, San Antonio, TX
Alexander Laubert's Books, Falls Church, VA
Interim Books, Bremerton, WA
Comstock's Bindery & Bookshop, Seattle, WA
Old Favorites Bookshop Ltd, Toronto, ON, Canada

Beverages

Marian L Gore Bookseller, San Gabriel, CA
Barbara L Feret, Northampton, MA
The Wine & Food Library, Ann Arbor, MI

Bibles & Bible Study. See Religion & Theology

Bibliography

The Ravenstree Co, Yuma, AZ
Live Oak Booksellers, Arcadia, CA
Talisman Press, Booksellers & Publishers, Georgetown, CA
Antiquus Bibliopole, San Francisco, CA
The Brick Row Book Shop, San Francisco, CA
Bernard M Rosenthal Inc, San Francisco, CA
Alan Wofsy Fine Arts, San Francisco, CA
Harmon Books, San Jose, CA
The Antiquarium, Bethany, CT
David Ladner Books, Hamden, CT
Chiswick Bookshop Inc, Sandy Hook, CT
Oak Knoll Books, New Castle, DE
Thomas W Burrows, Bookseller, Downers Grove, IL
Leonard Hoffnung Books, Martinton, IL
Gary L Steigerwald Bookseller, Bloomington, IN
Maury A Bromsen Associates Inc, Boston, MA
Robert L Merriam, Conway, MA
Elmcress Books, Hamilton, MA
Harold M Burstein, Antiquarian, Waltham, MA
Jeffrey D Mancevice Inc, Worcester, MA
Exnowski Enterprises, Warren, MI
Melvin McCosh Bookseller, Excelsior, MN
The Book House Booksellers, Minneapolis, MN
James & Mary Laurie Booksellers, Saint Paul, MN
Victor Tamerlis, Mamaroneck, NY
Kraus Periodicals Co, Millwood, NY
W Graham Arader III, New York, NY
Barnstable Books Inc, New York, NY
De Simon Company, New York, NY
Jonathan A Hill, Bookseller, New York, NY
H P Kraus Books, New York, NY
S R Shapiro Co, Books for Libraries, New York, NY
Alfred F Zambelli, New York, NY
Oceanside Books Unlimited, Oceanside, NY
Richard Cady Rare Books, Port Chester, NY
Paulette Greene, Rockville Centre, NY
W Graham Arader III, King of Prussia, PA
Bruce McKittrick, Rare Books, Philadelphia, PA
W Graham Arader III, Houston, TX
George H Tweney, Books, Seattle, WA
The Old Book Home, Spokane, WA
St Nicholas Books, Toronto, ON, Canada
Michael Davey Bookseller, Weston, ON, Canada

Biography

Book City of Burbank, Burbank, CA
The Book Cellar, Fullerton, CA
Merlin's Bookshop, Isla Vista, CA
Hollywood Book City, Los Angeles, CA
Hollywood Book Service, Los Angeles, CA
Pettler & Lieberman, Booksellers, Los
 Angeles, CA
Buckabest Books & Bindery, Palo Alto, CA
The Albatross Book Store, San Francisco, CA
Antiquus Bibliopole, San Francisco, CA
Lion Bookshop, San Francisco, CA
Book Swap, Solana Beach, CA
Okman's Happy Endings, Woodland Hills,
 CA
Collectors' Center, Rare Books, Denver, CO
Robert Shuhi—Books, Morris, CT
I-Am-I-Books, Orange, CT
Park Road Bookshop, West Hartford, CT
Mandala Books, Daytona Beach, FL
Lucile Coleman, Books, A-to-Z Service,
 North Miami, FL
The Old Bookshop, Palm Beach, FL
Aceto Bookmen, Sarasota, FL
Yesteryear Bookshop Inc, Atlanta, GA
Memorable Books, Stone Mountain, GA
Yesterday, Chicago, IL
Richard S Barnes & Co, Books, Evanston, IL
Kennedy's Bookshop, Evanston, IL
Storeybook Antiques & Books, Sycamore, IL
Richard Owen Roberts Booksellers,
 Wheaton, IL
The Source Bookstore, Davenport, IA
Gale Books, Marshalltown, IA
Green Dragon Bookstore, Wichita, KS
Lillian Berliawsky—Books, Camden, ME
Osee H Brady Books, Assonet, MA
Irving Galis, Marblehead, MA
Ellie Panos Books, Whitman, MA
George Tramp—Books, Jackson, MI
Exnowski Enterprises, Warren, MI
Harry B Robinson Book Search Service,
 Columbia, MO
Addison's Bookstore, Springfield, MO
M F Duffy—Books, Las Vegas, NV
Evelyn Clement—Dealer in Old Books,
 Franklin, NH
Book Farm, Henniker, NH
Cranford Antique Exchange, Cranford, NJ
Acres of Books, Trenton, NJ
Main Street Booksellers, Brooklyn, NY
Nationwide Book Service, Brooklyn, NY
Pioneer Book Service, Brooklyn, NY
H C Roseman Bookseller, Brooklyn, NY
Lorraine Galinsky, Cold Spring Harbor, NY
Argosy Bookstore Inc, New York, NY
Gramercy Book Shop, New York, NY
Temares Family Books, Plandome, NY

The Ancient Page, Asheville, NC
The Browsery, Greensboro, NC
Duttenhofer's Book Treasures, Cincinnati,
 OH
Publix Book Mart, Cleveland, OH
T J McCauley Books, Langhorne, PA
Big John's Bookroom, Meshoppen, PA
Book Search Service, Pittsburgh, PA
The Tuckers, Pittsburgh, PA
Dale W Starry Sr—Bookseller, Shippensburg,
 PA
Old Bookstore, Nashville, TN
Jennie's Book Nook, Alexandria, VA
Books, Then & Now, Madison, WI
Constant Reader Bookshop Ltd, Milwaukee,
 WI
Renaissance Book Shop Inc, Milwaukee, WI
Burton Lysecki Books, Winnipeg, MB,
 Canada
Batta Bookstore, Toronto, ON, Canada
Great Northwest Book Co, Toronto, ON,
 Canada
Northland Books, Saskatoon, SK, Canada

Biology

Tolliver's Books, Los Angeles, CA
Lubrecht & Cramer, Monticello, NY

Birds. *See* Ornithology

Black Studies

Bibliomania, Berkeley, CA
Richard Gilbo—Books, Carpenteria, CA
Third World Ethnic Books, Los Angeles, CA
Harvey Dan Abrams—Booksellers, Atlanta,
 GA
David McCord Books, Atlanta, GA
P R Rieber, Thomasville, GA
Herbert Biblo Bookseller, Chicago, IL
McBlain Books, Des Moines, IA
Willis Van Devanter Books, Poolesville, MD
George Tramp—Books, Jackson, MI
Bauman Rare Books, Atlantic City, NJ
Richard T Jordan Antiquariat, Flushing, NY
American Library Service, New City, NY
Maiden Voyage Books, New York, NY
Nudel Books, New York, NY
Graedon Books Inc, New Hope, PA
The Americanist, Pottstown, PA
Louis Ginsberg—Books & Prints, Peters-
 burg, VA

Books about Books

Marshal Vance Publisher-Bookseller, Forrest
 City, AR

Books about Books (cont.)

Harold B Diamond—Bookseller, Burbank, CA
Books Et Cetera, Chico, CA
The Book Cellar, Fullerton, CA
California Book Auction Galleries, Los Angeles, CA
Dawson's Bookshop, Los Angeles, CA
Kenneth Karmiole, Bookseller Inc, Los Angeles, CA
Zeitlin & Ver Brugge Booksellers, Los Angeles, CA
Robert Perata Books, Oakland, CA
Christophe Stickel Fine Books & Autographs, San Francisco, CA
Wade Lillywhite Books, Santa Ana, CA
Tiger's Tale Bookshop, Santa Clara, CA
The Antiquarium, Bethany, CT
The Book Block, Cos Cob, CT
Preston C Beyer Fine Literary Property, Stratford, CT
Oak Knoll Books, New Castle, DE
AABS-Atlanta Antiquarian Booksellers, Atlanta, GA
Jacqueline Levine Books, Savannah, GA
Thomas W Burrows, Bookseller, Downers Grove, IL
John William Martin—Bookseller, La Grange, IL
Leonard Hoffnung Books, Martinton, IL
Gary L Steigerwald Bookseller, Bloomington, IN
Midnight Bookman, West Lafayette, IN
Gail Klemm—Books, Ellicott City, MD
Robert L Merriam, Conway, MA
Rebecca B Desmarais Rare Books, Framingham, MA
Elmcress Books, Hamilton, MA
Dwyer's Bookstore Inc, Northampton, MA
Leaves of Grass, Ann Arbor, MI
The Book House Booksellers, Minneapolis, MN
James & Mary Laurie Booksellers, Minneapolis, MN
David R Spivey Fine Books & Prints, Kansas City, MO
Colophon Bookshop, Epping, NH
David L O'Neal, Antiquarian Booksellers Inc, Peterborough, NH
Wilsey Rare Books, Montclair, NJ
Joseph J Felcone Inc, Rare Books, Princeton, NJ
Abacus Books, Santa Fe, NM
Ancient City Bookshop, Santa Fe, NM
Bev Chaney Jr, Books, Croton-on-Hudson, NY
De Simon Company, New York, NY
Leo Weitz—Herbert E Weitz, New York, NY

Richard Cady Rare Books, Port Chester, NY
A Collector's List, Rockville Centre, NY
Howard O Berg, Devils Lake, ND
Enterprise Books, Ripley, TN
The Wilson Bookshop, Dallas, TX
Limestone Hills Bookshop, Glen Rose, TX
Joe Petty—Books, Victoria, TX
Louis Ginsberg—Books & Prints, Petersburg, VA
Waves Press & Bookshop, Richmond, VA
The Bookpress Ltd, Williamsburg, VA
The Old Book Home, Spokane, WA
Pegasus Books & Press, Vashon, WA
Village Bookstore, Toronto, ON, Canada
Gail Wilson—Bookseller, Toronto, ON, Canada
William P Wolfe Inc Rare Books, Montreal, PQ, Canada

Botany. See Gardening & Horticulture; Natural History

Broadsides

Don E Burnett, East Greenwich, PA

Business. See Economics & Business

Calligraphy

Samuel W Katz, Los Angeles, CA
Chiswick Bookshop Inc, Sandy Hook, CT
Richard's Readers, Tennyson, IN
Midnight Bookman, West Lafayette, IN
Dwyer's Bookstore Inc, Northampton, MA

Canadiana

McLaughlin's Books, Chico, CA
Family Bookstore, Whittier, CA
Country Lane Books, Collinsville, CT
Lawrence F Golder Rare Books, Collinsville, CT
Douglas N Harding, Wells, ME
Michael Ginsberg Books Inc, Sharon, MA
Trotting Hill Park Antiquarian Booksellers, Springfield, MA
Richard Fitch Old Maps & Prints & Books, Santa Fe, NM
J N Bartfield Books Inc, New York, NY
Yankee Peddler Bookshop, Pultneyville, NY
Springwater Books & Antiques, Springwater, NY
Michael Dunn Books, Newport, VT
Heritage Books, Calgary, AB, Canada
Tom Williams Books, Calgary, AB, Canada
Academic Books, North Vancouver, BC, Canada

Stephen C Lunsford Books, North Vancouver, BC, Canada
Bishop-Williams, Vancouver, BC, Canada
Bond's Bookshop, Vancouver, BC, Canada
William Hoffer Bookseller, Vancouver, BC, Canada
Johnson & Small Booksellers, Victoria, BC, Canada
Pandora's Books Ltd, Altona, MB, Canada
Pioneer Books, Steinbach, MB, Canada
Antiquarian Books, Winnipeg, MB, Canada
Burton Lysecki Books, Winnipeg, MB, Canada
Arctician Books, Fredericton, NB, Canada
The Caledonian, Sussex, NB, Canada
Schooner Books Store, Halifax, NS, Canada
Thoth's Bookshops Ltd, Wolfville, NS, Canada
Madonna House Bookshop, Combermere, ON, Canada
Nostalgia Books, Guelph, ON, Canada
John Rush Books, Hamilton, ON, Canada
Marven Somer Bookseller, Hamilton, ON, Canada
John W Smith Books, Hensall, ON, Canada
Kuska House, Kingston, ON, Canada
C & E Books, Kitchener, ON, Canada
Attic Books, London, ON, Canada
Mrs A L Ashton, Ottawa, ON, Canada
Book Bazaar, Ottawa, ON, Canada
J Patrick McGahern—Books Inc, Ottawa, ON, Canada
The Bookstore, Peterborough, ON, Canada
Headley Hannelore Old & Fine Books, Saint Catharines, ON, Canada
Acadia Bookstore, Toronto, ON, Canada
The Alphabet Bookshop, Toronto, ON, Canada
Hugh Anson-Cartwright, Toronto, ON, Canada
Batta Bookstore, Toronto, ON, Canada
Canadiana House, Toronto, ON, Canada
Great Northwest Book Co, Toronto, ON, Canada
Dora Hood's Book Room Ltd, Toronto, ON, Canada
D & E Lake Ltd Old & Rare Books, Toronto, ON, Canada
Longhouse Bookshop Ltd, Toronto, ON, Canada
William Nelson Books, Toronto, ON, Canada
North Toronto Coins Ltd, Toronto, ON, Canada
Old Favorites Bookshop Ltd, Toronto, ON, Canada
Joseph Patrick Books, Toronto, ON, Canada
Michael Davey Bookseller, Weston, ON, Canada
Librairie O Vieux Bouquins, Drummondville, PQ, Canada
I Ehrlich, Montreal, PQ, Canada
Helen R Kahn Antiquarian Books, Montreal, PQ, Canada
Librairie D'Antan, Montreal, PQ, Canada
Librairie Encyclopedique, Montreal, PQ, Canada
Librairie Faubourg—Quebec, Canadiana, Montreal, PQ, Canada
Librairie Quebecoise, Montreal, PQ, Canada
Westmount Parnassus, Montreal, PQ, Canada
William P Wolfe Inc Rare Books, Pointe-Claire, PQ, Canada
Philip Lozinski, Canadian Branch Reg'd, Saint Bruno, PQ, Canada
Jean Gagnon, Quebec, PQ, Canada
Northland Books, Saskatoon, SK, Canada

Cartography. *See* Maps, Atlases & Cartography

Catholica

Daniel H Deutsch PhD—Books, Pasadena, CA
Valley Bookshop, Galena, IL
Renaissance Book Shop Inc, Milwaukee, WI
Madonna House Bookshop, Combermere, ON, Canada

Chess & Checkers

Dale A Brandreth Books, Hockessin, DE
Oscar Shapiro, Washington, DC
Old Editions Bookshop, Buffalo, NY
Rivendell Bookshop Ltd, New York, NY
Charlotte F Safir Books, New York, NY
Justin G Schiller Ltd, New York, NY
Peter Tumarkin Fine Books Inc, New York, NY
University Place Bookshop, New York, NY
Fred Wilson—Books, New York, NY

Children's Books

Antiquarian Shop, Scottsdale, AZ
Ruby D Kaufman, Tempe, AZ
The Ravenstree Co, Yuma, AZ
Marshall Vance Publisher-Bookseller, Forrest City, AR
The Book Baron, Anaheim, CA
Carol Docheff—Bookseller, Berkeley, CA
James Hansen Books, Carlsbad, CA

Children's Books (cont.)

The Memory Box, Corona Del Mar, CA
Danville Books, Danville, CA
Alpha Books, Encino, CA
The Book Harbor, Fullerton, CA
Ralston Popular Fiction, Fullerton, CA
Jack London Bookstore, Glen Ellen, CA
American Fragments, Goleta, CA
Merlin's Bookshop, Isla Vista, CA
La Mesa Bookstore, La Mesa, CA
The Book Nest, Los Altos, CA
California Book Auction Galleries, Los
  Angeles, CA
Hollywood Book City, Los Angeles, CA
Alfred Kronfeld Bookseller, Los Angeles, CA
Vagabond Books, Los Angeles, CA
West Los Angeles Book Center, Los Angeles,
  CA
Curious Book Shoppe, Los Gatos, CA
Joyce Book Shops Offices, Martinez, CA
James G Leishman—Bookseller, Menlo Park,
  CA
Rik Thompson—Books, Milpitas, CA
Valley Book City, North Hollywood, CA
J & J Berger Booksellers, Oakland, CA
Gull Book Shop, Oakland, CA
Edward M Herny, Bookseller, Oakland, CA
Marvin Stanley Booksellers, Oakland, CA
Book Carnival, Orange, CA
Book Case Books, Pasadena, CA
G F Gustin Jr Books, Pasadena, CA
The Beautiful & the Unusual, Redondo
  Beach, CA
Grady's Books, Redwood City, CA
The Bookie Joint, Reseda, CA
Libra Books, Reseda, CA
Gammage Cup Books, Sacramento, CA
Richard L Press Fine & Scholarly Books,
  Sacramento, CA
Happy Booker, San Bernardino, CA
Carlos Canterbury Bookstore, San Carlos,
  CA
Golden Hill Antiquarian Books & Antiques,
  San Diego, CA
Acorn Books, San Francisco, CA
The Albatross Book Store, San Francisco, CA
Antiquus Bibliopole, San Francisco, CA
Arkadyan Books & Prints, San Francisco,
  CA
The Bookstall, San Francisco, CA
Maelstrom, San Francisco, CA
Perry's Antiques & Books, San Jose, CA
The Novel Experience, San Luis Obispo, CA
Grapevine Antiques & Books, San Mateo,
  CA
George Deeds Book Finder, San Pedro, CA
Carl Blomgren Books, San Rafael, CA
Mandrake Bookshop, San Rafael, CA

Book Vault, Santa Ana, CA
Drew's Bookshop, Santa Barbara, CA
Helan Halbach—Bookseller, Santa Barbara,
  CA
Virginia Burgman, Santa Rosa, CA
Chimney Sweep Books, Scotts Valley, CA
L S Kaiser Books—Chimney Sweep Books,
  Scotts Valley, CA
Book Swap, Solana Beach, CA
Bonnie Denver Books, Stockton, CA
Garcia-Garst, Bookseller, Turlock, CA
Calico Cat Bookshop, Ventura, CA
Okman's Happy Endings, Woodland Hills,
  CA
Collectors' Center, Rare Books, Denver, CO
Old Corner Bookshop, Fort Collins, CO
The Prospector, Littleton, CO
The Cache, Loveland, CO
The Collective—Millet & Simpson Antiquar-
  ian Booksellers, Pueblo, CO
Whitlock Farm Booksellers, Bethany, CT
Country Lane Books, Collinsville, CT
John Woods Books—(Out of Print), Coven-
  try, CT
Extensive Search Service, Danielson, CT
Gilann Books, Darien, CT
R & D Emerson, Falls Village, CT
William & Lois Pinkney Antiquarian Books,
  Granby, CT
Antique Books, Hamden, CT
Jumping Frog, Hartford, CT
Jan & Larry Malis, New Canaan, CT
Pharos Books-Fine First Editions, New
  Haven, CT
I-Am-I-Books, Orange, CT
The Raven Bookshop, Pawcatuck, CT
Blue Star Bookstore, Putnam, CT
Kathleen & Michael Lazare, Sherman, CT
Barbara Farnsworth Bookseller, West
  Cornwall, CT
Park Road Bookshop, West Hartford, CT
Turkey Hill Books, Westport, CT
Tappin Book Mine, Atlantic Beach, FL
Gilbert K Westgard II, Boynton Beach, FL
Book Warehouse Inc, Coral Gables, FL
Robert A Hittel—Bookseller, Fort Lauder-
  dale, FL
Alla T Ford Rare Books, Lake Worth, FL
Demerara Book Service, Miami, FL
Lewis Antiques, Micanopy, FL
Lucile Coleman, Books, A-to-Z Service,
  North Miami, FL
The Old Bookshop, Palm Beach, FL
Wallace A Robinson, Saint Petersburg, FL
Horse Trader Antique Mall, Athens, GA
David McCord Books, Atlanta, GA
Cooper's Books, Decatur, GA
G S Herron Books, Rome, GA
Memorable Books, Stone Mountain, GA

P R Rieber, Thomasville, GA
Pacific Book House, Honolulu, HI
Tusitala Bookshop, Kailua, HI
The Yesteryear Shoppe, Nampa, ID
Barrington Old Bookshop, Barrington, IL
Estate Books, Berkeley, IL
H Popinski Books, Berwyn, IL
Booklegger's, Chicago, IL
Old Print Store, Chicago, IL
Yesterday, Chicago, IL
Richard S Barnes & Co, Books, Evanston, IL
Bookman's Alley, Evanston, IL
Kennedy's Bookshop, Evanston, IL
Thomas J Joyce & Co, Geneva, IL
Titles Inc, Highland Park, IL
Cogitator Books, Libertyville, IL
Joyce Klein Bookseller, Oak Park, IL
Valerie Kraft, Fine Books, Prospect Heights,
  IL
Bookstall of Rockford, Rockford, IL
James Dowd—Bookseller, Saint Charles, IL
Family Book Exchange, Springfield, IL
Storeybook Antiques & Books, Sycamore, Il
Mary F Wendell Books, White Hall, IL
Caveat Emptor, Bloomington, IN
Sycamore Books, Clayton, IN
The Bookstack, Elkhart, IN
Forest Park Bookshop, Fort Wayne, IN
Back Tracts Inc, Indianapolis, IN
Erasmus Books, South Bend, IN
Mason's Rare & Used Books, Wabash, IN
Gil O'Gara, Des Moines, IA
The Haunted Bookshop, Iowa City, IA
Andromeda Bookshop, Maquoketa, IA
Gale Books, Marshalltown, IA
Pied Piper Bookstore, Wichita, KS
George Brosi Bookseller, Berea, KY
Shawk's Green Dome Antiques, Lexington,
  KY
Old Louisville Books, Louisville, KY
Cottonwood Books, Baton Rouge, LA
A Collector's Book Shop, New Orleans, LA
The Mathom Bookshop & Bindery, Augusta,
  ME
Book Pedlars, Brunswick, ME
Dolphin Bookstore, Camden, ME
Frederica De Beurs Books, Dexter, ME
Bedford's Used Books, Ellsworth, ME
Book Cellar, Freeport, ME
Charles L Robinson Rare Books, Manchester,
  ME
Harland H Eastman Books & Prints,
  Springvale, ME
F P Wood Books, Springvale, ME
Douglas N Harding, Wells, ME
Dragoman Books, Annapolis, MD
Marilyn Braiterman, Baltimore, MD
Kelmscott Bookshop, Baltimore, MD
Deeds Bookshop, Ellicott City, MD

Gail Klemm—Books, Ellicott City, MD
Doris Frohnsdorff, Gaithersburg, MD
The Old Printed Word, Kensington, MD
Drusilla's Books, Lutherville, MD
Henrietta's Attic, Salisbury, MD
Imagination Books, Silver Spring, MD
Second Life Books, Adams, MA
Osee H Brady Books, Assonet, MA
Jean S McKenna Old, Scarce, Out-of-Print
  Books, Beverly, MA
Boston Book Annex, Boston, MA
Bromer Booksellers Inc, Boston, MA
Buddenbrooks Books Inc, Boston, MA
Choreographica, Boston, MA
Horse in the Attic Bookshop, Brookline, MA
Book & Tackle Shop, Chestnut Hill, MA
The Barrow Bookstore, Concord, MA
Irene's Bookshop, Gardner, MA
The English Bookshop, Gloucester, MA
Ten Pound Island Book Co, Gloucester, MA
Elmcress Books, Hamilton, MA
Robert & Barbara Paulson Books,
  Huntington, MA
Peter L Masi—Books, Montague, MA
D R Nelson & Co, Booksellers, New
  Bedford, MA
The Book Collector, Newton, MA
Suzanne Schlossberg, Newton, MA
Saxifrage Books, Salem, MA
Books, South Egremont, MA
Second Fiddle Bookshop, Southbridge, MA
Trotting Hill Park Antiquarian Booksellers,
  Springfield, MA
John R Sanderson PhD—Antiquarian Books,
  Stockbridge, MA
Harold M Burstein, Antiquarian, Waltham,
  MA
Roger F Casavant, Wayland, MA
Twice Sold Tales, Wellfleet, MA
Ellie Panos Books, Whitman, MA
Murray Books, Wilbraham, MA
Isaiah Thomas Books & Prints, Worcester,
  MA
James M Babcock Bookseller, Algonac, MI
West Side Bookshop, Ann Arbor, MI
Marion the Antiquarian Librarian, Auburn
  Heights, MI
Bygone Book House, Dearborn, MI
Curious Bookshop, East Lansing, MI
Memory Aisle, Grand Rapids, MI
Grub Street—A Bookery, Grosse Pointe Park,
  MI
Bernard A Margolis—Books, Monroe, MI
Yesterday's Books, Oak Park, MI
Treasures from the Castle, Rochester, MI
House of Trivia, Williamston, MI
J & J O'Donoghue Books, Anoka, MN
Biermaier's B H Books, Minneapolis, MN
The Current Company, Minneapolis, MN

Children's Books (cont.)

S & S Books, Saint Paul, MN
Mary Twyce Antiques & Books, Winona, MN
Books & Stuff, Pearl, MS
Marvelous Books, Ballwin, MO
Columbia Books, Columbia, MO
Grunewald Klaus—Bookdealer, Kansas City, MO
ABC Theological Index, Springfield, MO
Shirley's Old Bookshop, Springfield, MO
Barjon's Books & Graphics, Billings, MT
The Book Exchange, Missoula, MT
Mostly Books, Omaha, NE
1023 Booksellers, Omaha, NE
Book Barn, South Sioux City, NE
Book Stop III, Las Vegas, NV
Donato's Fine Books, Las Vegas, NV
Emery's Books, Contoocook, NH
Evelyn Clement—Dealer in Old Books, Franklin, NH
Cranford Antique Exchange, Cranford, NJ
Oz & Ends Book Shoppe, Kenilworth, NJ
Collectors' Corner, Tenafly, NJ
Hobbit Rare Books, Westfield, NJ
Chafey's Old & Rare Books, Albuquerque, NM
Great Southwest Books, Santa Fe, NM
Margolis & Moss, Santa Fe, NM
Nicholas Potter, Bookseller, Santa Fe, NM
Page One Books, Albany, NY
Reston's Booknook, Amsterdam, NY
Denbry Books, Bronx, NY
Mahoney & Weekly, Buffalo, NY
Lorraine Galinsky, Cold Spring Harbor, NY
Croton Book Service—Sportsman's Book Service, Croton-on-Hudson, NY
Berry Hill Bookshop, Deansboro, NY
J Norman Books 'n Tobacco, Depew, NY
N & N Pavlov, Dobbs Ferry, NY
Bernice Weiss—Rare Books, Eastchester, NY
Ingeborg Quitzau the Edmeston Trader, Edmeston, NY
As You Like It Bookshop, Elma, NY
M & M Halpern Bookdealers, Flushing, NY
Xerxes Books, Glen Head, NY
H & R Salerno, Hauppauge, NY
Daniel Hirsch, Hopewell Junction, NY
North Shore Books Ltd, Huntington, NY
Janus Books, Huntington Station, NY
With Pipe & Book, Lake Placid, NY
Littwin & Feiden, Mamaroneck, NY
Pages, Mount Kisco, NY
Appelfeld Gallery, New York, NY
C Virginia Barnes, New York, NY
Books 'n Things, New York, NY
Books of Wonder, New York, NY
William G Boyer, New York, NY

James Cummins Bookseller Inc, New York, NY
Peter Thomas Fisher—Bookseller, New York, NY
Ralph D Gardner, New York, NY
Golden Griffin Bookshop, New York, NY
Gryphon Bookshop, New York, NY
Renate Halpern Galleries Inc, New York, NY
Kim Kaufman Bookseller, New York, NY
Elliot Klein Ltd, New York, NY
Riverow Bookshop, Owego, NY
Temares Family Books, Plandome, NY
Fiddler's Folly, Pleasant Valley, NY
Collector's Antiques Inc, Port Washington, NY
Yankee Peddler Bookshop, Pultneyville, NY
Ang & Lill's Collector's Corner, Rochester, NY
Lyrical Ballad Bookstore, Saratoga Springs, NY
Southampton Book Co, Southampton, NY
Jim Hodgson Books, Syracuse, NY
Hoffman Lane Books, Troy, NY
Trojan Books, Troy, NY
Ben Franklin Bookshop & Printery, Upper Nyack, NY
Aleph-Bet Books, Valley Cottage, NY
The Backroom Bookstore, Webster, NY
Avonlea Books, White Plains, NY
Perry's Books, Carthage, NC
B L Means—Rare Books & First Editions, Charlotte, NC
Chelsea Antiques, Durham, NC
Wentworth & Leggett Rare Books, Durham, NC
The Browsery, Greensboro, NC
Grandpa's House, Troy, NC
Pacificana, Jamestown, NC
Akron Books, Akron, OH
The Bookseller Inc, Akron, OH
Old Bookstore, Akron, OH
Stagecoach Antiques, Akron, OH
Tally Ho Studio, Canton, OH
Barbara Agranoff Books, Cincinnati, OH
Attenson Antiques & Books, Cleveland, OH
Susan Heller Books, Cleveland, OH
Peter Keisogloff Books, Cleveland, OH
Publix Book Mart, Cleveland, OH
Miran Arts & Books, Columbus, OH
Karen Wickliff Books, Columbus, OH
Maran Enterprises, Harrison, OH
Doris Davis Books, Hudson, OH
Maggie McGiggles Antiques, Mentor, OH
Ada Book Stall, Ada, OK
Aladdin Book Shoppe, Oklahoma City, OK
Old Weird Herald's, Portland, OR
The Manuscript, Salem, OR
99-E Antique-Used, Woodburn, OR
D Sedenger Galleries, Huntingdon Valley, PA

Hobson's Choice, Jenkintown, PA
T J McCauley Books, Langhorne, PA
Molly Kirwan Books, Meadow Lands, PA
Bernard Conwell Carlitz, Philadelphia, PA
Book Search Service, Pittsburgh, PA
Schoyer's Books, Pittsburgh, PA
Terry Harper Bookseller, Rouseville, PA
Valley Books, Sayre, PA
Dale W Starry Sr—Bookseller, Shippensburg, PA
Marie Fetrow, York, PA
Don E Burnett, East Greenwich, RI
Sign of the Unicorn Bookshop, Peace Dale, RI
S Clyde King Rare & Out-of-Print Books, Providence, RI
The Wayside Bookshop, Westerly, RI
Tom Scott Firebooks, Oak Ridge, TN
Big D Books & Comics, Dallas, TX
David Grossblatt Bookseller, Dallas, TX
The Ole Moon & Other Tales, Dallas, TX
Books Etc, Fort Worth, TX
Zane Grey's West, Keene, TX
Antiquarian Book Mart, San Antonio, TX
Collector's Museum & Market, Taft, TX
Book Cellar, Temple, TX
Bygone Books Inc, Burlington, VT
Brick House Bookshop, Morrisville, VT
The Unique Antique, Putney, VT
Economy Books, Alexandria, VA
Book Ends, Arlington, VA
Jo Ann Reisler Ltd, Vienna, VA
Interim Books, Bremerton, WA
Antiques & Art Associates, Seattle, WA
Bibelots & Books, Seattle, WA
David Ishii Bookseller, Seattle, WA
Edward D Nudelman Children's & Illustrated Antiquarian Books, Seattle, WA
House of Yesterday Antiques, Spokane, WA
Dora Hood's Book Room Ltd, Toronto, ON, Canada
Mostly Mysteries Books, Toronto, ON, Canada

China

Cecil Archer Rush, Baltimore, MD
China Book Gallery, Minneapolis, MN
Noah Albay Company, New York, NY
Deecee Books, Nyack, NY

Cinema

The Scriptorium, Beverly Hills, CA
Book City of Burbank, Burbank, CA
Aladdin Books & Memorabilia, Fullerton, CA
Merlin's Bookshop, Isla Vista, CA

Hollywood Book City, Los Angeles, CA
Hollywood Book Service, Los Angeles, CA
Paul Hunt, Los Angeles, CA
Pettler & Lieberman, Booksellers, Los Angeles, CA
Third World Ethnic Books, Los Angeles, CA
Vagabond Books, Los Angeles, CA
West Los Angeles Book Center, Los Angeles, CA
Paul Romaine—Books, Chicago, IL
The Athenaeum, Evanston, IL
Omega Books, Northampton, MA
Leo Loewenthal, Dover, NJ
H C Roseman Bookseller, Brooklyn, NY
M & M Halpern Bookdealers, Flushing, NY
Richard T Jordan Antiquariat, Flushing, NY
J N Herlin Inc, New York, NY
Arthur H Minters Inc, New York, NY
Richard Stoddard Performing Arts Books, New York, NY
The Bookseller Inc, Akron, OH
Tally Ho Studio, Canton, OH
Hampton Books, Newberry, SC
Gasoline Alley Antiques, Seattle, WA
Old Seattle Paperworks, Seattle, WA

Circus & Carnival

Valley Book City, North Hollywood, CA
Robert Kuhn Antiques—Autographs, San Francisco, CA
J & J Lubrano, South Lee, MA
Richard Stoddard Performing Arts Books, New York, NY
The Unique Antique, Putney, VT

Civil War

Guidon Books, Scottsdale, AZ
Ostby's Americana, Bellflower, CA
Danville Books, Danville, CA
Xanadu Galleries Co, Glendale, CA
The Book Habit, San Marcos, CA
Book Swap, Solana Beach, CA
A Blue Moon Books & Records, Clearwater, FL
C R Sanders Jr, Saint Augustine, FL
John Rybski Bookseller, Chicago, IL
Avatar Books, Moline, IL
James Dowd—Bookseller, Saint Charles, IL
Historical Newspapers & Journals, Skokie, IL
Book Barn, Walnut, IL
Donald S Mull, Louisville, KY
The Mount Sterling Rebel, Mount Sterling, KY
A Collector's Book Shop, New Orleans, LA
Ark-La-Tex Book Co, Shreveport, LA

Civil War (cont.)

Old Quenzel Store, Port Tobacco, MD
W D Hall, East Longmeadow, MA
Frank E Reynolds Bookseller, Newburyport, MA
John K King Books, Detroit, MI
Don's Bookstore & Black Letter Press, Grand Rapids, MI
J E Sheldon Fine Books, Hastings, MI
Exnowski Enterprises, Warren, MI
Ken Crawford Books, North Saint Paul, MN
ABC Theological Index, Springfield, MO
The Bookworm, Corning, NY
Carriage House Books, Kirkwood, NY
Yankee Peddler Bookshop, Pultneyville, NY
The Ancient Page, Asheville, NC
Carolina Bookshop, Charlotte, NC
Wentworth & Leggett Rare Books, Durham, NC
Broadfoot's Bookmark, Wendell, NC
Maggie McGiggles Antiques, Mentor, OH
Irving M Roth, Antiques, Norwalk, OH
William H Powers, Export, PA
Battlefield Bookshop, Gettysburg, PA
Obsolescence, Gettysburg, PA
Molly Kirwan Books, Meadow Lands, PA
Robert C Salathe, Mount Penn, PA
Patrick T Conley—Books, Cranston, RI
Frank J Williams, Lincolniana, Hope Valley, RI
James S Pipkin Old & Rare Books, Rock Hill, SC
F M Hill—Books, Kingsport, TN
Old Bookstore, Nashville, TN
Frederick W Armstrong Bookseller, Stephenville, TX
The Memorabilia Corner, Norfolk, VA
Louis Ginsberg—Books & Prints, Petersburg, VA
Collectors' Old Bookshop, Richmond, VA
Appleland Books, Winchester, VA
Olin O Evans, Woodstock, VA
Bookworm & Silverfish, Wytheville, VA
Culpepper & Hanson Bookseller, Tacoma, WA
Appalachian Bookshop, Bluefield, WV

Classical Languages

Krown & Spellman, Booksellers, Los Angeles, CA

Classical Studies

The Ravenstree Co, Yuma, AZ
Robert Allen Books, Altadena, CA
Harold B Diamond—Bookseller, Burbank, CA

Libra Books, Reseda, CA
Boleriem Books, San Francisco, CA
Henry A Clausen Bookshop, Colorado Springs, CO
James M W Borg Inc, Chicago, IL
Thomas W Burrows, Bookseller, Downers Grove, IL
The Athenaeum, Evanston, IL
Cogitator Books, Libertyville, IL
The Source Bookstore, Davenport, IA
B & B Smith—Booksellers, Mount Airy, MD
Imagination Books, Silver Spring, MD
University Book Reserve, Hull, MA
Grub Street—A Bookery, Grosse Pointe Park, MI
George Tramp—Books, Jackson, MI
Book Stop III, Las Vegas, NV
Book Farm, Henniker, NH
Bauman Rare Books, Atlantic City, NJ
Tom Davies Bookstore, Albuquerque, NM
Ancient City Bookshop, Santa Fe, NM
Willis Monie Books, Cooperstown, NY
Jerry Granat Manuscripts, Hewlett, NY
Paulette Rose Ltd, New York, NY
William Salloch, Ossining, NY
Richard Cady Rare Books, Port Chester, NY
Chris Fessler Bookseller, Theresa, NY
The Backroom Bookstore, Webster, NY
Chelsea Antiques, Durham, NC
Mid-America Books, Memphis, TN
Avenue Bookshop, Ottawa, ON, Canada
The Alphabet Bookshop, Toronto, ON, Canada
Atticus Books, Toronto, ON, Canada

Coins. See Numismatics

Color Plate Books

Irving Keats, Carmel, CA
Trophy Room Books—Big Game Hunting Books, Encino,CA
Cherokee Bookshop Inc, Los Angeles, CA
Michael S Hollander Rare Books, San Rafael, CA
The Old Print Gallery, Washington, DC
Collector's World, Atlanta, GA
Valerie Kraft, Fine Books, Prospect Heights, IL
Taylor Clark's Inc, Baton Rouge, LA
Douglas N Harding, Wells, ME
Leonard Balish, Englewood, NJ
J N Bartfield Books Inc, New York, NY
K Gregory, New York, NY
Albert Gutkin, New York, NY
Harmer Johnson Books Ltd, New York, NY
Irving Zucker Art Books, New York, NY
High Ridge Corner, Rye, NY
Tally Ho Studio, Canton, OH
Tamerlane Books, Havertown, PA

Comedy. *See* Humor

Comics

Fantasy Illustrated, Garden Grove, CA
Book Sail, Orange, CA
Extensive Search Service, Danielson, CT
The Old Bookshop, Jacksonville, FL
Books & Art Prints Store, Miami, FL
Geppi's Comic World, Baltimore, MD
Omega Books, Northampton, MA
House of Trivia, Williamston, MI
Old Weird Herald's, Portland, OR
Big D Books & Comics, Dallas, TX
Geppi's Crystal City Comics, Arlington, VA
Ken Mitchell Books, Willowdale, ON,
    Canada

Communism

Scattergood Books, Berkeley, CA
Harry B Robinson Book Search Service,
    Columbia, MO
M & M Halpern Bookdealers, Flushing, NY
L J Ryan—Scholarly Books, Columbus, OH

Cookery & Gastronomy

Appletree Books, Williford, AR
The Book Cellar, Fullerton, CA
The Book Harbor, Fullerton, CA
Merlin's Bookshop, Isla Vista, CA
California Book Auction Galleries, Los
    Angeles, CA
Caravan Bookstore, Los Angeles, CA
Book Case Books, Pasadena, CA
Rochelle R Ronketty Bookseller, Pasadena,
    CA
The Beautiful & the Unusual, Redondo
    Beach, CA
The Bookie Joint, Reseda, CA
The Bookstall, San Francisco, CA
Marian L Gore Bookseller, San Gabriel, CA
Calico Cat Bookshop, Ventura, CA
Okman's Happy Endings, Woodland Hills,
    CA
The Haunted Bookshop, Iowa City, IA
Willis Van Devanter Books, Poolesville, MD
Book & Tackle Shop, Chestnut Hill, MA
Barbara L Feret, Northampton, MA
Ellie Panos Books, Whitman, MA
The Wine & Food Library, Ann Arbor, MI
Bygone Book House, Dearborn, MI
Barbara J Rule Books, Rochester, MI
Millard S Cohen, Saint Louis, MO
The Question Mark, Albany, NY
Page One Books, Buffalo, NY
Hector's, Eastchester, NY
A Collector's Library, Hilton, NY
Janus Books, Huntington Station, NY

M M Einhorn Maxwell Books—At the Sign
    of the Dancing Bear, New York, NY
Charlotte F Safir Books, New York, NY
Riverow Bookshop, Owego, NY
Wentworth & Leggett Rare Books, Durham,
    NC
Publix Book Mart, Cleveland, OH
Maran Enterprises, Harrison, OH
99-E Antique-Used, Woodburn, OR
Old Bookstore, Nashville, TN
Montrose Bookshop, Houston, TX
Comstock's Bindery & Bookshop, Seattle,
    WA
House of Yesterday Antiques, Spokane, WA
The Old Book Home, Spokane, WA
Dancing Bear Antiquarian Bookshop &
    Paperback Exchange, Milwaukee, WI
Renaissance Book Shop Inc, Milwaukee, WI
Pomona Book Exchange, Rockton, ON,
    Canada

Costumes

Albert Gutkin, New York, NY
R L Shep, Lopez, WA

Crafts

Alpha Books, Encino, CA
Just Books and . . . , Sacramento, CA
Books in Transit, Turlock, CA
Lois St Clair, Van Nuys, CA
Okman's Happy Endings, Woodland Hills,
    CA
Collectors' Center, Rare Books, Denver, CO
AABS—Atlanta Antiquarian Booksellers,
    Atlanta, GA
Memorable Books, Stone Mountain, GA
Mary Chapman Bookseller, College Park,
    MD
Edward Morrill & Son Inc, Boston, MA
Ellie Panos Books, Whitman, MA
Exnowski Enterprises, Warren, MI
Edward C Fales Old & Rare Books & Manu-
    scripts, Salisbury, NH
Hector's, Eastchester, NY
Timothy Trace, Peekskill, NY
Wentworth & Leggett Rare Books, Durham,
    NC
Maran Enterprises, Harrison, OH
Douglas Gunn—Books, Wooster, OH
The Tuckers, Pittsburgh, PA
Auld Stone Bookshop, Glasgow, VA
R L Shep, Lopez, WA

Criminology

Town & Gown Book Co, Dutch Flat, CA
Patterson Smith, Montclair, NJ
Hoffman Research Services, Rillton, PA

Dance

Fain's First Editions, Pacific Palisades, CA
Buckabest Books & Bindery, Palo Alto, CA
Book Warehouse Inc, Coral Gables, FL
Larry Laws Bookstore, Chicago, IL
Buddenbrooks Books Inc, Boston, MA
Choreographica, Boston, MA
William J Cassidy, Kansas City, MO
Leo Loewenthal, Dover, NJ
H C Roseman Bookseller, Brooklyn, NY
Books 'n Things, New York, NY
M M Einhorn Maxwell Books—At the Sign
  of the Dancing Bear, New York, NY
Richard Stoddard Performing Arts Books,
  New York, NY
Lyrical Ballad Bookstore, Saratoga, Springs,
  NY
Cesi Kellinger, Bookseller, Chambersburg, PA

Decorative Arts

Cynthia Elyce Rubin, Charlestown, MA
The Wine & Food Library, Ann Arbor, MI
Timothy Mawson, New York, NY
St Nicholas Books, Toronto, ON, Canada

Detective Fiction. *See* Mystery & Detective Fiction

Discovery & Exploration. *See* Voyages, Exploration & Discovery

Dogs

Paula Sterne—Books, West Redding, CT
Fur Fin Feather Books, Lansing, IL
Kathleen Rais Books, Bloomington, IN
Gunnerman Books, Auburn Heights, MI
Highwood Bookshop, Traverse City, MI
Sydney R Smith Sporting Books, Canaan, NY
Chang Tang Books, Peekskill, NY
Carol Butcher, Youngstown, OH
The Ken-L-Questor, Newberg, OR
Arabest Bookshop, Big Bend, WI
Sportsman's Cabinet, Manotick, ON, Canada
Bibliography of the Dog, Montreal, PQ,
  Canada

Dolls

Paul A Ruddell Books—Hobby House Press
  Inc, Cumberland, MD
Bird's Nest, Missoura, MT

Drama. *See* Theater & Drama

Drawings

Barbara Leibowits, Graphics Ltd, New York,
  NY
Bruce P Ferrini, Rare Books, Akron, OH

Economics & Business

Harold J Mason Inc, Phoenix, AZ
Pacific Book Supply Co, Farmersville, CA
Abbey Bookshop, Los Angeles, CA
Bennett & Marshall, Los Angeles, CA
William Bledsoe, Bookseller, San Carlos, CA
Boleriem Books, San Francisco, CA
Mandrake Bookshop, San Rafael, CA
B & L Rootenberg Fine & Rare Books,
  Sherman Oaks, CA
Richard Adamiak, Chicago, IL
Kenneth Nebenzahl Inc, Chicago, IL
John Rybski Bookseller, Chicago, IL
Carmel Bookshop, Lapel, IN
Buddenbrooks Books Inc, Boston, MA
A E Maxted, Cohasset, MA
Robert & Barbara Paulson Books,
  Huntington, MA
Peter L Masi—Books, Montague, MA
Robert H Rubin Books, Stoughton, MA
Western Hemisphere Inc, Stoughton, MA
M & S Rare Books Inc, Weston, MA
William J Cassidy, Kansas City, MO
S Millman, Brooklyn, NY
Noah Albay Company, New York, NY
Bookfinder's General Inc, New York, NY
Hive of Industry, Booksellers, Easton, PA
Hoffman Research Services, Rillton, PA
Brandywine Books, Saxton, PA
Lincoln Book Shoppe Inc & Lincoln Out-of-
  Print Book Search Ltd, Foster, RI
Leonard Dixon Bookstore, San Antonio, TX

Education

Pacific Book Supply Co, Farmersville, CA
Gale Books, Marshalltown, IA
West Side Bookshop, Ann Arbor, MI
Acres of Books, Trenton, NJ
The Backroom Bookstore, Webster, NY
Harvey Abrams—Books, State College, PA

Engineering

Merlin's Bookshop, Isla Vista, CA
Tolliver's Books, Los Angeles, CA
Charles E Gardiner, Bayside, NY
Stevens & Co Books Inc, New York, NY

Ephemera

Argus Books & Graphics, Sacramento, CA
Ex Libris, New York, NY

Paulette Rose Ltd, New York, NY
Irving M Roth, Antiques, Norwalk, OH
Lincoln Book Shoppe Inc & Lincoln Out-of-
Print Book Search Ltd, Foster, RI
Louis Ginsberg—Books & Prints, Peters-
burg, VA
McDuffie's Old Books, Spokane, WA

Erotica

The Book Cellar, Fullerton, CA
The Beautiful & the Unusual, Redondo
Beach, CA
Cecil Archer Rush, Baltimore, MD
Exnowski Enterprises, Warren, MI
C J Scheiner Books, Brooklyn, NY
J B Rund, New York, NY

Ethnic Studies

Sun Dance Books, Los Angeles, CA
Haight Street Bookshop, San Francisco, CA
T N Luther Books, Shawnee Mission, KS
Exnowski Enterprises, Warren, MI
Renate Halpern Galleries Inc, New York,
NY
Great Northwest Book Co, Toronto, ON,
Canada

Evolution

Canterbury Bookshop, Los Angeles, CA
Scientia, Books in Science & Medicine,
Minneapolis, MN
Jerry Ray Books, Bowling Green, OH

Falconry

William R Hecht, Scottsdale, AZ
W J Bookunter, Denver, CO
Paul J Drabeck, Bronx, NY

Farming. *See* Agriculture

Feminism. *See* Women

Film. *See* Cinema

Fine Arts

George K Oppenheim, Berkeley, CA
Kurt L Schwarz, Los Angeles, CA
Northwest Books, Oakland, CA
Richard L Press Fine & Scholarly Books,
Sacramento, CA
Eldorado Books, San Francisco, CA

AABS—Atlanta Antiquarian Booksellers,
Atlanta, GA
The Athenaeum, Evanston, IL
Christopher's Book Room, Bloomington, IN
Artistic Endeavors, Boston, MA
Maury A Bromsen Associates Inc, Boston,
MA
Cynthia Elyce Rubin, Charlestown, MA
Dinkytown Antiquarian Bookshop, Minne-
apolis, MN
Lucien Goldschmidt Inc, New York, NY
S R Shapiro Co, Books for Libraries, New
York, NY
Weyhe Art Books Inc, New York, NY
Irving Zucker Art Books, New York, NY
Susan Heller Books, Cleveland, OH
Karen Wickliff Books, Columbus, OH
Maran Enterprises, Harrison, OH
Glenn Armitage, Miamisburg, OH
Cesi Kellinger, Bookseller, Chambersburg, PA
Geoffrey Steele Inc, Lumberville, PA
Olympia Books, Philadelphia, PA
Lincoln Book Shoppe Inc & Lincoln Out-of-
Print Book Search Ltd, Foster, RI
M Taylor Bowie Bookseller, Seattle, WA

Fine Printing. *See* Press Books & Fine Printing

Firearms, Guns & Weapons

Valley Book City, North Hollywood, CA
Aviation Bookmobile—Mil-Air Photos &
Books, Norwalk, CA
Just Books and . . . , Sacramento, CA
N Flayderman & Co Inc, New Milford, CT
Paula Sterne—Books, West Redding, CT
Yesteryear Bookshop Inc, Atlanta, GA
Creedmoor Bookstore, Chicago, IL
Donald R Doerres, Wilton, IA
Red River Books, Shreveport, LA
Gustave H Suhm Book-Tique, Westfield, MA
Global Book Research, Belding, MI
Bygone Book House, Dearborn, MI
Ray Russell—Books, Rochester, MI
Highwood Bookshop, Traverse City, MI
Paul J Drabeck, Bronx, NY
Melvin Marcher, Oklahoma City, OK
Sam Laidacker, Bloomsburg, PA
William H Powers, Export, PA
Franklin M Roshon, Pottstown, PA

Folklore

Marshall Vance Publisher-Bookseller,
Forrest City, AR
Carol Docheff—Bookseller, Berkeley, CA
The Book Cellar, Fullerton, CA

Folklore (cont.)

Stephen Scharoun, Newburyport, MA
Twice Sold Tales, Wellfleet, MA
The Dawn Treader Book Shop, Ann Arbor, MI
Charlie Brown's Book-Gallerie, Brooklyn, NY
Elliot Klein Ltd, New York, NY
Rivendell Bookshop Ltd, New York, NY
Serpent & Eagle Books, Oneonta, NY
Lyrical Ballad Bookstore, Saratoga Springs, NY
L J Ryan—Scholarly Books, Columbus, OH
The Country Bookshop, Plainfield, VT
Benjamin Koenig's Country Bookshop, Plainfield, VT
Irene Rouse—Bookseller, Alexandria, VA
Glynis Barnes, Toronto, ON, Canada

Food. See Cookery & Gastronomy

Foreign Languages

George K Oppenheim, Berkeley, CA
George Frederick Kolbe Fine Numismatic Books, Crestline, CA
Hyman & Sons Rare Books, Los Angeles, CA
Samuel W Katz, Los Angeles, CA
Tolliver's Books, Los Angeles, CA
Joyce Book Shops Offices, Martinez, CA
Gull Book Shop, Oakland, CA
"Otento" Books, San Diego, CA
Marian L Gore Bookseller, San Gabriel, CA
Old Corner Bookshop, Fort Collins, CO
Red Horse at Ybor Square, Tampa, FL
Cooper's Books, Decatur, GA
Bern Wheel, Books, Oak Park, IL
The Haunted Bookshop, Iowa City, IA
Dolphin Bookstore, Camden, ME
Dragoman Books, Annapolis, MD
Hardford Coins, Baltimore, MD
Gail Klemm—Books, Ellicott City, MD
C & M Hutchinson, Green Harbor, MA
Philip Lozinski Scholarly Books, Westport, MA
State Street Bookshop, Ann Arbor, MI
Collectors' Corner, Tenafly, NJ
The Book Barn, Canandaigua, NY
Ex Libris, New York, NY
Peter Thomas Fisher—Bookseller, New York, NY
Richard C Ramer Old & Rare Books, New York, NY
Charlotte F Safir Books, New York, NY
University Place Bookshop, New York, NY
Weyhe Art Books Inc, New York, NY
Alfred F Zambelli, New York, NY

Hoffman Lane Books, Troy, NY
Albert J Phiebig Inc, White Plains, NY
Duttenhofer's Book Treasures, Cincinnati, OH
Maggie McGiggles Antiques, Mentor, OH
The Battery Book Shop, Nashville, TN
Mostly Mysteries Books, Toronto, ON, Canada
Philip Lozinski, Canadian Branch Reg'd, Saint Bruno, PQ, Canada

Freemasonry

University Book Exchange, Lowell, MA
Anthony G Ziagos Bookseller, Lowell, MA
Carolina Bookshop, Charlotte, NC
Irving M Roth, Antiques, Norwalk, OH

French History & Literature

Lucien Goldschmidt Inc, New York, NY
Le Valois Rare Books, New York, NY
Paulette Rose Ltd, New York, NY
Mary S Rosenberg, New York, NY
Liberty Rock Book Shoppe, Sloatsburg, NY
Akron Books, Akron, OH
Librairie Encyclopedique, Montreal, PQ, Canada

Fur Trading

Beaver Books, Daly City, CA
Ray Russell—Books, Rochester, MI
Joseph Patrick Books, Toronto, ON, Canada

Gardening & Horticulture

Marshall Vance Publisher-Bookseller, Forrest City, AR
Appletree Books, Williford, AR
Black Swan Books, Sacramento, CA
The Bookstall, San Francisco, CA
L S Kaiser Books—Chimney Sweep Books, Scotts Valley, CA
Calico Cat Bookshop, Ventura, CA
Robert Shuhi—Books, Morris, CT
Barbara Farnsworth Bookseller, West Cornwall, CT
Carroll Miner Robinson Old Books, Palm Beach, FL
Yesteryear Bookshop Inc, Atlanta, GA
Charlotte's Web Antiques, Monkton, MD
Second Life Books, Adams, MA
Robin Wilkerson Books, Auburndale, MA
Savoy Books, Salem, MA
The Wine & Food Library, Ann Arbor, MI

Edward C Fales Old & Rare Books & Manuscripts, Salisbury, NH
Hurley Books, Westmoreland, NH
Elisabeth Woodburn, Hopewell, NJ
Woodstock Ink, Placitas, NM
Albert Gutkin, New York, NY
Timothy Mawson, New York, NY
Robert E Underhill, Poughkeepsie, NY
Wentworth & Leggett Rare Books, Durham, NC
George D Brown—Books, Toledo, OH
G A Bibby Books, Gold Hill, OR
Molly Kirwan Books, Meadow Lands, PA
Anchor & Dolphin Books, Newport, RI
Pomona Book Exchange, Rockton, ON, Canada
Hortulus, Toronto, ON, Canada
Mostly Mysteries Books, Toronto, ON, Canada

Gastronomy. *See* Cookery & Gastronomy

Genealogy

Ostby's Americana, Bellflower, CA
Sharp's Bookstore, North Hollywood, CA
Howard Karno Books Inc, Santa Monica, CA
The Collective—Millet & Simpson Antiquarian Booksellers, Pueblo, CO
Old Mystic Bookshop, Old Mystic, CT
Aceto Bookmen, Sarasota, FL
G S Herron Books, Rome, GA
Dickey Books, Wichita, KS
Goodspeed's Bookshop Inc, Boston, MA
M Douglas Sackman, Deerfield, MA
James M Babcock Bookseller, Algonac, MI
Paul Henderson Books, Nashua, NH
Bookfinder—World-Wide Booksearch, Sea Isle City, NJ
C Virginia Barnes, New York, NY
Robert C Salathe, Mount Penn, PA
Dale W Starry Sr—Bookseller, Shippensburg, PA
Fortunate Finds Bookstore, Warwick, RI
The Book Shelf, Cleveland, TN
Tuttle Antiquarian Books Inc, Rutland, VT
Jennie's Book Nook, Alexandria, VA
Appalachian Bookshop, Bluefield, WV
Librairie D'Antan, Montreal, PQ, Canada

Geography

Mount Eden Books & Bindery, Hayward, CA
Robert Ross & Co, Woodland Hills, CA
Kenneth Nebenzahl Inc, Chicago, IL
The Antiquarian Shop, Stevens Point, WI
The Odd Book, Wolfville, NS, Canada

Geology & Mining

Ken Prag Paper Americana, Burlingame, CA
Mount Eden Books & Bindery, Hayward, CA
Hollywood Bookshop, Los Angeles, CA
Tolliver's Books, Los Angeles, CA
James G Leishman—Bookseller, Menlo Park, CA
Hammon's Archives & Artifacts, Sacramento, CA
Peri Lithon Books, San Diego, CA
The Book Habit, San Marcos, CA
The King's Market—Books & Prints, Boulder, CO
The Court Place Antiquarian Bookshop, Denver, CO
The Prospector, Littleton, CO
Geological Book Center, Falls Village, CT
Thomas Minckler Art & Books, Billings, MT
The Antiquarian Shop, Stevens Point, WI
Poe Bookshop, Mayaguez, PR

German History & Literature

Mary S Rosenberg, New York, NY
Peter Tumarkin Fine Books Inc, New York, NY
Akron Books, Akron, OH
Obsolescence, Gettysburg, PA

Graphic Arts

Albion Fine Prints, Berkeley, CA
Regent Street Books, Berkeley, CA
Sarkis Shmavonian Books & Prints, Berkeley, CA
California Book Auction Galleries, Los Angeles, CA
Richard L Press Fine & Scholarly Books, Sacramento, CA
Stonehill's Antiquarian Books, Champaign, IL
Carlson & Turner Books, Portland, ME
Pan Books & Graphics, Catskill, NY
Ex Libris, New York, NY
Arthur H Minters Inc, New York, NY

Greek History & Literature

David Ladner Books, Hamden, CT
John Bridge, Stamford, CT
Ex Libris Etcetera, Dover, NH

Guns. *See* Firearms, Guns & Weapons

History

Albion Fine Prints, Berkeley, CA
Vernon Howard Books, Burlingame, CA
Taylor Coffman Bookseller, Cambria, CA
Town & Gown Book Co, Dutch Flat, CA
Pacific Book Supply Co, Farmersville, CA
Xanadu Galleries Co, Glendale, CA
Merlin's Bookshop, Isla Vista, CA
Abbey Bookshop, Los Angeles, CA
California Book Auction Galleries, Los
   Angeles, CA
Cherokee Bookshop Inc, Los Angeles, CA
Dawson's Bookshop, Los Angeles, CA
"Otento" Books, San Diego, CA
Lion Bookshop, San Francisco, CA
Howard Karno Books Inc, Santa Monica, CA
Robert Ross & Co, Woodland Hills, CA
Henry A Clausen Bookshop, Colorado
   Springs, CO
Collectors' Center, Rare Books, Denver, CO
The Hermitage Antiquarian Bookshop,
   Denver, CO
Antique Books, Hamden, CT
Jan & Larry Malis, New Canaan, CT
I-Am-I-Books, Orange, CT
Park Road Bookshop, West Hartford, CT
Q M Dabney & Co Inc, Washington, DC
Book Warehouse Inc, Coral Gables, FL
Books & Art Prints Store, Miami, FL
Farley's Old & Rare Books, Pensacola, FL
Aceto Bookmen, Sarasota, FL
Red Horse at Ybor Square, Tampa, FL
AABS — Atlanta Antiquarian Booksellers,
   Atlanta, GA
The Old Book Scout — Jim McMeans, At-
   lanta, GA
Memorable Books, Stone Mountain, GA
Marshall Field & Co, Chicago, IL
Abraham's Books, Evanston, IL
Richard S Barnes & Co, Books, Evanston, IL
Kennedy's Bookshop, Evanston, IL
Historical Newspapers & Journals, Skokie,
   IL
Richard Owen Roberts Booksellers,
   Wheaton, IL
The Bookstack, Elkhart, IN
Lillian Berliawsky — Books, Camden, ME
B & B Smith — Booksellers, Mount Airy, MD
Shirley Balser 16th-20th Century Paintings,
   Prints & Books, Pikesville, MD
Books of Colonial America, Wheaton, MD
Second Life Books, Adams, MA
Philip Lozinski Scholarly Books, Westport,
   MA
George Tramp — Books, Jackson, MI
Ray Russell — Books, Rochester, MI
Exnowski Enterprises, Warren, MI
Melvin McCosh Bookseller, Excelsior, MN

The Book House Booksellers, Minneapolis,
   MN
Ross & Haines Old Books Co, Wayzata, MN
William M Hutter, Ocean Springs, MS
Glenn Books Inc, Kansas City, MO
R Dunaway, Bookseller, Saint Louis, MO
Anthony Garnett — Fine Books, Saint Louis,
   MO
Addison's Bookstore, Springfield, MO
Old Number Six Book Depot, Henniker, NH
Arthur Stiles, Hollis, NH
Richardson Books, Camden, NJ
Milton Kronovet, Lakewood, NJ
Acres of Books, Trenton, NJ
The London Bookshop, Albany, NY
Editions, Boiceville, NY
Old Editions Bookshop, Buffalo, NY
American Library Service, New City, NY
Noah Albay Company, New York, NY
Bookfinder's General Inc, New York, NY
Lion Heart Autographs Inc, New York, NY
James Lowe Autographs Ltd, New York, NY
Leona Rostenberg & Madeleine B Stern —
   Rare Books, New York, NY
Charlotte F Safir Books, New York, NY
Leo Weitz — Herbert E Weitz, New York, NY
Riverow Bookshop, Owego, NY
Colonial Out-of-Print Book Service, Pleasant-
   ville, NY
Collector's Antiques Inc, Port Washington,
   NY
Wentworth & Leggett Rare Books, Durham,
   NC
The Browsery, Greensboro, NC
Esther Isaacson, Velva, ND
Acres of Books Inc, Cincinnati, OH
L J Ryan — Scholarly Books, Columbus, OH
Kendall G Gaisser, Booksellers, Toledo, OH
Holland's Bookstore, Portland, OR
Lillian Kennedy Bookseller, Portland, OR
Longfellow's Book & Record Store, Port-
   land, OR
Robert F Batchelder, Ambler, PA
Book Haven, Lancaster, PA
Big John's Bookroom, Meshoppen, PA
Bernard Conwell Carlitz, Philadelphia, PA
Charles Sessler Inc, Philadelphia, PA
The Tuckers, Pittsburgh, PA
Lincoln Book Shoppe Inc & Lincoln Out-of-
   Print Book Search Ltd, Foster, RI
Merlin's Closet Inc, Providence, RI
Fortunate Finds Bookstore, Warwick, RI
Hampton Books, Newberry, SC
Burke's Bookstore, Inc, Memphis, TN
Mid-America Books, Memphis, TN
Colleen's Books & Things, Houston, TX
Jennie's Book Nook, Alexandria, VA
The Memorabilia Corner, Norfolk, VA
W B O'Neill — Old & Rare Books, Reston, VA

Books, Then & Now, Madison, WI
Spectrum Books & Records, Milwaukee, WI
The Antiquarian Shop, Stevens Point, WI
Johnson & Small Booksellers, Victoria, BC,
  Canada
Pandora's Books Ltd, Altona, MB, Canada
Pioneer Books, Steinbach, MB, Canada
Hugh Anson-Cartwright, Toronto, ON,
  Canada
Batta Bookstore, Toronto, ON, Canada
The Map Room, Exploration House, To-
  ronto, ON, Canada
Librairie D'Antan, Montreal, PQ, Canada
Librairie Faubourg — Quebec, Canadiana,
  Montreal, PQ, Canada

History, American

Van Allen Bradley Inc, Scottsdale, AZ
Serendipity Books Inc, Berkeley, CA
The Brick Row Book Shop, San Francisco,
  CA
Eldorado Books, San Francisco, CA
Transition Books, San Francisco, CA
Drew's Bookshop, Santa Barbara, CA
W J Bookunter, Denver, CO
William Reese Co, New Haven, CT
Avis & Rockwell Gardiner, Stamford, CT
Barry Scott, Stonington, CT
Barbara Farnsworth Bookseller, West
  Cornwall, CT
Cedric L Robinson, Bookseller, Windsor, CT
Yesteryear Bookshop Inc, Atlanta, GA
John Rybski Bookseller, Chicago, IL
Burkwood Books, Urbana, IL
Back Tracts Inc, Indianapolis, IN
F M O'Brien Old Book Shop, Portland, ME
Starr Book Co Inc, Boston, MA
Starr Bookshop Inc, Cambridge, MA
George Robert Minkoff Inc, Great Bar-
  rington, MA
Magnalia Americana, North Amherst, MA
Howard S Mott Inc, Sheffield, MA
Harold M Burstein, Antiquarian, Waltham,
  MA
Roger F Casavant, Wayland, MA
M & S Rare Books Inc, Weston, MA
Leaves of Grass, Ann Arbor, MI
Angelescu Book Service, Detroit, MI
Leland N Lien Bookseller, Minneapolis, MN
The Antiquarium, Omaha, NE
David L O'Neal, Antiquarian Booksellers
  Inc, Peterborough, NH
Heinoldt Books, Egg Harbor City, NJ
Past History, Lincroft, NJ
Joseph J Felcone Inc, Rare Books, Princeton,
  NJ
R A Petrilla, Booksellers, Roosevelt, NJ

Chafey's Old & Rare Books, Albuquerque,
  NM
Chaparral Books of Santa Fe, Santa Fe, NM
De La Pena Books, Santa Fe, NM
The London Bookshop, Albany, NY
L W Currey Rare Books Inc, Elizabethtown,
  NY
Wantagh Rare Book Co, Neversink, NY
Appelfeld Gallery, New York, NY
Carnegie Bookshop Inc, New York, NY
Stanley Gilman, New York, NY
S R Shapiro Co, Books for Libraries, New
  York, NY
Trebizond Rare Books, New York, NY
Nathaniel Cowen, Woodstock, NY
The Ancient Page, Asheville, NC
Sam Laidacker, Bloomsburg, PA
Battlefield Bookshop, Gettysburg, PA
R F Perotti, Rare Books, State College, PA
Patrick T Conley — Books, Cranston, RI
S Clyde King Rare & Out-of-Print Books,
  Providence, RI
W Thomas Taylor — Bookseller, Austin, TX
Montrose Bookshop, Houston, TX
George H Tweney, Books, Seattle, WA
Culpepper & Hanson Bookseller, Tacoma,
  WA
Arthur Wharton Books, Toronto, ON,
  Canada

History, Ancient

Krown & Spellman, Booksellers, Los
  Angeles, CA
John Bridge, Stamford, CT
B & B Smith — Booksellers, Mount Airy, MD
William H Schab Gallery Inc, New York, NY
Chris Fessler Bookseller, Theresa, NY
Akron Books, Akron, OH
The Allegory Bookshop, Woodstock, VT
Great Bridge Books Inc, Chesapeake, VA

History, English

The Ravenstree Co, Yuma, AZ
Serendipity Books Inc, Berkeley, CA
West Los Angeles Book Center, Los Angeles,
  CA
The Brick Row Book Shop, San Francisco,
  CA
Eldorado Books, San Francisco, CA
Transition Books, San Francisco, CA
Drew's Bookshop, Santa Barbara, CA
Maurice F Neville Rare Books, Santa Bar-
  bara, CA
William Reese Co, New Haven, CT
C A Stonehill Inc, New Haven, CT
Barry Scott, Stonington, CT

History, English (cont.)

Barbara Farnsworth Bookseller, West Cornwall, CT
The Bookfinders Inc, Miami Beach, FL
James M W Borg Inc, Chicago, IL
The London Bookshop, Chicago, IL
Van Norman Book Co, Galesburg, IL
Kelmscott Bookshop, Baltimore, MD
Starr Book Co Inc, Boston, MA
Starr Bookshop Inc, Cambridge, MA
George Robert Minkoff Inc, Great Barrington, MA
Irving Galis, Marblehead, MA
Stephen Scharoun, Newburyport, MA
Howard S Mott Inc, Sheffield, MA
Roger F Casavant, Wayland, MA
Hartfield Fine & Rare Books Ann Arbor, MI
Leaves of Grass, Ann Arbor, MI
Emery's Books, Contoocook, NH
John Hendsey, Bookseller, Epping, NH
Chafey's Old & Rare Books, Albuquerque, NM
The London Bookshop, Albany, NY
Roy W Clare, Getzville, NY
Charles Garvin Rare Books, Ithaca, NY
Appelfeld Gallery, New York, NY
Belanske & Levinger Inc, New York, NY
Trebizond Rare Books, New York, NY
Nathaniel Cowen, Woodstock, NY
Susan Heller Books, Cleveland, OH
Thomas Macaluso Rare & Fine Books, Kennett Square, PA
Murray Hudson—Books & Maps, Dyersburg, TN
W Thomas Taylor—Bookseller, Austin, TX
Montrose Bookshop, Houston, TX
Culpepper & Hanson Bookseller, Tacoma, WA

History, European

Volkoff & Von Hohenlohe, Santa Barbara, CA
Old Quenzel Store, Port Tobacco, MD
Leland N Lien Bookseller, Minneapolis, MN
Springwater Books & Antiques, Springwater, NY
The Ancient Page, Asheville, NC
William H Allen, Bookseller, Philadelphia, PA
Kuska House, Kingston, ON, Canada
D & E Lake Ltd Old & Rare Books, Toronto, ON, Canada
Librairie O Vieux Bouquins, Drummondville, PQ, Canada
Librairie Quebecoise, Montreal, PQ, Canada

Horses

Out-of-State Book Service, San Clemente, CA
Glover's Books, Lexington, KY
Ishtar Books, Canton, MA
Steve Finer—Books, Turners Falls, MA
Sydney R Smith Sporting Books, Canaan, NY
Bookfinder's General Inc, New York, NY
Bucephalus Books, New York, NY
James Cummins Bookseller Inc, New York, NY
Lyrical Ballad Bookstore, Saratoga Springs, NY
October Farm, Raleigh, NC
Tally Ho Studio, Canton, OH
The Ken-L-Questor, Newberg, OR
Arabest Bookshop, Big Bend, WI
Old Favorite Bookshop Ltd, Toronto, ON, Canada

Horticulture. See Gardening & Horticulture

Humanities

Ark Bookshop, Berkeley, CA
Taylor Coffman Bookseller, Cambria, CA
Ten O'Clock Books, Elkgrove, CA
Dianco International, Mill Valley, CA
Elliot's Books, Out of Print Specialists, Northford, CT
Joseph O'Gara Bookseller, Chicago, IL
Thomas W Burrows, Bookseller, Downers Grove, IL
Leekley Book Search, Winthrop Harbor, IL
Q M Dabney & Co, Rockville, MD
Pangloss Bookshop, Cambridge, MA
Philip Lozinski Scholarly Books, Westport, MA
The Book House Booksellers, Minneapolis, MN
Walter J Johnson Inc, Norwood, NJ
John C O'Connor, Tenafly, NJ
Chip's Bookshop Inc, New York, NY
Ideal Bookstore, New York, NY
International University Booksellers Inc, New York, NY
William H Schab Gallery Inc, New York, NY
William Salloch, Ossining, NY
The Good Times Bookshop, Port Jefferson, NY
Annemarie Schnase Antiquarian Bookseller & Publisher, Scarsdale, NY
Hammer Mountain Book Halls, Schenectady, NY
Howard O Berg, Devils Lake, ND
Douglas Gunn—Books, Wooster, OH

Holland's Bookstore, Portland, OR
Detering Book Gallery, Houston, TX
William Hoffer Bookseller, Vancouver, BC, Canada

Humor

Marshall Vance Publisher-Bookseller, Forrest City, AR
Apollo Book Shop, Costa Mesa, CA
Merlin's Bookshop, Isla Vista, CA
Pettler & Lieberman, Booksellers, Los Angeles, CA
West Los Angeles Book Center, Los Angeles, CA
The Bookie Joint, Reseda, CA
Jumping Frog, Hartford, CT
McBride First Editions, Hartford, CT
A Blue Moon Books & Records, Clearwater, FL
Wallace A Robinson, Saint Petersburg, FL
Bookman's Alley, Evanston, IL
Pied Piper Bookstore, Wichita, KS
Omega Books, Northampton, MA
Books & Stuff, Pearl, MS
Lorraine Galinsky, Cold Spring Harbor, NY
Ada Book Stall, Ada, OK
Book Stall, Norman, OK
Shawnee Book Stall, Shawnee, OK
Big D Books & Comics, Dallas, TX
Collector's Museum & Market, Taft, TX
Nostalgia Plus, Richmond, VA
The Comic Character Shop, Seattle, WA
Gasoline Alley Antiques, Seattle, WA

Hunting, Fishing & Angling

Jack Bailes—Books, Eureka Springs, AR
Adams Angling Books & Paraphernalia, Berkeley, CA
McLaughlin's Books, Chico, CA
Aviation Bookmobile—Mil-Air Photos & Books, Compton, CA
Trophy Room Books—Big Game Hunting Books, Encino, CA
Valley Book City, North Hollywood, CA
Five Quail Books, Rancho Santa Fe, CA
Just Books and . . . , Sacramento, CA
Family Bookstore, Whittier, CA
The Prospector, Littleton, CO
Angler's & Shooter's Bookshelf, Goshen, CT
A Cabinet of Books, Watertown, CT
Fleuron Books, Longboat Key, FL
Carroll Miner Robinson Old Books, Palm Beach, FL
P R Rieber, Thomasville, GA
Creedmoor Bookstore, Chicago, IL
Fur Fin Feather Books, Lansing, IL

The Bookstack, Elkhart, IN
Bedford's Used Books, Ellsworth, ME
Bunkhouse Books, Gardiner, ME
The Printers' Devil, Arlington, MA
Kenneth Andersen—Books, Auburn, MA
Book & Tackle Shop, Chestnut Hill, MA
The Open Creel, Palmer, MA
Bryant's, Provincetown, MA
Gustave H Suhm Book-Tique, Westfield, MA
Gunnerman Books, Auburn Heights, MI
Global Book Research, Belding, MI
Memory Aisle, Grand Rapids, MI
Highwood Bookshop, Traverse City, MI
Callahan & Co Booksellers, Temple, NH
Ernest S Hickok, Summit, NJ
The Question Mark, Albany, NY
Paul J Drabeck, Bronx, NY
Sydney R Smith Sporting Books, Canaan, NY
A Collector's Library, Hilton, NY
Carriage House Books, Kirkwood, NY
James Cummins Bookseller Inc, New York, NY
Wildwood Enterprises, Old Forge, NY
High Ridge Corner, Rye, NY
Morris Heller, Swan Lake, NY
George D Brown—Books, Toledo, OH
Carol Butcher, Youngstown, OH
Melvin Marcher—Bookseller, Oklahoma City, OK
Ernest L Sackett, Grants Pass, OR
William H Powers, Export, PA
R F Selgas Sporting Books, Hershey, PA
Molly Kirwan Books, Meadow Lands, PA
Franklin M Roshon, Pottstown, PA
F M Hill—Books, Kingsport, TN
Gary L Estabrook—Books, Vancouver, WA
The Antiquarian Shop, Stevens Point, WI
Sportsman's Cabinet, Manotick, ON, Canada

Illuminated Manuscripts. *See* Manuscripts, Medieval & Illuminated

Illustrated Books. *See* Art; Color Plate Books; Press Books & Fine Printing

Incunabula & Early Printing

Bennett & Marshall, Los Angeles, CA
California Book Auction Galleries, Los Angeles, CA
Caravan Bookstore, Los Angeles, CA
William & Victoria Dailey, Los Angeles, CA
Heritage Bookshop Inc, Los Angeles, CA
Kenneth Karmiole, Bookseller Inc, Los Angeles, CA

Incunabula (cont.)

Samuel W Katz, Los Angeles, CA
Krown & Spellman, Booksellers, Los
Angeles, CA
O P Reed Jr, Los Angeles, CA
Kurt L Schwarz, Los Angeles, CA
James G Leishman—Bookseller, Menlo Park,
CA
Book Sail, Orange, CA
William P Wreden, Books & Manuscripts,
Palo Alto, CA
John Roby, San Diego, CA
Meyer Boswell Books, San Francisco, CA
John Howell—Books, San Francisco, CA
Frank L Kovacs Archaeology Books, San
Francisco, CA
Jeremy Norman & Co Inc, San Francisco,
CA
Randall House, San Francisco, CA
Bernard M Rosenthal Inc, San Francisco, CA
L S Kaiser Books—Chimney Sweep Books,
Scotts Valley, CA
Rudolph William Sabbot—Natural History
Books, Woodland Hills, CA
W J Bookunter, Denver, CO
The Antiquarium, Bethany, CT
Whitlock Farm Booksellers, Bethany, CT
The Book Block, Cos Cob, CT
R & D Emerson, Falls Village, CT
Angler's & Shooter's Bookshelf, Goshen, CT
C A Stonehill Inc, New Haven, CT
Laurence Witten Rare Books, Southport, CT
Second Story Books, Washington, DC
Rare Books, Maps & Prints, Saint Augustine,
FL
Lighthouse Books, Saint Petersburg, FL
Harvey Dan Abrams—Booksellers, Atlanta,
GA
Julian Burnett Books, Atlanta, GA
H Popinski Books, Berwyn, IL
Hamill & Barker, Chicago, IL
Kenneth Nebenzahl Inc, Chicago, IL
Harry L Stern Ltd, Chicago, IL
Richard Owen Roberts Booksellers,
Wheaton, IL
Gary L Steigerwald Bookseller, Bloomington,
IN
Barnette's Books, South Bend, IN
Philatelic Bibliopole, Louisville, KY
Winter Farm Books, Pittsfield, ME
Chirurgical Bookshop, Baltimore, MD
Cecil Archer Rush, Baltimore, MD
Second Story Books, Bethesda, MD
The Old Printed Word, Kensington, MD
Ars Libri Ltd, Boston, MA
Atlantic Book Service, Boston, MA
Bromer Booksellers Inc, Boston, MA
Maury A Bromsen Associates Inc, Boston,
MA

Goodspeed's Bookshop Inc, Boston, MA
Brookline Village Books & Prints, Brookline,
MA
Hingham Book House, Hingham, MA
Gordon Totty—Scarce Paper Americana,
Lunenburg, MA
The Rendells Inc, Newton, MA
Isaiah Thomas Books & Prints, Worcester,
MA
Jeffrey D Mancevice Inc, Worcester, MA
James M Babcock Bookseller, Algonac, MI
The Wine & Food Library, Ann Arbor, MI
Einer Nisula—Rare Books, Okemos, MI
The Current Company, Minneapolis, MN
Oudal Bookshop, Minneapolis, MN
The Bookseller—Columbia, Columbia, MO
D Halloran Books, Saint Louis, MO
Mostly Books, Omaha, NE
Bauman Rare Books, Atlantic City, NJ
Leonard Balish, Englewood, NJ
P M Bookshop, Plainfield, NJ
Witherspoon Art & Bookstore, Princeton,
NJ
Hobbit Rare Books, Westfield, NJ
Albert Saifer, West Orange, NJ
Far Country Bookstore, Albany, NY
Reston's Booknook, Amsterdam, NY
Lawrence Feinberg Rare Books & Manu-
scripts, Brooklyn, NY
Mahoney & Weekly, Booksellers, Buffalo,
NY
John C Huckans Rare Books—Pan American
Books, Cazenovia, NY
N & N Pavlov, Dobbs Ferry, NY
Fly Creek Bookstall, Fly Creek, NY
Biblion Inc, Forest Hills, NY
Theoria Scholarly Books, Forest Hills, NY
Roy W Clare, Getzville, NY
Charles Dvorak—Book Dealer, Glen Head,
NY
Xerxes Books, Glen Head, NY
Victor Tamerlis, Mamaroneck, NY
Antiquarian Booksellers' Center, New York,
NY
C Virginia Barnes—Bookseller, New York,
NY
J N Bartfield Books Inc, New York, NY
Martin Breslauer Inc, New York, NY
Carnegie Bookshop Inc, New York, NY
James Cummins Bookseller Inc, New York,
NY
Peter Thomas Fisher—Bookseller, New
York, NY
Lathrop C Harper Inc, New York, NY
Jonathan A Hill, Bookseller, New York, NY
H P Kraus Books, New York, NY
William H Schab Gallery Inc, New York,
NY
Justin G Schiller Ltd, New York, NY
E K Schreiber, New York, NY

S R Shapiro Co, Books for Libraries, New York, NY
Peter Tumarkin Fine Books Inc, New York, NY
University Place Bookshop, New York, NY
Weyhe Art Books Inc, New York, NY
William Salloch, Ossining, NY
Southampton Book Co, Southampton, NY
Springwater Books & Antiques, Springwater, NY
Trojan Books, Troy, NY
Stagecoach Antiques, Akron, OH
Barbara Agranoff Books, Cincinnati, OH
Ohio Bookstore, Cincinnati, OH
Paul H North Jr, Columbus, OH
Ohio Bookhunter, Mansfield, OH
Aladdin Book Shoppe, Oklahoma City, OK
Blue Dragon Book Shop, Ashland, OR
The Family Album, Glen Rock, PA
Thomas Macaluso Rare & Fine Books, Kennett Square, PA
Bernard Conwell Carlitz, Philadelphia, PA
Schuylkill Book & Curio Shop, Philadelphia, PA
Schoyer's Books, Pittsburgh, PA
F Thomas Heller Rare Books, Swarthmore, PA
Walter Axelrod, Providence, RI
Noah's Ark Book Attic, Greenwood, SC
W Thomas Taylor—Bookseller, Austin, TX
Ray S Walton—Rare Books, Austin, TX
David Grossblatt Bookseller, Dallas, TX
Journey, Seattle, WA
Pegasus Books & Press, Vashon, WA
Spaightwood Galleries, Madison, WI
Hortulus, Toronto, ON, Canada
The Map Room, Exploration House, Toronto, ON, Canada

Industry & Labor

Bibliomania, Berkeley, CA
William Bledsoe, Bookseller, San Carlos, CA
Boleriem Books, San Francisco, CA
Carmel Bookshop, Lapel, IN
Timothy Trace, Peekskill, NY
Graedon Books Inc, New Hope, PA

Interior Design

The Court Place Antiquarian Bookshop, Denver, CO
Richard E Donovan, Endicott, NY
Weyhe Art Books Inc, New York, NY

Irish History & Literature

House of Books, Anaheim, CA
Chimney Sweep Books, Scotts Valley, CA

J & J O'Donoghue Books, Anoka, MN
The Bookmailer, Minneapolis, MN
Rivendell Bookshop Ltd, New York, NY
Liberty Rock Book Shoppe, Sloatsburg, NY
Cumberland Literary Agency, Nashville, TN
Aislinn: Irish Books & Research, Bennington, VT
Auld Stone Bookshop, Glasgow, VA
J Patrick McGahern—Books, Inc, Ottawa, ON, Canada

Japan

Hammon's Archives & Artifacts, Sacramento, CA
Cecil Archer Rush, Baltimore, MD
Noah Albay Company, New York, NY

Judaica & Hebraica

Harold B Diamond—Bookseller, Burbank, CA
The Bookie Joint, Reseda, CA
David Ladner Books, Hamden, CT
George A Bernstein, Brooklyn, NY
Louis Ginsberg—Books & Prints, Petersburg, VA
Yesterday's Memories Book & Old Record Shop, Milwaukee, WI

Juveniles. See Children's Books

Korea & Vietnam

Rair Literature, Encinitas, CA
Richard T Jordan Antiquariat, Flushing, NY

Labor History. See Industry & Labor

Landscape Architecture

Landscape Books, Exeter, NH
John H Stubbs Rare Books & Prints, New York, NY
Anchor & Dolphin Books, Newport, RI
Hortulus, Toronto, ON, Canada

Latin America

Harold B Diamond—Bookseller, Burbank, CA
Abbey Bookshop, Los Angeles, CA
Samuel W Katz, Los Angeles, CA
Sun Dance Books, Los Angeles, CA
Libros Latinos, Redlands, CA
The Brick Row Book Shop, San Francisco, CA

Latin America (cont.)

Haight Street Bookshop, San Francisco, CA
Howard Karno Books Inc, Santa Monica, CA
David Ladner Books, Hamden, CT
A Blue Moon Books & Records, Clearwater, FL
Vivian Kantor, Bookseller, Gainesville, FL
Demerara Book Service, Miami, FL
Lighthouse Books, Saint Petersburg, FL
David McCord Books, Atlanta, GA
John Rybski Bookseller, Chicago, IL
McBlain Books, Des Moines, IA
Maury A Bromsen Associates Inc, Boston, MA
George Tramp—Books, Jackson, MI
Ken Lopez Bookseller, Englewood, NJ
Jane Zwisohn Books, Albuquerque, NM
De La Pena Books, Santa Fe, NM
Lawrence Feinberg Rare Books & Manuscripts, Brooklyn, NY
Pan American Books, Cazenovia, NY
El Cascajero, The Old Spanish Book Mine, New York, NY
Richard C Ramer Old & Rare Books, New York, NY
S R Shapiro Co, Books for Libraries, New York, NY
Arthur Scharf, Travel Books, Pittsburgh, PA
Clark Wright Bookdealer, Waxahachie, TX

Law

Roy Bleiweiss Fine Books, Berkeley, CA
Town & Gown Book Co, Dutch Flat, CA
The Beautiful & the Unusual, Redondo Beach, CA
Boleriem Books, San Francisco, CA
Meyer Boswell Books, San Francisco, CA
W J Bookunter, Denver, CO
Fred B Rothman & Co, Littleton, CO
Q M Dabney & Co Inc, Washington, DC
Richard Adamiak, Chicago, IL
Q M Dabney & Co, Rockville, MD
A E Maxted, Cohasset, MA
Magnalia Americana, North Amherst, MA
Robert H Rubin Books, Stoughton, MA
Western Hemisphere Inc, Stoughton, MA
Oceana Publications Inc, Dobbs Ferry, NY
Bookfinder's General Inc, New York, NY
Sterling Valley Antiquities at Homestead Antiques, Syracuse, NY
Brandywine Books, Saxton, PA
Patrick T Conley—Books, Cranston, RI
Louis Ginsberg—Books & Prints, Petersburg, VA
D & E Lake Ltd Old & Rare Books, Toronto, ON, Canada

Linguistics

Theoria Scholarly Books, Forest Hills, NY
Bookfinder's General Inc, New York, NY
Atticus Books, Toronto, ON, Canada

Literary Criticism

Dickson Street Bookshop, Fayetteville, AR
The Invisible Bookman, Berkeley, CA
The Book Cellar, Fullerton, CA
G F Gustin Jr Books, Pasadena, CA
Transition Books, San Francisco, CA
Drew's Bookshop, Santa Barbara, CA
221 Books, Westlake Village, CA
David Ladner Books, Hamden, CT
John William Martin—Bookseller, La Grange, IL
Cogitator Books, Libertyville, IL
William S Johnson Books, Indianapolis, IN
Melvin McCosh Bookseller, Excelsior, MN
James & Mary Laurie Booksellers, Minneapolis, MN
Main Street Booksellers, Brooklyn, NY
Lorraine Galinsky, Cold Spring Harbor, NY
Book 'n Things, New York, NY
Chip's Bookshop Inc, New York, NY
Gramercy Book Shop, New York, NY
Glenn Armitage, Miamisburg, OH
T J McCauley Books, Langhorne, PA
The Tuckers, Pittsburgh, PA
Patrick T Conley—Books, Cranston, RI
Lincoln Book Shoppe Inc & Lincoln Out-of-Print Book Search Ltd, Foster, RI
Constant Reader Bookshop Ltd, Milwaukee, WI
Avenue Bookshop, Ottawa, ON, Canada
Atticus Books, Toronto, ON, Canada

Literature

Harold B Diamond—Bookseller, Burbank, CA
The Novel Experience, San Luis Obispo, CA
Booked Up Inc, Washington, DC
Marshall Field & Co, Chicago, IL
Douglas D Martin, Chicago, IL
James & Mary Laurie Booksellers, Minneapolis, MN
7 Terrace Drive, Hastings-on-Hudson, NY
Littwin & Feiden, Mamaroneck, NY
Antiquarian Booksellers' Center, New York, NY
Barnstable Books Inc, New York, NY
John F Fleming Inc, New York, NY
Ralph D Gardner, New York, NY
Stanley Gilman, New York, NY
Jonathan A Hill, Bookseller, New York, NY

Anna Sosenko Inc, New York, NY
Daniel Stokes, New York, NY
The Allegory Bookshop, Woodstock, VT
Great Bridge Books Inc, Chesapeake, VA

Literature, American

Van Allen Bradley Inc, Scottsdale, AZ
Robert Allen Books, Altadena, CA
Serendipity Books Inc, Berkeley, CA
James Hansen Books, Carlsbad, CA
William P Wreden, Books & Manuscripts,
 Palo Alto, CA
Maxwell Hunley, Pasadena, CA
Robert Larkin Link Bookseller, Redding, CA
The Brick Row Book Shop, San Francisco,
 CA
Eldorado Books, San Francisco, CA
Transition Books, San Francisco, CA
Drew's Bookshop, Santa Barbara, CA
Pepper & Stern—Rare Books Inc, Santa
 Barbara, CA
W J Bookunter, Denver, CO
William Reese Co, New Haven, CT
Avis & Rockwell Gardiner, Stamford, CT
Barry Scott, Stonington, CT
Barbara Farnsworth Bookseller, West
 Cornwall, CT
Cedric L Robinson, Bookseller, Windsor, CT
Yesteryear Bookshop Inc, Atlanta, GA
Pacific Book House, Honolulu, HI
John Rybski Bookseller, Chicago, IL
Burkwood Books, Urbana, IL
Back Tracts Inc, Indianapolis, IN
F M O'Brien Old Book Shop, Portland, ME
Starr Book Co Inc, Boston, MA
In Our Time, Cambridge, MA
Starr Bookshop Inc, Cambridge, MA
George Robert Minkoff Inc, Great Bar-
 rington, MA
Magnalia Americana, North Amherst, MA
Savoy Books, Salem, MA
Pepper & Stern—Rare Books, Inc, Sharon,
 MA
Howard S Mott Inc, Sheffield, MA
Harold M Burstein, Antiquarian, Waltham,
 MA
Roger F Casavant, Wayland, MA
M & S Rare Books Inc, Weston, MA
Leaves of Grass, Ann Arbor, MI
Angelescu Book Service, Detroit, MI
Leland N Lien Bookseller, Minneapolis, MN
Addison's Bookstore, Springfield, MO
The Antiquarium, Omaha, NE
David L O'Neal, Antiquarian Booksellers
 Inc, Peterborough, NH
Antic Hay Books, Fairfield, NJ
Past History, Lincroft, NJ

Joseph J Felcone Inc, Rare Books, Princeton,
 NJ
R A Petrilla, Booksellers, Roosevelt, NJ
Chafey's Old & Rare Books, Albuquerque,
 NM
Chaparral Books of Santa, Fe, Santa Fe, NM
The London Bookshop, Albany, NY
L W Currey Rare Books Inc, Elizabethtown,
 NY
Wantagh Rare Book Co, Neversink, NY
Appelfeld Gallery, New York, NY
William G Boyer, New York, NY
Carnegie Bookshop Inc, New York, NY
Gramercy Book Shop, New York, NY
Trebizond Rare Books, New York, NY
Liberty Rock Book Shoppe, Sloatsburg, NY
Nathaniel Cowen, Woodstock, NY
The Ancient Page, Asheville, NC
Old Oregon Bookstore, Portland, OR
Sam Laidacker, Bloomsburg, PA
James S Jaffe, Rare Books, Haverford, PA
George S MacManus Co, Philadelphia, PA
The Americanist, Pottstown, PA
R F Perotti, Rare Books, State College, PA
Patrick T Conley—Books, Cranston, RI
S Clyde King Rare & Out-of-Print Books,
 Providence, RI
The Wayside Bookshop, Westerly, RI
W Thomas Taylor—Bookseller, Austin, TX
Montrose Bookshop, Houston, TX
George H Tweney, Books, Seattle, WA
Culpepper & Hanson Bookseller, Tacoma,
 WA
Terry Rutherford Bookseller, Vancouver, BC,
 Canada
Steven Temple, Toronto, ON, Canada
Arthur Wharton Books, Toronto, ON,
 Canada

Literature, Canadian

William Hoffer Bookseller, Vancouver, BC,
 Canada
Steven Temple, Toronto, ON, Canada
Arthur Wharton Books, Toronto, ON,
 Canada

Literature, English

The Ravenstree Co, Yuma, AZ
Robert Allen Books, Altadena, CA
Serendipity Books Inc, Berkeley, CA
James Hansen Books, Carlsbad, CA
West Los Angeles Book Center, Los Angeles,
 CA
William P Wreden, Books & Manuscripts,
 Palo Alto, CA
Maxwell Hunley, Pasadena, CA

Literature, English (cont.)

Robert Larkin Link Bookseller, Redding, CA
The Brick Row Book Shop, San Francisco, CA
John Parke Custis Booksellers, San Francisco, CA
Eldorado Books, San Francisco, CA
Transition Books, San Francisco, CA
A S Fischler—Rare Books, San Jose, CA
Drew's Bookshop, Santa Barbara, CA
Maurice F Neville Rare Books, Santa Barbara, CA
Pepper & Stern—Rare Books Inc, Santa Barbara, CA
William Reese Co, New Haven, CT
C A Stonehill Inc, New Haven CT
Barry Scott, Stonington, CT
Barbara Farnsworth Bookseller, West Cornwall, CT
The Bookfinders Inc, Miami Beach, FL
Pacific Book House, Honolulu, HI
James M W Borg Inc, Chicago, IL
The London Bookshop, Chicago, IL
Van Norman Book Co, Galesburg, IL
Kelmscott Bookshop, Baltimore, MD
Starr Book Co Inc, Boston, MA
In Our Time, Cambridge, MA
Starr Bookshop Inc, Cambridge, MA
George Robert Minkoff Inc, Great Barrington, MA
Irving Galis, Marblehead, MA
Stephen Scharoun, Newburyport, MA
Savoy Books, Salem, MA
Pepper & Stern—Rare Books Inc, Sharon, MA
Howard S Mott Inc, Sheffield, MA
Roger F Casavant, Wayland, MA
Hartfield Fine & Rare Books, Ann Arbor, MI
Leaves of Grass, Ann Arbor, MI
Anthony Garnett—Fine Books, Saint Louis, MO
Addison's Bookstore, Springfield, MO
Emery's Books, Contoocook, NH
John F Hendsey, Bookseller, Epping, NH
Antic Hay Books, Fairfield, NJ
R A Petrilla, Booksellers, Roosevelt, NJ
Chafey's Old & Rare Books, Albuquerque, NM
The London Bookshop, Albany, NY
Charles Garvin Rare Books, Ithaca, NY
Appelfeld Gallery, New York, NY
Belanske & Levinger Inc, New York, NY
Gramercy Book Shop, New York, NY
Trebizond Rare Books, New York, NY
Liberty Rock Book Shoppe, Sloatsburg, NY
Nathaniel Cowen, Woodstock, NY
Susan Heller Books, Cleveland, OH
Old Oregon Bookstore, Portland, OR
James S Jaffe, Rare Books, Haverford, PA
Thomas Macaluso Rare & Fine Books, Kennett Square, PA
George S MacManus Co, Philadelphia, PA
The Wayside Bookshop, Westerly, RI
Murray Hudson—Books & Maps, Dyersburg, TN
W Thomas Taylor—Bookseller, Austin, TX
Montrose Bookshop, Houston, TX
Culpepper & Hanson Bookseller, Tacoma, WA
Terry Rutherford Bookseller, Vancouver, BC, Canada
Steven Temple, Toronto, ON, Canada

Literature, Foreign

Peter Thomas Fisher—Bookseller, New York, NY
The Americanist, Pottstown, PA

Literature, 17th Century

Ark Bookshop, Berkeley, CA
Alan Wofsy Fine Arts, San Francisco, CA
Ximenes: Rare Books Inc, New York, NY

Literature, 18th Century

Ark Bookshop, Berkeley, CA
Alan Wofsy Fine Arts, San Francisco, CA
Deborah Benson Bookseller, West Cornwall, CT
Hartfield Fine & Rare Books, Ann Arbor, MI
Ken Lopez Bookseller, Englewood, NJ
Daniel Hirsch, Hopewell Junction, NY
Ximenes: Rare Books Inc, New York, NY
Palinarus Antiquarian Books, Philadelphia, PA
Woodspurge Books, Spartanburg, SC
Ken Leach, Brattleboro, VT

Literature, 19th Century

Sarkis Shmavonian Books & Prints, Berkeley, CA
John Parke Custis Booksellers, San Francisco, CA
Alan Wofsy Fine Arts, San Francisco, CA
Deborah Benson Bookseller, West Cornwall, CT
Lucile Coleman, Books, A-to-Z Service, North Miami, FL
A Collector's Book Shop, New Orleans, LA
Boston Book Annex, Boston, MA
Ahab Rare Books, Cambridge, MA
The Dawn Treader Book Shop, Ann Arbor, MI

Hartfield Fine & Rare Books, Ann Arbor, MI
Don Allen, Three Oaks, MI
Daniel Hirsch, Hopewell Junction, NY
Johnson & O'Donnell, Rare Books, Liverpool, NY
Paul P Appel, Mount Vernon, NY
James Cummins Bookseller Inc, New York, NY
Paulette Greene, Rockville Centre, NY
Johnson & O'Donnell Rare Books Ltd, Syracuse, NY
The Scribbling Bookmonger, West Shokan, NY
Woodspurge Books, Spartanburg, SC
Limestone Hills Bookshop, Glen Rose, TX
Norumbega Books, Houston, TX
Ken Leach, Brattleboro, VT
David Mason Books, Toronto, ON, Canada

Literature, 20th Century

Peninsula Booksearch, Burlingame, CA
Richard Gilbo—Books, Carpenteria, CA
Sal Noto—Books, Cupertino, CA
Danville Books, Danville, CA
P F Mullins Books, Encinitas, CA
William Riley—Books, Kensington, CA
The Book Nest, Los Altos, CA
O P Reed Jr, Los Angeles, CA
The Scholarly Bookfinders, Los Angeles, CA
Sylvester & Orphanos, Los Angeles, CA
Book Carnival, Orange, CA
Fain's First Editions, Pacific Palisades, CA
Libra Books, Reseda, CA
Chloe's Bookstore, Sacramento, CA
Atticus Books, San Diego, CA
Wahrenbrock's Book House, San Diego, CA
Arkadyan Books & Prints, San Francisco, CA
Transition Books, San Francisco, CA
Alan Wofsy Fine Arts, San Francisco, CA
Harmon Books, San Jose, CA
Perry's Antiques & Books, San Jose, CA
Joseph the Provider Books, Santa Barbara, CA
Maurice F Neville Rare Books, Santa Barbara, CA
Sebastopol Book Shop, Sebastopol, CA
Bay Side Books, Soquel, CA
Lois St Clair, Van Nuys, CA
James M Dourgarian, Bookman, Walnut Creek, CA
Gilann Books, Darien, CT
Pharos Books-Fine First Editions, New Haven, CT
Deborah Benson Bookseller, West Cornwall, CT
Demerara Book Service, Miami, FL

Lucile Coleman, Books, A-to-Z Service, North Miami, FL
Memorable Books, Stone Mountain, GA
Richard S Barnes & Co, Books, Evanston, IL
Bookman's Alley, Evanston, IL
Thomas J Joyce & Co, Geneva, IL
Titles Inc, Highland Park, IL
Leekley Book Search, Winthrop Harbor, IL
The Haunted Bookshop, Iowa City, IA
Dickey Books, Wichita, KS
S-T Associates, Louisville, KY
A Collector's Book Shop, New Orleans, LA
Quill & Brush Bookstore, Bethesda, MD
Firstborn Books, Galesville, MD
Steven C Bernard First Editions, Rockville, MD
Allston Bookshop, Allston, MA
Boston Book Annex, Boston, MA
E Wharton & Co, Boston, MA
In Our Time, Cambridge, MA
Waiting for Godot Books, Cambridge, MA
Joseph A Dermont Fine Books, Onset, MA
The Dawn Treader Book Shop, Ann Arbor, MI
Don's Bookstore & Black Letter Press, Grand Rapids, MI
Dinkytown Antiquarian Bookshop, Minneapolis, MN
Columbia Books, Columbia, MO
H L Prosser Bibliophile, Professional Appraiser & Collector, Springfield, MO
Colophon Bookshop, Epping, NH
Stephen Koschal Autographs & Signed Books, Verona, NJ
Nicholas Potter, Bookseller, Santa Fe, NM
Bev Chaney Jr, Books, Croton-on-Hudson, NY
Roy Young Bookseller, Dobbs Ferry, NY
Bernice Weiss—Rare Books, Eastchester, NY
L W Currey Rare Books Inc, Elizabethtown, NY
Richard E Donovan, Endicott, NY
Riverrun, Hastings-on-Hudson, NY
Daniel Hirsch, Hopewell Junction, NY
Johnson & O'Donnell, Rare Books, Liverpool, NY
Paul P Appel, Mount Vernon, NY
Ampersand Books, New York, NY
Jordan Davies, Books, New York, NY
Gotham Book Mart & Gallery Inc, New York, NY
Gryphon Bookshop, New York, NY
Glenn Horowitz Bookseller Inc, New York, NY
House of Books Ltd, New York, NY
Kim Kaufman Bookseller, New York, NY
Maiden Voyage Books, New York, NY
Isaac Mendoza Book Co, New York, NY
Arthur H Minters, Inc, New York, NY

Literature, 20th Century (cont.)

James C Morel Fine Books, New York, NY
Bradford Morrow Bookseller, New York, NY
Pageant Book and Print Shop, New York, NY
Phoenix Bookshop, New York, NY
Carney Books, Oneonta, NY
Bibliomania, Schenectady, NY
Kevin T Ransom — Bookseller, Snyder, NY
Ridge Books, Stone Ridge, NY
Johnson & O'Donnell Rare Books Ltd, Syracuse, NY
Hoffman Lane Books, Troy, NY
Crows Nest Antique Mall, Durham, NC
H E Turlington Books, Pittsboro, NC
The Asphodel Bookshop, Burton, OH
Glenn Armitage, Miamisburg, OH
Longfellow's Book & Record Store, Portland, OR
D Sedenger Galleries, Huntingdon Valley, PA
J Howard Woolmer — Rare Books, Revere, PA
Merlin's Closet Inc, Providence, RI
Limestone Hills Bookshop, Glen Rose, TX
Gutenberg's Folly: Rare & Scholarly Books, San Antonio, TX
Daedalus Bookshop, Charlottesville, VA
The Associates — Modern First Editions, Falls Church, VA
M Taylor Bowie Bookseller, Seattle, WA
Robert L Brown Bookmonger, Seattle, WA
The Antiquarian Shop, Stevens Point, WI
Windhover Books, Vancouver, BC, Canada
Pioneer Books, Steinbach, MB, Canada
Mrs A L Ashton, Ottawa, ON, Canada
The Alphabet Bookshop, Toronto, ON, Canada
Batta Bookstore, Toronto, ON, Canada

Little Magazines

Sand Dollar Books, Albany, CA
Phoenix Bookshop, New York, NY

Magic & Conjuring

Aladdin Books & Memorabilia, Fullerton, CA
Valley Book City, North Hollywood, CA
Samadhi — Metaphysical Literature, Newberry, FL
J & J Lubrano, South Lee, MA
Steve Finer — Books, Turners Falls, MA
The Village Booksmith, Hudson Falls, NY
C Virginia Barnes — Bookseller, New York, NY
Richard Stoddard Performing Arts Books, New York, NY
C B Yohe — Conjuring Books, Bethel Park, PA

Manuscripts, Literary

Sand Dollar Books, Albany, CA
The Scriptorium, Beverly Hills, CA
Black Sun Books, New York, NY
John F Fleming Inc, New York, NY
Gotham Book Mart & Gallery Inc, New York, NY

Manuscripts, Medieval & Illuminated

Ben Sackheim — Rare Books & Fine Art, Tucson, AZ
Michael S Hollander Rare Books, San Rafael, CA
C A Stonehill Inc, New Haven, CT
Laurence Witten Rare Books, Southport, CT
Martin Breslauer Inc, New York, NY
Philip C Duschnes Inc, New York, NY

Maps, Atlases & Cartography

Roy V Boswell — Antiquarian Books & Maps, Fullerton, CA
Manuel Urrizola Old & Rare Maps & Atlases, Los Angeles, CA
Argonaut Bookshop, San Francisco, CA
Robert Ross & Co, Woodland Hills, CA
Branford Rare Book & Art Gallery, Branford, CT
Cartographics, North Stonington, CT
Avis & Rockwell Gardiner, Stamford, CT
The Old Print Gallery, Washington, DC
The Globe, Chicago, IL
Robert W Thompson — Books, Chicago, IL
Douglas N Harding, Wells, ME
Richard Fitch Old Maps & Prints & Books, Santa Fe, NM
W Graham Arader III, New York, NY
Albert Gutkin, New York, NY
H P Kraus Books, New York, NY
The Old Print Shop Inc, New York
Richard C Ramer Old & Rare Books, New York, NY
High Ridge Corner, Rye, NY
W Graham Arader III, King of Prussia, PA
William G Mayer Antiques, Pittsburgh, PA
Murray Hudson — Books & Maps, Dyersburg, TN
W Graham Arader III, Houston, TX
Cartographica, Houston, TX
The Map Room, Exploration House, Toronto, ON, Canada

Maritime. *See* **Nautical**

Mathematics

Merlin's Bookshop, Isla Vista, CA
Tolliver's Books, Los Angeles, CA
The Bookstall, San Francisco, CA
Bookfinder's General Inc, New York, NY
Stevens & Co Books Inc, New York, NY
Elgen Books, Rockville Centre, NY

Medicine

Bennett & Marshall, Los Angeles, CA
Samuel W Katz, Los Angeles, CA
Zeitlin & Ver Brugge Booksellers, Los
  Angeles, CA
Dianco International, Mill Valley, CA
The Beautiful & the Unusual, Redondo
  Beach, CA
John Howell—Books, San Francisco, CA
Jeremy Norman & Co Inc, San Francisco,
  CA
Howard Karno Books Inc, Santa Monica, CA
Edwin V Glaser Rare Books, Sausalito, CA
B & L Rootenberg Fine & Rare Books,
  Sherman Oaks, CA
The Court Place Antiquarian Bookshop,
  Denver, CO
The Antiquarium, Bethany, CT
Lawrence F Golder Rare Books, Collinsville,
  CT
John Woods Books—(Out of Print), Coven-
  try, CT
John M Skutel Rare Books, Fairfield, CT
Robert C Demarest Bookseller, Naples, FL
The Haunted Bookshop, Iowa City, IA
Chirurgical Bookshop, Baltimore, MD
Folkways Scholarly Books, Bethesda, MD
Old Hickory Bookshop Ltd, Brinklow, MD
E Donbullian Back Number Magazine Com-
  pany, Greenbelt, MD
The Antiquarian Scientist, Amesbury, MA
The Collector's Library, Arlington, MA
The Printer's Devil, Arlington, MA
Book & Tackle Shop, Chestnut Hill, MA
Newburyport Rare Books, Newburyport,
  MA
Second Fiddle Bookshop, Southbridge, MA
Trotting Hill Park Antiquarian Booksellers,
  Springfield, MA
Jeffrey D Mancevice Inc, Worcester, MA
The Science Bookshelf, Ann Arbor, MI
The Bookmailer, Minneapolis, MN
Scientia, Books in Science & Medicine,
  Minneapolis, MN
The Antiquarium, Omaha, NE
Old Number Six Book Depot, Henniker, NH
The Chatham Bookseller, Madison, NJ

Walter J Johnson Inc, Norwood, NJ
Lawrence Feinberg Rare Books & Manu-
  scripts, Brooklyn, NY
Hector's, Eastchester, NY
Biblion Inc, Forest Hills, NY
Roy W Clare, Getzville, NY
Karl Schick, Hartsdale, NY
Emil Offenbacher, Kew Gardens, NY
Argosy Bookstore Inc, New York, NY
Bookfinder's General Inc, New York, NY
Lathrop C Harper Inc, New York, NY
Jonathan A Hill, Bookseller, New York, NY
International University Booksellers Inc,
  New York, NY
Oscar Schreyer Books, New York, NY
Elgen Books, Rockville Centre, NY
Sterling Valley Antiquities at Homestead
  Antiques, Syracuse, NY
Chelsea Antiques, Durham, NC
Old Galen's Books, Durham, NC
Wentworth & Leggett Rare Books, Durham,
  NC
Autos & Autos—Book Dept, Elizabeth City,
  NC
Miran Arts & Books, Columbus, OH
Kendall G Gaisser, Booksellers, Toledo, OH
Bernard Conwell Carlitz, Philadelphia, PA
Bruce McKittrick, Rare Books, Philadelphia,
  PA
Schuylkill Book & Curio Shop, Philadelphia,
  PA
F Thomas Heller Rare Books, Swarthmore,
  PA
Old South Books, Memphis, TN
William Orbelo, San Antonio, TX
Louis Ginsberg—Books & Prints, Peters-
  burg, VA
McDuffie's Books, Opportunity, WA
McDuffie's Old Books, Spokane, WA
W Bruce Fye Antiquarian Medical Books,
  Marshfield, WI
Renaissance Book Shop Inc, Milwaukee, WI

Medieval Manuscripts. *See*
Manuscripts, Medieval &
Illuminated

Medieval Studies

Bernard M Rosenthal Inc, San Francisco, CA
Alfred F Zambelli, New York, NY
William H Allen, Bookseller, Philadelphia,
  PA
Avenue Bookshop, Ottawa, ON, Canada

Metaphysics. *See* **Occult &**
Metaphysics

Mexico

Abbey Bookshop, Los Angeles, CA
Samuel W Katz, Los Angeles, CA
Third World Ethnic Books, Los Angeles, CA
Tolliver's Books, Los Angeles, CA
The Brick Row Book Shop, San Francisco, CA
De La Pena Books, Santa Fe, NM
Frontier America Corporation, Bryan, TX
Joshua David Bowen, San Antonio, TX

Middle East

Hyman & Sons Rare Books, Los Angeles, CA
The Bookie Joint, Reseda, CA
Richard L Press Fine & Scholarly Books, Sacramento, CA
McBlain Books, Des Moines, IA
Asian Rare Books Inc, New York, NY
Noah Albay Company, New York, NY
S R Shapiro Co, Books for Libraries, New York, NY
W B O'Neill — Old & Rare Books, Reston, VA

Military

Aviation Bookmobile — Mil-Air Photos & Books, Compton, CA
New Albion Bookshop, Fairfax, CA
The Book Harbor, Fullerton, CA
Cherokee Bookshop Inc, Los Angeles, CA
The Globe Bookstore, Los Angeles, CA
Paul Hunt, Los Angeles, CA
West Los Angeles Book Center, Los Angeles, CA
Dianco International, Mill Valley, CA
Aviation Bookmobile — Mil-Air Photos & Books, Norwalk, CA
Just Books and . . . , Sacramento, CA
The Book Habit, San Marcos, CA
Book Vault, Santa Ana, CA
The Court Place Antiquarian Bookshop, Denver, CO
Lawrence F Golder Rare Books, Collinsville, CT
Robert Shuhi — Books, Morris, CT
N Flayderman & Co Inc, New Milford, CT
Stephen Auslender, Wilton, CT
Q M Dabney & Co Inc, Washington, DC
Tappin Book Mine, Atlantic Beach, FL
Eugene F Kramer, Jacksonville, FL
Farley's Old & Rare Books, Pensacola, FL
Historical Bookshelf Ltd, Plantation, FL
C R Sanders Jr, Saint Augustine, FL
Red Horse at Ybor Square, Tampa, FL

Collector's World, Atlanta, GA
Yesteryear Bookshop Inc, Atlanta, GA
H Popinski Books, Berwyn, IL
Kennedy's Bookshop, Evanston, IL
Bookstall of Rockford, Rockford, IL
Mason's Rare & Used Books, Wabash, IN
Q M Dabney & Co, Rockville, MD
Attic Books, Wheaton, MD
Gordon Totty — Scarce Paper Americana, Lunenburg, MA
Global Book Research, Belding, MI
Bygone Book House, Dearborn, MI
Ray Russell — Books, Rochester, MI
Ross & Haines Old Books Co, Wayzata, MN
ABC Theological Index, Springfield, MO
Page One Books, Buffalo, NY
Croton Book Service — Sportsman's Book Service, Croton-on-Hudson, NY
Carriage House Books, Kirkwood, NY
Bookfinder's General Inc, New York, NY
Peter Hlinka Historical Americana, New York, NY
The Military Bookman, New York, NY
Verkuilen Ager, Rochester, NY
Talbothays Books, Somers, NY
Jacques Noel Jacobson Jr Collectors — Antiquities Inc, Staten Island, NY
Lion Harvey Books, Wappingers Falls, NY
The Bookseller Inc, Akron, OH
Heritage Bookstore, Columbus, OH
J D S Books, Dayton, OH
Kendall G Gaisser, Booksellers, Toledo, OH
The Looking Glass, Worthington, OH
99-E Antique-Used, Woodburn, OR
William H Powers, Export, PA
Battlefield Bookshop, Gettysburg, PA
T J McCauley Books, Langhorne, PA
Molly Kirwan Books, Meadow Lands, PA
Brandywine Books, Saxton, PA
The Battery Book Shop, Nashville, TN
Tom Munnerlyn Books, Austin, TX
Antiquarian Book Mart, San Antonio, TX
William Orbelo, San Antonio, TX
Bookhouse, Arlington, VA
Schaefer Association, Arlington, VA
The Memorabilia Corner, Norfolk, VA
Louis Ginsberg — Books & Prints, Petersburg, VA
W B O'Neill — Old & Rare Books, Reston, VA
Interim Books, Bremerton, WA
Comstock's Bindery & Bookshop, Seattle, WA
Constant Reader Bookshop Ltd, Milwaukee, WI
Dancing Bear Antiquarian Bookshop & Paperback Exchange, Milwaukee, WI
Marven Somer Bookseller, Hamilton, ON, Canada

John W Smith Books, Hensall, ON, Canada
Headley Hannelore Old & Fine Books, Saint
  Catharines, ON, Canada
North Toronto Coins Ltd, Toronto, ON,
  Canada
Peter L Jackson—Military Books & Prints,
  Weston, ON, Canada

Miniature Books

Marshall Vance Publisher-Bookseller, Forrest
  City, AR
Lorson's Books & Prints, Fullerton, CA
Dawson's Bookshop, Los Angeles, CA
Alla T Ford Rare Books, Lake Worth, FL
Doris Frohnsdorff, Gaithersburg, MD
Bromer Booksellers Inc, Boston, MA

Modern Literature. *See* Literature, 20th Century

Mormons

The Book Cellar, Fullerton, CA
Wahrenbrock's Book House, San Diego, CA
Walt West Books, Provo, UT
Scallawagiana Books, Salt Lake City, UT

Mountains & Mountaineering

Live Oak Booksellers, Arcadia, CA
Vernon Howard Books, Burlingame, CA
Dawson's Bookshop, Los Angeles, CA
The Bookstall, San Francisco, CA
The King's Market—Books & Prints, Boul-
  der, CO
George Brosi Bookseller, Berea, KY
Kenneth Andersen—Books, Auburn, MA
Michael Dunn Books, Newport, VT
Appalachian Bookshop, Bluefield, WV
Tom Williams Books, Calgary, AB, Canada

Music

J B Muns, Books, Berkeley, CA
Vernon Howard Books, Burlingame, CA
Graeme Vanderstoel, El Cerrito, CA
Oscar Shapiro, Washington, DC
Omni Graphic Media Co, Hollywood, FL
The Bookfinders Inc, Miami Beach, FL
AABS-Atlanta Antiquarian Booksellers,
  Atlanta, GA
Book Search Service, Avondale Estates, GA
The Athenaeum, Evanston, IL
Dolphin Bookstore, Camden, ME
Firstborn Books, Galesville, MD
Imagination Books, Silver Spring, MD

Buddenbrooks Books Inc, Boston, MA
J & J Lubrano, South Lee, MA
Angelescu Book Service, Detroit, MI
Don Allen, Three Oaks, MI
Harry B Robinson Book Search Service,
  Columbia, MO
Book Barn, South Sioux City, NE
J & J Hanrahan, Portsmouth, NH
Bel Canto Bookshop, Metuchen, NJ
Vi & Si's Antiques, Clarence, NY
Academy Bookstore, New York, NY
Books 'n Things, New York, NY
Broude Brothers Limited, New York, NY
Jolly Roger Records & Music Books, New
  York, NY
Lion Heart Autographs Inc, New York, NY
James Lowe Autographs Ltd, New York, NY
Anna Sosenko Inc, New York, NY
Wurlitzer-Bruck, New York, NY
Colonial Out-of-Print Book Service, Pleasant-
  ville, NY
Annemarie Schnase Antiquarian Bookseller
  & Publisher, Scarsdale, NY
Liberty Rock Book Shoppe, Sloatsburg, NY ,
Lion Harvey Books, Wappingers Falls, NY
Kendall G Gaisser, Booksellers, Toledo, OH
Robert F Batchelder, Ambler, PA
Leonard Dixon Bookstore, San Antonio, TX
The Allegory Bookshop, Woodstock, VT
Book Bazaar, Ottawa, ON, Canada

Mystery & Detective Fiction

Janus Books Ltd, Tucson, AZ
The Book Baron, Anaheim, CA
Bibliomania, Berkeley, CA
New Albion Bookshop, Fairfax, CA
New Albion Rare Books, Fairfax, CA
Montroe Books, Fresno, CA
Ralston Popular Fiction, Fullerton, CA
Bryan Barrett Books, Hayward, CA
The Silver Door, Hermosa Beach, CA
Pettler & Lieberman, Booksellers, Los
  Angeles, CA
Vagabond Books, Los Angeles, CA
West Los Angeles Book Center, Los Angeles,
  CA
Rik Thompson—Books, Milpitas, CA
J & J Berger Booksellers, Oakland, CA
Book Carnival, Orange, CA
Book Sail, Orange, CA
Book Case Books, Pasadena, CA
Libra Books, Reseda, CA
The Mermaid—Books, Richmond, CA
Adams Avenue Bookstore, San Diego, CA
The Albatross Book Store, San Francisco, CA
Helan Halbach—Bookseller, Santa Barbara,
  CA

Mystery & Detective Fiction (cont.)

Pepper & Stern—Rare Books Inc, Santa Barbara, CA
Virginia Burgman, Santa Rosa, CA
Mainly Mysteries, Sherman Oaks, CA
The Court Place Antiquarian Bookshop, Denver, CO
Extensive Search Service, Danielson, CT
Blue Star Bookstore, Putnam, CT
McFarland Books, Tampa, FL
Lonnie E Evans—Books, Savannah, GA
Beasley Books, Chicago, IL
Douglas D Martin, Chicago, IL
Richard S Barnes & Co, Books, Evanston, IL
Yellowstone Books, Villa Park, IL
Forest Park Bookshop, Fort Wayne, IN
A Collector's Book Shop, New Orleans, LA
Andrew B W MacEwen and Aimee B MacEwen, Stockton Springs, ME
Key Books, Baltimore, MD
Imagination Books, Silver Spring, MD
Attic Books, Wheaton, MD
Buddenbrooks Books Inc, Boston, MA
R H Kristiansen Rare Books, Boston, MA
Starr Book Co Inc, Boston, MA
Pepper & Stern—Rare Books, Inc, Sharon, MA
The Dawn Treader Book Shop, Ann Arbor, MI
The Fine Books Co & David Aronovitz—Books, Rochester, MI
J & J O'Donoghue Books, Anoka, MN
S & S Books, Saint Paul, MN
Sykes & Flanders Old & Rare Books, Weare, NH
Nationwide Book Service, Brooklyn, NY
Claude Held, Buffalo, NY
7 Terrace Drive, Hastings-on-Hudson, NY
H & R Salerno, Hauppauge, NY
Charles Garvin Rare Books, Ithaca, NY
Isaac Mendoza Book Co, New York, NY
Oceanside Books Unlimited, Oceanside, NY
Bengta Woo, Plainview, NY
Paulette Greene, Rockville Centre, NY
Bibliomania, Schenectady, NY
Kevin T Ransom—Bookseller, Snyder, NY
Kolyer Publications, Stony Brook, NY
The Book Swappers, Wantagh, NY
Esther Isaacson, Velva, ND
Outdoorsman Bookshelf, Dayton, OH
Lois Ward—Books, Reynoldsburg, OH
McClintock's Books, Warren, OH
Mystery Manor Books, Huntingdon Valley, PA
Big John's Bookroom, Meshoppen, PA
S Clyde King Rare & Out-of-Print Books, Providence, RI
The Wayside Bookshop, Westerly, RI

James S Pipkin Old & Rare Books, Rock Hill, SC
Limestone Hills Bookshop, Glen Rose, TX
Waves Press & Bookshop, Richmond, VA
Bibelots & Books, Seattle, WA
Robert L Brown Bookmonger, Seattle, WA
Comstock's Bindery & Bookshop, Seattle, WA
Pegasus Books & Press, Vashon, WA
West's Booking Agency, Elm Grove, WI
Beckoning Cat Bookshop, Menasha, WI
Castalia Books, Milwaukee, WI
Terry Rutherford Bookseller, Vancouver, BC, Canada
Pandora's Books Ltd, Altona, MB, Canada
Attic Books, London, ON, Canada
Batta Bookstore, Toronto, ON, Canada
Mostly Mysteries Books, Toronto, ON, Canada
Passages, Toronto, ON, Canada

Mythology

Carol Docheff—Bookseller, Berkeley, CA
The Book House Booksellers, Minneapolis, MN
Charlie Brown's Book-Gallerie, Brooklyn, NY
Rivendell Bookshop Ltd, New York, NY
Lyrical Ballad Bookstore, Saratoga Springs, NY

Natural History

William R Hecht, Scottsdale, AZ
Adams Angling Books & Paraphernalia, Berkeley, CA
Richard Gilbo—Books, Carpenteria, CA
Xanadu Galleries Co, Glendale, CA
Tolliver's Books, Los Angeles, CA
Black Swan Books, Sacramento, CA
J & J House Booksellers, San Diego, CA
Olinghouse & Tyson Booksellers & La Querencia Press, San Diego, CA
John Howell—Books, San Francisco, CA
Rudolph William Sabbott—Natural History Books, Woodland Hills, CA
The King's Market—Books & Prints, Boulder, CO
W J Bookunter, Denver, CO
The Prospector, Littleton, CO
The Antiquarium, Bethany, CT
Whitlock Farm Booksellers, Bethany, CT
Robert Shuhi—Books, Morris, CT
William Reese Co, New Haven, CT
A Cabinet of Books, Watertown, CT
Demerara Book Service, Miami, FL

The Old Book Scout—Jim McMeans, Atlanta, GA
Whistles in the Woods, Rossville, GA
P R Rieber, Thomasville, GA
Creedmoor Bookstore, Chicago, IL
N Fagin Books, Chicago, IL
Kenneth Nebenzahl Inc, Chicago, IL
Mason's Rare & Used Books, Wabash, IN
Petersen Book Co, Davenport, IA
Taylor Clark's Inc, Baton Rouge, LA
Patricia Ledlie—Bookseller, Buckfield, ME
Charles L Robinson Rare Books, Manchester, ME
Bedford's Used Books, Ellsworth, ME
Saxifrage Books, Salem, MA
The Science Bookshelf, Ann Arbor, MI
George Tramp—Books, Jackson, MI
Harry B Robinson Book Search Service, Columbia, MO
Gallery of the Old West, Big Fork, MT
Arthur Stiles, Hollis, NH
Sykes & Flanders Old & Rare Books, Weare, NH
Bauman Rare Books, Atlantic City, NJ
Woodstock Ink, Placitas, NM
Owl Pen—Books, Greenwich, NY
Janus Books, Huntington Station, NY
Broadwater Books, Lewiston, NY
Irving Zucker Art Books, New York, NY
Lubrecht & Cramer, Monticello, NY
J N Bartfield Books Inc, New York, NY
K Gregory, New York, NY
Albert Gutkin, New York, NY
Maiden Voyage Books, New York, NY
Robert E Underhill, Poughkeepsie, NY
The Book Chest Inc, Rockville Centre, NY
Elgen Books, Rockville Centre, NY
Morris Heller, Swan Lake, NY
Wentworth & Leggett Rare Books, Durham, NC
Susan Heller Books, Cleveland, OH
Melvin Marcher—Bookseller, Oklahoma City, OK
The Oklahoma Bookman, Yukon, OK
G A Bibby Books, Gold Hill, OR
D Sedenger Galleries, Huntingdon Valley, PA
John E Deturck, Mount Penn, PA
Terry Harper Bookseller, Rouseville, PA
John Johnson Natural History Books, North Bennington, VT
Bookhouse, Arlington, VA
Mary Hosmer Lupton, Charlottesville, VA
Olin O Evans, Woodstock, VA
Comstock's Bindery & Bookshop, Seattle, WA
W O Moye—Bookseller, Seattle, WA
John L Polley—Bookseller, Seattle, WA
The Shorey Bookstore, Seattle, WA
Pomona Book Exchange, Rockton, ON, Canada

The Map Room, Exploration House, Toronto, ON, Canada

Nautical

Apollo Book Shop, Costa Mesa, CA
Caravan Bookstore, Los Angeles, CA
"Otento" Books, San Diego, CA
John Roby, San Diego, CA
The Albatross Book Store, San Francisco, CA
Bob Finch, Books, Torrance, CA
The Court Place Antiquarian Bookshop, Denver, CO
Alfred W Paine—Books, Bethel, CT
Old Mystic Bookshop, Old Mystic, CT
Tappin Book Mine, Atlantic Beach, FL
Wake-Brook House Books, Fort Lauderdale, FL
The Old Bookshop, Palm Beach, FL
Julian Burnett Books, Atlantic, GA
Jacqueline Levine Books, Savannah, GA
Cross Hill Books, Bath, ME
Bedford's Used Books, Ellsworth, ME
Starr Book Co Inc, Boston, MA
Brookline Village Books & Prints, Brookline, MA
W D Hall, East Longmeadow, MA
Edward J Lefkowicz Inc, Fairhaven, MA
The English Bookshop, Gloucester, MA
Ten Pound Island Book Co, Gloucester, MA
Elmcress Books, Hamilton, MA
Howland & Co, Jamaica Plain, MA
Neath the Elms, Marblehead, MA
Magnalia Americana, North Amherst, MA
West Side Bookshop, Ann Arbor, MI
Bygone Book House, Dearborn, MI
Robert M O'Neill, Rare Books, Warner, NH
Charles E Gardiner, Bayside, NY
Caravan-Maritime Books, Jamaica, NY
Bookfinder's General Inc, New York, NY
Bayview Books & Bindery, Northport, NY
Susan Heller Books, Cleveland, OH
Green Dolphin Bookshop, Portland, OR
T J McCauley Books, Langhorne, PA
Cantrell's Books, North East, PA
The Current Company, Bristol, RI
The Wayside Bookshop, Westerly, RI
Kitemaug Books, Spartanburg, SC
William Orbelo, San Antonio, TX
Craftsbury Common Antiquarian, Craftsbury Common, VT
Interim Books, Bremerton, WA
Comstock's Bindery & Bookshop, Seattle, WA
The Shorey Bookstore, Seattle, WA
Constant Reader Bookshop Ltd, Milwaukee, WI
Nautica Booksellers, Halifax, NS, Canada
The Odd Book, Wolfville, NS, Canada

New England. *See* **Americana: New England**

New York

Jens J Christofferson Rare Books, Mamaroneck, NY
New York Bound Bookshop, New York, NY
Wildwood Enterprises, Old Forge, NY
Riverow Bookshop, Owego, NY
Yankee Peddler Bookshop, Pultneyville, NY
Lyrical Ballad Bookstore, Saratoga Springs, NY
Edward J Monarski Antiquarian Books, Syracuse, NY
Sterling Valley Antiquities at Homestead Antiques, Syracuse, NY
Hoffman Lane Books, Troy, NY

Newspapers & Newspaper History

Stanley Gilman, New York, NY
The Tuckers, Pittsburgh, PA
Hughes', Williamsport, PA
Don E Burnett, East Greenwich, RI

Northwest. *See* **Americana: Northwest**

Numismatics

George Frederick Kolbe Fine Numismatic Books, Mission Viejo, CA
Hardford Coins, Baltimore, MD
House of Trivia, Williamston, MI
High Ridge Corner, Rye, NY
Irving M Roth, Antiques, Norwalk, OH

Nutrition. *See* **Cookery & Gastronomy**

Occult & Metaphysics

Unusual Books, Bakersfield, CA
Book City of Burbank, Burbank, CA
AIDE, Cardiff, CA
Bookpost, Cardiff, CA
Alpha Books, Encino, CA
Monroe Books, Fresno, CA
The Book Harbor, Fullerton, CA
Cherokee Bookshop Inc, Los Angeles, CA
Hollywood Book City, Los Angeles, CA
Sharp's Bookstore, North Hollywood, CA
Bailey Search Service, Redondo Beach, CA
The Albatross Book Store, San Francisco, CA
Maelstrom, San Francisco, CA

Book Vault, Santa Ana, CA
Tiger's Tale Bookshop, Santa Clara, CA
Sebastopol Book Shop, Sebastopol, CA
Collector's Center, Rare Books, Denver, CO
A Blue Moon Books & Records, Clearwater, FL
Book Warehouse Inc, Coral Gables, FL
Mandala Books, Daytona Beach, FL
Books & Art Prints Store, Miami, FL
Samadhi—Metaphysical Literature, Newberry, FL
Barrington Old Bookshop, Barrington, IL
Joan Marie Bruna, Cicero, IL
Imagination Books, Silver Spring, MD
The Book Bear, West Brookfield, MA
Memory Aisle, Grand Rapids, MI
Oudal Bookshop, Minneapolis, MN
S & S Books, Saint Paul, MN
Barjon's Books & Graphics, Billings, MT
Book Stop III, Las Vegas, NV
Bump's Barn Bookshop, Ashland, NH
Evelyn Clement—Dealer in Old Books, Franklin, NH
Charlie Brown's Book-Gallerie, Brooklyn, NY
U S Games Systems Inc, New York, NY
Samuel Weiser Inc, New York, NY
Bump's Books, Scarsdale, NY
Ben Franklin Bookshop & Printery, Upper Nyack, NY
Duttenhofer's Book Treasures, Cincinnati, OH
Richard P Germann, Willard, OH
Blue Dragon Book Shop, Ashland, OR
Holland's Bookstore, Portland, OR
The Gateway, Ferndale, PA
Molly Kirwan Books, Meadow Lands, PA
Book Search Service, Pittsburgh, PA
F Thomas Heller Rare Books, Swarthmore, PA
Leonard Dixon Bookstore, San Antonio, TX
Collector's Museum & Market, Taft, TX
Cosmic Aeroplane Books, Salt Lake City, UT
Mary Hosmer Lupton, Charlottesville, VA
Thoth's Bookshops Ltd, Wolfville, NS, Canada
Ben Abraham Books, Toronto, ON, Canada

Oceanography

Sarkis Shmavonian Books & Prints, Berkeley, CA
Tolliver's Books, Los Angeles, CA
Cedric L Robinson, Bookseller, Windsor, CT
Mandala Books, Daytona Beach, FL
Guideways Inc, Fernandina Beach, FL
Southampton Book Co, Southampton, NY

Oil

Red River Books, Shreveport, LA
Michael Gibbs Books, State College, PA
Ernest C Miller, Warren, PA
Colleen's Books & Things, Houston, TX
Louis Ginsberg—Books & Prints, Petersburg, VA

Orientalia

Jerrold G Stanoff Rare Oriental Book Co, Aptos, CA
Graeme Vanderstoel, El Cerrito, CA
Bennett & Marshall, Los Angeles, CA
Dawson's Bookshop, Los Angeles, CA
James Normile—Books, Los Angeles, CA
Kurt L Schwarz, Los Angeles, CA
J & J House Booksellers, San Diego, CA
The Compass Bookstore, San Francisco, CA
Cecil Archer Rush, Baltimore, MD
Hirschtritt's "1712," Silver Spring, MD
Xerxes Books, Glen Head, NY
Samuel Weiser Inc, New York, NY
Chris Fessler Bookseller, Theresa, NY
Blue Dragon Book Shop, Ashland, OR
The Gateway, Ferndale, PA
William H Allen, Bookseller, Philadelphia, PA
Tuttle Antiquarian Books Inc, Rutland, VT

Original Art for Book Illustration

Childs Gallery, Boston, MA
Black Sun Books, New York, NY
Books of Wonder, New York, NY

Ornithology

R M Schramm, Tucson, AZ
Tolliver's Books, Los Angeles, CA
Petersen Book Co, Davenport, IA
Janus Books, Huntington Station, NY
Albert Gutkin, New York, NY
The Oklahoma Bookman, Yukon, OK
John Johnson Natural History Books, North Bennington, VT

Oziana

Peninsula Booksearch, Burlingame, CA
Oz & Ends Book Shoppe, Kenilworth, NJ
Books of Wonder, New York, NY

Performing Arts

Harold B Diamond—Bookseller, Burbank, CA
Graeme Vanderstoel, El Cerrito, CA
Libra Books, Reseda, CA
Haight Street Bookshop, San Francisco, CA
Robert Kuhn Antiques—Autographs, San Francisco, CA
Lion Bookshop, San Francisco, CA
Howard Karno Books Inc, Santa Monica, CA
John Makarewich, Books, Van Nuys, CA
Okman's Happy Endings, Woodland Hills, CA
William F Hale—Books, Washington, DC
Larry Laws Bookstore, Chicago, IL
Artistic Endeavors, Boston, MA
Leo Loewenthal, Dover, NJ
La Scala Autographs Inc, Plainsboro, NJ
Richard T Jordan Antiquariat, Flushing, NY
Academy Bookstore, New York, NY
Anna Sosenko Inc, New York, NY
Richard Stoddard Performing Arts Books, New York, NY
Strand Bookstore, New York, NY
John Cashman Books, Sea Cliff, NY
Liberty Rock Book Shoppe, Sloatsburg, NY
Publix Book Mart, Cleveland, OH
Joshua David Bowen, San Antonio, TX
R L Shep, Lopez, WA
Westmount Parnassus, Montreal, PQ, Canada

Periodicals

Roskie & Wallace Bookstore, San Leandro, CA
Harrington's, Cos Cob, CT
E Donbullian Back Number Magazine Company, Greenbelt, MD
Kraus Periodicals Co, Millwood, NY
Albert J Phiebig Inc, White Plains, NY
Cameron's Book Store, Portland, OR
North Toronto Coins Ltd, Toronto, ON, Canada

Petroleum. *See* Oil

Philately

Philatelic Bibliopole, Louisville, KY
House of Trivia, Williamston, MI
The Memorabilia Corner, Norfolk, VA

Philosophy

Richard Gilbo—Books, Carpenteria, CA
The Book Cellar, Fullerton, CA
The Book Harbor, Fullerton, CA
Merlin's Bookshop, Isla Vista, CA
Canterbury Bookshop, Los Angeles, CA

Philosophy (cont.)

J & J House Booksellers, San Diego, CA
Antiquus Bibliopole, San Francisco, CA
Volkoff & Von Hohenlohe, Santa Barbara, CA
The Hermitage Antiquarian Bookshop, Denver, CO
AABS-Atlanta Antiquarian Booksellers, Atlanta, GA
Barrington Old Bookshop, Barrington, IL
Richard Adamiak, Chicago, IL
Abraham's Books, Evanston, IL
Richard Owen Roberts Booksellers, Wheaton, IL
Christopher's Book Room, Bloomington, IN
The Haunted Bookshop, Iowa City, IA
Dickey Books, Wichita, KS
John Gach Books Inc, Columbia, MD
Starr Book Co Inc, Boston, MA
Starr Bookshop Inc, Cambridge, MA
A E Maxted, Cohasset, MA
University Book Reserve, Hull, MA
Robert H Rubin Books, Stoughton, MA
State Street Bookshop, Ann Arbor, MI
Melvin McCosh Bookseller, Excelsior, MN
Harry B Robinson Book Search Service, Columbia, MO
Grunewald Klaus — Bookdealer, Kansas City, MO
Anthony Garnett — Fine Books, Saint Louis, MO
Hummingbird Books, Albuquerque, NM
Editions, Boiceville, NY
Theoria Scholarly Books, Forest Hills, NY
Karl Schick, Hartsdale, NY
Academy Bookstore, New York, NY
Noah Albay Company, New York, NY
Alfred F Zambelli, New York, NY
Colonial Out-of-Print Book Service, Pleasantville, NY
Chris Fessler Bookseller, Theresa, NY
Ben Franklin Bookshop & Printery, Upper Nyack, NY
The Backroom Bookstore, Webster, NY
The Browsery, Greensboro, NC
De Anima: Books in Psychology, Bowling Green, OH
Duttenhofer's Book Treasures, Cincinnati, OH
Holland's Bookstore, Portland, OR
The Epistemologist, Scholarly Books, Bryn Mawr, PA
Molly Kirwan Books, Meadow Lands, PA
William H Allen, Bookseller, Philadelphia, PA
F Thomas Heller Rare Books, Swarthmore, PA
Constant Reader Bookshop Ltd, Milwaukee, WI
Spectrum Books & Records, Milwaukee, WI
Atticus Books, Toronto, ON, Canada
D & E Lake Ltd Old & Rare Books, Toronto, ON, Canada

Photography

J B Muns, Books, Berkeley, CA
Sarkis Shmavonian Books & Prints, Berkeley, CA
Book City of Burbank, Burbank, CA
Aviation Bookmobile — Mil-Air Photos & Books, Compton, CA
The Book Harbor, Fullerton, CA
Talisman Press, Booksellers & Publishers, Georgetown, CA
California Book Auction Galleries, Los Angeles, CA
Davis & Schorr Art Books, Los Angeles, CA
Hollywood Book City, Los Angeles, CA
Stephen White's Gallery of Photography, Los Angeles, CA
Zeitlin & Ver Brugge Booksellers, Los Angeles, CA
Valley Book City, North Hollywood, CA
Aviation Bookmobile — Mil-Air Photos & Books, Norwalk, CA
Carl Blomgren Books, San Rafael, CA
Virginia Burgman, Santa Rosa, CA
Old Book & Photo — Russell Norton, New Haven, CT
R W Smith — Bookseller, New Haven, CT
John S Craig Photographic Historian, Norwalk, CT
Charles B Wood III Inc, Antiquarian Booksellers, South Woodstock, CT
Bickerstaff & Barclay, Washington, DC
A Blue Moon Books & Records, Clearwater, FL
Book Warehouse Inc, Coral Gables, FL
David McCord Books, Atlanta, GA
The Athenaeum, Evanston, IL
Titles Inc, Highland Park, IL
E F Keenan Books, Lake Bluff, IL
G & C Enterprises, Lafayette, LA
Ars Libri Ltd, Boston, MA
Temple Bar Bookshop, Cambridge, MA
William T Gavin, Leominster, MA
Trotting Hill Park Antiquarian Booksellers, Springfield, MA
Steve Finer — Books, Turners Falls, MA
Grub Street — A Bookery, Grosse Pointe Park, MI
Wenzel Books, New Troy, MI
Bump's Barn Bookshop, Ashland, NH
Carry Back Books, Haverhill, NH
Leo Loewenthal, Dover, NJ
De La Pena Books, Santa Fe, NM
Nicholas Potter, Bookseller, Santa Fe, NM

Far Country Bookstore, Albany, NY
The Question Mark, Albany, NY
Pan Books & Graphics, Catskill, NY
M & M Halpern Bookdealers, Flushing, NY
H & R Salerno, Hauppauge, NY
Carriage House Books, Kirkwood, NY
Academy Bookstore, New York, NY
Howard D Daitz — Photographica, New York, NY
Bevan Davies Books, New York, NY
Ex Libris, New York, NY
Leonard Fox Ltd, New York, NY
Huckleberry Designs, New York, NY
Lee & Lee Booksellers Inc, New York, NY
Janet Lehr Inc, New York, NY
James Lowe Autographs Ltd, New York, NY
Arthur H Minters Inc, New York, NY
Nudel Books, New York, NY
The Witkin Gallery, New York, NY
Yankee Peddler Bookshop, Pultneyville, NY
Bump's Books, Scarsdale, NY
Bibliomania, Schenectady, NY
Lion Harvey Books, Wappingers Falls, NY
The Book Gallery, White Plains, NY
Alrich Co, Cincinnati, OH
Robert Richshafer, Cincinnati, OH
Susan Heller Books, Cleveland, OH
Miran Arts & Books, Columbus, OH
The Family Album, Glen Rock, PA
Stephen Shuart Photographic Books, Kane, PA
Bernard Conwell Carlitz, Philadelphia, PA
Hoffman Research Services, Rillton, PA
Hampton Books, Newberry, SC
Photo-Eye, Austin, TX
T W Tingle Rare & Out-of-Print Books, Austin, TX
Frontier America Corporation, Bryan, TX
Louis Ginsberg — Books & Prints, Petersburg, VA
Cipriano's Books, Kennewick, WA
Comstock's Bindery & Bookshop, Seattle, WA
McDuffie's Old Books, Spokane, WA

Physics

Celestial Books, La Canada, CA
Tolliver's Books, Los Angeles, CA
Daniel H Deutsch PhD — Books, Pasadena, CA
The Bookstall, San Francisco, CA
Richard T Jordan Antiquariat, Flushing, NY
Stevens & Co Books Inc, New York, NY

Poetry

Dickson Street Bookshop, Fayetteville, AR
The Invisible Bookman, Berkeley, CA

Ralston Popular Fiction, Fullerton, CA
William Riley — Books, Kensington, CA
John B Nomland Booksellers, Los Angeles, CA
Pettler & Lieberman, Booksellers, Los Angeles, CA
West Los Angeles Book Center, Los Angeles, CA
Maxwell Hunley, Pasadena, CA
Robert Larkin Link Bookseller, Redding, CA
Chloe's Bookstore, Sacramento, CA
Atticus Books, San Diego, CA
Bay Side Books, Soquel, CA
The Prospector, Littleton, CO
Jumping Frog, Hartford, CT
McBride First Editions, Hartford, CT
Hugh Miller, Bookseller, New Haven, CT
Pharos Books — Fine First Editions, New Haven, CT
Turkey Hill Books, Westport, CT
Books & Art Prints Store, Miami, FL
Lucile Coleman, Books, A-to-Z Service, North Miami, FL
Bookman's Alley, Evanston, IL
Dickey Books, Wichita, KS
The Mathom Bookshop & Bindery, Augusta, ME
Dragoman Books, Annapolis, MD
Deeds Bookshop, Ellicott City, MD
Nouveau Rare Books, Jackson, MS
Addison's Bookstore, Springfield, MO
Book Barn, South Sioux City, NE
Bert Babcock — Bookseller, Derry, NH
Book Farm, Henniker, NH
Leo Loewenthal, Dover, NJ
Acres of Books, Trenton, NJ
Lorraine Galinsky, Cold Spring Harbor, NY
Bernice Weiss — Rare Books, Eastchester, NY
7 Terrace Drive, Hastings-on-Hudson, NY
Academy Bookstore, New York, NY
Bookfinder's General Inc, New York, NY
Books 'n Things, New York, NY
Jordan Davies, Books, New York, NY
Gramercy Book Shop, New York, NY
Glenn Horowitz Bookseller Inc, New York, NY
James Lowe Autographs Ltd, New York, NY
James C Morel Fine Books, New York, NY
Phoenix Bookshop, New York, NY
Daniel Stokes, New York, NY
A Collector's List, Rockville Centre, NY
The Backroom Bookstore, Webster, NY
The Browsery, Greensboro, NC
Duttenhofer's Book Treasures, Cincinnati, OH
The Looking Glass, Worthington, OH
Authors of the West, Dundee, OR
Hobson's Choice, Jenkintown, PA
T J McCauley Books, Langhorne, PA
Book Cellar, Temple, TX

Poetry (cont.)

Cosmic Aeroplane Books, Salt Lake City, UT
Jennie's Book Nook, Alexandria, VA
Irene Rouse—Bookseller, Alexandria, VA
Great Northwest Book Co, Toronto, ON,
 Canada

Political Science

Pacific Book Supply Co, Farmersville, CA
Abbey Bookshop, Los Angeles, CA
Hollywood Book Service, Los Angeles, CA
William Bledsoe, Bookseller, San Carlos, CA
Harmon Books, San Jose, CA
Volkoff & Von Hohenlohe, Santa Barbara,
 CA
Historical Bookshelf Ltd, Plantation, FL
The Old Book Scout—Jim McMeans, At-
 lanta, GA
Memorable Books, Stone Mountain, GA
Richard Adamiak, Chicago, IL
Kenneth Nebenzahl Inc, Chicago, IL
Paul Romaine—Books, Chicago, IL
Kennedy's Bookshop, Evanston, IL
Second Life Books, Adams, MA
As You Like It Bookshop, Elma, NY
Noah Albay Company, New York, NY
Bookfinder's General Inc, New York, NY
Leona Rostenberg & Madeleine B Stern—
 Rare Books, New York, NY
Deecee Books, Nyack, NY
White House Books, Boyertown, PA
Schaefer Association, Arlington, VA

Presidents & Presidency

Herbert Biblo Bookseller, Chicago, IL
Irving Galis, Marblehead, MA
Stephen Koschal Autographs & Signed
 Books, Verona, NJ
Jerry Granat Manuscripts, Hewlett, NY
Herbert B Lazarus, Ossining, NY
Robert F Batchelder, Ambler, PA

Press Books & Fine Printing

Marshall Vance Publisher-Bookseller, Forrest
 City, AR
Peninsula Booksearch, Burlingame, CA
Irving Keats, Carmel, CA
Bennett & Marshall, Los Angeles, CA
Barry R Levin Science Fiction & Fantasy
 Literature, Los Angeles, CA
James G Leishman—Bookseller, Menlo Park,
 CA
The Eclectic Gallery, Mill Valley, CA
Robert Larkin Link Bookseller, Redding, CA

J & J House Booksellers, San Diego, CA
The Brick Row Book Shop, San Francisco,
 CA
John Scopazzi Books, San Francisco, CA
Transition Books, San Francisco, CA
A S Fischler—Rare Books, San Jose, CA
The Eclectic Gallery, Sausalito, CA
John Makarewich, Books, Van Nuys, CA
J E Reynold, Bookseller, Willits, CA
The Book Block, Cos Cob, CT
Barry Scott, Stonington, CT
Bromer Booksellers Inc, Boston, MA
In Our Time, Cambridge, MA
Rebecca B Desmarais Rare Books,
 Framingham, MA
Hartfield Fine & Rare Books, Ann Arbor, MI
Dale Weber Books, Rochester, MI
Much Loved Books, Southfield, MI
James & Mary Laurie Booksellers, Minneap-
 olis, MN
Richard Flamer Bookseller, Omaha, NE
Wilsey Rare Books, Montclair, NJ
Bernice Weiss—Rare Books, Eastchester, NY
7 Terrace Drive, Hastings-on-Hudson, NY
Black Sun Books, New York, NY
Jordan Davies, Books, New York, NY
Philip C Duschnes Inc, New York, NY
Greenwich Books Ltd, New York, NY
William B Liebmann, New York, NY
Richard Cady Rare Books, Port Chester, NY
Joseph F Scheetz—Antiquarian Books,
 Youngstown, OH
James S Jaffe, Rare Books, Haverford, PA
Hobson's Choice, Jenkintown, PA
Graedon Books Inc, New Hope, PA
Kitemaug Books, Spartanburg, SC
W Thomas Taylor—Bookseller, Austin, TX
Ray S Walton—Rare Books, Austin, TX
Cipriano's Books, Kennewick, WA
Journey, Seattle, WA

Printing & Printing History

Marshall Vance Publisher-Bookseller, Forrest
 City, AR
Books & The Collector Arts, Encino, CA
Kenneth Karmiole, Bookseller Inc, Los
 Angeles, CA
John Slattery Books & Prints, Palo Alto, CA
William P Wreden, Books & Manuscripts,
 Palo Alto, CA
Oak Knoll Books, New Castle, DE
Midnight Bookman, West Lafayette, IN
Dwyer's Bookstore Inc, Northampton, MA
Glenn Books Inc, Kansas City, MO
John F Hendsey, Bookseller, Epping, NH
David L O'Neal, Antiquarian Booksellers
 Inc, Peterborough, NH
Wilsey Rare Books, Montclair, NJ

L W Currey Rare Books Inc, Elizabethtown, NY
De Simon Company, New York, NY
Alfred F Zambelli, New York, NY
The Wilson Bookshop, Dallas, TX
The Bookpress Ltd, Williamsburg, VA

Prints

Sergio Old Prints, San Francisco, CA
Estampe Originale, Saratoga, CA
Allison Gallery Inc, Coventry, CT
Cartographics, North Stonington, CT
The Museum Gallery Bookshop, Southport, CT
The Old Print Gallery, Washington, DC
Childs Gallery, Boston, MA
Ernest S Hickok, Summit, NJ
David Tunick Inc, New York, NY
Irving Zucker Art Books, New York, NY
Bruce P Ferrini, Rare Books, Akron, OH
W O Moye — Bookseller, Seattle, WA
McDuffie's Old Books, Spokane, WA

Psychiatry & Psychology

Ruby D Kaufman, Tempe, AZ
Albion Fine Prints, Berkeley, CA
Regent Street Books, Berkeley, CA
AIDE, Cardiff, CA
Pacific Book Supply Co, Farmersville, CA
Merlin's Bookshop, Isla Vista, CA
John Makarewich, Books, Van Nuys, CA
The King's Market — Books & Prints, Boulder, CO
Book Warehouse Inc, Coral Gables, FL
AABS-Atlanta Antiquarian Booksellers, Atlanta, GA
Memorable Books, Stone Mountain, GA
Abraham's Books, Evanston, IL
Storeybook Antiques & Books, Sycamore, IL
Richard Owen Roberts Booksellers, Wheaton, IL
The Haunted Bookshop, Iowa City, IA
J Hood Bookseller, Lawrence, KS
Folkways Scholarly Books, Bethesda, MD
John Gach Books Inc, Columbia, MD
Buddenbrooks Books Inc, Boston, MA
Starr Book Co Inc, Boston, MA
A E Maxted, Cohasset, MA
The Book Bear, West Brookfield, MA
Carriage-Barn Books and Antiques, Williamstown, MA
The Antiquarium, Omaha, NE
Book Stop III, Las Vegas, NV
Acres of Books, Trenton, NJ
Karl Schick, Hartsdale, NY
Academy Bookstore, New York, NY

Pageant Book and Print Shop, New York, NY
Colonial Out-of-Print Book Service, Pleasantville, NY
The Backroom Bookstore, Webster, NY
De Anima: Books in Psychology, Bowling Green, OH
Jerry Ray Books, Bowling Green, OH
The Epistemologist, Scholarly Books, Bryn Mawr, PA
Hoffman Research Services, Rillton, PA
F Thomas Heller Rare Books, Swarthmore, PA
Renaissance Book Shop Inc, Milwaukee, WI

Radical Literature

Scattergood Books, Berkeley, CA
Beasley Books, Chicago, IL
Leekley Book Search, Winthrop Harbor, IL
Rena & Merwin L Orner, Tenafly, NJ
Salt of the Earth Bookstore Ltd, Albuquerque, NM

Radio & Telegraphy

Aviation Bookmobile — Mil-Air Photos & Books, Compton, CA
Aviation Bookmobile — Mil-Air Photos & Books, Norwalk, CA
Donald R Doerres, Wilton, IA
Huckleberry Designs, New York, NY
A'Gatherin', Wynantskill, NY
Radiographics Books, Cleveland Heights, OH

Railroadiana

Ken Prag Paper Americana, Burlingame, CA
Caravan Bookstore, Los Angeles, CA
Hammon's Archives & Artifacts, Sacramento, CA
Collectors' Center, Rare Books, Denver, CO
The Prospector, Littleton, CO
Whistles in the Woods, Rossville, GA
Valley Bookshop, Galena, IL
Donald R Doerres, Wilton, IA
Bygone Book House, Dearborn, MI
South Jersey Magazine, Millville, NJ
Charles E Gardiner, Bayside, NY
Frederick Arone Railroad Items, Dobbs Ferry, NY
George D Brown — Books, Toledo, OH
Antiques & Artifacts, Noti, OK
Trackside Books, Houston, TX
Comstock's Bindery & Bookshop, Seattle, WA

Railroadiana (cont.)

Old Seattle Paperworks, Seattle, WA
The Antiquarian Shop, Stevens Point, WI

Reference Books

Harold J Mason Inc, Phoenix, AZ
Harold B Diamond—Bookseller, Burbank, CA
Talisman Press, Booksellers & Publishers, Georgetown, CA
Hollywood Book Service, Los Angeles, CA
Cartographics, North Stonington, CT
O G Lansford, Powersville, GA
Ars Libri Ltd, Boston, MA
Exnowski Enterprises, Warren, MI
Five Dog Books, Reno, NV
Richard T Jordan Antiquariat, Flushing, NY
Daniel Hirsch, Hopewell Junction, NY
Kraus Periodicals Co, Millwood, NY
W Graham Arader III, New York, NY
Leonard Fox Ltd, New York, NY
W S Heinman, New York, NY
Kim Kaufman Bookseller, New York, NY
Ursus Books Ltd, New York, NY
Paulette Greene, Rockville Centre, NY
W Graham Arader III, King of Prussia, PA
William G Mayer Antiques, Pittsburgh, PA
Valley Books, Sayre, PA
W Graham Arader III, Houston, TX
Comstock's Bindery & Bookshop, Seattle, WA
Northland Books, Saskatoon, SK, Canada

Religion & Theology

Allenson-Breckinridge Books, Geneva, AZ
American Bookstore, Fresno, CA
Krown & Spellman, Booksellers, Los Angeles, CA
Sharp's Bookstore, North Hollywood, CA
Marvin Stanley Booksellers, Oakland, CA
The Bookie Joint, Reseda, CA
Virginia Burgman, Santa Rosa, CA
Chimney Sweep Books, Scotts Valley, CA
L S Kaiser Books—Chimney Sweep Books, Scotts Valley, CA
Henry A Clausen Bookshop, Colorado Springs, CO
A Blue Moon Books & Records, Clearwater, FL
Book Warehouse Inc, Coral Gables, FL
Mandala Books, Daytona Beach, FL
Books & Art Prints Store, Miami, FL
Farley's Old & Rare Books, Pensacola, FL
O G Lansford, Powersville, GA
Opportunity Books, Lewiston, ID

Barrington Old Bookshop, Barrington, IL
Joseph O'Gara Bookseller, Chicago, IL
Book Barn, Walnut, IL
Richard Owen Roberts Booksellers, Wheaton, IL
Mason's Rare & Used Books, Wabash, IN
Gale Books, Marshalltown, IA
Old Louisville Books, Louisville, KY
Henrietta's Attic, Salisbury, MD
The Catholic Book Collector, Bellingham, MA
A E Maxted, Cohasset, MA
The English Bookshop, Gloucester, MA
University Book Reserve, Hull, MA
Angelescu Book Service, Detroit, MI
George Tramp—Books, Jackson, MI
Oudal Bookshop, Minneapolis, MN
S & S Books, Saint Paul, MN
Books & Stuff, Pearl, MS
Harry B Robinson Book Search Service, Columbia, MO
ABC Theological Index, Springfield, MO
Addison's Bookstore, Springfield, MO
Barjon's Books & Graphics, Billings, MT
Celtic Cross Books, Westmoreland, NH
Hurley Books, Westmoreland, NH
Rare Book Co, Freehold, NJ
Richard T Jordan Antiquariat, Flushing, NY
Theoria Scholarly Books, Forest Hills, NY
Bookfinder's General Inc, New York, NY
Elliot Klein Ltd, New York, NY
Samuel Weiser Inc, New York, NY
Alfred F Zambelli, New York, NY
Colonial Out-of-Print Book Service, Pleasant-ville, NY
Liberty Rock Book Shoppe, Sloatsburg, NY
Chris Fessler Bookseller, Theresa, NY
Ben Franklin Bookshop & Printery, Upper Nyack, NY
The Ancient Page, Asheville, NC
The Book Mart, Asheville, NC
Wentworth & Leggett Rare Books, Durham, NC
L J Ryan—Scholarly Books, Columbus, OH
Karen Wickliff Books, Columbus, OH
Lois Ward—Books, Reynoldsburg, OH
Douglas Gunn—Books, Wooster, OH
Ron Bever, Edmond, OK
Hive of Industry, Booksellers, Easton, PA
Schuylkill Book & Curio Shop, Philadelphia, PA
The Tuckers, Pittsburgh, PA
Patrick T Conley—Books, Cranston, RI
Noah's Ark Book Attic, Greenwood, SC
James S Pipkin Old & Rare Books, Rock Hill, SC
Mid-America Books, Memphis, TN
Cumberland Literary Agency, Nashville, TN
The Book Shoppe, Salt Lake City, UT

Cosmic Aeroplane Books, Salt Lake City, UT
Great Bridge Books Inc, Chesapeake, VA
Zen Americana, Manassas, VA
Comstock's Bindery & Bookshop, Seattle, WA
Stroud Theological Booksellers, Williamsburg, WV
Constant Reader Bookshop Ltd, Milwaukee, WI
Renaissance Book Shop Inc, Milwaukee, WI
Ben Abraham Books, Toronto, ON, Canada

Renaissance History & Literature

Krown & Spellman, Booksellers, Los Angeles, CA
Bernard M Rosenthal Inc, San Francisco, CA
The Antiquarium, Bethany, CT
Laurence Witten Rare Books, Southport, CT
Jeffrey D Mancevice Inc, Worcester, MA
Lawrence Feinberg Rare Books & Manuscripts, Brooklyn, NY
Leona Rostenberg & Madeleine B Stern — Rare Books, New York, NY
E K Schreiber, New York, NY
Alfred F Zambelli, New York, NY
William Salloch, Ossining, NY

Revolutionary War

Guthman Americana, Westport, CT
John Rybski Bookseller, Chicago, IL
Historical Newspapers & Journals, Skokie, IL
George Tramp — Books, Jackson, MI
Heinoldt Books, Egg Harbor City, NJ
Harold Nestler, Waldwick, NJ
Graedon Books Inc, New Hope, PA

Russia

Scattergood Books, Berkeley, CA
John Slattery Books & Prints, Palo Alto, CA
William S Johnson Books, Indianapolis, IN
Deecee Books, Nyack, NY
Old Oregon Bookstore, Portland, OR
Book Search Service, Pittsburgh, PA
P T Mallahan Bookseller, Bellevue, WA
Kuska House, Kingston, ON, Canada

Scholarly Literature

Ark Bookshop, Berkeley, CA
Roy Bleiweiss Fine Books, Berkeley, CA
Harold B Diamond — Bookseller, Burbank, CA
The Book Cellar, Fullerton, CA

Hollywood Book Service, Los Angeles, CA
Antiquus Bibliopole, San Francisco, CA
The Holmes Book Company, San Francisco, CA
Wade Lillywhite Books, Santa Ana, CA
Howard Karno Books Inc, Santa Monica, CA
The Court Place Antiquarian Bookshop, Denver, CO
The Hermitage Antiquarian Bookshop, Denver, CO
Elliot's Books, Out of Print Specialists, Northford, CT
Park Road Bookshop, West Hartford, CT
AABS-Atlanta Antiquarian Booksellers, Atlanta, GA
Stonehill's Antiquarian Books, Champaign, IL
Thomas W Burrows, Bookseller, Downers Grove, IL
Abraham's Books, Evanston, IL
Leonard Hoffnung Books, Martinton, IL
Leekley Book Search, Winthrop Harbor, IL
The Mathom Bookshop & Bindery, Augusta, ME
Ars Libri Ltd, Boston, MA
Brookline Village Books & Prints, Brookline, MA
C & M Hutchinson, Green Harbor, MA
Michael Ginsberg Books Inc, Sharon, MA
The Current Company, Minneapolis, MN
Glenn Books Inc, Kansas City, MO
Thomas Minckler Art & Books, Billings, MT
Leslie Poste, Geneseo, NY
Academy Bookstore, New York, NY
Barnstable Books Inc, New York, NY
Bookfinder's General Inc, New York, NY
The Good Times Bookshop, Port Jefferson, NY
Karen Wickliff Books, Columbus, OH
Kendall G Gaisser, Booksellers, Toledo, OH
McClintock's Books, Warren, OH
Douglas Gunn — Books, Wooster, OH
Book Search Service, Pittsburgh, PA
The Current Company, Bristol, RI
Sewards' Folly, Books, Providence, RI
Dupriest's Bookshop, Columbia, SC
Heartwood Used Books, Charlottesville, VA
Avol's Bookstore, Madison, WI
Raymond Dworczyk, Rare Books, Milwaukee, WI
The Alphabet Bookshop, Toronto, ON, Canada

Science

Zeitlin & Ver Brugge Booksellers, Los Angeles, CA
The Bookstall, San Francisco, CA

Science (cont.)

AABS-Atlanta Antiquarian Booksellers, Atlanta, GA
The Antiquarian Scientist, Amesbury, MA
Jeffrey D Mancevice Inc, Worcester, MA
The Science Bookshelf, Ann Arbor, MI
The Chatham Bookseller, Madison, NJ
Lawrence Feinberg Rare Books & Manuscripts, Brooklyn, NY
Theoria Scholarly Books, Forest Hills, NY
Roy W Clare, Getzville, NY
Karl Schick, Hartsdale, NY
Quality Book Service—T Emmett Henderson, Middletown, NY
Lathrop C Harper Inc, New York, NY
Jonathan A Hill, Bookseller, New York, NY
H P Kraus Books, New York, NY
William H Schab Gallery Inc, New York, NY
Richard P Germann, Willard, OH
The Epistemologist, Scholarly Books, Bryn Mawr, PA
Hive of Industry, Booksellers, Easton, PA
Bruce McKittrick, Rare Books, Philadelphia, PA
McDuffie's Books, Opportunity, WA
McDuffie's Old Books, Spokane, WA
Atticus Books, Toronto, ON, Canada
Steven Temple, Toronto, ON, Canada
Arthur Wharton Books, Toronto, ON, Canada

Science & Technology

Ark Bookshop, Berkeley, CA
Harold B Diamond—Bookseller, Burbank, CA
Aviation Bookmobile—Mil-Air Photos & Books, Compton, CA
Pacific Book Supply Co, Farmersville, CA
Bennett & Marshall, Los Angeles, CA
William & Victoria Dailey, Los Angeles, CA
Samuel W Katz, Los Angeles, CA
Dianco International, Mill Valley, CA
Aviation Bookmobile—Mil-Air Photos & Books, Norwalk, CA
John Roby, San Diego, CA
John Howell—Books, San Francisco, CA
Maelstrom, San Francisco, CA
Mandrake Bookshop, San Rafael, CA
Book Vault, Santa Ana, CA
Edwin V Glaser Rare Books, Sausalito, CA
B & L Rootenberg Fine & Rare Books, Sherman Oaks, CA
John Makarewich, Books, Van Nuys, CA
The King's Market—Books & Prints, Boulder, CO
Antique Books, Hamden, CT

Elliot's Books, Out of Print Specialists, Northford, CT
Charles B Wood III Inc, Antiquarian Booksellers, South Woodstock, CT
A Cabinet of Books, Watertown, CT
Book Warehouse Inc, Coral Gables, FL
Richard G Uhl, Lantana, FL
Kenneth Nebenzahl Inc, Chicago, IL
Kennedy's Bookshop, Evanston, IL
Bookstall of Rockford, Rockford, IL
Pied Piper Bookstore, Wichita, KS
Frederica De Beurs Books, Dexter, ME
Key Books, Baltimore, MD
Old Hickory Bookshop Ltd, Brinklow, MD
E Donbullian Back Number Magazine Company, Greenbelt, MD
Shirley Balser 16th-20th Century Paintings, Prints & Books, Pikesville, MD
C & M Hutchinson, Green Harbor, MA
Steve Finer—Books, Turners Falls, MA
M & S Rare Books Inc, Weston, MA
Global Book Research, Belding, MI
The Current Company, Minneapolis, MN
Scientia, Books in Science & Medicine, Minneapolis, MN
Emery's Books, Contoocook, NH
Evelyn Clement—Dealer in Old Books, Franklin, NH
Walter J Johnson Inc, Norwood, NJ
John C O'Connor, Tenafly, NJ
Woodstock Ink, Placitas, NM
George A Bernstein, Brooklyn, NY
As You Like It Bookshop, Elma, NY
Biblion Inc, Forest Hills, NY
Emil Offenbacher, Kew Gardens, NY
Bookfinder's General Inc, New York, NY
International University Booksellers Inc, New York, NY
Lion Heart Autographs Inc, New York, NY
Stevens & Co Books Inc, New York, NY
Elgen Books, Rockville Centre, NY
Annemarie Schnase Antiquarian Bookseller & Publisher, Scarsdale, NY
Hoffman Lane Books, Troy, NY
The Haunted Bookshop, Durham, NC
Old Galen's Books, Durham, NC
Autos & Autos—Book Dept, Elizabeth City, NC
Jerry Ray Books, Bowling Green, OH
Acres of Books Inc, Cincinnati, OH
Shaw-Banfill Books, Columbus, OH
Holland's Bookstore, Portland, OR
Longfellow's Book & Record Store, Portland, OR
Robert F Batchelder, Ambler, PA
Bernard Conwell Carlitz, Philadelphia, PA
Schuylkill Book & Curio Shop, Philadelphia, PA
The Tuckers, Pittsburgh, PA

The Americanist, Pottstown, PA
F Thomas Heller Rare Books, Swarthmore, PA
The Current Company, Bristol, RI
Burke's Bookstore Inc, Memphis, TN
Old South Books, Memphis, TN
The Jenkins Co, Rare Books, Austin, TX
Leonard Dixon Bookstore, San Antonio, TX
R M Weatherford — Books, Monroe, WA
Comstock's Bindery & Bookshop, Seattle, WA
McDuffie's Old Books, Spokane, WA
Atticus Books, Toronto, ON, Canada
Gail Wilson — Bookseller, Toronto, ON, Canada

Science Fiction & Fantasy

The Book Baron, Anaheim, CA
Carol Docheff — Bookseller, Berkeley, CA
Harold B Diamond — Bookseller, Burbank, CA
New Albion Bookshop, Fairfax, CA
New Albion Rare Books, Fairfax, CA
Monroe Books, Fresno, CA
Fantasy Illustrated, Garden Grove, CA
Bryan Barrett Books, Hayward, CA
Merlin's Bookshop, Isla Vista, CA
Barry R Levin Science Fiction & Fantasy Literature, Los Angeles, CA
West Los Angeles Book Center, Los Angeles, CA
Rick Thompson — Books, Milpitas, CA
Valley Book City, North Hollywood, CA
Book Carnival, Orange, CA
Bailey Search Service, Redondo Beach, CA
The Bookie Joint, Reseda, CA
Libra Books, Reseda, CA
"Otento" Books, San Diego, CA
The Albatross Book Store, San Francisco, CA
Jeremy Norman & Co Inc, San Francisco, CA
Pepper & Stern — Rare Books Inc, Santa Barbara, CA
Book Swap, Solana Beach, CA
Extensive Search Service, Danielson, CT
Blue Star Bookstore, Putnam, CT
Alla T Ford Rare Books, Lake Worth, FL
McFarland Books, Tampa, FL
Thomas J Joyce & Co, Geneva, IL
Caveat Emptor, Bloomington, IN
S-T Associates, Louisville, KY
Steven C Bernard First Editions, Rockville, MD
Attic Books, Wheaton, MD
Buddenbrooks Books Inc, Boston, MA
R H Kristiansen Rare Books, Boston, MA
Pepper & Stern — Rare Books Inc, Sharon, MA

The Dawn Treader Book Shop, Ann Arbor, MI
The Science Bookshelf, Ann Arbor, MI
Curious Bookshop, East Lansing, MI
George Tramp — Books, Jackson, MI
The Fine Books Co & David Aronovitz — Books, Rochester, MI
J & J O'Donoghue Books, Anoka, MN
S & S Books, Saint Paul, MN
Books & Stuff, Pearl, MS
Hall's Bookshop, Crystal City, MO
H L Prosser Bibliophile, Professional Appraiser & Collector, Springfield, MO
Book Stop III, Las Vegas, NV
Donato's Fine Books, Las Vegas, NV
Far Country Bookstore, Albany, NY
Reston's Booknook, Amsterdam, NY
Nationwide Book Service, Brooklyn, NY
Claude Held, Buffalo, NY
L W Currey Rare Books Inc, Elizabethtown, NY
As You Like It Bookshop, Elma, NY
Anton Gud, Elmhurst, NY
7 Terrace Drive, Hastings-on-Hudson, NY
H & R Salerno, Hauppauge, NY
Janus Books, Huntington Station, NY
Charles Garvin Rare Books, Ithaca, NY
Books of Wonder, New York, NY
Huckleberry Designs, New York, NY
Isaac Mendoza Book Co, New York, NY
Rivendell Bookshop Ltd, New York, NY
Paulette Greene, Rockville Centre, NY
Ben Franklin Bookshop & Printery, Upper Nyack, NY
The Book Swappers, Wantagh, NY
Esther Isaacson, Velva, ND
Old Bookstore, Akron, OH
Tally Ho Studio, Canton, OH
Duttenhofer's Book Treasures, Cincinnati, OH
Comics & Company, Columbus, OH
Maran Enterprises, Harrison, OH
McClintock's Books, Warren, OH
99-E Antique-Used, Woodburn, OR
S Clyde King Rare & Out-of-Print Books, Providence, RI
Merlin's Closet Inc, Providence, RI
The Wayside Bookshop, Westerly, RI
Big D Books & Comics, Dallas, TX
Collector's Museum & Market, Taft, TX
Cosmic Aeroplane Books, Salt Lake City, UT
Allbooks, Fairfax, VA
Nostalgia Plus, Richmond, VA
Interim Books, Bremerton, WA
The Book Exchange, Marysville, WA
Comstock's Bindery & Bookshop, Seattle, WA
John L Polley — Bookseller, Seattle, WA
Culpepper & Hanson Bookseller, Tacoma, WA

Science Fiction & Fantasy (cont.)

Pegasus Books & Press, Vashon, WA
Beckoning Cat Bookshop, Menasha, WI
Castalia Books, Milwaukee, WI
Renaissance Book Shop Inc, Milwaukee, WI
Spectrum Books & Records, Milwaukee, WI
William Matthews Bookseller, Fort Erie, ON, Canada
Mostly Mysteries Books, Toronto, ON, Canada
Passages, Toronto, ON, Canada
Arthur Wharton Books, Toronto, ON, Canada

Small Press Books

Bernard A Margolis—Books, Monroe, MI
Edward C Fales Old & Rare Books & Manuscripts, Salisbury, NH
Harold Nestler, Waldwick, NJ
Bernice Weiss—Rare Books, Eastchester, NY
Fly Creek Bookstall, Fly Creek, NY
Cosmic Aeroplane Books, Salt Lake City, UT

Social Sciences

Harold J Mason Inc, Phoenix, AZ
Harold B Diamond, Burbank, CA
Town & Gown Book Co, Dutch Flat, CA
New Albion Bookshop, Fairfax, CA
Alfred Kronfeld Bookseller, Los Angeles, CA
William Bledsoe, Bookseller, San Carlos, CA
Maelstrom, San Francisco, CA
Mandrake Bookshop, San Rafael, CA
Jan & Larry Malis, New Canaan, CT
Elliot's Books, Northford, CT
Vivian Kantor, Bookseller, Gainesville, FL
Caveat Emptor, Bloomington, IN
Folkways Scholarly Books, Bethesda, MD
Q M Dabney & Co, Rockville, MD
University Book Reserve, Hull, MA
Robert H Rubin Books, Stoughton, MA
Western Hemisphere Inc, Stoughton, MA
Carriage-Barn Books and Antiques, Williamstown, MA
Old Number Six Book Depot, Henniker, NH
Walter J Johnson Inc, Norwood, NJ
Editions, Boiceville, NY
S Millman, Brooklyn, NY
Theoria Scholarly Books, Forest Hills, NY
Ideal Bookstore, New York, NY
Strand Bookstore, New York, NY
Deecee Books, Nyack, NY
Hammer Mountain Book Halls, Schenectady, NY
Wentworth & Leggett Rare Books, Durham, NC

L J Ryan—Scholarly Books, Columbus, OH
Karen Wickliff Books, Columbus, OH
Douglas Gunn—Books, Wooster, OH
Hive of Industry, Booksellers, Easton, PA
Art Carduner, Philadelphia, PA
The Tuckers, Pittsburgh, PA
Hoffman Research Services, Rillton, PA
Lincoln Book Shoppe Inc & Lincoln Out-of-Print Book Search Ltd, Foster, RI
The Old Book Home, Spokane, WA
Renaissance Book Shop Inc, Milwaukee, WI
D & E Lake Ltd Old & Rare Books, Toronto, ON, Canada
Arthur Wharton Books, Toronto, ON, Canada

Sociology

Pacific Book Supply Co, Farmersville, CA
Kurt L Schwarz, Los Angeles, CA
The Bookie Joint, Reseda, CA
John Makarewich, Books, Van Nuys, CA
Memorable Books, Stone Mountain, GA
Kenneth Nebenzahl Inc, Chicago, IL
Abraham's Books, Evanston, IL
A E Maxted, Cohasset, MA
Patterson Smith, Montclair, NJ
Richard T Jordan Antiquariat, Flushing, NY
International University Booksellers Inc, New York, NY
Jerry Ray Books, Bowling Green, OH
Hoffman Research Services, Rillton, PA
Gail Wilson—Bookseller, Toronto, ON, Canada

South. *See* Americana: South

Southwest. *See* Americana: Southwest

Sporting

Collectors' Center, Rare Books, Denver, CO
Arthur M Griffiths, Johnstown, CO
Robert Shuhi—Books, Morris, CT
Paula Sterne—Books, West Redding, CT
E Tatro—Bookseller, Wethersfield, CT
Book Warehouse Inc, Coral Gables, FL
Fleuron Books, Longboat Key, FL
Carroll Miner Robinson Old Books, Palm Beach, FL
Sullivan Sporting Books, Chicago, IL
Fur Fin Feather Books, Lansing, IL
Valerie Kraft, Fine Books, Prospect Heights, IL
Kathleen Rais Books, Bloomington, IN
Charlotte's Web Antiques, Monkton, MD

Kenneth Andersen — Books, Auburn, MA
The Charles Daly Collection, Cambridge, MA
Barbara J Rule Books, Rochester, MI
D Halloran Books, Saint Louis, MO
John F Hendsey, Bookseller, Epping, NH
Joseph J Felcone Inc, Rare Books, Princeton, NJ
Richard E Donovan, Endicott, NY
With Pipe & Book, Lake Placid, NY
American Library Service, New City, NY
J N Bartfield Books Inc, New York, NY
James Cummins Bookseller Inc, New York, NY
Albert Gutkin, New York, NY
Hennessey's Bookstore, Saratoga Springs, NY
Hoffman Lane Books, Troy, NY
Susan Heller Books, Cleveland, OH
Outdoorsman Bookshelf, Dayton, OH
Maran Enterprises, Harrison, OH
Tamerlane Books, Havertown, PA
T J McCauley Books, Langhorne, PA
Hoffman Research Services, Rillton, PA
Harvey Abrams — Books, State College, PA
Zen Americana, Manassas, VA
Renaissance Book Shop Inc, Milwaukee, WI

Stock Market & Wall Street

Family Bookstore, Whittier, CA
Ron Bever, Edmond, OK

Technology

AABS-Atlanta Antiquarian Booksellers, Atlanta, GA
Whistles in the Woods, Rossville, GA
The Chatham Bookseller, Madison, NJ
Patterson Smith, Montclair, NJ
Harold Nestler, Waldwick, NJ
Battlefield Bookshop, Gettysburg, PA

Textiles

Mary Chapman Bookseller, College Park, MD
Harvey W Brewer, Closter, NJ
Renate Halpern Galleries Inc, New York, NY
R L Shep, Lopez, WA

Theater & Drama

The Ravenstree Co, Yuma, AZ
The Invisible Bookman, Berkeley, CA
Vernon Howard Books, Burlingame, CA
New Albion Bookshop, Fairfax, CA

Ralston Popular Fiction, Fullerton, CA
Xanadu Galleries Co, Glendale, CA
Hollywood Book Service, Los Angeles, CA
Pettler & Lieberman, Booksellers, Los Angeles, CA
Vagabond Books, Los Angeles, CA
West Los Angeles Book Center, Los Angeles, CA
Valley Book City, North Hollywood, CA
Buckabest Books & Bindery, Palo Alto, CA
Maxwell Hunley, Pasadena, CA
Robert Larkin Link Bookseller, Redding, CA
J & J House Booksellers, San Diego, CA
"Otento" Books, San Diego, CA
Helan Halbach — Bookseller, Santa Barbara, CA
Jumping Frog, Hartford, CT
McBride First Editions, Hartford, CT
Book Warehouse Inc, Coral Gables, FL
The Athenaeum, Evanston, IL
Bookman's Alley, Evanston, IL
Dolphin Bookstore, Camden, ME
Starr Book Co Inc, Boston, MA
J & J Lubrano, South Lee, MA
John R Sanderson PhD — Antiquarian Books, Stockbridge, MA
Nouveau Rare Books, Jackson, MS
Cranford Antique Exchange, Cranford, NJ
Nationwide Book Service, Brooklyn, NY
Lorraine Galinsky, Cold Spring Harbor, NY
Bernice Weiss — Rare Books, Eastchester, NY
Jerry Granat Manuscripts, Hewlett, NY
Books 'n Things, New York, NY
Broude Brothers Limited, New York, NY
Gramercy Book Shop, New York, NY
Glenn Horowitz Bookseller Inc, New York, NY
Jolly Roger Records & Music Books, New York, NY
M M Einhorn Maxwell Books — At the Sign of the Dancing Bear, New York, NY
Phoenix Bookshop, New York, NY
A Collector's List, Rockville Centre, NY
The Browsery, Greensboro, NC
T J McCauley Books, Langhorne, PA
The Unique Antique, Putney, VT
J B F Yoak, Jr, Charlestown, WV
Great Northwest Book Co, Toronto, ON, Canada

Theology. *See* Religion & Theology

Trade Catalogues

Albert Books, Lexington, KY
Peter L Masi — Books, Montague, MA
De Simon Company, New York, NY

Travel

Sarkis Shmavonian Books & Prints, Berkeley, CA
Vernon Howard Books, Burlingame, CA
New Albion Rare Books, Fairfax, CA
Monroe Books, Fresno, CA
Wayne G Kostman Books, Glendora, CA
Symposium Bookseller, Long Beach, CA
Abbey Bookshop, Los Angeles, CA
Bennett & Marshall, Los Angeles, CA
Heritage Bookshop Inc, Los Angeles, CA
The Scholarly Bookfinders, Los Angeles, CA
Manuel Urrizola Old & Rare Maps & Atlases, Los Angeles, CA
John Slattery Books & Prints, Palo Alto, CA
"Otento" Books, San Diego, CA
John Howell—Books, San Francisco, CA
Jeremy Norman & Co Inc, San Francisco, CA
Sergio Old Prints, San Francisco, CA
Helan Halbach—Bookseller, Santa Barbara, CA
Fred A Berk, Studio City, CA
Robert Ross & Co, Woodland Hills, CA
The Court Place Antiquarian Bookshop, Denver, CO
Branford Rare Book & Art Gallery, Branford, CT
Lawrence F Golder Rare Books, Collinsville, CT
The Book Block, Cos Cob, CT
Avis & Rockwell Gardiner, Stamford, CT
Booked Up Inc, Washington, DC
William F Hale—Books, Washington, DC
Mandala Books, Daytona Beach, FL
The Old Bookshop, Palm Beach, FL
Harry L Stern Ltd, Chicago, IL
Robert W Thompson—Books, Chicago, IL
The Athenaeum, Evanston, IL
Richard S Barnes & Co, Books, Evanston, IL
The Source Bookstore, Davenport, IA
Charles L Robinson Rare Books, Manchester, ME
Nathan Copeland Bookseller, Portland, ME
Marilyn Braiterman, Baltimore, MD
Kelmscott Bookshop, Baltimore, MD
Maury A Bromsen Associates Inc, Boston, MA
Buddenbrooks Books Inc, Boston, MA
Hurst & Hurst, Cambridge, MA
W D Hall, East Longmeadow, MA
Newburyport Rare Books, Newburyport, MA
Magnalia Americana, North Amherst, MA
Second Fiddle Bookshop, Southbridge, MA
Murray Books, Wilbraham, MA
Don Allen, Three Oaks, MI
Book Barn, South Sioux City, NE

Sykes & Flanders Old & Rare Books, Weare, NH
Richardson Books, Camden, NJ
Hummingbird Books, Albuquerque, NM
George A Bernstein, Brooklyn, NY
John C Huckans Rare Books—Pan American Books, Cazenovia, NY
Lorraine Galinsky, Cold Spring Harbor, NY
As You Like It Bookshop, Elma, NY
Charles Dvorak—Book Dealer, Glen Head, NY
Xerxes Books, Glen Head, NY
Janus Books, Huntington Station, NY
W Graham Arader III, New York, NY
Richard B Arkway Inc, New York, NY
J N Bartfield Books Inc, New York, NY
Book Ranger, New York, NY
James Cummins Bookseller Inc, New York, NY
Albert Gutkin, New York, NY
Renate Halpern Galleries Inc, New York, NY
Jonathan A Hill, Bookseller, New York, NY
Janet Lehr Inc, New York, NY
Richard C Ramer Old & Rare Books, New York, NY
Trebizond Rare Books, New York, NY
Ximenes: Rare Books Inc, New York, NY
Irving Zucker Art Books, New York, NY
Bayview Books & Bindery, Northport, NY
High Ridge Corner, Rye, NY
Chris Fessler Bookseller, Theresa, NY
Acres of Books Inc, Cincinnati, OH
Doris Davis Books, Hudson, OH
Green Dolphin Bookshop, Portland, OR
Tamerlane Books, Havertown, PA
W Graham Arader III, King of Prussia, PA
Charles Sessler Inc, Philadelphia, PA
Arthur Scharf, Travel Books, Pittsburgh, PA
The Tuckers, Pittsburgh, PA
Terry Harper Bookseller, Rouseville, PA
Murray Hudson—Books & Maps, Dyersburg, TN
The Jenkins Co, Rare Books, Austin, TX
Frontier America Corporation, Bryan, TX
W Graham Arader III, Houston, TX
Richard H Adelson, Antiquarian Bookseller, North Pomfret, VT
Louis Ginsberg—Books & Prints, Petersburg, VA
W B O'Neill—Old & Rare Books, Reston, VA
The Manuscript Company of Springfield, Springfield, VA
The Bookpress Ltd, Williamsburg, VA
Henry Stevens, Son & Stiles, Williamsburg, VA
M Taylor Bowie Bookseller, Seattle, WA
W O Moye—Bookseller, Seattle, WA
John L Polley—Bookseller, Seattle, WA

George H Tweney, Books, Seattle, WA
Acadia Bookstore, Toronto, ON, Canada
Batta Bookstore, Toronto, ON, Canada
D & E Lake Ltd Old & Rare Books, Toronto, ON, Canada

Typography

George Robert Kane Books, Santa Cruz, CA
Chiswick Bookshop Inc, Sandy Hook, CT
Barry Scott, Stonington, CT
Midnight Bookman, West Lafayette, IN
Gail Klemm — Books, Ellicott City, MD
James & Mary Laurie Booksellers, Minneapolis, MN
David L O'Neal, Antiquarian Booksellers Inc, Peterborough, NH
Hurley Books, Westmoreland, NH
W Thomas Taylor — Bookseller, Austin, TX

Voyages, Exploration & Discovery

Sarkis Shmavonian Books & Prints, Berkeley, CA
Beaver Books, Daly City, CA
New Albion Rare Books, Fairfax, CA
The Book Cellar, Fullerton, CA
Caravan Bookstore, Los Angeles, CA
Wahrenbrock's Book House, San Diego, CA
The Compass Bookstore, San Francisco, CA
Frank L Kovacs Archaeology Books, San Francisco, CA
Jeremy Norman & Co Inc, San Francisco, CA
Bob Finch, Books, Torrance, CA
Alfred W Paine — Books, Bethel, CT
Branford Rare Book & Art Gallery, Branford, CT
Kenneth Nebenzahl Inc, Chicago, IL
Robert W Thompson — Books, Chicago, IL
Maury A Bromsen Associates Inc, Boston, MA
Edward J Lefkowicz Inc, Fairhaven, MA
Magnalia Americana, North Amherst, MA
Bay Books & Prints, Big Fork, MT
Emery's Books, Contoocook, NH
Sykes & Flanders Old & Rare Books, Weare, NH
Heinoldt Books, Egg Harbor City, NJ
Stephen Koschal Autographs & Signed Books, Verona, NJ
George A Bernstein, Brooklyn, NY
Charles Dvorak — Book Dealer, Glen Head, NY
Richard B Arkway Inc, New York, NY
J N Bartfield Books Inc, New York, NY
Bayview Books & Bindery, Northport, NY
Alrich Co, Cincinnati, OH

Robert Richshafer, Cincinnati, OH
Terry Harper Bookseller, Rouseville, PA
Ray S Walton — Rare Books, Austin, TX
John Johnson Natural History Books, North Bennington, VT
M Taylor Bowie Bookseller, Seattle, WA
W O Moye — Bookseller, Seattle, WA
Joseph Patrick Books, Toronto, ON, Canada
The Map Room, Exploration House, Toronto, ON, Canada

West. *See* Americana: West

Whales and Whaling

Whaling Research, Berkeley, CA
Alfred W Paine — Books, Bethel, CT
David Ladner Books, Hamden, CT
Bookfinders of Hawaii, Hilo, HI
Robert F Lucas, Blandford, MA
Edward J Lefkowicz Inc, Fairhaven, MA
D R Nelson & Co, Booksellers, New Bedford, MA
S Clyde King Rare & Out-of-Print Books, Providence, RI

Wines

The Book Cellar, Fullerton, CA
California Book Auction Galleries, Los Angeles, CA
Marian L Gore Bookseller, San Gabriel, CA
G & C Enterprises, Lafayette, LA
Barbara L Feret, Northampton, MA
The Wine & Food Library, Ann Arbor, MI
Millard S Cohen, Saint Louis, MO
Louis Ginsberg — Books & Prints, Petersburg, VA
The Old Book Home, Spokane, WA

Witchcraft

The Antiquarium, Bethany, CT
Roy W Clare, Getzville, NY
Ben Abraham Books, Toronto, ON, Canada

Women

Bibliomania, Berkeley, CA
The Book Cellar, Fullerton, CA
Samuel W Katz, Los Angeles, CA
Boleriem Books, San Francisco, CA
Old Books, Brunswick, ME
Second Life Books, Adams, MA
Starr Book Co Inc, Boston, MA
E Wharton & Co, Boston, MA

NAME INDEX

Albert Books, Lexington, KY
Albion Fine Prints, Berkeley, CA
Aldredge Bookstore, Dallas, TX
Aleph-Bet Books, Valley Cottage, NY
Alicat Gallery, Yonkers, NY
Allbooks, Fairfax, VA
The Allegory Bookshop, Woodstock, VT
Don Allen, Three Oaks, MI
R R Allen — Books, Knoxville, TN
Robert Allen Books, Altadena, CA
William H Allen, Bookseller, Philadelphia, PA
Allenson-Breckinridge Books, Geneva, AZ
Allison Gallery Inc, Coventry, CT
Allston Bookshop, Allston, MA
Aloha Book Corner, Kaneohe, HI
Jerry Alper Inc, Eastchester, NY
Alpha Books, Encino, CA
The Alphabet Bookshop, Toronto, ON, Canada
Alrich Co, Cincinnati, OH
Al's Old & New Bookstore, Wichita, KS
Alta California Bookstore, Laguna Beach, CA
American Bookstore, Fresno, CA
American Fragments, Goleta, CA
American Library Service, New City, NY
American Library Service South, Margate, FL
American Southwest Books, Amarillo, TX
The Americanist, Pottstown, PA
Amitin's Bookshop, Saint Louis, MO
Ampersand Books, New York, NY
Anacapa Books, Berkeley, CA
Anchor & Dolphin Books, Newport, RI
Ancient City Bookshop, Santa Fe, NM
The Ancient Page, Asheville, NC
Kenneth Andersen — Books, Auburn, MA
Andover Square Books, Knoxville, TN
Andromeda Bookshop, Maquoketa, IA
Ang & Lill's Collector's Corner, Rochester, NY
Angelescu Book Service, Detroit, MI
Angler's & Shooter's Bookshelf, Goshen, CT
Anian Books, Nanaimo, BC, Canada
Hugh Anson-Cartwright, Toronto, ON, Canada
Antic Hay Books, Fairfield, NJ
Antiquarian Book Mart, San Antonio, TX
Antiquarian Books, Winnipeg, MB, Canada
Antiquarian Booksellers' Center, New York, NY
The Antiquarian Old Book Store, Portsmouth, NH
The Antiquarian Scientist, Amesbury, MA
Antiquarian Shop, Scottsdale, AZ
The Antiquarian Shop, Stevens Point, WI
The Antiquarium, Bethany, CT
The Antiquarium, Omaha, NE
Antique Books, Hamden, CT

Antique Prints, Oceanview, DE
Antiques & Art Associates, Seattle, WA
Antiques & Artifacts, Noti, OK
Antiquus Bibliopole, San Francisco, CA
Apollo Book Shop, Costa Mesa, CA
Appalachian Bookshop, Bluefield, WV
Paul P Appel, Mount Vernon, NY
Appelfeld Gallery, New York, NY
Applegate Books, Medford, OR
Appleland Books, Winchester, VA
Appletree Books, Williford, AR
Arabest Bookshop, Big Bend, WI
W Graham Arader III, New York, NY
W Graham Arader III, King of Prussia, PA
W Graham Arader III, Houston, TX
Arctician Books, Fredericton, NB, Canada
Argonaut Bookshop, San Francisco, CA
Argosy Bookstore Inc, New York, NY
Argus Books & Graphics, Sacramento, CA
Ark Bookshop, Berkeley, CA
Arkadyan Books & Prints, San Francisco, CA
Ark-La-Tex Book Co, Shreveport, LA
Richard B Arkway Inc, New York, NY
Glenn Armitage, Miamisburg, OH
Frederick W Armstrong Bookseller, Stephenville, TX
Arnold's of Michigan, Traverse City, MI
Frederick Arone Railroad Items, Dobbs Ferry, NY
Ars Libri Ltd, Boston, MA
Artistic Endeavors, Boston, MA
As You Like It Bookshop, Elma, NY
Mrs A L Ashton, Ottawa, ON, Canada
Asian Rare Books Inc, New York, NY
The Asphodel Bookshop, Burton, OH
The Associates — Modern First Editions, Falls Church, VA
The Athenaeum, Evanston, IL
Atlantic Book Service, Boston, MA
Attenson Antiques & Books, Cleveland, OH
Attic Books, Newark, DE
Attic Books, Wheaton, MD
Attic Books, London, ON, Canada
The Attic Inc, Hodges, SC
Atticus Books, San Diego, CA
Atticus Books, Toronto, ON, Canada
Bart Auerbach Ltd, New York, NY
Auld Stone Bookshop, Glasgow, VA
Authors of the West, Dundee, OR
Autos & Autos — Book Dept, Elizabeth City, NC
Avatar Books, Moline, IL
Avatar Books & Records, Clearwater, FL
Avenue Bookshop, Ottawa, ON, Canada
Aviation Bookmobile — Mil-Air Photos & Books, Compton, CA
Aviation Bookmobile — Mil-Air Photos & Books, Norwalk, CA

Avis & Rockwell Gardiner, Stamford, CT
Avocational, Ephrata, PA
Avol's Bookstore, Madison, WI
Avonlea Books, White Plains, NY
Axelrod—Music Inc, Providence, RI
Walter Axelrod, Providence, RI
Bert Babcock—Bookseller, Derry, NH
James M Babcock Bookseller, Algonac, MI
Back Tracts Inc, Indianapolis, IN
The Backroom Bookstore, Webster, NY
Jack Bailes—Books, Eureka Springs, AR
Bailey Search Service, Redondo Beach, CA
Baldwin's Book Barn, West Chester, PA
Leonard Balish, Englewood, NJ
Shirley Balser 16th-20th Century Paintings, Prints & Books, Pikesville, MD
Barjon's Books & Graphics, Billings, MT
Conway Barker—Autograph Dealer, Dallas, TX
C Virginia Barnes—Bookseller, New York, NY
Glynis Barnes, Toronto, ON, Canada
Richard S Barnes & Co, Books, Evanston, IL
Barnette's Books, South Bend, IN
Barnstable Books Inc, New York, NY
Charles Baron, Bronx, NY
Bryan Barrett Books, Hayward, CA
Barrington Old Bookshop, Barrington, IL
The Barrow Bookstore, Concord, MA
J N Bartfield Books Inc, New York, NY
Bartlett Street Bookstore, Medford, OR
Robert F Batchelder, Ambler, PA
Batta Bookstore, Toronto, ON, Canada
The Battery Book Shop, Nashville, TN
Battlefield Bookshop, Gettysburg, PA
Bauman Rare Books, Atlantic City, NJ
Bauman Rare Books, Philadelphia, PA
Bay Books & Prints, Big Fork, MT
Bay Side Books, Soquel, CA
Bayou Books Inc, Gretna, LA
Bayview Books & Bindery, Northport, NY
Mary Beth Beal, Chicago, IL
Doug Bearce, Salem, OR
Beasley Books, Chicago, IL
Beatty Bookstore, Seattle, WA
Beaufort Book Co, Beaufort, SC
The Beautiful & the Unusual, Redondo Beach, CA
Beaver Books, Daly City, CA
Beckham's Bookshop, New Orleans, LA
Beckoning Cat Bookshop, Menasha, WI
Bedford's Used Books, Ellsworth, ME
Deanna Beeching Bookseller, Harrisburg, PA
Bel Canto Bookshop, Metuchen, NJ
Belanske & Levinger Inc, New York, NY
Walter R Benjamin Autographs Inc, Hunter, NY
Bennett & Marshall, Los Angeles, CA

Deborah Benson Bookseller, West Cornwall, CT
Howard O Berg, Devils Lake, ND
J & J Berger Booksellers, Oakland, CA
Fred A Berk, Studio City, CA
Carl Sandler Berkowitz, Chester, NY
Lillian Berliawsky—Books, Camden, ME
Steven C Bernard First Editions, Rockville, MD
F A Bernett Inc, Larchmont, NY
Michael E Bernholz Antiques & Books, Hillsborough, NC
George A Bernstein, Brooklyn, NY
Berry Hill Bookshop, Deansboro, NY
Ken Bessinger, Milford, DE
Between the Lines, Bloomington, IN
Ron Bever, Edmond, OK
Preston C Beyer Fine Literary Property, Stratford, CT
G A Bibby Books, Gold Hill, OR
Bibelots & Books, Seattle, WA
Herbert Biblo Bookseller, Chicago, IL
Bibliography of the Dog, Montreal, PQ, Canada
Bibliomania, Berkeley, CA
Bibliomania, Schenectady, NY
Biblion Inc, Forest Hills, NY
Bickerstaff & Barclay, Washington, DC
Biermaier's B H Books, Minneapolis, MN
Big Bookstore, Detroit, MI
Big D Books & Comics, Dallas, TX
Big John's Bookroom, Meshoppen, PA
Binkin's Book Center, Brooklyn, NY
Bird's Nest, Missoula, MT
The Bishop of Books, Wheeling, WV
Bishop-Williams, Vancouver, BC, Canada
Roger Black, Pomfret, CT
Black Sun Books, New York, NY
Black Swan Books, Sacramento, CA
Warren Blake Bookseller, Fairfield, CT
William Bledsoe, Bookseller, San Carlos, CA
Roy Bleiweiss Fine Books, Berkeley, CA
Blitz Books, Weaverville, CA
Carl Blomgren Books, San Rafael, CA
Blue Dragon Book Shop, Ashland, OR
A Blue Moon Books & Records, Clearwater, FL
Blue Star Bookstore, Putnam, CT
Bluestem Books, Lincoln, NE
Bob's Bookshop, Appelton, WI
Bohling Book Co, Lawton, MI
Boise Book Mart, Boise, ID
Boleriem Books, San Francisco, CA
Nelson Bond, Roanoke, VA
Bond's Bookshop, Vancouver, BC, Canada
J C Bonnette Bookseller, Fair Oaks, CA
Book & Tackle Shop, Chestnut Hill, MA
Book Barn, Walnut, IL

Book Barn—Victorian House, Stockton Springs, ME
Book Barn, South Sioux City, NE
The Book Barn, Canandaigua, NY
The Book Baron, Anaheim, CA
Book Bazaar, Ottawa, ON, Canada
The Book Bear, West Brookfield, MA
The Book Block, Cos Cob, CT
Book Carnival, Orange, CA
Book Case Books, Pasadena, CA
The Book Cellar, Fullerton, CA
Book Cellar, Freeport, ME
Book Cellar, Temple, TX
Book Center—Dave Henson, Books, Santa Ana, CA
The Book Chest Inc, Rockville Centre, NY
Book City of Burbank, Burbank, CA
The Book Collector, Newton, MA
Book Company, Pasadena, CA
The Book End, Monterey, CA
Book Ends, Arlington, VA
The Book Exchange, Missoula, MT
The Book Exchange, Marysville, WA
The Book Exchange, Spokane, WA
Book Farm, Henniker, NH
Book Forum, Denver, CO
The Book Gallery, White Plains, NY
The Book Habit, San Marcos, CA
The Book Harbor, Fullerton, CA
Book Haven, Lancaster, PA
The Book House Booksellers, Minneapolis, MN
The Book Lady, Savannah, GA
Book Look, Warwick, NY
Book Mark, Philadelphia, PA
The Book Mart, Asheville, NC
Book Mart Annex, San Antonio, TX
The Book Nest, Los Altos, CA
Book Pedlars, Brunswick, ME
Book Ranger, New York, NY
Book Sail, Orange, CA
Book Search Service, Avondale Estates, GA
Book Search Service, Pittsburgh, PA
The Book Shelf, Cleveland, TN
The Book Shoppe, Salt Lake City, UT
Book Stall, Cincinnati, OH
Book Stall, Norman, OK
Book Stop III, Las Vegas, NV
Book Swap, Solana Beach, CA
The Book Swappers, Wantagh, NY
Book Vault, Santa Ana, CA
Book Warehouse Inc, Coral Gables, FL
Book World, Petoskey, MI
Booked Up Inc, Washington, DC
Booketeria, San Antonio, TX
Bookfinder, Sea Isle City, NJ
Bookfinder's General Inc, New York, NY
The Bookfinders Inc, Miami Beach, FL
Bookfinders of Hawaii, Hilo, HI

Bookhouse, Arlington, VA
The Bookie Joint, Reseda, CA
Booklegger's, Chicago, IL
The Bookmailer, Minneapolis, MN
Bookman's Alley, Evanston, IL
Bookpost, Cardiff, CA
The Bookpress Ltd, Williamsburg, VA
Books & Art Prints Store, Miami, FL
Books & Birds, Coventry, CT
Books & Stuff, Pearl, MS
Books & The Collector Arts, Encino, CA
Books-by-Mail, Albuquerque, NM
Books Et Cetera, Chico, CA
Books Etc, Fort Worth, TX
Books in Transit, Turlock, CA
Books of Colonial America, Wheaton, MD
Books of Wonder, New York, NY
Books on File, Guttenberg, NJ
Books, South Egremont, MA
Books, Then & Now, Madison, WI
Booksearch, San Antonio, TX
The Bookseller—Columbia, Columbia, MO
The Bookseller Inc, Akron, OH
Booksellers Ltd, Wheeling, WV
Booksellers Row, Chicago, IL
Books 'n Things, New York, NY
Books 'n Things, East Greenville, PA
Booksource, Swarthmore, PA
The Bookstack, Elkhart, IN
Bookstall of Rockford, Rockford, IL
The Bookstall, San Francisco, CA
Bookstop Albuquerque, Albuquerque, NM
The Bookstore at Depot Square, Englewood, NJ
The Bookstore, Peterborough, ON, Canada
W J Bookunter, Denver, CO
The Bookworm, Corning, NY
Bookworm & Silverfish, Wytheville, VA
James M W Borg Inc, Chicago, IL
Boro Book Store, Brooklyn, NY
Boston Book Annex, Boston, MA
Meyer Boswell Books, San Francisco, CA
Roy V Boswell—Antiquarian Books & Maps, Fullerton, CA
Joshua David Bowen, San Antonio, TX
E R Bowes Books, Vancouver, BC, Canada
M Taylor Bowie Bookseller, Seattle, WA
William G Boyer, New York, NY
Van Allen Bradley Inc, Scottsdale, AZ
Osee H Brady Books, Assonet, MA
Marilyn Braiterman, Baltimore, MD
Dale A Brandreth Books, Hockessin, DE
Brandywine Books, Saxton, PA
Branford Rare Book & Art Gallery, Branford, CT
Brattle Book Store, Boston, MA
Martin Breslauer Inc, New York, NY
Harvey W Brewer, Closter, NJ
Brick House Bookshop, Morrisville, VT

The Brick Row Book Shop, San Francisco, CA

John Bridge, Stamford, CT

Michel Brisebois Librairie, Montreal, PQ, Canada

Broadfoot's Bookmark, Wendell, NC

Broadwater Books, Lewiston, NY

Broken Kettle Books, Akron, IA

Bromer Booksellers, Inc, Boston, MA

Maury A Bromsen Associates Inc, Boston, MA

Brookline Village Books & Prints, Brookline, MA

George Brosi Bookseller, Berea, KY

Broude Brothers Limited, New York, NY

George D Brown—Books, Toledo, OH

Robert K Brown, New York, NY

Robert L Brown Bookmonger, Seattle, WA

Charlie Brown's Book-Gallerie, Brooklyn, NY

Browsers' Bookshop, Olympia, WA

The Browsery, Greensboro, NC

Joan Marie Bruna, Cicero, IL

Bryant's, Provincetown, MA

Bucephalus Books, New York, NY

Buckabest Books & Bindery, Palo Alto, CA

Buddenbrooks Books Inc, Boston, MA

Bump's Barn Bookshop, Ashland, NH

Bump's Books, Scarsdale, NY

Bunkhouse Books, Gardiner, ME

Bunter Books, Winnetka, IL

Virginia Burgman, Santa Rosa, CA

Burke's Bookstore Inc, Memphis, TN

Burkwood Books, Urbana, IL

Norm Burleson Bookseller, Spartanburg, SC

Don E Burnett, East Greenwich, RI

Julian Burnett Books, Atlanta, GA

Thomas W Burrows, Bookseller, Downers Grove, IL

Harold M Burstein, Antiquarian, Waltham, MA

Carol Butcher, Youngstown, OH

Bygone Book House, Dearborn, MI

Bygone Books Inc, Burlington, VT

C & E Books, Kitchener, ON, Canada

A Cabinet of Books, Watertown, CT

Dirk Cable Bookseller, Pasadena, CA

The Cache, Loveland, CO

Cadenza Booksellers, Smithtown, NY

Richard Cady Rare Books, Port Chester, NY

The Caledonia, Sussex, NB, Canada

Calico Cat Bookshop, Ventura, CA

California Book Auction Galleries, Los Angeles, CA

Callahan & Co Booksellers, Temple, NH

Camelot Books, Springfield, VA

Cameron's Book Store, Portland, OR

Canadiana House, Toronto, ON, Canada

Canterbury Bookshop, Los Angeles, CA

Carlos Canterbury Bookstore, San Carlos, CA

Cantrell's Books, North East, PA

Caravan Bookstore, Los Angeles, CA

Caravan-Maritime Books, Jamaica, NY

Art Carduner, Philadelphia, PA

Bernard Conwell Carlitz, Philadelphia, PA

Carlson & Turner Books, Portland, ME

Carmel Bookshop, Lapel, IN

Carney Books, Oneonta, NY

Carolina Bookshop, Charlotte, NC

Carriage-Barn Books and Antiques, Williamstown, MA

Carriage House Books, Kirkwood, NY

Carry Back Books, Haverhill, NH

Cartographica, Houston, TX

Cartographics, North Stonington, CT

Roger F Casavant, Wayland, MA

John Cashman Books, Sea Cliff, NY

Barry Cassidy Rare Books, Sacramento, CA

William J Cassidy, Kansas City, MO

Castalia Books, Milwaukee, WI

Jo Ann & Richard Casten Antique Maps, Wading River, NY

The Catholic Book Collector, Bellingham, MA

Caveat Emptor, Bloomington, IN

Celestial Books, La Canada, CA

The Cellar Bookshop, Detroit, MI

Celtic Cross Books, Westmoreland, NH

Chafey's Old & Rare Books, Albuquerque, NM

Bev Chaney Jr, Books, Croton-on-Hudson, NY

Chang Tang Books, Peekskill, NY

Chaparral Books of Santa Fe, Santa Fe, NM

Chapel Hill Rare Books, Carrboro, NC

Chapman & Berryman Booksellers, Los Angeles, CA

Mary Chapman Bookseller, College Park, MD

Charlotte's Web Antiques, Monkton, MD

The Chatham Bookseller, Madison, NJ

Chelmsford, Chelmsford, MA

Chelsea Antiques, Durham, NC

Cherokee Bookshop Inc, Los Angeles, CA

Childs Gallery, Boston, MA

Chimney Sweep Books, Scotts Valley, CA

China Book Gallery, Minneapolis, MN

Chip's Bookshop Inc, New York, NY

Chirurgical Bookshop, Baltimore, MD

Chiswick Bookshop Inc, Sandy Hook, CT

Chloe's Bookstore, Sacramento, CA

Choreographica, Boston, MA

Christian Classics Inc, Westminster, MD

Peggy Christian Bookseller, Los Angeles, CA

Jens J Christoffersen Rare Books, Mamaroneck, NY

Christopher's Book Room, Bloomington, IN

Doris Davis Books, Hudson, OH
Ernest Davis, Harrodsburg, KY
Davis & Schorr Art Books, Los Angeles, CA
The Dawn Treader Book Shop, Ann Arbor, MI
Dawson's Bookshop, Los Angeles, CA
De Anima: Books in Psychology, Bowling Green, OH
Frederica De Beurs Books, Dexter, ME
Deecee Books, Nyack, NY
Deeds Bookshop, Ellicott City, MD
George Deeds Book Finder, San Pedro, CA
De La Pena Books, Santa Fe, NM
Robert C Demarest Bookseller, Naples, FL
Demerara Book Service, Miami, FL
Denbry Books, Bronx, NY
Denning House, Salisbury Mills, NY
Bonnie Denver Books, Stockton, CA
Joseph A Dermont Fine Books, Onset, MA
De Simon Company, New York, NY
Rebecca B Desmarais Rare Books, Framingham, MA
Detering Book Gallery, Houston, TX
John E Deturck, Mount Penn, PA
Daniel H Deutsch PhD—Books, Pasadena, CA
Harold B Diamond—Bookseller, Burbank, CA
Dianco International, Mill Valley, CA
Dickey Books, Wichita, KS
Dickson Street Bookshop, Fayetteville, AR
Dinkytown Antiquarian Bookshop, Minneapolis, MN
Leonard Dixon Bookstore, San Antonio, TX
Carol Docheff—Bookseller, Berkeley, CA
Dr Nostalgia, Lynchburg, VA
Donald R Doerres, Wilton, IA
Dolphin Bookshop, New York, NY
Dolphin Bookstore, Camden, ME
Donato's Fine Books, Las Vegas, NV
E Donbullian Back Number Magazine Company, Greenbelt, MD
Richard E Donovan, Endicott, NY
Don's Bookstore & Black Letter Press, Grand Rapids, MI
James M Dourgarian, Bookman, Walnut Creek, CA
James Dowd—Bookseller, Saint Charles, IL
Downtown Bookshop, Jacksonville, FL
Paul J Drabeck, Bronx, NY
Dragoman Books, Annapolis, MD
Drew's Bookshop, Santa Barbara, CA
Emily Driscoll, Shepherdstown, WV
Drusilla's Books, Lutherville, MD
M F Duffy—Books, Las Vegas, NV
R Dunaway, Bookseller, Saint Louis, MO
Elizabeth F Dunlap, Books & Maps, Saint Louis, MO
Michael Dunn Books, Newport, VT

D N Dupley, Book Dealer, Omaha, NE
Dupriest's Bookshop, Columbia, SC
Philip C Duschnes Inc, New York, NY
Duttenhofer's Book Treasures, Cincinnati, OH
Charles Dvorak—Book Dealer, Glen Head, NY
Raymond Dworczyk, Rare Books, Milwaukee, WI
Dwyer's Bookstore Inc, Northampton, MA
Dykes, Jeff—Western Books, College Park, MD
Dyment Books—Scholars' Bookstore, Ottawa, ON, Canada
E & S Summerhouse Books, Dayton, WY
East Coast Books, Wells, ME
Harland H Eastman Books & Prints, Springvale, ME
Echo Books, Arlington, MA
The Eclectic Gallery, Mill Valley, CA
The Eclectic Gallery, Sausalito, CA
Economy Books, Alexandria, VA
J S Edgren, Carmel, CA
J S Edgren, Los Angeles, CA
Editions, Boiceville, NY
Educo Services International Ltd, Valhalla, NY
Egg Harbor Books, Egg Harbor City, NJ
I Ehrlich, Montreal, PQ, Canada
El Cascajero, The Old Spanish Book Mine, New York, NY
El Paisano Books, Albuquerque, NM
Eldorado Books, San Francisco, CA
Eldorado Comics, Cherry Hill, NJ
Elgen Books, Rockville Centre, NY
Elliot's Books, Out of Print Specialists, Northford, CT
Elmcress Books, Hamilton, MA
Elmwood Bookshop, East Bridgewater, MA
Dorothy Elsberg, West Stockbridge, MA
F P Elwert, Rutland, VT
Elysian Fields Booksellers, Elmhurst, NY
R & D Emerson, Falls Village, CT
Emery's Books, Contoocook, NH
The English Bookshop, Gloucester, MA
Enterprise Books, Ripley, TN
Entropy Books, Pleasant Ridge, MI
The Epistemologist, Scholarly Books, Bryn Mawr, PA
Louis Epstein, Hollywood, CA
Erasmus Books, South Bend, IN
Erie Book Store, Erie, PA
Gary L Estabrook—Books, Vancouver, WA
Estampe Originale, Saratoga, CA
Estate Book Sales, Washington, DC
Estate Books, Berkeley, IL
Lonnie E Evans—Books, Savannah, GA
Olin O Evans, Woodstock, VA
Ex Libris, New York, NY

Ex Libris Etcetera, Dover, NH
Exnowski Enterprises, Warren, MI
Extensive Search Service, Danielson, CT
F & I Books, Santa Monica, CA
N Fagin Books, Chicago, IL
Fain's First Editions, Pacific Palisades, CA
Edward C Fales Old & Rare Books & Manuscripts, Salisbury, NH
The Family Album, Glen Rock, PA
Family Book Exchange, Springfield, IL
Family Bookstore, Whittier, CA
Fantasy Illustrated, Garden Grove, CA
Far Country Bookstore, Albany, NY
Farley's Old & Rare Books, Pensacola, FL
Barbara Farnsworth Bookseller, West Cornwall, CT
Lawrence Feinberg Rare Books & Manuscripts, Brooklyn, NY
Joseph J Felcone Inc, Rare Books, Princeton, NJ
A B Fenner Books, Clute, TX
Barbara L Feret, Northampton, MA
Malcolm M Ferguson, Concord, MA
Ferndale Books, Ferndale, CA
Bruce P Ferrini, Rare Books, Akron, OH
Chris Fessler Bookseller, Theresa, NY
Marie Fetrow, York, PA
Fiddler's Folly, Pleasant Valley, NY
Bob Finch, Books, Torrance, CA
The Fine Books Co & David Aronovitz — Books, Rochester, MI
Fine Print, Tampa, FL
Steve Finer — Books, Turners Falls, MA
Firstborn Books, Galesville, MD
A S Fischler — Rare Books, San Jose, CA
C G Fisher — Books, Cobleskill, NY
Peter Thomas Fisher — Bookseller, New York, NY
Richard Fitch Old Maps & Prints & Books, Santa Fe, NM
Five Dog Books, Reno, NV
Five Quail Books, Rancho Santa Fe, CA
Richard Flamer Bookseller, Omaha, NE
N Flayderman & Co Inc, New Milford, CT
John F Fleming Inc, New York, NY
Frances Flenett, Brooklyn, NY
Fletcher's Books, Salado, TX
Fleuron Books, Longboat Key, FL
Fly Creek Bookstall, Fly Creek, NY
T T & Jean Foley — Antiques, Paris, IL
Folkways Scholarly Books, Bethesda, MD
Alla T Ford Rare Books, Lake Worth, FL
Forest Park Bookshop, Fort Wayne, IN
Fortunate Finds Bookstore, Warwick, RI
Fox Book Co, Tacoma, WA
Fox Hill Books, Palmer, MA
Leonard Fox Ltd, New York, NY
Ben Franklin Bookshop & Printery, Upper Nyack, NY

Harry A Franklin Gallery, Beverly Hills, CA
James Fraser, Burlington, VT
Howard Frisch, Livingston, NY
Doris Frohnsdorff, Gaithersburg, MD
Frontier America Corporation, Bryan, TX
Susan Frost, Austin, TX
Fuller's Books, West Haven, CT
Fur Fin Feather Books, Lansing, IL
Herbert Furse — Bookman, Glenview, IL
W Bruce Fye Antiquarian Medical Books, Marshfield, WI
G & C Enterprises, Lafayette, LA
John Gach Books Inc, Columbia, MD
Jean Gagnon, Quebec, PQ, Canada
Kendall G Gaisser, Booksellers, Toledo, OH
Gale Books, Marshalltown, IA
Lorraine Galinsky, Cold Spring Harbor, NY
Irving Galis, Marblehead, MA
Gallery of the Old West, Big Fork, MT
Galvez Books & Silver Inc, Pensacola, FL
Gammage Cup Books, Sacramento, CA
Garcia-Garst, Bookseller, Turlock, CA
Charles E Gardiner, Bayside, NY
Ralph D Gardner, New York, NY
Anthony Garnett — Fine Books, Saint Louis, MO
Charles Garvin Rare Books, Ithaca, NY
Gasoline Alley Antiques, Seattle, WA
Max Gate Books, Kankakee, IL
The Gateway, Ferndale, PA
William T Gavin, Leominster, MA
Gem Antiques, New York, NY
Genesee Bookshop, Rochester, NY
Geological Book Center, Falls Village, CT
Geppi's Comic World, Largo, FL
Geppi's Comic World, Baltimore, MD
Geppi's Comic World, Silver Spring, MD
Geppi's Comic World Inc, Alexandria, VA
Geppi's Crystal City Comics, Arlington, VA
Lois Gereghty Books, Sepulveda, CA
V F Germack, Professional Photography Collectors, New York, NY
Richard P Germann, Willard, OH
Ghent Bookworm, Norfolk, VA
Michael Gibbs Books, State College, PA
Gilann Books, Darien, CT
Richard Gilbo — Books, Carpenteria, CA
Franklin Gilliam: Rare Books, Charlottesville, VA
Stanley Gilman, New York, NY
Louis Ginsberg, Petersburg, VA
Michael Ginsberg Books Inc, Sharon, MA
G F Glaeve Art & Books, Mount Horeb, WI
Edwin V Glaser Rare Books, Sausalito, CA
Glenn Books Inc, Kansas City, MO
Global Book Research, Belding, MI
The Globe, Chicago, IL
Globe & Anchor Book Co, Saint Augustine, FL

Le Valois Rare Books, New York, NY
Philip G Le Van Bookseller, Allentown, PA
Barry R Levin Science Fiction & Fantasy Literature, Los Angeles, CA
Jacqueline Levine Books, Savannah, GA
Harry A Levinson Rare Books, Beverly Hills, CA
Lewis Antiques, Micanopy, FL
R E Lewis Inc, San Rafael, CA
Liberty Rock Book Shoppe, Sloatsburg, NY
Libra Books, Reseda, CA
Librairie Bookshop, New Orleans, LA
Librairie D'Antan, Montreal, PQ, Canada
Librairie Encyclopedique, Montreal, PQ, Canada
Librairie Faubourg—Quebec, Canadiana, Montreal, PQ, Canada
Librairie O Vieux Bouquins, Drummond-ville, PQ, Canada
Librairie Quebecoise, Montreal, PQ, Canada
Libros Latinos, Redlands, CA
William B Liebmann, Bronx, NY
Leland N Lien Bookseller, Minneapolis, MN
Lighthouse Books, Saint Petersburg, FL
Wade Lillywhite Books, Santa Ana, CA
Limestone Hills Bookshop, Glen Rose, TX
Lincoln Book Shoppe Inc & Lincoln Out-of-Print Book Search Ltd, Foster, RI
Robert Larkin Link Bookseller, Redding, CA
Lion Bookshop, San Francisco, CA
Lion Heart Autographs Inc, New York, NY
Little Hundred Gallery, Charlotte, NC
Littwin & Feiden, Mamaroneck, NY
Live Oak Booksellers, Arcadia, CA
Lloyd Books, Washington, DC
Lock Stock & Barrel Shop, Dalton, PA
The London Bookshop, Chicago, IL
The London Bookshop, Albany, NY
Jack London Bookstore, Glen Ellen, CA
Long Island Book Center, Hempstead, NY
Judith R Long, Marietta, GA
Longfellow's Book & Record Store, Port-land, OR
Longhouse Bookshop Ltd, Toronto, ON, Canada
The Looking Glass, Worthington, OH
L S Loomer Antiquarian Books, Windsor, NS, Canada
Ken Lopez Bookseller, Englewood, NJ
Lord Randall Book & Print Shop, Marshfield, MA
Lorson's Books & Prints, Fullerton, CA
James Lowe Autographs Ltd, New York, NY
Richard A Lowenstein, Mahopac, NY
Leo Lowenthal, Dover, NJ
Philip Lozinski, Canadian Branch Reg'd, Saint Bruno, PQ, Canada
Philip Lozinski Scholarly Books, Westport, MA

Ernest Lubbe, Books, San Francisco, CA
J & J Lubrano, South Lee, MA
Lubrecht & Cramer, Monticello, NY
Robert F Lucas, Blandford, MA
Stephen C Lunsford Books, North Vancou-ver, BC, Canada
Mary Hosmer Lupton, Charlottesville, VA
T N Luther Books, Shawnee Mission, KS
Lyrical Ballad Bookstore, Saratoga Springs, NY
Burton Lysecki Books, Winnipeg, MB, Canada
M & S Rare Books Inc, Weston, MA
Thomas Macaluso Rare & Fine Books, Kennett Square, PA
McBlain Books, Des Moines, IA
McBride First Editions, Hartford, CT
T J McCauley Books, Langhorne, PA
McClintock's Books, Warren, OH
David McCord Books, Atlanta, GA
Melvin McCosh Bookseller, Excelsior, MN
McDonald's Bookshop, San Francisco, CA
McDuffie's Books, Opportunity, WA
McDuffie's Old Books, Spokane, WA
Andrew B W MacEwen and Aimee B Mac-Ewen, Stockton Springs, ME
McFarland Books, Tampa, FL
J Patrick McGahern—Books Inc, Ottawa, ON, Canada
Maggie McGiggles Antiques, Mentor, OH
Laurence McGilvery, La Jolla, CA
McGrath's Book Collector, Muskogee, OK
Jean S McKenna Old, Scarce, Out-of-Print Books, Beverly, MA
Bruce McKittrick, Rare Books, Philadelphia, PA
McLaughlin's Books, Chico, CA
George S MacManus Co, Philadelphia, PA
Mike Maddigan, Cedar Rapids, IA
Madonna House Bookshop, Combermere, ON, Canada
Maelstrom, San Francisco, CA
Magnalia Americana, North Amherst, MA
Magus' Bookstore, Seattle, WA
Mahoney & Weekly, Booksellers, Buffalo, NY
Maiden Voyage Books, New York, NY
Main Street Books, Annapolis, MD
Main Street Booksellers, Brooklyn, NY
Mainly Mysteries, Sherman Oaks, CA
John Makarewich, Books, Van Nuys, CA
Jan & Larry Malis, New Canaan, CT
P T Mallahan Bookseller, Bellevue, WA
G B Manasek Inc, Chicago, IL
Jeffrey D Mancevice Inc, Worcester, MA
Mandala Books, Daytona Beach, FL
Mandrake Bookshop, San Rafael, CA
Robert W Mann Rare Books, San Diego, CA
Manning's Books, San Francisco, CA

New Albion Bookshop, Fairfax, CA
New Albion Rare Books, Fairfax, CA
New Englandiana, Bennington, VT
New York Bound Bookshop, New York, NY
Newburyport Rare Books, Newburyport, MA
J & T Nie Booksellers, Tucson, AZ
Niles & Silver, Santa Monica, CA
99-E Antique-Used, Woodburn, OR
Einer Nisula—Rare Books, Okemos, MI
Noah's Ark Book Attic, Greenwood, SC
John B Nomland Booksellers, Los Angeles, CA
J Norman Books 'n Tobacco, Depew, NY
Jeremy Norman & Co Inc, San Francisco, CA
James Normile—Books, Los Angeles, CA
John E Norris, Paoli, PA
Paul H North Jr, Columbus, OH
North Shore Books Ltd, Huntington, NY
North Toronto Coins Ltd, Toronto, ON, Canada
Northland Books, Saskatoon, SK, Canada
Northwest Books, Oakland, CA
Norumbega Books, Houston, TX
Nostalgia Books, Guelph, ON, Canada
The Nostalgia Factory, Newport, RI
Nostalgia Plus, Richmond, VA
Sal Noto—Books, Crestline, CA
Nouveau Rare Books, Jackson, MS
The Novel Experience, San Luis Obispo, CA
Nudel Books, New York, NY
Edward D Nudelman Children's & Illustrated Antiquarian Books, Seattle, WA
Oak Knoll Books, New Castle, DE
F M O'Brien Old Book Shop, Portland, ME
Obsolescence, Gettysburg, PA
Oceana Publications Inc, Dobbs Ferry, NY
Oceanside Books Unlimited, Oceanside, NY
John C O'Connor, Tenafly, NJ
October Farm, Raleigh, NC
The Odd Book, Wolfville, NS, Canada
J & J O'Donoghue Books, Anoka, MN
Emil Offenbacher, Kew Gardens, NY
Gil O'Gara, Des Moines, IA
Joseph O'Gara Bookseller, Chicago, IL
Ohio Bookhunter, Mansfield, OH
Ohio Bookstore, Cincinnati, OH
The Oklahoma Bookman, Yukon, OK
Okman's Happy Endings, Woodland Hills, CA
Olana Gallery, Brewster, NY
Old Book & Photo—Russell Norton, New Haven, CT
Old & Rare Literature, Kalamazoo, MI
The Old Book Corner, Racine, WI
The Old Book Home, Spokane, WA
The Old Book Scout—Jim McMeans, Atlanta, GA

Old Books, New Orleans, LA
Old Books, Brunswick, ME
The Old Bookshop, San Francisco, CA
The Old Bookshop, Jacksonville, FL
The Old Bookshop, Palm Beach, FL
The Old Bookshop, Morristown, NJ
Old Bookstore, Northampton, MA
Old Bookstore, Akron, OH
Old Bookstore, Nashville, TN
Old Corner Bookshop, Fort Collins, CO
Old Editions Bookshop, Buffalo, NY
Old Favorites Bookshop, Locust Hill, ON, Canada
Old Favorites Bookshop Ltd, Toronto, ON, Canada
Old Galen's Books, Durham, NC
Old Hickory Bookshop Ltd, Brinklow, MD
Old Louisville Books, Louisville, KY
Old Mill Books, Charleston, SC
Old Mystic Bookshop, Old Mystic, CT
Old New York Bookshop, Atlanta, GA
Old Number Six Book Depot, Henniker, NH
Old Oregon Bookstore, Portland, OR
The Old Print Gallery, Washington, DC
The Old Print Shop Inc, New York
Old Print Store, Chicago, IL
The Old Printed Word, Kensington, MD
Old Quenzel Store, Port Tobacco, MD
Old Seattle Paperworks, Seattle, WA
Old South Books, Memphis, TN
Old Weird Herald's, Portland, OR
Olde Soldier Book, Poolesville, MD
The Ole Moon & Other Tales, Dallas, TX
Olinghouse & Tyson Booksellers & La Querencia Press, San Diego, CA
Ollie's Books, Memphis, TN
Olympia Books, Philadelphia, PA
Omega Books, Northampton, MA
Omni Graphic Media Co, Hollywood, FL
Once Upon a Time Books, Roslyn Heights, NY
1023 Booksellers, Omaha, NE
David L O'Neal, Antiquarian Booksellers Inc, Peterborough, NH
Robert M O'Neill, Rare Books, Warner, NH
W B O'Neill—Old & Rare Books, Reston, VA
The Open Creel, Palmer, MA
George K Oppenheim, Berkeley, CA
Frank Opperman, Rochester, NY
Opportunity Books, Lewiston, ID
William Orbelo, San Antonio, TX
Origin Books, Minneapolis, MN
Rena & Merwin L Orner, Tenafly, NJ
Orsay Books, New York, NY
Ostby's Americana, Bellflower, CA
"Otento" Books, San Diego, CA
Simon Ottenberg, Booksellers, Seattle, WA
Oudal Bookshop, Minneapolis, MN

Red Horse at Ybor Square, Tampa, FL
Red River Books, Shreveport, LA
Robert H Redding Books, Sequim, WA
O P Reed Jr, Los Angeles, CA
William Reese Co, New Haven, CT
Regent Street Books, Berkeley, CA
Jo Ann Reisler Ltd, Vienna, VA
Renaissance Book Shop Inc, Milwaukee, WI
Renaissance Book Shop Inc—General Mitchell Field, Milwaukee, WI
The Rendells Inc, Newton, MA
Renrel Books, Lauderhill, FL
Reston's Booknook, Amsterdam, NY
Frank E Reynolds Bookseller
J E Reynolds, Bookseller, Willits, CA
Paul C Richards, Templeton, MA
Richard's Readers, Tennyson, IN
Richardson Books, Camden, NJ
Richardson, Mentor-on-the-Lake, OH
Robert Richshafer, Cincinnati, OH
Ridge Books, Stone Ridge, NY
P R Rieber, Thomasville, GA
William Riley—Books, Kensington, CA
Jack D Rittenhouse, Books, Albuquerque, NM
Rivendell Bookshop Ltd, New York, NY
Riverow Bookshop, Owego, NY
Riverrun, Hastings-on-Hudson, NY
Richard Owen Roberts Booksellers, Wheaton, IL
A G Robinson Bookman, Pontiac, MI
Carroll Miner Robinson Old Books, Palm Beach, FL
Cedric L Robinson, Bookseller, Windsor, CT
Charles L Robinson Rare Books, Manchester, ME
Harry B Robinson Book Search Service, Columbia, MO
Ruth E Robinson Books, Morgantown, WV
Wallace A Robinson, Saint Petersburg, FL
John Roby, San Diego, CA
Rockland Bookman, Cattaraugus, NY
Rogers Park Used Bookstore, Chicago, IL
Paul Romaine—Books, Chicago, IL
Ron-Dot Bookfinders, Greensburg, OH
Rochelle R Ronketty Bookseller, Pasadena, CA
B & L Rootenberg Fine & Rare Books, Sherman Oaks, CA
Paulette Rose Ltd, New York, NY
Rose Tree Inn Bookshop, Tombstone, AZ
H C Roseman Bookseller, Brooklyn, NY
Mary S Rosenberg, New York, NY
Fred A Rosenstock—Books & Arts, Denver, CO
Bernard M Rosenthal Inc, San Francisco, CA
Franklin M Roshon, Pottstown, PA
Roskie & Wallace Bookstore, San Leandro, CA

Ross & Haines Old Books Co, Wayzata, MN
Robert Ross & Co, Woodland Hills, CA
Frederic L Rosselot, Nyack, NY
Leona Rostenberg & Madeleine B Stern—Rare Books, New York, NY
Irving M Roth, Antiques, Norwalk, OH
Fred B Rothman & Co, Littleton, CO
Irene Rouse—Bookseller, Alexandria, VA
Cynthia Elyce Rubin, Charlestown, MA
Robert H Rubin Books, Stoughton, MA
Joseph Rubinfine, Pleasantville, NJ
Paul A Ruddell Books—Hobby House Press Inc, Cumberland, MD
Barbara J Rule Books, Rochester, MI
J B Rund, New York, NY
Cecil Archer Rush, Baltimore, MD
John Rush Books, Hamilton, ON, Canada
Ray Russell—Books, Rochester, MI
Terry Rutherford Bookseller, Vancouver, BC, Canada
L J Ryan—Scholarly Books, Columbus, OH
John Rybski Bookseller, Chicago, IL
S & S Books, Saint Paul, MN
S-T Associates, Louisville, KY
Rudolph William Sabbot—Natural History Books, Woodland Hills, CA
Ernest L Sackett, Grants Pass, OR
Ben Sackheim—Rare Books & Fine Art, Tucson, AZ
M Douglas Sackman, Deerfield, MA
Albert Saifer, West Orange, NJ
Charlotte F Safir Books, New York, NY
Lois St Clair, Van Nuys, CA
St Nicholas Books, Toronto, ON, Canada
Robert C Salathe, Mount Penn, PA
H & R Salerno, Hauppauge, NY
William Salloch, Ossining, NY
Salt of the Earth Bookstore Ltd, Albuquerque, NM
Samadhi—Metaphysical Literature, Newberry, FL
Peggy & Harold Samuels, Corrales, NM
San Francisciana Shop, San Francisco, CA
Sand Dollar Books, Albany, CA
C R Sanders Jr, Saint Augustine, FL
John R Sanderson PhD—Antiquarian Books, Stockbridge, MA
Santa Monica Book Bazaar, Santa Monica, CA
Savoy Books, Salem, MA
Saxifrage Books, Salem, MA
Scallawagiana Books, Salt Lake City, UT
Scarlet Letter Books & Prints, New Milford, CT
Scattergood Books, Berkeley, CA
William H Schab Gallery Inc, New York, NY
Schaefer Association, Arlington, VA
William L Schafer Books & Prints, Ridley Park, PA

Index

This general subject index covers Chapters 1 through 20. The "Directory of Collections and Sources," Part V, contains the following separate indexes: Name Index (p. 284) to Chapter 25, "Rare Book and Manuscript Libraries"; and Index of Specialties (p. 497) and Name Index (p. 552) to Chapter 26, "Dealers in Antiquarian Books and Manuscripts."